SITTING DUCKS
&
PEEPING TOMS

SITTING DUCKS
&
PEEPING TOMS

Michael I. Draper

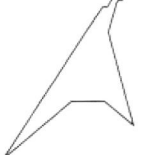

Copyright © 2011 by Michael I Draper

Published in the United Kingdom by

Air-Britain (Historians) Ltd
Victoria House,
Stanbridge Park,
Stapleford Lane,
Staplefield,
West Sussex RH17 6AS

www.air-britain.com

Edited by Douglas A. Rough

Distributed by:
Air-Britain (Historians) Ltd
Sales Department:
41 Penshurst Road
Leigh,
Tonbridge,
Kent TYN11 8HL

Correspondence regarding this publication to:
Michael. I. Draper
The Old Chapel
Nether Wallop
Hampshire SO20 8EU

All Rights Reserved. No part of this book may be reproduced, stored in a retrieval system or transmitted, in any form or by any means, electronic, mechanical, photocopying, recording or otherwise, without the prior permission of Air-Britain (Historians) Ltd

ISBN 978-0-85130-407-6

Printed in Poland
www.polskabook.co.uk

Origination: Susan Bushell

On 23 December 2006 and during the course of researching this book Richard Gordon (formerly Senior Project Engineer with M.L. Aviation Ltd) passed away.

This book serves as a testament to the assistance that he freely gave.

Contents

Introduction and Acknowledgements		ix
Abbreviations		xi
Chapter 1	The Pioneer Days	1
	Royal Aircraft Establishment (RAE) 'AT', Sopwith 'AT', RAE 1921 Target, RAE LARYNX, Fairey IIIF 'Queen'.	
Chapter 2	Queen Bee	17
	de Havilland Queen Bee	
Chapter 3	Beyond Queen Bee	51
	OR.29, OR.48 & OR.57, Airspeed Queen Wasp, Airspeed AS.37, General Aircraft Ltd GAL.35, Miles M.10, Miles Queen Martinet, Percival P.8 & P.8A, P.21& P.21A, Curtiss Queen Seamew and Supermarine Spitfire Drone	
Chapter 4	Unmanned Target Glider Trials	67
	RAE glider series, IMA 16 & 32, IMA Swallow, Air Service Training C-4, Brooklands TG, Slingsby T.19 & T.39.	
Chapter 5	Post-War Drone Conversions	91
	Avro Lancaster U.11, Avro Lincoln U.5, Fairey Firefly U.8/9, Gloster Meteor U.15/16/21 (D.15/16/21), Supermarine Swift, Folland Gnat Mk.6, English Electric Canberra U.10/D.14, and de Havilland Sea Vixen D.3	
Chapter 6	Jindivik & Stiletto	143
	Government Aircraft Factories Jindivik 102, 103, 104, Beech MQM-107/SD.2 Stiletto	
Chapter 7	Targets for the Royal Navy	165
	Arsenal 5501, Northrop MQM-36A (KD2R-5) Shelduck, MQM-74A/C Chukar I/II, Meteor Mirach 100/5	
Chapter 8	Unmanned Targets for the Army	221
	Auster B2, B3, ML Aviation Ltd, ML U-120D Midget, Short MATS-B, Short Skeet 1 & Skeet 2, Meggitt Banshee 300, 400, 500, CATS-Banshee, Meggitt Voodoo, Flight Refuelling Ltd (FRL) ASAT	

Chapter 9	Surveillance Drones for the Army …………………………………………	287
	Northrop MQM-57A (AN/USD-1), Canadair CL-89 Midge, BAe Phoenix, Hermes 450, Watchkeeper, Lockheed-Martin Desert Hawk, Honeywell T-Hawk	
Chapter 10	The UAV Revolution ……………………………………………………	323
	EADS/IAI Eagle, EADS Quadrocopter, EADS Scorpio-6, Boeing-InSitu ScanEagle, Mi-Tex Buster, General Atomics Aeronautical Systems Inc Predator	
Chapter 11	Other UAVs ………………………………………………………………	337
	MATS-A, AEL/Meggitt Snipe, RCS4024 Heron, BAe Stabileye, XRAE-1/FRL Raven, Cranfield A-3, Intora Firebird, ML Sprite, Westland Mote, Wisp, Wideye & Sharpeye plus BAe Systems range	
Appendix 1	Weapons & Systems ………………………………………………………	354
	Bristol Bloodhound, BAe Rapier, Short Blowpipe, Short Javelin plus naval weapons used against Shelduck, Chukar & Mirach. *Also Bofor guns.*	
Appendix 2	Units Equipped with Missiles used against Unmanned Aerial Targets ………	358
	Royal Air Force Regiment, Royal Artillery, Territorial Army & Volunteer Reserve, Miscellaneous Units.	
Appendix 3	Principle Ranges …………………………………………………………	362
	Aberporth, Benbecula, Cleave, Falkland Islands, Larkhill, Llanbedr, Manorbier & Castlemartin, NAMFI, Otterburn, Sennelager, Shoeburyness, Stiffkey, Thorney Island, Watchet, West Freugh, Weybourne, Suffield.	
Selected Bibliography………………………………………………………………………		367
Index ………………………………………………………………………………………		368

Introduction & Acknowledgements

Some years ago when I chose to write a book on the Nigeria-Biafra air war, a colleague – who lived in Nigeria throughout that 30-month civil war – questioned my decision. "A book? Maybe an article or two but surely there's not enough material for a book!" As it turned out the text had to be severely edited so as to fit between the covers. In much the same vein, one could easily be forgiven for applying the same obscure logic towards the complex subject of this book.

A straw poll would no doubt question the extent to which unmanned aircraft – UAVs – have served the British military forces. Yet in sheer numbers alone, the total Shelduck, Chukar, and Skeet target drones account for over 2,000 units, all of which were allocated identities within the standard military sequences. Add to this several hundred MATS-B, Banshee, Jindivik and various lesser types and the total grows to quite astonishing proportions. Yet, apart from a series of articles written by the author for BARG 'Roundel', few attempts appear to have been made to chronicle the development and track the individual histories of these aircraft.

This book therefore attempts to fill a gap in two ways. First, it offers coverage of all known target or drone aircraft operated by (or on behalf of) British forces, or developed against a military contract. But a fine dividing line emerges; do we include towed-targets such as the 'Rushton Sleeve'? No! Do we therefore exclude other powerless vehicles such as the towed glider targets of IML and Air Service Training? No! The rationale is perhaps not immediately clear, other than the simplistic fact that one resembles an aircraft, the other does not. One may just as well compare a rose with a sausage!

Second, the book attempts to list individual histories of each unmanned aircraft operated by the British armed forces. An exacting task by any standard, but what sets targets and drones apart from most other military aircraft is the stark reality that many simply did not have a history – and by the very call of their nature, many were lost on their first flight! Indeed, on a number of occasions, an airframe's total flight time can be measured only in seconds!

It has been a long and often frustrating journey to bring this book to fruition. More years than I care to admit have passed since I first had the notion of writing a book on such an overtly esoteric subject. And for much of that time I have ploughed a lonely furrow; a solitary pastime which, on occasions, was certainly not without immense difficulty. For a long time the Fleet Air Arm viewed Shelducks and Chukars as simply "ship's equipment or stores" whilst the Army Air Corps have looked upon targets and drones as mere "bits of Royal Artillery kit". For many years neither considered targets and drones to be part of their respective heritage and therefore made no real attempt to keep detailed records or archives. Thankfully views have since changed, but sadly much of the Royal Navy Pilotless Target Association (RNPTA) records held at Portland were lost when that base closed. Similarly little of the Army's early records have survived and it is with enormous gratitude that a number of former officers have gladly described their time on drones, especially Lt Col (Ret'd) 'Jim' Cooke, who managed the introduction of MQM-57A (AN/USD-1) and also Major (Ret'd) David Potts who headed up the Phoenix Trials Unit. Thankfully, both were willing to spend time recalling their service experiences.

Despite the recent growth in the use of UAVs, the sector is still relatively small – the annual ParcAberporth Exhibition & Symposium tended to resemble an old boys reunion – and most who work within the sector know each other. Many have become used to my constant quest for minutiae and have willingly responded. One service provider of target drones even issued an instruction that airframe log-books of destroyed aircraft should not be discarded until the author had inspected them! Amongst those who have assisted over the years are Lt Col (Ret'd) Dennis Robson and Bill Munday, both of Short Brothers Air Services Ltd, Mel Porter and Julian Dean of Cobham plc/Flight Refuelling Ltd, and Bill Longley of Tasuma Ltd. Jeremy Graham kindly fleshed out the bones of the Westland series of VTOL UAVs; Bill Blaine (formerly of Ferranti Ltd) made available his personal files on Ferranti's Phoenix proposals whilst Mark Agnew recounted the early trials of Phoenix. Julian Hasinski, of EADS, added new information on the JUEP trials as did David Bromley of the Air Warfare Centre UAV Battlelab.

Barry Guess of BAe Systems helped to locate pictures from the Group archives. My former colleagues at IPC Media's Aeroplane Monthly, including Nick Stroud and Phil Jarrett, have supplied other photographs from their respective archives. Geoff Wakeham opened up some important doors at RNAS Culdrose; Lee Howard explored FAA files held by the Yeovilton Museum under the stewardship of Jerry Shore. David Hatchard at Southampton's Solent Sky Museum offered encouragement and a few surprises – including a search in the Museum's stores for a couple of dusty boxes that turned out to contain a pair of long-forgotten IMA 4ft gliders.

Over the years Nick Chester and Reg Whittear, both of the Royal Navy's Pilotless Target unit, have provided key information whilst the Fleet Target Group (and its successor, 792 Squadron at Culdrose) have been especially accommodating with straightforward answers to complex questions. Former 728B Flight pilot Lt David Prothero was equally helpful in recounting his days flying Firefly and Meteor drones at Hal Far.

Former colleagues of the much-lamented British Aviation Research Group (BARG) including Dave Allen and especially Trevor Stone (who trawled through the records of Aerial Targets Ltd), have been constantly helpful. John Tipp's research of drone Firefly individual aircraft histories was first published in 1983, in BARG 'Roundel'. Much of that is repeated within these pages. Jim Halley and the late Ray Sturtivant, both of Air-Britain, have been a constant source of encouragement and detail. Clive Lynch helped with details of the Australian Meteor U.15 operations and Malcolm Fillmore provided vital details on Tiger Moth conversions to Queen Bees. Phil Butler willingly shared his vast knowledge, especially of home-grown gliders. Eddie Fuller helped with sightings of Shelducks at RAE Farnborough whilst details of individual Lincoln U.5 conversions have been provided by Alan Williams. Air-Britain's AB-IX network has brought answers to some searching queries; Terry Bowcutt, Andrew Horrex, Bernard Martin and Joe Barr have been especially helpful in providing answers to the author's questions. Chris Swan and Mike Rice also added important detail.

Two authors willingly allowed me to quote from their works. Wendy Mills, author of *Target Rolling* provided much insight into the Llanbedr side of the story, especially of the Meteor and Firefly operations. William Harrison allowed the author to rely heavily on his book *Fairey Firefly* for background material on the Firefly U.8 and U.9. Much of the information in this book is quoted directly from Bill's recommended work. Of the Jindivik story Simon Matthews provided information on late-production aircraft. Ken Elliott helped with observations of imported Jindiviks at Southend; Idwal Williams, Chris Smith and Tony Townsend were encouraged to recall their days at Aberporth and Llanbedr respectively.

Peter Amos has very kindly allowed me to quote from his much-acclaimed work on Miles Aircraft and at the same time pointed me towards Colin Mills and Susan Thompson, both of whom were involved in early Blowpipe target trials and helped to fill in details of that hitherto unpublicised episode.

It should also be recorded that, without the help of Ken Munson, former Editor of *Jane's Unmanned Aerial Vehicles and Targets*, this book would be considerably weaker on content and illustrations.

A word about individual aircraft histories should also be mentioned. These have been compiled by the author over many years of research but, as mentioned earlier, it is regrettable that many Royal Navy records have been lost. Much was destroyed when the Fleet Target Group transferred from Portland to Culdrose and no records have survived for the period prior to January 1981. Whilst this has not affected Chukar histories to a large degree – the author was allowed access to daily flight records since that date – it has affected the depth of detail on earlier Shelduck operations. Similarly (and somewhat typically!) the Army, for a long time, did not keep records on what was termed as "expendable equipment", but over the past 25 or so years the author has been allowed remarkable access to Larkhill and Manorbier as well as aircraft log books, maintenance records and "Camp" reports for Manorbier, Hebrides and Falkland Islands' operations. Battery Commanders from 18 Battery, RA and 22 Battery, RA also allowed the author access to historical records of UAV operations, especially those pertaining to Kosovo and the Gulf War periods. S/Sgt John Adam and Sgt Mark Wilkinson were also helpful in relating their experiences.

One final acknowledgement is to my friend of long-standing, Douglas Rough who has an unbelievably unique ability to unearth obscure information from equally obscure sources. Douglas also took on the role of mentoring an "undisciplined author" and his opinions on many aspects of this book have been greatly appreciated.

Lastly, the author is grateful to Chris Warn for undertaking the onerous, but essential, role of proof-reading.

Author's Note

In chronicling the use of unmanned vehicles in British service it has been the author's sole intention to focus upon the development and operational aspects as an "air vehicle airframe" rather than "how it works". The history of radio-control, much through trial and error in the earliest days, is a truly complex story, as is the subject of modern unmanned systems and associated software. Such a history would be too great for inclusion here but would be worthy of a separate work.

In recent times, UAVs have played an increasingly important role in Iraq and Afghan-Pakistan theatres – and indeed continue to do so. Sensitivity therefore surrounds their operational role and theatre deployment and it is for these reasons alone that certain details of current military UAVs have been purposely excluded.

Short Bros Ltd

The very success of Short Bros & Harland within its chosen field of aircraft and missile design as well as aerial target design and operation brings the company name to the fore throughout this book. Short Brothers (Rochester & Bedford) Ltd was formed in 1919 and became a public company in December 1935. On 2 June 1936, Short & Harland Ltd was created as a joint venture between Short Brothers (Rochester & Bedford) Ltd and Harland & Wolf. The Rochester facility was closed in June 1946 and on 5 November 1947 the company title was re-styled as Short Bros & Harland Ltd. Thirty years later, in 1977, the company name was simplified to Short Bros Ltd.

Throughout this book the author has used the terms "Short" and "Shorts" which, although technically incorrect, have become a widely-acceptable term to describe the company.

Chapter Notes

Use of extensive chapter notes has been made for two principal reasons. Firstly, a number of previously published statements have proved to vary and the author has tried to explain the rationale for the opinions shown in this book where inclusion in the main text would be distractive. Secondly, the author has, as far as possible, quoted his original source for information to support details within the main text.

Abbreviations

ACTC	Approved for Conversion to Components
ACTD	Advanced Concept Technology Demonstration
AMDP	Air Member for Development & Production
ADR	Aircraft Direction Room
AGS	Advanced Ground System
AMF(L)	Allied Mobile Force (Land Element)
AWC	Air Warfare Centre
BATES	Battlefield Artillery Target Engagement System
BBOC	Brought Back On Charge
B&TU	Base & Training Unit
CAA	Civil Aviation Authority
canx	cancelled
CASTOR	Corps Airborne Stand-Off Radar
CIA	Central Intelligence Agency (US)
Cr	Crashed
DEC	Directorate of Equipment Capability
Del/Deld	Delivered
DERA	Defence Evaluation & Research Agency
DTGW	Directorate, Trials Guided Weapons
DH	de Havilland Aircraft Co Ltd
Dptd	Departed
DTD	Director of Technical Development (Air Ministry)
f/f	First flight (or flown)
FOAS	Future Offensive Air System
GCS	Ground Control Station (or System)
GPS	Global Positioning System
GRP	Glass-reinforced plastic
GSR	General Staff Requirement
HALE	High-altitude, long endurance
HMS	His (Her) Majesty's Ship/Station
ICE	Image Collection and Exploitation
IED	Improvised Explosive Device
IFTU	Intensive Flying Training Unit
ISTAR	Intelligence, Surveillance, Target Acquisition & Reconnaissance.
JUEP	Joint UAV Experimentation Programme
LMM	Lightweight Multi-role Missile
MAGIC ATOLS	Microwave And GPS Integrated Cooperative Automatic TakeOff and Landing System.
MALE	Medium-altitude, long endurance
MATS-	Model Aircraft Target System-*
MDI	Miss-Distance Indicator
MGW3	Missiles & Guided Weapons (Branch 3)
Mkrs	Makers (or manufacturer)
MPRD	Metal & Produce Recovery Depot
MLRS	Multiple Launch Rocket System
MUAV	Mini Unmanned Air Vehicle
MWC	Maritime Warfare Centre
NATO	North Atlantic Treaty Organisation
NEC	Network Enabled Capability
nms	Nautical miles
OEF	Operation Enduring Freedom
RA	Royal Artillery
RAE	Royal Aircraft Establishment
Regd	Registered
res	reserved
RFA	Royal Fleet Auxiliary
RIAT	Royal International Air Tattoo
RIW	Repaired In Works
RNARY	Royal Navy Aircraft Repair Yard
RNPTA	Royal Navy Pilotless Target Association
RPH	Remotely-piloted helicopter
RPV	Remotely-piloted vehicle
Scr	Scrapped
SOC	Struck off charge
tfd	transferred
TDV	Technology Demonstrator Vehicle
T&EE	Test & Evaluation Establishment
TFH	Total Flying Hours
TI/TIs	Trial installation/s
TOC	Taken onto charge
TUAV	Tactical Unmanned Air Vehicle
UAV	Unmanned (or uninhabited) Air Vehicle
UCAV	Unmanned (or uninhabited) Combat Air Vehicle
UCLA	Uncommanded (or uncontrolled) Loss of Altitude
unkn	unknown
UOR	Urgent Operational Requirement
VISTA	Visual Intelligence, Surveillance and Target Acquisition
W/o	Written-off

Some sources have interpreted MATS- to imply Military Aircraft Target System.

Apart from the characteristic rolled-up sleeves and cloth cap this RAE worker offers the perfect posture of a pall-bearer! In this view of an 'RAE 1921 Aerial Target' what appears to be a serial '3152' is displayed across the rudder and which relates to a Grahame-White G.W.XV. Note the railway-type wheels on the trolley. (FAST Collection)

Chapter 1
The Pioneer Days

"My idea of Archie Low was to put him in a room with his feet up on the mantelpiece, and make him think out his ideas". That was how General Pitcher recalled one inspired boffin who could have changed the course of the First World War.[1]

WHAT PITCHER WAS ALLUDING TO was the contribution from the fertile brain of Professor Archibald M. Low, a versatile and vivid personality and the creator of Britain's first remotely-powered (air) vehicle (RPV). More precisely, Pitcher was reflecting on the circumstances that led to Low's work on radio control as well as what Low himself described as a "queer little monoplane with an unsuitable Gnome engine". Even Low's own assessment could not have been more accurate, but then the aeroplane's sole purpose was to pioneer a series of wireless experiments. In truth, what Low was secretly developing was an unmanned, radio-controlled aeroplane intended to be packed with explosives. It was the very stuff of fiction. As Low's biographer later wrote: "He was on the verge of one of the greatest war discoveries of the century, but the damnable part of it was that he discovered it in the wrong war. The mistake was that Archie Low always did everything too soon, with the result that half the world did not believe that any of it could be true."

The over-riding motivation for developing a successful unmanned aeroplane at the height of World War One was a means of combating the German Zeppelins which, by 1916, were carrying out regular air raids over southern and eastern England. They appeared to be untouchable and it was against that unlikely backdrop that led the Air Ministry to envisage a small aeroplane fitted with a "wireless controlling mechanism and carrying, instead of a crew, a large explosive charge." The machine would then be sent off and steered remotely into any desired objective, notably a Zeppelin.

Archibald Low had already worked on several projects for the Air Ministry's General Caddell.[2] That work had been carried out at his Chiswick workshop and it therefore came as little surprise that Caddell should ask if it was possible

---
1 *He Lit The Lamp*, Ursula Bloom, biography of Professor Archibald Low.
2 Archibald Low was, in fact, working on an Artillery Corps project to design the very first electronic range finder, based on the principles of radar. Although he had been an Associated Professor of Physics at the Royal Ordnance College he was distanced from the scientific community by continuing to use the term Professor throughout his life.

Professor Archibald M Low was, in many respects, the epitome of the inventor so often portrayed in comic strip as the "eccentric professor". His wireless experiments during the First World War led to the first radio-controlled unmanned aeroplane. (Reproduced from He Lit The Lamp *by Ursula Bloom.)*

that an aircraft's rudder and elevator could be controlled remotely. Low, as he always did when a tempting challenge was being offered, readily agreed to create and build a design that would meet Caddell's requirement. In the meantime General Sir David Henderson, the then Director-General of Military Aeronautics, told the inventor, "Well, Low, you must think of some thundering lie to conceal our ideas of attack and bombing. Let's call it the Aerial Target (AT). Everyone will think that it is merely intended as a target for our guns or 'planes."

Some sources suggest that the AT was built in Low's Chiswick workshop but Low's own recollection was that it was built in a hangar at Brooklands. Wherever it was built, it was, to say the very least, something of a hybrid; constructed largely out of wood and tin, the aeroplane was fitted with a lower wing salvaged from a B.E.2c and with an oversized propeller taken from an S.E.5.

Low's wireless control equipment was equally primitive. It consisted of a spark transmitter and a receiver to switch a relay which, in turn, operated a mechanism permitting the sequential selection of up/down and left/right commands using, for its time, a remarkably advanced rudder and elevator servo.

Nobody, of course, chose to doubt Low's expertise and skill in wireless technology, but few admired his ability to build a suitable aeroplane to test his theory. In fairness to Low, it was never designed to actually fly – only to be used for ground-running tests. Unfortunately, and undoubtedly as a consequence of the aeroplane's hybrid nature, satisfactory results were often frustrated, especially as excessive airframe vibration caused serious interference with Low's primitive radio control system. The ground trials, which took place in 1916, are said to have come to an unfortunate conclusion during a demonstration to senior Army and Navy officials at Laffan's Plain, Farnborough when Low's AT careered across the ground in a series of uncontrolled manoeuvres and almost decimated the assembled guests.[3]

It has to be said that the Laffan's Plain incident does not appear to be corroborated by any official evidence. Similarly, there is some doubt as to the location of these early tests. According to Low his equipment was conveyed to Upavon and test-flown there on 21 March 1917, his aircraft having been launched from a pneumatic catapult mounted on the back of a lorry. (It is unsure what aeroplane Low refers to – his "queer little aeroplane that was never intended to be flown" or an early version of the later AT.) Low goes on to admit that, because he was not a qualified pilot, he was not permitted to control the aeroplane directly. Instead he operated the radio transmitter on the orders of a pilot who

---

3   As originally reported by Aeroplane, 21 December 1921 and much later recounted in an Aeroplane Monthly (July 1988) article by D.W. Allen.

What is thought to be Archibald Low's original 'Aerial Target'. If so, then this rare view is likely to have been taken inside the RFC Experimental Works. (Newton & Company, via Malcolm Fillmore)

The 1917 RAE AT seen under construction and approaching what is clearly the finishing stage. (FAST Collection)

stood outside the lorry in which the ground equipment was installed. The pilot was Henry (later Sir Henry) Seagrave. The aircraft was launched satisfactorily and climbed steeply, but after carrying out an almost complete loop the AT crashed into the ground within 30ft of the launch lorry.[4]

The Upavon incident does bear some surprising similarities to the circumstances described as having taken place at Laffan's Plain – except that Low's aeroplane did not fly at Farnborough. Considering the degree of secrecy that these experiments were being conducted under it is hardly surprising that some reports are rather vague.

Despite the Upavon crash, it seems that official support remained relatively undaunted. Sir David Henderson decided that the Royal Flying Corps Experimental Works should be established and that Archibald Low should be appointed its Commanding Officer. The Works was located at Feltham, Middlesex and Low, in turn, appointed around thirty men including, it is said, jewellers, carpenters and aircraftsmen. By now Low had become enlisted in the Royal Flying Corps, initially with the rank of Second-Lieutenant and shortly afterwards, that of Captain.

It was at Feltham that Low built his first flyable 'Aerial Target'. He was given considerable assistance from the Royal Aircraft Factory at Farnborough although Low was not, it seems, the sole contender in developing an AT. Several private companies were also approached to design and build prototype RPVs. Certainly the Sopwith Aviation Company designed and built a small biplane with a four-wheel undercarriage arrangement whilst Lincoln-based Ruston Proctor & Co Ltd entered the fray with a single wire-braced monoplane although the latter is believed never to have flown.

The Sopwith AT, as it became known, was a 14ft wingspan biplane, thought to have also been erected in the Experimental Works at Feltham by a small number of Sopwith employees and Royal Aircraft Factory staff. Sopwith used an unusual four-wheeled undercarriage which was an attempt to ensure take-off in a straight line. Low's radio apparatus was installed in the fuselage towards the tail and behind the fuel, batteries and explosives bay. The aerials were strung around the wings and fuselage.[5] The power unit selected for the Sopwith AT was a 35hp A.B.C. horizontally-opposed two-cylinder Gnat engine.

To help protect the sensitive radio equipment it was fitted into a glass-topped wooden box and suspended on rubber supports. The box contained all of the relays, receiver and the Key system which acted as an interference filter. Unfortunately during the final erection stage the aircraft tipped and sustained damage to the bottom starboard wing and upper port wing. It is likely that the damaged airframe was then moved from Feltham to Brooklands for repair but in the end the work was not carried out and the project was abandoned.[6]

How far Sopwith had progressed with its AT programme is hard to judge, but it is evident that the concept was developed into the larger Sopwith Scout project. This may be associated with a contemporary report that four aircraft, numbered A8970-A8973, were stored at Brooklands in May 1917. They were described at the time as Sopwith "Small Scouts with warping wings" and they were stored without engines, albeit the same source stating that their intended powerplants were 50hp Gnome engines. That tends to

---

4   Ursula Bloom, *He Lit The Lamp*.

5   *Sopwith – The Man & His Aircraft*, Harleyford.
6   *Sopwith Aircraft 1912-1920*, by H.F. King, Putnam.

The Sopwith company was asked to assist in the radio-controlled experiments of Professor Archibald Low and build an experimental machine to prove his apparatus. It was erected in sheds at Feltham, Middlesex by a small number of Sopwith employees and Royal Aircraft Factory employees. In circumstances not fully known, but possibly during the final assembly stage, the aircraft sustained damage to the wings as is clearly visible in this view. As a result, the project was later abandoned. (Bruce Robertson Collection)

suggest that a small production batch of ATs was built, but never completed nor flown. The decision to abandon the project may have been influenced by an opinion within some ministerial circles that radio control would have a more direct application to motor-boat trials which, when failures in experiments occurred, did not result in a complete wreck. Whatever the case, Sopwith's involvement in unmanned aircraft development, unlike experiments at the Royal Aircraft Factory, progressed no further.

Work at the Royal Aircraft Factory did progress. Widely applauded for his design of the S.E.5A, Henry P. Folland assumed design leadership for what was termed as the Royal Aircraft Factory 1917 AT although most of the work was originated by Folland's assistant, Harry 'Joe' Preston.[7] Several variations were put forward before a final design was selected. It was a small shoulder-wing monoplane which, to ensure lateral stability, featured a wing with a generous dihedral. At the same time Granville Bradshaw of A.B.C. Motors Ltd – who had gained considerable fame by designing the well-proven 45hp Gnat engine – had designed a throwaway engine specifically for use in the RPV. Bradshaw's engine was a 35hp horizontally-opposed twin-cylinder version of the Gnat with a run life of about two hours. Lightweight and inexpensive, the engine allowed research and development to progress to a new phase.

It is believed that six examples of Folland's design were constructed at Farnborough in early 1917 and allocated the serials A8957-A8962. As each aircraft was completed it was conveyed, out of prying eyes, to the Experimental Works at Feltham where, under much secrecy, they were fitted with Low's wireless gear and tested on the ground. The first complete aircraft was despatched from Farnborough to Feltham on 5 June 1917 whilst at Northolt engineers had begun laying out a specially-designed launch track consisting of an initial 15 metres (50 feet) of horizontal track followed by a 30-metre (100 foot) incline.[8]

The first flight of a Farnborough-built AT took place at Northolt on 6 July 1917 and is thought to have involved A8957. According to the official report of the test, the machine rose from the carriage about half way down the track and immediately began to climb at a very steep angle. The angle increased until the nose was pointed vertically upwards. The machine then turned over on its back and dived vertically to the ground about 30 yards to the right of the track. The "elevators down" signal had been sent and may not have been received, as there was no appreciable flattening out of the climb. The accident was thought almost certainly to have been due to the machine being more tail-heavy than had been evident in the model tests. Subsequent thoughts on the cause considered it possible that the real cause was the large overshoot to be expected in an uncontrolled transition of this kind.

A second trial was carried out at Northolt on 25 July but ended in a crash because the change in tail setting of 2°, as compared with the previous trial, trimmed the machine at a speed considerably higher than it could reach in the length of the track. A third trial, on 28 July with an intermediate tail setting, also ended in failure because the engine cut out halfway down the track. It continued firing in an irregular manner and the machine which had, at halfway, attained a speed of nearly 40mph steadily decelerated. It left the track at about 30mph and the undercarriage broke up almost immediately. When the machine was travelling at its highest speed, it was still standing level on its supports which indicated that the tail setting was fairly accurate.

---

7   Harry E. 'Joe' Preston joined Henry Folland at Farnborough in 1915. When Folland moved to Nieuport, 'Joe' Preston joined him there and later followed him to Gloster Aircraft Ltd. When Folland Aircraft Ltd was formed in 1937 Preston became the company's Chief Engineer and Designer. He retired from Folland in October 1950.

8   It has been reported that the last of the RAE ATs (A8962) was later converted to a piloted aircraft by No. 3 (Western) Aircraft Depot at Bristol. Given the serial B8962 it was eventually sold to Ron Shelley of Billericay, Essex and broken up.

If, as is suspected, the markings on the rear fuselage of this RAE 1921 Target represent the number "11" then this view is likely to be of the aircraft that was launched off Stronghold on 3 September 1924. Two aircraft (numbers 11 and 12) are known to have been positioned aboard the destroyer and in this view a second Target can be seen just above the ship's pennant number. The catapult track was 60ft in length with a track gauge of 6ft. Two systems of propulsion were tried, the first, through suitable rope reeving, used a 'bag' of sea water dropping over the side of the ship, its impact with the sea being the mode of arresting the trolley. The development from this was the use of a container – also filled with sea water, probably the same bag – falling through the ammunition trunk of the destroyer's for'ard gun turret which had been removed to accommodate the catapult structure.

They had W/T controlling gear fitted to enable them to receive just four signals: Turn to Port; Fly straight; Turn to Starboard and Cut the Engine. Target No.11 was launched at 13:35 and took-off without any appreciable oscillation. However, owing to high winds at 1,500ft – gusting up to 35mph – the aircraft drifted some 30 miles off course and became lost to observers aboard 'Stronghold'. Eventually it ditched, out of sight and out of control, in shallow water some three miles off Selsey Bill. Although given up as lost it was later salvaged by fisherman and brought into shore. (FAST Collection)

No further flights were attempted despite three machines being available. The trials had demonstrated the difficulty of achieving successful take-off and climb with an elevator fixed in a pre-determined position.

By the end of 1918 the war had ended and the RFC Experimental Works disbanded. Archibald Low, in the meantime, had applied in January 1918 for a patent associated with his pioneering radio-control design. For security reasons the application was delayed by the Patents Office for almost a year. Patent specification No. 244258 in A.M. Low's name was finally accepted on 10 December 1918.

RAE 1921 'Aerial Target'

With the return to peace, the story of unmanned flight might well have ended. But less than six months after the Armistice the Naval Anti-Aircraft Gunnery Committee declared, in a letter to the Air Ministry dated 6 May 1919, a need to develop an aerial target for gunnery practice. What was unusual in this request was that the Navy saw, as a key factor, the development of an unmanned target aircraft for a series of planned experimental firings in the Portsmouth area. Quite how the Air Ministry reacted to the Navy's request does not seem to have been recorded but just two months later, in July 1919, the Admiralty urged the Air Ministry to make immediate enquiries in the USA where self-propelled unmanned aircraft were known to already exist. Whether or not any enquiries were made is again unclear; the Admiralty certainly thought not and in May 1920 again pressed the Air Ministry for more positive action.

It was true, of course, that the Americans had pursued the quest for a reliable unmanned aircraft, but like British attempts, they had met with little success. Few designs were ever flown; even less reached the initial build stage. There was also the factor of Britain's postwar financial constraints which prevented the purchase of American aircraft. Furthermore, the Air Ministry argued that the US product that had caught the attention of the naval gunnery planners was an "aerial torpedo" controlled by a gyroscope rather than a radio-controlled aircraft. But the notion appeared to fall onto deaf ears and instead the Air Ministry suggested that a new committee be set up under the Director of Research to resume the development of radio-controlled aircraft.

By the end of 1920 work had restarted on the development and provision of a simple automatic pilot, consisting of a gyroscopic rudder control and a crude control

The Pioneer Days 5

of elevator in response only to height by means of an aneroid and an air log to control range. The work was being carried out at the Instrument Development Establishment at Biggin Hill. In the meantime engineers at Farnborough began to work on a suitable aeroplane design and what became known as the RAE 1921 Aerial Target was, with minor alterations, remarkably similar to Folland's 1917 Aerial Target. It might even be fair to assume that the unflown examples left after the 1917 tests were rebuilt and suitably modified to meet the Admiralty's requirement. One change was the replacement of the unreliable ABC-Gnat engine with a 45hp Siddeley-Deasy (later Armstrong Siddeley) Ounce twin-cylinder engine.[9]

The most marked external difference between the original RAE 1917 AT and the new 1921 was in the re-designed fin and wing. It was also noteworthy that the 1921 design did not feature an undercarriage. The revised design had a wing-span of 23ft (7.01m), length 18ft (5.49m) and a launch weight of 630lb (285kg). It was designed to carry a 200lb (90kg) payload at a speed of 103mph (165km/hr) at 6,000ft (1,830m). Nobody seemed to question why an 'Aerial Target' should need to carry a 200lb payload and it is likely that the true objective of the RAE Farnborough technicians was to continue development of an 'Aerial Torpedo' (or flying-bomb). So, in the final analysis, was the RAE 1921 Target the true genesis of the flying-bomb – subsequently developed with such devastating menace by the Germans in WWII as the Fieseler FzG-76 (V-1) 'Doodle Bug'? The evidence more than implies that indeed it probably was.

A landmark was reached in October 1921 when a simple gyro rudder control was fitted to a Bristol F.2B fighter and flight-tested at RAE Farnborough. At the same time a single control wireless telegraphy (W/T) set was fitted and arranged to steer the aircraft in response to signals transmitted by radio from a ground command unit. The system, developed by Farnborough's Instrument & Photographic Flight, was not wholly successful to start with – but it did work and, for the first time in the UK, an aircraft was manoeuvred by wireless control from the ground to a distance of two or three miles.[10]

The next stage was to build a multi-channel radio system and fit it into a DH.9A; the selector being arranged to light lamps to indicate correct functioning, rather than operating the controls.

By the summer of 1922 the new RAE AT was ready for flight trials. The Admiralty had already selected HMS *Stronghold* for launch trials, but at the time the destroyer was still on active duty. Instead, the aircraft carrier HMS *Argus* was used for the initial flight trials for which a set of launch rails was laid along the carrier's deck. The first attempted launch took place on 13 July 1922 but the AT failed to get airborne. A second attempt fared better in that the AT did manage to get airborne but only to fall into the sea, having not been released from its launch trolley at the right moment. Despite the loss of the first AT a second aircraft was prepared for launch on 31 August but that too crashed into the sea. On that occasion the cause was put down to "violent lateral oscillation that followed the transition from the horizontal launch rails and the climb-out with a fixed elevator".

Following the loss on 31 August it was decided to launch into the climb from an inclined catapult, known as a 'flying-off platform'. The catapult, set at about 30°, was mounted on the bows of HMS *Stronghold* which, by September 1923, was ready to succeed *Argus*. The launch catapult worked simply by dropping a large water-filled bag vertically downwards into the sea, allowing the aircraft to accelerate up the catapult's track to a much-increased velocity.[11]

The first flight trial of an RAE Target off *Stronghold* took place on 12 September 1923 with a Fairey IIID (N9641) camera-carrying seaplane flying alongside. After flying satisfactorily for just over four minutes the aircraft turned to starboard, immediately rolled and finally nose-dived into the sea. Both wings broke off during the dive and although later recovered, the aircraft was totally wrecked.[12]

In preparation for further flight trials two new RAE Target aircraft were taken down to Portsmouth Dockyard on 29 October. Flights resumed on 7 November but, despite the wing fittings having been strengthened in the light of the previous flight, the aircraft crashed into the sea after 4 mins 20 secs. Although the aircraft was badly damaged the wings had remained intact.

Another RAE AT was taken by road to Portsmouth on 3 December but before it was flown the RAE asked for a delay to allow more remedial work to be carried out. Engineers had attributed the 7 November accident to either a faulty gyroscope or that the gyro had toppled, an unfortunate but regular occurrence with the simple gyros of the day. It underlined the need for a great deal more work to be done before the gyroscopic control mechanism could ensure a stable climb-away. With no sign, therefore, of any immediate flights taking place, the Admiralty seized the moment to send *Stronghold* to Pembroke Docks for a refit.[13]

By the end of February 1924 *Stronghold* was ready to return to service. RAE despatched a modified AT to Portsmouth Dockyard on 18 February in preparation for a resumption of trial flights. The flight took place four days later and this time the launch and climb-out was well-controlled although it took 2½ minutes for the AT to reach 2,000ft. Observers aboard the destroyer watched the aircraft fly a straight line for seven miles at a steady speed of around 85-90kts but then lost sight of it in the haze. The aircraft had been instructed to turn to starboard through 220° for the return straight flight back and, according to plan, the aircraft – having now been airborne for almost eight minutes – came back into view. However, what happened next was most certainly unplanned. The return flight was anything but straight; initially, it was seen to dive from a steep bank, then it levelled out briefly before entering a climb and performing a perfect, albeit unintentional, loop. What then followed was later described as "5½ minutes of wild and

---

9 The Instrument Development Establishment was later absorbed into the RAE as the Instrument & Photographic Flight (I & P Flt).
10 46th Wilbur Wright Memorial Lecture by George W.H. Gardner July 1958.
11 National Archives ADM116/2388
12 The date has also been reported (officially) as 13 September 1923. However National Archives' documents suggest that the launch took place on 12 September.
13 RAE Trial Report BA.482; National Archives AVIA6/1475/43A. Also ADM116/2388

HMS Stronghold *(H50) with an RAE Aerial Torpedo (Target) on its launch ramp. This aircraft appears to carry the marking '7' suggesting that it might be a different aircraft to that depicted on page 5. Just visible on the forward deck is a second AT. These trials enjoyed a fair degree of success considering that the entire unmanned flying element was still at an extremely early stage.*

uncontrolled manoeuvres, the aircraft turning, diving, climbing and stalling between 1,500-2,000ft. Finally, it collided with the tail of the accompanying camera-ship seaplane and dived vertically into the sea." Other than some fragments of wood and fabric, nothing worthy of recovery was visible. Only the propeller survived – it was embedded in the Fairey IIID's tailplane![14]

Back at Farnborough attention once again focused upon the gyroscope. Modifications included the introduction of an anti-topple mechanism to the rudder gyro whilst RAE engineers also removed any superfluous weight, including the exhaust pipes and carburettor muffs, to bring the overall weight down to 520lbs. Two such modified aircraft were then conveyed to Portsmouth on 2 June 1924 ahead of the next test-flight which took place at sea on 6 June.

The first aircraft launched successfully although it drifted slightly to port in the climbout. A turn took place at the correct time but it was then seen to be turning too fast and instead of changing course by 200°, it did so by 280°. Observers on *Stronghold* lost sight of it at that stage but other observers aboard the nearby HMS *Sturdy* managed to keep the aircraft in sight for the second pre-planned turn.

After several minutes observers on both ships had lost visual contact, and with no further sign of the aircraft, the test was abandoned and the ships sailed for their home base. Then, at some 9½ miles from the launch position, the aircraft was seen floating in the water and fully intact. After it was hauled aboard engineers discovered that the clock had run its full course and had even switched off the engine according to plan. The flight had proved to be much more successful than initially perceived. It also proved that the diagnosis reached after the previous flight had been correct and this, in turn, encouraged the RAE to consider a further test-flight under direct wireless control rather than a preset clockwork system.[15]

The seventh launch of an AT took place off *Stronghold* on 3 September 1924. By now advances in technology had brought about a significant improvement in stability and control. A multi-channel radio control, operating on a frequency of 267kHz, had been set up to give four commands: turn to port, fly straight, turn to starboard and cut engine. Aerial Target No.11 was launched successfully and obeyed all commands transmitted from the Fairey IIID 'shepherd' aircraft flying alongside. However, the flight lasted for just 12 minutes – cut short due to an unexpected in-flight engine failure after which the AT glided in to a safe sea landing with little damage.[16]

Two further launches of ATs took place in 1924; on 12 September and 16 October. For these flights two wireless transmitters were made available, one aboard the 'shepherd' aircraft and the other installed on board *Stronghold*. Both flights went ahead without serious incident as did the tenth, and final flight, on 26 February 1925. It lasted for 39 minutes during which time a standard transmitter on board HMS *Castor* sent 43 separate radio commands, all of which were received and acted upon. The AT landed safely and was picked up virtually undamaged.

Through ten test flights over a near three-year period, the RAE 1921 AT marked a significant milestone in successfully achieving remotely-controlled flight. Radio equipment had matured to an extent that it was now considerably more reliable than the engine, which remained a source of anxiety. What the AT also demonstrated was that, for some

---

14 RAE Trial Report BA.489; National Archives AVIA6/1475/70A

15 RAE Trial Report BA.500; National Archives AVIA6/1475/94A
16 RAE Trial Report BA.514; National Archives AVIA6/1475/146A

applications of unmanned flight, remote radio control was not necessary. An aircraft could, if designed as a flying bomb, be controlled solely by autopilot. That aspect of unmanned flight led directly to a more formidable unmanned design and one that was seen as perhaps even attaining production status. That was the RAE 'LARYNX'.

RAE 'LARYNX'

By the time that the Pilotless Aircraft Committee was formed in mid-1927 work on unmanned aircraft at Farnborough had gathered some pace. Instruments & Aerodynamics Department had already begun work on a new design back in September 1925 and by mid-1927 two prototypes were complete. Given the name 'LARYNX' – a somewhat ambiguous derivation of its intended purpose: a "**L**ong-**R**ange gun with L**ynx** engine" – it was fitted with a 200hp Armstrong Siddeley Lynx Mk.IV engine and was capable of carrying a 250lb warhead over a range of 300 miles. The airframe was a mid-wing monoplane with a tubular-shaped fuselage and cruciform tail unit. Larger than the RAE's AT, LARYNX also featured significant improvements in guidance accuracy by using a magnetic compass to monitor the rudder gyro, and an air log to measure the distance flown.

Flight trials of LARYNX began in mid-1927 with a series of planned launches from HMS *Stronghold*, the same destroyer that had been involved in the trials of the RAE 1921 Target. First sign of activity occurred on 11 July when RAE Farnborough's low-angle 5° catapult was taken down to Portsmouth and fitted onto the destroyer's forward deck. (Although Farnborough's catapult was a low-angled example, it appears to have been installed with a greater upwards angle). The ship then sailed for Devonport. Four days later two LARYNX aircraft left Farnborough in crates and were conveyed by road to RAF Cattewater, Plymouth where they were assembled for loading aboard *Stronghold*.[17]

Before any trial flights took place the launcher and aircraft trolley were tested by catapulting three large weights into the sea. By early afternoon on 20 July 1927 conditions for a launch looked good; the wind was suitable, visibility was fine and the sea calm. The course was marked out as a straight line offshore along the north Devon and Cornwall coastline with four direction-finding (D/F) stations set up at regular intervals along the coast.

The manner in which LARYNX was monitored in flight was immensely significant. The course of the aircraft was plotted by making D/F observations on radio transmissions from the aircraft. The pitch of the interrupted C.W. transmission was then used as a measure of engine speed and at intervals signals were interrupted by the air log, thereby enabling distance and speed to be readily deduced. This was probably the first application in the UK of the use of radio telemetry from an aircraft.

The first attempted launch suffered a potentially disastrous mechanical failure. Just before launching LARYNX 1 mechanics undertook an engine test at full throttle; some last minute adjustments were made by a junior member of the RAE team but as he did so the trolley carrying the aircraft collapsed forward and the aircraft crashed off the catapult. The propeller disintegrated, the container of titanium tetrachloride burst and the young mechanic was propelled (by the tailplane) over the edge of a six-foot high packing case – head-first onto the steel deck. The destroyer was steaming into wind and much of the titanium tetrachloride smoke went down the ventilating shafts and made its way throughout the ship, depositing hydrochloric acid on its way. Mercifully, the mechanic, G.W.H. Gardner, survived without serious injury.[18]

The second attempt was more successful. LARYNX was launched on 1 September and climbed to its pre-arranged height and turned onto its pre-determined course. However, it is thought that on launch the aerial weight struck the sea and broke off so it was not possible to track the aircraft. It failed to complete the length of the course and crashed prematurely but it was not until 11 days later that wreckage was recovered off the Cornish coast. Local fishermen were greatly concerned as to the fate of the pilot and George Gardner was sent down to St Ives. He recovered the wreckage and brought it back to Farnborough – reportedly in the guard's van of a train yet managed to avoid making any statement as to the kind of aircraft it came from.[19]

Inspection of the wreckage back at Farnborough put the cause of the crash down to either some form of engine failure or by a failure of the chain drive to the generator and compressor.

Back at Farnborough, RAE technicians prepared two more LARYNX for a further flight trial in August 1927. The two aircraft (reported as No.2 and No.3) were conveyed to Portsmouth and taken on board HMS *Stronghold* on Friday, 26 August 1927. The destroyer sailed two days later and arrived off Swansea on 29 August, putting to anchor about two miles offshore. For several days the trials team was hindered by hazy weather but by 1 September the conditions had improved; the weather was good, clear sky and a light westerly wind. The first of the two aircraft was assembled on the catapult although checking wing settings, instruments and other items in the preparation for launch took around 2½ hours.

LARYNX No.2 was launched satisfactorily but shortly afterwards began to display considerable instability before it too crashed prematurely into the sea. The trial was abandoned and *Stronghold* returned to Portsmouth.

As a result of the August 1927 trial LARYNX underwent some minor modifications, including a change of dihedral angle and a 20% increase in rudder area. The first of the modified LARYNX, No.3, was test-flown along a course off the north Cornish coast during the afternoon of 15 October 1927 with the objective of allowing the aircraft to fly some

---

17 RAF Cattewater was the stretch of water at the mouth of the River Plym, on the eastern side of Plymouth Ho. It was opened in February 1917 as a Royal Naval Air Station but with the formation of the Royal Air Force in 1918 the base became RAF Cattewater. Eventually the site was upgraded and re-named RAF Mount Batten on 1 October 1928.

18 It may be unfair to describe G.W.H.Gardner as simply a mechanic (as quoted from the trials report). It is more than likely that this was the young scientist, George (later Sir George) Gardner, destined to become RAE's Director 1955-1959. He is known to have been closely involved in LARYNX launch trials.

19 As related by George W.H.Gardner in his 46th Wilbur Wright Memorial Lecture and reproduced in the Journal of the Royal Aeronautical Society, July 1958.

Left: *A direct development of the 1921 AT was the RAE LARYNX, of which at least twelve were built and flight-tested over a two-and-a-half year period. These three views depict LARYNX No.3 just prior to being launched from the low-angle catapult on HMS* Stronghold *in October 1927. Clearly evident in this view are the neat lines of LARYNX and the early adoption of black and white striping for unmanned aircraft. (FAST Collection: RAE8986)*

Right: *LARYNX No.3 on the low-angle catapult, portraying the catapult trolley and track details. The central girder is the support rail for the telescopic tube power unit. The ramp atop the port track rail operates the trigger releasing the aircraft from the trolley. (FAST Collection: RAE8987*

Left: *The men forming the RAE research team are recognised as (left to right) A. Stratton, P.A. Cooke, G.W.H. Gardner (later to become Sir George Gardner and Director of RAE 1955-1959), G.J.R. Joyce, P. Salmon (Head of RAE Main Drawing Office), W. Andrews, J. Grosert (Manager of RAE Flight Workshops), R. King, C. Crowfoot (Manager of RAE Fitting Shop) and E. Cox. (FAST Collection: RAE8988)*

The Pioneer Days

96 miles at 1,500ft. The launch was good and it settled onto its pre-determined track but after a few minutes observers lost sight of LARYNX 3 as it entered haze. However signals received back from the aircraft, giving position and distance, confirmed that the aircraft had actually exceeded its target distance by 12 miles and that its speed had been calculated as 193mph (310km/hr). A search of the likely crash area failed to locate any sign of the aircraft and it was given up as lost. Three days later, however, a coastguard's boat, off St. Ives, picked up one wing still attached to a fractured spar.

Setting aside the lack of success so far, LARYNX did have in its favour the fact that it had achieved a very high performance for its time. The main factor in this was, of course, the engine, but equally important was the particularly low-drag cowling and the absence of any undercarriage.

Following the August 1927 trial the Pilotless Aircraft Committee turned its attention to extending the range of LARYNX up to 250 miles and exploring the possibilities of it releasing a bomb before its flight was terminated. To some extent this changed the role of LARYNX from an 'unmanned flying-bomb' to an 'unmanned bomber' and considerable debate centred on whether the bomb load should be carried internally or externally. In the end the decision was taken to house the bomb inside the aircraft and also to have it detonated on impact. For trials purposes, that had the added advantage of being able to pinpoint the location of the remains of the aircraft after the weapon had exploded. But the question of how to maintain safety and secrecy over a 250-mile flight meant that such a trial was virtually impracticable within the British Isles. The Pilotless Aircraft Committee was therefore led to consider testing LARYNX over desert territory, a factor that also allowed the proving of the weapon from a technical point of view. The decision to conduct long-range tests also had a bearing on the number of aircraft required which was estimated to involve two aircraft for preliminary short-range overland tests in Britain and six for tests over the full range.

In the meantime one further set of flight trials took place between Lyme Bay and Start Bay in September 1928. Two aircraft (a third was held back as a reserve) were taken to Portland and loaded aboard HMS *Thanet*. The first of the Autumn 1928 launches took place on 10 September. The aircraft launched satisfactorily and maintained its intended course until the flight terminated some 1½ miles from its objective. As was so often the case, despite a search of the sea area no sign of any wreckage was found. The second LARYNX was prepared for launch the following day, but during a pre-launch engine run-up the aircraft moved forward and slowly crashed off the launcher. It was not seriously damaged but was clearly unable to be flown. The trials were suspended and one decision taken in the light of the incident was to use a 'throw-away' trolley for all subsequent launches.

The 1928 flight trials had proven inconclusive but plans were now well advanced to test LARYNX under hot desert conditions. These were originally timed for April 1929 and to be conducted by the RAF, but later set back to August 1929. There is some evidence that some members of the P.A.C. argued that LARYNX still needed to be tested overland and over distances of between 50 and 200 miles before any desert trials could be considered.[20] However, they were overruled although, as a compromise, it was agreed to set aside a week (8-15 May 1929) to allow for a short series of overland flight trials to take place.

For the initial overland trial the RAE trials team set up camp at Blacknor Fort Battery, west of Portland where the Range was just 5 miles. On that occasion observers were aboard an airborne Supermarine Southampton flying-boat which loitered just offshore. The first launch took place on 14 May 1929 and it is possible that at least one other took place during the next day or so.[21]

Immediately after the Portland trials final preparations were made for shipping aircraft, weapons and other materials to Iraq. Interestingly, although LARYNX would perform its intended role as a "flying-bomb" with explosives in the (normally) empty payload section, the RAE technicians chose to forgo the radio-control feature and install gyroscopes instead.

Reflecting the continuing need for utmost secrecy, the launch and target sites could hardly have been at more remote spots. Chosen by the AOC Iraq, the launch site was at RAF Shaibah, the most westerly of several RAF out-stations around Basrah. The target was established out to the west, in the Mesopotamian Desert, at a point about six miles north-west of Sulman Fort, giving a range of about 200 miles whilst avoiding the local nomadic Iraqi tribesmen.

Five LARYNX aircraft were shipped out to Iraq and consigned to RAF Shaibah in two batches, the first consignment containing crated aircraft LARYNX 3 and 4 plus tooling and spares, a catapult, launch trolley as well as six phosphorus bombs and two high-explosive bombs. (The choice of phosphorus bombs was made so as to create a smoke cloud when the aircraft crashed and thereby assist in locating it). The shipment departed the UK on 20 June 1929 and arrived at Basrah a month later. The second shipment left the UK on 19 July and included the remaining three LARYNX 5, 6 and 7.[22]

The first of five live launches was scheduled for 31 August. Most of the preparations had been carried out throughout the previous day, including hoisting LARYNX 3 into position on the catapult. Since the catapult was outside the barbed-wire camp perimeter, a guard of RAF personnel remained close by throughout the night.[23]

At 7.30am the engine was run to maximum revs and then throttled down to allow the catapult cordite charge to be inserted. The RAF Officer charged with the pre-launch phase checked his navigational calculations and instrument settings, opened the throttle, closed the safety switch in the firing circuit and then pulled the starting pin for the air log. Unfortunately, in his anxiety to avoid running the engine at full throttle for longer than was necessary, he took hold of the air log lanyard with one hand and the safety switch with the other, but his hands were oily from the engine exhaust. When he moved both hands simultaneously, the hand

---

20 National Archives ADM116/2388
21 National Archives AIR5/444
22 The first batch of LARYNX was numbered individually, eg '1', '2', '3' etc. Identities for those aircraft built for the 1929 trials did not continue the sequence; instead the series reverted to '1' although for the latter series '-29' was added, eg '3-29', '4-29' etc.
23 National Archives AIR5/444

holding the lanyard slipped and the pin failed to come out but, believing everything to be all right, the Launch Controller duly closed the firing switch to launch LARYNX.

The ground crew realised instantly that LARYNX had launched with the air log inoperative and fully expected the aircraft to fly on until the fuel was exhausted. What was more worrying was that the safety pin in the bomb fuse could not be withdrawn during the flight as had been intended.

The initial launch of LARYNX had narrowly avoided disaster. The safety valve on the catapult had blown violently, bursting open the shield over the vent and thereby dropping the pressure to such an extent that, having intended to launch at 98mph, the actual launch speed was at least 15mph less. Nevertheless, it had taken off without any apparent lateral disturbance albeit only just above stalling speed and after several hundred yards it began to climb, entering a right turn as it did so, precisely according to plan.

Although from the launch site LARYNX was last seen gathering speed and heading off towards the target, it had been planned to monitor its progress by the OC 84 Squadron who was airborne in a Westland Walrus. He managed to keep LARYNX in sight for about twelve miles and at one time was flying level with it at 2,800ft.

Surprisingly, nobody quite knew the precise fuel consumption of LARYNX and whilst everybody fully expected LARYNX 3 to overshoot the target, the question remained as to by how much. The spotter aircraft was instructed to search up to 60 miles beyond the target but because the smoke bomb had been unable to detonate the actual crash had not been seen and the desert terrain made it difficult for a thorough search. After a while the search was called off and LARYNX 3 was declared lost.

The second trial launch took place two weeks later, on 13 September, and involved LARYNX 4. Like the first launch, the aircraft was 'live' with a phosphorus bomb on board. It launched without any lateral disturbance but failed to gain any height for the first 200 yards causing it to narrowly avoid rising ground. After a while the aircraft did start to gain height, enough for the airborne observers to keep it in view for about 15 miles and at its planned height of 3,000ft.

Twenty-five minutes after launch, a W/T message was received from observers at Jalibah reporting that the LARYNX had crashed nearby. The Jalibah party not only heard the aircraft approach but also saw a column of smoke from the aircraft's phosphorus bomb. An inspection of the wreckage revealed that LARYNX had apparently dived into the ground almost vertically. It had flown for exactly 60 miles but was about three miles south of the direct line to the target. Further inspection revealed that the engine had stopped before the crash.

When it came to launching the third LARYNX, on 17 September, technicians had by then realised that a higher launch speed was paramount. The cordite was re-calculated and at 9.20am LARYNX 5 was successfully launched. It rose instantly and climbed rapidly before turning, as planned, after 20 seconds and eventually levelling out at around 3,000ft. But on this occasion the en route observers aboard the Wapiti never caught sight of it, nor did the ground observers positioned near the target point at Sulman.

Disappointingly, a prolonged air search along the planned course line throughout the day revealed no sign of the LARYNX.

Throughout the next few days the small 84 Squadron Detachment continued to carry out an air search for the missing LARYNX, searching an area to a point about 100 miles from Shaibah. Then, on 20 September, wreckage was spotted in a remote area of the desert, just 27 miles from the launch point. When a ground team reached the site they were surprised to discover that the wreckage was not of LARYNX 5 but of LARYNX 3 that had been lost on 31 August. Three days after finding the wreckage of LARYNX 3 another airborne search party, whilst returning to base, discovered the wreck of LARYNX 5 lying in the desert about five miles beyond the crash site of LARYNX 3. Subsequent examination of LARYNX 5 revealed that the bomb had, in fact, exploded but more importantly there were clear signs that the engine oil had overheated, a factor that undoubtedly led to an engine seizure. The same symptoms were found in the recovered wrecked engines of LARYNX 3 and LARYNX 4.

Before any further LARYNX flights were attempted, RAF technicians sought to solve the overheating problem by creating additional air vents around the oil tank housing. It was also agreed that further flights would cruise at 8,000ft where the air temperature was at least 10° lower.[24]

1 October was set for the fourth trial launch, the aircraft selected being LARYNX 6. As it was intended to fly the aircraft at a much higher altitude the launcher pressure was increased slightly to give the aircraft a launch speed of around 105mph. However, when the charge was fired the safety valve blew with such violence that the launch pressure dropped and the aircraft left the catapult at a considerably lower speed than intended. LARYNX 6 lost height immediately and flew for barely more than 50 yards before hitting the ground. Thankfully, the bomb did not detonate, having not been made 'live' and after removing it the damaged aircraft was dismantled and packed for return to the UK.

After the abortive launch of LARYNX 6, there was some discussion about whether or not to launch the remaining aircraft. The fact that one flight had successfully delivered the bomb close to the target might have proved the concept to be sound but not sufficiently to declare an outstanding success. On the other hand, the engine overheating problem had apparently been solved but the mods had not tried and fully tested. Thus, and with some degree of haste, it was decided to launch LARYNX 7 around 10.45am on 3 October.

With the loss of LARYNX 6 in mind the launch speed was set back to 90mph. LARYNX 7 took off well and set course as planned. Observers aboard 84 Squadron's patrolling Wapiti picked it up and kept the unmanned aircraft in view for about 22 miles. They confirmed that it was successfully flying at 8,000ft but that was the last anybody saw of it; the ground observers at Sulman heard nothing and a second airborne observer at Sulman did not see it either. The trials team had little alternative but to return to England without finding it. In fact, LARYNX 7 was never found.

---

24 National Archives AIR5/536

RAE LARYNX
Individual Aircraft Histories

It is believed that a total of 12 LARYNX was built over a two-year period. All were identified by single number identities and the following details are based on available evidence. Exact details relating to co-locating identities to fates etc, however, remain unconfirmed.

No.1 (1927) First flown 20.7.27 from HMS *Stronghold*. Crashed into the Bristol Channel.

No.2 (1927) Believed first flown 1.9.27. Lost without trace; presumably crashed into the Bristol Channel.

No.3 (1927) First flown 15.10.27 and flew for 112 miles before ditching.

No.4 (1927) Believed first flown 10.9.28 from HMS *Thanet* and crashed in the English Channel between Lyme Bay and Start Bay.

No.5 (1927) Believed damaged 11.9.28 aboard HMS *Thanet*. Returned to Farnborough. Fate unknown.

No.1-29 Probably launched and lost over Blacknor Fort Range, Portland 14.5.29.

No.2-29 Possibly launched and lost over Blacknor Fort Range, Portland 14/15.5.29.

No.3-29 Despatched ex-UK by ship to Iraq 15.6.29. First flown 31.8.29 at Shaibah. Initially disappeared but found on 20.9.29 (during search for 5-29). Aircraft had crashed 32 miles from Shaibah, Iraq.

No.4-29 Despatched ex-UK by ship to Iraq 15.6.29. First flown 13.9.29 at Shaibah. Flew a distance of 60 miles before crashing 12 miles south-east of Jalibah, Iraq.

No.5-29 Despatched ex-UK by ship to Iraq 15.6.29. First flown 17.9.29 at Shaibah. Initially disappeared but found on 23.9.29. Flew a distance of 27 miles. Recovered and conveyed back to UK. Used for (ground-based) engine tests at Farnborough.

No.6-29 Despatched ex-UK by ship to Iraq 15.7.29. First flown 1.10.29 at Shaibah. Stalled and crashed shortly after launch due to failure of the catapult safety valve.

No.7-29 Despatched ex-UK by ship to Iraq 15.7.29. First flown 3.10.29 at Shaibah. Disappeared and never found.

RAE Larynx No 6-29 is seen lying in the Iraqi desert shortly after crashing due to a failure of the launch catapult safety valve on 1 October 1929. (Wal Anker)

The Iraq trials effectively marked the end of LARYNX. A development, fitted with a 'Serval' type of air-cooled engine and referred to as LARYNX II, was considered. Progress on the design reached a wind-tunnel testing phase in October 1929 with a 1/5th scale metal body. Tests were discontinued in February 1930 when it became clear that the projected re-design of the engine would have necessitated some radical changes to the body design.[25]

More than anything else, LARYNX provided ample evidence that the concept of a radio-controlled pilotless aeroplane was truly achievable. It had a top speed of around 200mph at sea level and a range of 200 miles but LARYNX was not, in fact, radio-controlled; it was operated by an automatic pilot. And what was clearly emerging towards the end of the 1920s was a dual requirement. Firstly a pilotless aircraft that could act as a real target for Army and Naval gunners and, secondly (with a bomb load of 250lb), a pilotless aerial torpedo that could be fired off to destroy enemy shipping.

Naval Gunnery Targets
Bomber versus Battleship

Setting aside the Admiralty's key role in the development of controlled unmanned flight, for many years there existed a raging 'bomber versus battleship' controversy that had divided defence chiefs of the day. Quite what sparked the controversy in the first instance does not appear to have been officially recorded but it may well have been influenced by the Admiralty who firmly believed that the Royal Navy was the senior service. Whatever the case, their Lordships did eventually manage to convince the Air Staff of the need to develop an aerial target that could realistically simulate a bombing or torpedo attack against its battleships. That decision, which the Naval and Air Staffs suspected would finally lead to settling the argument one way or the other, was finally taken in 1930 but it had taken almost eleven years to reach that conclusion.

The earliest recorded evidence for raising the need for a "W/T controlled aircraft" is contained within a memorandum dated 6 May 1919 and which originated from the Naval Anti-Aircraft Gunnery Committee. The note, in effect, was simply a request for unmanned aircraft to be used as targets for a series of experimental naval firings in the Portsmouth area, the Committee explained. No official

---
25 When the Iraq team returned to the UK, technicians at RAE Farnborough bench-tested a LARYNX engine to extreme temperatures to confirm that overheating of oil had been the major contributory factor. It was discovered that the oil would not overheat to such a degree to cause the engine to fail. The root problem was more likely to have been the formation of vapour locks in the fuel system.

record suggests that this request was ever responded to, which might well explain the fact that it was repeated just two months later. This time the Admiralty urged the Air Ministry to make enquiries in the USA where self-propelled target aircraft were known to exist. Again, whether or not the Air Ministry made any enquiries is unclear; certainly the Admiralty thought not and in May 1920 pressed the Air Ministry for a "great deal more positive action".

More than anything else it was the strict post-war financial constraints that precluded the purchase of American aircraft. The Air Ministry also countered that the US product referred to by the Admiralty was an 'aerial torpedo' and controlled by a gyroscope rather than a radio-controlled target aircraft. Any suggestion of 'buying American' therefore fell on deaf ears at the Air Ministry. But the Air Ministry did respond by strongly urging that a committee be set up under the Director of Research to develop the overall concept of radio-controlled aircraft.

The new Committee very soon agreed to explore several types: firstly, a gyro-controlled missile flying on a steady course at a constant speed for a given distance. Secondly, an aerial target, but one that was inherently stable and capable of radio control up to 20 miles and, finally, the Committee decided to pursue an aerial torpedo intended to be dropped from an aircraft under radio control and with a range of 10 miles. This project, it was argued, could be either powered or unpowered. Their Lordships at the Admiralty, in the meantime, began to express a lack of patience and rather than await the results of exploring small-scale unmanned aircraft began to consider the possibilities of using a real, full-size aeroplane as a representative target for gunnery training.

Traditional gunnery training for anti-aircraft purposes was carried out by two different methods. One was to tow a drogue behind a normal aircraft, the drogue being fixed to the end of a length of cable which might well extend to 1,000 feet in length. The second method was in "aiming off" whereby a manned aircraft was used for target practice but that gunners laid off a certain number of degrees instead of aiming directly at it.

Clearly both methods were equally unsuitable in assessing the capability of ships' gunners and in response to the continued demands from the Admiralty for a suitable target aircraft, as well as the recommendations from the Director of Research, the Air Ministry agreed to develop an unmanned aircraft specifically for naval gunnery practice. The basic principles of automatic pilot had already been tried and tested, both in Britain and the USA, but the use of wireless control of an automatic pilot was an untried variation, either on an aeroplane or even a land vehicle.

If the concept of launching an unmanned aircraft and controlling it at a certain altitude were not complex enough the very thought of adding altitude control posed even greater difficulties. The first aircraft designed around Air Ministry requirements was therefore adapted only to attain a fixed altitude and then to be manoeuvred back and forth along such pre-determined lines required by the gunners until the aircraft was either successfully shot down or its fuel was exhausted. But flying at a predetermined height – which for fear of losing a valuable aircraft in cloud was usually set at 5,000 feet – still provided conditions that, in many ways, were rather artificial. Similarly, the pilotless aircraft presented itself as a relatively easy target whereas a genuine bombing attack would likely be carried out by enemy aircraft flying at, say 15,000 feet. At that height the enemy would virtually be invisible to ships' gunners.

Development of pilotless aircraft might well have been halted at this stage had it not been for the awareness that a number of nations were known to be already developing torpedo-carrying aircraft, the very nature of which meant flying at low-altitude and attacking a ship on the beam. Until pilotless aircraft could be developed to fully re-enact a manned aircraft the question of whether ships' gunners could bring down a torpedo-carrying aircraft before dropping its weapon, would largely go unanswered. Aircraft carriers were also being developed between the wars and designed to carry a squadron of fighter/light-bomber aircraft. Again, it was difficult to determine whether or not anti-aircraft gunners could bring down high-speed aircraft either before or during a diving attack against the ship.[26]

RAE & the Fairey Queen

Having finally accepted the limitations of existing targets, pilotless or otherwise, the Air Staff's reaction was to propose the development of a "realistic, unmanned, powered target aeroplane" that would be "required to simulate torpedo, level and dive-bombing attacks as well as high-altitude bombing attacks". The first step was taken in October 1930 when the responsibility for the project – by now referred to as Project "Queen Bee" – was passed to the Royal Aircraft Establishment where, on 8 October, the Pilotless Aircraft Committee met. The main aspect of the Committee's meeting was to discuss the best means of meeting the Air Staff's requirements in developing a full-size aircraft plus a suitable catapult-launcher. What the Air Staff insisted upon was that the target should be capable of not only being launched from ships' catapults, but also, if it survived the ship's defensive gunfire, of safely landing on the sea afterwards.

RAE Farnborough's Physics & Instrument (P & I) Department had, for a number of years, experimented with pilotless aircraft – both powered and unpowered – but as Britain entered a period of financial recession, so work progressed at a relatively slow pace. However, Farnborough's scientists had developed a new autopilot and radio control system that allowed a move away from a specially-designed wireless-controlled aircraft – as was, for example, standard practice in the USA – to being able to modify an existing aircraft. When RAE designers within P & I Department (re-styled Instrument & Photographic (IAP) Department in 1930), came to select an existing design their first choice was the Fairey IIIF. Choosing the IIIF had two advantages; not only was the IIIF still in production but there was already a tried and tested floatplane variant suitably equipped for catapulting off a ship's deck.

Beneath a veil of strict secrecy three brand-new Fairey IIIF Mk.IIIBs were allocated to Farnborough for conversion to unmanned configuration. The first, S1490, was flown in from Fairey's Heath Row factory on 10 November 1930 to become the prototype for what was by now being referred to at Farnborough as the Fairey Queen – or more pedantically

---

26 National Archives AVIA6/2588

Three Fairey IIIFs were converted to "Queens" in 1931/32 to become the first true radio-controlled target aircraft. The first ship-launched pilotless test flight by a Fairey Queen took place in January 1932 when S1536 (pictured above on its catapult) was launched from HMS Valiant. The aircraft managed twenty-five seconds of flight before it struck the sea and was destroyed. (FAST Collection)

by some as the "Faërie Queen" *(sic)*. A second Fairey IIIF, S1497, was ferried from Martlesham Heath to Farnborough on 26 May 1931 whilst the last of the trio, S1536, flew in from Fairey's Hamble plant on 22 July 1931.[27]

Two further Fairey IIIF Mk.IIIs were loaned to Farnborough's IAP Department to allow a sequence of associated trials to take place. S1317 began a series of launches from the RAE catapult on 24 February 1931 before undertaking various radio transmission-receiver tests as well as wireless and instrument trials work. The other Fairey IIIF, Mk.IVB K1698, arrived at Farnborough from Henlow on 27 April 1931 although remaining unused until 12 June when IAP Flight used it for other radio trials and long-distance investigations.

Although it did involve some complex work, converting the standard Fairey IIIF into an unmanned Fairey Queen was a relatively straightforward affair. The original Pilot's Assister principles were embodied in a completely new set of automatic equipment that provided automatic stabilization in pitch and yaw, and the ability to perform fast and slow turns in either direction during climbing, level flight or in a dive. The same control enabled the aircraft to glide at any desired approach attitude and speed, and marked the occasion that designers were beginning to achieve what clearly was the first British fully manoeuvrable automatic pilot. One other modification was necessary; because no

aileron control was to be provided the three Fairey IIIFs had their wing dihedral increased by 10°, a change that gave the Fairey Queen a distinctly peculiar appearance.

Fitted with a standard wheeled undercarriage and equipped with the first set of W/T apparatus, the first of RAE's Fairey Queens to be completed was S1497. It was cleared for flight trials on 13 July 1931 although trials did not start until September 1931, all flights having a pilot and observer on board. Early flights were not without problems. Under automatic control, including wireless-controlled flights, the Fairey IIIF experienced some difficulty with the automatic pitch/yaw control after a catapult launch. There was another and potentially more difficult problem in assessing the most suitable landing approach speed and attitude – too fast or too slow and at a wrong angle of attack were factors that could cause a stall and crash. Some work was carried out on a standard float-equipped Fairey IIIF at the MAEE at Felixstowe where a system was devised and tested for managing the elevator control at the point of touchdown. The speed of the approach glide was set so that sudden application of full elevator would destroy all vertical velocity. The length of the trailing aerial was chosen to indicate the height required for this manoeuvre and when the aerial weight struck the sea, the 'full elevator' manoeuvre was automatically initiated. It was therefore only necessary to send one signal to glide and turn the aeroplane into wind; the rest was automatic.

The second Fairey Queen conversion, S1536, incorporated a number of modifications to alleviate some of the problems that had emerged in tests with S1497. The second Fairey Queen was also fitted with a four-bladed

---

[27] The identities of Farnborough's three Fairey Queen conversions have often been wrongly quoted. Two other Fairey IIIF identities have been variously quoted as S1532 and S1796 but these are believed to be incorrect.

propeller (in place of a standard two-bladed) and made its first flight at Farnborough on 6 November 1931.

As 1932 dawned, Fairey Queen S1536 was ferried to Gosport on 7 January, later moving on to Lee-on-Solent where it was fitted with floats and cine-camera recording apparatus before embarking aboard HMS *Valiant* for unmanned flight trials. Several manned flights were carried out before any unmanned trial was attempted, the first of which took place on 12 January when it was noted that immediately after engaging the automatic controls the aircraft began yawing and pitching. However, on that occasion a partial engine failure brought the flight to a premature conclusion. Some adjustments were made to the automatic control equipment and a second test flight was made on 13 January with a third on the following day. Further flights were carried out on 17th, 19th and 21st, each flight gradually resolving a newly-reported snag. On the last of these flights S1536 responded to 60 commands at up to six miles range, thus setting the scene for the first pilotless flight.

Bad weather prevented further flights for nine days. Then, on 30 January, *Valiant* took up a position some ten miles south-west off the Nab Tower and S1536 was launched later in the day to mark the first Fairey Queen unmanned flight. Unfortunately it did not go without incident; immediately after leaving the catapult the aircraft went out of control and crashed into the sea, having managed to achieve just eighteen seconds of pilotless flight. The cause of the crash was later traced to the adopted method of achieving longitudinal control through the elevator, which was by means of an accelerometer-monitored gyroscope.[28]

Back at Farnborough modifications were made to the remaining Fairey Queens before any further flight tests were attempted. S1497 was selected for the next trial and was flown from Farnborough to Gosport on 4 April 1932, later being transported to Lee-on-Solent for fitting of floats and a much-enlarged fin. This second Fairey Queen made its first (manned) flight in modified form on 12 April. The weather on that morning was quite appalling, conditions that affected the automatic controls to such an extent that no useful observations could be obtained. Later in the day, when the weather had improved, a second (manned) flight was achieved during which the aircraft showed signs of becoming unstable in automatic mode. This situation continued to dog test flights over the next few days although, after each flight, attempts to correct the snags were carried out. Eventually, on 19 April, it was decided to go ahead with a pilotless launch. S1497 was catapulted off *Valiant* and climbed to about 200ft when its starboard wing dropped and the aircraft dived almost vertically into the sea.

Recovery crews were quickly to the scene and managed to secure a tow rope to the severely-damaged aircraft and drag it back to *Valiant*. The wreck was later returned to Farnborough for examination after which the RAE decided that the cause of the accident was the inability of the automatic control system to hold on rudder which would have counter-acted the yaw that developed during the launch.[29]

After two embarrassing failures there was, quite understandably, some reticence towards attempting any further pilotless flights. Some consideration was given to having a pilot fly the aircraft to a safe height whereupon he would bale out and the aircraft would continue under radio control. The idea was not taken up and eventually the decision was taken to try a third launch and a fully pilotless flight.

Although S1497 was completely rebuilt, it was decided to turn to the third and final Fairey Queen conversion (S1490) for continued flight tests. During the course of its conversion to Queen status, S1490 had incorporated all of the various modifications raised during the earlier flight trials. It was also fitted with a specially-designed and much-enlarged all-moving rudder before making a successful initial flight at Farnborough on 9 August 1932. Just over a week later, on 18 August, it was flown to Gosport and then sent on to Lee-on-Solent by road where it was fitted with float undercarriage.

Several manned flights were carried out from Lee-on-Solent before HMS *Valiant* arrived at Spithead on 31 August. Several wireless control flights were also made in order to check out transmission range etc before S1490 was hoisted aboard *Valiant* in the afternoon of 9 September in preparation for its first pilotless flight. A long spell of bad weather caused frustrating delays and not until 14 September did conditions improve. Pilotless Fairey Queen S1490 was launched from *Valiant* just south-east of the Isle of Wight and, apart from the starboard wing dropping slightly and the aircraft yawing slightly to port, the flight went well. The flight was, on this occasion, fairly brief at only nine minutes as the objective was simply to test the launch and alighting phases in unmanned mode. S1490 landed about 800 yards from *Valiant* allowing a recovery crew to row out and tow the aircraft back without difficulty. Back aboard *Valiant* an inspection revealed some minor damage to the undercarriage struts and fittings. A second unmanned flight was therefore abandoned and S1490 was, instead, towed back to Lee-on-Solent and returned to RAE Farnborough.[30]

After a further brief period of trials with normal undercarriage fitted, S1490 was offered to the Admiralty for a series of live firing trials in the Mediterranean. S1490 was ferried from Farnborough to Gosport on 14 December 1932 and 14 days later embarked aboard HMS *Courageous* in Portsmouth docks. The carrier sailed for Gibraltar on 2 January where the Fairey Queen was offloaded and picketed out in the open to await the arrival of HMS *Valiant*. Although *Valiant* was not long in arriving a lengthy spell of bad weather prevented any live shoots until the end of the month. As soon as the weather cleared, two preliminary (manned) flights were carried out – the first on 24 January to confirm the rate of descent on the glide, whilst a second, on 30 January, provided a check that the automatic gear was functioning correctly in flight. A radio range test (between

---

28 S1536 made a number of manned flights from Lee-on-Solent between 12 January and 21 January 1932. The two pilots involved were Flt Lt Vincent and Flt Lt Ryde, with Mr G.W.H.Gardner on board each flight as observer. Some reports suggest that S1536 was first launched off HMS *Valiant* on 21 January 1932 and then crashed on its second launch nine days later. It is believed that the first unmanned flight took place on 30 January.

29 Fairey Queen S1497 carried out flights from Lee-on-Solent on 12 April, 13 April, 15 April and 17 April prior to its crash.
30 Fairey Queen S1490 carried out manned flights from Lee-on-Solent on 23 August, 24 August, 25 August, 26 August, 31 August and 9 September prior to its crash.

The third and final Fairey Queen was S1490, used for trials aboard HMS Valiant. *This view is thought to have been taken on 14 September 1932 when it sustained some damage to the undercarriage struts and fairings. (FAST Collection)*

the aircraft and HMS *Valiant* and HMS *Malaya*) also confirmed the wireless equipment to be working satisfactorily. Later in the day the Queen was flown under wireless control to 10,000ft and successfully maintained level flight for about an hour. Before the day was out the aircraft embarked aboard *Valiant* for a gunnery and torpedo exercise in Tetuan Bay, planned for the next day.

The sea was rough on the morning in question and with a fresh wind blowing across the course some doubt was expressed as to whether the Fairey Queen would be able to land safely. That, argued the Commander-in-Chief, was "totally immaterial" as the aircraft was "unlikely to survive the guns of the Home Fleet" anyway. The exercise was therefore allowed to proceed.

S1490 flew for one-and-a-half hours and, despite a heavy barrage – said to have involved as many as 420 shells – from the Fleet's big guns, including those of the battleships HMS *Nelson* and *Rodney*, it managed to escape totally unscathed. The aircraft landed safely and was later retrieved by *Valiant*. In what might have been seen as a demonstration of pure spite, the two-hour exercise certainly underlined the Navy's need to improve its ship-to-air gunnery capability – it also underlined the value of a pilotless target aircraft.

During February 1933 S1490 carried out more unmanned flights as a target, again for *Nelson* and *Rodney*. Just as before, both ships fired off their massive 4.7-inch guns whilst *Warspite* and *Malaya* opened up with 4-inch guns, but yet again S1490 survived. Quite what was now being said about the usefulness of an unmanned target aircraft or – and for that matter perhaps more importantly – the accuracy of ships' gunners remains unrecorded.

It is believed that with the end of the Gibraltar exercise the Fairey Queen was shipped back aboard HMS *Courageous* to Portsmouth where it was offloaded on 25 March, conveyed to Lee-on-Solent and restored to standard land undercarriage configuration. However S1490's stay in the UK was brief. It was chalked for more gunnery trials off Malta and allocated to HMS *Eagle* on 14 April for a two-month detachment.

The anti-aircraft trials took place to the east of Malta during May 1933 once S1490 had been transferred to HMS *London*. On the first day of the trials the weather clamped in badly but had cleared sufficiently for flight the next day. Catapulted off *London*, the aircraft attained 8,600ft in 45 minutes but the rate of climb was poor and the planned altitude of 10,000 feet was abandoned and the aircraft was kept at 8,600 feet. The guns of HMS *Sussex* fired 58 rounds of 4-inch calibre HE during the Fairey Queen's first run of around 3½ minutes. Most of the shell bursts were short of the target. A second run was made at the same height and at a range of five miles. *Sussex* again opened fire and after the 19th shot S1490 began a slow right-hand flat spin, eventually hitting the sea. The flight had lasted 55 minutes and after hitting the sea the aircraft sank after just three minutes.[31]

---

31 Some sources state that S1490 was shot down, not by HMS *Sussex*, but by HMS *Shropshire*

16   Sitting Ducks and Peeping Toms

A very fine air-to-air study of K8640/'66' flying in pilotless mode. Queen Bees operated with either floats or normal wheeled undercarriage. Some reports suggest that a normal undercarriage variant was referred to as a Queen Bee Mk.1 whilst the float-equipped was a Mk.2. However no official reference of this has been found. (Charles E. Brown)

Chapter 2

Queen Bee

OF ALL THE AERIAL TARGETS produced in the United Kingdom, probably the most widely-known is the de Havilland Queen Bee, viewed upon by many as simply an unmanned version of the Tiger Moth. There has to be some sympathy towards such a comparison but in fact the Queen Bee was, by many standards, quite a different aeroplane to its ubiquitous cousin.

Drawing on experience gained by the Fairey Queens, the Pilotless Aircraft Committee formally agreed to evaluate an unmanned version of the Tiger Moth at a meeting on 21 December 1932. It was not a spur-of-the-moment decision; the Committee had already approached de Havilland's Resident Technical Officer for details of a seaplane variant, not just of the Tiger Moth but also of the DH.60 Gipsy Moth. What the Committee proposed was to have a Tiger Moth suitably configured, and strengthened, for launching off a catapult at 65mph and into a cross-wind of up to 10mph. A further proposal was to have the aircraft built with a wooden fuselage which, apart from making it lighter, cheaper and possibly even stronger, would increase its chances of survival should it come down in the sea. The planners faced a dichotomy; a wooden structure directed the Committee towards the Gipsy Moth but the Tiger Moth's wings were far stronger and more likely to take the strains of pilotless operations. The final result was therefore something of a compromise, fusing a standard DH.60 fuselage with DH.82A wings. What emerged was designated the DH.82 Queen Bee.[1]

So despite sharing the same designation as the ubiquitous Tiger Moth, the DH.82 Queen Bee was more accurately the ultimate variation of the DH.60 So much so that when production of Moth Majors ended at Hatfield in 1935 all of the incomplete fuselages were diverted to a new Queen Bee production line and fitted with Tiger Moth wings, tail

---

1 Queen Bee has frequently been referred to as the DH.82B but this reference (in connection with the Queen Bee) is erroneous and that this designation was applied to a 'one-off' development of the DH.82A Tiger Moth that sought to rectify various criticisms of the DH.82 and DH.82A. An original de Havilland report (dated June 1939) covers preliminary stressing for a development prototype of the Tiger Moth. A later report (dated August 1939) reveals that the DH.82B had a wider fuselage (by 3–4 inches), a wider track (6–8 inches) with Hornet Moth-type gear, brakes and tailwheel; also increased engine power (Gipsy Major III), a larger fin, revised rudder, trim control by elevator trim tabs and a larger fuel tank. An AID weight report, dated 30 September 1939, is known to exist and this would coincide perfectly with the first flight of the "New Tiger Moth" (under Class B conditions, E-11) on 1 October 1939. It is virtually certain therefore that the designation DH.82B solely applies to aircraft E-11, c/n 1989. Queen Bee, on the other hand, is constantly referred to simply as a 'DH.82 Queen Bee' in official de Havilland records.

surfaces, engine mountings and undercarriage parts.[2] In fairness, to describe Queen Bee as a marriage of Moth Major and Tiger Moth is altogether too simplistic. There were other differences, many being quite major modifications that were standard only to the production Queen Bee. They involved a much strengthened fuselage to withstand the strain of catapult launches; the entire rear fuselage was reinforced to protect the integrity of the tail unit. Flying controls and instruments were fitted to the front cockpit only although the mixture control was deleted, as was the trimmer control. The rear cockpit, into which was fitted the radio receiver and automatic controls, was covered by removable fairings. A shelf was fitted behind the front instrument panel carrying two accumulators for the radio and auto-controls whilst the relay equipment was installed in the luggage compartment. Other changes involved replacing the original 19-gallon fuel tank with one having a capacity of 24 gallons. No fuel gauge was fitted to the Queen Bee and the top of the fuel tank was protected against accidental damage during slinging operations by a plywood covering. An 'Eclipse' hand-starting gear was installed on the starboard side of the engine and operated through a throw-out clutch. Often mistaken for a generator was a windmill-driven air compressor fitted neatly into the port wing bay and, finally, to aid recovery operations at sea, Queen Bee was fitted with built-in handling lines, slinging and salvage gear.[3]

It was, of course, standard practice that at some early stage a clear and defined Specification was raised by the Air Ministry. In fact the first Specification associated with Queen Bee was Spec. 18/33 which called for a design adaptation of the de Havilland Moth.[4] Whether in response to this, or to proposals by the Pilotless Aircraft Committee is unclear, but Farnborough had briefly evaluated one of 'E' Flight/RAE's DH.60M Moth 'hacks' (K1876) in early January 1933 in a target role.[5]

A Contract Letter for one Queen Bee prototype (Contract 232902/33C/C.4b) was issued on 8 February 1933, followed by an Instruction To Proceed, received at Hatfield on 23 March. This accounted for prototype K3584 (c/n 5027) which is believed to have made its initial flight during the following month although it had none of the (then) highly secret auto controls and radio equipment fitted. This first flight was therefore a manned flight with a test pilot aboard.[6]

The wireless control system for Queen Bee was designed and developed at RAE Farnborough. The airborne R1088A receiver was a simple four-valve set and fitted well into the Queen Bee cockpit. On the other hand, the ground base station, a mobile M11 unit, stood almost six feet high and weighed 1,500lb. The transmission frequency range used was within the 160-180Kcs (Long Wave) which required an aerial some 250ft high.

The M11 unit was operated by a nine push-button process, each button initiating a single command: left turn, right turn, straight ahead, climb, level flight, glide, dive, navigation lights on and navigation lights off. The autopilot was set at standard rates for each manoeuvre, e.g. rate one turns, climb at 400 feet-per-minute and to limit normal operating height to 9,000ft.

Although the Admiralty was the prime driver in Queen Bee development it was agreed jointly by the Admiralty and the Air Ministry to set up an evaluation unit at Farnborough. Officially formed on 1 April 1934, it was given the title 'The Gunnery Co-operation Flight', and whilst in some circles seen as an Admiralty-controlled Flight it was, in fact, under the control of the RAE and as if to underline its collaborative nature the Flight consisted of personnel drawn from both Services, as follows:[7]

Commanding Officer Flight:	1 Lt Cdr, Signals RN
Officer i/c Flying	1 Flt Lt, RAF
Second Pilot	1 Flying Officer, RN
Engineering Officer	1 Flt Lt (E) RAF
i/c Wireless Queen Bee	1 commissioned telegraphist, RN 1 Petty Officer telegraphist, RN
i/c Automatic controls	1 Sergeant, RAF 1 LAC Instrument Maker, RAF
Maintenance Staff	1 Flt Sgt, Ships Group 1 Aircraft fitter 1 Aircraft rigger

It had always been the intention that, once initial trials had been completed, four early-production Queen Bees would be despatched to Malta for the Mediterranean Fleet with four to be retained in the UK for the Home Fleet. These aircraft were to be taken from the first two orders (Contracts 262684/33 and 295738/33) which involved twelve aircraft. The remaining four Queen Bees were to be held in reserve although two, K3597 and K3598, were earmarked for shipboard trials. The two Queen Bees in question, coded '2' and '3' respectively, were flown from Farnborough to Roborough on 12 January 1934 where they were dismantled,

---

2   According to de Havilland's Production Record book, aircraft allocated c/ns 5000-5049 were originally intended to be built as Mk.III Gipsy Moth; c/ns 5050-5200 were originally allocated to production of Moth Major.

3   *The Tiger Moth Story* by Alan Bramson and Neville Birch (Air Review Ltd 1964)

4   Several Specifications were issued during the Queen Bee development phase. Spec 35/34 was designed to meet the requirements laid out in Spec 18/33 and against which two Contracts (370807/34 and 388676/35) were raised whilst Air Ministry Specification 20/35 covered the full-scale production of Queen Bee.

5   'E' Flight, RAE received two DH.60M Moths on 28 January 1931 when K1876 and K1877 were flown in from Stag Lane for use as 'hacks' although both were occasionally used for various trials. One other aircraft may have been involved: Janic Geelan, in his book *Moths, Majors and Minors* (NZ Aviation Press) states that a standard DH.60 Moth Major was delivered to Farnborough so that testing could begin before 13 January 1933. However, Geelan does not identify the aircraft involved.

6   Most published works offer 5 January 1935 as the date that the Queen Bee prototype made its first flight. However, as the Individual Aircraft Histories show, by then at least 13 Queen Bees had been built and delivered. The date, although widely quoted, must be incorrect and is thought to be a much-perpetrated mis-type of 1933.

7   National Archives AIR2/1346/62A; Minutes of the 34th Meeting of the Pilotless Aircraft Co-Ordination Committee.

18   Sitting Ducks and Peeping Toms

K4229/'10' was delivered to RAE Farnborough 30 May 1934 and remained on RAE charge for almost three years. Taken on 14 January 1935, this view clearly shows the wind-driven compressor attached by an arm to the port side of the fuselage and which took full advantage of the propeller slipstream. (FAST Collection)

conveyed to Mount Batten, fitted with floats and prepared for embarkation aboard HMS *Orion*.[8]

Orion sailed several days later and after making several wireless check flights K3597/'2' was flown out and hoisted aboard on 26 January; three days later it was launched by catapult. Conditions for launching Queen Bee from a ship's catapult had been well thought out beforehand whereupon it was agreed that there should be no wind down the catapult and, more importantly, no crosswind at the point of actual launch. However, there was on this occasion a fairly strong wind blowing and in a move to counteract that, the ship was steered directly downwind at a speed equal to that of the wind. Deckhands kept an eye on the ship's funnel smoke until it was seen to rise vertically at which point the order to launch was given.

K3597 was catapulted off without problem and after 35 seconds the first signal to maintain a climb was transmitted. At first the Queen Bee failed to respond but then did so on the second attempt and steadily gained height, entering cloud at about 2,000ft. A number of further commands were transmitted and the aircraft responded to each. Then, with the aircraft about a mile away and flying across the ship's stern, it stopped responding to transmissions. The Queen Bee's emergency landing device automatically cut in and the aircraft entered a slow left turn and landing glide. K3597 landed downwind but in a heavy swell; it bounced badly twice causing the undercarriage struts to collapse but it came to a stop resting on its floats and the right way up. Two factors then handicapped its retrieval, one being the sea condition but more importantly the fact that the ship's crew members were complete novices at handling aircraft in a salvage operation. The result was that K3597 sustained irreparable damage in the process of getting it back on board.

While investigations into the failure of the wireless gear got under way, HMS *Orion* sailed for Portland where a second series of test flights were planned. With a Short Southampton as escort, Queen Bee K3598/'3' was flown to Portland on 31 January and over the next few days carried out several flights to try and replicate the earlier difficulties. Unlike its unfortunate sister aircraft, K3598 behaved quite normally and a number of valuable lessons were learnt from the experience. On 6 February K3598 was restored to landplane configuration, transported by road to Chickerell aerodrome, erected and flown back to Farnborough two days later.

Whether or not the January 1934 series of trials marked the first occasion that a Queen Bee was flown remotely and unmanned is unclear. The first pilotless flight certainly took place in the English Channel and off HMS *Orion*. George W.H. Gardner who, at the time, was a member of Farnborough's Physics & Instruments Department, later described the event as follows:

"The aeroplane was successfully launched from the ship's catapult and various manoeuvres were satisfactorily executed until, when the aircraft was flying at low height in a slow right turn and gradually losing height, it was found impossible to get any response to further signals. The aircraft continued to fly in a wide circle and at one critical point appeared to be about to crash into the bridge of the ship. The

---

8 National Archives AIR2/1346/80A; "Queen Bee Trials with HMS *Orion*".

Chief of Air Staff and many other senior officials were on the bridge and tension built up rapidly. The Control Officer continued to press buttons, most of the Naval officers who were in familiar surroundings ran for cover, an RAE official laughed hysterically, while the Chief of Air Staff stood his ground but slowly turned up the collar of his greatcoat. The tension relaxed when the aeroplane just missed the ship and eventually crashed into the sea a short distance away. Tape records of the transmission showed that when the trouble began, the ship's transmitter had started to send a continuous signal and continued to do so until the end. This was subsequently found to be due to a key which had become stuck in the main transmitter circuit."[9]

Apart from one or two relatively minor incidents the Queen Bee trials, conducted mainly by RAE Farnborough, passed without serious incident and eventually the Air Ministry displayed sufficient confidence in Queen Bee to stage a demonstration to the national and aeronautical Press. The event, which took place at Farnborough on 26 June 1935, was completely successful, the remote control system working perfectly. K4227, the seventh production Queen Bee, performed a perfect take-off and a safe landing.

For the Farnborough press demonstration, K4227 had operated with a wheeled undercarriage but most of the early examples were float-equipped and allocated as gunnery targets for the Royal Navy. Queen Bees were launched from a catapult and one of the pre-flight actions was to spin up the controlling gyroscope using an external supply of compressed air. With all controls centralized the aircraft was then launched. Once airborne a winch box ran out a trailing aerial to enable contact with the M11 operator. The on-board compressor, by then, was producing sufficient airflow to operate the gyroscope. However, the operator had to keep the Queen Bee within his sight as there was no other indication of knowing where the aircraft was or what it was doing.

In the event of a naval operator losing sight of his aircraft or a close shell-burst disrupting the wireless contact, Queen Bee had an in-built safety feature which was immediately triggered. Having received no new instructions for some time, the remote control would close the throttle and initiate a left-hand descending turn followed by the "glide" sequence. It was then left to chance that the aircraft would survive what should have been a gentle landing on a calm sea.

Much of the development of Queen Bee was conducted, in the first instance, by RAE Farnborough civilian staff assisted by RAF service pilots. During the course of development a handful of service Engineering and Signals officers (and other ranks) were attached to the Queen Bee development team. These, together with the pilots, formed the nucleus of the first pilotless aircraft unit which, when development was complete, broke away from the RAE. The role of the new unit was to assemble and test-fly Queen Bees and to initially operate them for gunnery exercises.[10]

In November 1935 the decision was taken to equip three Queen Bee flights early in the following year. No 1 Gunnery Co-operation Flight would be based at Lee-on-Solent to operate with the Fleet Air Arm; another Flight would be based in Malta and the third at Biggin Hill for deployment to Watchet. The central point of the Queen Bee operation was to be the Base and Training Unit which would begin to move to Henlow on 1 October 1936 to come under No.1 (GES) Wing.

Delivery of true production Queen Bees got under way at the end of 1936, all of the early aircraft being ferried to the Base Training Unit at Henlow where pre-service modification work was carried out. By 10 May 1937 sufficient numbers were available to form Queen Bee Flight as part of HQ Training Command. A handful of aircraft were later transferred to Watchet on 26 July 1937 and flying commenced the following day. These Queen Bees were fitted with floats and launched by catapult out over the sea. The first such launch at Watchet took place on 3 August, involving K8661, and although some minor damage was sustained during the subsequent landing, the seaplane tender *Radstock* managed to retrieve the aircraft and return it to Watchet harbour.

The distinction of becoming the first gunnery unit to fire live ammunition against a Queen Bee fell to the men of the 170th Battalion, 61st Finsbury Rifles, Anti-Aircraft Brigade, RA. The event occurred on 6 August 1937 when 1 AACU's K8642 was catapulted from Watchet. The 61st Finsbury Rifles had yet to master the art of actually shooting an aircraft down and K8642 survived to fly another day.

In the meantime the Henlow-based Base & Training Unit, the hub of Queen Bee support operations, was re styled as the Pilotless Aircraft Section in January 1937. The unit later became part of 43 Maintenance Unit and held the responsibility for storing, servicing and preparing aircraft for service issue. Eventually, the P.A.S. was re-titled Pilotless Aircraft Unit and moved to St. Athan, Glamorgan.

Although much of Queen Bee's work was to provide a target for the Army, there was an equally key role in providing the same service for the Royal Navy. To meet that requirement the carrier HMS *Argus* was refitted at Portsmouth, during the Autumn of 1938, as a depot ship for Queen Bee operations and fitted with a launch catapult. (When *Argus* was re-commissioned, on 28 May 1938, it became the first ship to be commissioned on the new Fleet Air Arm basis and was allocated to work with both the Home Fleet and the Mediterranean Fleet.)

It was always intended that the Fleet Air Arm's Fleet Requirements Unit (as it then was) and the RAF's 2 Anti-Aircraft Co-operation Unit would both use *Argus* as a parent ship. In the event, the FRU never received any Queen Bees; 2 AACU did receive them but they remained land-based at Lee-on-Solent, until 5 May 1939, when they transferred to Gosport and later to Roborough.

The temporary deployments of Queen Bees aboard *Argus* did raise an interesting scenario inasmuch that there was never any RAF Headquarters unit as such allocated to *Argus* and there were very few RAF officers on board. There was, however, a complement of RAF fitters and riggers simply because the Navy had no skilled ratings available. As a result, while the Queen Bee was normally operated by an RAF unit, when operating from *Argus* they came under the control of a naval Officer, Lt Cdr R.A. Peyton.

---

9 Alan Bramson and Neville Birch, *The Tiger Moth Story*.
10 National Archives AVIA54/526

Incident at the Jubilee Review

One of the most impressive of Royal Navy Fleet Reviews was held in the Spithead on 16 July 1935 to mark the Jubilee of King George V and Queen Mary. Their Majesties reviewed the Fleet from the Royal Yacht *Victoria and Albert* which sailed through the Fleet during the early afternoon an hour or so ahead of a massed flypast of FAA aircraft. The evening produced an impressive firework display, followed by a succession of searchlight displays that lasted until midnight.

At 0615, on the following morning, several ships started the movement of the Fleet out to sea for exercises and at 0800 HMY *Victoria and Albert* led the 1st and 2nd Battle Squadrons out of Spithead to the guarded area to the south-east of the Isle of Wight.

At some point within the 'red flagged' area the light cruiser HMS *Achilles* (the only ship of the 2nd Cruiser Squadron that could carry two seaplanes) launched one of its two Queen Bees for a live firepower demonstration. Reports state that it inadvertently dived into the sea immediately after leaving the ship's catapult.

A second Queen Bee was launched from *Achilles*. The aircraft appeared to perform satisfactorily and was later targeted by the three 4.7-inch guns of HMS *Rodney*. The *Daily Telegraph*'s naval reporter described the event thus: "*Tongues of flame pierced the dun-coloured clouds of cordite smoke, and the sky was filled with balls of black cotton-wool, clustered thickly about the target. For a time it seemed as if the Queen Bee bore a charmed life. Again and again shells appeared to burst right in her path, but she flew on unconcernedly. Suddenly a ball of smoke developed just below her, and I saw a large fragment break off from the lower wing. Bravely the wounded machine attempted to climb above this terrible barrage, but it was too late. She began to circle, suddenly checked, side-slipped badly, and then shot down into a nose-dive. She crashed into the water, and by the time a destroyer had raced to the scene not a vestige of wreckage remained afloat.*"

Such rich journalese was later challenged by the weekly *Aeroplane* whose eye-witness saw the incident quite differently. "*The second Queen Bee which had been launched successfully was kept flying about for some considerable time. Control was handed over to a Naval Officer who had not had so much experience in handling these flying targets as some of the Farnborough experts have had. There was no question at all that the 4.7-inch anti-aircraft guns of HMS* Rodney *did eventually hit the Queen Bee and remove a portion of the starboard lower wing. But the Queen Bee still remained in the air and flying strongly.*

The clouds were quite low and the machine was only at about 600 feet. The officer in charge of the controls therefore took it back to the end of the run and began to turn it round in readiness for another shoot. As a result of the damaged wing, it lost considerable height on the turn, but was just picking up when it hit the water. According to informed opinion this might not have happened had one of the specialists in Queen Bees been playing with the buttons …"

So it would appear that this extraordinary demonstration of firepower, laid on especially for the benefit of Their Majesties, involved the complete loss of, not two, but only one Queen Bee – the first aircraft which nobody doubted had crashed immediately after launch due to, it is believed, a faulty engine. In fact, official records do support the *Aeroplane's* report by recording Queen Bee K4227 as being lost on 17 July 1935. No other Queen Bee is reported to have been lost on that date and so presumably the damaged aircraft was retrieved and subsequently repaired.

(From contemporary reports in the *Daily Telegraph* and *Aeroplane*, issue 31 July 1935.)

Two Queen Bee Flights ('Z' and 'Y') were formed within 1 Anti-Aircraft Co-operation Unit during April 1938. Three more Queen Bee Flights ('X', 'W' and 'V') were formed in May 1939 and dispersed around the country in time for the Summer Artillery Practice Camps.

One of the new Flights marked its arrival at Burrowhead, Wigtownshire on 10 May 1939 when a ten-vehicle convoy completed a two-day journey from Biggin Hill. This was 'W' Flight, 1 AACU, deployed to Scotland to lodge with No.2 Heavy Aircraft Practice Camp (2 HAAPC).

'W' Flight's first live Queen Bee 'shoot' took place on 7 June 1939 with a Queen Bee operating out of Burrowhead. These aircraft were float-configured, launched by catapult and at the end of each sortie were landed in the Solway Firth where they were met and made secure by an RAF launch based in Isle of Whithorn harbour. A small steam coaster, the *Crescent*, which had been leased by the RAF, was deployed to pick up the Queen Bee and tow it to the Isle of Whithorn where it was then hoisted on to the pier.

Getting the aircraft back to base was a time-consuming operation. Fitters and riggers removed the wings and floats which were stowed aboard a 3-ton truck. The floats were then replaced by a standard wheeled undercarriage and with the tail skid secured to the rear of the truck the Queen Bee was towed on its own wheels along public roads back to Burrowhead. On its arrival the whole process was reversed; wings were refitted, undercarriage removed and floats reinstated before the Queen Bee could be lifted on to the catapult and made ready for the next launch.[11]

The original intention had been to deploy 'W' Flight to Burrowhead temporarily until permanent facilities were completed at Kidsdale, two miles to the north-west and that the Flight would only be deployed to the area until the end of the Royal Artillery Territorial camp season in September 1939. Permanent buildings at Kidsdale were expected to be completed by May 1940 in time for the 1940 Summer Camp season, but the outbreak of war in September 1939 changed all of that and instead 'W' Flight remained in situ until 1 December when Flight

---
11 *The RAF in Galloway*, by A.T.Murchie (G.C.Book Publishers Ltd, 1992 ISBN 1 8723540 40 2)

HQ, stores and personnel moved into still-incomplete buildings at Kidsdale.

Flights continued to be launched from Burrowhead until May 1940 by which time a system for operating Queen Bee off a grass airstrip had been fully approved, thus allowing all future radio-controlled sorties to be from the Kidsdale grass airfield.

Other UK-based Queen Bee Flights also converted to aircraft with standard wheel undercarriage. At Cleave, the change was especially welcomed by 'V' Flight, 1 AACU. At the end of each fortnight's training, the Territorial Army gunners were, if weather allowed, given the opportunity to shoot live at a Queen Bee. On most occasions the aircraft managed to escape relatively unscathed and was later landed on the sea, close to a lighter, whose crew's role was to recover it and, in theory, bring it back to Padstow or Appledore docks for the road journey back to Cleave. In practice, and with a sea swell ever present off the Cornish coast, the aircraft invariably tipped on to its nose and sank. At best, the engine was salvaged, given anti-corrosion treatment and repaired.

Having aircraft with a standard undercarriage brought another benefit. The changeover allowed 'V' Flight to undertake a manned flight to accurately determine cloudbase height, together with wind speed and direction at the planned flight level, factors that were vital to the ground controller. Prior to any pilotless sortie, the weather flight was normally undertaken by the Flight's Commander, F/Lt Minifie although on a number of occasions a tug pilot was co-opted from 'G' Flight.

Preparing a Queen Bee for take-off from a grass airfield initially involved tethering it to a secure point before the engine was fully run up. The tether was then severed to allow a controlled take-off. Bringing Queen Bee back to base was not without its complications although the principle was generally similar to landing on water. The operator, using a tripod-mounted sight, would bring the aircraft to land visually. Allowing for wind, the aircraft could be accurately positioned on approach at the correct landing speed. When the "glide" command was transmitted the throttle closed and the aircraft descended until at about 20 feet, at which point the bob weight on the 25ft trailing aerial made contact with the ground. That signalled the ignition to shut off automatically (usually at about 10ft from the ground), the gyro was caged and the 'up elevator' was set in two distinct movements.[12]

In May 1942 the Pilotless Aircraft Unit moved a short distance along the Welsh coast, from St. Athan to Manorbier, to become the Central Depot for Queen Bee storage, routine maintenance and issue of aircraft to AACU Flights. But Queen Bee production had effectively ceased during the Spring of 1941 and Manorbier's stock of Queen Bees was beginning to dwindle fast to such an extent that operating units were facing a dire shortage of airworthy aircraft.

By July 1942 the question of resuming Queen Bee production had become increasingly urgent but it came at a time when de Havilland's Hatfield plant was fully committed, raising the likelihood of sub-contracting. Some consideration was given to transferring production to Morris Motors Ltd at their Cowley plant especially in the light of a contract for 50 aircraft thought to have been part of a 'reverse' Lend-Lease arrangement having been placed with this sub-contractor. But in the event, the US order was cancelled and de Havilland chose instead to sub-contract Queen Bee production to Scottish Aviation Ltd (SAL). The Prestwick-based company was awarded a contract (Acft/2398/C.20(b)) on 18 August 1942 involving 150 aircraft but these too were sub-contracted to a Glasgow furniture manufacturers, Messrs Morris and The West of Scotland Furniture Company. Building and assembly took place in the old SMT facility at 39, West Campbell Street, Glasgow.[13]

To enable jigs etc to be constructed, one Queen Bee (V4772) was loaned to SAL, from 21 October 1942, to act as a pattern aircraft. Production eventually began at Glasgow around 1 February 1943 and completed aircraft were conveyed by road to Prestwick for flight-testing and delivery, mostly to 19 MU at St. Athan.

In the meantime some doubt was being expressed over the viability of operating Queen Bee aircraft as aerial targets. Not long after deliveries of Scottish Aviation-built examples got under way, the Ministry of Aircraft Production reviewed the situation and as a result cut the existing Queen Bee programme back. The Ministry cancelled the final 90 SAL Queen Bees and deferred acceptance dates on those aircraft that remained contracted.

The shortage of Queen Bees had an effect at 1 AACU whose operations were progressively run down during 1942; 'W' Flight and 'T' Flight were disbanded in April 1942, followed by 'Y' Flight in August and 'U' Flight in October 1942. The remaining Flights ('V', 'X' and 'Z') were re-titled 1618, 1621 and 1620 Flights respectively but all three of these Flights were later disbanded in December 1943. 1618 Flight was absorbed into 639 Squadron whilst 1620 and 1621 Flights were absorbed by 595 Squadron.

The decision to cut back on production had been taken in the face of only a handful of Queen Bees being still operational at the turn of 1943 and most of those were either shot down or damaged beyond repair within a few months – V4788 on 23 January, P5770 (1621 Flt) on 2 February, P4761 (1618 Flt) on 7 February, P4805 (1AACU) on 18 February, P4700 (PAU) on 5 March, P4680 (1618 Flt) on 4 April and P5737 (1618 Flt) on 6 August 1943. RAF Mediterranean Command reported, on 31 March, the loss of L7721, L7761, P4708, P4715, P4748, P4753 and P4760 although these were probably written-off some considerable time beforehand. One of the Malta-based

---

12 The bob-weighted trailing aerial had a marked effect on Sqdn Ldr Pearce, the first Commanding Officer of RAF Cleave. Before the war he had been involved in early Queen Bee trials with the Pilotless Aircraft Section at Henlow. It was at Henlow where Pearce discovered that the trailing aerial had an unnerving habit of springing back towards the aircraft after contact with the ground. To avoid being "lashed about the back of the head" Pearce insisted on always wearing an appropriate tin helmet when test-flying Queen Bees. It was, by most accounts, quite a bizarre sight.

13 There has been much speculation over activities at 39, West Campbell Street. According to contemporary Post Office Business Directories for the period the premises were owned by the S.M.T. Co (Scottish Motor Traction). It may well be therefore that the warehouse was formerly used as a coachwork repair or manufacturing shop. Other reports simply suggest that the Queen Bees were assembled in a former Glasgow bus garage.

Queen Bees was said to have been the subject of curious incident that occurred on 23 June 1940. F/Lt William 'Timber' Woods was returning to base aboard his Gladiator N5531 'Hope' after encountering a formation of Italian Air Force MC.200 fighters escorting a wave of bombers. Woods is said to have collided with a Queen Bee as he prepared to land after the skirmish. If the report is accurate then that might explain the fate of L7759.

Another Malta-based Queen Bee, P4709, was used as a communications 'hack' at Hal Far for several years whilst back in the UK several others (including K8654, P4685, P4788 and V4750) soldiered on with the Pilotless Aircraft Unit for some time along with some of the LF-serialled Scottish Aviation-built examples. In what seems to have been an unprecedented move – presumably aimed at alleviating the shortage of serviceable aircraft – 16 standard RAF Tiger Moths were allocated to Manorbier for conversion to Queen Bee configuration although strictly speaking these differed considerably from the production Queen Bee. In the event only nine (N6648, N6722, N9161, R5106, R5147, T6104, T6863, T6867 and T7239) were converted. Paradoxically, two Queen Bees (P4709 and P4760) were converted to 'Tiger Moth' configuration at the Royal Naval Aircraft Repair Yard at Fayid, Egypt. The 'conversion' probably involved nothing more than removing the radio-control equipment and installing a second seat. Both were later used as general 'hacks' by 775 Squadron at Dekheila, Egypt.

By mid-1944 virtually all of the surviving Queen Bees – including many examples with just delivery hours on their books – were being held in long-term storage at Manorbier. All of these were finally struck off RAF charge on 12 November 1946 and sold off to civil buyers, twenty-two being purchased by Rollason Aircraft Ltd although none were civilianized. Instead Rollasons denuded them of all serviceable Tiger Moth components and the stripped fuselages were then reportedly stored at Redhill for some years until finally being burned there in what was later described as a "bonfire night bonanza"! Similarly the six Queen Bees (LF789, 790, 800, 801, 803 and 831) sold to the Redhill and Kenley-based British Air Transport of Whyteleafe were also stored in a Redhill perimeter blister hangar although at least two (LF789 and LF790) were used as instructional airframes for a time (until November 1949) by the locally-based College of Aeronautical Engineering.[14]

Apart from the example sold to the US during the War, only one Queen Bee (V4760) ever progressed to civilian status. This was LF858 which was stored under cover at Old Warden for more than 30 years. Eventually restored to flying condition, it was registered as G-BLUZ to joint owner Barrie Bayes of Little Gransden, Bedfordshire. Its initial post-restoration flight was made (manually!) by Norman Whistler at Meppershall airfield, Bedfordshire on 22 October 1986 but it continued to have a chequered life when it was sold at a Phillips auction for £34,000 to an unknown South African buyer who failed to pay up. It was

When Hessell Tiltman of Airspeed was designing the Queen Wasp he was lunching with the directors of de Havilland and discussing the Queen Bee. He told them of a story he had heard at Martlesham of one Bee pilot who had gone up to monitor a radio controlled flight on the clear understanding that transmission would cease at 12.00 in time for lunch in the Mess.

At noon the character of the transmission changed markedly; the aeroplane was gyrating about the sky in a most unpleasant fashion with the unfortunate pilot feeling less and less interested in lunch. After 20 minutes of this he decided that he had no wish to scrub out the cockpit so he switched off and landed, ashen faced. He hurried to the Mess to find the control officer at the end of his second pint, having switched off the transmission at the agreed hour.

Further tests were carried out and it was found that as the control transmission ceased, the radio picked up a dance band programme from Radio Paris, converting the signal into aerobatic commands quite unknown to the Central Flying School.

The de Havilland men had not heard of this, but a Group Captain at the table said, "Yes, I can confirm it, I was the pilot."

(Extract from *The Test Pilots* by Don Middleton.)

subsequently acquired by Colin Knowles and John Flynn and flown under the auspices of the aptly named Bee Keepers Group. Painted in an overall camouflage scheme, it was still current with the Group in June 2009 and maintained at RAF Henlow.[15]

Queen Bee Colour Schemes

When demonstrated to the Press on 27 June 1935, Queen Bee K4227 appeared in an overall silver finish with red outer wing panels. Serials and code letters were in black. This became the standard scheme for all production Queen Bees.

A number of Queen Bee aircraft that operated from ships were later repainted in an overall scheme, suspected to be a drab green.

At least one Queen Bee (L5894) operated in a standard overall earth/green camouflage scheme although this may have been repainted for a specific occasion.

---

14 The British Air Transport-owned examples were noted by M.J. Hardy at the time (see *Aeroplane Monthly*, April 1987). It could be that the reference to Rollason-owned examples, reportedly stored at Redhill and which ended their days in a "bonfire night bonanza" were in fact the BAT aircraft.

15 LF858 was one of three Queen Bees (the others being LF798 and LF823) originally sold off to South Wales Airways of Brigend, Glamorgan. Little is known of this operator although a South West Airways Ltd had been formed in March 1931 to take over the business of Robert Thomas of The Bridge End (sic), Glamorgan, a joy-riding business originally formed in 1927. Although South West Airways began flying instruction courses in 1934, it appears to have become dormant in 1936. The author assumes that the company name was used to offer credence to a tender for cheap aircraft spares as it was likely that all Queen Bees sold post-war were effectively dismantled for components, given the transferability of certain parts and engine.

Units Operating Queen Bees

Home Aircraft Depot (HAD)
RAF Henlow
Originally formed at Henlow, Bedfordshire in April 1926. Renamed RAF Henlow 2.2.39 and became 13 MU 1.6.39.

No.2 Aircraft Storage Unit
No.2 ASU had been formed 2.8.32 as the Aircraft Storage Section, Cardington, Bedfordshire where it became No.2 ASU in 1933 and subsequently redesignated 26 Equipment Unit on 10.2.38 (later re-titled 26 MU), see below.

RAF Maintenance Units
4 MU   HQ Ickenham, Middlesex. (Repair). Appears to have been at various locations, eg Cowley, Oxfordshire for repair of Queen Bee aircraft.
5 MU   Kemble, Gloucestershire (Storage Unit)
6 MU   Brize Norton, Oxfordshire (Storage Unit)
8 MU   Little Rissington, Gloucestershire (Storage Unit)
10 MU Hullavington, Wiltshire (Storage Unit)
12 MU Kirkbride, Cumberland (Storage Unit)
13 MU Henlow, Bedfordshire (see Home Aircraft Depot)
18 MU Dumfries, Dumfriesshire (Storage Unit)
19 MU St. Athan, Glamorgan (Storage Unit)
20 MU Aston Down, Gloucestershire (Storage & Preparation Unit)
26 MU Cardington, Bedfordshire (Repair Unit)
27 MU Shawbury, Shropshire (Storage Unit)
32 MU St Athan, Glamorgan (Repair and Servicing)
34 MU Monkmoor, Shrewsbury, Shropshire (Salvage Centre)
36 MU Sealand, Flintshire (Packing Depot). To 47 MU 1.5.40
47 MU Sealand, Flintshire (Packing Depot). Formerly 36 MU
48 MU Hawarden, Flintshire (Storage Unit)
50 MU Oxford, Oxfordshire (Repair and Salvage)
52 MU Pengham Moors, Cardiff, Glamorgan (Packing Depot)
54 MU Cambridge, Cambridgeshire (Repair and Salvage)
67 MU Taunton, Somerset (Repair and Salvage)
76 MU Wroughton, Wiltshire (Packing Depot)
78 MU Bynea, Glamorgan (Repair and salvage)

No.1 Gunnery Co-operation Flight, RAF
The Gunnery Co-operation Flight was formed on 1.4.34 at Farnborough as an experimental Flight under RAE control and attached to the School of Photography. The Flight is reported to have deployed to Kalafrana, Malta 6.5.34, returning to Farnborough 23.6.34. In the meantime, on 26.5.34, the GCF became a service Flight (in 70 Group) and probably at that stage was re-titled No.1 Gunnery Co-Operation Flight.

To Lee-on-Solent 13.6.35 and embarked HMS *Achilles* two days later. Returned to Farnborough (date not known). On 23.9.35 moved again to Lee-on-Solent and sailed 4.1.36 aboard SS *Orontes* to the Mediterranean. Arrived at Port Said, Egypt 15.1.36. Returned to Lee-on-Solent 27.4.36 (although elements are thought to have re-styled 2 Gunnery Co-operation Flt). Briefly to Novar, near Inverness between 20.9.36 and 12.10.36.

Transferred to No.17 Group 1.1.37 and disbanded into No.2 Anti-Aircraft Co-operation Unit 15.2.37.

No.2 Gunnery Co-operation Flight, RAF
Pilotless Aircraft Development Flight
Prior to being formed, the Pilotless Aircraft Co-operation Committee described "The planned 2nd Gunnery Co-operation Flight" as being inappropriately named and sought to have the Flight titled "Pilotless Aircraft Development Flight". Whilst this may have been agreed by the Committee, it was not formally taken up.

No.2 Gunnery Co-operation Flt was officially formed at Farnborough 1.5.36 (within 22 Group, RAF), although the unit appears to have emerged out of No.1 GCF 3.4.36 at Alexandria and moved to Kalafrana 7.4.36 before being transferred to Mediterranean Command 11.8.36.

On 1.3.37 it was redesignated **No.3 Anti-Aircraft Co-operation Unit**.

24 (Training) Group, RAF
Formed at RAF Halton Camp, Buckinghamshire 10.7.36 within RAF Training Command. On 27.5.40 the unit was transferred to RAF Technical Training Command and re-styled 24 (Technical Training) Group.

Base & Training Unit, Henlow (B&TU)
Pilotless Aircraft Section (PAS)
Pilotless Aircraft Unit (PAU)
The **Base & Training Unit** was established as the central point of Queen Bee operations and began to move into Henlow on 1.10.36. The unit was re-designated as the **Pilotless Aircraft Section** on 31.1.37. Became part of 13 MU 'A' Squadron within 43 Group, RAF. Based at Hawkinge, Kent from 15.2.40 (where it received Queen Bees K8654, L7760, N1828, P4682, P4708, P4710, P4747, P4753-56, P4761-63, P4767-70, P4777-80, P4797, P4800, P4802, P4815, P5741-47). On 29.2.40 PAS passed to 22 Group, RAF until 22.6.40 when moved to St. Athan as part of 70 Group, RAF.

Re-styled **Pilotless Aircraft Unit** at St. Athan 12.40. Moved to Manorbier 5.5.42 and took on the role of a Central Depot from where aircraft were readied for issue to independent Flights. Aircraft operated by the PAU were coded 'R2-' towards the latter stages. Disbanded at Manorbier 15.3.46

Queen Bee Flight
No.1 Anti-Aircraft Co-operation Unit, RAF
Queen Bee Flight was formed at Henlow 10.5.37 as part of 1 Anti-Aircraft Co-operation Unit (1 AACU). Moved to Watchet 27.7.37. On 16.9.37 re-titled **'D' Flight, 1 Anti-Aircraft Co-operation Unit** and transferred to Biggin Hill, Kent same day. Moved to Farnborough 11.4.38 and transferred from 11 Group to 22 Group, RAF.

The Unit contained numerous permanently detached Flights, the towed target Flights being lettered 'A' to 'S' and the pilotless aircraft Flights from 'T' to 'Z', although formed in reverse order. The Queen Bee element of 'D' Flight was re-titled 'Z' Flight/1AACU.

Details of further Queen Bee Flights formed within 1 AACU are as follows:

'Z' Flight/1AACU
1620 (Anti-Aircraft Co-operation) Flight
'Z' Flight was formed at Farnborough 11.4.38 by re-naming 'D' Flight, 1AACU. Moved to Watchet (summer camp) 14.5.38; to Henlow 3.10.38; to Watchet 13.5.39 (with a brief detachment to Barnstaple 27.11.39 – c9.12.39); to Aberffraw 30.10.40 (station renamed Bodorgan 15.5.41) to work with No.4 HAAPC (Heavy Aircraft Anti-Aircraft Practice Camp) at Ty Croes. With the disbandment of 1AACU on 1.10.42 'Z' Flight was re-designated **1620 (Anti-Aircraft Co-operation Flight)** on 1.11.42 in 70 Group to Co-operate with No.7 HAAPC (Heavy Anti-Aircraft Practice Camp) at Ty Croes although some official documents describe the unit as 1620 (Queen Bee) Flight. Disbanded 1.12.43 when incorporated into 595 Squadron.

'Y' Flight/1AACU
Formed at Henlow 11.4.38 as a Pilotless Aircraft Flight. Moved to Manorbier 29.6.38 (summer camp); returned to Henlow 4.10.38. Then back to Manorbier 15.5.39 to work with No.3 HAAPC (Heavy Aircraft Anti-Aircraft Practice Camp) at Manorbier. Remained at Manorbier until disbanded 16.8.42 due to a shortage of pilotless aircraft.

'X' Flight/1AACU
1621 (Anti-Aircraft Co-operation) Flight
Formed at Henlow 15.5.39 as a Pilotless Aircraft Flight. Moved to Weybourne, Norfolk next day. Transferred to Watchet, Somerset 14.9.39 (and operated a detachment at Barnstaple between 21.11.39 – 9.12.39). Transferred (gradually) to Aberporth from 3.9.40 to work with No.1 HAAPC (Heavy Aircraft Anti-Aircraft Practice Camp) at Aberporth. Flight re-designated **1621 (Anti-Aircraft Co-operation) Flight)** on 1.11.42 in 70 Group to Co-operate with No. 1 HAAPC (Heavy Anti-Aircraft Practice Camp) at Aberporth although some official documents describe the unit as 1621 (Queen Bee) Flight. Disbanded 1.12.43 when incorporated into 595 Squadron.

'W' Flight/1AACU
The nucleus of 'W' Flight deployed to Kidsdale on 8.5.39 although the Flight was not officially formed until 16.5.39, at Henlow. Based at Kidsdale initially, the Flight operated aircraft from Burrowhead Landing Ground. Disbanded 18.4.42 due to a shortage of pilotless aircraft.

'V' Flight/1AACU
1618 (Anti-Aircraft Co-operation) Flight
Formed at Cleave 14.5.39 as a Pilotless Aircraft Flight to work with No.6 HAAPC (Heavy Aircraft Anti-Aircraft Practice Camp) at Cleave. Flight re-designated **1618 (Anti-Aircraft Co-operation Flight** 1.11.42 in 70 Group to Co-operate with No.6 HAAPC (Heavy Anti-Aircraft Practice Camp) at St. Agnes although some official documents describe the unit as 1618 (Queen Bee) Flight. Disbanded 1.12.43 when incorporated into 639 Squadron.

'U' Flight/1AACU
1619 (Anti-Aircraft Co-operation) Flight
Formed at St Athan 15.8.40 as a Pilotless Aircraft Flight. Moved to Morfa Towyn 15.9.40 to work with No.7 HAAPC (Heavy Aircraft Anti-Aircraft Practice Camp) at Tonfanau. Disbanded 30.10.42 owing to a shortage of pilotless aircraft. (Was to have been re-titled **1619 (Anti-Aircraft Co-operation) Flight** at Towyn on 1.11.42. However the Flight never formed for reasons shown above.)

'T' Flight/1AACU
Formed at Farnborough 21.1.41 as a Pilotless Aircraft Flight. Moved to Weybourne 25.2.41 (although personnel transferred 4-10.2.41) to work with No.5 HAAPC (Heavy Aircraft Anti-Aircraft Practice Camp) at Weybourne. First two Queen Bee aircraft were delivered to the Flight on 25.2.41. Disbanded at Weybourne 29.4.42 owing to a shortage of pilotless aircraft.

RAF School of Naval Co-operation
No.2 Anti-Aircraft Co-operation Unit
The origins of the School of Naval Co-operation extend back to 30 July 1917 with the official opening of the H.M. Naval Seaplane Training School at Lee-on-Solent. Re-designated No.209 Training Depot Station in April 1918 but the title only lasted until June 1919 when changed to RAF and Naval Co-operation School. Another change took place in August 1920 when the School was re-titled School of Naval Co-operation and Air Navigation. Finally, on 19 April 1923 it became the RAF School of Naval Co-operation.

In September 1932 major changes took place at Lee-on-Solent when work began on an airfield to supplement the sea-plane station. The first use of the airfield was when Queen Bees K4226 and K4227 landed from Farnborough before embarking on HMS *Achilles*.

At this point the School of Naval Co-operation reorganized and brought together a number of Flights based at Gosport whilst the School's Queen Bees were transferred to Gunnery Co-operation Flights (see earlier).

No.2 Anti-Aircraft Co-operation Unit was formed at Lee 15.2.37 from No.1 Gunnery Co-operation Flight and 'A' (Co-operation) Flight of the School of Naval Co-operation. Moved to Gosport 5.5.39 and transferred from 17 Group to 16 Group. No.2 AACU's four flights provided both land and water-based aircraft for gunnery practice.

'A' Flight (Attached to unit HQ). Re-styled **1622 (Anti-Aircraft Co-operation) Flight** 14.2.43.

'B' Flight disbanded at Gosport 1.10.40

'C' Flight To Mount Batten 16.2.39; to St. Eval 27.4.40; to Cleave 16.8.40. Re-styled **1623 (Anti-Aircraft Co-operation) Flight** 14.2.43 and believed moved to Roborough 14.6.43.

'D' Flight To Eastchurch 16.2.39; to Gosport 4.9.39; to Donibristle 17.4.40; to Gosport 3.41; to Detling 11.6.41 until 14.2.43 (briefly detached to Ipswich 4.42).

Re-styled **1624 (Anti-Aircraft Co-operation) Flight** 14.2.43.

No.3 Anti-Aircraft Co-operation Unit, RAF
Formed at Kalafrana, Malta 1.3.37 from No.2 Gunnery Co-operation Flight. The unit had two Flights:

'A' Flight at Hal Far with Swordfish for sleeve towing and marking, and 'B' Flight at Kalafrana with Queen Bee.

'B' Flight detached to Alexandria 23.8.37 – 19.10.37, -.38 to 28.6.38, 3.10.38 to 21.12.38 and briefly from 5.5.39.

Disbanded at Kalafrana 19.9.40, aircraft being dispersed to other Squadrons, including 202, 775, 805 and 830.

No.4 Anti-Aircraft Co-operation Unit, RAF
Formed at Seletar, Singapore 1.8.38 in Far East Command. Transferred to Kalang 24.4.40; to Seletar (possibly on 10.2.41) and on to Tengah 15.2.41. Detached to Batu Pahat 2.1.42. With the advance of Japanese forces in 1941 4 AACU aircraft carried out attacks against enemy columns heading southwards through Malaysia. No aircraft remained active at the end of 1.42.

Singapore became occupied by Japanese forces from 15.2.42 and 4 Anti-Aircraft Co-operation Unit was officially disbanded at Mingaladon 28.3.42.

Other Anti-Aircraft Co-operation Flights were formed during the war (and numbered 1622-1634) but none operated pilotless aircraft.

Operational & Deployment Bases
Batu Pahat, Johor, Malaya
Burrow Head, Wigtownshire
Cleave, Cornwall
Hawkinge, Kent
Kalang, Malaya
Kalafrana, Malta
Kidsdale, Wigtownshire
Lee-on-Solent, Hampshire
Manorbier, Pembrokeshire
Mount Batten, Devon
Seletar, Singapore
Tengah, Singapore
Watchet, Somerset
Weybourne, Norfolk

Queen Bee Production & Histories

De Havilland DH.82 Queen Bee Production

Contract	Date	Serial Range	Allotment Date	Quantity	Remarks
232902/33	8.2.33	K3584		1	Built by de Havilland at Hatfield
262684/33		K3597-K3598 K4044-K4046 K4226-K4229		9	Built by de Havilland at Hatfield
295738/33		K4293-K4294, K4545		3	Built by de Havilland at Hatfield
370807/34		K5059-K5060		2	Built by de Havilland at Hatfield
388676/34		K5100-K5114, K5118		16	Built by de Havilland at Hatfield
463036/35		K8632-K8673 L5888-L5911		66	Built by de Havilland at Hatfield
694957/37		L7720-L7729 L7745-L7764		30	Built by de Havilland at Hatfield
767330/38		N1818-N1847		30	Built by de Havilland at Hatfield
962680/38		P4677-P4716 P4747-P4781 P4788-P4822 P5731-P5749 P5767-P5775		138	Built by de Havilland at Hatfield
B55389/39		V4742-V4772 V4787-V4805		50	Built by de Havilland at Hatfield
		V4806-V4827 V4852-V4876 V4889-V4909 V4926-V4966 V4995-V5006		(125)	Planned production by de Havilland Aircraft at Hatfield, Herts. Cancelled December 1939
Acft/945/C.38		DP114-DP163		(50)	Planned production by Morris Motors, Cowley. Cancelled April 1941
Acft/2398/C.20(b)	18.8.42	LF779-LF803 LF816-LF839 LF857-LF867		60	Built by Scottish Aviation Ltd at 39, West Campbell Street, Glasgow.
		LF868-LF882 MV572-MV606 MV618-MV657		(90)	Planned production by Scottish Aviation Ltd Cancelled December 1943
Total				405 built	265 Cancelled

Unconfirmed reports suggest that those Queen Bees within the DPxxx range were earmarked for the USA as part of a 'reverse Lend-Lease' arrangement. In the event none was built; all being cancelled as shown.

Note: Two de Havilland Tiger Moths (c/ns 3500 & 3501) were ordered against Contract 419031/35 and allocated serials K8336 & K8337 respectively. They were supplied ex-factory without engines and are thought to have been built for trials associated with finalizing the Queen Bee specification. Details on how and when they were used remains obscure but on 29 October 1936 both were issued to No. 2 Aircraft Storage Section at Cardington where they remained until 30 January 1939 when they were transferred to 6 MU Brize Norton for continued storage. Shortly afterwards K8337 was downgraded to instructional status (as 1505M) and allocated, on 1 June 1939, to Stepney Men's Institute in London E.1. K8336 was similarly downgraded as 1506M and allocated to Brighton Technical College on 12 June. Both of these airframes later passed on to No. 3 School of Technical Training at Blackpool on 21 November and 1 December 1939 respectively.

Queen Bee – Individual Aircraft Histories

Note that, in many instances, when aircraft are shown as being returned to de Havilland there is rarely any officially recorded indication as to whether this is to Stag Lane or Hatfield. Only where the location is definitely known is it stated.

Contract 232902/33.
1 aircraft built by de Havilland Aircraft Co Ltd at Hatfield

K3584 (c/n 5027) Retained by de Havilland initially; Del Stag Lane to Farnborough 26.4.33 for 'E' Flt, RAE. To I&P Flt, RAE but returned to Stag Lane 4.5.33. To RAE 8.5.33; to Gosport 9.5.33; believed flight-tested with floats 11.5.33 and returned to RAE same date. To Gosport 5.12.33 and flown 9.12.33 & 11.12.33. Returned to RAE 12.12.33. Ferried to Stag Lane 25.4.34. for mods. Finally SOC 7.2.35, having been reduced to spares.

Contract 262684/33.
9 aircraft built by de Havilland Aircraft Co Ltd at Hatfield

K3597 (c/n 5038) Del to RAE Farnborough 17.10.33. Coded '2'. DBR during trials at Mount Batten, Plymouth 29.1.34. Returned to the manufacturer and reduced to spares. Parts used in K4293 (c/n 5089). SOC 14.3.34.

K3598 c/n (5039) Del to RAE Farnborough 20.10.33. Coded '3' for control trials and catapult trials at Lee from 12.12.33. To Packing Depot, Sealand 10.4.34 and issued to Hal Far 2.5.34. Reportedly used by No.1 Gunnery Co-operation Flt, Calafrana 5.34. Returned to RAE Farnborough 29.8.34. To Packing Depot 25.10.34 but issued to School of Naval Co-operation 21.12.34. Reported to have been used on St Lucia, West Indies 1.35. Returned to de Havilland charge 22.3.35; released to RAE Farnborough 2.9.35. Issued to Gibraltar 7.3.36 for 1 Gunnery Co-operation Flt. Shot down off Gibraltar 17.4.36. SOC 4.6.36 (TFH 84.02)

K4044 (c/n 5044) Del to RAE Farnborough 19.2.34. Coded '4'. To Packing Depot, Sealand 10.4.34 and shipped to Gunnery Co-operation Flt, Hal Far (TOC 2.5.34) (still as '4'). To de Havilland charge 9.11.34. Allotted to RAE 8.4.35; delivered 11.4.35. To School of Naval Co-operation 12.6.35 (Del 19.6.35). Crashed into the sea and sank 28.6.35. (TFH 76.40)

K4045 (c/n 5045) Del to RAE Farnborough 19.2.34. (Probably coded '5'.) To Packing Depot, Sealand 24.4.34 and shipped to Gunnery Co-operation Flt, Hal Far (TOC 17.5.34). Returned to RAE charge 29.8.34 and to de Havilland 5.11.34. Issued to School of Naval Co-operation 1.1.35. Tfd to A & AEE 25.3.35 (although active at Farnborough 5.35) until 12.6.35 when issued to School of Naval Co-operation. Crashed 26.6.35. (TFH 56.55)

K4046 (c/n 5046) Del to RAE Farnborough 19.2.34. To Packing Depot, Sealand 24.3.34 prior to issue to Gunnery Co-operation Flt, Hal Far 17.5.34. Coded '6'. Returned to RAE charge 29.8.34; to de Havilland 5.11.34. Released to School of Naval Co-operation 1.1.35. To RAE charge 8.3.35 but returned to Sch of Nav. Co-op. 28.3.35. Crashed into the sea and sank 29.5.35. (TFH 45.05)

K4226 (c/n 5048) Del to RAE Farnborough 12.5.34. To Lee 25.6.34 for HMS *Achilles*. (Del to Mount Batten, Plymouth 6.7.34.) To School of Naval Co-operation for Gunnery Co-operation Flt. Coded '7'. (Reportedly to St Lucia, West Indies 1.35.) Crashed into the sea during a gunnery exercise 16.2.35. (TFH 30.55)

K4227 (c/n 5049) Del to RAE Farnborough 22.5.34. To Lee 25.6.34 for HMS *Achilles*. (Del to Mount Batten,

Like many early Queen Bees, K4227 was used on trials at RAE Farnborough. Note how on these early production-examples the serial presentation was hyphenated. The photograph is thought to have been taken on 28 June 1935. Within a month K4227 was lost during the 1935 Jubilee Review. (Daily Express Neg. No.48683)

Brand-new Queen Bee K5101 was delivered, as were so many early-production examples, to RAE Farnborough. This view was probably taken circa August 1935 before it was released to No.1 Gunnery Co-operation Flight. (M.I. Draper Archive)

Plymouth 6.7.34.) To School of Naval Co-operation 30.1.35 for trials in HMS *Pegasus*. To de Havilland 6.2.35; Returned to RAE charge 12.6.35. Allocated (and ferried) to Gunnery Co-operation Flt 2.7.35. Coded '8'. Crashed into the sea off Portsmouth 17.7.35. (TFH 41.00)

K4228 (c/n 5050) Del to RAE Farnborough 28.5.34; to Gunnery Co-operation Flight, Farnborough. Hit by AA fire; crashed and sank off Invergordon 9.34. SOC 12.2.35.

K4229 (c/n 5051) Del to RAE Farnborough 30.5.34. To Home Aircraft Depot 11.2.37. To Packing Depot, Sealand 3.10.38 for shipment to 3 AACU, Malta. SOC 31.3.43. At some stage it was coded '10'.

Contract 295738/33.
3 aircraft built by de Havilland Aircraft Co Ltd at Hatfield

K4293 (c/n 5089) Retained by the manufacturer (and incorporated parts from K3597 c/n 5038). Alternatively reported as TOC RAE Farnborough 14.8.34. Badly damaged when hit by "pom-pom" fire off Invergordon 9.34. Returned to the manufacturer for repair but SOC 12.2.35.

K4294 (c/n 5090) Del to RAE Farnborough c8.34. To School of Naval Co-operation and coded '12'. To St Lucia, West Indies 1.35. DBR repair in a crash 27.5.35.

K4545 (c/n 5099) Del to RAE Farnborough 17.12.34. To School of Naval Co-operation, Lee 1.1.35. Allocated (on loan) to de Havilland (location unkn) 22.3.35 until 2.8.35 when TOC by RAE. To 1 GCF, Gibraltar 3.3.36 but lost at sea during a firing exercise 9.4.36. (TFH 37.25)

Contract 370807/34.
2 aircraft built by de Havilland Aircraft Co Ltd at Hatfield

K5059 (c/n 5127) Del to RAE Farnborough 13.6.35. To School of Naval Co-operation, Lee-on-Solent 5.7.35. Allocated to de Havilland (location unkn) 13.9.35 until released to 2 ASU for storage 21.4.36. To 1 GCF 30.6.36. Coded 'B'. DBR 8.6.37. (TFH 69.45)

K5060 (c/n 5128) Del to RAE Farnborough 22.6.35. To 1 Gunnery Co-operation Flt 16.9.35. Shot down 15.2.36 during a naval gunnery exercise. (TFH 73.10)

Contract 388676/34.
16 aircraft built by de Havilland Aircraft Co Ltd at Hatfield

K5100 (c/n 5134) Del to RAE Farnborough 22.6.35. Crashed 31.7.35 (location unkn) and later reduced to produce. (TFH 17.10)

Left: *K4294 was allocated to the School of Naval Co-operation and given the code '12'. In these two views the aircraft is seen being launched from the ship's catapult and later being retrieved virtually undamaged by the ship's hoist. (M.I. Draper Archive)*

Queen Bee K5112/'A' (of No.1 Gunnery Co-operation Flight) displays an 'alpha' code as it is being towed back to ship after a successful sortie. (M.I. Draper Archive)

K5101 (c/n 5135) Del to RAE Farnborough 5.7.35. To 1 Gunnery Co-operation Flt, L-o-S 16.9.35. Coded '16'. Shot down at sea during a gunnery exercise 15.2.36, location unknown. (TFH 70.35)

K5102 (c/n 5136) Del to RAE Farnborough 17.6.35. To 1 Gunnery Co-operation Flt, Lee 3.12.35. To 2 ASU for storage 28.7.37 until 13.8.37 when released to the Home Aircraft Depot, Henlow. To 1 Anti-Aircraft Co-operation Unit 3.9.37. Crashed into the sea off Watchet, Som 20.7.38. (TFH 78.15)

K5103 (c/n 5137) Del to RAE Farnborough 7.8.35. To 1 Gunnery Co-operation Flt 16.9.35. Coded '18'. Crashed into the sea 19.2.36. (TFH 57.50)

K5104 (c/n 5153) Del to RAE Farnborough 4.8.35. To 2 Gunnery Co-operation Flt, 25.2.36. Crashed off Malta 3.2.37. (TFH 39.50)

K5105 (c/n 5154) Del to RAE Farnborough 4.8.35. Allocated to 1 Gunnery Co-operation Flt, 11.1.35. Crashed on landing 10.3.36. SOC 12.5.36. (TFH 134.20)

K5106 (c/n 5155) Del to 2 ASU, Cardington for storage 30.9.35. Released to 2 GCF 12.3.36. Damaged beyond economical repair off Malta 18.2.37. (TFH 51.55)

K5107 (c/n 5156) Del to 2 ASU, Cardington for storage 1.10.35. Released to 2 GCF 12.3.36 and coded '26'. Lost at sea 5.10.37. Presumably with 3AACU after unit title change. (TFH 59.40)

K5108 (c/n 5157) Del to 2 ASU, Cardington for storage 14.11.35. Released to 2 GCF 13.3.36. Crashed into the sea and sank, Malta 11.2.37. (TFH 33.35)

Queen Bee K5114/'20' is carefully hoisted by a hand-operated portable gantry onto the catapult trolley at Jersey Brow, Farnborough. The trolley can be seen to the right in collapsed mode. All flights from Farnborough were carried out with a wheeled undercarriage but in this view the undercarriage is seen discarded at the left forefront. That suggests that this may have been a trial matching of aircraft to launch trolley prior to it being trial-launched from the coastal catapult at Watchet, Somerset in September 1935. In pre-WWII times, it is quite astonishing to see how overt such activities appear to have been at Farnborough with a small group of schoolchildren watching the proceedings from the bank on the left, again suggesting that the timing of this view may have been towards the end of the school summer holiday. (FAST Collection)

Queen Bee 29

Left: *RAE Farnborough's K5114/'20' awaits launch preparation at the Watchet coastal catapult on 21 September 1935. Judging by the threatening appearance of the clouds over the Bristol Channel, launch has been postponed and the cockpit area covered by a protective tarpaulin – curiously, marked 'K4044'. (FAST Collection)*

K5109 (c/n 5158) Del to RAE Farnborough 2.9.35. To 1 Gunnery Co-operation Flt, 29.1.36. Believed returned to manufacturer 31.8.36 until 22.4.37 when TOC by 2 ASU for storage. Released to 24 Group, Henlow 5.2.38 and TOC 27.5.38 by 1 AACU. Crashed 21.7.38. (TFH 45.50)

K5110 (c/n 5159) Del to 2 ASU, Cardington for storage 10.9.35. Released to 2 GCF 13.3.36, coded '28', and shipped to Malta. Damaged beyond economical repair in a crash 11.2.37. (TFH 22.35)

K5111 (c/n 5160) Del to 2 ASU, Cardington for storage 23.9.35. Released to 2 GCF 13.3.36 and shipped to Malta. Crashed and sank off Malta 18.2.37. (TFH 22.05)

K5112 (c/n 5161) Del to 2 ASU, Cardington for storage 26.9.35. Released to 1 GCF 8.7.36 and coded 'A'. Damaged beyond repair 18.6.37. (TFH 63.50)

K5113 (c/n 5162) Del to RAE Farnborough 15.8.35. To Base & Training Unit, Henlow 9.10.36. To Packing Depot, Sealand and shipped to Malta. TOC at Hal Far 11.3.37. Sank during a naval shoot 2.8.37. (TFH 92.35)

K5114 (c/n 5163) Del to RAE Farnborough 16.8.35; coded '20'. To Base & Training Unit, Henlow 9.10.36. To Packing Depot, Sealand and shipped to Malta. TOC at Hal Far 11.3.37. Sank during a naval shoot 4.8.37. (TFH 60.10)

K5118 (c/n 5164) Del to RAE Farnborough 30.8.35. To Base & Training Unit, Henlow 9.10.36. To Packing Depot, Sealand 24.3.37 for shipment to Malta. TOC by 3 AACU 5.5.37. Crashed 6.8.37. (TFH 33.50) At some stage it was coded 'A'.

Lower three illustrations: *K8632/'C' was later repainted in what appears to be an overall drab green scheme with the code letter reduced and repositioned to the fin. Although the fuselage seems to have escaped fairly lightly, this series of three pictures depict K8632 being recovered from the sea after its final sortie on 2 June 1937 when it was damaged beyond repair. (M.I. Draper Archive)*

K8633/'D' (of No.1 Gunnery Co-operation Flight) is seen being hoisted aboard HMS Prince of Wales *for anti-aircraft gunnery practice. Interestingly this photograph is dated 27 November 1941, despite the fact that it was damaged beyond repair on 31 May 1937. (Central Press Photos Ltd)*

**Contract 463036/35.
66 aircraft built by
de Havilland Aircraft Co Ltd at Hatfield**

K8632 (c/n 5165) Del to RAE Farnborough 4.8.36. To 1 Gunnery Co-operation Flt, Lee-on-Solent 19.8.36. Coded 'C'. Damaged beyond repair 2.6.37. (TFH 45.10)

K8633 (c/n 5166) Del to RAE Farnborough 11.8.36. To 1 Gunnery Co-operation Flt, Lee-on-Solent 27.8.36 and later coded 'D'. Damaged beyond repair 31.5.37.

K8634 (c/n 5167) Del to RAE Farnborough 12.8.36. Allotted to 1 Gunnery Co-operation Flt, Lee-on-Solent 14.9.36. Tfd to 3AACU, Hal Far 30.7.37 and TOC 4.8.37. Wrecked when blown off its catapult 18.10.37. (TFH 33.00)

K8635 (c/n 5168) Del to RAE Farnborough 15.8.36. To Base & Training Unit, Henlow 9.10.36. Allocated to Packing Depot, Sealand 19.2.37 and shipped to Malta for 3 AACU, TOC 11.3.37. Crashed 31.10.38. (TFH 70.25)

K8636 (c/n 5169) Del to 2 ASU Cardington 1.9.36 for storage until released to Base & Training Unit, Henlow 31.8.37. To 2 AACU, Lee-on-Solent 4.10.37. Wrecked in a crash 3.6.38. (TFH 33.40)

K8637 (c/n 5170) Del to 2 ASU Cardington 25.9.36 for storage until released to GC Flt HAD 9.4.37 and TOC 20.4.37. Allocated to Packing Depot, Sealand 6.8.37 for despatch to Alexandria for 3AACU, to whom it was allotted 26.8.37. SOC 14.3.39. (TFH 54.00)

K8638 (c/n 5171) Del to DTD, RAE Farnborough 17.8.36 until 14.9.36 when tfd to 2 ASU Cardington. Released to 24 Group B & TU, Henlow, 24 Grp 30.8.37 until 8.10.37 when tfd to 2AACU. Returned to B & TU 25.10.37 and on to 4EO for de Havilland 27.1.38. Issued to 26 MU 8.9.38 and released to 24 Group, Henlow 12.10.38. Tfd to 1 AACU (22 Group) 5.5.39. Believed SOC 22.1.40.

K8639 (c/n 5172) Del to 2 ASU Cardington 1.9.36 for storage until released to 24 Group B & TU, Henlow 22.9.37. To 2 AACU, 17 Group 26.10.37. Crashed 16.6.38; SOC 3.8.38. (TFH 23.30)

K8640 (c/n 5173) Del to DTD, RAE Farnborough 25.8.36; tfd to 2 ASU Cardington 18.9.36 for storage. To 24 Group B & TU, Henlow 30.11.37. To 2 AACU 16.6.38. Coded '66'. Shot down 21.3.39 during a gunnery exercise whilst operating from HMS *Coventry*. (TFH 103.40).

K8641 (c/n 5174) Del to DTD, RAE Farnborough 17.8.36; tfd to 2 ASU Cardington 2.10.36 for storage. To 24 Group B & TU, Henlow 8.3.37. To 1 AACU 6.8.37 but SOC 20.8.37 as a result of being shot down by AA fire same date. (TFH 16.25)

K8642 (c/n 5175) Del to DTD, RAE Farnborough 25.8.36 for fitting of special Queen Bee equipment for No.2 GCF; tfd to 2 ASU Cardington 24.9.36 for storage. To 24 Group B & TU, Henlow 8.3.37. To 1 AACU 27.7.37 and coded '39'. SOC 20.8.37 as a result of a crash. (TFH 16.25).

K8643 (c/n 5176) Del to DTD, RAE Farnborough 25.8.36; tfd to 2 ASU Cardington 7.9.36 for storage. To 24 Group B & TU, Henlow 10.3.37. Allocated to Sealand Packing Depot 29.7.37 for shipment to Malta. To 3 AACU 2.9.37 but crashed 27.1.38. (TFH 25.00)

K8634 was taken onto 3 CAAC charge at Hal Far, Malta on 4 August 1937. During a six-week period (ending 16 October 1937) the aircraft managed to survive the guns of HMS Coventry *only to be written-off when blown off its catapult during a severe gale on the night of 17/18 October. Just visible is the overall camouflage scheme and the serial displayed within an unpainted block. (M.I. Draper Archive)*

DH.82 Queen Bee K8645 was allocated to 2 Anti-Aircraft Co-operation Unit and is seen here in May 1938 about to be winched aboard its mother ship. Although the damage appears to be fairly minimal, it was deemed irrepairable and K8645 was struck off charge on 1 October 1938. (M.I. Draper Archive)

K8644 (c/n 5177) Del to DTD, RAE Farnborough 25.8.36, coded '41'; tfd to 2 ASU Cardington 24.9.36 for storage. To 24 Group B & TU, Henlow 8.3.37. To Sealand Packing Depot 12.8.37 and shipped to Malta. To 3 AACU, Hal Far 2.9.37. Crashed and sank 6.4.38. (TFH 27.25)

K8645 (c/n 5178) Del to DTD, RAE Farnborough 25.8.36; tfd to 2 ASU Cardington 2.10.36 for storage. To 24 Group B & TU, Henlow 29.7.37. To 2 AACU, Lee-on-Solent 28.8.37. SOC 1.6.38 as a result of a crash. (TFH 35.55)

K8646 (c/n 5179) Del to DTD, RAE Farnborough 25.8.36; tfd to 2 ASU Cardington 22.10.36 for storage. To 24 Group B & TU, Henlow 13.8.37. To 2 AACU (17 Grp) 31.8.37. SOC 29.9.37 after lost at sea. (TFH 16.50)

K8647 (c/n 5180) Del to 2 ASU Cardington 25.9.36 for storage. To 24 Group B & TU, Henlow 14.9.37. To Sealand Packing Depot 8.11.37 for shipment to Malta. To 3 AACU 3.12.37. Crashed 27.4.38. (TFH 12.05)

K8648 (c/n 5181) Del to DTD, RAE Farnborough 17.8.36; tfd to 2 ASU Cardington 2.10.36 for storage. To 24 Group B & TU, Henlow 8.3.37. To 1 AACU 6.8.37 but SOC 20.8.37 as a result of a crash. (TFH 16.25)

K8649 (c/n 5182) Del to 2 ASU Cardington 8.10.36 for storage. To Gunnery Co-op Flt, Henlow 9.4.37; TOC by HAD 20.4.37; to 2 AACU 23.8.37. SOC 10.1.38 after crashing into the sea. (TFH 24.00)

K8650 (c/n 5183) Del to 2 ASU Cardington 7.10.36 for storage. To Gunnery Co-op Flt, HAD 20.4.37; to 2 AACU 23.8.37. SOC 21.9.37 following a crash (TFH 12.00)

K8651 (c/n 5184) Del to 2 ASU Cardington 8.10.36 for storage. To Gunnery Co-op Flt, HAD 20.4.37; to 1 AACU 30.8.37. SOC 3.6.38 after being completely wrecked. (TFH u/k)

K8652 (c/n 5185) Del to 2 ASU Cardington 12.10.36 for storage. To 24 (Training) Gp, Henlow 22.9.37. To Sealand Packing Depot 15.11.37 for shipment to Malta. Allocated to 3 AACU 3.12.37 and coded "54" but no further details known.

K8653 (c/n 5186) Del to 2 ASU Cardington 17.10.36 for storage. To 24 Grp TGCU, Henlow 15.11.37. To Sealand Packing Depot 6.1.38 for shipment to Malta. Allocated to 3 AACU 11.2.38. SOC 14.6.38 following a crash. (TFH 19.15)

K8654 (c/n 5187) Del to 2 ASU Cardington 12.10.36 for storage. Released to DTD de Havilland 2.11.37. To AMDP at RAE Farnborough 6.1.39. To 24(T) Grp 3.4.39. To PAS, Hawkinge 22.2.40, later Manorbier. To de Havilland for Repairs in Works 8.7.45 but re-Cat.E 25.7.45 and SOC same date.

K8655 (c/n 5188) Del to 2 ASU Cardington 17.10.36 for storage. To 2 AACU 22.10.37 as a reserve aircraft for HMS *Pegasus*. SOC 8.6.38. (TFH 24.25)

K8656 (c/n 5189) Allocated to 2 ASU 13.10.36 but TOC at Henlow 30.11.36. To 24 Grp B&TU 8.11.37; to Sealand Packing Depot 13.1.38 for shipment to Malta. Allocated to 3 AACU 11.2.38. Crashed and sank off Malta 19.4.39.

K8657 (c/n 5190) Allocated to 2 ASU 13.10.36 and TOC 27.10.36. To 24 Grp B&TU 4.11.37. To Sealand Packing Depot 6.1.38 for shipment to Malta. Allocated to 3 AACU 11.2.38. Crashed off Malta 10.6.38. (TFH 13.25)

K8658 (c/n 5191) Allocated to 2 ASU 13.10.36 and TOC 22.10.36. To 24 Grp B&TU 4.11.37 TOC 25.10.37). To Sealand Packing Depot 5.1.38 for shipment to Malta. Allocated to 3 AACU 11.2.38 and coded '58'. Damaged Beyond Repair 13.6.39. (TFH 36.45)

K8659 (c/n 5192) Allocated to HAD 13.10.36. To Sealand Packing Depot 20.3.37 for shipment to Malta. Allocated to 3 AACU 24.4.37 (TOC 3.5.37). Crashed off Malta 21.9.37. (TFH 20.00?)

K8660 (c/n 5193) Allocated to HAD 13.10.36 (TOC 29.10.36). To Sealand Packing Depot 24.3.37 for shipment to Malta. TOC by 3 AACU 5.5.37 but crashed at sea 6.10.37, possibly off Aboukir, Egypt. (TFH 26.10)

K8661 (c/n 5194) Allocated to HAD 13.10.36 (TOC 10.11.36). To 1 AACU Biggin Hill 27.7.36. Dived into the beach at Watchet 2.9.37; SOC 11.10.37.

K8662 (c/n 5195) Allocated to 2 ASU 3.11.36 (TOC 13.11.36). To 24 Grp B&TU, Henlow 4.11.37 (TOC 25.10.37). To Sealand Packing Depot 17.12.37 for shipment to Malta. Allocated to 3 AACU 12.1.38. Crashed off Malta 24.10.38. (TFH 28.15)

K8663 (c/n 5196) Allocated to 2 ASU 3.11.36 (TOC 13.11.36). To 24 Grp B&TU 4.11.37 (TOC 25.10.37). To 17 Gp 29.11.37 and TOC by 2AACU 10.2.38. Crashed 5.7.38 and SOC same date. (TFH 27.10)

K8664 (c/n 5197) Allocated to (and TOC) 2 ASU 11.11.36. To B&TU (24 Gp), Henlow 8.11.37 (TOC 15.11.37). To 22 Gp 8.4.38 and TOC by 1AACU Farnborough 4.5.38. SOC 25.8.38 after sustaining direct gunfire. (TFH 15.30)

K8665 (c/n 5198) Allocated to 2 ASU 17.11.36 (TOC 30.11.36). To 24 Gp B&TU, Henlow 8.11.37 (TOC 23.11.37). Conveyed to Sealand Packing Depot 17.1.38 for shipment to Malta. TOC by 3 AACU 11.2.38. Crashed 16.6.38. (TFH 10.30)

32 Sitting Ducks and Peeping Toms

K8666 (c/n 5199) Allocated to 2 ASU 11.11.36 (TOC 4.12.36). To 24 Gp B&TU, Henlow 8.11.37 (TOC 29.11.37). TOC by 2 AACU 29.6.38. SOC 25.3.39 after being shot down during gunnery trials with HMS Coventry. (TFH 58.20)

K8667 (c/n 5200) Allocated to 2 ASU 24.11.36 (TOC 5.12.36). To 24 Gp B&TU 8.11.37 (TOC 15.11.37). TOC by 1 AACU 4.5.38. SOC 6.7.38 as a complete wreck, circumstances remaining unkn.

K8668 (c/n 5201) Crashed on a test-flight at Welwyn, Hertfordshire 16.12.36. Probably retained at Hatfield for repair until allocated to 24 'T' Gp HAD 15.3.37. SOC 26.1.40 following a crash.

K8669 (c/n 5202) Allocated to 2 ASU 24.11.36 (TOC 18.12.36). To 24 Gp B&TU 3.12.37; to 22 Gp 8.4.38 but returned to 24 Gp Henlow 4.5.38. TOC by 2 AACU 6.5.38. TOC by PAU 3.4.41. To 1 AACU 1.10.41 but damaged in a flying accident 27.12.41. Declared Cat.B 2.1.42; repaired, issued to 19 MU 19.2.42 and released to PAU 14.3.42. Declared Cat.E 1.4.42 and SOC 31.8.42.

K8670 (c/n 5203) Allocated to 1 AACU/22 Gp 11.5.38. To 24 Gp 8.10.38. To 4 MU (de Havilland) 22.11.38 until 2.10.39 when tfd to 5 MU (TOC 16.10.39). Released to PAU 12.8.40. To 1 AACU 24.9.40. To 34 MU 1.12.40 and declared Cat.B 11.12.40 (SAS/de Hav). Destroyed in a flying accident 21.11.40.

K8671 (c/n 5204) Allocated to 2 ASU 11.12.36 (TOC 4.2.37). To 24 Gp B&TU 1.12.37; to 2 AACU Lee-on-Solent 27.4.38 but SOC 21.6.38 following a crash. (TFH 27.35)

K8672 (c/n 5205) Allocated to 2 ASU 11.12.36 (TOC 10.2.37). To 24 Gp B&TU 30.11.37. To 1 AACU 6.5.38 but returned to Henlow 28.9.38. Allocated to 4 MU de Havilland 22.11.38 until released to 6 MU 4.9.39. To PAU 1.8.41. Sustained Cat.E damage 31.8.42.

K8673 (c/n 5206) Allocated to 2 ASU 11.12.36 (TOC 10.2.37). To 24 Gp B&TU 30.11.37. To 1 AACU 6.5.38; to PAS, Henlow 28.9.38 but downgraded to Inst status 15.11.38 as 1182M, remaining at Henlow. On 11.1.39 it was transferred to 13 MU which might reflect its ultimate fate.

L5888 (c/n 5207) Allocated to 2 ASU 11.3.37 (TOC 18.3.37). To 6 MU 24.1.39; to 12 MU (date unkn). TOC by PAS 6.6.40; to 1 AACU 22.8.40. To de Havilland 17.5.41 until 20.8.41 when returned to PAU. To 1 AACU 22.10.41 probably for 1618 Flt. Lost height and landed in sea off Cleave and sank 15.12.42. (Known to have been coded '390', probably with PAS/PAU.)

L5889 (c/n 5208) Allocated to 2 ASU 11.3.37 (TOC 18.3.37). To 6 MU 24.1.39; to 12 MU (date unkn). TOC by PAS 6.6.40; to 1 AACU 2.9.40 but shot down and sank off Burrow Head 11.9.40. (TFH 27.55)

L5890 (c/n 5209) Allocated to 2 ASU 11.3.37 (TOC 25.3.37). To 6 MU 24.1.39; to 12 MU (date unkn); to 18 MU 1.8.40. Released to PAU 26.2.41 until 6.3.41 when del to 27 MU. Released to 1 AACU 8.5.41. Shot down in the sea off Burrow Head 20.7.41 (or 26.7.41) and SOC 4.10.41. (TFH 38.05)

L5891 (c/n 5210) Allocated to 2 ASU 11.3.37 (TOC 25.3.37). To 6 MU 24.1.39; to 12 MU (date unkn). Released to PAU

3 AACU Queen Bee K8662/'56' suffered a major mishap during an artillery shoot off Malta on 24 October 1938. Judging by the extent of the visible damage it does tend to pose the question as to why so much effort went into rescuing the aircraft. In the event K8662 was written-off as damaged beyond repair. (M.I. Draper Archive)

Left and below left: *The gathering of smartly turned out military and civilian guests suggests that K8669 is being used for a live demonstration. The aircraft is immaculately presented and possibly at an early stage of its life. (British Aerospace Neg. No 21910B, plus M.I. Draper Archive)*

10.6.40. To 'Y' Flt/1 AACU 7.9.40. Sustained Cat B damage 2.4.41. After repairs TOC by PAU 19.7.41. To 1 AACU 17.3.42 but crashed into the sea off Burrow Head 13.4.42 presumably after hit by AA fire.

L5892 (c/n 5211) Allocated to 2 ASU 11.3.37 (TOC 5.4.37). To 6 MU 24.1.39; to 12 MU (date unkn). TOC by PAS 6.6.40; to 1 AACU 10.9.40 but shot down into the sea off Burrow Head 1.10.40. SOC 1.11.40. (TFH 38.45)

L5893 (c/n 5212) Allocated to 2 ASU 11.3.37 (TOC 5.4.37). To 6 MU 24.1.39;

Below: *Queen Bee L5894/'305' sits on the Weybourne catapult being prepared for launch. Overseeing the preparations is Prime Minister Winston Churchill and Secretary of State for War Captain D. Margesson. L5894 was issued to No.1 Anti-Aircraft Co-operation Unit (1AACU) in May 1941 and was shot down off Weybourne on 18 June 1941. The camouflage scheme is noteworthy and may well have been specially applied for the occasion. (Imperial War Museum, Neg No. 10307)*

to 12 MU (date unkn); to 18 MU 1.8.40. Released to PAU 23.7.41 and coded '378'. TOC by 1 AACU 22.10.41. Rolled after catapult launch and crashed into sea off Manorbier 18.12.41. SOC 27.12.41.

L5894 (c/n 5213) Allocated to 2 ASU 6.4.37 (TOC 13.4.37). To 6 MU 24.1.39; to 12 MU (date unkn); to 18 MU 1.8.40. Released to PAU 23.2.41 until 13.5.41 when tfd to 1 AACU; coded '305'. Shot down off Weybourne 18.6.41 and SOC 25.6.41. (TFH 14.55)

L5895 (c/n 5214) Allocated to 2 ASU 6.4.37 (TOC 28.4.37). To 6 MU 24.1.39; to 12 MU (date unkn); to 18 MU 1.8.40. Released to PAU 26.6.42. To 'X' Flt/1 AACU 16.8.42. Shot down off Aberporth 24.9.42.

L5896 (c/n 5215) Allocated to 2 ASU 6.4.37 (TOC 13.4.37). To 6 MU 24.1.39; to 12 MU (date unkn); to 18 MU 1.8.40. Released to PAU 26.2.41 until 6.3.41 when tfd to 27 MU. Released to 1 AACU 1.5.41. To 54 MU 12.5.41 possibly for repair. Released to PAU 20.8.41 although spent a brief period (12-22.9.41) at 19 MU. To 1 AACU 10.2.42. Shot down off Pentre Gwyddel, Anglesey 25.7.42. SOC 18.8.42.

L5897 (c/n 5216) Allocated to 2 ASU 6.4.37 (TOC 28.4.37). To 6 MU 24.1.39; to 12 MU (date unkn); to 18 MU 1.8.40. Released to PAU 11.7.41 until 30.9.41 when to 1 AACU. Cat.B 25.11.41; repaired by de Havilland 1.12.41-28.1.42. To 19 MU 9.2.42; released to PAU 14.3.42. To 1AACU 15 (or 18).4.42. Stalled and spun into ground at Yfrwd-Uchaf, nr Aberporth 24.9.42.

L5898 (c/n 5217) Allocated to 2 ASU 6.4.37 (TOC 5.5.37). To 6 MU 24.1.39; to 12 MU (date unkn); to 18 MU 1.8.40. Released to PAU 18.8.41 and coded '383'. To 1 AACU 17.10.41. Cat.B 8.4.42; repaired by de Havilland at Hatfield 11.4.42-2.5.42. To 19 MU 27.5.42; released to PAU 28.6.42. To 'V' Flt/1 AACU 8.9.42 but DBR in heavy landing at Cleave 17.11.42.

L5899 (c/n 5218) Allocated to 2 ASU 6.4.37 (TOC 5.5.37). To 6 MU 24.1.39; to 12 MU (date unkn); to 18 MU 1.8.40. Released to PAU 30.12.40 until 26.2.41 when to 'Y' Flt/1 AACU. Crashed into the sea 4.4.41 after catapult launch from Manorbier. SOC 1.6.41.

L5900 (c/n 5219) Allocated to 2 ASU 4.5.37 (TOC 20.5.37). To 24 Grp Henlow 5.2.38; to 22 Grp for 1 AACU 27.5.38; returned to Henlow 28.9.38. Allocated to 4 MU Hatfield (DH) 22.11.38; released to 5 MU 16.10.39. To 13 MU 6.12.39. To PAS 1.3.40 and coded '327'. To 1 AACU 3.7.40. Damaged 3.8.40 and conveyed by 50 MU team to DH 14.8.40. To 19 MU 8.2.41; released to PAU 1.5.41. To 1 AACU 23.10.41. Dived into the sea off Burrow Head 4.12.41.

L5901 (c/n 5220) Allocated to 2 ASU 4.5.37 (TOC 31.5.37). To 24 Grp Henlow 5.2.38; to Packing Depot 26.5.38 for shipment to Seletar. Used by 4 AACU. Crashed into the sea near HMS *Suffolk* off Singapore 21.3.39. (TFH 40.35)

L5902 (c/n 5221) Allocated to 2 ASU 4.5.37 (TOC 20.5.37). To 24 Grp Henlow 5.2.38; to Packing Depot 26.5.38 for shipment to Seletar. Used by 4 AACU. Unaccounted for after the fall of Singapore on 15.2.42.

L5903 (c/n 5222) Allocated to 2 ASU 4.5.37 (TOC 25.5.37). To 24 Grp Henlow 5.2.38; to Packing Depot 26.5.38 for shipment to Seletar. Used by 4 AACU. Damaged beyond economical repair 21.3.39. (TFH 51.40)

L5904 (c/n 5223) Allocated to 2 ASU 25.5.37 (TOC 1.6.37). To 24 Grp Henlow 25.2.38; to Packing Depot 24.5.38 for shipment to Seletar. Used by 4 AACU. Request for SOC made by 4 AACU 22.8.41

L5905 (c/n 5224) Allocated to 2 ASU 25.5.37 (TOC 9.6.37). To 24 Grp B&TU 18.3.38; to 2 AACU 16.6.38. Crashed 1.7.38 and SOC same date. (TFH 14.50)

L5906 (c/n 5225) Allocated to 2 ASU 25.5.37 (TOC 14.6.37). To 24 Grp B&TU 18.3.38; to 2 AACU 23.7.38. Crashed 20.10.38 and SOC same date. (TFH 23.50)

L5907 (c/n 5226) Allocated to 2 ASU 25.5.37 (TOC 24.6.37). To 24 Grp B&TU 19.3.38; to 2 AACU 21.7.38. Crashed 13.10.38 and SOC same date. (TFH 18.35)

L5908 (c/n 5227) Allocated to 2 ASU 12.6.37 (TOC 30.6.37). To 24 Grp B&TU 18.3.38; to 2 AACU 23.7.38. Shot down by HMS *Coventry* and sank 22.3.39; SOC same date. (TFH 43.25)

L5909 (c/n 5228) Allocated to 2 ASU 12.6.37 (TOC 21.6.37). To 24 Grp B&TU 29.3.38; to Packing Depot 14.7.38 on allocation to 22 Grp but allocation cancelled. To 2 AACU 3.9.38. SOC 25.10.38 following a crash. (TFH 23.20)

L5910 (c/n 5229) Allocated to 2 ASU 12.6.37 (TOC 10.7.37). To 24 Grp B&TU 18.3.38; to Packing Depot 19.7.38 on allocation to 22 Grp but allocation cancelled. To 2 AACU 3.9.38. SOC 11.10.38 following a crash, details unkn. (TFH 15.35)

L5911 (c/n 5230) Allocated to 2 ASU 12.6.37 (TOC 19.7.37). To 24 Grp B&TU 29.7.37; to Packing Depot 14.7.38 on allocation to 22 Grp but allocation cancelled. To 2 AACU 26.10.37. SOC 21.6.38 following a crash. (TFH 26.20)

L5902 was one of a number of Queen Bees despatched to 4 AACU in Singapore. Most of the unit's aircraft were lost and unaccounted for when Singapore fell to invading Japanese forces in February 1942. In this view, taken at Hatfield in May 1937, the Queen Bee is somewhat dwarfed by the DH.91 Albatross E-2. (British Aerospace, Neg. No 86H)

**Contract 694957/37.
30 aircraft built by de Havilland
Aircraft Co Ltd at Hatfield**

L7720 (c/n 5231) Allocated to 26 MU 5.3.38 (TOC 25.3.38). To Henlow 1.2.39; to 36 MU 3.6.39. Allocated for shipment to Seletar 6.7.39. Bounced on landing on rough sea and overturned at Beting Kusa, Singapore 19.7.41. SOC 22.8.41.

L7721 (c/n 5232) Allocated to 26 MU 5.3.38 (TOC 21.3.38). To 13 MU 17.2.39; to 36 MU 3.6.39. Allocated to RAF Malta 7.6.39. reported to have been used by 805 Squadron at Fayid, Egypt where it suffered an engine failure on 30.8.42. Later SOC 31.3.43.

L7722 (c/n 5233) Allocated to 26 MU 5.3.38 (TOC 25.3.38). To 13 MU 9.11.38; to 36 MU 3.6.39. Allocated for shipment to Seletar 6.7.39. Unaccounted for after the fall of Singapore on 15.2.42.

L7723 (c/n 5234) Allocated to 26 MU 25.3.38 (TOC 24.3.38). To 13 MU 2.2.39; to 36 MU 3.6.39. Allocated to RAF Malta 7.6.39. Reportedly damaged after floats collapsed on landing off Malta 24.10.39. SOC 31.3.43. (Card has reference "E1(b) are arranging for aircraft to be tfd to Admiralty.")

L7724 (c/n 5235) Allocated to 26 MU 25.3.38 (TOC 31.3.38). To 13 MU 24.1.39; to 36 MU 3.6.39. Allocated for shipment to Seletar 6.7.39. Unaccounted for after the fall of Singapore on 15.2.42.

L7725 (c/n 5236) Allocated to 26 MU 25.3.38 (TOC 6.4.38). To 13 MU 23.1.39; to 36 MU 3.6.39. Allocated for shipment to Seletar 6.7.39. Unaccounted for after the fall of Singapore on 15.2.42.

L7726 (c/n 5237) Allocated to 26 MU 5.3.38 (TOC 6.4.38). To 13 MU 2.2.39; to 36 MU 3.6.39. Allocated for shipment to Seletar 6.7.39. Unaccounted for following the fall of Singapore on 15.2.42.

L7727 (c/n 5238) Allocated to 26 MU 5.3.38 (TOC 20.4.38). To 6 MU 24.1.39; to 12 MU (date unkn); to 18 MU 2.8.40. Released to PAU 23.2.41. To 1 AACU 20.4.41. Hit by AA; glided into cliffs 2nms north of Aberporth 16.6.41. SOC 27.6.41.

L7728 (c/n 5239) Allocated to 26 MU 25.3.38 (TOC 20.4.38). To 13 MU 2.2.39. Released to 1 AACU 1.7.39. Shot down into the sea off Watchet 3.8.39.

L7729 (c/n 5240) Allocated to 26 MU 4.4.38 (TOC 14.5.38). To 24 Grp, Henlow 30.6.38. To 1 AACU 3.8.38. Overturned after landing in the sea (location unkn) 9.9.38 and SOC. (TFH 24.40)

L7745 (c/n 5241) Allocated to 26 MU 25.3.38 (TOC 23.4.38). To 6 MU 24.1.39; to 12 MU (date unkn); to 18 MU 2.8.40. Released to PAU 30.12.40. To 1 AACU 3.3.41. Shot down into the sea off Burrow Head 7.4.41. SOC 1.6.41. (TFH 23.30)

L7746 (c/n 5242) Allocated to 26 MU 4.4.38 (TOC 23.4.38). To 6 MU 24.1.39; to 12 MU (date unkn); to 18 MU 2.8.40. Released to PAU 30.12.40. To 1 AACU 6.3.41. Shot down into the sea off Burrow Head 26.3.41. SOC 7.5.41. (TFH 17.05)

L7747 (c/n 5243) Allocated to 26 MU 4.4.38 (TOC 14.5.38). To 24 Grp Henlow 2.7.38. To 17(T) Grp for 2 AACU 23.8.38. Shot down 23.3.39 during an exercise with HMS *Coventry* and sank. (TFH 28.40)

L7748 (c/n 5244) Allocated to 26 MU 12.4.38 (TOC 28.4.38). To 6 MU 24.1.39; to 12 MU (date unkn); to 18 MU 2.8.40. Released to PAU 26.6.42; to 'V' Flt/1 AACU 20.8.40. Sustained Cat.E damage 28.8.42 when stalled on landing at Cleave.

L7749 (c/n 5245) Allocated to 26 MU 12.4.38 (TOC 9.5.38). To 24 Grp Henlow 2.7.38. To 1 AACU (22 Grp) 18.8.38. Crashed into the sea 20.6.39 and SOC. (TFH 31.05)

L7750 (c/n 5246) Allocated to 26 MU 12.4.38 (TOC 12.5.38). To 24 Grp Henlow 30.6.38. To 1 AACU (22 Grp) 18.8.38. Hit by AA and Crashed into the sea 3nms west of Watchet 25.5.39. (TFH 38.25)

Queen Bee L7728 was one of many that saw service with 1 AACU. It is seen here at the point of leaving the catapult launcher at Watchet, Somerset on 3 August 1939 for a shoot at the nearby Royal Artillery Camp at Williton. Only minutes after this picture was taken L7228 sustained a direct hit and dived into the sea. (M.I Draper Archive)

L7751 (c/n 5247) Allocated to 26 MU 12.4.38 (TOC 2.5.38). To 24 Grp Henlow 1.7.38. To 1 AACU (22 Grp) 23.8.38. To 4 MU (de H) for repairs 29.11.38; later to 6 MU 18.8.39. Released to PAU 17.1.42. To 1 AACU 9.3.42. Control lost after take-off from Aberporth 4.8.42; Crashed into a field. SOC 31.8.42.

L7752 (c/n 5248) Allocated to 26 MU 14.5.38 although TOC 12.5.38. To 24 Grp Henlow 2.7.38. To 1 AACU (22 Grp) 5.9.38. Overturned on landing, location unkn, and sank 4.7.39. SOC 11.8.39.

L7753 (c/n 5249) Allocated to 26 MU 3.5.38 (TOC 11.5.38). To 24 Grp Henlow 2.7.38. To 2 AACU (17 Grp) 5.10.38. To 4 MU (de H) for repairs 24.5.39; later to 19 MU 15.2.40. Released to PAU 30.9.40. To 1 AACU 21.10.40. Overshot on landing at Kidsdale 24.4.41 and hit hangar. SOC 5.5.41.

L7754 (c/n 5250) Allocated to 26 MU 3.5.38 (TOC 16.5.38). To 24 Grp Henlow 1.7.38. To 2 AACU (17 Grp) 5.10.38. Crashed 8.11.38, location unkn and SOC. (TFH 25.40)

L7755 (c/n 5251) Allocated to 26 MU 3.5.38 (TOC 16.5.38). To 2 AACU (17 Grp) 11.8.38. To 13 MU Henlow 1.4.39; to 4 MU (de H) 1.9.39; to 6 MU 22.6.40. Released to PAU 10.8.40; to 1 AACU 28.9.40. Crashed into the sea off Cleave during a storm 15.10.40.

L7756 (c/n 5252) Allocated to 26 MU 14.5.38 (TOC 16.5.38). To 2 AACU (17 Grp) 11.8.38. Ro 13 MU Henlow 1.4.39. Released to 2 AACU 26.10.39; to 1 AACU 21.12.39. Crashed into the sea off Burrow Head 8.5.40. SOC 28.6.40. (TFH 27.15)

L7757 (c/n 5253) Allocated to 26 MU 14.5.38 (TOC 16.5.38). To 24 Grp Henlow 17.8.38. To 2 AACU (17 Grp) 6.10.38. SOC 8.11.38. (TFH 29.45)

L7758 (c/n 5254) Allocated to 26 MU 14.5.38 (TOC 16.5.38). To 24 Grp Henlow 17.8.38. To 2 AACU (17 Grp) 2.12.38. Shot down during an exercise with HMS *Coventry*. SOC 24.3.39. (TFH 17.30)

L7759 (c/n 5255) Allocated to 26 MU 14.5.38 (TOC 19.5.38). To 24 Grp Henlow 17.8.38. Allocated to Packing Depot 10.10.38 for 3 AACU (allocated 16.12.38). and shipped to Malta for catapult trials at Kalafrana. Request for SOC raised 7.40. SOC 4.8.40.

L7760 (c/n 5256) Allocated to 26 MU 14.5.38 (TOC 24.5.38). Allocated to 24 Grp Henlow 30.8.38. To PAS Hawkinge 22.2.40. To 1 AACU 8.5.40. To 4 MU (de H) 8.7.40; to 20 MU 23.11.40. Released to PAU 17.2.41. To 'T' Flt/1 AACU 24.2.41. Control was lost off Weybourne 8.4.41; flew out to sea. SOC as 'missing'. (TFH 92.00)

L7761 (c/n 5257) Allocated to 26 MU 18.5.38 (TOC 24.5.38). To 24 Grp Henlow 12.9.38. To 36 MU 25.11.38. Allotted to 3 AACU 11.1.39 and shipped to Malta as a replacement aircraft. Damaged by AA and overturned on landing in Mediterranean 14.6.39. Presumably recovered and repaired as later reported overturned during a forced-landing in a ploughed field 12.3.42 and taken to the Royal Navy Aircraft Repair Yard at Fayid, Egypt. SOC 31.3.43.

L7762 (c/n 5258) Allocated to 26 MU 18.5.38 (TOC 24.5.38). To 24 Grp Henlow 12.9.38. To 36 MU 25.11.38. Allotted to 3 AACU 11.1.39 and shipped to Malta as a replacement aircraft. Shot down into the sea and sank off Malta 5.1.40. SOC 11.1.40.

L7763 (c/n 5259) Allocated to 26 MU 18.5.38 (TOC 25.5.38). To 24 Grp Henlow 11.9.38. To 36 MU 25.11.38. Allotted to 3 AACU 11.1.39 and shipped to Malta as a replacement aircraft. DBR in heavy landing on sea 22.6.39.

L7764 (c/n 5260) Allocated to 26 MU 18.5.38 (TOC 25.5.38). To 24 Grp Henlow 12.9.38. To 36 MU 25.11.38. Allotted to 3 AACU 11.1.39 and shipped to Malta as a replacement aircraft. Overturned alighting on the sea off Malta 22.8.39 and sank. SOC 8.9.39

Contract 767330/38.
30 aircraft built by de Havilland Aircraft Co Ltd at Hatfield

N1818 (c/n 5261) Allocated to 26 MU 16.8.38 (TOC 2.9.38). To 13 MU 1.2.39. Allocated to Pilotless Aircraft Flight, St Athan but no evidence of delivery. Briefly to RAE Farnborough 31.8.39-5.8.40 then to 19 MU; tfd to 32 MU 20.8.40. To 1 AACU 30.9.40. To DH 10.11.40 until 11.3.41 when del to 19 MU. Released to PAU 1.5.41. SOC 28.10.40.

N1819 (c/n 5262) Allocated to 26 MU 16.8.38 (TOC 2.9.38). To 13 MU 1.2.39. Released to 2 AACU 8.5.39. Shot down and sank 15.6.39, location unkn. (TFH 11.05)

N1820 (c/n 5263) Allocated to 26 MU 16.8.38 (TOC 3.9.38). To 13 MU 8.11.38. Released to 2 AACU 31.3.39. SOC 26.5.39 after being shot down. Salvaged in wrecked condition. (TFH 24.45)

N1821 (c/n 5264) Allocated to 26 MU 16.8.38 (TOC 3.9.38). To 13 MU 24.11.38. Released to 2 AACU 8.5.39. SOC 16.6.39 after being shot down and sank. (TFH 16.20)

N1822 (c/n 5265) Allocated to 26 MU 30.8.38 (TOC 2.9.38). To 13 MU 21.1.39. Released to 2 AACU 8.5.39. SOC 16.6.39 after being shot down and sank, location unkn. (TFH 25.55)

N1823 (c/n 5266) Allocated to 26 MU 30.8.38 (TOC 8.9.38). To 13 MU 24.1.39. Released to 2 AACU 25.5.39. SOC 21.6.39 after being lost at sea, location unkn. (TFH 10.25)

N1824 (c/n 5267) Allocated to 26 MU 30.8.38 (TOC 8.9.38). To 13 MU 24.1.39. Released to 2 AACU 25.5.39. SOC 4.7.39 after crashing, location unkn. (TFH 16.30)

N1825 (c/n 5268) Allocated to 26 MU 14.9.38 (TOC 12.9.38). To 24 Gp Henlow 11.10.38. To 1 AACU 5.5.39. SOC 2.40. (TFH 19.45)

N1826 (c/n 5269) Allocated to 26 MU 14.9.38 (TOC 16.9.38). To 24 Gp Henlow 11.10.38. To 1 AACU 5.5.39. To 13 MU 23.11.39. To 20 MU 10.10.40. Released to PAU 23.12.40. To 1 AACU 14.3.41. SOC 2.6.41 after being lost at sea, location unkn.

N1827 (c/n 5270) Allocated to 26 MU 14.9.38 (TOC 17.9.38). To 24 Gp Henlow 11.10.38. To 1 AACU 1.2.39. SOC 20.6.39 after a crash, location unkn.

N1828 (c/n 5271) Allocated to 26 MU 14.9.38 (TOC 17.9.38); released to 24 Gp Harlow and Del 11.10.38. To 1 AACU 1.2.39; to 4 MU for repair by DH 21.11.39. Allocated to 10 MU Hullavington 29.1.40 (TOC 1.3.40); released to PAS Hawkinge 21.3.40. To 1 AACU 12.9.40 but sustained Cat.C damage 11.9.40. To 4 MU (de Hav.) 30.9.40 and stored until 23,4,41 when released to 19 MU St Athan. Tfd to PAU 15.5.41. Crashed at Ty Croes, Anglesey 16.8.41. Cat.E.

N1829 (c/n 5272) Allocated to 26 MU 14.9.38 (TOC 19.9.38); released to 24 Grp Harlow 12.10.38 Del 11.10.38). 1 AACU 24.1.39 (TOC Farnborough 26.1.39). To 4 MU (DH) 5.9.39 (TOC 18.9.39) probably for repairs. Allocated to 6 MU 25.2.40 (TOC 22.4.40) and released to PAU St

A line-up of brand-new Queen Bees at Hatfield and awaiting delivery to 26 Maintenance Unit, Cardington in September 1938. The first two aircraft are N1826 and N1828 but the other three are unidentifiable – possibly N1827, N1829 and N1830. (M.I. Draper Archive)

Athan 10.8.40. To 'V' Flt/1 AACU 18.9.40. Shot down off Cleave 6.5.41.

N1830 (c/n 5273) Allocated to 26 MU 17.9.38 (TOC 19.9.38). Tfd to 13 MU 9.11.38 (TOC 8.11.38); released to 17(T) Grp for 2 AACU 1.5.39 (although TOC by 2AACU 31.3.39). Shot down into the Mediterranean 5.6.39.

N1831 (c/n 5274) Allocated to 26 MU 17.9.38 (TOC 20.9.38). Tfd to 13 MU 9.11.38 (TOC 24.1.39); released to 2 AACU 11.5.39 (TOC 25.5.39). Crashed 5.7.39.

N1832 (c/n 5275) Allocated to 26 MU 17.9.38 (TOC 23.9.38). Tfd to 13 MU 9.11.38 (TOC 9.11.38); transferred to 36 MU 2.5.39 (TOC 3.5.39). TOC RAF Seletar 6.7.39 for 4 AACU. Crashed at Pulau Tekong, Singapore 3.10.40. SOC 19.11.40.

N1833 (c/n 5276) Allocated to 26 MU 17.9.38 (TOC 22.9.38). Released to 24 Gp Henlow 12.10.38 (TOC 11.10.38). Issued to 1 AACU 24.1.39 (TOC 26.1.39), coded '108'. SOC whilst with 'Y' Flt, Manorbier, probably in 8.39.

N1834 (c/n 5277) Allocated to 26 MU 17.9.38 (TOC 22.9.38). Released to 24 Gp Henlow 12.10.38 (TOC 11.10.38). To 22(AC)Gp 2.5.39 for 1 AACU (TOC 5.5.39); to 'V' Flt. Conducted an AA Co-operation sortie for 2hrs 13.7.39 before alighting on rough sea. Salvaged by 'WD Western Hill' but despite only suffering one small hole in the port float the aircraft was wrecked by heavy sea.

N1835 (c/n 5278) Allocated to 26 MU 20.9.38 but allocation canx. To 24Gp Henlow 8.10.38 (TOC 6.10.38). Tfd to 36 MU 19.11.38 (TOC 25.11.38). TOC by RAF Depot, Malta 12.1.39. Later released to 3 AACU, coded '100'. Crashed into the Mediterranean after catapult launch from HMS *Penelope* 13.2.39. SOC 13.3.39.

N1836 (c/n 5279) Allocated to 26 MU 20.9.38 (TOC 27.9.38). To 24Gp Henlow 12.10.38 (TOC 11.10.38). To 22(AC)Gp 2.5.39 for 1 AACU (TOC 5.5.39) and coded '100'. To 4 MU (DH) 21.11.39. Tfd to 6 MU 25.2.40 (TOC 23.5.40). To PAU 13.8.40. To 1 AACU 24.9.40. Crashed on landing at Aberporth 1.12.40. To 36 MU 4.12.40 and SOC 15.12.40.

N1837 (c/n 5280) Allocated to 26 MU 20.9.38 (TOC 28.9.38). To 24Gp Henlow 12.10.38 (TOC 11.10.38). To 22(AC)Gp 2.5.39 for 1 AACU (TOC 5.5.39). To 'W' Flight. Crashed on landing off Burrow Head 20.7.39 and sank.

N1838 (c/n 5281) Allocated to 26 MU 28.9.38. To 24Gp Henlow 8.10.38 (TOC 6.10.38). To 36 MU 19.11.38 (TOC 25.11.38). Allotted to 3 CAACU, Malta 11.1.39. Crashed into the sea 16.2.40, location unkn, after loss of radio contact. SOC 17.2.40.

N1839 (c/n 5282) Allocated to 26 MU 28.9.38 but allocation canx. To 24Gp Henlow 8.10.38 (TOC 7.10.38). To 36 MU 19.11.38 (TOC 25.11.38). Allotted to 3 CAACU, Malta 11.1.39. Shot down into the Mediterranean by HMS *Sussex* 27.6.39.

N1840 (c/n 5283) Allocated to 26 MU 28.9.38 but allocation canx. To 24Gp Henlow 8.10.38 (TOC 6.10.38). To 36 MU 28.11.38 (TOC 25.11.38). Allotted to 3 CAACU, Malta 11.1.39. Crashed into the sea 30.6.39 after radio control was lost during a sortie with HMS *Sussex*.

N1841 (c/n 5284) Allocated to 26 MU 30.9.38 but allocation canx. To 24Gp Henlow 8.10.38 (TOC 12.10.38). To 1 AACU 24.1.39 (TOC 1.2.39). Shot down by AA fire off Watchet 7.6.39.

N1842 (c/n 5285) Allocated to 26 MU 30.9.38 but allocation canx. To 24Gp Henlow 8.10.38 (TOC 12.10.38). To 22(AC) Gp 2.5.39 for 1 AACU (TOC 5.5.39). Shot down by AA fire off Burrow Head, Wigtown 15.8.39.

N1843 (c/n 5286) Allocated to 26 MU 30.9.38 but allocation canx. To 24Gp Henlow 8.10.38 (TOC 14.10.38). To 22(AC) Gp 2.5.39 for 1 AACU (TOC 5.5.39). Damaged by AA fire 1.8.39 but sank after landing off Burrow Head.

N1844 (c/n 5287) Allocated to 26 MU 14.10.38 (TOC 15.10.38). To 22(AC) Gp 2.5.39 for 1 AACU (TOC 5.5.39). Spun into the sea off Weybourne 27.6.39. SOC 26.6.39.

N1845 (c/n 5288) Allocated to 26 MU 14.10.38 (TOC 25.10.38). To 22(AC) Gp 2.5.39 for 1 AACU (TOC 5.5.39). Crashed into the sea off Weybourne 2.8.39 after the aerial struck the ground and radio control was subsequently lost. To 13 MU for repair 16.12.39. Issued to 20 MU 17.5.40; released to PAU 11.10.40. To 1 AACU 9.3.42. Cat.E 29.4.42. SOC.

N1846 (c/n 5289) Allocated to 24Gp Harlow 14.10.38 (TOC 10.1.39). Allocated to 36 MU 24.4.39 but allocation canx. To 22(AC) Gp 2.5.39 for 1 AACU (TOC 5.5.39), coded '118'. Hit by AA fire and broke up off Weybourne 2.8.39.

N1847 (c/n 5290) Allocated to 24Gp Harlow 2.11.38 (TOC 31.10.38). Allocated to 36 MU 24.4.39 but allocation canx. To 22(AC) Gp 2.5.39 for 1 AACU. Crashed into the sea off Weybourne 5.7.39 after radio control was lost. (TFH 8.15)

Contract 962680/38.
138 aircraft built by de Havilland Aircraft Co Ltd at Hatfield

P4677 (c/n 5291) Allocated to 13 MU 17.2.39 (TOC 10.2.39). Tfd to 36 MU 5.7.39 (TOC 1.7.39). Tfd to Far East charge 21.9.39. Unaccounted for after the fall of Singapore on 15.2.42.

P4678 (c/n 5292) Allocated to 13 MU 17.2.39 (TOC 17.2.39). Tfd to 36 MU 5.7.39 (TOC 4.7.39). Tfd to Far East charge 21.9.39. Unaccounted for after the fall of Singapore on 15.2.42.

P4679 (c/n 5293) Allocated to 13 MU 17.2.39 (TOC 13.2.39). Released to 1 AACU 12.7.39 for 'Z' Flt as an attrition replacement. TOC de Havilland 28.1.41. Issued to PAU St Athan 26.6.41. To 1 AACU 7.8.41. Dived into the ground at Aberporth 5.9.41.

P4680 (c/n 5294) Allocated to 13 MU 17.2.39 (TOC 13.2.39). Released to 1 AACU 12.7.39 for 'Z' Flt as an attrition replacement. TOC de Havilland 2.1.41. Issued to 19 MU 8.5.41 and on to PAU St Athan 16.5.41. To 1 AACU 1.7.41; to PAU 25.3.42; to 1 AACU 15.4.42 and issued to 1618 Flight 31.12.42. Crashed on landing at Cleave 4.4.43.

Performing a radio-controlled landing was never a straightforward affair. Controllers at RAF Cleave, on the north Cornish coast, had to contend with up- and down-draughts as the Queen Bee crossed Coombe Valley on final approach. Then, as the Queen Bee approached the landing area and the trailing aerial came into contact with the ground, the joy-stick was automatically pulled back and engine power was cut. Inevitably the landing would be followed by a series of "broncoed" bounces leading to the aircraft tipping on to its nose. P4700 experienced such a situation at Cleave (F/Lt W. A. "Bill" Young)

P4681 (c/n 5295) Allocated to 13 MU 17.2.39 (TOC 17.2.39). Transferred to 36 MU 5.7.39 (TOC 4.7.39). Transferred to Far East charge 21.9.39. Unaccounted for after the fall of Singapore on 15.2.42.

P4682 (c/n 5296) Allocated to 13 MU 17.2.39 (TOC 24.2.39). Released to 1 AACU 12.7.39 (TOC 3.7.39) for 'X' Flt as an attrition replacement. To 4 MU (de Hav.) 21.11.39; to 10 MU 29.1.40 (TOC 1.3.40). To PAS Hawkinge 21.3.40; to 1 AACU 22.8.40. Crashed into the sea off Cleave 6.9.40.

P4683 (c/n 5297) Allocated to 13 MU 17.2.39 (TOC 17.2.39). Tfd to 36 MU 5.7.39 (TOC 1.7.39). Tfd to Far East charge 21.9.39. Unaccounted for after the fall of Singapore on 15.2.42.

P4684 (c/n 5298) Allocated to 13 MU 17.2.39 (TOC 24.2.39). Released to 1 AACU 12.7.39 (TOC 12.7.39) for 'X' Flt as an attrition replacement. Shot down off Watchet 22.7.40. SOC 2.9.40.

P4685 (c/n 5299) Allocated to 13 MU 17.2.39 (TOC 24.2.39). Released to 1 AACU 12.7.39 (TOC 14.7.39) for 'X' Flt as an attrition replacement. Cat.B/FA 24.10.40; to de Havilland 11.11.40. Issued to 19 MU 7.6.41; released to PAU St Athan 22.7.41. To 1 AACU 30.9.41; Returned to PAU 6.8.42. To 'X' Flt Aberporth 8.9.42. Cat.B/FA 21.1.43 (with 1621 Flt). To 19 MU 11.4.43. Delivered by 48 MU to Bodorgan for 1620 Flt 15.4.43 but due to an allotment error it was ferried on to PAU Manorbier later same day. (TOC by PAU 20.4.43). To 1618 Flt 9.5.43; to 67 MU 27.9.43. Reported Cat.B at de Havilland 7.10.43. Awaiting collection 18.12.43 but sustained minor damage in a flying accident 8.1.44. To 67 MU 22.1.44 for repair and ret'd to PAU 9.2.44. Sustained Cat.B damage 23.8.44; to de Havilland for repair 31.8.44 but SOC 8.1.45.

P4686 (c/n 5300) Allocated to 13 MU 17.2.39 (TOC 3.3.39). Released to 2 AACU 12.7.39 (TOC 17.7.39) as an attrition replacement. To PAU 22.11.40; to 1 AACU 15.12.40. Crashed into the sea off Aberporth 3.1.41. SOC 4.3.41. (TFH 56.55)

P4687 (c/n 5301) Allocated to 13 MU 17.2.39 (TOC 7.3.39). Released to 2 AACU 12.7.39 (TOC 17.7.39) as an attrition replacement. Hit trees during a piloted take-off from a forced-landing near Marlow, Buckinghamshire 22.7.39. SOC 10.39.

P4688 (c/n 5302) Allocated to 13 MU 17.2.39 (TOC 7.3.39). Released to 1 AACU 12.7.39 (TOC 17.7.39) as an attrition replacement. Forced-landed near Manorbier 14.8.39 and presumably not repaired. SOC at the Census 21.6.47.

P4689 (c/n 5303) Allocated to 13 MU 17.2.39 (TOC 7.3.39). To 36 MU 19.7.39 (TOC 24.7.39). TOC at Malta 14.10.39. Ditched off Malta 26.12.39.

P4690 (c/n 5304) Allocated to 13 MU 17.2.39 (TOC 10.3.39) for issue to 1 AACU. Seriously damaged during a piloted forced-landing near Shillington, Bedfordshire 23.5.39. Presumably not repaired. SOC 21.12.39.

P4691 (c/n 5305) Allocated to 13 MU 17.2.39 (TOC 7.3.39). Released to 1 AACU 12.7.39 (TOC 17.7.39) as an attrition replacement. Crashed 24.10.39, details unknown. SOC 2.40. (TFH 12.15)

P4692 (c/n 5306) Allocated to 13 MU 25.2.39 (TOC 7.3.39). To 36 MU 19.7.39 (TOC 25.7.39) for issue to 3 AACU. TOC at Malta 14.10.39. Ditched off Malta 26.12.39. SOC by HQ Malta 30.12.39.

P4693 (c/n 5307) Allocated to 13 MU 25.2.39 (TOC 7.3.39). To 36 MU 19.7.39 (TOC 26.7.39) for issue to 3 AACU. TOC at Malta 14.10.39. Damaged by AA fire 23.12.39 and crashed on approach to Malta and repaired locally. Crashed and burnt out in Malta 9.2.40.

P4694 (c/n 5308) Allocated to 13 MU 17.2.39 (TOC 7.3.39). To 36 MU 19.7.39 (TOC 27.7.39) for issue to 3 AACU. TOC at Malta 14.10.39. SOC 22.9.42 probably for spares recovery; the engine (No. 82334-143137) being tfd to FAA Queen Bee P4709.

P4695 (c/n 5309) Allocated to 13 MU 25.2.39 (TOC 7.3.39). To 2 AACU 25.7.39. To PAU 22.11.40; to 1 AACU 12.12.40. SOC 25.2.41, probably as a result of crashing into the sea 2.2.41.

P4696 (c/n 5310) Allocated to 13 MU 25.2.39 (TOC 24.3.39). To 1 AACU 4.8.39 (TOC 31.7.39) as an attrition replacement. SOC 2.10.40, details unknown. (TFH 11.00)

P4697 (c/n 5311) Allocated to 13 MU 25.2.39 (TOC 24.3.39). To 1 AACU 28.7.39 (TOC 31.7.39) as an attrition replacement. To 'V' Flt. Crashed in a field at Bradworthy, Devon 24.4.40 after the W/T aerial had been shot away. SOC 2.5.40.

P4698 (c/n 5312) Allocated to 13 MU 25.2.39 (TOC 24.3.39). To 1 AACU 28.7.39 (TOC 31.7.39) as an attrition replacement. Crashed into the sea off Burrow Head 11.8.39.

P4699 (c/n 5313) Allocated to 19 MU 9.3.39 for storage (TOC 16.3.39). TOC at Henlow 15.8.39 and issued to 1 AACU 30.10.39. Crashed on take-off from Kidsdale during a piloted sortie 31.10.39. Presumably not repaired. SOC 31.12.40.

P4700 (c/n 5314) Allocated to 19 MU 9.3.39 for storage (TOC 16.3.39). TOC at Henlow 15.8.39 and issued to 1 AACU 30.10.39. To 13 MU 8.1.40 for repair; to 4 MU (de Havilland) 5.3.40. Allocated to 5 MU 5.8.40 (TOC 2.8.40); released to PAU 5.12.40. To 'V' Flt/1 AACU 12.2.41. Cat.B/FA 4.4.41. To PAU 27.8.41; to 1 AACU 13.1.42. Ferried St Athan to 'U' Flt 15.1.42. Damaged 19.2.42 when it crashed one mile beyond the airfield. Declared Cat.B 1.3.42. To PAU 19.4.42; to 'Y' Flt, 1 AACU 30.7.42. To PAU Manorbier 6.8.42. RIW de Havilland 1.9.42. To PAU 27.10.42. Crashed into the sea off Manorbier 5.3.43.

P4701 (c/n 5315) Allocated to 19 MU 9.3.39 for storage (TOC 23.3.39). To Henlow 15.8.39 and issued to 1 AACU 24.11.39. To 13 MU for repair 5.1.40; to 4 MU (DH) 5.3.40. Issued to 20 MU 29.8.40 (TOC 25.8.40). Released to PAU 11.10.40; to 1 AACU 19.11.40. Crashed into the sea 25.2.41. (TFH 36.25)

P4702 (c/n 5316) Allocated to 19 MU 9.3.39 for storage (TOC 18.4.39). To Henlow 15.8.39 and issued to 1 AACU 9.12.39. To 4 MU (de Hav) 23.2.40. Allocated to 5 MU 10.8.40 (TOC 2.8.40). Released to PAU 8.11.40; to 1 AACU 12.12.40. Shot down off Aberporth 2.1.41. SOC 4.3.41.

P4703 (c/n 5317) Allocated to 19 MU 9.3.39 for storage (TOC 18.4.39). To Henlow 15.8.39 and issued to 1 AACU 16.1.40. Damaged by AA fire off Burrow Head 23.2.40; forced-landed in the sea but sank before recovery. (TFH 15.35)

P4704 (c/n 5318) Allocated to 19 MU 9.3.39 for storage (TOC 23.3.39). To PAS Henlow 24.9.39; TOC by 1 AACU 1.3.40. Swung on take-off from Kidsdale and hit trees 12.4.40. SOC 13.4.40.

P4705 (c/n 5319) Allocated to 19 MU 9.3.39 for storage (TOC 23.3.39). To PAS Henlow 24.9.39; TOC by 1 AACU 30.11.39. Shot down off Manorbier 10.7.40. (TFH 19.10)

P4706 (c/n 5320) Allocated to 19 MU 9.3.39 for storage (TOC 23.3.39). TOC by PAS Henlow 15.8.39 and issued to 1 AACU 30.11.39. To de Havilland 28.11.40; to PAU 23.3.41; to 1 AACU 13.5.41. Possible accident 6.6.41. Cat.B 11.6.41 at de Havilland. To PAU St Athan 20.8.41. Crashed into the sea off Cleave 27.3.42. SOC 31.8.42.

P4707 (c/n 5321) Allocated to 19 MU 9.3.39 for storage (TOC 18.4.39). TOC by PAS Henlow 24.9.39 and issued to 1 AACU 12.1.40. Hit by AA fire 10.4.40 and crashed into the sea off Cleave. SOC 15.4.40.

P4708 (c/n 5322) Allocated to 19 MU 9.3.39 for storage (TOC 18.4.39). TOC by PAS Henlow 24.9.39; to PAS Hawkinge 22.2.40. To 36 MU 7.3.40 and issued to Malta 5.4.40. Tfd to the Admiralty and reported at Royal Navy Aircraft Repair Yard, Fayid, Egypt 8.42-9.42. SOC 31.3.43.

P4709 (c/n 5323) Thought to have been issued to PAU until tfd to 3 AACU. Bounced heavily on landing at Hal Far, Malta 13.3.40. Repaired. Tfd to the FAA (probably in the Middle East) as a Queen Bee c1940. Tfd to the FAA and TOC by RNAS Fayid, Egypt 28.8.41. To 775 Sqdn, Dekheila, Egypt and coded '8' 12.41. To RNARY Fayid 9.43 and converted to "Tiger Moth" standard; air-tested 28.9.43. Ret'd to 775 Sqdn 11-43 (until 3.44). Reported back at RNARY Fayid 1945 and used as a communications 'hack' by Lt. P.W.Brooks RN until 2.46. No other details known until SOC at Hal Far 11.8.48. (See also engine details for Queen Bee P4694.)

P4710 (c/n 5324) Allocated to 19 MU 9.3.39 for storage (TOC 18.4.39). To 13 MU 24.10.39; to PAS Hawkinge 22.2.40. To 1 AACU 26.4.40. Shot down off Burrow Head 26.4.40. SOC 6.6.40 (TFH 15.10)

P4711 (c/n 5325) Allocated to 19 MU 30.3.39 for storage (TOC 4.4.39). To PAS 27.8.40; to 'V' Flt/1AACU 14.9.40. To de Havilland 5.10.40 for repairs, after which to 19 MU 23.6.41. Released to PAU St Athan 23.7.41 but SOC 27.12.41 after damaged in a forced landing near Llangybi, Cardigan 18.12.41.

P4712 (c/n 5326) Allocated to 19 MU 30.3.39 for storage (TOC 1.4.39). To PAS 27.8.40; to 1AACU 18.9.40. To de Havilland 29.10.40 for repairs, after which to PAU St Athan 27.12.40. To 1AACU 1.3.41. Shot down near Kidsdale 11.10.41. SOC 20.10.41

P4713 (c/n 5327) Allocated to 19 MU 30.3.39 for storage (TOC 1.4.39). To 32 MU 21.10.40 but released to PAU two days later. To 1AACU 5.11.40. Shot down by rockets off Aberporth, Cardigan 17.12.40. SOC 4.3.41.

P4714 (c/n 5328) Allocated to 19 MU 30.3.39 for storage (TOC 4.4.39). To PAU 26.9.40 and on to 1 AACU 28.9.49. Crashed near Cleave 17.4.41. To DH for repairs 26.4.41 but probably not repaired. SOC at Census 1.4.42.

P4715 (c/n 5329) Allocated to 19 MU 30.3.39 for storage (TOC 18.4.39). To 13 MU 24.10.39; to 36 MU 5.1.40. TOC Mediterranean Command 5.4.41 for 3 AACU. Tfd to the Admiralty and reported with 775 Squadron, Dekheila, Egypt 8.41. Struck water during a test flight at Port Said, Egypt 18.4.42 and declared Cat.Z. Eventually SOC 31.3.43.

P4716 (c/n 5330) Allocated to 19 MU 30.3.39 for storage (TOC 18.4.39). To 13 MU 24.10.39. Released to PAS 22.2.40. To 1 AACU 3.5.40. Lost height and hit a lake on approach to Cleave 8.7.40. SOC 20.7.40.

P4747 (c/n 5331) Allocated to 19 MU 30.3.39 for storage (TOC 19.4.39). Released to PAS Henlow 4.12.39; to Hawkinge, Kent 24.2.40. To 1 AACU 3.7.40. Possibly sustained damage as with 50 MU 8.9.40 and later to DH 16.10.40. To 19 MU 8.2.41; released to PAU 20.2.41. To 1 AACU 20.3.41. Crashed into the sea off Manorbier 27.6.41. SOC 6.8.41.

P4748 (c/n 5332) Allocated to 19 MU 30.3.39 for storage (TOC 19.4.39). To 13 MU 24.10.39; to 36 MU 12.1.40. TOC by 3 AACU Malta 4.3.40. SOC 31.3.43, circumstances unkn.

P4749 (c/n 5333) Allocated to 19 MU 30.3.39 for storage (TOC 13.4.39). To PAU 18.10.40; to 1 AACU 9.11.40. Damaged 20.4.41; to DH 22.4.41 for repair. To PAU 7.8.41. With 1 AACU at 31.12.41 Census. Shot down off Burrow Head 13.2.42.

P4750 (c/n 5334) Allocated to 19 MU 30.3.39 for storage (TOC 13.4.39). Released to PAU 2.10.40; to 1 AACU 21.10.40. Damaged 3.5.41; to DH for repair 4.5.41. To PAU 12.9.41; to 1 AACU 19.9.41. Crashed into the sea 2nm north of Bude, Cornwall 7.3.42. SOC 31.8.42.

P4751 (c/n 5335) Allocated to 19 MU 30.3.39 for storage (TOC 13.4.39). Released to PAU 10.10.40; to 1 AACU 16.10.40. Crashed into the sea off Cleave 25.2.42 and SOC same date.

P4752 (c/n 5336) Allocated to 19 MU 30.3.39 for storage (TOC 13.4.39). Released to PAU 14.10.40; to 1 AACU 21.10.40. Shot down off Burrow Head 3.2.41. SOC 4.3.41. (TFH 25.45)

P4753 (c/n 5337) Allocated to 19 MU 30.3.39 for storage (TOC 19.4.39). Released to HAD 20.10.39; to PAS Henlow 1.2.40; to PAU Hawkinge 24.2.40. To 36 MU 7.3.40 and later reported at Malta 6.4.40 for 3 AACU. SOC 31.3.43.

P4754 (c/n 5338) Allocated to 19 MU 30.3.39 for storage (TOC 19.4.39). To 13 MU 24.10.39; released to PAS Hawkinge 22.2.40. To 1 AACU 26.4.40. Shot down off Burrow Head and sank 6.5.40.

P4755 (c/n 5339) Allocated to 19 MU 30.3.39 for storage (TOC 20.4.39). To 13 MU 10.10.39; released to PAS Hawkinge 22.2.40. To 1 AACU 7.5.40. Crashed on landing off Burrow Head and sank 30.5.40. SOC 28.6.40. (TFH 27.40)

P4756 (c/n 5340) Allocated to 19 MU 19.4.39 for storage (TOC 25.4.39). To 13 MU 10.11.39; released to PAS Hawkinge 22.2.40. To 1 AACU 7.5.40. Hit a hut on landing at Kidsdale 9.5.40. SOC 13.5.40.

P4757 (c/n 5341) Allocated to 19 MU 30.3.39 for storage (TOC 25.4.39). Released to PAU St Athan 1.11.40; to 1 AACU 13.11.40. To SAS/DH 11.3.41 until 6.4.41 when to 19 MU. Released to PAU 15.5.41; to 1 AACU 13.6.41. Again to SAS/DH 18.8.41 until 3.10.41 when to 19 MU. Released to PAU 2.11.41; to 1 AACU 13.1.42; to PAU 7.3.42. Crashed on approach to Towyn, Conway 16.4.42.

P4758 (c/n 5342) Allocated to 19 MU 30.3.39 for storage (TOC 25.4.39). Released to PAU St Athan 29.1.40; to 1 AACU 25.9.40. Crashed 20m south of Burrow Head 10.12.40 after control was lost in bad weather.

P4759 (c/n 5343) Allocated to 19 MU 30.3.39 for storage (TOC 28.4.39). Released to PAU St Athan 30.11.40; to 1 AACU 15.1.42. Crashed into the sea off Ty Croes, Anglesey 16.4.42.

P4760 (c/n 5344) Allocated to 19 MU 19.4.39 for storage (TOC 25.4.39). To 13 MU 10.11.39; released to PAS Henlow 1.2.40. To 36 MU 1.3.40 and allocated for shipment to Malta. TOC Med Command 5.4.40. Reported at Royal Navy Aircraft Repair Yard, Fayid 9.42 where it was converted to "Tiger Moth" standard issued to 775 Squadron, Dekheila 10.42. Reportedly sustained damage to prop and engine bearers when it swung to port and struck a building at Ta Kali 3.3.45. Officially SOC 31.3.45.

P4761 (c/n 5345) Allocated to 19 MU 19.4.39 for storage (TOC 25.4.39). To 13 MU 10.11.39; released to PAS Hawkinge 22.2.40. To 1 AACU 15.5.40. Sustained damage in a flying accident 19.5.40 and conveyed to 4 MU (DH) 24.5.40. To 20 MU 27.9.40; to PAU 11.10.40. To 1 AACU 6.11.40; to 'X' Flt Aberporth 21.10.41. Returned to DH for repairs (date unknown); aw/cn 19.4.43. To 19 MU 1.5.43; later released to 1618 Flt. To PAU 8.9.43 but wrecked 7.12.43 in a forced-landing near Cardigan, West Wales (which suggests a possible allocation to 1618 Flt).

P4762 (c/n 5346) Allocated to 19 MU 19.4.39 for storage (TOC 25.4.39). To 13 MU 10.11.39. Released to PAS Hawkinge (date unknown); to Henlow 1.3.40. To 1 AACU 15.6.40. Glided into the sea off Burrow Head and sank 24.5.40. (TFH 21.50)

P4763 (c/n 5347) Allocated to 19 MU 19.4.39 for storage (TOC 27.4.39). To 13 MU 10.11.39; released to PAS Hawkinge 20.2.40. To 1 AACU 15.5.40. Failed to answer signals and crashed on landing at Kidsdale 3.6.40. SOC 6.6.40.

P4764 (c/n 5348) Allocated to 19 MU 30.3.39 for storage (TOC 2.5.39). Released to PAU 1.11.40; to 1 AACU 8.11.40. Noted with 'V' Flt/a AACU 12.41. Crashed at Langtree, Devon 10.7.42. SOC 31.7.42.

P4765 (c/n 5349) Allocated to 19 MU 30.3.39 for storage (TOC 2.5.39). Returned to DH 6.2.41; to 19 MU 3.3.41. Released to PAU 20.4.41; to 1 AACU 15.5.41. Crashed into the sea off Tonfanau, Carmarthenshire 23.6.41.

P4766 (c/n 5350) Allocated to 19 MU 30.3.39 (TOC 28.4.39). Released to PAU 1.11.40; to 1 AACU 19.1.41 Shot down off Burrow Head 3.2.41. (TFH 31.25)

P4767 (c/n 5351) Allocated to 19 MU 19.4.39 (TOC 27.4.39). Released to PAS Henlow 24.11.39; to Hawkinge 24.2.40. To 1 AACU 18.11.40. To SAS/DH 26.2.41; to PAU St. Athan 4.7.41. To 1 AACU 28.9.41. Crashed near Newborough Warren, Isle of Anglesey 22.10.41. Initially Cat.B; re-Cat.E and SOC 30.10.41.

P4768 (c/n 5352) Allocated to 19 MU 19.4.39 (TOC 27.4.39). Released to PAS Henlow 5.12.39; to Hawkinge 24.2.40. To 1 AACU 3.7.40. Shot down off Manorbier 3.9.40.

P4769 (c/n 5353) Allocated to 19 MU 19.4.39 (TOC 27.4.39). Released to PAS Henlow 24.11.39; to Hawkinge 24.2.40. To 1 AACU 17.6.40; to 4 MU/de Hav

21.7.40 for Cat.3 repairs. To 20 MU 17.12.40. Sustained Cat.E damage 7.7.41 and SOC 23.7.41.

P4770 (c/n 5354) Allocated to 19 MU 19.4.39 (TOC 11.5.39). Released to PAS Henlow 24.11.39; to Hawkinge 24.2.40. To 1 AACU 3.6.40. Hit by AA 3.7.40; engine cut; landed off Burrow Head but sank. SOC 2.9.40 (TFH 20.30)

P4771 (c/n 5355) Allocated to 19 MU 30.3.39 (TOC 10.5.39). Released to PAU 29.11.40; to 1 AACU 10.2.41. Shot down off Ty Croes, Isle of Anglesey 26.1.42. SOC 5.2.42.

P4772 (c/n 5356) Allocated to 8 MU 19.4.39 but canx and re-allocated to 19 MU 10.5.39 (TOC same date). Released to PAU 9.12.40; to 1 AACU 15.1.41. To SAS/DH 18.3.41; Returned PAU 4.7.41. To 1 AACU 23.9.41. To DH as Cat.B 30.11.41. Repaired by 31.1.42. To 19 MU 9.2.42; released to PAU 14.3.42. To 1AACU 5.4.42. Crashed at Sandy Cove, Cornwall 4.6.42. SOC 19.6.42.

P4773 (c/n 5357) Allocated to 8 MU 19.4.39 but canx and re-allocated to 19 MU 10.5.39 (TOC 4.5.39). Released to PAU 29.11.40; to 1 AACU 9.1.41. Crashed on landing at Aberporth 12.1.41.

P4774 (c/n 5358) Allocated to 8 MU 19.4.39 (TOC 10.5.39). Released to PAU Manorbier 2.3.43. To 1620 Flight 23.3.43. To PAU 29.7.43. Sustained Cat.B damage 15.8.43. Recorded still at Manorbier 21.3.46. Sold 4.9.47, details not known.

P4775 (c/n 5359) Allocated to 8 MU 19.4.39 but canx and re-allocated to 19 MU 10.5.39 (TOC 4.5.39). Released to PAU 29.11.40; to 1 AACU 10.2.41. Shot down at Ty Croes 26.1.42.

P4776 (c/n 5360) Allocated to 8 MU 19.4.39 but canx and re-allocated to 19 MU 10.5.39 (TOC 5.5.39). Released to PAU 29.11.40; to 1 AACU 12.2.41. Shot down off Aberporth 7.3.41. SOC 1.6.41. (TFH 9.00)

P4777 (c/n 5361) Allocated to 19 MU 19.4.39 (TOC 11.5.39). Released to PAS Henlow 5.12.39; to PAS Hawkinge 22.2.40. To 1 AACU 3.6.40; to 4 MU (DH) 26.7.40. To 20 MU 1.12.40; released to PAU 17.12.40. To 1 AACU 12.2.41. Damaged during a forced landing near Aberporth 26.2.41. SOC 12.5.41.

P4778 (c/n 5362) Allocated to 19 MU 19.4.39 (TOC 11.5.39). Released to PAS Henlow 5.12.39; to PAS Hawkinge 24.2.40. To 1 AACU 3.7.40. Shot down off Manorbier 7.8.40. SOC 4.3.41.

P4779 (c/n 5363) Allocated to 19 MU 19.4.39 (TOC 11.5.39). Released to PAS Henlow 5.12.39; to PAS Hawkinge 24.2.40. To 1 AACU 3.6.40. Shot down off Burrow Head 7.6.40. SOC 28.6.40. (TFH 23.45)

P4780 (c/n 5364) Allocated to 19 MU 19.4.39 (TOC 11.5.39). Released to PAS Henlow 5.12.39; to PAS Hawkinge 22.2.40. To 1 AACU 18.7.40; to SAS/DH 12.11.40. To PAU St Athan 13.3.41; to 1 AACU 12.5.41. Flying accident 13.6.41. Repaired but later shot down off Weybourne 12.12.41.

P4781 (c/n 5365) Allocated to 8 MU 19.4.39 (TOC 11.5.39). Released to PAU 8.11.40; to 1 AACU 9.1.41. Sustained extensive damage 22.1.41 when radio contact was lost before crashing at Perunain, nr Swansea. To DH 28.1.41 but declared unrepairable and SOC 20.2.41. (TFH 11.45)

P4788 (c/n 5366) Allocated to 8 MU 19.4.39 (TOC 4.5.39). Released to PAU 27.7.42; Returned to 8 MU 31.12.42. To PAU 11.2.43. Sustained Cat.B damage 27.3.43; conveyed to 78 MU 4.3.43. To PAU 8.9.43; to 1620 Flt 28.10.43. To RAF Manorbier 12.12.43. SOC 26.4.45, details unknown.

P4789 (c/n 5367) Allocated to 8 MU 19.4.39 (TOC 8.5.39). Released to PAU 3.10.41; to 1 AACU 8.12.41. Sustained Cat.B damage 27.12.41; to DH for repairs 2.1.42. To 19 MU 19.2.42; to PAU 14.3.43; to 1 AACU 11.4.42. Shot down at Ty Croes 1.8.42.

P4790 (c/n 5368) Allocated to 8 MU 19.4.39 (TOC 28.6.39). Released to PAU 18.6.41; to 1 AACU 12.8.41. Crashed on landing at Aberporth 21.11.41. Initially Cat.B but SOC 17.12.41.

P4791 (c/n 5369) Allocated to 8 MU 19.4.39 (TOC 8.5.39). Released to PAU 3.10.41. Sustained Cat.B damage 6.12.41; to DH for repair. To 1 AACU 13.2.42. Crashed off Burrow Head 25.3.42. SOC 28.3.42.

P4792 (c/n 5370) Allocated to 8 MU 19.4.39 (TOC 8.5.39). Released to PAU 18.6.41; to 63 MU 17.9.41; Returned 1AACU (date unkn). Crashed on landing at Weybourne 17.11.41. Unaccounted for at 1943 Census; possibly reduced to spares at DH.

P4793 (c/n 5371) Allocated to 8 MU 19.4.39 (TOC 8.5.39). Released to PAU 18.6.41; to 1 AACU 22.7.41. Crashed into the sea off Anglesey 23.9.41. Declared Cat.B but SOC 1.4.42.

P4794 (c/n 5372) Allocated to 8 MU 19.4.39 (TOC 8.5.39). Released to PAU 3.10.41 and coded '396'; to 1 AACU 28.10.41. Sustained Cat.B damage 8.12.41; to DH for repair 15.12.41. To 19 MU 18.2.42; to PAU 14.3.42; to 1 AACU 14.5.42. Crashed on landing at Aberporth 25.7.42.

P4795 (c/n 5373) Allocated to 8 MU 19.4.39 (TOC 12.5.39). Released to PAU 18.6.41. To 1 AACU 7.8.41. Crashed into the sea off Towyn 1.11.41. SOC 27.11.41.

P4796 (c/n 5374) Allocated to 8 MU 19.4.39 (TOC 8.5.39). Released to PAU 25.6.41. To 1 AACU 12.8.41. Shot down into Cardigan Bay 19.6.42.

P4797 (c/n 5375) Allocated to 8 MU 19.4.39 (TOC 16.5.39). To 13 MU 12.1.40. Released to PAS Hawkinge 24.2.40. To 1 AACU 18.7.40. Damaged 21.8.40; to 4 MU (DH) 26.8.40 for repair. Allocated to 19 MU 8.11.40 (TOC 9.1.41); released to PAU 20.2.41. To 1 AACU 8.4.41. To DH 10.5.41 for repair; to 19 MU 17.9.41 and released to PAU 26.9.41. Cat.B damage 19.1.42; repaired and to 19 MU 28.3.42. To PAU 31.3.42. To 1 AACU 11.6.42; to 'X' Flt/1 AACU 4.9.42. Crashed off Aberporth 26.9.42.

P4798 (c/n 5376) Allocated to 8 MU 19.4.39 but canx and issued to 10 MU 26.5.39 (TOC 13.5.39). Released to PAU 19.6.41; to 1 AACU 11.8.41. Crashed near Kidsdale 16.10.41. SOC 26.10.41.

P4799 (c/n 5377) Allocated to 8 MU 19.4.39 but canx and issued to 10 MU 20.5.39 (TOC 13.5.39). Released to PAU 3.10.41; to 1 AACU 8.12.41. Crashed off Burrow Head 23.2.42. SOC 31.8.42.

P4800 (c/n 5378) Allocated to 8 MU 19.4.39 but canx and issued to 10 MU 26.5.39 (TOC 18.5.39); to 13 MU 12.1.40. Released to PAS Hawkinge 24.2.40; later to 1 AACU. Shot down off Burrow Head 15.8.40. SOC 2.9.40.

P4801 (c/n 5379) Allocated to 8 MU 19.4.39 but canx and issued to 10 MU 26.5.39 (TOC 18.5.39); to 1 AACU 12.12.40. Shot down off Aberffraw, Isle of Anglesey 26.2.41. SOC 7.3.41.

P4802 (c/n 5380) Allocated to 8 MU 19.4.39 but canx and re-issued to 10 MU

26.5.39 (TOC 23.5.39); to 13 MU 25.1.40. Released to PAS Hawkinge 24.2.40; to 1 AACU 25.7.40. Crashed on landing off Manorbier 25.10.40.

P4803 (c/n 5381) Allocated to 6 MU 19.5.39 (TOC 23.5.39). Released to PAU 6.5.41; to 1 AACU 13.5.41. To 76 MU 13.7.41. Shot down off Aberporth 19.7.41. To DH 22.7.41 as Cat.B for repair but SOC 25.7.41.

P4804 (c/n 5382) Allocated to 6 MU 10.5.39 (TOC 16.5.39). To Henlow 25.7.39; to 1 AACU 7.9.39. Cat.2 flying accident 2.12.40; to DH 15.12.40 for repair. To PAU 3.4.41; to 1 AACU 27.5.41. Shot down off Aberporth 4.9.41.

P4805 (c/n 5383) Allocated to 6 MU 10.5.39 (TOC 23.5.39). To 1 AACU 7.11.41 and coded '379'. Cat.B crash 10.1.42; to DH for repair. To 19 MU 28.3.42; released to PAU 31.3.42. To 1 AACU 11.6.42. Crashed into the sea off Anglesey 18.2.43.

P4806 (c/n 5384) Allocated to 6 MU 10.5.39 (TOC 23.5.39). Released to PAU 21.5.41; to 1 AACU 2.7.41. Cat.B damage 26.3.42. RIW DH 6.4.42. To 19 MU 11.5.42; to PAU 27.7.42; to 1618 Flight 22.12.42. Crashed on landing at Cleave, Cornwall 7.3.43. SOC 18.3.43.

P4807 (c/n 5385) Allocated to 6 MU 10.5.39 (TOC 23.5.39). Released to PAU 6.5.41; to 1 AACU 10.6.41. Shot down off Burrow Head 12.7.41. SOC 6.8.41.

P4808 (c/n 5386) Allocated to 6 MU 10.5.39 (TOC 23.5.39). Released to PAU 21.5.41; to 1 AACU 1.7.41. Crashed 2mls north of Cleave 27.3.42. SOC 7.4.42.

P4809 (c/n 5387) Allocated to 6 MU 10.5.39 (TOC 23.5.39). Released to PAU 21.5.41; to 1 AACU 5.7.41. Shot down off Tonfanau 1.11.41. SOC 1.12.41.

P4810 (c/n 5388) Allocated to 6 MU 10.5.39 (TOC 23.5.39). Released to PAU 9.7.41; to 1 AACU 23.9.41. Cat.B 11.7.42 (or 14.7.42). To 1620 Flt 31.12.42. To 34 MU as Cat.E1.MR. Sold 'as is' to W.A. Rollason, Croydon 23.11.46 against Authority 41G/103701.

P4811 (c/n 5389) Allocated to 6 MU 10.5.39 (TOC 23.5.39). Released to PAU 6.5.41; to 1 AACU 13.6.41. Shot down at Ty Croes 14.8.41.

P4812 (c/n 5390) Allocated to 6 MU 10.5.39 (TOC 23.5.39). Released to PAU 6.5.41; to 1 AACU 8.6.41. Dived into the sea off Burrow Head 18.8.41.

P4813 (c/n 5391) Allocated to 6 MU 10.5.39 (TOC 26.5.39). Released to Henlow 25.7.39; to 2 AACU 26.10.39; to 1 AACU 21.12.39. To 4 MU/DH 4.5.40 for repairs; to 20 MU 19.9.40; released to PAU 11.10.40. To 1 AACU 28.10.40; to DH for repair 2.10.40. To PAU 13.4.41; to 1 AACU 25.6.41. Crashed on landing at Weybourne 2.7.41. Initially Cat.B but re-cat Cat.E 16.7.41 and SOC.

P4814 (c/n 5392) Allocated to 20 MU 20.5.39 (TOC 31.5.39). Released to PAU 14.8.40; to 1 AACU 24.9.40. Crashed into the sea off Aberporth 13.1.41; SOC 4.3.41. (TFH 20.05)

P4815 (c/n 5393) Allocated to 20 MU 26.5.39 (TOC 5.6.39). Released to PAS Hawkinge 6.3.40; to 1 AACU 23.7.40. To DH for repair 18.9.40 (following a crash 29.8.40). To 19 MU 3.2.41; released to PAU 20.2.41. To 1 AACU 6.4.41. Crashed immediately after launch at Manorbier 5.7.41. SOC 15.7.41.

P4816 (c/n 5394) Allocated to 20 MU 26.5.39 but canx and instead to DH 30.6.39. To 8 MU 24.5.40; to PAU 8.11.40; to 1 AACU 14.12.40. Shot down off Anglesey 3.5.41

P4817 (c/n 5395) Allocated to 20 MU 26.5.39 (TOC 31.5.39). Released to PAS St Athan 26.8.40.; to 1 AACU 28.9.40. Sustained Cat.B damage 5.11.41; to DH 11.11.41 for repair. To PAU 9.12.41; to 1 AACU 8.3.42. Crashed on approach to Towyn 23.3.42. SOC 30.3.42.

P4818 (c/n 5396) Allocated to 20 MU 26.5.39 (TOC 5.6.39). Released to PAU 14.8.40; to 1 AACU 10.9.40. Shot down off Burrow Head 25.9.40. SOC 1.11.43. (TFH 15.45)

P4819 (c/n 5397) Allocated to 20 MU 26.5.39 (TOC 31.5.39). Released to PAU 11.10.40; to 1 AACU 28.10.40. Shot down off Aberporth 9.1.41. SOC 4.3.41. (TFH 23.50)

P4820 (c/n 5398) Allocated to 20 MU 26.5.39 (TOC 13.6.39). Released to PAS 26.8.40; to 1 AACU 3.4.42. Crashed on approach to Cleave 23.8.42. SOC 31.8.42.

P4821 (c/n 5399) Allocated to 20 MU 26.5.39 (TOC 13.6.39). Released to PAS 26.8.40; to 1 AACU 25.9.40. Spun into the sea off Cleave 19.11.40. SOC 3.12.40. (TFH 9.45)

P4822 (c/n 5400) Allocated to 20 MU 26.5.39 (TOC 31.5.39). Released to PAS 26.8.40; to 1 AACU 28.2.41. Sank off Burrow Head 7.3.41. SOC 2.4.41. (TFH 32.50)

P5731 (c/n 5401) Allocated to 6 MU 20.6.39 (TOC 7.6.39). Released to PAU 9.7.41; to 1 AACU 19.9.41. Shot down near Aberporth 3.10.41. (TFH 10.20)

P5732 (c/n 5402) Allocated to 6 MU 20.6.39 (TOC 7.6.39). Released to PAU 6.5.41; to 1 AACU 26.6.41. Shot down off Ty Croes Range, Anglesey 1.8.41.

P5733 (c/n 5403) Allocated to 6 MU 20.6.39 (TOC 7.6.39). Released to PAU 9.7.41; to 1 AACU 19.9.41. Dived into the ground at Aberporth 17.10.41. SOC 28.10.41.

P5734 (c/n 5404) Allocated to 6 MU 20.6.39 (TOC 12.6.39). Released to PAU 21.5.41; reportedly allocated to RAF Odiham 5.7.41 but shot down off Aberporth 20.7.41, probably whilst with 1AACU. SOC same date.

P5735 (c/n 5405) Allocated to 6 MU 20.6.39 (TOC 12.6.39). Released to PAU 23.5.41; to 1 AACU 7.8.41. Crashed into the sea off Aberporth 18.9.41. SOC 1.4.42.

P5736 (c/n 5406) Allocated to 6 MU 20.6.39 (TOC 19.6.39). To 13 MU 3.8.39; released to 1 AACU 8.9.39. To 4 MU/DH 20.7.40 for repair. To 20 MU 15.11.40; released to PAU 17.12.40; to 1 AACU 12.2.41. Shot down off Aberporth 8.4.41. SOC 1.6.41. (TFH 44.50)

P5737 (c/n 5407) Allocated to 6 MU 20.6.39 (TOC 12.6.39). Released to PAU 16.7.41; to 1 AACU 1.10.41. Cat.B FA 6.1.42; to DH for repair. To 19 MU 19.2.42; released to PAU 31.3.42.; to 1 AACU 14.5.42. Cat.B at DH 26.2.43. To 1618 Flt 18.5.43; to 1620 Flt 9.7.43. Crashed near Bodorgan, Anglesey 6.8.43.

P5738 (c/n 5408) Allocated to 6 MU 20.6.39 (TOC 13.6.39). Released to PAU 23.5.41; to 1 AACU 22.7.41. Crashed off Ty Croes 20.8.41 after control was lost.

P5739 (c/n 5409) Allocated to 6 MU 20.6.39 (TOC 27.6.39). Tfd to 13 MU 25.7.39; to 1 AACU 21.12.39. Shot down off Cleave 2.7.40. SOC 5.8.40. (TFH 12.30)

P5740 (c/n 5410) Allocated to 6 MU 20.6.39 (TOC 19.6.39). Tfd to 13 MU 25.7.39; to 2 AACU 26.10.39; to 1 AACU

Set against the rolling Cornish countryside, the depicted scene belies the fact that Britain was at war. Queen Bee P5743 is prepared for a pilotless sortie from RAF Cleave and displays an interesting diamond-shaped marking on the upper rear fuselage that seems to have been applied to late-production aircraft. (F/Lt W.A. "Bill" Young)

21.12.39. Shot down off Cleave 17.6.40. SOC 5.8.40. (TFH 17.45)

P5741 (c/n 5411) Allocated to 5 MU 20.6.39 (TOC 13.6.39). Tfd to 13 MU 12.1.40; to PAS Hawkinge 24.2.40. To 1 AACU 3.7.40. To 4 MU/DH for repair 2.8.40. To 20 MU 9.12.40; released to PAU 26.2.41; to 1 AACU 5.5.41. Sustained Cat.B damage 15.6.41; to DH for repair; to PAU 20.8.41. To 19 MU 30.9.41; to 1 AACU 31.12.41 or 13.1.42. Cat.E 20.1.42. SOC 31.8.42.Released to PAU 23.5.41; to 1 AACU 7.8.41. Shot down off Aberporth 20.1.42. SOC 1.4.42.

P5742 (c/n 5412) Allocated to 5 MU 20.6.39 (TOC 20.6.39). Released to PAS Hawkinge 18.3.40; to Y Flt/1 AACU 7.9.40. Landed in the sea off Manorbier and damaged beyond repair during salvage 14.10.40. SOC 29.10.40.

P5743 (c/n 5413) Allocated to 5 MU 20.6.39 (TOC 21.6.39). Released to PAS Hawkinge 18.3.40; to 'V' Flt/1 AACU 25.7.40 and possibly coded '316'. To 50 MU 11.9.40; to 4 MU/DH 17.9.40; to 19 MU 24.11.40. To PAU 3.12.40. Dived into the ground 3miles north of St. Athan 2.1.41. SOC 11.1.41.

P5744 (c/n 5414) Allocated to 5 MU 20.6.39 (TOC 19.6.39). Released to PAS Hawkinge 18.3.40; to 1 AACU 16.8.40. Shot down off Burrow Head 4.9.40. SOC 1.11.40. (TFH 19.20)

P5745 (c/n 5415) Allocated to 5 MU 20.6.39 (TOC 19.6.39). Released to PAS Hawkinge 18.3.40; to 'V' Flt/1 AACU 17.10.40. To DH 24.4.41 (following an accident 19.4.41); to PAU 24.8.41; to 1 AACU 13.1.42. Crashed into the sea off Aberporth 14.2.42.

P5746 (c/n 5416) Allocated to 5 MU 20.6.39 (TOC 21.6.39). Released to PAS Hawkinge 18.3.40; to 1 AACU 16.8.40. To 4 MU/DH 18.9.40; to PAU 6.6.41; to 1 AACU 11.8.41. Shot down off Burrow Head 26.2.42.

P5747 (c/n 5417) Allocated to 5 MU 26.6.39 (TOC 27.6.39). Released to PAS Hawkinge 18.3.40; to 1 AACU 29.8.40. Crashed off Manorbier 4.12.40 after radio control was lost in cloud.

P5748 (c/n 5411) Allocated to 5 MU 20.6.39 (TOC 27.6.39). Released to PAU 12.8.40; to 'V' Flt/1 AACU 14.9.40. Crashed off Cleave 23.9.40 after engine cut.

P5749 (c/n 5419) Allocated to 5 MU 20.6.39 (TOC 27.6.39). Released to PAU 12.8.40; to 1 AACU 25.9.40. To DH 17.10.40; to PAU 20.5.41; to 1 AACU 4.7.41. Crashed on landing at Aberporth 5.8.42.

P5767 (c/n 5420) Allocated to 24 Grp, Henlow 20.6.39 (TOC 29.6.39). To 1 AACU 21.8.39. Spun into the ground 13.10.39 (location unknown). SOC 29.10.39.

P5768 (c/n 5421) Allocated to 24 Grp, Henlow 20.6.39 (TOC 29.6.39). To 1 AACU 21.8.39. Shot down into the sea 29.9.39 (location unknown). SOC 29.10.39.

P5769 (c/n 5422) Allocated to 24 Grp, Henlow 20.6.39 (TOC 29.6.39). To 2 AACU 17.8.39. To PAU 22.11.40; to 1 AACU 12.12.40. Shot down off Aberffraw, Anglesey 22.2.41. SOC 2.4.41. (TFH 79.20)

P5770 (c/n 5423) Allocated to 24 Grp, Henlow 20.6.39 (TOC 29.6.39). To 2 AACU 17.8.39. To PAU 22.11.40; to 1 AACU 10.1.41. To DH 28.1.41; returned to PAU 4.7.41. Cat.B 31.10.41; to DH for repair 7.11.41. To PAU 9.12.41. Again, to DH 31.12.41 for repair; to PAU 28.1.42. To 1 AACU 17.3.42. Cat.B 4.4.42; to DH for repair 15.4.42. To 19 MU 29.5.42; to PAU 28.6.42; to 'U' Flt/1 AACU 16.8.42. Cat.B 23.1.43 (by which time with 1621 Flt/1 AACU). Crashed on landing at Aberporth 23.1.43. SOC 2.2.43.

P5771 (c/n 5424) Allocated to 6 MU 23.6.39 (TOC 3.7.39); to Henlow 18.8.39; to 1 AACU 30.11.39. To 4 MU/DH 16.3.40; to 5 MU 18.8.40; released to PAU 9.11.40. Crashed off Manorbier 16.6.42.

P5772 (c/n 5425) Allocated to 6 MU 23.6.39 (TOC 3.7.39); released to PAS Henlow 17.8.39. Hit wall in forced landing

44 Sitting Ducks and Peeping Toms

in fog at Trawsfynydd, North Wales 19.2.40. The aircraft was being piloted at the time. SOC 9.3.40.

P5773 (c/n 5426) Allocated to 6 MU 1.7.39 (TOC 3.7.39); released to PAS Henlow 17.8.39; to 1 AACU 1.3.40. Stalled and Crashed near Kidsdale 7.3.40. SOC 17.3.40.

P5774 (c/n 5427) Allocated to 13 MU 4.7.39 (TOC 6.7.39); released to 1 AACU 9.9.39. DBR in heavy landing at Kidsdale 12.1.40. SOC 19.1.40.

P5775 (c/n 5428) Allocated to 13 MU 4.7.39 (TOC 7.7.39); released to 1 AACU 8.9.39. Shot down off Burrow Head 19.10.39. SOC 29.10.39.

**Contract B55389/39.
50 aircraft built by de Havilland Aircraft Co Ltd at Hatfield**

V4742 (c/n 5429) Allocated to PAU 15.12.40 but TOC at 19 MU 23.12.40 until 2.1.41 when released to PAU and coded '382'. To 'Y' Flt/1 AACU 26.2.41. To PAU 12.8.41. Cat.B damage 24.10.41 (possibly with 1 AACU). Crashed into the sea off Burrow Head 2.4.42 after radio control was lost.

V4743 (c/n 5430) Allocated to PAU 15.12.40 but TOC at 19 MU 23.12.40 until 24.2.41 when released to T Flt/1 AACU. Glided into the beach 2mls west of Weybourne 22.4.41 after the r/t aerial was shot away. SOC 29.4.41. (TFH 17.15)

V4744 (c/n 5431) Allocated to PAU 15.12.40 but TOC at 19 MU 1.1.41; to PAU 21.1.41. To 'Y' Flt/1 AACU 27.2.41. Overturned after landing on the sea and sank off Manorbier 22.10.41 after radio control was lost. SOC 3.11.41.

V4745 (c/n 5432) Allocated to PAU 15.12.40 but TOC at 19 MU 1.1.41; to PAU 2.1.41. To 1 AACU 4.4.41. DBR after undercarriage collapsed in heavy landing at Towyn 9.7.41. Initially Cat.B but SOC 27.7.41.

V4746 (c/n 5433) Allocated to 19 MU 23.12.40 (TOC 1.1.41); released to PAU 13.1.41. To 1 AACU 3.3.41. Crashed into the sea off Towyn 21.4.41 after radio control was lost. SOC 1.6.41. (TFH 13.55)

V4747 (c/n 5434) Allocated to 19 MU 23.12.40 (TOC 3.1.41); released to PAU 13.1.41; to 'Y' Flt/1 AACU 20.3.41. To PAU 28.3.42. Sustained damage c1.10.43; to DH for repair; returned to PAU 31.12.43. SOC 29.5.44, details unrecorded.

V4748 (c/n 5435) Allocated to 20 MU 1.1.41 (TOC 12.1.41); released to PAU 22.5.41. To 1 AACU 5.7.41. Sustained Cat.B damage 31.8.41; to DH for repair 4.9.41. To PAU 1.11.41; to 1 AACU 19.12.41. Shot down off Manorbier 14.2.42.

V4749 (c/n 5436) Allocated to 20 MU 1.1.41 (TOC 9.1.41); released to PAU 30.6.41. To 1 AACU 24.8.41. Flew into a hill at Stackpool Pier, Pembrokeshire 9.3.42 after radio control was lost. SOC 19.3.42.

V4750 (c/n 5437) Allocated to 20 MU 1.1.41 (TOC 15.1.41); released to PAU 30.6.41. To DH 23.10.41; returned to PAU 15.12.41; to 1 AACU 8.2.42. Sustained Cat.B damage 25.2.42; to DH for repair. To PAU 31.3.42; to 1 AACU 11.6.42. Cat.B damage 23.6.42; to DH for repair 7.7.42. To PAU 25.9.42. Allocated to 1618 Flt 18.11.42. Damaged in heavy landing at Manorbier 23.8.43 whilst with PAU. To DH 24.8.43. Aw/Cn 16.11.43; to PAU 19.11.43. Written-off 14.1.44 and SOC same date.

V4751 (c/n 5438) Allocated to 20 MU 1.1.41 (TOC 2.2.41); released to PAU 30.6.41. To 1 AACU by 31.12.41 Census. Undercarriage collapsed after stalling on landing at Weybourne 26.3.42. SOC 4.4.42 as unrepairable.

V4752 (c/n 5439) Allocated to 20 MU 1.1.41 (TOC 2.2.41); released to PAU 6.7.41. To 1 AACU 19.9.41. Sustained Cat.B damage 5.11.41; to DH for repair 11.11.41; to PAU 9.12.41. To 1 AACU 9.3.42. On 5.6.42 V4752 was recorded with Sunbeam-Talbot (almost certainly at the Talbot factory in London) with Cat.B damage. Transferred to DH 27.6.42. Aw/Cn 22.8.42; to PAU 7.9.42; to 'V' Flt/1 AACU 16.10.42. Crash-landed at Woodford, nr Cleave 18.12.42 after radio control was lost.

NB. The Sunbeam and Talbot motor companies merged on becoming part of the Rootes Group in 1935. During WW2 Rootes devoted much factory space to military vehicle and bomber production as well as aircraft airframe and engine work.

V4753 (c/n 5440) Allocated to 20 MU 1.1.41 (TOC 17.1.41); released to PAU 30.6.41. To 1 AACU 5.9.41. Dived into the sea ½ n.mile west of Towyn 28.11.41 after radio control was lost. SOC 1.12.41.

V4754 (c/n 5441) Allocated to 19 MU 4.1.41 (TOC 6.2.41); released to PAU 20.2.41. To 1 AACU 16.4.41. Sustained Cat.B damage 26.6.41; to DH for repair 1.7.41; to 19 MU 21.10.41; to PAU 1.11.41; to 1 AACU 14.4.42. Shot down by AA fire in Cardigan Bay 1.7.42.

V4755 (c/n 5442) Allocated to 19 MU 4.1.41 (TOC 24.2.41); released to PAU 21.3.41. To 1 AACU 12.5.41 Lost radio control after being hit by AA off Weybourne 2.7.41. SOC 5.11.41. (TFH 18.25)

V4756 (c/n 5443) Allocated to 19 MU 4.1.41 (TOC 6.2.41); released to PAU 20.2.41. To 1 AACU 17.3.41; to PAU 23.12.41; to 'Z' Flt/1 AACU 5.8.42. Crashed at Bryngollon Farm, Llanerchymedd, Anglesey 28.10.42 after radio control was lost.

V4757 (c/n 5444) Allocated to 19 MU 4.1.41 (TOC 6.2.41); released to PAU 21.2.41; to 'T' Flt/1 AACU 20.3.41. Flew into the sea off Weybourne 5.5.41 after the engine failed immediately on take-off. SOC 3.9.41. (TFH 12.20)

V4758 (c/n 5445) Allocated to 19 MU 4.1.41 (TOC 6.2.41); released to PAU 18.5.41; to 1 AACU 1.7.41. Sustained Cat.B damage 10.1.42; to DH for repair 21.1.42. To 19 MU 28.3.42; to PAU 31.3.42. Damaged by AA off Manorbier and crashed on approach 28.7.42.

V4759 (c/n 5446) Allocated to 19 MU 4.1.41 (TOC 6.2.41); released to PAU 21.2.41; to 1 AACU 16.4.41. Dived into the sea off Manorbier 18.8.41 after radio control was lost (which suggests that it had returned to PAU charge). SOC 6.4.42.

V4760 (c/n 5447) Allocated to PAU 18.1.41 (TOC 20.2.41); to 1 AACU 20.4.41. Damaged 21.5.41; to DH 22.5.41 for repair. To PAU 20.8.41; to 19 MU 10.9.41; to PAU 22.9.41. To 52 MU 28.11.41 until 16.12.41 when sold to the USA. Stored in US until overhauled. Reg'd N2726A 1955 to Hayward Leland Productions Inc, Burbank, CA. Flown in the film 'Spirit of St.Louis' (in Pathé News colour scheme as 'NC726A') . To Paul Mantz & Frank Tallman, t/a Tallmantz CA. To Johan M Larsen, Minneapolis, and stored at the Minnesota Aircraft Museum, Flying Cloud Airport, MN. Reg'd 1977 to Eugene O ('Gene') Kunde, St Paul, MN. Stored North Bend, nr Seattle (2002); reg'd to Fred A Bahr of Issaquah, WA 10.7.02 (reserved 6.3.02); reg'd to Port Townsend Aero Museum, Chimacum, Port Ludlow, WA 20.8.02. Undergoing a lengthy rebuild.

V4761 (c/n 5448) Allocated to PAU 18.1.41 (TOC 6.2.41). To 1 AACU 2.3.41.

Queen Bee 45

Few Queen Bees managed to survive into the post-war years and even fewer progressed to flyable condition. V4760 enjoyed a unique post-war life in the USA as a film prop before it began a lengthy restoration at Port Townend Aero Museum. These views clearly illustrate the method of construction in wood and metal. (Jerry Thuotte)

V4767 (c/n 5454) Allocated to PAU 18.1.41 (TOC 15.2.41). To 1 AACU 4.4.41. Crashed into the sea 1mile off Cromer 16.9.41 after losing control due to AA hit. SOC 5.11.41. (TFH 18.15)

V4768 (c/n 5455) Allocated to 19 MU 23.1.41 (TOC 15.2.41). Released to PAU 21.2.41; to 1 AACU 16.4.41. Broke up on landing in the sea off Manorbier 18.8.41 due to damage by AA. SOC 1.4.42.

V4769 (c/n 5456) Allocated to 19 MU 23.1.42 (TOC 19.2.41). Released to PAU 20.3.41; to 1 AACU 15.5.41; to PAU 30.6.41. Hit a tree on take-off from Towyn 7.7.41. (Reportedly conveyed to DH for repairs which were completed on 17.1.42 and returned to PAU 17.2.42. However no further details are recorded; it was not reported at the 1943 Census and finally SOC at the 21.6.47 Census).

V4770 (c/n 5457) Allocated to 19 MU 23.1.41 (TOC 15.2.41). Released to PAU 21.2.41; to 'Y' Flt/1 AACU 22.4.41. Dived into the sea off Manorbier 10.6.42 after being hit by AA. SOC 31.8.42.

V4771 (c/n 5458) Allocated to 19 MU 23.1.41 (TOC 15.2.41). Released to PAU 21.2.41; to 'W' Flt/1 AACU 17.4.41. DBR 6.5.41 when it failed to take-off and hit a hedge at Kidsdale.

V4772 (c/n 5459) Allocated to 19 MU 23.1.41 (TOC 19.2.41). Released to PAU 21.2.41; to 1 AACU 22.4.41. Sustained Cat.B damage 10.9.41; to DH 17.9.41. To PAU 1.11.41. To DH Hatfield 24.8.42; tfd to Prestwick-based Scottish Aviation Ltd 21.10.42 (as a pattern aircraft for Queen Bee production.). To 19 MU 7.9.44 for long-term storage. Sold 21.11.46 to W.A. Rollason, Croydon.

V4787 (c/n 5460) Allocated to 19 MU 25.1.41 (TOC 19.2.41). Released to PAU 21.2.41; to 1 AACU 2.7.41. Sustained Cat.B damage 30.8.41; to DH 9.9.41 for repair. To 19 MU 1.11.41; to PAU 2.11.41; to 1 AAVU 19.12.41. Crashed off Manorbier 18.4.42 after radio control was lost due to AA hit.

V4788 (c/n 5461) Allocated to 20 MU 9.2.41 (TOC 21.2.41). Released to PAU

Damaged 9.4.41; to DH for repair, returning to PAU 20.8.41. To 1 AACU 10.2.42. Cat.B again 24.2.42; to DH 4.3.42 for repairs. To 19 MU 12.4.43; released to 1618 Flt 14.10.43. Sustained Cat.B damage 2.12.43; repaired by 5.2.44. To 19 MU 26.2.44 for storage. Sold to W.A.Rollason, Croydon 18.12.46 under Authority 41G/103701.

V4762 (c/n 5449) Allocated to PAU 18.1.41 (TOC 6.2.41). To 1 AACU 9.4.41. Spun into the sea 3miles north of Aberporth 19.6.41 after radio control was lost on launch. SOC 4.10.41.

V4763 (c/n 5450) Allocated to PAU 18.1.41 (TOC 10.2.41). To 'U' Flt/1 AACU 18.3.41. Recorded as passing to PAU 19.12.41 but also reported as damaged by AA and glided into the sea off Towyn 6.5.41 and not recovered. Eventually SOC at the 1.4.42 Census.

V4764 (c/n 5451) Allocated to PAU 18.1.41 (TOC 15.2.41). To 'Z' Flt/1 AACU 18.3.41. Damaged 21.6.41; to DH 27.6.41 as Cat.B. To 19 MU 17.9.41; to PAU 22.9.41; to 1 AACU 25.2.42. Sustained Cat.B damage 4.3.42; to DH 8.3.42 for repair. To 19 MU 22.4.42; to PAU 28.6.42. To 'Z' Flt/1 AACU 9.9.42. Landed in rough sea and sank off Ty Croes 12.12.42 after radio control was lost.

V4765 (c/n 5452) Allocated to PAU 18.1.41 (TOC 10.2.41). To 1 AACU 13.3.41. Written-off 5.4.41, probably hit by 3.7" shell; glided into the sea off Burrow Head. SOC 1.6.41.

V4766 (c/n 5453) Allocated to PAU 18.1.41 (TOC 15.2.41). To PAU 15.2.41; to 'Z' Flt/1 AACU 19.3.41. DBR 4.7.41 after hitting rocks on Aberffraw beach, Anglesey after radio control was lost. SOC 21.7.41.

46   Sitting Ducks and Peeping Toms

22.5.41; to 1 AACU 2.7.41. Sustained Cat.B damage 13.3.42; to DH 24.3.42 for repair. To 19 MU 25.4.42; to PAU 28.7.42; to 'X' Flt/1 AACU 15.10.42. Crash-landed at Brynhoffnant, Cardigan 23.1.43 after the radio jammed when hit by AA.

V4789 (c/n 5462) Allocated to 20 MU 9.2.41 (TOC 21.2.41). Released to PAU 22.5.41; to 1 AACU 4.7.41. Sustained Cat.AC damage 12.4.42; to DH 23.4.42 for repair. To 19 MU 11.6.42; to PAU 28.6.42; to 'X' Flt/1AACU 13.8.42. Shot down by AA off Aberporth 29.8.42.

V4790 (c/n 5463) Allocated to 20 MU 9.2.41 (TOC 21.2.41). Released to PAU 22.5.41; to 1 AACU 4.7.41. Dived into a hill nr Towyn 18.11.41 after radio control was lost. SOC 27.11.41.

V4791 (c/n 5464) Allocated to 20 MU 9.2.41 (TOC 22.2.41). Released to PAU 22.5.41; to 1 AACU 11.8.41. Sustained Cat.B damage 5.12.41; to DH for repair 15.12.41; to PAU 31.1.42. To 19 MU 9.2.42; to PAU 14.3.42; to 1 AACU 1.5.42. Dived into the ground at Aberffraw, Anglesey 10.9.42 after radio control was lost.

V4792 (c/n 5465) Allocated to 20 MU 9.2.41 (TOC 22.2.41). Released to PAU 30.6.41; to 1 AACU 11.8.41. Sustained Cat.B damage 25.7.42; to DH 10.8.42 for repair; to PAU 11.10.42. On 5.12.42, after radio control was lost on take-off, it glided into the sea off Manorbier and sank.

V4793 (c/n 5466) Allocated to 20 MU 9.2.41 (TOC 24.2.41). Released to PAU 22.5.41; to 1 AACU 22.7.41. Destroyed by fire on 24.2.42 when it flew into Mt. Snowdon after radio control was lost. SOC 25.2.42.

V4794 (c/n 5467) Allocated to 19 MU 15.2.41 (TOC 26.2.41). Released to PAU 20.3.41; to 'U' Flt/1 AACU 15.5.41. Flew into sea 10miles north of Towyn 6.10.41 after radio control was lost. (TFH 9.45)

V4795 (c/n 5468) Allocated to 19 MU 16.2.41 (TOC 26.2.41). Released to PAU 20.3.41; to 1 AACU 8.5.41. To PAU 25.3.42; to 'X' Flt/1 AACU 14.5.42. Crashed into the sea off Aberporth 19.8.42 after radio control was lost. SOC 31.8.42.

V4796 (c/n 5469) Allocated to 19 MU 15.2.41 (TOC 1.3.41). Damage necessitated a return to DH 7.4.41 for repair. To PAU 1.8.41; to 1 AACU 5.9.41. A flying accident 3.2.42 required a return to DH for repair 8.2.42. To 19 MU 28.3.42; to PAU 31.3.42. Hit by AA and spun into the sea in Cardigan Bay 19.6.42.

V4797 (c/n 5470) Allocated to 19 MU 21.2.41 (TOC 1.3.41). Released to PAU 6.4.41; to 'T' Flt/1 AACU 28.5.41. Shot down by rockets off Weybourne 18.6.41. SOC 25.6.41.

V4798 (c/n 5471) Allocated to 19 MU 21.2.41 (TOC 5.3.41). Released to PAU 6.4.41; to 1 AACU 13.5.41. Declared Cat.B 25.6.41; to DH 1.7.41 for repair; to PAU 20.8.41; to 19 MU 12.9.41; to PAU 22.9.41; to 1 AACU 8.12.41. Shot down into the sea off Burrow Head 3.2.42. SOC 31.8.42.

V4799 (c/n 5472) Allocated to 19 MU 21.2.41 (TOC 6.3.41). Released to PAU 6.4.41; to 1 AACU 28.5.41. Hit by AA 3.8.41 causing engine to cut and hitting a hedge on landing near Weybourne. SOC 17.8.41.

V4800 (c/n 5473) Allocated to 19 MU 21.2.41 (TOC 11.3.41). Released to PAU 6.4.41; to 1 AACU 27.5.41. Shot down and sank 1mile off Cleave 20.8.41.

V4801 (c/n 5474) Allocated to 19 MU 2.3.41 (TOC 11.3.41). Released to PAU 15.5.41; to 1 AACU 1.7.41. Disappeared off Cleave 24.3.42; believed hit by AA causing radio control to be lost.

V4802 (c/n 5475) Allocated to 19 MU 2.3.41 (TOC 11.3.41). Released to PAU 21.4.41; to 1 AACU 2.6.41. Sustained Cat.B damage 2.8.41; to DH for repair 18.8.41. To 19 MU 1.11.41; released to PAU 10.12.41; to 1 AACU 27.2.42. Shot down by AA and dived into the sea off Aberporth 7.3.42.

V4803 (c/n 5476) Allocated to 19 MU 6.3.41 (TOC 11.3.41). Released to PAU 20.4.41; to 1 AACU 12.5.41. Shot down by AA and crashed into a cliff 2miles west of Aberporth 11.7.41. SOC 3.9.41. (TFH 14.35)

V4804 (c/n 5477) Allocated to 19 MU 6.3.41 (TOC 11.3.41). Released to PAU 21.4.41; to 1 AACU 19.6.41. To DH 5.9.41 for attention; to 19 MU 12.11.41. Released to PAU 10.12.41; to 1 AACU 8.6.42. Glided into the sea and sank off Aberporth 11.6.42 following damage by AA and losing radio control.

V4805 (c/n 5478) Allocated to 19 MU 6.3.41 (TOC 19.3.41). Released to PAU 15.5.41; to 1 AACU 27.6.41; to PAU 1.8.41. DBR 23.10.41 after hitting a bank whilst lost in haze at Hell's Mouth Landing Ground, nr Llangraw,. SOC 5.11.41.

Contract Acft/2398/C.20(b)
150 aircraft contracted to Scottish Aviation Ltd (and sub-contracted to Messrs Morris & The West of Scotland Furniture Co.)

(Unconfirmed reports suggest that the first 75 aircraft were sequentially allocated c/ns SAL100 to SAL174 inclusive. Note also that all aircraft were built at Glasgow and conveyed by road to Prestwick for initial flight and delivery.)

LF779 TOC by 19 MU 19.10.43 for storage; released to PAU Manorbier 21.11.43. Cat.E/FA 24.3.44.

LF780 TOC by PAU Manorbier 9.12.43. Cat.E/FA 18.4.44.

LF781 TOC by PAU Manorbier 9.12.43. Cat.E/FA 28.7.45. SOC 2.8.45.

LF782 TOC by PAU Manorbier 9.12.43. Cat.E/FA 15.6.44.

LF783 Allocated to PAU Manorbier 29.12.43; TOC 31.12.43. Cat.E/FA 20.3.44.

LF784 TOC by 19 MU 14.1.44 for storage; released to PAU Manorbier 24.5.45. Cat.E/FA 11.10.45. SOC 25.10.45.

LF785 TOC by 19 MU 12.2.44 for storage; released to PAU Manorbier 31.5.44. Cat.E/FA 1.11.45. SOC 29.11.45.

LF786 TOC by 19 MU 19.1.44 for storage. Sustained Cat.B damage in a flying accident 24.1.44 (details unknown) and later "repaired in works" (again, location etc unknown). Awaiting collection 15.7.44 and probably released to PAU Manorbier. Sold to W.A. Rollason, Croydon 20.12.46 under Authority 41G/103707. Fate unknown.

LF787 TOC by 19 MU 28.1.44 for storage. Released to PAU 24.5.44. SOC 30.8.45, details unknown.

LF788 TOC by 19 MU 19.1.44 for storage. To PAU Manorbier 24.5.45. Sold to W.A. Rollason, Croydon 5.12.46 under Authority 41G/103701. Fate unknown.

LF789 TOC by 19 MU 10.2.44 for storage. To PAU Manorbier 23.8.45 and coded 'R2-K'. To 19 MU 10.3.46. Sold to Redhill and Kenley-based British Air Transport, Whyteleafe, Surrey 26.11.46 under Authority 41G/103729. Noted semi-derelict in College of Aeronautical

Queen Bee 47

Engineering storage hangar, Redhill 1949. Subsequently reported as being stored at Droylesden, Lancashire and at Hadfield, Derbyshire. Later noted carrying false marks 'K3584'. Currently on static display at the de Havilland Aircraft Heritage Centre at London Colney, Hertfordshire, fully-restored and painted as LF789.

LF790 TOC by 19 MU 14.2.44 for storage. Sold to Redhill and Kenley-based British Air Transport, Whyteleafe, Surrey 26.11.46 under Authority 41G/103729. Noted semi-derelict in College of Aeronautical Engineering storage hangar, Redhill 1949. Fate unknown.

LF791 TOC by 19 MU 10.2.44 for storage. Sold to W.A. Rollason, Croydon 26.11.46 under Authority 41G/103701. Fate unknown.

LF792 TOC by 19 MU 17.2.44 for storage. Sold to Straight Corporation, Weston-super-Mare 5.12.46 under Authority 41G/103699. Fate unknown.

LF793 TOC by 19 MU 14.2.44 for storage. Sold to Field Aircraft Services 1.7.47 under Authority 41G/104269. Fate unknown.

LF794 TOC by 19 MU 18.2.44 for storage. Sold to W.A. Rollason, Croydon 2.12.46 under Authority 41G/103701. Fate unknown.

LF795 TOC by 19 MU 28.2.44 for storage. Sold to Field Aircraft Services 3.7.47 under Authority 41G/104269. Fate unknown.

LF796 TOC by 19 MU 28.2.44 for storage. Sold to Field Aircraft Services 1.7.47 under Authority 41G/104269. Fate unknown.

LF797 TOC by 19 MU 6.3.44 for storage. Sold to Field Aircraft Services 3.7.47 under Authority 41G/104269. Fate unknown.

LF798 TOC by 19 MU 18.3.44 for storage. Sold to South Wales Airways, Laleston, Bridgend 24.1.47 under Authority 41G/103700. Fate unknown.

LF799 TOC by 19 MU 18.3.44 for storage. Sold to Field Aircraft Services 1.7.47 under Authority 41G/104269. Subsequent movements and fate unknown.

LF800 TOC by 19 MU 21.3.44 for storage. Sold to Redhill and Kenley-based British Air Transport 26.11.46 under Authority 41G/103729. Noted semi-derelict in College of Aeronautical Engineering storage hangar, Redhill 1949. Fate unknown.

LF801 TOC by 19 MU 21.3.44 for storage. Sold to Redhill and Kenley-based British Air Transport 26.11.46 under Authority 41G/103729. Fuselage noted with the College of Aeronautical Engineering, Redhill 1949 with code 'R2-M' (which suggests use by Pilotless Aircraft Unit).

LF802 TOC by 19 MU 27.3.44 for storage. Sold to Field Aircraft Services 3.7.47 under Authority 41G/104269. Fate unknown

LF803 TOC by 19 MU 30.3.44 for storage. Sold to British Air Transport 26.11.46 under Authority 41G/103729. Fuselage noted with the College of Aeronautical Engineering, Redhill 1949. No further details.

LF816 TOC by 19 MU 5.4.44 for storage. Sold to W.A. Rollason, Croydon 16.12.46 under Authority 41G/103701. Fate unknown.

LF817 TOC by 19 MU 8.5.44 for storage. Written-off in a flying accident 6.6.45; SOC 6.7.45.

LF818 TOC by 19 MU 6.4.44 for storage. Sold to W.A. Rollason, Croydon 7.12.46 under Authority 41G/103702. Fate unknown.

LF819 TOC by 19 MU 3.5.44 for storage. Sold to W.A. Rollason, Croydon 26.6.47 under Authority 41G/104270. Fate unknown.

LF820 TOC by RAF Manorbier 12.5.44 for storage. Written-off in a flying accident 4.5.45.

LF821 TOC by 19 MU 28.5.44 for storage. Sold to W.A. Rollason, Croydon 23.12.46 under Authority 41G/103701. Fate unknown.

LF822 TOC by 19 MU 7.5.44 for storage. Sold to Field Consolidated 27.11.46 under Authority 41G/103747. Fate unknown.

LF823 TOC by 19 MU 26.4.44 for storage. Sold to South Wales Airways, Bridgend 6.1.47 under Authority 41G/103700. Fate unknown.

LF824 TOC by 19 MU 11.5.44 for storage. Sold to W.A. Rollason, Croydon 18.11.46 under Authority 41G/103701. Fate unknown.

LF825 TOC by PAU Manorbier 12.5.44. PAU notified a Cat.E flying accident 18.12.44. No further details.

LF826 TOC by 19 MU 14.5.44 for storage. Released to PAU 9.11.45. To 19 MU 9.4.46. Sold to W.A. Rollason, Croydon 7.12.46 under Authority 41G/103701. Fate unknown.

LF827 TOC by 19 MU 14.5.44 for storage. Sold to W.A. Rollason, Croydon 16.11.46 under Authority 41G/104701. Fate unknown.

LF828 TOC by 19 MU 28.5.44 for storage. Sold to W.A. Rollason, Croydon 20.6.47 under Authority 41G/104270. Fate unknown.

LF829 TOC by 19 MU 13.6.44 for storage. Sold to W.A. Rollason, Croydon 13.12.46 under Authority 41G/103701. Fate unknown.

LF830 TOC by 19 MU 10.6.44 for storage. Sold to Field Consolidated 27.11.46 under Authority 41G/103747. Fate unknown.

LF831 TOC by 19 MU 22.6.44 for storage. Sold to British Air Transport 23.11.46 under Authority 41G/103729. Noted semi-derelict in College of Aeronautical Engineering storage hangar, Redhill 1949. No further details.

LF832 TOC by 19 MU 22.6.44 for storage. Sold to W.A. Rollason, Croydon 2.7.47 under Authority 41G/104270. No further details.

LF833 TOC by 19 MU 19.6.44 for storage. Sold to Straight Corporation, Weston-super-Mare 13.12.46 under Authority 41G/103699. Fate unknown.

LF834 TOC by PAU 17.6.44. To 19 MU 10.3.46. Sold to W.A. Rollason, Croydon 27.11.46 under Authority 41G/103701. Fate unknown.

LF835 TOC by PAU 24.6.44. PAU notified a Cat.E flying accident 3.8.45. No further details.

LF836 TOC by PAU 24.6.44. PAU notified a Cat.E flying accident 24.5.45. SOC 17.7.45.

LF837 Probably TOC by 19 MU (date unkn) for storage. Sold to W.A. Rollason, Croydon 16.6.47 under Authority 41G/104270. Fate unknown.

LF838 TOC by 19 MU 6.7.44 for storage. Sold to W.A. Rollason, Croydon 12.12.46

under Authority 41G/103701. Fate unknown.

LF839 TOC by 19 MU 17.7.44 for storage. Sold to W.A. Rollason, Croydon 18.6.47 under Authority 41G/104270. Fate unknown.

LF857 TOC by 19 MU 21.7.44 for storage. Sold to W.A. Rollason, Croydon 29.11.46 under Authority 41G/103701. Fate unknown.

LF858 TOC by 19 MU 17.7.44 for storage. Sold to South Wales Airways, Bridgend, Glamorgan 16.12.46 under Authority 41G/103700. Noted stored in a blister hangar at Old Warden 11.52. Eventually sold to EMK Aeroplane Ltd/ John Evetts and moved to their workshop at Whitehall Farm, Benington, Herts 4.83. Civilianised (and rebuilt) by EMK at Watton-on-Stone. Reg'd **G-BLUZ** to Barry Bayes, Cranfield 9.4.85. Later in 1985 moved to Standalone Farm, Meppershall, Beds with Brinkley Light Aircraft Services. 3-month Permit to Fly issued 20.9.86. First post-restoration flight 22.10.86 at Meppershall. Re-reg'd 9.2.96 to Colin I. Knowles & John Flynn (trustees of The Bee Keepers Group, Hitchin). Still current in 6.09, operating as LF858.

LF859 TOC by 19 MU 24.7.44 for storage. Sold to W.A. Rollason, Croydon 8.7.47 under Authority 41G/104270. Fate unknown.

LF860 TOC by 19 MU 8.8.44 for storage. Sold to W.A. Rollason, Croydon 11.6.47 under Authority 41G/104270. Fate unknown.

LF861 TOC by 19 MU 4.8.44 for storage. Sold to W.A. Rollason, Croydon 30.6.47 under Authority 41G/104270. Fate unknown.

LF862 TOC by 19 MU 17.8.44 for storage. Released to PAU 28.5.45. Sustained Cat.A damage 14.12.45 when, during an engine run-up at Manorbier, the anchor rope broke causing the aircraft to run away and tip up. It is unlikely that repairs were carried out as it was SOC 3.7.46

LF863 TOC by 19 MU 31.8.44 for storage. Released to PAU 23.8.45. To 19 MU 9.4.46. Sold to Straight Corporation, Weston-super-Mare 6.12.46 under Authority 41G/103699. Fate unknown.

LF864 TOC by 19 MU 31.8.44 for storage. Sold to Field Consolidated 27.11.46 under Authority 41G/103747. Fate unknown.

LF865 TOC by 19 MU 31.8.44 for storage. SOC 31.5.46; further details not known.

LF866 TOC by 19 MU 8.9.44 for storage. SOC(MR) 7.7.45; further details not known.

LF867 TOC by 19 MU 30.9.44 for storage. Sold to W.A. Rollason, Croydon 9.7.47 under Authority 41G/104270. Fate unknown.

LF868-LF882 Cancelled 12.43 and not built.

MV572-MV606, MV618-MV657 All cancelled 12.43 and not built.

The Pilotless Aircraft Unit also converted and operated a number of Tiger Moths that had been converted to 'Queen' configuration and which involved the following nine aircraft:

DH.82A Tiger Moth converted to unmanned configuration.

N6648 (c/n 3952) *(Taken on charge at 10 MU 20.3.39; released to 30 ERFTS 7.6.39. To 22 EFTS 15.10.39. Crashed at Barton 4.6.40. Conveyed to DH for repairs 10.6.40 after which issued to 38 MU 2.9.40. Undated allocation to 1 AACU (and may not have therefore been delivered).)*
Allocated to PAU 6.8.42. 'Converted to Queen Bee 22.11.43'. SOC 30.6.44 as Cat.E1.

N6722 (c/n 3995) *(Previously used as a Tiger Moth by 4 Coastal Patrol Flight and 6EFTS.)*
Allocated to PAU 30.6.43. 'Converted to Queen Bee 22.11.43'. Crashed on landing at Manorbier 12.6.44.

N9161 (c/n 82280) *(Taken on charge at 27 MU 27.8.39; released to Horsham St Faith Station HQ 20.8.41. To 20 EFTS 20.9.41; to 18 EFTS 28.1.42. Crashed 17.5.43 and conveyed to Lundy & Atlantic Coasts Air Lines, Barnstaple for repairs 25.5.43 after which issued to 10 MU 26.6.43.)*
Released to PAU charge 17.9.43. 'Converted to Queen Bee 22.11.43'. Tfd to 1606 Flight 7.12.43. Wrecked as a result of a forced-landing at Bodorgan, Anglesey 12.4.44. SOC 9.5.44.

R5106 (c/n 82988) Allocated to PAU 21.9.43. 'Converted to Queen Bee 22.11.43'. Written-off in a crash 29.10.45.

R5147 (c/n 83029) Allocated to PAU 23.6.43. 'Converted to Queen Bee 22.11.43'. Sustained damage after striking a mast on landing at Manorbier 30.7.43. SOC during Census 21.6.47.

T6104 (c/n 84571) Allocated to PAU 1.7.43. 'Converted to Queen Bee 22.11.43'. Seriously damaged during a forced-landing at Hill Farm, Manorbier 23.10.43; SOC 16.11.43.

T6863 (c/n 85110) Allocated to PAU 4.7.43. 'Converted to Queen Bee 22.11.43'. Shot down off Manorbier 11.12.43.

T6867 (c/n 85114) Allocated to PAU 28.6.43. 'Converted to Queen Bee 22.11..43' Shot down off Manorbier 10.9.43 but not SOC until the 21.6.47 Census.

T7239 (c/n 83729) Allocated to PAU 1.7.43. 'Converted to Queen Bee 22.11.43'. Written-off in a crash on 24.3.44.

848.—Queen Bee Aircraft—Disposal
(A. E. 3858/44.—17 Feb. 1944.)

Queen Bee aircraft are no longer required as pilotless targets. Any such aircraft held, are in future to be called Tiger Moths, and used as such. Any special radio or other equipment peculiar to their use as target aircraft should be returned to store depots.

On 17 February 1944, Admiralty Fleet Orders (AFO848/44) marked the official end of the Queen Bee in Royal Navy service. From that date all related remote control gear was to be removed and that aircraft should be thereafter referred to as Tiger Moth.

The Pilotless Aircraft Unit also had a number of DH.82A Tiger Moth aircraft on strength. It is highly likely that most, if not all, were earmarked for conversion to unmanned configuration but in the event none was converted:

L6936 (c/n 3571) Allocated to PAU 17.9.43 possibly for conversion to Queen Bee. Not converted and re-issued to Lundy & Atlantic Coasts Air Lines, Barnstaple for repairs 7.12.43.

T6519 (c/n 84860) Allocated to PAU 8.7.44. Issued to 38 MU 8.1.46.

T6683 (c/n 84983) Allocated to PAU 21.9.43 possibly for conversion to Queen Bee. Not converted and instead transferred to Glider Pilot Exercise Unit, Thruxton, Hampshire 7.12.43.

T6770 (c/n 85057) Allocated to PAU 21.9.43 possibly for conversion to Queen Bee. Not converted and instead transferred to Glider Pilot Exercise Unit, Thruxton, Hampshire 7.12.43.

T7694 (c/n 84088) Allocated to PAU 17.9.43 possibly for conversion to Queen Bee. Not converted and instead transferred to 274 Squadron, Detling, Essex 21.6.44.

DE132 (c/n 85202) Allocated to PAU 10.7.43. Transferred to 80 Squadron, Detling, Essex 15.6.44.

DF117 (c/n 85866) Allocated to PAU 25.8.44. Issued to 20 MU Aston Down, Gloucestershire 10.4.46.

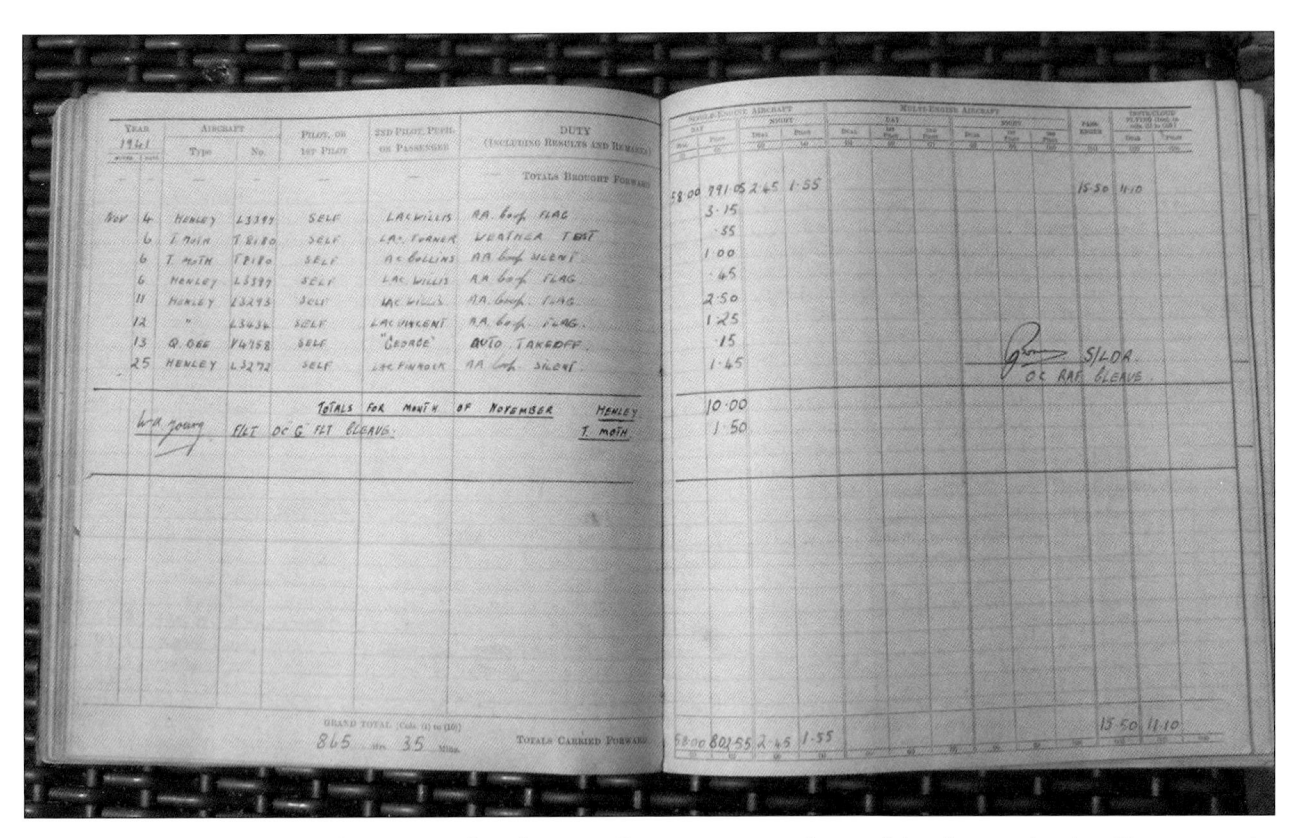

Before 'V' Flight, 1 AACU launched a Queen Bee drone from RAF Cleave, it was routine for one of the pilots to undertake a 15-minute weather test flight in order to determine the cloud base level. The log-book of F/Lt W.A. "Bill" Young reveals that such a flight was performed on 13 November 1941 aboard V4758. Of interest is that the aircraft was launched under automatic control and as if to underline the fact the co-pilot is entered as "George"!

Queen Bee Bomber

For a brief period in 1941 some consideration was given to ascertain whether pilotless aircraft could operate in an offensive role and in conjunction with the newly-formed Fighter Experimental Establishment a short series of experiments were carried out at Middle Wallop. Two special Queen Bees were prepared at the Pilotless Aircraft Unit at Manorbier and flown down to Middle Wallop on 5 June and 11 June 1941 respectively. Each aircraft was fitted with VHF and Indentification Friend or Foe (IFF) in addition to the Queen Bee's standard equipment. However when it became clear that the additional weight would make it difficult to fly above 5,000ft, the Queen Bee receiver and relay set was removed and replaced by a TR9 radio set. A final modification was the fitting of screened plugs to avoid unwanted interference.

A bomb rack was fitted beneath each of the Queen Bees and test flights revealed no difficulty in releasing bombs by remote signal. Trial flights, most of which were flown under automatic control, took place from Middle Wallop between 14-17 June 1941, totalling 48.25 flying hours. A further series of tests was carried out at Portkerry, eight miles east of St Athan. However the notion of unmanned Queen Bees in a remotely-controlled bombing role was not proceeded with and the aircraft were returned to the Pilotless Aircraft Unit.

Chapter 3
Beyond Queen Bee

A SIGNIFICANT FACTOR in the general improvement of both Army and Naval gunnery training techniques in the years immediately preceding World War II can probably be attributed to the de Havilland Queen Bee – Britain's first realistic 'live' anti-aircraft target to be used operationally. However, rapid development of front-line aircraft in terms of speed and manoeuvrability brought about an urgent need for an equally higher-performance aerial target. The military planners of the day clearly recognised the need in that, between 1935 and 1938, three separate Operational Requirements were established. Two of these Requirements led directly to the issue of Specifications, against which a number of designs were tendered. One was not proceeded with.

Details of these ORs and their subsequent Specifications are summarised below, together with a further wartime Specification issued to cover the conversion of Miles Martinet aircraft into target drones.

Operational Requirements Involving Drone Aircraft 1935-1938

Operational Requirement	Date	Description	Specifications
OR.29	1935	Queen Bee replacement	Specification Q.32/35
OR.48	1937	High-speed FAA target	Specification Q.8/37
OR.57	1938	Wireless-controlled target	Not proceeded with

Specifications Involving Drone Aircraft 1935-1943

Spec Reference	Date	Description	Specifications
Q.32/35	1935	Radio-controlled target (Alternatives)	Airspeed AS.30 Queen Wasp Miles M.10 project Percival P.8 & P.8A Gull Six
Q.8/37	1937	High-speed FAA target	Airspeed AS.37 General Aircraft Ltd GAL. 35 Percival P.21 & P.21A
Q.12/38	1939	Radio-controlled target	–
Q.10/43	1943	Radio-controlled target	Miles M.50 Queen Martinet

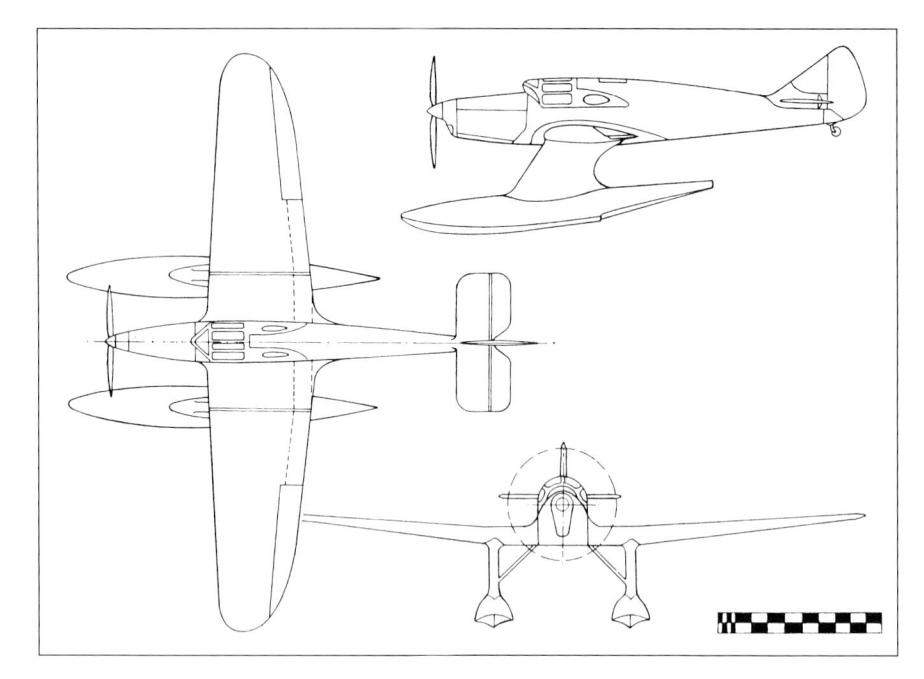

Illustration on page 51: *An early view of Queen Wasp K8887, possibly taken at Portsmouth shortly after completion. The graceful lines of the Queen Wasp led to one considered opinion that the aircraft was "too good-looking to be shot down". (Imperial War Museum, Neg. No MH5068, via Ken Munson.)*

Left: *Miles M.10*

Specification Q.32/35

Operational Requirement 29 led directly to Air Ministry Specification Q.32/35 which in the broadest sense was simply a straightforward successor to Queen Bee. Apart from calling for a high-performance aircraft, the Specification also demanded that it be small enough to be stowed aboard, and launched from, a warship. Folding wings were seen to be an obvious advantage as was the ability to convert from wheel to float undercarriage – a factor that enabled the new aircraft to serve as a target for both Army and Navy gunners. Ease of handling on catapults both at sea and ashore were other key factors that tendering companies were asked to consider.

Three companies (Airspeed, Miles and Percival) responded to Q.32/35 each with outline designs and estimated performance criteria but only the Airspeed submission progressed to flight status and subsequent selection.

Miles M.10

Phillips & Powis (Miles Aircraft Ltd) at Woodley, Berkshire had first explored radio-controlled, unmanned flight to meet an Air Ministry enquiry for a Miles M.3D Falcon Six to be fitted with radio-control for a series of projected experimental trials at RAE Farnborough. The aircraft was also to have been fitted with an Onions undercarriage but which could be adapted to take floats if necessary.[1] It seems that Miles later adapted the design to meet Q.32/35 when an airframe, allocated the c/n 279, was described as a "Queen Wasp mock-up based on the M.3D".

The Miles M.10 was especially noteworthy in that it was the first, and only, seaplane proposal designed by the company.

In many respects it strongly resembled what became the M.11 Whitney Straight albeit with float undercarriage. Against Air Ministry Contract 498568/36 two M.10 prototypes were ordered and allotted c/ns 433 and 482. On 17 April 1936, they were allocated the serials K8889 and K8890 respectively. However, in the event neither prototype was built and after some 120 design man-weeks had been expended on the M.10, the project was cancelled in favour of the Airspeed proposal. No evidence is to hand that the 'Queen Wasp mock-up' was completed either.[2]

Proposed known dimensions	
Span	35.0 ft
Length	25.0 ft

Percival Type H (P.8 & P.8A)

The submission by Percival Aircraft Ltd of Luton, Bedfordshire to Specification Q.32/35 was allocated the manufacturer's designation, Percival Type H. In the same manner that Miles had adapted an existing design, Percival took the Gull Six and modified it sufficiently to meet the Air Ministry's requirements. Subsequently, when Percival retrospectively revised their system of Type Numbers, the Type H became the Percival P.8 whilst a twin-float version of the P.8 was designated P.8A.[3]

The submission by Percival was not successful.

Proposed known dimensions & performance	
Span	37 ft
Length	25 ft 1 in (P.8 landplane)
	26 ft 10 in (P.8A Seaplane)
Gross weight	2,500 lb
Cruising speed	165 mph

---

1 Designed by John H. Onions, the undercarriage design was based on oleo-pneumatic shock-absorber struts which were designed to allow extremely heavy landings, lessening the likelihood of causing serious damage. The struts were manufacturered by Ribbesford Company Ltd of Wolverhampton. (Further details are featured in Flight 19 December 1935.)

2 *Miles Aircraft – The Early Years 1926-1939* by Peter Amos (Air-Britain Historians, 2009)

3 *Aeroplane Spotter*, February 7 1948

The first prototype Airspeed Queen Wasp made its first flight on 11 June 1937, just 13 weeks from the issue of drawings. At the end of the month it appeared at the RAF Display at Hendon for which it carried the identity '4'. (Aeroplane)

Airspeed AS.30 Queen Wasp

It has been suggested – albeit perhaps rather "tongue in cheek" – that when Airspeed's design team submitted a proposal to meet Q.32/35 there was a proposal to refer to the aircraft as the Airspeed 'Clay Pigeon'. It was, of course, truly apt but in the event much wiser counsel stepped in and the Airspeed AS.30 was more appropriately named the Queen Wasp. Paradoxically, there was also a view that Airspeed's design was infinitely too good-looking to be shot down!

Designed by the company's Chief Designer, Hessell Tiltman, the Queen Wasp was a single-bay biplane, constructed mainly of wood and with the fuselage built in three sections. The forward section was a crafted strong spruce and ply assembly which provided the centre sections for upper and lower mainplanes and carried the welded steel tubular engine mounting. On the lower centre section were the strong points for the undercarriage mounting and the forward catapult spools. The rear fuselage was a semi-monocoque structure of spruce longerons and stiffeners, ply-covered on the top surface merging into the ply-covered fin, which was built integrally with the rear fuselage.

The mainplanes, which were sharply tapered, were of plywood-covered construction, with fabric-covered slotted flaps and ailerons. The tailplane was of similar construction, with rudder and elevators of fabric-covered spruce.

The smallest and cheapest engine available with the ability to meet the required performance was the Wolseley Scorpio Mk.2 but following the decision to close down the Wolseley aero engine plant the Queen Wasp was redesigned to take the 350hp Armstrong Siddeley Cheetah IX seven-cylinder radial engine.

The basic control system was based on an air-powered gyro directing pneumatic servos to the rudder and elevators, although no elevator control was used in automatic flight. Coded Morse signals from the transmitter were fed into the gyro by pneumatic pistons and limited throttle control was available in three positions: fully open, cruise power and closed. The whole concept of pilotless flight was remarkably advanced at this time, with an array of fail-safe devices to cope with every predictable malfunction. To land the Queen Wasp 'landing glide' was selected on the control panel, and as the speed dropped to the correct figure a servo motor lowered the flaps. The landing sequence was then initiated by the use of a trailing aerial (which was controlled automatically from the airspeed indicator) so that when the aircraft descended to a height whereby the weight touched the ground, the contacts on the aerial were closed and this in turn selected 'elevators up' and switched off the gyro.[4]

The Air Ministry had required tenders to be submitted as quickly as possible; Hessell Tiltman therefore established a special drawing office in London Road, Portsmouth so that work could proceed without the day-to-day distraction of the main factory. The move paid off and the prototype flew just nine months after design work started.

Two prototypes were ordered; K8887 with a standard land undercarriage and K8888 with floats. K8887 was first flown at Airspeed's Portsmouth Airport base on 11 June 1937, piloted by George Errington and before the month was out was publicly exhibited in the new and experimental park at the Hendon RAF Display. After completing

---
[4] *Airspeed – The Company and its Aeroplanes* by D.H.Middleton (Terence Dalton, 1982)

The second prototype Queen Wasp, K8888, was built with float undercarriage and made its first flight off Lee-on-Solent cOctober 1937 before embarking on HMS Pegasus *for piloted catapult trials. In December 1937 it passed to the Maritime Aircraft Experimental Establishment for performance trials. The attractiveness of the Queen Wasp was certainly enhanced with floats.*

manufacturer's tests at Portsmouth K8887 was flown to IAD Flt/RAE Farnborough on 9 October 1937 for several months of piloted catapult and radio-controlled flight trials. In fact K8887 spent much of its early life at Farnborough when, throughout 1938 and 1939, further work included the testing of wireless transmission equipment as well as exploring stalling characteristics, take-offs and landings, carburettor tests and auto-mixture controls.

The second Queen Wasp prototype (K8888) was completed with float undercarriage and made its first flight off Lee-on-Solent, Hampshire. Shortly afterwards, in November 1937, it was transferred to HMS *Pegasus* (formerly *Ark Royal*) for a series of piloted catapult trials although it was soon converted to a standard wheeled undercarriage and delivered to RAE Farnborough, on 13 April 1938, for similar trials.

K8888 was first flown at Farnborough on 20 April when it underwent general handling and engine tests with the RAE's ER Flight although it was officially allocated to IAD Flight. On the following day K8888 was prepared for its first catapult launch from Farnborough's catapult, located at Jersey Brow, just to the west of the main hangar area. The launch met with disastrous results but a lucky escape for the Farnborough test pilot, Flt Lt McDougall.

McDougall climbed into the cockpit through the starboard door and clambered over the lowered backrest to his seat. The catapult was fired and the Queen Wasp rose gracefully into the air, dived slightly, touched a wheel on the grass and bounced again to drop the other wheel. The wing tip then struck the ground and dug in, the aircraft then rolling into the inverted position, disintegrating as it went. Onlookers, fearing a fire, rushed over to rescue the pilot and found him shouting for release from the rear fuselage. Unfortunately before launch he had failed to replace the backrest sufficiently far enough for the retaining catches to fully engage and as the aircraft was fired from the catapult and rose from the launch trolley the pilot's seat collapsed backwards whereupon he lost the ability to control the

Spinning Trials – Queen Wasp – RAE Farnborough

"The centre-of-gravity position in the Queen Wasp with full equipment was situated aft, and when the time came for the spinning tests I was warned that the aircraft might behave dangerously. The first anti-spinning parachute to be used in this country was therefore fitted in case of emergency. By pulling a handle I could release the parachute, which would trail out behind on 50 feet or so of strong wire, slowing me up and helping me out of the spin. Another lever released the chute from the aircraft.

After each successful spinning test, the scientists moved the centre-of-gravity position farther back, and the loading was well to the rear when I put the Wasp into a spin for the last time. I have always been liable to giddiness after about five turns in any spin, and I have never relied upon my confused senses for recovery. My method was to place the controls in the right position and wait for the aircraft to recover itself. It had always worked before, but this particular day the Wasp failed entirely to respond to the controls. I pushed the controls over to the opposite position to the spin, but nothing happened except that the Wasp continued to spin faster and faster. I pump-handled the stick backwards and forwards, the final method a pilot uses before he bales out, but the Wasp still spun.

I was getting too low now to play about any longer. I needed what height there was left, to try the tail parachute. I pulled the lever. Immediately there was a slight jerk, and then a steady tugging at the tail that dragged the Wasp smoothly out of the spin. In level flight again with the engine on, I pulled the release handle and the parachute drifted free. The tail parachute had worked perfectly."

The Dangerous Skies by Air Commodore A.E.Clouston, DSO, DFC, AFC and Bar. (Cassell & Co Ltd, 1954)

54   Sitting Ducks and Peeping Toms

K8887 – A Vertical Stall

Hessell Tiltman, designer of the Queen Wasp, recalled a strange incident during stalling trials. Test-pilot George Errington asked him to fly with him so that he could demonstrate an unusual phenomenon. George said, "I would like you to look over the side: we are at 2,000ft heading into wind over the leeward side of the aerodrome. I shall now close the throttle and pull the stick back until the angle of incidence is on the other side of the stall."

Tiltman saw the air speed indicator reading drop to 45mph and, gradually, to zero. "In the meantime we were losing height rapidly. Errington assured me that we were under proper control which he demonstrated by applying full aileron. The machine responded by rocking gently as it would do under normal flying conditions. Errington had to apply full throttle to reach the aerodrome; we just skimmed the hedge!"

"Whilst we were in the super-stalled condition we must have descended vertically, indeed I think we were going astern in the ten-knot wind. During the descent the attitude was normal, say, plus five to ten degrees, but the angle of attack must have been nearer eighty degrees. This counfounded the theory that highly tapered wings are unstable in the stall and tend to drop sharply."

It was possible to reproduce the phenomenon on K8887, but not on K8888 or later production models, which attracted adverse comments from pilots who found that the stalling characteristics of the Queen Wasp were, predictably, rather vicious.

(Extract from *The Test Pilots* by Don Middleton.)

---

aircraft. Mercifully McDougall survived the crash almost uninjured but the aircraft was wrecked although not, it seems, irreparably. Taken back by road to Airspeed's Portsmouth factory in June 1938, it was painstakingly rebuilt and later returned to Farnborough on 23 February 1939 for further trials.

An initial production order (Contract 968560/38) for 65 examples (serialled between P5441 and P5565), was followed by a second, and larger, order involving 258 aircraft (with serials ranging between V5010 and V5361). With the promise of large-scale production Airspeed opened a small factory at Langstone Harbour, under the control of Tom Laing, one of the original Airspeed executives. Construction of the first batch began there with initial deliveries to the Pilotless Aircraft Unit at Manorbier commencing in April 1940. However, after just five Queen Wasps had been built, the two Contracts were cancelled and production was immediately halted. No further examples were built.

There were a number of reasons for abandoning the Queen Wasp programme, including, it must be said, some unsatisfactory aspects of its flight characteristics. Only one Queen Wasp is known to have operated away from Manorbier, that being P5445 which was issued to 1 Anti-Aircraft Co-operation Unit. Eventually a lack of spares grounded the survivors and all were struck off RAF charge in July 1943.

Few would deny the attractiveness of the Queen Wasp design which was said to have later influenced two further designs – the Airspeed AS.38 communications aircraft and the AS.50 Trainer (to Spec T.24/40). However, neither of these was developed beyond the drawing-board and the company diverted its war effort to much more urgent requirements.

Dimensions		
Span		31 ft (9.45 m); wings folded 12 ft (3.65 m)
Overall length	(landplane)	24 ft 4 in (7.42 m)
	(seaplane)	29 ft 1 in (8.85 m)
Overall height	(landplane)	10 ft 1 in (3.05 m)
	(seaplane)	13 ft (3.96 m)
Loaded weight	(landplane)	3,500 lb (1,588 kg)
	(seaplane)	3,800 lb (1,724 kg)
Performance		
Max speed at 8,000 ft (2,438 m)		172 mph (277 km/h)
Cruising speed at 10,000 ft (3,048 m)		151 mph (243 km/h)
Service ceiling		20,000 ft (6,096 m)

Airspeed AS.30 Queen Wasp Contracts & Production					
Contract	Date	Serial Range	Allotment Date	Quantity	Remarks
489567/36		K8887/K8888	17.4.36	2	Prototypes
968560/38		P5441-P5455 P5496-P5525 P5546-P5565	7.1.39	65	Only P5441-P5445 built. Remaining 60 aircraft cancelled.
B.55388/39		(V5010-V5057) (V5073-V5112) (V5131-V5180) (V5206-V5240) (V5262-V5306) (V5322-V5361)	--.12.39	258	All Cancelled

Queen Wasp K8888 was seriously damaged at RAE Farnborough 21 April 1938. Reports suggest that the aircraft was wrecked. However, it was returned to Airspeed and rebuilt. Later, on 20 March 1941 it overturned on landing at Manorbier but again appears to have ben repaired. Its ultimate fate is said to have occurred on 7 July 1943 when it sustained serious damage in a flying accident. This view is believed to have been of the Farnborough incident which, if accurate, certainly suggests that the aircraft was wrecked. Was it really rebuilt after this?

Airspeed AS.30 Queen Wasp – Individual Aircraft Histories

Contract 489567/36
2 Prototypes built by Airspeed Ltd at Portsmouth

K8887 f/f 11.6.37. Del Portsmouth-Farnborough 9.10.37 for handling trials with 'A' Flt, RAE. Later to 'IAD' Flt, RAE and on to 'E' Flt, RAE 3.1.38. Ferried to Lee-on-Solent 21.3.38. Reported at MAEE Felixstowe, Suffolk 6.38 for radio-controlled seaplane trials and catapult trials aboard HMS *Pegasus*. Returned to Farnborough 28.7.38. To Portsmouth 21.4.39 for engine mods; Returned to Farnborough 8.5.39 (presumably from Martlesham Heath with landplane undercarriage) for 'IAD' Flt, RAE (also used by 'A' Flt on handling trials). To Airspeed, Portsmouth 13.6.39 for fitting of modified cowling. Allocated to MAEE Felixstowe 12.7.39 but ret'd to RAE (date unkn). To Airspeed 4.10.39. To RAE 29.12.39. Allocated to 19 MU St Athan, Glamorgan 5.8.40 but thought to have been destroyed before delivery in a Luftwaffe air-raid on Portsmouth, believed 12.8.40, when Ju-88As of KG51 attacked the area. SOC 21.8.40.

K8888 f/f off Lee-on-Solent c10.37; to HMS *Pegasus* for piloted catapult trials. Del to MAEE 16.12.37 for performance tests. Allocated to A&AEE Martlesham Heath, Suffolk and fitted with standard undercarriage. Ferrried to Farnborough 13.4.38 for 'ER' Flt, RAE. Later to 'IAD' Flt, RAE but seriously damaged in a crash at Farnborough 21.4.38. To Airspeed, Portsmouth by road 2.6.38 for rebuild; returned Portsmouth-Farnborough 23.2.39. Test-flown 19.4.39 and used for w/t tests with 'IAD' Flt, RAE 20.4.39; also by 'A' Flt, RAE for "research handling" 24.4.39.; to Airspeed, Portsmouth 18.5.39 for modified cowling. To RAE 13.6.39 for aerodynamic tests. To Lee-on-Solent 26.6.39; to MAEE 12.7.39 for handling trials; to Lee-on-Solent 22.8.39, reportedly for fitment of slotted wings. To Pilotless Aircraft Unit, St Athan 26.12.40. Overshot on landing and overturned at Manorbier 20.3.41. Sustained serious damage.
To Portsmouth, Southsea & Isle of Wight Aviation Ltd, Portsmouth for rebuild. Awaiting collection 30.4.42 and allocated to 19 MU 27.5.42. Sustained serious damage in a flying accident 7.7.43. SOC 27.7.43.

Contract 968560/38
65 production aircraft to be built by Airspeed Ltd at Portsmouth

P5441 f/f 29.3.40. Del to Pilotless Aircraft Section (PAS), Hawkinge 19.4.40 for installation of automatic control equipment and flight-tests. To RAE Farnborough 22.5.40; to Airspeed, Portsmouth 1.6.40. To Pilotless Aircraft Unit (PAU) 22.2.41. SOC 27.7.43.

P5442 f/f 18.5.40. Del to PAU, St Athan 2.6.42. SOC 27.7.43.

P5443 Del to PAU, St Athan. Probably SOC 27.7.43.

P5444 Del to PAU, St Athan. SOC 27.7.43.

P5445 Del to 1 Anti-Aircraft Co-operation Unit, possibly at Farnborough. To PAU, St Athan. Crashed into the sea 15.9.42.

P5446-P5450 Reported as partially built but never completed. Those aircraft that were under construction at the time of cancellation reportedly broken up on the site of the former Hayling Island aerodrome.

Specification Q.8/37E

In order to meet Operational Requirement OR.48 the Air Ministry issued, on 18 June 1937, Specification Q.8/37E. Manufacturers were invited to tender for a "special type of aeroplane for use as an anti-aircraft target automatically controlled and directed by wireless". It was to be capable of landing, taxiing or being towed on water but not to be fitted with floats. Take-off from water was not a requirement. It was also required to have an aircraft sufficiently strong to withstand being catapulted into the air. Wooden construction was preferred and that the aircraft's wings would fold.

It was also stipulated that the prototype was required to have standard land undercarriage, which was to be readily detachable and attachable. Finally, the Air Ministry called for the aircraft to be designed around the 205hp de Havilland Gipsy Six Mk.II engine.

At least three manufacturers accepted the invitation to tender. Luton-based Percival Aircraft Ltd offered its Type T design (later and retrospectively designated Type P.21 with P.21A and P.22 as variations) whilst General Aircraft Ltd, at Hanworth aerodrome, Feltham, Middlesex offered the GAL.35, an unusual mid-wing monoplane with a single float and pylon-mounted engine.

The third of the manufacturers to respond to Q.8/37E was Airspeed Ltd of Portsmouth who completed preliminary design work on the AS.37 project during August 1937. Designed outwardly as a radio-controlled flying-boat the AS.37 was to have been powered by a single 205hp de Havilland Gipsy Six II engine as requested in the Specificaton.

The engine was housed in an over-wing nacelle directly above the pilot's cabin and drove a tractor propeller. A cantilever wing, which merged neatly into the fuselage hull, was also designed to fold for shipboard stowage. For land-based operations a standard tricycle undercarriage was planned.

None of the proposals was developed beyond the design stage.

Airspeed AS.37 dimensions	
Span	28 ft (9.30 m); wings folded 14 ft (4.3 m)
Length	25 ft 7 in (7.8 m)
Wing area (including hull chines)	156 sq ft (14.5 m²)

General Aircraft GAL.35 dimensions	
Span	30 ft 6 in (8.5 m), wings folded 15 ft 6 in (4.72 m)
Length	26 ft 8 in (8.13 m)

Specification Q.12/38

In continuing its search for a new aerial target aircraft the Air Ministry planners had, by the end of 1938, turned their sights away from floatplanes and instead focused upon a new landplane. With Operational Requirement OR.57 specifically in mind, the Air Ministry issued Specification

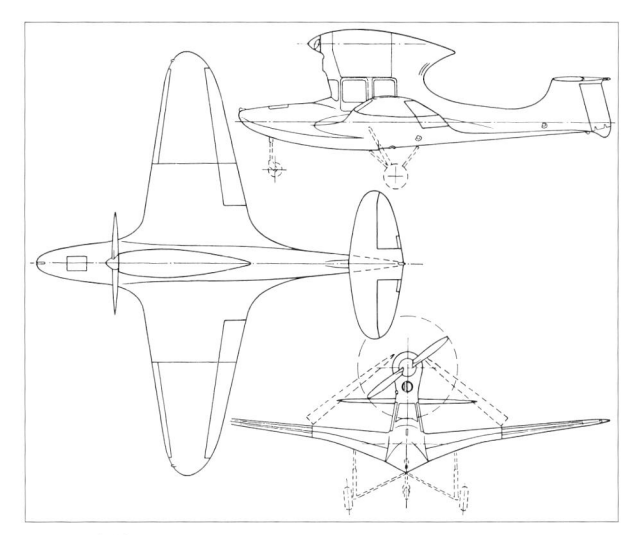

Airspeed AS.37

Q.12/38 on 21 March 1939 with a strong recommendation that any proposed tender be based around the Bristol Mercury VIII engine

Q.12/38 was required to make pilotless take-offs and landings on a standard aerodrome and for this purpose it was expressly requested that a tricycle undercarriage be fitted. Control would be effected by ailerons and elevator only and it was this that led the Air Ministry to suggest that the undercarriage be of a Stearman-Hammond type whereby the nose wheel is interconnected with the aileron control. Not that the notion of a seaplane variant was entirely ruled out and the Air Ministry certainly envisaged possible development of a floatplane version to follow later.

Intended performance requirements were fairly exacting. The seaplane variant, for example, was expected to maintain a minimum speed of 250mph at 10,000 feet.

The Specification was abandoned before any manufacturers were invited to tender.

World War II

The outbreak of World War II and the immediate call-up underlined an urgent need to provide suitable targets for training thousands of raw recruits, many of whom had never handled a gun let alone received any basic tuition. By the end of 1939, by which time the War was just over three months old, the Directorate of Training, in looking for a means of training gunners in ground-to-air firing, began to show an interest in amateur designers and operators of radio-controlled model aeroplanes. Aware of a need for the tightest of security measures, the Directorate's first move was to place a carefully worded advertisement in the contemporary magazine 'Wireless World', seeking experienced model aircraft builders and operators. Amongst those modellers who responded, two emerged as likely candidates.[5]

The more promising of the two was a Mr C. Jeffries of Shirley, Warwickshire who had already built and flown a large radio-controlled model. Jeffries was immediately invited to travel down to London for a meeting at Adastral House on 5 February 1940, during which Air Ministry

---

5   National Archives AVIA15/2633

planners outlined their precise requirements. They called for a model aeroplane capable of simulating a low-level attack on an aerodrome; dimensions were seen as a 10ft wingspan, length of 8ft, an operating speed of around 50mph and an operational endurance of about 30 minutes within a radius of a mile. Jeffries believed that he could develop a larger version of his own radio-controlled model but raised a snag that he would find difficult to overcome. Along with every other modeller throughout the country, his licence had been cancelled as part of wartime restrictions. Furthermore, his radio transmitter had been confiscated under special orders of the Director of Post & Communications.

The Air Ministry, in not seeking conflict with the D of P & P, chose to nominate Aladdin Industries Ltd of Greenford, Middlesex, with whom Jeffries was an employee, as the primary contractor. By November 1940 Aladdin had started work on the projected model target aircraft and had charged Jeffries with the role of designer and developer. The company even funded work on the model which by then had grown to 10ft span and expected to be capable of achieving 150mph, to have an operational height of between 3,000 and 5,000 feet and an endurance of some 2 hours.

Flight-testing was arranged through Fairey Aviation Ltd who gave permission to use the company's Great West aerodrome at Heath Row (later becoming London (Heathrow) Airport. Under the watchful gaze of Admiralty representatives and members of the Pilotless Aircraft Committee, the initial test flight took place during the evening of Friday, 20 June 1941. The official onlookers were less than impressed; the model failed to achieve its designed airspeed and after just 5 minutes it refused to respond to any further radio commands. After achieving a height of only 400 feet it gently glided down to earth about 4nm downwind of the aerodrome.

The Aladdin-Jeffries demonstration was an embarrassment to designer and builder, but it failed to dissuade military planners of the need to pursue the notion of model aircraft as aerial gunnery targets. So much so that, on 11 July, it was decided to place an order for two Denny A-2 target aircraft from the USA under Lease-Lend terms. But production of the A-2 had only just begun and it was not until the end of 1942 that the two examples were shipped to the RAE at Farnborough. By that time the Admiralty had long lost interest in model aircraft as gunnery targets, although those charged with aerodrome defence had maintained an interest in the project.[6]

In the meantime the Manchester-based company, F.Hills & Sons, had also worked on a balsa-wood model target aircraft. Developed in parallel with the Aladdin-Jeffries project, the Hills' design was flight-tested at RAF Kidsdale, Wigtownshire on 28 November 1941. Powered by an Aspin 10cc engine (developing 18hp) this 20ft span aircraft achieved a speed of 100-120mph. It was controlled by a standard Queen Bee transmitter.

What is believed to be the model built by C. Jeffries of Aladdin Industries Ltd and demonstrated at Fairey Aviation's Great West aerodrome at Heath Row in June 1941. The concept was not adopted after the one example failed to impress. (National Archives, AVIA15/2633)

Although the Hills' model had performed better than the Aladdin-Jeffries example, the manufacturer chose to completely re-design it. By the Autumn of 1942 a second prototype was ready for test-flight. It was smaller but fitted with a 40hp twin-cylinder air-cooled Praga engine. Rather curiously, the second example was, like its predecessor, a biplane design but without any interplane struts. Furthermore it was designed to take-off from land as opposed to being catapulted from a launcher. This second design was identified by the manufacturer as "Target Aeroplane No. FH/35/1".

An official demonstration was arranged at Manorbier airfield on Saturday, 24 October 1942. In attendance was a team from RAE Farnborough and by most accounts the flight was successful. The RAE observers declared a wish to see gyroscopic controls fitted to the model but at the same time voiced frustration at the length of time that it was taking to develop model target aircraft. Examples of the Denny A-2 had, by then, arrived from the USA and flight tests were already being carried out at Manorbier. Partially as a result of these tests, the Hills aircraft was dropped, as was the Aladdin-Jeffries project. Also, as a result of these tests, no further progress was made in developing the Denny A-2 into an operational aerial target in the United Kingdom.

Specification Q.10/43

Miles M.28, M.47, M.49, M.49A & M.50 Queen Martinet

Airspeed's Queen Wasp had been cancelled in mid-1940 and for two years no real effort had been made towards producing a full-sized pilotless target aircraft. The Queen Bee was still in active service but its performance had become increasingly unrealistic in terms of speed alone. However, the quest for a Queen Bee successor was re-visited in 1942 and led to the issue of a combined Naval and Air Staff Requirement, OR.119, calling for a high-speed twin-engined target-towing aircraft with a provision for the towing of target gliders. OR.119 led directly to Specification Q.9/42 against which the Miles M.33 Monitor was submitted, but the prototype-to-production phase was likely to be a lengthy process.

In the meantime the Admiralty also began to consider operating target aircraft in a manner already tried, tested and adopted by the Americans. It involved what the Americans

---

6 The Denny A-2 was a product of Reginald Denny who, in the USA in the 1930s, created many radio-controlled flying models and later opened a shop on Hollywood Boulevard called 'Reginald Denny Hobby Shops'. The shop evolved into the 'Radioplane Company' which became synonymous worldwide with the dersign and construction of target drones.

termed as a 'shepherd' and a 'sheep' aircraft; the former being a manned airborne control post that was controlling the latter, an unmanned drone, in mid-air and from a safe distance. Hitherto, of course, Queen Bees and other target aircraft had been controlled in flight by a ground-based pilot.

The US Navy had proved the two-aircraft target system using a Beech JRB-1 as an airborne drone director – a controlling 'shepherd' aircraft. Such was the interest being shown by their Lordships that a Naval Party was formed and sent out to the USA for training in drone equipment and procedures. The Party's other task was to arrange for the supply of necessary control equipment and bring it back to Britain.[7]

Back in the UK, the Admiralty drew up a list of suitable types for conversion to drones and take on the role of 'sheep" – the Gladiator II, the Westland Lysander III/IIIA and even the Miles Master were suggested. For the 'shepherd' role, the Admiralty put forward the Fairey Fulmar and the Boulton Paul Defiant.[8]

By December 1942's meeting of the DNAD the Lysander had been ruled out on the grounds that it was not available in sufficient numbers, if at all. Similarly, only a limited number of Gladiator IIs could be obtained. But the lack of availability of any other suitable types that were flapless, and had a fixed undercarriage and fixed props, prompted the Admiralty to re-consider the Gladiator II and, by using the American drone equipment (when it arrived in the UK) convert up to 25 examples into 'sheep' aircraft. Four Fairey Fulmars would fulfil the 'shepherd' role. There was even some consideration given to asking RAE Farnborough to fit the Airspeed Queen Wasp undercarriage to a Gladiator and at the same time fit tail-hooks. One thing that was agreed, however, was that the first 'sheep and shepherd' unit would be based at either RNAS Hatston or RNAS Twatt, both in the Orkney Islands.

As a direct result of these deliberations the Air Ministry drew up a fresh Specification, Q.10/43, which called for a high-performance radio-controlled pilotless aircraft. No mention of 'sheep' and 'shepherd' appeared and the Admiralty eventually agreed to adopt Q.10/43 as an ultimate staff requirement but, as a short-term measure, sought to acquire a number of Queen Bees, currently on order for the Army.

The Admiralty envisaged its ultimate requirement for a high-speed unmanned target aircraft as a single-seat aircraft roughly the size of a Hawker Typhoon. It needed to achieve 300kts at 12,000ft in level flight. It was also to be capable of diving at 75° and have an endurance of around 3½ hours. Curiously, it seems that the Specification was never actually written up; instead the Air Ministry officially approached Phillips and Powis Aircraft Ltd towards the end of 1942 to seek the likelihood of that company producing an aircraft that could meet the Admiralty's short-term need pending the design of a high-speed target.

George Miles chose to respond with two separate proposals, one based on the ability to supply almost immediately, the other designed solely around high performance. The first of these designs, the Miles M.47, was to be powered by a simple, cheap, mass-produced engine giving 220hp at its normal operational height. But such an engine was not available and as a temporary measure it was proposed to install a 250hp supercharged de Havilland Gipsy Queen engine. In this guise it was referred to as the M.47A. With the wings, twin fins and rudders identical to the Miles M.28, the M.47A was really no more than a re-design of the M.28. A fixed undercarriage, tail-skid and provision for a teardrop canopy, however, set the two designs more apart.

Miles' second proposal to meet Q.10/43 was the M.49. Powered by the same engine proposed for the M.47, it had a wingspan of only 21ft 6in and a provision for a teardrop canopy. Of note was the M.49's undercarriage; it consisted of two main skids, each fitted with a pair of jettisonable wheels for take-off, and a fixed tail-skid. Also of note was the fact that the M.49 had a tall, single fin and rudder with two circular endplates at the tips of the tailplanes. In terms of performance, the M.49 was designed to be 100mph faster than the M.47, capable of reaching 300mph (see page 60).

Not long after completing design work of the M.49, George Miles held a series of discussions with the Minister of Aircraft Production. What emerged was a third proposal, this again being based on the M.28 but fitted with a 250hp de Havilland Gipsy Queen engine and a retractable tricycle undercarriage.

Although all three designs had been submitted to both the Ministry of Aircraft Production and the Admiralty, events began to move at a quicker pace. An easier, and more favoured, option was soon realised and that was to modify the standard Miles M.25 Martinet I to drone configuration, especially as a number of the former were in storage and new-build examples were also being put straight into storage. Thus emerged the M.50 Queen Martinet and this marked the end of the M.47 and the M.49, both of which were discontinued.[9]

The to-ing and fro-ing of aircraft selection came to an end on 7 April 1943 when the Admiralty finally agreed to accept the Queen Martinet to fulfil the role of an unmanned 'sheep', but only on the understanding that a naval aeroplane, ie the Fairey Fulmar, be operated in a 'shepherd' role.[10]

Externally the converted Queen Martinet remained virtually unchanged. The main changes were structural to take the additional equipment which increased the all-up weight to 6,780lb. Other changes involved introducing the Mercury 26 or 32 which differed from the corresponding Mercury 25 or 30 engine in the Martinet I in two respects: the Queen Martinet had no manual mixture adjustment but was provided with an auxilliary drive to operate the auto-control hydraulic system. The Martinet's 12-volt (with two pole DC) supply was replaced by a 24-volt DC supply, with the autopilot and communications equipment negatively earthed to the aircraft frame. There were other minor internal changes.[11]

The first two prototype Queen Martinets were EM500 and PW979, both of which were originally built as standard

---

7 Although a large quantity of equipment was requested, the Party later revised its requirement downwards and eventually cancelled it on the realisation that British equipment was better.
8 National Archives AVIA15/1749/SB39870/RDInst2(a)

9 Peter Amos, *Miles Aircraft – The Early Years*.
10 National Archives AVIA 15/1749
11 Technical Note IAP.971, held at the National Archives.

Martinet production was severely cut back towards the end of World War II at which time production switched to the Queen Martinet. The drone variant had a very brief service life. RH122, the first production Queen Martinet, is thought to have acted as a target with the Pilotless Aircraft Unit for just three months before being returned to the manufacturer for Cat.B repairs. There are, as yet, no known in-operational use photos. Similarly, no individual squadron codes seem to have been allotted, let alone applied (Imperial War Museum, Neg. No MH5040)

Martinets but allocated to Miles Aircraft in January and July 1944 for conversion. However, it is thought that another Martinet, LR244, was used for earlier trial flights. These trials indicated the possibility of using equipment intended for the cancelled Airspeed Queen Wasp programme but unfortunately stocks were insufficient to cover the Queen Martinet programme and further production was not possible. No other suitable equipment was available in the UK and so a mission was sent to the USA to examine the air pick-off systems, successfully operated by the USAAF and US Navy. It seems that a sufficient number of units were ordered, although what arrived was a later design of auto-

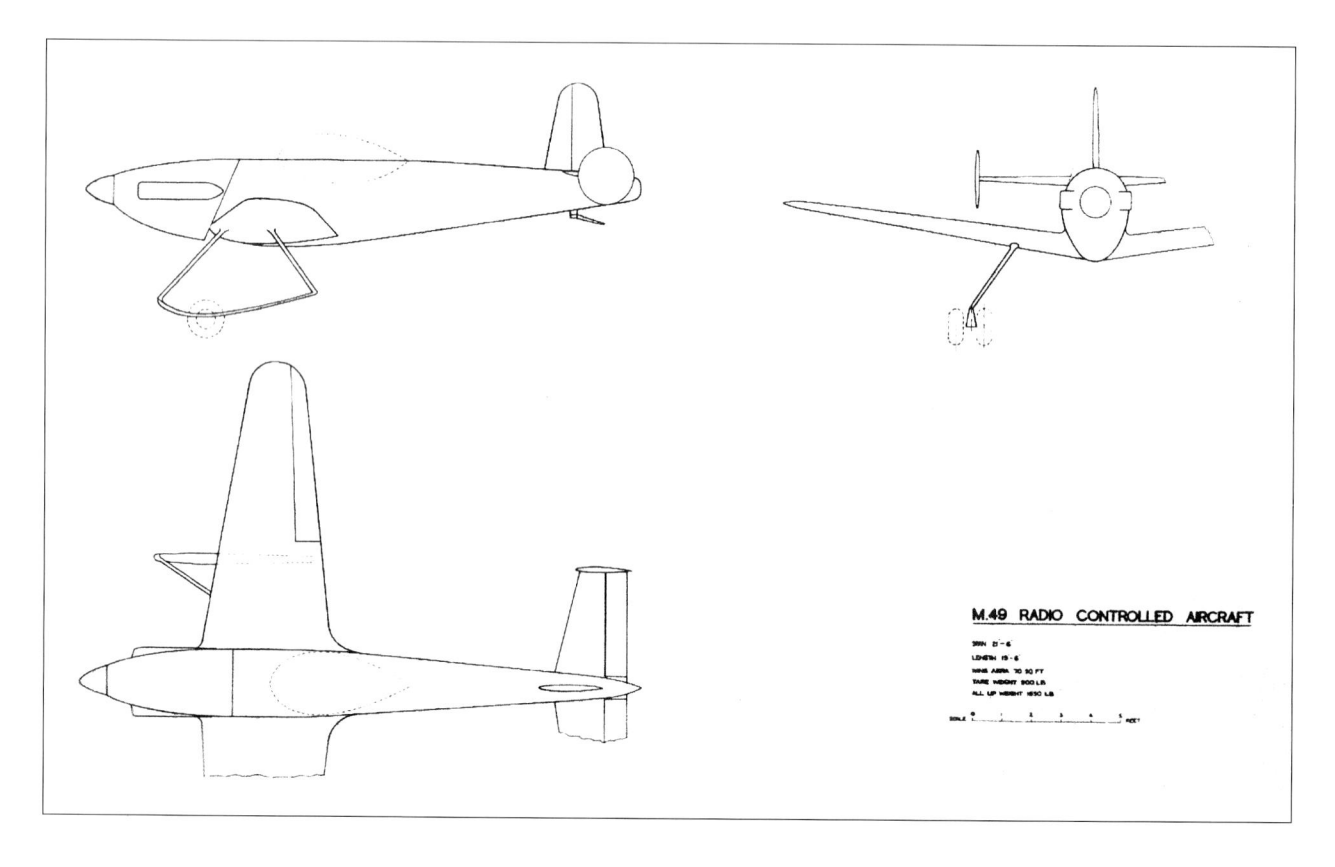

60 Sitting Ducks and Peeping Toms

With cancellation of the Queen Martinet programme in August 1947, a number of incomplete fuselages were stored in a series of buildings on the south-east corner of Woodley airfield. They remained stored until August 1955 when they were finally burnt, possibly at the Miles' Sports Ground at Sonning, judging by the rugby goalposts in the background. The same fate may well have befallen VF100-103. (David Kynaston)

pilot which embodied an electric pick-off and which had not proved wholly satisfactory in American service.[12]

Because the auto-pilot system required much development the Queen Martinet programme was never straightforward and became dogged by complex and lengthy flight trials. All of the flight-testing took place at Farnborough and was carried out jointly by the RAE's IAP and Radio Departments. The latter was responsible for radio equipment, control boxes and relay sets while IAP Department was responsible for developing the automatic pilot, instrumentation, control operation and conducting the flight trials.[13]

Production of Queen Martinets at Woodley was covered by amending an existing contract (Aircraft/1690) for standard M.25 Martinet I target-towing aircraft. This contract had originally accounted for the production of 300 aircraft but was later cut back and amended. The amendment called for 58 aircraft (RH122-RH148 and RH162-RH192) to be completed as Queen Martinets instead. A second contract (Acft/5338/C.23) called for a further 30 Queen Martinets (within the VF-range). However this contract also suffered from cancellations and only seven aircraft can be confirmed as built.[14]

Apart from new-build Queen Martinets, a number of standard Martinets were converted to drone configuration against Contract Acft/127/CB.9(a). This contract involved an initial batch of six conversions although the total number of conversions to Queen Martinet (alongside normal production aircraft) eventually reached twenty.[15]

Virtually the entire Queen Martinet output (production and conversions) was placed into long-term storage at 12 MU Kirkbride, Cumberland; others were temporarily stored at 113 Sub-Storage Site at RAF Market Harborough, Leicestershire (the Site being an offshoot of 273 MU at Polebrook, Northamptonshire.). Four examples (RH123, RH125-RH127) were released to the Pilotless Aircraft Unit at Manorbier but they were for evaluational purposes rather than for issue as 'live' targets. Four others (RH169, RH182, RH185 & RH186) were transferred to Royal Navy charge in May 1946 and allocated to 773 Naval Air Squadron Pilotless Aircraft Unit (PAU).

773 Squadron reformed at Lee-on-Solent during June 1945 as a Pilotless Aircraft Unit (PAU) under the command of Lt Cdr(E) Peter Richmond. Only a handful of pilots were posted to 773 and there was little flying activity at first. One of those pilots was Lt(A) Douglas Harley, RNVR, who was waiting to be deployed to the Far East, hostilities having ceased in Europe. But with the sudden surrender of Japanese forces Harley was quickly re-posted to 773, a posting which he queried by demanding to know why a pilotless aircraft squadron should have a need for experienced pilots!

The role of 773 Squadron would be to operate a fleet of 'shepherd' and 'sheep' aircraft. A small number of Mosquito B.XXVs (including KA930, KA940 and KB670) were taken on charge at Lee-on-Solent to operate in a 'shepherd' role. At least one 773 pilot underwent Twin-Engine Conversion on Oxfords and Beauforts with 762 Squadron at RNAS

---

12 There is some doubt as to whether LR244 could be considered as a full Queen Martinet conversion. The later prototypes (EM500 & PW979) have traditionally been considered as the true Queen Martinet prototypes.

13 National Archives AVIA 6/16125

14 By an apparent quirk of fate, when Contract Aircraft/1690 (involving 300 M.25 Martinet TT.1) was issued on 3 October 1943 the manufacturer was still Phillips & Powis Aircraft Ltd. Two days later, on 5 October, the company was re-titled Miles Aircraft Ltd.

15 The original six aircraft are reported to have been HN945, HP168, HP272, HP277, HP310 and HP487 although HP168 and HP487 were later replaced on-contract by HN909 and HP222.

Miles M.50 Queen Martinet I Production

Contract	Date	Serial Range	Allotment Date	Quantity	Remarks
		LR244		1	Queen Martinet pattern a/c
		EM500 & PW979		2	Prototypes
Acft/1690		RH122-RH148, RH162-RH192	3.10.43	58	
		RH193-RH205, RH218-RH259, RH273-RH315, RH329-RH365		135	Cancelled
Acft/5338/C23(c)		VF100-VF103 VF104-VF110	11.4.45	11	Reportedly diverted to RN
		VF111-VF133		23	VF113-133 canx 26.3.46; VF110-112 later canx also.

In addition some 20 standard Martinets are recorded as converted to Queen Martinet between June 1945 and January 1947. In order of conversion they were: HN909, MS741, HP222, MS928, EM434, NR599, NR387, JN662, JN290, MS723, HP277, EM496, HP310, MS730, MS847, HN945, HP272, MS515, EM518 and MS778. However see Individual Aircraft Histories for further details.

Total production: 69 new-build aircraft, plus 3 prototypes and 20 conversions.

Dale, Pembrokeshire followed by a Mosquito Conversion Course with 704 Squadron this time at RNAS Ford, Sussex. 773's pilots spent a brief period in August/September 1945 at Manorbier on a pilotless aircraft familiarization course flying Queen Bees "hands off" and witnessing Queen Bee drone operations. What did become clear, however, was that Lee-on-Solent was not the wisest choice of locations. The precise role of 773 Squadron was never widely publicised but word soon got out, eventually reaching the Lee-on-Solent Station Commander. "There'll be no bloody unmanned aircraft let loose around my Station" was his alleged response and as nobody on the Squadron was prepared to risk countering the word of the Station Commander, 773 was transferred to RNAS Brawdy, the (as yet unused) "remotest and wildest" outstation in Pembrokeshire, Wales. The pending move to Brawdy was, in reality, no coincidence but indeed pre-planned. Brawdy was ideal as it was a recently acquired (1 January 1946) Royal Naval Air Station. It was otherwise deserted, in close proximity to RNAS Dale with Mosquito facilities as well as the nearby Radar Unit at Kete and, finally, was surrounded by dedicated training and trials airspace.

The actual movement from Lee-on-Solent to Brawdy took place on 27 March 1946. Although it was known that 773 Squadron's drone aircraft would be the Miles Queen Martinet it was not until mid-May 1946 that the first of four aircraft (RH185) was delivered in from Woodley. It must be assumed that 773's aircraft were delivered with drone equipment already installed; they were certainly fully painted in the adopted Queen Martinet scheme which was an overall drab yellow.

The Squadron immediately began establishing operational procedures with the Mosquito and Queen Martinet. Much of the work out of Brawdy involved formation flying, radio range testing and general handling of the Queen Martinet which, once airborne, was flown under radio control but with a pilot on board in a 'no hands' manner.

It is doubtful if any of 773 Squadron's Queen Martinets were ever flown in true pilotless mode. One former pilot has recalled that because of the aircraft's over-bearing torque and swing on take-off, fully unmanned radio-controlled flights – while certainly contemplated – were never attempted. In the event, and with Britain no longer at war, plans for a Fleet Air Arm drone Squadron were shelved and the unit was disbanded at RNAS Brawdy at the end of September 1946.

No evidence has come to light to suggest that the 89 Queen Martinet conversions ever performed their intended role as target drones. It seems hardly credible that such an amount of time, effort and funding should have been expended on a fleet that was condemned to permanent storage. The final chapter closed on 7 August 1947 when all Queen Martinets were struck off charge and scrapped.

Miles M.50 Queen Martinet I dimensions and performance	
Span	39 ft 0 in
Length	30 ft 11 in
Height	11 ft 7 in
Wing area	242 sq ft
Max speed	221 mph at sea-level; 240 mph at 5,800 ft
Cruising speed	199 mph at 5,000ft
Stalling speed	83 mph (with flaps up); 62 mph (with flaps down)
Duration	5 hours

Miles M.50 Queen Martinet – Individual service histories

Note: The use of 'f/f' in the following histories indicates a 'confirmed post construction' first flight date. The term 'flown' indicates a date when aircraft were first flown by named test pilots. The majority of the latter are also likely to be first flight dates but have not been confirmed as such.

EM500 Retained by Miles Aircraft Ltd, Woodley, Berkshire 27.1.44 for trial installation of drone equipment. Flown by Miles Asst. test pilot Flt Lt Hugh Kennedy 23.11.44. To RAE Farnborough 29.11.44 for flight trials. Sustained Cat.4 damage 26(or 28).4.46 when it made a heavy landing during flight trials. Flown by Sqn Ldr M.C. Adderley of Instrument Flt, RAE Farnborough. To Miles for Cat.B repair. Engine removed 21.3.47 (by 2MPRD). Airframe declared Cat.E2 scrap and allotted to 49MU and 'burnt on site' (at either Woodley or Faygate), recorded as 7.5.47 on paperwork.

PW979 Allocated to Miles Aircraft Ltd, Woodley, Berkshire 7.7.44 (on loan until 20.7.45) for trial installation of drone equipment. 2nd prototype M.50. To PAU 9.8.45; to RAE Farnborough 14.12.45 for flight trials. SOC 28.10.46. Engine removed 21.3.47 and sent by road to 2 Metal Produce & Recovery depot (2MPRD), Eaglescliffe, Stockton-on-Tees. Airframe declared as Cat.E2 scrap and allotted to 49MU, RAF Faygate, Sussex 25.5.47 and 'burnt on site' (at either Woodley or Faygate), recorded as 7.5.47 on paperwork.

Contract Aircraft/1690

Contract 1690 originally accounted for 300 M.25 Martinet TT.1 (RG882-RG929, RG948-RG997, RH113-RH148, RH162-RH205, RH218-RH259, RH273-RH315 and RH329-RH365) but the contract was subsequently amended. The first 107 aircraft (to RH121) were built as Martinet TT.1 but the remaining 193 were re-allocated as Queen Martinet. In the event only 58 were built, the final 135 being cancelled.

RH122 Deld to PAU Manorbier 21.3.46 (although unit disbanded 15.3.46). Declared Cat.B and retd to Woodley for repair 4.6.46. To 12 MU Kirkbride 2.5.47. SOC 22.10.47 and scrapped by 2 Metal Produce & Recovery Depot (2MPRD).

RH123 Departed Woodley 1420/19.12.45 for Manorbier (flown by 2FP pilot S/l R F Clarke), but after 75mins the engine failed, probably due to fuel starvation. Aircraft was ditched 100 yds from the shore of Langland Bay, Swansea. Pilot managed to get out and swim around for 20 mins but rescuers could not reach him due to the strong currents and he was swept out to sea and drowned. During salvage operation RH123 turned upside down and was severely damaged. SOC 18.2.46.

RH124 Twice 'test' flown, by Hugh Kendall, 2.4.46. Departed Woodley 1430/19.12.45 for Manorbier (flown by 2FP pilot) The fuel drained unevenly during the flight and the pilot considered diverting to St. Athan before fault rectified itself and flew on to Manorbier, landing c1550. To 12 MU Kirkbride 10.5.46. SOC 7.8.47.

RH125 Passed fit for service 5.45. Departed Woodley 1415/19.12.45 for Manorbier (flown by W/O N Aspinall, 2FP). After 1hr the engine failed due to fuel starvation. Forced-landed (with u/c retracted but flaps down) at 1520 in a field at Pencoed, Glamorgan. Sustained Cat.B damage to wing undersides and fuselage. Pilot unhurt.Retd to Woodley for repair 31.1.46. Test flown (by H. Kendall) 30.8.46. Aw/Cn 5.9.46 and deld to 12 MU 18.9.46. SOC 7.8.47.

RH126 Departed Woodley 1430/19.12.45 for Manorbier (flown by a 2 FP pilot) but after 35 mins landed normally at Aston Down due to fuel drainage problems. Hugh Kendall flew M.28 Mercury G-AGVX to Aston Down 31.1.46 to collect RH126, which he flew back to Woodley same day. On 20.2.46, while flown by Kendall on a 'Fuel system test', the engine failed after 75mins due to fuel starvation when changing over fuel tanks. (This was later deemed to have been an inherent design deficiency in the M.50 fuel system.) Kendall attempted a wheels up landing in a field nr White Waltham but undershot due to the strong wind; noted in his log book as 'Engine cut belly landing.' Retd to Woodley 21.2.46 for Cat.B repair. Test flown by Kendall 9.9.46 & 10.9.46. Aw/Cn 12.9.46 and deld to 12 MU Kirkbride 3.10.46. SOC 7.8.47.

RH127 Deld to Manorbier 19.12.45. Retd to Woodley for repair 4.6.46; tst-flown (Kendall) 18.11.46. Aw/Cn 1.5.47. Deld to 12 MU same date. SOC 20.10.47 and scrapped by 2 MPRD.

RH128 Allocated to 12 MU Kirkbride 16.12.45 and stored. SOC 7.8.47.

RH129 Retained at Woodley on allocation to CRD. Allocated to Miles, Woodley 1 (or 19).12.45, Miles Aircraft on allocation 19.12.45. SOC as scrap 26.11.46.

RH130 Allocated to 12 MU 13.12.45 and stored. SOC 7.8.47.

RH131 Flown 5.4.46 (two flights) by Hugh Kendall. Allocated to 12 MU Kirkbride 17.4.46 and stored. SOC 7.8.47.

RH132 Flown 8.4.46 (two flights) by Hugh Kendall. Allocated to 12 MU Kirkbride 17(or 18).4.46 and stored. SOC 7.8.47.

RH133-RH134 Allocated to 12 MU 17.10.46 and stored. SOC 7.8.47.

RH135 To RAF Market Harborough, Leicestershire 6.2.46 (for 113 Sub-Storage Depot). To 12 MU 14.6.46. SOC 7.8.47.

RH136 To RAF Market Harborough 6.2.46 (for 113 Sub-Storage Depot). To 12 MU 13.6.46. SOC 7.8.47.

RH137 To RAF Market Harborough 6.2.46 (for 113 Sub-Storage Depot). To 12 MU 14.6.46. SOC 7.8.47.

RH138 To RAF Market Harborough 6.2.46 (for 113 Sub-Storage Depot). To 12 MU Kirkbride 20.6.46. SOC 7.8.47.

RH139-RH140 To RAF Market Harborough 6.2.46 (for 113 Sub-Storage Depot). To 12 MU Kirkbride 14.6.46. SOC 7.8.47.

RH141-RH142 To RAF Market Harborough 6.2.46 (for 113 Sub-Storage Depot). To 12 MU Kirkbride 20.6.46. SOC 7.8.47.

RH143 To RAF Market Harborough 18.2.46 (for 113 Sub-Storage Depot). To 12 MU Kirkbride 26.6.46. SOC 7.8.47.

RH144 To RAF Market Harborough 6.2.46 (for 113 Sub-Storage Depot). To 12 MU Kirkbride 26.6.46. SOC 7.8.47.

RH145 To RAF Market Harborough 18.2.46 (for 113 Sub-Storage Depot). To 12 MU Kirkbride 9.7.46. SOC 7.8.47.

RH146 To RAF Market Harborough 18.2.46 (for 113 Sub-Storage Depot). To 12 MU 26.6.46. SOC 7.8.47.

RH147 To 12 MU 17.4.46. Returned to CRD Miles 20.5.46. SOC 7.8.47.

RH148 & RH162 Both flown by Hugh Kendall 9.2.46. Both to RAF Market Harborough 18.2.46 (for 113 Sub-Storage Depot). To 12 MU Kirkbride 9.7.46. SOC 7.8.47.

RH163 Flown 9 and 11.2.46 by Hugh Kennedy. To RAF Market Harborough (for 113 Sub-Storage Depot) 18.2.46. Returned to Woodley (date unkn) and test flown again by Kendall 21.6.46. To 12 MU Kirkbride 9.7.46. SOC 7.8.47.

RH164 Flown 24.6.46 by Hugh Kendall. To RAF Market Harborough 18.2.46 (for 113 Sub-Storage Depot). Returned to Woodley (date unkn) and test flown again by Kendall 24 & 25.6.46. To 12 MU Kirkbride 9.7.46. SOC 7.8.47.

RH165 Flown 12.2.46 by Hugh Kendall. To RAF Market Harborough 18.2.46 (for 113 Sub-Storage Depot). To 12 MU Kirkbride 16.7.46. Returned to Woodley (date unkn) and test flown again by Kendall 21.6.46. To 12 MU Kirkbride 16.7.46. SOC 7.8.47.

RH166 Flown 12.2.46 by Hugh Kendall. To RAF Market Harborough 18.2.46 (for 113 Sub-Storage Depot). Returned to Woodley (date unkn) and test flown by Kendall 21.6.46.To 12 MU Kirkbride 22.7.46. SOC 7.8.47.

RH167 Flown 4,8 & 10.7.46 by Hugh Kendall. To 12 MU Kirkbride 22.7.46. SOC 7.8.47.

RH168 Flown 2.7.46 by Hugh Kendall. To 12 MU Kirkbride 23.7.46. SOC 7.8.47.

RH169 Flown 4.4.46 by Hugh Kendall. To RNAS St Davids, Pembrokeshire 16.7.46. Actually allocated to nearby RNAS Brawdy for 773 Sqdn PAU. 773 Sqdn disbanded at Brawdy 30.9.46. SOC 7.8.47.

RH170 Flown 1.3.46 by Hugh Kendall. Further test flights recorded by him 2 & 3.7.46. To 12 MU Kirkbride 25.7.46. SOC 7.8.47.

RH171 Flown 27 & 28,2,46 by Hugh Kendall. Further test flight by him on 12.7.46. To 12 MU Kirkbride 25.7.46. SOC 7.8.47.

RH172 Flown 1.3.46 by Hugh Kendall. Further test flight by him on 9.5.46. To 12 MU Kirkbride 14.5.46. SOC 7.8.47.

RH173 To 12 MU Kirkbride 25.7.46. SOC 7.8.47.

RH174 Flown 7.3.46 by Hugh Kendall. To 12 MU Kirkbride 26.7.46. SOC 7.8.47.

RH175 To 12 MU Kirkbride 10.5.46. SOC 7.8.47.

RH176 To 12 MU Kirkbride 26.7.46. SOC 7.8.47.

RH177 Flown 12.12.45 by Hugh Kendall and again on 31.7.46. To 12 MU Kirkbride 19.8.46. SOC 7.8.47.

RH178 Flown 14.3.46 by Hugh Kendall. To 12 MU Kirkbride 19.8.46. SOC 7.8.47.

RH179 Flown 19.12.45 by Hugh Kendall and again on 16.5.46. To 12 MU Kirkbride 22.5.46. SOC 7.8.47.

RH180 Flown 15 & 18.7.46 by Hugh Kendall. To RAF Market Harborough, Leicestershire 18.2.46 (for 113 Sub-Storage Depot). Returned to Woodley (date unkn) and test flown by Kendall 1,8 & 9.8.46. To 12 MU Kirkbride 21.8.46. SOC 7.8.47.

RH181 Flown 15 & 18.7.46 by Hugh Kendall. To 12 MU Kirkbride 26.7.46. SOC 7.8.47.

RH182 Flown 17.5.46 by Hugh Kendall. Diverted to Admiralty charge 26.5.46; to RNAS St Davids, Pembrokeshire 28.5.46 for 773 Sqdn STU at nearby RNAS Brawdy. Sustained damage when it dropped its starboard wing on landing 30.7.46 (pilot Sub Lt H.W. Grinstead RN). 773 Sqdn disbanded at Brawdy 30.9.46. SOC 7.8.47.

RH183 Flown 16.5.46 by Hugh Kendall. To 12 MU Kirkbride 22.5.46. SOC 7.8.47.

RH184 Flown 22.2.46 by Hugh Kendall. To 12 MU Kirkbride 10.5.46. SOC 7.8.47.

RH185 Flown 1.3.46 & 10.5.46 by Hugh Kendall. Flown Woodley-RNAS Brawdy, Pembrokeshire 15.5.46 by Sub Lt D. Harley RNVR on delivery to 773 Sqdn PAU. Officially diverted to Admiralty charge 16.5.46. Flown Brawdy-Woodley 28.5.46 by Harley (Sub Lt Bond, passenger) to collect RH182. Believed retd to Brawdy same day by Sub Lt Bond. 773 Sqdn disbanded at Brawdy 30.9.46. SOC 7.8.47.

RH186 Flown 22.2, 7.3 & 10.5.46 by Hugh Kendall. Flown Woodley-RNAS Brawdy 15 or 16.5.46 on delivery to 773 Sqdn PAU. Officially diverted that day to Admiralty charge. 773 Sqdn disbanded 30.9.46. SOC 7.8.47.

Notable 773 Sqdn Trials Flights by Sub Lt Harley in RH186:

21.5.46 50 minutes solo local flying

22.5.46 35 mins Glide & Landings plus equipment monitor/operator passenger. 45 mins flying as 'Sheep' in Controlling Formation with 'Shepherd' Mosquito B.XXV KA940 plus equipment monitor/operator passenger. 25 mins in Controlling Formation with 'Sheep' Queen Martinet.

31.5.46 45 mins of Radio Controlled landings. Sub Lt Harley + equipment monitor/operator passenger.

7.6.46 30 mins of Radio Controlled landings. Sub Lt Harley + equipment monitor/operator passenger.

RH187 Flown 1.3.46 by Hugh Kendall. To 12 MU Kirkbride 31.5.46. SOC 7.8.47.

RH188 Flown 14.3 & 4.5.46 by Hugh Kendall. To 12 MU Kirkbride 10.5.46. SOC 7.8.47.

RH189 Flown 3.4.46 by Hugh Kendall. To 12 MU Kirkbride 12.6.46. SOC 7.8.47.

RH190 Flown 11.3 & 23.5.46 by Hugh Kendall. To 12 MU Kirkbride 31.5.46. SOC 7.8.47.

RH191 Flown 6.4.46 by Hugh Kendall. To 12 MU Kirkbride 19.4.46. SOC 7.8.47.

RH192 To 12 MU Kirkbride 18.4.46. SOC 7.8.47.

(Note that although the remaining RH-serialled allocations were ostensibly cancelled, two entries in test pilot Hugh Kendall's Flying Log Book record the following flights:

8.4.47 222 Queen Martinet test flight (10 mins)

8.4.47 225 Queen Martinet test flight (10 mins)

Unfortunately Kendall does not show prefix letters but the only British contenders are RH222 & RH225. This might imply aircraft built but not accepted by the Ministry of Supply (MoS) which came into being in April 1946.)

**Contract Aircraft/5338/C.23(c)
34 aircraft**

VF100-VF103 Reportedly diverted to the Fleet Air Arm.

VF104 Del to 12 MU Kirkbride 17.4.46. SOC 7.8.47.

VF105 Flown 16.4.46 by Hugh Kendall. Del to 12 MU Kirkbride 24.4.46. SOC 7.8.47.

VF106 Del to 12 MU Kirkbride 30.4.46. SOC 7.8.47.

VF107 Del to 12 MU Kirkbride 7.5.46. SOC 7.8.47.

VF108 Flown 8.5.46 by Hugh Kendall. Del to 12 MU Kirkbride 14.5.46. SOC 7.8.47.

VF109 Flown 21.5.46 by Hugh Kendall. Del to 12 MU Kirkbride 31.5.46. SOC 7.8.47.

VF110 Flown 5.6.46 by Hugh Kendall. Del to 12 MU Kirkbride 20.6.46. SOC 7.8.47.

VF111-VF133 were canx and not built.

However at least eleven uncompleted fuselages were stored at Woodley until August 1955 when they were finally burnt.

M.50 Queen Martinet conversions from M.25 Martinet

EM434 Test flown 22.7.46. Awaiting collection Woodley 30.7.46. To 12 MU Kirkbride 21.8.46. SOC 7.8.47.

EM496 Aw/cn Woodley 3.10.46 but flown Woodley-12 MU Kirkbride 3.10.46 (Flt Lt G. Smith). SOC 7.8.47.

EM518 Flown 18.11.46 by Hugh Kendall. Aw/cn Woodley 23.1.47; to 12 MU Kirkbride 26.3.47. SOC 7.8.47.

HN909 To 12 MU Kirkbride 18.6.45 (as a TT.1, ex 3 Air Gunnery School, Castle Kennedy, Wigtownshire). Surviving records do show that HN909 was allotted for conversion to Queen Martinet and it may well have been returned from 12 MU to Miles at Woodley, converted, test-flown and returned to 12 MU. However no dates are available to substantiate this apart from being SOC 7.8.47 along with all other Queen Martinets.

HN945 Aw/cn Woodley 24.10.46; to 12 MU Kirkbride 28.10.46. SOC 7.8.47.

HP222 Aw/cn Woodley 24.5.46; to 12 MU Kirkbride 8.7.46. SOC 7.8.47.

HP272 Aw/cn Woodley 24.10.46; to 12 MU Kirkbride 12 or 19.11.46. SOC 7.8.47.

HP277 Aw/cn Woodley 8.9.46; to 12 MU Kirkbride 12 or 20.9.46. SOC 7.8.47.

HP279 Martinet TT.I. Sustained a flying accident at 10 Air Gunnery School (AGS), Barrow-in-Furness 24.7.45, assessed as Cat.E and SOC two days later. However it is recorded as Brought Back On Charge (BBOC) (date unkn) and sent to Miles at Woodley for conversion to Queen Martinet. Flown 22.7.46 and 30.8.46 by Hugh Kendall and recorded by him as a Queen. No more details.

HP310 Aw/cn Woodley 3.10.46; to 12 MU Kirkbride same date. SOC 7.8.47.

JN290 Flown 23 & 24.8.46 by Hugh Kendall. Aw/cn Woodley 6.9.46; to 12 MU Kirkbride 3.10.46. SOC 7.8.47.

JN662 Aw/cn Woodley 28.8.46; to 12 MU Kirkbride 30.8.46. SOC 7.8.47.

MS515 Aw/cn Woodley 24.10.46; to 12 MU Kirkbride 26.11.46. SOC 7.8.47.

MS723 Flown 30.8.46 by Hugh Kendall. Aw/cn Woodley 5.9.46; to 12 MU Kirkbride 10.9.46. SOC 7.8.47.

MS730 Aw/cn Woodley 3.10.46; to 12 MU Kirkbride 5.10.46. SOC 7.8.47.

MS741 Flown 22 & 23.8.46 by Hugh Kendall. Aw/cn Woodley 6.9.46; to 12 MU Kirkbride 20.9.46. SOC 7.8.47.

MS778 Flown 29.10 & 8.11.46 by Hugh Kendall. Aw/cn Woodley 23.1.47; to 12 MU Kirkbride 18.2.47. SOC 7.8.47.

MS847 Flown 23.9.46 by by Hugh Kendall. To 12 MU Kirkbride 15.10.46. SOC 7.8.47.

NR387 Flown 23.9.46 by Hugh Kendall. Aw/cn Woodley 19.8.46; to 12 MU Kirkbride 30.8.46. SOC 7.8.47.

NR599 Flown 16.7.46 by Hugh Kendall. Aw/cn Woodley 22.7.46; to 12 MU Kirkbride 21.8.46. SOC 7.8.47.

Queen Seamew

The American Curtiss-Wright SO3C-1 entered service with the US Navy in 1942 but its performance had proved to be unsatisfactory, a factor that led to their early withdrawal from front-line service. A number were subsequently returned to the manufacturer's Columbus, Ohio factory and converted into radio-controlled targets under the designation SO3C-1K.

Under the USA Lend-Lease programme some 30 SO3C-1K Seamew drones were procured by the British Purchasing Commission under Requisition BAC/N-1857. They were destined for service with the Fleet Air Arm and given the name Queen Seamew Mk.I and known to have been ferried to the Royal Navy depot at Roosevelt Field, New York. Whether or not they had already been converted or the intention was to convert them to drone configuration at Roosevelt Field remains uncertain. The 30 were allocated serials JX663-JX669, JZ771-JZ774 and KE286-KE304 although how many, if any, were ever shipped to the UK is again unknown. There is some available evidence to suggest that the first 12 (JX663-JX669, JZ771-JZ774, KE286) were in fact delivered to the UK and whilst the British Air Commission Statistical Delivery Summary reveals that all, with the exception of KE304, were shipped to the UK it is strongly suspected that, in reality, none of the remaining 18 were shipped. The exception, as recorded in the Air Commission Summary – KE304, is known to have crashed in the USA during an early flight test.[16]

The following 30 SO3C-1 & SO3C-3 aircraft were struck off US Navy charge at Roosevelt Field, presumably being those intended for conversion to RN Queen Seamews:

---

16 *Air Arsenal North America – Aircraft for the Allies 1938-1945 Purchases and Lend-Lease* by Phil Butler with Dan Hagedorn (Midland Publishing 2004) plus additional comment by Phil Butler.

Above: *Spitfire Vb BL773 lies to one side of ML Aviation Ltd's facility at White Waltham. Although allocated for conversion to a high-speed drone there remains some doubt how far the conversion had progressed before the programme was cancelled. (ML Aviation Ltd Archives, courtesy The Museum of Berkshire Aviation).*

Left: *What is believed to be the remote-control panel fitted to the cockpit of Spitfire Vb BL773. (ML Aviation Ltd Archives, courtesy The Museum of Berkshire Aviation)*

31.1.45: BuAer 4735
31.3.45: BuAer 4828, 4835, 4837, 4839, 4846, 4847, 4856, 4876, 04180, 04275, 04280, 04281, 04287, 04292, 04330, 04332, 04346, 22012 and 22019.
30.4.45: BuAer 4826, 4877, 04171, 04189, 04270, 04271, 04294, 04309, 04310 and 22016.

Supermarine Queen Spitfire

Little is known about the proposal to re-configure a Spitfire to a drone. ML Aviation at White Waltham, Berkshire was certainly contracted to explore the possibility of adapting the Spitfire as a high-speed target drone and one aircraft, a Mk. Vb (BL773), was allocated to ML Aviation in 1944.

The aircraft was certainly worked upon and photographic evidence shows that it was fitted with drone equipment, reportedly originally acquired for the Queen Martinet programme. However, whilst reports suggest that the Spitfire drone may have completed a series of ground tests at White Waltham, no firm evidence has been found to suggest that it was ever flown as such.

It is also possible that a second Mk.Vb, BM923 which was allocated to ML Aviation on 11 February 1946, was also earmarked for drone development work but, again, there is no firm evidence to suggest any conversion work was carried out.[17]

---

17 An exhaustive search was made through the ML Aviation Archive, held by Berkshire Museum, but no details found.

Chapter 4
Unmanned Target Glider Trials

When, in February 1920, the Naval Anti-Aircraft Gunnery Committee (NAAGC) first floated the notion of suspending (or dropping) a target glider from a kite balloon at 2,000-3,000ft – or simply towing it behind a destroyer – nobody could have imagined that it would take six years to come up with a suitable and satisfactory answer. The first step taken by the NAAGC was to make an official request to the Director of Research who, several weeks later, on 26 March 1920, re-directed the request to RAE Farnborough as a formal Requirement to design and test a suitable system for naval gunnery practice. The resultant design, it was suggested, could be either a monoplane or biplane of around 20ft span but capable of gliding at between 60 and 90mph for about three minutes.

Scientists at RAE Farnborough worked initially on a number of model gliders and by July 1920 had completed one ¼-scale model, with five others and three ½-scale models under construction. Tests revealed that a full-scale version would weigh around 96lb and could achieve a glide angle of 1:14 at 70mph. Precisely when flight trials began is uncertain. What is known is that two Bristol F.2B Fighters (F4675 & F4329) were used for "aerial target" tests with 'B' Flight, RAE from 14 August 1920 onwards. Farnborough's movement log records further flights on 8 November whilst F4675 is noted as "glider-dropping" on 11 November. Tests continued into the new year but not every flight met with success. On Monday 3 January 1921 a pair of 2ft span gliders were dropped from 3,000ft; both fell in a spiral, achieving only 25 and 35 seconds of flight respectively.

Four more gliders were built and in an attempt to improve performance they were all fitted with a gyro-controlled rudder system after a torpedo gyro had been tested on one of the Bristol Fighters. Two of these gliders, with an 8ft span, were conveyed to the Marine & Armament Experimental Establishment site on the Isle of Grain where three Farnborough-based Bristol F.2B Fighters (F4329, F4675 and F4728) were positioned on 28 April. On the same date a series of glider-drop tests was carried out but they failed to perform satisfactorily. The first glider was lost almost immediately after release at 3,500ft (and at 85mph). The glider climbed for a few seconds, banked to port, then to the right before entering a spiral dive into the sea. It disintegrated on impact and sank.

The second of the pair was launched at a lower airspeed of 75mph and proved satisfactory. An observer (aboard a Bristol F.2B "chase plane") calculated the rate of descent to be 1:7 at a speed of 70mph and that it had glided for 260 seconds before landing on the water. Other observers on the ground formed the opinion that the glider would be a visible target from about three miles. The results were encouraging but the glider had oscillated quite considerably in its descent and more work on flying controls was necessary.

In the meantime two DH.9As (E865 and E870) were delivered to Farnborough where they were re-configured with a locally-designed glider-launching cradle on the upper wing. After a test-flight at Farnborough on 20 May 1921, the first of the re-configured DH.9As (E870) was cleared to join the glider trials programme and a second series of test flights was

Target gliders were produced in some quantity during the initial post-war years. This example of a 32ft IMA target glider was operated by the Royal Navy and is seen from a Miles Martinet camera ship. Note the high V-strut on the nose and the central landing skid beneath the fuselage. (Aeroplane Neg. No.12096/15)

As part of its 8ft target glider development programme, RAE Farnborough tested a number of scale models. In this view a half-scale model is mounted on top of a Bristol F.2B Fighter. 'B' Flt, RAE employed two F.2Bs (F4329 & F4675) on glider-dropping trials during the summer and autumn of 1920. (The late J.D.Oughton Collection, via Phil Butler)

carried out at Grain on 25 May 1921. These again involved 8ft span models but with a reduced rudder control. Again results were not wholly satisfactory. The first of the two gliders was actually released from a Bristol Fighter at 3,000ft but immediately went into a nose dive and fell almost vertically into the sea – in virtually the same circumstances as happened on the 28 April test. For the second launch of the day, a glider was released from DH.9A E870 at a height of 3,500ft. For a few seconds the glider flew as intended but it too entered a spin and dived vertically into the water. The cause of both accidents was attributed to the gyro mechanism.[1]

---
1 It is likely that the Bristol F.2B involved on the 13 May 1921 trial was F4675 with DH.9A E746 acting as "chase-plane"

There was another factor which, though unrelated, was thought to have had a bearing on the outcome of these trials. The two launch aircraft had flown from Farnborough to Grain with the gliders in their upper-wing launch cradles. Both pilots had reported considerable difficulty in landing their aircraft with the glider in position. It was likely, therefore, that when carrying a 16ft glider (the projected full-scale Admiralty version) a much larger launch aircraft was required. In the meantime plans by Farnborough to produce up to twenty 16ft gliders were put on hold until a suitable launch aircraft could be located.

By now DH.9A E865 had joined the trials programme and on 13 June it was flown to Grain where it carried out test flights on 14 June and 16 June before returning to Farnborough the following day. A third glider-drop test took place at the end

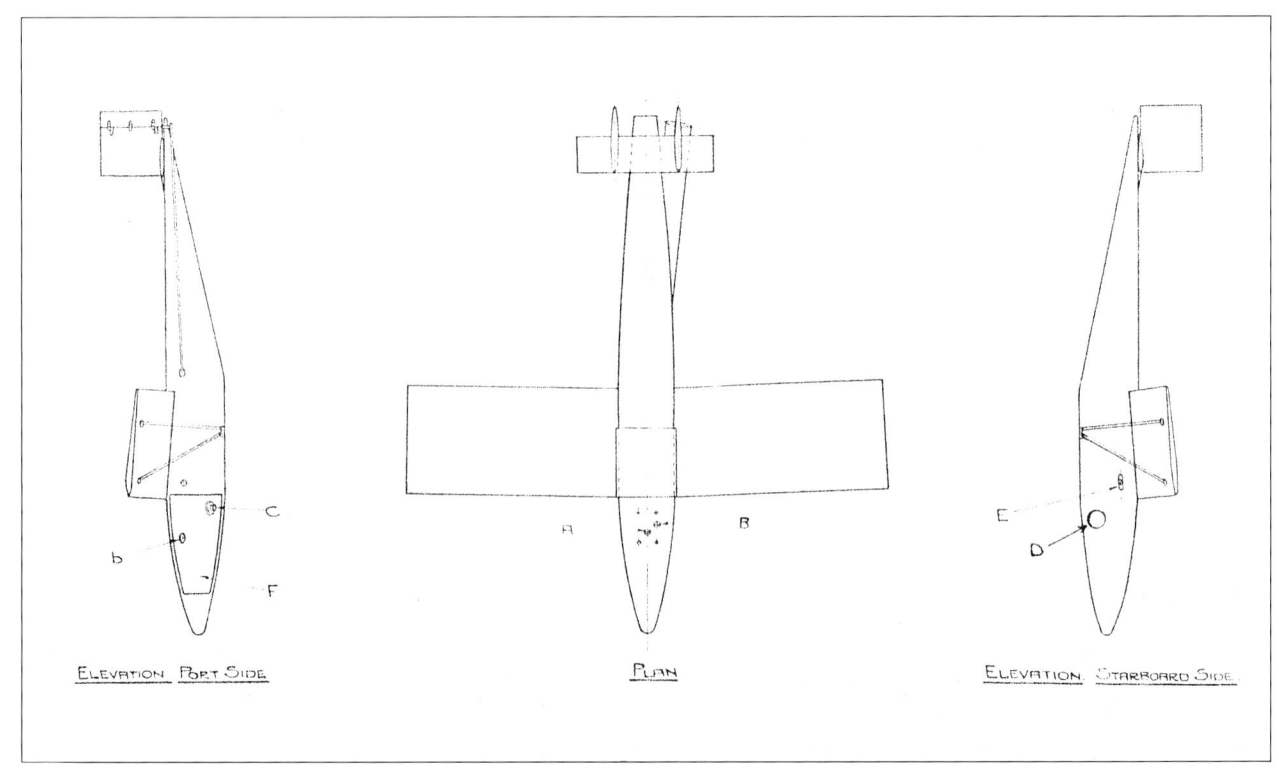

Three-view arrangement of the RAE 8ft (span) Glider with gyro rudder control. Note the twin fin and rudder.

68   Sitting Ducks and Peeping Toms

of June 1921. For this the problematic spring-operated gyro had been modified so that the observer aboard the DH.9A could start the gyro before the glider was actually launched. (Hitherto the gyro starter and the glider-release mechanism were one control). To increase their visibility, the gliders were painted in specific schemes; the upper surfaces, fin and rudder of "Glider No.1" were painted overall black whilst "Glider No.2" had the same areas painted in a vermilion.[2]

The first of the two launches on 30 June went more or less to plan. The independent control to start the gyro before the glider's release functioned perfectly and at last a satisfactory launch procedure was beginning to evolve. Launched at 77mph the glider landed, after 3 minutes 11 seconds of flight, 1½ miles to the north of the Nore lightship but unfortunately it suffered a broken wing on landing. The second glider performed equally well; both were salvaged from the water and taken back to Farnborough by road for repair and minor modification.[3]

Although the desired in-service target glider was the 16ft-span version, full-scale production remained a low priority.[4] There were still too many problems to overcome, none more so than the pilot's difficulty in controlling the launch aircraft with a glider in its launch cradle. One of the DH.9As was fitted with a dead weight – equivalent to the weight of a 16ft glider – on the top wing. That simply underlined the need for a larger launch aircraft. In the meantime, of the six 8ft gliders originally sanctioned by the Department of Research, all had been either lost or severely damaged and so in order to maintain permanent availability of six serviceable 8ft gliders, more examples were sanctioned. Construction resumed at Farnborough on July 18 at the rate of two per week but the modifications built into these resulted in a slight increase in weight. Four of the modified examples were therefore conveyed to Grain for a further set of tests on 11 August 1921. Despite the difficulties experienced with the DH.9A the same launch aircraft were used. All four gliders were launched at 3,000ft off Sheerness on a 68° line between Garrison Point and the Nore Lightship. (In fact, only the first two gliders were from the production batch of twenty; the second pair were rebuilt earlier examples). A summary of the glide-distances achieved on 11 August is as follows:

Flight	Glide (yards)	Remarks
1	7,090	Wings broke off on impact
2	6,280	One wing broke off on impact
3	Nil	Spun in and sank
4	7,290	Wings broke off on impact

The fact that three of the landings resulted in extensive damage became a cause for concern and resulted in a strengthening of the strut bracing on subsequent gliders.

With the likelihood of further flight trials the RAE dispatched ten crated gliders (numbered P1 to P10) by road from Farnborough to the Isle of Grain on 24 November 1921. A lack of available aircrew and a bout of bad weather delayed the next test for ten days. Eventually, on 5 December,

---

2 Trial Report; National Archives AIR2/200/67a
3 Trial Report; National Archives AIR2/200/67a
4 Minutes of Progress meeting; National Archives AIR2/200/68a

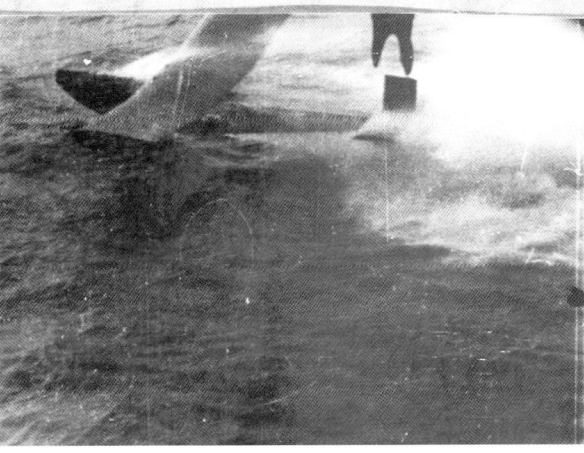

Four stills from a filmed flight test of a RAE 18ft (span) Glider, showing the launch and landing sequences.

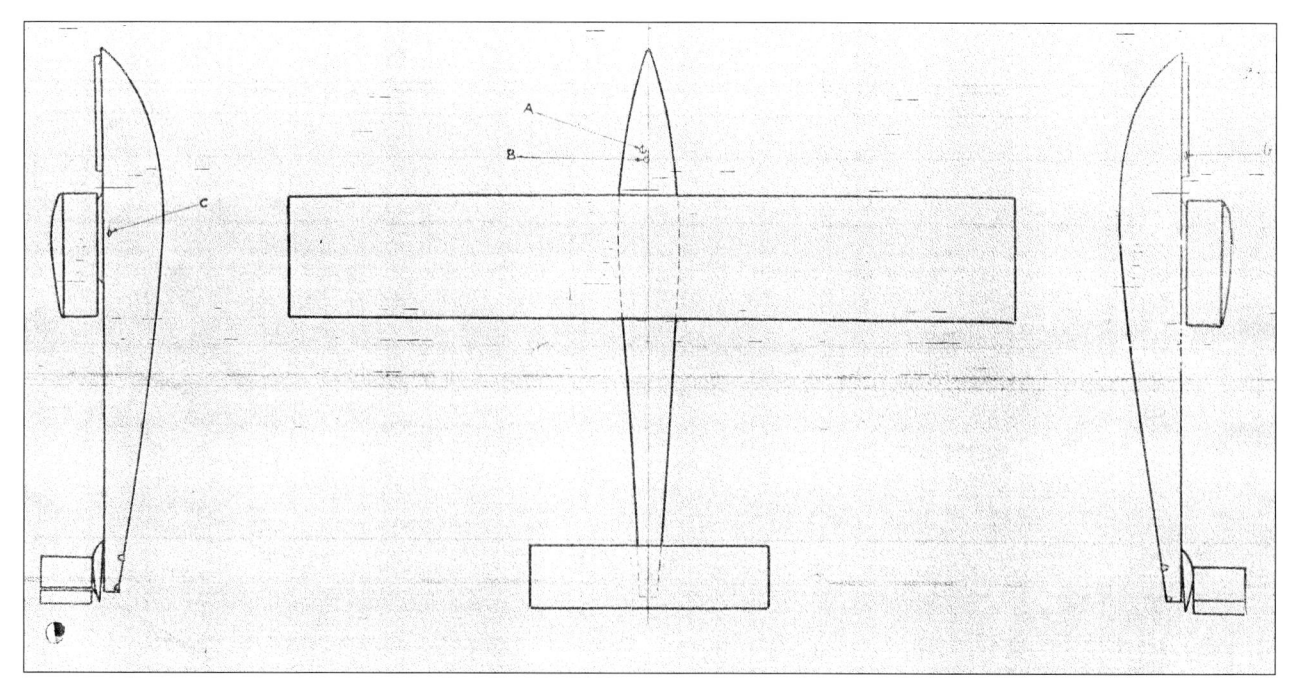

Three-view arrangement of the 18ft span RAE Glider with gyro rudder control. The fuselage underside is noticeably more curved than its earlier designs. Note also the wing is mounted on a central pylon.

flights resumed with a launch from the DH.9A. Although the flight went well and, the fuselage was safely rescued, the wings were destroyed and lost. No further flights were made until 16 December when three more launches were carried out. The first of the day (Glider No. P.4) was launched from 2,000ft and at a speed of 81mph. The glider performed satisfactorily although for about 20 seconds it was seen to enter a steep dive as it encountered the DH.9A's slipstream but then recovered and began a normal gliding angle.[5]

The second drop of the day involved Glider P.3 from a similar height and speed but immediately after launch it entered a wide right-handed spiral as if it had lost gyro control. After one complete turn the angle of glide became steeper until it entered a spin and struck the water just 50yards from Sheerness Pier. The final launch (Glider P.9) failed to launch after the lever which pulled the ring of the gyro release fractured. Aircraft and glider returned to the airfield.

What was beginning to emerge from these tests were two factors. Firstly, there was an opinion that the glider needed to be fitted with a gyro that allowed greater freedom of movement in vertical and horizontal planes. Secondly, a larger wing area was needed, not just for improving the landing technique, but also to improve longitudinal stability and allow it to recover from peculiar attitudes resulting from air disturbance.

A demonstration to the Admiralty took place on the Isle of Grain on 20 February 1922 when the first two gliders (P1 and P2) were air-launched. Both were launched from the RAE's two DH.9As (E865 and E870) and both gliders performed reasonably well, convincing the Admiralty representatives that progress, albeit at a rather slow pace, was finally being achieved.

At Farnborough more modifications were embodied into production gliders, including a slight alteration in the tail setting to compensate for the new stronger (and rounded) wing struts. Two of the modified gliders were flown to Grain on 5 April 1922 (aboard the two DH.9As). Only one launch was achieved; the second glider had sustained slight damage before flight and was returned to Farnborough for repair.[6]

The one flight on 5 April was successful. So much so that testing moved on to the next phase – a demonstration of reliability under true service conditions. For these trials it was decided to transfer operations to RAF Gosport and six gliders were conveyed down from Farnborough. The first flights from Gosport took place on 15/16 August 1922 when all six were launched from DH.9As on a line from Bembridge Point to the Nab Tower.[7]

One of the pilots brought in to conduct these early glider trials was F/O Cecil Bouchier. He later described the glider as having "a wingspan of about 10 or 12ft, and was painted pillar-box red. It was designed to be carried piggyback on a two-seater DH.9A, attached aft by a steel rod to the fuselage, and in front by a quick-release mechanism to the top wing, just above and in front of the pilot's head."

"Often I would fly this contraption down to Gosport, with Garner (later Sir Harry Garner and eventually Principal Director, Scientific Research (Air) at the MoS.) When the Royal Navy ships out to sea reported they were ready to engage in live firing target practice, we would take off. Then, when we were at a good height and position in relation to the ships, Garner would fire a Verey light as a signal that we were about to release the target. The release was always exciting. After I had throttled down and lost some speed, Garner would activate the quick-release mechanisms, and the red monoplane, like a huge bird, would rise vertically above our heads, then gently stall and go into a long, slow glide downwards to the sea – its slight involuntary movements to

---
5 Trial Report; National Archives AIR2/200/94a

6 Trial Report; National Archives AIR2/200/108B

7 Trial Report by Captain, HMS *Excellent*; National Archives AIR2/200/117B. The DH.9As E865 and E870 continued to be used as the launch aircraft and made three flights each on this date.

right and left always corrected by its gyro-controlled rudder. As soon as it had been released, I would get out of the live firing area pronto and from a safe distance we would watch the red monoplane's eventual fall into the sea."[8]

A summary of the initial 1922 Gosport flights reveals that not all of the flights were successful:

Flight	Glide time (mins/sec)	Remarks
1	2.27	Salvaged. One wing broken off on landing
2	–	Spiral nose-dive into sea
3	3.25	'Zig-zag' glide. Wings broke off on landing
4	2.45	Gyro failed. Crashed and sank
5	–	Nose-dived after launch. Sank
6	2.00	Salvaged. One wing broke off on landing

Clearly the programme had suffered another set-back and the Admiralty spectators were not over-impressed. Not only that but it soon became apparent (in their report to the Director of Research) that the Admiralty was no longer interested in the type of target glider that had been first specified back in 1920. That Requirement had called for a glider to glide directly towards the ship at 45°, to be reasonably accurate, and that a straight glide was preferred to a spiral. But RAE technicians argued that the Admiralty representatives' assessment of the 16 August flight demonstration was based on observing flights at right angles to the line of flight. In other words the Admiralty, it seemed, was no longer regarding the target glider as representing an attack by a torpedo-carrying aircraft. In a response to the criticism from the Admiralty, RAE Farnborough announced to the Air Ministry's Research Controlled Aeroplane Committee that, if the Admiralty wanted a glider simply to shoot at from long range and at a high angle of fire, then it would be possible to produce a non-gyro-controlled 9ft span glider at relatively little cost and without much of a delay.

From what clearly had become a showdown between the Admiralty and RAE Farnborough emerged, not a 9ft glider, but a full-size 18ft span glider. The overall weight had increased to 270lb and the wing area to 54sq ft. The wings were unbraced but with dihedral and tapering thickness over the outer thirds of the span. The hull was designed with a V-entry and a single step so that the glider could land on water undamaged. Wing-tip floats were also fitted. Although RAE had suggested dispensing with a gyro the 18ft glider was fitted with a spring-driven gyroscope in order to move the rudder through 5° and so be able to correct any departure from course.

Initial flight trials of the 18ft glider took place over the Nab Tower on 15 January 1924. Two gliders (Nos. 1 and 2) were tested. Despite all of the difficulties experienced by the pilots conducting earlier test launches, Glider No.1 was taken down to Gosport on the launching DH.9A (E870) some five days beforehand and stored. No.2 was conveyed in the same manner on the day of the test and therefore became the first to be released.

From 3,000ft the first launch went well; the glider settled quickly onto its glidepath without any excessive pitching. Only a slight crosswind caused it to drift slightly off line and after 3 minutes 22 seconds the glider alighted on water close to the Nab Tower. (The only hitch had occurred as a result of conflicting instructions issued to the pilot launching the glider and those given to the Admiralty observers watching from aboard the destroyer HMS *Sharpshooter*. Because of the mix-up *Sharpshooter* was moored 3½ miles upwind and therefore those on board had an extremely poor view of the glide)!

The second launch fared little better. In an attempt to have the glider complete its glide close to *Sharpshooter* it was launched about four miles away. In the meantime the wind had increased causing the glider to trim much quicker and thereby come down at a steeper angle. It hit the sea about two miles short of 'Sharpshooter' after a glide lasting 2 minutes 8 seconds.

Both gliders were retrieved and taken back to Farnborough where they were repaired. At the same time the tail setting was altered by 1° to improve the glide angle. Flight tests were carried out using these two gliders off Portsmouth on 5 March 1924. (It had been intended to carry out these trials at Grain but the RAF Marine Aircraft Experimental Unit was in the process of transferring to Felixstowe to become the Marine Aircraft Experimental Establishment, on 1 April 1924. Consequently facilities at Grain were then due to close). Only one launch took place (from DH.9A E870 with F.2B F4675 as observer platform)

Apart from Queen Bee, suitable aerial targets for training purposes were in very short supply and often the need led to some rather strange alternatives. In this 1940 view, men of the Home Guard practice shooting down "an enemy aircraft" on fields at Osterley, Middlesex. A chalked swastika is just visible beneath the wing. (Michael I Draper Collection)

---

8 *Spitfires in Japan*, a memoir by AVM Sir Cecil 'Boy' Bouchier. (Global Oriental, 2005)

Summary of RAE 18ft Glider Trials by Glider Target Unit, Gosport 1925-1926

Date	Trial	Launcher Aircraft	Glider No.	Launch Alt. (ft)	Glide (min/sec)	Remarks
8.10.25	1	Walrus N9506	?	3,000	4.30	
30.11.25	2	Walrus N9506	?			Landed short of target
30.11.25	3	Walrus N9506	?			Crashed on shore
8.2.26	4	Blackburn N9586	?	1,500	1.28	1st launch by Blackburn
12.3.26	5	Blackburn N9586	?	2,000	3.21	
25.3.26	6	Blackburn N9586	?	1,200	1.50	
25.3.26	7	Blackburn N9586	?	1,200	2.10	
9.4.26	8	Blackburn N9586	No.1	1,200	1.05	Pilot released glider too early in error
16.4.26	9	Blackburn N9586	No.3	3,400	3.15	
4.6.26	10	Blackburn N9586	No.4	2,000	3.25	
14.6.26	11	Blackburn N9586	No.4	2,000	3.45	
16.6.26	12	Blackburn N9586	No.3	1,000	1.45	
6.7.26	13	Blackburn N9586	No.3	800	1.31	
29.7.26	14	Blackburn N9586	No.3	1,000	1.25	
29.7.26	15	Blackburn N9586	No.1	1,000	1.25	
4.8.26	16	Blackburn N9586	No.3	1,000	1.53	
5.8.26	17	Blackburn N9586	No.2	1,000	1.30	
16.8.26	18	Blackburn N9586	No.2	1,000	1.47	
17.8.26	19	Blackburn N9586	No.3	1,000	1.34	Erratic flight
	20-22					No details
–	23	–	–	–	–	Not launched

and it went well; from a launch height of 3,000ft the glider achieved a duration of 4minutes 49seconds and a glide angle of 1:9.[9]

In the meantime, although progress seemed painfully slow, the Admiralty was at last expressing some pleasure at the prospect of getting a satisfactory target glider. The next phase was to plan actual live firing trials. But the Admiralty planners now seriously questioned the use of the DH.9A as a launch platform – not because of its unsuitably in handling larger gliders but simply because it was neither a naval aircraft nor a deck-landing aircraft. Their Lordships preferred to launch from an Avro Bison, Blackburn Blackburn or a Westland Walrus.

Few Bisons were available but a Walrus (N9502) was on RAE Farnborough charge and readily available. An examination showed that the existing launch cradle fixed to the DH.9As did fit the Walrus with ease which, considering the Walrus was based on the DH.9A, was hardly surprising. But N9502 was then earmarked for radiator experiments with RAE's Engine Research Flight so one of 420 Flight's aircraft (N9506) was transferred instead from Gosport to Farnborough's Aerodynamics Flight for modification. N9506 arrived at Farnborough on 11 October 1924 and made its initial flight, with the glider-carrying cradle fitted, on 22 January 1925.

Exactly how many launches were made with the Walrus is hard to determine. It certainly made an "aerial target" flight on 5 March 1925 and several others before its final recorded flight on 13 May. By then a second Blackburn Mk.I, N151, had been allocated to Farnborough where Equipment Flight modified it for glider launching and test-flew it on 11 May. Both aircraft were then flown back to Gosport on 19 June (although N151 was later replaced by a Blackburn Blackburn Mk.II, S1057.) One rather unusual development took place at this time when, despite the gliders being officially the property of the Admiralty, the RAF formed, in April 1925, a Glider Target Unit to whom the gliders were allocated.[10]

1925 saw several other flights involving 18ft gliders with mixed results. On 8 October one such glider was launched south-west of the Nab Tower but observers aboard HMS

---

9 RAE Trial Report BA486, dated 11 February 1924; National Archives AIR2/200/170A

10 Blackburn Mk.1 N151 had arrived at Farnborough from Brough on 19 September 1924 but appears not to have been flown again until 5 May 1925.

Summary of RAE 18ft Glider 'Shrapnel' Trials in conjunction with HMS *Tiger* 1926

Date	Trial	Launcher Aircraft	Glider No.	Launch Alt. (ft)	Glide (min/sec)	Remarks
12.10.26	24	Blackburn N9586	No.4	1,200	1.36	Dummy run only
16.10.26	25	Blackburn N9586	No.1	1,400	2.23	Broadside salvo of 8 13.5" guns fired. Glider hit and crashed into the centre-deck turret of HMS *Tiger*
16.10.26	26	Blackburn S1057	No.2	1,400	2.30	Double salvo at 5-second interval fired; glider not hit and landed in the sea beyond HMS *Tiger*
16.10.26	27	Blackburn N9586	No.3	1,300	0.36	Salvo from each turret; 3.4 seconds interval. Glider entered a steep spiral dive due to the gyro not functioning
16.10.26	28	Blackburn S1057	No.4	1,200	1.39	Quadruple salvo attempted but only one turret fired. Glider not hit and landed in the sea short of, and ahead of, HMS *Tiger*
18.10.26	29	Blackburn N9586	No.2	1,250	2.44	Broadside guns fired; glider hit by two bullets; glide not affected and landed short of HMS *Tiger*
18.10.26	30	Blackburn S1057	No.4	1,400	2.22	Broadside guns fired; glider not hit and landed beyond HMS *Tiger*
19.10.26	31	Blackburn S1057	No.2	1,450	2.46	Not fired at due to bad weather – difficult for gunners to keep sight of target
19.10.26	32	Blackburn N9586	No.4	1,650	2.36	Not fired at, having been released when the ship's "WAIT" signal was displayed
20.10.26	33	Blackburn S1057	No.4	1,450	0.44	Not fired at. Glider descended steeply and crashed, possibly due to a frozen reducing valve
21.10.26	34	Blackburn N9586	No.2	1,400	1.54	Broadside guns fired; glider hit by 31 bullets and as a result entered a steep dive and crashed

Sharpshooter lost sight of it until the glider hit the sea. Two more flights took place in Stokes Bay on 30 November, the first landing short whilst the second crashed onto shoreline rifle butts.

At the turn of 1926 the Westland Walrus launch platform was replaced by the Blackburn II in which the pilot had control of the launch mechanism. The first flight involving the Blackburn was only a practice launch principally for the pilot's benefit. It took place on 8 February. The launch proved satisfactory especially since the pilot had an improved and uninterrupted forward view from the Blackburn. Trial flights continued throughout the summer of 1926, as summarised in the table.

Towards the end of August 1926 the Admiralty finally felt the time had come to test the effect of shrapnel from a ship's turret gun against the 18ft glider. The ship chosen to make the first live firings was the battlecruiser HMS *Tiger* (with the destroyer HMS *Stronghold* acting as a "spectator platform".) The objective was to simulate the use of a heavy ship's main armament by firing shrapnel with a time fuse against a low-flying aircraft.

The series of test flights began on 12 October with what effectively was a dummy run. It also offered the opportunity to test a new glider release cradle that had been fitted to Blackburn Mk.II N9586. Unfortunately the cradle's release mechanism failed and the aircraft was flown back to Gosport with the glider still attached. An inspection afterwards revealed that although the release gear worked with a static load the clearances were insufficient when in-flight air forces on the glider were applied. An immediate modification solved the issue but it did delay the start of the live firing trials for several days.

The first of four glider drops on 16 October led to one of those occasions when things can sometimes not go quite to plan. Glider No.1 had been released at 1,400ft and quickly settled on to a straight and steady glide, as intended, towards 'Tiger'. The cruiser's broadside gun opened fire with a salvo of eight shrapnel shells. When the cordite smoke cleared the glider was seen to be dropping steadily past the ship's bow at a height of approximately 200ft. It continued for a few seconds, then turned to starboard, kept turning through 270° and promptly crashed into the centre-deck turret gun! When the

What appears to be an RAE 18ft Target Glider sits atop an unidentified Fairey IIIF, probably circa 1926. The identity '9' would suggest that more of these gliders were built than is implied in the trials reports. (Air Pilot AP1245, via Peter Kirk)

wreckage was examined two shrapnel pieces were found, one in the front spar port wing and the other in the rear fuselage.

Four launches against live firings were achieved on 16 October which marked the introduction of a second Blackburn launch aircraft (S1057). The second test of the day went well with Glider No.2 coming under fire but escaping unscathed and landing in the sea close to 'Tiger'. The third launch ended in disaster when, after just 36 seconds, the glider entered a spiral dive and crashed into the sea. The fourth, and final, flight of the day was intended to face a heavy barrage – a quadruple salvo from 'Tiger''s 13.5" guns but in the event only one turret actually fired. Again, the glider survived and landed in the sea close to 'Tiger'.

The loss of gliders (Nos. 1 and 3) left the Glider Target Unit somewhat short of serviceable gliders. Replacements were requested but the Admiralty was by now starting to wonder if further trials were likely to prove anything. Target gliders had clearly demonstrated their effectiveness as a gunnery target and the October 1926 series of trials had allowed the Navy to gain considerable experience.

It had taken six years of tests and trials to convince the Admiralty of the merits of employing target gliders. But in the final analysis little came out of it as the Admiralty began, as it had done in the past, to dither. In July 1928 RAE Farnborough produced six more gliders and conveyed them to Gosport but, it seems, they were never used. The Admiralty had, in the meantime, come to the conclusion that, at 62mph, the target glider was far too slow for simulating a torpedo aircraft attack against a ship. Undoubtedly there was some disappointment at Farnborough where, instead of further developing the free-flying target glider, attention turned towards seeking an improved type of towed target capable of being towed far behind and below the aeroplane and better suited for target practice.

RAE 6ft Machine-Gun Target Gliders

Whilst trials of 18ft target gliders were progressing satisfactorily the Admiralty had also become aware of developments in the US involving smaller gliders specifically for use as aerial machine-gun targets. The Admiralty's

Summary of RAE 6ft Glider Trials by Glider Target Unit, Gosport 1926

Date	Trial	Launcher Aircraft	Glider No.	Launch Alt. (ft)	Glide (min/sec)	Remarks
27.8.26	1	Fairey IIID S1015	2	3,200	3.27	
27.8.26	2	Fairey IIID S1015	4	3,000	7.00 ?	
27.8.26	3	Fairey IIID S1015	4	3,000	2.00	
27.8.26	4	Fairey IIID S1015	2	3,100	3.35	Wing damaged in landing
8.10.26	5	?	3	2,100	4.40	Port elevator damaged on landing
8.10.26	6	?	4	3,000	?	Glider entered cloud; not seen again

interest in this concept prompted a note to the Air Ministry (on 28 July 1925) suggesting that up to four experimental gliders be built together with a mounting/launching frame that would fit onto a Fairey IIID.[11]

Response by the Air Ministry was positive and led again to a formal request that RAE Farnborough design and build four (later increased to six) gliders with a maximum 6ft wingspan. Unlike the larger 18ft gliders there was no requirement for gyro-controlled rudders. The Instruction To Proceed was issued on 1 October 1925.

Farnborough completed the six 6ft gliders by mid-1926. The only difficulty encountered was in modifying a launch frame to fit the Mk.II variant of the Fairey IIID. It had been intended to use RAF Gosport's IIID S1011 as a launch platform but the launch frame had been designed to fit an earlier version of the IIID. The frame was therefore later fitted to IIID S1015 while S1011 returned to Gosport on 29 January 1926.

Two sets of flight-trials took place involving a total of six flights, all using the Fairey IIID launcher and with a Blackburn Fleet Spotter carrying an observer.[12]

The gliders (numbered 1 to 6) enjoyed mixed results. From a tactical point of view the first two air-launches (involving Gliders 1 and 2) were considered to be successful although neither glider achieved a steady glide and both were damaged on ditching. (No.2 was later made serviceable by fitting it with the wings from No.3 but went on to break several ribs during a later ditching). The third and fourth launches were good although the fourth glider crashed inland. Unfortunately from a trial point of view the "attacking" aircraft was poorly positioned and the pilot failed to see the glider. Of the final two launches the first was successfully engaged with a camera gun by the observer in the parent aircraft whilst the last glider to be launched entered cloud and was never seen again.

A second series of live shrapnel firing trials involved HMS *Tiger* and began with a dummy run on 12 October 1926 to test a new glider release cradle fitted to a Blackburn Mk.II. Unfortunately the cradle's releasing mechanism proved faulty and the aircraft returned to Gosport where it was later discovered that the release gear worked under a static load but that the clearances were insufficient with in-flight air forces on the glider. Therefore the first firing trial was not conducted until 16 October and by using a Blackburn Mk.I. Four gliders were involved and between them conducted ten launches between 16-20 October, the results of which were fairly mixed. A summary of the firing trials appears above.[13]

World War II

When the Admiralty turned its attention away from using large free-falling gliders as targets, development switched instead to towed banners, or drogue targets. In many respects, of course, any resemblance between a drogue and an aircraft was purely imaginative; indeed it has even been said, no doubt partially in jest, that one may just as well

---
11 National Archives AIR5/417
12 National Archives AIR5/547
13 Collated from National Archives AIR5/547

Above: *Stress-testing of 32ft target glider fuselages at Merton. Note that the main undercarriage wheel has already been fitted. (Lines Brothers Ltd.)*

Above and below: *32ft target gliders under construction at IMA's Merton works. The fuselages were of duralumin and steel construction. (Lines Brothers Ltd.)*

Above: *Production of wings for 32ft target gliders at Merton, Surrey. Extreme accuracy was essential, a factor that IMA had developed during its pre-war modeling period. (Lines Brothers Ltd.)*

Unmanned Target Glider Trials 75

compare a rose with a sausage! True, the drogue has a shape that vaguely resembles a fuselage but one of an aircraft's most important features is its wing – and the drogue does not have one.

Using a drogue target was seen to have another disadvantage in that its speed was restrictive. Speed was solely dependent on the power of the towing aircraft and there were also limits to the strain which calico or silk would withstand.

At a very early stage in World War II it soon became clear that, to achieve any degree of success, Light Anti-Aircraft gunners had to practice against a target that represented a modern aircraft. Attention therefore began to revert to target gliders, several types of which were produced throughout the war, principally by one South London company, International Model Aircraft Ltd.

Lines Bros Ltd
International Model Aircraft Ltd

International Model Aircraft Ltd – IMA Ltd for short – had been formed in December 1931 as a subsidiary of Lines Bros Ltd, a company universally known for producing dolls and wooden rocking horses. The new company was registered to two model aircraft enthusiasts, Charles Wilmot and Joseph Mansour, who soon began making the first flying model aeroplanes. A separate factory was built next to Lines' existing plant at Merton, Surrey and when the plastics industry began to develop the Merton factory became the centre of the group's injection moulding activities from which emerged the FROG range of model aircraft.

Lines Bros Ltd later developed the Tri-ang toy range, at which point the company absorbed IMA Ltd and production of model aircraft was transferred to the Tri-ang Works in Morden Road, Merton, London SW19. Despite the take-over, International Model Aircraft continued to operate under its own name and Lines Bros Ltd became the sole concessionaire.

IMA's production and output was not immediately affected by the outbreak of war and it was not until 1941 that the company began to experience difficulty in obtaining raw materials. Production then dropped dramatically but IMA's expertise in model aircraft became the focus of a renewed demand for small target gliders.

The idea was not a new one; before the war, in Britain and in other countries, experiments had been carried out with small target gliders, but most of the designs met with little success. In fact, the US industry had abandoned the notion of target gliders altogether. In Britain, trial and error led eventually to a workable target glider.

The first target glider that could be described as operationally successful was IMA's first design, a 6ft 3in-span example which became known officially as the Free Flying Glider Mk.1. It was of wooden construction with a balsa monocoque fuselage and fabric-covered wings and tail unit. Launched by a hand winch, it featured an auto-rudder control that held the glider in a straight line during the tow-up. Right rudder was automatically applied on release from the tow-line (usually at about 300ft) which then allowed the glider to circle down-wind at about 40mph. WREN operators were trained to handle the gliders and also to carry out minor repairs made necessary by crashes or bullets, although some fuselage damage necessitated a return to the Merton works.

Initial flights had been carried out with a balsa wood model of only 2ft span, which was towed behind a car at speeds of up to 80mph. From results obtained, balsa models of 4ft- and 8ft-span were then built and again test-flown, firstly behind cars and, later on, by aircraft. The first successful release of a glider was made on 9 September 1942 with a 4ft model towed by a Hawker Hart flown by a Gp Capt J. Noakes. The glider behaved satisfactorily but the Admiralty demanded a higher towing speed and suggested a Boulton-Paul Defiant be used for further trials.

By the end of the year the Admiralty had awarded IMA Ltd a contract (3B/70456/Ep593/42) to cover the development of a series of larger Target Gliders. The company worked closely with RAE Farnborough's Aero Flight on two initial designs based on an original concept by Lt.Cdr Stanley Bell, a Volunteer Reserve naval officer. (Bell was also appointed the co-ordinator of the Target Glider project.)

Test-flights began at Worminghall aerodrome on 16 December 1942 when several trial tows were made from behind a Lagonda sports car. The first air-towed flight came on the following day when the same gliders were towed by Defiant TT.1 DS139 (which had been acquired by RAE Farnborough on a 3-month loan). The air-tows were not without difficulties as in almost every instance the gliders became prematurely airborne after bouncing during the ground run and then getting caught in the Defiant's slipstream.

Towards the end of 1942 the responsibility for target glider development passed to the Director of Technical Development, Ministry of Aircraft Production, although Bell remained the key link person. One of Bell's more imaginative initiatives was to modify two gliders to more accurately represent enemy aircraft. They were re-modelled to look like a Focke-Wulf Condor and a Heinkel He111. Although test-flights were satisfactory the concept was never adopted.

In March 1943 IMA Ltd acquired the use of an empty hangar at Thame airfield where the company very quickly began assembly of six 8ft gliders (referred to as Type A) and three 16ft gliders (two Type A and one Type B).[14] The 16ft Type B gliders were sub-contracted to Slingsby Sailplanes Ltd and built under that manufacturer's designation, Slingsby T.19. Slingsby built six examples of the 16ft gliders: one Type B1 (metal skin); four Type B2s (all-wood) and one Type B3 (steel tubing fuselage)). The six T.19s were allocated manufacturer's c/ns SSK/FF/19 to SSK/FF/24 respectively. Tests proved that the Slingsby T.19 could be towed at speeds up to 250mph (402km/hr).[15]

For some time it had been felt that the Defiant was not the ideal tug aircraft and an alternative was sought. On 3 March 1943 a Miles Martinet TT.1 HP428 was ferried in to Thame as a possible replacement. A trial tow carried out three days later using a 16ft Glider displayed no signs of instability from the glider and confirmed that the Defiant be

---

14 Some confusion could arise over these designations. IMA described the basic 8 ft glider as a Type A. The 16 ft glider was also described as Type A as well as a Type B although it is uncertain quite what constituted a Type A 16 ft glider.

15 The six T.19s were allocated manufacturer's fuselage numbers SSK/FF/19 to SSK/FF/24 respectively, following on from a batch of sub-contracted Hengist troop-carrying gliders.

Two views of the IMA 16ft target glider, possibly seen at RNAS Twatt towards the end of the war. Of note is the ROYAL NAVY legend on the fin and the serial LB283 on the nose but styled as 283/A on the fin, the prefix letters presumably being a reference to Lines Bros. (via Geoff Wakeham)

replaced. However HP428 was fitted with the older B-Type wind-driven winch and as a consequence the Martinet was replaced by another example, HP216, which had a more practical electrical winch. In the meantime, on 20 March, IML was awarded a contract (SB46561/C.20(a)) for 100 gliders (later reduced to 79) to consist of seventy-five 16ft (Type B3) and four 32ft examples. The first three 16ft gliders from this contract (identified as A1, A2 and A3) were test-flown from Oakley airfield on 17 June 1943, using the Miles Martinet HP216 as the tug but by July 1943 it was becoming increasingly evident that at 10,000' the 16ft Glider might well be too small a target to see, let alone shoot down.

A second prototype 32ft Target Glider was flown at Oakley on 24 March 1944. The flight itself was satisfactory

Left: *Several 32ft target gliders were employed on flight trials at A&AEE Boscombe Down. This example exhibits severe damage to the starboard wing. (A&AEE; Neg No.7693B)*

Right: *In order to improve flying characteristics one 32ft target glider was fitted with neat-looking undercarriage fairings. (A&AEE: Neg. No.8457/4)*

Unmanned Target Glider Trials   77

The main hangar at Buttocks Booth, Moulton (Sywell aerodrome) shows eight complete Brooklands 32ft Target Gliders, all unpainted. The nearest example has the c/n BAL 642 handwritten on the forward section. These are Mk.II versions which were constructed of light alloy instead of steel as on the Mk.I – something that Lt Cdr Bell advised (see page 81). The 32ft Target Glider had a length of 26ft 5in (7.92m) and a height of 6ft 3in (1.83m). The outer wing section had a dihedral of 6°. (Brooklands Aviation Ltd.)

but the glider's wings collapsed on landing. Two more 32ft examples (designated Type C) were test-flown on 5 April; these were lightweight all-wood versions (serialled C5 and C7), the latter fitted with a parallel wing and a single tow-point. On 17 April the Royal Navy Experimental Unit (RNEU) test-flew another variation, this being an all-metal glider with fabric-covered wings, tailplane and fin. It was designated Type D and carried the identity D2. Unfortunately during the take-off run the two wing wheels and the front wheels seized. Some damage was also sustained by the main airframe, so much so that during the approach to land the glider hit the ground with its nose and was completely wrecked.

The all-metal 32ft Winged Glider (as the Target Glider was now being referred to) suffered another failure when the hitherto unflown D1 was test-flown on 18 April. During the take-off the starboard wing lifted causing it to run only on the port wing. The tug observer, in realising a potential disaster, cut the tow cable; the glider was then seen to yaw to port before straightening itself and finally going into a climb. At 200ft it partially stalled, entered a shallow dive, and ultimately struck the ground nose first. The glider was a total write-off.

By June 1944 initial development work on the 16ft and 32ft gliders effectively ended the first trials phase. Contract SB46561/C.20a – which had covered the manufacture and initial development – was succeeded by three new Contracts. Aircraft/4281/C.20(a) was awarded to IMA Ltd for mock-up & trial installation work; 4282/C.20(a) to Lines Bros Ltd for further experimental work on winged targets and 3391/C.20(a), also to Lines Bros, for the production of 16ft and 32ft gliders for the Royal Navy. The order clearly overrode

A finished, fully-painted Brooklands Target Glider is posed for the photographer. On the fuselage top can be seen the Brooklands Aviation Ltd c/n BAL848 and also a Sywell Repair Facility identification SRF26, the precise meaning of which remains obscure. (Brooklands Aviation Ltd.)

78   Sitting Ducks and Peeping Toms

Above: *Amongst units equipped with the 32ft Winged Target was 728 Squadron Fleet Requirements Unit at RNAS Hal Far, Malta (HMS* Falcon*) and who offered a target facility for Royal Navy ships operating in the area. Seen here, on a short tow, is a Winged Target behind 728 Squadron Short Sturgeon TT.2 TS486 '591/(HF)'. The picture is undated but the Sturgeon is known to have been on 728 Squadron strength between January 1952 and November 1954. (Douglas A. Rough Collection).*

Right: *Women made up a large proportion of the Brooklands Aviation workforce. This view of a wing at the welding stage illustrates the structure and obvious strength in the design of the Target Glider wing. (Brooklands Aviation Ltd.)*

Below: *Just how much punishment a 32ft Winged Target could absorb and yet still return safely is well-illustrated in this view, taken at RNAS Ford (HMS* Peregrine*) on 8 October 1952. 771 Squadron Fleet Requirements Unit was based at Ford and equipped with Short Sturgeon TT.2 for sleeve and winged target towing. (Douglas A. Rough Collection)*

Unmanned Target Glider Trials   79

A Royal Navy 16ft target glider under tow. This is a later-production example with a four-digit serial (prefixed by LB) on the nose. The long landing skid is particularly evident in this air-to-air view. (Aeroplane)

any concerns expressed by the Admiralty as to whether the 16ft glider was sufficiently visible at medium altitude.

Not all winged target production was for the Navy. At the same time that the new production contracts had been awarded to Lines Bros a requirement was raised by R.D.Arm.3(c) for 40 16ft and 20 32ft gliders. Twenty of the 16ft examples were ordered on behalf of the Gunnery Wing School of Anti-Aircraft Artillery, the remainder being sent to the Ministry of Aircraft Production for experimental purposes and to be held in reserve. Similarly the 32ft gliders were allocated to MAP for similar purposes. These were all added to Contract Aircraft/3391/C.20(a) although the actual quantity of 16ft gliders delivered against this contract appears to have only involved twelve: nine to 595 Squadron's satellite base at RAF Carew Cheriton and three to No.2 Group Support Unit at Swanton Morley.

By mid-1946 production of the 16ft and 32ft Winged Gliders was in full swing although by now they were being referred to as Target Gliders; TG.1 and TG.II respectively. Constructed in a comparative light mix of steel and fabric and with improved streamlining meant that the performance of the tug aircraft – usually a Miles Martinet – was unaffected to any great extent. For many tug pilots take-off and landing proved to be an interesting business, though not apparently as tricky as one might have expected. At take-off, the pilot simply had to be very careful to fly steadily and to climb at prescribed speeds; for landing, however, the tug pilot took his instructions over the radio from another pilot who was seated in a runway control vehicle. The system worked very well, and even gliders that had been badly shot up were usually landed successfully.

What did give concern was the speed achieved by a Miles Martinet towing a glider which had, by now, become unrepresentative of a 'realistic target'. A series of exploratory high-speed tow trials, involving both 16ft TG.I and 32ft TG.II gliders, was conducted at the Airborne Forces Experimental Establishment at Beaulieu. Oversaw by a group of Royal Navy officers these trials examined the characteristics of high-speed towing behind a Mosquito TT.39 of the Establishment's 'A' Flight'. At first, the TG.I appeared to be the more successful of the two, the TG.II Mk.2 (as it was now regarded) revealing a number of structural weaknesses. Several incidents of the fin attachment to the rear fuselage failing were recorded and also instances of skin buckling along the fuselage centre section as well as an unintended alteration of the tailplane incidence after assembly due to an apparent weakness in the transport joint. Finally, there were recorded instances of an alteration in the outer wing dihedral, caused by an inherent slackness of the wing root attachment. In view of these difficulties the TG.II was, for a time, restricted to tow-speeds not exceeding 200 knots (376 km/hr).

Remedial work proved to be relatively simple. Described as 'Mod 10', TG.II gliders were retro-fitted with a modified fuselage transport joint as well as stringers at the fuselage centre section and a new bolt fitment into the wing root. These effectively solved many of the snags and a strengthening of the tail unit attachment to the fuselage and a slight shortening of the fin enabled the TG.II to be towed at speeds of 220-250knots (414-470km/hr). In time, the TG.II became the preferred version of Target Glider and production of the smaller TG.I ceased. By 1948 large-scale production of the TG.II Mk.II glider was underway. Precisely how many 32ft target gliders were supplied to the British forces remains unclear as surviving manufacturer's records offer confused details. Orders for up to 5,000 TG.II Mk.2 gliders are known to have been placed, against several contracts: 6/AIR/5942/CB.8(a); 6/AIR/6704/CB.8(a) and 6/AIR/7243/CB.8(a) but details of precisely how many were built by Lines Bros Ltd are sketchy. One batch (c/ns 2253-2900) is known to have been delivered between July 1951 and October 1952.

A fine air-to-air shot of a Royal Navy 32ft target glider under tow. The underwing markings are especially noteworthy, as is the serial 1500 on the lower fin. (Aeroplane)

Lt Cdr Stanley Bell, RNVR

The pivotal figure in the development of 16ft and 32ft winged target gliders was a Royal Navy Volunteer Reserve officer, Lt. Cdr Stanley Bell. It was Bell who not only created the concept of a towed target glider but also designed its basic shape and pattern. When, in mid-1942, he presented his concept the response by the Admiralty was both positive and immediate. Indeed, within a very short time, Bell was given virtually a free hand to manage the project.

Much of the development of IMA Ltd's target gliders was carried out by RAE Farnborough and Lt.Cdr Bell had to work closely with both the RAE and the manufacturer. When overall responsibility for development passed to the Ministry of Aircraft Production, Bell remained in a key position. But the relationship between Bell and the RAE was never a cosy one.

By most accounts Bell's relationship with IMA Ltd – and its associate company, Lines Bros Ltd – was almost constantly fraught. He frequently found the opportunity to criticise both and the situation was not made any easier when Bell instructed IMA Ltd to sub-contract a batch of target gliders to Slingsby Sailplanes Ltd. That decision was made by Bell without, it seems, notifying the M.A.P.

At one of the regular Whitehall progress meetings, on 2 June 1944, those present learnt that on several occasions 32ft gliders had suffered minor accidents during routine test flying. One of the causes was said to be a faulty winch but Bell doubted this to be the case. He also expressed grave disquiet at the high weight of the target glider and refused to accept any responsibility for the (then) present design which he claimed was completely at variance to his first proposals. To alleviate the problem, he argued, a lighter Mk.2 variant should be developed. Bell also voiced other concerns, none less than questioning the wisdom of Lines Bros being allowed to go-ahead with jigging and tooling for target glider production. Bell's request for a Mk.2 was turned down.

The relationship between Bell and Lines Bros Ltd deteriorated rapidly and concerns were beginning to be expressed as to whether Bell should remain the link person. Matters became increasingly delicate after Bell had not only chosen to sub-contract work to Slingsby Sailplanes but also instructed IMA Ltd to sub-contract work to other companies, including CB Projections. CB Projections, it was later discovered, was Clare & Bell, ie Lt Cdr Bell's peacetime company. That was later viewed as an "undesirable" situation as was Bell's refusal to meet a request from IMA to carry out other MAP development work in the partially unused glider hangar at Thame. Bell's instructions and threats were by now coming thick and fast; he was even reported to have threatened to get the Ministry of Labour to close the factory. Matters finally came to a head when IMA discovered Bell going through their private correspondence.

It was left to Research & Development (Naval) Branch to raise the alarm after they too complained of the impossible attitude of Bell on all matters concerned with targets. There was, they claimed, only one way to resolve the situation – "that Lt.Cdr Bell be posted away from Thame".

(*Source:* National Archives AVIA15/1807 & 1808)

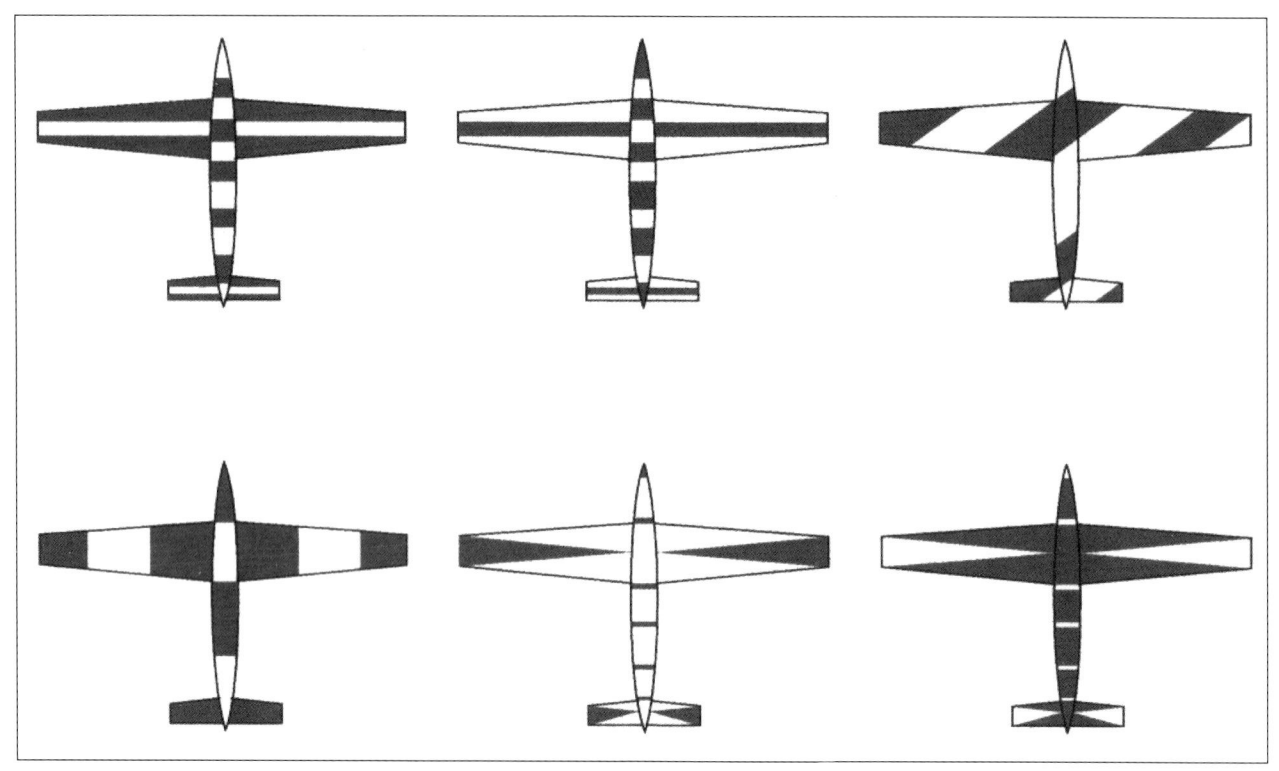

The RAE put forward six alternative proposals for Target Glider schemes. All show variations based on a standard target colours of black and yellow although other colour schemes were also considered.

The major constructor of TG.II Mk.2 gliders was Brooklands Aviation Ltd who was sub-contracted to build at least 3,000 and which became known as the Brooklands Winged Target Mk.2. Production was established at Brooklands' Buttocks Booth facility at Moulton, near Northampton with an initial 600 built against Contract 6/Air/5791/CB.8(a) with deliveries taking place between 7 November 1951 and 27 June 1952. Although they were not issued serials in the normal format, Brooklands allocated construction numbers BAL1 to BAL600 inclusive. A second contract (6/Air/6307/CB.8(a)) involved a further 1,474 examples, allocated c/ns BAL601-BAL871 and BAL/SRF872 to BAL/SRF2074. A third final contract (6/Air/10298/CB.9(b)) accounted for c/ns BAL/SRF2136 to BAL/SRF2226 with deliveries commencing on 12 November 1954. This final contract may well have involved a modified variant as a series of flight trials was conducted at Boscombe Down in August 1954. Deliveries of gliders from Contract 10298 are thought to have extended well into 1955.[16]

The TG.II MK.2 effectively marked the end of target glider production by either International Model Aircraft Ltd or Lines Bros Ltd although Lines did announce a new target glider at the 1948 SBAC Show, held that year for the first time at Farnborough. Displayed on the company's stand was a half-scale model of what was being marketed as the Lines LB-1 target glider. The full-scale version was to have a 12ft wing-span and for take-off it had an 8hp two-stroke, horizontally-opposed engine. No evidence has been found that suggests the LB-1 was ever placed in production.

Winged Target Glider Colour Schemes

Devising a standard colour scheme for target gliders proved to be a fairly lengthy process. The initial suggestion was of black and white vertical stripes the length of the fuselage whilst the wing was to be white with a one-third chord wide black stripe spanning across the wing. This pattern was repeated on the tailplane and fin.

It was later suggested that upper surfaces should be in a temperate land camouflage scheme to avoid detection on the ground. The suggestion was not taken up but the subject of top-surfaces did give rise for much discussion. The RAE put forward six different top-surface schemes but the Admiralty argued that any scheme should be totally dissimilar from a standard target-towing aircraft. Thus any combination of black and yellow, or diagonal patterns, was deemed unacceptable. To evaluate the effect of various colours and to determine the most effective, ten 16' Gliders were repainted (in pairs) and, in October 1943, sent to RNAS Twatt (in the Shetland Isles) for flight trials. The variations were as follows:

(i) Bright red undersurfaces
(ii) Bright yellow undersurfaces
(iii) Red & yellow undersurfaces
(iv) Red and aluminium or white
(v) Black and aluminium or white

The view taken by those involved in the Twatt trials was that not one of the colour variations was wholly satisfactory.

---

16 Buttocks Booth was actually on the edge of Sywell aerodrome and was also known as the Sywell Repair Facility. The facility also undertook repairs of damaged RAF aircraft.

Ironically, the overall opinion was in favour of reverting to a yellow and black striped pattern.

IMA Swallow Project

At the same time that they were developing the 16ft and 32ft target gliders, IMA Ltd became heavily involved with the country's Combined Operations staff on a project cloaked in the utmost secrecy.

In June 1942 the Combined Operations staff began forward planning for forthcoming landings on enemy coastlines. What was being considered was a method of shielding the approach of landing craft by providing dense smoke screens between the approaching waves of assault craft and the enemy defences. Various methods were freely available, including smoke shells, smoke canisters and smoke-laying aircraft but all of these had inherent difficulties.

In an attempt to find a viable alternative a Staff Requirement was issued. Though simple almost to the extreme, the Requirement suggested that the solution lay in a small pilotless aircraft that could act as a "smoke-laying device capable of being catapulted from a Landing Craft Tank (LCT) or a Landing Ship Tank (LST)." To give an idea of the scale of things, the Requirement stated that 1,000 were to be produced by 1 April 1943.

With almost every other aircraft manufacturer heavily committed to producing full-sized aircraft and components, IMA Ltd was allocated the task of developing the small craft. From an early stage the project was given the name 'Swallow' but precisely who drew up the initial basic design is difficult to determine. Minutes of regular meetings ascribe it to "having been designed by the Admiralty" but what is known is that the go-ahead was effectively given on 24 September 1942 by way of a Minute from the Naval Armament Research & Development Department to the Ministry's Department of Armament Development.

Real progress on the 'Swallow' project began on 26 October 1942 when L/Cdr Neville Shute Norway of the Miscellaneous Weapons Department (MWD) outlined the aircraft's design and its launch catapult to a gathering of scientists at RAE Farnborough where much of the development work was to be carried out. The catapult had been designed to accelerate Swallow to 80mph (128.7 km/hr) air-speed by approximately 6g. Norway then went on to describe the Swallow design as being a small aircraft of 19ft (5.79m) wingspan and with a fully-loaded weight of 780lbs (353.8kg). Propulsion was by means of slow-burning cordite rockets that had been designed for a skimming projectile experiment, since abandoned. With Swallow in mind Woolwich Arsenal carried out a number of experiments, at first with propellant charges of gunpowder and later with cordite-filled rockets specially developed at Woolwich. Four rockets provided a thrust of 200lbs (90.7kg) for 40 seconds. After they burnt out the craft would then glide along a pre-determined course. "It was needed to fly straight for 1¼ miles (2.01km) and then to produce smoke for any ¼ mile (0.4km) of flight excluding the first ¼ mile. Swallow should have a maximum speed of 140mph (225.3km/hr); lateral and directional control to be achieved by a Mark VIB Gyro whilst longitudinal control would be by means of a clockwork mechanism. The latter was also designed to start the Gyro, the firing units and the smoke".[17]

The first rocket-powered glider was built at IMA's Merton, Surrey works in 1941. These were made for the Admiralty and preceded the German "Doodle Bug" flying bomb by several years. This view shows the glider fuselage interior, the top of the fuselage having been detached. The rocket was carried in the fuselage below the wing in a bakelized paper tube, and held in position by a steel clip. Finally, a balance weight of 20oz (0.57kg) was fitted in the extreme nose. (Lines Brothers Ltd)

Apart from the initial examples – which were all-wood – Swallow was of mixed wood and metal construction with a wing span of 19ft (5.79m) and an overall length of 12ft 3in (3.73m). The nacelle housed a 300lb (136.1kg) SCI unit, fitted snugly into the steel-tube nacelle which also held a Mk.IVB gyro control unit, air bottle and racks for rockets. It was plywood covered. The wing was intended to fold back for stowage and had a spruce main spar with stiffened plywood ribs and ailerons. From the centre section, a pair of box frame booms carried the tail assembly in which the clockwork device was installed to actuate the elevators at the end of a flight. The underside of the nacelle was of steel sheet due to the proximity of the racks for four rockets. Each rocket consisted of five wrapped charges which gave a thrust of approximately 50lbs (22.7kg) each and which had been provided by the Low Pressure Ballistics Section of Woolwich Arsenal. The SCI was held in place by two steel straps and was protected by a nose pressing made of impregnated buckram.[18]

By the time of the October 1942 meeting, the Admiralty (via the Ministry of Works & Production) had placed two

---

17 National Archives AVIA15/1788
18 This description, from National Archives, first appeared in an article by James J Halley, published in *Aviation News* 4-17 November 1983.

orders (each involving 12 Swallows) with IMA. These early examples were made entirely of wood and the first prototype was test-launched on 2 November 1942 from a specially-constructed catapult at Worthy Down, near Winchester. The catapult consisted of 75ft (22.86m) of normal catapult rails with a trolley. The trolley was driven by PAC Type J rockets that had been developed for anti-aircraft use. Up to twenty rockets could be fitted but the number used depended very much on wind direction, wind force and air temperature. For much of the time the number of rockets used for launch was deduced by trial and error. They were fired by pulling a plug from the side of the nacelle – naturally from a safe distance. This act fired both the Swallow's internal rockets and the catapult firing sequence.

Definitive flight trials of the Swallow began at Worthy Down (referred to as HMS *Kestrel* by the Admiralty) on 19 December 1942. Sixteen rockets were used on the trolley to launch the first Swallow which burned for 20 seconds but after a steep climb away from the catapult the aircraft stalled and spun into the ground.

Ten days later, a second flight was attempted. This time the elevator was set for a flatter climb out. Two charges exploded four seconds after launch but, again, the Swallow flew into the ground. By 10 February 1943 seven Swallows had been launched at Worthy Down although only the first could be described as having been successful. Flight No.3 had hit a new snag. Water from the deceleration ram, which stopped the trolley, had been thrown up at the Swallow, causing it to stall. No.4 lost its fin on launching, hit the ground, bounced into the air again and crashed 3,000ft (914.4m) further on. The next two were catapulted at too low a speed and as a result both hit the ground in front of the catapult. No.7 also hit the ground but flew on at low level for another 300yards (30.5m). No.8 had a rocket fail to fire and crashed; No.9 also touched the ground but flew on for some distance. Slow motion film revealed that the blast of the launching rockets had affected the airflow over the tailplane causing vibration which in turn had altered the tail setting. After some modifications, No.10 flew just over 1,000yds (914.4m) at a height of around 150ft (45.72m).

The first series of tests revealed the need for major modifications before flight-testing resumed. These included stiffening the booms by steel tubes from the back of the nacelle to halfway along the booms. The mountings of the SCI were also strengthened and the shape of the fins was changed from oval to square. It is likely that several of the later aircraft were built to what, in its modified state, was anticipated as the production standard. Other improvements involved a fuselage construction of seven laminations of resin-impregnated paper pressed to shape, with an interior 1/8th-inch ply keel and bulkheads. Wing, tailplane and fin attachments were 'Cellomold' plastic mouldings anchored to both skin and bulkheads.

IMA Swallow was a well-kept secret during its early development stage. This example, an early prototype, reveals the oval fin shape that Swallow originally featured. It is seen on its launching catapult at Worthy Down, near Winchester. The lanyard was for firing the rockets but was later replaced by an electrical firing system. (via Tony Dowland)

Despite the development of wooden construction, IMA was also exploring new materials and began to develop a completely new method of manufacture, making extensive use of plastics and therefore offering a very high strength-weight ratio. But there were other difficulties. When the results of the initial flight-trials were fully-analyzed, few doubted whether any of the first ten flights had actually reached adequate air speed. At low temperatures (around 32°F/0°C), the observers noted that the propulsive rocket thrust picked up very slowly, suggesting that there was a link between poor acceleration and low atmospheric conditions. When flight trials were resumed the propulsive rockets were kept at around 70°F/21°C until the last possible moment.

Perhaps of greater significance was the fact that the last of the initial test flights (No.10) had taken place on 23 March 1943; the projected target requirement of 1,000 examples by 1 April was clearly not going to happen. In fact the target date had long since been abandoned.

While modifications were taking place, LCT Mk.V 2119 had been made available at Northney for a second series of flight trials and by mid-July had been fitted with a catapult at Portsmouth Dockyard. She was ready for action on 1 November 1943 when the first of a new series of tests began.

The second series of trials were carried out at Warren Farm on Hayling Island, to the east of Portsmouth, where there were marshes and mudflats to soften the Swallow's controlled crashes. As the LCT proceeded at a stately 5kts, Swallow was catapulted and climbed steeply away, levelled out and flew for about 20 seconds. The flight offered promise but on the next trial (No.12) the aircraft lost a fin and dived into the water. The following launch faired equally poorly after it is thought to have fouled the catapult as the Swallow rolled and then spiraled into the mud. Flight No.14, on 10 December, was more successful; the aircraft climbed normally and arrived in the target area as did the following test which performed a perfect 40-second flight.

At this point the trials moved west to the mouth of the River Beaulieu, LCT 2119 operating from Lepe Hard. Flight No.16 dived into the sea after a rocket burst. No.17 climbed to 100ft (30.48m) but then dived into the mud whilst No.18 flew 1,600yds (1,463m) but was 10° off target.

No.19 was a more successful flight and laid a very good smoke curtain except that it was 100ft (30.48m) too high. This trial was back at Northney and the Swallow landed in a small pond on Warren Farm. A gyro failure on the next launch caused the aircraft to spin into the water while No.21 was satisfactory apart from the fact that due to the acceleration, the smoke control jammed and not a puff appeared!

The next few launches were good and Swallow performed well but on Flight 26 (17 April 1944) one rocket failed to fire, broke loose and hit the tail, causing the aircraft to crash. 27 and 28 had opposite problems, the first laying smoke too high and the other flying into the ground by being too low. No.29 went out of control and No.30, carried out at Lepe, rolled after launch, probably as a result of incorrectly crossing controls during assembly.

Despite the concept of smoke-laying ahead of any allied invasion still very much a desired tactic, Swallow – after some thirty test flights – was clearly not yet in a position to go to war. An alternative 'quick-fix' involved fitting smoke-laying equipment in the bomb-bays of RAF Boston IVs. Thus when the Allied armies invaded the Normandy beaches they did so in the wake of smoke-laying manned aircraft rather than unmanned examples operating off the leading landing craft. As it transpired, Swallow had been too late for D-Day and, on 5 July 1944, the Admiralty met to consider its plans for unmanned aircraft for future operations. In the Far East, landings were likely on the Malayan and Burmese coasts and planning was well advanced for an invasion of Malaya. However, only one Boston had been lost while laying smokescreens off the Normandy beachhead and if this could be carried out at such low cost by Bostons in the face of all the flak that the so-called 'Atlantic Wall' could throw at them, there seemed little point in continuing development of a pilotless smoke-laying aircraft which would only be used in the Far East where the amount of anti-aircraft flak located around the chosen landing point would be much less.

Despite the feelings of the Admiralty towards Swallow, some flight testing did continue and whilst they performed perfectly well with good smoke screens laid, Flight 34 – on 1 September 1944 – proved to be the last. The rocket glider project, from which much had been learnt, was abandoned.

R.F.D. Mk.1 Towed Target

During the First World War R.F.Dagnall undertook a study of flotation gear of various sorts and in 1918 constructed some of the earliest rubber dinghies. At the same time he developed a sound knowledge of lighter-than-air craft, skills that he put to use after the war when he began to manufacture dinghies and a series of gliders from a small works in Stoke Road, Guildford, Surrey. The various glider designs that emerged from Guildford did so with designations based on the designer's initials.

In 1930 Dagnall began marketing a primary glider based on the German Zögling but with a number of design improvements. Four years later, in July 1934, he formed a limited company under the title R.F.D. Co Ltd, and in 1936 moved into a new factory built in pleasant semi-rural surroundings in Catteshall Lane, Godalming. From here a number of projects emerged, including a towed target glider. Sadly, however, Dagnall never saw many of his company's target gliders in service; he died in 1942 whilst still in his late-fifties.

R.F.D's first entry into the target glider sector came just after the end of World War II with the RFD Mk.1 towed target. The glider was a high-wing design of 26ft (7.92m) span and 75ft sq ft wing area. What made this design so unique was the twin-boom fuselage and triple fixed-fin layout. It was designed for both ground-to-air and air-to-air practice, and made up of interchangeable components of resin-bonded birch plywood on a spruce and pine structure. Resistance to damage from heavy-calibre ammunition proved to be good. The target was designed to be towed off and landed either on grass or a concrete runway, the landing being made by towing it down on to the ground, at which point a trigger skid under the mainplane centre-section

The RFD Winged Target Mk.1 was unveiled at the 1951 Farnborough Show. Few can doubt that it appears a complex and unusual design – as does the tubular display stand that supports it. The first deliveries were made to Boscombe Down in October 1951. (via Ken Munson)

A contemporary advertisement for the RFD Winged Target Mk.1 shows well the twin-boom fuselage arrangement and the unusual triple fin. This advertisement appeared in November 1951 and it is interesting to see the company referred to as RFD Air Target Ltd.

released the tow-lines and caused a 6ft tail parachute to deploy.

The RFD Mk.1, however, was not without its problems. Because of the mix of materials used in its construction, the RFD Target Glider had to be fitted with a separate radar deflector. In reality, the real snag with the RFD Mk.1 was revealed during early flight tests when its maximum towing speed proved to be only 240kts. As a result, a number of minor modifications were carried out and eventually the RFD Target was capable of being towed up to speeds of 365kt (676 km/hr) and reaching a height of 24,000ft (7,315m).[19]

First deliveries of RFD Winged Target Mk.1s involved a development batch of ten against Contract 6/Air/6005. All were completed between 8-17 October 1951 and were identified simply by single letters 'A' to 'J' for evaluational purposes.[20]

Although adopted by the Services as an aerial target the quantity produced appears fairly low, probably not exceeding 250 units. The full extent of Winged Target Mk.1 production remains obscure; known details are:

6/Air/8156/CB.9(b) 10: c/ns 31-40; Del 17.9.52
6/Air/8571/CB.9(b) 10: c/ns 41-50; Del 10-13.10.52

---

19 *Flight*, 6 May 1956. However, *Indian & Eastern Engineer Journal* (July 1954 issue) claimed that the RFD target glider "had a maximum tow-speed of up to Mach 0.7 or 450-500mph at height".
20 It is likely that these gliders were delivered to A&AEE Boscombe Down for flight performance trials. National Archives WO32/13355/121A refers to nine RFD target gliders arriving at Boscombe Down on 22 October 1951.

6/Air/8591/CB.9(b) 42: c/ns 51-76, 78-79, 82-86 and 100-108.

Details of production beyond Contract 8591 (dated 31 August 1953) are unknown but deliveries of the twin-fuselage towed glider are thought to have extended well into 1955.

One other user of RFD Winged Target gliders was the Royal Australian Air Force. Ten examples were acquired (A88-1 to A88-10) and these were used by 30 Squadron RAAF for towing behind converted Beaufighters, mainly for Army AA practice over the Holsworthy, NSW firing range. A trial for air-to-air gunnery also took place, at Laverton, but it was not regarded as a success and the fighters eventually reverted to shooting at towed drogue targets.[21]

R.F.D. Dart Target

One other development by R.F.D. Co Ltd was the Dart target which was announced at the 1955 Farnborough Show and derived its name from its resemblance to a paper dart. Cruciform wings of 4ft span were fitted and the overall length was approximately 12ft. Balance weights were contained in a 4ft tube of approximately 4" diameter which projected forward, and radar reflectors were situated at the tail end. Construction in the simplest form of Dart was plywood, with a metal backbone. The maximum weight was approximately 150lb and in the USA speeds of approximately 450 knots were achieved. Details of production, if any, remain unknown.

Specification WT1/RDL3

In September 1952 Specification WT1/RDL3 was issued. It called for a high-speed glider with a minimum span of 25ft – that being the minimum target size to which contemporary gun sights could be set.

Several manufacturers responded with tenders and at least three designs reached a flying prototype stage. A third design, produced by the innovative Miles Aircraft company, was test-flown in model form only on at least two occasions.

Slingsby Type 39

Against Air Ministry Specification WT1/RDL.3, Slingsby Sailplanes Ltd designed and submitted the Type 39 glider. Of all-wood construction, the Type 39 was an unconventional design comprising a swept-wing and twin fuselages which were 6ft apart. The retractable tricycle undercarriage was similarly non-standard as the mainwheels retracted into the fuselage booms whilst the nosewheel – actually a nose skid – retracted into the wing. The undercarriage retraction, tail parachute and tip drogue releases were all electrically operated. Twin towing positions were mounted at the nose of each fuselage.

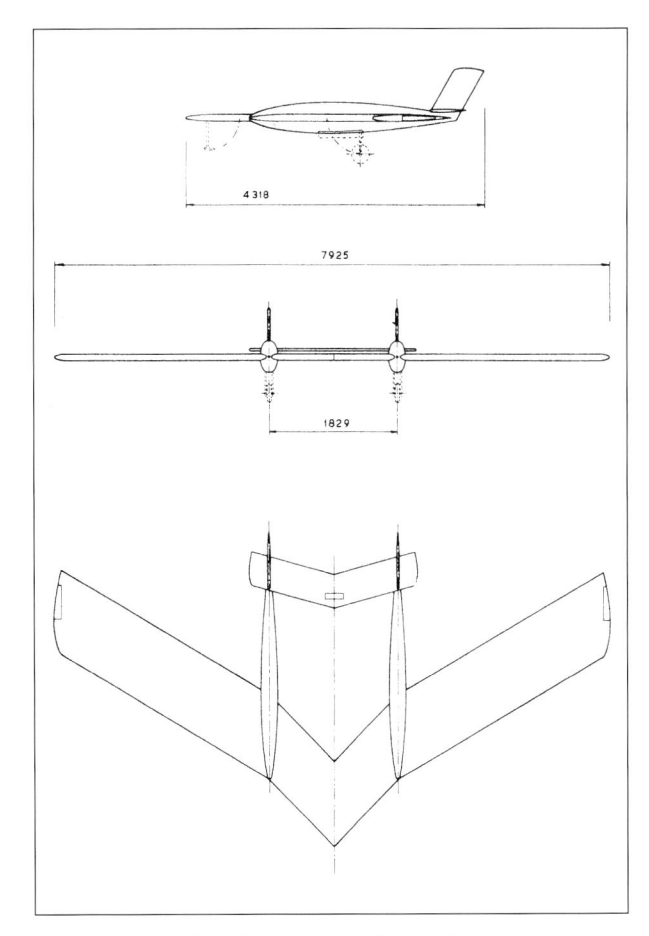

---

21 It is possible that the RFD glider underwent several trial modifications A demonstration of an RFD target glider with a 30ft span wing was given to a Swedish delegation at RNAS Ford on 19 September 1951. There was a likelihood that the Swedish Government would place an order. (National Archives WO32/13355/120A)

3-view drawing of the Slingsby Type 39 Target Glider.

The 26ft span wing was of NACA66008 section and with a sweepback of 30° created a design very different to any other project conceived by Slingsby. Type 39 remained purely a project and was never built, in common with its primary competitor from Elliots of Newbury in 1952.

Slingsby Type 39 specifications	
Wing span	26 ft 0 in (7.92 m)
Length	14 ft 2 in (4.32 m)
Wing Area	98.5 sq ft (9.14 m²)
Aspect Ratio	6.8
Weight (Tare)	425.6 lb (193.0 kg)
Weight (All-up)	500 lb (226.8 kg)

(For details of the Slingsby Type 19 target glider, see under Lines Bros Ltd.)

Eon Target Glider

Elliotts of Newbury Ltd began manufacturing furniture after the 1914-18 war in an old established joinery works in Newbury which had been operating since the mid 19th Century. During the Second World War this furniture manufacturer became involved in glider production through its membership of the Airspeed Horsa Group Firms'. This gave the firm all the necessity approvals. Elliotts retained their involvement in glider production for a number of years after the war. As Elliotts did not have a design organisation, all of the design work was contracted out to the design consultants Aviation & Engineering Products Ltd.

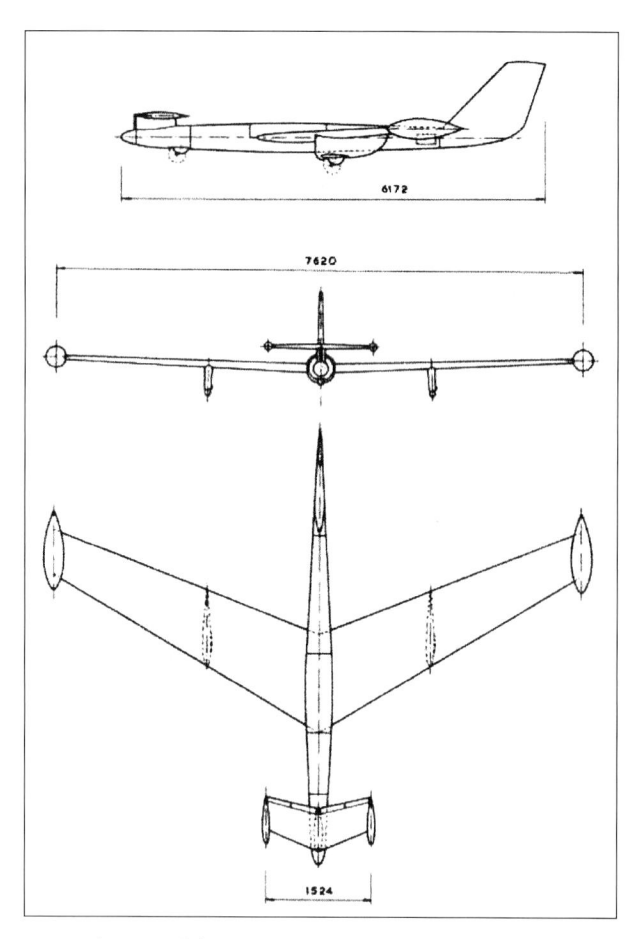

3-view drawing of the EoN Target Glider proposal.

In 1952, and in response to Air Ministry Specification WT1/RDL.3, Elliotts submitted an unmanned target glider design. It was intended to construct the glider using a mix of spruce and ply although at an early stage it was proposed to build it in an alternative plastic construction of the Asbestos-Phenolic type.[22]

The EoN target glider was a "tail-first" canard design with twin towing points located at the tips of the front stabilizer. The glider had a semi-retractable tricycle undercarriage, operated from pitot pressure which allowed the wheels to drop when the speed decreased for landing. A braking parachute was to be located in the fuselage forward of the fin and this was to be released by the action of the nosewheel on landing.

The EoN target glider submission was not selected and all design work ceased immediately.

EoN Target Glider specifications	
Wing span	25 ft 0 in (7.62 m)
Length	20 ft 3 in (6.17 m)
Wing Area	81.3 sq ft (7.56 m²)
Aspect Ratio	7.7
Weight (Tare)	694 lb (314.8 kg)
Weight (All-up)	750 lb (340.2 kg)

---

22 There have been reports that Elliotts' target glider was allocated the designation Type 9; even moreso originally described as the Type AP.9. However, there is some doubt about the authenticity of such designations and the EoN Type 9 should be correctly attributed to the Kendall K.1 sailplane which was built by Elliotts.

Air Service Training C4
Brooklands Aviation Towed Target

Known principally for training pilots for the State-operated airline, BOAC, Air Service Training Ltd also ran an Aircraft Division at Hamble which carried out various aircraft repairs and gas-turbine engine installations. For a brief period the Division was involved in the design and construction of a towed target glider.

Designed by Professor E.J. Richards, MA, BSc, FRAeS of Southampton University, the AST C4 was a high-speed gunnery-target capable of being towed to high subsonic speeds – up to Mach 0.9. Described as of 'bat-like' appearance and with a wingspan of 25ft (7.62m) the delta-form centre section was bounded by two swept fins, outboard of which were two swept rectangular wing panels. A small fuselage provided an aiming datum for the attacking aircraft and housed sundry equipment, including – if required – a radar responder and a firing error indicator unit. The undercarriage was of a tricycle type, the bases of the fins housing outboard wheels. When the nose-wheel touched down a braking parachute was automatically deployed from a housing compartment at the rear of the target. At the same moment, the 1,000ft (304.8m) towing cable was released.

The airframe itself consisted of a metal shell with a Sebalkyd resin filling. One innovative factor was a self-trimming linkage, so designed that as speed increased the drag of the flat plate overcame a spring and moved the central elevator downwards and so making the target more nose-down in flight.[23]

The prototype C4, or 'flying-wing' as it become known at Hamble, successfully made its first flight in August 1953. It was later exhibited at the SBAC Show at Farnborough.

It is doubtful if any construction of the C4 took place at Hamble; instead production was sub-contracted to Brooklands Aviation Ltd at which stage the C4 became known as the Brooklands Aviation High-Speed Towed Target although at the 1954 Farnborough Show, Air Service Training revealed that the company had produced "a number of prototype C4s, mostly showing progressive minor modifications". Brooklands Aviation is known to have built six prototypes of the High-Speed Towed Target at its Buttocks Booth facility.[24]

One of the six Brooklands prototypes was statically displayed at the 1954 SBAC Farnborough show whilst at the same time the other five, all finished in a black and yellow scheme, were being tested and evaluated at the A. & A.E.E. at Boscombe Down. Test results showed that the ideal towed take-off speed was around 150mph (241.4km/hr) and once airborne the High-Speed Target would assume a position some 300ft (91.4m) beneath the tug. Because of its design and smooth finish to all surfaces, the drag factor was significantly reduced so that quick climbs to 4,000ft (1,219m) could be easily achieved. During one test the target was towed by a Meteor at 535mph (861km/hr) at 30,000ft (9,144m) – faster than any previous target had

---

23 *Flight*, 18 September 1953
24 Professor Richards was a retained consultant to Brooklands Aviation Ltd

Several examples of target gliders were built by Brooklands Aviation Ltd. This High-Speed target, identified as No.1, is thought to have been taken at Boscombe Down. (A&AEE; Neg No. 8573/1)

been towed. There were plans to tow it up to 650mph (1,046km/hr), behind a Canberra, but no evidence can be found that this was ever achieved.[25]

The extent to which the Brooklands High-Speed Towed Target was used post-1954 is unrecorded. However, at the 1955 SBAC Farnborough show Air Service Training announced that deliveries of its C4 high-speed towed target had already started, but no figures were released to support the claim.

A direct development of the C4 was exhibited, in model form only, at the 1955 Paris Air Salon. The revised design had twin, swept fins on the cut-off tips of its true delta wing. The towing bridle was attached to the tips of the "canard" nose plane, and a trimming surface was provided at the trailing edge of the main surface. The new design, which was intended to be towed by a Hawker Hunter, also had a swept nose-fin. Yet again, there is no evidence of it entering production.

---

25 As reported by the *Northampton Evening Telegraph*, 14 September 1954.

A later example of the Brooklands Aviation High-Speed Winged Target, No.6, shows a neat undercarriage fairing. The wording on the nose reads "TO LOWER U/C RELEASE BOLT SLOWLY". (A&AEE; Neg No. 9022/C)

Miles Aircraft Towed Target

In September 1952 Miles Aircraft produced a prototype design to meet Specification WT1/RDL3. Designed to be towed behind a Supermarine Swift at speeds up to 450mph, the glider was never allocated a company Type Number and was only produced as a ¼-scale model to check the aerodynamic configuration. The model, built of wood and plastic, made its first flight at Shoreham on 18 November 1952 when it was towed behind the company's Aerovan Mk.6 G-AKHF. The first aerial tow revealed the glider to have some adverse flying characteristics but both tug and glider managed to land back at Shoreham with the glider only sustaining minor damage.[26]

---

26 *Miles Aircraft – The Wartime Years* by Peter Amos; (to be published by Air-Britain Historians; reproduced by kind permission.)

After repairs and modifications to the canard-wing's angle of dihedral a second flight took place on 5 January 1953, again behind the Aerovan. On that occasion the target glider's behaviour was much improved but in the end the glider failed to reach production status and work was halted.

Miles Aircraft Towed Target specifications	
Wing span	25 ft 0 in (7.62 m)
Length	26 ft 8 in (8.13 m)
Wing area	104 sq ft (9.67 m²)

Chapter 5

Post-War Drone Conversions

Less than a year since the guns of World War II fell silent, Winston Churchill – and with his customary oratorical skill – described the division between the Western powers and the Soviet Union as an "Iron Curtain". Churchill introduced the defining term in a speech, given in Missouri in March 1946, at a time when large segments of Britain's armed forces were demobilizing. There was, it seemed, little need for widespread training of gunners and as if to underline that fact virtually all of the RAF's surviving Queen Bee target aircraft, most of which were being held in long-term storage, were about to be declared obsolete and sold off. Similarly the RAF's stock of Queen Martinets, also held in storage, were struck off charge and scrapped.

It must, therefore, seem to be something of a paradox that just as the RAF had withdrawn its entire fleet of unmanned aerial targets, so dawned a new Cold War era dominated by modern guided weapons – all of which would require an aerial target for trials and training. But Queen Bee and Queen Martinet were far from adequate and when Operational Requirement 272 (OR.272) was drawn up it underlined the need for a series of new target drones, larger, considerably faster and much more sophisticated than any previous examples.

By 1947, of those weapon systems being proposed for the UK's post-war strategic defences, three projects were far more advanced than others. They were *Red Hawk,* an air-to-air missile (later referred to as *Blue Sky* and which subsequently entered RAF service as the Fireflash) and two versions of a ground-to-air missile, code-named *Red Heathen.*

Red Heathen was initially sponsored jointly by the Army and the Air Staffs, both of whom had agreed on the required performance criteria. The Army, however, wanted it based on a mobile launcher for rapid deployment whilst the Air Force preferred static mountings for the defence of airfields. In time *Red Heathen* led to two separate (and independent) programmes: *Red Duster* (developed by Bristol Aircraft as Bloodhound I for the RAF) and *Red Shoes* (developed by English Electric as Thunderbird I for the Army).

Out of OR.272 emerged Specification E.7/48 which called for a large, full-scale, pilotless target aircraft. Unlike previous practices of inviting tenders from industry, the UK instead turned its attention directly to Australia where the Government Aircraft Factory had proposed a larger and definitive target variant of its prototype Pica project. This was seen as offering the only real opportunity for acquiring a dedicated target aircraft to meet E.7/48. (See Chapter 6)

By the Spring of 1951 target requirements for the UK's strategic missile test programmes were completely re-assessed and the following serves to outline anticipated target requirements over the timescales shown:

Pilot-Controller "Jock" Kyle prepares to command Meteor U.16 WH284 to take-off on an unmanned test-flight from Flight Refuelling's Tarrant Rushton base. WH284 was used on initial U.16 development and was the first U.16 to be delivered to Llanbedr, on 30 June 1960. Four months later, on 7 November 1960 – and as nature intended – it was shot down by an air-to-air missile. (Cobham plc Archive)

Seaslug	
1953-54	Trials at Aberporth using drogues as targets
Jul 1954	Trials against Jindivik aircraft; rate one direct hit per week
1955	Continuation trials using drogues and Jindivik aircraft; rate one hit per week.

Red Shoes (Thunderbird I)	
Jan 1952	Balloons at 10,000 ft (3,050 m) from naval vessels off Aberporth
Apr 1952	Slow-speed targets (at least 2 hours endurance) at Aberporth.
Oct 1952	Jindivik aircraft at Aberporth; six direct hits per year for at least two years.

Red Duster (Bloodhound I)	
1952-53	Balloons with radar response of at least 20 m^2
Oct 1953	32 ft winged targets
1954	65 weapons to be fired against Jindivik aircraft, targets flown at 300-500 kts (345-575 mph) at between 10,000-40,000 ft (3,050-12,190 m).

RTV-1 (Rocket Test Vehicle No 1)	
Dec 1951	Fixed balloons and towed targets
Jun–Dec 1952	OQ-3 up to 10,000' (3.050m) at 100 kts (115.2mph).
1953	Not yet decided.

Blue Sky (Fireflash)	
1953-54	Trials at Aberporth using drogues as targets
Jun 1952 – Jun 54	120 sorties against targets of which 30 to be Jindivik aircraft.

Red Hawk (Firestreak)	
Jul-Dec 1953	15 sorties in 6 months against high-speed target up to 60,000 ft (18,290 m). Suggested drone conversion of DH.98 Mosquito.
1954	Five sorties per month using the same drone type as in 1953.

Lancaster Target Drone

Although the Australian Jindivik was being jointly developed to (and likely to meet) E.7/48 as a suitable target, by mid-1951 it was increasingly evident that testing and production of Jindiviks in time to meet the start of missile tests was an unrealistic set of expectations. As a consequence the RAE was tasked to explore an alternative opportunity for producing suitable stop-gap full-size target aircraft. The most obvious solution was to convert surplus RAF heavy bombers into target drones, the first consideration being the Avro Lancaster B.1. The first real evidence of this came on 20 July 1951 when Lancaster B.1 PA343 was officially allotted to Air Service Training Ltd for conversion to an unmanned drone.[1]

There is little doubt that Air Service Training had the design capacity for converting the Lancaster to drone configuration and the company even entered into some hard negotiations for the use of a hangar at Lasham, sufficiently large to allow three conversions at a time. However, not everybody was convinced and PA343 remained at Farnborough pending the issue of a definite contract. When the contract for conversion work was eventually awarded it went instead to Flight Refuelling Ltd. Farnborough's PA343 was immediately ferried to Tarrant Rushton on 23 October 1951, followed much later by a second Lancaster B.1 (PA474) on 26 May 1952. A third Lancaster, NN801 – having completed unconnected trials work with the de Havilland company – was ferried to Flight Refuelling's Dorset base for long-term storage until drone equipment became available.[2]

Apart from the Lancaster, several other types were also selected for possible conversion to target drones, including the Fairey Firefly and Gloster Meteor. By January 1953 these had evolved into more than just a possibility when the RAE's Guided Weapons Department estimated the UK's target drone requirement as involving 160 Jindiviks (or Meteor drones), 49 Firefly drones and 44 Lancaster drones. Such was the growing urgency of the situation that provisional contracts were placed for 40 Fireflies, 50 Jindiviks and 20 Lancasters.

Assessing how many target aircraft were required became a constantly testing exercise for Air Ministry planners. For most of the missile programmes it was difficult to maintain the original time frames. Some programmes fell seriously behind schedule whilst in other instances requirements simply changed. Nevertheless, when, in February 1953, the RAE re-assessed likely target shoot-downs the overall requirement had changed little. The 1953 estimates were as follows:

---

1 The concept of converting redundant full-size bombers into unmanned drones was not entirely new. In June 1944 Maj-Gen James H. Doolittle, USAAF approved plans for flying war-weary B-17 Fortresses as unmanned drone bombers (re-designated Boeing BQ-7) against German targets in north-west Europe, notably the V-1 sites and U-Boat pens. Stripped of all combat armament and non-essential equipment, these aircraft were loaded with more than twice the normal B-17 bomb-load. Because the remote control system was insufficient for take-off, each aircraft was flown initially by a volunteer pilot and flight engineer. At 2,000ft the crew would transfer control to an accompanying CQ-17 'mother ship', arm the payload, and then bale out via the cockpit canopy (removed before take-off). The CQ-17 would then direct the drone on to its target.

Assignment of BQ-7 drones was given to the USAAF 562nd Bomber Squadron who positioned aircraft to the remote airfield at RAF Fersfield, Norfolk. The first drone mission (under Operation 'Aphrodite') was flown on 4 August 1944 when four BQ-7s were directed against V-1 sites in northern France. Eight more missions (including one by a BQ-8, a drone conversion of a USN PBY-1 Liberator) were flown during August and September 1944. The last of 13 'Aphrodite' missions from the UK (which, in total, involved at least 22 aircraft) took place on 1 January 1945. None of the missions were successful and after the final mission, when two BQ-7s were shot down by flak before reaching their target of Oldenburg power station, Operation 'Aphrodite' was deemed unfeasible and abandoned.

2 National Archives AVIA54/700/E4 & E42

Red Shoes (Thunderbird I)

Year	Jindivik or Meteor	Firefly	Lancaster
1953	–	–	–
1954	3	2½	1
1955	8	2	1
1956	7	2	2
1957	8	1	2

Red Duster (Bloodhound I)

Year	Jindivik or Meteor	Firefly	Lancaster
1953	–	–	–
1954	3	3	1
1955	8	2	1
1956	7	2	2
1957	8	1	2

Seaslug

Year	Jindivik or Meteor	Firefly	Lancaster
1953	–	–	–
1954	4	3	–
1955	8	6	–
1956	8	–	–
1957	–	–	2

Blue Sky (Fireflash)

Year	Jindivik or Meteor	Firefly	Lancaster
1953	–	2	–
1954	2	11	5
1955	7	1½	2½
1956	–	–	–
1957	–	–	–

Red Dean

Year	Jindivik or Meteor	Firefly	Lancaster
1953	–	–	–
1954	–	–	–
1955	–	4	–
1956	16	–	–
1957	28	–	5

Blue Jay (Firestreak)

Year	Jindivik or Meteor	Firefly	Lancaster
1953	–	–	–
1954	3	4	–
1955	27	2	7
1956	5	–	10
1957	–	–	–

Lancaster B.1 PA474 was one of several earmarked for conversion to unmanned drone configuration. However, all proved to be unfit for conversion and PA474 subsequently found its way to the College of Aeronautics at Cranfield where it was used for icing research, as evidenced by the aerofoil mounted on the fuselage roof. Ultimately '474 returned to RAF charge as part of the Battle of Britain Memorial Flight. (Dave Welch Collection)

Lancaster Target Drone – Individual Aircraft Histories

PA343 Allocated to drone conversion programme 20.7.51 towards end of suppressed aerial trials at RAE Farnborough. Stored at RAE until ferried to Tarrant Rushton 23.10.51 for conversion against Contract 6/Acft/7278/CB.9(a). SOC as Cat.5 (Scrap) 30.11.53 and disposed of to PEE Shoeburyness.

PA474 Ferried to Tarrant Rushton 26.5.52 for conversion to drone configuration. Partially converted with fitment of Mk.9 autopilot.

At the curtailment of drone programme allocated to College of Aeronautics 11.11.53 for boundary-layer research. Ferried Tarrant Rushton to Cranfield 8.3.54.

Some published sources quote conflicting dates. In an *Air Pictorial* article Michael Burns states that PA474 arrived at Tarrant Rushton on 27 May 1952 and later ferried to Cranfield on 7 March 1954.*

Total drone requirements for the period 1953-1957 period therefore amounted to 156 Jindiviks, 49 Fireflies and 43½ Lancaster aircraft.

In the meantime Flight Refuelling had begun to experience difficulties with the Ultra-modified throttle box. This, together with concerns over the rising costs of converting redundant Lancasters, effectively rendered the Lancaster as unsuitable. As it turned out PA343 was the first, and only, example to be converted to drone standard – reportedly with the designation Lancaster U.11. It was test-flown at Tarrant Rushton on five occasions by company pilot Tom Marks with Maurice Jenkins as Flight Engineer. But the Lancaster drone project was never to proceed any further. The pure cost of conversion and the physical difficulties involved had proved to be the catalyst in bringing the Lancaster drone programme to a premature end. Most of those aircraft selected for conversion had already been rejected by Flight Refuelling for various reasons, including the fact that a number were showing early signs of corrosion. Ironically some of these Lancasters had notched up less than ten airframe flying hours since new.[3]

Outstanding work needed to bring PA474 up to full drone standard was promptly abandoned and nine other Lancaster B.1s earmarked for conversion – at least five of which (NX624, NX625, NX628, NX630 and NX688) were in long-term storage at 22 MU Silloth – were stood down. The other aircraft earmarked for conversion involved Lancaster B.1 TW661 in storage at 34 MU Market Drayton, an unidentified B.1 at 38 MU Llandow and a single B.7 in store at 22 MU Silloth. One other Lancaster B.1, NN801 had already been transferred from de Havilland charge and flown to Tarrant Rushton for long-term storage.

Avro Lincoln U.5

Rejection of Lancaster as a possible drone conversion led directly to a decision, taken in October 1953, to consider the Avro Lincoln instead and once again Flight Refuelling was contracted to undertake the conversion work.[4] Within a few weeks, on 29 October, Lincoln B.2 RF538 was ferried from 20 MU Aston Down to Tarrant Rushton to become the first prototype U.5 drone. (A second Lincoln B.2 was added to the programme on 6 May 1954 when RF561 was also flown to Tarrant Rushton although it was later found to be unsuitable and rejected.)

Between 23 September 1954 and 8 March 1956 over 30 redundant Lincoln B.2s, all earmarked for drone conversion, were ferried from various Maintenance Units to A.V.Roe Ltd's satellite engineering facility at Langar, Nottinghamshire for reconditioning. Most of the Lincolns available proved to be in a much better condition than the rejected Lancasters but the cost of bring them up to a fully serviceable condition had been grossly underestimated. There was also another, and perhaps even greater, growing concern and that was the very thought of having unmanned Lancasters or Lincolns flying around the vicinity of guided weapon ranges. They were, after all, still regarded as very large aeroplanes! Nevertheless, the Lincoln drone was considered to be a suitable target for testing the fuse for *Blue Sky* and to counter any concerns of unmanned Lincolns flying in UK airspace, an early decision was taken to stage *Blue Sky* trials in Woomera, Australia where Range facilities were infinitely better than those available at the UK Ranges.

By the end of 1954 the Ministry of Supply was forced to admit that the Lincoln drone programme had slipped some three months behind schedule and that the first three conversions would not be available until July 1955 at the earliest. But once the first three had departed for Australia delivery of further Lincoln drones was then expected to follow at the rate of three per month. In the meantime, Lincoln B.2 RF395, one of a number of candidate drone conversions being gathered at Langar for reconditioning, was flown to Tarrant Rushton on 10 March 1955. The aircraft, which joined the U.5 flight programme, embarked upon a series of urgent taxi trials, circuits and landings, to prove a differential braking system for drone Lincolns. By the end of the year the Air Ministry had written an outline Specification for the Lincoln drone which, as Spec D.171D&P, was issued on 9 December 1955.

RF395 became the U.5 Trial Installation aircraft and thus effectively the prototype drone Lincoln. Under its new guise it made its initial test-flight at Tarrant Rushton on 29 February 1956 (or 16 June 1956).[5] By 30 November, when

---

3 One of the factors said to have proved especially difficult was the fact that the Lancaster's wings flexed too much for the tip-mounted cameras to record near misses. Michael G Burns (*Aircraft Modelworld*, Nov 1989 issue) goes on to say that after the drone conversion programme was cancelled PA474 was converted by Flight Refuelling to carry rocket launchers below the outer wing for experiments with rockets and missiles. This, too, was cancelled, it being impossible to accurately launch missiles from a wing which flexed 10"-12" in flight.

4 The initial conversion work was carried out against Contract 6/Acft/9971/CB.24(a)

5 There are conflicting dates published for the initial U.5 flight. Barry Jones ("Meteor"), for example, states 29 February 1956.

Royal Air Force Avro Lincoln B.2 aircraft transferred to the Ministry of Supply for storage and reconditioning by A.V.Roe at Langar prior to U.5 drone conversion by Flight Refuelling Ltd against Contract 6/Acft/10876/CB.24(a).

Serial	Transferred to Ministry of Supply	Ferried to AVRO Langar for storage	From
RE372	unkn	unkn	unkn
RE376	11 January 1955	20 June 1955	38 MU Llandow
RE380	11 January 1955	c18 May 1955	38 MU Llandow
RE394	–	23 September 1954	45 MU Kinloss
RE395	10/16 January 1955	3 October 1955	15 MU Wroughton
RE417	19 January 1955	21 June 1955	20 MU Aston Down
RE421	19 January 1955	8 July 1955	20 MU Aston Down
RF357	19 January 1955	19 September 1955	20 MU Aston Down
RF361	13 January 1955	14 February 1955	20 MU Aston Down
RF364	13 December 1954	10 December 1954	10 MU Hullavington
RF367	19 January 1955	15 February 1955	44 MU Edzell
RF370	15 January 1955	15 February 1955	23 MU Aldergrove
RF396	10 July 1955	c30 September 1955	15 MU Wroughton
RF400	19 January 1955	9 March 1955	44 MU Edzell
RF404	13 January 1955	22 April 1955	20 MU Aston Down
RF417	13 January 1955	c14 February 1955	23 MU Aldergrove
RF426	19 January 1955	7 October 1955	20 MU Aston Down
RF427	19 January 1955	26 April 1955	44 MU Edzell
RF455	18 January 1955	29 March 1955	44 MU Edzell
RF458	19 January 1955	13 April 1955	44 MU Edzell
RF463	19 January 1955	7 March 1955	44 MU Edzell
RF473	6 January 1955	29 March 1955	10 MU or 44 MU
RF477	11 January 1955	10 November 1955	38 MU Llandow
RF480	10 January 1955	30 June 1955	44 MU Edzell
RF483	17 December 1954	17 December 1954	5 MU Kemble
RF484	30 December 1954	12 January 1955	5 MU Kemble
RF499	unkn	unkn	unkn
RF501	19 January 1955	unkn	20 MU Aston Down
RF502	unkn	unkn	unkn
RF504	16 January 1955	–	–
RF505	25 April 1955	5 March 1956	20 MU Aston Down
RF506	11 January 1955	12 January 1955	38 MU Llandow
RF515	15 January 1955	–	–
RF517	25 April 1955	8 March 1956	20 MU Aston Down
RF519	–	11 July 1954	RAE West Freugh
RF520	10 January 1955	14 June 1955	15 MU Wroughton
RF535	–	27 September 1954	20 MU Aston Down

Note that RE394, RF519 and RF535 were already on Ministry of Supply charge at the time of being allocated to the conversion programme. Neither RF504 nor RF515 were flown to Langar; both remained in storage at 23 MU Aldergrove

Plans for converting surplus Lincoln B.2 bombers to drone configuration became a drawn-out and frustrating exercise. Among those earmarked for conversion was RF417 seen here in open storage at 23 MU Aldergrove in January 1955 just prior to being ferried to Langar for an intended refurbishment. (Phil H Butler)

it made its final flight as a U.5, it had accrued some 64 flying hours.[6]

Despite much work carried out by Flight Refuelling, the Lincoln U.5 programme was subsequently abandoned. The company had already embarked upon a programme of converting surplus Meteor F.4s to drone standard and these were viewed as being a suitable alternative to the Lincoln U.5. All of the refurbished Lincolns stored at Langar were sold off to International Alloys Ltd in October 1958 as scrap.

Firefly U.8 and U.9

The need for a medium-speed drone to act as a target for projected Blue Sky trials was first raised during mid-1951 and from the outset the selected aircraft was seen as a conversion rather than developing an entirely new design. Three types were seriously considered for conversion to drone configuration, the Blackburn Firebrand TF.5, Fairey Firefly Mk.5 and the Vickers-Supermarine Seafire F.17. The Seafire, of which approximately 70 were readily available for conversion, was very quickly ruled out owing to its narrow undercarriage base and its relatively small radar echoing area. Moreover, the Seafire was a single-seat aircraft, a factor that was likely to present difficulties when installing and testing drone equipment.[7]

Serious consideration was given to the Firebrand TF.5, so much so that one example, EK658, was ferried from RNAS Lee-on-Solent to RAE Farnborough on 18 January 1952 for a series of evaluation flights. As it turned out, only two flights were made before the aircraft was returned to Lee on 29 January. The Firebrand was rejected, not because of any adverse flying characteristics – it proved to be extremely docile to fly and, according to the Ministry of Supply some "81 Firebrands could be had for the asking" – but because the RAE assessed Firebrand to have a serious drawback. It had no provision for a second occupant. That factor alone, in the same way that affected the Seafire, would have created difficulties in the fitment and adjustment of drone equipment. On the other hand, Firefly had a large second cockpit and by removing unwanted radio equipment sufficient room could be made available for most of the autopilot and still allow an observer to be carried.

Unlike many wartime designs, the Firefly had continued to be developed post-war. The unarmed Firefly AS.6 anti-submarine version had entered service with the Fleet Air Arm as late as 1951 and remained in service until replaced by the Gannet AS.1 in 1956. But the Gannet was found to be too heavy for the light aircraft carriers and, as an interim measure in fulfilling the anti-submarine search role, Fairey further developed the Firefly into the AS.7 variant. Powered by a Griffon 59 engine with the original chin radiator, the interim version was fitted with an elliptical wing form based upon the Mk.1 and to improve directional stability a taller fin and rudder was incorporated. Understandably, the AS.7 was never considered the ideal aircraft for its intended role and consequently a number were later converted to a trainer role (for the training of observers and radar operators). These were re-designated T.7 and involved little more than simply having the arrester hook removed.

Development of the Firefly as an unmanned target drone was first discussed seriously at a meeting held at Hayes on 8 April 1952. At Fairey's instigation, the gathering involved RAE representatives and Fairey's design staff. The main topic focused around the need for a new target drone aircraft and the possibility of fitting an autopilot plus associated equipment into a Firefly AS.7. RAE representatives preferred

---

6 RF395 remained at Tarrant Rushton long after the U.5 programme was cancelled, eventually being sold to Hounslow scrap dealer R.J.Coley Ltd on 8 July 1959.
7 National Archives AVIA54/1278/E21

Seen from behind the fence at Fairey Aviation's Ringway facility, Firefly U.8 WM859 seemed to spend more of its life in storage than in operational service. (Phil Butler)

the aircraft to be capable of also operating manually with an observer aboard to calibrate the autopilot, probably before each controlled flight took place. In short, the conversion meant stripping the rear cockpit compartment and installing radio control, autopilot and trials instrumentation units, including cameras mounted in special nacelles fitted to the aircraft's wing-tips. Finally, and to save weight, much of the standard, but now unnecessary, items such as wing-folding mechanism, flame dampers, water/methanol system, heaters etc would be removed.[8]

Immediately after the Hayes meeting, six standard AS.7 aircraft (WJ147 and WJ149 to WJ153) were taken "off contract" and converted to what became termed as the Firefly T.8. Work on the first four aircraft was officially completed on 24 September 1952, after which WJ151 was delivered to RAE Farnborough a month later for a series of comprehensive flight tests. The second aircraft, WJ147, was flown to Llanbedr on 25 October where Short Brothers and Harland's Flying Services Division maintained a unit on behalf of the Ministry of Supply. With a check pilot on board, WJ147 was then used for developing remote control techniques until, by the end of 1953, its behaviour and speed could be controlled from nearby Aberporth. (WJ147 later had the distinction of making the first unmanned flight by a Firefly drone, at Llanbedr on 3 February 1954 when it undertook what was officially referred to as a "Q Trial". The Llanbedr controllers tried three times to land the aircraft and on the third attempt the aircraft ground-looped although little damage was sustained as a result.) Three other prototypes were also flown to Farnborough for drone or chase duties: WJ149 (on 12 November 1952), WJ150 (6 January 1953) and WJ152 (22 January 1953).[9]

By mid-1953 the Air Ministry was sufficiently confident of progress that, on 16 July, it issued Specification D.140P to cover production of what was now being termed Firefly U.8. Conversions to full drone standard began immediately, the first of which involved one of the Farnborough prototypes (WJ150) that had been returned to Fairey's White Waltham facility for conversion. WJ150 had been earmarked for a series of tests at RAE Llanbedr and was ferried there on 12 November 1953. (WJ150 was subsequently shot down on a sortie from Llanbedr on 7 April 1954.) In the meantime another of the prototypes (WJ151) was converted to a 'partial U.8' standard at Stockport, work being completed on 14 December 1953.

Although the initial "full" drone conversion had been carried out at White Waltham, most of the development work took place at Hayes with flight-testing at White Waltham. The first two aircraft used in these trials were two Mk.7 conversions, WJ216 and WJ217. Both were later re-designated as Mk.7D drone test beds.

Because of the urgency of the drone equipment, the conversion arrangements for the initial six aircraft for pilotless operation were not the most suitable from an operating point of view. A pure conversion programme using existing aircraft was therefore not embarked upon, and instead components and details surplus to the requirements of the original Firefly T.7 contract were used to produce an improved layout of equipment and controls. In view of the operating difficulties experienced with the initial six conversions it was decided that, on production aircraft, the equipment layout would be revised within the limitations of the basic design.

The first contract for true production Firefly drones accounted for 34 aircraft, designated Firefly U.8. However, the first two production aircraft were, in fact, conversions of aircraft on the T.7 line, contracts for which had been significantly curtailed. The remaining U.8s emerged from the AS.7 jigs at Fairey's Stockport works in late-1953.

Early production aircraft were fitted with 11-inch diameter camera nacelles on each wing-tip as part of the weapon assessment gear. These cameras were electrically actuated and designed to photograph 'near misses' of intercepting missiles. Later, with the introduction of a larger and improved camera, a new nacelle of 16-inch diameter was fitted although it was designed to be interchangeable with the smaller type. The larger nacelle also accommodated, in alternative rear fairings, homing devices for several new missiles then under development.

The Firefly U.8 was capable of being flown manually with a crew of pilot and observer, or by remote control from

---

8 *Fairey Firefly – The Operational Record* by William Harrison (Airlife Publishing 1992 ISBN 1 85310 196 6))
9 Details and dates from a series of articles on the Fairey Firefly by John Tipp, first published in *Roundel* (BARG 1983/1984). Individual Aircraft Histories originate from the same source.

Fully-operational Firefly U.8 WM890 is seen in the static aircraft display at a 1957 show. It was finally lost on a target operation off Llanbedr on 31 October 1957. (Lee Howard Collection)

the ground. The control equipment, developed by the RAE, included a Mk.9 autopilot that could be monitored and adjusted by radio and which operated the controls by electric actuators. Actuators also operated the undercarriage, flaps, propeller and throttle. A deck arrester hook, which had been deleted from the standard Firefly T.7, was re-introduced as a convenient method of shortening the landing run after pilotless sorties. The propeller was locked for 2,600rpm and, as was the original intention, all other unnecessary equipment was removed.

In many respects RAF Llanbedr was an ideal location for unmanned target aircraft operations. Relatively remote, Llanbedr already had a long association with gunnery training. 5 Civilian Anti-Aircraft Co-operation Unit (5 CAACU), had, since forming at Llanbedr in 1951, served the Army Ranges at Tonfannau and Ty Croes. The Unit was operated by civilian contractor Short Brothers & Harland Ltd and equipped with Mosquito TT.35 and Meteor TT.8 target-tugs. But operating manned and unmanned aircraft simultaneously from the same airfield became a growing concern. As a consequence the Royal Air Force element was eventually phased out and 5 CAACU disbanded at the end of 1957. At the same time Short Brothers, who employed ex-service pilots and engineers, added an Air/Ground Radio Section and an Autopilot Section to their Llanbedr-based Aircraft Engineering Section. And with the Air Force, having vacated the airfield, the civilianisation of Llanbedr was now complete and RAF Llanbedr became RAE Llanbedr.[10]

On 29 September 1955 Llanbedr's U.8 WM886 became the first Firefly to be destroyed by an air-launched guided and controlled missile. The missile was fired by an RAF Venom – probably by one of the two DH Propeller Co's Venom F.2s (WL813 and WL820) which at the time were being used on Firestreak missile development trials. At the time of the shoot-down, it was rather unkindly rumoured that to ensure success the Firefly was aimed at the missile rather than the missile at the Firefly![11]

By the time that the Ministry of Supply was in need of a follow-on order for Firefly drones both the AS.7 and U.8 had been phased out of production. Large quantities of AS.7s, then in storage, appear to have been overlooked and instead a decision was taken to convert 40 surplus standard Firefly AS.4s and AS.5s. Air Ministry Specification D.168D&P covered the conversion and was issued, on 19 August 1955 to Fairey Aviation who became solely responsible for the conversions. The new variant was given the designation Firefly U.9 with WB257 serving as the prototype. After making its first flight at Ringway on 6 April 1956, it was used for testing all of the changes required in converting aircraft to U.9 standard.

All prospective U.9 conversions were flown into Ringway and then conveyed by road to Fairey's Stockport facility for conversion. They were then conveyed back to Ringway for flight-testing. Development trials, which were carried out at Ringway with assistance from a design team from Fairey's Heston-based Guided Weapons Division, effectively began when the first "production" U.9 (WB416) flew from Ringway on 13 December 1956. WB416 later embarked

---

10 The title 5 CAACU was formally transferred to a new Unit (within 25 Group RAF) at Woodvale on 1 January 1958.

11 *Ibid.* William Harrison

98   Sitting Ducks and Peeping Toms

Firefly U.9 drone mission procedure at Hal Far as recollected by former 728B Flight pilot, Lt David Prothero, RN

Setting-Up

Each drone was given a number of 'setting-up' flights when the aircraft was operated as if it were an unmanned flight, but with one pilot in the front seat, ready to take over if anything went wrong, and a second pilot in the rear, originally observer's seat, equipped with two screwdrivers ready to make adjustments to the potentionmeters as necessary. After a faultless setting-up flight a drone was serviceable for a drone flight.

Pitch-Platform

The drones were fitted with an autopilot and automatic throttle. The associated gyroscope known as the 'pitch-platform' included a number of fixed 'attitudes' which included: TAKE-OFF, CLIMB, CRUISE, FAST CRUISE, TURN RIGHT, TURN LEFT, DESCEND and LAND. The required 'attitude' could be selected from the ground by radio signal, eg if CLIMB was selected the signal would tilt the pitch-platform a certain number of degrees down. The auto-pilot would then move the elevators up so that the aircraft assumed a climbing attitude bring ing the pitch-platform back to a horizontal position and the throttle would react to maintain a pre-determined speed. In TAKE-OFF and LAND the rudder controller and pitch controller could send signals to move respectively, the rudder left or right, and the elevators up or down. A command called DESTROY cut the engine and applied full nose-up elevator (to create a stall and a spin straight down).

Control Positions

The control box which selected 'attitudes' was in the Aircraft Direction Room (ADR) next to a display on which the radar-derived positions of the drone and shepherd were plotted. Four control positions, connected to the ADR by cable, were established on the airfield – one on the extended centerline at the downwind end of the runway for the rudder controller on landings; one on the roof of the ADR for the pitch controller on take-offs, and one to the side of the runway opposite the point at which the drone was expected to touch down., for the pitch controller on landings. The positions were weather-proof sockets into which the controllers could plug their control boxes. The positions were manned by pilots who were in radio contact with each other and with the pilot of the shepherd.

Drone Take-off

The shepherd aircraft and drone taxied out together. The shepherd took-off and orbited in a position near the downwind end of the runway. The pilot who had taxied the drone lined it up on the centre of the runway, engaged the autopilot and auto-throttle, got out, checked the cockpit, closed the canopy and left the drone. After checking with the other controllers that the elevators and rudder were responding correctly, the controller in the ADR first checked with Air Traffic Control and then selected TAKE-OFF. .

The rudder controller kept the drone straight. The TAKE-OFF was such that the drone became airborne automatically, but the pitch controller was able to adjust the attitude if necessary.

Drone Flight

When the drone was comfortably airborne the controller in the ADR selected CLIMB, making the drone adopt the preset climbing attitude, raise the undercarriage and flaps. The throttle moved so that the drone reached and then maintained the preset climbing speed. The shepherd left his orbiting position and flew in loose formation on the drone which was turned out to sea. On reaching the desired height, the ADR controller selected CRUISE, followed – if a higher speed was wanted – by FAST CRUISE. The shepherd was able to confirm speed and height. The shepherd was vectored away to a safe position once the drone had been established on the track required for the missile firing run. After the missile had been fired the shepherd was vectored on the drone to make a visual inspection. A missile was not programmed to hit the drone but pass in close proximity so that it could be photographed by the cameras on the wing-pods. If the drone was undamaged it was manoeuvered by the ADR Controller to be on the extended centre-line of the runway at a particular height and a particular distance from touchdown. LAND was then selected at which the drone adopted the landing attitude, lowered its undercarriage, flaps and hook, with the throttle maintaining a preset approach speed. The shepherd checked the wheels, flaps and hook were down, that the drone was in stable flight and broke away.

Landing

The rudder controller at the up-wind end of the runway kept the drone on the centerline (with the aid of binoculars. The controls were probably reversed so that application of RIGHT on the control box moved the rudder left and thus moved the drone to the controller's right). The pitch controller at the downwind end of the runway adjusted the drone's attitude so that it remained on the required glide slope, the throttle automatically maintaining the correct speed until the drone touched down and caught a wire. (Two wires laid across the runway were attached to heavy chains on each side of the runway. The chains ran from the wires towards the up-wind end of the runway so that retardation was slight to begin with but steadily increased.)

HMS *Girdle Ness* Seaslug Trials

The Gunnery Log of HMS *Girdle Ness* records the progress of Seaslug trials that took place at Marsaxlokk Bay, off Malta, during 1957-1961. Extracts show the following:

28.11.57 "Missile PP11 loaded 1130. Drone airborne 1245. Missile fired 1355 through cloud at approaching target drone. Missile beam-rode; hit drone. Bits seen breaking off but drone continued to fly and landed at Hal Far safely. Port pod camera and wing badly damaged."

9.7.58 "Missiles PF29 & PF30 fired. Satisfactory. Drone launched 1546. Missile PP28 fired 1614. MDI recorded very close to drone. Missile broke up and exploded at 27,500yds (25,146m)."

30.7.58 "Missiles PG14 & PG15 ready to fire as a salvo but Firefly drone crashed on take-off from Hal Far. Trial abandoned." **(See Firefly U.9 VX429)**

17.9.58 "At 1540 fired PG33 & PG34 as a salvo with 3 seconds interval. A successful firing. Missile beam rode, the first missile hit the target at 34 seconds and at 17,000yds (15,545m) range; the second continued to beam ride and broke up at 53 seconds at 28,000 yds (25,603m). The drone carried on flying for another 5 minutes. It was obviously very unstable and eventually crashed into the sea." **(See Firefly U.9 VT463)**

23.7.59 "Missile SC14 fired at Firefly drone. Drone crashed on landing at Hal Far." **(See Firefly U.9 VH130)**

25.8.59 "Missile SC35 destroyed the drone." (SC signifies a missile with warhead.)

29.3.60 "Missile SD12 fired at target drone. Drone sustained direct hit." **(See Meteor U.15 VT104)**

11.5.60 "Meteor drone took-off from Hal Far 1211 but crashed into the sea immediately after take-off. A second Meteor drone took-off at 1450 but that too crashed into the sea after take-off." **(See Meteor U.15s VT110 & VT243)**

12.5.60 "Missile SD15 fired from centre barrel to Flight Plan AT16. Drone hit at 15,000 yds (13,716m) at 32,000ft (9,754m)." (SD signifies a Seaslug missile and AT an Acceptance Trials round.) **(See Meteor U.15 VT310)**

25.5.60 "Intended to fire Missile SD13 at target drone but aircraft was destroyed by order after it developed a swing to the right." On the same date "Missile SD16 hit its target at 15,000yds (13,716m) and at 10,000ft (3.050m)." **(See Firefly U.9 VT470; also Firefly U.9 WB245)**

19.8.60 "Missile SD32 fired at 1001. Drone sustained direct hit." **(See Firefly U.9 VT493 but see also VT481)**

30.11.61 "Missile SD79 (warhead) fired at 1533. Meteor drone sustained direct hit." **(Drone identity unknown)**

Firefly U.9 WB373/597 was delivered to 728B Flight on 13 September 1958 but only lasted just over seven weeks before being shot down on 4 November 1958. In this view much of the fabric on the rudder has been blown away. This might have led to its crash, implying that it is seen on its final unmanned flight. (Lt David A. Prothero RN)

The prototype Firefly U.9, WB257, posed for the official photographer at Ringway in April 1956, immediately prior to making it initial flight on 6 April 1956. Clearly visible in these two views are the wing-tip mounted cameras as part of the weapon assessment system.(Crown Copyright RTP28764A & RTP28764E, via P.H.Butler)

upon, and again under Fairey's direction, remote-control trials at Llanbedr ahead of the start of operations there in October 1957.[12]

When the Royal Navy proposed to adopt the Firefly U.9 for drone operations there was a suggestion that the operating unit should be 771 Squadron for no other reason than the Squadron's crest depicted three drone bees![13]

Sensible though it was, the suggestion of reforming 771 Squadron was not adopted simply because, apart from the administrative burden, their Lordships did not favour raising the standard for a new Squadron. Instead, the new unit was formed as a Flight and as it was to based in Malta, it was styled – apparently more for the sake of convenience than for any other reason – as 728B Flight, therefore becoming associated with the existing Hal Far-based 728 Squadron albeit only a loose association.[14]

In fact, 728B Flight was formed at RNAS Stretton, near Warrington, on 13 January 1958. The location was chosen due to its close proximity to both Fairey's Ringway factory and RAE Llanbedr where some limited experience of the U.9 variant had been achieved.[15]

728's pilots and ground ratings – most of whom were qualified on Firefly T.7 – were drafted in from 796 Squadron at Culdrose and spent September and October 1957 at Llanbedr gaining first-hand experience on air and ground-control drone operations. The Flight's first two Firefly U.9s, VT487 and WB341, were delivered to Stretton on 3 February 1958. Three more, VT461, VT483 and VT493, followed on 11 February; WB307 on 14 February, and a final pair, VX418 and VX429, on 20 & 21 February respectively. Some of these aircraft were newly-converted examples; others were former Llanbedr aircraft which, having been declared surplus, had been returned to Fairey Engineering for storage.

After a brief working-up period, 728B Flight began moving out to Hal Far, Malta towards the end of February 1958. Personnel and aircraft were ferried from the UK, via RNAS Yeovilton and Ford in time for the Flight to be officially established at Hal Far on 1 March 1958. After settling in, 728B concentrated initially on working-up to their primary role of providing targets for HMS *Girdle Ness*. The first Firefly U.9 pilotless sortie was flown successfully on 8 July 1958. By Christmas Eve – the end of 1958 operations – the Flight

---

12 *Ibid.* William Harrison
13 Conversation with Lt David A. Prothero RN (Retd), former pilot with 728B Flight.
14 728 Squadron had long been associated with the Mediterranean area. Formed at North Front, Gibraltar on 1 May 1943 as a Fleet Requirements Unit, the Squadron later moved to Luqa, Malta in mid-1945 before settling in at Hal Far on 1 January 1946. By the late-1950s, apart from a pair of Sea Devon C.20s, 728 operated aircraft solely for offering target facilities to both the Mediterranean Fleet and, increasingly, to Army anti-aircraft batteries and the RAF Regiment. In 1958 the Squadron's target-towing Short Sturgeon TT.3s were superceded by Meteor TT.20s.

15 The first U.9 conversion, WB410, had been delivered to Llanbedr on 9 July 1957 and the first U.9 sortie was performed there by VX421 three months later, on 8 October. The last of 40 Firefly U.9 conversions departed Fairey's Ringway base on 3 July 1959.

Post-War Drone Conversions 101

728B Flight Firefly U.9 VT481/595 acts as a 'shepherd' for unmanned U.9 VT485/592 (nearest the camera) off the island of Malta. VT485 was later written-off in a landing accident at Hal Far on 25 August 1959. (Lt David A. Prothero RN)

reported a stock of ten serviceable aircraft, having lost thirteen others – five shot down during trials, three others failed to get airborne, two suffered mechanical failures and three were seriously damaged in landing accidents. For a unit seen by some to exist for the unique purpose of losing its aircraft, its accident record was considered to be quite exemplary!

728B Flight Firefly U.9 Code Sequence

The Flight was allocated a code sequence between '590' and '599'. Known examples are:

Code	Serial	Period
'590'	VT487	Feb 1958 – Jul 1958
	VT470	Jul 1959 – May 1960
'591'	VT497	Feb 1958 – Aug 1958
	WB257	??.??.?? – May 1960
'592'	VT485	??.??.?? – Aug 1959
	WB245	Sep 1959 – May 1960
'593'	WB341	Feb 1958 – Jul 1958
	VT364	Dec 1958 – Aug 1960*
	WB347	Nov 1958 – Sep 1960*
'594'	WB257	Dec 1958 – ??.??.??
'595'	VT481	Feb 1958 – Aug 1960
	WB331	Aug 1960 – Sep 1961
'596'	VX427	Nov 1958 – Jul 1959
	WB410	Oct 1959 – Aug 1960
	VT430	Aug 1960 – Sep 1961
'597'	WB373	Sep 1958 – Nov 1958
	VT413	Oct 1960 – Nov 1961
'598'	VH130	Sep 1958 – Jul 1959
	WB391	Sep 1960 – Nov 1961
'599'	WB365	Jul 1959 – Oct 1960

* No definite explanation can be found as to why two Firefly U.9s appear to have been allocated the code '593' during the same period. It is possible that one of the two was a First Immediate Replacement (FIR) aircraft and quickly brought into service as '593' whilst the original '593' was undergoing repairs, only to become the replacement FIR aircraft. As such it would have been test-flown on a fairly regular basis. However, this remains conjecture.

In reality – and contrary to popular belief – the objective of drone operations was always to bring the unmanned aircraft safely back to base where the photographic evidence captured by its wing-tip pod cameras could determine the true accuracy of any missile engagement. Missile trials were frequently conducted with unarmed missiles; had they been armed then under normal circumstances, proximity fused-missiles would have destroyed the target.

Radio command of pilotless Firefly missions was exercised from the ground but for most of the time the aircraft was out of sight from its ground controllers, a factor that created particular difficulties. In addition to continual radar surveillance, watch was also maintained on the pilotless drone by an accompanying "shepherd" Firefly, whose pilot relayed information back to ground control.[16]

The Firefly drone was programmed to fly a pre-computed flight pattern, the sequence of which could only be varied so far as the time factor was concerned, via the autopilot and airspeed control. The equipment converted the demands from ground control into variations of attitude, manoeuvre, height, speed etc, in addition to maintaining the normal flight stability of the aircraft. Another vital component of the Control and Engagement system was the telemetry, which provided the ground controller necessary flight information such as airspeed, rate of climb, altitude and engine speed.

Getting an unmanned Firefly off and back to the ground was the responsibility of two controllers, both of whom were fully-qualified pilots. The Azimuth controller stood at one end of the runway and kept the aircraft correctly aligned by means of two buttons – for right and left rudder actuation – while the Pitch controller had his "box of tricks" to one side of the runway and selected the appropriate regime to govern the height of the aircraft.

---
16 *Aeroplane*, 28 November 1958. (Temple Press Ltd)

102 Sitting Ducks and Peeping Toms

Landing the U.9 was never an easy operation for several reasons. At low speed the aircraft suffered from what pilots described as "inadequate controllability" despite the realisation that the Firefly was designed for a piloted three-point deck landing. That was difficult enough; even more so for pilots attempting to land an unmanned drone in the same manner from outside the cockpit. On occasions some pilots elected to make a "wheeler" landing at a higher speed and in a level attitude, but that was made more difficult by the Firefly's excessive torque (especially noticeable on take-off). But a "wheeler" landing brought about an added difficulty as the arrestor hook was not sufficiently long enough to engage the runway arrester wires.[17]

Although 728B received Meteor U.15 and U.16 drones from mid-1960, the Firefly U.9 remained on strength even though all were officially returned to Ministry of Aviation charge on 26 July 1960. Nevertheless Firefly drone sorties continued out of Hal Far throughout 1960 and 1961. The last losses came on 23 November 1961 when one was shot down by a Scimitar F.1 (off HMS *Centaur*) and another by a Sea Vixen (off HMS *Ark Royal*). Four days later 728B won the dubious distinction of losing the last Firefly U.9 in Royal Navy service when WB391 was shot down off Malta by the guns of HMS *Duchess*. Shortly afterwards, on 2 December 1961, 728B Flight – albeit many were by now referring to it unofficially as 728B Squadron – was disbanded.[18]

---

[17] Squadron mechanics managed to overcome this by extending the arrestor hook. It was achieved by adding a Sea Hawk "sting" hook to the original "V" frame of the Firefly. In fact, the first U.9 to have a modified hook was fitted with a genuine Sea Hawk hook, taken from an aircraft that had earlier ditched offshore. With only a slight modification to the airframe, the enlarged hook effectively solved the problem.

[18] Most published accounts describe the Firefly and Meteor operation as being 728B Squadron. However, it was always known officially as 728B Flight. Pilot's log-books etc were always stamped '728B Flight'.

Firefly U.8 Conversions from AS.7 – Individual Aircraft Histories

WJ147 (c/n F8757) Converted to "partial T.8" at Hayes; completed 24.9.52. To CS(A) charge 2.10.52 and ferried to Llanbedr 28.10.52 for flight tests. To FAC White Waltham 3.11.52 (for fitting of 6cm oscillator equipment). Flight-tested 19.11.52; returned to Llanbedr for flight trials 25.11.52. Returned to Hayes 24.2.53 for conversion to "full T.8"; Del to RAE Farnborough 8.1.54 for flight trials. To Shorts, Aberporth 21.4.54 for experimental drone flying tests. Returned to FAC (Ringway) 21.7.54 for long-term storage, followed by Cat.4 overhaul 8.6.55. Retained by FAC for trials (replacing WM856) from 23.2.56. Converted to U.8 standard at Stockport 21.2.58; to Ringway 15.4.58 for flight-testing (in association with Ferranti). Allocated to "Ready For Use" pool 28.11.58. Collected by Shorts 20.11.59 and ferried to Llanbedr. Lost on target operations 20.7.60.

WJ149 (c/n F8759) Converted to T.8 24.9.52. To CS(A) charge 1.10.52 at White Waltham. Ferried to RAE Farnborough 12.11.52 for check tests prior to ferry back to FAC 16.1.53 for conversion to "full T.8" standard. To RAE 14.10.53 for Drone Development tests; Del to Shorts, Llanbedr 25.10.53 as a development aircraft. Damaged on take-off 11.5.54; Returned to FAC 1.9.54 for storage. Cat.4 repairs began 9.6.55. Test-flown Ringway 22.8.56; flown to Anthorn AHU 1.10.56 for long-term storage; ferried to Shorts, Llanbedr 27.5.57 as a "shepherd" aircraft and coded "C". Returned to FAC Ringway 15.4.58 for conversion to "full U.8". Test-flown 8.1.59; del to Shorts, Llanbedr 20.3.59 but lost on target operations 26.11.59. SOC 12.1.60.

WJ150 (c/n F8760) Converted to T.8 at Hayes 24,9.52 and TOC by CS(A) 2.10.52 at White Waltham. To RAE Farnborough 6.1.53 for trials. Returned to Fairey, White Waltham 4.8.53 for modification to U.8. Upon completion Returned to RAE Farnborough 4.11.53 for final tests. Collected by Shorts and ferried to Llanbedr 12.11.53 for drone trials. 1st pilotless flight made 3.2.54 but destroyed by direct missile hit 7.4.54 on its 2nd pilotless flight. SOC 29.4.54.

WJ151 (c/n F8761) Converted to T.8 at Hayes 24.9.52 and TOC by CS(A) 10.10.52. To RAE Farnborough 24.10.52. Returned to FAC 11.5.53 for fitting of dummy camera nacelles. Del to RAE for further trials 11.8.53. Ferried to FAC Stockport 27.10.53 for conversion to "partial U.8" and f/f as such 2.12.53. Del to RAE Farnborough 14.12.53 for drone development trials. To FAC Ringway 5.2.54 for fitting of heat source pods etc; test-flown 25.5.54. Del to de Havilland Propellers 18.6.54 for heat source trials more tests. Returned to FAC Ringway 8.4.57. To Shorts, Llanbedr 12.6.57 to act as "shepherd" aircraft for U.8s. Returned to FAC Ringway 22.4.58 for conversion to "full T.8". Returned to Shorts 20.11.59 but lost on operations 27.11.59. SOC 12.1.60.

WJ152 (c/n F8762) Converted to T.8 at White Waltham 1.10.52 and TOC by CS(A) 2.10.52. To RAE Farnborough 22.1.53 for trials and adjustment of various items of stores. Del to Shorts, Llanbedr 23.2.53 for more tests. Returned to FAC White Waltham 11.1.54 for further mods, becoming a "semi-drone". Collected by Shorts and ferried to Aberporth 19.5.54 for drone flights. To FAC Ringway 18.5.55 for mods; test-flown 30.4.56 before del to Anthorn AHU 1.6.56 for long-term storage. Released to Shorts, Llanbedr 27.5.57 for use as a "shepherd" aircraft and coded 'A'. Sustained starboard undercarriage collapse on landing 21.11.57. To FAC Ringway 15.4.58 for repair and mods to "full U.8" standard. Test-flown 18.12.58. To Shorts, Llanbedr 19.3.59 for target operations. Written-off 26.11.59.

WJ153 (c/n F8763) Converted to T.8 at White Waltham 1.10.52 and TOC by CS(A) 2.10.52. To RAE Farnborough 3.7.53 for drone development trials. Del to Shorts, Llanbedr 5.8.53 for trials of drone equipment. (Temporarily exhibited at SBAC Farnborough 9.53.) Damaged at Llanbedr 15.12.53 when nose-tipped. Resumed trials 4.54 after repairs. Suffered engine failure 23.4.54 and forced-landed. Declared Cat.E(components) and SOC at 34 MU Stoke Heath 21.10.54.

WM810 (c/n F8887) Issued to Shorts 1.2.55 for drone development. To Anthorn AHU 31.5.55 for long-term storage until 2.2.56 when collected by Fairey for mod to full U.8 standard. Del to Llanbedr 14.11.56 for target ops and coded 'A'. Cat.4 damaged on landing at

Llanbedr 23.11.56; to Fairey 27.3.57. Returned to Llanbedr 26.7.57. Cat 4 damage (date u/k); to Fairey, Ringway 4.11.57 for repair. To Llanbedr 17.7.58.

Sustained Cat.3 damage at Llanbedr 9.10.59. Lost on operations out of Llanbedr 27.11.59.

WM823 (c/n F8900) Issued to Shorts at Llanbedr 27.5.57 for target ops. Crash-landed 20.6.57. Declared Cat.5 and SOC 15.8.57. Scrapped.

Firefly U.8 Production Aircraft – Individual Aircraft Histories

WM856 (c/n F.8911) f/f Ringway 14.2.54. Dispatched from Ringway 26.2.54 presumably to Llanbedr for radar trials (with Ferranti). Returned to FAC/Ringway 7.7.54 for minor inspection but remained until 23.2.56 when replaced by WJ147. Remained at Ringway until 26.11.56 when called by Shorts for target ops at Llanbedr. Cat 3 damage sustained in landing 1.3.56. Repaired on site. 1st pilotless sortie 10.1.57, again on 15.1.57, 17.1.57, 11.2.57, 27.2.57 and finally on 1.3.57 when at 1108 it took-off Llanbedr; handed-over to Aberporth control 1121A and returned to Llanbedr control 1226A for landing. Rejoined circuit 1230A but crashed onto the runway at 1241A. Cat.3 but repaired on site. Lost on operations 4.3.58 when it crashed into the sea. SOC 26.3.58.

WM857 (c/n F8912) f/f Ringway 22.2.54. Held in short-storm storage until 31.3.54 when Del to GWTW (Shorts) at Llanbedr 27.4.54 (via Chester) for experimental flying; returned to Ringway 1.5.54 for fitting of oscillator. Flown to Llanbedr 7.5.54, it later returned to Ringway (from Aberporth) 21.7.54 and placed into short-term storage. Modified by Fairey before re-delivery to Shorts at Aberporth 25.11.54 for drone development work. To Fairey/Ringway 11.1.56 for mods; returned to Llanbedr 13.7.56 and performed pilotless flights on 28.7.56, 2.11.56, 5.11.56, 6.11.56 before crashing pilotless into the sea 9.11.56; SOC 30.1.57.
(NB: Llanbedr records show WM857 as also making a pilotless flight on 20.5.56.)

WM858 (c/n F8913) f/f Ringway 26.3.54. Held in short-term storage until 21.7.54 when issued to Shorts (Aberporth) for experimental flying. To FAC Ringway 21.12.54 for rectification. To Anthorn AHU store 23.3.55; to FAC Ringway 31.1.56 for mods to full U.8 standard – completed 23.8.56. To RAE Llanbedr 17.10.56; to Shorts, Llanbedr 20.11.56 for drone use. Made initial pilotless flight 18.12.56 but crashed into Tremadoc Bay, Grwnedd during its 2nd unmanned flight 19.12.56. SOC 30.1.57.

WM859 (c/n F8914) f/f Ringway 7.4.54. Held in short-term storage until 21.7.54 when delivered to RAE Aberporth for experimental flying. To FAC Ringway for mods 18.1.55. To Anthorn AHU store 28.3.55; to FAC Ringway for mods up to full U.8 standard. To Anthorn AHU store 1.6.56; to FAC Ringway for mods 13.12.56. To Shorts, Llanbedr 3.4.57. Damaged on landing 3.5.57. Declared Cat.5(c) and reduced to components. SOC 19.6.57 and scrapped.

WM860 (c/n F8915) f/f Ringway 21.4.54. Held in short-term storage until 21.7.54 when delivered to Aberporth (for RAE Llanbedr) for experimental flying although first unmanned flight did not take place until 25.5.55. To FAC Ringway 30.6.55 in connection with Firefly 5 conversion programme until 16.7.56; Del to Llanbedr 18.7.56 and performed four unmanned flights, on 10.9.56, 14.9.56 and 18.9.56 before sustaining major damage in a pilotless landing 1.10.56. SOC 20.3.57.

WM861 (c/n F8916) f/f Ringway 9.4.54. Held in storage until delivered to Shorts, Llanbedr 19.1.55 for drone use. First pilotless flight made on 18.2.55 but failed to return from mission. SOC 22.3.55.

WM862 (c/n F8917) f/f Ringway 16.5.54. Held in storage 3.6.54 until 21.10.54 when issued to Anthorn AHU. Returned to FAC Ringway 26.1.55 for mods to full U.8 standard. To Anthorn AHU 25.4.55; Returned to FAC Ringway 6.12.55 for mods. To Anthorn AHU 1.6.56. Returned to FAC Ringway 5.10.56 for retrospective mods. To Shorts, Llanbedr 4.3.57 for target ops. Crashed into the sea 29.3.57. SOC 3.4.57.

WM863 (c/n F8918) f/f Ringway 14.6.54. Held in short-term storage until 26.10.54 when delivered to Anthorn AHU. Returned to FAC Ringway 16.12.54 for mods to full U.8 standard. To Shorts, Llanbedr 22.2.55 for trials. Performed pilotless sorties on 16.3.55, 24.3.55, 25.3.55 before sustaining Cat.4 damage in a pilotless (and wheels-up) landing at Llanbedr 11.5.55; to FAC Ringway by road 25.9.55 for repairs/mods. Repaired by 15.10.56; ferried to Llanbedr 6.11.56. Sustained wing damage by missile strike 21.11.56 but repaired locally and next unmanned flight on 30.11.56. Further flights were made on 19.12.56 and 2.1.57 before lost into the sea on 9.1.57. SOC 30.1.57.

WM880 (c/n F8935) f/f Ringway 17.6.54. Held in short-term storage until 11.10.54 when delivered to Anthorn AHU. Returned to Ringway 19.4.56 for mods. To RAE Llanbedr 22.10.56. Crashed into the sea 29.11.56 on its 1st pilotless sortie. SOC 30.1.57.

WM881 (c/n F8936) f/f Ringway 24.6.54. Held in short-term storage until 12.10.54 when flown to Anthorn AHU. Returned to FAC Ringway 19.6.56 for mods. Issued to Shorts, Llanbedr 18.2.57. Crashed into the sea 29.3.57. SOC 3.4.57.

WM882 (c/n F8937) f/f Ringway 22.7.54. Flown to White Waltham 31.8.54 presumably ahead of SBAC Farnborough. On 25.10.54 issued to Anthorn AHU. Returned to FAC Ringway 13.6.56 for major mods. Del to Shorts, Llanbedr 21.3.57. Cat.4 damaged on landing

A fine air-to-air study of Firefly U.8 WM888 over Cardigan Bay. In this view the aircraft is manned and flying in 'clean' configuration, ie without camera pods etc. '888 was later lost in a take-off accident on 12 March 1957 for what was its first pilotless sortie. (Lt David A. Prothero RN)

104 Sitting Ducks and Peeping Toms

24.4.57 and repaired at Ringway from 20.5.57. Returned to Llanbedr 3.2.58. Damage to prop & engine on 3.11.58 was assessed as Cat.5. SOC 19.12.58.

WM883 (c/n F8938) f/f Ringway 25.8.54. Held in short-term storage until 22.10.54 when issued to Anthorn AHU. Returned to FAC Ringway for mods 5.6.56. Del to Shorts, Llanbedr 14.1.57. Lost on target operations 26.3.57. SOC 1.4.57.

WM884 (c/n F8939) f/f Ringway 5.9.54. Held in short-term storage until 26.10.54 when flown to Anthorn AHU. Returned to FAC Ringway for mods (date unkn). Del to Shorts, Llanbedr 8.5.57. Sustained Cat.4 damage 17.6.57; Returned to FAC Ringway 6.7.57 by road for repair. Del to Shorts, Llanbedr 2.5.58. Lost on target operations 26.11.59. SOC 12.1.60.

WM885 (c/n F8940) f/f Ringway 29.12.54. Allocated to RAE Llanbedr 5.1.55 but sent to RAE Farnborough 3.3.55. To Llanbedr (date unkn) and made 1st pilotless flight 10.6.55. Lost over Cardigan Bay at 1943hrs, 21.6.55 on its 2nd pilotless flight. SOC 27.6.55.

WM886 (c/n F8941) f/f Ringway 10.2.55. Delivered to Shorts/Aberporth 18.3.55 and made 1st pilotless flight from Llanbedr on 24.5.55. A 2nd unmanned flight took place on 26.8.55 but was shot down on 5.9.55 (or 29.9.55).

WM887 (c/n F8942) f/f Ringway 22.2.55. TOC by CS(A) at FAC Ringway 11.3.55 for trials. Delivered to GWTW (Shorts)/Llanbedr 19.5.55 and made 1st pilotless flight 18.7.55. Further unmanned flights were made on 19.7.55, 21.7.55, 28.7.55, 23.8.55, 5.9.55, 9.7.56, 11.7.56 (twice), 18.7.56, 20.7.56, 23.7.56, 25.7.56, 28.8.56, 29.8.56, 30.8.56, 4.9.56, 5.9.56, 12.9.56, 18.9.56, 19.9.56, 20.9.56, 23.10.56 before being lost into the sea 2.11.56. SOC 30.1.57.

WM888 (c/n F8943) f/f Ringway 18.2.55. Declared "ready for use" 31.3.55; delivered to Llanbedr by an RAF pilot 9.6.55. Sustained Cat.3 damage at Llanbedr 21.6.56 during trials; repaired on site by 20.11.56 when issued to Shorts/Llanbedr for target ops. Crashed into sand-dunes during take-off from Llanbedr 12.3.57 on what was 1st pilotless sortie. SOC 20.3.57.

WM889 (c/n F8944) f/f Ringway 13.3.55. Flown to Anthorn AHU 29.4.55 for storage; returned to FAC Ringway 8.10.56 for mods. To Shorts/Llanbedr 27.11.56 for target ops and flew 1st unmanned sortie 20.12.56. Made further pilotless flights on 1.1.57, 11.1.57, 15.1.57, 18.1.57, 6.2.57 (twice) until it crashed 14.2.57 on its 8th pilotless sortie. SOC 20.3.57.

WM890 (c/n F8945) f/f Ringway 23.3.55. Flown to Anthorn AHU 17.5.55 for storage; returned to FAC Ringway 23.10.56 for mods. To Shorts/Llanbedr 10.12.56 for target ops. Damaged 12.2.57 and again 3.6.57, repaired on site on both occasions. Finally lost on operations 31.10.57; SOC 26.11.57.

WM891 (c/n F8946) f/f Ringway 26.4.55. Delivered to Llanbedr 17.6.55 (possibly via Anthorn AHU). 1st pilotless flight 23.9.55; again on 28.9.55 before sustaining damaged in pilotless landing 27.10.55; repaired on site by Shorts. Flown pilotless on 9.4.56 & 11.6.56 before crashing at Llanbedr 15.6.56. Subsequently broken down to components 21.6.56 and SOC 30.10.56.

WM892 (c/n F8947) f/f Ringway 22.5.55. Delivered to Llanbedr 28.6.55 where 1st pilotless flight took place 31.10.55. Made further unmanned flights on 10.11.55, 16.11.55, 17.11.55, 8.12.55, 27.2.56, 5.3.56 (twice), and 25.6.56. Suffered engine failure on approach to Llanbedr 15.10.56 during a manned sortie. Crash-landed and caught fire; pilot and observer escaped unhurt. Remains removed to 54 MU scrapyard; SOC 7.3.57.

WM893 (c/n F8948) f/f Ringway 25.5.55. Delivered to Llanbedr 7.9.55 as replacement for WM886. Flew pilotless sorties on 14.5.56, 15.6.56, 25.6.56, 27.6.56 until crashed 21.8.56, sustaining Cat.4R damage. Not repaired and conveyed to P&EE Foulness for ground trials by the Southern NATSU 9.12.56. SOC by GWTW 7.3.57.

WM894 (c/n F8949) f/f Ringway 4.7.55. Stored "at readiness" at Ringway until delivered to RAE Llanbedr 1.11.55. 1st pilotless sortie made 5.3.56; again on 7.3.56, 9.3.56 but lost over Cardigan Bay 25.5.56. SOC 31.5.56.

WM895 (c/n F8950) f/f Ringway 13.7.55. Stored "at readiness" at Ringway until delivered to RAE Llanbedr 26.3.56. Crashed on 1st pilotless sortie 30.5.56; declared Cat.5 (Components) 21.6.56. SOC 30.10.56.

WM896 (c/n F8951) f/f Ringway 31.8.55. Stored "at readiness" at Ringway; to Anthorn AHU 27.10.55.

Returned to FAC Ringway for mods 25.10.56 before delivery to Shorts, Llanbedr 13.12.56. Crashed into the sea 12.2.57 on its 1st pilotless sortie. SOC 18.2.57.

WM897 (c/n F8952) f/f Ringway 13.9.55. Stored "at readiness" at Ringway; to Anthorn AHU 27.10.55. Returned to FAC Ringway 29.10.56 for mods. To Shorts, Llanbedr 31.12.56 for target operations. Lost 25.3.57. SOC 1.4.57.

WM898 (c/n F8953) f/f Ringway 7.10.55. Flown to Anthorn AHU store 25.10.55. Returned to FAC Ringway for mods 9.11.56. To Shorts, Llanbedr 22.1.57 for target ops. 1st pilotless sortie 19.2.57 but sustained a direct hit by Fireflash missile 26.2.57 and crashed into the sea. SOC 7.3.57.

WM899 (c/n F8954) f/f Ringway 18.10.55. Flown to Anthorn AHU store 1.11.55. Returned to FAC Ringway for mods 27.11.56. Del to Shorts, Llanbedr 24.4.57 for target ops. Damaged on landing 13.5.57. To FAC Ringway by road 10.7.57 as Cat.4. After repairs re-delivered to Llanbedr 26.11.57 for target ops. Crashed 10.3.58; remains dumped at Llanbedr. SOC 26.3.58.

WP351 (c/n F8955) f/f Ringway 8.11.55. To C(A) charge 30.12.55 and stored at Ringway. Released to Shorts/Llanbedr 4.6.56 for target ops. 1st pilotless sortie 3.7.56; again on 10.7.56, 26.7.56 but crashed on landing at Llanbedr 27.7.56 after its 4th pilotless flight. SOC 30.11.56.

WP352 (c/n F8956) f/f Ringway 8.12.55. To C(A) charge 30.12.55 and stored at Ringway. Released to Shorts/Llanbedr 4.6.56 for target ops. 1st pilotless sortie 6.7.56; further flights 9.7.56, 26.9.56, 10.10.56, 11.10.56, 12.10.56, 15.10.56 but destroyed over Aberporth Range 18.10.56.

WP353 (c/n F8957) f/f Ringway 31.1.56. To C(A) charge 17.2.56 and stored at Ringway. Released to Shorts/Llanbedr 27.6.56 for drone ops. 1st pilotless sortie 26.7.56 but damaged in poor landing. Repairs eventually completed by 12.11.56 when it made 2nd pilotless flight. Seriously damaged in a crash-landing at Llanbedr 13.11.56; SOC 20.3.57.

WP354 (c/n F8958) f/f Ringway 5.3.56. To C(A) charge 26.3.56 and stored at Ringway 20.4.56. Released to Shorts/Llanbedr 13.7.56 for target ops. Crashed into the sea 10.9.56 during its 1st pilotless sortie. SOC 20.9.56.

Firefly U.9 Conversions – Individual Aircraft Histories

VH130 (c/n F8029) Transferred to CS(A) charge (whilst at RDU Anthorn) 29.9.55. To Fairey, Hamble 9.57 for re-conditioning. To Fairey, Ringway 19.9.57 for conversion to U.9; f/f as U.9 15.5.58. To 728B Flight, Hal Far 2.9.58 and coded '598'. Written-off 23.7.59 when arrestor wire parted during a pilotless landing following a live Seaslug missile trial.

VH134 (c/n F8033) Transferred to CS(A) charge (whilst at RDU Anthorn) 29.9.55. To Fairey, Hamble for re-conditioning. To Fairey, Ringway 15.7.57 for conversion to U.9; f/f as U.9 28.3.58. To RAE Llanbedr 14.4.58; ferried to Hal Far 21.8.58 for 728B Flight. Written-off 31.10.58 when ditched on take-off from Hal Far.

VT364 (c/n F8274) Transferred from RDU Anthorn to Fairey, Hamble 2.3.56 for re-conditioning. To Fairey, Ringway 10.9.57 for conversion to U.9; f/f as U.9 18.6.58. To 728B Flight, Hal Far as '593' 4.12.58 (ferried Ringway-Llanbedr-Culdrose-Hal Far, with WB257). Crashed on landing at Hal Far 26.8.60.

VT370 (c/n F8280) Transferred from RDU Anthorn to Fairey, Hamble 2.3.56 for re-conditioning. To Fairey, Stockport/Ringway 31.5.57 for conversion to U.9; f/f as U.9 7.3.58. To 728B Flight, Hal Far 20.8.58 (arrived 21.8.58). Declared a write-off after undercarriage collapsed during a ground loop 3.11.58.

VT372 (c/n F8282) Transferred from RDU Anthorn to Fairey, Hamble 24.5.55 for re-conditioning. To Fairey, Ringway 2.7.56 for conversion to U.9; f/f as U.9 1.3.57. To RAE Llanbedr 28.8.57. Crashed on landing at Llanbedr 13.1.58.

VT403 (c/n F8303) Transferred to CS(A) charge (whilst at RDU Anthorn), date unkn. To Fairey, Hamble 2.3.56 for re-conditioning. To Fairey, Ringway 26.8.57 for conversion to U.9.; f/f as U.9 12.5.58. Allocated to 728B Flight and departed Yeovilton for Malta 2.9.58 but swung off runway on take-off due to tailwheel being unlocked. Further swings after becoming airborne, aborted, applied severe rudder to avoid control tower and parked Sea Venoms. Struck ground travelling sideways, undercarriage collapsed, tip tanks caught fire and aircraft burnt out. Crew (Mr C.J. Kiss & REM H.D. Joyce) suffered slight burns. (Officially VT403 was on Ferry Flight, Yeovilton charge at the time.)

VT413 (c/n F8313) Transferred to permanent CS(A) charge (whilst at RDU Anthorn) 29.9.55. To Fairey, White Waltham 9.12.55 for conversion to U.9. To Fairey, Ringway 22.10.56; to RAE Llanbedr 7.57 but returned to Ringway 14.8.57 (and later exhibited at SBAC Farnborough 9.57). To Shorts, Llanbedr 16.12.57 but returned to Fairey, Ringway 9.6.58 for Cat.4 repairs. To Yeovilton 13.10.60 in transit to Malta for 728B Flight, Hal Far (arrived 14.10.60) and coded '597'. Shot down off Malta 23.11.61 by either a Sea Vixen from HMS *Centaur* or a Scimitar from HMS *Ark Royal* (see VT430). (TFH as U.9 61:25)

VT430 (c/n F8330) Transferred to permanent CS(A) charge (whilst at RDU Anthorn) 9.5.55. To Fairey, Hamble 26.5.55 for re-conditioning. To Fairey, Ringway 27.4.56 for conversion to U.9; f/f as U.9 10.1.57. To Shorts Llanbedr 16.6.57 and coded 'V'. Flown to Fairey, Ringway 9.1.59. To 728B Flight, Hal Far as '596' 27.8.60. Shot down off Malta 23.11.61 by either a Sea Vixen from HMS *Centaur* or a Scimitar from HMS *Ark Royal* (see VT413). (TFH as U.9 284.45)

VT441 (c/n F8341) Transferred to permanent CS(A) charge (whilst at RDU Anthorn), 29.9.55. To Fairey, Hamble 2.3.56 for re-conditioning. To Fairey, Ringway 21.6.57 for conversion to U.9; f/f as U.9 14.3.58. To 728B Flight, Hal Far 7.10.58. Shot down off Malta 26.11.58 by guns of HMS *Duchess*.

VT461 (c/n F8345) Transferred to permanent CS(A) charge (whilst at RDU Anthorn), date n/k. To Fairey, Hamble 23.5.55 for re-conditioning. To Fairey, Ringway 21.8.56 for conversion to U.9; f/f as U.9 22.5.57. To RAE Llanbedr 29.8.57. Ditched into sea 6 miles SW of Bardsey Island 29.11.57 after losing control. Reportedly recovered and repaired and deld Ringway-Stretton 11.2.58 (with VT461 & VT493) for 728B Flight. Fate unkn.

VT463 (c/n F8347) Transferred to permanent CS(A) charge (whilst at RDU Anthorn), 29.9.55. To Fairey, Hamble 2.3.56 for re-conditioning. To Fairey, Ringway 3.1.57 for conversion to U.9; f/f as U.9 22.10.57. To AHU Stretton 11.2.58. To 728B Flight, Hal Far by 5.58. Sustained damage to starboard undercarriage 23.5.58. Later shot down off Malta 17.9.58. (The HMS *Girdle Ness* Gunnery Report states that two missiles (PG33 & PG34) were fired as a salvo at 3secs intervals. The first missile hit the target at 34secs and at 17,000yard range. The second missile continued to beam ride and broke up at 53secs at c28,000yards. The drone carried on flying for another 5 minutes; it was obviously very unstable and eventually crashed into the sea.)

VT470 (c/n F8354) Transferred to permanent CS(A) charge (whilst being re-conditioned at Hamble), 5.3.57 in exchange for VT380. To Fairey, Ringway 31.5.57 for conversion to U.9; f/f as U.9 9.1.59. To Yeovilton 3.7.59 en route to 728B Flight, Hal Far. Coded '590'. Shot down off Malta 25.5.60 by Seaslug missile SD16. SOC 26.8.60.

VT481 (c/n F8365) Transferred to permanent CS(A) charge (whilst at RDU Anthorn), 29.9.55. To Fairey, Hamble 20.1.56 for re-conditioning. To Fairey, Ringway 27.11.56 for conversion to U.9; f/f as U.9 4.10.57. To AHU Stretton 11.2.58. To 728B Flight, Hal Far 2.58. Coded '595'. Shot down off Malta 19.8.60 possibly by Seaslug missile SD32 (but see also VT493). SOC 26.8.60.

VT485 (c/n F8369) Transferred to permanent CS(A) charge (whilst at RDU Anthorn), 29.9.55. To Fairey, Hamble 27.11.56 for re-conditioning. To Fairey, Ringway 7.10.57 for conversion to U.9; f/f as U.9 4.6.58. To 728B Flight, Hal Far as '592'. Written-off 25.8.59 when it belly-landed on the Hal Far runway following an undercarriage failure. At the time it was being piloted by Lt TCJ Martins RN and REM1 F.Smith).

VT487 (c/n F8371) Transferred to permanent CS(A) charge (whilst at RDU Anthorn), 29.9.55. To Fairey, Hamble 8.2.56 for re-conditioning. To Fairey, Ringway 28.2.57 for conversion to U.9; f/f as U.9 22.11.57. To AHU Stretton 28.1.58. To 728B Flight, Hal Far 3.2.58 as '590'. Written-off 8.7.58 when the undercarriage collapsed during a pilotless landing at Hal Far.

VT493 (c/n F8377) Transferred to permanent CS(A) charge (whilst at RDU Anthorn), 29.9.55. To Fairey, Hamble 17.5.56 for re-conditioning. To Fairey, Ringway 11.3.57 for conversion to U.9; f/f as U.9 30.12.57. Deld to 728B Flight, Stretton 11.2.58. Shot down off Malta 19.8.60 possibly by Seaslug missile SD32 (but see also VT481).

VT494 (c/n F8378) Transferred to permanent CS(A) charge (whilst at RDU Anthorn), 9.5.55. To Fairey, Hamble 25.5.55 for re-conditioning. To Fairey, Ringway 7.5.56 for conversion to U.9; f/f as U.9 24.1.57. To Shorts, Llanbedr 20.6.57. Sustained Cat.4 damage in a ground-looped landing at Llanbedr 15.11.57. Conveyed to RNAY Donibristle 15.4.58 but struck off charge.

VT497 (c/n F8381) Transferred to permanent CS(A) charge (whilst at RDU Anthorn), 29.9.55. To Fairey, Hamble 26.3.56 for re-conditioning. To Fairey, Ringway 27.11.56 for conversion to U.9; f/f as U.9 15.10.57. To AHU Stretton 14.1.58. Ferried to Fairey, Ringway for mods 27.1.58; returning to Stretton 3.2.58 (with WB341). Ferried Stretton-Ford-Bordeaux-Istres-Nice-Hal Far 17-18.2.58 for 728B Flight. Coded '591'. Written-off 4.8.58 when it missed the wire, ground-looped and caught fire at Hal Far. SOC 10.12.58.

VX416 (c/n F8432) Transferred to permanent CS(A) charge (whilst at RDU Anthorn), 2.6.54. To Fairey, Hamble 21.6.55 for re-conditioning. To Fairey, Ringway 21.9.56 for conversion to U.9; f/f as U.9 19.6.57. To Shorts, Llanbedr 26.9.57. Damaged on landing 4.3.58. To Fairey, Ringway by road 16.6.58 for Cat.4 repair. To RN charge at Ringway 15.7.60; air-tested 5.10.60 and deld to Yeovilton 13.10.60 and on to Hal Far 14.10.60. TOC by 728B Flight 17.10.60 as '599' for Seaslug trials. Shot down during Fleet gunner practice off Malta 8.11.61. (TFH as U.9 79:00).

VX418 (c/n F8434) Transferred to permanent CS(A) charge (whilst at RDU Anthorn), 29.9.55. To Fairey, Hamble 13.1.56 for re-conditioning. To Fairey, Ringway 9.11.56 for conversion to U.9; f/f as U.9 5.9.57. Deld to Stretton 20.2.58 for 728B Flight. Sustained major damage at Hal Far 2.6.58 when the prop struck the ground on take-off due to the brakes having been left on. Flown by Lt PA McKern & LREM RA McKinney. SOC 26.11.54.

VX421 (c/n F8437) Transferred to permanent CS(A) charge (whilst at RDU Anthorn), 9.5.55. To Fairey, Hamble 23.5.55 for re-conditioning. To Fairey, Ringway 31.5.56 for conversion to U.9; f/f as U.9 18.2.57. To RAE Llanbedr 19.7.57. Crashed on approach to land 7.11.57. SOC 5.12.57.

VX427 (c/n F8443) Transferred to permanent CS(A) charge (whilst at RDU Anthorn), (date unkn). To Fairey, Hamble 2.3.56 for re-conditioning. To Fairey, Ringway 13.11.57 for conversion to U.9; f/f as U.9 12.6.58. To 728B Flight, Hal Far 20.11.58 and coded '596'. Sustained

728B Flight Firefly U.9 VT487/590 suffered a starboard undercarriage collapse on landing at Hal Far on 8 July 1958. Although the damage does not look too serious, the aircraft was actually written-off as a result. (Lt David A. Prothero RN)

Flaps down, arrestor hook down and Firefly U.9 VT487 is all set to land at Hal Far at the end of a pilotless sortie. Whilst on this occasion the drone has escaped being shot down, there still remained the tricky business of performing an unmanned landing. (Lt David A. Prothero RN)

Firefly U.9 VX427/596 was due to act as a target for a live Seaslug trial on 30 July 1958 but ground-looped during its take-off run from Hal Far. The Maltese summer climate clearly had an effect on naval ratings' standard dress issue. (Lt David A. Prothero RN)

Post-War Drone Conversions 107

Firefly U.9 WB257/591 suffered an unintended undercarriage retraction during a pilotless take-off at Hal Far on 2 May 1959. The Hal Far fire section was quick in spreading foam to avoid a fire from the aircraft's full fuel tanks while ground crew prepare to retrieve the aircraft off the runway. WB257 was eventually shot down on 25 May 1960. (Lee Howard Collection)

Cat.5 damage 21.7.59 when it ground-looped at Hal Far after parting with the arrestor wire during a pilotless landing. Remains to Hal Far dump.

VX429 (c/n F8445) Transferred to permanent CS(A) charge (whilst at RDU Anthorn), 29.9.55. To Fairey, Hamble 9.6.56 for re-conditioning. To Fairey, Ringway 13.3.57 for conversion to U.9; f/f as U.9 24.1.58. To AHU Stretton 21.2.58. To 728B Flight, Hal Far 21.2.58. Sustained Cat.5 damage 30.7.58 when it ground-looped at Hal Far at slow speed during take-off for an intended live Seaslug missile trial. SOC 10.12.58.

WB245 (c/n F8471) Transferred to permanent CS(A) charge (whilst at RDU Anthorn), 29.9.55. To Fairey, Hamble 15.5.56 for re-conditioning. To Fairey, Ringway 11.4.57 for conversion to U.9; f/f as U.9 12.2.58. To RAE Llanbedr 11.3.58 and coded 'J'. Flown to Fairey, Ringway 9.1.59. To 728B Flight, Hal Far 11.9.59 as '592/B'. Crashed on take-off at Hal Far 25.5.60 for an intended live Seaslug trial. SOC 26.5.60.

WB257 (c/n F8483) Transferred to permanent CS(A) charge 16.7.51 and retained by the manufacturer as a trials' aircraft. To Fairey, Ringway (ex AHU Abbotsinch) 2.5.55 for conversion to U.9 prototype; f/f as U.9 6.4.56. Displayed at SBAC Farnborough 1-9.9.56. To RAE

Firefly U.9 WB257 was subsequently repaired and returned to 728B Flight strength, still as '591'. It flew a number of unmanned drone sorties, including this one viewed from an accompanying 'shepherd' aircraft which shows the lines of the U.9 to their best. (Lt David A. Prothero RN)

Farnborough 6.3.58. To 728B Flight, Hal Far 4.12.58 (ferried Ringway-Llanbedr-Culdrose-Hal Far as 'Navair 594'.), later coded '594'; later re-coded '591'. Sustained damage at Hal Far 2.5.59 when the undercarriage retracted during a radio-controlled take-off run (Lt RG Gordon). Repaired but shot down off Malta 25.5.60. SOC 26.8.60.

WB307 (c/n F8525) Transferred to permanent CS(A) charge (whilst at RDU

Anthorn), 29.9.55. To Fairey, Hamble 11.5.56 for re-conditioning. To Fairey, Ringway 7.1.57 for conversion to U.9; f/f as U.9 22.11.57. To AHU Stretton 28.1.58. To 728B Flight, Hal Far 14.7.58. Shot down off Malta 16.9.58. SOC 10.12.58.

WB331 (c/n F8536) To Fairey, Hamble (ex RDU Anthorn) for re-conditioning 25.7.56. To Fairey, Ringway 3.5.57 for conversion to U.9; f/f as U.9 4.3.58. To Shorts, Llanbedr 28.3.58 and coded 'F'. Flown to

Fairey, Ringway 8.1.59. To 728B Flight, Hal Far 27.8.60 as '595' for Seaslug acceptance trials. Reported as crashed on landing at Hal Far 26.9.60 and presumably repaired. Shot down off Malta by HMS *Lion* 2.9.61. (TFH as U.9 208:50).

WB341 (c/n F8546) Transferred to permanent CS(A) charge (whilst at RDU Anthorn), 29.9.55. To Fairey, Hamble 17.5.56 for re-conditioning. To Fairey, Ringway 28.2.57 for conversion to U.9; f/f as U.9 2.12.57. Deld to AHU Stretton 3.2.58 for 728B Flight and coded '593'. Sustained Cat.5 damage during an exceptionally heavy pilotless landing at Hal Far 30.7.58. SOC 10.12.58 and dumped at Luqa 2.59.

WB347 (c/n F8552) Transferred to permanent CS(A) charge (whilst at RDU Anthorn), 29.9.55. To Fairey, Hamble 24.1.57 for re-conditioning. To Fairey, Ringway 21.12.57 for conversion to U.9; f/f as U.9 17.9.58. To Yeovilton 20.11.58 and ferried to Hal Far (via Orange and Cagliari 26-27.11.58) for 728B Flight. Coded '593'. Shot down by HMS *Eastbourne* 9.9.60. (TFH as U.9 77:10).

WB350 (c/n F8555) Transferred to permanent CS(A) charge (whilst at RDU Anthorn), 29.9.55. To Fairey, Hamble 12.7.56 for re-conditioning. To Fairey, Ringway 24.5.57 for conversion to U.9; f/f as U.9 14.2.58. To RAE Llanbedr 2.4.58 and coded 'L'. Flown to Fairey, Ringway 8.1.59; returned to Llanbedr 2.6.60 (still as 'L'). Shot down off Llanbedr by Firestreak missile 26.7.60.

WB365 (c/n F8570) Transferred to permanent CS(A) charge (whilst at RDU Anthorn), 29.9.55. To Fairey, Hamble 10.1.57 for re-conditioning. To Fairey, Ringway 21.10.57 for conversion to U.9; f/f as U.9 6.10.58. To Yeovilton 29.6.59 and to 728B Flight, Hal Far 3.7.59. Coded '599'. Shot down by HMS *Tiger* off Malta 6.10.60. (TFH as U.9 68.25).

WB373 (c/n F8578) Transferred to permanent CS(A) charge (whilst at RDU Anthorn), 29.9.55. To Fairey, Hamble 20.2.57 for re-conditioning. To Fairey, Ringway 8.12.57 for conversion to U.9; f/f as U.9 14.7.58. To Malta, via Yeovilton 10.9.58 and Orange 12.9.58. To 728B Flight, Hal Far 13.9.58 as '597'. Shot down off Malta 4.11.58. SOC 10.12.58.

WB374 (c/n F8579) Transferred to permanent CS(A) charge (whilst at RDU Anthorn), 9.5.55. To Fairey, Hamble 26.6.55 for re-conditioning. To Fairey, Ringway 22.6.56 for conversion to U.9; f/f

Firefly U.9 WB331/595 was one of several 728B Flight aircraft that had seen service at Llanbedr. In this pilotless sortie view the former Llanbedr code 'F' is very much in evidence. (Lee Howard Collection)

as U.9 28.3.57. To Shorts, Llanbedr 26.7.57 and coded 'H'. Flown to Fairey, Ringway 31.12.58; to ARS Yeovilton 22.7.60 (still as 'H'); arrived at Hal far 29.7.60 for 728B Flight. Shot down by Seaslug missile off Malta 7.10.60.

WB391 (c/n F8588) Transferred to permanent CS(A) charge 22.6.55 (whilst undergoing re-conditioning at Fairey, Hamble) To Fairey, Ringway 17.5.56 for conversion to U.9; f/f as U.9 1.2.57. To Shorts, Llanbedr 26.7.57. Sustained Cat.4 damage when it crashed on landing at Llanbedr 17.2.58. To Fairey, Ringway 12.6.58 for repair. Noted at Yeovilton 27.9.60 en route to Malta. To 728B Flight 28.9.60 and coded '598'. Shot down off Malta 27.11.61 by HMS *Duchess*. (TFH as U.9 131.40)

WB392 (c/n F8589) Transferred to permanent CS(A) charge (date unkn) whilst undergoing re-conditioning at Fairey, Hamble 1955. To Fairey, Ringway 12.9.56 for conversion to U.9; f/f as U.9 26.8.57. To Shorts, Llanbedr 12.2.58 and coded 'Z'. Flown to Fairey, Ringway 20.1.59. To 728B Flight 27.9.60. Shot down off Malta 6.10.60 by HMS *Tiger*. (TFH as U.9 127.55)

WB394 (c/n F8591) Transferred to permanent CS(A) charge (whilst at RDU Anthorn), 22.6.55. To Fairey, Hamble 17.10.56 for re-conditioning. To Fairey, Ringway 22.7.57 for conversion to U.9; f/f as U.9 18.4.58. Ferried Ringway-Hal Far (via Ford, Orange, Cagliari) 20-21..8.58 for 728B Flight. Damaged at Hal Far 12.10.58 when it inadvertently made a wheels-up landing. Shot down off Malta 3.11.58. SOC 10.12.58.

WB402 (c/n F8599) Transferred to permanent CS(A) charge (whilst at RDU Anthorn), 9.5.55. To Fairey, Hamble 26.5.55 for re-conditioning. To Fairey, Ringway 20.8.56 for conversion to U.9; f/f as U.9 11.4.57. To RAE Llanbedr 26.7.57. Written off 30.1.58 after failing to respond to turn commands and ditched into the sea 2m west of Bardsey Island. SOC 14.2.58.

WB410 (c/n F8607) Transferred to permanent CS(A) charge (whilst at RDU Anthorn), 9.5.55. To Fairey, Hamble 23.5.55 for re-conditioning. To Fairey, Ringway 16.4.56 for conversion to U.9; f/f as U.9 13.12.56. To Shorts, Llanbedr 9.7.57 and coded 'K'. Flown to Fairey, Ringway 31.12.58; to 728B Flight (via Yeovilton) 5.10.59 and coded '596/K'. Destroyed when landed at Hal Far with no hook 25.8.60. SOC 30.8.60.

WB411 (c/n F8608) Transferred to permanent CS(A) charge (whilst at RDU Anthorn), 29.9.55. To Lee-on-Solent 6.2.57; to Fairey, Hamble 20.2.57 for re-conditioning. To Fairey, Ringway 4.12.57 for conversion to U.9; f/f as U.9 10.11.58. To 728B Flight 25.6.59 and coded '596'. Shot down 25.8.60.

WB416 (c/n F8613) Transferred to permanent CS(A) charge (whilst at RDU Anthorn), 9.5.55. To Fairey, Hamble 18.5.55 for re-conditioning. To Fairey, Ringway 5.10.55 for conversion to U.9; f/f as U.9 13.12.56. To A&AEE 28.8.57 for blower tunnel tests of trial installation jettisonable camera pods. To Fairey, Ringway 3.9.57; to RAE Llanbedr 15.10.57 for development trials. Returned to Fairey, Ringway 18.10.57. To RAE Llanbedr 14.11.57 until 30.1.58 when returned to Fairey, Ringway for mock-up and trial installation of mods. Sold for scrap to H.H. Bushell & Co 21.7.61.

Firefly U.9 WB416 was allocated to A&AEE on 28 August 1957 for trials of jettisonable camera pods. Seen here two days later, outside the Blower Tunnel at Boscombe Down, WB416 is being worked on with the entire aircraft at a 10° bank to starboard. (via Boscombe Down Aviation Collection.)

Firefly T.7 – 'Shepherd' Aircraft

WJ188 Transferred to C(A) charge 1.3.58 for use by Shorts. Ferried Lossiemouth-Llanbedr 4.3.58 for 'target & shepherd' duties. Coded 'T' and painted grey overall. Released by GW(A) 3.10.60; briefly to 728B Flight, later Returned to GW(A) charge at Llanbedr. Released 24.1.61; sold to Hants & Sussex Aviation 8.11.61 and departed Llanbedr by road 16.11.61, presumably to Portsmouth.

WM764 Transferred to C(A) charge 1.3.58 for use by Shorts. Ferried Lossiemouth-Llanbedr 4.3.58 for 'target & shepherd' duties. Released by GW(A) 27.10.57 and sold as scrap 24.8.60 to H.H.Bushell & Co.

WM767 Transferred to C(A) charge 1.3.58 for use by Shorts. Ferried Lossiemouth-Llanbedr 4.3.58. To FAC Ringway 4.58 for mods. To Llanbedr as 'chase & shepherd' duties; coded 'O' and painted grey overall. SOC by GW(A) 3.10.60. Sold to Hants & Sussex Aviation 8.11.61 and departed Llanbedr by road 16.11.61, presumably to Portsmouth.

WJ188/T was one of several Firefly T.7s used at Llanbedr for 'shepherd' duties. Unlike the drone Fireflies, these T.7s retained their folding wing capability. (Lee Howard Collection)

Firefly T.7 WM767/O rests outside Llanbedr's main hangar. Just barely visible in the background is one of several Firefly U.8 converted from a standard Mk. AS.7.(Lee Howard Collection)

Meteor Drone Conversions

1954 unfolded with Jindivik so far behind schedule that there were genuine fears of Armstrong-Siddeley closing down its Viper engine production line.[19]

The delay was felt mostly among those RAE planners charged with developing a suitable target aircraft for Britain's new generation of strategic missiles. Not only was the delay frustrating but there was a widely-held view that the effectiveness of Britain's defences could suffer a detrimental effect due to lack of suitable target aircraft – not just for trials and testing but also for working-up to operational state. Of course, some warning signs had already been raised early on in Jindivik's development and as a consequence the go-ahead had been given to convert a number of Firefly AS.5 and AS.7 aircraft into target drones. But Firefly was seen very much as a stop-gap and with no immediate sign of getting Jindivik back onto schedule, the requirement for a high-speed target drone became an increasingly urgent issue. Some consideration had been given to converting a number of de Havilland Mosquitoes to drones but that concept was dropped on the realisation that early Meteor variants, fast approaching retirement, would soon become available. As early as July 1953 several examples were earmarked for conversion to what was now being described as the Meteor U.15. RA421 was already being used by Flight Refuelling Ltd at Hurn (in conjunction with Portsmouth Aviation Ltd) and RA479, then with RAE Farnborough. Both were part of the CS(A) Fleet and both were available to become the 1st and 2nd prototypes respectively. CS(A) had three other F.4s available, viz VZ389 at Fairey's, White Waltham and RA420 and RA438, both at A&AEE Boscombe Down.[20]

In the meantime those same RAE planners charged with finding a suitable high-speed drone concluded that the Meteor was probably the most likely contender for a 'quick-fix' high-speed drone conversion and in mid-1954 RAE was commissioned to undertake a series of test programmes using a modified two-seat Meteor T.7 (VW413). Fitted with an Ultra throttle-control unit in order to evaluate the Meteor's true potential as an unmanned target aircraft, the first exploratory flight took place at Farnborough on 2 September 1954, with Flt Lt E. F. Pennie (Deputy OC Flying, Unmanned Operations, Llanbedr) in command and with Gordon Hamm of Ultra Ltd in the rear seat. A number of other automatic system components were flight-tested in the same aircraft before the Meteor was ready to fly as a fully-fledged drone. Eventually, on 17 January 1955, the first pilotless take-off under automatic control was made with Pennie at the controls (acting as a Safety Pilot) and Mr E. Summerhayes as observer.

Results of these initial tests were sufficiently encouraging to warrant the go-ahead in converting further Meteors. With factory-fresh Hawker Hunter F.1s now entering first-line service with Fighter Command, relatively large numbers of Meteor F.4s had become available. Gloster Aircraft Ltd was the obvious first choice to carry out the conversion work but that company was fully committed to Javelin production, as well as producing late mark Meteors.

As a sub-contractor of Meteor night-fighters, Armstrong-Whitworth was in the same situation as Glosters, so the Ministry turned to Flight Refuelling Ltd (FRL) and awarded the Tarrant Rushton-based company overall responsibility for the Meteor Drone programme.

It was, of course, not the first time that FRL had become involved in converting aircraft to drone status. Several years earlier the company had been engaged on a programme to convert nine Lancaster B.1s into drones. As it turned out the Lancaster, after just one conversion had been test-flown, proved unsuitable for drone operation. FRL was then contracted to convert up to 33 Lincolns into drones but the Lincoln proved equally unsuitable. Both programmes were cancelled but FRL had gained much knowledge in drone conversion work.

Meteor U.15

Meteor F.4s began to arrive at Tarrant Rushton in quantity towards the end of January 1955 by which time the initial conversion, RA421 (by now re-designated U.15), had made its initial test flight albeit with a pilot on board. It went on to achieve a fully automatic, ground-controlled, take-off from Tarrant Rushton, on Sunday, 11 March 1955, although the landing was made under the control of the pilot. By the end of the month the same aircraft completed the cycle by making the first ground-controlled landing, but not without incident. The Meteor landed too heavily, causing the undercarriage to be pushed upwards through the wings, causing extensive damage. As a precautionary measure, all subsequent test flights carried a Safety Pilot.[21]

Conversion of the basic aircraft to pilotless configuration involved the installation of a radio link, an autopilot and trials instrumentation equipment. This included a camera system capable of recording the final stages of an attacking missile's flight towards the target. Cameras were carried in wing-tip pods, each containing two Wretar units developed by the Weapons Research Establishment in Australia. This camera covered the hemispherical field of vision of 180° and each pair was mounted to give all-round coverage with one viewing above the wing and one below. The converted drone could be flown either as a pilotless target under radio control from the ground, as a radio controlled aircraft carrying a pilot for air testing the systems, for training new pilots or ground controllers, or as a normal piloted aircraft with the autopilot etc inoperative.

Although the Air Ministry drew up a Specification (Spec D.173D&P) it seems not to have been widely circulated within the industry as Flight Refuelling had already been awarded a contract (6/Acft/15570/CB.24(b)) to cover conversions of just over twenty U.15s. Just two years after the first Meteor F.4s had arrived for conversion, the initial delivery of a fully-converted U.15 drone to Llanbedr

---

19 The line was geared for producing 80 Viper engines in 1953 but a lack of any further orders threatened its closure. Restarting the line would have proved expensive.

20 In fact RA479 was placed into storage at 38 MU until released back to Farnborough for drone aerial tests. It eventually joined the U.15 programme in September 1956. The other three F.4s were placed into storage at 33 MU until July 1954 when they were all conveyed to Flight Refuelling for conversion in July 1954.

21 RA421 was subsequently repaired and later despatched to Australia. (See individual aircraft histories.)

Captured by the wing-tip camera, a Seaslug missile passes close enough to a 728B Flight Meteor U.15 that a 'hit' would have been recorded. (via Lt David A. Prothero RN)

occurred on 29 January 1957 when VT110 was ferried in from Tarrant Rushton. It marked the end of a long and often frustrating desire by those at Llanbedr to operate jet-powered unmanned target aircraft.

Training at Llanbedr began immediately after the arrival of VT110, under the guidance of the Ministry of Supply with RAF pilots detached from IAP Flight, RAE Farnborough. The responsibility for aircraft servicing and the supply of civilian pilots and ground controllers was taken on by Short Bros.

The U.15 was officially declared operational on 17 July 1958 when RA432 made the first pilotless sortie over Cardigan Bay. It acted as a target for a 'Red Shoes' (Thunderbird) missile to be fired from the nearby Aberporth Range but ironically on the day the missile failed to fire and the drone Meteor returned unscathed to Llanbedr after 33 minutes. By the end of the year eight more U.15 sorties were completed with only one loss; VT135/L dived into the sea on 18 December 1958 after 'land-glide' had been selected on return from a sortie against a Seaslug missile at 30,000ft (9,144m).

U.15s completed 60 unmanned sorties at Llanbedr during 1959, the majority of which acted as targets for Thunderbird and Bloodhound missiles. The very first firing of a RAF Bloodhound by the service was made on 22 July 1959 and resulted in the loss of U.15 VT338/B. Apart from serving as targets for the Aberporth Range, the Llanbedr-based drones were also made available for No.1 Guided Weapons Development Squadron at RAF Valley which initially operated Swift F.7s with Fireflash beam-riding missiles. The Squadron later converted to Javelins equipped with IR-guided Firestreak missiles, the first live firing of which was made by a GWDS Javelin FAW.7 on 21 December 1959. That engagement led to the shooting down of U.15 VW293/M.[22]

---

22 *Air Clues*, February 1978.

In the same manner that several Firefly T.7s were employed as 'shepherd' aircraft for Firefly U.8 sorties, so Llanbedr received a Meteor T.7 to accompany Meteor targets in a similar role. WA662 was delivered in to Llanbedr from Bovingdon on 17 March 1958 having latterly operated with the Fighter Command Communications Squadron. As it transpired WA662 was to serve that role at Llanbedr for over 25 years.

One Meteor U.15, VT196, was delivered to Llanbedr on 27 February 1959, and was used for special tasking. It spent most of its life on development trials and the testing of special aerials etc. Prior to its arrival it had spent time with the A&AEE Boscombe Down having had telemetry and a beeped throttle system installed. That allowed it to be used at Llanbedr for work-up training in preparation for the arrival of Jindivik drones, resulting in it becoming affectionately, but aptly, referred to as a 'Meteorvik'. Later, a 24-channel telemetry system was used allowing 'shepherd' aircraft to be used only in the event of a telemetry failure or for the need of air-to-air inspection of missile damage to the drone.

At the same time that drone Meteors were entering service at Llanbedr, so a similar operation was getting underway in Australia. A joint UK/Australia trials team, based at Salisbury, Southern Australia – the Long Range Weapons Establishment – had originally been formed in 1947 with the sole objective of developing and testing a range of intercontinental ballistic missiles. A base airfield was later established at Edinburgh Field, whilst the Test Range was nearly 300 miles (483m) away at Woomera. The Australian operation was supported by a Ministry of Supply team from the UK, initially to establish requirements for operating target drones. The selection of Meteor U.15 as a target aircraft at the Woomera Missile Range, probably more than anything else, reflected the delay in getting Jindivik fully operational.

By 1955 the LRWE began to take on the responsibility for developing a wider range of general weapons testing and in reflecting this, together with the declining role of ballistic missiles, the unit's title was amended to become the Weapons Research Establishment (WRE).

The first U.15 to be shipped to Australia was EE524, which was converted by Flight Refuelling, prepared for shipment by 47MU at Hawarden, and which arrived at Melbourne docks in July 1955 before being officially taken onto RAAF charge at No.1 Air Depot at Laverton. It later positioned to Edinburgh Field. (Further U.15 conversions for use in Australia involved: EE521, RA367, RA371, RA398, RA417, RA421, RA430, RA433, RA438, RA441, RA454, RA457, RA473, VT105, VT106, VT112, VT113, VT118, VT130, VT139, VT142, VT168, VT175, VT177, VT179, VT184, VT187, VT191, VT192, VT197, VT219, VT220, VT222, VT226, VT230, VT256, VT259, VT262, VT270, VT286, VT289, VT294, VT316, VT319, VT329, VT330, VT334, VW266, VW273, VW275, VW303, VW308, VW781, VW791, VZ386, VZ389, VZ401, VZ403, VZ407 and VZ414.)

The Meteor U.15 was declared fully operational in Australia on 17 May 1957 when VT187 made the first pilotless sortie out of Evett's Field, Woomera. The flight proved trouble-free and by most accounts successful when it was destroyed by a Fireflash missile after 29 minutes. The second pilotless sortie over the Woomera Range, with U.15 VW275, took place on 24 July 1957; on that occasion the drone was successfully engaged by a Blue Jay (Firestreak) missile but managed to return to base unscathed after 51 minutes.[23]

All of the drone Meteors sent to Woomera were allocated to the Air Trials Unit until 31 March 1958 when the ATU was split into No.1 Air Trials Unit and No.2 Air Trials Unit based at Woomera and Edinburgh Field respectively. The Royal Australian Air Force operated the aircraft as a service to a succession of numbered Joint Service Trials Units (JSTU) which were tasked with the development and proving of various weapons systems.[24]

Back in the UK, the Royal Navy also took a firm interest in the U.15 and on 20 May 1959 the first navalised example, VT110, was flown from Tarrant Rushton to Llanbedr where pilots seconded to 728B Flight began conversion training. The Flight was, of course, already operating Firefly U.9 targets from its base at Hal Far, Malta and throughout the early trials period at Llanbedr, and later at Hal Far, RAE Llanbedr not only gave technical support but also made available a number of Meteors on loan. The first operational unmanned flight of a Royal Navy U.15 took place on 29 March 1960 when VT110/655 acted as a target for a Seaslug missile fired from HMS *Girdle Ness*.

Meteor U.16

Despite the continuing availability of redundant F.4s, an early decision was taken to switch to converting Meteor F.8s to drone configuration. Specification D.174D&P was issued to cover the F.8 conversion into what was designated U.16.[25] There were a number of advantages in selecting the F.8. With the earlier U.15 the autopilot and allied drone equipment had to be installed where space permitted, but in the U.16 considerable structural alterations were introduced to cater for the specific and demanding requirements of target aircraft operations. This improved the aircraft's flexibility as a target, whilst retaining the original performance figures. With the need for a pre-trial servicing of the control equipment, the nose section of the fuselage was lengthened by 30in to provide a compartment for the radio control and autopilot equipment. A forward-hinged door provided access to these units. To increase the endurance, important with development trials, the existing fuel system was augmented by an additional 95-gallon (431 litres) tank in the fuselage. The cameras were installed in slim-line wing-tip nacelles, these being jettisonable and recoverable to enable vital film records of the trial to be retrieved should the target be damaged. The recovery system,

Landing a Meteor U.15 after an unmanned sortie was never a straightforward affair. In this sequence 728B Flight Meteor U.15 '657' has been perfectly lined up for landing but the ground controller misjudged the angle of descent and it landed on rough ground just ahead of the start of the runway. (via Lt David A. Prothero RN)

installed in a detachable section of the outer wing inboard of the camera nacelle, comprised a parachute system, a buoyancy bag and a homing beacon similar to SARBE. On command the wing-tip and its nacelle could be jettisoned and separated from the mainplane which initiated the parachute sequence. In the event the system was never used due to recovery problems.

The system used for controlling the Meteor U.16 in flight was originally developed by RAE Farnborough and became standard in all UK target drones, including the Jindivik. A built-in safety factor – in the event of loss of signal – put the drone into orbit, climbing or descending to a safety altitude of 5,000ft (1,524m) where it remained until the transmitter was changed or the fault rectified. Command destroy was instantaneous if required; it simply actuated the control surfaces and caused the aircraft to plunge into the sea.

The Meteor U.16 was fitted with an Elliott B4 autopilot and to provide performance and navigational information to the pilot and navigator, the drone was provided with a

---

23 Although VT187 flew the first pilotless sortie at WRE, it had previously made at least sixteen flights of various durations with a safety pilot on board – the first such flight being on 10 December 1956.
24 1 ATU was subsequently disbanded on 30 September 1967 when range ferry and recovery duties were taken over by Short Bros & Harland Air Services Ltd. 2 ATU became a non-flying unit on 10 December 1969 and finally disbanded on 27 February 1970.
25 Spec D.174D&P was originally raised on 2 January 1956 but progressively updated (with Issue 2) on 21 August 1958 and finally (Issue 3) on 7 July 1959.

So proficient was Flight Refuelling at converting Meteor F.8s into U.16s that at one stage production outstripped Llanbedr's requirements. FRL was therefore contracted (against KK/F/0149/CB.24(a)) to store completed U.16s at Tarrant Rushton. This splendid line-up of a dozen U.16s is believed to have been taken on 20 March 1963. (Flight Refuelling Ltd)

telemetry system which repeated the aircraft's flight instrument readings. Transponder beacons could be fitted to assist tracking. Infra-red seeking missiles required a heat source to home onto, so the Meteor could carry flares in clusters of three under each engine nacelle which could be fired either in a salvo or in sequence on command. Wing drop tanks were not usually fitted on the Meteor drone, but the wing-tank attachments were often used to carry extra trials equipment such as smoke generators, chaff dispensers and TV camera, etc.[26]

Despite the improvements of the U.16 over the U.15, the former was not without its problems. Early test flights in pilotless mode revealed that it had a tendency to over-bank. Its rate of climb was also very poor; in fact so poor that, after becoming operational, the U.16 could only make one circuit of the so-called Aberporth Range "race-track" at 35,000ft (10,668m) before lack of fuel forced its return to Llanbedr. What compounded the problem even further was that the Firestreak development trials required a high-speed target operating at a minimum of 40,000ft (12,192m).[27]

There were other problems, including the delay at Elliot Brothers in producing essential items of drone equipment – including the autopilots – and as a consequence the U.16 programme slipped by some six months behind the original schedule. The first U.16 was eventually delivered to Llanbedr on 30 June 1960 when WH284 (which had the first jig-built extended nose) – was ferried in from Tarrant Rushton. WK926, the second U.16, – but which was in fact the first production aircraft – was delivered in on 18 July 1960 and these two Meteors were used to establish operational procedures for the U.16. WK926 flew the type's first pilotless sortie on 12 September 1960, signalling the retirement of

the Firefly U.8. Later, on 24 November, WK926 became the first drone to undertake a trial at 40,000ft (12,192m). It was also the first drone to be landed by the pilot from the cell, aided by the PAR Controller, after being airborne for a record 89 minutes. Having taken off in bright and clear weather, a sudden deterioration had obscured the airfield for landing but when the technicians found the aircraft it was stationery on the runway – and sitting astride the centerline! Unfortunately, this remarkable U.16 was destroyed later in the day by a GWTS Firestreak missile.

More problems with the U.16 came to a head in mid-1961 when three aircraft were lost in quick succession. WA982 crashed into Cardigan Bay on 9 May after the telemetry transmission and command receiver failed. A week later VZ514 suffered a similar problem and was inadvertently destroyed by command, followed by a third similar incident involving WA775. In order to find a solution one of Llanbedr's U.16s (WH320) was returned to Flight Refuelling for investigation. The problem seemed to be associated with the missile tracking system and after modifications were made to WH320, and other U.16s, no further incidents were recorded.

In late-1960 Meteor U.16s began to supplement U.15s with 728B Flight. The Flight's first U.16, WF716, was taken on charge on 18 October 1960 when it landed at Hal Far, Malta but the first pilotless flight by a 728B Flight U.16 was not made until 11 October 1961, by WE932. However the U.16's naval career was cut short when 728B was disbanded on 2 December 1961.[28]

---

26 *Air Clues*, February 1978.
27 National Archives AIR27/10076

28 Since its formation 728B Flight had achieved 153 pilotless sorties flown (on Firefly U.9, Meteor U.15 & U.16 and Canberra U.10) in a total of 147.30 flying hours. However, against this must be added some 2,345 hours of test-flying and approximately 300 hours spent ferrying aircraft out from the UK. A total of 52 aircraft passed through the Flight.

Flight Testing D.16 WK800

When Meteor D.16 WK800 was loaned to Marshall of Cambridge Engineering Ltd for Radar Vector Miss Distance Indicator (RVMDI) modifications, company pilot F/Lt Tim Mason was the only pilot in the UK with relevant type experience. It therefore fell to him to undertake all of the test-flying. Nevertheless he needed to spend a brief period at Llanbedr for refresher-training on RAE's Meteor T.7.

Back at Cambridge, Tim Mason undertook two flight-test sorties aboard WK800 to prove that all was well with the aircraft. The flights included relighting of the engines and a spot of asymmetric flying at low speed and high power. Declared fully fit, the Meteor was then towed into Marshall's hangar for trial installation work, including ten additional radomes – two transmitters top and bottom of the centre fuselage and eight at the extremities – for the RVMDI, a TV camera in the nose, a datalink and, later, a TV Miss Distance Indicator.

Flying restarted in January 1987 with threshold speeds raised just in case the 5% of wing area lost to the wing-tip radomes reduced lift. Flights revealed no significant change to stalling speeds and the only noticeable effect reported by Mason was the severe turbulence and noise generated by the top nose radome. As a result it was decided to restrict flying to 400kts maximum. Rates of roll, stick force per g and critical speeds all proved satisfactory. All of the kit worked as planned and the trials team in their caravan received good close-up TV pictures of themselves from unnecessary, but enjoyable, low passes over the top!

Mason flew WK800 to RAE Farnborough for a brief series of ground tests using a dummy Rapier missile. A detachment to Llanbedr then followed where Mason conducted sixteen enjoyable but unremarkable test-flights. The real work took place back at Cambridge where a number of flights checked the accuracy of the test kits. That involved flying at 55ft along the two-mile length of RAE Bedford's runway – passing inches from a dummy missile mounted on a 55ft pole while the ground kinetheodolites measured precise separation. On board recorders also marked each metal drain cover as the aircraft passed over them. Further accurate flying and navigation was needed on a track between the former RAF airfields at Waterbeach and Ridgewell to assess recording instruments in the ground caravan. After landing Mason was told that he had crossed the track numerous times but had remained within 200yds of it!

For a while WK800 was grounded for fitting of wing-tip TV cameras and all remaining test-flying was carried out at Llanbedr, using the nearby Aberporth Range. One incident almost threatened the entire trial.

At the end of a sortie and after the Range Controller reported no change in the favourable weather at Llanbedr, Mason decided to complete some optional test points, after which he planned to make a smart visual landing back at Llanbedr. With minimum fuel remaining Mason called the airfield but was horrified to learn that the cloud base was by then just 200-300ft and reducing. Mason debated whether to close down one engine to save fuel but the short distance to Llanbedr made this a marginal benefit in spite of the lengthy radar circuit. The Llanbedr controller provided Mason with an immaculate Ground Controlled Approach (GCA) talk-down and Mason picked out the runway lights at half-a-mile out and landed safely, albeit with fuel tanks virtually empty.

Mason's involvement ended with the last of his RVMDI-related flights at Llanbedr in July 1988.

Meteor U.17, U.18 & U.19

The continuous availability of redundant Meteor F.8s meant that the U.16 programme was never under any threat. However, not all of those Meteors in storage were found to be suitable candidates. In August 1961 a team of engineers from Flight Refuelling inspected no less than 52 redundant Meteor F.8s then in storage at 33 MU Lyneham. Quite a few were ruled out at first glance for a variety of reasons, eg VZ477 had a non-standard flight-refuelling probe and system fitted whilst WK738 turned out not to have an original rear fuselage. Others were rejected for a variety of reasons. On the other hand, the Meteor drone conversion programme was, at one stage, not just restricted to F.4s and F.8s. By April 1956 there was intent to develop further Marks of pilotless Meteors as U Marks 17, 18 and 19. Issued in April 1957, Specification D.187D&P called for the conversion of Meteor NF.11s into what was to be officially designated the Meteor U.17 drone. Hawker Siddeley's de Havilland Division was appointed prime contractor but in the end the programme was abandoned as were similar plans to convert NF.12s and NF.14s into Meteor U.18s and U.19s.

Meteor U.21 & U.21A

The Meteor U.21 and U.21A variants were produced specifically to operate as targets over the Australian Woomera Range and as such had equipment fits that differentiated them from the Aberporth Range-specific U.16s. Although not publicly announced until March 1961, the U.21 programme began in early-1960 when Flight Refuelling Ltd modified two U.16s and shipped them to Melbourne. The two aircraft, WK797 and WE960 were crated and shipped separately (departing Tarrant Rushton by road on 5 April 1960 and 26 May 1960 respectively). Both aircraft were consigned to The Fairey Aviation Company of Australasia's facility at Bankstown, Sydney although there is some doubt as to whether both actually arrived there initially. It seems that WK797 was re-assembled at AD Laverton and then flown direct to Edinburgh Field where it was held by Maintenance Squadron until 21 April 1961 when released to 1ATU for flight trials. Conversely WE960 *was* conveyed to FAC at Bankstown on 6 July 1960 for re-assembly. It is possible that WE960 was converted to U.21 standard immediately after arrival in Australia – or equally possible that it had been converted to U.21 by Flight Refuelling before departing the UK. Certainly this was not so for WK797 which was later upgraded to U.21 standard by FAC using a kit supplied by Flight Refuelling and subsequently test-flown before being ferried to where Fairey's Special Projects Division completed the equipment fits.

In the meantime Flight Refuelling began work on converting eight Meteor F.8s, the first of which, WL136, made its initial post-conversion (manned) flight at Tarrant Rushton on 31 May 1961, a full year after WK797 and WE960 had been despatched to Australia. Although converted in the first instance to a basic U.16, WL136 was, in fact, upgraded to U.21 standard at Tarrant Rushton and indeed may well have been fully upgraded before it made its initial flight. This is borne out by the fact that it departed Tarrant Rushton in crates just one week afterwards en route to Australia.[29] The remaining seven Meteors were simply converted to U.16 standard by Flight Refuelling and then shipped out (as U.16s) for Fairey Aviation Company to modify them to U.21 using kits supplied by Flight Refuelling. The last of the eight U.16s for Australia (VZ455) left Tarrant Rushton in crates in January 1962.[30]

The first unmanned Meteor U.21 sortie at Woomera Range took place on 11 December 1962, the aircraft involved being WK797.

Concurrent with the U.21 programme, the Fairey Aviation Company of Australasia was awarded a contract to convert surplus RAAF Meteor F.8s for Woomera Range duties. The first batch involved ten F.8s that were officially purchased by WRE (ex-RAAF) on 17 October 1960. They involved A77-422, A77-510, A77-802, A77-851, A77-855, A77-863, A77-872, A77-876, A77-882, A77-884 and A77-885. One further example was purchased by WRE on 21 December 1960 (A77-873). All were converted to drone configuration at Fairey's Bankstown facility using kits supplied by Flight Refuelling but to differentiate them from the ex-UK aircraft the former RAAF examples were designated U.21A. After basic conversion was completed at Bankstown they were ferried to Edinburgh Field for the final installation of control and engagement equipment.

The initial U.21A conversion (A77-884) was first flown on 1 November 1961 but it was not until 19 February 1963 that the first U.21A unmanned sortie over Woomera Range took place. Ironically, on that occasion the aircraft (A77-855) suffered a control malfunction and crashed before any missile interception could be made.[31]

1963 saw the final retirement of the Meteor F.8 in RAAF service when the last three aircraft serving with 38 Squadron Communications Flight at RAAF Richmond were withdrawn from service. All three (A77-157, A77-193 and

---

29 WE960 and WK797 (plus a further eight 'production' U.21s) were shipped out in an overall grey primer scheme and repainted in the special Woomera scheme after arrival.
30 The U.16/U.21 programme for Australia can be summarized by referring to the Contract details. WK797 and WE960 were both originally converted to U.16s against Contract KD/N/04/CB7(c), a contract that covered large-scale U.16 production for UK usage. Both aircraft were then allocated to the packing company, R & J Park Ltd, against Contract KK/F/067/CB7(c) for shipment to Australia. The eight production U.21s were originally converted to U.16 against Contract KK/F/097/CB24(a). No other U.16s appear to have been placed against this Contract. All eight aircraft appear to have been shipped to Australia against the same contract of KK/F/0150/CB24(a).
31 It would not be unfair to record that information on Australian U.16 & U.21 operations are fairly scant in many respects and often condractictory. As for the U.21A programme, the RAAF Status Cards did not always record the RAF/RAAF serial tie-up. Trevor E. Stone, who researched the Australian Meteor drones in 1981 (for Military Aviation Review) managed at the time to confirm most of the identities but was only able to conclude that A77-157, 207, 422 and 510 were formally WE889, WE905, WF750 and WH251 – although not necessarily in that order. It is unsure whether subsequently published details draw upon newly-researched confirmatory material or has simply converted Stone's conclusion as "fact".

In addition, considerable variances in dates and details occur when comparing RAF Movement Cards (Form AM78s) with Ministry of Supply/Aviation records and also with Flight Refuelling's records. In assembling individual aircraft movements the author has increasingly relied upon MoS/MoA records and Tarrant Rushton Tower Movement Logs.

A77-207) were sold to WRE for drone conversion on 15 February 1963. This brought total U.21A production to 15 aircraft.

In the meantime the stock of U.15s available for drone duty at Woomera had dwindled considerably during 1962/63, so much so that the final U.15 pilotless sortie was completed on 15 November 1963. From then onwards all pilotless Meteor sortie requirements were met by U.21s or U.21As.

Considering the growing shortage of Meteor drones it seems odd that, in May 1969, Flight Refuelling was put on notice to receive two ex-Australia sourced Meteors and U.21 WL136 and U.21A A77-876 were duly sent back to the UK. Quite why these two aircraft were shipped back is unclear but both were converted to U.16 standard and later delivered to Llanbedr. A77-876 reverted to its original identity, WK800.

Just three years later, by which time the WRE stock of U.21/U.21A had been fully expended, an urgent need for more drone Meteors was met by Flight Refuelling modifying two former Llanbedr U.16s (VZ554 & WF685) to Australian requirements and shipping them out in 1973.[32] There is no available evidence to suggest that these two aircraft were re-designated U.21 but to be compatible with the Woomera Range equipment the work carried out by Flight Refuelling must have put them into a very similar state. These two aircraft were the last pilotless Meteors to be operated in Australia.[33]

Throughout their operational use at Woomera, Meteor drones (including the later U.21 & U.21A) made 477 pilotless sorties. Most of those aircraft shot down over the Range had been destroyed by Bloodhound and Thunderbird missiles while to a lesser extent Seaslug and Firestreak trials accounted for others. Towards the end of 1968 and throughout 1969 a series of Rapier trials took place at Woomera Range and which accounted for the loss of a number of U.21s and U.21As. In 1972 21 Joint Services Trials Unit returned to Australia to conduct a series of Rapier trials in tropical conditions at Darwin.[34]

In the course of these trials one Meteor U.21 was destroyed (thought to be WF659). In February 1973 another Trials Unit (23 JSTU) was assembled at Woomera to test the Rapier/Blindfire system. This trial involved Meteors as unmanned targets, these undoubtedly being the modified U.16s VZ554 and WF685. It was one of these two that conducted the last Meteor drone flight in Australia in June 1974.[35] The final tally showed that a total of 59 Meteors had been destroyed in flight by various missiles and another 22 had crashed through malfunctions. By 1975 the Evett's Field service (which, of course, also involved Jindivik target drones) was wound down and disbanded.[36]

The final chapter on drone Meteor operations began in 1983 with an attempt to produce a non-optical system that would provide the same standard and detail of information as provided by the Ampor Cameras. Meteor U.16 WK800 – by now re-designated D.16 – was allocated to Marshall of Cambridge Engineering Ltd and modified to carry a Radar Vector Miss-Distance-Indicator (RVMDI) designed by Cambridge Consultants Ltd. Initial flight-tests were carried out from Cambridge until transferred to Llanbedr where WK800 made its first post-mods pilotless flight from there on 7 December 1988. This marked the first unmanned Meteor sortie for some seven years.

In the meantime Llanbedr's other U.16, WH453, was finally taken off the Llanbedr flying roster on 10 October 1990. Almost 14 years earlier WH453 had the distinction of making the last Meteor flight out of Tarrant Rushton. Grounded at Llanbedr WH453 ended its days as a static engine test-bed and a source of spares for the much-travelled WK800.

Meteor Drone Colour Schemes

The prototype U.15 (RA421) and a number of early production conversions were initially finished in an overall silver scheme; almost the only distinguishing features between these and standard F.4 variants was a small black

---

32 There is much contradiction over published accounts of the U.21 programme. WL136 is often referred to as the first U.21 conversion and which is known to have made its initial post-conversion flight at Tarrant Rushton on 31 May 1961. Yet by then two aircraft allocated to the U.21 programme (WK797 and WE960) had already been shipped out to Australia. WE960 was received by Fairey Aviation on 6 July 1960 and re-assembled. The RAAF aircraft logbook describes WE960 as 'U Mark 21 (Prototype)' from the outset. However, it is also possible that, bearing in mind these two aircraft were converted to U.16 against a separate contract and even shipped out against a different contract, they were initially converted to U.16 but with variations to make them suitable for conditions at Woomera but not brought up to full U.21 status until after arrival in Australia. That would explain the announcement that delivery of eight "Mark 16s for 21s" did not commence until a full year later.
33 A candidate customer for the two U.16s is 23 JSTU which had arrived at Woomera by February 1973 for a series of Rapier trials which lasted until early 1975. It should also be noted that Flight Refuelling referred to two 'hybrid' U.16s being converted to U.16As. Whilst this is probably an unofficial designation – and perhaps even an in-house FRL creation – the only two 'hybrid' U.16s were VZ554 and WF685. Both these aircraft were shipped to Australia in their UK designate colour scheme of red and yellow.
34 21 JSTU initially arrived at Woomera in mid-1967, followed by Rapier equipment in October 1967. According to Peter Morton ("Fire Across the Desert") "21 JSTU was a diverse team of 70 servicemen from various Army regiments, the RAF Regiment and the Australian Army Guided Weapons Trials Unit. The trials began in December 1967". When the trials were completed in 1969 21 JSTU transferred to Singapore where a series of Rapier proving trials took place in a humid tropical climate. The return of 21 JSTU in January 1972 was a short trials programme called 'Advocate' but was described as more of a sales pitch to the Australian Forces who were considering purchasing Rapier". Morton also records that "two Rushton towed-targets and a Meteor were destroyed in seven successful launches, with only one failure". In 1976, Australia signed a contract with BAC for the supply of Rapier missiles.
35 Although Rapier was initially successful it suffered a handicap in that its optical system needed good weather to function. BAC, having designed its radar-tracked PT428 system later joined up with Marconi Space and Defence Systems to produce a new ancillary radar, known initially as DN181 and later as Blindfire. 34 Rapiers were fired during the evaluation trial of which 26 were deemed successful, either by direct hits, near misses or deliberate 'turn-aways'.
36 This coincided with the end of Meteor operations at WRE. During the mid-1970s two Meteor TT.20s (WD646 & WD767) were operated by Short Bros & Harland on behalf of WRE to present towed targets for Seawolf, Rapier and Blowpipe missiles. Both aircraft were later donated to Australian museums in July 1975, as had been the WRE Meteor T.7 WA680 in January 1975.

An extremely eye-pleasing view of 728B Flight Meteor U.15 VT104/656 during a sortie from Hal Far. (Lt David A. Prothero RN)

radome on top of the fuselage, some distance behind the cockpit, and wingtip-mounted camera pods.

One Meteor U.15 (RA479) had black and white horizontal stripes applied along the fuselage and fin for camera calibration tests.

Subsequently production aircraft were repainted in an overall signal red colour scheme with rescue yellow topsides. Those aircraft operated in Australia had a standard scheme of white overall with red applied to the nose, the forward engine nacelles, outer wing upper and rear fuselage side surfaces although in practice there were many variations of this.

728B Flight Meteor Code Sequence

Meteor U.15s and U.16s were allocated individual codes within the sequence '655' to '659'. Known examples are:

'655'	VT291	U.15	Jan 1961 – Oct 1961
	WK870	U.16	Nov 1960 – Nov 1961
'656'	VT104	U.15	Sep 1959 – Mar 1960
	WE932	U.16	Mar 1961 – Nov 1961
'657'	VT310	U.15	Dec 1959 – May 1960
	VT107	U.15	Sep 1960 – Oct 1961
'658'	RA375	U.15	Apr 1960 – May 1960
	RA387	U.15	May 1960 – Aug 1960
	WF716	U.16	Oct 1960 – Nov 1961

Several 728B Flight Meteor U.15s inherited from RAE Llanbedr retained their Llanbedr code letters.

Meteor U.15 – Individual Service Histories

(Note that histories only relate to the period as a U.15 variant. Details of former service life as a standard F.4 variant are excluded.)

Official dates of allocations are as recorded by MoD and MoS but which are frequently at odds with actual movements as recorded in the Tarrant Rushton control tower logs. However, the last-mentioned has been used as the primary source for transfers.

The following details relate only to those U.15 aircraft that were operated by wholly British units. Aircraft operated by the WRE/RAAF at Woomera, Australia are listed later.

Note that five Meteors (RA387, VT268, VW258, VW276 and VZ417) in long-term storage at 12 MU Kirkbride were flown back to Tarrant Rushton for continued storage against Contract KK/F/058/CB.24(b), probably because Kirkbride was closing down.

RA373 Transferred to MoS charge 27.3.56 ex-storage at 8 MU. Ferried Little Rissington-Tarrant Rushton 25.10.56 but flown to 12 MU Kirkbride 4.4.57 for storage. Flown back to Tarrant Rushton 7.1.58 for conversion to U.15 against Contract 6/Acft/15570/CB.24(b). (TFH 620.33). Del to Llanbedr 10.3.59 and coded 'X'. First drone sortie 22.4.59. Crashed into the sea following a missile strike 4.5.59. SOC 30.9.59. (TFH 1.57 pilotless)

RA375 Transferred to MoS charge 28.3.56 ex-storage at 38 MU. Ferried Llandow-Tarrant Rushton 25.6.56 (TFH 883.50) but flown to 12 MU Kirkbride 28.3.57 for storage. Re-del to Tarrant Rushton 7.11.57 for conversion to U.15 against Contract 6/Acft/15570/CB.24(b). (TFH 888.00). Del to Llanbedr 22.4.58 and coded 'F'. To FRL 9.1.59 for mods (TFH 989.30) against Contract 6/Acft/10925/CB.24(b)), returning to Llanbedr 28.4.59. First drone sortie 8.7.59. Damaged in crash 30.9.59; ret to FRL for repair. Issued on loan to 728B Flight; Dptd Llanbedr 21.3.60 as "NAVAIR375" to Hal Far. Arrived Hal Far 22.3.60 and coded '658'. Ferried Hal Far-Llanbedr 13.4.60 (replaced by VT243, ex-Tarrant Rushton). Written-off 6.5.60 when inadvertently received self-destruct command from ground controller, causing it to crash into the sea whilst on approach to Llanbedr. The aircraft was undergoing an XTV trial at the time and on its 13th pilotless flight.

RA387 Transferred to MoS charge 28.3.56 ex-storage at 38 MU. Ferried Llandow-Tarrant Rushton 16.11.56. Dptd to 12 MU Kirkbride 25.7.57 for storage. Flown back to Tarrant Rushton 2.6.59 for continued storage. (TFH 1207.20). To U.15

118   Sitting Ducks and Peeping Toms

against Contract 6/Acft/15570/CB.24(b). Del ex T. Rushton 3.5.60 to 728B Flight via Yeovilton. Arrived Hal Far 9.5.60; coded '658'. Allocated to RAE Llanbedr 14.4.60 but returned to 728B Flight 3.5.60 (still as '658'). Written-off 9.8.60 when it ditched into the sea after losing control at 10,000', having earlier survived a near miss by a Seaslug missile at 31,500'.

RA397 Transferred to MoS charge 28.3.56 ex-storage at 8 MU. Ferried Little Rissington-Tarrant Rushton 14.9.56 but flown to 12 MU Kirkbride 4.4.57 for storage. Flown back to Tarrant Rushton 7.1.58 for conversion to U.15 against Contract 6/Acft/15570/CB.24(b). (TFH 650.21). Del to Llanbedr 10.2.59 and coded 'O'. First drone sortie 16.3.59. Destroyed by command 28.7.59 after becoming unstable in flight during a Seaslug missile trial and on its 5th pilotless sortie. (TFH (pilotless) 3:02)

RA415 Transferred to MoS charge 28.3.56 ex-storage at 33 MU. Ferried Lyneham-Tarrant Rushton 16.7.56. (TFH 379.32). Dptd 28.3.57 to 12 MU Kirkbride for storage. Flown back to FRL Tarrant Rushton 7.11.57 for conversion to U.15 against Contract 6/Acft/15570/CB.24(b). Del to Llanbedr 22.4.58 and coded 'L'.

Crashed 5.9.58 after a suspected roll unit failure whilst on a piloted flight. The aircraft yawed during a radio-controlled landing (due to malfunctioning roll unit) when the wing struck the top of a hangar before hitting the ground. The pilot was seriously injured. This aircraft had not made any pilotless flights since conversion to U.15. SOC 8.10.58.

Meteor U.15 RA415/L was the subject of a rather spectacular accident at Llanbedr on 5 September 1958. RAE pilot F/O Frank Johnson was carrying out an air-test which included a number of approaches controlled from Llanbedr's ground control station. On one approach the autopilot aileron control "ran away" causing the Meteor to yaw seriously before putting it into a roll motion. The aircraft was only at 100ft (30m) at the time and by the time that Frank Johnson had disconnected the autopilot the Meteor's wing struck the roof of Llanbedr's main hangar, leaving a lengthy scar as it did so. It then hit the ground and slid into another hangar where it finally came to rest. Despite sustaining serious injuries F/O Johnson survived the accident and later returned to flying duties on 11 April 1960, eventually becoming a First Officer with Cambrian Airways on Viscounts and BAC-111s. Meteor RA415 was considered a write-off and was later struck off charge. (Photographs and log-book kindly loaned by Eve Johnson.)

Post-War Drone Conversions

RA420 Allocated to Flight Refuelling 20./.54 for conversion to U.15, ex-storage at 33 MU. Conveyed Lyneham-Tarrant Rushton by road 23.7.54. (TFH 309.45). Reported del to Llanbedr 19.9.57 or 29.7.60 and coded 'T'. First pilotless sortie 24.3.61; final flight 19.2.62. Used primarily as a development aircraft. (TFH (pilotless) 1:14)

RA432 Transferred to MoS charge 27 or 28.3.56 whilst in storage at 12 MU. Ferried Kirkbride-Tarrant Rushton 17.12.57 for conversion to U.15 against Contract 6/Acft/15570/CB.24(b). (TFH 719.49). Dptd to Llanbedr 23.6.58 and coded 'T'. First pilotless sortie 17.7.58. Returned to FRL for mods 29.5.59 (TFH 842.15) against Contract 6/Acft/10925/CB.24(b)); re-del to Llanbedr 30.7.59. Written-off 25.4.60. (TFH (pilotless) 10:06)

RA439 Transferred to MoS charge 27 or 28.3.56 whilst in storage at 12 MU. Ferried Kirkbride-Tarrant Rushton 10.7.56 but returned to 12 MU 4.4.57 for storage. Flown back to Tarrant Rushton 9.1.58 for conversion to U.15 against Contract 6/Acft/15570/CB.24(b). (TFH 867.54). Del to Llanbedr 3.7.58 and coded 'V'. Returned to FRL for mods 8.1.59 (TFH 903.05) against Contract 6/Acft/10925/CB.24(b)) until 4.5.59 when re-del to Llanbedr. First pilotless sortie 24.7.59. Written-off 9.12.59. SOC 12.1.60. (TFH (pilotless) 4:14)

RA442 Transferred to MoS charge 27.3.56, ex-storage at 38 MU. Ferried Llandow-Tarrant Rushton 1.7.56 but transferred to 12 MU Kirkbride 4.4.57. Flown back to Tarrant Rushton 9.1.58 for conversion to U.15 against Contract 6/Acft/15570/CB.24(b). (TFH 468.31). Del to Llanbedr 5.3.59 and coded 'J'. First pilotless sortie 14.4.59.

Crashed into the sea 23.4.59 in unestablished circumstances during a 'Yellow Temple' trial. RA442 was on its 2nd pilotless flight at the time. (TFH (pilotless) 0:55).

RA479 Transferred to RAE 2.7.54 (ex-storage at 38 MU) for drone aerial tests. To 20 MU 2.3.55. Ferried Aston Down-Tarrant Rushton 17.9.56 to join U.15 programme. (TFH 391.55). Del to Llanbedr 19.9.57. To FRL 10.6.58; Returned to Llanbedr 16.6.58. Coded 'E'. Returned to FRL 24.3.59 for mods; again ferried Llanbedr-Tarrant Rushton 20.11.59 for full conversion to U.15 against Contract 6/Acft/15570/CB.24(b). (TFH 596.15). Allocated to 728B Flight 24.5.60 but allotment cancelled and flown to Llanbedr 21.6.60. Used as a development aircraft. First pilotless sortie 29.6.60. Written-off 30.6.60. SOC 11.7.60. (TFH (pilotless) 1:52).

VT104 Transferred to MoS charge 7.1.55 ex-storage at 38 MU. Ferried Llandow-Tarrant Rushton 8.7.55 to join the U.15 programme. (TFH 728.45) To Shorts, Belfast 23.1.57 for storage. Ferried Belfast-Tarrant Rushton 4.11.58 for conversion against Contract 6/Acft/15570/CB.24(b). (TFH 731.50). Del to Llanbedr 19.8.59 but not coded. Allocated to 728B Flight 9.9.59; arrived Hal Far 10.9.59 (via Châteauroux, Orange, Pisa, Rome) and coded '656'. Written-off 29.3.60 when hit by non-warhead Seaslug missile SD12 off Malta. SOC 29.6.60.

VT107 Transferred to MoS charge 25.3.56, ex-storage at 38 MU. Ferried Llandow-Tarrant Rushton 30.7.56 for conversion to U.15 against Contract 10925. (TFH 775.05). Allocated to the Royal Navy 22.9.60 for 728B Flight; arrived Hal Far 30.9.60 and coded '657'. Port mainplane found severely damaged by missile strike 17.1.61. Port mainplane replaced and flown to UK. Dptd Hal Far to FRL, Tarrant Rushton 10.3.61 for camera alignment. To Yeovilton 27.4.61 and possibly returned to Hal Far. Shot down by a missile off Malta 4.10.61. SOC 11.10.61.

VT110 Transferred to MoS charge 7.1.55, ex-storage at 33 MU. Ferried Lyneham-Tarrant Rushton 2.5.55 for conversion to (interim) drone standard. (TFH 644.05). Transferred to Contract 13737 15.10.56. To Llanbedr 24.1.57 for trials; returned to FRL for mods 20.2.57. Del to Llanbedr 1.4.57 for further trials; returned to FRL 29.4.57 for mods. To Short Bros & Harland 26.9.57 for trials; to FRL 6.11.57 for mods; to S & H 13.1.58 for trials; to FRL 1.4.58 for Tls; to S & H 4.6.58 for radar trials; ferried Llanbedr-Tarrant Rushton 11.9.58 for bringing up to full U.15 standard against Contract 6/Acft/15570/CB.24(b). (TFH 705.35). Del to S & H, Llanbedr 17.6.59 for FAA pilot-training and onward ferry to 728B Flight. Dptd Llanbedr 8.7.59 as "NAVAIR 55" to Yeovilton; arrived Hal Far 10.7.59 (via Châteauroux, Orange, Pisa, Pratica di Mare) and coded '655'. Shot down off Malta 11.5.60. SOC 29.6.62.

VT135 Transferred to MoS charge 7.1.55 ex-storage at 38 MU. Ferried Llandow-Tarrant Rushton 26.3.56 for conversion to U.15. (TFH 688.15). Del to Llanbedr 26.9.58 and coded 'L'. First pilotless sortie 18.12.58 but crashed 1½ miles off Harlech beach after 37 minutes, towards the end of a Seaslug missile trial flight. SOC 30.12.58

VT196 Arrived at Tarrant Rushton by road 25.9.56 (ex Div of Mech Engineering, Ottawa (National Research Council)) for conversion to U.15. (TFH 384.55). Allocated to Short & Harland same date for tests of ground control. Del to Llanbedr 27.2.59 and coded 'U'. First pilotless sortie 15.11.62. Fitted with a Jindivik autopilot, it was used as a telemetry development aircraft until written-off 9.2.63. (TFH (pilotless) 1:11). *(Note that the flight on 9.2.63 marked the occasion of the final U.15 flight.)*

VT243 Ferried 12 MU Kirkbride-Tarrant Rushton 25.7.56 to join U.15 programme against Contract 10925. (TFH 978.50). Del to 12 MU 18.6.57 for storage. Flown back to Tarrant Rushton 28.5.59 and converted to U.15 against Contract 6/Acft/15570/CB.24(b). Dptd Tarrant Rushton 21.4.60 for ferry to 728B Flight (arrived Hal Far 22.4.60). Shot down off Malta 14.12.60.

VT268 Transferred to MoS charge 27.2.56 ex-storage at 38 MU. Ferried Llandow-Tarrant Rushton 8.10.56 to join U.15 programme. (TFH 339.25). To 12 MU 24.4.57 for storage. Flown back to Tarrant Rushton 29.6.59 for continued storage. Converted to U.15 against Contract 6/Acft/15570/CB.24(b). Dptd 13.7.60, arrived Hal Far same date. Allocated to 728B Flight 14.9.60. Shot down off Malta 7.3.61. SOC 29.3.61.

VT282 Transferred to MoS charge 27.3.56 ex-storage at 32 MU. Ferried Kirkbride-Tarrant Rushton 14.9.56 for conversion to U.15. (TFH 441.55). Dptd to 12 MU 28.3.57; ferried Kirkbride-Tarrant Rushton 17.12.57. To U.15 against Contract 6/Acft/15570/CB.24(b). Del to Llanbedr 1.5.58 and coded 'Z'. To FRL 13.1.59 for mods (TFH 556.05) against Contract 6/Acft/10925/CB.24(b)); Returned to Llanbedr 28.4.59. To 728B Flight. First pilotless sortie 25.7.60. Shot down off Malta 8.9.60. SOC 13.9.60. (TFH (pilotless) 6.59)

VT291 Transferred to MoS charge 28.3.56 ex-storage at 38 MU. Del to Flight Refuelling 25.6.56 for conversion to U.15. Del to Llanbedr 20.4.59 and coded 'S'. Overshot roller landing at Llanbedr 30.4.59. ROS. To FRL for mods 11.10.59; Returned to S&H 20.11.59. Allocated to 728B Flight 10.1.61; arrived Hal Far 13.1.61. Shot down off Malta 5.10.61. SOC 11.10.61.

VT310 Transferred to MoS charge 27.3.56 ex-storage at 12 MU. Ferried Kirkbride-Tarrant Rushton 14.9.56 to join U.15 programme. (TFH 796.50). To 12 MU

Meteor U.15 VT310/657 of 728B Flight is seen flying unmanned over the Mediterranean. It was eventually shot down by a Seaslug missile (Lt David A. Prothero RN)

for storage 28.5.57; flown back to Tarrant Rushton 14.5.59. To U.15 against Contract 6/Acft/15570/CB.24(b). Dptd to Llanbedr 2.11.59 but not coded. Dptd Llanbedr 17.12.59 as 'NAVAIR657' to Yeovilton. Arrived Hal Far 20.12.59 for 728B Flight and coded '657'. Shot down off Malta 12.5.60 by Seaslug missile SD15 from HMS *Girdle Ness*. Drone hit at 15,000 yds (13,716m) at 32,000ft (9,754m).

VT332 Transferred to MoS charge 27.3.56 ex-storage at 12 MU. Ferried Kirkbride-Tarrant Rushton 14.9.56 to join U.15 programme. (TFH 738.55). Dptd to 12 MU 24.4.57; flown back to Tarrant Rushton 28.5.59. To U.15 against Contract 6/Acft/15570/CB.24(b). Del to Llanbedr 4.2.60 and coded 'X'. First pilotless sortie 15.3.60. Written-off 16.3.60 when it crashed into the sea on a low-level sortie caused by a loss of radio communications during a "Yellow Temple" trial flight. VT332 was on its 2nd pilotless flight at the time. SOC 24.3.60. (TFH (pilotless) 0:47)

VT338 Transferred to MoS charge 27.3.56 ex-storage at 38 MU. Ferried Llandow-Tarrant Rushton 30.8.56 for conversion to U.15. (TFH 514.00). Del to Llanbedr 9.12.58 and coded 'B'. First pilotless sortie 15.1.59. Destroyed by command 22.7.59 after it stopped responding to signals to turn. This was during a Bloodhound missile trial and on its 6th pilotless flight. (TFH (pilotless) 3:59)

VW258 Transferred to MoS charge 27.3.56 ex-storage at 38 MU. Ferried Llandow-Tarrant Rushton 8.10.56 to join U.15 programme. (TFH 734.15). Ferried to 12 MU 21.5.57 (F/O F Johnson) for storage; flown back to Tarrant Rushton 15.6.59 for continued storage. Converted to U.15 against Contract 6/Acft/15570/CB.24(b). Ferried Tarrant Rushton-Llanbedr 15.8.60 (F/O F Johnson) and coded 'J'. First pilotless sortie 31.8.60; last sortie at Llanbedr 3.10.60. (4:15 pilotless hours at Llanbedr). Transferred to 728B Flight 10.10.60 and arrived at Hal Far 19.10.60. Shot down off Malta 14.12.60.

VW276 Transferred to MoS charge 27.3.56 ex-storage at 38 MU. Del to Flight Refuelling 8.10.56 to join U.15 programme. (TFH 909.25) To 12 MU 28.5.57; flown back to Tarrant Rushton 29.6.59 for continued storage. To U.15 against Contract 6/Acft/15570/CB.24(b). Del to Llanbedr 8.6.60 and coded 'T'. First pilotless sortie 20.6.60. Written-off during a Firestreak missile trial flight 20.7.60 after control was lost due to a fault with the range controller. The aircraft was on its 12th pilotless sortie and spiralled into the sea off Aberporth. (TFH (pilotless) 8.16).

VW280 Transferred to MoS charge 7.1.55 ex-storage at 12 MU. Ferried Kirkbride-Tarrant Rushton 4.8.55 for

Meteor U.15 VZ415/A made its first pilotless sortie on 28 July 1959 and served at Llanbedr until May 1960 when it sustained Cat.4 damage in a landing accident. In this view, the pilot is seen disembarking after taxying out to the runway for lining-up before launching on a pilotless sortie. By this time '415 had successfully completed 28 pilotless sorties out of Llanbedr, each sortie being recorded with a 'broomstick' logo beneath the cockpit area. (Short Bros & Harland Negs J.8.6949K and J.8.6950M)

Post-War Drone Conversions   121

conversion to U.15. (TFH 909.25). Originally destined for delivery to Australia but damaged when it caught fire whilst being dismantled at Tarrant Rushton 25.10.56. Repaired on site. Conv. to U.15 and del to Llanbedr 31.12.58 (or 31.10.58) and coded 'P'. Used for development purposes. Sustained Cat.4 damage in a heavy landing at Llanbedr 9.4.59 whilst on its first pilotless sortie. To FRL 8.7.59 for repairs. Returned to S&H 25.4.60. Written-off 2.6.60. (TFH (pilotless) 10:00).

VW285 Transferred to MoS charge 27.3.56 ex-storage at 33 MU. Ferried Lyneham-Tarrant Rushton 16.7.56 for conversion to U.15. (TFH 675.55). Dptd to 12 MU 27.6.57 for storage; flown back to Tarrant Rushton 5.5.59. and converted to U.15 against Contract 6/Acft/15570/CB.24(b). Del to Llanbedr 10.9.59 and coded 'X'. First pilotless sortie 30.9.59. Written-off 16.12.59. (TFH (pilotless) 3:08).

VW293 Transferred to MoS charge 7.1.55 ex-storage at 38 MU. Ferried Llandow-Tarrant Rushton 23.3.56 for conversion to U.15. (TFH 504.05). Dptd to 12 MU 28.3.57 for storage. Ferried Kirkbride-Tarrant Rushton 17.12.57. To U.15 against Contract 6/Acft/15570/CB.24(b). Dptd to Llanbedr 16.6.58 and coded 'M'. First pilotless sortie 23.7.58. Ferried Llanbedr-Tarrant Rushton 29.5.59 for mods against Contract 15643; Returned to Llanbedr 30.7.59. Shot down 21.12.59 by a Firestreak from a 1GWDS Javelin FAW.7. (TFH (pilotless) 5:37).

VW299 Transferred to MoS charge 23.3.56 ex-storage at 12 MU. Ferried Kirkbride-Tarrant Rushton 3.8.56 to join U.15 programme. (TFH 683.35). Dptd to 12 MU 24.4.57 for storage; flown back to Tarrant Rushton 11.5.59 for conversion against Contract 6/Acft/15570/CB.24(b). Dptd to Llanbedr 22.9.59 and coded 'H'. First pilotless sortie 1.12.59. Written-off 7.4.60. (TFH (pilotless) 10:09).

VZ415 Transferred to MoS charge 7.1.55 ex-storage at 38 MU. Ferried Llandow-Tarrant Rushton 23.3.56 for conversion to U.15. (TFH 511.00). Dptd to 12 MU 4.4.57 for storage; flown back to Tarrant Rushton 31.12.57. To U.15 against Contract 6/Acft/15570/CB.24(b). Del to Llanbedr 20.7.59 and coded 'A'. First pilotless sortie 28.7.59. First sortie for Thunderbird 3.5.60. Crashed on landing at Llanbedr 18.5.60 in adverse weather conditions at the end of a Thunderbird trial and its 42nd pilotless sortie. To FRL for Cat.4 repairs 11.8.60. To 728B Flight 7.2.61 (arrived Hal Far 10.2.61). Shot down off Malta 30.10.61. (TFH (pilotless) 27.42).

VZ417 Flown Kirkbride-Tarrant Rushton 4.6.59 (ex-12 MU store) for conversion to U.15 against Contract 6/Acft/15570/CB.24(b). (TFH 963.40). Delivered Tarrant Rushton-Hal Far 25.5.60 for Flight. Shot down 24.8.60.

Meteor U.15 Drones to Australia

Note that, apart from the 30 above conversions, an additional 61 Meteor U.15 drones were converted by Flight Refuelling Ltd for shipment to Australia.

EE521 Ferried High Ercall-Tarrant Rushton 23.9.54 (ex-33 MU Store) for conversion to U.15 (TFH 661.15). Dptd Tarrant Rushton 3.1.56 to 47 MU Hawarden for packing and shipment to Australia. Taken onto charge 7.3.56. Crashed on take-off 8.9.58 following an autopilot failure at the start of an intended Thunderbird sortie over Woomera Range. SOC 22.10.58.

EE524 Del to Flight Refuelling 30.6.54 (ex-215 AFS, Finningley) for Cat.4 repairs (against Contract 9225) but transferred to the U.15 programme 5.7.54. (TFH 794.40) Dptd Tarrant Rushton 6.4.55 to 47 MU Hawarden for packing and shipment to Australia aboard SS *Lodestone*. Taken onto RAAF charge 18.7.55 at 1 Aircraft Depot, Laverton (or 30.8.55). Official records state that "on 16.12.57 to be used as a source of spares on completion of trials." Approved for Conversion to Components (ACTC) by RAAF 25.3.58; SOC by Air Ministry 31.1.59. *(There remains some uncertainty as to whether EE524 was actually converted to U.15 status.)*

RA367 Ferried Kirkbride-Tarrant Rushton 10.6.55 (ex-12 MU) for conversion to U.15. (TFH 265.25). Handed over to R & J Park Ltd (date unkn) for packing (against Contract 12932). Departed UK by ship to Australia 25.5.56. To Fairey Aviation 12.6.56. Taken onto RAAF charge 25.7.56; to 1 AD 8.7.57. To Edinburgh 26.3.58; later to 1 ATU (by 12.3.59). Undercarriage torn off during a heavy landing at Evett's Field 17.3.59 after a Bloodhound sortie. Not repaired and SOC 6.9.60.

RA371 Ferried High Ercall-Tarrant Rushton 7.7.55 (ex-29 MU) for conversion to U.15. (TFH 355.25). Dptd Tarrant Rushton 1.5.56 to 47 MU Hawarden for packing. Dptd UK by ship to Australia 1.5.56. To Fairey Aviation 17.9.56; Taken onto RAAF charge 19.9.56. To Edinburgh 8.6.59; to 1 ATU 12.5.60. Shot down at Woomera by a Seaslug missile 23.2.61. SOC 4.5.61.

RA398 Ferried Llandow-Tarrant Rushton 16.5.55 (ex-38 MU) for conversion to U.15. (TFH 961.25). Handed over to R & J Park Ltd 20.6.56 for packing (against Contract 12932). Shipped to Australia aboard SS *Moreton Bay*. Taken onto RAAF charge 7.9.56; to Fairey Aviation 17.5.57. To Edinburgh 26.8.59; to 1 ATU 12.5.60. Crashed 2.11.60 due to autopilot malfunction after 11 mins flight for a Thunderbird sortie. SOC 23.2.61.

RA417 Ferried to Tarrant Rushton 12.7.54 (ex-Gloster Aircraft Ltd) for conversion to U.15. (TFH 116.05). Dptd Tarrant Rushton 6.4.55 to 47 MU Hawarden for packing. Shipped to Australia aboard SS *Nordic* ex-Liverpool 23.6.55. Taken onto RAAF charge at 1AD 16.8.55; to ATU 29,3,56, Seriously damaged when the undercarriage collapsed on landing at Woomera 13.7.56. SOC by RAAF 25.2.58 (or 25.3.58); SOC by the Air Ministry 8.5.58.

RA421 Ferried Hurn-Tarrant Rushton 16.9.53 (ex-Portsmouth Aviation Ltd) for conversion to Prototype U.15 (TFH 202.25); f/f (manned) 21.10.54; first fully automatic take-off 11.3.55; first fully automatic landing -.4.55. Trials aircraft until handed over to R & J Park Ltd 7.9.56 (TFH 248.20) for packing; departed UK by ship 11.9.56 to Australia. Taken onto RAAF charge 22.11.56 at Fairey Aviation; to Edinburgh 21.12.59; 1 ATU 22.8.60. Destroyed by Bloodhound missile at Woomera 10.4.63. SOC 20.5.63.

RA430 Ferried Lyneham-Tarrant Rushton 13.9.54 (ex-33 MU) for conversion to U.15. (TFH 593.35). Departed Tarrant Rushton 9.11.55 to 47 MU for packing; dptd UK 9.12.55 aboard SS *Grel Marion* to Melbourne. Taken onto RAAF charge at 1 AD 6.3.56; air-tested at Laverton 2.7.56. Ferried Laverton-Edinburgh 19.7.56 for ATU. Broke-up during a crash-landing 4m NE of Evett's Field 22.7.58 as a result of losing azimuth control at the start of an intended Thunderbird sortie. SOC 20.8.58 or 10.10.58.

RA433 Ferried Little Rissington-Tarrant Rushton 4.7.55 (ex-8 MU) for conversion to U.15. (TFH 633.50). Handed over to R & J Park Ltd 6.7.56 for packing (against Contract 12932); dptd UK 26.7.56 aboard SS *Cymric*. Taken onto RAAF charge 13.9.56; to Fairey Aviation 11.5.57; to Edinburgh 17.12.58. Shot down by a Thunderbird missile over Woomera Range 17.6.59. SOC 2.7.59.

RA438 Conveyed by road Lyneham-Tarrant Rushton 20.7.54 (ex-33 MU) for conversion to U.15. (TFH 292.00). Dptd Tarrant Rushton 9.11.55 to 47 MU Hawarden for packing; dptd Liverpool docks 20.12.55 aboard SS *Theseus* to Melbourne. Taken onto RAAF charge at 1 AD 9.2.56; ferried Laverton-Edinburgh for 1 ATU 3.8.56. Port undercarriage leg collapsed on landing at Evett's Field 22.10.58 after a Bloodhound sortie. Repaired but later shot down on Woomera Range 2.7.59 by a Thunderbird missile. SOC 23.7.59.

RA441 Ferried Llandow-Tarrant Rushton 13.4.55 (ex-38 MU) for conversion to U.15. (TFH 445.50). Handed over to R & J Park Ltd 9.4.56 for packing (against Contract 12932); dptd UK 15.5.56 aboard SS *Perim*. Taken onto RAAF charge 28.6.56; to 1 AD 15.7.56. To Edinburgh 27.5.57; 1 ATU 24.5.58. Shot down by a Bloodhound missile at 15,000ft over Woomera Range 21.11.58. SOC 12.12.58.

RA454 Ferried Llandow-Tarrant Rushton 2.5.55 (ex-38 MU) for conversion to U.15. (TFH 805.43). Handed over to R & J Park Ltd 27.7.56 for packing (against Contract 12932). Shipped ex-UK 3.7.56 aboard SS *Chindwara*. To Fairey Aviation 25.6.56; taken onto RAAF charge 23.10.56; to Edinburgh 16.3.60; to 1 ATU 8.5.61. Rolled 2 mins after take-off from Evett's Field 13.4.62 and crashed into Lake Koolimilka (adjacent to Evett's Field). Cause: autopilot failure. SOC 22.5.62.

RA457 Ferried Little Rissington-Tarrant Rushton 6.10.54 (ex-8 MU) for conversion to U.15 (TFH 843.15). Dptd Tarrant Rushton 24.11.54 to 47 MU Hawarden for packing. To Liverpool docks 12.12.54 for shipment aboard SS *Chindwara*. Taken onto RAAF charge at 2 AD 4.2.55; ferried Laverton-Edinburgh 24.2.55; to ATU 7.3.55. SOC 25.2.58 for component recovery on 25.3.58.

RA473 Ferried Lyneham-Tarrant Rushton 13.4.55 (ex-33 MU) for conversion to U.15. (TFH 734.15). Dptd Tarrant Rushton 3.2.56 to 47 MU for packing; to Liverpool docks 19.3.56 for shipment aboard SS *Tasmania Star*. Taken onto RAAF charge at 1 AD 17.5.56; to Edinburgh 28.11.57 for 1 ATU. Damaged during Woomera Range sortie 3.12.58 (target for two Bloodhound missiles). Shot down by a Bloodhound missile at Woomera Range on 11.2.59. SOC 10.3.59.

VT105 Ferried Kirkbride-Tarrant Rushton 27.7.55 (ex-12 MU) for conversion to U.15. (TFH 1070.30). Handed over to R & J Park Ltd 28.3.56 for packing (against Contract 12932). Shipped ex-UK aboard SS *Flamenco*. Taken onto RAAF charge 18.5.56; to 1 AD 5.2.57; to Edinburgh 27.5.57. Shot down by a Seaslug missile at Woomera Range 24.3.59. SOC 16.4.59.

VT106 Ferried High Ercall-Tarrant Rushton 13.6.55 (ex-29 MU) for conversion to U.15. (TFH 329.40). Handed over to R & J Park Ltd 5.9.56 for packing (against Contract 12932). Dptd UK by ship 22.9.56. Taken onto RAAF charge 22.11.56 at Fairey Aviation; to Edinburgh 20.8.59 for 1 ATU. Shot down at Woomera 26.5.60 by a Thunderbird missile. SOC 27.6.60.

VT112 Ferried Llandow-Tarrant Rushton 6.7.55 (ex-38 MU) for conversion to U.15. (TFH 956.15). Handed over to R & J Park Ltd 21.11.56 for packing (against Contract 12932). Dptd UK 29.11.56 aboard SS *Patonga*. Taken onto RAAF charge 18.5.57; to Fairey Aviation 10.8.57; to Edinburgh 2.10.59 for 1 ATU. Shot down over Woomera Range by a Seaslug missile 7.9.61. SOC 8.10.61.

VT113 Ferried Kirkbride-Tarrant Rushton 10.6.55 (ex-12 MU) for conversion to U.15. (TFH 566.20). Handed over to R & J Park Ltd 10.12.56 for packing (against Contract 12932). Shipped ex-UK 19.12.56 aboard SS *Largs Bay*. Taken onto RAAF charge 19.4.57; to Fairey Aviation 13.8.57; to Edinburgh 1.12.59; to 1 ATU 3.5.61. Shot down by a Bloodhound 2 missile over Woomera Range 15.11.63. SOC 29.1.64. (This marked the last U.15 to be shot down).

VT118 Ferried Little Rissington-Tarrant Rushton 6.6.55 (ex-8 MU) for conversion to U.15. (TFH 590.50). Handed over to R & J Park Ltd 11.4.56 for packing (against Contract 12932). Shipped ex-UK 15.5.56 aboard SS *Perim*. To 1 AD 28.6.56; taken onto RAAF charge 22.2.57; to Edinburgh 27.5.57; to ATU 8.1.58. Shot down by a Thunderbird I missile at Woomera Range 19.9.58. SOC 22.10.58.

VT130 Ferried Kirkbride-Tarrant Rushton 13.6.55 (ex-12 MU) for conversion to U.15. (TFH 817.55). Handed over to R & J Park Ltd 1.5.56 for packing (against Contract 12932). Shipped ex-UK 25.5.56 aboard SS *Port Ourtis*. Taken onto RAAF charge 22.2.57; to Fairey Aviation 24.4.57; to Edinburgh 3.8.59; 1 ATU 12.5.60. Damaged in abortive take-off from Evett's Field 21.4.61 for an intended Seaslug trial. Next unmanned flight 5.12.62, and again on 6.12.62 & 19.2.63. Crashed on landing 5.3.63, believed in piloted mode as location reported as Woomera airfield. SOC 14.5.63.

VT139 Ferried High Ercall-Tarrant Rushton 27.6.55 (ex-29 MU) for conversion to U.15. (TFH 1199.05). Handed over to R & J Park Ltd 6.6.56 for packing (against Contract 12932). Shipped ex-UK 28.6.56 aboard SS *Nuddea*. Taken onto RAAF charge 3.9.56; to Fairey Aviation 11.10.56; to Edinburgh 22.1.59. Shot down by a Thunderbird I missile at Woomera Range 15.7.59. SOC 17.8.59!

VT142 Ferried Llandow-Tarrant Rushton 19.7.55 (ex-38 MU) for conversion to U.15. (TFH 2.04). Handed over to R & J Park Ltd 19.9.56 for packing (against Contract 12932). Shipped ex-UK 13.10.56 aboard SS *Tasmania Star*. Taken onto RAAF charge at Fairey Aviation 10.12.56; to Edinburgh 23.4.59. Shot down by a Bloodhound missile 35,000ft over Woomera Range 28.4.60; SOC 25.5.60.

VT168 Ferried Moreton Valence-Tarrant Rushton 15.10.54 (ex-repairs at Gloster Aircraft Ltd) for conversion to U.15 (TFH 890.45). Dptd Tarrant Rushton 6.12.54 to 47 MU Hawarden for packing. Shipped ex-UK 17.2.55 aboard SS *Huntsbrook*. Taken onto RAAF charge 3.5.55 at 1 AD; to ATU 18.8.55. ACTC 25.2.58; SOC 25.3.58.

VT175 Ferried Kirkbride-Tarrant Rushton 6.7.55 (ex-12 MU) for conversion to U.15. (TFH 440.51). Handed over to R & J Park Ltd 13.2.56 for packing (against Contract 12932) but possibly re-issued to 47 MU 15.2.56. Shipped ex-UK aboard SS *Tregenna*. Taken onto RAAF charge 9.5.56; to 1 AD 15.6.56 and test-flown after assembly at Laverton 26.7.56. To ATU 7.11.56. On 9.9.58 sustained direct hit on the port pod by a Thunderbird 1 missile on Woomera Range and crashed during the subsequent landing. SOC 22.10.58.

VT177 Ferried Llandow-Tarrant Rushton 5.5.55 (ex-38 MU) for conversion to U.15. (TFH 962.40). Handed over to R & J Park

Post-War Drone Conversions 123

Ltd 9.7.56 for packing (against Contract 12932). Shipped ex-UK 26.7.56 aboard SS *Cymric*. Taken onto RAAF charge 13.9.56; to Fairey Aviation 9.9.58; to Edinburgh 28.11.58 for 1 ATU. Shot down by a Seaslug missile at Woomera Range 26.6.59. SOC 15.7.59.

VT179 Ferried Llandow-Tarrant Rushton 29.6.55 (ex-38 MU) for conversion to U.15. (TFH 3.15). Handed over to R & J Park Ltd 12.8.56 for packing (against Contract 12932). Shipped ex-UK 2.8.56. Taken onto RAAF charge 8.11.56; to Fairey Aviation 12.11.56; to Edinburgh 18.9.58. Shot down by a Thunderbird missile 25.6.59. SOC 15.7.59.

VT184 Ferried Kirkbride-Tarrant Rushton 22.6.55 (ex-12 MU) for conversion to U.15. (TFH 964.50). Handed over to R & J Park Ltd 21.9.56 for packing (against Contract 12932). Shipped ex-UK 13.10.56 aboard SS *Tasmania Star*. Taken onto RAAF charge at Fairey Aviation 10.12.56; to Edinburgh 10.5.59. Shot down by a Thunderbird missile 17.7.59. SOC 17.8.59.

VT187 Ferried Llandow-Tarrant Rushton 14.9.54 (ex-38 MU) for conversion to U.15. (TFH 382.15). Departed Tarrant Rushton 6.9.55 to 47 MU Hawarden for packing and shipment to Melbourne. Dptd UK 4.10.55 aboard SS *Stirlingshire*. Taken onto RAAF charge 29.11.56 at 1 AD; to Edinburgh 28.3.56. Shot down by a Fireflash missile 7.5.57. SOC 21.1.58.

VT191 Ferried Lyneham-Tarrant Rushton 16.6.55 (ex-33 MU) for conversion to U.15. (TFH 742.35). Handed over to R & J Park Ltd 19.9.56 for packing (against Contract 12932). Shipped ex-UK aboard SS *Moreton Bay*. To Fairey Aviation 13.7.59; to Edinburgh 5.9.59; to 1 ATU 12.5.60. Shot down by a Thunderbird I missile over Woomera Range 17.5.60. SOC 27.6.60.

VT192 Ferried Kirkbride-Tarrant Rushton 16.5.55 (ex-12 MU) for conversion to U.15. (TFH 460.30). Departed Tarrant Rushton 19.6.56 to 47 MU Hawarden for packing and shipment. Departed UK 19.6.56 aboard SS *Southern Prince*. Taken onto RAAF charge at Fairey Aviation 6.11.56; to Edinburgh 3.3.60; to 1 ATU 18.5.61. Crashed 14.6.62 during a pilotless approach to Evett's Field) due to a control failure 32mins after take-off for an intended Thunderbird sortie. SOC 13.7.62.

VT197 Ferried Kirkbride-Tarrant Rushton 4.8.55 (ex-12 MU) for conversion to U.15. (TFH 728.35). dptd Tarrant Rushton 17.5.56 to 47 MU Hawarden for packing and shipment. Taken onto RAAF charge 8.10.56 at Fairey Aviation; to Edinburgh 23.4.59; to 1 ATU 12.5.60. Shot down by a Thunderbird missile 19.5.60. Also recorded as 'ACTC 27.6.60' and SOC same date.

VT219 Ferried Llandow-Tarrant Rushton 14.4.55 (ex-38 MU) for conversion to U.15. (TFH 546.05). Handed over to R & J Park Ltd 14.5.56 for packing (against Contract 12932). Shipped ex-UK 30.5.56 aboard SS *Wairangi*. Taken onto RAAF charge 27.7.56; to 1 AD 24.1.58; to Edinburgh 19.6.68 for 1 ATU. Presumed to have been hit during a Seaslug sortie 8.4.59 and declared 'missing'; last seen heading south-east over Woomera Range. SOC 21.4.59.

VT220 Ferried Kirkbride-Tarrant Rushton 4.7.55 (ex-12 MU) for conversion to U.15. (TFH 1047.10). Handed over to R & J Park Ltd 19.3.56 for packing (against Contract 12932). Shipped ex-UK 12.4.56 aboard SS *Flamenca*. Taken onto RAAF charge 18.5.56. To 1 AD 13.9.57; to Edinburgh 22.11.57. Shot down by a Bloodhound missile over Woomera Range 21.1.59. SOC 12.2.59.

VT222 Ferried Little Rissington-Tarrant Rushton 19.4.55 (ex-8 MU) for conversion to U.15. (TFH 375.50). Handed over to R & J Park Ltd 23.11.56 for packing (against Contract 12932). Shipped ex-UK 29.11.56 aboard SS *Patonga*. Taken onto RAAF charge 18.5.57. To Fairey Aviation 6.8.59; to Edinburgh 16.4.59; to 1 ATU 12.5.60. Shot down by a Bloodhound missile over Woomera Range 26.5.60. SOC 27.6.60.

VT226 Ferried Kirkbride-Tarrant Rushton 14.9.54 (ex-12 MU) for conversion to U.15. (TFH 560.50). Dptd Tarrant Rushton 10.10.55 to 47 MU Hawarden for packing and shipment. Departed UK 4.11.55 aboard SS *South Africa Star* to Melbourne. Taken onto RAAF charge 29.12.55 at 1 AD; to Edinburgh 13.8.56 for ATU. Shot down by a Bloodhound missile on Woomera Range 22.7.58 although also recorded as relegated to training duties by 19.6.58. SOC 10.10.58.

VT230 Ferried Kirkbride-Tarrant Rushton 6.7.55 (ex-12 MU) for conversion to U.15. (TFH 609.05). To 47 MU Hawarden 22.3.56 for packing and shipment. Dptd UK (date unkn) aboard SS *Trelyon*. Taken onto RAAF charge 26.6.56 at 1 AD; to Edinburgh 26.7.57. Shot down 27.11.58 by a Bloodhound missile at 35,000ft over Woomera Range. SOC 18.12.58.

VT256 Ferried Llandow-Tarrant Rushton 6.9.55 (ex-38 MU) for conversion to U.15. (TFH 1113.00). Dptd Tarrant Rushton 28.2.56 to 47 MU for packing (against Contract 12932). Dptd UK (date unkn) aboard SS *Trelyon*. Taken onto RAAF charge 26.6.56 at 1 AD 29.6.56; to Edinburgh 26.7.57; to ATU 6.3.58. Seriously damaged 8.10.58 after port tyre burst and starboard undercarriage collapsed on landing, presumably at Evett's Field, at the end of a Fireflash sortie. SOC 14.5.59.

VT259 Conveyed by road Boscombe Down-Tarrant Rushton 5.5.54 (ex-A&AEE) for conversion to U.15. (TFH 185.00). Dptd Tarrant Rushton 3.1.56 to 47 MU Hawarden for packing and shipment. Dptd UK 16.2.56 aboard SS *Clan MacDougall* to Mebourne. Taken onto RAAF charge 3.4.56 at 1 AD; to Edinburgh 25.2.58; 1 ATU 12.3.59. On 8.4.59 lost control in Evett's Field circuit and crashed. Relegated to ACTC 14.5.59. and SOC same date.

VT262 Ferried High Ercall-Tarrant Rushton 11.7.55 (ex-29 MU) for conversion to U.15. (TFH 310.20). Dptd Tarrant Rushton 3.2.56 to 47 MU Hawarden for packing and shipment. Dptd UK 4.4.56 aboard SS *Ajana* to Melbourne. Taken onto RAAF charge 30.5.56; to 1 AD 22.6.56; Edinburgh 26.2.58; 1 ATU 12.2.59. Shot down by a Bloodhound missile on Woomera Range 29.5.59. SOC 30.6.59.

VT270 Ferried Kirkbride-Tarrant Rushton 19.4.55 (ex-12 MU) for conversion to U.15. (TFH 369.15). Handed over to R & J Park Ltd 24.8.56 for packing (against Contract 12932). Shipped ex-UK 7.9.56 aboard SS *Dwelo*. Taken onto RAAF charge 8.11.56; to Fairey Aviation 12.11.56; to Edinburgh 23.7.58. Shot down by a Bloodhound missile at 35,000ft over Woomera Range 20.7.59. SOC 17.8.59.

VT286 Ferried Llandow-Tarrant Rushton 7.6.55 (ex-38 MU) for conversion to U.15. (TFH 915.05). Handed over to R & J Park Ltd 16.5.56 for packing (against Contract 12932). Shipped ex-UK 30.5.56 aboard SS *Wairangi*. Taken onto RAAF charge 27.7.56. To Fairey Aviation 9.10.57; to Edinburgh 26.3.59. Crashed 2 mins after pilotless take-off from Evett's Field 13.5.59 for an intended Thunderbird sortie. SOC 8.6.59.

VT289 Ferried Kirkbride-Tarrant Rushton 27.7.55 (ex-12 MU) for conversion to U.15. (TFH 799.00). To 47 MU Hawarden 6.3.56 for packing and shipment aboard SS *Trelyon*. Taken onto RAAF charge 26.6.56 at 1 AD; to Edinburgh 31.1.58; 1

ATU 12.3.59. Destroyed over Woomera Range 27.5.59 when hit by a Thunderbird missile. SOC 30.6.59.

VT294 Ferried Kirkbride-Tarrant Rushton 4.7.55 (ex-12 MU) for conversion to U.15. (TFH 433.20). Handed over to R & J Park Ltd (date unknown) for packing (against Contract 12932). Shipped ex-UK 12.12.56 aboard SS *Largs Bay*. Taken onto RAAF charge 19.4.57 and believed stored before being received by Fairey Aviation Co, Bankstown 4.11.59 for assembly. Allocated to Base Sqdn, Edinburgh 14.12.59 and ferried Bankstown-Richmond same date; ferried Richmond-Canberra-Laverton-Nhill-Edinburgh 8.2.60. Crashed during an intended Seaslug trial at Woomera Range 21.4.61 after control was lost at 22,000ft. and aircraft dived into the ground. SOC 28.6.61.

VT316 Ferried Llandow-Tarrant Rushton 13.4.55 (ex-38 MU) for conversion to U.15. (TFH 679.30). Dptd Tarrant Rushton 19.6.56 to 47 MU Hawarden for packing. Shipped ex-UK aboard SS *Limerick*. Taken onto RAAF charge 8.10.56 at Fairey Aviation; to Edinburgh 8.6.59. Lost control over Woomera Range 21.4.60 after 36 mins flight and 70 miles out; 'destroy' signal sent. SOC 20.5.60.

VT319 Ferried High Ercall-Tarrant Rushton 24.11.54 (ex-29 MU) for conversion to U.15. (TFH 954.45). Handed over to R & J Park Ltd 4.6.56 for packing (against Contract 12932). Shipped ex-UK 28.6.56 aboard SS *Nubbea*. Taken onto RAAF charge 3.9.56. To Fairey Aviation 11.10.56; to Edinburgh 6.2.59; 1 ATU 12.5.60. Shot down at Woomera Range 25.5.60 by one of two Thunderbird missiles fired. SOC 27.6.60.

VT329 Ferried Little Rissington-Tarrant Rushton 30.6.55 (ex-8 MU) for conversion to U.15. (TFH 322.40). Handed over to R & J Park Ltd 2.11.56 for packing (against Contract 12932). Shipped ex-UK 17.11.56 aboard SS *Perim*. Taken onto RAAF charge 14.1.57; to Fairey Aviation 22.1.57; to Edinburgh 14.8.59; 1 ATU 12.5.60. Hit and damaged over Woomera Range 20.5.60 but repaired. Shot down by a Seaslug missile at Woomera Range 2.5.61. SOC 17.5.61.

VT330 Ferried Llandow-Tarrant Rushton 20.7.55 (ex-38 MU) for conversion to U.15. (TFH 786.40). Handed over to R & J Park Ltd 10.2.56 for packing (against Contract 12932) and shipment to Australia. Taken onto RAAF charge 9.5.56. Reportedly f/f at Laverton after assembly 10.9.56. Shot down over Woomera Range by a Bloodhound 2 missile 17.5.61. SOC 8.6.61.

VT334 Ferried Llandow-Tarrant Rushton 20.7.55 (ex-38 MU) for conversion to U.15. (TFH 474.05). Handed over to R & J Park Ltd 5.3.56 for packing (against Contract 12932) and shipment to Australia aboard SS *Pinjarra*. Taken onto RAAF charge 14.5.56; to 1 AD 2.11.56; to ATU 29.11.56. Crashed 28.3.58 after pilotless take-off from Evett's Field for an intended Thunderbird sortie. SOC 23.5.58.

VW266 Ferried Kirkbride-Tarrant Rushton 16.5.55 (ex-12 MU) for conversion to U.15. (TFH 351.55). Handed over to R & J Park Ltd 5.3.56 for packing (against Contract 12932) and shipment to Australia aboard SS *Pinjarra*. Taken onto RAAF charge 14.5.56; to 1 AD 15.6.56; to Fairey Aviation 9.7.56; 1 AD 22.1.57; ATU 20.2.57. Shot down by a Bloodhound missile on Woomera Range 22.7.58. SOC 22.10.58.

VW273 Ferried Llandow-Tarrant Rushton 25.7.55 (ex-38 MU) for conversion to U.15. (TFH 679.40). Dptd Tarrant Rushton 26.3.56 to 47 MU for packing and shipment to Australia aboard SS *Theseus*. Taken onto RAAF charge 4.7.56 at 1 AD; to ARDU 13.6.57; Edinburgh 28.1.58. Lost control in Evett's Field circuit and crashed at the end of a Seaslug sortie 2.12.59. SOC 28.1.60.

VW275 Ferried Kirkbride-Tarrant Rushton 14.9.54 (ex-12 MU) for conversion to U.15. (TFH 839.25). Dptd Tarrant Rushton 6.9.55 to 47 MU Hawarden for packing and shipment. Dptd Liverpool docks 4.10.55 aboard SS *Stirlingshire*. Taken onto RAAF charge 29.11.55 at 1 AD; to Edinburgh 28.3.56 for ATU. On 24.2.58 and at the end of a Bloodhound sortie, VW275 sustained undercarriage collapse on landing at Evett's Field. SOC

VW303 Conveyed by road Baginton-Tarrant Rushton 3.5.56 (ex-Dunlop Rubber Co.) for conversion to U.15. (TFH 364.35). Handed over to R & J Park Ltd 5.11.56 for packing (against Contract 12932). Shipped aboard SS *Perim*. Taken onto RAAF charge 14.1.57; to Fairey Aviation 22.1.57; to Edinburgh 3.8.59; to 1 ATU 12.5.60. Shot down by Seaslug missile at Woomera Range 11.4.61. SOC 12.5.61.

VW308 Ferried Martlesham Heath-Tarrant Rushton 1.9.54 (ex-A.I.E.U) for conversion to U.15. (TFH 185.00). Handed over to R & J Park Ltd for packing (against Contract 12932). Shipped ex-UK aboard SS *Cymric*. Taken onto RAAF charge 3.4.56 at 1 AD; to Edinburgh 28.8.57; 1 ATU 16.7.58. Crashed after performing an uncontrolled climb and roll during a Fireflash sortie at Woomera Range 20.11.58. SOC 12.12.58.

VW781 Conveyed by road Lyneham-Tarrant Rushton 27.8.54 (ex-33 MU) for conversion to U.15. (TFH 27.04). Handed over to R & J Park Ltd for packing (against Contract 12932). Shipped ex-UK aboard SS *Cymric*. Taken onto RAAF charge 3.4.56 at 1 AD; to Edinburgh 18.6.57; 1 ATU 8.7.58. Destroyed at Woomera Range 21.10.58 by a Fireflash missile. SOC 10.11.58.

VW791 Transferred 8 MU to Tarrant Rushton (date unkn) for conversion to U.15. Dptd UK 31.1.57 aboard SS *Port Alma*. Taken onto RAAF charge 18.3.57; to Fairey Aviation for storage. To Edinburgh 21.4.60; to 1 ATU 16.10.61. Shot down by a Thunderbird missile at Woomera Range 18.4.63. SOC 20.5.63.

VZ386 Ferried Llandow-Tarrant Rushton 14.6.55 (ex-38 MU) for conversion to U.15. (TFH 530.05). Handed over to R & J Park Ltd 28.9.56 for packing (against Contract 12932). Shipped ex-UK 18.10.56 aboard SS *Hacienda*. Taken onto RAAF charge 12.12.56 at Fairey Aviation; to Edinburgh 22.1.60; 1 ATU 3.4.62. Shot down by a Thunderbird missile at Woomera Range 9.8.63. SOC 10.9.63.

VZ389 Conveyed by road Lyneham-Tarrant Rushton 16.7.54 (ex-33 MU Store) for conversion to U.15 (TFH 149.40). Dptd Tarrant Rushton 9.11.55 to 47 MU Hawarden for packing. To Liverpool docks 6.1.56 and shipped aboard SS *Clan Shaw*. Taken onto RAAF charge 27.2.56 at 1 AD; ferried Laverton-Edinburgh 20.8.56; ATU 12.3.57. Shot down by a Bloodhound missile at Woomera Range 31.7.58. SOC 10.9.58.

VZ401 Ferried Lyneham-Tarrant Rushton 21.6.55 (ex-33 MU) for conversion to U.15. (TFH 393.05). Handed over to R & J Park Ltd 26.9.56 for packing (against Contract 12932). Shipped ex-UK 18.10.56 aboard SS *Hacienda*. Taken onto RAAF charge 12.12.56 at Fairey Aviation; to Edinburgh 23.12.59; 1 ATU 22.8.60. Shot down by a Thunderbird missile at Woomera Range 19.4.62. SOC 22.5.62.

VZ403 Ferried Farnborough-Tarrant Rushton 28.4.54 (ex-RAE) for conversion to U.15 (TFH 403.20). Dptd Tarrant Rushton 17.7.56 to 47 MU Hawarden for packing and shipment to Australia. Taken onto RAAF charge 21.12.56; to Fairey Aviation 22.1.57; to Edinburgh 6.2.59. Destroyed over Woomera Range by a Seaslug missile 12.11.59. SOC 1.12.59.

VZ407 Ferried Lyneham-Tarrant Rushton 13.9.54 (ex-33 MU) for conversion to U.15. (TFH 468.25). Dptd Tarrant Rushton 10.10.55 to 47 MU for packing. To Liverpool docks 4.11.55 for shipment aboard SS *South Africa Star*. Taken onto RAAF charge 29.12.55 at 1 AD; to Edinburgh 8.5.56; ATU 22.6.56. Flew into the ground 16.9.58 after a reported auto transition failure during a Seaslug sortie. SOC 22.10.58.

VZ414 Ferried Little Rissington-Tarrant Rushton 28.6.55 (ex-8 MU) for conversion to U.15. (TFH 260.15). Handed over to R & J Park Ltd 30.7.56 for packing (against Contract 12932). Shipped ex-UK aboard SS *Chandawla*. Taken onto RAAF charge 23.10.56 at Fairey Aviation; to Edinburgh 2.2.60. SOC 6.9.60.

Meteor U.16 – Individual Service Histories

(Note that histories only relate to the period as a U.16 variant. Details of former service life as a standard F.8 variant are excluded.)

VZ445 Conveyed by road Aston Down-Tarrant Rushton (ex-storage at 20 MU) 11.3.59 for conversion to U.16 against Contract KD/N/04/CB.24(a). (TFH 350.15). Ferried Tarrant Rushton-Llanbedr 3.2.61 (F/O F Johnson) (TFH 358.10) and coded 'E'. Destroyed 16.5.61. SOC 18.5.61.

VZ448 Conveyed by road Lyneham-Tarrant Rushton (ex-storage at 33 MU) 11.10.61. Originally allocated to Flight Refuelling for spares use only but added to the U.16 programme 21.11.67 against Contract KK/F/893/CB24(a); f/f 20.5.69. Issued to SB&H 27.5.69 and del Llanbedr next day and coded 'H'. Shot down 1973, details unknown.

VZ455 See U.21 Individual Aircraft Histories.

VZ485 Conveyed by road Aston Down-Tarrant Rushton (ex-storage at 20 MU) 9.3.59 for conversion to U.16 against Contract KD/N/04/CB.24(a). (TFH 799.15). Del to Llanbedr 3.11.60 and coded 'V'. Expended 25.1.61. SOC 31.1.61.

VZ503 See U.21 Individual Aircraft Histories.

VZ506 Conveyed by road Aston Down-Tarrant Rushton (ex-storage at 20 MU) 9.4.59 for conversion to U.16 against Contract KD/N/04/CB.24(a). (TFH 289.40). Del to Llanbedr 19.12.60 (TFH 293.12) and coded 'H'. Expended 25.1.61. SOC 31.1.61.

VZ508 Conveyed by road Kemble-Tarrant Rushton (ex-storage at 5 MU) 11.2.72 for conversion to U.16. f/f (as U.16) 19.7.73 as 'R1'. Deld to Llanbedr 1.8.73.

VZ513 Del Lyneham-Tarrant Rushton 17.10.61 (ex-storage at 33 MU) for cannibalization as spares but possibly later stored at Merryfield. Added to the U.16 programme 21.11.67 against Contract KK/F/893/CB24(a); f/f 14.8.69. Del to Llanbedr 27.8.69. No further details known.

VZ514 Conveyed by road Aston Down-Tarrant Rushton (ex-storage at 20 MU) 17.4.59 for conversion to U.16 against Contract KD/N/04/CB.24(a). (TFH 1202.55). Del to RAE Llanbedr 4.1.61 (TFH 1206.10) and coded 'A'. Crashed into Cardigan Bay 7m NW of Llanbedr 15.5.61 when it was "inadvertently destroyed" following a problem with the telemetry transmission and command receiver. The aircraft was engaged in Firestreak trials and this was its 5th pilotless sortie.

VZ551 Conveyed by road Aston Down-Tarrant Rushton (ex-storage at 20 MU) 5.3.59 for conversion to U.16 against Contract KD/N/04/CB.24(a). (TFH 835.40). Del to Llanbedr 4.11.60 (TFH 840.25) and coded 'F'. Destroyed 26.1.61. SOC 31.1.61.

VZ554 Conveyed by road Lyneham-Tarrant Rushton (ex-storage at 33 MU) 24.10.61 for cannabilsation. Added to U.16 programme 21.11.67 for Llanbedr against Contract KK/F/893/CB24(a). Allotted to FRL 13.3.70 for "post design services installation work". Later allocated to Woomera 30.3.73 for missile trials, possibly due to all U.21/U.21As having been expended. (See also WF685).

WA756 Conveyed by road Kirkbride-Tarrant Rushton 1.4.60 (ex-storage at 12 MU) for conversion to U.16 against Contract KK/F/0149. (TFH 840.30). Del to Llanbedr 6.6.61 and coded 'L'. Lost 23.6.61, details not known. SOC 29.6.61

WA775 Ferried Defford-Tarrant Rushton (ex-Royal Radar Establishment) 29.11.55. Converted to prototype U.16 against Contract 6/Acft/12736/CB.7(b). (TFH 227.10). f/f 22.10.56. To Cranfield 23.4.58; Returned to FRL 3.6.58. Against Contract KD/N/04/CB.24(a) it was brought up to "Issue 3 standard of Spec D.174P" (as a replacement for WK660 which was deleted from the programme – see WA982.) (TFH 388.30) Del to Llanbedr 6.2.61. Crashed into Cardigan Bay 7½ miles NW of Llanbedr 18.5.61 after being inadvertently destroyed following a problem with the telemetry transmission and command receiver. The aircraft was engaged in Firestreak trials on what was its first pilotless sortie.

WA842 Conveyed by road Aston Down-Tarrant Rushton (ex-storage at 20 MU) 3.4.59 for conversion to U.16 against Contract KD/N/04/CB.24(a). (TFH 1010.00). Del to Llanbedr 14.11.60 (TFH 1035.35) and coded 'E'. Expended 22.1.61. SOC 25.1.61.

WA982 Ferried Farnborough-Tarrant Rushton (ex-NGTE) 10.7.59 for conversion to U.16 against Contract KD/N/04/CB.24(a). (TFH 179.50). Due to the unsuitability of 982's fuel system the conversion used the wings of WK660. Del to Llanbedr 17.1.61 (TFH 184.10) and coded 'X'. Written-off 9.5.61 when it crashed into Cardigan Bay 22m SW of Llanbedr following a problem with the telemetry transmission and command receiver. The aircraft was engaged in Firestreak trials and this was its first pilotless sortie. SOC 12.5.61.

WA991 Conveyed by road Lyneham-Tarrant Rushton 24.10.61 (ex-storage at 33 MU) for cannibalization. Stored at Merryfield. Added to U.16 programme 21.11.67 against Contract KK/F/893/CB24(a); f/f 19.11.68. Del to Llanbedr 1.4.69 and coded 'F'. No further details.

WE867 Conveyed by road Hullavington-Tarrant Rushton 16.11.61 (ex-storage at 33 MU) for conversion to U.16. (TFH 232.00). Test-flown 21.5.63. Allocated to Flight Refuelling 27.5.63. Transferred to Contract KK/F/0149 and del to Llanbedr 23.4.64; coded 'V'. Declared Cat.4R 14.10.64. Rtnd to FRL 15.9.65 to be broken down for spares. SOC 23.9.65.

To Tarrant Rushton scrap compound 3.11.67; still extant 5.68.

WE872 Conveyed by road Kirkbride-Tarrant Rushton 30.10.59 (ex-storage at 12 MU) for conversion to U.16. (TFH 752.00). Del to Llanbedr 8.2.62 (TFH 756.37) and coded 'J'. Destroyed 15.11.62. SOC 30.11.62.

WE902 See U.21 Individual Aircraft Histories.

WE915 Ferried Kirkbride-Tarrant Rushton (ex-12 MU) 26.2.59 for conversion to U.16 against Contract KD/N/04/CB.24(a). (TFH 1266.10). Del to Llanbedr 19.8.60 (TFH 1270.15) and 'F'. Shot down 14.10.60. SOC 20.10.60.

WE932 Conveyed by road Kirkbride-Tarrant Rushton 5.11.59, ex-storage at 12 MU, for conversion to U.16 against Contract KK/F/052. (TFH 770.0). Ferried Tarrant Rushton-Yeovilton 14.3.61 for del'y to Malta. Arrived Hal Far 16.3.61 for 728B Flight and coded '656'. (1st pilotless flight 11.10.61). Dptd Hal Far 20.11.61 to RAE Llanbedr (after 6 pilotless sorties) and coded 'E' (or 'D'). Expended 23.2.62.

WE934 Del to Flight Refuelling 3.8.54 (or 19.5.53), ex-storage at 33 MU, for high altitude in-flight refuelling trials; later allocated as 2nd prototype U.16 31.10.55 against Contract 6/Acft/12736/CB.7(b). (TFH 431.46); f/f as U.16 15.4.56. Del to Llanbedr 7.2.62 and coded 'C'. Expended 14.5.62. SOC 18.5.62.

WE960 See U.21 Individual Aircraft Histories.

WE962 Conveyed by road Hullavington-Tarrant Rushton 2.3.61, ex-storage at 33 MU, for conversion to U.16. Del to Llanbedr 21.3.62. Expended 18.4.62.

WF659 See U.21 Individual Aircraft Histories.

WF681 Conveyed by road Hullavington-Tarrant Rushton 6.10.61, ex-storage at 33 MU, for conversion to U.16. (TFH 650.35). Del to Llanbedr 12.9.63. Expended 13.3.64.

WF685 Del to Flight Refuelling 6.10.61, ex-storage at 33 MU for cannibalization. Added to the U.16 programme 21.11.67. Del to Llanbedr 8.5.69 and coded 'U'; later 'T'. Returned to FRL 16.10.72 for preparation for transfer to WRE Woomera. (See also VZ554.)

WF706 Conveyed by road Lyneham-Tarrant Rushton 22.11.61, ex-storage at 33

Meteor WH286 was the final U.16 conversion by Flight Refuelling Ltd and had 1 Squadron RAF markings applied to reflect its past service. It was delivered to Llanbedr on 26 August 1975. (Flight Refuelling Ltd)

MU for conversion to U.16. (TFH 523.05). Added to Contract KK/F/0149 and test-flown 21.8.63. Placed into long-term storage at FRL 28.8.63. Del to Llanbedr 11.1.65 and coded 'J'. Destroyed at Llanbedr 27.9.65. SOC 22.10.65.

WF707 Conveyed by road Kirkbride-Tarrant Rushton 12.11.59, ex-storage at 12 MU for conversion to U.16, against Contract KK/F/052. (TFH 334.10). Del to Llanbedr 27.2.61 and coded 'A'. Expended 9.6.61.

WF711 Ferried Kemble-Tarrant Rushton 17.2.72, ex-storage at 5 MU for conversion to U.16. Del to Llanbedr 5.11.73. No further details.

WF716 Conveyed by road Aston Down-Tarrant Rushton (ex-20 MU Store) 1.4.59 for conversion to U.16 against Contract KD/N/04/CB.24(a). (TFH 402.55). Allocated to 728B Flight 11.10.60 (departed T. Rushton 12.10.60; arrived Hal Far 18.10.60, the Flight's 1st U.16.) Coded '658'. Completed 2 unmanned sorties before allocated to Llanbedr 20.11.61; arrived 30.11.61 and coded 'B'. Lost 30.4.62, (or 20.2.62) details not known.

WF741 Conveyed by road Kirkbride-Tarrant Rushton 16.11.59, ex-storage at 12 MU for conversion to U.16 against Contract KK/F/052. (TFH 806.35). Del to Llanbedr 5.10.61 and coded 'H'. Sustained Cat.3 damage 26.10.61. Repaired by 5.2.62. Lost 20.2.62, details not known.

WF743 Conveyed by road Lyneham-Tarrant Rushton 15.11.61 (ex-storage at 33 MU) for conversion to U.16. Del to RAE Llanbedr 9.5.63. Expended 24.6.64. SOC 6.5.64.

WF751 Del to Tarrant Rushton 29.4.60 (ex-storage at 12 MU) for conversion to U.16. (TFH 697.30). Ferried Tarrant Rushton-Llanbedr 25.1.62 (F/O F.Johnson). Expended 9.5.62.

WF755 Conveyed by road Aston Down-Tarrant Rushton (ex-storage at 20 MU) 6.9.60 for conversion to U.16. (TFH 1073.50). Placed in short-term storage at Tarrant Rushton 22.9.61-9.1.62 (with WK693). Del to Llanbedr 1.2.62 and coded 'V'. Expended 12.4.62.

WF756 Del to Tarrant Rushton 9.5.60 (ex-storage at 12 MU) for conversion to U.16. (TFH 709.00). Del to Llanbedr 25.1.62 and coded 'P'. Expended 12.3.62.

WH258 Conveyed by road Aston Down-Tarrant Rushton (ex-storage at 20 MU) 24.3.59 for conversion to U.16 against Contract KD/N/04/CB.24(a). (TFH 461.40). Del to Llanbedr 3.10.60 (TFH 465.55) and coded 'N'; later 'E'. Expended 4.11.60.

WH284 Ferried Chilbolton-Tarrant Rushton (ex-Folland Aircraft trials aircraft) 3.2.59 for conversion to U.16 against Contract KD/N/04/CB.24(a). (TFH 683.56). Del to Llanbedr 30.6.60 (TFH 717.45) and coded 'E'. Lost 9.11.60, details unkn.

WH286 Ferried Chivenor-Tarrant Rushton 16.5.72, ex-229 OCU for conversion to (the final) U.16. Del to Llanbedr 26.8.75. No further details.

WH309 Conveyed by road Lyneham-Tarrant Rushton 26.10.61 (ex-storage at 33 MU) for conversion to U.16 against Contract KK/F/0153/CB.24(a). (TFH 456.05). Del to Llanbedr 16.2.63 and coded 'F'. SOC 13.3.72 but this is probably

Post-War Drone Conversions 127

a "catch-up" date for a much earlier loss (See also WH372, WH373 & WH420).

WH315 Conveyed by road Kirkbride-Tarrant Rushton 3.3.60, ex-storage at 12 MU for conversion to U.16 against Contract KK/F/0149, (TFH 825.15). Del to Llanbedr 26.5.61 and coded 'A'. Written off 4.7.61 when it crashed into the sea 7½miles SW of Llanbedr after the aircraft's throttles closed. A faulty throttle actuator was found to be the cause. The aircraft was on its 5th pilotless sortie and engaged in Thunderbird trials.

WH320 Conveyed by road Aston Down-Tarrant Rushton (ex-20 MU Cat.4R) 7.4.59 for conversion to U.16 against Contract KD/N/04/CB.24(a). (TFH 103.50) Del to Llanbedr 20.12.60 (TFH 108.25) and coded 'N'. To FRL 12.6.61, returning to Llanbedr 22.8.61. To FRL 25.8.66 for UHF aerial TI, returning to Llanbedr 25.1.68. To FRL 28.5.70 for installation of landing lights, returning to Llanbedr 23.6.70. Shot down over the Aberporth range 15.8.79 by a Sky Flash missile fired by a 29 Squadron Phantom FGR.2.

WH344 Conveyed by road Kirkbride-Tarrant Rushton 13.4.60, (ex-12 MU), for conversion to U.16 against Contract KK/F/052. (TFH 782.05). Ferried Tarrant Rushton-Llanbedr (F/O F Johnson) 28.6.61 and coded 'O'. Destroyed 27.10.61, details not known.

WH349 Conveyed by road Kirkbride-Tarrant Rushton 28/29.3.60 (ex-storage at 12 MU) for conversion to U.16 against Contract KK/F/052. (TFH 441.00) Del to Llanbedr 4.7.61 and coded 'E'. Expended 17.11.61.

WH359 Conveyed by road Kirkbride-Tarrant Rushton 16.3.60 (ex-storage at 12 MU) for conversion to U.16 against Contract KK/F/0149. (TFH 879.00). Del to Llanbedr 19.6.61 and coded 'V'. Expended 20.7.61.

WH365 Conveyed by road Kirkbride-Tarrant Rushton 26.3.60 (ex-storage at 12 MU) for conversion to U.16 against Contract KK/F/0149. (TFH 928.35). Del to Llanbedr 16.6.61 and coded 'H'. Expended 2.10.61.

WH369 Conveyed by road Kirkbride-Tarrant Rushton 23.11.59 (ex-storage at 12 MU) for conversion to U.16 against Contract KK/F/052. (TFH 690.00). Del to Llanbedr 21.2.61 for assessment of new Control Relay Unit. Returned to FRL 15.6.62. Re-del to Llanbedr 21.3.63 and coded 'T'. Expended 19.4.63.

WH372 Conveyed by road Aston Down-Tarrant Rushton (ex-20 MU Store) 17.3.59 for conversion to U.16 against Contract KD/N/04/CB.24(a). (TFH 551.50). Del to Llanbedr 10.1.61 (TFH 555.25) and coded 'H'. To FRL 12.3.62 for Cat.4R repair; Returned to Llanbedr 31.8.62. To FRL 7.5.63 for repair; Returned to Llanbedr 4.2.64 and coded 'J'. SOC 13.3.72 but this is probably a "catch-up" date for a much earlier loss (See also WH309, WH373 & WH420).

WH373 Conveyed by road Hullavington-Tarrant Rushton 9.2.61 (ex-storage at 33 MU) for conversion to U.16. Ferried Tarrant Rushton-Llanbedr (F/O F. Johnson) 2.7.62 and coded 'M'. To FRL 31.5.68 for mods; Returned to Llanbedr 9.6.69. SOC 13.3.72

WH376 Conveyed by road Hullavington-Tarrant Rushton (in damaged condition) 23.3.61 (ex 33 MU store) for conversion to U.16. Del to RAE Llanbedr 5.6.62. Expended 9.2.63.

WH381 Conveyed by road Kirkbride-Tarrant Rushton 13.11.59 (ex-storage at 12 MU) for conversion to U.16 against Contract KK/F/052. (TFH 861.00). Allocated as development aircraft; Del to Llanbedr 2.10.62 for trials. Coded 'G'. To FRL 15.3.63 for TIs; Returned to Llanbedr 2.2.66. SOC 13.3.72 but this is probably a "catch-up" date for a much earlier loss (See also WH372, WH373 & WH420).

WH419 Conveyed by road Aston Down-Tarrant Rushton 19.12.61 (ex-storage at 20 MU) for conversion to U.16. (TFH 744.25) Test-flown 9.2.63; transferred to Contract KK/F/0149. Del to Llanbedr 8.7.64. Expended 20.9.65.

WH420 Conveyed by road Kirkbride-Tarrant Rushton 19/20.11.59 (ex-storage at 12 MU) for conversion to U.16. (TFH 650.00). Del to Llanbedr 7.12.61 and coded 'S'. To FRL 12.12.68 for mods; Ret to Llanbedr 23.10.69. To A&AEE 4.9.70 for DN181 (Blindfire) trials. To RAE Llanbedr 21.12.70 (still as 'S'). SOC 13.3.72.

WH453 Conveyed by road Kemble-Tarrant Rushton 17.4.72 (ex-storage at 5 MU) for conversion to U.16; f/f 18.3.74; Del to RAE West Freugh 9.8.74 (or 21.8.74). To Llanbedr 6.1.75 and coded 'L'; returned to FRL 13.9.76 for upgrade/mods (TR logs state Llanbedr to Tarrant Rushton 8.10.76). Test-flown 19.11.76 and del Tarrant Rushton-Llanbedr 26.11.76. (This marked the final flight of a Meteor at Tarrant Rushton.) Removed

from flying duty 10.10.90 and used as a static engine test airframe; also as a spares source for Llanbedr's last remaining flyable Meteor U.16/D.16 WK800. Departed Llanbedr 18.1.05 for restoration at the Bentwaters Cold War Museum, Suffolk for restoration to F.8 standard by the Bentwaters Aviation Society.

WH460 See U.21 Individual Aircraft Histories.

WH469 Conveyed by road Hullavington-Tarrant Rushton 31.10.61 (ex-storage at 33 MU) for conversion to U.16. (TFH 673.00) Transferred to Contract KK/F/0149 for storage at FRL. Del to Llanbedr 28.3.64. Destroyed 27.4.65.

WH499 Conveyed by road Aston Down-Tarrant Rushton (ex-20 MU Store) 2.3.59 for conversion to U.16 against Contract KD/N/04/CB.24(a). (TFH 301.40). Del to Llanbedr 22.9.60 (TFH 308.15) and coded 'Z'. Expended 9.11.60.

WH500 Conveyed by road Kirkbride-Tarrant Rushton 9.11.59 (ex-storage at 12 MU) for conversion to U.16 against Contract KK/F/0149. (TFH 1149.00). Del to Llanbedr 19.5.61 and coded 'E'. Expended 16.6.61.

WH505 Conveyed by road Kirkbride-Tarrant Rushton 28/29.3.60 (ex-storage at 12 MU) for conversion to U.16 against Contract KK/F/052. (TFH 900.05). Del to Llanbedr 14.9.61 and coded 'B'. Destroyed 27.10.61.

WH506 Conveyed by road Kirkbride-Tarrant Rushton 21.11.59 (ex-storage at 12 MU) for conversion to U.16 against Contract KK/F/0149. (TFH 773.00). Del to Llanbedr 24.5.61 and coded 'V'. Expended 12.6.61.

WH509 Conveyed by road Lyneham-Tarrant Rushton (in damaged condition) 7.3.61 (ex-storage at 33 MU) for repair & conversion to U.16. Ferried Tarrant Rushton-Llanbedr (F/O F Johnson) 6.4.62. Expended 3.8.62.

WK648 Conveyed by road Lyneham-Tarrant Rushton 1.11.61 (ex-storage at 33 MU) for conversion to U.16. (TFH 776.00). Del to Llanbedr 30.4.63. Expended 1.10.63.

WK660 Ferried Wroughton-Tarrant Rushton 21.4.59 (ex-15 MU) for conversion to U.16 against Contract KD/N/04/CB.24(a). (TFH 275.15). Declared unsuitable for conversion and replaced on contract by WA775. SOC 28.7.59. (See also WA982). (WK660 was the Aden 30mm cannon trials aircraft and probably had non-standard mods to the fuselage.)

WK675 Conveyed by road Lyneham-Tarrant Rushton 8.11.61 (ex-storage at 33 MU) for conversion to U.16. Del to Llanbedr 28.3.63. Destroyed 3.7.63.

WK693 Conveyed by road Aston Down-Tarrant Rushton 7.9.60 (ex-storage at 20 MU) for conversion to U.16. (TFH 495.15). Placed in short-term storage at Tarrant Rushton 22.9.61-9.1.62 (with WF755). Del to Llanbedr 1.2.62. SOC 8.3.62.

WK709 Conveyed by road Lyneham-Tarrant Rushton (in damaged condition) 28.3.61 (ex-storage at 33 MU) for repair & conversion to U.16. Del to Llanbedr 5.7.62. Expended 20.3.63.

WK710 See U.21 Individual Aircraft Histories.

WK716 Conveyed by road Lyneham-Tarrant Rushton 7.12.61 (ex-storage at 33 MU) for conversion to U.16. (TFH 1260.15). Del to Llanbedr 11.11.63. Destroyed 27.5.64.

WK717 Conveyed by road Kirkbride-Tarrant Rushton 2.11.59 (ex 12 MU Store) for conversion to U.16 against Contract KK/F/0149. (TFH 681.00). Del to Llanbedr 25.5.61 and coded 'X'. Expended 12.6.61.

WK721 Conveyed by road Lyneham-Tarrant Rushton 27.10.61 (ex-storage at 33 MU) for conversion to U.16. (TFH 855.40). Del to Llanbedr 25.3.63. Shot down 11.11.63.

WK729 Conveyed by road to Tarrant Rushton 28/29.4.60 (ex-12 MU) for conversion to U.16 against Contract KK/F/0149. (TFH 973.45). Del to Llanbedr 23.10.61 and coded 'Z'. Expended 27.1.62.

WK731 Conveyed by road Lyneham-Tarrant Rushton 14.12.61 (ex-storage at 33 MU) for conversion to U.16. (TFH 923.20). Test-flown 30.7.63. Transferred to Contract KK/F/0149 and del to Llanbedr 25.8.64 and coded 'T'. Shot down 22.9.66.

WK737 Conveyed by road Lyneham-Tarrant Rushton 5.1.62 (ex-storage at 33 MU) for conversion to U.16. (TFH 800.50). Del to Llanbedr 22.10.63. Shot down 13.7.64.

WK738 Conveyed by road Lyneham-Tarrant Rushton 13.10.61 (ex-storage at 33 MU) for conversion to U.16. Del to Llanbedr 11.12.69. SOC 13.3.72.

WK743 Conveyed by road Lyneham-Tarrant Rushton (in damaged condition) 16.2.61 (ex-storage at 33 MU) for repair & conversion to U.16. Del to Llanbedr 8.4.62 and coded 'B'. Destroyed 12.7.62.

WK744 Conveyed by road Lyneham-Tarrant Rushton 2.11.61 (ex-storage at 33 MU) for conversion to U.16. (TFH 876.40). Del to Llanbedr 13.2.63 and coded 'V'. Badly damaged 9.3.63 when it bounced very heavily on landing at Llanbedr in heavy rain. It had just completed its 1st pilotless sortie and engaged in a Seaslug missile trial. SOC as Cat.5(s) 12.3.63.

WK745 Conveyed by road Lyneham-Tarrant Rushton 23.11.61 (ex-storage at 33 MU) for conversion to U.16. (TFH 820.20). Test-flown 19.8.63; placed into storage at FRL 23.8.63 against Contract KK/F/0149. Del to Llanbedr 8.12.64. Destroyed 23.9.65.

WK746 Conveyed by road Lyneham-Tarrant Rushton 12.12.61 (ex-storage at 33 MU) for conversion to U.16 against Contract KK/F/0149. (TFH 971.55). Test-flown 27.11.63 and possibly del to Llanbedr 5.12.63. Then perhaps transferred to Contract KK/F/0149 and returned to Tarrant Rushton. Del to Llanbedr 7.12.65 and coded 'E'. Expended 2.11.66 during a course of trials.

WK747 Conveyed by road Lyneham-Tarrant Rushton 30.11.61 (ex-storage at 33 MU) for conversion to U.16 against Contract KK/F/0149. (TFH 1270.20). Test-flown 8.8.63. Del to Llanbedr 9.11.64 and coded 'D'. Still current in 1973 but no further details.

WK783 Conveyed by road Lyneham-Tarrant Rushton 5.12.61 (ex-storage at 33 MU) for conversion to U.16 against Contract KK/F/0149. Test-flown 27.6.63. Del to Llanbedr 23.6.64 and coded 'Z'. Destroyed 6.11.64.

WK784 Conveyed by road Lyneham-Tarrant Rushton 16.3.61 (ex-storage at 33 MU) for conversion to U.16. (TFH 535.30). Del to Llanbedr 15.5.62 and coded 'E'. Lost 27.9.62.

WK789 Conveyed by road Lyneham-Tarrant Rushton 6.12.61 (ex-storage at 33 MU) for conversion to U.16. (TFH 614.00). Del to Llanbedr 18.10.63 and coded 'P'. Sustained Cat.4 damage in a crash-landing 10.3.64. To FRL for repair. Returned to Llanbedr 20.8.65 and coded 'Z'. Later destroyed 27.3.69 but apparently not SOC until 13.3.72.

WK790 Conveyed by road Lyneham-Tarrant Rushton (in damaged condition) 24..2.61 (ex-storage at 33 MU) for repair & conversion to U.16. Del to Llanbedr 14.3.62 and coded 'P'. Failed to become airborne during pilotless take-off from Llanbedr 2.8.62 and destroyed by fire. SOC 5.12.62.

WK793 Conveyed by road Lyneham-Tarrant Rushton (in damaged condition) 29.3.61 (ex 33 MU store) for conversion to U.16. Del to Llanbedr 15.6.62 and coded 'C'. Destroyed 15.11.62

WK795 Conveyed by road Lyneham-Tarrant Rushton 24.11.61 (ex-storage at 33 MU) for conversion to U.16. (TFH 779.00). Test-flown 24.5.63; transferred to Contract KK/F/0149. Del to Llanbedr 29.4.64 and coded 'J'. Shot down 23.9.64.

WK797 See U.21 Individual Aircraft Histories.

WK799 Conveyed by road Lyneham-Tarrant Rushton 9.3.61, ex-storage at 33 MU, for conversion to U.16, Del to Llanbedr 13.4.62. Destroyed 7.2.63.

WK800 Returned to UK from Australia by road/sea c5.69, having operated in Australia as U.21A A77-876. Re-converted to U.16 by FRL against Contract K24A/18/CB24(a). "Weighed on conversion" 8.7.71 after its 9th and final test flight. Del Tarrant Rushton-Llanbedr 26.7.71 and coded 'Z'. Re-designated D.16 on system change. To Marshall of Cambridge Engineering Ltd 7.4.83 for fitment of Radar Vector Miss Distance Indicator (RVMDI) against Contract A3a/129, later positioning to Farnborough for RVMDI trials. Ferried to Llanbedr 25.8.87 for major servicing. Returned to MCE Ltd, Cambridge 23.11.87 for on-going RVMDI trial. Ferried to Llanbedr 27.6.88 for pilotless RVMDI trial. Sustained damage when it struck the barrier during an aborted pilotless take-off from Llanbedr 19.4.89. Returned to service after repair 13.2.91. Retired from flying with Llanbedr's pending closure and ferried Llanbedr to Boscombe Down 11.10.04 to mark its final flight. Sold to Trevor E. Stone 2008; loaned to Boscombe Down Aviation Collection 1.09.

WK807 Conveyed by road Lyneham-Tarrant Rushton 23.2.61 (ex storage at 33 MU) for conversion to U.16. Del to Llanbedr 1.8.62 and coded 'B'. Rtnd to FRL 7.6.68 presumably for upgrade mods; Rtnd

Meteor U.16 WK807 with a sensor pod beneath the port wing. (Arthur Pearcy, via Jennifer M Gradidge)

Llanbedr 24.4.69. SOC after destruction advised by letter dated 13.3.72.

WK812 Conveyed by road Kirkbride-Tarrant Rushton 1.4.60 (ex-storage at 12 MU) for conversion to U.16 against Contract KK/F/052. (TFH 355.00). Del to Llanbedr 3.3.61 and coded 'F'. Expended 9.11.61. SOC 14.11.61.

WK852 Conveyed by road Kirkbride-Tarrant Rushton 16.3.60 (ex-storage at 12 MU) for conversion to U.16 against Contract KK/F/0149. (TFH 975.10). Del to Llanbedr 6.6.61. Expended 20.7.61.

WK855 Conveyed by road Lyneham-Tarrant Rushton 7.11.61 (ex-storage at 33 MU) for conversion to U.16. (TFH 868.10). Del to Llanbedr 21.3.63 and coded 'X'. Lost on operations 6.9.63. SOC 17.9.63.

WK859 Conveyed by road Lyneham-Tarrant Rushton 26.10.61 (ex-storage at 33 MU) for conversion to U.16. (TFH 1365.15). Del to Llanbedr 28.2.63 and coded 'Z'. Lost on operations 16.10.63. SOC 1.1.64.

WK867 Conveyed by road Aston Down-Tarrant Rushton (ex-storage at 20 MU) 14.4.59 for conversion to U.16 against Contract KD/N/04/CB.24(a). (TFH 868.30) Del to Llanbedr 17.11.60 (TFH 892.15) and coded 'Z'. Expended 29.9.61.

WK870 Conveyed by road Aston Down-Tarrant Rushton (ex-storage at 20 MU) 11.3.59 for conversion to U.16 against Contract KD/N/04/CB.24(a). (TFH 551.49) Dptd Tarrant Rushton 29.11.60 to Hal Far for 728B Flight (TFH 554.55) and coded '655'. To Yeovilton 16.11.61. To Llanbedr 29.11.61. Expended 1.2.62.

WK877 Conveyed by road Lyneham-Tarrant Rushton 20.12.61 (ex-storage at 33 MU) for conversion to U.16. (TFH 799.45). Del to Llanbedr 7.6.63. Destroyed over the Aberporth range 27.9.66 during the course of trials.

WK879 See U.21 Individual Aircraft Histories.

WK883 Conveyed by road Lyneham-Tarrant Rushton 5.1.62 (ex-storage at 33 MU) for conversion to U.16. (TFH 738.00). Del to Llanbedr 13.8.63 and coded 'A'. Destroyed 23.8.65.

WK885 Conveyed by road Lyneham-Tarrant Rushton 14.3.61 (ex-storage at 33 MU) for conversion to U.16. Del to Llanbedr 2.7.62. Lost 29.8.63.

WK911 Conveyed by road to Tarrant Rushton 9.11.61 for conversion to U.16. (TFH 12369.20). Del to Llanbedr 17.12.62. Destroyed 22.8.63.

WK925 Conveyed by road Aston Down-Tarrant Rushton (ex-storage at 20 MU) 19.3.59 for conversion to U.16 against Contract KD/N/04/CB.24(a). (TFH 568.55) Del to Llanbedr 12.9.60 (TFH 572.05) and coded 'V'. Expended 19.10.60.

WK926 Ferried Pershore-Tarrant Rushton 19.12.58 (ex-RRE) for conversion to U.16. (TFH 590.30) Del to Llanbedr 18.7.60 (TFH 594.20) and coded 'H'. SOC 12.12.60.

WK932 Conveyed by road Lyneham-Tarrant Rushton 9.1.62 (ex-storage at 33 MU) for conversion to U.16. (TFH 1204.15). Del to Llanbedr 1.1.64. Destroyed 28.5.64.

WK941 Ferried Chivenor-Tarrant Rushton 15.5.72 for conversion to U.16; f/f 7.6.74; Del to Llanbedr 11.7.74 and coded 'T'. No further details.

WK942 Del Kirkbride-Tarrant Rushton 4.5.60 (ex-storage at 12 MU) for conversion to U.16, Ferried Tarrant Rushton-Llanbedr 23.10.61 (F/O F Johnson). Expended 22.2.62.

WK949 Conveyed Lyneham-Tarrant Rushton (in damaged condition) 14.2.61 (ex-storage at 33 MU) for conversion to U.16. Del to Llanbedr 1.3.62. Destroyed by command 27.3.62 after suffering an in-flight failure of an oleo micro-switch, resulting in undercarriage failing to retract and directional control minimal. Crashed into sea 28 miles (45km) WSW of Llanbedr. The aircraft was on its 2nd pilotless sortie and engaged on Bloodhound missile trials.

WK971 Conveyed by road Lyneham-Tarrant Rushton 29.11.61 (ex-storage at 33 MU) for conversion to U.16. (TFH 1221.00). Test-flown 30.9.63; transferred to Contract KK/F/0149. Del to Llanbedr 21.10.65 but overshot on landing and sustained damage. Repaired and coded 'V'. Crashed at Llanbedr 22.2.67.

The operational life of Meteor U.16 WK855/X was less than a year. Delivered to Llanbedr in March 1963, it was later lost on a drone sortie on 6 September 1963. (Arthur Pearcy, via Jennifer M Gradidge)

130 Sitting Ducks and Peeping Toms

WK980 Conveyed by road Kirkbride-Tarrant Rushton 22.4.60 (ex-storage at 12 MU) for conversion to U.16 against Contract KK/F/052. (TFH 240.20). Del to RAE Llanbedr 28.7.61 and coded 'A'. Sustained Cat.3 damage 26.9.61; repaired by 12.3.62. Again declared Cat.3 4.4.62. Repaired but expended 10.10.62.

WK989 Conveyed by road Lyneham-Tarrant Rushton 13.12.61 or 31.12.61 (ex-storage at 33 MU) for conversion to U.16. (TFH 696.50). Test-flown 20.12.63 and placed into storage at FRL 7.1.64 against Contract KK/F/0149. Del to Llanbedr 7.1.66. Expended during the course of trials 21.6.66.

WK993 Conveyed by road Kirkbride-Tarrant Rushton 7.4.60 (ex-storage at 12 MU) for conversion to U.16. (TFH 616.40). Del to Llanbedr 19.6.61 and coded 'X'. Expended 12.10.61.

WK994 Conveyed by road Kirkbride-Tarrant Rushton 13.4.60 (ex-storage at 12 MU) for conversion to U.16 against Contract KK/F/052. (TFH 816.20). Del to Llanbedr 4.7.61 and coded 'C'. Expended 23.1.62.

WL110 Conveyed by road Lyneham-Tarrant Rushton 1.3.61 (ex-storage at 33 MU) for conversion to U.16. Del to Llanbedr 26.4.62 and coded 'E'. Lost on operations 19.11.62.

WL111 Conveyed by road Lyneham-Tarrant Rushton 20.12.61 (ex-storage at 33 MU) for conversion to U.16. (TFH 754.05). Del to Llanbedr 1.8.63 and coded 'V'. Destroyed 29.1.64.

WL124 Del Kirkbride-Tarrant Rushton 13.4.60 (ex-storage at 12 MU) for conversion to U.16. (TFH 813.20). Del to Llanbedr 17.12.61 and coded 'O'. Expended 23.8.63.

WL127 Conveyed by road Kirkbride-Tarrant Rushton 4.5.60 (ex 12 MU) for conversion to U.16. (TFH 905.00) Ferried Llanbedr-Yeovilton 30.10.61 on allocation to 728B Flight but not flown to Hal Far. Temporarily stored at Yeovilton Re-allocated to Llanbedr 14.11.61 and ferried there 20.11.61. Coded 'F'. Destroyed 9.2.63.

WL134 Conveyed by road Lyneham-Tarrant Rushton 28.11.61 (ex-storage at 33 MU) for conversion to U.16. (TFH 890.05). Del to Llanbedr 8.6.64. SOC after destruction advised by letter dated 13.3.72.

WL136 See U.21 Individual Aircraft Histories.

WL160 Del Kirkbride-Tarrant Rushton 28/29.3.60 (ex-storage at 12 MU) for conversion to U.16. (TFH 534.20). Del to Llanbedr 3.8.61 and coded 'P'. Expended 27.10.61.

WL162 Del Kirkbride-Tarrant Rushton 22.4.60 (ex-storage at 12 MU) for conversion to U.16. (TFH 813.45). Del to Llanbedr 2.11.61 and coded 'P'. Expended 19.1.62.

WL163 Conveyed by road Lyneham-Tarrant Rushton (in damaged condition) 21.3.61 (ex 33 MU store) for conversion to U.16. Del to Llanbedr 30.5.62 and coded 'X'. Destroyed 15.11.62.

The following Meteor F.8s were included in the U.16 programme but cannibalized at Tarrant Rushton for spares use only:

VZ439 Del to Tarrant Rushton 11.10.61 (ex-storage at 33 MU) to act as spares for the U.16 programme. Sold as scrap to B.A. Taylor (Metals), West Bromwich 9.9.69.

VZ458 Del to Tarrant Rushton 13.10.61 (ex-storage at 33 MU) to act as spares for the U.16 programme. Sold as scrap to B.A. Taylor (Metals), West Bromwich 9.9.69.

VZ462 Del to Tarrant Rushton 18.10.61 (ex-storage at 33 MU) to act as spares for the U.16 programme.

VZ520 Del to Tarrant Rushton 2.10.61 (ex-storage at 33 MU) to act as spares for the U.16 programme. Sold as scrap to B.A. Taylor (Metals), West Bromwich 9.9.69.

VZ530 Del to Tarrant Rushton 18.10.61 (ex-storage at 33 MU) to act as spares for the U.16 programme. (See WE925)

WA781 Del to Tarrant Rushton 28.9.61 (ex-storage at 33 MU) to act as spares for the U.16 programme. SOC as scrap 3.69.

WA850 Del to Tarrant Rushton 6.10.61 (ex-storage at 33 MU) to act as spares for the U.16 programme. SOC as scrap 3.69.

WA984 Del to Tarrant Rushton 4.10.61 (ex-storage at 33 MU) to act as a spares source for the U.16 programme.

WE881 Del to Tarrant Rushton 2.10.61 (ex-storage at 33 MU) to act as a spares source for the U.16 programme. Subsequently sold as scrap to B.A. Taylor (Metals) 9.9.69.

WE919 Del to Tarrant Rushton 4.10.61 (ex-storage at 33 MU) to act as a spares source for the U.16 programme. Subsequently sold as scrap to B.A. Taylor (Metals), West Bromwich 9.9.69.

WE925 Del to Tarrant Rushton 10.10.61 (ex-storage at 33 MU) to act as a spares source for the U.16 programme. Subsequently acquired by the Wales Aircraft Museum and conveyed by from road Tarrant-Rushton-Cardiff Airport c1979. (Composite aircraft with parts from VZ530). To Classic Jet Aircraft Group, Loughborough by 10.90. At East Midlands Aeropark by 3.99.

WE946 Del to Tarrant Rushton 20.10.61 (ex-storage at 33 MU) to act as a spares source for the U.16 programme. SOC as scrap 3.69

WF646 Del to Tarrant Rushton 16.10.61 (ex-storage at 33 MU) to act as a spares source for the U.16 programme.

WH281 Del to Tarrant Rushton 12.10.61 (ex-storage at 33 MU) to act as spares for the U.16 programme. SOC as scrap 3.69.

WK660 Ferried Wroughton-Tarrant Rushton 21.4.59 (ex-storage at 15 MU) for conversion to U.16, but cannibalized for spares. SOC 28.7.59. *(There is some evidence to suggest WK660 may have been converted to U.21 standard and released to R & J Park Ltd 4.4.60 for packing and shipment to Australia. However this remains unconfirmed.)*

Post-War Drone Conversions   131

Meteor U.21 – Individual Service Histories

Although the serials of those aircraft converted to U.21 are known, there remains some doubt as to their prior U.16 status. It is believed that Flight Refuelling converted one example (WL136) to U.21 leaving FAC of Australasia Pty Ltd to subsequently modify the remaining seven production examples. Of the two prototype U.21s that had earlier been sent to Australia, one (WE960) was processed through FAC Bankstown whilst the other (WK797) is thought to have been sent direct to Edinburgh Field. Ten U.21s operated with the WRE and these are believed to be the extent of U.21 conversions:

VZ455 Conveyed by road Aston Down-Tarrant Rushton 20.9.60 (ex-20 MU). for conversion to U.16 against Contract KK/F/097/CB24(a). (TFH 682.30). To R & J Park Ltd 25.1.62 for packing and shipment. Dptd UK 22.2.62 to Australia. To Fairey Aviation; to Edinburgh 21.6.62; allocated to 1 ATU 18.4.63 (dispatched 6.5.63, arrived 7.5.63). Shot down by a Thunderbird missile on Woomera Range 18.6.63. Approved for conversion to scrap 22.7.63.

VZ503 Conveyed by road Aston Down-Tarrant Rushton 13.9.60 (ex-20 MU). for conversion to U.16 against Contract KK/F/097/CB24(a). (TFH 846.20). Allotted to Bankstown 22.9.61; to R & J Park Ltd 27.10.61 for packing. Dptd UK 16.11.61 by ship to Australia. To Fairey Aviation; to Edinburgh 18.5.62; 1 ATU 1.11.62. Shot down by a Thunderbird missile on Woomera Range 6.2.64. SOC 7.5.64.

WE902 Conveyed by road Aston Down-Tarrant Rushton 15.9.60 (ex-20 MU). for conversion to U.16. (TFH 603.05). Allotted to Bankstown 28.6.61; to R & J Park Ltd 7.7.61 for packing. Dptd UK 10.7.61 by ship to Australia. To Fairey Aviation; Edinburgh 2.10.61; 1 ATU 26.7.62. Shot down at 26,000ft over Woomera by a Seaslug 2 missile 30.10.64. SOC 14.1.65.

WE960 Conveyed by road Aston Down-Tarrant Rushton 25.2.59 (ex-20 MU) for conversion to U.16 against Contract KD/N/04/CB7(c). To R & J Park Ltd 26.5.60 for packing against Contract KK/F/067/CB7(c). Dptd UK 30.5.60 by ship to Australia. Rec'd by Fairey Aviation 6.7.60; modified to U.21 prototype and allotted to ARDU 16.11.60 for flight trials (actual movement 27.1.61); ferried ARDU-Edinburgh 3.2.61) for Base Sqdn; to Maintenance Sqdn 7.2.61 for acceptance checks and mods. Ferried to 1 ATU Woomera 22.11.61 for preliminary trials; ret to Maint Sqdn 7.12.61 for final 'auto-flight' mods. Conveyed to 1ATU 12/13.2.62. Ret to Maint. Sqdn 4.2.63 for servicing and autopilot check. Ferried to 1ATU 17.4.63. Shot down by a Thunderbird missile at Woomera Range 26.11.63. Approved for conversion to components/scrap 29.1.64.

WF659 Conveyed by road Aston Down-Tarrant Rushton 9.9.60 (ex-20 MU) for conversion to U.16 against Contract KK/F/097/CB24(a). (TFH 1614.55). Allocated to R & J Park Ltd 22.9.61 for packing against Contract KK/F/050/CB24(a); handed over 5.10.61. Dptd UK 16.11.61 by ship to Australia. To Fairey Aviation 21.3.62; to Edinburgh 27.3.62; 1 ATU 3.4.62; 2 ATU 12.6.65. Destroyed 18.2.72 during a pilotless sortie over Woomera Range.

WH460 Conveyed by road Aston Down-Tarrant Rushton 2.9.60 (ex-20 MU). for conversion to U.16 against Contract KK/F/097/CB24(a). (TFH 1408.05). Allocated to R & J Park Ltd 18.8.61 for packing against Contract KK/F/0150/CB24(a); handed over 1.9.61. Shipped to Australia. Allotted to Fairey Aviation, Bankstown 22.9.61; to Edinburgh 2.2.62; 1 ATU 15.3.62. Destroyed by a Rapier missile 5,200ft (1,585m) over Woomera Range 28.5.69.

WK710 Conveyed by road Aston Down-Tarrant Rushton 13.9.60 (ex-20 MU). for conversion to U.16 against Contract KK/F/097/CB24(a). (TFH 875.40). Allocated to R & J Park Ltd 8.12.61 for packing and shipment to Australia against Contract KK/F/0150/CB24(a). Dptd UK 19.1.62. To Edinburgh 29.5.62; 1 ATU 11.7.63. Destroyed after unintentionally hit by a Rapier missile over Woomera Range 6.2.69.

WK797 Allocated to FRL 9.12.58 for conversion to U.16 against Contract KD/N/04/CB7(c). Ferried Lyneham-Tarrant Rushton 20.4.59 (ex-33 MU), Released to R & J Park Ltd 4.4.60 for packing against

Above: *Meteor U.21 VZ503 displays the standard red and white 'Australia' scheme as well as the clean lines of this one-time front-line fighter.*

Left: *Meteor U.21 WH460 seen immediately after re-assembly in Australia but awaiting its new paint scheme. (via Jennifer M. Gradidge)*

Contract KK/F/067/CB7(c). Dptd UK 6.5.60 aboard SS *Pinjara*; arrived at Base Sqdn, Edinburgh 14.6.60. To 1 ATU 21.4.61. Crashed 8.2.63 after control was lost during a Bloodhound sortie at Woomera Range. SOC 22.4.63.

WK879 Conveyed by road Aston Down-Tarrant Rushton 15.9.60 (ex-20 MU). for conversion to U.16 against Contract KK/F/097/CB24(a).

(TFH 808.00). To R & J Park Ltd 14.11.61 for packing against Contract KK/F/0150/CB24(a). Dptd UK 27.11.61 by ship to Fairey Aviation, Australia. To Edinburgh 4.5.62; 1 ATU 29.11.62. Shot down by a Bloodhound 2 missile at Woomera Range 17.10.63.

WL136 Conveyed by road Aston Down-Tarrant Rushton 20.9.60 (ex-20 MU). for conversion to U.16 against Contract

KK/F/097/CB24(a). (TFH 691.00). Modified to U.21 and f/f 31.5.61. To R & J Park Ltd 6.6.61 for packing and shipment. Test-flown in Australia 28.9.61. Allocated to Fairey (Australia) 2.10.61. Struck off RAAF Charge 9.8.67 (ex 2 ATU) on transfer to WRE charge. Rtnd to UK and arrived at Tarrant Rushton 5.10.70. Believed converted to U.16 and del to Llanbedr 20.12.71 for trials. Coded 'W'. No further details.

Meteor U.21A A77-422 was one of a number of former RAF/RAAF Meteor F.8s converted to drone status for operations over the Woomera Range. A77-422 (originally WF750) displays the larger engine intake that was standard to this mark of Meteor and is seen outside the Fairey Australia Company facility at Bankstown awaiting fitment of a full set of aerials. (via Jennifer M. Gradidge)

Meteor U.21A – Individual Service Histories

Fairey also converted 15 former RAAF Meteor F.8s to U.21A standard, as follows:

A77-157 Originally del to RAAF (ex-WE889) 19.12.51. Sold to WRE/MoA 15.2.63. To Fairey for conversion to U.21A. To 1 ATU 28.2.64. Transferred from RAAF to WRE charge 4.4.67. Destroyed by Rapier missile over Woomera Range 16.9.69.

A77-193 Originally del to RAAF (ex-WE969) 2.12.51. Sold to WRE/MoA 15.2.63. To Fairey for conversion to U.21A. To 1 ATU 28.1.64. Sustained Cat.5 damage 3.4.64, possibly as a result of a Thunderbird missile strike over Woomera Range. SOC 14.5.64.

A77-207 Originally del to RAAF (ex-WH251) 8.3.51. Sold to WRE/MoA 15.2.63. To Fairey for conversion to U.21A. Allicated to Base Sqdn, Edinburgh

28.5.63 (delivered 25.7.63). Transferred from RAAF to WRE charge 11.4.67. Destroyed by (unknown) missile at Woomera Range 18.11.71.

A77-422 Originally del to RAAF (ex-WF750) 18.12.51. Sold to WRE 17.10.60. To Fairey Aviation for conversion to U.21A. To Maint. Sqdn, Edinburgh 6.2.62. To 1 ATU 15.3.62; to 2 ATU 27.8.65; to WRE Woomera 31.7.67. Crashed within Woomera Range 4.8.69 after just 9 mins flight into an intended Rapier missile trial.

A77-510 Originally del to RAAF (ex-WE905) 18.12.51. In use at Edinburgh Field by Maint Sqdn and 2 ATU as an F.8 until sold to WRE 17.10.60. Retained at Edinburgh until allotted to Fairey 18.9.61 (despatched 6.10.61; received 12.10.61)

for conversion to U.21A. Issued to Base Sqdn, Edinburgh 14.12.62 (actually received 9.4.63) and received by 1 ATU 5.8.64. Transferred from RAAF to WRE charge 11.4.67. Destroyed at 6,300ft (1,920m) over Woomera Range by a Rapier missile 12.11.68.

A77-802 Originally del to RAAF (ex-WA998) 24.4.52. Sold to WRE 17.10.60; to Fairey for conversion to U.21A. Allocated to Edinburgh Field (ex FAC) 25.10.62 (actually received 1.11.62). To 1 ATU 8.10.63. Transferred from RAAF to WRE charge 11.4.67. Destroyed by a Rapier missile over Woomera Range 16.9.69.

A77-851 Originally del to RAAF (ex-WK683) 20.8.52. Sold to WRE 17.10.60.

To Fairey for conversion to U.21A. To Base Sqdn, Edinburgh 4.9.62. Undercarriage damaged on landing at Evett's Field 13.6.63 after a Bloodhound sortie over Woomera. Not repaired; SOC 8.1.64 and later scrapped at Edinburgh Field 10.65. Cockpit section extant at SA Aviation Museum in Mk.8 guise.

A77-855 Originally del to RAAF (ex-WK728) 20.8.52. Sold to WRE 17.10.60. To Fairey for conversion to U.21A. Crashed at Woomera Range 19.2.63 due to loss of control 21 mins into a Thunderbird sortie.

A77-863 Originally del to RAAF (ex-WK730) 20.8.52. Sold to WRE 17.10.60. To Fairey for conversion to U.21A. Issued to 1 ATU 15.3.62 (actually delivered 21.3.62); 2 ATU 12.6.65. WRE Woomera 14.9.67 or 14.9.67. During a Rapier missile trial at Woomera Range 14.2.69 control was lost after 5 mins at 3,000ft (914m) during a high bank turn. Crashed within Range boundary.

A77-872 Originally del to RAAF (ex-WK792) 29.3.53. Sold to WRE 17.10.60. To Fairey for conversion to U.21A. To Base Sqdn, Edinburgh 21.6.62. Destroyed by a Seaslug 2 missile 32,000ft (9,754m) over Woomera Range 28.5.65.

A77-873 Originally del to RAAF (ex-WK796) 29.3.53. Sold to WRE 21.12.60. To Fairey for conversion to U.21A. Issued to Base Sqdn 20.5.62 (received 13.6.62); to 1 ATU 26.6.63 (delivered 1.7.63). Transferred from RAAF to WRE charge 11.4.67. Destroyed by (unidentified) missile at Woomera Range 30.11.71.

A77-876 Originally del to RAAF (ex-WK800) 3.5.53. Sold to WRE 17.10.60. To Fairey for conversion to U.21A. Last recorded flight in Australia 11.67 (presumably Woomera-Evett's Field for storage). Returned to UK c5.69 and converted to U.16 WK800 (later re-des'd D.16). See U.16 Individual Histories for further details.

A77-882 Originally del to RAAF (ex-WK937) 23.8.53. Sold to WRE 17.10.60. To Fairey for conversion to U.21A. Issued to Edinburgh 18.5.62 (received 5.6.62). To 1 ATU 26.6.63 (although not del'd until

Prior to each unmanned Meteor sortie over Woomera Range, a photographic record was taken of aircraft and mission details. On this occasion Meteor U.21A A77-207 is recorded before performing "Trial MU475" on 18 November 1971, a trial that resulted in '207 sustaining a direct missile hit. The tail section, which at first glance appears remarkably complete, was later recovered from the Range. (via John Hopton)

30.1.64). Destroyed by a Seaslug 2 missile at Woomera 13.10.65.

A77-884 Originally del to RAAF (ex-WK931) 25.9.53. Sold to WRE 17.10.60. To Fairey for conversion to U.21A. To Edinburgh 15.11.61; Base Squadron 7.12.61. Destroyed by a Thunderbird missile 30,000ft (9,144m) over Woomera Range 3.11.65.

A77-885 Originally del to RAAF (ex-WK973) 16.10.53. Sold to WRE 17.10.60. To Fairey for conversion to U.21A. To Base Squadron 11.5.62. Undercarriage collapsed during pilotless landing 4.4.63 at Evett's Field after a Thunderbird sortie. On 20.6.63 it was reported as "in process of being written-off". Later reported as re-assembled in reasonably complete condition and used for fire-fighting at Edinburgh Field 10.65.

Supermarine Swift Drone

As mentioned earlier, by the mid-1950s, and with modern missile systems entering front-line service, it was generally accepted that the Meteor drone was based on an outdated design. One front-line fighter that had failed to attain widespread usage was the Supermarine Swift. Overshadowed by the Hawker Hunter, many production Swifts were surplus to requirements.

On 18 October 1955 Fairey Aviation Ltd was awarded a contract (6/Acft/12692/CB.9)) to raise a design study to convert surplus Supermarine Swift fighters into high-speed drones.

Design work started at Hayes and Swift F.1 WK248, which had spent its entire life on Ministry of Supply charge, was earmarked for the initial conversion. Whether or not WK248 was ever conveyed to Hayes is uncertain; it is doubtful that it did but in the event the conversion never took place and the contract was officially cancelled on 4 February 1957. By that time WK248 had been sold to the College of Aeronautics at Cranfield.

Folland Gnat Drone

Plans to develop the Folland Gnat into a high-speed target drone were certainly given some consideration but thought never to have reached any further than the late discussion stage.

It is unclear how and where the Gnat (described in some company archive material as the Gnat Mk.6) would be built or converted. It was also unclear who the contractor would have been. However Short Brothers & Harland did prepare a Preliminary Design project, known as the Short P.D.35 and which was described at the time as a high-speed target drone based on the Gnat. No further details are known.

Similarly, unconfirmed reports suggest that a study was made into the possibility of having an unmanned Gnat attached to an under-wing pylon of a Vulcan bomber. It has been said that several test-flights were made with a Gnat T.1 in extreme close formation with a Vulcan but the concept was never developed.

Canberra Drone Conversions

With the growing threat posed by Soviet nuclear-armed bomber force throughout the 1950s the need to develop a credible guided missile response became increasingly urgent. At the same time came an equally urgent requirement for a suitable unmanned target aircraft to act in a training and development role. The only target aircraft that could be considered as available was the joint Australian/British Jindivik but in terms of speed and size the Jindivik was never a realistic option. The Meteor U.15 was also an option but it was based on an outdated design and also too small to be an appropriate target to meet future requirements. Said to produce a radar image ten times larger than a Jindivik, the Canberra represented a more authentic target and attention therefore turned to the conversion of standard Canberra aircraft into drone configuration.

Air Ministry Specification D.169D&P, was issued on 17 August 1955 to cover the conversion of existing Canberra

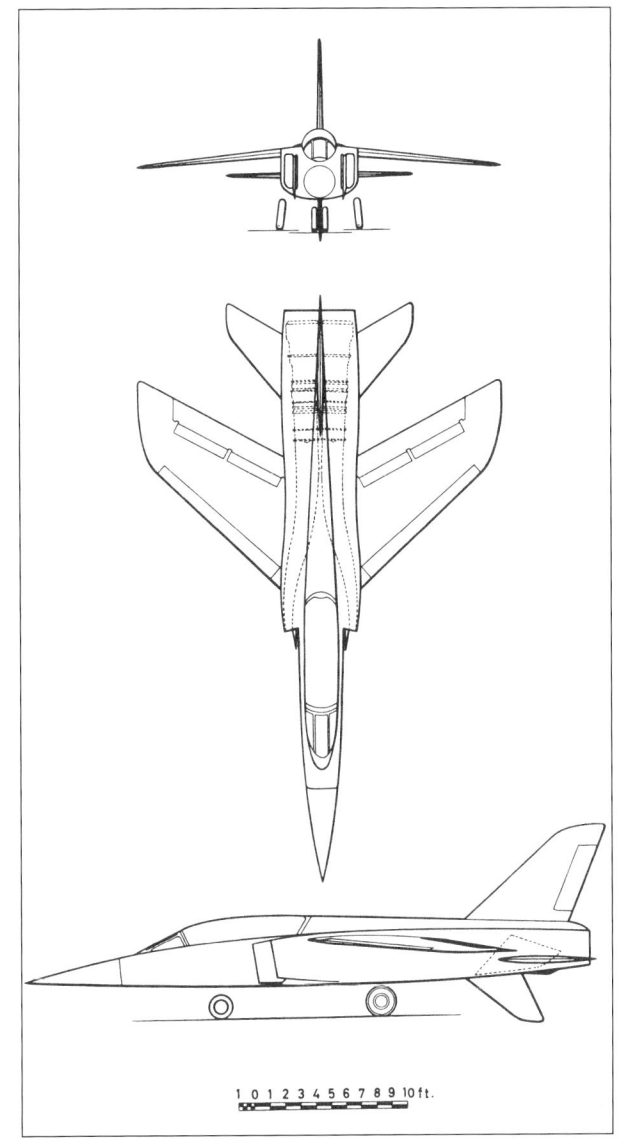

3-view drawing of the proposed Gnat 6 drone

B.2s to U.10s for operation at the Weapons Research Establishment Range at Woomera. There were few demands within the Specification; performance of the U.10 would be the same as the B.2 and the radio control system would be capable of operating under all conditions of flight at a range of up to at least 100 nautical miles at 10,000 ft altitude. Engines and other 'life' items were to have at least 100 hours remaining.

Apart from producing aircraft of its own design, Short Brothers & Harland Ltd had secured a number of contracts to modify, overhaul and maintain large numbers of Royal Navy Sea Hawks, Scimitars and Sea Venoms at the Aircraft Yard at Sydenham. Shorts had also entered sub-contract manufacturing and had won contracts to produce 150 English Electric Canberras.[37] The PR.9 variant of the Canberra represented a major redesign and was solely the responsibility of Shorts. With Flight Refuelling Ltd fully engaged on the Meteor drone programme, it was perhaps

---

37 The 150 aircraft (allocated c/ns SH.1610 to SH.1759) consisted of 60 Mk. B.2s, 49 B.6s and 41 PR.9s, although the final 18 PR.9s were subsequently cancelled.

For many it must have been considered a crime to purposely re-configure such a graceful and iconic aeroplane solely for the purpose of shooting it down. U.10 WH733 displays the fine lines of the Canberra whilst test-flying out of Belfast in July 1959. (Short Bros & Harland Ltd.)

not surprising therefore that the Canberra drone programme was awarded to Short Bros.

At the initial stage the projected Canberra drone was referred to by Shorts as Preliminary Design 31 (PD.31) but as the project developed so the company designation Short SC.4 was adopted. The allocation of aircraft to the drone programme certainly underlined the Canberra's mixed pedigree; the first B.2 to be ferried to Shorts for conversion (WJ624) was a Handley Page-built whilst the second (WJ987) was from a batch sub-contracted to Avro. Both served as the U.10 conversion prototypes, the first of which to fly being WJ624 which took to the air at Belfast on 11 June 1957. All initial flight-testing was conducted with test pilot D.R. Turley-George on board as at that stage there was no ground link, the aircraft being flown by a supervisory control panel instead of normal controls. This panel, which was fitted in production U.10s for check flights, carried a series of control buttons with associated indicator lamps, generally similar to those available to the ground master controller in pilotless operations. The second prototype U.10, WJ987, made its first flight on 4 February 1958 and later made the first ground-controlled flights albeit with a check pilot on board. High-altitude trials were later conducted by Alex Roberts who took WJ624 up to 56,700ft.

Go-ahead for the conversion of 16 Canberra B.2s to U.10s was given on 21 March 1958 with the issue of revised Specification D.169D&P.2. All, including the second prototype (WJ987), were fitted with a long-range fuel tank in the bomb bay to enable aircraft to be ferried out to Australia. The first target operation by a Canberra over the Woomera Range took place in June 1959 and by November 1965 when the target service ended, 12 of the 17 delivered were shot down. The remaining five malfunctioned and crashed.

Conversions of drone Canberras was not restricted to the U.10. Under the company designation Short SC.6, a further six Canberra B.2s were later converted to U.14 standard; these were similar to the U.10 except for the fitting of hydraulic servo-assisted controls (as on the Canberra PR.9). The U.14 (subsequently re-designated D.14) was specifically allocated to the Fleet Air Arm for use by 728B Flight at Hal Far, Malta as part of the on-going Seacat and Seaslug missile trials programme.[38]

WH720 undertook the Squadron's first pilotless sortie on 3 August 1961; the first loss to a missile occurred on 6 October 1961 when HMS *Girdle Ness* successfully shot WH921 down. However, Canberra operations at Hal Far were surprisingly brief. A short but intensive period of missile guidance system trials ended when the Squadron disbanded in December 1961. The surviving five aircraft were flown back to Pershore for long-term storage and eventually disposed of as scrap.

728B Flight Canberra Code Sequence

Canberra U.14s (later D.14s) were allocated individual codes within the sequence '590' to '595', as follows:

'590'	WH921	U.14	May 1961 – Oct 1961
'591'	WD941	U.14	Jun 1961 – Dec 1961
'592'	WH720	U.14	July 1961 – Dec 1961
'593'	WJ638	U.14	Aug 1961 – Dec 1961
'594'	WH704	U.14	Sep 1961 – Dec 1961
'595'	WH870	U.14	Sep 1961 – Dec 1961

Canberra Drone Colour Schemes

All Canberra U.10s and U.14s were finished, as per Specification D.169 D&P.2, in an overall matt white scheme for delivery, with standard service markings and black anti-reflection finish in the regions necessary for the optical recording installation. Wide black bands were also applied around the outer part of each wing.

U.10 prototypes WJ624 and WJ987 both carried black/white/black stripes around the rear fuselage whilst flight-testing in the UK.

---

38 Service designations for Unmanned aircraft were changed from "U" to "D" in mid-1962 at a time when the Wessex Mk. HU.5 (Helicopter Utility) was issued. Theoretically this should have involved surviving Meteor U.15s, U.16s and later U.21 conversions being re-designated D.15, D.16 and D.21. However it seems that operators paid little more than lip service to the change and for reasons of convenience the author has referred to the original designation throughout unless original source material has shown otherwise.

728B Flight Canberra U.14 WH921 is the subject of much attention from ground crews at Hal Far. WH921 was delivered to the Flight in May 1961 and was shot down by a Seaslug missile on 6 October 1961. (via Robin A. Walker)

Canberra U.10 Conversions – Individual Aircraft Histories

WD929 Allocated to Short Bros, Belfast 12.7.57-15.7.57 and then to Rochester 15.7.57-30.5.59 (although these dates are not necessarily movement dates). Ferried Warton to Shorts Belfast 15.7.57. Flown to West Malling 17.7.57 for conversion to U.10 at Rochester under Contract 6/Aircraft/12392/CB6(b). Conveyed by road to Southend post-conversion and later flown to Belfast 20.1.59. Grounded temporarily until 14.4.59 when test-flying commenced. Ferried Belfast-Benson 19.5.59 and temporarily used by the RAF Handling Squadron at Boscombe Down. Allocated to the WRE 30.5.59 and departed UK (date unknown) using RAAF call-sign VM-HDS for onward delivery to Australia. Allocated to Base Sqdn, Edinburgh 11.6.59. Destroyed by missile 15.10.59 whilst with No.1 ATU.

WD951 Transferred from 15 Squadron to Controller (Aircraft) charge 30.4.57 and ferried Hawarden to Belfast 3.5.57. Grounded after 22.7.57 for conversion to U.10; f/f as U.10 28.7.58 and delivered Belfast to Bedford same date and using RAAF call-sign VM-HMP. Ferried Warton to Belfast 20.10.58 (using a Shorts call-sign) and immediately grounded. Re-commenced flying 10.2.59 and ferried Belfast-Benson 10.3.59 and later temporarily used by the RAF Handling Squadron at Boscombe Down. Delivered to Australia late-3.59 (using RAAF call-sign VM-HDR). Allocated to Base Squadron, Edinburgh 3.4.59. Believed seriously damaged by a missile 20.7.59; reported at 1ATU 12.9.59 awaiting write-off.

WD961 Transferred from 15 Squadron to Controller (Aircraft) charge 26.4.57 and ferried Harwarden to Belfast same date. Grounded after 18.7.57 for conversion to U.10; f/f as U.10 7.9.58. Delivered Belfast to Bedford 12.9.58. Returned to Belfast 3.10.58. Delivered Belfast-Benson 24.11.58 (using RAAF call-sign VM-HDP) for onward delivery to Australia. Allocated to Base Sqdn, Edinburgh 18.12.58. Notified as unserviceable 12.3.59. Reported at 1ATU 19.6.59 awaiting write-off, possibly following a missile strike on 9.6.59.

WH652 Ferried from 23 MU Aldergrove to Belfast 19.9.60 and transferred to MOA charge same date. Grounded for conversion to U.10; f/f as U.10 12.12.61. Delivered Belfast-Aldergrove 23.2.62 (using the RAAF call-sign VM-HDH) for onward delivery to Australia. Reported with Maintenance Sqdn, Edinburgh 10.3.62 and later to 1 ATU 31.5.63. Destroyed by a Thunderbird 2 missile at Woomera 12.2.64.

WH705 Ferried from 15 MU Wroughton to Belfast 29.9.60 and transferred to MOA charge same date. Grounded for conversion to U.10; f/f as U.10 19.4.62. Delivered Belfast-Lyneham 4.7.62 (using the RAAF call-sign VM-HDW) for onward delivery to Australia. Reported with Base Sqdn, Edinburgh 26.7.62. To 2 ATU 22.5.63; to 1 ATU 3.3.64. Destroyed by a Seaslug missile at Woomera 28.4.65.

WH710 Ferried from Marshall of Cambridge to Belfast 22.7.58 and immediately grounded. Briefly test-flown 14.12.59 prior to conversion to U.10; f/f as U.10 9.8.60. Delivered Belfast-Benson 30.9.60 (using RAAF call-sign VM-HDP) and onward delivery to Australia. Reported with Base Sqdn, Edinburgh 3.11.60. To 1 ATU 25.1.62. Thought to have crashed whilst returning from a target sortie over Woomera. Noted in the Woomera scrap compound for several years in the mid-1960s.

WH729 Transferred from 9 Squadron to MoA charge 8.10.57 and ferried Aldergrove-Belfast 11.10.57. Grounded until test-flown 5.58 & 6.58. Again grounded after 4.7.58 for conversion to U.10; f/f as U.10 20.10.59. Delivered Belfast-Benson 5.11.59 using RAAF call-sign VM-HDU but returned to Belfast 16.11.59. Delivered out to Benson again 18.11.59 for onward delivery to Australia. Reported with Base Sqdn, Edinburgh 2.12.59. To 1 ATU 12.5.60. Destroyed by a Bloodhound 2 missile 14.4.65 (or 14.4.64).

WH733 Transferred from 57 Squadron to Controller (Aircraft) charge 8.10.57 and ferried Binbrook-Belfast same date. Immediately grounded until test flown thoroughly during 4.58. Again grounded after 29.4.58 for U.10 conversion; f/f as U.10 30.6.59. Delivered Belfast-Benson 18.9.59 using RAAF call-sign VM-HDT 18.9.59 and onward delivery to Australia. Reported with Base Sqdn, Edinburgh 2.10.59. Notified as awaiting write-off 11.12.59, following a landing accident 30.11.59.

WH742 Ferried Binbrook-Belfast 22.11.57 and transferred to Controller (Aircraft) charge 25.11.57. Grounded until test-flown throughout 6.58. Again grounded after 20.6.58 for U.10 conversion; f/f as U.10 11.12.59. Delivered

Post-War Drone Conversions 137

Belfast-Lyneham 24.12.59 using RAAF call-sign VM-HDW for onward delivery to Australia. Reported with Base Sqdn, Edinburgh 4.1.60; to 1 ATU 1.7.60. Notified 26.7.62 as "recommended for write-off" being hit by a Thunderbird 2 missile 17.7.62.

WH860 Transferred from 15 MU to MoA charge 23.9.60 and ferried Wroughton-Belfast same date. Immediately grounded for U.10 conversion; f/f as U.10 9.1.62. Delivered Belfast-Lyneham 5.4.62 (using RAAF call-sign VM-HDZ) for onward delivery to Australia. To No.1 ATU. Destroyed by a Seaslug 2 missile 24.11.64.

WH885 Transferred from 23 MU to MoA charge 29.9.60 and ferried Aldergrove-Belfast same date. Immediately grounded for U.10 conversion; f/f as U.10 10.4.62. Delivered Belfast-Lyneham 21.5.62 (using RAAF call-sign VM-HDM) for onward delivery to Australia. Destroyed in an accident 1.4.64.

WJ604 Transferred from 9 Squadron to Controller (Aircraft) charge 8.10.57 and ferried Aldergrove-Belfast 11.10.57. Grounded until test-flown 5.58. Again grounded after 30.5.58 for conversion to U.10; f/f as U.10 20.11.59. Delivered Belfast-Benson 9.12.59 (using RAAF call-sign VM-HDV) for onward delivery to Australia. Destroyed due to control failure 18.2.64.

WJ621 Transferred from 33 MU to Controller (Aircraft) charge 13.3.58 and ferried Benson-Belfast same date. Grounded until test flown throughout 8.58. Again grounded after 25.8.58 for U.10 conversion; f/f as U.10 22.1.60. Delivered Belfast-Benson 2.3.60 (using RAAF call-sign VM-HDX) for onward delivery to Australia. To 1 ATU. Crashed on approach (location unkn) 17.12.64. Cat.5

WJ623 Transferred from 15 MU to Controller (Aircraft) charge 7.3.58 and ferried Wroughton-Belfast same date. Grounded until test flown in 10.58 & 11.58. Again grounded after 13.11.58 for U.10 conversion; f/f as U.10 11.3.60. Delivered Belfast-Benson 24.5.60 (using RAAF call-sign VM-HDY) for onward delivery to Australia. Later to WRE Edinburgh Field, Australia. Destroyed by a Bloodhound 2 missile 10.12.63 (although reported still at Edinburgh 1965).

WJ624 To Shorts Belfast 6.9.55; to MOA charge 9.12.55 for initial development work on U.10 programme. Converted to U.10 and f/f at Belfast 11.6.57. Initially no ground link was used, the aircraft being flown by a pilot who operated a supervisory control panel. To RAE Bedford 13.1.58 for trials and also at Boscombe Down at times during 1958. To RAE Llanbedr 15.10.59 for evaluation. Later converted to U.14 at RAE Llanbedr. Last recorded flight 18.10.61. Derelict at Belfast by 1964.

WJ987 Transferred to Controller (Aircraft) charge 23.11.56 and ferried Aldergrove-Belfast same date. Detached to Valley 29.11.56 to 26.1.57 (and reportedly at Boscombe Down during 1958) after which it was grounded at Belfast 21.4.58 and not flown again until 5.1.59. Converted to U.10 but reportedly as variously f/f as such 1.1.58 or 5.2.59. Ferried Belfast-Bedford 3.2.58; returned to Belfast 21.4.58 and not flown again until 5.1.59. (WJ987 is recorded as the first 'production U.10' and therefore the first flight date of 1.1.58 is more likely.) Delivered Belfast-Benson 25.2.59 (using RAAF call-sign VM-HDQ) for onward delivery to Australia. Reported as being delivered to WRE Edinburgh Field, Australia 14.3.59. Destroyed by a missile 17.10.59.

WK107 Transferred to MoA charge 29.9.60 and ferried Aldergrove-Belfast the same date. Immediately grounded for U.10 conversion; f/f as U.10 25 or 28.1.62. Delivered Belfast-Lyneham 6.3.62 (using RAAF call-sign VM-HDL). Noted at WRE Edinburgh Field 2.63 but later destroyed by a Thunderbird 2 missile 17.11.65.

WK110 Transferred to Controller (Aircraft) charge 13.3.59 and ferried Binbrook-Belfast the same date. Grounded after 6.5.59 for conversion to U.10; f/f as U.10 20.4.60. Delivered Belfast-Benson 30.5.60 (using RAAF call-sign VM-HDZ) for onward delivery to Australia. Destroyed by a Bloodhound 2 missile 23.11.62.

Note that Canberra B.2 **WJ609** was ferried from Binbrook to Belfast on 8.10.57 and immediately grounded. It was test flown during 4.58, 5.58 and 10.58 before being grounded on 14.10.58 for conversion to U.10. However the conversion was not completed and the aircraft was next flown on 7.9.59 when it was ferried Belfast to Llanbedr, as a B.2.

The Canberra U.10 was a development by Short Brothers & Harland and involved conversions from a standard B.2 variant. WJ987 has been variously described as the 2nd Prototype and the 1st production example. Whatever the case, everything that is overtly graceful about a Canberra is more than evident in this air-to-air shot, taken during an early test-flight. (Short Brothers & Harland Ltd. Neg. No. AC.8.3073H)

Canberra U.14 Conversions – Individual Aircraft Histories

WD941 23 MU Store to Shorts Belfast 3.5.60 for conversion to U.14; f/f 27.4.61 (as U.14). Del to Lyneham 6.6.61; rec'd by 728B Flight, Hal Far 9.6.61 and coded '591'. To Pershore 11.12.61 (arrived 12.12.61) for storage. Broken-up on site 10.63.

WH704 15 MU Store to Shorts Belfast 15.6.60 for conversion to U.14; f/f Aldergrove 4.7.61. To 728B Flight 5.9.61 (rec'd 6.9.61) as '594'. To Pershore 5.12.61 for storage. SOC 20.9.63 for apprentice training; later for fire practice. Broken up at Pershore 9.65.

WH720 15 MU Store to Shorts Belfast 10.5.60 for conversion to U.14; f/f 18.5.61. To 728B Flight 3.7.61 (Del Lyneham-Hal Far 7.7.61) as '592'. First pilotless sortie 3.8.61. To Pershore 5.12.61 for storage. SOC 20.9.63 & sold as scrap to R.J. Coley 10.63.

WH876 f/f 10.8.61 (as U.14). Del to 728B Flight 14.9.61 as '595'. To Pershore 3.12.61 for storage. Restored to (virtual) B.2 standard at Pershore for A&AEE. Issued to A&AEE as a B.2(mod).

WH921 f/f 28.3.61 (as U.14). To 728B Flight 25.5.61 as '590'. Damaged 24.7.61. Repaired but shot down off Malta 6.10.61 by Seaslug missile from HMS *Girdle Ness*.

WJ638 To Shorts, Belfast 30.5.60 for conversion to U.14; f/f 13.6.61 (as U.14). To 728B Flight 9.8.61 as '593'. To Pershore 12.12.61 for storage. Restored to B.2 status by RRE Pershore for A&AEE; issued to A&AEE 27.6.62. To Predannack 5.1.78.

Note that Canberra U.10 **WJ624** *was converted to U.14 standard at RAE Llanbedr.*

Sea Vixen D.3 (and QF-100 Super Sabre)

To many industry observers, the Sea Vixen D.3 was perhaps the ultimate of drone conversions.[39] Transforming the standard shipboard fighter to a pilotless drone promised, probably for the first time, to be straightforward process, the conversion being based around a Universal Drone Pack (UDP), a remote control package jointly designed and developed by Flight Refuelling Ltd, GEC and Marconi-Elliot. What made the UDP so effective was that it combined all of the necessary remote control equipment needed to convert an aircraft to drone configuration but that its greatest value was the relative ease of fitting it into any aircraft type by simply taking the space normally occupied by the pilot's ejection seat. (Conversions of Meteors had proven to be both expensive and complex because the drone equipment had to be fitted into various points around the aircraft's structure.)

Conversion of Sea Vixen to drone configuration was a two-stage process. Firstly, all unnecessary equipment and weight (including guns and radar) was removed, that being the responsibility of RAE Farnborough. The second stage, that of actually installing the remote control equipment and all related items, was contracted to Flight Refuelling Ltd at Tarrant Rushton. Flight Refuelling fitted the UDP into the space made available by removing the observer's cockpit, thus leaving the pilot's seat in situ and allowing the aircraft to be flown conventionally if and when required.

The first sign of any activity came about on 25 January 1972 when an 899 Squadron Sea Vixen FAW.1 (XJ580) was ferried from Yeovilton to Llanbedr to allow pilots and engineers to familiarize themselves with the type. Over the next few days four more (XJ524, XJ579, XJ608 and XS577) followed for the same purpose. One factor realised almost immediately was the need to install heavier-duty arrestor wires across the airfield's main runway.

In the meantime, and with no official Requirement or Specification having yet been issued, XN649 was flown to Tarrant Rushton where it would act as a 'pattern' aircraft. Several months later, on 5 July, one of Lee-on-Solent's instructional airframes (XJ482/A2598) was conveyed by road to Tarrant Rushton to act as a static rig for the Universal Drone Pack (later moving to Wimborne when Tarrant Rushton was closed).

Initially, the Sea Vixen drone programme involved the conversion of three prototypes and 22 'production' D.3s and within a short period other redundant Sea Vixens were gathered at Farnborough where their suitability for conversion was assessed before being placed into what was hoped to be short-term storage there.[40] However, real progress was slow and installation work at Tarrant Rushton did not really get under way until mid-1975 by which time some doubts were already being expressed over the lack of sensitivity in the Sea Vixen's control systems.[41]

In the meantime some activity had taken place. The first of two Sea Vixen FAW.2s, XP924, was flown to Llanbedr on 4 June 1973 to carry out 'shepherding' duties on a number of Jindivik sorties. The same aircraft was also involved in tracking trials and pilot continuation training as was the second aircraft, XP920, which arrived at Llanbedr in August 1973.

The first prototype drone conversion, XN657, eventually made its first flight at Tarrant Rushton 11 May 1979 with the appropriate marking 'TR-1'. A second conversion, XP924 (marked as 'TR-2') followed, just before Tarrant Rushton closed as an active airfield. All drone conversion work was then transferred to Hurn at which time the third conversion, XS577 (and what was considered as the first production example), was still uncompleted.

XN657 logged 129 test flying hours with Flight Refuelling before being ferried to Llanbedr on 9 July 1981, still marked as 'TR-1', to undergo various trial flights. In the meantime the conversion programme, dogged by rising

---

[39] The Sea Vixen drone was originally referred to as a Sea Vixen U.3 but was later dropped and more correctly designated D.3 following the adoption of the letter 'U' for Utility aircraft; the 'D' simply relating to Drone.

[40] At least 30 Sea Vixen FAW.2s were earmarked for conversion and spares etc: XJ482, XJ494, XJ524, XJ560, XJ572, XJ579, XJ580, XJ602, XJ608, XN649, XN652, XN653, XN657, XN658, XN683, XN688, XN694, XN696, XN697, XN700, XN705, XN706, XN707, XP920, XP924, XP925, XP956, XS577, XS580 and XS587.

[41] *The de Havilland Sea Vixen* by Tony Buttler (Air-Britain Historians 2007).

The third and final Sea Vixen D.3 conversion was XS577, seen here touching down at Bournemouth-Hurn. Its colour scheme looks decidedly 'gawdy' when compared to its former naval finish.

In many respects, converting Sea Vixen into an unmanned drone was fairly straightforward as a result of it being based around the Universal Drone Pack (UDP). This was a remote control package jointly designed and developed by Flight Refuelling Ltd, GEC and Marconi-Elliot to fit neatly into the space created by removing the pilot's ejection seat. (GEC-Marconi)

financial costs, dragged on slowly until Autumn 1983 when all work at Hurn was eventually halted. Just three aircraft had been converted although these did continue test flying at both Hurn and Llanbedr.

Llanbedr did receive its first true Sea Vixen D.3 when XP924 was flown in from Hurn on 6 January 1986. But there were no immediate plans for it to be flown in full drone mode; instead it was to be flown at all times with a safety pilot in order to assess the full implications of Sea Vixen as a drone.[42]

Reflecting on events that led to cancellation of the Sea Vixen drone, Lt. C. S. (Bill) Drake RN (Retd) has described how he received a call from the Lieutenant-Colonel in charge of the Rapier missile programme. The purpose of the call was to find out when he could expect to use Sea Vixen for live firing trials. Drake, having been appointed to DTGW just days beforehand was understandably unable to offer a satisfactory answer.[43]

Lt. Drake writes: "The very idea of a Sea Vixen drone gave me food for thought. I immediately dropped all else and started probing. I found that the (Sea Vixen) project was still under development although it had been promised to users for months; moreover production had been authorized ahead of completion of development without receiving Safety and Acceptance Clearance by the Range Authority at Aberporth. Aberporth was adamant that it was unacceptable to operate such a heavy and high-speed aircraft within Rapier range of the Range head at Aberporth, as the fallout due to a missile hit or an accident was a serious risk to the facility, and it was obvious that there had been insufficient consultation at the outset. I then ordered an inspection of all the Sea Vixens and found that many were little more than wrecks when they had been discarded by the Royal Navy in 1972, for example one had its tail booms sawn off. The cost assumptions were therefore hopelessly incorrect as each successive aircraft would need greater corrective work. On the evidence I proposed cancellation of all but two development aircraft to be used solely with a safety pilot for operator training and not as a target. This was welcomed by

---

42 Wendy Mills, *Target Rolling*.
43 *A Bit of a Tiff* by Lt. C. S. (Bill) Drake RN (Retd) C.Eng. MIERE. MBIM

The Sea Vixen D.3 programme suffered frustrating delays and eventual cancellation. Converted from FAW.2 to D.3 configuration at Tarrant Rushton, XP924 emerged in a rather stark red and white scheme. Although it was later delivered to Llanbedr in January 1986 it did so solely for storage purposes. Eventually it was flown out of Llanbedr in August 1996 as G-CVIX. (British Aerospace; Weybridge-Bristol Division; Neg. No WH18875)

the head of Instrumentation & Trials Department at RAE Farnborough and I went ahead as planned.".

In the final analysis a number of factors worked against the Sea Vixen drone conversion, none more so than the imposed financial economies which had prevented the installation of a back-up system. Sea Vixen D.3 did have its positive points. It was large enough to offer the 'attacking' aircraft a good radar return but on the other hand, the twin-boom arrangement potentially blocked a heat-seeking missile's 'view' of the jet pipe. However, the Sea Vixen's greatest weakness was simply that it lacked the ability to fly at supersonic speeds, nor was it equipped with reheat, a key aspect when offering a realistic heat signature to an infra-red air-to-air missile.[44]

Apart from rising conversion costs there were, in the end, too many other difficulties that arose and many of those problems could not easily be overcome. The programme was therefore abandoned.

Although Jindivik was still available at Llanbedr albeit operating more as a means of providing a towed-body decoy target, the cancellation of Sea Vixen D.3 left a gap in providing a high-speed, truly realistic full-sized target. Several visits were made by DTGW personnel to Holloman Air Force Base, New Mexico and the Naval Weapons Center at China Lake to sample at first hand the US QF-86 drone operation. At the time Sperry Flight Systems Inc was undertaking the development and conversion of a number of former USAF F-100D/F Super Sabres to drones, against a contract awarded in August 1979, as replacements for the QF-86 fleet. Convinced that the QF-100 could serve as a replacement for the dogged Sea Vixen programme, the British delegation accepted a formal offer by the USAF to release between 24 and 30 QF-100s to the UK. The offer was clearly taken seriously as shortly afterwards a team from Sperry Flight Systems took up temporary residence at Llanbedr and Aberporth to help prepare and establish the British QF-100 operation. In the meantime the US – in preparing to place further orders for QF-100 drones and being much more stringent on their contractors than the British -chose to go out to tender. As a result Sperry lost out to a competitor, reputedly because the alternative bid was based on using cheaper 'Mexican' labour. The successful bidder was TRACOR/Flight Systems Division who went on to convert several hundred QF-100s. Despite the fact that Britain was "ready to go" with the QF-100 drone, the MoD was, it appears, unwilling to open up talks with an alternative provider and as a result any notion of British-operated drone Super Sabres faded to nothing.[45]

---

44 *Ibid*. Tony Buttler

45 *Ibid*. Lt. C. S. (Bill) Drake RN (Retd) C.Eng. MIERE. MBIM

Sea Vixen D.3 Conversions – Individual Aircraft Histories

XN657 (c/n 10089) Transferred from long-term storage at RNAY Belfast to RAE Llanbedr 15.3.73 (received at Llanbedr 19.4.73) for further long-term storage pending conversion to drone standard. Struck off RN charge 9.5.73. To Flight Refuelling at Tarrant Rushton 6.11.73 (received at Tarrant Rushton 7.11.73). Coded 'TR-1' and converted to prototype D.3; f/f as such 11.5.79 in a red/yellow scheme. Returned to RAE Llanbedr (still as 'TR-1') for completion of drone test-flying. Written off charge at Llanbedr 24.7.84; derelict by 8.88 and reduced to spares by 1989. Sectioned on fire dump c1991/93; cockpit section at Hanningfield Metals, Stock, Essex 1998. To M. Long, Yateley, Hants and extant 2004.

XP924 (c/n 10125) Transferred from long-term storage at RNAY Belfast to RAE Llanbedr 4.6.73. Struck off RN charge 12.11.73. Noted in storage at Farnborough 9.76 but reported back at Llanbedr by 5.77. Arrived at Tarrant Rushton 11.10.77 (reportedly from Farnborough) and remained until at least 7.79 under conversion to D.3 with code

'TR-2' (and red/yellow scheme). With FRL/ Yeovilton by 31.7.82 but in long-term storage at Hurn by 6.84. Flown to Llanbedr 6.1.86 and stored. Flown to Swansea Airport 2.8.96 for the 'Wings Over Wales' Museum having been registered G-CVIX 26.2.96. Ferried Swansea-Bournemouth (Hurn) 29.5.00 for De Havilland Aviation. Current and active.

XS577 (c/n 10135) Ferried to Llanbedr 26.1.72 (presumably ex-Yeovilton). Struck off RN charge 15.2.72. To RAE Farnborough 16.8.72 and stored until despatched to FRL at Tarrant Rushton 2.4.76 and converted to D.3 with code 'TR-3'. Returned to RAE Farnborough 10.1.78 but noted at Llanbedr 6.78 as 'TR-3'. With FRL at Hurn by 1980 for radar trials (until at least 1.85). Placed in long-term storage at Hurn until flown to Llanbedr (c1.86) but stored by 9.91. To T&EE Llanbedr by 11.93 (still in storage). Up for tender 11.95 and moved to Sharnford, Leics by 3.96. Nose section to Phoenix Aviation, Bruntingthorpe, Leics on 4.3.97.

Other aircraft associated with the Sea Vixen D.3 programme:

XJ494 (c/n 10021) Ferried Boscombe Down-Tarrant Rushton 19.2.74. To Farnborough 11.4.76 for long-term storage. Sold 4.12.83.

XJ524 (c/n 10033) Ferried to Llanbedr 28.1.72. To Farnborough 8.11.72 for long-term storage. To Tarrant Rushton 7.4.77. Conv to TT standard. Damaged c28.7.78 in runway overrun during taxying tests.

XJ560/8142M (c/n 10042) To Farnborough by 3.77 for long-term storage. Ex-storage 12.2.79 and conveyed by road to RAE Bedford 25.2.79 for arrestor hook trials.

XJ572 (c/n 10054) Ferried to Llanbedr 21.11.73. To Farnborough 6.6.75. Allocated to Catterick as 8803M 23.2.84.

XJ579 (c/n 10061) Ferried to Llanbedr 26.1.72; to Boscombe Down 11.7.72. To Farnborough (by road) 21.12.75. Broken up at Farnborough 3.84. Nose section passed to Midland Air Museum, Coventry 14.9.92.

XJ580 (c/n 10062) Ferried to Llanbedr 25.1.72. To Farnborough and in open storage by 6.73. To Tarrant Rushton 10.1.80. Written off charge 15.5.84. Subsequently purchased by Sea Vixen Society and mounted outside Somerford Road Industrial Park, Christchurch 17.12.84. To Tangmere Military Museum by road 27.6.00.

XJ602/A2622 (c/n 10069) Ferried Culdrose-Hurn 15.5.79 for long-term storage. Broken up c3.84 by Bradbury's of Bournemouth.

XJ608 (c/n 10075) Ferried to Llanbedr 7.2.72. To HAS Hatfield (via Belfast) 17.7.72. To Tarrant Rushton 8.10.74. To Farnborough 7.4.77 for long-term storage. Ex-storage for checks and engine runs 26.2.79. To Bedford 7.6.79; to Llanbedr 29.6.79. To FRL Hurn 3.11.81 for long-term storage. Disposed of to North Luffenham by road 20.3.84.

XN649 (c/n 10081) Ferried Yeovilton-Tarrant Rushton 25.1.72. To Farnborough 7.3.73 for long-term storage (in 'Q' Shed). Broken up by 5.84.

XN652 (c/n 10084) Ferried Boscombe Down-Farnborough 31.7.72. To Llanbedr 11.1.74. To Bedford c2-11.78. To Farnborough 6.2.79 for long-term storage. To Tarrant Rushton 15.5.80. Disposed of to Catterick as 8817M 4.84.

XN653 (c/n 10085) To Farnborough (date unknown) for long-term storage. Noted flying there 14.3.79 but returned to store. Broken up 7.84.

XN658/8223M (c/n 10090) Conveyed Halton-Farnborough by 10.76 for long-term storage. Derelict by 12.83.

XN688/8141M (c/n 10096) Conveyed to Farnborough by road 15.4.77 for long-term storage. Broken up c5.90.

XN696 (c/n 10104) Ferried Yeovilton-Tarrant Rushton 5.2.74. To Farnborough 28.2.76 for long-term storage. Sold 2.84.

XN697/A2623 (c/n 10105) Ferried Culdrose-Hurn 18.12.78. Scrapped 3.84.

XN700/8138M (c/n 10108) Conveyed Halton-Farnborough by road and re-assembled 10.1.77. Reduced to spares 12.83.

XN705/8225M (c/n 10113) Conveyed Abingdon-Farnborough by road 7.77.

XN706/A2613 (c/n 10114) Conveyed Lee-on-Solent to Farnborough 9.1.76. Reduced to spares 12.83.

XN707/8144M (c/n 10115) Conveyed Halton-Farnborough 27.3.77 for long-term storage. Ex-storage 13.2.79 and placed on RAE dump 2.79.

XP920 (c/n 10121) Ferried to Llanbedr 20.8.73. To Farnborough 30.6.76. Reduced to spares 12.83.

XP925 (c/n 10126) Ferried Yeovilton-Tarrant Rushton 4.2.74. To Farnborough 25.1.76. Broken up 6.84.

XP956 (c/n 10130) Ferried Boscombe Down-Tarrant Rushton 22.2.74. To Farnborough 22.1.76. reduced to spares 12.83.

XS580 (c/n 10138) Ferried Yeovilton-Tarrant Rushton 4.2.74. To Farnborough 5.4.76. To FR Wimborne by road 4.4.76 for D.3 systems development. SOC 19.11.81 and reduced to spares by 12.83.

XS587 (c/n 10145) Ferried Yeovilton-Tarrant Rushton 5.2.74. To Farnborough 11.1.76. To Tarrant Rushton 5.6.78. To Llanbedr 13.8.79 for crew training. Returned to Tarrant Rushton.

RIP – Sea Vixen drone. Two prospective drone conversions (XJ602 and XN697) were burnt at Hurn on 5 April 1984 as part of the final scrapping process by breaker G.W. & L.M. Bradbury & Co. XN697 is seen here the following morning waiting to be removed to the breaker's yard. (Michael I Draper)

A92-621, a Jindivik 103BL, is captured by the Llanbedr photographer at the point of leaving its launch trolley. '621 achieved 23 recoverable flights before being lost 4 June 1975 on its 24th flight. (via Tony Doyle)

Chapter 6
Jindivik and Stiletto

The long shadow of Nazi Germany's V-weapons and a deepening Cold War against the Soviet Union created an increasingly nervous backdrop to post-war Europe. Anxious to develop a range of modern technological weapon systems, the British Government took the first steps towards establishing a joint British-Australian missile range in the Australian outback almost immediately after World War II had ended. The initial move was made by Britain in February 1946 and after a series of meetings the Long Range Weapons Board of Administration was set up and an area at Woomera, South Australia, nominated as the weapons testing Range. The project came into formal existence on 1 April 1947.

Setting up a missile test range was of course paramount but what also emerged at an early stage was an equal need to develop a high-speed pilotless target aircraft. Again, the project became a joint British-Australian venture with the UK having responsibility for development of the engine, the automatic control equipment and the remote control links whilst the airframe would be designed and built in Australia. Another decision taken during this initial phase was that the prototypes would be piloted versions for use primarily in matching aircraft and automatic control system characteristics. From the outset, it was also agreed that take-off would be from a detachable trolley and that landing would be on retractable skid undercarriage. These factors were written into an outline Air Ministry Specification, E.7/48.

Approval to proceed on the design and construction of both pilotless (Project B) and piloted (Project C) versions was passed on 4 June 1948, involving six Project B and two Project C aircraft. Production commenced at the Government Aircraft Factory at Fisherman's Bend, Melbourne. The two projects were also named as Jindivik (Project B) and Pika (Project C). The first Pika was completed in October 1950 and transported from Fisherman's Bend to Woomera aboard a Bristol 170. Taxying trials commenced on 29 October and two days later the Pika made its first flight with GAF Test Pilot, John Miles at the controls.[1]

Between them, the two Pika prototypes completed a total of 214 flights, amounting to a total just short of 100 flying hours. The final test flight by a Pika was carried out on 29 June 1954.

---

1 National Archives AVIA54/526

Jindivik and Stiletto   143

By the time that the first Jindivik was signed off for flight, all six prototypes had been delivered to Evett's Field airstrip at Woomera. Eventually, on 28 August 1952, one of the prototypes (carrying the simple identity B-5) made a successful maiden flight. Ironically, it ended with the drone being written-off on landing after experiencing transmission difficulties between it and the accompanying Meteor "shepherd" aircraft.

Although Jindivik had been developed around Specification E.7/48 the UK had issued a second Specification in 1949, U.22/49, being much more stringent than E.7/48. Technical evolution of Jindivik was extremely rapid; so much so that Jindivik 2 design work had begun even before the first prototype Jindivik 1 had flown. U.22/49 led directly to Jindivik 2 which, in reality, was the true production version. It was powered by the more powerful Armstrong Siddeley Viper ASV.3 engine which allowed a maximum speed up to Mach 0.85 and an increased Jindivik's operational ceiling to 48,000ft. An initial order for ten production aircraft was placed in October 1951 which accounted for four Jindivik 2s plus a further six Mk.1 prototypes (with Adder engines). The first quantity order for production Jindivik 2 aircraft was placed in early-1952 and accounted for fifty aircraft for the RAAF.

A summary of Jindivik production is provided below.

Export Orders

In 1957 the Royal Swedish Air Force Board became the first overseas user with a purchase of ten Jindivik 2 variants. It is reported that the order was negotiated by Fairey Aviation Ltd who also acted as European agents for Jindivik. The Swedish Jindiviks were operated at a missile range on the Arctic Circle in Northern Sweden.

A number of sources have quoted useage by the US Navy. Certainly the manufacturer received, from the US

Jindivik Production

Variant	Total	Serial Ranges	Remarks
Jindivik 1	12	B-1 to B-12 initially A92-1 to A92-12	Armstrong-Siddeley Adder engine. F/F 28.8.52.

All 12 aircraft were initially marked as B1 to B12. Although they were re-allocated in the A92- range only B-7 to B-12 are known to have been repainted. It has been reported that production of Jindivik 1 accounted for 14 aircraft.

Variant	Total	Serial Ranges	Remarks
Jindivik 2	114	A92-21 to A92-110 S.1 to S.10 (Sweden) A92-111 to A92-124	Viper ASV.3 engine. F/F 11.12.53.

Construction Numbers reportedly run consecutively from 1 to 114. Three aircraft (A92-87, A92-90 & A92-111) were subsequently converted to Jindivik 2A (see below)

Variant	Total	Serial Ranges	Remarks
Jindivik 2A	(3)	(A92-87, A92-90, A91-111)	Jindivik 2 with extended span wings and modified intake. F/F 18.9.58.

All three Jindivik 2A aircraft were conversions of Jindivik 2. It is possible that other Jindivik 2s were later converted to 2As.

Variant	Total	Serial Ranges	Remarks
Jindivik 2B	76	A92-201 to A92-276	Jindivik 2 with Viper ASV.8 engine. F/F 8.10.59

The total of 76 includes Jindivik 102BL aircraft that were supplied to the UK Ministry of Defence
Construction numbers are reported to run consecutively from 115 to 190.

Variant	Total	Serial Ranges	Remarks
Jindivik 3	10	A92-301 to A92-310	Jindivik 2B with Viper ASV.11 engine. F/F 12.5.61

These aircraft are reported to have been issued c/ns 120, 124,125, 152, 156, 158, 161, 163, 166 & 168 respectively but these numbers clash with Jindivik 2B aircraft.
A92-303 was subsequently converted to Jindivik 3A and re-serialled A92-400.

Variant	Total	Serial Ranges	Remarks
Jindivik 3A	146	A92-401 to A92-546	Jindivik 3 with new autopilot and other improvements; F/F 10.11.61

The total includes Mk. 103AL for the UK and Mk.203A for the Royal Australian Navy. A number of aircraft were earmarked for the US Navy (and referred to as Jindivik 303A). Construction numbers reportedly run consecutively from 1 to 146.

Variant	Total	Serial Ranges	Remarks
Jindivik 3B	126	A92-601 to A92-674 A92-701 to A92-740 N11-741 to N11-752	Jindivik 3A with internal mods for higher speed at low-level, F/F 22.1.70. Production included 90 Jindivik 103B for the UK; 27 Jindivik 203B for the Royal Australian Navy and 9 Jindivik 203B for WRE, Woomera.

Construction Numbers are reported to run consecutively from 1 to 126.

Variant	Total	Serial Ranges	Remarks
Jindivik 4A	34	A92-801 to A92-816 A92-901 to A92-918	Rolls-Royce Viper Mk.201 jet engine Entered production March 1981.

The serial range A92-801 onwards are referred to as Jindivik 104AL.

Navy, a Letter of Intent which may have even suggested a requirement of some 42 Jindivik 3As. In July 1962 three Jindivik 3s were airfreighted aboard a RAAF C-130A Hercules from Edinburgh to the US Navy Pacific Missile Range at Point Mugu, California. Personnel from 1ATU accompanied the aircraft and carried out eleven trials and demonstration sorties at Point Mugu. One of the Jindiviks was flown to a height of 65,000ft – then a record altitude for a pilotless aircraft.

During 1963 the Jindivik was again demonstrated to the US Navy when a series of 18 flights were made on San Nicholas Island, offshore from Point Mugu (and some 75 miles south-west of Los Angeles). Clearly impressed with Jindivik, the US Navy planned a purchase of 42 aircraft in two batches; 12 to be delivered by 1964 and a further 30 in 1966/67. Production of the initial twelve aircraft proceeded in the light of the Letter of Intent.

Jindivik A92-68 was shipped to the UK in mid-1957 after being exhibited at the Paris Air Show. Whether or not it ever flew at Llanbedr is uncertain but it certainly acted as a pattern aircraft for Fairey Aviation's engineers. This view shows A92-68 at the 1958 Farnborough Air Show. (Arthur Pearcy)

UK Usage

Although Jindivik was very much a joint UK/Australian project it was not until March 1955 that the Ministry of Supply confirmed an order for ten Jindivik 2s. Deliveries to the UK were expected to commence in early-1956 at the rate of 2 or 3 per month.[2] Subsequently, the order was increased to fifteen, by which time the British variant had been designated Jindivik 102. However, various snags that emerged during early test flights in Australia created serious delays in the production schedule.

In the meantime Fairey Aviation had been contracted to undertake a study of the Jindivik's systems and to design and make necessary modifications as well as taking on the role of assembly, testing and arranging, in co-operation with the RAE. All flight trials would be carried out at Llanbedr. Some early Jinidivik trials work was also carried out by Shorts at Rochester when Sturgeon TT.2 VR371 was fitted with Elliotts' autopilot equipment. Flight trials are believed to have taken place out of West Malling during June 1955.

In order to help Fairey Aviation to become fully familiarized with Jindivik, A92-68 was shipped to the UK in June 1957, immediately after being exhibited at the Paris Air Salon. Much of the subsequent modification work was carried out at Fairey's Weapons Division at Heston to meet an eventual Specification D.202D&P, issued by the Air Ministry on 6 August 1959. Ground-testing was carried out at Fairey's White Waltham base.

Although the first batch of Jindiviks arrived in the UK as complete aircraft (i.e. with engines and control systems already fitted), modifying Jindivik for UK operations proved to be far more complex than was at first thought.

---
2   National Archives AVIA54/1282 ; memorandum dated 16 March 1955

A92-107 was part of the initial UK order for Jindivik Mk.102, accounting for 15 aircraft but is something of a mystery ship. No record of any flights in the UK have been recorded and it was written-off on 30 June 1960, a very early stage in Llanbedr operations.

A92-119 seen at Llanbedr on 20 December 1960. The modification to the rear fuselage is believed to be an electrically-powered heat source being evaluated on Jindivik after earlier trials on Firefly U.8 found that aircraft's generator was not powerful enough. (RAE Llanbedr; Neg. No. FOR161.)

Consequently, Fairey Aviation was faced with having to concede a delay in deliveries and in-service dates slipped badly. The first Jindivik 102 (A92-105) was not cleared for flight until late-1959 and not delivered from White Waltham to Llanbedr until Monday, 4 January 1960.

Official handover of A92-105 took place in March 1960. Engine runs started on 3 March and, finally, on 21 June 1960 '105 made the first flight by a Jindivik in the UK. All of the early flights were aimed at obtaining CA release, again a process not without difficulties after faulty telemetry wiring was discovered.

Having missed the original planned in-service date of November 1959, the Ministry of Aviation was forced to announce that the first live target would not be available until July 1960 at the earliest. But the July deadline came and CA release had still not been obtained; even more worrying was that two Jindiviks (A92-105 and A92-107) had already been lost in familiarisation and proving flights. It must have been with some relief when the first operational sortie by a Jindivik eventually took place on 4 November 1960 when A92-104 made what was in fact the 9th Jindivik flight out of Llanbedr.

In Australia, the decision had long been taken to replace the Adder engine with the more powerful Viper ASV.3 engine. This had given rise to the Jindivik Mk.2 which had made its first flight back in December 1953. Progressive development

Jindivik 2B A92-210 was used for various trials in the UK. Associated mods and special equipment included a 10" passive microwave reflector and transponders for enhancing radar acquisition; a flare-heated source and towed infra-red flare for simulating the jet efflux of a larger aircraft and podded cameras that gave full spherical coverage for recording the attitude and miss-distance of attacking missiles. (Fairey Aviation)

146   Sitting Ducks and Peeping Toms

Above: Jindivik 103AL A92-436 achieved 56 flights by 9 February 1972 when it was written-off. The aircraft was recovered and re-assembled. This view was taken on 11 May 1972. (FAST Collection)

Right: Jindivik 102B A92-274 sustained a direct hit on 10 May 1965 and lost half of its fin area. It still managed to make a safe landing at Llanbedr and was later repaired. It was eventually destroyed on 27 September 1966 whilst making its 38th flight (National Archives, Ref. AVIA13/1384)

of the Mk.2 led, in October 1959, to the 2B with a Viper ASV.8 engine. An Anglicized version of the Jindivik 2B was developed to meet Specification D.208D&P (issued on 30 March 1960) and which became known as the 102B.

First examples of the Jindivik 102B had been expected to be delivered to Llanbedr in January 1961. However, as was the case with the Jindivik 2, early flight-tests in Australia were not wholly successful and the 2B also experienced a number of problems. Modifications to the 2B delayed the first flight until 19 July 1961 and service entry was put back by almost a year. The first official delivery of a 102B to the UK took place on 18 August when A92-207 was received at Llanbedr where it made its initial UK flight on 10 November 1961. In the meantime Government Aircraft Factory had begun flight-testing an uprated Jindivik 3 variant.

Merger and corporate changes within the Fairey Company during 1961 meant that Jindivik modification and acceptance work would be transferred to Fairey Engineering's plant at Ringway. An eventual total of 64 Jindivik 102Bs were delivered to the UK, the final 29 of which were shipped to Ringway as bare airframes and where they were fitted with Bristol Siddeley Viper 8 turbojets, British autopilot, radio and telemetry equipment. Most, if not all, Jindiviks were air-freighted from Adelaide, initially by Air Ferry (British United Airways) to Southend until June 1962 when Cunard Eagle Airlines (later British Eagle) took over the MoD contract.

During its service life at Llanbedr, Jindivik 102B accounted for 967 sorties, the last surviving example (A92-255) being lost on 5 December 1967 on its 79th flight.[3]

Jindivik 3 had made its first flight in Australia on 12 May 1961 – some three months before Llanbedr received its first 102B. An uprated Viper ASV11 turbojet powered the Jindivik 3 although the limitations of its automatic control system restricted its maximum operating ceiling to 55,000ft. Only ten Jindivik 3s were built before GAF introduced the Jindivik 3A with a new automatic pilot, an AC system and more versatile radar and infra-red augmentation equipment. In order to raise the maximum operational ceiling a Jindivik 3A was fitted with an auxiliary rocket motor and, in exploring the possibility of very high altitude operations, a height of 67,000 ft was achieved during flight-testing.

---

3 Some sources suggest that it was lost on its 81st sortie.

Jindivik and Stiletto   147

Demonstrating its ability to act as a target tower Jindivik 103AL A92-442 is carefully suspended from the roof of the "Bristol" hangar at Aberporth on 15 June 1967. (FAST Collection)

The increased performance of Jindivik 3A – especially its ability to fly above 60,000' – was well received in the UK as the operational requirement for Sea Slug 2 or Red Top called for an altitude of 65,000'. However there was a question mark over whether it was capable of maintaining an above-60,000 ft altitude for a sufficient length of time or, for that matter, whether or not Jindivik 3A was fully controllable at over 60,000 ft.

The MoD had considered buying the French CT.41 instead and it is possible that ten examples were ordered for evaluational purposes. A further concern, expressed within the MoD as early as January 1961, was that owing to design problems in Australia deliveries of Jindivik 103A were unlikely to start before mid-1962. In fact the target delivery date was never likely to have been met. To provide a necessary stop-gap until 103A was available the MoD placed a repeat order for 102Bs as an interim measure aimed at overcoming an expected deficiency in UK Jindivik stocks. Based on contemporary loss rates, the UK required at least 43 aircraft but in view of the need to run down the holding of 102Bs the requirement was reduced to just 30, although in the event the interim order accounted for just 14 airframes.

The first (of 64) Jindivik 103A to fly at Llanbedr was A92-416; it entered service there in November 1964. (In fact, total stockholding was eventually 65 including the indigenous "LLANBEDR 1", assembled at Llanbedr from spare parts.) A total of 1,548 flights were made in the UK by Llanbedr's Jindivik 103A fleet.

Specification UD.243D&P was issued by the Air Ministry on 1 October 1963 to cover an improved version of the 3A for the UK. Thus emerged the Jindivik 103BL, 50 of which were shipped to the UK.

Specification D.257D&P was issued on 20 March 1967 to cover development and production of what became variously the "600 Series" or the "700 Series". Their serials became the determinant factor although officially all were designated Jindivik 103BL.

Fifty "600 series" aircraft (A92-610 to A92-635, A92-651 to A92-674) were delivered to the UK and accounted for 1,187 flights. The last of these was lost on 1 March 1983 when A92-664 – the only Jindivik until then to have made over 100 flights – was lost on its 133rd flight. The "700 series" accounted for 40 aircraft (A92-701 to 740) to which can be added a second indigenous example identified as "LLAN2".

Although the Jindivik's performance had exceeded its original expectations the unit cost was, in fact, relatively high. As a consequence the Ministry of Defence began, in 1977, to consider alternatives and attention was focused on the Beech MQM-107 jet-powered, zero-launch parachute-recovered system as an eventual replacement for Jindivik. This action appeared to prompt GAF to re-examine the cost of producing Jindivik and when, eventually, the Jindivik 4 was put forward as a contender it did so with a considerable cost-saving.

The Mk.4 Jindivik suffered a lengthy period of design and development. One of the contributory factors involved a Universal Drone Pack (UDP) that had been developed by Marconi. It was designed to fit into most service aircraft and the decision was taken to re-design Jindivik 4's electronics to use the UDP, but it led to a number of technical difficulties.

The Jindivik 4 was also fitted with its own Flight Control Computer and the aircraft's structure was strengthened to

Jindivik A92-729 was one of 90 Mk. 103BL variants supplied to the UK against two contracts. In August 1986 it was temporarily detached to RAE Farnborough for a series of ground tests. Eventually A92-729 went on to achieve 135 flights, being lost on 30 Sepotember 1992. (FAST Collection)

increase the *g* limit to +6. The new version was also fitted with a generator in place of an alternator and improved electronics allowed space for a larger fuel tank. A number of other design improvements were built into Jindivik 4, for which the Anglo-Australian Jindivik Mk.4 Development Project provided the financing for two prototypes. The first of these (N11-800) was delivered to Jervis Bay in March 1981 where it underwent initial flight trials; a second prototype (N11-801) joined the development programme in April 1982. It is probably fair to suggest that development of the Mk.4 was carried out solely in the light of a UK order, placed in 1980, for 40 aircraft. However, in a further cost-saving exercise, that order was later reduced to just 15. The fifteen Mk.104As were serialled A92-802 to A92-816. The first production example (A92-802) was initially retained in Australia for continued development trials; thus the first delivery to Llanbedr involved A92-803.

Since its introduction in 1960, Jindivik had been continually improved and updated and the 104A represented the ultimate variant. For low altitude work, it was fitted with Mk.9 wingtip pods each containing two cameras, a microwave reflector and a small amount of fuel. For high-altitude work it retained the Mk.9 pods but was fitted with 80-inch wing extensions outboard of the pod. A ventral fin was also fitted for high-altitude flying and maximum turn rate configurations.

Drone Operations at Llanbedr

All target operations at Llanbedr from take-off to landing were completely automatic. Three operating channels were used with separate frequencies so that simultaneous operation of three target aircraft could be carried out if required. Each channel could be used to operate either Meteor U.16 or Jindivik without any equipment or additional preparation being needed.

The rate of Jindivik operations at Llanbedr was determined to a large extent by the speed of ground handling and the availability of runways. One of the firmest rules at Llanbedr was that as far as possible unmanned target aircraft did not fly over land. The main runway therefore, which ran north to south across the peninsula, was most frequently used for take-off and landing in either direction.

The second runway, which ran roughly east to west, was used for take-off only in a westerly direction and out to sea. The remaining runway at Llanbedr was not used for Pilotless operations. In the days of the Firefly U.8 drone it was the "arrestor" runway with sets of cables which caught the extended deck-hook of the Firefly on landing.

RAE News, December 1966

The main hangar at Llanbedr was always a hive of activity with numerous Jindiviks undergoing regular checks and maintenance. In this 1965 view Jindivik 103ALs A92-415, A92-419 and A92-456 are readily identifiable as is Mk. 102B A92-255 seen complete but without its nose cone. (BAC Guided Weapons Division)

Jindivik and Stiletto 149

A sequence of views depicting Jindivik 104AL A92-808 taking-off from Llanbedr on 30 August 2000 and later landing back at its base. Jindivik took-off with the aid of an undercarriage trolley but which was discarded on the point of lift-off. For landing Jindivik used a built-in skid undercarriage that on touchdown provided quite a display as sparks fly off the skid. Once the aircraft became stationary it was hoisted by crane and lowered onto its take-off trolley for transporting back to the hangar. A92-808 was one of several Jindiviks repainted in a black scheme. (Falcon Aviation Photographs)

The microwave reflectors, together with transponders, allowed Jindivik to be used for trials of active, semi-active or beam-riding missiles. Heat sources, including infra-red flare packs mounted on the rear fuselage provided a low-frequency IR output. Provision was also made for a recoverable towed target to be carried beneath each wing, the TOW bodies carrying either active radar, in-flight commanded IR flares, or forward-looking Luneburg lens cameras. Cameras with wide-angle lenses were also fitted to the wingtip pods, these having an all-round viewing capability. By fitting rearward-looking prisms to the lower cameras Jindivik was also able to record missile performance when towed targets were being used. To simulate different types of aircraft, Plessey Microwave Ltd developed a Semi-active Artificial Radar Target (SART) for operation in a towed configuration using Jindivik as the towing aircraft.

By using Jindivik to tow a target meant that the drone aircraft was itself not the target – albeit often an attractive one from the firer's point of view. The actual target was towed at a distance of between 40 and 200ft behind the Jindivik, the longer tow being reserved for live warhead rounds. The tows were configured either as IR targets or as radar targets.[4]

Having cut back rather drastically its original order for Jindivik 104A, it was perhaps not surprising that a requirement for additional aircraft soon emerged. However, the initial fifteen were the last Jindiviks to be built and although now out of production Jindivik was still very much active at Llanbedr. The on-going UK requirement for additional aircraft could likely have ensured production well

---

4   *Air Clues*, October 1985 issue

The main hangar at RAE Llanbedr on 30 August 2000 showing Jindivik 104ALs A92-807 (left) and ZJ492 (right). A92-807 was later re-serialled as ZJ488. (Falcon Aviation Photographs)

into the 1990s but the Australian manufacturer – now re-styled as Aerospace Technologies Australia (ASTA) – was not so keen to re-open the production line. With no other contender available a rather unexpected deal was negotiated.

Brooklands Aviation Ltd, based at Old Sarum, Wiltshire had established a production facility for the Edgely EA-7 Optica. The company was trying to secure a large order from Australia which would ensure the company's future. One of the terms of the deal involved a set-off arrangement whereby Brooklands Aviation would establish a Jindivik assembly line at Old Sarum. At the final stage of negotiating, Brooklands suffered a serious setback when its Old Sarum factory was destroyed by fire on the night of 16/17 January 1987, the circumstances of which have never, to this day, been fully explained. Arson was strongly suspected to have been the primary cause but nobody was ever charged, or indeed arrested. The fire, however, signalled the end of any plans to assemble Jindiviks in the UK.[5]

Eventually ASTA agreed to re-open the Jindivik line to meet a final order from the MoD. Jindivik 104A A92-809 was air-freighted back to Australia in mid-1994 to act as a pattern aircraft for what became the "900 Series" batch.

Total Jindivik 104A procurement by the UK accounted for 33 examples; 15 in the "800" series" and 18 in the "900 series". Most of these were subsequently placed on the UK Military Aircraft Register on 26 June 1997 within the range ZJ482 to ZJ513.

Llanbedr received an overall total of 267 Jindiviks and if the number of sorties achieved is any measure then Jindivik was without doubt the most successful target drone to operate in the UK. Milestones in Jindivik's service life included the 1,000th sortie which took place on 22 June 1965 (by A92-259), the 2,000th on 12 June 1968 (by A92-437); the 3,000th on 3 February 1975 (by A92-610); the 4,000th on 12 December 1981 (by A92-716); the 5,000th on 15 January 1988 (by A92-733) and the 6,000th on 30 October 1992 (by A92-737). As at 1 September 2001 sorties had accounted for 7,738 Jindivik flights in the UK. Virtually all Jindivik operations were performed at Llanbedr; the exception being a small number of trials conducted across the Hebrides Range.[6]

---

6   *Target Rolling* by Wendy Mills

It has been a long-established practice to record the number of sorties achieved by individual aircraft. In the case of Jindiviks each sortie was marked by an image of a bat with outstretched wings. This view shows markings applied to A92-731 as at 30 August 2000. This drone was eventually lost on its 180th flight. (Falcon Aviation Photographs)

---

5   As related to the author by Simon Matthews.

Jindivik and Stiletto   151

Drone Control at Llanbedr

A Master Controller sited in the Llanbedr Control Tower had overall responsiblity for a target drone sortie. He took into consideration weather limitations for take-off and landing and from his desk was able to delegate control to his team who were dispersed at various points on the airfield.

The en-route "pilot" and "navigator" were located in one of the three control cells – the unit had a two-targets-at-once capability – equipped with radar and a full control panel. The take-off operator, in his mobile site, was positioned behind the drone and steered it in azimuth until airborne. For landing, another azimuth operator at the other end of the runway, and assisted by a vertical graticule in his sight-binoculars, controlled the aircraft's heading relative to the runway centre-line. The pitch operator was located in a fixed site on the left of the runway and used an up/down control to transmit small variations in the pitch attitude of the drone, again assisted by sight-binoculars. (In the case of the Meteor drone the pitch operator also operated the fuel-off switch.)

In the drone itself one-third brake was automatically actuated on touch-down and full brake was applied on reaching 80 knots. The target drone was given full radar surveillance by ATC, and given a Precision Approach Radar talk-down on a two-degree glide-path by the ATC Controller. He transmitted his speech to the "pilot" in the cell, who flew the aircraft until pitch and azimuth operators took over visually.

Jindivik was unique in that it used a conventional aircraft runway but had no undercarriage. At launch it started its take-off run mounted on a three-wheeled steerable trolley that was left behind once flying speed was reached. On completion of the sortie Jindivik landed back on the runway using a retractable skid – which created a somewhat spectacular shower of sparks!

Arthur Pearcy, *Aviation News*, 3 February 1978

During 1991 a decision was taken to evaluate Jindivik operations from a mobile Ground Station. The Hebrides Range was selected for the trial and an exploratory flight was made from Benbecula airfield on 21 May 1991 (by A92-810). Meteor U.16 WK800 was specially fitted with drop-tanks to allow it to act as a "shepherd" to the Jindivik.

Although the results of the trial were encouraging no action was taken immediately afterwards and a second series of flights later took place between 29 January and 30 October 1992. These flights, over two separate periods, involved A92-803, A92-804, and A92-810. Again no decision was taken to operate Jindivik in the Outer Hebrides. However the question was again raised in 1994. The issue had come about on that occasion due to the inability to increase the size of the Aberporth (Cardigan Bay) danger area (due to it being bounded by the Welsh land mass to the East, Irish airspace to the west and major trans-Atlantic airways to the north and south). The restriction meant that it would become difficult to trial those higher performance AAMs due in service in the late-1990s over the Aberporth Range. Some consideration had been given to testing these missiles across the Royal Artillery Range at Hebrides but the Range lacked a suitable locally-based target aircraft. So yet again a Jindivik 104A (A92-807) was positioned to Benbecula from where it made one evaluation flight on 21 September 1994. However the scenario of Jindivik operating in the Hebrides was not ideal and the aircraft was returned to Llanbedr. No plans to operate Jindivik anywhere other than Llanbedr was considered further.

Since 1951 the responsibility for operating target drones at Llanbedr had been held by Short Brothers. The company had overseen the introduction of Firefly, Meteor and Jindivik drones, but in October 1979 their contract had come to an end. It was awarded instead to Bournemouth-based Airwork Services and was to run initially for five years. Responsibility for running Llanbedr airfield was taken on by Airwork in 1982 but only until 1990 when it was announced that Airwork's submission had failed to secure a second term. The Llanbedr contract was instead awarded to FR/SERCO, a company jointly owned by FR Aviation and SERCO who were already operating RNAS Yeovilton, RAE West Freugh and RAF Swinderby. At the same time FR/SERCO also picked up contracts to operate RAF Woodvale and RAF Shawbury. Each contract was led by one or the other of the two companies; at Llanbedr it was to be FR Aviation with a start-date of 1 April 1991. The FRA/SERCO contract was renewed for another five years in 1998 but was ended slightly prematurely in 2002 when, on 1 July, the entire operation became the responsibility of QinetiQ.

The final flight of a Jindivik from Llanbedr was undertaken by ZJ496 (A92-901). The aircraft returned safely and is now preserved at the FAST Museum, Farnborough. The withdrawal of Jindivik was sudden and in the event some aircraft held in storage at Llanbedr had never been assembled. In what seems to have been an incredulous move all surviving Jindiviks – including those that had never flown – were sold for scrap in February 2005.

Whether or not the withdrawal marked the the end of Jindivik in the UK remains to be seen. Cardigan Bay, into which some 200 Jindiviks ended their lives, is now the centre of an increasingly active scallop industry. The process involves trawling nets along the seabed, a process that led one Aberporth veteran to later remark, rather laconically, "Goodness only knows how many Jindiviks are likely to be dragged up over the next few years!"

Jindivik – Individual Histories of UK-operated aircraft

A92-68 c/n 48 Mk.102. Exhibited at Paris Air Salon, Le Bourget 1957; later to UK and shown at SBAC Farnborough 9.57; presumably part of the UK "Ministry of Defence" order. Known to have made two flights in Australia prior to shipment to Europe but was never flown in the UK. Retained by Fairey at White Waltham until c1973 when conveyed to Llanbedr for storage. By mid-1974 it was repainted as 'A92-480' and placed on gate-guardian duty at Llanbedr.

1st Contract:
15 Jindivik Mk. 102

A92-102 Lost on 5.10.61 on its 14th flight.

A92-103 Lost on 28.3.62 on its 16th flight.

A92-104 First operational flight 4.11.60 ("ex Fairey Aviation, Ringway") The last of 25 flights was made on 19.7.61.

A92-105 UK marks **XN808** allocated 2.7.59; cancelled 12.8.59. Delivered to Ringway-Llanbedr by road 4.1.60. Underwent engine-runs 3.3.60; lost on its 1st flight 21.6.60 when it crashed into the sea off Barmouth with fuel starvation. (TFH 0.59hrs)

A92-106 UK marks **XN809** allocated 2.7.59; cancelled 12.8.59. Delivered to Llanbedr 12.2.60; taxi-trials 22.4.60; f/f 26.4.60. Sustained Cat.4 damage 24.3.61 (8th flight) when it landed with skid retracted. Repaired. Shot down by a GWTS Firestreak missile 4.10.61. 10 Flights.

A92-107 Lost at Llanbedr on 30.6.60; details unknown and not thought to have flown.

A92-108 Lost on 17.7.61 on its 9th flight.

A92-109 Lost on 19.12.61 on its 21st flight.

A92-110 Lost on 22.12.60 on its 5th flight.

A92-119 Lost on 20.2.61 on its 7th flight.

A92-120 Lost on 27.2.61 on its 6th flight.

A92-121 Lost on 28.3.61 on its 16th flight

A92-122 Lost on 6.7.61 on its 3rd flight.

A92-123 Lost on 5.7.61 on its 2nd flight.

A92-124 Lost on 31.7.61 on its 6th flight.

2nd Contract:
50 Jindivik Mk.102B

A92-204 f/f 19.7.61. On 25.7.61 (and on its 4th sortie) it was recorded as being "unstable in climb" due to elevator trim snag. (Jindivik Flight 98). On its 10th sortie (Jindivik Flt 127), on 22.9.61, it suffered a telemetry failure and on its 14th sortie (Jindivik Flt 142) on 14.3.62 the JPT Telemetry was u/s causing the drone to drift. Shot down 15.5.62 during its 18th sortie.

A92-205 Retained by BAC as a Development Aircraft. Incident recorded 3.11.61 on 2nd sortie (Jindivik Flt 142) when an instrument fault caused failure to accept fast glide. On 10.4.63 it failed to disengage from the trolley in an aborted take-off for what would have been its 11th sortie. Crashed 22 or 26.5.64 after loss of elevator control (on its 17th flight).

A92-206 Acceptance dates at Llanbedr not known and may have been retained by BAC. It was eventually destroyed in the course of trials on 6 Oct 1966 and on its 6th flight.

A92-207 Received at Llanbedr 18.8.61. Shot down 25.3.63 on 15th sortie.

A92-208 Received at Llanbedr 5.9.61. Crashed on approach to Llanbedr 1.11.61 after completing its 2nd sortie.

A92-209 Received at Llanbedr 6.9.62. Shot down 21.3.63 by Thunderbird Mk.1 472 on its 10th sortie. (Also recorded as f/f 6.6.62 – Jindivik Flight 215.)

A92-210 Displayed statically at SBAC Farnborough Sept 1961. Received at Llanbedr 29.6.62. Destroyed by command 17.12.62 on its 15th sortie.

A92-211 Received at Llanbedr 2.10.61. Shot down 5.6.62 during its 7th (or 8th) sortie.

A92-212 Received at Llanbedr 19.10.61. Shot down 1.6.62 during its 13th sortie.

A92-213 Received at Llanbedr 3.11.61 but shot down 13.4.62 on its 1st sortie.

A92-214 Received at Llanbedr 7.11.61. Shot down 30.5.62 on its 8th sortie.

A92-216 Received at Llanbedr 5.12.61. Shot down 17.4.62 on its 4th sortie.

A92-217 Received at Llanbedr 12.12.61. On 12.7.62, during its 4th sortie (Jindivik Flt 220) a faulty carbon pile voltage regulator caused a "Signal Fail Orbit." Shot down 29.8.62 on its 7th sortie.

A92-218 Received at Llanbedr 14.1.63. Undertook its 1st sortie on 6.5.63 (Jindivik Flt 366) but sustained telemetry difficulties due to no histogram signals. Landed safely. On 22.10.63 and on its 25th sortie (Jindivik Flt 498) an incident described as "Signal Fail Orbit" occurred. Its 26th sortie, on 15.11.63, was aborted due to it not accepting straight commands. Shot down 17.1.64 on its 30th sortie.

A92-220 Received at Llanbedr 2.2.62. Shot down 17.4.63 on its 15th sortie.

A92-223 Observed at Southend 29.7.60 as inbound air-freight from Australia. Received at Llanbedr 9.2.62. Accidentally lost on its 1st sortie 13.7.62 due to equipment failure.

A92-225 Observed at Southend 29.7.60 as inbound air-freight from Australia. Received at Llanbedr 14.1.63. Its 1st sortie (Jindivik Flt 350) on 17.4.63 was marred by a telemetry fault causing commands not to be accepted. Landed safely. Its 2nd sortie, on 22.4.63 (Jindivik Flt 357) saw an autopilot fault causing the aircraft to be sluggish in starboard turns. Shot down 23.4.63 on its 3rd sortie. Rebuilt for 'gate guardan' duty at Aberporth.

A92-227 Observed at Southend 29.7.60 as inbound air-freight from Australia. Received at Llanbedr 29.4.63. Destroyed by command on its 1st sortie due to equipment failure in flight on 4.7.63.

A92-228 Observed at Southend 22.9.60 as inbound air-freight from Australia. Received at Llanbedr 15.5.63. Shot down 21.8.63 during its 5th sortie.

A92-230 Observed at Southend 22.9.60 as inbound air-freight from Australia. Received at Llanbedr 20.6.62. Shot down 9.7.62 on its 1st sortie.

A92-232 Observed at Southend 22.9.60 as inbound air-freight from Australia. Received at Llanbedr 5.4.62. Shot down 8.5.63 on its 2nd sortie.

A92-233 Received at Llanbedr 20.6.62. On 17.4.63, and during its 13th sortie (Jindivik Flt 349) a transmitter fault caused unsteady telemetry. Landed safely. Shot down 15.5.63 on its 21st sortie.

A92-235 Received at Llanbedr 7.6.62. Shot down 25.3.63 on its 3rd sortie.

A92-236 Received at Llanbedr 12.6.62. Shot down 28.8.62 on its 3rd sortie.

A92-237 Received at Llanbedr 7.6.62. Accidentally lost after being destroyed by command on 1.3.63 whilst on its 1st sortie.

A92-238 Received at Llanbedr 16.7.62. Undertook its 1st sortie 4.9.62 (Jindivik Flt 238) but suffered a snag with the fuel transfer system. Landed safely. Another incident occurred on 3.4.63 (9th sortie, Jindivik Flt 342) when the VSI telemetry and roll angle was u/s. Landed safely. The loss of telemetred ASI was again reported on 26.4.63 (12th sortie, Jindivik Flt 360) and again on 2.9.63 (31st sortie, Jindivik Flt 451) when telemetry was interfered with by control transmissions. Shot down 11.10.63 on its 37th sortie.

A92-239 Received at Llanbedr 16.7.62. Destroyed by command 13.9.62 on its 1st **(or 2nd)** sortie.

A92-240 Received at Llanbedr 21.8.62. On 6.11.62 take-off was aborted (for its 1st sortie when the aircraft came off the trolley on the runway. Shot down 18.3.63 by Thunderbird Mk.1 480 on its 2nd sortie.

A92-241 Exhibited at SBAC Farnborough show 1962. Received at Llanbedr 23.10.62. Sustained auto-pilot problems on 1.2.63 (during its 1st sortie, Jindivik Flt 298) causing a lack of throttle. Shot down by Thunderbird Mk.1 458 18.3.63 on its 5th sortie.

A92-242 Received at Llanbedr 14.9.62. Shot down by Thunderbird Mk.1 340 19.2.63 on its 15th sortie.

A92-243 Received at Llanbedr 11.10.62. On 30.11.62 (on its 2nd sortie; Jindivik Flt 275) it suffered loss of control and telemetry after landing. Shot down 12.3.63 on its 6th sortie by Thunderbird Mk.1 445.

A92-244 Received at Llanbedr 11.10.62. Its 1st sortie, on 13.11.62, was aborted due to it failing to disengage from the trolley. On 4.12.62, on its 5th sortie (Jindivik Flt 281), the JPT telemetry was u/s with a fuel warning. On 18.4.63 it landed at Llanbedr (after its 15th sortie, Jindivik Flt 354) with its landing skid in the retracted position. As at 30.9.64 it was with Fairey Engineering Ltd for repair. Subsequently destroyed by command 26.10.66 after sustaining in-flight damage by gunfire on its 16th sortie.

A92-245 Received at Llanbedr 7.12.62. Shot down by Thunderbird Mk.1 475 21.2.63 on its 2nd sortie.

A92-246 Received at Llanbedr 5.2.63. Shot down 17.4.63 on its 4th sortie.

A92-247 Received at Llanbedr 29.4.63. Destroyed by command 20.8.63 due to equipment failure in flight during its 19th sortie.

A92-248 Noted at Adelaide 7.4.62 (with '249) being loaded aboard BUA DC-4 G-APNH. Arrived at Southend 16.4.62 as air-freight. Received at Llanbedr 6.5.63. Destroyed by command (on land) 24.6.63 on its 3rd sortie.

A92-249 Noted at Adelaide 7.4.62 (with '248) being loaded aboard BUA DC-4 G-APNH. Arrived at Southend 16.4.62 as air-freight. Received at Llanbedr 15.5.63. Shot down 13.4.64 during its 27th sortie.

A92-250 Received at Llanbedr 19.6.63. Shot down 25.10.63 during its 15th **(or 16th)** sortie.

A92-251 Received at Llanbedr 19.6.63. Shot down 23.8.63 during its 2nd sortie.

A92-252 Received at Llanbedr 5.7.63. Destroyed by command 28.8.63 during its 3rd sortie due to equipment failure in flight.

A92-253 Received at Llanbedr 16.8.63. On 22.10.63 it sustained "Signal fail orbit" during its 8th sortie (Jindivik Flt 500). On its 13th sortie, on 13.11.63, a servo control failure caused pitching up in left turns but again was landed safely. During its 23rd sortie, on 19.2.64, (Jindivik Flt 577) it sustained a telemetry failure in flight whilst on 20.3.64 it suffered a "Signal Fail Operated" during its 26th sortie (Jindivik Flt 600). Shot down 5.5.64 during its 34th sortie.

A92-254 Received at Llanbedr 31.7.63. Suffered an engine flame-out on 10.9.63 during its 2nd sortie (Jindivik Flt 461) but landed safely. Destroyed by command 21.10.63 during its 8th sortie due to equipment failure in flight.

A92-255 Built 5.62. Received at Llanbedr by road (ex-Ringway) 23.9.63. Lost on 5.12.67 on its 79th flight. (Also quoted as 81st flight.)

An example marked as "A92-255" (and in reality a composite airframe of sundry spare parts) is displayed at Aberporth Missile Park. Reported with the Defence Science & Technology Laboratory, Aberporth. It is likely that this is now with DPA/QinetiQ at Boscombe Down for apprentice use.

A92-256 Received at Llanbedr 10.9.63. Destroyed by command 25.10.63 during its 3rd sortie due to equipment failure in flight.

A92-257 Received at Llanbedr 13.11.63. Destroyed 24.6.66 on its 65th flight in the course of trials.

A92-258 Received at Llanbedr 4.11.63. Destroyed by command 25.10.66 (on its 73rd flight) after sustaining damage by gunfire.

A92-259 Received at Llanbedr 8.11.63. Lost on 7.10.65 on its 30th flight.

A92-260 Received at Llanbedr 2.12.63. 1st sortie flown 17.12.63 (Jindivik Flt 528) but suffered a faulty destroy receiver during the flight. Lost on 13.7.67 on its 32nd flight.

A92-261 Received at Llanbedr 9.12.63. Lost on 11.5.65 on its 27th flight.

A92-262 Received at Llanbedr 18.12.63. Shot down 13.5.64 during its 16th sortie.

3rd (Interim) Contract:
14 Jindivik Mk.102B

A92-263 Received at Llanbedr 7.1.64. Lost on 22 Oct 1964 on its 9th flight.

A92-264 Received at Llanbedr 12.2.64. Destroyed by command 10.4.64 during its 1st sortie following an in-flight equipment failure.

A92-265 Arrived at London-Heathrow 8.11.62 as air-freight from Australia. Received at Llanbedr 12.2.64. Shot down 16.4.64 during its 3rd sortie.

A92-266 Arrived at London-Heathrow 8.11.62 as air-freight from Australia. Received at Llanbedr 25.3.64. Lost on 14.5.65 on its 51st flight.

A92-267 Arrived at London-Heathrow 8.11.62 as air-freight from Australia. Received at Llanbedr 25.3.64. Shot down 20.10.64 on its 6th flight.

A92-268 Arrived at London-Heathrow 8.11.62 as air-freight from Australia. Received at Llanbedr 16.4.64. Destroyed 16.10.64 on its 6th flight as a result of an "accidental loss"

A92-269 Arrived at London-Heathrow 8.11.62 as air-freight from Australia. Received at Llanbedr 16.4.64. Lost on 12.2.65 on its 18th flight.

A92-270 Arrived at London-Heathrow 3.12.62 as air-freight from Australia. Received at Llanbedr 1.5.64. Destroyed by command 4.11.64 on its 1st flight.

A92-271 Arrived at London-Heathrow 3.12.62 as air-freight from Australia. Received at Llanbedr 1.5.64. Reported as lost on 6.7.64 on its 1st sortie.

A92-272 Arrived at London-Heathrow 6.2.63 as air-freight from Australia. Received at Llanbedr 3.6.64. Lost on 14.4.67 on its 61st flight.

A92-273 Arrived at London-Heathrow 6.2.63 as air-freight from Australia. Received at Llanbedr 3.7.64. Destroyed 5.11.64 on its 5th flight following a malfunction in the height lock.

A92-274 Arrived at London-Heathrow 1.4.63 as air-freight from Australia. Received at Llanbedr 22.7.64. Sustained damage to fin area 10 May 1965 but landed Llanbedr safely. Eventually destroyed 27.9.66 during the course of trials and on its 38th flight.

A92-275 Received at Llanbedr 8.9.64. Lost on 21.4.65 on its 17th flight.

A92-276 Arrived at London-Heathrow 1.4.63 as air-freight from Australia. Received at Llanbedr 9.10.64. Lost on 12.5.65 on its 7th flight.

4th Contract:
65 Jindivik Mk.103AL

A92-415 Lost on 15.3.67 on its 39th flight.

A92-416 Arrived at London-Heathrow 3.12.62 as air-freight from Australia. To Llanbedr (date unkn). Lost on 25.3.66 on its 23rd flight.

A92-417 Shot down by a Sea Dart missile 11.6.69.

A92-419 Arrived at London-Heathrow 6.2.63 as air-freight from Australia. Lost on 17.7.67 on its 71st flight.

A92-420 Lost on 24.9.65 on its 4th flight.

A92-421 Lost on 21.7.70 on its 42nd flight.

A92-424 Lost on 12.10.65 on its 15th flight.

A92-425 Crashed on 1.12.65 (on its 14th flight) after taking-off from Llanbedr at 11:18A but engine flamed-out when passing through 7000'.

A92-426 Lost on 31.8.65 on its 3rd flight.

A92-427 Arrived at London-Heathrow 19.7.63 as air-freight from Australia. Lost on 14.6.67 on its 27th flight.

A92-428 Lost on 19.9.67 on its 31st flight.

A92-429 Lost on 22.12.70 on its 43rd flight.

A92-430 Lost on 18.1.66 on its 12th flight.

A92-431 Destroyed on 21.7.66 (on its 19th flight) and in the course of trials from Llanbedr.

A92-434 Crashed at Llanbedr (Runway 18) after carrying out a sortie to Spec GW.411 at Ty Croes on 19.12.66 (and on its 15th flight).

A92-435 Crashed during the course of trials from Llanbedr 27.4.66 and on its 4th flight. An accidental loss.

A92-436 Arrived at London-Heathrow 2.12.63 as air-freight from Australia. Lost on 9.2.72 on its 56th flight.

A92-437 Arrived at London-Heathrow 2.12.63 as air-freight from Australia. On 12.6.68 it flew the 2,000th UK Jindivik sortie at Llanbedr. Lost on 22.7.70 on its 47th flight.

A92-438 Arrived at London-Heathrow 2.12.63 as air-freight from Australia. Lost on 18.10.67 on its 64th flight.

A92-441 Lost on 17.5.68 on its 18th flight.

A92-442 Arrived at London-Heathrow 31.12.63 as air-freight from Australia. Lost on 16.6.70 on its 7th flight.

A92-443 Arrived at London-Heathrow 31.12.63 as air-freight from Australia. Lost on 4.2.69 on its 18th flight.

A92-446 Lost on 19.7.71 on its 68th flight.

A92-447 Arrived at London-Heathrow 23.1.64 as air-freight from Australia. Lost on 18.9.70 on its 21st flight.

A92-448 Arrived at London-Heathrow 23.1.64 as air-freight from Australia. Crashed 27.9.66 on its 5th flight after failing to turn onto final approach to Llanbedr or to respond to 'DESTROY' command and crashed into a hillside at Pont Afon Gan.

A92-449 Arrived at London-Heathrow 6.4.64 as air-freight from Australia. Lost on 25.8.69 on its 7th flight.

A92-452 Arrived at London-Heathrow 6.4.64 as air-freight from Australia. Lost on 5.1.67 on its 2nd flight.

A92-453 Arrived at London-Heathrow 6.4.64 as air-freight from Australia. Lost on 11.7.67 on its 13th flight.

A92-454 Lost on 8.9.67 during its 17th flight.

A92-455 Lost on 17.8.67 during its 10th flight.

A92-456 Lost on 9.2.68 during its 29th flight.

A92-457 Lost on 20.10.67 during its 12th flight.

A92-458 Lost on 10.5.72 during its 43rd flight.

A92-461 Lost on 10.10.68 during its 22nd flight.

A92-462 Lost on 24.4.69 during its 14th flight.

A92-466 Lost on 8.7.69 during its 25th flight.

A92-467 Lost on 26.8.70 during its 37th flight.

A92-470 Arrived at London-Heathrow 18.11.64 as air-freight from Australia. Lost on 20.1.72 during its 40th flight.

A92-471 Arrived at London-Heathrow 18.11.64 as air-freight from Australia. Lost on 21.5.68 during its 1st flight.

A92-472 Arrived at London-Heathrow 18.11.64 as air-freight from Australia. Lost on 18.8.71 during its 66th flight.

A92-473 Arrived at London-Heathrow 14.4.65 as air-freight from Australia. Lost on 13.1.72 during its 59th flight.

A92-476 Arrived at London-Heathrow 14.4.65 as air-freight from Australia. Lost on 13.4.70 during its 23rd flight.

A92-477 Arrived at London-Heathrow 14.4.65 as air-freight from Australia. Lost on 21.7.70 during its 40th flight.

A92-478 Lost on 9.10.68 during its 6th flight.

A92-479 Lost on 1.7.69 **(or 17.7.69)** during its 4th flight.

A92-480 Lost on 6.12.67 during its 6th flight.

A92-487 Lost on 23.2.68 during its 3rd flight.

A92-488 Lost on 6.12.67 during its 6th flight.

A92-489 Lost on 18.9.67 during its 5th flight.

A92-490 Lost on 5.6.68 during its 30th flight.

A92-491 Lost on 19.7.67 during its 1st flight.

A92-533 Lost on 21.4.72 during its 20th flight.

A92-534 Lost on **6.6.72** during its 33rd flight.

A92-535 Lost on 13.9.71 during its 10th flight.

A92-536 Lost on 3.6.72 during its 11th flight.

A92-537 Lost on 10.2.71 during its 7th flight.

A92-538 Lost on 5.7.72 during its 13th flight.

A92-539 Lost on 16.5.72 during its 3rd flight.

A92-540 Lost on 4.2.72 during its 18th flight.

A92-541 Lost on 27.2.73 during its 30th flight.

A92-542 Lost on 25.10.71 during its 11th flight.

A92-543 F/F 6.6.72. Lost on 17.6.75 off Aberporth during its 75th flight. (The last Jindivik 103A in UK service.)

A92-544 Lost on 6.9.71 during its 1st flight.

A92-545 Lost on 21.6.73 during its 34th flight.

A92-546 Lost on 3.5.72 during its 8th flight.

5th Contract:
50 Jindivik Mk.103BL

A92-610 Flew the 3,000th UK Jindivik sortie on 3.2.75 (with 15,000 commemorative covers on board). Lost on 13.10.75 during its 31st flight.

A92-611 Lost on 19.6.73 during its 3rd flight.

A92-612 Shot down by an AIM-7 Sparrow air-to-air missile on 13.1.76 during its 35th flight.

A92-613 Lost on 5.3.74 during its 12th flight.

A92-614 Lost on 25.10.72 during its 8th flight.

A92-615 Lost on 18.6.74 during its 12th flight.

A92-616 Lost on 18.3.75 during its 28th flight.

A92-617 Lost on 24.1.74 during its 1st flight.

A92-618 Lost on 11.3.74 during its 4th flight.

A92-619 In May 1970 became the first Jindivik 103B to be delivered to Llanbedr. Lost on 8.4.71 during its 1st flight.

A92-620 Lost on 1.9.75 during its 30th flight.

A92-621 Lost on 4.6.75 during its 24th flight.

A92-622 Lost on 22.11.72 during its 6th flight.

A92-623 Lost on 20.12.72 during its 7th flight.

A92-624 Lost on 8.11.72 during its 8th flight.

A92-625 Lost on 14.4.78 during its 43rd flight.

A92-626 Lost on 16.10.72 during its 2nd flight.

A92-627 Lost on 5.2.74 during its 16th flight.

A92-628 Lost on 18.5.73 during its 7th flight.

A92-629 Lost on 13.3.74 during its 18th flight.

A92-630 Lost on 4.6.73 during its 20th flight.

A92-631 Lost on 22.3.74 during its 23rd flight.

A92-632 Lost on 26.11.75 during its 38th flight.

A92-633 Lost on 26.9.74 during its 9th flight.

A92-634 Lost on 5.4.77 during its 10th flight.

A92-635 Lost on 8.3.77 during its 53rd flight.

A92-651 Lost on 5.2.75 during its 12th flight.

A92-652 Lost on 19.2.75 during its 4th flight.

A92-653 Lost on 13.5.76 during its 29th flight.

A92-654 Lost on 13.10.75 during its 5th flight.

A92-655 Lost on 3.9.75 during its 17th flight.

A92-656 Lost on 20.10.75 during its 3rd flight.

A92-657 Lost on 9.7.76 during its 20th flight.

A92-658 Lost on 11.10.78 during its 22nd flight.

A92-659 Lost on 13.5.76 during its 9th flight.

A92-660 Lost on 5.9.77 during its 41st flight.

A92-661 Lost on 9.7.76 during its 9th flight.

A92-662 Lost on 22.12.76 during its 15th flight.

A92-663 Lost on 16.6.77 during its 23rd flight.

A92-664 First UK Jindivik to complete 100 sorties. The 100th sortie was made on 10.7.81 when it performed an exercise with the Royal Navy at RAE Aberporth Range. Lost 1.3.83 during its 133rd flight.
 'A92-664' (composite) later at Maes Artro Craft Village. Subsequently to The Military Aircraft Collection, Welshpool and finally to Boscombe Down Aviation Collection.

A92-665 Lost on 6.3.78 during its 53rd flight.

A92-666 Lost on 23.11.79 during its 75th flight.

A92-667 Lost on 1.6.77 during its 23rd flight.

A92-668 Lost on 24.6.80 during its 51st flight.

A92-669 Lost on 25.10.78 during its 17th flight.

A92-670 Lost on 1.12.81 during its 77th flight.

A92-671 Lost on 21.5.79 during its 25th flight.

A92-672 Lost on 25.11.81 during its 75th flight.

A92-673 Lost on 26.4.79 during its 7th flight.

A92-674 Noted at Adelaide Airport 2.3.74 awaiting airfreight to UK by British Eagle Britannia. Lost on 16.1.79 during its 3rd flight.

6th Contract:
40 Jindivik Mk.103BL

A92-701 Lost on 24.1.80 during its 2nd flight.

A92-702 Lost on 30.7.78 during its 11th flight.

A92-703 Lost on 18.10.82 during its 32nd flight.

A92-704 Lost on 28.1.82 during its 10th flight.

A92-705 Lost on 1.11.88 during its 111th flight.

A92-706 Lost on 14.5.91 when it crashed one mile south of Llanbedr and during its 171st flight. Remains returned to Llanbedr and 'reconstructed' for investigation. Later scrapped.

A92-707 Lost on 18.12.86 during its 98th flight.

A92-708 Lost on 20.8.80 during its 125th flight.

Believed to be assembled from a number of redundant Jindiviks, this example – photographed at Caernarfon in 2009 – represents an attempt to convert it into a replica of a piloted version. (Tom Singfield)

Crashed on landing at Llanbedr 28.8.80 due to poor visibility. Later used for ground trials at Llanbedr until rescued by Bristol Aeroplane Collection, Kemble.

A92-709 Lost on 28.5.82 during its 23rd flight.

A92-710 Lost on 9.5.82 during its 14th flight.

A92-711 Lost on 20.7.87 during its 107th flight.

A92-712 Lost on 20.3.81 during its 4th flight.

A92-713 Lost on 22.4.81 during its 4th flight.

A92-714 Lost on 1.7.83 during its 14th flight.

A92-715 Lost on 29.7.83 during its 18th flight.

A92-716 On 12.12.81 flew the 4,000th Jindivik UK sortie. Lost on 14.7.82 during its 14th flight.

A92-717 Lost on 9.5.82 during its 9th flight.

A92-718 Lost on 30.7.82 during its 11th flight.

A92-719 Lost on 17.7.89 during its 126th flight.

A92-720 Lost on 21.4.86 during its 69th flight.

A92-721 Lost on 19.6.84 during its 13th flight.

A92-722 On 31.1.92 became the first UK Jindivik to reach 200 flights. Crashed into Cardigan Bay 20.6.93 after sustaining a hit by a Rapier surface-to-air missile during its 265th flight.

A92-723 Lost on 3.7.87 during its 67th flight.

A92-724 Lost on 7.12.83 during its 7th flight.

A92-725 Lost on 21.2.85 during its 21st flight.

A92-726 Lost on 25.3.91 during its 160th flight.

A92-727 Lost on 11.4.86 during its 10th flight.

A92-728 Lost on 3.3.86 during its 21st flight.

A92-729 Lost on 30.9.92 during its 135th flight.

A92-730 Lost on 5.8.87 during its 33rd flight.

A92-731 Issued to DTEO Llanbedr. Repainted in "half-black" scheme and carried dual identity A92-731 and ZJ483 (allocated 27.6.97). Lost on 11.1.01 during its 180th flight.

A92-732 Lost on 10.8.89 during its 60th flight.

A92-733 On 15.1.88 flew the 5,000th UK Jindivik sortie. Lost on 9.1.90 during its 45th flight.

A92-734 Lost on 16.2.89 during its 23rd flight.

A92-735 Lost on 17.10.89 during its 28th flight.

Jindivik and Stiletto

Jindivik A92-902 being towed out of Llanbedr's main hangar on 30 August 2000 in order to be positioned for a specially-posed line-up photograph that later featured on the cover of Wendy Mills' book on the history of Llanbedr airfield, "Target Rolling". (Falcon Aviation Photographs)

A92-737 On 30.10.92 made the 6,000th UK Jindivik sortie. Issued to DTEO Llanbedr. Re-allocated as ZJ482 27.6.97. Shot down by a Sea Dart surface-to-air missile 22.9.98 during its 85th flight.

A92-738 Lost on 11.5.90 during its 19th flight.

A92-739 Lost on 2.8.90 during its 20th flight.

A92-740 Lost on 27.6.95 during its 89th flight.
Sundry parts later reported as being at Caernarfon Airport Airworld Museum.

7th Contract:
15 Jindivik Mk.104AL

A92-802 Noted with RAE Llanbedr 27.4.84; with DERA Llanbedr. Lost on 11.5.88 during its 12th flight.

A92-803 Re-allocated as ZJ484 27.6.97. Lost 29.1.04

A92-804 Noted with DTEO Llanbedr 6.5.98. Re-allocated as ZJ485 27.6.97; Lost on 26.8.97 during its 86th flight.

A92-805 Noted with DTEO Llanbedr 6.5.98 despite being re-allocated as ZJ486 27.6.97. Completed 78 flights as at 1.9.01. At end of Jindivik era conveyed to RAF Stafford for storage. Last noted Mar 2003. Believed since scrapped although parts have been reported at Baldonnel.

A92-806 Noted with DTEO Llanbedr 6.5.98. Re-allocated as ZJ487 27.6.97. Completed 154 flights as at 1.9.01. Later handed over to the Caernarfon Museum at Gynedd, Wales. Lost 13.02.03 (195 flights).

A92-807 Noted with DTEO Llanbedr 6.5.98. Re-allocated as ZJ488 27.6.97. Completed 137 flights as at 1.9.01. Lost on 18.6.02 during its 173rd flight.

A92-808 Noted with DTEO Llanbedr 6.5.98. Repainted in black overall scheme. Re-allocated as ZJ489 27.6.97. Completed 175 flights as at 1.9.01.

Reported as undergoing rebuild at Caernarfon Airworld Museum 2008.

A92-809 Noted with DTEO Llanbedr 6.5.98. Re-allocated as ZJ490 27.6.97. Returned to Australia to act as a pattern aircraft (by ASTA) when production line re-opened to meet new UK/MoD order for Series 900 aircraft. Completed 5 flights as at 1.9.01.

A92-810 Noted with DTEO Llanbedr 6.5.98. Re-allocated as ZJ491 27.6.97. Completed 96 flights as at 1.9.01.

A92-811 Lost on 28.3.96 during its 23rd flight.

A92-812 Lost on 27.3.96 during its 13th flight.

A92-813 Noted with DTEO Llanbedr 6.5.98. Re-allocated as ZJ492 27.6.97. Completed 75 flights as at 1.9.01. Lost 13.2.03 on its 100th flight.

A92-814 Noted with DTEO Llanbedr 6.5.98. Re-allocated as ZJ493 27.6.97. Completed 49 flights as at 1.9.01. At end of Jindivik era conveyed to RAF Stafford for storage. Reported at the RAF Museum Reserve Collection at Cosford

A92-815 Noted at Avalon 22.6.88; noted with DTEO Llanbedr 6.5.98. Re-allocated as ZJ494 27.6.97. As at 1.9.01 had not yet flown.

A92-816 Noted at Avalon 22.6.88; noted with DTEO Llanbedr 6.5.98. Re-allocated as ZJ495 27.6.97. As at 1.9.01 had not yet flown. Written-off 15.2.03 but reported as under repair 4.03.

7th Contract:
18 Jindivik Mk.104AL

A92-901 Noted with DTEO at Llanbedr 6.5.98. Re-allocated as ZJ496 27.6.97. Completed 18 flights as at 1.9.01. At end of Jindivik era conveyed to Boscombe Down for storage before transfer to Farnborough Air Sciences Trust (FAST) and conveyed to Farnborough 10.5.05.

A92-902 Noted with DTEO at Llanbedr 6.5.98. Re-allocated as ZJ497 27.6.97. Completed 1 flight as at 1.9.01. Lost 12.10.04.

A92-903 Re-allocated ZJ498 27.6.97. As at 1.9.01 had not yet flown. At end of Jindivik era conveyed to RAF Stafford for storage, having been allocated to the RAF Museum. Scrapped at Conifer Metals c2.05.

Despite having operated in the UK with Australian identities, a number of late-production Jindiviks were re-allocated British military serials within the normal sequence. ZJ486 was originally delivered as A92-805 but is seen here at Llanbedr on 30 August 2000 wearing its British marks. (Falcon Aviation Photographs)

A92-904 Re-allocated ZJ499 27.6.97. As at 1.9.01 had not yet flown. At end of Jindivik era conveyed to RAF Stafford for storage. Scrapped at Conifer Metals c2.05.

A92-905 Re-allocated ZJ500 27.6.97. As at 1.9.01 had not yet flown. At end of Jindivik era conveyed to RAF Stafford for storage. Scrapped at Conifer Metals c2.05.

A92-906 Re-allocated ZJ501 27.6.97. As at 1.9.01 had not yet flown. At end of Jindivik era conveyed to RAF Stafford for storage. Scrapped at Conifer Metals c2.05.

A92-907 Re-allocated ZJ502 27.6.97. As at 1.9.01 had not yet flown. At end of Jindivik era conveyed to RAF Stafford for storage. Scrapped at Conifer Metals c2.05.

A92-908 Re-allocated ZJ503 27.6.97. F/f 10.04. Displayed on launch trolley in compound opposite Llanbedr gate until at least 11.09.

A92-909 Re-allocated ZJ504 27.6.97. As at 1.9.01 had not yet flown. At end of Jindivik era conveyed to RAF Stafford for storage. Scrapped at Conifer Metals c2.05.

A92-910 Re-allocated ZJ505 27.6.97. As at 1.9.01 had not yet flown. At end of Jindivik era conveyed to RAF Stafford for storage. Scrapped at Conifer Metals c2.05.

A92-911 Re-allocated ZJ506 27.6.97. As at 1.9.01 had not yet flown. At end of Jindivik era conveyed to RAF Stafford for storage. Scrapped at Conifer Metals c2.05.

A92-912 Re-allocated ZJ507 27.6.97. As at 1.9.01 had not yet flown. At end of Jindivik era conveyed to RAF Stafford for storage. Scrapped at Conifer Metals c2.05.

A92-913 Re-allocated ZJ508 27.6.97. As at 1.9.01 had not yet flown. At end of Jindivik era conveyed to RAF Stafford for storage. Scrapped at Conifer Metals c2.05.

A92-914 Re-allocated ZJ509 27.6.97. As at 1.9.01 had not yet flown. At end of Jindivik era conveyed to RAF Stafford for storage. Scrapped at Conifer Metals c2.05.

A92-915 Re-allocated ZJ510 27.6.97. As at 1.9.01 had not yet flown.

A92-916 Re-allocated ZJ511 27.6.97. As at 1.9.01 had not yet flown.

A92-917 Re-allocated ZJ512 27.6.97. As at 1.9.01 had not yet flown. At end of Jindivik era conveyed to RAF Stafford for storage. Scrapped at Conifer Metals c2.05.

A92-918 Re-allocated ZJ513 27.6.97. As at 1.9.01 had not yet flown. At end of Jindivik era conveyed to RAF Stafford for storage. Scrapped at Conifer Metals c2.05.

A92-LLAN-1 Built entirely from spare parts; f/f 4.10.72. Lost 23.1.74 on its 37th flight. Later repaired for static display at Llanbedr.

A92-LLAN2 Constructed from spare parts of Series 700 aircraft at Llanbedr and described as a Mk.103B; f/f Feb 1993. Suffered Cat.5 damage 12.11.96 during a night take-off from Llanbedr for what would have been its 67th flight.

Llanbedr's engineers proved to be resourceful when, from serviceable parts salvaged from damaged Jindiviks and obsolete items from the phasing out of Jindivik 103A, an additional 'home-built' Jindivik 103A was completed in 1972. A92-LLAN-1, always known as 'Llanbedr One', was successfully flown on 4 October 1972 and survived intact until brought down by a Sparrow air-to-air missile 15 months later on its 37th sortie. Later repaired, it was statically displayed at the entrance to Llanbedr airfield for a number of years. (Falcon Aviation Photographs)

An unusual, but interesting, view of a Jindivik 104AL. Clearly visible attached to underwing pylons are two SART (Semi-Active Radar Target) towed augmentation systems, specifically designed to decoy I/J band radar guided missiles engaging the Jinidivik target. Also visible is a pack of what appear to be six A23 Infra-Red Flares in a pack strapped to the underside rear fuselage.

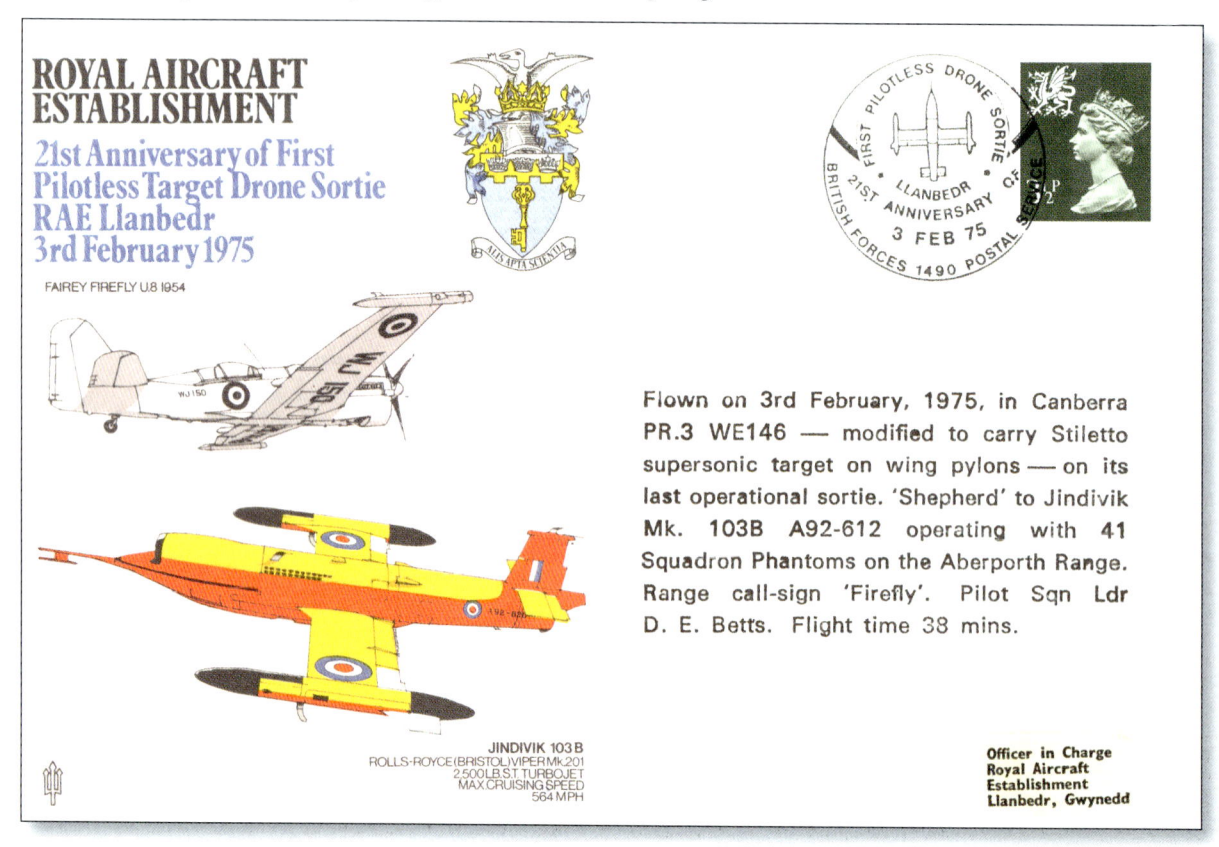

To mark the 21st anniversary of the first pilotless target drone sortie at RAE Llanbedr, a special First Day Cover was issued on 3 February 1975 and flown inside the Stiletto-equipped Canberra PR.3 WE146. Interestingly, the cover drawing depicts Firefly U.8 WJ150 whereas the first unmanned sortie was in fact flown by WJ147.

160 Sitting Ducks and Peeping Toms

The Beech Stiletto drone made its first flight in the UK on 28 June 1968 when carried beneath the wing of a Llanbedr-based Canberra. The Stiletto in question was an inert Dummy which was test-fired shortly afterwards, on 30 July. A second inert dummy was never used and was stored at Llanbedr for a number of years. When Llanbedr was closed Inert Dummy Stiletto No.2 was transferred to the RAF Museum Reserve Store at Stafford, where Tom MacGhee photographed it on 2 February 2000. (Tom MacGhee)

Beech/Short Stiletto

Jindivik was never, from the outset, designed to be a truly high-speed, ie supersonic, target drone. Therefore when, in 1965, a British Requirement for a high-altitude, high-speed target was issued, the MoD had little alternative but to source from the USA. Driven by both the Royal Navy and the Royal Air Force, who both needed a Mach 2 target capable of presenting at 50-60,000ft for training and practice firings of Sea Slug and Bloodhound respectively, the Beechcraft AQM-37A was adopted as the UK's first supersonic target drone. The initial contract involved a literally "off-the-shelf" purchase.

The AQM-37 (then designated XKD2B-1) had been the winner of a 1959 joint USN/USAF design competition for a supersonic air-launched expendable target drone, designed for air-to-air weapons evaluation and pilot training. Powered by a Rocketdyne twin-chamber liquid hypergolic bi-propellant rocket engine, it was first successfully launched from a F-3B Demon on 31 May 1961 at the PMTC, Point Mugu Test Range in California. In a subsequent launch, in 1965, from an F-4B flying at Mach 1.3 and 47,000ft, it demonstrated a 91,000ft altitude capability and attained Mach 2.8. The success of the canard-configured drone can be measured by the fact that, by 1968, some 1,500 had been delivered to the US Navy for use with F-4, A-4 and F-8 fighters since becoming fully operational in September 1963.[7]

AQM-37A was optimized for Mach 2 at 70,000ft but to achieve that speed at lower altitudes in order to meet British requirements the drone needed additional thrust. By replacing the AQM-37A's dual chamber motor with a single chamber unit enabled the increase in power at a lower altitude, this being the first step at transforming AQM-37A into Stiletto.

In US service, AQM-37A was a genuine one-shot – a 'fire and forget' – device with a timed 'aerodynamic' (ie canards hard down) means of achieving flight termination. As it was planned to operate the drone within the confines of Cardigan Bay, a degree of azimuth control and an explosive break-up system capable of being commanded by the Aberporth Range, was paramount. That led to other modifications: a telecommand to effect the azimuth control (height and speed were preset), range-radar compatible transponders, a British EMI T44/1 telemetry transmitter and, finally, a 15V explosive-destruct WREBUS flight termination system.

Under the terms of the MoD contract, Beech supplied the main fuselage and motor section with a new single chamber motor and with space for an explosive charge to be installed between the fuel and the oxidizer bulkheads. Re-design and manufacture of the nose section to accommodate the UK-specific instrumentation package was carried out at Belfast by Short Brothers' Aircraft Division under the designation, Short SD.2 Stiletto. Stiletto therefore was an "Irish-ised" version of the Beech AQM-37A, referred to by Beech as the Model 1072.

Stiletto was never designed to be ground-launched. Instead it was launched from a Canberra based at Llanbedr.

---

7 The XKB-2B1 was re-designated AQM-37A in September 1963. The manufacturer's basic designation for the US Navy variant was Beech Model 1019.

At the same time as Shorts was re-designing the AQM-37A, the company began to modify, under a separate MoD contract, Canberra PR.3 WE146 which had been selected as the first launch vehicle. After various modifications carried out at Belfast, including the fitting of a modified AS.30 pylon, the Canberra was officially re-designated Short SD.1 and it went on to achieve 30 operational launches. Over the years three further Canberras were modified to SD.1 standard: B.2 WE121 (15 launches); B.2/TT.18(P) WH734 in 1977 (89 launches) and B.2/TT.18(P) WK128 in 1978 (185 launches).[8]

The first procurement of SD.2 Stiletto drones involved just fifteen units, serialled KC001-KC015. All were delivered as complete units. The ready-fuelled rear sections went direct to RAE Llanbedr for which base support was provided by Shorts, whilst the forward sections were shipped to Shorts' Queen's Island for modification and additions.

The first test round was delivered by Shorts to Llanbedr where, on 28 June 1968, the first flight of a Canberra carrying a Stiletto drone took place. On 30 July the same Canberra performed the first release, albeit on both flights the Stiletto involved was purely an inert dummy example. The first live firing of a Stiletto drone took place on Friday, 2 August 1968, involving Stiletto KC002. Launched at 55,000ft the drone flew for 28 nautical miles at an average speed of Mach 1.4 before the flight was terminated by a commanded explosive destruct.[9] The flight was purely designed to determine the capabilities of the guidance system, telemetry, beacons and tele-commands. The flight was an outstanding success. (It is believed that this Stiletto – and the next two – retained the original AQM-37A two-stage motor.) The crew of the Llanbedr-based Canberra on that occasion were Sq/Ldr B.J.S. Knight OC Flying, RAE Llanbedr and Flt/Lt C. Westwood, the only uniformed pilots on site – all the others being contract pilots.

Stiletto development trials continued throughout 1968/69 and by late-1970 the "Irish-ised" target drone was finally declared operational and formally entered the Aberporth-Llanbedr target inventory. (There is some conflicting detail on the extent of the Stiletto development programme – or at least the original intentions. One source claimed that all of the first batch of target drones (KC001-KC015) were to be used for research and development, but the trials were so successful that operational presentations were introduced early. By the time of the last R&D release in January 1972 no fewer than seven operational releases had been undertaken.)

The first true operational presentations as a free flying target drone (ie to be fired at) were on 16 November and 7 December 1970 for an RAF Bloodhound and an RN Sea Slug respectively. However, on both occasions, and for a variety of reasons, neither weapon was fired. The first live intercept was on 17 December 1970 by a Bloodhound.

Sea Slug and Bloodhound remained the primary users of Stiletto until research and development trials of Sea Dart began in 1974; in-service firings of Sparrow later began in 1979. From the 1980s onwards, RAF Phantom FG.1s and FGR.2s were the primary customer for Stiletto at Aberporth. Subsequently Tornado F.3s began using Stiletto as a target for Sidewinder and Skyflash. The final presentation was made on 16 November 1999 for a Skyflash fired by a Tornado F.3. In total, some 108 Stiletto targets were released at Aberporth – 11 for R&D and 97 as operational targets.

The success of Stiletto presentations at Aberporth led both the Navy and the RAF to consider using the target elsewhere, away from Aberporth. In time, some Stiletto launches were made over the Outer Hebrides Range but mostly such launches took place on the high seas, in exercise or temporary danger areas, such as Saxa Vord and Gibraltar. On reflection, this must be viewed as having been an expensive – and on occasion a wasteful – use of Stiletto. Stiletto could only be launched by Llanbedr-based Canberras and operating away from the Aberporth Range meant that the telecommand and WREBUS flight termination systems could not be used. (On such occasions the explosive destruct was retained but modified to operate on a timer.) The first launch away from Aberporth took place in 1973 and despite the relatively high cost, such 'off-Range' launches continued for RAF presentations until 1998.

Although the basic AQM-37A failed to fully meet the original 1965 Requirement a batch of ten examples was ordered from the US manufacturer in August 1974 in what, in all probability, must be seen as a cost-saving measure. These targets (serialled KP001-KP010) differed from the standard AQM-37A in that they were fitted with a Shorts' autopilot developed specifically for Stiletto. (Despite the difference in dates, it is just possible that these ten targets were allocated British serials XZ900-XZ909. The allocation was made on 4 October 1976 against Contract NGW11B/573 but there is no evidence to suggest the serials were ever applied.) Subsequently a further thirty such targets (given the manufacturer's designation Beech Model 1095 and serialled KP011 to KP040) were purchased. All forty were used between 1976 and 1983 for 'off-Range' Royal Navy presentations.

In 1983 the standard AQM-37A was succeeded by a modified drone, being a combination of the Stiletto single-chamber motor/fuselage but with a standard (ie "non-Irishised") AQM-37A nose section. Being neither an AQM-37A nor a Stiletto, the new variant became known as the Hybrid Mk.1. The first fifteen examples were serialled KC136 to KC150 which had originally been intended to have been standard Stiletto drones. A further 76 Hybrid Mk.1s (serialled HM001 to HM076) were produced under the manufacturer's designation Beech Model 1108.

One other Stiletto variant was produced to meet a specific (but undisclosed) requirement. As a result a one-off purchase was made involving three Beech AQM-37C (Model 1113) target drones. They did, however, have Shorts-provided modifications to provide safety circuits independent of the control circuitry. Known as the Hybrid Mk.2, two were expended in 1992 and the third in 1995. None of the Hybrid Mk.1s or Mk.2s were used over the Aberporth Range; all were expended off-Range.[10]

---

8 A full description of Stiletto was first published in *Flight International*, issue dated 11 September 1969.

9 The date of the first Stiletto launch has also been quoted as 1 August 1968.

10 Some reports suggest that the purchase involved more than three examples, and possibly as many as eight were involved. If true, it is

An unidentifiable Beech Stiletto drone forms part of the Ulster Aviation Society Collection at Long Kesh, Northern Ireland. This view, taken on 14 September 2010, shows it to be in company with other aircraft closely related to the Province. (Peter Hughes)

Stiletto, in its various forms, remained in active service until 2000. The final release from a Llanbedr-based Canberra took place on 25 October 2000 and involved a Hybrid Mk.1.

Operationally, Stiletto proved to be an outstanding success and remained in active service for some thirty years. There were few, if any, reported misgivings although, in 1968, the Hybrid Mk.1 variant did become the focus of an incident that was both curious and politically explosive – literally! On 24 March 1968, and whilst operating a scheduled Cork to London service, an Aer Lingus Viscount 803 (EI-AOM) had crashed into the Irish Sea off Tuskar Rock, County Wexford. The cause of the crash was, at the time, unexplained and, in fact, no confirmed cause of the accident has ever been disclosed. The circumstances gave rise to a number of suggested causes, many of which were later disproved. However, when the rear fuselage of Hybrid Mk.1 HM042 was later washed up on the Irish coast it offered firm evidence to those conspiracy theorists in Ireland that "things from Aberporth" frequently strayed into Irish airspace. Ironically, at the time of the crash Stiletto had yet to make its initial flight in UK airspace and the theorists were left to assume that some other Aberporth-based target, or missile, had caused the crash. The conspiracy theorists may still have it otherwise but any mystery relating to the Viscount crash has nothing to do with Aberporth. 24 March 1968 was a Sunday and Aberporth was closed!

The British Government has consistently denied any involvement in the Viscount crash and a subsequent re-opening of the enquiry led investigators to report that a failure of the Viscount's port tailplane was the likely cause. The conspiracy theories, however, live on.

Beech AQM-37/Stiletto Procurement

Excluding the inert dummy used for initial flight tests, total procurement of Stiletto target drones (and their variations) amounted to 367 units. The breakdown of variants, showing original Beech construction numbers and the appropriate Beech Model Number, is as follows:

Variant	Model	Serial (c/n)	No
Stiletto Mk.1	1072	KC001-KC055	55
Stiletto Mk.2	1072	KC056-KC110	55
Stiletto Mk.2	1072	KC111-KC135	25
Stiletto Mk.2	1072	KC151-KC220	70
Stiletto Mk.2	1072	JP001-JP028	28
AQM-37A	1095	KP001-KP040	40
Hybrid Mk.1	1072a	KC136-KC150	15
Hybrid Mk.1	1108	HM001-HM076	76
Hybrid Mk.2	1113	JE001-JE003	3

Beech AQM-37/Stiletto Code Sequence

When AQM-37s left the Beech production line they did so as complete units but when they arrived in the UK the nose section was removed and sent to Shorts for 'Irishification' whilst the main fuselage and motor section was despatched either to Llanbedr or to the Propellants, Explosives and Rocket Motor Establishment (PERME) at Westcott, Bucks for storage and/or fuelling. For a variety of reasons it became difficult to later match the original nose section with its 'proper' fuselage at Llanbedr. An added complication was that nose sections were often configured as 'special/specific to task'. Different projects frequently required different augmentation and instrumentation fits whereas essentially the rear fuselage sections were identical.

---

likely that these were part of a 2005/06 purchase of AQM-37C for RAF Typhoon firings of AMRAAM at the QinetiQ Hebrides Range. The launch aircraft were USAF-supplied Lockheed F-16s.

The size of the Stiletto drone can be fully appreciated when seen attached to the underwing pylon of a Canberra. In this instance the target drone is attached to the specially-modified Canberra PR.3 WE146, the first of several such conversions referred to as the Short SD.1.

To overcome these difficulties one of the Shorts' employees at Llanbedr, J. 'Dusty' Rhodes, introduced, towards the end of 1974, a unique code sequence for Stiletto drones nose sections. The system was first used for the three target drones released in 1975, involving Stiletto Mk.1s KC039/X, KC038/Z and KC043/Y, in that order. Once the single-letter sequence had been consumed, the system moved on to AA–AZ; BA–BZ etc and through to at least HD. The final Stiletto release of 1999 is known to have involved JP014/HC, on 16 November. A similar code system existed for the Hybrid target drones but these used a simple numerical sequence, eg HM060 '26' and HM033 '29'. Unfortunately no complete record of Stiletto or Hybrid codes appears to have survived and the only known examples (together with launch/expenditure dates) are as follows: KC114/CJ (5.6.85); KC115/CK (20.8.85); KC116/CL (15.4.85); KC117/CM (17.9.85); KC118/CN; KC119/CP (9.5.86); KC120/CW (13.5.86); KC121/CS (13.5.86); KC122/CT (8.5.86); KC123/CU (15.5.86); KC124/CQ (15.5.86); KC125/CV; KC126/CO (11.6.86); KC127/CR (16.6.86) and KC128/CX.

Other launch dates involve HM001 (18.6.85); HM002 (11.2.86); HM003 (18.10.85) and HM004 (12.11.85)[11]

Two examples of Beech Stiletto remain extant, one being Mk.2 KC200 which is part of the FAST Collection at Farnborough; the other is with the Ulster Aviation Society Collction at Long Kesh.

---

11 Details of construction numbers and variations compiled from DERA Aberporth archives. However records held at the FAA Museum Yeovilton indicate that HM001-008 and KC137-150 were Hybrid Mk.2s. The author has considered the Aberporth details to be correct.

164 Sitting Ducks and Peeping Toms

Chapter 7
Targets for the Royal Navy

THE PERIOD 1945–1955 opened with the Royal Navy, not for the first time, becoming increasingly concerned at the manner in which gunnery practice at sea was being performed. The concern was especially felt in the Far East where, since the fall of Singapore in 1942 – and the loss of the resident Queen Bee Flight there – aerial target facilities had become the sole domain of a small number of dedicated target-towing RAF Squadrons. Concerns were equally felt in the Middle East and in UK waters where no suitable aerial target aircraft was available since Queen Bee had been withdrawn, Queen Martinet was still at a development stage and the high-speed Queen Spitfire project had been abandoned. It was not an ideal situation and as a consequence, as early as November 1945, the Royal Navy raised a requirement for a small pilotless target aircraft.[1]

Aware that no British project was under consideration, Admiralty planners began to focus upon an American drone, the Naval Aircraft Factory TD2N-1 Gorgon IIIB. This was an air-launched target powered by a Westinghouse 9.5in turbojet and had made its first successful powered flight in August 1945. But the programme had run into difficulties because of problems with the drone's engine and in March 1946, after only 12 had been built, the TD2N-1 programme was cancelled.

There was, in fact, one British project that showed some promise. In 1947 Fairey Aviation was developing its "Stooge" ballistic missile and it was suggested that a 7ft jet-propelled equivalent could be developed as a target for the Admiralty. However the proposal was not taken up: it was perhaps a little too sophisticated for what their Lordships wanted. What the Admiralty was really calling for was "the provision of a small inexpensive target for operation and use by ships and anti-aircraft units for their own tracking and firing practices, particularly when air co-operation and target towing is not available." This eventually translated into Naval/General Staff Requirement NA.3, issued on 7 March 1949.

Later in the year, the Air Ministry also declared an interest in a small, low-speed pilotless target aircraft when Specification U.25/49 was issued on 24 November. Involving just the design and construction of a single prototype, U.25/49 did encompass all of the naval requirements outlined in Spec NA.3 but the important factor was that the aircraft should be "as small and as cheap as possible" and, according to an amendment issued on 19 June 1950, could "account for an existing, or new, piston or jet engine of British manufacture". A second amendment,

XW999 was the last of the first batch of Northrop Chukar D.1 target drones, delivered to the UK in December 1971. Sitting on its suitably restrained zero-launcher, fully-fuelled and connected the drone is virtually ready for launch in this October 1972 view. XW999 survived its time as a target and currently resides with the Cornwall At War Museum, Davidstowe Moor.

---

1 National Archives ADM1/20348

All present and correct! The fact that a British soldier stands in the foreground and a naval officer can be seen in the background suggests that Arsenal 5501 No.49 was one of the drones used for the A&AEE 'Trial 331' at Aberporth during July-September 1952. The trial led to a decision by the Admiralty to acquire further Arsenal 5501 drones. The similarity between the Arsenal 5501 and the German V-1 'Doodle-Bug' is clearly evident in this view. (National Archives AVIA54/921)

on 5 March 1951, reflected a need "for steady flight when control signals are not being passed to the aircraft".

Fairey Aviation are known to have undertaken a design study for U.25/49 but stopped work immediately after the Specification was cancelled in favour of a new Specification, U.120D. Announced by the Air Ministry on 28 September 1951, U.120D again reflected the requirements of both the Navy and Army but for a variety of reasons U.120D became a long and drawn out affair and which was ultimately dogged by failure.[2]

Meanwhile a Ministry of Supply mission had visited the US in 1951 with the object of obtaining detailed information on all American pilotless targets. At the time, the mission was looking specifically for targets that would meet Naval Requirement NA.3 and recommended that the D.G.D purchase a quantity of Radioplane KD2R-2 (OQ-19) drones. In response the D.G.D. made an immediate bid for 36 KD2R-2s under the Military Defence Aid Programme.

If, by ordering American target drones, the Admiralty was seen as having found a suitable solution then naval planners were very soon disappointed. The KD2R-2 did not have an 'out-of-sight' autopilot; nor was it capable of operating from a zero-length launcher, factors that were essential to meet Navy requirements. KD2R-2 also proved unsuitable for medium calibre anti-aircraft firings and as a consequence the bid was cancelled.[3] To add to the Admiralty's growing frustration there was a realisation that the U.120D target drone would not be available until late-1954/early-1955 at the very earliest. What the Admiralty really wanted was a quick fix solution. This came from an unexpected source and not without a degree of irony.

Arsenal 5501

The French Arsenal de l'Aèronautique had developed a small, radio-controlled monoplane powered by a pulse-jet based on the Fieseler FzG-76 – more widely known as the V-1 'Doodle Bug' flying bomb. Designated ARS 5501 and named 'Bernadette', it only differed externally from the V-1 by having twin fins, a nose probe radio aerial and stabilizers on the trailing wing edges, near the tips. It was ramp-fired with the assistance of two solid-fuel booster rockets on a mobile sled.

The 5501's motor was again a development of the FzG-76 pulse-jet and gave the Bernadette a speed of around 325mph for a duration of approximately 30 minutes. In performance terms, it could climb to 13,000ft in 10 minutes. Descent was controlled either by parachute or by firing braking rockets when a few metres from the ground to absorb the landing shock, these being operated by a proximity fuse.

Towards the late-Spring of 1952 a Ministry of Supply technical mission, under Air Commodore Silyn Roberts, visited the CERES Test Range at Ile du Levant, in Southern France. A series of test flights had been arranged to evaluate a new autopilot system and to measure the effect of re-launching an aircraft immediately after recovery. An added factor was the question of plotting a target aircraft with ship's instruments.

French-owned aircraft were used on these flights, the first of which took place on 8 May 1952 (with 5501 No.20). The flight, which only lasted 10 minutes, was cut short following the failure of the revised autopilot. Two further flights were carried out on the following day with aircraft Nos. 19 and 25 and whilst both were engaged by ships lying offshore neither drone was hit and both were recovered satisfactorily. Four more flights (involving No.35 on 13 May, No.50 on 14 May and two by No.25 on 15 May) completed the series. The final flight, on 15 May, involved re-launching No.25 immediately after recovery. It flew satisfactorily for 27 minutes, thereby achieving one of the trial's objectives.

Setting aside the test with the new automatic pilot, all of the flights had proved successful and steps were immediately taken to acquire a small quantity for further trials in the UK. Six examples of the 5501B variant were purchased by the Ministry of Supply and air-freighted to Aberporth for what was termed as 'Trial 331' between July and September 1952. This trial, conducted by an A&AEE Detachment, was to establish the drone's radar response.

---

2 See Chapter 8 for further details on the U.120D programme.
3 Apart from KD2R-2 not meeting all of the Navy's requirements, there is some doubt as to whether the purchase would have been allowed to go ahead. UK fiscal restrictions concerning dollar transactions were in place at the time.

Flt	Date	Flight Designation	Duration Mins/Secs	Remarks
1	23.7.52	RAF-1	15.00	Satisfactory flight but aircraft purposely ditched because of close proximity to coast-line and some doubt as to drone's exact course.
2	13.8.52	RN-1	21.00	Cause of flight termination unknown
3	14.8.52	RN-2	00.30	Port rocket motor blew a release plate after a hang fire. The flame from this vent covered the intake to the pulse jet and caused a break in combustion. Belly-landed onto the sea, bounced and then broke up.
4	22.8.52	ARMY-1	00.15	A "Hang Fire" occurred in starboard rocket motor. Unbalanced thrust knocked off the end of the fuel jettison pipe. The aircraft caught fire and dived into the sea. According to the official post-flight report it was "a magnificent spectacle!"
5	5.9.52	ARMY-2	03.00	Satisfactory launch but when attempting a climbing turn the aircraft started to turn but immediately entered a spiral dive into the sea.

Although interest in the 5501 was strongest from the Admiralty it was still viewed as an aircraft that could meet a tri-service requirement. The Aberporth trial was therefore organised around various flight patterns to reflect specific needs by the Royal Navy, the Army and finally the RAF.

As it turned out only five (of six) planned flights were achieved during the trial period. One each on behalf of the Navy and Air Force were satisfactory; some data was obtained from one Army flight. What the flights did reveal was that a mean average speed of 215kt was achievable but that for gunnery purposes the target only had an effective range duration of twenty minutes.[4]

Details of the five flights are given in the table at the top of the page.

Over at the Admiralty, their Lordships were quietly delighted with the outcome of the Aberporth trial and as a result the Gunnery Division was encouraged to push for the purchase of further aircraft. The trial also encouraged the Admiralty to form a special Pilotless Target Aircraft Unit (PTAU).

The choice of a location for the Navy's PTAU meant that the Navy's Arsenal drones would rarely, if ever, be seen in the UK. Reliably good weather conditions for long periods throughout the year helped planners to decide on placing the unit on the island of Malta. The location was also ideal for ships working-up and testing their guns whilst en route to the Far East.

A small group of air personnel was quickly assembled and given basic training, firstly in Paris and later at the Ile du Levant Missile Test Range. The new unit proceeded to Malta on 28 July 1953 and set up a summer base at Fort Benghaisa, situated above Hassans Cave on Benghaisa Point at the end of Marsaxlokk Bay. The first two Arsenal 5501B targets were air-freighted in from Villacoublay on 15 August, followed by a second pair two days later.

The launch site could not have been better suited; it was close to the edge of a sheer cliff some 180 feet above sea

---

4 National Archives AVIA54/921

Arsenal 5501B No.66 represents one of the batch of target drones purchased by the Admiralty for the Pilotless Target Aircraft Unit at Fort Benghaisa, Malta. The location was ideal for offering Royal Navy ships en route to the Far East with an opportunity to carry out gunnery practice under 'live' conditions. This 1953 view shows the aircraft on its launch ramp receiving last-minute attention before firing. (National Archives ADM1/24884)

level. Catapult launches were aided by rockets attached to each side of the fuselage. Immediately after the launch carriages automatically detached from the aircraft and descended by parachute into the sea, to be recovered later by naval divers.

Scheduled for 21 August 1953, the first flight by a British Arsenal 5501B did not go quite as planned. Take-off was set at 1330. Technicians, having worked throughout the night to prepare both launcher and aircraft, received a message from the Hal Far SATCO just 45 minutes before the scheduled launch time stating that the launch had, in fact, been prohibited by order of the Island's Governor and the Director of Civil Aviation. By the time that somebody managed to verify whether or not the message was not a hoax, zero hour had passed.

The prohibition order did subsequently prove to be false and a revised launch time of 1430 was set. The normal pre-launch cycle of checks began one hour beforehand but air pressure was building up too slowly and the launch time passed with the target's fuel tank insufficiently pressurized. Launch was again delayed, to 1530.

At 1530 minus 15 seconds the pulse jet was fired but as it did so the quick release connector on the air pressure starting line became disconnected and the engine stopped. (This was later found to be a manufacturer's fault by not supplying the correct starting hose.) A quick on-the-spot repair was carried out and at 1545 the aircraft was again ready for launch.

For a second time the engine was fired but after just thirteen seconds the main power switch for the radio and W/T transmitters in the control vehicle failed. The aircraft should have launched two seconds later but at the critical moment the engine was stopped. The cause of the power failure was very quickly traced to vibration through the solid rock structure of the launch site, caused by the engine running at full power. To avoid any repetition of a power failure technicians re-wired the power switch so that it was locked in the 'ON' position and the target was again declared ready to launch at 1605.

At 1605 the engine was again started; full power selected and the drone was finally, and successfully, catapulted off its launch ramp. The launching carriage jettisoned cleanly into the sea and the target drone was then ordered to climb and

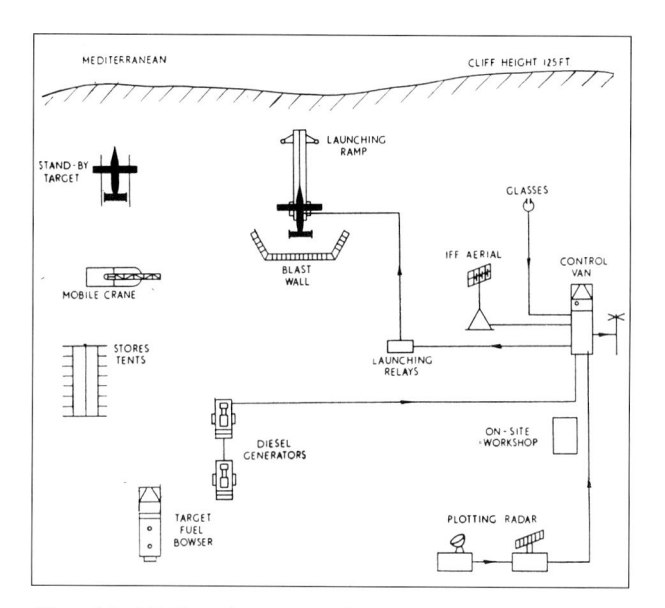

Plan of the PTA launch site at Benghaisa Point, Malta.

level out at 5,000 feet. The target performed perfectly and was later recovered from the sea close to the launch site. Arsenal 5501B was declared fully operational.

Plotted by radar, the Arsenal 5501 targets were flown at any height from 2,000 to 20,000 feet up to a range of 20 miles from a control station situated in a large vehicle close to the launch site. On completion of a mission the target was then flown directly overhead the recovery vessel, RFA *Sea Salvor*. The engine was stopped on command, a recovery parachute automatically allowing the target to descend slowly into the sea from which it was rescued intact by the recovery vessel. During the descent the fuel tank was depressurized by jettisoning any remaining fuel so that maximum buoyancy was available in the water. After recovery the target was washed, serviced and made ready for the next launch.

Speed and endurance of the 5501 varied with height since constant thrust from the pulse jet was obtained by the automatic fuel regulator at all heights – a factor never achieved by the Germans with the V-1. Speed at 10,000 ft was approximately 280 knots straight and level, and Royal Navy 5501s achieved an average endurance of about 40 minutes.

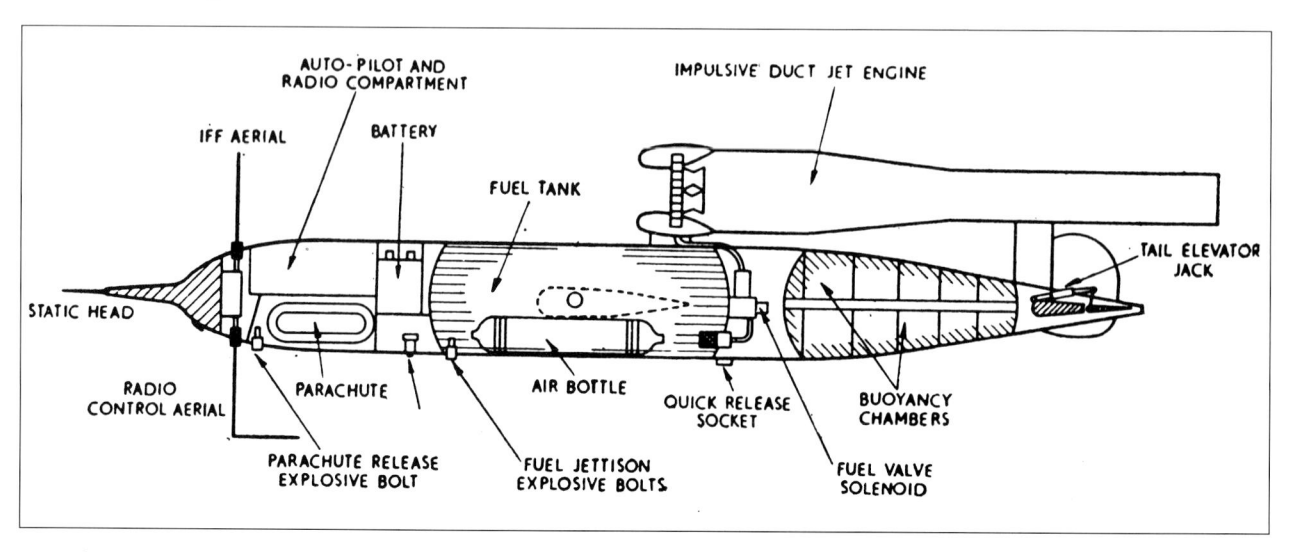

Arsenal 5501 interior arrangement.

Arsenal 5501B No.337 blasts off its launcher at Fort Benghaisa, Malta leaving a huge cloud of black exhaust smoke as it does so. Note that this example is fitted with wing-tip fuel tanks. (via Douglas A. Rough)

The initial operational trial period at HMS *Falcon* was satisfactorily completed by November 1953. The unit was temporarily suspended for the winter of 1953/54 until June 1954 when started again for the summer season. By now the decision was taken to try using Arsenal in a more flexible manner and attempt to operate targets from a launcher mounted on the deck of a ship. The cruiser HMS *Cumberland* was selected for a series of at least nine firing runs over three separate occasions off Gibraltar. Several Arsenal targets were deployed aboard *Cumberland* and the first launch took place on 13 July 1954. On the target's first run it sustained a close burst, causing it to turn away involuntarily; the aircraft was never seen again. On 20 July six firing runs were successfully achieved and on 1 September an Arsenal target managed two more successful runs. Several weeks later a number of Arsenal 5501s were launched from the same ship (this time under the aegis of the Ministry of Supply) as targets for RAF Meteors.

Considering its acquisition was very much a stop-gap measure, Arsenal 5501 proved to be a much more realistic target than any other aircraft previously used by British forces. Its speed did not approach speeds of contemporary jets but it did represent a vast improvement over any contemporary target towed behind a 'live' aircraft. More importantly, firing could be carried out with few restrictions as revealed when an Arsenal drone took part in a brief series of trials in August 1954 for the Ministry of Supply using a Meteor.

September 1954 marked the end of the trial period; operations were wound down on Malta and the Special PTA Trials Unit returned to the UK and was accommodated at RNAS Lee-on-Solent pending its return to Malta to set up a regular target service. In April 1955 the notion that the PTA unit should become part of Hal Far-based 728 Squadron was raised. There was, of course, much merit in the suggestion but it was not taken up and instead, in May 1955, the PTA Unit became an independent unit and re-titled Naval Experimental Pilotless Target Unit (NEPTU) under the control of Commanding Officer Lt/Cdr S.Timbs, RN.

In the meantime a second order for Arsenal 5501B targets was placed with the French manufacturer in the Spring of 1955. The order (against Contract 6/Acft/11782/CB.9(b) originally involved just 12 aircraft but the quantity was later increased to fifteen on 13 May 1955.) All were delivered direct to Malta.[5]

---
5 National Archives ADM1/26739

When the Arsenal target drone had completed its mission it was commanded back to the recovery site whereupon its engine would be cut, a recovery parachuite automatically deployed, and allowed to gently descend into the sea. During the descent the fuel tank would depressurize by jettisoning any remaining fuel so to increase the buoyancy factor. Arsenal 5501 No.78 is seen floating in the Mediterranean and about to winched out of the water at the end of another successful sortie – or an unsuccessful one if you're a ship's gunner! (via Douglas A. Rough)

The Arsenal 5501B target drone proved to be satisfactory in service. So much so that towards the end of 1955 the launching site at Fort Benghaisa was redesigned so as to allow two launching ramps to be used. But the Admiralty still had its eye firmly focused on the ML U-120D drone which was still undergoing flight trials in the UK. However not all the U-120D trials were wholly satisfactory and it was only continued Admiralty interest in the U-120D that had effectively kept that programme alive despite it losing favour with the War Office. *(See Chapter 8)*

The problems that dogged the U-120D drone ultimately proved too difficult to solve and even the Admiralty began to lose interest. So much so that, in mid-1957, the Admiralty chose to end its support of the U-120D programme. After five years of on-going trials the U-120D had proved incapable of meeting naval requirements. The two factors that had finally tipped the Admiralty's opinion was the autopilot system which had never functioned satisfactorily and the simple fact that the U-120D's speed was well below expectation. When the RAE issued its final assessment report on U-120D it was quite damning and even went as far as recommending the purchase of American target drones. Coincidentally, another report, which originated from the Director of the Gunnery Division and dated 17

Targets for the Royal Navy   169

December 1957, had come to the same conclusion and went further to suggest that a number of Radioplane OQ-19s, previously purchased by the Ministry of Supply but which had been held in store at Aberporth for a number of years, should be transferred to the Admiralty to replace the ill-fated U-120D and also as a successor to the Arsenal 5501B.

KD2R-5/MQM-36A Shelduck

To this day it still remains uncertain whether the stored and un-used MoS OQ-19 drones were in fact ever transferred to the Royal Navy. It is strongly suspected that they were not transferred since the Admiralty had decided that if it was to purchase American target drones, then it would buy newer models directly from the American manufacturer. That decision led to the acquisition of Northrop-Radioplane's highly-successful KD2R-5 target drone, itself being a development of the OQ-19, the origin of which dated back to the last few months of World War II.

Encouraged by the US military forces as a replacement for its OQ-2, OQ-3 and OQ-14 target drones, Radioplane had completed a prototype of a new design in March 1945; it carried the company designation RP-18 and was, like its predecessors, a high-wing monoplane. But there any similarities ended. The RP-18 fuselage was rounded and constructed of aluminium; it had a one-piece wooden wing with leading-edge slots and the entire design was considerably more streamlined. The military readily adopted the new Radioplane design which, in US Army service became the OQ-17 and in US Navy service became known as the KDR-1.[6]

The OQ-17/KDR-1 was powered by the 35hp Righter 0-45-35 engine which, despite being an ideal engine for the aircraft in most respects, suffered severe reliability problems and production ended after just 430 examples had been built. The search for an alternative engine took Radioplane from the two-stroke Righter back to the 4-cylinder McCulloch 0-90-1 engine that had been used successfully on the OQ-6 series.

The McCulloch engine was considerably heavier and necessitated a redesign of the OQ-17 fuselage and wing. When the designers had finished they were faced with an almost totally new aircraft, now referred to by Radioplane as the RP-19. Adopted by the American forces the RP-19 was traditionally allocated two respective designations – the US Army OQ-19 and the KD2R for the US Navy.

The OQ-19/KD2R range marked the start of an astonishing production run that extended for over four decades during which time, under various guises and designations, the total units manufacturered rose to over 48,000. Including sub-contracted examples – a number of which were built by Helio at their Norwood, MA factory – the total eventually rose to over 55,000 examples. It proved to be the longest series production run in aviation history.

The first 150 OQ-19As built by Radioplane had wooden wings with leading-edge slots and two ailerons. Control surfaces on all OQ-19As consisted of ailerons and elevators only; the rudder was fixed.

---

[6] This was at a time when the US Army and US Navy were using completely different service designation systems.

Design of the OQ-19B and OQ-19D variants began concurrently in October 1949. The first launches were tested in April 1950 and the first air-launch test was accomplished in August 1950 when an OQ-19D was launched from a B-26 operating out of Holloman AFB. Within a month the research and development phase was complete and the first production OQ-19D was delivered in October 1950; the first production OQ-19B followed in May 1951.

The primary difference between the OQ-19B and the OQ-19D was that the former had a vertical gyro and could be flown out of sight of the ground pilot. A retrofit kit to convert OQ-19Ds into OQ-19Bs did become available in 1951 and many were subsequently modified in service.

In July 1952 the Radioplane Company was acquired by Northrop Aircraft Inc. No immediate effect was felt and Radioplane continued to function as an independent company until August 1957 when re-styled as the Radioplane Division of the Northrop Corporation. Not until 2 April 1962 did the Van Nuys facility become known as the Northrop Corporation – Ventura Division.

UK Contracts (Royal Navy)

In July 1957 the Director of the Gunnery Division (D.G.D.) – just prior to compiling its damning report on the U-120D – learnt that the US Navy had taken delivery of the Radioplane KD2R-5, a version of KD2R-2 fitted with an 'out-of-sight' autopilot and operable from a zero length launcher. KD2R-5 was, in effect, a fully developed alternative to the ill-fated U-120D. Furthermore, it was capable of flying at 228mph (191 kts) – compared to 140-150kts achieved by the U-120D.

Treasury approval for the purchase of U-120Ds had long been secured and a provision for the purchase of 30 U-120Ds had been contained in the 1956-57 defence estimates. That had come about largely as a result of plans by the RAF to withdraw its target-towing Beaufighter TT.Xs from Hong Kong as well as a planned British withdrawal from Ceylon, a situation that was to leave naval forces east of Suez with little, if any, opportunity for conventional anti-aircraft practice. So when, in July 1958, the Admiralty assessed its future requirement for gunnery practice, the situation was seen as follows:

Station	No of ships to use KD2R-5s	No of flights per year (plus Working-Up)	Total
East of Suez	15	30 + 15	45
Home & Mediterranean	50	100 + 50	150
Atlantic & West Indies	4	8 + 4	12
South Atlantic & South America	5	10 + 5	15
Total			222

From US Navy experience the average number of flights achieved by individual target aircraft, taking into account all causes of mortality, was just four. Therefore to achieve a total of 222 flights the Admiralty required a minimum of 55 drones – and that was only the requirement for conventional gunnery practice. What concerned naval planners more than anything else was the potential lack of suitably available targets to forces 'east of Suez' when Seaslug and the short-range 'Green Light' (later renamed Seacat) missiles entered service, the latter as a successor to 40mm guns. The July 1958 assessment went further to estimate requirements over the following few years as being five aircraft in the financial year 1961/62), 12 (1962/63), 20 (1963/64) and 25 (1964/65).[7]

On 22 December 1958, the Admiralty lodged a request for Treasury approval to spend £140,000 on 50 KD2R-5 target aircraft, 25 for delivery in the 1958/59 financial year and the remainder during the following financial year. The total costings were broken down as follows:

Item	Cost
50 Targets @ £1,600 each	£80,000
6 Zero length launchers @ £1,615 each	£9,690
6 sets of spares for launchers @ £310 each	£1,860
2 Ground support sets @ £11,600 each	£23,200
Spares for 50 Targets	£23,200
Transport	£9,650
Total	£140,000

All of these figures were still based on the experience of the US Navy and the average life of just four flights per aircraft. But by the time the initial contract was placed, costs had risen slightly and in order to work within the original fiscal estimates, the quantity of aircraft ordered was reduced to forty – ten to be allocated to the Commander-in-Chief, Far East Station, Singapore and the remainder being consigned to the Flag Officer Sea Training at Portland.[8]

The order for forty KD2R-5s (Contract KF/5R/01/CB.25(b)) was placed through Northrop/Radioplane's UK subsidiary agent, C.T. (London) Ltd on 18 February 1959 and by re-arranging delivery schedules against existing contracts, the manufacturer was able to fulfill the Admiralty order immediately. The first batch of KD2R-5 Shelduck targets was delivered virtually "off-the-shelf" although it is still unclear precisely where and when they were shipped to. Despite being shipped from the USA at the end of February 1959 the first recorded use of Shelduck took place in September 1959 when ten were taken to Larkhill and where crews were trained in operating the aircraft. What clouds the situation is that Northrop's records state that the first ten were shipped to Seletar whilst the remaining thirty went to RNAS Abbotsinch for storage. It is feasible that all were sent to Abbotsinch and that ten were despatched to Singapore once the Larkhill training period had finished. Alternatively, the initial ten may well have gone to Singapore where they were held in store for several months whilst crews worked up on another ten at Larkhill.

A second batch of ten Shelducks is said to have been sent out to Singapore in December 1959 where they joined the others at HMS *Terror* and help form a detached Flight of the newly-established Royal Navy Pilotless Target Aircraft (RNPTA) Squadron. The Flight operated from what was described at the time as the "smallest air station in existence, in the middle of the Naval base at Singapore. No runways, no hangars, just two large buildings at the side of the road

The Royal Navy Pilotless Target Association Squadron crest was highly apt and only required a change of wording when the RNPTA was re-styled as Fleet Target Group. (via Lee Howard)

leading to HMS *Terror* from the dockyard." The Shelducks were, of course, not launched from inside the dockyard; they were operated from HM Tug *Nimble*.[9]

The RNPTA had been formed at RNAS Portland in 1959 and operated out of a small facility situated on what was the main dockyard car park in the Naval Base. Squadron Headquarters and two Flights – 'A' and 'B' – were retained at Portland whilst two further Flights were detached overseas; 'C' Flight at Hal Far, Malta (formerly the Naval Experimental Pilotless Target Unit) and 'D' Flight at HMS *Terror*, Singapore. As well as the four Flights, the RNPTA established Equipment Holding Units at Gibraltar and Mombasa, Kenya to give the Royal Navy a worldwide aerial target service for ships' gun and short-range missile systems.

There was another aspect of Shelduck operations that was never widely publicised and which, although co-ordinated by RNPTA Headquarters at Portland, was very much an independent unit working with the Air Ministry and the Director of Gunnery Development. Based at Morice Yard, Plymouth and operating from HMS *Decoy* the offshoot unit acted as a form of trials unit and especially worked closely with Short Bros in the pre-service trials of Seacat missile.

The initial forty Shelducks, delivered to the Royal Navy in March 1959, were in standard production finish of overall dark red with white wings. They were unmarked although individually identified as 'UK1' to 'UK40' and not until 13 August 1959 were they allocated traditional military serials (XN862-XN876/XN893-917) within the standard

---

7   National Archives ADM1/26739
8   National Archives ADM1/26739

9   As reported by Lt Cdr R.D. Bateman, RN (Commanding Officer, PTA Squadron) in Flight Deck No.1 1965.

One of a batch of Northrop KD2R-5 Shelduck target drones purchased specifically for use in the Seacat missile acceptance trials. None was allocated standard series serials and operated with a UK-sequence number. 151 is seen being prepared for launch from HMS Decoy. (Short Brothers & Harland Ltd Neg. No.PED 1671-1)

sequence. Just ten days earlier it was officially announced that the Northrop KD2R-5 was officially named and designated Shelduck D.Mk.1 in British service although, rather curiously , the term Shelduck was adopted by other operators, including some US constituents in much the same manner that the term Dakota was widely adopted around the world for the C-47. More curious, however, is that the designation KD2R-5 was maintained by Northrop's sign-writers long after the official US designation changed to MQM-36A as part of the system change in September 1962.

Shelduck remained the Navy's basic ship-to-air target throughout the 1960s, but the need for a faster and more sophisticated target to meet equally sophisticated weapon systems led to the acquisition of Northrop's Chukar drone. Depending on the level of target service required, Shelduck and Chukar were jointly operated by the RNPT for some fifteen years.

Orders for KD2R-5/MQM-36A targets for British armed forces eventually took total procurement to just short of 1,000 units. Almost all of them were for the Royal Navy and, with the exception of a small batch of ten aircraft, all were built by Northrop's Ventura Division and delivered by ship to the UK.[10]

---

10 Shipment details etc extracted and collated from the files of Aerial Targets Ltd

KD2R-5 Shelduck XT308 poses before officers and men of the RNPTA for the unit's annual photograph. Note that Headquarters, 'A' and 'B' Flight were based at Portland. 'C' Flight was a permanent detachment in Malta and 'D' Flight similarly located in Singapore. XT308 represents the revised scheme of dark red but a white fin. Note also that the serial is in stencil-style, unlike all other lettering, suggesting that the serial was applied after delivery to the UK. XT305 was delivered ex-factory to Lee-on-Solent in September 1964 yet still carries the designation KD2R-5, despite the fact that the type was changed to MQM-36A some two years beforehand. (792 Squadron Archive)

The ten aircraft not built in the US were assembled in Italy as part of a sub-contract arrangement finalized in 1967. The deal between Northrop and Meteor S.p.A involved the Italian company producing, under licence, 94 sets of aerodynamic and avionic components for the MQM-36A (KD2R-5) target. Thirty of these aircraft were built for the Italian Navy who christened the aircraft as the NVM-1 (Northrop Ventura-Meteor 1). The remaining 64 targets were sold to various foreign forces, including ten for the Royal Navy and which were serialled XV828-XV837. These were shipped direct from the Italian factory to the RNPTA Detachment in Singapore during March 1968.[11]

The Malta-based 'C' Flight was disbanded in 1970 and the responsibility for serving ships in the Mediterranean was taken over by RNPTA Headquarters at Portland with deployments of target aircraft aboard ships of the Royal Fleet Auxilliary. Existing facilities at Portland were by now proving inadequate for the increase in operations. Design and construction of a complete target facility inside RNAS Portland was completed in October 1974 and in a move to reflect the wider range of target services being provided the RNPTA was re-titled Fleet Target group.[12]

In the Far East Shelduck operations had continued from either RFA *Typhoon* or HM Ships deployed to the area but with the more centralized role adopted by the Fleet Target group, the Singapore-based 'D' Flight returned to RNAS Portland in October 1974 and was formally disbanded.

By 1986 only 'B' Flight was operating Shelduck drones although by that time the Fleet Target group more often referred to it as 'Shelduck Flight'. Since the early-1980s, Chukar had became the Navy's standard aerial target and as Shelduck operations began to wind down so consideration was given to selling off some of the unflown examples. At least seven Shelducks (XZ750/751/753/754/ 757/763 & 796) were taken out of storage at Portsmouth, conveyed to Portland, assembled and prepared for a possible sale to the Abu Dhabi Government. However by September 1982 the Abu Dhabi military had lost interest in the Shelducks; the terms of the deal lapsed and the aircraft were returned to storage at Portsmouth.[13]

The end of UK Shelduck operations came in 1986. The penultimate deployment took 'B' Flight to the South Atlantic in January 1986 where six Shelducks were flown, two of which were lost in the process – XZ754 which crashed after refusing to climb after launch and ZA505 which was shot down. No more Shelduck sorties took place until 1 July 1986 when XZ794 and XZ795 provided targets in the Portland Exercise Area. These were the last Shelduck flights flown by the Royal Navy, the distinction of making the final flight rested with XZ794 which flew for 28 minutes before it was shot down.

The Fleet Target Group continued its aerial target operations solely with Chukar II although the Navy did turn to using MATS-A targets as close-range targets for weapons up to 40mm.[14]

---

11 Aerial Targets Ltd
12 One little-known aspect of the Fleet Target Group's naval operations was the use of small "Firefish" radio-controlled boats, used for more advanced surface gunnery exercises.
13 As recorded within the Movement & Deployment records of the Fleet Target Group, Portland
14 Despite its "Boys Toys" image, MATS-A proved an ideal target for

A number of Royal Navy Shelducks progressed to preservation status. XZ791 was held at Culdrose for several years until 29 June 2009 when it was collected for the 'Cornwall at War' Museum at Davidstowe Moor. In 1993 an unidentified example was donated to 1157 (Helston) Squadron, ATC who, after finding it too cumbersome to display, passed it on to 1225 (St Austell & District) Squadron, ATC at St Austell. Representing the Army's involvement in Shelduck, the Museum of Army Flying at Middle Wallop hold XZ795 whilst the Fleet Air Arm Museum at RNAS Yeovilton secured sundry sections to assemble a complete example which carried the ficticious serial XS574. Several other Shelducks were acquired by the Bournemouth Air Museum and re-assembled into one aircraft with the serial XR346 although these particular examples had little, or no, Royal Navy connection.

A summary of Shelduck contracts involving aircraft used by the Royal Navy is shown on page 174.

UK Contract Shipments (Royal Navy)

Deliveries of MQM-36A Shelduck targets to the Royal Navy were made from the USA direct to the recipient units. Known details are summarised in tabular form on pages 175–176.

Note that the serials XR818-XR842 (initially applied to "UK208-UK232") were subsequently added to Contract KK/T/09/CB25(b) when that contract was amended on 14 Feb 1962. The reason for this is not known but these 25 serials could correlate to the fact that a batch of 25 ("UK208-UK232") from Contract KK/T/05/CB25(b) were shipped to Plymouth in January 1962 and that these serials were later re-applied by amending the later contract. An earlier batch of 30 KD2R-5s shipped to Plymouth ("UK148-UK177") was never issued standard serial numbers.

The batch XV818-XV837 was divided between Northrop-built aircraft and sub-contractor Meteor SpA at Monfalcomne, Trieste. See Individual Histories for further details.

Not included in the table is the batch of MQM-36A XR447-XR450 whose origin is obscure.

KD2R-5/MQM-36A Shelduck Technical Data	
Power Plant	McCulloch 0-100-2 (2-cycle, 4-cylinder) gasoline engine
Wing Span (without pods)	11 ft 6 in (3.51 m)
Length overall	13 ft 4 in (4.08 m)
Height overall	2 ft 7 in (0.8 m)
Weight empty	233 lb (106 kg)
Max launch weight	466 lb (211 kg)
Max level speed	160 kt (184 mph; 296 km/h) at sea level 144 kt (166 mph; 267 km/h) at 7,000 ft
Max rate of climb	1,500 ft/min (457 m/min)
Service ceiling	15,000 ft (4,572 m)
Endurance at sea level	30 min

developing aimer skills, giving a challenging fighter-ground-attack simulation at very low cost, and requiring a team of two personnel to operate, it could be transported globally with ease.

Summary of Shelduck Contracts

Contract	Date	Serial Range	Allotment Date	Quantity	Remarks
KF/5R/01/CB25(b)	18.2.59	XN862-XN876 XN893-XN917	13.8.59	40	UK1-UK15 UK16-UK40
KF/5R/07/CB25(b)	3.5.60	XR148-XR162 XR185-XR209	6.9.60	40	UK96-UK110 UK111-UK135
KK/T/02/CB25(b)	9.5.61	–	–	30	UK148-UK177**
-		XR447-XR450	15.3.61	4	Obscure origin
KK/T/05/CB25(b)		XR818-XR842 XR861-XR890	29.1.62*	55	UK178-UK202 UK203-UK232
KK/T/09/CB25(b)	15.11.61	XR818-XR842	14.2.62*	25	UK233-UK257
KK/T/022/CB25(b)	23.7.62	XS246-XS257 XS273-XS290 XS294-XS311 XS335-XS346	4.5.62	60	
		XS352-XS381 XS398-XS408	31.7.62	41	
KK/T/36/CB25(b)	26.6.64	XT293-XT323 XT357-XT410	26.5.64	85	Originally allocated as XT293-330, XT357-403
KK/T/41/CB25(b)	8.3.65	XT685-XT703 XT717-XT747 XT931-XT947	26.2.65	100	C/ns in the range 6990–7306
		XT953-XT985	3.8.65		
KK/T/52/CB20(b)	2.5.67	XV818-XV837	7.4.67	20	
KK/T/55/CB20(c)		XW101-XW150 XW161-XW170	12.9.67	60	
KK/T/58/CB20(b)	3.1.69	XW444-XW478 XW492-XW516	18.9.68	60	
KK/T/59/CB20(b)***	3.1.69	XW571-XW580	13.12.68	10	
K20C/6/28/CBA2(c)	15.1.70	XW670-XW707 XW724-XW745	29.12.69	60	C/ns 7814-7873
K20C/97/CB20C6	24.2.71	XW941-XW980	19.2.71	40	C/ns 8040-8079
K/GW41B/186		XX850-XX879	27.10.72	30	C/ns 8150-8169
		XX923-XX941	27.4.73	19	C/ns 8185-8203
K/MGW/11B/372	16.9.74	XZ410-XZ425	4.9.74	16	
K/MGW/11B/493	9.10.75	XZ505-XZ518 XZ531-XZ546	30.9.75	30	C/ns 8356-8379, 8577-8582
K/MGW11B/597	22.7.76	XZ745-XZ774 XZ790-XZ811	6.7.76	52	C/ns 8638-8689
MGW11B/906	5.10.78	ZA500-ZA509 ZA525-ZA538	1.9.78	24	C/ns 8878-8901
Total				901	

* Note that the serial range XR818-XR842 was allocated (possibly in error) to targets with Build Numbers UK233-257, the serials having previously been allocated to Build Numbers UK178-202.
** Note also that Build Numbers UK148-177 (30) are not co-located with UK serials
*** Contract KK/T/59/CB20(b) also accounted for ten MQM-36A targets for use as pilot training ahead of Blowpipe trials. (See Chapter 8 – Targets For The Army)
Note also that a Shelduck was assembled at Portland from spare parts and given the serial XS574. The aircraft never flew and was displayed statically only. The serial is spurious and not an official allocation.

KD2R-5/MQM-36A Shelduck Target Shipments to the Royal Navy

Serial Batch	Total	Departure USA	Shipment Consigned to	Remarks
XN862-XN871	10	26 Feb 1959	RAF Seletar	Delivered as 'UK1' – 'UK10'
XN872-XN876 XN893-XN917	30	26 Feb 1959	RNAS Abbotsinch	Delivered as 'UK11' – 'UK40'
XR148-XR162	15	8 Aug 1960	RNPTA Portland	Delivered as 'UK96' – 'UK110'
XR185-XR194	10	27 Jul 1960	RNPTA Singapore	Delivered as 'UK111' – 'UK120'
XR195-XR209	15	?? ??? 1960	RNPTA Malta	Delivered as 'UK121' – 'UK135'
–	30	14 Sept 1961	HM Dockyard, Plymouth	Delivered as 'UK148'-'UK177'; operated in UK as '148' to '177'
XR818-XR828	11	21 Dec 1961	RNPTA Singapore	Delivered as 'UK178' – 'UK188'
XR829-XR832	4	21 Dec 1961	RNAS Hal Far, Malta	Delivered as 'UK189' – 'UK192'
XR833-XR842 XR861-XR862	12	19 Feb 1962	RNPTA Portland	Delivered as 'UK193' – 'UK204'
XR863-XR865	3	19 Feb 1962	RNPTA Hal Far, Malta	Delivered to the UK as 'UK205-UK207' for onward shipment to Malta
XR866-XR890	25	11 Jan 1962	HM Dockyard, Plymouth	Shipped as 'UK208' – 'UK232' and possibly operated as '208'-'232'
–	15	2 Apr 1962	RNPTA Portland	Shipped as 'UK233' – 'UK244' etc
–	5	12 Apr 1962	RNPTA Singapore	Possibly shipped via UK as 'UK245' – 'UK249'
–	5	2 Apr 1962	RNAS Hal Far, Malta	Possibly shipped via UK as 'UK253' – 'UK257'
XS246-XS257 XS273-XS288	28	28 Dec 1962	RNPTA Lee-on-Solent	
XS289-XS290	2	28 Dec 1962	RNPTA Singapore	Shipped to Singapore via UK
XS294-XS307	14	12 Feb 1963	RNPTA Singapore	Shipped to Singapore via UK
XS308-XS310	3	30 Jan 1963	RNPTA Lee-on-Solent	
XS311 XS335-XS346	13	8 Feb 1963	RNPTA Malta	Shipped to Malta via UK
XS352-XS381 XS398-XS408	41	Jan 1963	RNPTA Lee-on-Solent	
XT293-XT312 XT314 XT389-XT395	28	13 Sep 1964	RNPTA Lee-on-Solent	
XT313 XT315-XT323 XT409-XT410	12	19 Oct 1964	RNPTA Singapore	Shipped to Singapore via UK
XT357-XT388	32	1 Sep 1964	RNPTA Lee-on-Solent	
XT396-XT408	13	16 Sept 1964	RNPTA Singapore	Shipped to Singapore via UK
XT685-XT688	4	14 Oct 1965	RNPTA Singapore	Shipped to Singapore via UK
XT689-XT703 XT717	16	11 Oct 1965	RNPTA Lee-on-Solent	
XT718-XT723	6	29 Sept 1965	RNPTA Singapore	Shipped to Singapore via UK
XT724-XT747	24	8 Oct 1965	RNPTA Lee-on-Solent	

continued

KD2R-5/MQM-36A Shelduck Target Shipments to the Royal Navy *continued*

Serial Batch	Total	Departure USA	Shipment Consigned to	Remarks
XT931-XT940	10	14 Apr 1966	RNPTA Lee-on-Solent	
XT941-XT945	5	4 Apr 1966	RNPTA Singapore	Shipped to Singapore via UK
XT946-XT947 XT953-XT959 XT964	10	5 Jan 1966	RNPTA Singapore	Shipped to Singapore via UK
XT960-XT963 XT965-XT971 XT974	12	14 Jan 1966	RNPTA Lee-on-Solent	
XT972-XT973 XT975-XT985	13	10 Mar 1966	RNPTA Lee-on-Solent	
XV818-XV837	20	Mar 68	RNPTA Lee & Singapore	See Individual Histories for further details of this shipment.
XW101-XW134 XW145-XW150	40	10 July 1968	RNPTA Lee-on-Solent	
XW135-XW144 XW161-XW170	20	14 Aug 1968	RNPTA Singapore	Shipped to Singapore via UK
XW444-XW458	15	24 Jun 1969	RNPTA Singapore	Shipped to Singapore via UK
XW459-XW478 XW492-XW516	45	3 Jul 1969	RNPTA Lee-on-Solent	
XW670-XW674	5	31 July 1970	RNPTA Lee-on-Solent	
XW675-XW679	5	31 July 1970	Mombasa	Shipped to Mombasa via UK
XW680-XW683	4	31 July 1970	HMS *St Angelo*, Malta	Shipped to Malta via UK
XW684-XW687	4	31 July 1970	RAF Muharraq, Bahrain	Shipped to Bahrain via UK
XW688-XW699	12	31 July 1970	RNPTA Singapore	Shipped to Singapore via UK
XW700-XW707 XW724-XW745	30	23 Sept 1970	RNPTA Lee-on-Solent	
XW941-XW965	25	8 Dec 1971	15 MU Wroughton	
XW966-XW975	10	8 Dec 1971	HMS *Terror* (Singapore)	Shipped to Singapore via UK
XW976-XW980	5	8 Dec 1971	Mombasa	Shipped to Mombasa via UK
XX850-XX869	20	5 June 1973	RNAY Wroughton	
XX870-XX879	10	29 May 1973	RNPTA Singapore	Shipped to Singapore via UK
XX923-XX941	19	24 Jan 1974	RNAY Wroughton	
XZ410-XZ425	16	Dec 1974	RNAY Wroughton	
XZ505-XZ518 XZ531-XZ546	30	17 Mar 1976	RNAY Wroughton	
XZ745-XZ762	18	22 Dec 1976	RNAY Wroughton	
XZ763-XZ774 XZ790-XZ811	34	7 Feb 1977	RNAY Wroughton	
ZA500-ZA509 ZA525-ZA538	24	?	RNPTA Lee-on-Solent	
Total	897			

Shelduck XW513 is seen on its mobile launcher behind the RNPTA Squadron HQ at Portland in June 1972. The scheme is standard apart from the wing-tip tank artwork which depicts a Shelduck and the legend "RNPTA SQUADRON SHELDUCK" (Michael I Draper)

Colour Scheme and Markings

The first batch of Shelduck targets were delivered in an overall dark red scheme with white wings. The serial was applied in white to the mid-rear fuselage side and repeated in larger lettering on the upper wing surface.

Later delivereies retained the dark red scheme and white lettering but also had a white tailplane, fin and wing.

All Shelducks were delivered ex-factory with the service designation applied beneath the tailplane and appeared as either KD2R-5 or MQM-36A. In most instances serials were applied in the UK and in 'stencil-type' lettering. Contrary to standard practice many British serials were applied with a hyphen, eg XW-126, XW-513 whilst a number of aircraft from the batch XZ505-XZ518/XZ531-XZ546) operated with serials incorrectly marked as X2505-X2518 etc. (It is just possible that these were applied in the USA prior to delivery to the UK.) Towards the latter stages of Shelduck operations, aircraft appeared with Type D roundels and a ROYAL NAVY legend.

There were also other differences, most of which were local adaptations. Some early Shelducks with 'D' Flight, RNPTA had the three digits of their serial applied prominently on the fin, whilst Shelducks allocated to 'C' Flight at Malta had the Hal Far code 'HF' applied to the fin.

Other variations included the application of an RNPTA Squadron crest (as applied to XW513).

Royal Navy KD2R-5/MQM-36A Individual Aircraft Histories

Operational records for the 1974-1980 period appear not to have survived and may well have been destroyed during 1998 in the move (by the Fleet Target Group) from Portland to Culdrose. As a result a number of histories remain incomplete.

Note also that this section includes known details of Shelduck targets that were initially supplied to the RAE and the British Army. A number were later transferred to the Royal Navy but these transfers took place during the period for which official files have been lost and so details again remain incomplete.

Northrop construction numbers for many of the early Shelducks remain unrecorded. Northrop referred to these aircraft by their Customer Build numbers, eg UK1, UK2 etc.

Details of individual service histories for MQM-36As delivered as UK148-UK177 and UK208-257 are unknown.

Contract KF/5R/01/CB25(b)
40 Shelduck D.1

XN862 c/n UK1 Dptd USA 26.2.59 aboard SS *Glenville*. Consigned to the Naval Air Equipment Authority, Seletar. Damaged beyond repair when it flew into the sea 12.12.59 (on its 2nd flight). SOC 22.1.60.

XN863 c/n UK2 Shipped ex-USA (with XN862 etc). Lost at sea 23.11.59 when it sank less than 10 minutes after landing. SOC 26.11.59.

XN864 c/n UK3 Shipment details as XN862 etc. Crashed shortly after launch 9.2.60 and DBR. Recovered but reduced to spares. SOC 5.3.60.

XN865 c/n UK4 Shipment details as XN862 etc. Crashed into the sea 13.6.60 following recovery parachute failure. Reduced to spares; SOC 6.7.60. (6 Flights)

XN866 c/n UK5 Shipment details as XN862 etc. Conveyed to Portland (date unkn). Crashed (in the UK) 18.1.61 before the recovery 'chute had fully deployed, (13 Flights)

XN867 c/n UK6 Shipment details as XN862 etc. DBR 23.10.59 and later reduced to spares. SOC 26.11.59.

XN868 c/n UK7 Shipment details as XN862 etc. Conveyed to Portland 1960. Lost 3.8.60 during recovery at sea by HMS *Yarmouth*. SOC 10.8.60. (8 Flights)

XN869 c/n UK8 Shipment details as XN862 etc. Recovery 'chute failed to deploy on command 16.12.59 during a controller training flight; salvage impracticable due to navigational hazards. SOC 22.1.60 (7 Flights).

XN870 (c/n UK9) Shipment details as XN862 etc. Lost at sea 26.2.60. SOC 5.3.60. (6 Flights)

XN871 (c/n UK10) Shipment details as XN862 etc. Conveyed to Portland 1960. DBR 14.12.60 (details u/k) and reduced to salvage. (16 Flights; final flight 12.12.60). (TFH 10.20)

XN872 (c/n UK11) Departed USA 26.2.59 aboard SS *Pacific Stronghold*. Consigned to RNAS Abbotsinch. To Portland; f/f 23.6.60. DBR 19.1.61 on its 6th and final flight.

XN873 (c/n UK12) Shipment details as XN872 etc. To Portland 1960. Crashed into the sea 18.12.61. (12 Flights)

XN874 (c/n UK13) Shipment details as XN872 etc. Crashed 6.5.60 during a series of 3-inch rocket trials. Reduced to spares. SOC 6.7.60. (8 Flights)

XN875 (c/n UK14) Shipment details as XN872 etc. To Portland 1960. DBR 16.1.61 during rocket motor trials. A rocket struck the fuselage. Reduced to spares. (6 Flights)

XN876 (c/n UK15) Shipment details as XN872 etc. To Portland 1960. DBR 24.1.61 during rocket motor trials. (14 Flights)

XN893 (c/n UK16) Shipment details as XN872 etc. To Portland by 7.60. Lost at sea 3.2.61 when its recovery 'chute candled during rocket motor trials in UK waters. (6 Flights)

XN894 (c/n UK17) Shipment details as XN872 etc. Issued to RNPTA by 7.60; f/f at Larkhill 8.9.60 but crashed after the recovery 'chute failed to deploy during a Controller Training exercise. SOC 6.10.60. (TFH 0.20)

XN895 (c/n UK18) Shipment details as XN872 etc. DBR at Larkhill 9.5.60 during a Controller Training exercise and when the aircraft became visually lost and crashed before parachute deployed. Reduced to spares. (11 Flights)

XN896 (c/n UK19) Shipment details as XN872 etc. To RNPTA Portland; f/f 15.6.60 but lost on its 2nd flight, on 21.6.60, when it sank at sea after ditching. SOC 6.7.60.

XN897 (c/n UK20) Shipment details as XN872 etc. To RNPTA Portland; f/f 31.5.60. Crashed into the sea and sank 11.10.60 during a long- and close-range anto-aircraft firing exercise in UK waters. (TFH 2.25; 4 flights)

XN898 (c/n UK21) Shipment details as XN872 etc. To RNPTA Portland.; f/f 20.6.62. SOC 28.7.62 when it was lost to ship's radar at 10,000 yds and crashed. Wreckage was recovered but beyond economical repair.

XN899 (c/n UK22) Shipment details as XN872 etc. To RNPTA Portland; f/f 27.9.60. DBR 23.5.61 when it crashed and burst into flames, location unknown. (7 Flights)

XN900 (c/n UK23) Shipment details as XN872 etc. To RNPTA Portland; f/f 21.4.61 for long-range AA firing but was lost at sea off HMS *Gossamer* after 50 minutes.

XN901 (c/n UK24) Shipment details as XN872 etc. To RNPTA Portland by 1.61. DBR 23.5.61 after crashing into the sea. (6 Flights)

XN902 (c/n UK25) Shipment details as XN872 etc. To RNPTA Portland by 1.61; f/f 17.3.61. Crashed on launch from HMS *Tyne* 21.3.61 and sank. (TFH 0.30; 2 flights)

XN903 (c/n UK26) Shipment details as XN872 etc. To RNPTA Portland by 1.61. Crashed immediately after launch 19.6.62 and sank. SOC 11.7.62. (TFH 6.50; 13 flights)

XN904 (c/n UK27) Shipment details as XN872 etc. To RNPTA by 1.61; f/f 11.3.61. Lost at sea 22.3.61 (in UK waters). (TFH 0.14; 2 flights)

XN905 (c/n UK28) Shipment details as XN872 etc. To RNPTA; f/f 15.6.62. Crashed into the sea immediately after launch 19.6.62. SOC 11.7.62. (TFH 1.05; 2 flights)

XN906 (c/n UK29) Shipment details as XN872 etc. To RNPTA by 7.61; f/f 13.7.61. Crashed into the sea during long- and close-range firings 24.7.61. (2 flights)

XN907 (c/n UK30) Shipment details as XN872 etc. To RNPTA by 7.61. Shot down by anti-aircraft shell 10.2.62. Wreckage sank. (10 flights)

XN908 (c/n UK31) Shipment details as XN872 etc. To RNPTA Singapore by 7.60. Crashed into the sea and sank 12.8.60. (6 flights)

XN909 (c/n UK32) Shipment details as XN872 etc. To RNPTA Singapore by 7.60. Crashed into the sea off Singapore 4.8.60 after the target became visually lost. Never recovered. (7 flights)

XN910 (c/n UK33) Shipment details as XN872 etc. To RNPTA Singapore but was lost at sea during recovery trials 28.4.60. (3 flights)

XN911 (c/n UK34) Shipment details as XN872 etc. To RNPTA Singapore but was lost at sea during control trials 14.6.60. (3 flights)

XN912 (c/n UK35) Shipment details as XN872 etc. Stored until 7.60. To RNPTA Singapore by 7.60. To RNPTA Tengah by 1.61. Lost at sea 2.5.61 during rocket trials. (8 flights)

XN913 (c/n UK36) Shipment details as XN872 etc. Stored until 7.60. To RNPTA Singapore by 7.60. To RNPTA Tengah by 1.61. Crashed into the sea and sank 17.7.61 during medium- and close-range anti-aircraft firings. (6 flights)

XN914 (c/n UK37) Shipment details as XN872 etc. To RNPTA Singapore by 7.60. To RNPTA Tengah by 1.61. Shot down 11.4.61 and sank before recovery. (9 flights)

XN915 (c/n UK38) Shipment details as XN872 etc. Stored until 7.60. To RNPTA Singapore by 7.60. To RNPTA Tengah by 1.61. Lost at sea 11.4.61 after becoming visually lost in haze. Never recovered. (4 flights)

XN916 (c/n UK39) Shipment details as XN872 etc. Stored until 7.60. To RNPTA Singapore by 7.60. To RNPTA Tengah by 1.61. Lost at sea in the Far East 15.3.61 during a Fleet Gunnery Exercise. (2 flights)

XN917 (c/n UK40) Shipment details as XN872 etc. Stored until 7.60. To RNPTA Singapore by 7.60. To RNPTA Tengah by 1.61. Lost at sea 16.3.61 after breaking up in the air. (4 flights)

Contract KF/5R/07/CB25(b)
40 Shelduck D.1

XR148 (c/n UK96) Departed USA 8.8.60 aboard SS *Pacific Envoy*. Consigned to RNPTA Portland; f/f 31.10.60. Written-off 24.1.62 during a Controller Training flight. (8 flights)

XR149 (c/n UK97) Shipment details as XR148 etc. Crashed into the sea 14.2.62 during a trials flight. Fuselage recovered but considered not repairable. (12 flights)

XR150 (c/n UK98) Shipment details as XR148 etc.; f/f 31.10.60. Crashed 1.12.61 after radar contact was lost during an AA Firing & Tracking exercise. A search was carried out but the aircraft was never found. (5 flights)

XR151 (c/n UK99) Shipment details as XR148 etc; f/f 9.11.60 for a long- and close-range firing mission but crashed into the sea immediately after take-off. Recovered and later reduced to salvage. (TFH 0.00).

XR152 (c/n UK100) Shipment details as XR148 etc; f/f 9.11.60 for long- and close-range firings. Crashed and sank 11.3.61 immediately after launch from HMS *Tyne*. (TFH 0.32; 3 flights)

XR153 (c/n UK101) Shipment details as XR148 etc; f/f 16.3.61. Dived into the sea under full power and sank 2.8.61 during long- and close-range firings. (10 flights)

XR154 (c/n UK102) Departed USA 8.8.60 aboard SS *Pacific Envoy*. Consigned to RNPTA Portland; f/f 11.10.61. Crashed 10.7.62 during flight-training exercise. (TFH 1.50; 4 flights)

XR155 (c/n UK103) Departed USA 8.8.60 aboard SS *Pacific Envoy*. Consigned to RNPTA Portland; f/f 5.10.61. Crashed 14.2.62 during a trials exercise and sank before recovery.

XR156 (c/n UK104) Departed USA 8.8.60 aboard SS *Pacific Envoy*. Consigned to RNPTA Portland; f/f 6.10.61. Last of five recorded flights 22.5.62 but SOC 23.5.63 after crashing on take-off. (It is possible that the SOC date should be 1962 as this aircraft was not reported during the RN Census' of July 1962 and Jan 1963.)

XR157 (c/n UK105) Departed USA 8.8.60 aboard SS *Pacific Envoy*. Consigned to RNPTA Portland; f/f 20.1.62 for AA firing exercise during which it crashed into the sea.

XR158 (c/n UK106) Departed USA 8.8.60 aboard SS *Pacific Envoy*. Consigned to RNPTA Portland; f/f 5.2.62. Last of 7 recorded flights 13.6.62 on long-range AA firings. Not reported after this date and SOC 10.8.63 as "lost at sea".

XR159 (c/n UK107) Departed USA 8.8.60 aboard SS *Pacific Envoy*. Consigned to RNPTA Portland; f/f 20.3.62. Crashed into the sea 26.1.64 whilst operating with HQ Flight. SOC 11.2.64. (TFH 5.00; 5 flights)

XR160 (c/n UK108) Departed USA 8.8.60 aboard SS *Pacific Envoy*. Consigned to RNPTA Portland; f/f 15.3.62. Lost at sea 22.3.62 during long- and close-range firings. (2 flights)

XR161 (c/n UK109) Departed USA 8.8.60 aboard SS *Pacific Envoy*. Consigned to RNPTA Portland; f/f 15.3.62 on long- and close-range AA firings during which it crashed into the sea after recovery 'chute failed to operate.

XR162 (c/n UK110) Departed USA 8.8.60 aboard SS *Pacific Envoy*. Consigned to RNPTA Portland; f/f 20.6.62 on long- and close-range AA firings but during recovery in adverse sea state the mainplane broke away and the aircraft sank.

XR185 (c/n UK111) Departed USA 27.7.60 aboard SS *Pleasantville*. Consigned to RNPTA Singapore; f/f 22.4.61. Crashed into the sea 27.9.61 during medium-range AA firings. (2 flights)

XR186 (c/n UK112) Shipped ex-USA with XR185 etc. Consigned to RNPTA Singapore; f/f 22.4.61. Crashed 2.5.61 during rocket launching trials. (2 flights)

XR187 (c/n UK113) Shipped ex-USA with XR185 etc. Consigned to RNPTA Singapore; f/f 2.5.61. Crashed into the sea 4.12.61 during medium- and close-range AA firings. (4 flights)

XR188 (c/n UK114) Shipped ex-USA with XR185 etc. Consigned to RNPTA Singapore; f/f 2.5.61. DBR after crashing in the sea 27.9.61 during medium-range AA firings.

XR189 (c/n UK115) Shipped ex-USA with XR185 etc. Consigned to RNPTA Singapore; f/f 8.5.61. Last of 7 recorded flights 7.5.62 for medium-range AA firings. SOC 19.7.62 which suggests it crashed 7.5.62.

XR190 (c/n UK116) Shipped ex-USA with XR185 etc. Consigned to RNPTA Singapore; f/f 12.10.61. SOC 8.8.63 after being reduced to spares by 'D' Flight/RNPTA. (8 flights)

XR191 (c/n UK117) Shipped ex-USA with XR185 etc. Consigned to RNPTA Singapore; f/f 12.10.61. SOC 31.3.62 after crashing into the sea in the Far East 13.3.62. Only the mainplane was recovered.

XR192 (c/n UK118) Shipped ex-USA with XR185 etc. Consigned to RNPTA Singapore; f/f 9.10.61. Last of 8 recorded flights 13.3.62. SOC 19.7.62 as lost at sea whilst with 'D' Flight/RNPTA.

XR193 (c/n UK119) Shipped ex-USA with XR185 etc Consigned to RNPTA Singapore; f/f 12.10.61 for medium- and close-range AA firings. Final recorded flight 14.3.62 when lost at sea. SOC 19.3.62. (5 flights)

XR194 (c/n UK120) Shipped ex-USA with XR185 etc Consigned to RNPTA Singapore; f/f 14.3.62 for medium- and close-range AA firings. Reported by 'D' Flight/RNPTA as lost at sea. SOC 27.3.63.

XR195 (c/n UK121) Shipped USA to RNPTA, Hal Far, Malta -/60; f/f 18.5.61 for rocket-launching trials. Possibly to UK 16.4.63. SOC 25.6.63 possibly after a crash at sea 13.6.63. (TFH 5.30; 9 flights)

XR196 (c/n UK122) Shipped USA to RNPTA, Hal Far, Malta -/60; f/f 18.5.61 for rocket-launching trials. Extensively damaged 20.5.62 on its 5th flight. To UK 16.4.63 and repaired. Crashed into the sea immediately after launch 26.3.63. (TFH 2.30)

XR197 (c/n UK123) Shipped USA to RNPTA, Hal Far, Malta -/60; f/f 12.1.61 for air-to-air firings. Crashed into the sea 6.10.62 just 5 seconds after take-off. Not recovered.

XR198 (c/n UK124) Shipped USA to RNPTA, Hal Far, Malta -/60. Crashed into the sea and sank 29.3.62 during long-range AA firings. (5 flights)

XR199 (c/n UK125) Shipped USA to RNPTA, Hal Far, Malta -/60; f/f 25.10.61 on a trials flight. To UK 16.4.63. Destroyed by anti-aircraft fire B.E.R. 11.6.63. (TFH 3.50)

XR200 (c/n UK126) Shipped USA to RNPTA, Hal Far, Malta -/60; f/f 7.4.61. Reported in store at Hal Far 7.61-1.63. To UK 16.4.63. To Bahrain by 7.63. SOC 19.11.63, details not known. (Only 1 Flight recorded.)

XR201 (c/n UK127) Shipped USA to RNPTA, Hal Far, Malta -/60; f/f 5.4.61 on close-range AA firings but crashed into the sea and sank. (TFH 1.00)

XR202 (c/n UK128) Shipped USA to RNPTA, Hal Far, Malta -/60; f/f 13.1.61 on long- and close-range firings but jettisoned by recovery helicopter and sank.

XR203 (c/n UK129) Shipped USA to RNPTA, Hal Far, Malta -/60; f/f 9.11.60 on trial flight. Crashed into the sea and sank 13.4.61 during long- and close-range firings. (TFH 2.50; 6 flights)

XR204 (c/n UK130) Shipped USA to RNPTA, Hal Far, Malta -/60; f/f 12.1.62 on air-to-air firings. Final (and 6th) successful flight recorded 18.1.62. Crashed into the

The second UK Shelduck order involved another 40 drones, all shipped ex-US in mid-1960. The final 15 (XR195-XR209) were shipped direct to Malta to form 'C' Flight, RNPTA at Hal Far. Interestingly the Malta-based examples had the station code 'HF' applied to the fin and a 'Maltese Cross' insignia on the side of the fuselage. This, together with the non-standard style of lettering bears witness to the fact that they had their markings applied locally – indeed they arrived a month before the serial range was issued. XR206 is seen running at full power on the Hal Far launchpad, on 2 November 1960 whilst the 'pilot' can be seen at his station in the background. (HMS Osprey; neg.no G1571)

sea immediately after take-off 1.10.62. SOC 9.11.62. (TFH 4.40)

XR205 (c/n UK131) Shipped USA to RNPTA, Hal Far, Malta -/60. Noted at Hal Far 1.62 but written-off (by 7.62), date and details not known.

XR206 (c/n UK132) Shipped USA to RNPTA, Hal Far, Malta -/60; f/f 1.11.60. Crashed into the sea 23.2.61 during long-range anti-aircraft firings. 3 Flights. (Note that RN records show that XR206 was lost in the Mediterranean Sea 11.4.60 but this is believed to be an erroneous report.)

XR207 (c/n UK133) Shipped USA to RNPTA, Hal Far, Malta -/60; f/f 13.1.61. Sustained direct hit 11.8.61 during long- and close-range anti-aircraft firings. Half of the target was recovered from the sea for spares use. (2 flights)

XR208 (c/n UK134) Shipped USA to RNPTA, Hal Far, Malta -/60; f/f 18.5.61 as part of rocket-launching trials. Lost at sea 3.8.61 during long- and close-range AA firings when recovery 'chute candled. (2 flights)

XR209 (c/n UK135) Shipped USA to RNPTA, Hal Far, Malta -/60; f/f 18.1.62 on long-range AA firings. SOC 31.1.62, details not known.

Contract KK/T/02/CB25(b): 30 Shelduck D.1

Note that Shelducks built and delivered against this contract (UK148-UK177) were not issued serials within the standard sequence. Instead they carried just the digits of the 'build number', eg 148, 149 150 et seq. All 30 were shipped ex-Terminal Island, California 19.1.61 aboard SS *Colorado Star* and consigned to HMS *Decoy* at HM Dockyard, Plymouth. It is believed that all were expended during Sea Cat missile trials.

4 Shelduck D.1s of undetermined origin.

XR447 To RNPTA HQ Portland; f/f 16.6.61 on long- and close-range firings but crashed and later sank during recovery.

XR448 To RNPTA HQ Portland; f/f 13.7.61. Crashed 12.9.61 after recovery 'chute 'candled'. (2 flights)

XR449 To RNPTA HQ Portland; f/f 13.6.61. Crashed into the sea 16.6.61 after recovery 'chute 'candled'. (2 flights)

XR450 To RNPTA HQ Portland. Crashed on launch, date unconfirmed but SOC 25.7.62.

Contract KK/T/05/CB25(b): 55 Shelduck D.1

There is considerable confusion over this contract. In the Ministry of Defence Contracts Branch "serial ledger" the contract states that the block XR818-XR842/XR861-XR890 was allocated against this contract. However, documentation held by Aerial Targets Ltd indicated that the batch XR818-XR842 was allocated to Contract KK/T/09/CB25(b) on 14 February 1962.

XR818 (c/n UK178) Shipped ex-USA (Terminal Island, California) aboard SS *Mandeville* 21.12.61 to Singapore. Transferred to 'C' Flt/RNPTA Malta by 1.63. Crashed into the sea off Malta, date unconfirmed. SOC 6.3.63.

XR819 (c/n UK179) Shipped ex-USA (with XR818 etc) to Singapore. Transferred to 'C' Flt/RNPTA Malta by 1.63. Crashed into the sea off Malta, date unconfirmed. SOC 5.6.63.

XR820 (c/n UK180) Shipped ex-USA (with XR818 etc to Singapore. Transferred to 'C' Flt/RNPTA Malta by 11.62. Crashed off Malta, date unknown. SOC 20.11.62.

XR821 (c/n UK181) Shipped ex-USA (with XR818 etc) to Singapore. Transferred to 'C' Flt/RNPTA Malta by 11.62. Crashed into the sea off Malta 14.11.62. SOC 20.11.62. (TFH 1.00)

XR822 (c/n UK182) Shipped ex-USA (with XR818 etc) to Singapore. Transferred to 'C' Flt/RNPTA Malta by 1.63. Crashed off Malta, date and circumstances unknown. SOC 10.7.63.

XR823 (c/n UK183) Shipped ex-USA (with XR818 etc) to Singapore. Transferred to 'C' Flt/RNPTA Malta by 11.62. Crashed, date and circumstances unknown. SOC 9.11.62.

XR824 (c/n UK184) Shipped ex-USA (with XR818 etc) to Singapore. Transferred to 'C' Flt/RNPTA Malta by 10.62. Crashed on take-off 26.10.62 without gaining level flight. (TFH 0.00)

XR825 (c/n UK185) Shipped ex-USA (with XR818 etc) to Singapore. Transferred to 'C' Flt/RNPTA Malta by 1.63. Crashed, date and circumstances unknown. SOC 10.7.63.

XR826 (c/n UK186) Shipped ex-USA (with XR818 etc) to Singapore. No further details.

XR827 (c/n UK187) Shipped ex-USA (with XR818 etc) to Singapore. Crashed into the sea 10.11.62 in the Far East. SOC 22.11.62. (TFH 1.31)

XR828 (c/n UK188) Shipped ex-USA (with XR818 etc) to Singapore. Lost at sea in the Far East. SOC 13.3.63.

XR829 (c/n UK189) Shipped ex-USA (Brooklyn, New York) 21.12.61 aboard SS *Flygia* to Malta; consigned to RNAS Hal Far. Transferred to 'D' Flt/RNPTA by 7.62. Lost at sea in far East. SOC 15.10.62. (3 Flights)

XR830 (c/n UK190) Shipped ex-USA (with XR829 etc) to Malta; consigned to RNAS Hal Far. Transferred to 'D' Flt/RNPTA by 7.62. Crashed into the sea in the Far East 15.6.63. SOC 1.8.63. (TFH 9.50)

XR831 (c/n UK191) Shipped ex-USA (with XR829 etc) to Malta but transferred to Singapore. Written-off 22.1.63, details unknown.

XR832 (c/n UK192) Shipped ex-USA (with XR829 etc) to Malta but transferred to Singapore. Lost at sea in Far East 23.8.63. SOC 3.9.63. (TFH 1.30; 4 flights).

XR833 (c/n UK193) Shipped ex-USA (Terminal Island, California) 19.2.62 aboard SS *Columbia Star* to UK but transferred to Singapore. Lost at sea in Far East, date unknown. SOC 20.3.64.

XR834 (c/n UK194) Shipped ex-USA (with XR833 etc) to UK but transferred to Singapore. Lost at sea in Far East, date unknown. SOC 18.7.63. 5 flights.

XR835 (c/n UK195) Shipped ex-USA (with XR833 etc) to UK but transferred to Singapore. Lost at sea in Far East, date unknown. SOC 8.8.63. 2 flights.

XR836 (c/n UK196) Shipped ex-USA (with XR833 etc) to UK but transferred to Singapore. Lost at sea 23.8.63. SOC 3.9.63. (TFH 1.05; 3 flights)

XR837 (c/n UK197) Shipped ex-USA (with XR833 etc) to UK but transferred to Singapore. Lost at sea in Far East, date unknown. SOC 20.3.64.

XR838 (c/n UK198) Shipped ex-USA (with XR833 etc) to UK but transferred to Singapore. Lost at sea in Far East, date unknown. SOC 20.12.63.

XR839 (c/n UK199) Shipped ex-USA (with XR833 etc) to UK but transferred to Singapore. Lost at sea in Far East, date unknown. SOC 20.3.64.

XR840 (c/n UK200) Shipped ex-USA (with XR833 etc) to UK but transferred to Singapore. Lost at sea in Far East, date unknown. SOC 8.8.63. (2 flights)

XR841 (c/n UK201) Shipped ex-USA (with XR833 etc) to UK but transferred to Singapore. Lost at sea in Far East, date unknown. SOC 24.9.63. (2 flights)

XR842 (c/n UK202) Shipped ex-USA (with XR833 etc) to UK but transferred to Singapore. SOC 9.4.64, circumstances not known.

XR861 (c/n UK203) Shipped ex-USA (with XR833 etc) to RNPTA, Portland. Sank in Portland Exercise Area 20.9.62. SOC 22.9.62.

XR862 (c/n UK204) Shipped ex-USA (with XR833 etc) to RNPTA, Portland; f/f 24.5.62 for Flight & Controller Training. Crashed and sank in Portland Exercise Area 28.8.62. SOC 29.8.62. (3 flights)

XR863 (c/n UK205) Shipped ex-USA (with XR833 etc) to RNPTA, Portland. Crashed into the sea 6.12.62, details unkn. SOC 10.12.62. (TFH 0.20)

XR864 (c/n UK206) Shipped ex-USA (with XR833 etc) to RNPTA, Portland. Crashed into the sea immediately after launch 24.9.62. SOC 26.9.62.

XR865 (c/n UK207) Shipped ex-USA (with XR833 etc) to RNPTA, Portland. Lost at sea 14.12.62. SOC 17.12.62. (TFH 1.50; 3 flights.)

XR866 (c/n UK208) Shipped ex-USA (Wilmington, California) 11.1.62 aboard SS *Pacific Reliance* to HMS *Decoy*, HM Dockyard, Plymouth. Crashed into the sea 30.11.62, details unkn. SOC 3.12.62. (TFH 1.35)

XR867 (c/n UK209) Shipped ex-USA (with XR866 etc) to HMS *Decoy*, HM Dockyard, Plymouth. Noted at Portland 1.63-7.63. SOC 12.7.63, details unknown.

XR868 (c/n UK210) Shipped ex-USA (with XR866 etc) to HMS *Decoy*, HM Dockyard, Plymouth. f/f 10.10.62 but rolled on take-off, crashed and sank. (TFH 0.05)

XR869 (c/n UK211) Shipped ex-USA (with XR866 etc) to HMS *Decoy*, HM Dockyard, Plymouth. No record of RNPTA usage; further details unkn.

XR870 (c/n UK212) Shipped ex-USA (with XR866 etc) to HMS *Decoy*, HM Dockyard, Plymouth. No record of RNPTA usage. SOC 12.62.

XR871 (c/n UK213) Shipped ex-USA (with XR866 etc) to HMS *Decoy*, HM Dockyard, Plymouth. Noted in store at Lee-on-Solent 1.63-7.64. SOC 9.11.64 after crashing and sinking on its first flight. (TFH 0.45)

XR872 (c/n UK214) Shipped ex-USA (with XR866 etc) to HMS *Decoy*, HM Dockyard, Plymouth. Noted in store at Lee-on-Solent 1.63-7.64. SOC 10.12.64 when unable to recover aircraft. (TFH 0.35; 2 flights)

XR873 (c/n UK215) Shipped ex-USA (with XR866 etc) to HMS *Decoy*, HM Dockyard, Plymouth. f/f 10.10.62. Noted at Portland 1.63-1.64. Written-off when crashed into the sea 26.2.64. SOC 12.3.64 (TFH 0.45; 2 flights)

XR874 (c/n UK216) Shipped ex-USA (with XR866 etc) to HMS *Decoy*, HM

Targets for the Royal Navy   181

Not every launch was successful. Shelduck XW964 is seen rolling and diving under full power into the sea immediately after the JATO booster, seen to the upper right, was jettisoned. On such occasions flight duration was measured in only seconds and inevitably the target sank before it could be reached by recovery crews. (792 Squadron Archive)

Dockyard, Plymouth. To RNPTA. Lost at sea, details unknown. SOC 10.8.63.

XR875 (c/n UK217) Shipped ex-USA (with XR866 etc) to HMS *Decoy*, HM Dockyard, Plymouth. To RNPTA. SOC 11.7.63 after crashing on take-off, details unkn.

XR876 (c/n UK218) Shipped ex-USA (with XR866 etc) to HMS *Decoy*, HM Dockyard, Plymouth. Noted at Portland 1.63-7.63. SOC 12.11.63 after crashing in the sea whilst being operated by HQ Flt/RNPTA, Portland.

XR877 (c/n UK219) Shipped ex-USA (with XR866 etc) to HMS *Decoy*, HM Dockyard, Plymouth. Noted with RNPTA 1.63-7.63. SOC 24.10.63 after crashing into the sea immediately after launch on its maiden flight.

XR878 (c/n UK220) Shipped ex-USA (with XR866 etc) to HMS *Decoy*, HM Dockyard, Plymouth. Noted at Portland 1.63. SOC 10.6.63 after crashing into the sea.

XR879 (c/n UK221) Shipped ex-USA (with XR866 etc) to HMS *Decoy*, HM Dockyard, Plymouth. SOC 7.6.63 after crashing into the sea whilst operating with HQ Flt/RNPTA.

XR880 (c/n UK222) Shipped ex-USA (with XR866 etc) to HMS *Decoy*, HM Dockyard, Plymouth. Crashed into the sea within Portland Exercise Area 15.10.62 after a flare fitted to the fuselage exploded. SOC 18.10.62.

XR881 (c/n UK223) Shipped ex-USA (with XR866 etc) to HMS *Decoy*, HM Dockyard, Plymouth. Crashed into the sea within Portland Exercise Area 27.9.62. SOC 2.10.62.

XR882 (c/n UK224) Shipped ex-USA (with XR866 etc) to HMS *Decoy*, HM Dockyard, Plymouth. Lost at sea, details unknown. SOC 10.8.62.

XR883 (c/n UK225) Shipped ex-USA (with XR866 etc) to HMS *Decoy*, HM Dockyard, Plymouth. Noted at Portland 1.63-1.64. SOC 1.4.64.

XR884 (c/n UK226) Shipped ex-USA (with XR866 etc) to HMS *Decoy*, HM Dockyard, Plymouth. Noted at Portland 1.63-1.64. Crashed on take-off 29.5.64, details unkn. SOC 2.6.64. (TFH 4.05; 9 flights)

XR885 c/n UK227) Shipped ex-USA (with XR866 etc) to HMS *Decoy*, HM Dockyard, Plymouth. Noted in store at Lee-on-Solent 1.63-7.64. Issued to RNPTA Portland. Crashed into the sea 13.5.65, location unknown. SOC 18.5.65. (TFH 3.15; 4 flights)

XR886 (c/n UK228) Shipped ex-USA (with XR866 etc) to HMS *Decoy*, HM Dockyard, Plymouth. Initially stored at Lee-on-Solent. Crashed into the sea 13.11.62, details unkn.

XR887 (c/n UK229) Shipped ex-USA (with XR866 etc) to HMS *Decoy*, HM Dockyard, Plymouth. Noted in store at Lee-on-Solent 1.63-7.64. SOC 1.10.64, details unkn. (TFH 1.30; 2 flights)

XR888 (c/n UK230) Shipped ex-USA (with XR866 etc) to HMS *Decoy*, HM Dockyard, Plymouth but noted at Hal Far 1.63; later to Bahrain by 1.63. SOC 19.11.63, details unkn.

XR889 (c/n UK231) Shipped ex-USA (with XR866 etc) to HMS *Decoy*, HM Dockyard, Plymouth. To 'C' Flt/RNPTA Hal Far. Crashed into the sea off Malta immediately after take-off 25.10.62. SOC 9.11.62. (TFH 1.50)

XR890 (c/n UK232) Shipped ex-USA (with XR866 etc) to HMS *Decoy*, HM Dockyard, Plymouth. SOC 28.1.63 after crashing into the sea whilst operating with C Flt/RNPTA Hal Far.

**Contract KK/T/022/CB25(b):
60 Shelduck D.1**

XS246 Shipped ex-USA (Wilmington, California) 28.12.62 to Lee-on-Solent. TOC 4.3.63. To Portland by 7.63. SOC 16.4.64. (TFH 3.00; 5 flights)

XS247 Shipped ex-USA to Lee-on-Solent (with XS246 etc). To Portland by 7.63; f/f 25.2.64. Crashed into the sea 27.2.64. SOC 12.3.64.

XS248 Shipped ex-USA to Lee-on-Solent (with XS246 etc). To Portland by 7.63. Crashed immediately after launch on its first launch. SOC 24.10.63 (which may be crash date) (TFH 0.00)

XS249 Shipped ex-USA to Lee-on-Solent (with XS246 etc). TOC 4.3.63. To Portland by 7.63. SOC 19.11.63, details unkn.

XS250 Shipped ex-USA to Lee-on-Solent (with XS246 etc). To Portland by 7.63; f/f 5.11.63. Written-off 2.3.64 when recovery 'chute failed. SOC 12.3.64 (TFH 4.00).

XS251 Shipped ex-USA to Lee-on-Solent (with XS246 etc). TOC 4.3.63. To Portland by 7.63. SOC 12.11.63, no further details.

XS252 Shipped ex-USA to Lee-on-Solent (with XS246 etc). TOC 4.3.63. Noted at Lee 7.63. To Singapore by 7.64. Lost at sea in Far East. SOC 13.8.65. (5 flights)

XS253 Shipped ex-USA to Lee-on-Solent (with XS246 etc). TOC 4.3.63. Noted at Lee 7.63. To Singapore by 7.64. Lost at sea in the Far East. SOC 5.2.65.

XS254 Shipped ex-USA to Lee-on-Solent (with XS246 etc). Noted at Lee 7.63. To Singapore by 7.64. Crashed into the sea 17.9.65. (TFH 2.19; 7 flights)

XS255 Shipped ex-USA to Lee-on-Solent (with XS246 etc). Noted at Lee 7.63. To Singapore by 7.64. Lost at sea in the Far East. SOC 7.6.65. (2 flights)

XS256 Shipped ex-USA to Lee-on-Solent (with XS246 etc). Noted at Lee 7.63. To Singapore by 7.64. Lost at sea in the Far East. SOC 19.3.65. (8 flights)

XS257 Shipped ex-USA to Lee-on-Solent (with XS246 etc). TOC 4.3.63. Noted at Lee 7.63. To Singapore by 7.64. Lost at sea in the Far East. SOC 13.8.65. (4 flights)

XS273 Shipped ex-USA to Lee-on-Solent (with XS246 etc). TOC 4.3.63. Noted at Lee 7.63. To Portland by 1.64. SOC 16.4.64, details unkn. (TFH 3.00; 5 flights)

XS274 Shipped ex-USA to Lee-on-Solent (with XS246 etc). Noted at Lee 7.63. To Portland by 1.64. Destroyed by anti-aircraft fire 6.3.64 whilst on its first flight. SOC 16.4.64. (TFH 0.30)

XS275 Shipped ex-USA to Lee-on-Solent (with XS246 etc). Noted at Lee 7.63. To Portland by 1.64. Crashed into the sea 29.5.64. SOC 2.6.64. (TFH 1.50; 3 flights)

XS276 Shipped ex-USA to Lee-on-Solent (with XS246 etc). TOC 4.3.63. Noted at Lee 7.63. To Portland by 1.64. Lost at sea whilst out of sight. (TFH 2.55; 5 flights)

XS277 Shipped ex-USA to Lee-on-Solent (with XS246 etc). Noted at Lee 7.63. To Portland by 1.64. SOC 15.6.64 without having flown.

XS278 Shipped ex-USA to Lee-on-Solent (with XS246 etc). TOC 4.3.63. Noted at Lee 7.63. To Portland by 1.64. SOC 22.6.64, details unkn. (TFH 1.00; 1 flight)

XS279 Shipped ex-USA to Lee-on-Solent (with XS246 etc). Noted at Lee 7.63-7.64. To Portland by 1.65. Destroyed by missile 20.5.65. SOC 24.5.65. (TFH 4.10; 6 flights)

XS280 Shipped ex-USA to Lee-on-Solent (with XS246 etc) TOC 4.3.63. Noted at Lee 7.63-7.64. Rolled on initial launch and Crashed into the sea and sank. SOC 5.1.65. (TFH 0.00; 1 flight)

XS281 Shipped ex-USA to Lee-on-Solent (with XS246 etc). Noted at Lee 7.63-1.64. SOC 15.6.64 after crashing on its maiden flight. (TFH 0.35; 1 flight)

XS282 Shipped ex-USA to Lee-on-Solent (with XS246 etc). Noted in store at Lee 7.63-1.64. To RNPTA but w/o on first flight, date unkn. SOC 22.6.64. (TFH 0.30)

XS283 Shipped ex-USA to Lee-on-Solent (with XS246 etc). No record of RNPTA usage.

XS284 Shipped ex-USA to Lee-on-Solent (with XS246 etc). Noted in store at Lee 7.63-1.64. To RNPTA by 7.64. Dived into the sea and sank, date unknown. SOC 5.1.65. (TFH 4.30; 6 flights)

XS285 Shipped ex-USA to Lee-on-Solent (with XS246 etc). Noted in store at Lee 7.63-1.64. To RNPTA by 7.64. Crashed and broke up on hitting the sea, date unkn. SOC 31.3.65. (TFH 2.00; 4 flights)

XS286 Shipped ex-USA to Lee-on-Solent (with XS246 etc). Noted in store at Lee 7.63-1.64. SOC by RNPTA 15.6.64. (TFH 0.15; 1 flight)

XS287 Shipped ex-USA to Lee-on-Solent (with XS246 etc). Noted in store at Lee 7.63-1.64; to RNPTA by 7.64. Shot down by a missile, date unkn. SOC 5.1.65. (TFH 6.00; 7 flights)

XS288 Shipped ex-USA to Lee-on-Solent (with XS246 etc). Noted in store at Lee 7.63-7.64; to RNPTA by 1.65. Shot down by missile, date unkn. SOC 2.6.65. (TFH 3.00; 4 flights)

XS289 Shipped ex-USA 28.12.62 (Wilmington, California) aboard SS *Johannes Maersk* to PTA Unit, Naval Base, Singapore. Lost at sea in Far East. SOC 24.9.63.

XS290 Shipped ex-USA to RNPTA Singapore (with XS289 etc). Lost at sea in Far East. SOC 17.4.63.

XS294 Shipped ex-USA 12.2.63 (Wilmington, California) aboard SS *Jeppson Maersk* to RNPTA Singapore. Lost at sea in Far East. SOC 27.8.64. (22 flights)

XS295 Shipped ex-USA to RNPTA Singapore (with XS294 etc). Lost at sea in Far East. SOC 20.3.64.

XS296 Shipped ex-USA to RNPTA Singapore (with XS294 etc). Lost at sea in Far East 20.3.64. SOC 9.4.64.

XS297 Shipped ex-USA to RNPTA Singapore (with XS294 etc). Lost at sea in Far East. SOC 17.4.63.

XS298 Shipped ex-USA to RNPTA Singapore (with XS294 etc). Ready for flight 26.9.63. Reduced to spares and SOC 14.5.64.(TFH 2.15; 3 flights)

XS299 Shipped ex-USA to RNPTA Singapore (with XS294 etc). Crashed into the sea 1.8.64. SOC 5.8.64 (TFH 2.50; 3 flights)

XS300 Shipped ex-USA to RNPTA Singapore (with XS294 etc). Destroyed by a Seacat missile 27.4.65. (TFH 2.40; 8 flights)

XS301 Shipped ex-USA to RNPTA Singapore (with XS294 etc). Lost at sea in Far East. SOC 27.8.64 (2 flights)

XS302 Shipped ex-USA to RNPTA Singapore (with XS294 etc). No further details.

XS303 Shipped ex-USA to RNPTA Singapore (with XS294 etc). Damaged beyond repair by shellfire 5.4.65. SOC 9.4.65. (TFH 2.20; 8 flights)

XS304 Shipped ex-USA to RNPTA Singapore (with XS294 etc). Shot down by Seacat missile in Far East 7.4.65. (TFH 1.45; 4 flights)

XS305 Shipped ex-USA to RNPTA Singapore (with XS294 etc). Shot down by a Seacat missile in Far East 27.4.65. (TFH 4.55; 6 flights)

XS306 Shipped ex-USA to RNPTA Singapore (with XS294 etc). Crashed into the sea 25.3.65. (TFH 1.05; 2 flights)

XS307 Shipped ex-USA to RNPTA Singapore (with XS294 etc). f/f 2.10.64 but crashed into the sea after 40mins.

XS308 Shipped ex-USA 30.1.63 (Wilmington, California) aboard SS *Pacific Fortune* to Lee-on-Solent. TOC 28.3.63. Noted in store at Lee 7.63-7.64 SOC by RNPTA 5.1.65 after crashing into the sea on launch. (TFH 3.00; 4 flights)

Targets for the Royal Navy 183

XS309 Shipped ex-USA to Lee-on-Solent (with XS308 etc). TOC 28.3.63. Noted in store at Lee 7.63-7.64. To RNPTA by 1.65. Broke up when flown into the sea under power, date unkn. SOC 2.6.65. (TFH 3.00; 4 flights)

XS310 Shipped ex-USA to Lee-on-Solent (with XS308 etc). TOC 28.3.63. Noted in store at Lee 7.63-7.64. To RNPTA. Shot down by missile, date unkn. SOC 5.1.65. (TFH 0.24; 1 flight)

XS311 Shipped ex-USA 8.2.63 (Erie Bason, Brooklyn, New York) aboard SS *Florida* to Malta; consigned to PTA Unit, Hal Far. No further details.

XS335 Shipped ex-USA to RNPTA Hal Far (with XS311 etc). SOC 15.9.64. (TFH 1.40; 3 flights)

XS336-XS337 Shipped ex-USA to RNPTA Hal Far (with XS311 etc). No further details.

XS338 Shipped ex-USA to RNPTA Hal Far (with XS311 etc). SOC 15.7.64 whilst operating with C Flt/RNPTA Hal Far. (TFH 6.00; 7 flights)

XS339 Shipped ex-USA to RNPTA Hal Far (with XS311 etc). SOC 19.11.63.

XS340 Shipped ex-USA to RNPTA Hal Far (with XS311 etc). Possibly transferred to Portland. Sank on hitting the sea, date unkn. SOC 9.8.65. (TFH 4.00; 6 flights)

XS341 Shipped ex-USA to RNPTA Hal Far (with XS311 etc). No further details.

XS342 Shipped ex-USA to RNPTA Hal Far (with XS311 etc). To Portland by 7.64. SOC 7.12.64. (TFH 2.00; 2 flights)

XS343 Shipped ex-USA to RNPTA Hal Far (with XS311 etc). To Portland by 7.64. Destroyed by a missile 20.5.65. SOC 24.5.65. (TFH 4.25; 7 flights)

XS344 Shipped ex-USA to RNPTA Hal Far (with XS311 etc). To Portland by 7.64. SOC 1.10.64. (TFH 0.20; 1 flight)

XS345 Shipped ex-USA to RNPTA Hal Far (with XS311 etc). No further details.

XS346 Shipped ex-USA to RNPTA Hal Far (with XS311 etc). No further details.

Unknown Contract: 41 Shelduck D.1

XS352-XS357 Details of shipment, consignment and fates unkn.

XS358 TOC at Lee-on-Solent 1.8.62. To Portland by 7.64. Crashed into the sea on its first flight due to insufficient thrust on launch. SOC 26.10.64.

XS359 TOC at Lee-on-Solent 1.8.62. Noted at Lee 1.63-1.64. To RNPTA but SOC 15.6.64, details unkn. (TFH 2.40; 3 flights)

XS360 TOC at Lee-on-Solent 1.8.62. Noted at Lee 1.63-1.64. To RNPTA by 7.64; to Jufair (Bahrain) by 1.65. Crashed into the sea after recovery 'chute failed to operate, date unknown. SOC 28.6.65. (TFH 3.00; 6 flights)

XS361 TOC at Lee-on-Solent 1.8.62. Noted at Lee 1.63-1.64. To RNPTA by 7.64; to Jufair (Bahrain) by 1.65. Crashed into the sea after parachute separated from target. SOC 28.6.65. (TFH 1.00; 3 flights)

XS362 TOC at Lee-on-Solent 1.8.62. To Portland by 7.63. Lost at sea during post-flight recovery 8.10.63. SOC 24.10.63. (TFH 1.05)

XS363 TOC at Lee-on-Solent 1.8.62. To Portland by 7.63. Seriously damaged on launch 6.10.63. SOC 11.2.64 (TFH 0.45).

XS364 TOC at Lee-on-Solent 1.8.62. To Portland by 7.63. SOC 8.4.64, details unkn.

XS365 TOC at Lee-on-Solent 1.8.62. To Portland by 7.63. Lost at sea 8.10.63. SOC 24.10.63. (TFH 1.20)

XS366 TOC at Lee-on-Solent 1.8.62; f/f 3.7.63. Written-off when it dived into the sea 6.3.64. SOC 11.3.64 TFH 2.35; 7 flights).

XS367 TOC at Lee-on-Solent 1.8.62. Noted in store at Lee 1.63-1.64; to Portland by 7.64 (still unflown). SOC 10.12.64 (TFH 4.00; 6 flights)

XS368 TOC at Lee-on-Solent 1.8.62. To Portland and f/f 3.7.63. Crashed on launch 11.2.64. SOC 12.3.64. (TFH 1.45; 2 flights)

XS369 TOC at Lee-on-Solent 1.8.62. Noted in store at Lee until 1.64. To Portland but crashed on first flight after 55 mins. SOC 15.7.64.

XS370 TOC at Lee-on-Solent 1.8.62. Noted in store at Lee until 7.64. To Portland but broke up on impact with the sea after 5 minutes into its first flight. SOC 14.10.64.

XS371 TOC at Lee-on-Solent 1.8.62. Noted in store at Lee until 7.62. To Jufair (Bahrain) by 1.64; to Portland by 7.64. SOC 26.10.64 after crashing immediately a launch. (TFH 2.00; 4 flights)

XS372 No details known

XS373 TOC at Lee-on-Solent 1.8.62 and stored until 7.63. To Jufair (Bahrain) by 1.64. SOC 11.3.64 after completing 3 flights in the Persian Gulf Area.

XS374 TOC at Lee-on Solent 1.8.62 and stored until 7.63. To Jufair (Bahrain) by 1.64; to Portland by 7.64; to Jufair by 1.65. SOC 28.6.65 after crashing in the sea when recovery 'chute separated from aircraft. (TFH 3.00; 6 flights)

XS375 TOC at Lee-on-Solent 1.8.62 and stored until 7.63. To Jufair (Bahrain) by 1.64. SOC 15.7.64 after crashing on its first flight. (TFH 0.25)

XS376 Possibly f/f 11.10.63. Written-off when dived into the sea 12.2.64. SOC 11.3.64 (TFH 1.55; 2 flights)

XS377 TOC at Lee-on-Solent 1.8.62 and stored until 1.64. To Portland but SOC 22.6.64 after only one flight. (TFH 1.00)

XS378 TOC at Lee-on-Solent 1.8.62 and stored until 1.64. To Portland by 7.64. Shot down by a Seacat missile 6.10.64. SOC 8.10.64. (TFH 3.00; 5 flights)

XS379 No details known.

XS380 TOC at 1.8.62 and stored until at least 1.64. To Portland by 7.64. Crashed into the sea 8.8.64. SOC 13.8.64. (TFH 2.35; 5 flights)

XS381 TOC at Lee-on-Solent 1.8.62 and stored until at least 7.64. To Portland but crashed into the sea 6.10.64. SOC 8.10.64. (TFH 3.40; 4 flights)

XS398 TOC at Lee-on-Solent 2.8.62. To Portland by 1.63. Destroyed by Seacat missile 14.5.64. SOC 19.5.64. (TFH 8.50; 19 flights)

XS399 TOC at Lee-on-Solent 2.8.62. To Portland by 1.63. SOC 12.3.63 after lost at sea.

XS400 TOC at Lee-on-Solent 2.8.62. To Portland by 1.63. SOC 5.9.63. (5 flights)

XS401 TOC at Lee-on-Solent 2.8.62. To Portland by 1.63. SOC 19.4.63 after crashing on launch.

XS402 TOC at Lee-on-Solent 2.8.62. To Portland by 1.63. Lost at sea 6.2.64; SOC 11.2.64 (TFH 7.10)

XS403 TOC at Lee-on-Solent 2.8.62. To Portland by 1.63. SOC 18.2.63 after it crashed and sank. (TFH 0.45; 4 flights)

XS404 TOC at Lee-on-Solent 2.8.62. To Portland by 1.63. Lost in a crash at sea 5.5.64. SOC 11.5.64. (TFH 6.40)

XS405 TOC at Lee-on-Solent 2.8.62. To Portland by 1.63. SOC 16.4.64. (TFH 3.00; 5 flights).

XS406 TOC at Lee-on-Solent 2.8.62. To Portland by 1.63. SOC 12.7.63, details unkn.

XS407 TOC at Lee-on-Solent 2.8.62. To Portland by 1.63. SOC 5.3.63 after it crashed on take-off and sank.

XS408 TOC at Lee-on-Solent 2.8.62. To Portland by 1.63. Lost at sea 8.5.63; SOC 10.5.63. (TFH 1.32)

Contract KK/T/036/CB25(b): 85 Shelduck D.1

XT293-XT299 Shipped ex-USA (Wilmington, California) 14.9.64 aboard SS *Loch Gowan* to PTA Unit Store, Lee-on-Solent. (XT297 & XT299 were noted at HM Naval Base, Singapore 28.7.66 and which may suggest that this batch were transferred. No further details known.)

XT300 Shipped ex-USA to PTA Store, Lee-on-Solent (with XT293 etc) Crashed into the sea 24.3.66, details unkn. (TFH 2.30)

XT301 Shipped ex-USA to PTA Store, Lee-on-Solent (with XT293 etc) to PTA Unit, Lee-on-Solent. Lost at sea 15.11.67, details unkn.

XT302-XT303 Shipped ex-USA to PTA Store, Lee-on-Solent (with XT293 etc). No further details known.

XT304 Shipped ex-USA to PTA Store, Lee-on-Solent (with XT293 etc). Lost at sea 1.3.67, details unkn.

XT305 Shipped ex-USA to PTA Store, Lee-on-Solent (with XT293 etc). No further details known.

XT306 Shipped ex-USA to PTA Store, Lee-on-Solent (with XT293 etc). No further details known apart from XT306 noted at HM Naval Base, Singapore 28.7.66 and which may suggest others of this batch were transferred.)

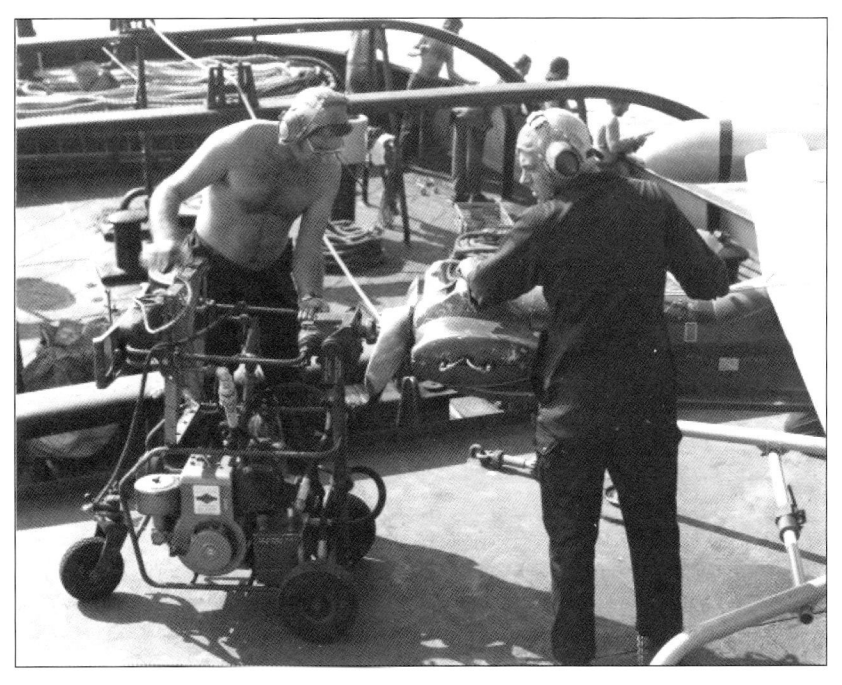

Ground crews aboard a Royal Navy destroyer prepare to fire the engine with a portable starter trolley. The trolley is positioned so that the coupling fits onto the propeller hub and thereby is able to spin the prop. In this age of Health & Safety the standard of protective equipment for the personnel and the close proximity of both men must be considered quite frightening. (RNPTA)

A different style of starter trolley is demonstrated outside the RNPTA Hangar at Portland. The expression on the engineer's face suggests that this may well have been his first attempt! (HMS Osprey Neg. No. 27806)

XT307 Shipped ex-USA to PTA Store, Lee-on-Solent (with XT293 etc). Lost at sea 15.11.67, details unkn.

XT308 Shipped ex-USA to PTA Store, Lee-on-Solent (with XT293 etc). No further details known.

XT309 Shipped ex-USA to PTA Store, Lee-on-Solent (with XT293 etc). Lost at sea 1.3.67, details unkn.

XT310 Shipped ex-USA to PTA Store, Lee-on-Solent (with XT293 etc). Crashed into the sea 10.7.67. (TFH 0.35)

XT311 Shipped ex-USA to PTA Store, Lee-on-Solent (with XT293 etc). Crashed into the sea 23.4.65. (TFH 0.20)

XT312 Shipped ex-USA to PTA Store, Lee-on-Solent (with XT293 etc). No further details known.

XT313 Shipped ex-USA (Terminal Island, California) 19.10.64 aboard SS *Bongainville* to RNPTA, Singapore. No further details known.

XT314 Shipped ex-USA to PTA Store, Lee-on-Solent (with XT293 etc). No further details known.

XT315-XT320 Shipped ex-USA to RNPTA Singapore (with XT313 etc). No further details known apart from XT315 being noted at HM Naval Base, Singapore 28.7.66 and 22.9.66.

XT321 Shipped ex-USA to RNPTA Singapore (with XT313 etc). Lost at sea 21.9.65, details unkn. (TFH 2.20)

XT322-XT323 Shipped ex-USA to RNPTA Singapore (with XT313 etc). No further details known. (Both were noted at HM Naval Base, Singapore 28.7.66.)

XT357-XT358 Shipped ex-USA (Terminal Island, California) 1.9.64 aboard SS *Colorado Star* to RNPTA Store, Lee-on-Solent. No further details known.

XT359 Shipped ex-USA to PTA Store, Lee-on-Solent (with XT357 etc). Lost at sea 6.4.66, details unkn. (TFH 2.30)

XT360-XT361 Shipped ex-USA to PTA Store, Lee-on-Solent (with XT357 etc). No further details known.

XT362 Shipped ex-USA to PTA Store, Lee-on-Solent (with XT357 etc). Shot down into the sea 9.3.66. (TFH 1.55)

XT363-XT365 Shipped ex-USA to PTA Store, Lee-on-Solent (with XT357 etc). No further details known.

XT366 Shipped ex-USA to PTA Store, Lee-on-Solent (with XT357 etc). Shot down into the sea 9.3.66. (TFH 3.00)

XT367 Shipped ex-USA to PTA Store, Lee-on-Solent (with XT357 etc). No further details known.

XT368 Shipped ex-USA to PTA Store, Lee-on-Solent (with XT357 etc). Shot down into the sea 8.3.66. (TFH 1.15)

XT369 Shipped ex-USA to PTA Store, Lee-on-Solent (with XT357 etc). No further details known.

XT370 Shipped ex-USA to PTA Store, Lee-on-Solent (with XT357 etc). Crashed into the sea 7.3.66. (TFH 3.00)

XT371-XT372 Shipped ex-USA to PTA Store, Lee-on-Solent (with XT357 etc). No further details.

XT373 Shipped ex-USA to PTA Store, Lee-on-Solent (with XT357 etc). Shot down into the sea 18.3.66. (TFH 1.45)

XT374 Shipped ex-USA to PTA Store, Lee-on-Solent (with XT357 etc). No further details known.

XT375 Shipped ex-USA to PTA Store, Lee-on-Solent (with XT357 etc). Crashed into the sea 23.4.65. (TFH 2.55)

XT376 Shipped ex-USA to PTA Store, Lee-on-Solent (with XT357 etc). No further details known.

XT377 Shipped ex-USA to PTA Store, Lee-on-Solent (with XT357 etc). Lost at sea 20.8.67, details unkn. (TFH 5.20)

XT378 Shipped ex-USA to PTA Store, Lee-on-Solent (with XT357 etc). No further details known.

XT379 Shipped ex-USA to PTA Store, Lee-on-Solent (with XT357 etc). Lost at sea 9.8.65, details unkn. (TFH 2.45)

XT380 Shipped ex-USA to PTA Store, Lee-on-Solent (with XT357 etc). Lost at sea 22.4.65, details unkn. (TFH 4.55)

XT381-XT382 Shipped ex-USA to PTA Store, Lee-on-Solent (with XT357 etc). No further details.

XT383 Shipped ex-USA to PTA Store, Lee-on-Solent (with XT357 etc). Shot down into the sea 22.3.66. (TFH 0.35)

XT384 Shipped ex-USA to PTA Store, Lee-on-Solent (with XT357 etc). Crashed into the sea 18.3.66, possibly on its first flight. (TFH 0.05)

XT385-XT386 Shipped ex-USA to PTA Store, Lee-on-Solent (with XT357 etc). No further details.

XT387 Shipped ex-USA to PTA Store, Lee-on-Solent (with XT357 etc). Shot down into the sea 21.3.66. (TFH 0.35)

XT388 Shipped ex-USA to PTA Store, Lee-on-Solent (with XT357 etc). No further details known.

XT389 Shipped ex-USA 14.9.64 (Wilmington, California) aboard SS *Loch Gowan* to PTA Store, Lee-on-Solent. No further details known.

XT390 Shipped ex-USA to PTA Store, Lee-on-Solent (with XT389 etc). Shot down into the sea 18.3.66, possibly on its first flight. (TFH 0.10)

XT391 Shipped ex-USA to PTA Store, Lee-on-Solent (with XT389 etc). No further details known.

XT392 Shipped ex-USA to PTA Store, Lee-on-Solent (with XT389 etc). Crashed into the sea 25.7.66. (TFH 1.25)

XT393-XT395 Shipped ex-USA to PTA Store, Lee-on-Solent (with XT389 etc). No further details known.

XT396-XT407 Shipped ex-USA (Terminal Island, California) 16.9.64 aboard SS *Fernview* to RNPTA, Singapore. No further details.

XT408 Shipped ex-USA to RNPTA, Singapore (with XT396 etc). Sunk at sea 18.5.65, details unkn. (TFH 0.15)

XT409-XT410 Shipped ex-USA (Terminal Island, California) 19.10.64 aboard SS *Bongainville* to RNPTA, Singapore. No further details known.

Contract KK/T/041/CB25(b): 100 Shelduck D.1

XT685-XT687 (c/ns 7268-7270) Shipped ex-USA (Wilmington, California) 14.10.65 aboard SS *Lica Maersk* to RNPTA Singapore. No further details apart from all three being noted at HM Naval Base, Singapore 28.7.66; XT686 only noted on 21.9.66.)

XT688 (c/n 7271) Shipped ex-USA (with XT685 etc) to RNPTA Singapore. Crashed 24.8.66, details unkn.

XT689 (c/n 7272) Shipped ex-USA (Wilmington, California) aboard SS 'Picardy' 8 or 11.10.65 to RNPTA Store, Lee-on-Solent. No further details known.

XT690 (c/n 7274) Shipped ex-USA (with XT689 etc) to RNPTA Store, Lee-on-Solent. Lost at sea 21.7.67, details unkn. (TFH 0.15)

XT691 (c/n 7275) Shipped ex-USA (with XT689 etc) to RNPTA Store, Lee-on-Solent. Lost at sea 2.8.67, presumably at launch on its first flight. (TFH 0.00).

XT692-XT693 (c/ns 7276,7281) Shipped ex-USA (with XT689 etc) to RNPTA Store, Lee-on-Solent. No further details known.

XT694 (c/n 7277) Shipped ex-USA (with XT689 etc) to RNPTA Store, Lee-on-Solent. Lost at sea 9.8.67, details unkn. (TFH 0.15)

XT695 (c/n 7273) Shipped ex-USA (with XT689 etc) to RNPTA Store, Lee-on-Solent. Written-off in Singapore 19.4.69

XT696-XT703, XT717 c/ns (7278-7280, 7282-7287) Shipped ex-USA (with XT689 etc) to RNPTA Store, Lee-on-Solent. No further details known.

XT718 (c/n 6990) Shipped ex-USA 29.9.65 (Wilmington, California) aboard SS *Jeppesen Maersk* to RNPTA, Singapore. Ditched in the sea 16.4.66, details unkn. (TFH 3.00)

XT719-XT721 (c/ns 6991, 6992, 7000) Shipped ex-USA (with XT718 etc) to RNPTA, Singapore. No further details known apart from XT719 & XT720 being noted at HM Naval Base, Singapore 28.7.66; XT720 only on 21.9.66.

XT722 (c/n 7001) Shipped ex-USA (with XT718 etc) to RNPTA, Singapore. Crashed into the sea 15.4.66, details unkn. (TFH 2.25)

XT723-XT725 (c/ns 6999, 6995, 6994) Shipped ex-USA (with XT718 etc) to RNPTA, Singapore. No further details known.

XT726-XT741 Shipped ex-USA (with XT689 etc) to RNPTA Store, Lee-on-Solent. No further details known. (XT741 was noted at HM Naval Base, Singapore 28.7.66 and which may suggest that more from this batch were transferred.)

Construction numbers for the above batch are:
XT726	6998	XT734	7002
XT727	6997	XT735	7020
XT728	6996	XT736	7009
XT729	6993	XT737	7010
XT730	7005	XT738	7008
XT731	7004	XT739	7011
XT732	7003	XT740	7012
XT733	7006	XT741	7013

XT742 (c/n 7015) Shipped ex-USA (with XT689 etc) to RNPTA Store, Lee-on-Solent. Lost at sea 11.67, details unkn.

XT743 (c/n 7014) Shipped ex-USA (with XT689 etc) to RNPTA Store, Lee-on-Solent. Lost at sea 13.7.67, details unkn.

XT744 (c/n 7017) Shipped ex-USA (with XT689 etc) to RNPTA Store, Lee-on-Solent. No further details known.

Contract KK/T/41/CB25(b) accounted for 100 Shelduck D.1s, the largest single UK order for the type. These were delivered between October 1965 and April 1966 and were supplied in the earlier scheme of all-red fuselage and fin. XT701 (c/n 7284) sits on its launcher in a darkened hangar, possibly at Yeovilton. (Flight Refuelling Ltd, Neg No. M2255C)

XT745 (c/n 7018) Shipped ex-USA (with XT689 etc) to RNPTA Store, Lee-on-Solent. Shot down 4.8.66, details unkn. (TFH 1.00)

XT746-XT747 (c/ns 7019, 7007) Shipped ex-USA (with XT689 etc) to RNPTA Store, Lee-on-Solent. No further details known.

XT931-XT934 (c/ns 7292-7295) Shipped ex-USA (Wilmington, California) 14.4.66 aboard SS *Dongedyk* to RNPTA Store, Lee-on-Solent. No further details known.

XT935 (c/n 7296) Shipped ex-USA (with XT931 etc) to RNPTA Store, Lee-on-Solent. Shot down by Seacat missile fired from HMS *London* 27.11.67.

XT936 (c/n 7297) Shipped ex-USA (with XT931 etc) to RNPTA Store, Lee-on-Solent. No further details.

XT937 (c/n 7298) Shipped ex-USA (with XT931 etc) to RNPTA Store, Lee-on-Solent. Shot down by Seacat missile fired from HMS *Eagle* 27.11.67.

XT938-XT940 (c/ns 7299-7301) Shipped ex-USA (with XT931 etc) to RNPTA Store, Lee-on-Solent. No further details known.

XT941 (c/n 7302) Shipped ex-USA (Wilmington, California) 4.4.66 aboard SS *Kingsville* to RNPTA Singapore. No further details.

XT942 (c/n 7303) Shipped ex-USA (with XT941 etc) to RNPTA Singapore. Destroyed by a direct missile hit 19.8.67.

XT943 (c/n 7304) Shipped ex-USA (with XT941 etc) to RNPTA Singapore. No further details.

XT944 (c/n 7305) Shipped ex-USA (with XT941 etc) to RNPTA Singapore. Crashed on take-off, No further details.

XT945 (c/n 7306) Shipped ex-USA (with XT941 etc) to RNPTA Singapore. No further details.

XT946-XT947/XT953-XT959 Shipped ex-USA (Wilmington, California) 5.1.66 aboard SS *Ellen Bakke* to RNPTA, Singapore. All were noted at HM Naval Base, Singapore 28.7.66 whilst only XT946, 947, 953, 954, 956 & 958 were noted in store 21.9.66. No further details known.

Construction numbers for the above batch are:
XT946	7016	XT956	7261
XT947	7265	XT957	7262
XT953	7258	XT958	7263
XT954	7259	XT959	7266
XT955	7260		

XT960 (c/n 7267) Shipped ex-USA (Wilmington, California) 14.1.66 aboard SS *Dintledyk* to RNPTA Store, Lee-on-

Targets for the Royal Navy 187

Solent. Destroyed by 4.5" shell 4.3.69, details unkn. (TFH 6.05)

XT961 (c/n 7268) Shipped ex-USA (with XT960 etc) to RNPTA Store, Lee-on-Solent. Lost at sea 4.5.69; further details unkn.

XT962-XT963 (c/n 7269-7270) Shipped ex-USA (with XT960 etc) to RNPTA Store, Lee-on-Solent. No further details known.

XT964 (c/n 7264) Shipped ex-USA (Wilmington, California) 5.1.66 aboard SS *Ellen Bakke* to RNPTA Singapore. No further details.

XT965-XT967 (c/ns 7271-7273) Shipped ex-USA (with XT960 etc) to RNPTA Store, Lee-on-Solent. No further details known.

XT968 (c/n 7274) Shipped ex-USA (with XT960 etc) to RNPTA Store, Lee-on-Solent. Shot down by a Seacat missile 29.4.69. (TFH 0.30)

XT969 (c/n 7275) Shipped ex-USA (with XT960 etc) to RNPTA Store, Lee-on-Solent. No further details.

XT970 (c/n 7276) Shipped ex-USA (with XT960 etc) to RNPTA Store, Lee-on-Solent. Lost at sea 27.3.68, details unkn.

XT971 (c/n 7277) Shipped ex-USA (with XT960 etc) to RNPTA Store, Lee-on-Solent. No further details.

XT972-XT974 (c/ns 7287, 7278, 7280) Shipped ex-USA (Wilmington, California) 10.3.66 aboard SS *Diemerdyk* to RNPTA Store, Lee-on-Solent. No further details known.

XT975 (c/n 7279) Shipped ex-USA (with XT972 etc) to RNPTA Store, Lee-on-Solent; f/f 28.1.68. Shot down by a Seacat missile off Singapore 10.5.69. (TFH 4.15; 7 flghts)

XT976-XT981 (c/n 7281-7286) Shipped ex-USA (with XT972 etc) to RNPTA Store, Lee-on-Solent. No further details known.

XT982 (c/n 7288) Shipped ex-USA (with XT972 etc) to RNPTA Store, Lee-on-Solent. Lost at sea 2.8.67, details unkn. (TFH 1.00)

XT983-XT985 (c/n 7289-7291) Shipped ex-USA (with XT972 etc) to RNPTA Store, Lee-on-Solent. No further details known.

Note that c/ns 7007/7017-7019 are known to have been supplied to the UK but the true serial-c/n co-location to XT747, XT744, XT745, and XT746 remains unconfirmed.

Contract KK/T/52/CB20(c): 20 Shelduck D.1

XV818-XV827 were shipped by Northrop to the UK in kit-form and consigned to RNPTA store at Lee-on-Solent, dates unknown. No further details known, apart from the following:

XV822 Crashed into the sea 2.4.69. (TFH 2.35)

Also ten MQM-36A target aircraft (XV828-XV837) sub-contracted by Northrop to Meteor SpA at Monfalcomne, Trieste. They departed Italy 20.3.68 aboard SS *Quirinale* and shipped direct to 'D' Flight/RNPTA at HM Naval Base, Singapore. Apart from the underlisted, no further details are known. However, all are believed to have been lost in the Far East.

XV828 damaged beyond repair by a Seacat missile off Singapore 3.2.69. (TFH 3.30; 5 flights).

XV829 Crashed immediately after launch 29.10.68.

XV834 Written-off in Singapore 2.69.

Contract KK/T/55/CB20(c): 60 Shelduck D.1

XW101 Shipped ex-USA (Wilmington, California) 10.7.68 aboard SS *Loch Royal* to Liverpool docks for onward delivery to PTA Unit, Lee-on-Solent. No further details known.

XW102 Shipped ex-USA to RNPTA Store, Lee-on-Solent (with XW101 etc). Ditched into the sea 6.10.70, details unkn. (TFH 4.55)

XW103 Shipped ex-USA to RNPTA Store, Lee-on-Solent (with XW101 etc); f/f 28.11.69. Run over by recovery ship off Bahrain 19.5.71. Target sunk. (TFH 3.00; 6 flights)

XW104-XW106 Shipped ex-USA to RNPTA Store, Lee-on-Solent (with XW101 etc). No further details known.

XW107 Shipped ex-USA to RNPTA Store, Lee-on-Solent (with XW101 etc). Shot down by Seacat missile 29.7.70. (TFH 4.30)

XW108-XW110 Shipped ex-USA to RNPTA Store, Lee-on-Solent (with XW101 etc). No further details known (although XW109 was noted at Portland 9.82.)

XW111 Shipped ex-USA to RNPTA Store, Lee-on-Solent (with XW101 etc). Destroyed by Seacat missile 2.70. (TFH 1.25; 3 flights)

XW112 Shipped ex-USA to RNPTA Store, Lee-on-Solent (with XW101 etc). No further details known.

XW113 Shipped ex-USA to RNPTA Store, Lee-on-Solent (with XW101 etc). Crashed into the sea 4.70, details unkn.

XW114 Shipped ex-USA to RNPTA Store, Lee-on-Solent (with XW101 etc). No further details known.

The change in designation from KD2R-5 to MQM-36A, which officially took place in June 1962, was finally reflected on the July 1968 delivery of XW-serialled Shelducks. XW126 is captured on a mobile stand behind the RNPTA hangar at Portland on 8 September 1969. Note the use of a hyphen in the serial presentation, a curious practice that was first used by de Havilland on Queen Bee drones. (Michael I Draper)

XW115 Shipped ex-USA to RNPTA Store, Lee-on-Solent (with XW101 etc). Shot down by a Seacat missile 26.9.72.

XW116 Shipped ex-USA to RNPTA Store, Lee-on-Solent (with XW101 etc). Lost when it sank before recovery 10.70. (TFH 4.50)

XW117 Shipped ex-USA to RNPTA Store, Lee-on-Solent (with XW101 etc). No further details.

XW118 Shipped ex-USA to RNPTA Store, Lee-on-Solent (with XW101 etc). Shot down by a Seacat missile 20.3.69. (TFH 1.40)

XW119 Shipped ex-USA to RNPTA Store, Lee-on-Solent (with XW101 etc). No further details known.

XW120 Shipped ex-USA to RNPTA Store, Lee-on-Solent (with XW101 etc). Crashed into the sea 4.70, details unkn.

XW121-XW122 Shipped ex-USA to RNPTA Store, Lee-on-Solent (with XW101 etc). No further details.

XW123 Shipped ex-USA to RNPTA Store, Lee-on-Solent (with XW101 etc). Damaged beyond repair 22.10.70, details unkn. (TFH 7.05)

XW124-XW125 Shipped ex-USA to RNPTA Store, Lee-on-Solent (with XW101 etc). No further details.

XW126 Shipped ex-USA to RNPTA Store, Lee-on-Solent (with XW101 etc). Shot down by a Seacat missile 26.10.70. (TFH 1.40)

XW127-XW128 Shipped ex-USA to RNPTA Store, Lee-on-Solent (with XW101 etc). No further details.

XW129 Shipped ex-USA to RNPTA Store, Lee-on-Solent (with XW101 etc). Shot down by a Seacat missile 25.4.69. (TFH 2.55)

XW130 Shipped ex-USA to RNPTA Store, Lee-on-Solent (with XW101 etc). Lost in the Portland Exercise Area 12.8.69. (TFH 1.00)

XW131-XW133 Shipped ex-USA to RNPTA Store, Lee-on-Solent (with XW101 etc). No further details.

XW134 Shipped ex-USA to RNPTA Store, Lee-on-Solent (with XW101 etc). Shot down by Seacat missile 26.10.70. (TFH 4.50)

XW135 Shipped ex-USA (San Pedro) 14.8.68 aboard SS *American Mail* to RNPTA Singapore. Crashed into the sea 4.70, details unkn. (TFH 6.35)

XW136 Shipped ex-USA to RNPTA Singapore (with XW135 etc). No further details known.

XW137 Shipped ex-USA to RNPTA Singapore (with XW135 etc). Crashed into sea on launch off Singapore 10.5.69. (TFH 0.37; 3 flights)

XW138-XW139 Shipped ex-USA to RNPTA Singapore (with XW135 etc). No further details known.

XW140 Shipped ex-USA to RNPTA Singapore (with XW135 etc)' f/f 12.12.68. Crashed immediately after launch off Singapore 10.5.69. Sank before recovery. (TFH 2.50; 4 flights)

XW141 Shipped ex-USA to RNPTA Singapore (with XW135 etc). known to have been shot down by HMS *Tartar* 22.2.71 (TFH 4.05)

XW142-XW143 Shipped ex-USA to RNPTA Singapore (with XW135 etc). No further details known.

XW144 Shipped ex-USA to RNPTA Singapore (with XW135 etc). Known to have crashed into the sea 23.2.71. (TFH 8.15)

XW145 Shipped ex-USA to RNPTA Store, Lee-on-Solent (with XW101 etc). No further details.

XW146 Shipped ex-USA to RNPTA Store, Lee-on-Solent (with XW101 etc). Shot down by Seacat missile 20.3.69. (TFH 0.35)

XW147 Shipped ex-USA to RNPTA Store, Lee-on-Solent (with XW101 etc). Shot down by Seacat missile c3.69. (TFH 3.10)

XW148 Shipped ex-USA to RNPTA Store, Lee-on-Solent (with XW101 etc). Destroyed by a 4.5″ shell 26.2.69 on (probably) its first flight. (TFH 0.10)

XW149 Shipped ex-USA to RNPTA Store, Lee-on-Solent (with XW101 etc). Shot down by Seacat missile 28.7.70. (TFH 7.55)

XW150 Shipped ex-USA to RNPTA Store, Lee-on-Solent (with XW101 etc). No further details.

XW161 Shipped ex-USA to RNPTA Singapore (with XW135 etc). No further details known.

XW162 Shipped ex-USA to RNPTA Singapore (with XW135 etc). No further details known.

XW163 Shipped ex-USA to RNPTA Singapore (with XW135 etc). Lost 8.69, details unknown. (TFH 0.20)

XW164-XW165 Shipped ex-USA to RNPTA Singapore (with XW135 etc). No further details known.

XW166 Shipped ex-USA to RNPTA Singapore (with XW135 etc). Crashed into the sea 3.69, details unknown.

XW167 Shipped ex-USA to RNPTA Singapore (with XW135 etc). Crashed into the sea 3.69, details unknown.

XW168 Shipped ex-USA to RNPTA Singapore (with XW135 etc). No further details known.

XW169 Shipped ex-USA to RNPTA Singapore (with XW135 etc); f/f 11.12.68. Rolled and dived into the sea off Singapore 10.5.69. (TFH 1.17; 3 flights)

XW170 Shipped ex-USA to RNPTA Singapore (with XW135 etc). No further details known.

Contract KK/T/58/CB20(c): 60 Shelduck D.1

XW444 Shipped ex-USA (Terminal island, California) 24.6.69 aboard SS *Zeeland* to PTA Squadron, HM Naval Base, Singapore. Shot down by a Seacat missile from HMS *Swan* 12.70. (TFH 2.45)

XW445-XW447 Shipped ex-USA to RNPTA Singapore (with XW444 etc). No further details.

XW448 Shipped ex-USA to RNPTA Singapore (with XW444 etc). Destroyed by Seacat missile 31.7.71. (TFH 1.20)

XW449 Shipped ex-USA to RNPTA Singapore (with XW444 etc). No further details known.

XW450 Shipped ex-USA to RNPTA Singapore (with XW444 etc). F/F 27.1.70. Sank in the sea off Singapore 2.71.

XW451 Shipped ex-USA to RNPTA Singapore (with XW444 etc). No further details known.

XW452 Shipped ex-USA to RNPTA Singapore (with XW444 etc). Shot down by Seacat missile 2.71.

XW453 Shipped ex-USA to RNPTA Singapore (with XW444 etc). F/F 28.1.70. Shot down 17.2.71. (TFH 3.05; 8 flights)

XW454 Shipped ex-USA to RNPTA Singapore (with XW444 etc). No further details known.

XW455 Shipped ex-USA to RNPTA Singapore (with XW444 etc). Lost at sea off Western Australia 7.12.70. (TFH 2.10)

XW456-XW458 Shipped ex-USA to RNPTA Singapore (with XW444 etc). No further details known.

XW459-XW478/XW492-XW516 Shipped ex-USA (Wilmington, California) 3.7.69 aboard SS *Pacific Northwest* to RNPTA Store, Lee-on-Solent (via London docks). No further details known.

XW460 Shipped ex-USA to RNPTA Store Lee-on-Solent (with XW459 etc). Ditched into the sea 10.72, details unkn. (TFH 1.34)

XW461 Shipped ex-USA to RNPTA Store Lee-on-Solent (with XW459 etc). No further details known.

XW462 Shipped ex-USA to RNPTA Store Lee-on-Solent (with XW459 etc). Lost at sea 19.10.71, details unkn. (TFH 0.50)

XW463 Shipped ex-USA to RNPTA Store Lee-on-Solent (with XW459 etc). No further details known.

XW464 Shipped ex-USA to RNPTA Store Lee-on-Solent (with XW459 etc). Conveyed Lee-on-Solent to Portland 2.70. Lost at sea 2.71. (TFH 1.00)

XW465 Shipped ex-USA to RNPTA Store Lee-on-Solent (with XW459 etc). Lost 10.72, details unkn. (TFH 7.30)

XW466-XW467 Shipped ex-USA to RNPTA Store Lee-on-Solent (with XW459 etc). No further details.

XW468 Shipped ex-USA to RNPTA Store Lee-on-Solent (with XW459 etc). Conveyed Lee-on-Solent to Portland 2.70. Destroyed by Seacat missile 8.2.71. (TFH 4.35)

XW469 Shipped ex-USA to RNPTA Store Lee-on-Solent (with XW459 etc). No further details known.

XW470 Shipped ex-USA to RNPTA Store Lee-on-Solent (with XW459 etc). Destroyed by Seacat missile 5.73 during an exercise off San Juan. (TFH 1.45; 4 flights)

XW471 Shipped ex-USA to RNPTA Store Lee-on-Solent (with XW459 etc). Conveyed Lee-on-Solent store to Portland 2.70.

XW472 Shipped ex-USA to RNPTA Store Lee-on-Solent (with XW459 etc). No further details known.

XW473 Shipped ex-USA to RNPTA Store Lee-on-Solent (with XW459 etc). Shot down by a Seacat missile fired from HMS *Londonderry*. (TFH 0.30)

XW474-XW476 Shipped ex-USA to RNPTA Store Lee-on-Solent (with XW459 etc). No further details.

XW477 Shipped ex-USA to RNPTA Store Lee-on-Solent (with XW459 etc). Shot down 5.11.71, details unkn. (TFH 1.05)

XW478 Shipped ex-USA to RNPTA Store Lee-on-Solent (with XW459 etc). No further details known.

XW492 Shipped ex-USA to RNPTA Store Lee-on-Solent (with XW459 etc). Shot down 8.11.71, details unkn. (TFH 0.05)

XW493 Shipped ex-USA to RNPTA Store Lee-on-Solent (with XW459 etc). No further details.

XW494 Shipped ex-USA to RNPTA Store Lee-on-Solent (with XW459 etc). Crashed into the sea 12.70, details unknown but presumably on its first flight. (TFH 0.10)

XW495-XW499 Shipped ex-USA to RNPTA Store Lee-on-Solent (with XW459 etc). No further details.

XW500 Shipped ex-USA to RNPTA Store Lee-on-Solent (with XW459 etc). Shot down 8.11.71, details unkn, but possibly on its first flight. (TFH 0.15)

XW501 Shipped ex-USA to RNPTA Store Lee-on-Solent (with XW459 etc). Ditched into the sea 4.11.72, details unkn.

XW502 Shipped ex-USA to RNPTA Store Lee-on-Solent (with XW459 etc). Lost 5.73 during an exercise off San Juan. (TFH 7.25; 12 flights)

XW503-XW504 Shipped ex-USA to RNPTA Store Lee-on-Solent (with XW459 etc). No further details.

XW505 Shipped ex-USA to RNPTA Store Lee-on-Solent (with XW459 etc). Conveyed Lee-on-Solent store to Portland 2.70. Destroyed by Seacat missile 8.2.71. (TFH 1.06)

XW506 Shipped ex-USA to RNPTA Store Lee-on-Solent (with XW459 etc). Conveyed Lee-on-Solent store to Portland 2.70.

XW507-XW508 Shipped ex-USA to RNPTA Store Lee-on-Solent (with XW459 etc). No further details.

Being hoisted out of the water tail-first – like a dronned rat – an RNPTA Shelduck reveals that the buoyancy bag had worked and by most accounts with little damage. After a complete washdown and a thorough inspection this Shelduck is likely to have lived for another day.

XW509 Shipped ex-USA to RNPTA Store Lee-on-Solent (with XW459 etc). Crashed into the sea 8.2.71. (TFH 1.15)

XW510-XW516 Shipped ex-USA to RNPTA Store Lee-on-Solent (with XW459 etc). No further details.

Contract KK/T/59/CB.20(c): 20 Shelduck D.1

XW571-XW580 Departed USA (Wilmington, California) aboard SS *Pacific Stronghold* 29.7.69. Shipped to London Docks; consigned to the PTA Unit, Lee-on-Solent although they appear to have been diverted to RAE Farnborough for storage and where XW575-XW580 were noted during 1972. No further details known apart from XW573/574/575 being transferred to the RNPTA in 9.76. XW578 was also operated by the Army, the remains of which were later disposed of to Larry Bax at Amesbury. It was subsequently acquired by the Bournemouth Aviation Museum and used in the restoration of XR346.

For details of MQM-36A Shelduck targets within the range XW594 to XW603, see Chapter 8.

Contract K20c/6/28/CBA2(c): 60 Shelduck D.1

XW670-XW673 (c/n 7814-7817) Departed USA (Wilmington, California) aboard SS *Moerdyke* 31.7.70. Shipped to UK; consigned to PTA Squadron, Lee-on-Solent. No further details known.

XW674 (c/n 7818) Shipped ex-USA to RNPTA Store, Lee-on-Solent (with XW670 etc). Lost at sea 4.12.74.

XW675 (c/n 7819) Shipped ex-USA (Terminal Island, California) 31.7.70 aboard SS *Maas Lloyd* to RNPTA Store, Mombasa. Crashed immediately after launch 10.72. (TFH 1.25)

XW676 (c/n 7820) Shipped ex-USA to RNPTA Store, Mombassa (with XW675 etc) Elevator control rod fouled the elevator during its initial flight 4.72, off Mombasa. Aircraft dived into the sea after parachute failed to deploy. Aircraft sank immediately. (TFH 0.10)

XW677-XW678 (c/n 7821-7822) Shipped ex-USA to RNPTA Store, Mombassa (with XW675 etc). No further details.

XW679 (c/n 7823) Shipped ex-USA to RNPTA Store, Mombassa (with XW675 etc). Crashed immediately after launch 10.72. (TFH 2.45)

XW680 (c/n 7824) Shipped ex-USA (Wilmington, California) 31.7.70 aboard SS *Goldstone* to RNPTA Malta. No further details known.

XW681 (c/n 7825) Shipped ex-USA to RNPTA Malta (with XW680 etc). In 5.73 JATO failed to detach on completion of thrust during an exercise off San Juan. Target rolled to the left, hit the sea and sank immediately. (TFH 5.10; 9 flights)

XW682 (c/n 7826) Shipped ex-USA to RNPTA Malta (with XW680 etc). Destroyed by Seacat missile 5.73. (TFH 5.55; 12 flights)

XW683 (c/n 7827) Shipped ex-USA to RNPTA Malta (with XW680 etc). No further details known.

XW684 (c/n 7828) Shipped ex-USA (Terminal Island, California) 31.7.70 aboard SS *Limburg* to RNPTA Store, RAF Muharraq, Bahrain 31.7.70. Shot down by 3" gunfire from ITS *Kahamoie* 12.70. (TFH 2.15)

XW685-XW687 (c/n 7829-7831) Shipped ex-USA to Bahrain (with XW684 etc). No further details.

XW688-XW691 (c/n 7832-7835) Shipped ex-USA (Wilmington, California) 31.7.70 aboard SS *Nicocine* to RNPTA Singpaore. No further details.

XW692 (c/n 7836) Shipped ex-USA (Wilmington, California) 31.7.70 aboard SS *Nicocine* to RNPTA Singapore. Lost at sea 1.72, details unknown. (TFH 0.25)

XW693 (c/n 7837) Shipped ex-USA (with XW692 etc). 5 minutes after a launch (in 5.73) it rolled into inverted flight; recovery 'chute was fired but it failed to open. Crashed into the sea and sank before recovery attempt. (TFH 9.40; 15 flights)

XW694 (c/n 7838) Shipped ex-USA (with XW692 etc). Crashed into the sea and sank before recovery 1.72. (TFH 5.25)

XW695 (c/n 7839) Shipped ex-USA (with XW692 etc). Crashed into the sea 1.72, details unkn. (TFH 0.30)

XW696 (c/n 7840) Shipped ex-USA (with XW692 etc). No further details known.

XW697 (c/n 7841) Shipped ex-USA (with XW692 etc); f/f 21.1.71. Shot down by Seacat missile off Mombasa 17.2.71.

XW698 (c/n 7842) Shipped ex-USA (with XW692 etc). No further details known.

XW699 (c/n 7843) Shipped ex-USA (with XW692 etc); f/f 4.1.71. Shot down by Seacat missile off Mombasa 17.2.71. (TFH 2.15; 3 flights)

XW700 (c/n 7844) Shipped ex-USA (Wilmington, California) 23.9.70 aboard SS *Pacific Ranger* to RNPTA Store, Lee-on-Solent. Sunk off Gibraltar 4.72 after sustaining engine failure and the recovery parachute failed to deploy. (TFH 5.20; 11 flights)

XW701 (c/n 7845) Shipped ex-USA (with XW700 etc). Hit by missile off Portland 4.72. Recovered but reduced to spares. (TFH 1.45; 3 flights)

XW702 (c/n 7846) Shipped ex-USA (with XW700 etc). Destroyed by missile 29.7.71.

XW703 (c/n 7847) Shipped ex-USA (with XW700 etc). Crashed into the sea 22.5.74, details unknown. (TFH 10.30)

XW704 (c/n 7848) Shipped ex-USA (with XW700 etc). Lost (circumstances not known) 22.7.71 (TFH 0.10)

XW705 (c/n 7849) Shipped ex-USA (with XW700 etc). Shot down by a missile 3.8.71. (TFH 3.35)

XW706 (c/n 7850) Shipped ex-USA (with XW700 etc). No further details known.

XW707 (c/n 7851) Shipped ex-USA (with XW700 etc). TOC Portland 15.12.70. Crashed into the sea off Portland 4.2.71, possibly on first flight. (TFH 0.25)

XW724 (c/n 7852) Shipped ex-USA (with XW700 etc). Recovery parachute failed to deploy on command off Gibraltar 4.72; aircraft glide-landed and recovered but declared uneconomical to repair. Reduced to spares. (TFH 3.15; 6 flights)

XW725-XW731 (c/ns 7853-7859) Shipped ex-USA (with XW700 etc). No further details known.

XW732 (c/n 7860) Shipped ex-USA (with XW700 etc). Lost 5.73 when it fell away from its parachute and plunged into the sea. Sank before recovery attempt. (TFH 5.50; 8 flights)

XW733-XW738 (c/ns 7861-7866) Shipped ex-USA (with XW700 etc). No further details known.

XW739 (c/n 7867) Shipped ex-USA (with XW700 etc). Shot down 26.11.71, details unknown. (TFH 0.43)

XW740 (c/n 7868) Shipped ex-USA (with XW700 etc). Sustained direct hit by Seacat missile off Portland 5.71. (TFH 2.00; 4 flights)

XW741 (c/n 7869) Shipped ex-USA (with XW700 etc). No further details known.

XW742 (c/n 7870) Shipped ex-USA (with XW700 etc). Sank before recovery 13.9.71, details unknown. (TFH 4.35)

XW743-XW745 (c/n 7871-7873) Shipped ex-USA (with XW700 etc). No further details known.

For details of MQM-36A Shelduck targets within the range XW803 to XW832, see Chapter 8.

Contract K20c/97/CB20C6: 40 Shelduck D.1

XW941-XW957 (c/ns 8040-8056) Departed USA (Terminal Island, California) 8.12.71 aboard SS *Falstria*. Consigned to 15 MU Wroughton. Further details not known.

XW958 (c/n 8057) Shipped ex-USA to 15 MU Wroughton (with XW941 etc). Damaged beyond repair 7.5.74, details unknown. (TFH 0.45)

XW959 (c/n 8058) Shipped ex-USA to 15 MU Wroughton (with XW941 etc). No further details.

XW960 (c/n 8059) Shipped ex-USA to 15 MU Wroughton (with XW941 etc). Received direct missile hit 19.5.74, details unkn. (TFH 2.10)

XW961 (c/n 8060) Shipped ex-USA to 15 MU Wroughton (with XW941 etc). Further details not known.

XW962 (c/n 8061) Shipped ex-USA to 15 MU Wroughton (with XW941 etc). Crashed into the sea 4.70, details unkn.

XW963 (c/n 8062) Shipped ex-USA to 15 MU Wroughton (with XW941 etc). Further details not known.

XW964 (c/n 8063) Shipped ex-USA to 15 MU Wroughton (with XW941 etc). Crashed immediately after launch 30.5.74, (TFH 2.20)

XW965 (c/n 8064) Shipped ex-USA to 15 MU Wroughton (with XW941 etc). Further details not known.

XW966-XW968 (c/ns 8065-8067) Shipped ex-USA (Terminal Island, California) 8.12.71 aboard SS *Falstria* 8.12.71. Consigned to MinTech for onward shipment to RNPTA, HMS *Terror* (PFPO 164), a storage unit in Singapore. Further details not known.

XW969 (c/n 8068) Shipped ex-USA (XW966 etc). Lost at sea 10.72, details unkn. (TFH 2.20)

XW970-XW975 (c/ns 8069-8074) Shipped ex-USA (with XW966 etc) Further details not known.

XW976 (c/n 8075) Shipped ex-USA (with XW966 etc) but consigned to MinTech for onward shipment to Naval Liaison Officer, Mombasa (BFPO 51). Shot down by Seacat missile 10.72. (TFH 1.30)

XW977-XW978 (c/ns 8076-8077) Shipped ex-USA (with XW966 etc) but consigned to MinTech for onward shipment to Naval Liaison Officer, Mombasa (BFPO 51). Further details not known.

XW979 (c/n 8078) Shipped ex-USA (with XW966 etc) but consigned to MinTech for onward shipment to Naval Liaison Officer, Mombasa (BFPO 51). Shot down by Seacat missile 10.72 (TFH 1.30)

XW980 (c/n 8079) Shipped ex-USA (with XW966 etc) but consigned to MinTech for onward shipment to Naval Liaison Officer, Mombasa (BFPO 51). Shot down 6.5.74, details unknown. (TFH 2.55)

Contract K/GW41B/186: 49 Shelduck D.1

XX850-XX860 (c/ns 8150-8160) Shipped ex-USA (Terminal Island, California) 5.6.73 aboard SS *Meonia*. Consigned to RNAY Wroughton. No further details known.

XX861 (c/n 8161) Shipped ex-USA (with XX850 etc) to RNAY Wroughton. Lost 12.12.77, details unkn.

XX862-XX869 (c/ns 8162-8169) Shipped ex-USA (with XX850 etc) to RNAY Wroughton. Further details unkn.

XX870 (c/n 8170) Shipped ex-USA (Terminal Island, California) 29.5.73 aboard SS *Gudrun Bakke* to RNAY Wroughton. Released to 'D' Flt/RNPTA Sqdn. Consigned to ANZUK Forces, Woodlands Garrison, Singapore. Lost 24.10.77, details unkn.

XX871 (c/n 8171) Shipped ex-USA (with XX870 etc) to RNAY Wroughton. Released to 'D' Flt/RNPTA Sqdn. Consigned to ANZUK Forces, Woodlands Garrison, Singapore.

XX872 (c/n 8172) Shipped ex-USA (with XX870 etc) to RNAY Wroughton. Released to 'D' Flt/RNPTA Sqdn. Consigned to ANZUK Forces, Woodlands Garrison, Singapore. With RNPTA Portland 9.82. Launched by 'B' Flt, FTG from RFA *Tidespring* 19.6.83 in the Falkland Islands area but crashed immediately after launch.

XX873-XX879 (c/ns 8173-8179) Shipped ex-USA (with XX870 etc) to RNAY Wroughton. Released to 'D' Flt/RNPTA Sqdn. Consigned to ANZUK Forces, Woodlands Garrison, Singapore. No further details known.

XX923-XX929 (c/ns 8185-8191) Shipped ex-USA (Terminal Island, California) 24.1.74 aboard SS *Axel Johnson* to RNAY Wroughton. No further details known.

XX930 (c/n 8192) Shipped ex-USA (with XX923 etc) to RNAY Wroughton. Crashed into the sea off Tonga 6.9.79. Possibly recovered and used in the rebuild of XX934.

XX931-XZ933 (c/n 8193-8195) Shipped ex-USA (with XX923 etc) to RNAY Wroughton. No further details known.

XX934 (c/n 8196) Shipped ex-USA (with XX923 etc) to RNAY Wroughton. Possibly rebuilt c1977 using the fuselage of XX930. Later destroyed 14.10.78.

XX935-XX941 (c/n 8197-8203) Shipped ex-USA (with XX923 etc) to RNAY Wroughton. No further details known.

Contract K/GW11B/372: 16 Shelduck D.1

Details of shipping from USA to UK are unknown. It is presumed that all were consigned to RNAY Wroughton.

XZ410 Lost 21.9.77, details unkn.

XZ411 No details known

XZ412 Lost 7.7.77, details unknown.

XZ413-XZ424 Known to have been exported ex-US 12.74. Operational details not known.

XZ425 Shipping and pre-1981 operational details not known. Shot down 1.2.82 by a Seawolf missile whilst operating from HMS *Brilliant* in the Plymouth Exercise area. (TFH 10.05; 19 flights)

Contract K/GW11B/493: 30 Shelduck D.1

XZ505 (c/n 8356) Shipped ex-USA (Terminal Island, California) 17.3.76 aboard SS *California Star*. Shipped to London Docks; consigned to RNAY Wroughton. On 4.3.81, whilst with 'A' Flt, FTG aboard RFA *Tidepool* in the Arabian Sea area it rolled to the left during a timed turn, crashed into the sea and sank. (TFH 4.40; 11 flights)

XZ506-XZ512 (c/ns 8357-8363) Shipped with XZ505 etc, consigned to RNAY Wroughton. No further details.

XZ513 (c/n 8364) Shipped ex-USA (with XZ505 etc) to RNAY Wroughton. To FTG by 9.82; final flight 9.2.83 with 'A' Flt, FTG from Portland when its recovery parachute appeared to 'candle' (TFH 7.00; 9 flights)

XZ514 (c/n 8365) Shipped ex-USA (with XZ505 etc) to RNAY Wroughton. No further details; presumed lost pre-1981.

XZ515 (c/n 8366) Shipped ex-USA (with XZ505 etc) to RNAY Wroughton. To FTG by 9.82 and named "GILBERT". Final flight 5.3.83 with 'B' Flt off Portland as part of 'STANAVFORLANT' (NATO Standing Naval Force Atlantic.) when, having proved to be difficult to fly, the flight was terminated. Only wreckage was found. (TFH 6.39; 12 Flights)

XZ516 (c/n 8367) Shipped ex-USA (with XZ505 etc) to RNAY Wroughton. No further details; presumed lost pre-1981.

XZ517 (c/n 8368) Shipped ex-USA (with XZ505 etc) to RNAY Wroughton. To FTG by 9.82. Final flight 3.3.83 with 'B' Flt off Portland as part of 'STANAVFORLANT' when, lost on radar, the flight was terminated. No wreckage was ever found. (TFH 4.20; 11 flights)

XZ518 (c/n 8369) Shipped ex-USA (with XZ505 etc) to RNAY Wroughton. No further details; presumed lost pre-1981.

XZ531-XZ532 (c/n 8370-8371) Shipped ex-USA (with XZ505 etc) to RNAY Wroughton. No further details; presumed lost pre-1981.

XZ533 (c/n 8372) Shipped ex-USA (with XZ505 etc) to RNAY Wroughton. To FTG. Final flight 24.1.81 with 'B' Flt in the Arabian Sea area when it displayed a hard left bias in flight. Recovered safely but reduced to spares. (TFH 9.20; 15 flights)

XZ534 (c/n 8373) Shipped ex-USA (with XZ505 etc) to RNAY Wroughton. Lost 17.1.78, details unkn.

XZ535-XZ540 (c/n 8374-8379)
XZ541-XZ546 (c/n 8577-8582)
Shipped ex-USA (with XZ505 etc) to RNAY Wroughton. No further details; presumed lost pre-1981.

Contract K/GW11B/597: 52 Shelduck D.1

Note that whilst these aircraft were consigned to RNAY Wroughton most were later transferred to RNAY Fleetlands for storage.

XZ745 (c/n 8638) Departed USA (Terminal Island, California) 22.12.76 aboard SS *Annie Johnson*. Shipped to London Docks; consigned to RNAY Wroughton. No further details.

XZ746 (c/n 8639) Shipped ex-USA (with XZ745 etc) to RNAY Wroughton. Shot down 22.4.81 by a Seacat missile whilst operating with 'A' Flt, FTG from RFA *Olna* in the Arabian Sea area. (TFH 2.35)

XZ747 (c/n 8640) Shipped ex-USA (with XZ745 etc) to RNAY Wroughton. Last flight 18.8.81 when operated by 'C' Flt, FTG from RFA *Olwen* in the Gulf area. Immediately after take-off the aircraft lost height until it landed heavily in the sea. Recovered but reduced to spares. (TFH 8.25; 18 flights)

XZ748 (c/n 8641) Shipped ex-USA (with XZ745 etc) to RNAY Wroughton; f/f 15.11.84 with 'B' Flt, FTG, location unkn, but fail-safed after 2 minutes. Recovered but not flown again.

XZ749 (c/n 8642) Shipped ex-USA (with XZ745 etc) to RNAY Wroughton. Shot down 11.10.81 whilst operating in the Irish Sea by 'B' Flt, FTG. (TFH 2.25; 3 Flights)

XZ750 (c/n 8643) Shipped ex-USA (with XZ745 etc) to RNAY Wroughton; f/f 23.5.83 in the Portland Exercise Area. Final flight on 9.9.83 in the North Atlantic when it suffered an engine failure whilst operating with 'A' Flt, FTG from HMCS *Preserver*. Recovered but never flown again. (TFH 1.40; 3 Flights)

XZ751 (c/n 8644) Shipped ex-USA (with XZ745 etc) to RNAY Wroughton; f/f 23.5.83 in the Portland Exercise Area. Final flight on 4.10.83 in the South Atlantic when it fail-safed whilst operating with 'A' Flt, FTG from RFA *Olwen*. Recovered safely but never flown again. (TFH 1.64; 3 Flights)

XZ752 (c/n 8645) Shipped ex-USA (with XZ745 etc) to RNAY Wroughton. No further details.

XZ753 (c/n 8646) Shipped ex-USA (with XZ745 etc) to RNAY Wroughton; f/f 8.6.83 in the South-West Approaches. Final flight on 30.9.85 in the South Atlantic whilst operating with 'A' Flt, FTG. Damaged in landing, recovered, but never flown again. (TFH 1.20; 2 flights)

XZ754 (c/n 8647) Shipped ex-USA (with XZ745 etc) to RNAY Wroughton; f/f 23.5.83 in the Portland Exercise Area. Second and last flight 11.6.85 with 'A' Flt, FTG in the Gibraltar Exercise Area.

XZ755 (c/n 8648) Shipped ex-USA (with XZ745 etc) to RNAY Wroughton. No further details.

XZ756 (c/n 8649) Shipped ex-USA (with XZ745 etc) to RNAY Wroughton; f/f 16.1.81 by 'B' Flt, FTG off RFA *Tidepool* in the Arabian Sea. Crashed 18.6.83 in the Falkland Islands immediately after launch from RFA *Tidespring*.

XZ757 (c/n 8650) Shipped ex-USA (with XZ745 etc) to RNAY Wroughton; f/f 6.10.83 by 'A' Flt, FTG off RFA *Olwen* in the South Atlantic. On the second flight of the day it flew erratically and fail-safed into the sea after 6 minutes. (TFH 0.50; 2 flights)

XZ758-XZ760 (c/n 8651-8653) Shipped ex-USA (with XZ745 etc) to RNAY Wroughton. Presumed w/o pre-1981.

XZ761 (c/n 8654) Shipped ex-USA (with XZ745 etc) to RNAY Wroughton; f/f 27.4.82 by 'B' Flt, FTG off RFA *Sir Geraint* off Ascension Island. Final flight 24.4.84, location unkn. Recovered but not flown again. (TFH 1.34; 4 flights)

XZ762 (c/n 8655) Shipped ex-USA (with XZ745 etc) to RNAY Wroughton; f/f 16.1.81 by 'B' Flt, FTG off RFA *Tidepool* in the Arabian Sea. Aircraft lost after 25 minutes after proving difficult to control.

XZ763 (c/n 8656) Shipped ex-USA (Terminal Island, California) 7.2.77 aboard

SS *San Francisco* to London Docks; consigned to RNAY Wroughton. Seriously damaged 24.4.84 by unspecified missile whilst operating with 'A' Flt, FTG. (TFH 6.29; 8 flights)

XZ764 (c/n 8657) Shipped ex-USA (with XZ763 etc); f/f 2.11.81 by 'B' Flt, FTG off Gibraltar. Final flight with 'A' Flt 12.11.85 in the Gibraltar Exercise Area. Recovered but not flown again. (TFH 2.29; 4 flights)

XZ765 (c/n 8658) Shipped ex-USA (with XZ763 etc) Made only one flight, on 11.11.85, with 'B' Flt, FTG in the Portland Exercise Area. (TFH 0.16)

XZ766 (c/n 8659) Shipped ex-USA (with XZ763 etc). Made only one flight, on 6.10.83, with 'A' Flt, FTG off RFA *Olwen* in the South Atlantic. Recovery parachute refused to deploy and aircraft crashed into a minefield after 10 minutes.

XZ767 (c/n 8660) Shipped ex-USA (with XZ763 etc); f/f 19.6.81 in the Portsmouth Exercise area. Shot down 26.3.83 by a Rapier missile whilst operating with 'A' Flt, FTG from RFA *Olna* in the Falkland Islands. (TFH 3.30; 6 flights)

XZ768 (c/n 8661) Shipped ex-USA (with XZ763 etc). Shot down by a Seawolf missile on 28.1.82 whilst with 'A' Flt, FTG, operating from HMS *Brilliant* off Plymouth. (TFH 3.05; 6 flights)

XZ769 (c/n 8662) Shipped ex-USA (with XZ763 etc); f/f 11.6.85 with 'A' Flt, FTG in the Gibraltar Exercise area. Final flight 13.11.85 off Gibraltar; recovered but not flown again. (TFH 2.43; 3 flights)

XZ770 (c/n 8663) Shipped ex-USA (with XZ763 etc). Made last of 14 flights on 11.6.85 when the recovery parachute deployed immediately after launch in the Gibraltar Exercise Area. Recovered but later scrapped. (TFH 7.25)

XZ771 (c/n 8664) Shipped ex-USA (with XZ763 etc); f/f 6.10.83 off RFA *Olwen* in the South Atlantic. Sustained direct missile strike 28.9.85 in the South Atlantic. (TFH 0.46; 2 flights)

XZ772 (c/n 8665) Shipped ex-USA (with XZ763 etc) Made its only flight on 30.9.83 from RFA *Olwen* in the South Atlantic; after 39 minutes it fail-safed into the sea.

XZ773 (c/n 8666) Shipped ex-USA (with XZ763 etc); f/f 28.9.83 with 'A' Flt, FTG from RFA *Olwen* in the South Atlantic. On 18.6.84 it was lost in the South Atlantic after being accidentally dropped by its Lynx recovery helicopter following a launch from RFA *Olna*. (TFH 2.43; 3 flights)

XZ774 (c/n 8667) Shipped ex-USA (with XZ763 etc) Made last of 12 flights on 7.3.83 when it was shot down by a Sea Sparrow missile whilst operating off Portland as part of 'STANAVFORLANT'.

(Note that whilst several NATO forces use Sea Sparrow, it was not adopted by the Royal Navy. It is likely, therefore, that XZ774 was destroyed by a ship of the Royal Netherlands Navy.)

XZ790 (c/n 8668) Shipped ex-USA (with XZ763 etc). Made last of 8 flights on 20.8.81 when, whilst operating with 'C' Flt, FTG from RFA *Olwen*, it was seen to lose height and then parachute into the sea. Recovered but later scrapped. (TFH 4.15; 8 flights)

XZ791 (c/n 8669) Shipped ex-USA (with XZ763 etc). Made just one flight in FTG service, on 15.11.84, with 'B' Flt, location unkn. Recovered and ret'd to Portland. Retained by FTG after move to Culdrose and allocated for preservation. Eventually collected by the 'Cornwall at War Museum' and conveyed to Davidstowe Moor airfield 26.9.09.

XZ792 (c/n 8670) Shipped ex-USA (with XZ763 etc). Made last of 12 flights on 13.11.85 when, whilst operating with 'A' Flt, FTG in the Gibraltar Exercise Area the engine failed after 4 minutes and it crashed into the sea. (TFH 7.31; 12 flights)

XZ793 (c/n 8671) Shipped ex-USA (with XZ763 etc). Made last of 7 flights on 6.10.81 when operating with 'C' Flt, FTG from RFA *Olwen* in the Gulf Zone. (TFH 5.20; 7 flights)

XZ794 (c/n 8672) Shipped ex-USA (with XZ763 etc). Made last of 6 flights on 17.6.84 when it was shot down whilst operating with 'B' Flt, FTG from RFA *Olna* in the South Atlantic. (TFH 2.36; 6 flights)

XZ795 (c/n 8673) Shipped ex-USA (with XZ763 etc); f/f 18.1.85 from HMS *Fearless* in mid-Atlantic. Second (and final) flight in South Atlantic 29.9.85, Recovered and repaired. Subsequently handed over to Museum of Army Flying, Middle Wallop for static display. (TFH 2.00; 2 flights)

XZ796 (c/n 8674) Shipped ex-USA (with XZ763 etc); f/f 23.5.83 in the Portland Exercise Area. Shot down 8.6.83 by a Sea Sparrow missile in the South-West Approaches. (TFH 1.08; 2 flights)

XZ797 (c/n 8675) Shipped ex-USA (with XZ763 etc); f/f 5.10.83 with 'A' Flt, FTG from RFA *Olwen* in the South Atlantic but lost radar and visual contact after 20 minutes. Recovery parachute deployed but aircraft never found.

XZ798 (c/n 8676) Shipped ex-USA (with XZ763 etc); f/f 8.11.81 with 'B' Flt, FTG for HMS *Arrow* in the Gibraltar Exercise Area. Lost on 13.11.85 whilst operating with 'A' Flt off Gibraltar. (TFH 2.29; 5 flights)

XZ799 (c/n 8677) Shipped ex-USA (with XZ763 etc); f/f 15.6.81 with 'C' Flt, FTG in the Portsmouth area. Named "BRILLIANT". W/o 25.3.83 during a flight from RFA *Olna* in the Falkland Islands when, after 57 minutes it became lost (visually) in low cloud and presumed crashed. The wreck has never been found. (TFH 4.12; 5 flights)

XZ800 (c/n 8678) Shipped ex-USA (with XZ763 etc). Lost on 27.4.82 during operations from RFA *Sir Geraint* off Ascension Island when after 10 minutes of flight airspeed dropped too low to sustain level flight and it dived into the sea. (TFH 12.42; 18 flights)

XZ801 (c/n 8679) Shipped ex-USA (with XZ763 etc); f/f 28.9.83 with 'A' Flt, FTG off RFA *Olwen* in the South Atlantic. Seriously damaged in the same area on 3.10.83; recovered but not repaired. (TFH 1.46; 2 flights)

XZ802 (c/n 8680) Shipped ex-USA (with XZ763 etc); f/f 30.9.83 with 'A' Flt, FTG off RFA *Olwen* but shot down after 10 minutes.

XZ803 (c/n 8681) Shipped ex-USA (with XZ763 etc); f/f 4.10.83 with 'A' Flt, FTG off RFA *Olwen* in the South Atlantic. Shot down 16.1.85 by a Seacat missile whilst operating from HMS *Fearless* in mid-Atlantic. (TFH 1.19; 2 flights)

XZ804 (c/n 8682) Shipped ex-USA (with XZ763 etc); f/f 23.8.83 with 'A' Flt, FTG off HMCS *Preserver* in the North Atlantic. Second and final flight off the same ship in the same area 9.9.83. (TFH 1.36; 2 flights)

XZ805 (c/n 8683) Shipped ex-USA (with XZ763 etc); f/f 23.8.83 with 'A' Flt, FTG off HMCS *Preserver* in the North Atlantic. Final flight 24.4.84, location unkn. (TFH 3.29; 4 flights)

XZ806 (c/n 8684) Shipped ex-USA (with XZ763 etc); f/f 9.9.83 with 'A' Flt, FTG off

Shelduck and Chukar target drones were operated concurrently by the RNPTA from 1971 to 1985. In this 1973 view Chukar I XW994 shows the effect of a heavy landing in the sea whilst all-red Shelduck D.1 XW943, in the background, looks very much the worse for wear and tear. (Royal Navy)

HMCS *Preserver* in the North Atlantic. Final flight 24.4.84, location unkn. (TFH 2:02; 3 flights)

XZ807 (c/n 8685) Shipped ex-USA (with XZ763 etc); f/f 23.8.83 with 'A' Flt, FTG off HMCS *Preserver*. Shot down 23.4.84 by a Rapier missile, location unkn. (TFH 1.07; 5 flights)

XZ808 (c/n 8686) Shipped ex-USA (with XZ763 etc). To FTG. Written-off 2.3.81 when, whilst operating with 'A' Flt, FTG off RFA *Tidepool* it became lost on radar at 6 miles and presumed crashed in the Arabian Sea. (TFH 2.50; 4 flights)

XZ809 (c/n 8687) Shipped ex-USA (with XZ763 etc); f/f 31.8.83 with 'A' Flt, FTG off HMCS *Preserver* in the North Atlantic. Lost on a sortie 23.4.84, details unkn. (TFH 0.55; 3 flights)

XZ810 (c/n 8688) Shipped ex-USA (with XZ763 etc) No further details, presumed lost pre-1983.

XZ811 (c/n 8689) Shipped ex-USA (with XZ763 etc). No further details, presumed lost pre-1983.

Contract MGW11B/906:
24 Shelduck D.1

Note that as a result of an MoD (Contracts Branch) administrative error the identities ZA525 to ZA535 were also allocated to MATS-B target drones. When the error was later realised the MATS-B targets were re-serialled as ZB525-ZB535.

ZA500 (c/n 8878) Shipped ex-USA 3.79 to FTG Store, Fleetlands; f/f 17.1.85 with 'A' Flt, FTG off HMS *Fearless* in Mid-Atlantic but shot down by a Seacat missile after 47 minutes.

ZA501-ZA503 (c/n 8879-8881) Shipped ex-USA to FTG Store, Fleetlands (with ZA500 etc). No further details.

ZA504 (c/n 8882) Shipped USA to FTG Store, Fleetlands (with ZA500 etc). To FTG and flew the last of 4 flights 30.9.85 in the South Atlantic.

ZA505 (c/n 8883) Shipped USA to FTG Store, Fleetlands (with ZA500 etc); f/f 16.1.85 (for 43 minutes) with 'A' Flt/FTG off HMS *Fearless* in the Mid-Atlantic Area. 2nd and final flight 17.1.86 in the South Atlantic when shot down. (TFH 2.09; 3 flights)

ZA506-ZA509 (c/n 8884-8887) Shipped USA to FTG Store, Fleetlands (with ZA500 etc). No further details.

ZA525 (c/n 8888) Shipped USA to FTG Store, Fleetlands (with ZA500 etc); f/f 18.1.85 with 'A' Flt, FTG off HMS *Fearless* in the Mid-Atlantic Area but shot down after 53 minutes by a Seacat missile.

ZA526-ZA531 (c/n 8889-8894) Shipped USA to FTG Store, Fleetlands (with ZA500 etc). No further details.

ZA532 (c/n 8895) Shipped USA to FTG Store, Fleetlands (with ZA500 etc); f/f 18.1.85 with 'A' Flt, FTG off HMS *Fearless* in the Mid-Atlantic Area but suffered a gyro failure after 5 minutes. Recovered safely. On its 3rd flight from *Fearless* (on 18.1.85) it was lost during the recovery process. (TFH 1.09; 3 flights)

ZA533-ZA538 (c/n 8896-8901) Shipped USA to FTG Store, Fleetlands (with ZA500 etc). No further details.

The second (of two) orders for Chukar I targets accounted for just 13 units, including XZ154 seen here on its zero-length launcher on 24 May 1976. The engine ignitor cable is attached to the top of the fuselage whilst the air-start hose is connected to lower fuselage. Not fitted is the JATO rocket motor. The wing-tip pylons are being used, in this instance, to carry flares, used on some sorties to provide additional visual and infra-red augmentation. (792 Squadron Archive)

MQM-74A Chukar I

The original design concept that led to the Chukar range was established by Northrop in late-1964. Preliminary designs were largely influenced by an advanced version of the Radioplane RP-76 rocket-powered vehicle. The new target, initially referred to by the Northrop-Ventura designation NV-105 had an inverted "Y" empennage with elevons, a 12-inch (30cm) diameter fuselage and a delta wing without ailerons. A Williams Research Corporation WR24 turbojet engine was fitted into the rear fuselage for which an airscoop was installed in the rear fuselage underside.

Design work on the prototype, the NV-105A, was completed in 1965. Four examples were built at the Van Nuys facility; one as a launch-test vehicle, the others as flight-test drones. For launching, the NV-105A test vehicles were fitted with two Mk.34 JATO rockets mounted on each side of the fuselage. Initial flight tests were carried out at the El Centro Range, California but an electrical connector failure caused one of the boosters not to ignite on the first flight and the target crashed immediately after take-off. Subsequent launches were more successful and led to interest from the US Navy.

Northrop designed the NV-105A as a lightweight target for anti-gunnery, surface-to-air, air-to-air missile training, and weapon systems evaluation. Production of the NV-105A began in 1966 against a US Navy contract by which time the aircraft had been designated MQM-74A. The name Chukar was adopted from the beginning and the MQM-74A became the Chukar D.I.

Chukar D.I entered operational use with the RNPTA Squadron in 1971 but production of Chukar I ended in 1973 by which time some 2,300 examples had been built, mostly for the US Navy. Against two separate contracts 23 examples were bought by the Ministry of Defence/Procurement Executive. 13 of these (XZ152-XZ164) were among the last examples of Chukar I to be manufactured.

Apart from a series of flights carried out at Aberporth few details are known of Chukar D.1 operational usage. The Aberporth flights, which consisted of 10 launches, took place between 7-16 June 1976 and were made by a Fleet Target Group Detachment. The Chukars (which included XW992, XZ155 and XZ159) flew presentations for the Aberporth shore-based Sea Dart system on 14 June, followed by air-to-air engagements with Red Top-equipped Lightnings on 15 June and by 29 Squadron Phantoms (Sparrow AAM) on 15/16 June. At least one Chukar was shot down by a Sparrow missile whilst another was destroyed when it impacted an adjacent launcher following an asymmetric JATO burn.[15]

---

15 Asymmetric JATO burns accounted for the loss of several Chukars during its long career as a target. On this occasion the Chukar impacted with an adjacent launcher and spread itself – and its fuel – over a large area of the Rangehead. Two of the launch crew suffered burns from the fuel spillage although both recovered satisfactorily.

Chukar D.2 XZ958, seen at the Portland Open Day 30 July 1978, displays the standard Chukar scheme applied to early deliveries. This was a more "orangy" base and with white fin and stabilizers. Note the construction number 0120 on the centre lower fuselage (Michael I Draper).

MQM-74C Chukar II

In 1973 Northrop introduced an improved version of the MQM-74A Chukar I with an uprated Williams WR24-7 jet engine giving increased power and improved performance. The new variant was placed into immediate production and adopted by the US Navy as the MQM-74C although it was more widely known as Chukar II. The first UK procurement of Chukar D.2, as it became known in British service, accounted for just ten examples (allocated serials XZ950-XZ959 on 24 December 1976). Most, if not all, of this batch were initially conveyed to RAE Aberporth to take part in the Royal Navy Chukar II formal acceptance trials. Five targets were launched across the Range over three days (24-26 April 1978); all were recovered safely.

Chukar D.2 entered British service in 1978 after the first batch, having completed acceptance trials, were conveyed from Aberporth to Portland to join the Fleet Target Group (formerly the RNPTA, re-titled in 1974).

Like its earlier version, Chukar D.2 was zero- launched from either a ground or ship-based platform using two jettisonable JATO rocket motors. The Chukar's own jet engine provided a 190lb (86.4kg) thrust at sea level and for flight profiles between 10,000 and 30,000' the target could fly at up to Mach 0.81, falling to Mach 0.72 at low level.

On-board autopilot and remote control equipment allowed Chukar to meet a wide variety of operating profiles, including an ability to operate out to 100 n.miles or at line-of-sight altitudes down to 200ft at relatively close range (although UK operations did not allow flight at lower than 1,000ft). A 'clean' Chukar, i.e. no external add-ons, could undertake steady state 4g manoeuvre turns.

Throughout its 33 years of continuous UK service Chukar D.2 underwent a number of modification-fits, mostly visual, infra-red and radar augmentation systems either incorporated internally or as wing-tip pylon attachments.

Most of these add-ons were, in the first instance, tested at RAE Aberporth. The first of these involved evaluating the role of Chukar as a target-towing drone with a trailed target that was being specially developed in the UK for Chukar. Over three days, 8-10 November 1982, five Chukars (XZ956, ZB708, ZD292, ZD301 and ZD302) were launched, two of which were launched "clean"; the other three with TOW fits. Apart from one of the "clean" Chukars (ZD301) being lost when it "nosed-over" the Aberporth cliff and crashed into the sea immediately after launch, all of the flights were successful. On each occasion the Chukars were accompanied by an RAE Llanbedr Hawk T.1 camera-ship.

Further development trials took place at Aberporth in April 1984 when a number of Chukars (ZA907, ZD674, ZD677, ZD680, ZD683 and ZD688) were launched for MDI and SART trials. The **M**iss **D**istance **I**ndicator became a standard fit for many of the UK's unmanned target aircraft, it being able to judge if a missile engagement was sufficiently close to determine a hit had the missile been live or fitted with a proximity fuse. On the other hand, SART – a **S**emi-**A**ctive **R**adar **T**arget – was a more complex system (having been originally developed for Jindivik but later modified to fit Chukar) and was a development of the system evaluated in November 1982.

SART was in fact a non-recoverable 4.5" diameter towed body which was streamed to a maximum of 500ft behind the Chukar. The SART pod was normally mounted onto the port wing-tip pylon, a dummy SART body being mounted on the starboard wing-tip to even the balance. SART had originally been developed for use with Jindivik and as a target for Sparrow AAMs, later being modified to suit Skyflash. When Sea Dart proved itself to be a somewhat voracious consumer of Chukar targets the SART concept was re-packaged and miniaturized (as the SART 5) to fit Chukar. Ultimately the MATRA/Marconi SART 5b Mk.2, a J-Band towed system specifically designed to decoy J-Band radar-guided missiles, became the standard SART kit for Chukar D.2 .

The SART trials carried out in April 1984 were simply early proving flights. Live presentations of SART-equipped Chukar D.2s began at Aberporth on 3-4 July 1984 when five Chukars (ZD674, ZD677, ZD680, ZD683 and ZD688) were deployed towing SART Mk.5 targets for Sea Dart missiles fired from HMS *Newcastle*. In time the primary role for the Fleet Target Group's Chukar D.2 fleet was to provide a target for Sea Dart by using a towed SART as standard kit.

Almost a year after the initial Sea Dart-Chukar trials, another series of trials took place at Aberporth to test the introduction of a PLUMER modification and to determine whether Chukar D.2 was suitable as a target for RAF Tornado ADV with Marconi A124 Foxhunter radar.

The PLUMER consisted of a 32.8-inch (833mm) long tubular steel-cased pod, 5-inch (127mm) diameter with an end nozzle so as to provide an augmented Infra-Red signature in the medium and long waveband. The pod was mounted on the port wing-tip. Fuel pumped into the PLUMER from the Chukar's own fuel tank was then burnt to provide a similar signature to that of the exhaust of a jet-powered aircraft. The PLUMER was triggered by an electro-explosive igniter fired by a command received by the Chukar. A second igniter was available if the first failed to ignite the fuel and once ignited the flame could be set to two levels, either full burn for signature generation or pilot light to conserve fuel. When fitted with a PLUMER pod on the port wing-tip, Chukars were usually fitted with a CHAFF/FLARE pod on the starboard wing-tip. Chukar D.2s fitted with a PLUMER were almost exclusively for RAF operations.

The PLUMER fit was evaluated at Aberporth between 22 April to 1 May 1985 when at least eleven Chukar D.2s (ZD308, ZD312, ZD314, ZD502, ZD530, ZD682, ZD687, ZE455, ZE456, ZE483 and ZE484) were launched off the Welsh Range. All of the Chukars were recovered satisfactorily.

Although most operational Chukar sorties were with regular Royal Navy shipboard deployments around the world, such as the South Atlantic, the Arabian Sea, the Gibraltar Exercise Area and, closer to home, in the South-West Approaches, there was an increasing tendency to use Chukar as a target for the Royal Air Force. Trial air-to-air "dummy" engagements began in February 1986 across the Aberporth Range using BAe Warton's Tornado development aircraft ZA254 as well as A&AEE's Tornado ADV ZA267 equipped with Skyflash AAMs. Later trials involved a Buccaneer S.2 from RAE Bedford. Chukar was deemed suitable as a target for live firings in February 1987 when a number of Chukars were launched off Aberporth to act as targets for 43 Squadron Phantoms, equipped with Skyflash and AIM-9 Sidewinders. At least two Chukars (ZD678 and ZE999) were shot down.

With the withdrawal of Shelduck in July 1986 and the decision to cease Medium Range 4.5-inch Range Anti-Aircraft Gunnery, the volume of operational work involving the Fleet Target Group decreased markedly. As a direct consequence, a major reduction in FTG strength subsequently took place in 1992 leaving just an HQ Flight and one operational Flight for overseas deployments. However, the increased demand for Chukar as a target for the RAF involved a number of examples being deployed to RAE Aberporth on a semi-permanent basis.

One of the most unusual Chukar operations took place at Aberporth in mid-1993. With the dismantling of the Berlin Wall and the reunification of Germany, the West German Luftwaffe acquired, virtually overnight, a wing of former East German Air Force MiG-29s together with an assortment of Soviet air-to-air missiles, including AA-8 (*'Aphid'*), AA-10 (*'Alamo'*) and AA-11 (*'Archer'*). The objective of the Aberporth trial was to demonstrate the safe carriage and release of these weapons; also to conduct firings with live seeker heads against targets across the Aberporth Range in order to assess the performance of the complete MiG-29 weapon system.[16]

One MiG-29 (29+20) was deployed from Preshen (on the German/Polish border) to RAF Valley on 4 May 1993. The first phase of the trial was simply to stage a "shake-down" so as to check that the MiG's systems were compatable with those on the Aberporth Range. The MiG-29 flew several sorties from Valley, including one with a 120 Squadron Nimrod MR.2P (XV226) before returning to Wittmund, German on 10 May.[17]

The second phase of the MiG-29 trial took place in July 1993. On that occasion two WTD-6 aircraft (MiG-29

A Chukar D.2 is carefully winched back onto the deck of HMS Regent *after being recovered from the sea. The Chukar shows a remarkable lack of damage.*

---

16 *Fireflash to Skyflash* by Mike Hollingsworth & Gordon Campbell Owen.
17 Aircraft details first published by BARG *British Aviation Review* June 1993.

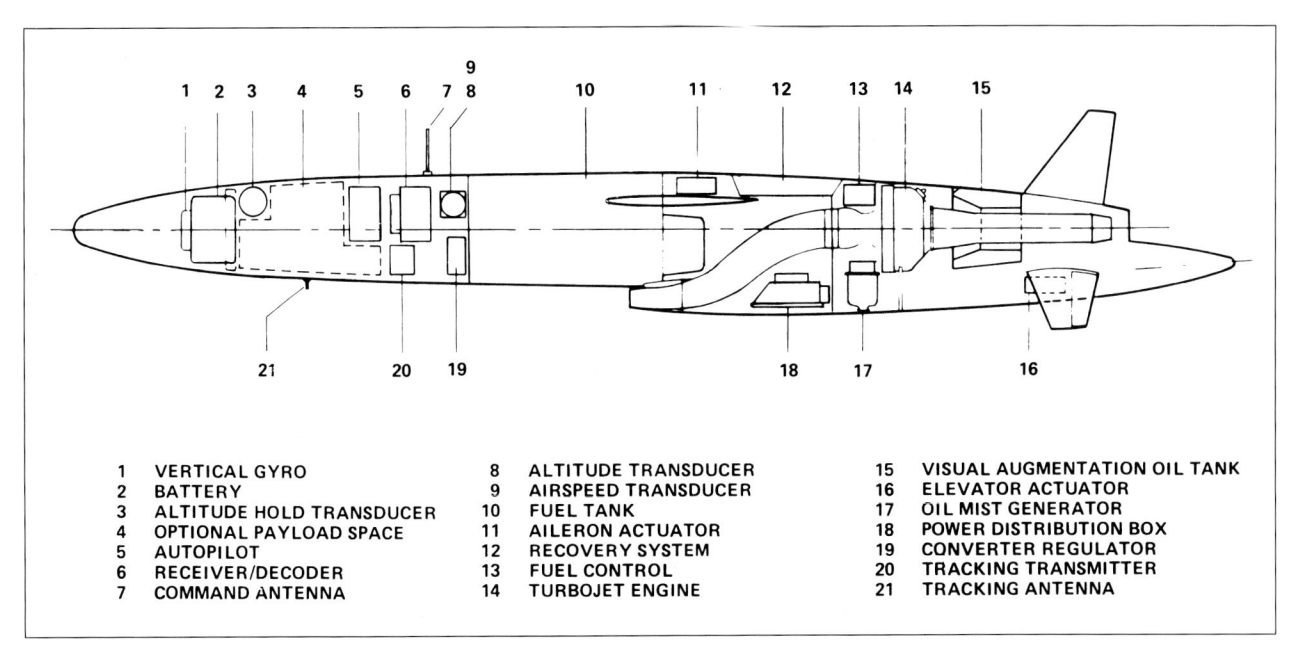

1	VERTICAL GYRO	8	ALTITUDE TRANSDUCER	15	VISUAL AUGMENTATION OIL TANK
2	BATTERY	9	AIRSPEED TRANSDUCER	16	ELEVATOR ACTUATOR
3	ALTITUDE HOLD TRANSDUCER	10	FUEL TANK	17	OIL MIST GENERATOR
4	OPTIONAL PAYLOAD SPACE	11	AILERON ACTUATOR	18	POWER DISTRIBUTION BOX
5	AUTOPILOT	12	RECOVERY SYSTEM	19	CONVERTER REGULATOR
6	RECEIVER/DECODER	13	FUEL CONTROL	20	TRACKING TRANSMITTER
7	COMMAND ANTENNA	14	TURBOJET ENGINE	21	TRACKING ANTENNA

Chukar D.2 general interior arrangement showing the basic configuration without ancilliary equipment.

29+18 and MiG-29UB 29+21) deployed to Valley on 5 July. Whilst Llanbedr launched several Jindiviks (in SART-mode) for the AA-10 AAM and other Jindiviks with TOW FLARE packs presented for AA-8 firings, Aberporth launched eight Chukar D.2s to provide air-to-air targets for the MiG's AA-11 missiles. The Chukar had been selected for the AA-11 in the belief that each firing was likely to result in a direct hit – and the loss of a Chukar was less of a financial burden to bear than that of a Jindivik! In the event, only one Chukar (ZE711) was actually shot down to what, on this occasion, could perhaps realistically be described as "enemy fire".

The MiG-29s used a variety of attack profiles against the targets, each sortie being accompanied by an RAE Llanbedr Hawk T.1 camera-ship. The results provided ample information necessary for an "In Service Clearance" for the German Air Force.

Despite the frequency of Chukar operations at RAE Aberporth, the Fleet Target Group remained headquartered in a small complex on a corner of RNAS Portland. Because of a restriction in available space at Portland most unflown Chukars were initially stored away at RNAY Fleetlands (and later at RNAY Wroughton) and only released to the Fleet Target Group at Portland as and when the Group required them. However, plans to close the Portland base were first mooted in 1996 and as a result the Fleet Target Group received warning of a transfer to RNAS Culdrose. Work started on a dedicated target workshop and administration facility as well as a separate storage facility in late 1997. The move to Culdrose finally took place in June/July 1998 and at the same time all Chukar D.2s held in storage elsewhere were also transferred to Culdrose.

Steps to seek a successor to Chukar II were first taken in 1997 when a new joint RN/RAF requirement was endorsed and put out to tender. What became termed as the Replacement Aerial Subsonic Target (RAST) was seen as possessing higher overall performance and a much-improved low level capability. The natural choice, in many respects, was the Northrop BQM-74C Chukar III, examples of which had been evaluated at Aberporth but it seemed the high procurement cost became a major prohibitive factor.[18] The winner of the RAST competition was the Italian company, Meteor, in partnership with GEC Marconi. Initial delivery of Mirach 100/5 target drones for tests and trials evaluation was in November 1998 and Mirach 100/5 finally entered service in April 2001 as the Chukar's successor.

Procurement of new-build Chukar D.I and Chukar D.2 targets for the Royal Navy eventually reached 250 examples. Several others were assembled from damaged or spare parts while a small number (thought to be eleven) were acquired, at the end of 1993 in the Middle East from a Northrop Detachment based in Saudi Arabia. These aircraft were taken onto charge and (following a request by the Fleet Target Group to MoD) were issued the serials ZH764-774 inclusive.

The last series of operational Chukar flights took place on 14/15 May 2001 when four targets (ZG631, ZG676, ZG684, ZH768) were launched from Aberporth for AIM-9L Sidewinder firings by Tornado F.3s of 111 Squadron. The 'honour' of making the final flight fell to ZH768 which survived two air-to-air attacks on the day and although it was not hit, the Chukar was not recovered; instead it was flown into the sea off Aberporth. Somehow it seemed too great an irony that what was procured solely as a subsonic target drone for the Royal Navy should finally fall to an attack by the RAF.

Colour Schemes

All Chukars operated in an overall orange factory-finish with white extremities: nose cone, wings, fin, tailplane and tail cone. Apart from the manufacturer's serial number

---

18 Aberporth archives record that "four Chukar III flights for non-firing trials by the GWS30/T909/Sea Dart system on HMS *Coventry*." These are recorded as the first flights in the UK by a Chukar III. Unfortunately no date is recorded, nor any aircraft identities. However one unconfirmed theory suggests that ZH250 & ZH251 were allocated to Chukar III for evaluation purposes.

MQM-74A Chukar I and MQM-74C Chukar II – UK Contracts

Contract	Contract Date	Serial Range	Allotment Date	Quantity	Remarks
K20C/115/CB20C6	16.7.71	XW990-XW999	17.6.71	10	MQM-74A/Chukar D.1
K/GW41B/286	17.12.73	XZ152-XZ164	29.11.73	13	MQM-74A/Chukar D.1
MGW11b/644/CB	3.2.77	XZ950-XZ959	24.12.76	10	MQM-74C/Chukar D.2
MGW11b/842/CB	12.6.78	ZA155-ZA164	12.5.78	10	MQM-74C/Chukar D.2
MGW11b/1028	2.4.79	ZA903-ZA912 ZA925-ZA929	15.3.79	15	MQM-74C/Chukar D.2
		ZA512-ZA516	11.7.79	5	MQM-74C/Chukar D.2

Due to a clerical error within MoD Contracts Branch the final five aircraft added to Contract 1028 were allocated with 'compromised' serials ZA512-ZA516. When the extent of this administrative mistake was fully appreciated the easy solution was to officially alter the prefix letters and ZA512-ZA516 were re-allotted as ZB512-516. However the incorrect serials had already been applied to the targets and never altered. In fact a number of these targets had already been expended by the time the error had been realised.

Contract	Contract Date	Serial Range	Allotment Date	Quantity	Remarks
ML22A/109	3.6.80	ZB695-ZB709	6.5.80	15	MQM-74C/Chukar D.2
ML22A/255	8.12.81	ZD290-ZD314	17.11.81	25	MQM-74C/Chukar D.2
	Amended 30.9.82	ZD530-ZD533 ZD550-ZD553	21.9.82	8	MQM-74C/Chukar D.2
ML22A/412	Not known	ZD500-ZD508 ZD521-ZD526	21.9.82	15	MQM-74C/Chukar D.2
ML22A/420	15.12.82	ZD674-ZD688	1.12.82	15	MQM-74C/Chukar D.2
ML11A/1331	Not known	ZE452-ZE466	18.4.84	15	MQM-74C/Chukar D.2
		ZE483-ZE490	18.6.84	8	MQM-74C/Chukar D.2
		ZE710-ZE724	29.10.84	15	MQM-74C/Chukar D.2
ML11A/1414	Not known	ZE988-ZE992 ZE996-ZE999	31.1.85	9	MQM-74C/Chukar D.2
ML11A/1489	Not known	ZF603-ZF617	19.12.85	15	MQM-74C/Chukar D.2

Although Contract ML11A/1489 was officially allocated the block ZF603-ZF617 on 19.12.85 the Fleet Target Group painted the aircraft as ZF603-607/619-628. This was a result of apparently confusing the manufacturer's number and placing the prefix ZF, eg ZF621 is known to have a Centre Fuselage Section No.621. It remains unconfirmed that those targets painted as ZF619-ZF628 were done so because their "c/ns" were 619-628. As a consequence Chukars ZF622 and ZF627 are 'compromised' with ZF622 PA-31 Navajo and an export Hawk T.64 for the Kuwaiti Air Force.

Contract	Contract Date	Serial Range	Allotment Date	Quantity	Remarks
ML11A/1573	Not known	ZG335-ZG349 ZG364-ZG368	11.12.86	20	MQM-74C/Chukar D.2
ML11A/1623	Not known	ZG630-ZG650 ZG665-ZG685 ZG693-ZG700	6.8.87	50	MQM-74C/Chukar D.2
?	Not known	ZH248-ZH251	28.2.90	4	MQM-74C/Chukar D.2

ZH248 and ZH249 are 'compromised' serials, being duplicated with part of an order for Vigilant T.1 gliders.

		ZH764-ZH774	4.1.94	11	MQM-74C/Chukar D.2
–	–	ZJ481	4.2.97	1	MQM-74C/Chukar D.2
Total				289	

Disposition of all Shelduck and Chukar drones could be seen at a glance by a constantly-updated wall-chart at the Fleet Target Groups's Portland HQ. The situation seen here, as of 31 March 1983, shows 25 Shelducks held at Portland, including two veterans XW109 and XX817, and 46 Chukar IIs. Six Shelducks were detached to RFA 'Olna' and four were permanently detached to Gibraltar. Of note is the fact that 29 Shelducks are shown as being in store at RNAY Fleetlands and whilst XZ804-807/809 are shown, the remaining 24 are accounted for by new aircraft ZA500-509/525-538 in crates and in storage but as yet not taken onto charge. (XZ808 had already been written-off on 2 March 1981 and it must be assumed that XZ810 and XZ811 had also been written-off when this wall chart was photographed. (Michael I Draper)

The situation one year on (31 March 1984) and the stock of Shelduck has marginally increased with six detached to RFA 'Olmeda'. Over the year, five of the most recent Shelduck delivery (ZA500, 504, 505, 525 & 532) have emerged from the Fleetlands Store (leaving nineteen still in store). Stocks of Chukar D.2 have been boosted by the arrival at Portland of fifteen new examples (ZD674-ZD688) over Christmas 1982 albeit fourteen have been removed over the 12-month period. ZA164, ZB705, ZD904, ZD291, ZD293, ZD501, ZD522-524, ZD526, ZD533, ZD550, ZD551 & ZD553 were all lost during exercises. Unexplained, however, is the absence of Chukar II ZD309. (Michael I Draper)

Targets for the Royal Navy 201

Chukar I Technical Data	
Power Plant	Williams WR24-6 (YJ400-WR400)
Wing Span	5 ft 6 in (1.69 m)
Length overall	11 ft 9 in (3.58 m)
Body diameter	1 ft 2 in (0.36 m)
Height overall	2 ft 3 in (0.70 m)
Weight empty	233 lb (106 kg)
Max launch weight	425 lb (192 kg)
Max level speed	425 kt (489 mph; 787 km/h) at 20,000 ft (6,100 m)
Max rate of climb	5,500 ft (1,676 m)/min
Service ceiling	40,000 ft (12,200 m)
Range at max speed	237 n miles (273 statute miles; 439 km)

Chukar II Technical Data	
Power Plant	Williams WR24-7 (J400-WR-401)
Wing Span	5 ft 8 in (1.73 m)
Length overall	12 ft 8.5 in (3.87 m)
Body diameter	1 ft 2 in (0.36 m)
Height overall	2 ft 4 in (0.71 m)
Weight empty	283 lb (128 kg)
Max launch weight	492 lb (223 kg)
Max level speed	515 kt (593 mph; 954 km/h) at 20,000 ft (6,100 m)
Max rate of climb	5,840 ft (1,780 m)/min with full fuel load
Service ceiling	40,000 ft (12,200 m)
Range at max speed	330 n miles (380 statute miles; 611 km)

(which appeared in white on the lower centre fuselage) all lettering was applied in black. Later examples were delivered in the same factory finish but with white restricted to nose and tail cones.

ZH248 and ZH249 (and probably others within this small batch) were painted in a markedly darker orange than standard UK Chukars.

Pre-launch checks for Chukar I XW996, on 14 November 1975, offer the chance to study the air-intake, the power distribution box and one of two oil-mist generators. Also clearly visible in this view is one of two JATO rocket motors strapped to the fuselage and used to launch the Chukar from a zero-length launcher. Each JATO rocket burnt for about one second and developed a nominal thrust of approximately 2,400lb (1,089kg). A spring-loaded ejector mechanism was incorporated in each carrier to force the carrier and spent JATO bottle down and away from the aircraft after rocket-motor burnout. (792 Squadron Archive)

MQM-74 Chukar
Individual Aircraft Histories

**Contract K20C/115/CB20C6:
10 Chukar I**

XW990-XW998 (c/n C1-C9) Shipped ex-USA (Berth 228D, Terminal Island, California) 8.12.71 aboard SS *Falstria* (Scan Star Lines). Conveyed to RNAY Wroughton and stored pending issue to RNPTA. Service details unkn except for XW994 below.

XW994 (c/n C5) Donated to FAAM date unknown and displayed. To RNAY Wroughton store 12.8.93. Returned to Yeovilton 30.11.99 and displayed in Cobham Hall.

XW999 (c/n C10) Shipped ex-USA (with XW990 etc) to RNAY Wroughton Service details unkn. Retained by 792 Sqdn, Culdrose for static display purposes. Eventually donated to the 'Cornwall at War Museum' and conveyed to Davidstowe Moor airfield 26.9.09.

**Contract K/GW41B/286:
13 Chukar I**

XZ152-XZ164 (c/n 0028-0040) Shipped ex-USA (Berth 231, Terminal Island, California) 6.3.74 aboard SS *Columbia Star* to London docks and on to RNAY Wroughton for storage pending issue to RNPTA. Service details not known.

**Contract MGW11B/644/CB:
10 Chukar II**

Note that Northrop records show XZ950-959 as having c/ns 0115-0124 running concurrently but observations by the author shows c/ns as listed below.

XZ950 (c/n 0119) Shipped ex-USA (Berth 231, Terminal Island, California) 2.12.77 aboard SS *Axel Johnson* to London docks and on to RNPTA Portland; f/f 24.4.78 at Aberporth. Shot down by a Sea Dart missile 25.3.80 whilst operating with 'B' Flt/RNPTA. (TFH 1.36; 3 flights)

XZ951 (c/n 0122) (Manufacturer's plate shows build date 30.9.77.) Shipped ex-USA (with XZ950 etc) Believed stored until 27.2.79 (or 27.2.78) when flown by 'B' Flt/RNPTA for 34 minutes. Although recovered safely no other flights are recorded.

XZ952 (c/n 0123) Shipped ex-USA (with XZ950 etc). Believed stored until 9.4.81 when flown by C Flt/RNPTA in the North Atlantic for 13 minutes. Although recovered safely no other flights are recorded.

XZ953 (c/n 0121) Shipped ex-USA (with XZ950 etc). Believed f/f 24.4.78 at Aberporth on a Chukar II trials flight. On 8.4.81, and operating in the Eastern Atlantic off RFA *Olwen* with B Flt/RNPTA during Exercise *Springtrain* target suffered 'lock problems' near firing ships and therefore terminated. (Other reports suggest the drone ran out of fuel.) Not found and presumed sunk. (TFH 3.35; 5 flights)

XZ954 (c/n 0124) Shipped ex-USA (with XZ950 etc). Believed f/f 24.4.78 at Aberporth on a Chukar II trials flight. Flown by "C" Flight; FTG from RFA *Olwen* 5.3.81 during Ex *Springtrain* but lost control at 14 miles and after 0.34hrs flight; recovery parachute deployed by command but aircraft not found and presumed sunk. (Other reports state that the drone dived under power into the Eastern Atlantic during Ex *Springtrain*.) (TFH 5.37; 8 flights)

XZ955 (c/n 0118) Shipped ex-USA (with XZ950 etc). Believed f/f 24.4.78 at Aberporth on a Chukar II trials flight. On 12.6.78 it was flown by "B" Flight but lost after 11mins. (TFH 0.37; 2 flights)

XZ956 (c/n 0115) (Manufacturer's plate shows build date 14.10.77.) Shipped ex-USA (with XZ950 etc); f/f 24.4.78 at Aberporth on a Chukar II trials flight. On 4.7.84 it was shot down by a Sea Dart missile whilst operating from RFA *Resource* by "B" Flight, FTG in the South-West Approaches. (TFH 8.05; 16 flights)

XZ957 (c/n 0117) (Manufacturer's plate shows build date 29.9.77.) Shipped ex-USA (with XZ950 etc); f/f 28.2.79 by 'B' Flt/RNPTA but lost after 7 minutes due to radar trouble.

XZ958 (c/n 0120) Shipped ex-USA (with XZ950 etc); f/f 12.7.78. On 28.2.79 it was shot down by a Sea Dart missile. (TFH 0.55; 2 flights)

XZ959 (c/n 0116) Shipped ex-USA (with XZ950 etc); f/f 13.7.78. On 26.3.80 it was shot down by a Sea Dart missile whilst operating with "B" Flight, FTG. (TFH 2.47; 5 flights)

**Contract MGW11B/842/CB:
10 Chukar II**

ZA155 (c/n 0197) Shipped ex-USA 8.3.79 to RNPTA Portland; f/f 27.6.79 with 'C' Flt, RNPTA but shot down by a Sea Slug 2 missile after just 9 minutes of flight.

ZA156 (c/n 0198) Shipped ex-USA (with ZA155 etc) to RNPTA Portland; f/f 27.6.79 with 'C' Flt, RNPTA. On 23.7.82, and whilst operating with 'A' Flt/RNPTA it was

An unidentified Chukar D.1 (from the XW990-999 batch) lies inverted in the water whilst a swimmer begins to secure it for recovery

Targets for the Royal Navy 203

shot down by a Sea Dart missile in the South-West Approaches. (Other reports state the date to be 22.7.82.) (TFH 4.59; 8 flights)

ZA157 (c/n 0199) Shipped ex-USA (with ZA155 etc) to RNPTA Portland; f/f 22.4.81 from RFA *Olna* in the Arabian Sea. On 30.4.81, and in the same area, it was lost after a probable error by the pilot. (TFH 2.04; 3 flights)

ZA158 (c/n 0200) Shipped ex-USA (with ZA155 etc) to RNPTA Portland and stored; f/f 28.6.79 by 'C' Flt/FTG. On 27.5.84, and whilst operating with 'A' Flt/FTG from RFA *Resource* in the Palma area it was shot down by a Sea Dart missile. (TFH 5.04; 9 flights)

ZA159 (c/n 0201) Shipped ex-USA (with ZA155 etc) to RNPTA Portland; f/f 28.6.79 by 'C' Flt/FTG. On 9.4.81 it was destroyed by a Sea Slug missile whilst operating in the North Atlantic from RFA *Olwen* by 'B' Flt/FTG during Exercise *Springtrain*. (TFH 1.57; 4 flights)

ZA160 (c/n 0202) Shipped ex-USA (with ZA155 etc) to RNPTA Portland and stored; f/f 27.8.80 by 'C' Flt/FTG. On 17.3.82 it was lost in the Arabian Sea whilst operating with 'A' Flt/FTG from RFA *Olna*. (TFH 2.40; 5 flights)

ZA161 (c/n 0203) Shipped ex-USA (with ZA155 etc) to RNPTA Portland; f/f 29.6.79 by 'C' Flt/FTG. On 19.9.79 it was destroyed by a Sea Slug 2 missile whilst operating with 'B' Flt/FTG. (TFH 1.31; 2 flights)

ZA162 (c/n 0204) Shipped ex-USA (with ZA155 etc) to RNPTA Portland and stored; f/f 27.3.80 by 'B' Flt/FTG. On 7.4.81 it was destroyed by a Sea Slug missile whilst operating in the North Atlantic from RFA *Olwen* by 'B' Flt/FTG during Exercise *Springtrain*. (TFH 3.01; 5 flights)

ZA163 (c/n 0205) Shipped ex-USA (with ZA155 etc) to RNPTA Portland and stored; f/f 31.3.81 by 'B' Flt/FTG from RFA *Olwen*. On 2.4.81, and operating from the same ship during Exercise *Springtrain* in the Bay of Biscay, it ran out of fuel and crashed into the sea. Not found and presumed sunk. (TFH 1.48; 2 flights)

ZA164 (c/n 0206) Shipped ex-USA (with ZA155 etc) to RNPTA Portland; f/f 29.6.79 by 'C' Flt/FTG. On 13.6.83, whilst operating from RFA *Tidespring* by 'B' Flt/FTG in the Falkland Islands HSF, it was lost after 2 minutes of flight, possibly due to a faulty altimeter.

**Contract MGW11B/1028:
20 Chukar II**

ZA903 (c/n 0183) Departed USA by ship 22.2.80. Consigned to RNAS Portland and stored; f/f 24.3.82 by 'B' Flt/FTG. On 29.10.88, whilst operating with 'A' Flt/FTG in the South-West Approaches it was shot down by a missile from HMS *Liverpool*. (TFH 8.20; 17 flights)

ZA904 (c/n 0184) Shipped ex-USA (with ZA903 etc) to RNPTA Portland and stored; f/f 31.5.82 by 'STO' Flt/FTG. On 12.6.83, whilst operating with 'B' Flt/FTG in the Falkland Islands it was shot down by a Sea Dart missile from HMS *Southampton*. (TFH 3.41; 6 flights)

ZA905 (c/n 0185) Shipped ex-USA (with ZA903 etc) to RNPTA Portland; f/f 28.7.80 by 'C' Flt/FTG. On 7.4.81, whilst operating with 'B' Flt/FTG (in the Eastern Atlantic) from RFA *Olwen* it was shot down by a Sea Slug missile during Exercise *Springtrain*. (TFH 1.09; 2 flights)

ZA906 (c/n 0186) Shipped ex-USA (with ZA903 etc) to RNPTA Portland and stored; f/f 8.4.81 by 'B' Flt/FTG from RFA *Olwen*, during Exercise *Springtrain* (in the Eastern Atlantic) but was shot by a Sea Slug missile down after 35 minutes of flight.

ZA907 (c/n 0187) Shipped ex-USA (with ZA903 etc) to RNPTA Portland and stored; f/f 30.4.81 by 'A' Flt/FTG off RFA *Olna* in the Arabian Sea area. On 3.7.84 it was lost over the Aberporth Range for HMS *Newcastle* but crashed into the sea due to a failure of the recovery parachute. (TFH 4.48; 8 flights)

ZA908 (c/n 0188) Shipped ex-USA (with ZA903 etc) to RNPTA Portland and stored; f/f 17.10.82 by 'A' Flt/FTG in the Falkland Islands. On 26.2.83 it was lost in the Portland area (during an NR4113 JATO trial) when the recovery parachute failed to deploy. (TFH 0.56; 2 flights)

ZA909 (c/n 0189) Shipped ex-USA (with ZA903 etc) to RNPTA Portland and stored; f/f 17.2.82 by 'A' Flt/FTG. On 29.4.82 it was lost in the South-West Approaches, whilst operating with 'STO' Flt/FTG from RFA *Grey Rover*. The likely cause was icing-up. (TFH 1.35; 3 flights)

ZA910 (c/n 0190) Shipped ex-USA (with ZA903 etc) to RNPTA Portland and stored; f/f 8.4.81 by 'B' Flt/FTG from RFA *Olwen* as part of Exercise *Springtrain*. Although damaged on this flight it was recovered and later reduced to spares. (Other reports state it was lost in the East Atlantic)

ZA911 (c/n 0191) Shipped ex-USA (with ZA903 etc) to RNPTA Portland and stored; f/f 18.10.82 by 'A' Flt/FTG. On 2.8.85, whilst operating with 'B' Flt/FTG in the Arabian Sea area, the recovery conditions were unsuitable and the target was flown into the sea. (TFH 4.24; 7 flights)

ZA912 (c/n 0192) Shipped ex-USA (with ZA903 etc) to RNPTA Portland and stored; f/f 9.4.81 by 'C' Flt/FTG. On 30.9.81, whilst operating with 'A' Flt/FTG from RFA *Tidespring* in the South-West Approaches it was shot down by a Sea Dart missile. (TFH 1.31; 2 flights)

ZA925 (c/n 0209) Shipped ex-USA (with ZA903 etc) to RNPTA Portland and stored; f/f 30.9.81 with 'A' Flt/FTG from RFA *Tidespring*. On 31.3.82, whilst operating from HMS *Glamorgan* it was 'abandoned in flight after 48 minutes.' (TFH 2.45; 4 flights)

ZA926 (c/n 0210) Shipped ex-USA (with ZA903 etc) to RNPTA Portland and stored; f/f 17.5.82 from RFA *Grey Rover*. Second and final flight on 17.10.82 from RFA *Olmeda* in the Falkland Islands but shot down after 12 minutes. (TFH 0.50; 2 flights)

ZA927 (c/n 0211) Shipped ex-USA (with ZA903 etc) to RNPTA Portland and stored; f/f 9.12.81 by 'B' Flt/FTG in the Western Approaches but shot down after 30 minutes.

ZA928 (c/n 0212) Shipped ex-USA (with ZA903 etc) to RNPTA Portland and stored; f/f 25.4.81 from RFA *Olna* in the Arabian Sea. Flight was terminated after 48 minutes but no recovery parachute was deployed. The target was (reportedly) retrieved by HMS *Newcastle* but later ditched. It is possible that the target simply ran out of fuel.

ZA929 (c/n 0213) Shipped ex-USA (with ZA903 etc) to RNPTA Portland and stored; f/f 31.5.82. On 25.8.82, and operating with 'A' Flt, FTG off HMS *Newcastle* in the South-West Approaches it was shot down by a Sea Dart missile after 14 minutes. (TFH 1.06; 2 flights)

(ZB512) ZA512 Shipment details not known. f/f 8.8.82 from HMS *Liverpool* in the South-West Approaches but shot down by a Sea Dart missile after 15 minutes.

(ZB513) ZA513 Shipment details not known. f/f 29.9.81 with 'A' Flt, FTG off RFA *Tidespring* in the South-West Approaches. Next flown 1.10.81 in the same area from the same ship but destroyed by a Sea Dart missile after 27 minutes. (TFH 1.04; 2 flights)

(ZB514) ZA514 Shipment details not known. f/f 30.9.81 from RFA *Tidespring* in the South-West Approaches. Second and final flight from RFA *Tidespring* 1.4.82 in support of HMS *Ariadne* but target crashed during the launch phase (when the flotation drogue appears to have deployed.) Never found. (TFH 0.56; 2 flights)

(ZB515) ZA515 Shipment details not known. f/f 31.5.82 with 'B' Flt, FTG but destroyed by a Sea Dart missile after 23 minutes. (Other unit reports state that this shoot-down took place on 26.5.82.)

(ZB516) ZA516 Shipment details not known. f/f 1.4.82 with 'B' Flt/FTG from RFA *Tidespring* in support of HMS *Ariadne*. Lost 7.8.82 as 'destroyed'. (Believed to have crashed immediately after launch but other reports suggest it was shot down by a Sea Dart missile. The TFH would suggest the former.) (TFH 0.48; 3 flights)

Contract ML22A/109: 15 Chukar II

ZB695 (c/n 0229) Shipped ex-USA (Pier 228, Wilmington, California) 2.9.80 aboard SS *Axel Johnson* to RNPTA Portland. f/f 11.6.81 with 'B' Flt, FTG off Portland. Destroyed 16.9.89, possibly due to a controller error, in the South-West Approaches and whilst operating with 'B' Flt, FTG. (TFH 1.06; 2 flights).

ZB696 (c/n 0230) Shipped ex-USA (with ZB695 etc). f/f 31.3.81 with 'C' Flt, FTG off RFA *Olwen*. Final flight 20.10.82 with 'B' Flt, FTG off RFA *Grey Rover* in the South-West Approaches. The flight was terminated after 18 minutes possibly due to missile damage; sank before recovery. (TFH 3.20; 6 flights).

ZB697 (c/n 0231) Shipped ex-USA (with ZB695 etc). f/f 31.3.81 with 'C' Flt, FTG off RFA *Olwen*. Final flight 1.4.82 with 'B' Flt, FTG off RFA *Tidespring* in support of HMS *Ariadne*. After 12 minutes and 20 miles out the target disappeared, presumed shot down. (TFH 1.36; 3 flights).

ZB698 (c/n 0232) Shipped ex-USA (with ZB695 etc). f/f 2.4.81 with 'C' Flt, FTG in the Bay of Biscay off RFA *Olwen* but parachute inadvertently deployed after 34 minutes and 28 miles out. Target never found.

ZB699 (c/n 0233) Shipped ex-USA (with ZB695 etc). f/f 7.4.81 with 'C' Flt, FTG off RFA *Olwen* but shot down by a Sea Slug missile after 15 minutes.

Serious damage sustained to the fuel tank area was sufficient to declare Chukar D.2 ZB700 beyond economical repair. At the time of the strike, on 29 September 1981, ZB700 was making its first, and last, flight.

ZB700 (c/n 0234) Shipped ex-USA (Pier 228 Wilmington, California) 3.3.81 aboard SS *Margaret Johnson* to RNPTA Portland. f/f 29.9.81 with 'A' Flt, FTG off RFA *Tidespring* in the South-West Approaches. Recovered safely although damaged and never flown again. (TFH 0.51; 1 flight)

ZB701 (c/n 0235) Shipped ex-USA (with ZB700 etc). f/f 19.11.81 with 'A' Flt, FTG off RFA *Olwen* in the Gulf Zone (Arabian Sea) but was shot down after 26 minutes.

ZB702 (c/n 0236) Shipped ex-USA (with ZB700 etc). f/f 1.10.81 off RFA *Tidespring* in the South-West Approaches. Second (and final) flight 14.5.82 from RFA *Grey Rover* when shot down by Sea Dart missile after 44 minutes. (TFH 1.31; 2 flights)

ZB703 (c/n 0237) Shipped ex-USA (with ZB700 etc). f/f 21.10.82 with 'B' Flt, FTG off RFA *Grey Rover* in the South-West Approaches. Shot down 17.3.83 in the Falkland Islands whilst operating with 'A' Flt, FTG off RFA *Olna*. (TFH 0.45; 3 flights)

ZB704 (c/n 0238) Shipped ex-USA (with ZB700 etc). f/f 19.11.81 with 'A' Flt, FTG off RFA *Olwen* in the Gulf Zone. Crashed 19.4.84 immediately after launch from RFA *Tidespring* in the South Atlantic due to a slow JATO burn. (TFH 2.30; 5 flights)

ZB705 (c/n 0239) Shipped ex-USA (with ZB700 etc). f/f 31.3.82 with 'B' Flt, FTG off RFA *Tidespring*. Lost on 7.12.83 whilst operating off RFA *Olna* in the South Atlantic, just 9 minutes from launch and 23 miles out. Target never found. (TFH 3.08; 6 flights)

ZB706 (c/n 0240) Shipped ex-USA (with ZB700 etc). f/f 19.11.81 with 'A' Flt, FTG off RFA *Olwen* in the Gulf Zone. Final flight 7.8.82 off HMS *Liverpool* in the South-West Approaches when the flotation drogue deployed during launch causing it to crash into the sea. (TFH 0.50; 2 flights)

ZB707 (c/n 0241) Shipped ex-USA (with ZB700 etc). f/f 19.11.81 with 'A' Flt, FTG off RFA *Olwen* in the Gulf Zone. Lost on 23.7.82 whilst operating with 'A' Flt in the South-West Approaches. Target began to behave erratically and recovery 'chute commanded after 17 minutes. Target never found. (TFH 1.54; 4 flights)

ZB708 (c/n 0242) Shipped ex-USA (with ZB700 etc). f/f 17.3.82 with 'A' Flt, FTG off RFA *Olna* in the Arabian Sea. Final flight 21.3.83 with 'A' Flight off RFA *Olna* in the Falkland Islands. The flight was terminated after 26 minutes due to an 'Air Raid Warning Yellow'. Target never found. (TFH 4.23; 7 flights)

ZB709 (c/n 0243) Shipped ex-USA (with ZB700 etc). f/f 20.11.81 with 'C' Flt, FTG off RFA *Olwen* in the Gulf Zone. Shot down 19.10.82 by a Seawolf missile in the Falkland Islands whilst operating off RFA *Olmeda*. (TFH 1.43; 3 flights)

Contract ML22A/255 (Part 1): 25 Chukar II

ZD290 (c/n 0306) Shipped ex-USA (Pier 228, Wilmington, California) 18.2.82 aboard SS *Axel Johnson* to RNPTA Portland. f/f 23.1.83 with 'B' Flt, FTG off RFA *Tidespring* in the Falkland Islands.

Lost on 12.6.83 in the same area, possibly due to icing up in flight. (TFH 1.03; 2 flights)

ZD291 (c/n 0307) Shipped ex-USA (with ZD290 etc) to RNPTA Portland. f/f 25.8.82 with 'A' Flt, FTG off HMS *Newcastle* in the South-West Approaches. Shot down by a Sea Dart missile fired by HMS *Southampton* 12.6.83 whilst operating with 'B' Flt, FTG off RFA *Tidespring* in the Falkland Islands. (TFH 2.46; 4 flights)

ZD292 (c/n 0308) Shipped ex-USA (with ZD290 etc) to RNPTA Portland. f/f 25.8.82 with 'A' Flt, FTG off HMS *Newcastle* in the South-West Approaches. Lost on 14.1.86 when recovery was abandoned due to sea state in the South-West Approaches. (TFH 4.42; 8 flights)

ZD293 (c/n 0309) Shipped ex-USA (with ZD290 etc) to RNPTA Portland. f/f 21.10.82 with 'B' Flt, FTG off RFA *Grey Rover* in the South-West Approaches but made a shallow launch. Recovery parachute deployed immediately; target recovered but damaged in process. Lost on 21.4.83 on its 2nd flight when operating from RFA *Olwen* off Gibraltar when it crashed immediately after launch due to port JATO failure. (TFH nil; 2 launches)

ZD294 (c/n 0310) Shipped ex-USA (with ZD290 etc) to RNPTA Portland. f/f 20.10.82 with 'B' Flt, FTG off RFA *Grey Rover* in the South-West Approaches but proved difficult to fly. Lost after 18 minutes when it made a heavy impact with the sea.

ZD295 (c/n 0311) Shipped ex-USA (with ZD290 etc) to RNPTA Portland. f/f 23.1.83 with 'B' Flt, FTG off RFA *Tidespring* in the Falkland Islands. Shot down by a Sea Dart missile 28.7.84 in the South-West Approaches. (TFH 3.22; 6 flights)

ZD296 (c/n 0312) Shipped ex-USA (with ZD290 etc) to RNPTA Portland. f/f 20.1.83 with 'B' Flt, FTG off RFA *Tidespring* in the Falkland Islands. Lost two days later, details unclear. (TFH 0.59; 2 flights)

ZD297 (c/n 0313) Shipped ex-USA (with ZD290 etc) to RNPTA Portland. f/f 24.1.83 with 'B' Flt, FTG off RFA *Tidespring* in the Falkland Islands but destroyed after 42 minutes.

ZD298 (c/n 0314) Shipped ex-USA (with ZD290 etc) to RNPTA Portland. f/f 23.1.83 with 'B' Flt, FTG off RFA *Tidespring* in the Falkland Islands but ran out of fuel after 43 minutes. Target was found by helicopter but sank before recovery.

ZD299 (c/n 0315) Shipped ex-USA (with ZD290 etc) to RNPTA Portland. f/f 23.1.83 with 'B' Flt, FTG off RFA *Tidespring* in the Falkland Islands but seriously damaged in the recovery process. Reduced to spares. (TFH 0.31; 1 flight)

ZD300 (c/n 0316) Shipped ex-USA (Pier 228, Terminal Island, Los Angeles, California) 5.8.82 aboard SS *Columbia Star* to London docks and on to RNPTA Portland. f/f 19.1.83 with 'B' Flt, FTG off RFA *Tidespring* in the Falkland Islands but shot down after 13 minutes.

ZD301 (c/n 0317) Shipped ex-USA (with ZD300 etc). f/f 9.11.82 with 'HQ' Flt, FTG at Aberporth as part of a JATO & TOW trial. 'Nosed-over' the cliff and crashed into the sea immediately after launch.

ZD302 (c/n 0318) Shipped ex-USA (with ZD300 etc). f/f 8.11.82 with 'HQ' Flt, FTG at Aberporth as part of a JATO & TOW trial. Final flight 25.11.87 in the South-West Approaches when it was flown into the sea which was too rough for recovery. (TFH 7.56; 12 flights)

ZD303 (c/n 0328) Shipped ex-USA (with ZD300 etc). f/f 20.3.83 with 'A' Flt, FTG off RFA *Olna* in the Falkland Islands. Shot down 21.3.83. (TFH 1.10; 2 flights)

ZD304 (c/n 0329) Shipped ex-USA (with ZD300 etc). f/f 15.11.82 with 'A' Flt, FTG off HMS *Bristol* in the South-West Approaches but lost after nine minutes.

ZD305 (c/n 0330) Shipped ex-USA (with ZD300 etc). f/f 15.11.82 with 'A' Flt, FTG off HMS *Bristol* in the South-West Approaches but lost after 11 minutes.

May 1987 and seven Chukar IIs of 'A' Flight, Fleet Target Group are positioned on the deck, the first two of which are ZE991 and ZD302. Of note is the standard orange overall (less nose cone) scheme of all except ZD302 which has white wings with orange ailerons and orange tailplane with white elevons. (792 Squadron Archive)

ZD306 (c/n 0331) Shipped ex-USA (with ZD300 etc). f/f 14.11.82 with 'A' Flt, FTG off HMS *Bristol* in the South-West Approaches but shot down after 24 minutes.

ZD307 (c/n 0332) Shipped ex-USA (with ZD300 etc). f/f 14.11.82 with 'A' Flt, FTG off HMS *Bristol* in the South-West Approaches but ran out of fuel at long-range after 43 minutes.

ZD308 (c/n 0333) Shipped ex-USA (with ZD300 etc). f/f 21.2.83 with 'A' Flt, FTG. Final flight 14.1.86 in the South Atlantic when shot down by the RAF. (TFH 5.11; 8 flights)

ZD309 (c/n 0334) Shipped ex-USA (with ZD300 etc). f/f 19.3.83 with 'A' Flt, FTG off RFA *Olna* in the Falkland Islands. Final flight 4.12.84 in the South Atlantic when, after 24 minutes the target disappeared. (TFH 0.54; 3 flights)

ZD310 (c/n 0353) Departed Los Angeles 5.3.83 aboard a Flying Tiger Line Boeing 747F; arrived Heathrow 0630/6.3.83. Conveyed to RNPTA Portland by road; f/f 4.7.83 with 'A' Flt, FTG' in the South-West Approaches. Shot down 27.4.84 in the South Atlantic whilst operating off RFA *Tidespring* (TFH 1.30; 2 flights)

ZD311 (c/n 0354) Air-freighted Los Angeles to Heathrow (with ZD310 etc); f/f 6.12.83 with 'B' Flt, in the South Atlantic off RFA *Olna*. Shot down 14.2.87 in the South-West Approaches. (TFH 3.01; 6 flights)

ZD312 (c/n 0355) Shipped ex-USA (with ZD300 etc); f/f 17.11.83 with 'A' Flt, FTG' off RFA *Olmeda* in the Far East. Lost on 18.10.86 in the Cape Finisterre area whilst operating with 'A' Flt. (TFH 2.18; 5 flights)

ZD313 (c/n 0356) Shipped ex-USA (with ZD300 etc); f/f 6.12.83 with 'B' Flt, FTG' in the South Atlantic off RFA *Olna*. Shot down 20.10.85 in the South-West Approaches (TFH 0.48; 2 flights)

ZD314 (c/n 0357) Shipped ex-USA (with ZD300 etc); f/f 3.10.83 with 'B' Flt, FTG off Gibraltar. Lost on 14.7.88 when it crashed immediately after launch from Aberporth. (TFH 6.04; 10 flights)

Contract ML22A/412: 15 Chukar II

ZD500 Shipment details unkn; f/f 20.4.83 from RFA *Olwen* off Gibraltar. Shot down 11.2.86 whilst operating with 'B' Flt, FTG in the Gulf area. (TFH 2.56; 5 flights)

ZD501 Shipment details unkn; f/f 25.4.83 from HMS *Alacrity* off Gibraltar. Lost on 28.9.83 when it ditched immediately after launch from RFA *Olwen* in the South-West Atlantic. (TFH 0.46; 2 flights)

ZD502 Shipment details unkn; f/f 19.4.83 from RFA *Olwen* off Gibraltar. Lost on 17.10.87 in the South-West Approaches when it was deliberately flown into the sea which was too rough for normal recovery. (TFH 4.41; 9 flights)

ZD503 Shipment details unkn; f/f 18.4.84 with 'A' Flt, from RFA *Tidespring* in the South Atlantic. Lost 19.2.89 in the South-West Approaches when, with 'B' Flt, it was shot down. (TFH 4.06; 10 flights)

ZD504 Shipment details unkn; f/f 25.4.83 with 'B' Flt, from HMS *Alacrity* off Gibraltar. Lost 16.9.89 in the South-West Approaches when, with 'B' Flt, it was never recovered from a standard sortie. (TFH 6.42; 11 flights)

ZD505 Shipment details unkn; f/f 3.10.83 with 'B' Flt off Gibraltar. Lost 20.4.84 when with 'A' Flt, in the South Atlantic it was lost immediately after launch from RFA *Tidespring* due to a slow JATO burn. (TFH 0.11; 2 flights)

ZD506 Shipment details unkn; f/f 29.9.83 with 'A' Flt, from RFA *Olwen* in the South West Atlantic. Lost 19.5.84 in the South-West Approaches when, with 'B' Flt aboard RFA *Gold Rover*, it was shot down by a Sea Dart missile. (TFH 1.40; 3 flights)

ZD507 Shipment details unkn; f/f 6.2.84 with 'A' Flt in the Gibraltar Exercise Area. Shot down 13.6.87 in the South-West Approaches. (TFH 4.30; 7 flights)

ZD508 Shipment details unkn; f/f 25.4.83 with 'B' Flt, from HMS *Alacrity* off Gibraltar. Lost in the South Atlantic 18.4.84 when the recovery parachute failed to deploy after a mission off RFA *Tidespring* with 'A' Flt, FTG. (TFH 2.09; 3 flights)

ZD521 Shipment details unkn; f/f 21.4.83 from RFA *Olwen* off Gibraltar. Lost 18.7.87 in the South-West Approaches due to an unserviceable coder controller. (TFH 4.06; 10 flights)

ZD522 Shipment details unkn; f/f 19.4.83 from RFA *Olwen* off Gibraltar. Lost off Gibraltar 18.7.83, circumstances unkn. (TFH 0.28; 2 flights)

ZD523 Shipment details unkn; f/f 28.9.83 from RFA *Olwen* in the South-West Atlantic but shot down by a Sea Dart missile after 28 minutes.

ZD524 Shipment details unkn; f/f 26.4.83 from HMS *Glasgow* off Gibraltar but shot down by a Sea Dart missile after 14 minutes.

ZD525 Shipment details unkn; f/f 19.4.83 from RFA *Olwen* off Gibraltar. Shot down 4.12.84 in the South Atlantic. (TFH 1.57; 4 flights)

ZD526 Shipment details unkn; f/f 4.7.83 in the South-West Approaches. Shot

It took a team of eight to manually lift a Chukar from its trolley and on to the launcher by using specially-made cradle bars. Chukar D.2 ZD532 is seen aboard HMS Falmouth *in the Gulf Area on 27 April 1984. Later on this date the Chukar was launched for a 56 minute flight and recovered satisfactorily. (Royal Navy)*

down 23.10.83 by a Sea Dart missile off Gibraltar. (TFH 1.14; 2 flights)

Contract ML22A/255 (Part 2): 8 Chukar II

ZD530 (c/n 0383) Air-freighted Los Angeles to Heathrow (with ZD310 etc). f/f 21.3.84 with 'B' Flt in the Indian Ocean. Lost 19.3.88 in the South-West Approaches 1 minute after launch due to a failure of the Pitch TDU. (TFH 2.01; 6 flights)

ZD531 (c/n 0384) Air-freighted Los Angeles to Heathrow (with ZD310 etc). f/f 20.4.83 from RFA Olwen off Gibraltar. Lost 19.5.84 in the South-West Approaches when the recovery parachute failed to deploy immediately after launch from RFA Gold Rover whilst operating with 'B' Flt. (TFH 0.35; 2 flights)

ZD532 (c/n 0385) Air-freighted Los Angeles to Heathrow (with ZD310 etc). f/f 26.4.83 from HMS Glasgow off Gibraltar. Last flight 12.2.86 in the Gulf area during which it sustained heavy damage. Recovered but reduced to spares. (TFH 3.30; 5 flights)

ZD533 (c/n 0386) Air-freighted Los Angeles to Heathrow (with ZD310 etc). f/f 19.4.83 from RFA Olwen off Gibraltar. Lost 9.12.83 in the South Atlantic whilst with 'B' Flt, FTG. Became lost on radar after 10 minutes and 30 miles from launch. Despite a search the aircraft was not found. (TFH 1.01; 3 flights)

ZD550 (c/n 0387) Air-freighted Los Angeles to Heathrow (with ZD310 etc). f/f 17.11.83 with 'A' Flt, FTG from RFA Olmeda in the Far East. Shot down 21.3.84 in the Indian Ocean. (TFH 1.12; 2 flights)

ZD551 (c/n 0388) Air-freighted Los Angeles to Heathrow (with ZD310 etc). f/f 4.7.83 with 'A' Flt, FTG in the South-West Approaches but shot down by a Sea Dart from HMS Nottingham after 14 minutes.

ZD552 (c/n 0389) Air-freighted Los Angeles to Heathrow (with ZD310 etc). f/f 19.4.83 from RFA Olwen off Gibraltar. Final flight 17.2.90 in the South-West Approaches when the engine died, the nose pitched down and the target crashed and sunk. (TFH 10.18; 16 flights)

ZD553 (c/n 0390) Air-freighted Los Angeles to Heathrow (with ZD310 etc). f/f 29.9.83 from RFA Olwen with 'A' Flt, FTG in the South-West Atlantic but crashed after 33 minutes, circumstances not known.

Contract ML22A/420: 15 Chukar II

ZD674 (c/n 0412) Shipped ex-USA (Port Jersey, New Jersey) 16.12.83 to RNPTA Portland (ship unknown). f/f 4.4.84 with 'Special' Flt, FTG at Aberporth. Damaged during recovery operation. (TFH 0.43; 1 flight)

ZD675 (c/n 0413) Shipped ex-USA (with ZD674 etc).; f/f 8.2.85 with 'A' Flt, FTG off RFA Regent in the Armilla area. Crashed 13.6.87 in the South-West Approaches with 'B' Flt when the recovery parachute failed to fully deploy. (TFH 2.47; 4 flights)

Chukar D.2 ZD680 was allocated to the Fleet Target Group Special Flight for development work at Aberporth in 1984. Later returned to Portland it was eventually shot down in the South-West Approaches in July 1987. (792 Squadron Archive)

ZD676 (c/n 0414) Shipped ex-USA (with ZD674 etc)' f/f 27.5.84 with 'A' Flt, FTG off RFA Resource in the Palma area but shot down by a Sidewinder missile after 35 minutes.

ZD677 (c/n 0415) Shipped ex-USA (with ZD674 etc); f/f 3.4.84 with 'Special' Flt, FTG at Aberporth. Final flight 20.10.85 when, with 'A' Flt, FTG it was shot down in the South-West Approaches. (TFH 2.05; 3 flights)

ZD678 (c/n 0416) Shipped ex-USA (with ZD674 etc); f/f 25.6.84 with 'A' Flt, FTG in the Gibraltar Exercise Area. Final flight 25.2.87 with 'B' Flt at Aberporth when shot down by the RAF. (TFH 3.06; 7 flights)

ZD679 (c/n 0417) Shipped ex-USA (with ZD674 etc); f/f 27.5.84 with 'A' Flt, FTG off RFA Resource in the Palma area but was shot down by a Sea Dart missile after 14 minutes.

ZD680 (c/n 0418) Shipped ex-USA (with ZD674 etc); f/f 2.4.84 with 'Special' Flt, FTG at Aberporth. Shot down 17.7.87 in the South-West Approaches whilst with 'B' Flt, FTG. (TFH 3.25; 6 flights)

ZD681 (c/n 0419) Shipped ex-USA (with ZD674 etc); f/f 20.6.84 with 'B' Flt, FTG off RFA Olna in the South Atlantic. Final flight 14.12.87 at Aberporth when it sustained major damage; recovered but reduced to spares. (TFH 3.59; 7 flights)

ZD682 (c/n 0420) Shipped ex-USA (with ZD674 etc); f/f 16.6.84 with 'B' Flt, FTG off RFA Olna in the South Atlantic. Final flight 10.3.89 with 'A' Flt at Aberporth but not recovered due to heavy sea state. (TFH 6.50; 10 flights)

ZD683 (c/n 0421) Shipped ex-USA (with ZD674 etc); f/f 2.4.84 with 'Special' Flt, FTG at Aberporth. Final flight 1.2.86 with 'A' Flt, FTG in the South-West Approaches when not recovered due to adverse weather conditions. (TFH 1.35; 3 flights)

ZD684 (c/n 0422) Shipped ex-USA (with ZD674 etc); f/f 25.5.85 with 'B' Flt, FTG in the South-West Approaches but destroyed after 34 minutes.

ZD685 (c/n 0423) Shipped ex-USA (with ZD674 etc); f/f 20.6.84 with 'B' Flt, FTG off RFA Olna in the South Atlantic. Final flight 16.10.86 with 'A' Flt in the Bay of Biscay when seriously damaged by a missile. Recovered but reduced to spares. (TFH 3.29; 6 flights)

ZD686 (c/n 0424) Shipped ex-USA (with ZD674 etc); f/f 28.9.84 with 'A' Flt, FTG but destroyed by a Sea Dart missile after 19 minutes.

ZD687 (c/n 0425) Shipped ex-USA (with ZD674 etc); f/f 16.6.84 with 'B' Flt, FTG off RFA *Olna* in the South Atlantic. Final flight 14.1.86 in the South Atlantic when it failed to get airborne and sank immediately after launch. (TFH 2.03; 4 flights)

ZD688 (c/n 0426) Shipped ex-USA (with ZD674 etc); f/f 2.4.84 with 'Special' Flt, FTG at Aberporth. Final flight 8.2.85 with 'A' Flt off RFA *Olwen* in the South-West Approaches when it was lost after 42 minutes, cause unkn. (TFH 1.44; 3 flights)

Contract ML11A/1331: 38 Chukar II

Northrop "Centre Fuselage Section Numbers" (c/ns) for the range ZE452-ZE466/ZE483-ZE490 are likely to be 0459-0481 in consecutive order but only those confirmed by sightings are listed.

Note that details of shipment etc are unrecorded, as indeed for all aircraft against subsequent contracts.

ZE452 f/f 11.2.86 with 'B' Flt, FTG in the Gulf area. Final flight 22.1.90 with 'A' Flt in the Gibraltar Exercise Area when, after 14 minutes, the target pitched down in a turn; recovery parachute deployed immediately but target not recovered. (TFH 1.15; 4 flights)

ZE453 f/f 5.11.86 with 'B' Flt, FTG in the Indian Ocean. Final flight 9.12.87 with 'A' Flt at Aberporth for the RAF but crashed after 8 minutes. (TFH 1.15; 4 flights)

ZE454 f/f 31.10.86 with 'B' Flt, FTG in the Indian Ocean. Shot down in the same area 6.11.86. (TFH 1.00; 2 flights)

ZE455 (c/n 0462) f/f 23.4.85 with 'B' Flt, FTG at Aberporth. Final flight 8.7.88 with 'A' Flt at Aberporth but sustained a flare problem one minute after launch and destroyed on command. (TFH 1.42; 4 flights)

ZE456 f/f 24.4.85 with 'B' Flt, FTG at Aberporth. Final flight 17.2.99 at Manorbier when the port JATO impacted on the port stabilizer after jettison. Flight became erratic at 500' at which point the recovery parachute was deployed on command. Target hit the sea after 30 seconds; only minor debris found afterwards.

ZE457 (c/n 0464) f/f 14.10.85 with 'B' Flt, FTG in the Gibraltar Exercise Area.

Chukar D.2 ZD683 (c/n 0421) was transferred to A&AEE Boscombe Down in March 1984 for various mod fits. This view, taken at Boscombe Down on 30 May 1985, shows the target fitted with an inert SART decoy target on its port wing-tip. The wording across the upper fin reads "Boscombe Down 13.5.85-31.5.85". (M.I. Draper Collection)

Chukar D.2 ZD683 (c/n 0421) blasts off from its launcher at Aberporth on 2 April 1984. On the port wing-tip pylon is a SART 5B non-recoverable decoy target whilst to offset this a dummy body is mounted on the starboard wing-tip.) It is likely that ZD683 was, on this occasion, taking part in a Sea Dart presentation for HMS Newcastle.*(RAE Aberporth; Neg. No 7636/2)*

Designed to enhance the IR signature of aerial targets, the plume burner is simply a tubular steel case from which aviation fuel from the Chukar's fuel tank is burnt to provide a similar signature to that of the exhaust of a jet-engined fighter. This example is seen attached to the port wing-tip of Chukar D.2 ZE455 c/n 0462.

Final flight 4.4.86 with 'A' Flt in the South Atlantic when lost after 46 minutes due to pilot error. (TFH 1.26; 2 flights)

ZE458 f/f 30.1.85 with 'B' Flt, FTG off RFA *Regent* in the Armilla area. Final flight 2.4.86 with 'A' Flt in the South Atlantic when shot down after 30 minutes (TFH 1.36; 3 flights)

ZE459 f/f 30.1.85 with 'B' Flt, FTG off RFA *Regent* in the Armilla area. Final flight 22.7.85 with 'A' Flt in the Gibraltar Exercise Area when the flotation gear proved inoperative and the target sank, (TFH 1.09; 3 flights)

ZE460 f/f 5.4.86 with 'A' Flt, FTG in the South Atlantic. Final flight 20.9.86 with 'B' Flt in the South-West Approaches when shot down after 16 minutes. (TFH 1.27; 3 flights)

ZE461 f/f 21.1.85 with 'B' Flt, FTG in the Gibraltar Exercise Area. Final flight 17.10.87 with 'A' Flt in the South-West Approaches when shot down after 16 minutes. (TFH 2.30; 4 flights)

ZE462 f/f 22.7.85 with 'A' Flt, FTG in the Gibraltar Exercise Area. Final flight 3.3.91 with 'A' Flt in the South-West Approaches when shot down after 35 minutes. (TFH 2.24; 7 flights)

ZE463 f/f 21.1.85 with 'B' Flt, FTG in the Gibraltar Exercise Area. Final flight 22.1.90 with 'A' Flt in the same area when it lost power one minute after take-off and ditched into the sea. Not recovered. (TFH 5.21; 9 flights)

ZE464 f/f 18.6.85 with 'B' Flt, FTG in the South Atlantic but lost after 23 minutes, probably due to icing.

ZE465 f/f 17.3.86 with 'A' Flt, FTG at Aberporth. Final flight 17.7.87 with 'B' Flt in the South-West Approaches when shot down after 12 minutes. (TFH 2.18; 4 flights)

ZE466 f/f 26.9.85 with 'A' Flt, FTG in the South Atlantic. Final flight 7.7.88 with 'A' Flt at Aberporth but lost when the recovery 'chute failed to open. (TFH 3.58; 6 flights)

ZE483 f/f 22.4.85 with 'B' Flt, FTG at Aberporth. Next, and final, flight 20.9.86 with 'B' Flt in the South-West Approaches when shot down after 16 minutes. (TFH 0.55; 2 flights)

ZE484 f/f 1.5.85 with 'B' Flt, FTG at Aberporth. Final flight 21.6.87 with 'A' Flt in the South Atlantic when lost after 37 minutes due to recovery 'chute failure. (TFH 1.34; 3 flights)

ZE485 f/f 12.2.86 with 'A' Flt, FTG at Aberporth. Final flight 8.4.89 with 'B' Flt in the South-West Approaches. The target proved sluggish on take-off and in the climb. After 33 minutes the recovery 'chute failed to deploy on demand and so the target was destroyed on command. (TFH 5.36; 11 flights)

ZE486 f/f 25.5.85 with 'B' Flt, FTG but shot down after 32 minutes by a proximity burst fired from a Sea Harrier. The target's recovery 'chute did deploy but the target was never found. (TFH 1.27; 3 flights)

ZE487 (c/n 0478) f/f 23.3.86 with 'B' Flt, FTG in the South-West Approaches. Final flight 13.1.91 with 'B' Flt in the South-West Approaches when not recovered due to severe weather conditions. (TFH 1.49; 4 flights)

ZE488 (c/n 0479) f/f 3.6.85 with 'A' Flt, FTG in the Gibraltar Exercise Area. Final flight 3.7.88 with 'B' Flt in the South-West Approaches when shot down after 24 minutes. (TFH 3.00; 5 flights)

ZE489 (c/n 0480) f/f 3.6.85 with 'A' Flt, FTG in the Gibraltar Exercise Area. Final flight 26.2.98 in the Indian Ocean when shot down after 11 minutes. (TFH 11.00; 22 flights)

ZE490 (c/n 0481) f/f 3.6.85 with 'A' Flt, FTG in the Gibraltar Exercise Area. Final flight 13.1.91 with 'B' Flt in the South-West Approaches when not recovered at the end of a normal flight due to adverse weather. (TFH 7.58; 13 flights)

ZE710 f/f 28.1.88 with 'B' Flt, FTG in the South-West Approaches. Final flight 3.9.90 with 'B' Flt in the same area when it was shot down (TFH 2.07; 4 flights)

ZE711 f/f 7.7.88 with 'A' Flt, FTG at Aberporth. Final flight 21.7.93 from Aberporth when shot down after 13 minutes by a German Air Force MiG-29 operating out of 'RAF Yockleton' (cover code for RAF Valley). (TFH 6.12; 14 flights)

ZE712 f/f 9.12.87 with 'A' Flt, FTG at Aberporth but crashed after 21 minutes.

ZE713 f/f 20.5.86 with 'A' Flt, FTG at Aberporth. Final flight 5.10.90 with 'B' Flt in the South-West Approaches when it ditched in the sea and sank. (TFH 5.21; 9 flights)

ZE714 f/f 15.1.88 with 'B' Flt, FTG in the South-West Approaches. Final flight 14.10.89 with 'B' Flt in the same area when it crashed after 33 minutes due to a controller error. (TFH 1.49; 3 flights)

ZE715 f/f 28.11.89 with 'A' Flt, FTG in the Caribbean. Final flight 13.1.91 with 'B' Flt in the South-West Approaches but shot down after 21 minutes. (TFH 0.32; 2 flights)

ZE716 f/f 21.5.86 with 'A' Flt, FTG at Aberporth. Final flight 24.6.89 with 'A' Flt in the South-West Approaches when it crashed after one minute, suspected cause being a faulty coder-controller. (TFH 3.27; 6 flights)

ZE717 f/f 4.7.88 with 'A' Flt, FTG at Aberporth but the JATO bottle struck the port elevator and the target flew into the water. Recovered and repaired. Final flight 5.7.88 with 'A' Flt at Aberporth when it was lost due to a controller error. (TFH 0.02; 2 flights)

ZE718 f/f 20.5.86 with 'A' Flt, FTG at Aberporth. Final flight 27.2.93 in the South-West Approaches when it was shot down after 35 minutes. (TFH 6.00; 11 flights)

ZE719 f/f 8.12.87 with 'A' Flt, FTG at Aberporth. Final flight 20.11.93 in the South-West Approaches when it was shot down after 12 minutes. (TFH 2.26; 6 flights)

ZE720 f/f 19.5.86 with 'A' Flt, FTG at Aberporth. Final flight 9.4.89 in the South-West Approaches when it was shot down after 30 minutes. (TFH 6.08; 10 flights)

ZE721 f/f 28.11.89 with 'A' Flt, FTG in the Caribbean. Final flight 28.11.96 at Aberporth when it crashed but lack of daylight precluded search. (TFH 2.41; 9 flights)

ZE722 f/f 28.11.89 with 'A' Flt, FTG in the Caribbean but shot down after 14 minutes.

ZE723 f/f 19.5.86 with 'A' Flt, FTG at Aberporth. Final flight 28.5.86 at Aberporth when lost immediately after launch. The JATO recovery 'chute is believed to have hit the target's tail. (TFH 1.10; 3 flights)

ZE724 f/f 20.9.86 with 'B' Flt, FTG in the South-West Approaches but destroyed by a missile after 15 minutes.

Contract ML11A/1331: 38 Chukar II

ZE988 f/f 14.7.86 with 'A' Flt, FTG in the Gibraltar Exercise Area. 2nd and final flight 6.10.86 (with 'B' Flt) in the same area but target crashed after 47 minutes. (TFH 1.27; 2 flights)

ZE989 f/f 3.3.86 with 'A' Flt, FTG in the Gibraltar Exercise Area. Final flight 24.11.87 in the same area but although the target landed satisfactorily the "ship ran it down" during the recovery process. (TFH 4.18; 7 flights)

ZE990 f/f 14.7.86 with 'A' Flt, FTG in the Gibraltar Exercise Area. Final flight 15.11.94 at Aberporth when shot down by a Sidewinder fired by a Sea Harrier. (TFH 2.25; 6 flights)

ZE991 f/f 29.10.86 with 'A' Flt, FTG at Aberporth as part of a VEGA trial. Final flight 25.11.87 with 'B' Flt in the South-West Approaches when shot down after 17 minutes. (TFH 2.25; 5 flights)

ZE992 f/f 12.2.86 with 'A' Flt, FTG at Aberporth for the RAF. Final flight 17.10.86 in the Cape Finisterre Area but target suffered engine seizure after 22 minutes and crashed. (TFH 2.41; 5 flights)

ZE996 f/f 17.3.86 with 'A' Flt, FTG at Aberporth. Final flight 10.10.87 with 'A' Flt in the South-West Approaches when the recovery parachute prematurely deployed. (TFH 3.07; 6 flights)

ZE997 f/f 25.3.87 with 'B' Flt, FTG in the South Atlantic. Final flight 8.2.88 with 'A' Flt in the Gibraltar Exercise Area when the parachute failed to deploy and the target crashed and sank. (TFH 2.21; 3 flights)

ZE998 f/f 28.9.87 with 'B' Flt, FTG in the North-West Approaches. Final flight 18.12.87 with 'A' Flt at Aberporth for the RAF when it was shot down after 11 minutes. (TFH 0.44; 3 flights)

ZE999 f/f 8.12.86 with 'A' Flt, FTG at Aberporth. 2nd and final flight 27.2.87, also at Aberporth, for the RAF when shot down after 5 minutes. (TFH 0.38; 2 flights)

Contract ML11A/1489: 15 Chukar II

ZF603 f/f 14.7.88 with 'A' Flt, FTG at Aberporth. Final flight 17.2.90 (with 'B' Flt) in the South-West Approaches when the parachute failed to open during the recovery stage. (TFH 3.36; 6 flights)

ZF604 f/f 21.4.90 with 'A' Flt, FTG in the South-West Approaches but shot down after 13 minutes.

ZF605 f/f 3.7.88 with 'B' Flt, FTG in the South-West Approaches. Final flight 22.1.90 with 'A' Flt in the Gibraltar Exercise Area when lost due to a Controller error. (TFH 1.36; 3 flights)

ZF606 f/f 14.7.88 with 'A' Flt, FTG at Aberporth. Final flight 17.2.90 with 'B' Flt in the South-West Approaches when shot down. (TFH 2.03; 4 flights)

ZF607 f/f 12.6.90 with 'B' Flt, FTG at Aberporth. 2nd and final flight 5.10.90 in the South-West Approaches when the recovery 'chute failed to deploy. (TFH 0.40)

ZF619 (ZF608) f/f 20.9.91 with 'A' Flt, FTG in the South-West Approaches. 2nd and final flight 24.1.92 with 'B' Flt in the Gibraltar Exercise Area when the ground station receiver failed. Target deployed recovery 'chute but it was never found and presumed sank. (TFH 1.02; 2 flights)

ZF620 (ZF609) f/f 24.5.88 with 'B' Flt, FTG at Aberporth. Final flight 2.10.92, location unkn, when the engine failed after 15 minutes but only the recovery 'chute was found. Presumed sunk. (TFH 2.16; 5 flights)

ZF621 (ZF610) (c/n 0621) f/f 25.5.88 with 'B' Flt, FTG at Aberporth. Final flight 4.6.94 in the South-West Approaches when the target was not recovered. (TFH 0.57; 3 flights)

ZF622 (ZF611) f/f 25.5.88 with 'B' Flt, FTG at Aberporth. Final flight 18.3.89 in the South-West Approaches when shot down. (TFH 1.08; 3 flights)

ZF623 (ZF612) f/f 30.10.88 with 'A' Flt, FTG in the South-West Approaches but shot down after 14 minutes.

ZF624 (ZF613) f/f 28.11.89 with 'A' Flt, FTG in the Caribbean but flew into a 'blind arc'; recovery 'chute deployed after 14 minutes but target never found. Presumed sank.

ZF625 (ZF614) f/f 1.3.92 with 'A' Flt, FTG in the South-West Approaches but unable to increase speed in flight and Crashed after 2 minutes.

ZF626 (ZF615) f/f 28.11.89 with 'A' Flt, FTG in the Caribbean. Final flight 25.2.95 in the South-West Approaches when it Crashed due to a loss of VEGA. Not recovered. (TFH 3.17; 11 flights)

ZF627 (ZF616) f/f 22.1.90 with 'A' Flt, FTG in the Gibraltar Exercise Area but shot down after 11 minutes.

ZF628 (ZF617) f/f 7.4.90 with 'B' Flt, FTG in the South-West Approaches. Final flight 13.1.91 with 'B' Flt in the same area when shot down after 10 minutes. (TFH 1.07; 3 flights)

Evidence of a clerical error by the RNPTA is provided by Chukar D.2 ZF625, seen facing to the right. The serial ZF626 is a corruption of its c/n 626 (visible on the fuselage side). When the RNPTA took this Chukar on charge the Portland technicians simply assumed that, as all the recent deliveries were prefixed ZF- the serial was ZF626. In fact it should have been ZF615. Also visible in this view are Chukar D.2s ZF619 (which should be ZF608) and ZF625 (which was officially allocated as ZF614).

Contract ML11A/1573: 20 Chukar II

ZG335 f/f 26.5.88 with 'B' Flt, FTG at Aberporth. Final flight 18.3.89 with 'B' Flt in the South-West Approaches when shot down. (TFH 1.19; 3 flights)

ZG336 f/f 2.7.88 with 'B' Flt, FTG in the South-West Approaches but lost after 7 minutes, possibly due to a lightning strike.

ZG337 f/f 26.10.96 in the South-West Approaches. Final flight 21.1.01 in the same area but pitched into the sea 2 seconds after launch. Not recovered. (TFH 3.18; 8 flights) (See also ZH773.)

ZG338 f/f 8.2.96 at Aberporth. Final flight 24.1.98 in the South-West Approaches when shot down after 10 minutes. (TFH 1.51; 5 flights)

ZG339 f/f 16.7.96 at Aberporth but shot down after 22 minutes.

ZG340 f/f 28.9.96 in the South-West Approaches but deliberately ditched after 13 minutes and not recovered due to bad sea state.

ZG341 f/f 29.10.88 with 'A' Flt, FTG in the South-West Approaches, possibly in support of HMS *York*. 2nd and final flight 8.4.89 in the same area but shot down after 22 minutes. (TFH 0.59)

ZG342 f/f 10.3.97 at Aberporth. Final flight 12.12.97 when shot down by a Sidewinder missile.

ZG343 f/f 7.2.96 at Aberporth. Final flight 31.10.99 in the South-West Approaches when the recovery 'chute deployed after two missiles fired. Not recovered and presumed sank. (TFH 1.12; 3 flights)

ZG344 f/f 25.10.00 in the North-West Approaches but although a Sea Dart missile missed the target was unable to be recovered and it flew into the sea after 13 minutes.

ZG345 f/f 18.1.97 with 'B' Flt, FTG in the South-West Approaches. Final flight 22.2.01 in the same area when shot down by a Sea Dart missile after 20 minutes. (TFH 1.51; 4 flights)

ZG346 f/f 28.9.96 in the South-West Approaches but shot down after 12 minutes.

ZG347 f/f 22.2.01 in the South-West Approaches. Recovered safely but not flown again and retained by 792 Sqdn for static display. Eventually donated to the 'Cornwall at War Museum' and conveyed to Davidstowe Moor airfield 26.9.09. (TFH 0.16; 1 Flight)

ZG348 f/f 18.1.97 in the South-West Approaches. Final flight 11.6.99 in the same area when shot down by a Sea Dart after 10 minutes. (TFH 0.58; 4 flights)

ZG349 f/f 26.7.97 in the South-West Approaches. Final flight 25.10.00 in the North-West Approaches when the starboard JATO failed to ignite and the target spiralled off the launcher and into the sea; destroyed in the process. (TFH 1.32; 4 flights)

ZG364 f/f 26.2.98 in the Indian Ocean. Final flight 27.3.99 in the South-West Approaches when the target made an uncommanded climb after the second presentation and during the height-recovery action the target impacted with the sea. Destroyed on impact. (TFH 2.12; 5 flights)

ZG365 f/f 9.11.96 in the South-West Approaches. On its 2nd flight in the same area on 9.5.99 the Controller lost the target after experiencing poor tracking. (2 flights)

ZG366 f/f 19.4.96 in the South-West Approaches but shot down after 16 minutes.

ZG367 f/f 10.3.97 at Aberporth. Final flight 15.2.99 at Manorbier but on reducing height from 1500' to 1000' the target lost height suddenly and hit the sea before the recovery 'chute could be deployed. (3 flights)

ZG368 f/f 24.7.98 in the South-West Approaches. Shot down 21.1.01 by a missile from HMS *Southampton* in the South-West Approaches. (TFH 1.35; 3 flights)

Contract ML11A/1623: 50 Chukar II

ZG630 f/f 24.6.90 in the South-West Approaches. Last flown 4.6.94 in the same area but not recovered. (TFH 2.26; 6 flights)

ZG631 f/f 9.11.96 in the South-West Approaches. Last flown 15.5.01 at Aberporth. Stored at Aberporth for several years until transferred to the FAST Museum at Farnborough in October 2008. (TFH 1.20; 4 flights)

ZG632 f/f 8.9.94 at Aberporth but fail-safed into the Irish Sea after 2 minutes and 12 miles out. Recovered. Final flight 25.2.95 when destroyed in the South-West Approaches.

ZG633 f/f 22.9.94 at Aberporth but lost to controlling radar and pilot after 5 minutes. Not recovered.

ZG634 f/f 25.1.91 in the South-West Approaches. Last flown 22.9.94 at Aberporth but recovered. No further details. (TFH 1.09; 3 flights)

ZG635 f/f 22.1.90 in the Gibraltar Exercise Area. Last flown 25.2.95 in the South-West Approaches but never recovered. (TFH 2.39; 7 flights)

ZG636 f/f 19.5.91 in the South-West Approaches with 'A' Flt, FTG but damaged by a missile after 25 minutes. Recovered but scrapped immediately afterwards.

ZG637 f/f 19.1.91 in the South-West Approaches. Destroyed by missile in the South-West Approaches 6.5.94. (TFH 1.10; 5 flights)

ZG638 f/f 7.10.91 in the West Indies Destroyed by missile in the South-West Approaches 21.1.01. (TFH 2.13; 5 flights)

ZG639 f/f 30.5.92 in the South-West Approaches. Last flown 4.6.94 in the same area when it failed to gain height above 3,500ft. Sortie ended after 17 minutes; target not recovered. (TFH 0.51; 3 flights)

ZG640 f/f 3.6.91 in the South-West Approaches but destroyed by missile after 7 minutes.

ZG641 f/f 5.11.94 in the South-West Approaches. Last flown 30.9.95 in the same area when the recovery parachute was unintentionally deployed after 7 minutes. Target not found. (TFH 0.48; 3 flights)

ZG642 f/f 15.11.91 in the South-West Approaches but destroyed after 14 minutes.

ZG643 f/f 30.5.92 in the South-West Approaches. Last flown 20.6.95 in the same area when the recovery parachute failed to deploy on command and the target was lost, presumed sunk. (TFH 1.59; 7 flights)

ZG644 f/f 11.5.96 in the South-West Approaches. Last flown 11.3.00 in the same area when shot down by a missile. (TFH 3.24; 8 flights)

ZG645 f/f 19.5.89 in the South-West Approaches. Shot down in the same area 18.5.90 (TFH 1.33; 3 flights)

ZG646 (c/n 0666) No record has been found of it ever having flown. Earmarked for preservation at Culdrose but eventually donated to Veritair Ltd for use as a training-aid to support Mirach recovery contract. Dumped at Cardiff airport May 2008 but gone by July 2009.

ZG647 f/f 19.5.89 with 'A' Flt, FTG in the South-West Approaches. Last flown 6.5.94 in the same area but it failed to climb during the JATO burn and crashed into the sea. (TFH 4.36; 13 flights)

ZG648 f/f 25.1.92 with 'B' Flt, FTG in the Gibraltar Exercise Area. 2nd and last flight 3.12.94 in the South-West Approaches, details not known. (TFH 1.01; 2 flights)

ZG649 f/f 27.2.93 in the South-West Approaches but shot down after 35 minutes.

ZG650 f/f 25.9.91 in the South-West Approaches. Last flown 9.6.98 in the same area. Failed to engage due to unserviceability of Sea Dart missile. Target was then flown into the sea (after 29 minutes) due to not being able to recover because of the bad sea state. (TFH 4.51; 10 flights)

ZG665 f/f 7.10.91 with 'B' Flt, FTG in the West Indies. 2nd (and final) flight in the South-West Approaches 21.7.95 when it was shot down (TFH 0.33; 2 flights)

ZG666 f/f 24.6.90 in the North-West Approaches. To Aberporth by 2.91 and w/o there, on 27.11.96, after losing height in a turn (due to Height Hold being u/s). Recovery was abandoned due to poor light. (TFH 2.57; 10 flights)

ZG667 f/f 29.2.92 in the South-West Approaches but destroyed by a missile after 37 minutes.

ZG668 f/f 7.10.91 with 'B' Flt, FTG in the West Indies. Its 2nd and last flight was made on 4.6.94 in the South-West Approaches when it was shot down after 15 minutes. (TFH 0.35; 2 flights)

ZG669 f/f 8.10.91 with 'B' Flt, FTG in the West Indies. On its 2nd flight, on 5.11.93, in the South-West Approaches it was not recovered due to an adverse sea state. (TFH 1.06; 2 flights)

ZG670 f/f 20.6.95 in the South-West Approaches but after 4 minutes the recovery parachute was commanded but failed to deploy. The target was destroyed on impact.

ZG671 f/f 19.2.91 with 'B' Flt, FTG at Aberporth. Flew again from Aberporth on 24.2.91 but shot down after 17 minutes. (TFH 0.33; 2 flights)

ZG672 f/f 4.9.90 in the South-West Approaches but performed a loop immediately after launch and JATO separation. Recovery parachute deployed and target recovered from the sea. Its 2nd flight took place 13.1.91 with 'B' Flt, FTG in the same area but was not recovered due to adverse sea state. (TFH 0.33; 2 flights)

ZG673 f/f 26.11.00 in the South-West Approaches; completed three presentations but attempts to recover target failed after 20 minutes of flight.

ZG674 f/f 22.4.90 with 'A' Flt, FTG in the South-West Approaches. Last flight in the same area 30.9.95 when it ditched after 1 minute from launch. (TFH 1.20; 5 flights)

ZG675 f/f 20.2.91 at Aberporth Range but destroyed by missile after 13 minutes.

ZG676 f/f 14.5.01 at Aberporth but shot down by a missile after 11 minutes. Wreckage later washed up at Pencriback and displayed in a Shropshire garden.

ZG677 f/f 6.7.96 in the South-West Approaches. Last flight in the same area 19.4.97 when it ditched 11 minutes after launch due to control difficulties. (TFH 0.55; 3 flights)

ZG678 f/f 30.9.95 in the South-West Approaches but lost after 40 minutes. Never found.

ZG679 f/f 31.10.99 in the South-West Approaches but lost after 19 minutes, details unkn.

ZG680 f/f 11.6.99 in the South-West Approaches but shot down by a Sea Dart missile after 11 minutes.

ZG681 (c/n 0729) f/f 25.7.98 in the South-West Approaches as a TOW target for a successful Sea Dart engagement. Last flown 12.6.00 in the North-West Approaches but lost after 4 minutes. (TFH 1.23; 4 flights)

ZG682 (c/n 0730) f/f 25.11.00 in the South-West Approaches; completed four presentations before ditching after 37 minutes.

ZG683 (c/n 0731) f/f 25.10.00 in the North-West Approaches but destroyed by a Sea Dart missile after 15 minutes.

ZG684 f/f 2.4.01 at Aberporth Range as a target for 111 Squadron Tornado 14.5.01 at Aberporth Range but lost after 8 minutes.

ZG685 f/f 20.11.93 in the South-West Approaches. Final flight 21.7.95 in the same area but shot down after 15 minutes. (TFH 1.31; 4 flights)

ZG693 f/f 29.1.01 over the Aberporth Range as a target for Sea Harrier FRS.2. Not recovered from the sea.

ZG694 f/f 30.11.97 in the South-West Approaches. 2nd and final flight 25.7.98 in the same area but lost after 16 minutes, circumstances unkn.

ZG695 (c/n 0736) f/f 25.11.00 in the South-West Approaches but ditched after 17 minutes and 20 miles from launch ship. Cause attributed to loss of telemetry.

ZG696 f/f 25.11.00 in the South-West Approaches but shot down by a missile fired from HMS *Exeter* after 19 minutes.

ZG697 f/f 10.6.97 at Aberporth but destroyed by a Sidewinder missile after 9 minutes.

ZG698 f/f 6.7.96 in the South-West Approaches. Final flight on 9.5.99 when shot down on its 2nd presentation. (TFH 2.15; 5 flights)

ZG699 f/f 26.11.96 at Aberporth Range but veered left immediately after launch and barrel-rolled. Recovered by parachute safely before level flight was achieved. Flown satisfactorily at Aberporth 28.11.96 but on 9.1.97 it was shot down off Aberporth after 10 minutes. (TFH 0.31; 3 Flights)

ZG700 f/f 30.9.95 in the South-West Approaches. Flown by FTG from Benbecula 28.6.97 but recovered safely. Final flight in the same area 9.6.98 when it ditched and not recovered due to adverse sea conditions. (TFH 2.01; 4 flights)

Miscellaneous Chukar II targets

The precise origin of ZH248-251 is unrecorded which implies that they may have been "acquired" or assembled from sundry undamaged spare components. The batch ZH764-ZH774 are the survivors

Targets for the Royal Navy   213

of a manufacturer's trial that took place in Saudi Arabia. At the end of this trial, and not wishing to return them to the USA, they were offered "as is" to the Royal Navy in late-1993. No record of former flight history (if any) was provided and after thorough inspections in the UK each target was accorded with "zero hours". One of these aircraft (ZH772) was initially "papered" as "Target 712" (which may suggest c/n 0712) but subsequently referred to by the Fleet Target Group as ZH772 after serials had been officially allocated.

ZJ481 is believed to have been an example assembled by the FTG from assorted spare parts and components and for which a new serial was allocated.

ZH248 (c/n 0720) f/f 19.7.90 with 'B' Flt, FTG at Aberporth. 2nd and final flight 9.11.96 when it 'tumbled' on an active TOW stream. The recovery 'chute was commanded at 1200' but the target was lost, believed destroyed.

ZH249 f/f 25.1.91 with 'A' Flt in the South-West Approaches but disappeared after 19 minutes. Never found.

ZH250-ZH251 No details known and no confirmation of existence available.

ZH764 f/f 30.11.97 in the South-West Approaches but rolled immediately after JATO separation. Target hit the water after recovery 'chute was commanded and sank.

ZH765 (c/n 0713) f/f 9.3.96 in the South-West Approaches but shot down by a Sea Dart missile after 25 minutes.

ZH766 (c/n 0733) f/f 29.1.01 at Aberporth but only one JATO fired. The target spiralled off the launcher and crashed into a field.

ZH767 f/f 25.11.95 in the South-West Approaches but after 14 minutes the engine RPM dropped to zero, target pitched down and crashed. Not recovered.

ZH768 f/f 5.10.98 at Aberporth. Final flight 15.5.01 from Aberporth as a target for a 111 Squadron Tornado F.3. Not recovered and flown into the sea. This was the final flight by a Chukar in British service.

ZH769 f/f 9.3.96 in the South-West Approaches but shot down by a Sea Dart after 11 minutes.

ZH770 f/f 27.11.96 at Aberporth. Final flight at Aberporth 4.11.98 when, after 13 minutes, the target ditched and not recovered. (TFH 1.22; 4 flights)

ZH771 f/f 26.11.96 at Aberporth when intercepted by a missile but recovery was abandoned due to failing light. (TFH 0.22)

ZH772 f/f 25.2.95 in the South-West Approaches but not recovered. (TFH 0.33)

ZH773 f/f 14.6.95 at Aberporth. Final flight 21.1.01 in the South-West Approaches when the target left the launcher but instantly pitched nose-down and dived into the sea after 2 seconds. Not recovered. (TFH 1.03; 4 flights)

ZH774 f/f 25.11.95 in the South-West Approaches but not recovered due to severe sea state. (TFH 0.27)

ZJ481 f/f 16.2.99 at Manorbier but descended rapidly after launch. Pitch-up was applied and the target stabilised but when a turn was initiated the target again lost height. The telemetry became spurious and the recovery 'chute was commanded at 350kts. Recorded flight-time of 1 minute. Retrieved from the sea and still extant at Culdrose; earmarked for preservation.

Looking exceptionally clean and pristine Chukar D.2 ZH765 (c/n 0713) is one of a batch of eleven targets that had survived a manufacturer's trial in Saudi Arabia and which were subsequently acquired by the Royal Navy. The meaning of the figure "5" on the rear fuselage is unknown but may have been associated with the earlier trials. (Royal Navy)

Mirach 100/5 ZJ609 made headlines in the Spanish press and a potential diplomatic incident when, in February 2009, it was washed up near La Coruna, conveyed to Ferrol naval base, and proclaimed to be an 'unidentified NATO missile'. This view, taken much earlier at Portland, shows it just after delivery to 792 Squadron. (Staffordshire Aviation Society)

Meteor Mirach 100/5

When, in 1997, the Ministry of Defence invited tenders for a successor for the Royal Navy's Chukar II targets, one key factor was said to be of paramount importance – a much higher overall performance with, especially, a much-enhanced low level capability than achieved with Chukar II. Naval planners favoured the Northrop BQM-74C Chukar III and there is some evidence to suggest that the American target was briefly evaluated at the Aberporth Range.[19] But when the time came for the MoD to select a target to meet what was by then termed as the Replacement Aerial Subsonic Target (RAST) – to meet both RAF and Royal Navy requirements – the target chosen was the Italian-designed Meteor Mirach 100/5. Chukar III, which Northrop had offered as a proposed partnership arrangement with GEC Marconi, was said to be simply too expensive. Ironically, the UK Mirach 100/5 was also produced in partnership with GEC Marconi.

Designed by Meteor Costruzioni Aeronautiche ed Elettroniche SpA in the late 1970s, the original Mirach 100 drone was initially conceived as a surveillance drone equipped with SIRAH, an automatic navigation system allowing the drone to be programmed to loiter over a battlefield. Reconnaissance, target location and acquisition, electronic warfare, defence saturation and strike were the designed primary roles of Mirach 100. Re-defining Mirach 100 as a straightforward target was always an obvious possibility but not a primary consideration.

As well as being ground launched, Mirach 100 was also designed for launching from an Agusta A.109A or from a specially-modified Aeritalia G222, the latter being capable of carrying up to six Mirach 100s. Launch customer for Mirach 100 was the Libyan Armed Forces with whom it entered service in a purely reconnaissance role in the early 1980s. For this the Libyan Mirachs were fitted with a modified nose-cone and under-fuselage ports to house surveillance cameras.

Production of the first sub-variant, the Mirach 100/2 target drone, began later at Meteor's Gorizia facility to meet a batch of orders from the Italian Army, Navy and Air Force. The first 100/2 entered service with the Italian Air Force (673° Squadriglia) at the Salto di Quirra Range in Sardinia in 1984. Additional orders subsequently took Mirach 100/2 production to 90 examples.

Further target sub-variants were supplied to France for operation at the Centre d'Essais des Landes (CEL) at Biscarosse and the Centre d'Essais de la Méditerranée (CEM). The French Mirach was given the designator 100/4, as were examples purchased by the German Navy for RAM missile training. Production of two further sub-variants, 100/4S (in 1993) and the 100/4E (in 1998) were specifically designed for the Spanish Army and Navy respectively and which were used at the CEDEA Test Range in Huelva for European Stinger and Aster 30 trials. NATO member countries Belgium, Denmark, Germany, Greece, Netherlands, Norway and the USA also made use of 100/4 targets at the NATO Missile Firing Installation (NAMFI) on the island of Crete.

---

19 According to reference contained within the Aberporth negative archive.

Under a 1995 Italian Ministry of Defence contract which called for an advanced multi-role threat simulation target system, Meteor developed the 100/5 variant and it was this version that was selected by Britain to meet its RAST Requirement. The prototype 100/5 was first flown in December 1996 and the first of an order for 32 examples for the Italian Navy was delivered in 2002, entering service at the Salto di Quirra Range.

The initial UK purchase for Mirach 100/5 targets was placed in June 1998 (Contract AARM1B/381) and involved three ground control systems and 39 aircraft which were allocated serials ZJ580-ZJ618 inclusive. What appeared to be an unusual quantity was explained by an allocation of 35 for the Royal Navy and four for the RAF. Deliveries to the UK began shortly afterwards, in November 1998, with a small number shipped to the UK to carry out flight and acceptance trials at Aberporth. These initial trials were not without problems and three Mirachs (ZJ580, ZJ581 and ZJ582) were lost in the process. However, as these losses occurred before formal acceptance of the drone, the Italian manufacturer agreed to fund replacements and which were allocated serials ZJ721-ZJ723. (A fourth attrition replacement later accounted for Mirach 100/5, ZJ724).

Subsequent production deliveries from Italy were made by road/sea, using specially-constructed "coffin" containers. All were consigned to the Fleet Target Group at RNAS Culdrose, with whom the Mirach 100/5 finally entered service in March 2001, just ahead of the last operational Chukar II flight.

All 39 Mirach 100/5s, including those lost during initial trials, were officially allocated to the Fleet Target Group. In November 2001 the Fleet Target Group was formally disbanded and 792 Naval Air Squadron was immediately re-commissioned at RNAS Culdrose on 29 November 2001 as the Royal Navy's aerial target service.

A second order for six Mirach 100/5s involved ZJ657-ZJ662, these being originally intended for use as air-to-air targets by the RAF and which brought the total RAF allocation to 10 aircraft. Despite being 'chalked' as RAF stock all, plus the earlier four (ZJ605, ZJ609, ZJ610 and ZJ612) were parented by 792 Squadron at Culdrose. In fact aircraft allocation was changed from time to time.

Many of the early flights on behalf of the RAF were, in reality, providing targets for development Tornado and Typhoon aircraft. A number of sorties were conducted at the NAMFI Range. Not until October 2006 did Mirach start to be deployed against front-line aircraft. The first live firing of an Advanced Short-Range Air-to-Air Missile (ASRAAM) by a front-line RAF Squadron aircraft was carried out on 26 February 2007 when a Coningsby-based Typhoon F.2 engaged a Mirach 100/5 in TOW configuration. This alone underlined the value of having an unmanned target drone towing a live target.

Royal Navy deployments of Mirach 100/5 were principally to serve as an aerial target system for the Sea Dart-equipped Type 42 Destroyer fleet. On occasions Mirach 100/5 has also acted as a target for FAA Sea Harrier FRS.2 Sidewinder air-to-air sorties. Standard deployment of Royal Navy Mirach 100/5s has been on board Type 42 destroyers although, like the Chukar D.2, they were also launched from ships of the 'Fort' or 'Rover' Class Royal Fleet Auxiliary (RFA).

Mirach was assisted on launch by two rockets that fall away once the drone is airborne. On completing its mission, Mirach was commanded to deploy its recovery parachute and after splashdown, the target is normally recovered by Lynx Helicopter, or if sufficiently close, by the ship's boat. A Royal Air Force Nimrod was usually present while the drone was flying to ensure the Range was clear at all times. Other Mirach sorties were made from land-based sites operated by QinetiQ at Aberporth and Benbecula, in the Hebrides.

Increasingly, Mirach operations switched to the Aberporth Range where the retrieval of downed Mirach 100/5 targets from the Cardigan Bay became the responsibility of Veritair Ltd. The company, based at Cardiff International Airport, had begun such operations out of Aberporth in 1996 on an ad hoc basis when helicopters had been used to pluck Chukar targets from the water. Later, when the company secured a £3m contract from Qinetiq to retrieve Mirach targets, the company introduced a sling process specifically designed for the purpose.

The formation of the Combined Aerial Target Service (CATS) at the end of 2006 effectively marked the end of the Royal Navy's target service as an independent unit. (See Chapter 8). 792 Squadron operations began to run down towards the end of 2008 with the final recorded sortie taking place early afternoon on 25 March 2009 when ZJ612 made a 45 minutes flight over the Hebrides Range.[20]

792 Squadron finally disbanded on 4 June 2009 and it had been expected that all Mirach 100/5 targets would be transferred to the Qinetiq facility at Aberporth, but the Aberporth Mirach 100/5s were built to a different

---

[20] Although this sortie is the last recorded flight it is thought that a further 792 Squadron Mirach deployment was made in May 2009 but no details appear to have been recorded and this therefore remains unconfirmed.

Mirach 100/5 UK Contracts

Serial Range	Allotment Date	Quantity	Remarks
ZJ580-ZJ618	3.11.98	39	ZJ580-604/606-608/611/613-618 procured for FTG/792 Sqdn, RN ZJ605/609-610/612 allocated to RAF
ZJ657-ZJ662	28.2.02	6	Procured for RAF use
ZJ721-ZJ723	31.1.03	3	Attrition replacements
ZJ724	18.11.03	1	Attrition replacement
ZJ775-ZJ776	3.11.04	2	792 Sqdn

specification to those operated by 792 Squadron. In the event the surviving stock of ten Mirachs (ZJ583, ZJ587, ZJ610, ZJ612, ZJ615, ZJ662, ZJ721, ZJ723, ZJ775 and ZJ776) were placed into long-term storage at RNAS Culdrose to await return to the manufacturer.

For details of Mirach 100/5 targets ZJ725-ZJ774 and ZZ450-ZZ499 see Chapter 8.

Colour Schemes

All Mirach 100/5 targets supplied to the UK were in what is officially described as "FIAT tractor orange". All lettering (warnings and instructions) were in white.

In 2003 six 100/5s (ZJ613-ZJ618) were repainted in a 'black' scheme to simulate Exocet missiles at extremely low altitude. They were presented as targets to the new Sea Dart missile with IR fuse.

The black paint simply increased "immissivety", i.e. it made the fuselage skin hotter at high speed which helped to fool the missile into thinking it was supersonic.

Two further examples (ZJ662 and ZJ724) were also painted in overall black scheme.

Mirach 100/5 Technical Data

Power Plant	One 1.57kN (353lb st) Microturbo TRS 18-1-201-1 turbojet
Wing Span	7 ft 6.6 in (2.30 m)
Wing Area	11.84 sq ft (1.10 m²)
Length overall	13 ft 4 in (4.08 m)
Height overall	2 ft 11 in (0.89 m)
Max payload	132.2 lb (60 kg)
Max launch weight from ramp	727 lb (380 kg)
Max Mach No	0.9
Max level speed	540 kt (621 mph; 1,000 km/h) at sea level
Operating height (min)	10 ft (3 m)
Operating height (max)	41,000 ft (12,500 m)
Max endurance	1 hr 30 min

792 Squadron's Mirach 100/5 ZJ613 displays the black and orange scheme that was applied to a number of 2002-build aircraft. Seen at Culdrose 28 September 2006. (Michael I Draper)

Meteor Mirach 100.5
Individual Aircraft Histories

All built by Meteor Costruzioni Aeronautiche ed Elettroniche SpA (Meteor CAE SpA) at Gorizia, Italy.
(Note that the first two digits of construction numbers indicate year of build. For targets built in 2000 (and beyond) the year is expressed in letters, eg AA=2000, AB=2001, AC=2002 etc.)

ZJ580 (c/n 98001) Arr Culdrose by road 18.1.99 (ex-Italy) for Fleet Target Group (FTG). f/f 1.12.99, later lost off RFA *Fort Victoria* 7.12.99 due to a 'failure to retrieve'.

ZJ581 (c/n 98002) Arr Culdrose 18.1.99 for FTG. Conveyed to Aberporth and f/f 30.7.99 but lost after 31mins due to a recovery parachute malfunction.

ZJ582 (c/n 99004) Arr Culdrose 26.11.99 for FTG. Conveyed to Aberporth and f/f there 3.4.01 but drone crossed the corridor safety boundary after 55 seconds. Abort command given; recovery parachute deployed but aircraft flying too fast for recovery. Parachute failed, aircraft ditched and broke up on impact. (TFH 1.05)

ZJ583 (c/n 99006) Arr Culdrose 26.11.99 for FTG. Stored and believed never to have flown. Still current at 792 Sqdn decommissioning 4.6.09 and currently awaiting collection and shipment back to Meteor, Italy.

ZJ584 (c/n 99008) Arr Culdrose 26.11.99 for FTG; f/f 3.6.01 off HMS *Exeter* in the South-West Approaches but began to perform two slow barrel rolls after 5 seconds due to differential alignment of JATO bottles. Recovered by parachute safely and picked up by Lynx from HMS *York* and returned to *Exeter*. Later returned to Culdrose with Cat.1 damage and repaired. Final flight 26.11.04 after which withdrawn from use 1.12.06 due to general damage. Presumably reduced to spares.

ZJ585 (c/n 99005) Arr Culrose 26.11.99 for FTG. Believed f/f 29.9.03 but later withdrawn from use 1.12.06 due to general damage. Presumably reduced to spares.

ZJ586 (c/n 99007) Arr Culdrose 26.11.99 for FTG. Lost at Manorbier 1.4.00 due to recovery parachute malfunction.

ZJ587 (c/n 99009) Arr Culdrose 26.11.99 for FTG. Used by FTG/792 Sqdn as a simulator but known to have flown 20.9.06. Still current at Squadron decommissioning 4.6.09 and currently awaiting collection and shipment back to Meteor, Italy.

ZJ588 (c/n AA020) Arr Culdrose by 5.00 for FTG. Launched off HMS *York* 24.10.01 in the South-West Approaches but shot down by a Sea Dart missile fired from HMS *Newcastle*.

ZJ589 (c/n AA021) Arr Culdrose by 5.00 for FTG. Launched off HMS *Newcastle* 8.3.03 in the South-West Approaches but shot down by a Sea Dart missile fired from HMNLS *Jacob van Heemskerck*.

ZJ590 (c/n AA022) Arr Culdrose by 5.00 for FTG. Destroyed by a Sea Dart missile fired from HMS *Edinburgh* 27.4.02 in the South-West Approaches.

ZJ591 (c/n AA023) Arr Culdrose by 5.00 for FTG; f/f 3.4.01 at Aberporth. Sustained damage 3.6.01 in a crash off HMS *Exeter*. Rtnd to Italy 20.5.02 for repair. Re-del to Culdrose (date unkn). Shot down 6.11.05 by a Sea Dart missile fired by HMS *Nottingham* or *Chatham* in the South-West Approaches.

ZJ592 (c/n AA024) Arr Culdrose by 5.00 for FTG; f/f 7.9.02 in the South-West Approaches. Shot down 6.9.03 by a Sea Dart missile fired from either HMS *Gloucester* or HMS *Newcastle*.

ZJ593 (c/n AA025) Arr Culdrose by 5.00 for FTG; f/f 2.6.01 in the South-West Approaches. Shot down off Hebrides Range 4.5.04 by a Sea Dart missile fired from HMS *Manchester*.

ZJ594 (c/n AA031) Arr Culdrose by 1.01 for FTG; f/f 3.6.01 off HMS *Exeter* in the South-West Approaches but failed to gain flight. Recovered from sea. Used for trials until allocated for EFA trials to replace ZJ603. Shot down 9.4.02 off the Hebrides Range by an AIM-120 AMRAAM missile fired by Warton-based EFA/Typhoon ZH590.

ZJ595 (c/n AA032) Arr Culdrose by 1.01 for FTG; f/f 23.2.02 off RFA *Black Rover* in the South-West Approaches but shot down by a Sea Dart missile fired from HMS *Nottingham* after 32mins.

ZJ596 (c/n AA033) Arr Culdrose by 1.01 for FTG; f/f 15.11.02 in the South-West Approaches but destroyed by a Sea Dart missile fired from HMS *Liverpool* after 44mins.

ZJ597 (c/n AA034) Arr Culdrose by 1.01; f/f 6.4.01 at Aberporth on a FTG Controller Training sortie. Lost 24.10.01 in the South-West Approaches after launch from HMS *York* when weather conditions exceeded target recovery limitations so ZJ597 was flown into the sea and destroyed.

ZJ598 (c/n AA035) Arr Culdrose by 1.01 for FTG. Damaged after falling off forklift during unloading at Aberporth 26.3.01. Rtnd to the manufacturer for repair. Re-deld to Culdrose by 5.11.05. Destroyed by a Sea Dart missile 9.5.06 fired from HMS *Exeter* over the Hebrides Range after 42mins of flight.

ZJ599 (c/n AA036) Arr Culdrose by 1.01 for FTG; f/f 8.3.03 from HMS *Newcastle* in the South-West Approaches but failed to gain height and dived into the sea after 9 seconds of flight. Not recovered.

ZJ600 (c/n AB043) Deld Italy to NAMFI Range, Crete 1.7.01. Later to 792 Sqdn Culdrose (date unkn). Shot down over Hebrides Range 18.6.05 by a Sea Dart missile fired from HMS *Exeter*. Possibly operating from HMS *Chatham* at the time.

ZJ601 (c/n AB044) Deld Italy to NAMFI Range, Crete 1.7.01. Later to 792 Sqdn Culdrose (date unkn). Launched on the Hebrides Range 5.11.05 for HMS *Exeter* but not recovered from sea until two weeks later for reasons unknown. Believed reduced to spares at Culdrose due to salt water corrosion.

ZJ602 (c/n AB045) Deld Italy to NAMFI Range, Crete 1.7.01. Later to 792 Sqdn Culdrose (date unkn). Launched in the South-West Approaches 5.11.05 for HMS *Gloucester* but after two presentations flown into the sea after 30mins and not recovered.

ZJ603 (c/n AB046) Deld direct Italy-Hebrides Range 1.7.01 for FTG. Lost over Hebrides 17.9.01 during EFA/Typhoon trials when recovery 'chute failed.

ZJ604 (c/n AB047) Deld direct Italy-Hebrides Range 1.7.01 for FTG. Lost over

Mirach 100/5 ZJ659 was given up as lost after it came down and sank in the sea off Benbecula. The sea around the Hebrides is not usually forgiving but on this occasion the target was washed ashore just 24 hours later. This view shows just how the fuselage filled with sand; note also the parachute release straps fully extended. (M.I.Draper Collection)

Hebrides Range 29.1.02 during EFA trials due to adverse sea state.

ZJ605 (c/n AB048) Deld direct Italy-Hebrides Range 1.7.01 for FTG. Shot down 15.2.05 over the QinetiQ Deep Sea Range off Benbecula by an AMRAAM missile fired by Typhoon ZH590/DA04.

ZJ606 (c/n AB058) Arr Culdrose 1.12.01 for 792 Sqdn. Flown to destruction in the South-West Approaches 16.6.02 after Sea Dart missile misfire from HMS *Edinburgh*. (May have been operating from HMS *Cardiff* at the time.)

ZJ607 (c/n AB059) Arr Culdrose 1.12.01 for 792 Sqdn. Shot down 15.6.02 in the South-West Approaches by a Sea Dart missile fired from either HMS *Cardiff* or HMS *Edinburgh*.

ZJ608 (c/n AB060) Arr Culdrose 1.12.01 for 792 Sqdn. Developed serious fuel leak and dptd UK 20.5.02 for return to manufacturer Rtnd to Culdrose (by 3.05). Destroyed by a Sea Dart missile 9.7.08 fired from HMS *Gloucester* in the South-West Approaches after 29mins.

ZJ609 (c/n AB061) Arr Culdrose 1.12.01 for 792 Sqdn. Lost in the South-West Approaches 30.10.07 after 32mins whilst acting as target for HMS *Edinburgh* and HMS *York*. Later washed up near La Coruna, north-west Spain c11.2.09 and conveyed to Ferrol Spanish naval base. No further details.

ZJ610 (c/n AB062) Arr Culdrose 1.12.01 for 792 Sqdn; f/f 1.10.03 over the Hebrides Range as RAF Tornado target. Recovered. Withdrawn from use 9.08 due to fuel contamination. Still current at Squadron de-commissioning 4.6.09 and currently awaiting collection and shipment back to Meteor, Italy.

ZJ611 (c/n AB063) Arr Culdrose 1.12.01 for 792 Sqdn. Lost 8.3.03 when, after launch from HMS *Newcastle* in the South-West Approaches, it banked sharply to port and flew into the sea approximately 800m behind the ship after 6 seconds of flight. Weather conditions prevented recovery and ZJ611 was destroyed by small-arms fire from the ship.

ZJ612 (c/n AB068) Arr Culdrose 13.6.02 for 792 Sqdn; f/f 1.10.03 over the Hebrides Range. Still current at Squadron de-commissioning 4.6.09 and currently awaiting collection and shipment back to Meteor, Italy.

ZJ613 (c/n AC069) Arr Culdrose 13.6.02 for 792 Sqdn; f/f 26.9.08 over the Hebrides Range as target for 41 Sqdn Typhoon but shot down by AMRAAM missile after 21mins of flight.

ZJ614 (c/n AC070) Arr Culdrose 13.6.02 for 792 Sqdn; f/f 19.4.07 over the Hebrides Range. On 19.9.08, target control was lost during 41 Sqdn Typhoon AMRAAM firings and target ditched. Recovered from sea but later scrapped at Culdrose.

ZJ615 (c/n AC071) Arr Culdrose 13.6.02 for 792 Sqdn. Repainted in 'black' scheme. Flown 19.9.08 over Hebrides Range as target for 41 Sqdn Typhoon. (This is believed to have been first flight). Still current at Squadron de-commissioning 4.6.09 and currently awaiting collection and shipment back to Meteor, Italy.

ZJ616 (c/n AC072) Arr Culdrose 13.6.02 for 792 Sqdn. Destroyed over the Hebrides Range 8.7.02 by a Sea Dart missile fired from HMS *Southampton*.

ZJ617 (c/n AC073) Arr Culdrose 13.6.02 for 792 Sqdn; f/f 8.7.02 over the Hebrides Range. Repainted in 'black' scheme. Destroyed by a Sea Dart missile fired from HMS *York* 6.09. (Precise date and location unkn).

ZJ618 (c/n AC074) Arr Culdrose 13.6.02 for 792 Sqdn; f/f 8.7.02 over the Hebrides Range but shot down by a Sea Dart missile fired from HMS *Southampton*.

ZJ657 (c/n AC075) Arr Culdrose 6.9.02 for 792 Sqdn. On 30.10.04 it was launched from HMS *Gloucester* but ship's Sea Dart weapon system malfunctioned and ZJ657 made a controlled ditching 1mile off the port bow 48*27'N, 012*23W. Attempts to recover target were thwarted by bad weather and it was SOC. Two years later it was found (by a Spanish trawler) floating off the Canary Islands.

ZJ658 (c/n AC076) Arr Culdrose 6.9.02 for 792 Sqdn. Destroyed 30.10.07 by a Sea dart missile fired from HMS *Edinburgh* or HMS *Liverpool*.

ZJ659 (c/n AC077) Arr Culdrose 6.9.02 for 792 Sqdn. Launched from Benbecula (Hebrides Range) 30.9.08 as a target for HMS *Manchester* but landed in rough seas, making recovery impossible. Destroyed by machine-gun fire from the ship's helicopter and sunk. Subsequently washed ashore 24 hours later and possibly returned to Culdrose and scrapped.

ZJ660 (c/n AC078) Arr Culdrose 6.9.02 for 792 Sqdn. Launched at Hebrides Range 12.4.07 as target for RAF Typhoon but suffered uncommanded engine shut-down after 12 seconds and recovered on shore. Sustained damage when parachute failed to detach and the target was dragged across shoreline. Returned to Culdrose (extant 23.10.07) but later scrapped.

ZJ661 (c/n AC079) Arr Culdrose 6.9.02 for 792 Sqdn. Destroyed 11.9.04 by Sea Dart missile fired from HMS *Nottingham* in the South-West Approaches.

ZJ662 (c/n AD134) Arr Culdrose 19.12.03 for 792 Sqdn. Repainted in 'black' scheme but not flown until 20.3.09. Still current at Squadron de-commissioning 4.6.09 and currently awaiting collection and shipment back to Meteor, Italy.

ZJ721 (c/n AD135) Arr Culdrose 19.12.03 for 792 Sqdn. Sustained damage

Targets for the Royal Navy

26.9.08 due to uncommanded parachute deployment on launch for 41 Sqdn Typhoon AMRAAM missile sortie over the Hebrides Range. Returned to Culdrose and stored. Still current at Squadron de-commissioning 4.6.09 and currently awaiting collection and shipment back to Meteor, Italy.

ZJ722 (c/n AD136) Arr Culdrose 19.12.03 for 792 Sqdn. Launched 28.1.09 in the South-West Approaches but entered the sea 30nm from the launch vessel. Despite an extensive search ZJ722 was not found and was declared sunk.

ZJ723 (c/n AD137) Arr Culdrose 19.12.03 for 792 Sqdn; f/f 12.4.07 over the Hebrides Range for Typhoon target. Recovered satisfactorily and returned to Culdrose. Still current at Squadron de-commissioning 4.6.09 and currently awaiting collection and shipment back to Meteor, Italy.

ZJ724 (c/n AC080) Arr Culdrose 19.12.03 for 792 Sqdn. Launched over Hebrides Range 26.9.08 as target for 41 Sqdn Typhoon but lost control and entered the sea 86nm from launch point. Not recovered immediately but later washed up on a beach on the Isle of Harris 19.10.08.

Mirach 100/5 ZJ662 displays the overall black scheme applied to a small of number of targets in 2003. Designed to simulate an Exocet misile at extremely low altitude, the black paint increased the target's 'immissivety', ie making the fuselage skin hotter at high speed and confusing the approaching missile to think it was supersonic. (Staffordshire Aviation Society)

ZJ775 (c/n AE169) Arr Culdrose 15.11.04 but found not to be to design standard and not taken onto charge. Still current at Squadron de-commissioning 4.6.09 and currently awaiting collection and shipment back to Meteor, Italy.

ZJ776 (c/n AE170) Arr Culdrose 15.11.04 but found not to be to design standard and not taken onto charge. Still current at Squadron de-commissioning 4.6.09 and currently awaiting collection and shipment back to Meteor, Italy.

"Poacher turned Gamekeeper!" Chukar D.2 targets were often used for deploying a towed target, in this instance the target is a Semi-Active Radar Target (SART) Mk.5. This is an augmentation system, specially designed to decoy J-Band radar-guided missiles engaging on the Chukar target. Although not precisely dated, this 1984 view is known to have been taken from Llanbedr's 'chase' Hawk T.1 XX145.

Chapter 8
Unmanned Targets for the Army

THE ARMY'S POST-WAR QUEST for an aircraft suitable for small-arms target practice proved to be a long and drawn-out process. After several years of frustrating indecision a development contract, based on a Ministry of Supply Requirement dated 1 May 1950, was finally awarded to Lines Brothers Ltd. It called for the design and construction of a dedicated powered target drone, referred to as Pilotless Target Aircraft No.2 Mk.1 but when Lines Brothers presented its case to the Ministry, the result proved to be no more than a so-called "Chinese" copy of the American-designed Radioplane OQ-3. Lines built three examples as well as two examples of an "anglicized" version of the OQ-3. The difference between the two versions was that the "Chinese OQ-3" retained the triangulated fuselage whilst the anglicized version featured a standard monocoque fuselage.[1]

For fixed-base operations, the Flight Refuelling Falconet I target drone was launched in an extremely unusual manner. A permanent circular runway strip (known as a 'carousel') had been constructed beside the Hebrides Range from which Falconet could be launched under its own power. Tethered to the centre of the circular runway Falconet needed three complete circuits of the runway to allow sufficient speed to gather and to allow the drone to lift off from the launch trolley – rather like the traditional "stone in a sling" fable. A distinct advantage of this method was Falconet's ability to take-off in any given wind direction. (Flight Refuelling Ltd. Neg. No 9272)

The War Office readily took to the concept and agreed to flight test the "Chinese" copy OQ-3s at the Manorbier Artillery Range in South Wales. The flights took place in September 1950 with the aircraft fitted with American Righter O-15-3 engines and American radio equipment but the outcome was not as successful as had been hoped.[2] As a consequence, the American components were replaced by British-made units but even then further trial results were not much better. One of the main problems had been with the recovery parachutes which had continually released too early although at the time it was thought that this may have been caused, not by a design fault, but by interference from a nearby ground radar station.

A third series of flight trials took place at the Stiffkey Artillery Range, Norfolk, in October 1950 and these, presumably without any interference, proved that the British radio equipment was, after all, as good as – if not better – than the American kit; so much so that the RAE recommended the production of 150 British-built OQ-3s.[3] Strict financial restrictions at the time prohibited the import

---
1 National Archives WO32/13355/8A
2 National Archives WO32/13355/8A
3 A bid was placed in 1945 for 2,400 Radioplane OQ-3 target drones to be supplied under Lend-Lease but it is highly doubtful that the bid was successful. However it does illustrate just how much the War Office wanted to acquire US target drones.

of American engines and so the choice fell to a British engine produced by A.B.C. Motors Ltd. This was a 276cc air-cooled, flat-twin engine which developed about 6hp and which was fitted a fixed-pitch wooden propeller. A contract was immediately placed for 150 engines.

The precise circumstances surrounding the OQ-3 situation, and the extent to which it featured in British use remains confusing. Even official documents are contradictory as there is some evidence to suggest that a quantity of American-built OQ-3s were indeed imported for the Army.[4] Certainly the Ministry of Supply had some examples on charge and made one OQ-3 available at RAE Farnborough on 19 September 1950 for inspection by a number of manufacturers who had been invited to tender for the run of 150 UK-built examples. Whether the MoS example was a genuine one or one of the "Chinese" copies still remains unclear.[5]

The notion that the MoS did acquire at least three OQ-3s is supported by the fact that serial numbers WF325, WF328 and WF332 were issued on 19 January 1950 to three OQ-3 targets against Contract 6/Acft/4354/GW.1 Of course, this could have been an allocation for the three "Chinese" copies. However, on the assertion that the OQ-3s, being essentially model aircraft, did not need to be issued with standard military serials, the allocation was later cancelled by Contracts Branch CB.9(c) on 24 January and re-allocated to Varsity T.1 aircraft.

Deadline for tenders was 31 October 1950 and deliveries of the 150 British-built OQ-3s were expected to start as soon as possible after selection with production eventually peaking at some eight aircraft per week. The sense of urgency was underlined by the fact that due to the type of ground equipment required in operating the drone as well as the absence of any experienced operator, the successful bidder was not expected to undertake flight trials.

Auster B3 Target
Pilotless Target Aircraft No.1

Two of the nine companies invited to tender, the Bristol Aeroplane Co Ltd and Handley-Page Ltd, chose not to submit a design, the latter claiming that a sub-contracted order for 100 Canberras had taken up all of the company's production facilities. Fairey Aviation Co Ltd tendered a bid costing some £83,400; Short Bros & Harland's bid amounted to £47,700, whilst Scottish Aviation Ltd's bid emerged at £30,000. Walsall-based Heliwells Ltd, who proposed to open a production line at Treforest, near Pontypridd, tendered a price of £17,850 whilst Slingsby Sailplanes Ltd tendered at £16,602. The difference between the highest and lowest price was quite extraordinary and a tender from Auster Aircraft was even lower – at £10,934 although Auster's tender was subsequently revised upwards.

After viewing the OQ-3 at Farnborough, Auster's Chief Designer immediately set about work on a slightly modified version under the manufacturer's designation Auster B2. Aerodynamic improvements built into the B2 offered the promise of better flying characteristics and at the same time led to a simplification of design and manufacture, thus reducing the cost of basic materials. It is likely that Austers built an example of the B2 although it is doubtful if it was ever actually flown.[6]

The Ministry of Supply chose not to proceed with the Auster B-2; instead the MoS accepted Auster's tender for a UK-built OQ-3 target and ordered 150 examples against Contract 6/Acft/5435/CB.8(a), placed on 20 November 1950. The Auster-built OQ-3 was allocated the company designation B3. The eventual cost of producing 150 B-3 targets rose to just over £60,000.[7]

The fuselage of the Auster B3 was of standard vee-section and housed the fuel tank, a recovery parachute and radio-control unit. The American (Type RC-57) receiver set was replaced by a British (R.221 Kit No.1) set, although the American (Type RC-56-A) transmitter system was retained. Should the target still be flying on the completion of a shoot, or if its limit of duration was being approached, the recovery parachute would automatically deploy, or when the ground operator pressed a button on the control box.

Auster B3 was launched by an American-designed Type A-2 catapult. Rubber shock cords placed under tension by a winch mechanism were sufficient to accelerate the target to flying speed. The target was mounted on the catapult with three fittings. The two front fittings were short tubes welded to the wing brace struts; these tubes fitted over short pins on the catapult car. The front fittings took none of the launching load. The rear fitting of the target was a small tube on the keel of the fuselage, which slid into a pin at the rear end of the catapult car; this pin took the full launching load.

A retrieving cable was attached to the car and the winch, with ratchet set, was wound until the car was in a fully retracted position and engaged an automatic spring trigger. Pulling a launch cable disengaged the holding mechanism and allowed the car and target to be propelled down the launcher. The car stopped at the end of the launcher; the target continued forward and flew away from the launch site.

It has always been thought that the American-designed catapults were manufactured in the UK but the Air Pilot, issued for the Auster B3, suggests that they were American-built and imported from the US. The manual contains a warning that the launcher "incorporates an American lighting system. Therefore the plug on the towing frame cannot, at present, be connected to an English prime mover. It cannot be towed at night."[8]

Production of the B3 began at the company's Rearsby plant in early 1951; the first delivery was made at the end of

---

[4] A War Office Situation Report dated 18 September 1951 states that "it is estimated that stocks of the OQ-3 would run out this year and as an interim measure, until the PTA Small arrives, 150 PTA No.2 Mk.I aircraft have been ordered." The reference to the PTA Small clearly relates to the eventual ML U-120D drone whilst the PTA No.2 Mk.1 is the Auster B3 drone, a British-built equivalent of the OQ-3. (National Archives WO32/13355/64A)

[5] According to a Situation report dated September 1951, "the Army have been using the American OQ-3 target. This is a small affair and is used for close-range sub-calibre firings. It is "tricky" in its control and must be close enough to be able to judge its altitude and control it. A British replacement is being built for the Army." (National Archives WO32/13355/64A)

[6] National Archives AVIA53/37
[7] National Archives WO/32/13355
[8] National Archives AIR10/7172

Three views showing an Auster B3 Target being prepared for launch. What is clearly evident in these pictures is the very close resemblance to the American Radioplane OQ-3, of which the B3 was a British-built version. Note the top-fuselage hinged panel is open and allowing good access to the aircraft's systems and fuel tank. Construction of the B3 Target was of a fabric-covered, steel tube-structured, high-wing monoplane – a description that just about covered everything that the Auster Aircraft Co built! (via Ian O'Neill)

April 1951 to the Army's Central Ordnance Depot at Donnington, near Wellington, Shropshire. (Some official sources show that the first delivery was made on 27 April 1951; other records show another delivery took place on 30 April.) A delay in the production of engines, radio equipment, propellers and parachutes badly affected Rearsby's output of B3s and it was not until 31 October that a second delivery (of nine examples) was made. Thereafter the delivery rate of targets to Donnington increased and the entire run was completed on 3 January 1953. Details of deliveries (showing only 149) can be summarised as follows:

30 April 1951	1 example
31 October 1951	9 examples
20 December 1951	10 examples
21 January 1952	10 examples
20 February 1952	6 examples
24 March 1952	12 examples
16 April 1952	18 examples
8 May 1952	14 examples
16 June 1952	6 examples
2 July 1952	8 examples
21 July 1952	10 examples
7 October 1952	9 examples
4 November 1952	12 examples
4 December 1952	12 examples
3 January 1953	12 examples

Of those delivered to Donnington, only the first 36 Auster B3s were earmarked for immediate issue; the remainder were placed in storage and issued later. The first service issues took place on 5 December 1951 when six examples were conveyed to the School of Artillery. What was effectively a final acceptance trial was conducted at Manorbier on the following day; the results proving to be fully satisfactory.

None of the Auster B3s were issued serials within the standard military sequence and the only known reference to individual identities are by the fuselage numbers which, according to manufacturer's records, ran sequentially from AUS100FF to AUS249FF.[9]

In British Army service the Auster B3 was never referred to as such; it was always known as the 'Pilotless Aircraft Target No.2 Mk.1' and built solely to meet Army Staff Requirement M105 in order to provide practice for Bren guns and light artillery. Precisely which Army units operated the B3 is fairly obscure although by 5 February 1952 twelve aircraft are known to have been on the strength of the School of Artillery at Manorbier. None had any external markings and all were in an identical scheme of red under-surfaces (wings and fuselage) and yellow top-surfaces.[10]

Normal operating height of the Auster B3 was at 2,500ft; it had an endurance of about one hour and a maximum speed of 110mph. After completing production of B3 target drones, the Rearsby design office began work on a follow-up project aimed at improving the B3's performance. Design work on the new variant, given the designation Auster C9, was wholly funded by the manufacturer. It was to be powered by a twin two-stroke Villiers-Talisman engine but despite the fact that B3 had performed admirably as a target, Austers could not persuade the military to show any interest in the C9. Surprisingly, considering its satisfactory service record, the War Office never placed a repeat order for the B3.

---

9 The only previously published source relating to the Auster B-3 (*Auster Production* by N.Ellison & R.MacDemitrea) claims that 149 Auster B-3 drones built. Indeed the details of deliveries shows only 149 aircraft delivered. However documents relating to target drones discovered during the clear-out (and closure) of BAC's Weybridge facility show that 150 were in fact built and quote the fuselage numbers shown. Quite why there was a rich archive of drone data at Weybridge is unclear.

10 It is quite likely that all 150 drones were allocated to the School of Artillery.

Fig. 3. Ground crew stations for starting

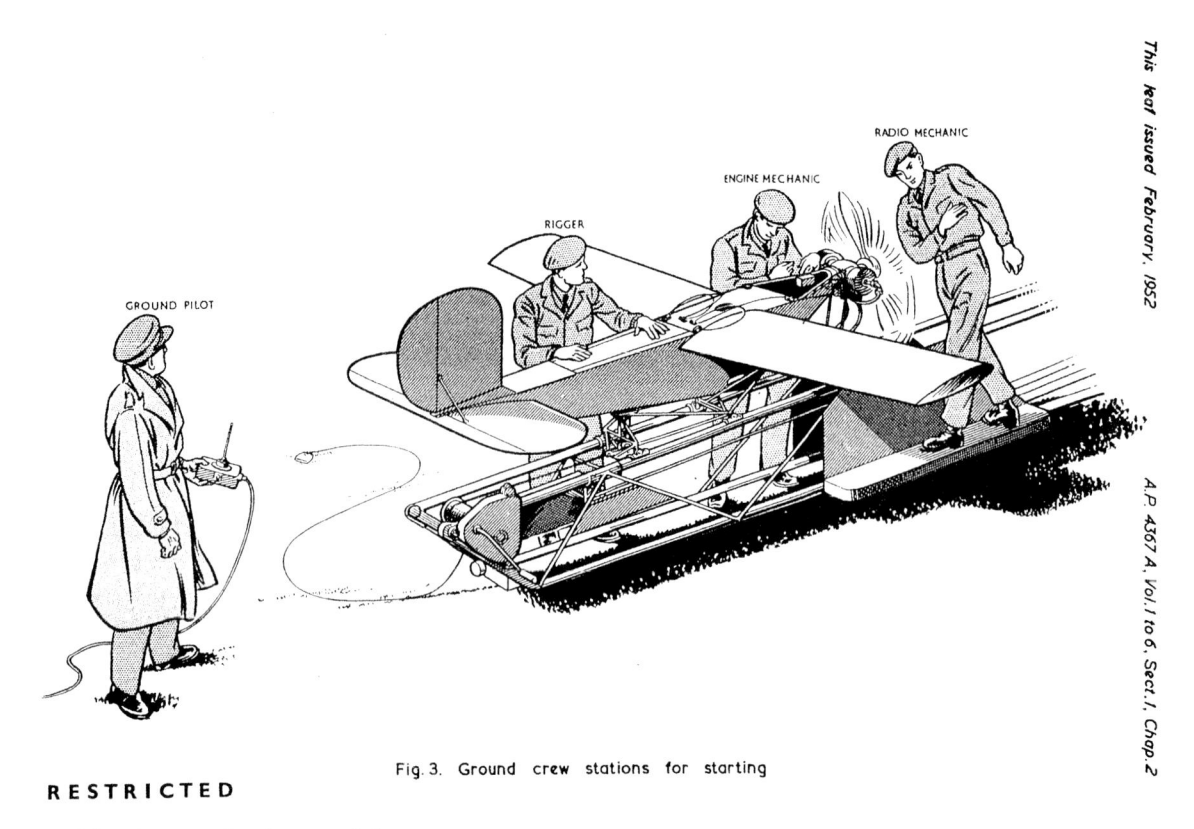

The manual for what was referred to as "Pilotless Target Aircraft No.2 Mk.1" – the Auster B3 – was issued in February 1952 and contained an illustration showing how the ground crew should position themselves for flight preparation. (Air Pilot 4367A; NA File AIR10/7172; reproduced courtesy of National Archives.)

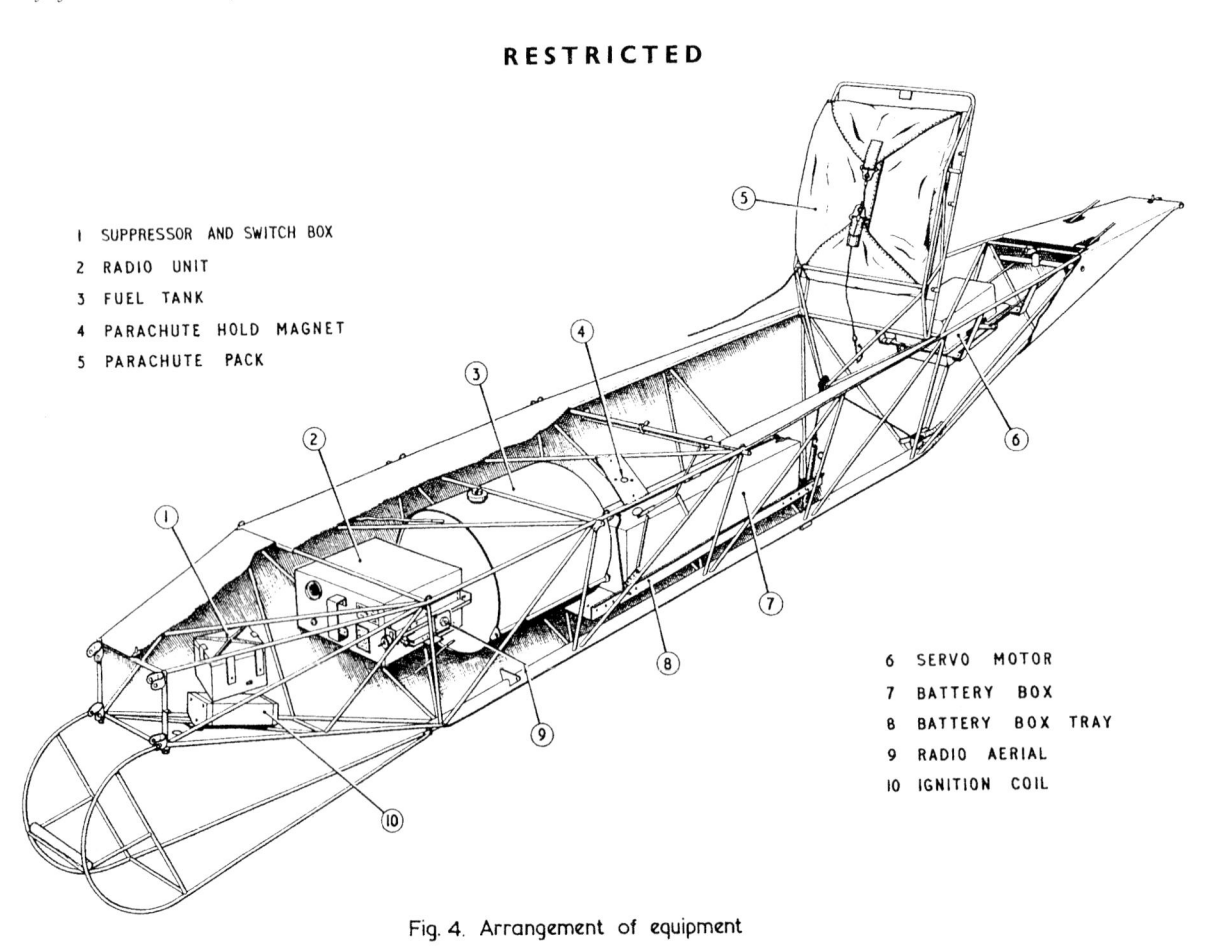

1 SUPPRESSOR AND SWITCH BOX
2 RADIO UNIT
3 FUEL TANK
4 PARACHUTE HOLD MAGNET
5 PARACHUTE PACK
6 SERVO MOTOR
7 BATTERY BOX
8 BATTERY BOX TRAY
9 RADIO AERIAL
10 IGNITION COIL

Fig. 4. Arrangement of equipment

The arrangement of equipment within the Auster B3 target is clearly illustrated in this drawing. The rather unusual tubular steel framework design is also notable and which tended to give this drone its distinctive shape. (Air Pilot 4367A; NA File AIR10/7172; reproduced courtesy of National Archives.)

224   Sitting Ducks and Peeping Toms

The original design by ML Aviation Ltd featured a "butterfly-style" tailplane. In this view an unpowered prototype has been fired from a catapult to test the basic flying characteristics. Despite the tracked vehicle and heavy Germanic-looking trench coat this view was taken on one of the Welsh Ranges (ML Aviation Archive)

Production only accounted for 150 aircraft and by the end of 1952 103 unflown targets were still available for use, a further 39 had been seriously damaged although of those only 17 were declared as written-off.

Having, it seems, ignored the development work carried out by Auster Aircraft, the process of selecting a successor to the B3/Pilotless Aircraft No.2 became a long and drawn out affair. It had begun with Specification U.25/49 which called for a "small and low-speed pilotless target aircraft and launching ramp". A key factor was that it should be "as small and as cheap as possible" but the basic U.25/49 was quickly amended (on 19 June 1950) to specify an existing (or new) piston or jet engine of British manufacture. Even then the Ministry Specification was open to further amendment when, on 5 March 1951, it reflected the need for steady flight when control signals are not being passed to the aircraft.

Tenders against U.25/49 were submitted by three companies: Fairey Aviation Ltd, ML Aviation Ltd (who submitted three alternative proposals) and Tiltman Langley Laboratories. Of the three submissions the one from Fairey was probably the most attractive.[11] However, the Specification was later cancelled and replaced by new Specification (U.120D), issued on 19 September 1951.

U.120D proposed the design and construction of a prototype, small low-speed pilotless target aircraft with launching ramps suitably adapted for both the Army and the Royal Navy (for whom Naval Requirement NA.3 had been issued).

ML Aviation U-120D 'Midget'

ML Aviation's association with unmanned target aircraft first emerged from a meeting with the Ministry of Supply in December 1950. The mood of the meeting was clearly positive as subsequent discussions led to ML being awarded a contract to design and build an aircraft to meet U.120D.

---

11 National Archives WO32/13355. Another known design was the Percival P.73, powered by a single pulsejet. There is no evidence that Percival Aircraft submitted the P.73

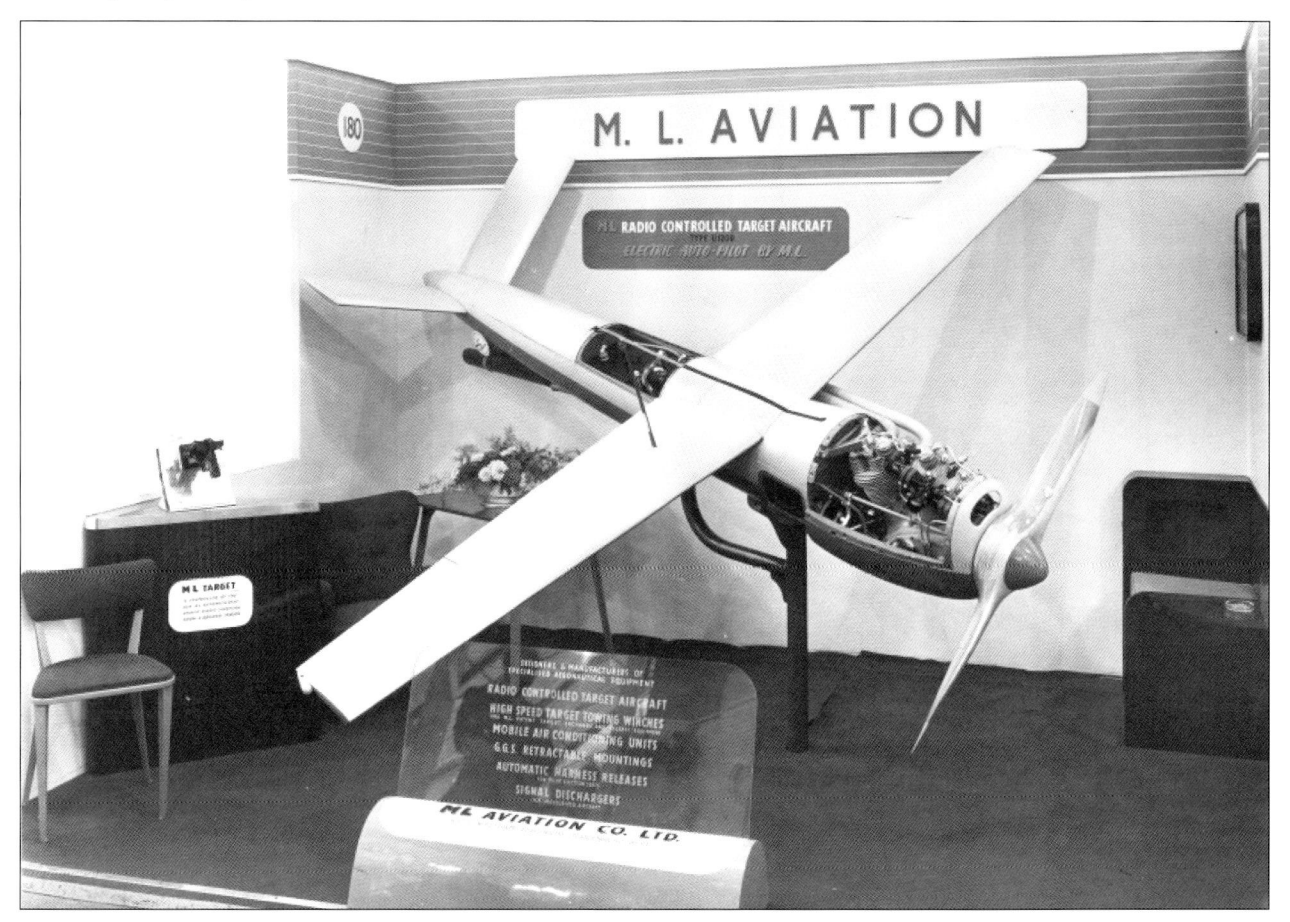

Stand 180 at the 1952 SBAC Farnborough Exhibition was the location for the first public airing of the U-120D Midget. This view clearly shows the butterfly tail arrangement. The neatness of the engine compartment is another noteworthy feature. (Larkin Brothers Ltd.)

Unmanned Targets for the Army 225

One of the initial U.120D prototypes after recovery in the Libyan desert. The flotation bag and parachute lines are clearly visible in this view. Note how the propeller has automatically stopped in the horizontal position in order to avoid damage on touchdown. (ML Aviation Archive; Neg. No.18982)

ML's design, insisted the Ministry, was that it be powered by a fuel-injected Vincent 65 bhp twin-cylinder, four-stroke engine, known as the Picador (a modified form of the motorcycle manufacturer's Vincent Rapide engine which had been specially developed to power Vincent's new Blackshadow bike.)

Design and construction of a first prototype took just over eighteen months. It was designed as a high-wing monoplane of stressed skin alloy structure with a wingspan of 12ft, overall length of 12.5ft and weighed 472lb.

Using a specially-built test model, an initial series of flight tests took place at Larkhill in early-1952. Not that true flight was ever achieved. The test vehicle was unpowered, and had just two small sections of aerofoil plus a 'butterfly' style fin. It was simply blasted off a catapult launcher to simulate a real launch. The first true prototype U-120D was first flown later in the year.[12]

Initial flight trials began in 1953, not in the UK, but on a Libyan desert Range about 50 miles south-east of Idris-el-Awal. More precisely the Range was close to the Beni Ulid road approximately 15 miles south of Tarhuna. Six aircraft were air-freighted out to Libya, none of which had (at that stage) been allocated standard service serial numbers; they were identified simply as "Target No.1", "Target No.2", Target No.3" et seq.

The first of the Libyan flights involved Target No.3 on 29 March 1953 but it ended in near disaster when the recovery parachute was deployed prematurely owing to a temporary loss of radio hold. Unfortunately the two main parachutes failed and the aircraft sustained serious damage on impact. (In the subsequent report it was suggested that the pilot's hand may have brushed the LEVEL push button whilst he was operating the BANK control knob. Later tests revealed that a slight depression on both buttons simultaneously caused a loss of radio contact. To avoid this re-occurring, the press buttons were replaced with tumbler switches.)

A second flight, on 8 April 1953 ended in almost identical circumstances although the loss of radio contact on that occasion was attributed to a loosening of two out of three bolts attaching the relay set to the aircraft's chassis.

Target No.4 was launched on 16 April 1953 in slightly adverse weather conditions, ie a 15mph side wind. The aircraft flew satisfactorily and was allowed to fly out of sight of the controller. Observers, meanwhile, kept watch through binoculars but the aircraft became lost in the sun and the aircraft subsequently flew into the ground.

The last of the Libyan flights involved Target No.6, on 6 May 1953. It was flown to an altitude of 4,000ft and successfully carried out several controlled turns, but just after five minutes of flight the engine was heard to falter as one cylinder began to cut out. Recovery parachutes were deployed but the aircraft descended in a nose-down attitude and sustained damage on impact.

A total of seven flights had been achieved in Libya and whilst launch and recovery techniques had worked effectively the overall performance of the ML aircraft was far from satisfactory. The surviving U-120Ds were airfreighted from Idris to Lyneham on 3/4 June 1953.[13]

---

12 National Archives AVIA18/1938

13 The drones were airfreighted back to the UK aboard Hastings C.1 WJ328.

ML U-120D XE725 in a "ready to launch" position. The launch platform appears to be of complex construction but was able to withstand the thrust of a zero-launch aircraft. This view, taken at Manorbier Range on 15 December 1953, is thought to have been specially posed rather than the aircraft being ready for launch. (A&AEE Neg. No.1754-1)

Despite the difficulties experienced in Libya, ML Aviation was awarded a contract (6/Acft/5535/CB.9(b)) for twenty U-120Ds together with a set of ground controls and operational equipment. The twenty aircraft were purchased specifically for development and assessment trials and were allocated serials XE722-XE735/XE749-XE754 on 10 July 1953. Interestingly, the contract included the six Libya trials aircraft and so Targets No.1 to 6 were retrospectively allocated the serials XE722-XE727 respectively.

Arrangements were made for a second series of flight trials, this time at the School of Anti-Aircraft Artillery Range at Manorbier. The object of these flights was to ensure that the U-120D was ready for C(A) release. Ahead of the start-date ML Aviation established a small service and repair facility at Manorbier and despatched by road five aircraft from White Waltham, the now-repaired XE725 & XE727 on 22 September 1953, followed by newly-built XE728, XE729 and XE731 on 9 October. Army personnel who had been trained as target operators were posted to Manorbier to act as controllers.

The Manorbier flights took place over a period of ten months. Details of the flights are as follows:

Flt	Date	Duration Mins/Secs	Remarks
1	2.10.53	2.00	Dived into the sea
2	9.10.53	2.00	Recovered
3	18.11.53	7.15	Recovered
4	2.12.53	3.30	Dived into the sea
5	12.12.53	2.30	Lost at sea
6	17.3.54	0.15	Recovered
7	7.4.54	0.13	Lost when it hit the sea
8	22.6.54	0.20	Hit ground; major damage
9	19.7.54	32.4	Minor damage on landing
10	13.8.54	20.0	Fuselage damaged

One of the U-120Ds, XE730, had been retained at White Waltham and underwent a number of modifications, including the fitting of a modified engine. Other changes

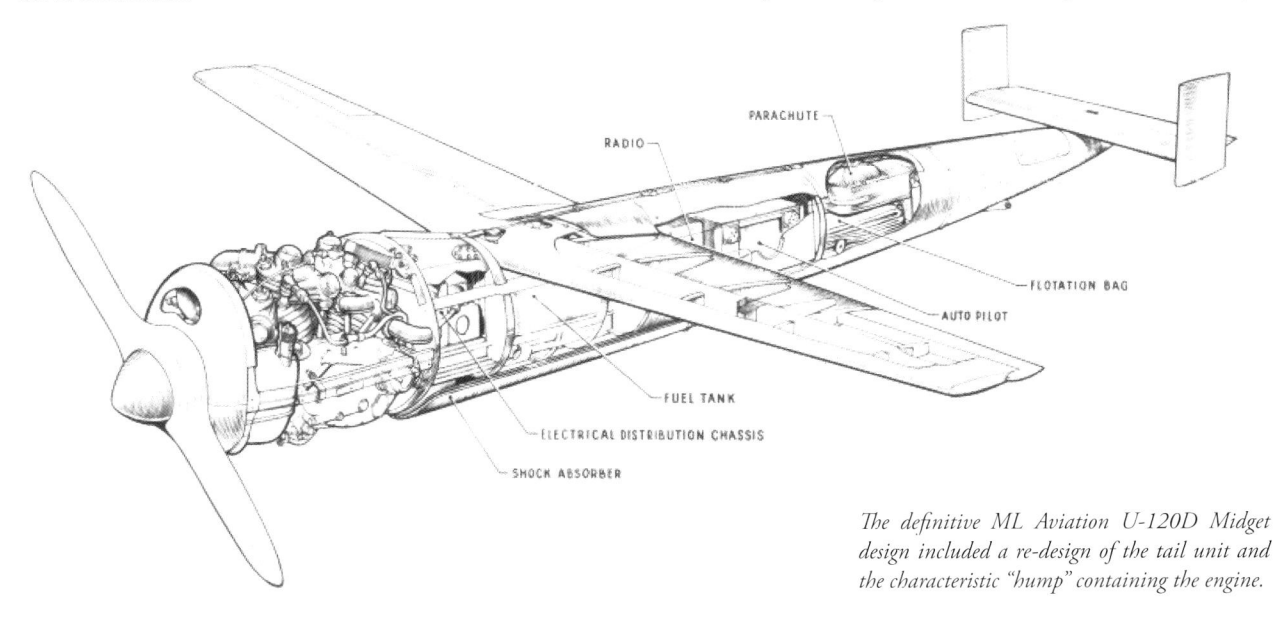

The definitive ML Aviation U-120D Midget design included a re-design of the tail unit and the characteristic "hump" containing the engine.

Unmanned Targets for the Army   227

made as a direct result of the Manorbier flights involved re-setting the ailerons at 3° negative incidence and extending the fins by 4¼ inches. The radio box was also ventilated to help cooling.

Whilst the Manorbier flight-trials proved that the U-120D's flying characteristics had improved, its overall performance was still poor when out of sight of the controller. The principal reason for this was that the autopilot system was considered to be very much under-developed for the task in hand. For that reason all flights were temporarily suspended on 20 August 1954. Several U-120Ds had been lost during the trial period and rather than risk losing more, an improved autopilot was fitted to a Provost T.1 for testing – with a pilot. In the meantime a second batch of six U-120D pre-production aircraft was ordered and allocated serials XG487-XG492 on 17 May 1954.

It was always intended that the U-120D would be operated by both the Army and the Navy but because of the growing concerns within senior Army circles over the problems affecting the drone – as well as a likely delay in it entering service – the War Office began to consider alternatives and, in October 1954, raised the possibility of using an American Northrop drone, especially as a number of surplus OQ-19s were known to be held in store at Aberporth. (These had been acquired for a series of guided-weapons trials but had never, in fact, been used.) But the Ministry of Supply offered them, not to the Army, but to the Admiralty as a stop-gap. However, the offer was rejected partly for the same reason that the KD2R-2 had been rejected several years earlier, but more so because the Admiralty believed U-120D to be "just around the corner".[14]

Under the auspices of the A&AEE test flights had resumed at Manorbier on 27 September 1954. These were designed to test a more simplified control system. A breakdown of these flights is as follows:

Flt	Date	Duration Mins/Secs	Remarks
1	27.9.54	32.54	Dived into the ground
2	1.11.54	0.33	Dived into the ground
3	10.12.54	6.33	Damaged
4	12.1.55	0.18	Damaged
5	19.1.55	27.56	OK
6	26.1.55	29.02	Minor damage

The initial two A&AEE flights (involving XE732 and XE733) both ended in disaster. The first was catapulted successfully and carried out a number of controlled manoeuvres and circuits for just over a half-hour but then, and whilst making a left turn, the aircraft's nose dropped and it dived near vertically into the ground. Subsequent inspection of the wreckage revealed that the elevators had been set at 8° up and this, together with a steep bank angle, had caused the port wing to stall. The second flight, on 1 November, also ended in disaster and somewhat prematurely after the aircraft failed to respond to a "Right Turn" command and promptly dived into the ground from 150 feet. In neither instance did the aircraft's recovery parachute deploy.

For Flight 3 the aircraft was fitted with a 2ft wing extension. Launch went without any problem but after just six minutes the recovery 'chutes deployed without command. The fourth flight, on 12 January 1955, was also launched successfully but when the aircraft was put into a gentle descent, the aircraft rolled rapidly. The controller immediately deployed the parachute but the drone was only 50ft above the ground and the heavy landing that followed caused irrepairable damage. The final two flights of this series were both terminated early due to engine misfirings.

It was very evident from the series of A&AEE test flights that the U-120D's overall performance was still marginal and, of greater significance, was far from meeting the fundamental requirements. Nevertheless the A&AEE arranged for two more test flights at Castlemartin Range, on 9 March and 1 April 1955. However, although they were airborne for some time, the flights were dogged by engine misfirings. Details were:

Flt	Date	Duration Mins/Secs	Remarks
7	9.3.55	43.25	OK
8	1.4.55	54.05	Damaged

Despite the difficulties experienced with the ML U-120D there was, rather surprisingly, still confidence that it would eventually meet the requirements – so much so that another series of flights took place at Castlemartin specifically to train enough new controllers to undertake flight-testing of production aircraft. A brief summary of these flights, all of which were conducted at Castlemartin, is as follows:

Flt	Date	Duration Mins/Secs	Remarks
1	11.6.55	1.50	
2	30.6.55	0.43	
3	7.7.55	0.05	
4	8.7.55	0.02	Destroyed on launch
5	21.7.55	–	'Chute deployed on launch
6	23.7.55	–	'Chute deployed on launch
7	25.7.55	1.50	
8	27.7.55	1.20	
9	4.8.55	1.12	
10	5.8.55	1.48	

One of the factors that dogged the U-120D programme was the aircraft's tendency to enter a roll too easily. Another, and more relevant factor, was the lack of auto control when the aircraft was out of sight to the controller. A new set of test flights was chalked in for September 1955 in order to test a new out-of-sight version of the autopilot but the

---

14 There appears to be some confusion surrounding British usage of the Northrop OQ-19 drone. There was certainly a 1952 Requirement for 23 OQ-19 drones for use at Aberporth on a series of guided-weapon trials which were due to start during the first quarter of 1953. A reference to the OQ-19's colour scheme (red undersurfaces and cream upper-surfaces) can be found in AVIA54/1988 although this does not necessarily relate to British OQ-19s. However, a further reference to the operation of OQ-19 appears in WO32/13355/325A which states that "OQ-19 has been flying at Weybourne and has many of the characteristics of U-120D".

XG491 represents the pre-production batch of U-120D target drones and survived the flight-trials programme long enough to be exhibited at the 1956 SBAC Farnborough Show. Note the serial applied beneath the port wing and what appears to be a revised colour scheme, presumably applied for the Farnborough Show. Note also the lack of engine exhausts which suggests that XG491 had perhaps by then become a non-flying static example. (Phil H. Butler, Neg.No M20329)

equipment was not ready in time and the series was cancelled.[15] In the meantime, and in a further attempt to improve the drone's flying characteristics, one aircraft was modified with smaller ailerons and test-flown at Castlemartin on 4 November 1955. The aircraft, thought to be XE749, performed well although it continued to show a tendency to roll. At the end of a long and straight flight the controller transmitted a "Left Turn" command to bring it back to base but the aircraft refused to respond and as it was rapidly reaching the limit of visual range the flight was terminated. The same aircraft made a second flight on 16 November, still with the reduced ailerons but this time with a reduction in the aileron gearing. The launch was satisfactory but the drone immediately went into a near-vertical climb and before the inevitable stall the recovery parachute was deployed, bringing it safely back to earth. On the third and final flight the rocket carrier position was adjusted to avoid repeating a steep climb-out. It worked and the drone flew a series of left and right turns without difficulty although the "roll oscillation" tendency was still very evident, but that was compensated by continually transmitting correction commands. After 40 minutes the flight was terminated safely.[16]

Flt	Date	Duration Mins/Secs	Remarks
11	4.11.55	12.07	Aileron span reduced by 5½ inches at outer edges.
12	16.11.55	0.31	Recovered safely
13	17.11.55	40.00	Recovered safely

At the same time as the Castlemartin test-flights were taking place, the Admiralty, still keen on acquiring U-120D, held a series of shipboard flight tests in the English Channel. The decision had been taken, in May 1955, to fit a catapult launcher on the aft deck of the destroyer HMS *Vigo* and by August work was complete. Three U-120Ds (including XE750 and XE751) were transferred from Manorbier to Portsmouth on 27 August and the first of several test launches took place on 1 September. In mid-Channel and stationary, *Vigo* launched XE751, but the flight failed to perform as planned. On the first attempt to launch, the port rocket failed to fire and although the starboard rocket fired normally the target was held back. Technicians discovered that a faulty connecting plug on the launcher had worked loose during the launch preliminaries. A second attempt was more successful and XE751 flew several turns around the ship at a radius of about a mile. After 8 minutes the controller steered the aircraft towards HMS *Charity* which was in attendance for observation purposes. The attitude of the aircraft as it turned proved difficult to control and XE751 began to enter a dive, at which point the controller pressed the 'parapop' command. He held it for some ten seconds but unfortunately the aircraft had already hit the sea.

HMS *Vigo* proceeded to the crash scene and began to search for the aircraft. Its position was located by the sight of an oil patch and parts of the propeller floating on the surface. The flotation bag, which had fully inflated, was seen to be just below the surface but by the time the ship was turned and in positioned to recover XE751, no trace of it could be found.

A second test flight was carried out off HMS *Vigo* on the following day, a flight which marked the maiden flight of XE750. On this occasion the ship was moving at 5kts and the aircraft was launched into a 25kt wind. The aircraft was flown in a flight profile very similar to the previous day's test but after just four minutes of flight, and without any command being transmitted, the recovery parachutes deployed and it landed in the sea. On this occasion the U-120D was successfully recovered but it sustained some damage in the process owing to the roughness of the sea and to the inexperience of the ship's crew in recovering downed aircraft. The cause of the premature recovery was thought to be a brief screening caused by the ship's superstructure. A third test took place on 5 September when the aircraft flew satisfactorily for ten minutes before making a routine recovery.

As far as the Admiralty was concerned, the *Vigo* trials were considered successful and the overall performance of

---

15 National Archives WO32/13355/427A
16 A&AEE U-120D Trials Report 6600/25 (National Archives WO32/13355)

ML U-120D
Individual Aircraft Histories

Contract 6/Acft/5535/CB.9(b):
20 Prototype & Pre-Production Targets

XE722 Written-off in Libya trials 1953 when it climbed steeply, stalled and crashed before the controller could recover it (precise date unkn).

XE723 Written-off in Libya trials 1953 when it dived into the ground immediately after launch (precise date unkn).

XE724 Written-off in Libya trials 29.3.53.

XE725 Used in Libya trials 1953. Sustained slight damage 8.4.53 but later repaired. Used for engine installation tests with modified Picador engine 1953.

XE726 Written-off in Libya trials 1953 (precise date unkn).

XE727 Used in Libya trials 1953. Sustained slight damage but later repaired by ML. Conveyed to Manorbier where, on 2.10.53, it was destroyed after diving into the sea.

XE728 Built 7.53. Dived into the sea off Manorbier 2.12.53.

XE729 Built 7.53. Lost at sea off Manorbier 12.12.53.

XE730 Built 8.53. Later modified to Mk.2 variant. Exhibited statically at SBAC Farnborough 9.1955. No further details

XE731 Built 8.53. Lost when it struck the sea off Manorbier 7.4.54.

XE732-XE735 Details not known but believed to have been w/o during flight trials at Manorbier 9.54 to 1.55.

XE749 Modified to Mk.2 variant. No further details.

XE750 f/f 2.9.55 off HMS *Vigo*

XE751 Written-off 1.9.55 whilst operating off HMS *Vigo*.

XE752-XE753 Modified to Mk.2 variant. No further details

XE754 No details.

XG487 Destroyed 8.7.55 during launch at Castlemartin.

XG488 Crashed at Castlemartin Range 25.7.55.

XG489-XG492 Believed all written-off at Castlemartin 1955 with the exception of XG491 which was exhibited statically at the 1956 SBAC Farnborough Show.

---

the U-120D offered no cause for concern. Indeed Admiralty observers had been favourably impressed by the post-flight lack of damage and the dryness of the equipment although the full extent of waterproofing was considered not wholly sufficient for extended naval operations. On the other hand, the DGD held totally different views of the U-120D and went as far as informing the Deputy Controller of Aircraft (Ministry of Supply) that he was becoming "greatly concerned over the U-120D progress and (that) greater vigour was called for."

In an attempt to overcome the "out-of-sight" autopilot problem, a newly-developed system was evaluated at White Waltham in an Auster AOP.6, VF627, on loan from the RAF. In tests the system worked perfectly and so seven U-120Ds were modified and a final series of trials took place in May 1956. Four of the U-120Ds were in a standard, non-waterproofed configuration whilst the remaining three (XE749, XE752, XE753) were fitted with modified waterproofing and other minor modifications – the latter now being referred to as U-120D Mk.2 variants.[17]

By July 1956 there were signs that the ML U-120D might achieve what it was designed to do. The Admiralty continued to show a keen interest in the U-120D and even announced, subject to a satisfactory demonstration of the U-120D's 'out-of-sight' capability (which the Navy had planned for September 1956), a willingness to order 50 production examples, followed by a further 150 over the next three years. The company's confidence in an Admiralty contract was underlined by displaying one example (XG491) on its stand at the 1956 Farnborough Show. But in the event the 'out-of-sight' demonstration was a catastrophic failure

and only succeeded in confirming just how unreliable the U-120D really was.

Another concern was that costs had risen alarmingly, much being attributable to the cost of the engines. In real terms the cost of each aircraft had risen from £2,015 to £3,150 while development costs were now running at some £6,000 per month. For the War Office it was becoming all too much to bear and, in October 1956, they announced that the Army was no longer interested in the U-120D.[18]

The failure of the 'out-of-sight' trial and the withdrawal of War Office support convinced the Admiralty that the U-120D was unlikely to meet its requirements. After five years since the original requirement was issued and an expenditure of £½million on research and development, the U-120D ended in failure. Work stopped immediately and RAE Farnborough was asked to undertake a post mortem on the entire project.[19]

Farnborough's investigation into the U-120D affair was damning. Not only was the autopilot constantly troublesome, the U-120D's speed was also below expectation, being able to operate at only between 140-150kts.

Losing the U-120D did nothing to lessen the Navy's need for a reliable aerial target; if anything it had become more urgent. In July 1957 the DGD learnt that the US Navy had taken delivery of the Radioplane KD2R-5, a new version of KD2R-2 that was fitted with an 'out-of-sight' autopilot, a zero length launcher and with a normal operational speed of 228mph. The KD2R-5 was, in effect, a fully developed, proven and ideal alternative to the U-120D. Ironically, but perhaps not surprisingly, the RAE report had recommended the purchase of Radioplane KD2R-5 targets. Coincidentally, another report, which originated from the Director of the

---

17 Contemporary reports state that the four non-waterproofed aircraft were XE731-XE734 but a Trials Report on the first series of Manorbier flights shows that XE731 was written-off on 7 April 1954.

18 National Archives WO32/13355/474A
19 National Archives ADM1/26739

Gunnery Division (and dated 17 December 1957) recommended the same action and even went on to suggest that a quantity of Northrop OQ-19 drones held in store by the Ministry of Supply should be released to the Admiralty.

RAE Larkhill Trials – MQM-36A (KD2R-5)

Not only did the withdrawal from the U-120D programme leave the Army without a dedicated target aircraft for weapons training, but also without plans to design and develop an alternative. Throughout the 1960s and early 1970s the Army's use of unmanned drone aircraft was almost entirely associated with battlefield surveillance. Not until the rapid development in portable surface-to-air missile systems (SAMs) did the Army demonstrate the need for a suitable unmanned aircraft specifically for target training.

The modern surface-to-air missile (SAM) come of age during the Vietnam War. Technological development of a simplistic and robust infra-red seeker head had offered the opportunity for an infantryman to hit back at a ground-attack aircraft. The catalyst had been the Soviet SA-7 "Grail" missile which, in Vietnam, had taken air defence to a new level. Almost overnight low-technology, prop-driven COIN aircraft had been rendered extremely vulnerable. In fact, anything that acted as a heat source was immediately vulnerable. But the threat of SA-7 was soon lessened by newly-adopted counter-measure tactics. The greatest source of heat from an aircraft is the exhaust and thus the attacker was at its greatest vulnerability only when flying away from its ground target. The missile had also to be fast enough to catch the attacker. Artificially-modulated heat sources and decoy flares offered the simplest countermeasures – and in most instances proved successful.

Western development of battlefield SAMs mirrored that of the Soviets. The direct equivalent of the SA-7 in the US was the General Dynamics FIM-43 Redeye and its successor, the FIM-92A Stinger. Stinger entered US Army service in 1981 and had the benefit of filtering out much countermeasure activity and intentionally distracted heat sources. (During the 1982 Falkland Islands conflict, the SAS used Stinger but in British hands its effect was, to some degree, disappointing.)

The most effective SAM in British infantry use during the 1970/80s, and which became the Army's standard battlefield missile, was the Short Blowpipe. Like its counterparts, Blowpipe was shoulder-launched and therefore highly mobile, but it was not a heat-seeking missile; it was

Despite an extensive search no description of the ML U-120D drone's colour scheme has surfaced. However, the widely-acclaimed comic, "Eagle", published an interesting cutaway drawing of a U-120D in its 22 January 1954 issue. There is, of course, no reason to doubt the authenticity of the colour scheme. (Hulton Press Ltd)

command-guided. Once the missile was launched the gunner directed the missile to its target by using a thumb-operated controller and a direct radio link. Simplistic up/down, left/right commands directed the missile to its target. What made Blowpipe stand out ahead of others was that it was designed from the outset to work best at head-on engagements, i.e. before the attacking aircraft had attacked. But Blowpipe required considerable skill and determination by the soldier to gain maximum effect.

In 1969 the Ministry of Technology contracted Short Bros to establish an aerial target operation to support Blowpipe development and field trials. A key requirement in assessing missile and target was that the expended missile should be recoverable for subsequent examination. Ranges at Manorbier, Aberporth and the Hebrides were such that the missile would end up in the sea and not be recoverable. Therefore the decision was taken to conduct trials on the Rocket Range at RAE Larkhill. Shorts made full use of RAE facilities and set up a base in two *Nissen* huts, situated on the edge of Salisbury Plain, and which served as a workshop and hangar respectively. The unit, manned by a small team of technicians led by Cyril 'Ollie' Oliver, also made use of RAE personnel including Radar Controller John Lees and Visual Controller Susan Thompson who made history by becoming the first British female controller.

The search for a suitable target for Blowpipe trials and subsequent in-service user-training began at an early stage in Blowpipe's development. In fact the choice was fairly academic and largely influenced in the knowledge that for a number of years the Royal Navy Pilotless Target Association (RNPTA) had made extensive use of the Northrop MQM-36A Shelduck target. The Army had also used Shelduck for training controllers selected for deployment on MQM-57A surveillance drones. (See Chapter 9). Ten ex-factory Northrop MQM-36A target drones (XW594-XW603) were delivered in 1969 to allow flying training to begin early in 1970.[20]

---

20 The ten MQM-36As were ordered against Contract KK/T/59/CB.20(b) which also included ten examples (XW571-XW580) for the Royal Navy Pilotless Target Association.

Unmanned Targets for the Army   231

Above: *From 1969 RAE Larkhill hosted a small pilotless aircraft unit formed to establish procedures for training drone pilots ahead of Short Blowpipe trials. Normally it was only the drone that was wrecked. In this instance KD2R-5 XW601 was being towed out to the Larkhill Range on 1 August 1973 when the towing vehicle hit an unseen rut and overturned. Initially drones were carried one at a time on a trailer behind a standard Land Rover but this arrangement was later superceded by a 3-ton lorry adapted to carry three drones. Note the hyphenated and stenciled serial style and that the overall dark red scheme extended across the fin. (RAE Larkhill Neg. No.6525, via Colin Mills)*

Left: *Seen at Larkhill on 30 November 1971 is the team of technicians that comprised the RAE Larkhill Pilotless Aircraft Unit along with one of its KD2R-5 (MQM-36A) drones. They are (left-to-right) Noel Ward, John Lees (controller), Susan Thompson (controller), Colin Mills, Cyril Oliver and team leader Keith Clayton. (via Colin Mills)*

Susan Thompson: Britain's First Female Controller

A love for aviation led Susan Thompson to take a job with the RAE at Larkhill where much of her work involved extrapolating and assessing data from trials held over the Larkhill Ranges. By the time that Short Bros set up their trials base at Larkhill she had gained her PPL and was therefore a natural choice to join the small team of RAE personnel as a Visual Controller.

The role of Visual Controller meant being responsible for launching the drone from just outside the Impact Area, ensuring that the JATO bottle was automatically dropped after several seconds, and then "flying" the drone up to its desired altitude and into the Impact Area. Control was then handed over to the Radar Controller who flew the aircraft across the Impact Area and within line of sight of the Blowpipe firer.

At the end of the flight, the Shelduck was flown back to the launch area whereupon control was handed back to the Visual Controller who positioned the aircraft over a landing area outside the Impact Area before giving the command to deploy the recovery parachute for a safe landing.

The ground-based flight control unit was basic to the extreme. The only flying surfaces fitted to Shelduck were ailerons and elevators and accordingly only two controls were necessary, in the form of two knobs. The elevator control knob was turned clockwise or anti-clockwide to put the drone into a climb or a descent. Being a qualified pilot, Susan Thompson found it unnatural to operate the drone's elevator by the turn of a knob. She managed to convince RAE technicians to replace the control knob with a "control column" onto the right-hand side of the control box. Flying a drone became as natural as flying a Tiger Moth.

Three views of one of RAE Larkhill's KD2R-5 (MQM-36A) drones launching at the Rocket Range on Larkhill on 13 May 1970. The launch process was established by the RAE trials unit. Once the engine was started it was fine-tuned remotely by a technician standing behind the port wing. The drone would then be "jacked-up" to launch attitude, the electric parachute hatch was engaged, parachute safety pins were removed as were the pins on the JATO bracket; the JATO was then connected at which stage the launch technician would retire to the firing-point to wait for the instruction from the drone's pilot to fire the JATO rockets. The JATO rocket motor produced a rather fearsome flame on launch but once sufficient height and speed had been attained so the expended JATO bottle fell away. Note that the drone carries the legend "MINISTRY OF TECHNOLOGY" AND "RAE LARKHILL". (RAE Larkhill Neg Series 5165)

Although these ten drones were standard MQM-36As (ie as operated by the Royal Navy's Pilotless Target Association) the RAE is believed to have installed some radio equipment necessary for British operations. A second shipment of MQM-36A Shelduck targets took place in March 1971, involving 30 aircraft. Again, these were consigned to RAE Farnborough for storage, having been earmarked as targets for the live Blowpipe missile trials. Targets were transferred to Larkhill as and when required; the first successful flight against a live Blowpipe missile took place on Friday 19 November 1971. The target drone was flown by Susan Thompson.

The initial RAE batch of twenty Shelducks retained their standard factory overall red finish with white wings, tailplane and fin but are known to have had the legend "MINISTRY OF TECHNOLOGY" and "RAE LARKHILL" applied to the mid-fuselage. Serials were applied beneath the tailplane in a stenciled fashion and with a hyphen, eg XW-594. The second batch were supplied with a similar overall red scheme but with a red fin and standard serial presentation.

RAE MQM-36A (KD2R-5) Individual Aircraft Histories

Contract KK/T/59/CB.20(b):
20 MQM-36A (10 of which ordered by MinTech for the RAE)

XW594-XW603 Departed USA July 1969 and shipped to UK; consigned to RAE Farnborough for use at Larkhill. Believed to have been expended during pilot training and Blowpipe trials 1969-1973

The remaining aircraft placed against this Contract were ordered for the Royal Navy PTA.

Contract K20c/65/CB20(b):
30 MQM-36A ordered by MinTech for the RAE

Note that this Contract was dated 24.7.70.

XW803 (c/n 7893) Departed USA (Wilmington, California) aboard SS *Kamperdyk* 10.3.71. Shipped to UK; consigned to RAE Farnborough. Noted in store there 1972; released to Army stocks, date unkn. Tfd to RNPTA, Portland 9.76. Further details unkn.

XW804 (c/n 7894) Shipped ex-USA with XW803 etc. Presumed lost during Blowpipe trials.

XW805-XW806 (c/n 7895-7896) Shipped ex-USA with XW803 etc. Noted in store at Farnborough 1972. Presumed lost during Blowpipe trials.

XW807 (c/n 7897) Shipped ex-USA with XW803 etc. Released to Army stocks, date unkn. Tfd to RNPTA, Portland 9.76. Crashed into the sea in the Portland

Exercise Area 11.11.85 when it fell off its recovery parachute. (TFH 6.21; 10 Flights)

XW808 (c/n 7898) Shipped ex-USA with XW803 etc. Noted in store at Farnborough 1972; released to Army stocks, date unkn. Tfd to RNPTA, Portland 9.76. Last recorded flight on 13.11.85 with 'A' Flt/RNPTA in the Gibraltar Exercise Area. (TFH 9.33; 17 Flights)

XW809-XW810 (c/n 7899-7900) Shipped ex-USA with XW803 etc. Presumed lost during Blowpipe trials.

XW811 (c/n 7901) Shipped ex-USA with XW803 etc. Noted in store at Farnborough 1972; released to Army stocks, date unkn. Tfd to RNPTA, Portland 9.76. Further details unkn.

XW812 (c/n 7902) Shipped ex-USA with XW803 etc. No further details although known to have been used in the rebuild of XW596 at Portland in 1977.

XW813 (c/n 7903) Shipped ex-USA with XW803 etc. Noted in store at Farnborough 1972. Tfd to RNPTA, Portland 9.76. Further details unkn.

XW814 (c/n 7904) Shipped ex-USA with XW803 etc. Presumed lost during Blowpipe trials.

XW815 (c/n 7905) Shipped ex-USA with XW803 etc. Noted in store at Farnborough 1972. Tfd to RNPTA, Portland 9.76. Further details unkn.

XW816 (c/n 7906) Shipped ex-USA with XW803 etc. Presumed lost during Blowpipe trials.

XW817 (c/n 7907) Shipped ex-USA with XW803 etc. Noted in store at Farnborough 1972. Tfd to RNPTA, Portland. Destroyed by a Rapier missile 18.6.83 over the Falkland Islands Range whilst operating from RFA *Tidespring*. (TFH 2.47; 5 Flights)

XW818 (c/n 7908) Shipped ex-USA with XW803 etc. Noted in store at Farnborough 1972. Tfd to RNPTA, Portland 9.76. Further details unkn.

XW819-XW820 (c/n 7909-7910) Shipped ex-USA with XW803 etc. Presumed lost during Blowpipe trials.

XW821 (c/n 7911) Shipped ex-USA with XW803 etc. Noted in store at Farnborough 1972. Tfd to RNPTA, Portland 8.76. Sustained extensive damage 13.11.85 when it flew into the sea whilst operating with 'A' Flt/FTG in the Gibraltar Exercise Area. (TFH 6.39; 7 Flights)

XW822-XW824 (c/n 7912-7914) Shipped ex-USA with XW803 etc. Presumed lost during Blowpipe trials.

XW825-XW827 (c/n 7915-7917) Shipped ex-USA with XW803 etc. Noted in store at Farnborough 1972. Tfd to RNPTA, Portland 8.76. Further details unkn.

XW828 (c/n 7918) Shipped ex-USA with XW803 etc. Noted in store at Farnborough 1972. Tfd to RNPTA, Portland 8.76. Crashed 25.3.83 immediately after launch from RFA *Olna* in the Falkland Islands.

XW829 (c/n 7919) Shipped ex-USA with XW803 etc. Presumed lost during Blowpipe trials.

XW830 (c/n 7920) Shipped ex-USA with XW803 etc. Noted in store at Farnborough 1972. Tfd to RNPTA, Portland 8.76. Further details unkn.

XW831 (c/n 7921) Shipped ex-USA with XW803 etc. Pressumed lost during Blowpipe trials.

XW832 (c/n 7922) Shipped ex-USA with XW803 etc. Noted in store at Farnborough 1972. Tfd to RNPTA, Portland 9.76. Further details unkn.

Sitting on its launch trolley KD2R-5 XW829 is being prepared for flight. The JATO rocket has yet to be fitted whilst just visible beneath the port wing is the starter trolley, specially designed by RAE Technician Les Van Hagen. The woman walking around the port wingtip is Susan Thompson, the UK's first fully-trained drone controller. (Via Colin Mills)

Short MATS-B & Short Skeet Target Drones

On several occasions Blowpipe had been test-fired against a towed Rushton "sleeve" target, trailing up to 5km behind a Canberra at the time. However, Blowpipe was designed to attack a head-on target and a towed target was hardly likely to replicate the profile of a head-on target. Apart from that and the hazardous operation of having manned aircraft fly across a live Range which worried Army planners, there was the added cost of Range time. Any form of towed target would always be uneconomical due to the tug aircraft having to operate from a distant airfield as well as being dependent on suitable weather conditions. There was also a cost factor that precluded the use of Blowpipe against the sophisticated Jindivik drone. In any case targets facing Blowpipe were not expected to last for more than two or three flights.

In many respects the trials at Larkhill demonstrated that the MQM-36A (KD2R-5) Shelduck drone was ideally suited for the Army's needs, but there was a drawback. The unit cost of buying Shelduck – even off the shelf – was high. What the planners within the Ministry of Defence's TGW3 Branch really wanted was a Weapons Training Package that was essentially a "cheap and nasty" aircraft and one which was relatively simple to operate.

The first steps towards a suitable target system were taken towards the end of 1973 when Ministry of Defence TGW3 Branch approached the manufacturer of Blowpipe, the Missile Systems Division of Short Brothers Ltd. The response was quick. By employing model aircraft technology and equipment Shorts managed to produce a relatively cheap, compact, radio-controlled target drone. The design was effectively the product of Ed Marshall who was personally responsible for all of the aerodynamic aspects. He

Positioned on its launcher and with its engine-start mesh safety shield in position, MATS-B ZA549 is ready for engine-start and test-flight. This view is taken behind the Short Brothers maintenance facility at Larkhill. (Michael I Draper)

also designed the propellor which, at the time, was of an untried size.

Three laminated prototypes were constructed at the company's Castlereagh, Belfast facility to test the target's aerodynamics. The first of the three was successfully test-flown at Ballykelly airfield in June 1975. Powered by a single-cylinder 123cc McCulloch engine the aircraft, by now referred to as MATS-B (Military Aircraft Target System), consisted of a 2.44m (8ft) long square-section fuselage, the forward half of which was constructed in aluminum and a rear portion in glass fibre. The whole length of the fuselage was divided into compartments to contain engine, recovery parachutes, batteries, a 5-litre fuel tank, electronics, 4 × 60second flares, elevator servo and radar reflector. The wing, spanning 3.35m (11ft), fin and all-moving tailplane, were built in fibreglass and filled with polyurethane foam.

The McCulloch engine, with its "over-sized" propeller, was also tested by Shorts' technicians although in a rather unconventional manner. Starting the engine required a "prop-swing", a procedure which, if carried out by hand, was thought likely to result in dire consequences – amputation of one's fingers being the obvious concern. On the first attempt they used a shortened broomstick with a cloth wrapped around the business end! It worked, despite being both unconventional and dangerous. But it did lead the same technicians to devise an alternative electric starter albeit a standard British Leyland Mini starter motor but with the brushes re-wired so as to reverse the direction of rotation. It was also fitted with a "spigot and dog clutch". Just as radical but probably less dangerous!

Unmanned Targets for the Army   235

All three MATS-B prototypes were tested to destruction during early flight trials at Ballykelly in 1975. The trials proved that the system was fundamentally successful and on the strength of that Shorts was awarded a development contract for twenty pre-production aircraft, all built specifically for testing over Army Ranges.

The first test firings of Blowpipe missiles had already taken place at the Larkhill Range but by the time the missile was ready for service entry facilities at the Range had changed considerably. Larkhill had become much more of an exercise area than a missile testing Range and the only available Range suitable for Blowpipe firings was now in the Outer Hebrides. All further MATS-B testing therefore took place at the Royal Artillery Range at Benbecula where Shorts set up a company "Camp" with a fully-equipped workshop and support facilities. MATS-B completed its acceptance tests in January 1977 at Benbecula in the Hebrides.

Short Brothers had been awarded a production contract for MATS-B in August 1976 which accounted for just 50 aircraft (XZ815-XZ840/XZ861-XZ884). But despite the success of the MATS-B trials there did remain one major controversy. The Army, in the meantime, had raised the question of who should operate MATS-B. With a few exceptions the Army had used drones mainly for battlefield surveillance, a role which was considered so vital that the Army should have total control. After all, a battlefield surveillance drone was seen as an essential piece of Army kit. On the other hand MATS-B existed solely to be shot at. It did not, claimed Army Chiefs, need an expensive and fully-trained soldier to go through the additional process of learning how to fly a 'model aeroplane' just so that another fully-trained soldier can shoot it down! There was, of course, an easy solution. The MoD chose to award Shorts with another contract, that of operating MATS-B on behalf of the Army. That put Shorts in an enviable situation – not only did the company build the missile and the designated target aircraft; it now took on the responsibility of operating it. As an integral part of Shorts' Flying Services Division (which itself was a direct offshoot of the Missile Systems Division) the company set up the Target Operations Group (TOG) which was established on the edge of Llanbedr airfield.

Early MATS-B target drones operated with the SHORTS legend on their fin and TOG beneath it – indicating use by the Target Operations Group at Llanbedr. ZA864, a well-battered example, has had its fibreglass rear fuselage repaired and its serial very crudely re-applied. (Michael I Draper)

Not long after MATS-B entered service with the TOG an aggravating flying problem developed which had not been evident in early test flights. Because the all-moving tailplane of the MATS-B was aerodynamically and statically balanced the continuous jolting from skid landings had caused servos to fail on a number of aircraft. Remedial action was speedily incorporated into new-build aircraft, which featured a fixed tailplane but with standard elevators operated by separate servos. At the same time Shorts took the decision to increase the capacity of the flare pack to include twelve flares, each lasting some 40 seconds. In its modified form the new version became known as the MATS-B Mk.1A and a 1978 order for 25 aircraft (ZA200-ZA214/ZA237-ZA246) was for the Mk.1A variant. A follow-on order, placed in 1979, for fifty aircraft (ZA806-ZA822/ZA837-ZA846/ZA859-ZA874/ZA893-ZA899) was also for the Mk.1A version as was a final contract for another 50 examples (allocated as ZA520-ZA535/ZA548-ZA564/ZA580-ZA596). (This final batch was the subject of a complex administrative mix-up. An error by MoD Contracts Branch created a large number of compromised serials and in order to resolve the error Contracts Branch advised that the blocks should be prefixed ZB- instead of ZA-. By the time that the error had been realised most of the aircraft had been built and delivered. They were therefore never corrected. But not only did MoD make an error. Shorts had forgotten to observe the "blacked-out" block after ZA564. Thus what should have been ZB580-596 in fact appeared with the serials ZA565-581 applied in error.)

Target Operations Group's base at Llanbedr came under threat during late 1980 when Shorts lost the tenure of the airfield. Not wishing to disrupt target operations the Ministry of Defence arranged for new premises to be made immediately available on the edge of Rollestone Camp at Larkhill and TOG moved in to its new home in April 1981. Other changes to the operational structure were about to take place. Since April 1980 Short Brothers had, through the TOG, operated MATS-B on behalf of the Army under a somewhat 'ad hoc' contractural arrangement. The terms were relatively simple: the contract lasted for a year and was funded through an 'on-cost' basis. That contract expired at the time of TOG's move to Larkhill and, following some pressure from Shorts, the contract was changed to a 'fixed-price' basis but to run for three years, i.e. from April 1981 until 30 April 1984. Five months later, in September 1981, the Target Operations Group was re-organised to become an independent subsidiary company of Short Brothers Ltd. TOG became Short Brothers Air Services Ltd under the leadership of Lt Col (Rtd) Dennis A. Robson.

Including prototypes, pre-production aircraft plus a small export order for twenty from the Malawi Armed Forces (which, incidentally, are thought never to have been flown) total MATS-B production amounted to 218. By the time that the last Army example (ZA596) had left Short's Castlereagh factory in November 1981 its successor, the Skeet, was just weeks away from service issue.

The Royal Artillery Range in the Hebrides was the primary site for Blowpipe firing but with Rapier and Lance missile-firing camps beginning to take place, the Hebrides Range had become overcrowded. There were few alternative sites to hand. The Otterburn Training Range in Northumberland, which had also been designated as suitable for Blowpipe training, was not yet developed with full support facilities. In any case Otterburn was much in demand for artillery practice and training. Larkhill, as mentioned earlier, had also become more of an Exercise Area. Army planners therefore turned their attention towards the old coastal Ranges at Manorbier, near Tenby in South Wales. Although facilities at Manorbier were poor and in need of considerable refurbishment, the work was quickly carried out and Manorbier became established as the principal Blowpipe Training Range. Just ahead of Skeet entering service SBAS established an on-camp base at Manorbier, operating as a satellite to the company's main base at Larkhill.

MATS-B had proved to be successful but its design had relied almost entirely on model aircraft technology; it had – perhaps rather surprisingly – been developed and flown straight from the drawing-board. Its successor, the Short Skeet, was the subject of a £½million development contract which included a series of wind tunnel, stress and climatic tests. One necessary change was the powerplant as the 123cc McCulloch engine had been phased out of production. In its place the Ministry of Defence encouraged Shorts to adopt the 274cc Normalair-Garrett Weslake twin-cylinder, two-stroke engine which had originally been specified for the frustrated Westland Wisp helicopter project. The major advantage of the Weslake engine was its very low vibration factor, a vital consideration when employing built-in fail-safe systems.

MATS-B Technical Data	
Power Plant	1 × 8.6 kW (11.5 hp) McCulloch 123cc single-cylinder, two-stroke piston engine, driving a two-blade propeller.)
Wing Span	11 ft 0 in (3.35 m)
Length overall	8 ft 0 in (2.44 m)
Payload	15 lb (6.8 kg)
Max launching weight	107 lb (48.5 kg)
Max level speed	126 mph (203 km/h)
Range	3.1 miles (5 km)
Maximum endurance	45 mins
Guidance & Control	7-Channel radio command guidance system (hand-held transmitter), in the 68MHz band. Aerodynamic control by servo-operated ailerons and all-moving tailplane (Mk.1), or elevators (Mk.1A)

Short Skeet I

Other than perhaps religion, few things are taken so seriously or venerated so highly as fieldsport traditions. This is especially true in the long-established area of shotgun shooting which, from game to clay, comes in a wide variety of guises. Among those is the strange and artificial discipline of 'Skeet Shooting'.

It was developed in the USA during the 1920s when a group of friends, in practising their quail shooting technique, laid down a basic format for a series of local competitions. In time, a set of rules was defined for this new discipline which consisted of a semi-circle of shooters facing targets fired from trap-houses across and from either side of the Range

Recovery of Short MATS-B target drone back to earth was achieved by three standard parachutes and which ensured a safe landing. (Short Brothers & Harland Ltd.)

area. For a long while the discipline had no name but was referred to as "semi-circle two trap shooting". An American magazine sought, through a competition, a name more suitable. The winner suggested "Skytt", a Scandanavian word meaning "shoot" and a quick Americanisation produced the term "skeet" – and it has remained ever since. Appropriately, some six decades later, Shorts adopted the name "skeet" for a new version of the MATS-B target.

Apart from the change of engine, Skeet incorporated a number of refinements over the MATS-B. Twin fuel tanks were introduced – the second tank being installed just aft of the wing mounting bolt so as to effectively increase duration from 45 minutes to 75 minutes at full throttle. An obvious consequence of increasing the available time over the Range led to the number of Pains-Wessex smoke flares being increased from 12 to 16. Skeet also introduced a single cruciform recovery parachute instead of a cluster of three small round parachutes as on MATS-B. Not unnaturally these refinements increased the overall weight of Skeet from 50kg to 63kg. Shorts therefore redesigned the wing albeit it remained exactly the same dimensions as for MATS-B. The most visible difference between MATS-B and Skeet could be found in the tail area. On Skeet the tailplane was moved aft and fitted directly beneath the fin. This change allowed the installation of a Racal Doppler Miss-Distance Indicator (MDI) to be installed in the rear fuselage section.

The first prototype Skeet made its initial test flight on 10 October 1978. By the time that development trials had been

The first prototype Short Skeet 1 target is seen ready for launch at RAE Llanbedr. The black and white scheme was applied only to the prototypes. (Short Bros Neg. No.79117-22)

completed, in September 1981, Skeet was proving to be almost fourteen times more reliable that MATS-B.

A single order for 300 Skeet aircraft had already been placed with Shorts, in June 1980. The quantity was fixed to meet an expected attrition rate of 100 aircraft per year over a three-year service contract. The serial allocation represented the largest single serial block since World War II and involved ZB715-ZB764, ZB778-ZB827, ZB847-ZB886, ZB900-ZB949, ZB970-ZB999 and ZD115-ZD164, ZD180-ZD209. (By a curious quirk of Irish logic the production department at Shorts' Belfast factory chose to ignore the serial prefix letters and instead of producing aircraft in the intended alpha-numeric sequence, allocated identities in a strictly numeric sequence. Therefore the first Skeet to be built was actually ZD**115**; the 300th and last Skeet I being ZB**999**!)

In order to meet the terms of the MoD contract (which stipulated first deliveries by the end of 1981) ZD115 was very speedily delivered to Larkhill just before the Christmas break; shortly afterwards it was transferred to the RAE West Freugh Range for acceptance tests.

Deliveries of Skeet I began in earnest during 1982. With stocks of MATS-B targets still in abundance all of the early deliveries – which consisted of batches of approximately a dozen units per month – were stored at Rollestone Camp, Larkhill. Eventually a consignment of 25 Skeets (ZD118/120-123/125-129/131-137/139-141/145/146/151/152 and 159) was despatched from Larkhill up to the Hebrides Range in August 1982 and a similar number was transferred to the Otterburn Range (including ZD117/130/138/143/149/150/156-158/160/164/180-182/184 and 186). Once again these aircraft were placed into storage until stocks of MATS-B were exhausted and it was not until January 1983 that Skeet finally entered service at Otterburn.

The establishment of a post-conflict Garrison Force in the Falkland Islands raised the question of providing live firing practice for Army Air Defence Batteries which had begun to rotate temporary deployments to the South Atlantic. The first of the postwar Camps on the Falklands was in fact manned by the Portland-based Royal Navy Fleet Target Group who positioned eight targets – a mix of Chukar I and II targets – in

Only the small-print identity '002' on the forward fuselage identifies this as the 2nd prototype Skeet 1 drone, seen on its launcher at Llanbedr. The stainless steel spinner was only fitted to the two Skeet prototypes and purely for aesthetic purposes only. (Short Bros Neg. No.79094-4)

238 Sitting Ducks and Peeping Toms

Preparation and launch of Skeet involved (1) re-setting the pneumatic launch "cage" to the start of the run, an operation usually requiring pure muscle power. (2) The aircraft is then guided on to the "cage". Note the protective foam sections still attached to the wing. (3) The smoke flares are fitted, in this instance, to the wing-tips. (4) recovery parachute is checked and secured and the final pre-flight action (5) involves starting the engine by using a standard Black & Decker drill with a screwdriver attachment that slots into the propeller hub. Health & Safety insisted on a protective wire mesh for the operator but the pilot, standing at the rear and steadying the drone in the full downwash, received no protection as he controls engine and flying controls. (6) shows Skeet on the point of release and under control of the pilot as it heads out over Manorbier Bay and finally (7) the loose parachute straps and the 'drogue tin' are evidence that the Skeet has recovered safely. By pure coincidence Shorts discovered that the dimensions of the 'drogue tin' were identical to a Heinz baked beans tin, thereby saving a considerable amount by not having to have a specially designed container! Note that the propeller is designed to stop in the horizontal position. This series of pictures depict Skeet 1s ZB741 and ZB781 at Manorbier on 16 April 1984. (Michael I Draper)

Unmanned Targets for the Army

October 1982. After a month the RNFTG was withdrawn and Short Brothers Air Services (SBAS) took over the Camp at San Carlos but rather than deploy new Skeet targets, Shorts despatched a number of MATS-B Mk.1A aircraft. Most of those taken down from Larkhill were unflown late-production examples – ZA531, ZA549, ZA554, ZA556, ZA559, ZA560, ZA562, ZA564, ZA566, ZA567, ZA570, ZA571, ZA577 and ZA578. Initially, they provided targets for the Rapier-equipped 58 Air Defence Battery, RA and later worked with another Rapier unit, 37 Squadron, RAF Regiment at Port Stanley. The Fleet Target Group returned to the Falklands at the end of January 1983 and remained there until November 1983 when Shorts took over for a second tour, again with MATS-B.

Few would doubt that the exclusive contract for operating targets was, for SBAS, a lucrative business; not only did Shorts build the targets but a subsidiary company operated them. However the competitive and conservative approach to military contracts in the 1980s inevitably brought changes. The contract for operating targets was put up for tender in 1984. RCA Flying Services Ltd succeeded in winning a new five-year contract and moved into Shorts' Rollestone Camp, Larkhill facility on 1 June 1984.[21]

When Short Brothers Air Services vacated Larkhill they took up temporary accomodation at Thruxton airfield where a repair and servicing facility was established. It proved to be a lean period for SBAS; although there was some support work for the parent company's overseas sales plus some missile development work at the West Freugh Range.

The changeover from SBAS to RCA had another effect as it finally marked the end of MATS-B operations. Ten flyable examples were passed over to Marconi (at Upavon) before being tested to destruction at Manorbier; two others (ZA220 & ZA535) were acquired by the author for long-term storage and eventual restoration. The remainder were conveyed to Short's new facility on the edge of Thruxton airfield where they were cannibalised for useful spares etc.

At the time of the handover from SBAS to RCA a total of 132 Skeet I targets was on charge. From the original order for 300, a further forty examples (ZB940-949,970-999) were yet to be delivered. At the normal attrition rate these 172 targets were expected to last for approximately eighteen months. There was therefore some hope that, as RCA was not a manufacturer, Shorts would continue to build Skeet targets and hopefully would win a follow-on contract, especially as the company had been developing an improved Skeet II target.

In many respects the follow-on order was almost assured, the relationship between Shorts and the MoD being long-established and an especially close one. However subsequent events were not quite so straightforward.

Skeet I was powered by a single Weslake 274-6 engine but for Skeet II it was proposed to use the more powerful Weslake 342. One Skeet, ZB743, was repainted in an overall grey scheme at Larkhill to act as a static test-bed for the new engine. However, the engine's manufacturer, Normalair-Garrett Ltd, had been taken over by Target Technology Ltd, builder of the BTT-3 Banshee target aircraft which also used the 342 engine. It was alleged at the time that when Shorts sought delivery of engines to start Skeet 2 production and to meet what was effectively a time-sensitive contract, the new engine was not available in the required quantities for at least nine months, due to "requirements by other customers". Shorts was therefore forced to concede that Skeet 2 was unlikely to avoid incurring time penalties. Ironically, the MoD decided to accept the time lapse but ordered "nine month's attrition" of stop-gap target aircraft. An even greater irony was that the choice of stop-gap fell to the TTL Banshee target.

The final Skeet I Camp began at Manorbier on 17 November 1987, in support of 21 Battery, RA and 46 Battery, RA. Five days later, Skeet II entered service. Its development had indeed been long and costly, not just financially but also in terms of allowing TTL to find sufficient production slots to supply Banshee target drones as a stop-gap.

Towards the end of 1986 RCA Flying Services' parent company – the RCA Corporation – had been the subject of a take-over by General Electric. But operating targets for the Army was not on General Electric's agenda. The Corporation therefore agreed to allow a management buy-out of the UK-based RCA Service Division. The buy-out was concluded on 29 January 1987 although one of the conditions was that the new company would retain the RCA name for six months afterwards. So, not until 31 July 1987 was there any visible evisence of a change; that came about when the Larkhill operation became a separate company, Serco Operations Ltd.

Short Skeet 2

In view of its proposed powerplant, Skeet 2 was originally referred to as the Skeet 342. It seemed a straightforward

---

21 One observer very close to the Target Industry of the day claimed that Shorts believed that they would automatically win a contract renewal and submitted a bid based upon their previous costings. RCA's bid, on the other hand, was based on what they believed the Ministry of Defence was thought to be looking for.

Skeet 2 featured some marked differences compared to Skeet 1. Most obvious is the "humped" nose area and the horizontal stabilizer fitted to the top of the fin. The prospective ZF801 awaits launch from the test & demonstration area on Larkhill Ranges. (Short Bros Neg. No.87217-7)

move to increase the engine power and two unflown Skeet 1s (believed to be ZB995 and ZB999) were re-engined and re-serialled Skeet 342-001 and Skeet 342-002. But during a series of engine-running tests it became evident that carburettor icing was becoming a serious problem. To overcome this, Skeet 2 was re-designed with an improved air intake which protruded above the fuselage and thus led to a modified top cowling. That gave Skeet 2 its characteristic 'humped' appearance to the engine compartment.

Skeet 1 had suffered from heavy torque and the increased engine proposed for Skeet 2 was likely to increase the torque factor even further. To counter this (and also to balance the effect of the revised forward fuselage shape) Shorts considered re-designing Skeet with a larger fin or, alternatively, adopt a dorsal fin arrangement. Instead, it was decided to retain the standard fin shape and size but to add a small "T-tail" which in turn helped to improve overall stability.

Auxiliary-powered Ford Sierra

Short Brothers Air Services very kindly agreed to loan to the author a late-production MATS-B, ZA573, as a static exhibit at the British Aviation Research Group (BARG) 1984 AGM. This particular MATS-B had an interesting pedigree, having not long beforehand returned from the Falkland Islands, one of the last MATS-B deployments before being succeeded by new Skeet 1 drones, a quantity of which are seen here, still in protective crepe-cardboard covers.

In order to convey the aircraft from Larkhill to the AGM at Sunningdale, the dismantled aircraft was loaded onto the roof of the author's car. The author then drove carefully through the Larkhill military complex until reaching the A303 dual carriageway at Amesbury. Turning onto the A303 gave an opportunity to increase speed but as the car reached 50-60mph so the increase in air-flow began to turn the propeller. Several moments later the unsilenced 123cc McCulloch engine fired into life. What the Larkhill engineers had failed to warn the author about was the likelihood of unburnt fuel still inside the engine. The unsilenced McCulloch engine is one of the noisiest of its type and created an extremely loud – and embarrassing – diversion until the fuel finally exhausted.

(Picture by Michael I Draper, 15 March 1984)

In the meantime the original target acceptance date for Skeet 2 service entry had slipped by two months. The original date of 18 May 1987 was unlikely to be met and was altered to 18 August without the imposed penalty of £90 per day as stipulated in the original MoD contract. Other factors that gave rise for concern included the fact that, following the award of the service contract to RCA/SERCO, Short Bros Air Services had lost its facility at Rollestone Camp, Larkhill. As a temporary measure, and being far from ideal, SBAS had taken temporary premises at Thruxton but with no Army service contract there was little available work apart from in-house sales support business. That led to a decision to build Skeet 2, not at Castlereagh, but at Thruxton instead. In turn, SBAS agreed a sub-contract arrangement with TASUMA (UK) Ltd to manufacture Skeet 2 fuselages at that company's facility at Verwood, Dorset. Final assembly was completed at new premises at Thruxton.[22]

The first four TASUMA-built fuselages (c/n F.001 to F.004) were delivered to Thruxton on 6 May 1987; six more (F.005 to F.010) followed on 3 June. From these, five aircraft (ZF801-804/807) were fully-rigged and departed Thruxton by road on 2 August to undergo MoD flight trials at West Freugh. Service acceptance trials were later carried out at Larkhill on 6 October, again with five aircraft (ZF801, 802, 807, 815 & 816). Apart from ZF816 crashing immediately after launch, the trial was successful and Skeet 2 was finally released for service.

Skeet 2 proved to be Shorts' final entry in the Target Drone sector. Some 400 examples were built at Thruxton before production ended in late-1991. It was superceded by the Meggitt Banshee, the target that had been ordered as a temporary stop-gap when Skeet 2 fell behind schedule. Banshee had become the Army's preferred target aircraft and was procured in large quantities. In the meanwhile the SBAS base at Thruxton was closed down in early 1992.

Skeet 1 Technical Data	
Power Plant	1 × 13.4 kW (18 hp) NGL WAM274-6 (274 cc) two-cylinder, two-stroke engine, driving a two-blade propeller.
Wing Span	11 ft 0 in (3.35 m)
Length overall	8 ft 11 in (2.72 m) including MDI aerial
Max launching weight	150 lb (68 kg)
Max level speed	150 mph (241 km/h)
Range	3.1 miles (5 km)
Maximum range under control	6.2 miles (10 km)
Endurance at max speed	1 hr 15 min

Skeet 2 Technical Data	
Power Plant	1 × 18.6 kW (25 hp) NGL WAEL 342 two-cylinder, two-stroke engine, driving a two-blade propeller.
Wing Span	11 ft 0 in (3.35 m)
Length overall	8 ft 11 in (2.72 m) including MDI aerial
Max launching weight	160 lb (72.6 kg)
Max level speed	161 mph (259 km/h)

---

22 TASUMA transferred their base to Blandford Forum after Skeet 2 production ended.

MATS-B – Contract & Production Summary

Contract	Date	Serial Range	Allotment Date	Quantity	Remarks
K/MGW IIB/510	N/k	XZ815-XZ840 XZ861-XZ884	19.8.76	50	MATS-B Mk.1
K/MGW IIB/799	N/k	ZA200-ZA214 ZA237-ZA246	8.6.78	25	MATS-B Mk.1A
K/MGW IIB/803	N/k	ZA806-ZA822 ZA837-ZA846 ZA859-ZA874 ZA893-ZA899		50	MATS-B Mk.1A
K/MGW IIB/1118	N/k	ZA520-ZA535 ZA548-ZA564 ZA580-ZA596		50	MATS-B Mk.1A

Note that this batch was originally allocated with 'ZA' serials (as above) but which were later discovered to have been duplicated with earlier allocations. A Ministry of Defence instruction to amend the prefix letters to 'ZB' was ignored as all had been built and delivered. The final block of aircraft was also given incorrect serials by the manufacturer who inadvertantly omitted the 'black-out' gap after ZA564. Refer to Individual Aircraft Histories for further details.

| Total | | | | 175 | |

MATS-B
Individual Aircraft Histories

Contract K/MGW 11B/510
50 MATS-B Mk.1

XZ815-XZ840 No details known

XZ861-XZ884 No details known

Contract K/MGW 11B/799
25 MATS-B Mk.1A

ZA200-204 No details known

ZA205 Known to have made 22 flights with total flying hours, 9.42. Its last flight was probably at Larkhill 29.7.82.

ZA206-208 No details known

ZA209 No details of individual flights have survived but its last flight is known to have been in the Hebrides when it landed in the sea. Recovered and later donated to the Museum of Army Flying, Middle Wallop.

ZA210-214 No details known

ZA237-246 No details known except that these are known to have been painted as ZA215-ZA224 in error as a result of the manufacturer forgetting to leave a blocked-out batch.

ZA220 First recorded flight 26.4.82 at the Hebrides Range. Final flight at Manorbier 5.2.83. Rtnd to Larkhill and stored. Acquired by the author for restoration and currently in long-term storage at Nether Wallop, Hants. Note that ZA220 was, in reality, allocated as ZA242.)

Contract K/MGW 11B/803:
50 MATS-B Mk.1A

ZA806 f/f 19.6.80 at Bovington as part of an Army demonstration. Later rtnd to Larkhill for transfer to Otterburn where, on 30.11.80, it sustained a direct missile hit. Some fragments were later recovered from the Range. (TFH 4.11; 18 Flights)

ZA807 f/f 8.2.81 at Otterburn. On 21.2.81 it crashed on its third presentation after severe pitching and rolling took the aircraft out of control.

ZA808 f/f 27.4.81 at West Freugh Test Range but later crashed on its second flight (on the same date) after carrying out a dummy firing run. (TFH 0.10; 2 Flights)

ZA809 f/f 26.5.80 at a TOG Camp in the Hebrides but fail-safed after launch and crashed into the sea. Not recovered.

ZA810 f/f 31.10.81 at Manorbier. Tfd to Otterburn in 2.82 but was rtnd to Manorbier by 4.82. On 8.5.82 the engine unexplainably cut over the Range and the aircraft crashed into the sea. (TFH 3.45; 7 Flights)

ZA811 f/f 13.6.80, possibly at Otterburn where it was operating during Jan 1981. To Manorbier but was lost there on 11.4.81 when it crash-landed and severely damaged the rear fuselage. Rtnd to Larkhill and repaired using parts salvaged from ZA532. On 21.8.82 it crashed at Otterburn; reasons unexplained.

ZA812 f/f 8.2.81 at Otterburn but sustained severe damage to rear fuselage and aileron rods on 21.2.81. Repaired and later conveyed to West Freugh for demonstrations of a 'head-on target from a soft target area' on 5.5.81 and 6.5.81. On 11.5.81 it was conveyed to Manorbier for an Ordnance Board trials flight before transfer to Larkhill where several flights were made to measure parachute descent rates. On 19.6.81 it was flown at West Freugh for a 'flashing-light' demonstration. On 10.7.81 it sustained a direct missile hit and destroyed. (TFH 4.48; 20 Flights)

ZA813 f/f 26.5.80, possibly at Llanbedr. Used for pilot training at Llanbedr throughout 7.80. Conveyed to Otterburn 1.81 where, on 7.2.81, it fail-safed in adverse weather conditions and was destroyed after being dragged by high winds across rough ground. (TFH 2.31; 14 Flights)

ZA814 f/f 24.1.81 at Otterburn but crashed immediately after launch after failing to respond to radio commands.

ZA815 f/f 21.2.81 at Otterburn but crashed after one minute following a severe control failure. Altitude proved too low for a parachute recovery.

ZA816 f/f 31.7.81 in the Hebrides. On 26.4.82 it sustained a direct missile hit over the Hebrides Range. (TFH 4.37; 11 Flights)

ZA817 f/f 8.7.81 in the Hebrides. On 9.7.81 it sustained a direct missile hit and was destroyed. (TFH 0.44; 2 Flights)

"Have company car – will travel!" When MATS-B was finally withdrawn from service in favour of the Skeet, Short Brothers Air Services set about having the surviving MATS-B drones written-off. The two best examples were earmarked by Shorts for the author, but "losing" a brace of target drones provided a considerable administrative difficulty as the Army could only officially write off target drones if they had been either shot down or destroyed beyond repair. Clearly MATS-Bs ZA220 and ZA535 had suffered neither fate and there was no guidance within "Operational Orders" that allowed the donation of two aircraft to a civilian. Eventually, Larkhill's Senior Equipment Officer came up with the answer; he decided to have certain sensitive items removed and the engines replaced with examples already declared unrepairable. This rendered both aircraft as unflyable and both were duly written-off. They were then conveyed by road from Larkhill to the author's home at Chandler's Ford on 5 June 1984. (Michael I. Draper)

ZA818 f/f 26.3.81 in the Hebrides. On 15.9.81 it suffered loss of control and fail-safed into the sea. Not recovered. (TFH 6.46; 15 Flights)

ZA819 f/f 9.6.81, location unkn. On 30.7.81 sustained a direct missile hit and was destroyed. (TFH 1.57; 5 Flights)

ZA820 f/f 30.3.81, location unkn. On 31.3.81 it sustained a direct missile hit on the 4th engagement of the day. (TFH 0.23; 2 Flights)

ZA821 No details known.

ZA822 f/f 26.3.81, location unkn, but sustained a direct missile hit after 9 minutes and on its second engagement.

ZA837 f/f 2.11.81. location unkn. On 28.4.82 the recovery parachute inadvertently deployed causing the aircraft to land in the sea. Not recovered. (TFH 2.38; 6 Flights)

ZA838 f/f 30.3.81, location unkn, but sustained a direct missile hit after 7 minutes and on its 2nd presentation.

ZA839 f/f 26.3.81, location unkn. On 30.3.81 it sustained a direct missile hit on its 3nd engagement of the day. (TFH 0.37; 2 Flights)

ZA840 f/f 28.10.80, location unkn. On 11.9.81 it sustained damage when all control "went haywire" immediately after launch. The recovery parachute deployed automatically but the damage was caused by being dragged along the ground. Repaired and test-flown 22.2.82. However it crashed on recovery due to it being too low for the recovery 'chute to fully deploy. Written-off.

ZA841 f/f 27.10.80 location unkn. On 30.3.81 the parachute deployed inadvertantly and it landed in the sea. Not recovered. (TFH 1.12; 4 Flights)

ZA842 f/f 9.10.80 at Larkhill Range. On 30.3.81 the engine cut in mid-flight and it landed in the sea. Not recovered. (TFH 6.45; 15 Flights)

ZA843 f/f 10.7.80 as part of a demonstration to Canadian Forces. After 5 minutes the aircraft failed to respond to controls and it crashed into the sea. Not recovered.

ZA844 f/f 14.10.80 but after 16 minutes the aircraft refused to 'trim right'. As a result it crashed on landing without aileron control. W/o.

ZA845 f/f 14.10.80. On 15.9.81 it sustained a direct missile hit and was destroyed. (TFH 6.42; 13 Flights)

ZA846 f/f 7.10.80 in the Hebrides as part of a demonstration for the Canadian Forces (after loss of ZA843). Remained in Hebrides until 30.10.80 when fuselage damaged during routine skid-landing. Repaired and next flown 25.3.81 but shot down after 8 minutes. (TFH 5.03; 11 Flights)

ZA847 f/f 7.10.80 as part of a demonstration for the Canadian Forces. Flown regularly until 30.10.80. Stored until 25.3.81 when flown (probably at the Hebrides Range) but destroyed by a missile on its second run. (TFH 5.06; 11 Flights)

ZA859 f/f 27.10.80 but landed after 10 minutes due to 'being sick'. Flown again on 28.10.80 but was shot down on its first presentation. (TFH 0.15; 2 Flights)

ZA860 f/f 10.10.80. On 14.10.80 the aircraft failed to respond to landing commands. The recovery parachute deployed and it landed in the sea. Not recovered.

ZA861 f/f 10.10.80 but suffered a control failure after just two minutes of flight. Parachute deployed too late and the aircraft crashed.

ZA862 No details known.

ZA863 f/f 26.4.82, location unkn. Flown again on 27.4.82 but landed due to sighting of a boat in the Range area. No record of any further flights.

ZA864 Known to have been operated at Manorbier and survived several forced-landings in the sea. Carried unorthodox "eye and shark's teeth" marking by the end of its life when scrapped at Larkhill.

ZA865 f/f 13.7.81 at the Hebrides 'LA2' Range. On 24.3.82 it crashed in the Hebrides after losing control during a pilot changeover ahead of landing.

ZA866 f/f 6.2.82 at Manorbier but crash-landed in the sea after 30 minutes. Initially w/o but later recovered from the beach and repaired. To Otterburn 8.82, Larkhill 10.82 and Manorbier 11.82. Final flight 8.12.82. Rtnd to Larkhill and SOC as scrap. (TFH 13.25; 24 Flights)

ZA867 No details of any flights are known. SOC Larkhill 29.5.84 as scrap.

ZA868 f/f 4.11.81 at West Freugh. Flown occasionally until 26.11.82 after which conveyed to Larkhill and SOC 29.5.84 as scrap. (TFH 2.47; 9 Flights)

ZA869 f/f 11.5.82, probably at the Hebrides Range. On 25.5.82 it crashed into the sea after the battery box lead broke in flight. (TFH 2.18; 5 Flights)

ZA870 f/f 23.7.81 at West Freugh. To Larkhill for demonstration flights to Zimbabwe Army 17.9.81. To Manorbier 9.81 and later demonstrated to French Army 13.10.81. Crashed at Manorbier 29.11.81 whilst approaching to land. (TFH 3.31; 7 Flights)

ZA871 f/f 31.10.81 at Manorbier. Crashed at Otterburn 30.1.82 after radio control was lost. (TFH 3.39; 7 Flights)

ZA872 f/f 13.11.81 at Manorbier. Shot down at Manorbier 25.3.81. (TFH 3.35; 8 Flights)

MATS-B ZA864 had landed in the sea so often that it became known as "Old Sharky" and was painted with teeth and an eye. (Michael I Draper)

ZA873 f/f 6.3.82 at Otterburn. Shot down 13.3.82. (TFH 0.41; 2 Flights)

ZA893 f/f 12.11.81 at Manorbier. Damaged 25.5.82; Rtnd to Larkhill for repair. To Otterburn where it crashed 23.10.82 in unknown circumstances. (TFH 3.58; 11 Flights)

ZA894 f/f 28.11.81 at Manorbier. Returned to Larkhill 12.81 before issue to Otterburn where, on 11.9.82, it was shot down. (TFH 2.13; 5 Flights)

ZA895 No details known.

ZA896 f/f 8.6.81 at the Hebrides Range. Lost in poor visibility 27.4.82 and presumed crashed into the sea. (TFH 2.20; 8 Flights)

ZA897 f/f 11.11.81 at the Hebrides Range. Crashed into the sea 26.5.82 after loss of radio control. (TFH 5.46; 11 Flights)

ZA898 f/f 6.2.82 at Manorbier. Written-off 16.2.82 when it crashed into the sea after the flare circuit failed and the pilot commanded the recovery 'chute to deploy over land but the 'chute failed to open. (TFH 1.45; 4 Flights)

ZA899 Believed conveyed to West Freugh and f/f 21.5.81. Engaged on a series of trials until late-7.81 when rtnd to Larkhill. To Manorbier where, on 31.10.81, the engine cut across the Range and it crashed into the sea. (TFH 3.56; 8 Flights)

Contract K/MGW11B/1118:
50 MATS-B Mk.1A

ZA520 (ZB520) Del ex-Castlereagh 23.2.81 by road to Larkhill. To Manorbier 10.81; f/f 3.10.81 but recovery parachute deployed after 23 minutes and the target crashed into the Irish Sea.

ZA521 (ZB521) Del to Larkhill (with ZA520 etc) To Manorbier 10.81; f/f 31.10.81. To Otterburn 1.82 but rtnd to Manorbier by 5.82. On 26.5.82 the pilot lost visual contact in poor weather and commanded recovery mode. Crashed into sea but recovered by boat. Conveyed to Larkhill but not repaired. (TFH 4.58; 10 Flights)

ZA522 (ZB522) Del to Larkhill (with ZA520 etc) To Manorbier; f/f 11.10.82. Shot down 14.10.82. (TFH 2.05; 4 Flights)

ZA523 (ZB523) Del to Larkhill (with ZA520 etc); f/f (probably at Larkhill) 20.5.81. To Manorbier where it sustained damage 6.9.82 after the controls began to respond slowly and the recovery 'chute was deployed on approach to land. Repaired and returned to Larkhill for storage. SOC early-1984.

ZA524 (ZB524) Del to Larkhill (with ZA520 etc) To West Freugh (date u/k) where f/f 23.7.81. To Manorbier where, on 12.11.81, it was shot down. (TFH 1.30; 3 Flights)

ZA525 (ZB525) Del ex-Castlereagh 13.4.81 by road to Larkhill. To Manorbier where f/f 14.10.82 but the engine cut after 18 minutes and '525 crashed into the sea. Not recovered.

ZA526 (ZB526) Del ex-Castlereagh (with ZA525 etc). f/f 6.1.82 (probably at Larkhill). To Otterburn; later to Manorbier where it was shot down (date unkn). (TFH 3.38; 8 Flights)

ZA527 (ZB527) Del ex-Castlereagh (with ZA525 etc) To Manorbier 10.82 where f/f 13.10.82. Later to Larkhill for storage. SOC 6.84. (TFH 5.13; 9 Flights)

ZA528 (ZB528) Del ex-Castlereagh (with ZA525 etc) To Manorbier where f/f 20.11.82. Final flight 8.12.82; to Larkhill for storage. SOC 6.84. (TFH 1.45; 4 Flights)

ZA529 (ZB529) Del ex-Castlereagh (with ZA525 etc) To Manorbier 9.82 where f/f 2.10.82. Shot down 1.11.82. (TFH 3.31; 6 Flights)

ZA530 (ZB530) Del ex-Castlereagh (with ZA525 etc) To Otterburn where f/f 13.3.82. Sustained serious damage at Otterburn 12.9.82. Rtnd to Larkhill and stored. SOC early-1984. (TFH 2.15; 10 Flights)

ZA531 (ZB531) Del ex-Castlereagh (with ZA525 etc). Air-freighted to Falkland Islands (ex-Brize Norton 12.11.82); f/f 19.11.82 at San Carlos. Shot down 20.11.82. (TFH 0.35; 2 Flights)

ZA532 (ZB532) Del ex-Castlereagh 1.6.81 by road to Larkhill. To Manorbier 5.82 where f/f 26.5.82. Air-freighted to the Falkland Islands 1.83 but further details unknown. (TFH 2.15; 4 Flights)

ZA533 (ZB533) Del ex-Castlereagh (with ZA532 etc) To Manorbier early-2.82 where f/f 11.2.82. Final flight at Manorbier 11.10.82 when it landed in the sea. Recovered and Rtnd to Larkhill where SOC 6.84. (TFH 5.32; 13 Flights)

ZA534 (ZB534) Del ex-Castlereagh (with ZA525 etc). To Manorbier early-2.82 where f/f 16.2.82. Crashed into the sea 8.5.82 after loss of radio link. (TFH 1.03; 3 Flights)

ZA535 (ZB535) Del ex-Castlereagh (with ZA525 etc). To Manorbier 5.82 where f/f 8.5.82. Final flight 9.12.82 after which fuselage cracks were discovered; Rtnd to Larkhill for repair. Stored until SOC 5.6.84. Handed-over to the author same date and conveyed to Chandler's Ford for storage. Currently stored at Nether Wallop, Hants. (TFH 3.08; 6 Flights)

ZA548 (ZB548) Del ex-Castlereagh (with ZA525 etc). To Manorbier 9.82 where f/f 11.10.82. Fail-safed after 2 minutes on 13.10.82 and crashed into the sea. Not recovered. (TFH 1.16; 3 Flights)

The Larkhill storage rack holds a number of repaired MATS-B, including ZA530, plus some unflown examples still wrapped in factory protective covering. (Michael I Draper)

ZA549 (ZB549) Del ex-Castlereagh (with ZA525 etc). Departed Brize Norton 12.11.82 as air-freight to Falkland Islands where, on 23.11.82, it was shot down (TFH 0.25; 1 Flight)

ZA550 (ZB550) Del ex-Castlereagh (with ZA525 etc). To Manorbier 9.82 where f/f 11.10.82. Fail-safed after 2 minutes on 13.10.82 and crashed into the sea. Not recovered. (TFH 1.16; 3 Flights)

ZA551 (ZB551) Del ex-Castlereagh 1.6.81 by road to Larkhill. To Manorbier c3.82 where f/f 23.4.82. Crashed 17.6.82 off Lulworth, Dorset during a series of demonstration flights. (TFH 3.09; 7 Flights)

ZA552 (ZB552) Del ex-Castlereagh (with ZA551 etc). To Manorbier 2.82 where f/f 11.2.82 but fail-safed after 20 minutes. The recovery 'chute failed to deploy and it crashed into the sea.

ZA553 (ZB553) Del ex-Castlereagh (with ZA551 etc). To Manorbier 2.82 where f/f 11.2.82 but after 19 minutes was commanded to recover by parachute. However the 'chute failed to deploy and it crashed into a nearby field.

ZA554 (ZB551) Del ex-Castlereagh 27.7.81 by road to Larkhill. To Falkland Islands (ex Brize Norton 12.11.82); f/f off San Carlos 19.11.82 but shot down after 15 minutes.

ZA555 (ZB555) Del ex-Castlereagh (with ZA554 etc). To Manorbier 2.82 where f/f 11.2.82. but after 3 minutes the pilot lost control and '555 crashed into the sea.

ZA556 (ZB556) Del ex-Castlereagh (with ZA554 etc). To Falkland Islands (ex Brize Norton 12.11.82). Further details unkn.

ZA557 (ZB557) No record of ever departing Castlereagh.

ZA558 (ZB558) Del ex-Castlereagh (with ZA532 etc). To Manorbier 2.82 where f/f 16.2.82 but shot down after 16 mins

ZA559 (ZB559) Del ex-Castlereagh (with ZA554 etc); f/f 8.7.82 at Larkhill. To Otterburn 9.82 where, on 11.9.82, it fail-safed out of sight to pilot. Landed on Range but never found. SOC as "stolen pending an investigation by Military Police". Subsequently found in a gully and restored to Army charge. Air-freighted to Falkland Islands 1.83 where it was shot down off San Carlos 12.1.83. (TFH 2.01; 5 Flights)

ZA560 (ZB560) Del ex-Castlereagh (with ZA554 etc). To Falkland Islands (ex Brize Norton 12.11.82); f/f off San Carlos 19.11.82 but shot down after 4 minutes.

ZA561 (ZB561) Del ex-Castlereagh (with ZA554 etc). No further details.

ZA562 (ZB562) Del ex-Castlereagh (with ZA554 etc). To Falkland Islands (ex Brize Norton 12.11.82); f/f off San Carlos 19.11.82. Shot down 20.11.82. (TFH 1.26; 3 Flights)

ZA563 (ZB563) Del ex-Castlereagh (with ZA554 etc). To Otterburn 9.82 where f/f 11.9.82 but crash-landed after 33 minutes due to fuel problems.

ZA564 (ZB564) Del ex-Castlereagh (with ZA554 etc). To Otterburn 10.82 where f/f 23.10.82. To the Falkland Islands briefly 1.83. Rtnd to Larkhill and on to Manorbier where, on 21.2.83, the flight controls malfunctioned and '564 flew into the sea. (TFH 3.33; 6 Flights)

ZA565 (ZB580) Del ex-Castlereagh (with ZA554 etc). To Manorbier 9.82 where f/f 30.9.82 but after 3 minutes it rolled to inverted position before diving into the ground.

ZA566 (ZB581) Del ex-Castlereagh (with ZA554 etc). To Falkland Islands (ex Brize Norton 12.11.82); f/f off San Carlos 23.11.82. Shot down 13.1.83. (TFH 1.21; 3 Flights)

ZA567 (ZB582) Del ex-Castlereagh (with ZA554 etc). To Falkland Islands (ex Brize Norton 12.11.82); f/f off San Carlos 23.11.82. On 13.1.83 control was lost one minute after launch and although it automatically fail-safed the 'chute opened too late and '567 smashed against rocks during the descent. (TFH 1.31; 3 Flights)

ZA568 (ZB583) Del ex-Castlereagh (with ZA554 etc). To Otterburn 9.82 where f/f 11.9.82. Final flight 23.10.82 when it was written-off in a crash following engine failure. (TFH 2.13; 6 Flights)

ZA569 (ZB584) Del ex-Castlereagh 18.9.81 by road to Larkhill. Fitted with flashing light mod 4.82 (for night engagements) and conveyed to West Freugh where f/f 20.4.82. Extensively tested until 3.3.83 when it failed to respond to signals and flew into the sea off West Freugh. (TFH 9.28; 22 Flights)

ZA570 (ZB585) Del ex-Castlereagh (with ZA554 etc). To Falkland Islands (ex Brize Norton 12.11.82); f/f off San Carlos 19.11.82 but flying controls began to malfunction after 20 seconds and it flew into the sea.

ZA571 (ZB586) Del ex-Castlereagh (with ZA554 etc). Stored until 7.82 when prepared for a Camp at Otterburn but further details unkn.

ZA572 (ZB587) Del ex-Castlereagh (with ZA569 etc). Stored until 7.82 when prepared for a Camp but no record of any flights exist and no further details known.

An early production MATS-B makes a straight presentation across a Range during the Army's annual manoeuvres in Norway. Despite the high-visibility of the target, especially against a clear sky, many MATS-B target drones carried out up to ten presentations during one flight and even then escaped to live another day. (Short Brothers plc Neg. No. CN78224-5)

ZA573 (ZB588) Del ex-Castlereagh (with ZA569 etc). Stored until 10.82 when prepared for a Camp but no record of any flights exists apart from it 'failing to leave launcher at San Carlos 6.12.82'. Rtnd to Larkhill and SOC 6.84 as scrap.

ZA574 (ZB589) Del ex-Castlereagh (with ZA569 etc). Modified at Larkhill 10.81 for a series of trials at West Freugh where f/f 4.11.81. Written-off 21.4.82 after loss of radio contact caused fail-safe mode to engage but made an excessively heavy landing (TFH 2.26; 5 Flights)

ZA575 (ZB590) Del ex-Castlereagh (with ZA554 etc). To Otterburn Range 1.82 where f/f 31.1.82 but plunged into the ground immediately after launch for reasons unkn.

ZA576 (ZB591) Del ex-Castlereagh (with ZA554 etc). To West Freugh c12.82 where f/f 6.12.82 but sustained minor damage during normal skid landing. There are no reports of it being repaired, or making any further flights. Presumed w/o at West Freugh.

ZA577 (ZB592) Airfreighted Castlereagh to West Freugh by company Skyvan 12.3.82 but no flights recorded. To Larkhill for preparation for a Falkland Islands camp; f/f at San Carlos 9.1.83. Shot down 12.1.83. (TFH 0.47; 2 Flights)

ZA578 (ZB593) Airfreighted Castlereagh to West Freugh by company Skyvan 12.3.82 but no flights recorded. To Larkhill for preparation for a Falkland Islands camp. Departed Brize Norton 12.11.82 and f/f at San Carlos 19.11.82 but shot down after 15 minutes.

ZA579 (ZB594) Del ex-Castlereagh 23.11.81 by road to Larkhill. To Otterburn 9.82 where f/f 12.9.82. On 15.9.82 target rolled to the inverted position after 15 minutes and flew into the ground. (TFH 0.33; 3 Flights)

ZA580-ZA581 (ZB595-ZB596) No record of delivery and/or flight has been found.

Skeet – Contract & Production Summary

Contract	Date	Serial Range	Allotment Date	Quantity	Remarks
HMG ML22a/1		ZB715-ZB764 ZB778-ZB827 ZB847-ZB886 ZB900-ZB949 ZB970-ZB999 ZD115-ZD164 ZD180-ZD209	19.5.80	300	Skeet Mk.1 ZD115-209 were built prior to ZB715-999. Built at Castlereagh, Belfast
ML11A/1500		ZF801-ZF850 ZF876-ZF895 ZF901-ZF950 ZF961-ZF990 ZG111-ZG160 ZG171-ZG190 ZG221-ZG270 ZG301-ZG330	10.11.86	300	Skeet Mk.2 ZF876-893 were built and delivered incorrectly marked as ZF851-868. All built by TASUMA and assembled at Thruxton
ML11A/1500 (Option)		ZH263-ZH277 ZH281-ZH290 ZH302-ZH316 ZH336-ZH344 ZH356-ZH366 ZH396-ZH410 ZH431-ZH440 ZH484-ZH498	1.6.90	100	Skeet Mk.2 All built by TASUMA and assembled at Thruxton
Total				700	

Short Skeet
Individual Aircraft Histories

**Contract HMG ML22a/1:
300 Skeet 1**

ZB715 Dptd Castlereagh 25.10.82, to Larkhill. TOC 8.11.82; f/f 24.3.84 at Manorbier. Shot down by missile 31.3.84. (TFH 1.22; 2 Flights)

ZB716 Dptd Castlereagh 25.10.82, to Larkhill. TOC 8.11.82; f/f 2.5.84 at Manorbier. On 12.5.84 it parachute-landed into the sea after 10 seconds of flight. Not recovered. (TFH 0.53; 3 Flights)

ZB717 Dptd Castlereagh 25.10.82, to Larkhill. TOC 8.11.82; f/f 17.9.83 at Otterburn. No further details.

ZB718 Dptd Castlereagh 25.10.82, to Larkhill. TOC 8.11.82. Stored until f/f 23.1.84 in the Falkland Islands. Rtnd to UK and stored. Damaged in landing in Norway 6.7.87 but repaired. On 14.11.87 the engine cut during a Javelin shoot at Manorbier with 103 TA Battery, RA. Landed in the sea but not recovered. (TFH 2.09; 3 Flights)

ZB719 Dptd Castlereagh 25.10.82, to Larkhill. TOC 8.11.82 but stored until f/f 3.10.83 in the Falkland Islands. Wrecked on 5.10.83 when it landed on rocks in an attempt to land. (TFH 2.23; 3 Flights)

ZB720 Dptd Castlereagh 25.10.82, to Larkhill. TOC 8.11.82 but stored until f/f 22.1.84 in the Falkland Islands but was lost at sea on its first flight. (TFH 1.13)

ZB721 Dptd Castlereagh 25.10.82, to Larkhill. TOC 8.11.82 but stored until f/f 22.10.83 at Manorbier. Conveyed to West Freugh and carried out a number of test-flights there during 1985. On 10.2.86 it was shot down by a Javelin missile during an exercise shoot by AMF(L) in Norway. (TFH 5.03; 8 Flights)

ZB722 Dptd Castlereagh 25.10.82, to Larkhill. TOC 8.11.82 but stored until f/f 16.4.84 at Manorbier. Visual sight lost in sea mist off Manorbier during a Blowpipe shoot with the Royal School of Artillery on 10.10.84. Believed crashed into the sea and sunk.

ZB723 Dptd Castlereagh 25.10.82, to Larkhill. TOC 8.11.82 but stored until f/f 3.10.83 in the Falkland Islands. On 5.10.83 crashed after control was lost. (TFH 1.51; 4 Flights)

ZB724 Dptd Castlereagh 25.10.82, to Larkhill. TOC 8.11.82 but stored until f/f 12.5.84 at Manorbier. On 11.3.86 it was shot down at Manorbier by a Blowpipe during a shoot with 21 Battery, RA.

ZB725 Dptd Castlereagh 25.10.82, to Larkhill. TOC 8.11.82 but stored until f/f 4.10.83 in the Falkland Islands. Later rtnd to UK but crashed at Manorbier 11.2.87 during a Javelin shoot with the Royal School of Artillery. The aircraft had failed to respond to signals; a parachute recovery was attempted but the drogue failed to open properly. Lost at sea. (TFH 6.05; 9 Flights)

ZB726 Dptd Castlereagh 25.10.82, to Larkhill. TOC 8.11.82 but stored until f/f 12.12.83 at Manorbier; parachute-landed into the sea after 54 minutes and sank.

ZB727 Dptd Castlereagh 25.10.82, to Larkhill. TOC 8.11.82 but stored until f/f 22.10.83 at Manorbier. On 24.3.84 it crashed into the sea off Manorbier; no other details known. (TFH 2.13; 4 Flights)

ZB728 Dptd Castlereagh 25.10.82 to Larkhill. TOC 8.11.82 but initially stored. Later shot down 7.11.85 by a Javelin missile of 10 Battery, RA at Manorbier.

ZB729 Dptd Castlereagh 25.10.82 to Larkhill. TOC 8.11.82 but stored until f/f 27.11.83 at Manorbier. Shot down at Manorbier 13.12.83, details unkn. (TFH 0.44; 2 Flights)

ZB730 Dptd Castlereagh 25.10.82 to Larkhill. TOC 8.11.82 but stored until f/f 14.7.84 at Otterburn. However it was shot down on its first flight by a Blowpipe of 103 Battery, TA. (TFH 0.20).

ZB731 Dptd Castlereagh 25.10.82 to Larkhill. TOC 8.11.82 but stored until f/f 24.3.84 at Manorbier. Crashed into the sea after 16 minutes of its first flight. No other details known.

ZB732 Dptd Castlereagh 10.12.82 to Larkhill. TOC 16.12.82 but stored until f/f 17.1.84 in the Falkland Islands. Shot down by 42 Air Defence Battery, RA after 49 minutes of its first flight.

ZB733-ZB734 Dptd Castlereagh 10.12.82 to Larkhill. TOC 16.12.82 and initially stored. No further details known.

ZB735 Dptd Castlereagh 10.12.82 to Larkhill. TOC 16.12.82 and initially stored; f/f 30.4.84 in the Falkland Islands. Rtnd to UK and on 14.2.87 was shot down at Otterburn during a Blowpipe shoot with 103 TA. (TFH 1.13; 2 Flights)

ZB736 Dptd Castlereagh 10.12.82 to Larkhill. TOC 16.12.82 and initially stored; f/f 14.4.84 at Manorbier but was shot down two days later. (TFH 1.05; 2 Flights)

ZB737 Dptd Castlereagh 10.12.82 to Larkhill. TOC 16.12.82 and initially stored. No further details known.

ZB738 Dptd Castlereagh 10.12.82 to Larkhill. TOC 16.12.82 and initially stored; f/f 24.3.84 at Manorbier. No further details known.

ZB739 Dptd Castlereagh 10.12.82 to Larkhill. TOC 16.12.82 and initially stored; f/f 2.4.84 at Manorbier. Shot down at Manorbier 8.5.84. (TFH 3.33; 5 Flights)

ZB740-ZB741 Dptd Castlereagh 10.12.82 to Larkhill. TOC 16.12.82 and initially stored. No further details known.

ZB742 Dptd Castlereagh 10.12.82 to Larkhill. TOC 16.12.82 and initially stored; f/f 22.1.84 in the Falkland Islands where, on 12.8.84, it was shot down by a Rapier during a shoot with 26 Sqdn, RAF Regt. (TFH 2.00; 4 Flights)

ZB743 Dptd Castlereagh 10.12.82 to Larkhill. TOC 16.12.82 and initially stored; f/f 23.5.84 in the Hebrides. Rtnd Larkhill for repair but relegated to Weslake engine test-bed. Later scrapped at Larkhill. (See ZD207)

ZB744 Dptd Castlereagh 10.12.82 to Larkhill. TOC 16.12.82 and initially stored; f/f 17.3.84 at Otterburn. Shot down the following day. (TFH 1.01; 2 Flights)

ZB745 Dptd Castlereagh 10.12.82 to Larkhill. TOC 16.12.82 and initially stored; f/f 18.11.85 in the Falkland Islands. Crashed into the sea on 15.1.86 after the engine cut during a shoot with 26 Sqdn, RAF Regt. (TFH 2.28; 2 Flights)

ZB746-ZB748 Dptd Castlereagh 10.12.82 to Larkhill. TOC 16.12.82 and initially stored. No further details known.

ZB749 Dptd Castlereagh 10.12.82 to Larkhill. TOC 16.12.82 and initially stored; f/f 15.11.85 at West Freugh but was damaged on landing. Repaired at Larkhill and conveyed to the Falkland Islands where, on 5.8.86, it was "shot down by radio interference" during a Rapier shoot with 16 Sqdn, RAF Regt.

ZB750 Dptd Castlereagh 18.2.83 to Larkhill. TOC 4.3.83 and initially stored; f/f 30.4.84 at Manorbier but crash-landed into the sea during its second flight on 2.5.84.

ZB751 Dptd Castlereagh 10.12.82 to Larkhill. TOC 16.12.82 and initially stored; f/f 26.10.85 at Manorbier but fail-safed into the sea on the following day during a Blowpipe shoot with 104 TA. Recovered and conveyed to Larkhill for repair/restoration. Rtnd to Manorbier but on 4.2.87 lost power during a Javelin shoot with 21 Battery, RA. Landed in the sea but not recovered. (TFH 2.51; 4 Flights)

ZB752 Dptd Castlereagh 10.12.82 to Larkhill. TOC 16.12.82 and initially stored; f/f 2.4.84 at Manorbier. Later tfd to Otterburn where, on 21.3.87, all electrics failed 10 seconds into flight during a Blowpipe shoot with 103 TA. W/o in a crash that followed.

ZB753 Dptd Castlereagh 18.2.83 to Larkhill. TOC 4.3.83 and initially stored; f/f 5.8.84 (or 8.5.84) in the Falkland Islands but crashed after 12 minutes of its first flight.

ZB754 Dptd Castlereagh 10.12.82 to Larkhill. TOC 16.12.82 and initially stored; f/f 2.4.84 at Manorbier but crash-landed into the sea on 8.5.84. (TFH 2.59; 3 Flights)

ZB755 Dptd Castlereagh 18.2.83 to Larkhill. TOC 4.3.83 and initially stored; f/f 16.4.84 at Manorbier. Rtnd Larkhill and fitted with a new engine but accidentally damaged in 9.85, requiring a new tail-block. Conveyed to the Falkland Islands 3.86 and flew on 16.3, 17.3 and 26.3.86. On the last date it fail-safed over the sea during a Javelin shoot with 43 Battery, RA. Not recovered. (TFH6.25; 9 Flights)

ZB756 Dptd Castlereagh 18.2.83 to Larkhill. TOC 4.3.83 and initially stored; f/f 31.3.84 at Manorbier. On 16.4.84 it was shot down over the Manorbier Range; further details unkn. (TFH 2.41; 3 Flights)

ZB757 Dptd Castlereagh 18.2.83 to Larkhill. TOC 4.3.83 and initially stored. On 3.11.83 it was deployed to the Hebrides for MESA trials and f/f 16.11.83 at West Freugh. Its last flight at West Freugh took place on 5.11.84 (for an MDI flight test) after which it was rtnd to Larkhill. On 10.2.86 it was shot down by a Javelin missile in Norway during an exercise with AMF(L) (TFH 3.17; 10 Flights)

ZB758-ZB759 Dptd Castlereagh 18.2.83 to Larkhill. TOC 4.3.83 and initially stored. No further details known.

ZB760 Dptd Castlereagh 18.2.83 to Larkhill. TOC 4.3.83 and initially stored. Conveyed to the Falkland Islands 4.84 where f/f 2.5.84 but came down in the sea after 55 minutes.

ZB761 Dptd Castlereagh 18.2.83 to Larkhill. TOC 4.3.83 and initially stored. Conveyed to the Falkland Islands 4.84 where f/f 2.5.84 but came down in the sea after 53 minutes.

ZB762 Dptd Castlereagh 18.2.83 to Larkhill. TOC 4.3.83 and initially stored. Conveyed to the Falkland Islands 4.84 where f/f 6.11.84 for a Rapier shoot with 14 Battery, RA. Made two further flights on this date but was shot down by a Rapier (Blindfire) missile on its 3rd flight. (TFH 2.11; 3 Flights)

ZB763 Dptd Castlereagh 18.2.83 to Larkhill. TOC 4.3.83 and initially stored. Conveyed to Manorbier where it f/f 17.4.84. Shot down at Manorbier 8.5.84. (TFH 1.40; 2 Flights)

ZB764 Dptd Castlereagh 18.2.83 to Larkhill. TOC 4.3.83 and initially stored. Conveyed to Otterburn where it f/f 14.2.87. On 28.2.87 it was shot down by a Blowpipe missile during a shoot with 102 TA.

ZB778 Dptd Castlereagh 18.2.83 to Larkhill. TOC 4.3.83 and initially stored; f/f 17.3.86 at Manorbier but was shot down by a Blowpipe missile after 48 minutes during a shoot with 21 Battery, RA.

Skeet 1 ZB778 made its first flight at Manorbier Range on 17 March 1986 but after just 48 minutes sustained a direct hit from a Blowpipe missile. This view shows exactly how it came back to earth – battered and wrecked. (Bill Munday)

ZB779 Dptd Castlereagh 18.2.83 to Larkhill. TOC 4.3.83 and initially stored. Conveyed to the Hebrides c7.12.85 where f/f 9.12.85. In 1.86 it made one flight at Otterburn and by 4.86 was at Manorbier where, on 11.4.86, it crashed on launch for a shoot with 43 Battery, RA. (TFH 1.46; 4 Flights)

ZB780 Dptd Castlereagh 18.2.83 to Larkhill. TOC 4.3.83 and initially stored; f/f 24.7.84 at the Hebrides Range for a Blowpipe shoot with the Royal School of Artillery but fail-safed into the sea after 54 minutes.

ZB781 Dptd Castlereagh 18.2.83 to Larkhill. TOC 4.3.83 and initially stored. No further details known.

ZB782 Dptd Castlereagh 18.2.83 to Larkhill. TOC 4.3.83 and initially stored.

Conveyed to the Falkland Islands where f/f 12.11.86. Rtnd UK but shot down at Manorbier 4.11.87 by a Javelin missile of 46 Battery, RA. (TFH 2.56; 4 Flights).

ZB783 Dptd Castlereagh 18.2.83 to Larkhill. TOC 4.3.83 and initially stored. Conveyed to the Falkland Islands; f/f 4.11.84 but shot down by a Rapier missile on its first flight during a shoot with 14 Battery, RA.

ZB784 Dptd Castlereagh 18.2.83 to Larkhill. TOC 4.3.83 and initially stored. No further details known.

ZB785 Dptd Castlereagh 3.83 Larkhill. TOC 29.3.83 and initially stored. Conveyed to the Falkland Islands where, on 9.11.84, it was shot down by a Rapier (Blindfire) missile during a shoot with 14 Battery, RA. (TFH 0.11; 1 Flight). (Note

In the compound outside Short Brothers Air Services' hangar at Rollestone Camp, Larkhill Skeet 1 ZB782 is fired up for an engine test-run. The engines were unsilenced and were often run at full throttle for up to 20-minute periods. Note how the stand is weighted down. (Michael I Draper)

that this was the first engagement using Blindfire against a Skeet target.)

ZB786 Dptd Castlereagh 3.83 to Larkhill. On charge 29.3.83 and initially stored; f/f 4.11.85 at Manorbier. Shot down 7.11.85 by a Javelin missile during a shoot with 10 Battery, RA. (TFH 3.55; 4 Flights)

ZB787 Dptd Castlereagh 3.83 to Larkhill. TOC 29.3.83 and initially stored; f/f 24.7.84 at the Hebrides Range. Subsequently rtnd Larkhill and later conveyed to the Falklands 12.85 where, on 24.1.86, it was parachute-landed at the end of a Javelin shoot with 10 Battery, RA but was written-off after being dragged across uneven ground by strong winds.

ZB788 Dptd Castlereagh 3.83 to Larkhill. TOC 29.3.83 and initially stored; f/f 18.11.85 at Manorbier. Shot down 11.12.85 by a Javelin missile during a shoot with the Royal School of Artillery, RA. (TFH 4.19; 4 Flights)

ZB789 Dptd Castlereagh 3.83 to Larkhill. TOC 29.3.83 and initially stored; f/f 15.7.84 at Otterburn. Later conveyed to Hebrides Range where, on 24.7.84, it fail-safed into the sea during a Blowpipe shoot with the Royal School of Artillery, RA.

ZB790 Dptd Castlereagh 3.83 to Larkhill. TOC 29.3.83 and initially stored; f/f 14.7.84 at Otterburn. Remained at Otterburn until 4.7.86 when shot down by a Blowpipe missile during a shoot with AMF(L) & 10 Battery, RA. (TFH 8.42; 8 Flights) (Note that this loss has also been reported as taking place over the Hebrides Range.)

ZB791 Dptd Castlereagh 3.83 to Larkhill. TOC 29.3.83 and initially stored; f/f 29.10.84 at the Hebrides Range but shot down by a Javelin missile during a shoot with the Javelin QA.

ZB792 Dptd Castlereagh 3.83 to Larkhill. TOC 29.3.83 and initially stored; f/f 23.7.84 at the Hebrides Range. Shot down over the same Range 16.7.85 by a Rapier missile during a shoot with 11 Battery, RA. (TFH 5.05; 6 Flights)

ZB793 Dptd Castlereagh 3.83 to Larkhill. TOC 29.3.83 and initially stored. No further details known.

ZB794 Dptd Castlereagh 3.83 to Larkhill. TOC 29.3.83 and initially stored; f/f 23.9.84 at Otterburn. Tfd to Manorbier 10.84 where, on 24.3.85, it was shot down by a Blowpipe missile during a shoot with the Royal School of Artillery, RA. (TFH 10.52; 11 Flights)

ZB795 Dptd Castlereagh 12.5.83 to Larkhill. TOC 20.5.83 and initially stored; f/f 21.5.85, location unknown. Briefly used in the Falkland Islands 3.86 and at Manorbier 5.86. Shot down at the Hebrides Range 4.7.86 by a Blowpipe missile during a shoot with AMF(L) & 10 Battery, RA. (TFH 10.01; 14 Flights)

ZB796 Dptd Castlereagh 12.5.83 to Larkhill. TOC 20.5.83 and initially stored; f/f 3.8.84 in the Falkland Islands. Destroyed 11.8.84 during a Rapier shoot with 26 Sqdn, RAF Regt when dragged across rocks by high winds after landing in the water at Ajax Bay. (TFH 1.02; 2 Flights)

ZB797 Dptd Castlereagh 12.5.83 to Larkhill. TOC 20.5.83 and initially stored; f/f 5.8.84 in the Falkland Islands. Lost at sea 11.8.84 after the engine cut during a Rapier shoot with 26 Sqdn, RAF Regt. (TFH 2.18; 5 Flights)

ZB798 Dptd Castlereagh 12.5.83 to Larkhill. TOC 20.5.83 and initially stored; f/f 15.1.86 in the Falkland Islands. Fail-safed into the sea on the same date (but on its 2nd flight of the day) during a Rapier shoot with 26 Sqdn, RAF Regt. (TFH 1.09; 2 Flights)

ZB799 Dptd Castlereagh 12.5.83 to Larkhill. TOC 20.5.83 and initially stored; f/f 5.8.84 in the Falkland Islands. Lost at sea 7.8.84 during a Rapier shoot with 46 Battery, RA. (TFH 0.59; 2 Flights)

ZB800 Dptd Castlereagh 12.5.83 to Larkhill. TOC 20.5.83 and initially stored; f/f 4.3.84 at Otterburn. Tfd to Manorbier but crashed after engine failure during a training flight with RCA, this being the first loss under a new RCA contract.

ZB801 Dptd Castlereagh 12.5.83 to Larkhill. TOC 20.5.83 and initially stored; f/f 5.8.84 in the Falkland Islands. Shot down 12.8.84 by a Rapier missile during a shoot with 26 Sqdn, RAF Regt. (TFH 4.13; 4 Flights)

ZB802 Dptd Castlereagh 12.5.83 to Larkhill. TOC 20.5.83 and initially stored; f/f 24.7.84 at the Hebrides Range. Believed not flown again until 16.7.85 when it crashed into the sea and sank off the Hebrides after not responding to transmissions during a Rapier shoot with 11 Battery, RA.

ZB803 Dptd Castlereagh 12.5.83 to Larkhill. TOC 20.5.83 and initially stored; f/f 12.8.84 in the Falkland Islands. No further details known until it was shot down 22.4.85 by a Blowpipe at Manorbier during a shoot with 46 Battery, RA.

ZB804 Dptd Castlereagh 12.5.83 to Larkhill. TOC 20.5.83 and initially stored. No further details known.

ZB805 Dptd Castlereagh 12.5.83 to Larkhill. TOC 20.5.83 and initially stored; f/f 24.9.84 (possibly in the Falkland Islands). Seriously damaged during a Blowpipe camp in the Falklands 10.11.84 but recovered and repaired at Larkhill. Next flown 30.8.86 at Otterburn; conveyed to the Hebrides but not flown there. Flown at Otterburn 29.1.87, 28.2.87 & 21.3.87. To the Falkland Islands 10.87, flown once and then returned to Larkhill. Finally shot down 6.2.88 by a Javelin missile during an exercise with 3 Commando RM in Norway. Believed recovered and returned to Larkhill where it was restored for pilot training. Prepared for flight 4.7.90 but thought not to have flown again. (TFH 7.35; 11 Flights)

ZB806 Dptd Castlereagh 12.5.83 to Larkhill. TOC 20.5.83 and initially stored; f/f 6.8.84 in the Falkland Islands. Seriously damaged during a Blowpipe camp in the Falklands 10.8.84 when it was dragged onto rocks by high winds after landing in the sea during a Rapier shoot with 26 Sqdn, RAF Regt. Recovered and repaired at Larkhill. Next flown 17.3.86 at Manorbier where it later crashed 11.4.86 during a Blowpipe shoot with 43 Battery, RA. (TFH 6.29; 6 Flights)

ZB807 Dptd Castlereagh 12.5.83 to Larkhill. TOC 20.5.83 and initially stored; f/f 6.11.84 at Otterburn. Conveyed to the Falkland Islands 12.85 but damaged during a parachute landing 20.1.86. Rtnd to Larkhill. Flown at Otterburn 22.11.86, possibly in the Hebrides 8.12.86 before rtnd to Otterburn 1.87 where, on 14.2.87, it was shot down by a Blowpipe during a shoot with 103 TA. (TFH 14.34; 15 Flights)

ZB808 Dptd Castlereagh 12.5.83 to Larkhill. TOC 20.5.83 and initially stored. Details of initial five flights unknown but known to have been lost on its 10th flight at Manorbier when fog and strong sun glare caused loss of visual control. Crashed into the sea and sunk.

ZB809 Dptd Castlereagh 12.5.83 to Larkhill. TOC 20.5.83; f/f 22.10.83 at Manorbier but no further details known.

ZB810 Dptd Castlereagh 12.5.83 to Larkhill. TOC 20.5.83 and initially stored;

f/f 4.11.84 at Ajax Bay, Falkland Islands. Shot down there 5.11.84 by a Rapier missile during a shoot with 14 Battery, RA. (TFH 1.43; 3 Flights)

ZB811 Dptd Castlereagh 12.5.83 to Larkhill. TOC 20.5.83 and initially stored; f/f 13.2.85 at Manorbier. Shot down at Manorbier 25.3.85 by a Blowpipe during a shoot with the Royal School of Artillery, RA. (TFH 2.15; 2 Flights)

ZB812 Dptd Castlereagh 12.5.83 to Larkhill. TOC 20.5.83 and initially stored; f/f 6.11.84 at Ajax Bay, Falkland Islands but shot down after 85 minutes by a Rapier of 14 Battery, RA.

ZB813 Dptd Castlereagh 20.6.83 to Larkhill. TOC 8.7.83 and initially stored; f/f 24.9.84, location unknown. On 22.4.85 the engine failed in flight during a Rapier shoot with 16 Sqdn, RAF Regt over the Falkland Islands Range. Crashed into the sea and sunk. (TFH 2.52; 4 Flights)

ZB814 Dptd Castlereagh 20.6.83 to Larkhill. TOC 8.7.83 and initially stored; f/f 10.9.84, possibly at Otterburn. On 10.8.85 it was shot down by a Rapier during a shoot with 37 Sqdn, RAF Regt. (TFH 3.46; 6 Flights)

ZB815 Dptd Castlereagh 20.6.83 to Larkhill. TOC 8.7.83 and initially stored; f/f 7.11.84 at Otterburn. Shot down there 24.11.84 by a Blowpipe during a shoot with 102 TA (TFH 1.21; 2 Flights)

ZB816 Dptd Castlereagh 20.6.83 to Larkhill. TOC 8.7.83 and initially stored; f/f 23.9.84 at Otterburn. Last flown there 20.7.85 before tfd to the Falkland Islands. Rtnd to Larkhill before issue to Manorbier where, on 17.10.87, it was shot down by a Javelin during a shoot with 104 TA. (TFH 10.05; 12 Flights)

ZB817 Dptd Castlereagh 20.6.83 to Larkhill. TOC 8.7.83 and initially stored; f/f 4.11.84 at Ajax Bay, Falkland Islands. Destroyed in a crash 7.11.84 when the engine cut on final landing approach after a Rapier shoot with 14 Battery, RA. (TFH 3.05; 4 Flights)

ZB818 Dptd Castlereagh 20.6.83 to Larkhill. TOC 8.7.83 and initially stored; f/f 6.11.84 at Otterburn, Last flew there 26.10.85. Tfd to Falkland Islands where, on 13.11.85, it was shot down by a Rapier during a shoot with 12 Battery, RA. (TFH 8.46; 8 Flights)

ZB819 Dptd Castlereagh 20.6.83 to Larkhill. TOC 8.7.83 and initially stored; f/f 5.11.84 at Otterburn; last flown there 20.7.85 before transfer to Falkland Islands. Sustained a direct hit by a Rapier over Ajax Bay 13.11.85 but missile fin only cut the skidpan in half and sliced open the electronic pack underside. Pilot managed to skid-land the aircraft with no further damage! Later rtnd to Larkhill. Shot down at Manorbier 28.5.86 by a Blowpipe during a shoot with 10 Battery, RA. (TFH 9.23; 12 Flights)

ZB820 Dptd Castlereagh 20.6.83 to Larkhill. TOC 8.7.83 and initially stored; f/f 2.11.84 at Ajax Bay, Falkland Islands. Wrecked on 11.11.84 just one minute after launch due to what was reported at the time as a *'pilot changeover cock up'*. (Officially ZB820 stalled and crashed during a Blowpipe shoot with 21 Battery, RA.) (TFH 1.22; 3 Flights)

ZB821 Dptd Castlereagh 20.6.83 to Larkhill. TOC 8.7.83 and initially stored; f/f 2.11.84 at Ajax Bay, Falkland Islands. Lost at sea after the controls stopped responding during a Rapier shoot with 14 Battery, RA. (TFH 2.58; 3 Flights)

ZB822 Dptd Castlereagh 20.6.83 to Larkhill. TOC 8.7.83 and initially stored; f/f 10.10.84 at Manorbier. On 29.4.85, and during a Blowpipe shoot with the Gibraltar Regiment, it was lost at sea as a result of either aileron jamming or radio failure. (TFH 8.32; 10 Flights)

ZB823 Dptd Castlereagh 19.8.83 to Larkhill. TOC 8.9.83 and initially stored; f/f 11.10.84 at Manorbier but crashed into the sea after 40 minutes on its 1st flight and after stalling in a turn. The flight was a training flight ahead of a Blowpipe shoot with 7th Royal Horse Artillery.

ZB824 Dptd Castlereagh 19.8.83 to Larkhill. TOC 8.9.83 and initially stored; f/f 16.4.84 at the Hebrides Range. Tfd to Manorbier where, on 9.10.84, it was shot down by a Blowpipe during a shoot with the Royal School of Artillery, RA. (TFH 1.30; 3 Flights)

ZB825 Dptd Castlereagh 19.8.83 to Larkhill. TOC 8.9.83 and initially stored; f/f 9.10.84 at Manorbier. On 10.12.84 it suffered an engine failure and crashed into the sea during a Blowpipe shoot with 46 Battery, RA. (TFH 3.19; 4 Flights)

ZB826 Dptd Castlereagh 19.8.83 to Larkhill. TOC 8.9.83 and initially stored; f/f 6.11.84 at Otterburn. Rtnd to Larkhill c3.85 and stored. To Manorbier c3.86 until 5.86 when to Larkhill. To the Falkland Islands 11.86. Sustained minor damage 9.11.87 and rtnd to Larkhill. Shot down 7.2.88 by a Javelin missile in Norway during an exercise shoot with AMF(L). (TFH 14.22; 15 Flights)

ZB827 Dptd Castlereagh 19.8.83 to Larkhill. TOC 8.9.83 and initially stored; f/f 26.11.84 at Manorbier. Shot down 18.4.85 by a Blowpipe during a shoot with 46 Battery, RA. (TFH 1.05; 2 Flights)

ZB847 Dptd Castlereagh 19.8.83 to Larkhill. TOC 8.9.83 and initially stored; f/f 6.2.85 in the Falkland Islands but at the pilot changeover phase it stalled and crashed, having achieved just three minutes of flight.

ZB848 Dptd Castlereagh 19.8.83 to Larkhill. TOC 8.9.83 and initially stored; f/f 6.11.84 at Otterburn. Tfd to the Hebrides 12.84 where it was shot down 16.7.85 by a Rapier during a shoot with 11 Battery, RA. (TFH 4.51; 6 Flights)

ZB849 Dptd Castlereagh 19.8.83 to Larkhill. TOC 8.9.83 and initially stored; f/f 7.11.84 at Otterburn but sustained slight damage on landing. Repaired and tfd to Hebrides where, on 12.9.85, the parachute deployed during a Javelin shoot with MGW3. Landed in the sea and sank. (TFH 2.29; 3 Flights)

ZB850 Dptd Castlereagh 19.8.83 to Larkhill. TOC 8.9.83 and initially stored; f/f 13.2.85 at Manorbier. Shot down there 18.4.85 by a Blowpipe during a shoot with 46 Battery, RA. (TFH 2.26; 3 Flights)

ZB851 Dptd Castlereagh 19.8.83 to Larkhill. TOC 8.9.83 and initially stored; f/f 26.11.84 at Manorbier but after 45 minutes debris was seen falling off the aircraft before it rolled out of control. It is thought that the wing became detached in flight.

ZB852 Dptd Castlereagh 19.8.83 to Larkhill. TOC 8.9.83 and initially stored; f/f 18.1.86 at Otterburn. Tfd to Manorbier 3.86 where, on 7.5.86, it was shot down by a Blowpipe during a shoot with 3 Commando RM. (TFH 7.15; 8 Flights)

ZB853 Dptd Castlereagh 19.8.83 to Larkhill. TOC 8.9.83 and initially stored; f/f 16.3.85, location unkn. At Otterburn 10.85. Shot down 4.7.86 over the Hebrides during a Blowpipe shoot with AMF(L) & 10 Battery, RA. Recovered and repaired for ground training with the serial ZB853(T). (TFH 2.31; 4 Flights)

ZB854 Dptd Castlereagh 19.8.83 to Larkhill. TOC 8.9.83 and initially stored; f/f

16.4.85, location unkn. Shot down 19.8.85 by a Rapier during a shoot with 30 Battery, RA. (TFH 10.41; 16 Flights)

ZB855 Dptd Castlereagh 19.8.83 to Larkhill. TOC 8.9.83 and initially stored; f/f 4.11.83 in the Hebrides. No further details known.

ZB856 Dptd Castlereagh 19.8.83 to Larkhill. TOC 8.9.83 and initially stored; f/f 10.2.85 in the Falkland Islands but shot down by a Rapier after 15 minutes during a shoot with 11 Battery, RA.

ZB857 Dptd Castlereagh 21.9.83 to Larkhill, arrived 23.9.83 and stored.; f/f 10.2.85, possibly in the Falkland Islands where it was later lost on 12.11.85 during a Rapier shoot with 12 Battery but as a result of radio interference. (TFH 6.49; 9 Flights)

ZB858 Dptd Castlereagh 21.9.83 to Larkhill, arrived 23.9.83 and stored.; f/f 23.4.85, location unkn. Shot down in the Hebrides 18.6.85 by a Javelin missile during a shoot with the Royal School of Artillery, RA. (TFH 7.36; 10 Flights)

ZB859 Dptd Castlereagh 21.9.83 to Larkhill, arrived 23.9.83 and stored; f/f 21.4.85, location unkn. Shot down 19.10.85 by a Blowpipe during a shoot with the Royal School of Artillery, RA. (TFH 5.02; 6 Flights)

ZB860 Dptd Castlereagh 21.9.83 to Larkhill, arrived 23.9.83 and stored; f/f 17.4.85, location unkn. Shot down 17.8.85 by a Blowpipe during a shoot with the 10 Battery, RA in the Falkland Islands. (TFH 11.53; 15 Flights)

ZB861 Dptd Castlereagh 13.10.83 to Larkhill, arrived 18.10.83 and stored; f/f 22.4.85 at Manorbier. Shot down on its first flight by a Blowpipe missile during a shoot with 46 Battery, RA..

ZB862 Dptd Castlereagh 13.10.83 to Larkhill, arrived 18.10.83 and stored; f/f 30.1.85, probably in the Falkland Islands where, on 7.2.85, it stalled on launch and crashed during a shoot with 11 Battery, RA. (TFH 3.28; 4 Flights)

ZB863 Dptd Castlereagh 13.10.83 to Larkhill, arrived 18.10.83 and stored; f/f 28.11.84 but reportedly crashed on its first flight. One report claims that after launch the engine gradually slowed down and eventually cut out after 4 minutes whereupon it crashed into the sea. The cause was described as either *"Alan's plug-cap mod"* or that the *"fuel pipe R-clips being fitted too high and tightly causing the pipe to collapse under vibration"*! Another report records that ZB863 suffered an engine cut and lost at sea over the Falkland Islands Range on 30.1.85 during a Rapier shoot with 63 Sqdn, RAF Regt.

ZB864 Dptd Castlereagh 13.10.83 to Larkhill, arrived 18.10.83 and stored; f/f 30.1.85, probably in the Falkland Islands. On 11.11.85 it was shot down by a Rapier missile during a shoot with 12 Battery, RA in the Falklands. (TFH 3.17; 4 Flights)

ZB865 Dptd Castlereagh 13.10.83 to Larkhill, arrived 18.10.83 and stored; f/f 6.2.85, probably in the Falkland Islands where, on 10.2.85, it was shot down by a Rapier missile during a shoot with 11 Battery, RA. (TFH 2.09; 3 Flights)

ZB866 Dptd Castlereagh 13.10.83 to Larkhil, arrived 18.10.83 and stored; f/f 12.3.86, probably at Manorbier. Shot down at Manorbier 6.5.86 by a Blowpipe missile during a shoot with 3 Commando RM. (TFH 9.15; 10 Flights)

ZB867 Dptd Castlereagh 13.10.83 to Larkhill, arrived 18.10.83 and stored; f/f 20.11.85, probably at Manorbier. Shot down at Manorbier on 12.12.85 by a Blowpipe during a shoot with 104 TA. (TFH 3.37; 4 Flights)

ZB868 Dptd Castlereagh 13.10.83 to Larkhill, arrived 18.10.83 and stored; f/f 31.1.85 in the Falkland Islands but made a forced-landing on Stanley airfield after 3 minutes. Engine later changed and re-flown 21.4.85. Suffered another engine failure in flight on 22.4.85 during a Rapier shoot with 16 Sqdn, RAF Regt and came down in the sea. Recovered by helicopter. Rtnd to Larkhill. On 11.2.87 it was shot down by a Javelin missile at Manorbier during a shoot with the Javelin QA. (TFH 1.05; 4 Flights)

ZB869 Dptd Castlereagh 13.10.83 to Larkhill, arrived 18.10.83 and stored; f/f 5.11.84 at Ajax Bay, Falkland Islands. On its 2nd flight of the day it was shot down by Rapier (Blindfire) during a shoot with 14 Battery, RA. (TFH 1.23; 2 Flights)

ZB870 Dptd Castlereagh 13.10.83 to Larkhill, arrived 18.10.83 and stored; f/f 3,5,85 as part of an MDI trial, possibly at Manorbier. It later crashed on 11.6.85 due to a transmission fault on its 7th flight, all of which are thought to have been trials flights. (TFH 4.08; 7 Flights)

ZB871 Dptd Castlereagh 13.10.83 to Larkhill, arrived 18.10.83 and stored; f/f 16.5.85 as part of an MDI trial flight (replacing ZB870 qv) and possibly at Manorbier. Final trial flight on 13.6.85. On 15.7.85 it fail-safed and parachute-landed in the sea during a Javelin shoot with the Royal School of Artillery, RA. Not recovered. (TFH 3.07; 7 Flights)

ZB872 Dptd Castlereagh 16.11.83 to Larkhill, arrived 23.11.83 and stored; f/f 29.4.85 as part of a series of MDI trial flights (until 16.5.85 at least), probably at Manorbier. Possibly used for training flights until 9.85 when recorded at the Hebrides Range. W/o 12.9.85 on the Hebrides Range when it stalled on an overshoot and made a heavy landing after the flare circuit failed in flight during a Blowpipe shoot with 21 Battery, RA. (TFH 16.25; 26 Flights)

ZB873 Dptd Castlereagh 16.11.83 to Larkhill, arrived 23.11.83 and stored. First flight is unkn as are details of first 18 flights. At Manorbier 4.86 where, on 6.5.86, it was shot down by a Blowpipe during a shoot with 3 Commando, RM (TFH unkn; 21 Flights).

ZB874 Dptd Castlereagh 16.11.83 to Larkhill, arrived 23.11.83 and stored; f/f 4.3.85, location unkn but intentionally fail-safed after 4 minutes due to radio interference. Noted at Manorbier 7.85. To the Falkland Islands 1.86. To Manorbier 10.87 where, on 28.10.87, it was shot down by a Javelin missile during a shoot with 46 Battery, RA. (TFH 12.59; 16 Flights)

ZB875 Dptd Castlereagh 16.11.83 to Larkhill, arrived 23.11.83 and stored; f/f 17.7.85, location unkn. On 16.1.86 it was shot down by a Rapier during a shoot with 26 Sqdn, RAF Regt in the Falkland Islands. (TFH 2.19; 3 Flights)

ZB876 Dptd Castlereagh 16.11.83 to Larkhill, arrived 23.11.83 and stored; f/f 9.10.84 at Manorbier. On 22.4.85 it was shot down by a Blowpipe during a shoot with 46 Battery, RA. (TFH 5.30; 5 Flights)

ZB877 Dptd Castlereagh 16.11.83 to Larkhill, arrived 23.11.83 and stored; f/f 7.11.85 at Manorbier but shot down after 18 minutes by a Javelin missile during a shoot with 10 Battery, RA.

ZB878 Dptd Castlereagh 16.11.83 to Larkhill, arrived 23.11.83 and stored. No further details known.

ZB879 Dptd Castlereagh 16.11.83 to Larkhill, arrived 23.11.83 and stored; f/f 9.4.86 at Manorbier where, on 7.5.86, it crashed into the sea after an in-flight engine failure during a Blowpipe shoot with 3 Commando RM (TFH 5.29; 7 Flights)

ZB880 Dptd Castlereagh 14.12.83 to Larkhill and stored; f/f 11.3.86 at Manorbier. Shot down at Manorbier 16.4.86 by a Blowpipe during a shoot with 43 Battery, RA. (TFH 4.21; 4 Flights)

ZB881 Dptd Castlereagh 14.12.83 to Larkhill and stored; f/f 15.1.86 in the Falkland Islands but fail-safed into the sea after 1 hour when the tail section fell off in flight during a Rapier shoot with 26 Sqdn, RAF Regt. It is possible that the aircraft sustained a direct hit by the missile.

ZB882 Dptd Castlereagh 14.12.83 to Larkhill and stored; f/f 6.8.86 but shot down after 21 minutes, details unkn.

ZB883-ZB884 Dptd Castlereagh 14.12.83 to Larkhill and stored. No further details known.

ZB885 Dptd Castlereagh 14.12.83 to Larkhill and stored. To the Falkland Islands where on 6.8.86 (and on its first flight) it was shot down by a Rapier missile during a shoot with 16 Sqdn, RAF Regt.

ZB886 Dptd Castlereagh 14.12.83 to Larkhill and stored. No further details known.

ZB900 Dptd Castlereagh 14.12.83 to Larkhill and stored. Reported to have crashed off Manorbier 22.4.85 when the port engine cylinder sheared off in flight during a Blowpipe shoot with 46 Battery, RA. Recovered and repaired and next flown in the Falkland Islands 14.4.87. Rtnd to UK and finally w/o at Manorbier 4.11.87 when the elevator fell off 2 minutes after launch (during a Javelin shoot with 46 Battery, RA) causing it to crash into the sea.

ZB901 Dptd Castlereagh 2.84 to Larkhill, arrived 20.2.84 and stored; f/f 18.9.85, location unkn. Flown in the Falkland Islands between 15.1.86 and 9.11.87. Rtnd to UK and later shot down 8.2.88 by a Javelin missile during a shoot with AMF(L) on exercise in Norway. Recovered and brought back to Larkhill; repaired for pilot training only. Known to have undergone a "pre-flight check" 4.7.90 but no further details recorded.

ZB902 Dptd Castlereagh 2.84 to Larkhill, arrived 20.2.84 and stored; f/f 18.4.85 at Manorbier. Shot down by a Blowpipe at Manorbier 8.5.85 during a shoot with 10 Battery, RA (TFH 4.42; 5 Flights)

Two Skeet 1 fuselages (ZB916 & ZB988) sit on the floor of the Larkhill maintenance facility on 14 August 1987 and awaiting repair. Both had just been unloaded following their return from operations in the Falkland Islands. Note how the Miss Distance Indicator (MDI) cover had a tendency to obliterate the final digit of the serial. (Michael I Draper)

ZB903 Dptd Castlereagh 2.84 to Larkhill, arrived 20.2.84 and stored; f/f 7.7.86 at the Hebrides Range but shot down after 15 minutes by a Javelin missile during a shoot with AMF(L) & 10 Battery, RA.

ZB904 Dptd Castlereagh 2.84 to Larkhill, arrived 20.2.84 and stored; f/f 4.3.85 in Norway during a Blowpipe exercise shoot with AMF(L) but brought down after 5 minutes due to 'Clansman interference'.

ZB905 Dptd Castlereagh 2.84 to Larkhill, arrived 20.2.84 and stored; f/f 4.3.85 in Norway. W/o 17.10.87 at Manorbier after experiencing a transmission problem during a shoot with 104 TA. Aircraft failsafed and crashed into the sea. Not recovered. (TFH 2.42; 6 Flights)

ZB906 Dptd Castlereagh 2.84 to Larkhill, arrived 20.2.84 and stored; f/f 10.2.86 in Norway but shot down after 21 minutes by a Javelin missile during an exercise shoot with AMF(L).

ZB907 Dptd Castlereagh 2.84 to Larkhill, arrived 20.2.84 and stored. No further details known.

ZB908 Dptd Castlereagh 2.84 to Larkhill, arrived 20.2.84 and stored; f/f 21.4.85 at Manorbier. Shot down by a Blowpipe at Manorbier 18.10.85 during a shoot with the Royal School of Artillery, RA. (TFH 1.30; 2 Flights)

ZB909 Dptd Castlereagh 2.84 to Larkhill, arrived 20.2.84 and stored; f/f 12.11.85 in the Falkland Islands. Crashed into the sea 13.11.85 after suffering engine failure in flight during a Rapier shoot with 12 Battery, RA. (TFH 1.09; 3 Flights)

ZB910 Dptd Castlereagh 2.84 to Larkhill, arrived 20.2.84 and stored; f/f 16.5.85, probably in the Hebrides as part of an MDI trial. Shot down off the Hebrides 18.6.85 by a Javelin missile during a shoot with the Royal School of Artillery, RA. (TFH 2.28; 3 Flights)

ZB911 Dptd Castlereagh 2.84 to Larkhill, rrived 20.2.84 and stored; f/f 28.4.85, location unkn. Damaged at Manorbier 17/18.10.85 when it fail-safed due to a pilot changeover error. Repaired at Larkhill and despatched to the Hebrides Range where it was shot down 17.11.87. (TFH 7.05; 11 Flights)

ZB912 Dptd Castlereagh 2.84 to Larkhill, arrived 20.2.84 and stored. No further details known.

ZB913 Dptd Castlereagh 2.84 to Larkhill, arrived 20.2.84 and stored; f/f 29.4.85, location unkn. Shot down 11.11.85 by a Rapier in the Falkland Islands during a shoot with 12 Battery, RA. (TFH 1.34; 3 Flights)

ZB914 Dptd Castlereagh 2.84 to Larkhill, arrived 20.2.84 and stored; f/f 3.5.85 at Manorbier. Shot down at Manorbier 4.11.85 by a Javelin missile during a shoot with 10 Battery, RA. (TFH 2.42; 3 Flights)

ZB915 Dptd Castlereagh 2.84 to Larkhill, arrived 20.2.84 and stored; f/f 19.10.85 at Manorbier but shot down on the 2nd flight of the day by a Blowpipe during a shoot with the Royal School of Artillery, RA. (TFH 1.17; 2 Flights)

ZB916 Dptd Castlereagh 3.84 to Larkhill, arrived 2.4.84 and stored; f/f 22.5.85 at Manorbier. Briefly flown in the Hebrides 7.86; later to Otterburn 2.87 and to Falkland Islands 7.87. Finally shot down 17.11.87 by a Javelin missile at Manorbier during a joint shoot with 21 Battery, RA and 46 Battery, RA (TFH 15.52; 18 Flights)

ZB917 Dptd Castlereagh 3.84 to Larkhill, arrived 2.4.84 and stored; f/f 21.5.85 at Manorbier. Shot down by a Rapier in the Falkland Islands 5.8.86 during a shoot with 16 Sqdn, RAF Regt. (TFH 4.37; 5 Flights)

ZB918 Dptd Castlereagh 3.84 to Larkhill, arrived 2.4.84 and stored. Believed f/f 6.5.85 but recorded as being shot down on that date by a Blowpipe during a shoot with 10 Battery,RA. Also recorded as being shot down at Manorbier 6.5.88 but later repaired for pilot training only.

ZB919 Dptd Castlereagh 3.84 to Larkhill, arrived 2.4.84 and stored; f/f 23.4.85 at Manorbier. To Otterburn 8.86; to Hebrides 12.86. To Manorbier 2.87 where, on 11.2.87, it was shot down by a Javelin missile during a shoot with the Javelin QA. (TFH 11.50; 14 Flights)

ZB920 Dptd Castlereagh 3.84 to Larkhill, arrived 2.4.84 and stored; f/f 22.4.85 at Manorbier. Shot down by a Javelin missile at Manorbier 6.11.85 during a shoot with 10 Battery, RA. (TFH 9.25; 9 Flights)

ZB921 Dptd Castlereagh 3.84 to Larkhill, arrived 2.4.84 and stored; f/f 26.10.85 at Manorbier. Shot down by a Javelin missile at Manorbier 6.11.85 during a shoot with 10 Battery, RA. (TFH 4.28; 5 Flights)

ZB922 Dptd Castlereagh 3.84 to Larkhill, arrived 2.4.84 and stored. No further details known.

ZB923 Dptd Castlereagh 3.84 to Larkhill, arrived 2.4.84 and stored; f/f 6.5.85 at Manorbier where, on 6.5.86, it was shot down by a Blowpipe during a shoot with 3 Commando RM. (TFH 11.24; 10 Flights)

ZB924 Dptd Castlereagh 3.84 to Larkhill, arrived 2.4.84 and stored; f/f 7.5.86 at Manorbier but was shot down after 12 minutes by a Blowpipe during a shoot with 3 Commando, RM

ZB925 Dptd Castlereagh 3.84 to Larkhill, arrived 2.4.84 and stored; f/f 8.9.86 at the Hebrides Range. Fail-safed and crashed into the sea on 29.7.86 during a joint shoot with AMF(L) & 10 Battery, RA. (TFH 0.50; 2 Flights)

ZB926 Dptd Castlereagh 3.84 to Larkhill, arrived 2.4.84 and stored; f/f 6.5.85 at Manorbier but was shot down after 1.06hrs by a Blowpipe during a shoot with 10 Battery.

ZB927 Dptd Castlereagh 17.5.84 to Larkhill, arrived 21.5.84 and stored; f/f 11.5.85 at Manorbier but stalled off the launcher without gaining true flight.

ZB928 Dptd Castlereagh 17.5.84 to Larkhill, arrived 21.5.84 and stored; f/f 6.5.86 at Manorbier. To the Hebrides 6.86 where, on 4.7.86, it was shot down by a Blowpipe during a shoot with AMF(L) & 120 Battery, RA. (TFH 5.02; 6 Flights)

ZB929 Dptd Castlereagh 17.5.84 to Larkhill, arrived 21.5.84 and stored; f/f 18.5.85 at the Falkland Islands Range but crashed into the sea after refusing to respond to radio commands. Not recovered.

ZB930 Dptd Castlereagh 17.5.84 to Larkhill, arrived 21.5.84 and stored; f/f 8.5.85 at Manorbier. Crashed 24.5.85 during a Blowpipe shoot with 104 TA, possibly due to engine failure. (TFH 4.58; 5 Flights)

ZB931 Dptd Castlereagh 17.5.84 to Larkhill, arrived 21.5.84 and stored; f/f 14.8.85 in the Falkland Islands. On 20.8.85 it crashed into the sea following loss of engine power during a Rapier shoot with 30 Battery, RA. (TFH 3.56; 5 Flights)

ZB932 Dptd Castlereagh 17.5.84 to Larkhill, arrived 21.5.84 and stored. No further details.

ZB933 Dptd Castlereagh 17.5.84 to Larkhill, arrived 21.5.84 and stored; f/f 16.3.86 in the Falkland Islands. Seriously damaged 26.3.86 when it stalled on launch during a Javelin shoot with 46 Battery, RA. Rtnd to UK and repaired. To Otterburn 10.86. To Manorbier 1.87 where, on 4.2.87, it was shot down by a Javelin missile during a shoot with 21 Battery, RA. (TFH 6.10; 9 Flights)

ZB934 Dptd Castlereagh 17.5.84 to Larkhill, arrived 21.5.84 and stored; f/f 7.7.86 in the Hebrides. To Otterburn 11.86 where it was shot down on 22.11.86. (TFH 2.58; 3 Flights)

ZB935 Dptd Castlereagh 17.5.84 to Larkhill, arrived 21.5.84 and stored. Details of flights etc unkn until rebuilt by SBAS at Thruxton 9.84. No further details known.

ZB936-ZB937 Dptd Castlereagh 17.5.84 to Larkhill; arrived 21.5.84 and stored. No further details known.

ZB938 Dptd Castlereagh 17.5.84 to Larkhill, arrived 21.5.84 and stored. Allocated to Shorts as a trials aircraft; f/f 7.11.84 at West Freugh as part of an MDI trial but visibility too poor for missile firing. To Manorbier for 'live' tests and flown 14.11.84, 26.11.84, 10.12.84 and 11.12.84. Rtnd to West Freugh; to Manorbier 5.85. Rtnd Larkhill 1.86 for normal issue. To Norway 2.86; to Falklands 3.86 (but unflown); to Manorbier where, on 22.5.86, it was shot down by a Blowpipe during a shoot with 10 Battery, RA. (TFH 10.30; 19 Flights)

ZB939 Dptd Castlereagh 17.5.84 to Larkhill, arrived 21.5.84 and stored; f/f 23.5.85 at Manorbier. To Otterburn 2.87. W/o 9.11.87 when the flare pack developed a fault and set the skid-pan alight. The battery, harness and parachute also caught fire but the pilot managed to land the aircraft normally, but on fire. Left to burn out. (TFH 8.27; 11 Flights)

Note that for aircraft ZB940 to ZB999 despatch/arrival dates are unknown. Aircraft were initially stored at Larkhill and unpacked as and when required. After unpacking, assembly and engine test Skeets were then taken onto charge (TOC). Only these dates are recorded.

ZB940 TOC 4.6.85. Conveyed to the Falkland Islands and f/f 9.8.85. W/o 10.8.85 during a Rapier shoot with 37 Sqdn, RAF Regt when the engine failed after 12 minutes of flight and it crashed into the sea. (TFH 1.27; 3 Flights)

ZB941 TOC 12.6.85. Conveyed to the Hebrides and f/f 13.8.85. Shot down by a Javelin missile during a shoot with MGW3. (TFH 4.10; 6 Flights)

ZB942 TOC 12.6.85; f/f 9.8.85, probably in the Hebrides. Shot down over the Hebrides Range 10.9.85 by a Blowpipe during a shoot with 21 Battery, RA. Repaired at Larkhill. Recorded as being conveyed to the Falklands 10.86 and to Norway 2.87 but not flown. To Manorbier by 10.87 where, on 14.11.87, it was shot down by a Javelin missile during a shoot with 103 TA. (TFH 6.05; 9 Flights)

ZB943 TOC 18.6.85; f/f 9.8.85 in the Falkland Islands but engine failed after

1.08hrs during a Rapier shoot with 37 Sqdn, RAF Regt. Crashed into the sea.

ZB944 TOC 15.8.85; f/f 10.9.85 in the Hebrides but shot down after 16 minutes by a Blowpipe during a shoot with 21 Battery, RA.

ZB945 TOC 15.8.85; f/f 16.9.85, possibly in the Hebrides. To Otterburn 3.86 and to Manorbier 4.86 where, on 8.4.86, it was shot down by a Blowpipe during a shoot with 43 Battery, RA. (TFH 6.53; 7 Flights)

ZB946 TOC 15.8.85; f/f 10.9.85 at the Hebrides Range. Shot down 12.9.85 by a Javelin missile during a shoot with MGW3. (TFH 1.34; 2 Flights)

ZB947 TOC 14.8.85; f/f 17.10.85 at Manorbier. W/o 3.2.87 when, during a Javelin shoot with 21 Battery, RA at Manorbier, it fail-safed into the sea. A faulty servo was suspected. (TFH 2.49; 5 Flights)

ZB948 f/f 16.9.85 at the Hebrides Range. Shot down 18.9.85 by a Blowpipe during a shoot with AMF(L). (TFH 1.55; 2 Flights)

ZB949 TOC 19.8.85; f/f 12.9.85 at the Hebrides Range but suffered engine failure during a shoot with 21 Battery, RA and landed in the sea. Recovered and repaired at Larkhill. Stored. To Otterburn 8.86; to Hebrides 12.86 where, on 17.11.87, it crashed into the sea after contact was lost during a joint Javelin shoot with 21 Battery, RA and 46 Battery, RA. (TFH 4.47; 7 Flights).

ZB970 f/f 16.9.85 at the Hebrides for a shoot with 21 Battery, RA but was shot down by a Blowpipe missile on the same flight.

ZB971 TOC 18.8.85; f/f 17.9.85 at Otterburn. To the Hebrides Range 7.86 where, on 8.7.86, it was shot down by a Javelin missile during a shoot with AMF(L) and 10 Battery, RA. (TFH 8.53; 8 Flights)

ZB972 TOC 19.8.85; f/f 17.9.85 at Otterburn. To Manorbier 4.86 but was later shot down 23.5.86 by a Blowpipe during a shoot with 10 Battery, RA. (TFH 6.07; 9 Flights).

ZB973 TOC 15.8.85; f/f 12.9.85 at the Hebrides Range but shot down after 10 minutes by a Blowpipe during a shoot with 21 Battery, RA.

ZB974 TOC 17.11.85; f/f 11.12.85 at Manorbier but fail-safed into the sea after 9 minutes during a Javelin shoot with the Royal School of Artillery, RA.

ZB975 TOC 14.11.85; f/f 19.11.85 at Manorbier where, on 11.3.86, it was shot down by a Blowpipe during a shoot with 21 Battery, RA. (TFH 5.28; 6 Flights)

ZB976 TOC 17.11.85; f/f 9.12.85 at Manorbier where, on 19.3.86, it fail-safed into the sea whilst pilots changed transmitter during a Blowpipe shoot with 21 Battery, RA. (TFH 5.11; 7 Flights)

ZB977 TOC 10.11.85; f/f 18.11.85 at Manorbier where, on 10.3.86, it was shot down by a Blowpipe during a shoot with 21 Battery, RA. (TFH 10.01; 11 Flights)

ZB978 TOC 16.11.85; f/f 12.12.85 at Manorbier where, on 3.2.86, it was shot down by a Javelin missile during a shoot with the Royal School of Artillery, RA. (TFH 1.44; 3 Flights)

ZB979-ZB980 Believed to have arrived at Larkhill 30.10.84, ex-Castlereagh. No further details known.

ZB981 Believed to have arrived at Larkhill 30.10.84, ex-Castlereagh. TOC 18.2.86; f/f 17.3.86 at Manorbier but was w/o in a heavy landing due to engine refusing to cut out. (TFH 1.07; 1 Flight)

ZB982 Believed to have arrived at Larkhill 30.10.84, ex-Castlereagh. TOC 8.4.86; f/f 10.5.86 at Manorbier for which the MDI was removed to allow a shoot for small-arms air defence. Landed safely without damage despite 28 runs across the firing area! On 23.5.86 it was shot down by a Blowpipe during a shoot with 10 Battery, RA. (TFH 3.14; 3 Flights)

ZB983 Believed to have arrived at Larkhill 30.10.84, ex-Castlereagh. TOC 21.2.86; f/f 17.3.86 at Manorbier but damaged when the engine cut after 3 minutes and it landed on rocks. Recovered and repaired. On its 2nd flight, on 11.4.86, the engine began to run on only one cylinder after 30 minutes. Attempted a parachute recovery but the main 'chute did not deploy. Landed in the sea beneath its drogue parachute. Not recovered. (TFH 0.33; 2 Flights)

ZB984 Believed to have arrived at Larkhill 30.10.84, ex-Castlereagh. TOC 1.4.86; f/f 7.5.86 at Manorbier where, on 28.5.86, it was shot down by a Blowpipe during a shoot with 10 Battery, RA. (TFH 3.22; 4 Flights)

ZB985 Believed to have arrived at Larkhill 30.10.84, ex-Castlereagh. TOC 18.2.86; f/f 11.3.86 at Manorbier but the engine cut during a Blowpipe shoot with 21 Battery, RA. Crashed into the sea. The cause was probably running out of fuel. (TFH 1.13; 1 Flight)

ZB986 Believed to have arrived at Larkhill 30.10.84, ex-Castlereagh. TOC 7.4.86; f/f 20.5.86 at Manorbier but was shot down after 41 minutes by a Blowpipe during a shoot with 10 Battery, RA.

ZB987 TOC 24.1.86; f/f 22.2.86 at Manorbier where, on 10.3.86, it rolled into the sea after 55 minutes during a Blowpipe shoot with 21 Battery, RA. (TFH1.57; 2 Flights)

ZB988 TOC 10.4.86; f/f 30.8.86 at Otterburn. To the Falkland Islands 7.87. Rtnd to UK and later w/o 8.2.88 when it hit a rock on landing during a Javelin exercise shoot in Norway with AMF(L). (TFH 6.13; 9 Flights).
   Note that ZB988 was the last Skeet to be lost in service.

ZB989 TOC 9.4.86; f/f 7.5.86 at Manorbier where, on 23.5.86, it was shot down by a Blowpipe during a shoot with 10 Battery, RA. It was later recovered and rebuilt but not flown again. (TFH 2.36; 4 Flights)

ZB990 TOC 10.4.86; f/f 23.5.86 at Manorbier but was shot down after 30 minutes by a Blowpipe during a shoot with 10 Battery, RA.

ZB991 TOC 7.6.86; f/f 29.7.86 at the Hebrides Range but was shot down after 43 minutes by a Javelin missile during a joint shoot with AMF(L) and 10 Battery, RA.

ZB992 TOC 18.6.86; f/f 5.8.86 in the Falkland Islands but was "shot down by radio interference" after 13 minutes during a Rapier shoot with 16 Sqdn, RAF Regt.

ZB993 f/f 10.10.85, location unkn. Next flown 28.7.86 at the Hebrides Range. To Otterburn where it was shot down 30.8.86 by a Blowpipe during a TA competition. (TFH 1.51, 3 Flights)

ZB994 Apart from being seen by the author at Thruxton on 19.10.88 with a fuselage inscription "QUASIE Mk.1", no other details are known.

ZB995 Used as an engine test-bed for Weslake 274-6 and re-serialled Skeet 342-001.

ZB996 TOC 7.5.86; f/f 22.5.86 at Manorbier where, on 23.5.86, it crashed

Unmanned Targets for the Army 255

into the sea during a Blowpipe shoot with 10 Battery, RA. The cause was suspected to have been a Clansman interfering with transmissions.

ZB997 TOC 18.8.88 as a training aircraft and believed marked as ZB997(T). No details of any flights recorded.

ZB998 TOC 14.5.86; f/f 6.8.86 in the Falkland Islands where, on 10.8.86, it was shot down by a Blowpipe during a shoot with 21 Battery, RA. (TFH 1.24; 2 Flights)

ZB999 Used as an engine test-bed for Weslake 274-6 and re-serialled Skeet 342-002.

ZD115 The first production Skeet. Arrived Larkhill 11.12.81 (ex Castlereagh). To West Freugh 1.82 and reported as w/o 8.2.82. Possibly rebuilt as reported flying at Otterburn 17.3.84. No further details known.

ZD116 Dptd Castlereagh 19.2.82 to Larkhill and stored; f/f 4.5.83 in the Falkland Islands. Crashed there 2.8.83 after engine failure in flight. (TFH 3.28; 5 Flights)

ZD117 Retained by Shorts at Castlereagh for tests. Dptd Castlereagh 25.10.82 to Larkhill and stored; f/f 17.9.83 at Otterburn. Rtnd to Larkhill 21.3.84. To the Hebrides 5.84 where, on 23.7.84, it was damaged beyond repair in a parachute landing following engine failure over the Range. (TFH 4.23; 6 Flights)

ZD118 Dptd Castlereagh 19.2.82 to Larkhill and stored. Departed Larkhill for Hebrides by road 24.8.82; f/f 14.11.83. To Larkhill 1984. To Manorbier where, on 17.10.87, it crashed into the sea after failsafing due to a transmitter problem, during a Javelin shoot with 104 TA. (4 Flights)

ZD119 Dptd Castlereagh 19.2.82 to Larkhill and stored; f/f 1.8.83 in the Falkland Islands but shot down after 40 minutes.

ZD120 Dptd Castlereagh 19.2.82 to Larkhill and stored; f/f 8.3.83 in the Hebrides. W/o 21.7.83, cause unkn. (TFH 1.25; 3 Flights)

ZD121 Dptd Castlereagh 19.2.82 to Larkhill and stored; f/f 7.3.83 in the Hebrides. W/o 21.7.83, cause unkn. (TFH 1.38; 4 Flights)

ZD122 Dptd Castlereagh 19.2.82 to Larkhill and stored; f/f 23.6.83 in the Hebrides but written-off 28.6.83. (TFH 1.54; 2 Flights)

ZD123 Dptd Castlereagh 19.2.82 to Larkhill and stored. To the Hebrides 24.8.82; f/f 18.4.83 in the Hebrides where, on 19.4.83, it was w/o. (TFH 0.38; 2 Flights)

ZD124 Dptd Castlereagh 19.2.82 to Larkhill and stored; f/f 14.2.84 at Manorbier. Believed w/o 24.3.84. (TFH 1.25; 2 Flights)

ZD125 Dptd Castlereagh 19.2.82 to Larkhill and stored. To the Hebrides by road 24.8.82 and w/o there c18.5.83. No further details.

ZD126 Dptd Castlereagh 19.2.82 to Larkhill and stored. To the Hebrides by road 24.8.82 where f/f 23.5.83 but no further details known.

ZD127 Dptd Castlereagh 19.2.82 to Larkhill and stored. To the Hebrides by road 24.8.82 where f/f 21.7.83 but shot down 22.7.83. (TFH 1.20; 3 Flights)

ZD128 Dptd Castlereagh 19.2.82 to Larkhill and stored. To the Hebrides by road 24.8.82 where f/f 19.4.83. No further details.

ZD129 Dptd Castlereagh 19.2.82 to Larkhill and stored. To the Hebrides by road 24.8.82 where f/f 8.3.83. W/o in a crash 11.3.83 after the pilot lost sight of it in a rainstorm. (TFH 2.16; 2 Flights)

ZD130 Dptd Castlereagh 19.2.82 to Larkhill and stored; f/f 23.3.83 at Manorbier. To Otterburn c2.84. To the Hebrides where, on 22.5.84, it stalled on launch and crashed. (TFH 11.06; 16 Flights)

ZD131 Dptd Castlereagh 19.2.82 to Larkhill and stored. To the Hebrides by road 24.8.82 where f/f 29.6.83 but crashed into the sea after 22 minutes. No further details.

ZD132 Dptd Castlereagh 2.4.82 to Larkhill and stored. To the Hebrides by road 24.8.82 but no record of any flights can be found.

ZD133 Dptd Castlereagh 2.4.82 to Larkhill and stored. To the Hebrides by road 24.8.82 where f/f 11.3.83. Crashed into the sea 21.4.83 after the engine failed over the Range. (TFH 1.28; 2 Flights)

ZD134 Dptd Castlereagh 2.4.82 to Larkhill and stored. To the Hebrides by road 24.8.82 where f/f 14.11.83. To Manorbier 11.84 where lost at sea 28.11.84 after engine failure in flight.

ZD135 Dptd Castlereagh 2.4.82 to Larkhill and stored. To the Hebrides by road 24.8.82 where f/f 21.7.83 but crashed into the sea after 17 minutes when engine failed over the Range.

ZD136 Dptd Castlereagh 2.4.82 to Larkhill and stored. To the Hebrides by road 24.8.82 where f/f 23.5.83. Shot down 20.6.83. (TFH 1.22; 3 Flights)

ZD137 Dptd Castlereagh 2.4.82 to Larkhill and stored. To the Hebrides by road 24.8.82 where f/f 19.4.83. Shot down 21.4.83. (TFH 1.50; 3 Flights)

ZD138 Dptd Castlereagh 2.4.82 to Larkhill and stored. To Otterburn but

Always ensure the landing strip is clear of barbed-wire fences! After being stored at Larkhill for almost fourteen months Skeet 1 ZD122 was conveyed to the Hebrides Range where it made its first flight. Shortly afterwards, on 28 June 1983, it was wrecked in a landing accident. This view of ZD122 was taken immediately after the crash. (Bill Munday)

crashed on its first flight, on 22.1.83, when control was lost after 3 minutes.

ZD139 Dptd Castlereagh 2.4.82 to Larkhill and stored. To Otterburn but tfd to the Hebrides where f/f 21.7.83. Shot down 14.11.83. (TFH 5.45; 6 Flights)

ZD140 Dptd Castlereagh 2.4.82 to Larkhill and stored. To the Hebrides by road 24.8.82 where f/f 26.7.84. Crashed into the sea 9.4.85 during a Rapier shoot with 53 Battery, RA due to engine failure. (TFH 2.16; 4 Flights)

ZD141 Dptd Castlereagh 2.4.82 to Larkhill and stored. To the Hebrides by road 24.8.82. No further details.

ZD142 Dptd Castlereagh 25.10.82 to Larkhill and stored. To Otterburn where f/f 17.9.83. Damaged 18.3.84, details unkn. Arrived Larkhill by road 21.3.84 with a 'broken back' fuselage. Scrapped at Larkhill. (TFH 2.41; 3 Flights)

ZD143 Dptd Castlereagh 25.10.82 to Larkhill and stored. To Manorbier where f/f 13.5.83. To Otterburn c9.83. Damaged in landing 14.7.84. To the Hebrides where, on 21.6.85, it was shot down by a Rapier during a shoot with 12 Air Defence Battery, RA. (TFH 11.04; 13 Flights)

ZD144 Dptd Castlereagh 2.4.82 to Larkhill and stored. To Otterburn where f/f 19.9.83. Last recorded flight 18.3.84. Rtnd to Larkhill by road 21.3.84. No further details. (TFH 2.13; 3 Flights)

ZD145 Dptd Castlereagh 2.4.82 to Larkhill and stored. To the Hebrides by road 24.8.82. No further details.

ZD146 Dptd Castlereagh 2.4.82 to Larkhill and stored. To the Hebrides by road 24.8.82 where f/f 20.4.83. Crashed 19.5.83, cause unkn. (TFH 3.42; 5 Flights)

ZD147 Dptd Castlereagh 4.5.82 to Larkhill and stored. To Manorbier where f/f 31.3.84. Shot down 16.4.84. (TFH 1.29; 2 Flights)

ZD148 Dptd Castlereagh 4.5.82 to Larkhill and stored. To the Falkland Islands where it was w/o after 8 minutes into its first flight, 5.5.83, cause unkn.

ZD149 Dptd Castlereagh 4.5.82 to Larkhill and stored. To Otterburn where f/f 23.10.82 but broke rear fuselage on landing. Rtnd Larkhill for repairs. Stored. To Manorbier where, on 12.5.84, it was shot down. (TFH 1.15; 2 Flights)

ZD150 Dptd Castlereagh 4.5.82 to Larkhill and stored. To Otterburn where f/f 22.1.83. Damaged 19.9.83 but no further flights made. (TFH 4.33; 5 Flights)

ZD151 Dptd Castlereagh 4.5.82 to Larkhill and stored. To the Hebrides where f/f 7.3.83. Shot down 21.4.83. (TFH 3.48; 5 Flights)

ZD152 Dptd Castlereagh 4.5.82 to Larkhill and stored. To the Hebrides by road 24.8.82 where f/f 22.5.84 but shot down after 23 minutes.

ZD153 Dptd Castlereagh 4.5.82 to Larkhill and stored. To Otterburn where f/f 17.9.83. Crashed 19.9.83. (TFH 4.30; 6 Flights)

ZD154 Dptd Castlereagh 4.5.82 to Larkhill and stored until 1.83 when air-freighted to the Falkland Islands; f/f 1.8.83. Shot down 10.8.85 by a Rapier during a shoot with 37 Sqdn, RAF Regt. (TFH 1.47; 3 Flights)

ZD155 Dptd Castlereagh 4.5.82 to Larkhill and stored. To Manorbier where f/f 6.5.83. To Otterburn and flown there 17.9.83. Rtnd to Larkhill 21.3.84. No other details. (TFH 1.05; 2 Flights)

ZD156 Dptd Castlereagh 7.6.82 to Larkhill and stored. No further details.

ZD157 Dptd Castlereagh 7.6.82 to Larkhill and stored. Early flight details unknown. To the Falkland Islands 3.86 where it was shot down by a Rapier during a shoot with 35 Battery, RA.

ZD158 Dptd Castlereagh 7.6.82 to Larkhill and stored. No further details.

ZD159 Dptd Castlereagh 7.6.82 to Larkhill and stored. To the Hebrides by road 24.8.82 where it f/f 11.3.83. W/o c18.5.83.

ZD160 Dptd Castlereagh 7.6.82 to Larkhill and stored. To Otterburn where f/f 22.1.83. Last recorded flight 20.2.83. (TFH 2.13; 4 Flights)

ZD161 Dptd Castlereagh 7.6.82 to Larkhill and stored. W/o at West Freugh 11.3.83 on what appears to have been its first flight. No further details.

ZD162 Dptd Castlereagh 17.8.82 to Larkhill, arrived 20.8.82 and stored. To Manorbier c3.83 where f/f 23.3.83. Shot down 9.4.83 (or 12.4.83). Wreckage returned to Larkhill and scrapped. (TFH 1.59; 2 Flights)

ZD163 Dptd Castlereagh 17.8.82 to Larkhill, arrived 20.8.82 and stored. To Manorbier where f/f 5.5.83. Shot down 17.5.83. (TFH 2.45; 4 Flights)

ZD164 Dptd Castlereagh 17.8.82 to Larkhill, arrived 20.8.82 and stored. To Otterburn where f/f 20.2.83. Known to have been conveyed Lyneham-Larkhill (date unkn) after Exercise 'Hardfell' in Norway. Shot down in the Falkland Islands 30.4.84. (TFH 2.11; 3 Flights)

ZD180 Dptd Castlereagh 17.8.82 to Larkhill, arrived 20.8.82 and stored. To Otterburn where f/f 5.3.83. To Manorbier where last flown 7.5.83. No further details. (TFH 5.03; 6 Flights)

ZD181 Dptd Castlereagh 17.8.82 to Larkhill, arrived 20.8.82 and stored. To Otterburn where f/f 19.5.83. Scrapped at Larkhill 1.6.83. (TFH 2.33; 5 Flights)

ZD182 Dptd Castlereagh 17.8.82 to Larkhill, arrived 20.8.82 and stored; f/f 5.11.83 at Manorbier but was shot down after 51 minutes.

ZD183 Dptd Castlereagh 17.8.82 to Larkhill, arrived 20.8.82 and stored; f/f 5.11.83 at Manorbier. Last recorded flight 13.12.83 at Manorbier. No further details (TFH 2.08; 5 Flights)

ZD184 Dptd Castlereagh 17.8.82 to Larkhill, arrived 20.8.82 and stored; f/f 12.3.83 at Otterburn. To Manorbier immediately afterwards. Last flight 9.5.83. Fate not known. (TFH 4.56; 6 Flights)

ZD185 Dptd Castlereagh 17.8.82 to Larkhill, arrived 20.8.82 and stored; f/f 23.7.83, location unkn. To Hebrides. Shot down 10.2.86 by a Javelin missile on Exercise in Norway during a shoot with AMF(L).

ZD186 Dptd Castlereagh 17.8.82 to Larkhill, arrived 20.8.82 and stored; f/f 5.3.83 at Otterburn. To Manorbier where it crashed on launch 12.5.83. (TFH 0.31; 2 Flights)

ZD187 Dptd Castlereagh 17.8.82 to Larkhill, arrived 20.8.82 and stored; f/f 12.3.83 at Otterburn. To Manorbier immediately afterwards where, on 16.5.83, it crashed into the sea. (TFH 3.23; 5 Flights)

ZD188 Dptd Castlereagh 17.8.82 to Larkhill, arrived 20.8.82 and stored; f/f 13.2.83 at Manorbier. Crashed into the sea 24.3.83. (TFH 1.38; 2 Flights)

ZD189 Dptd Castlereagh 17.8.82 to Larkhill, arrived 20.8.82 and stored; f/f 22.1.83 at Otterburn but sustained a direct missile hit after 50 minutes.

ZD190 Dptd Castlereagh 17.8.82 to Larkhill, arrived 20.8.82, and stored; f/f 17.1.84 in the Falkland Islands. On 23.1.84 engine cut over Range; crashed into the sea. (TFH 0.33; 2 Flights)

ZD191 Dptd Castlereagh 17.8.82 to Larkhill, arrived 20.8.82 and stored; f/f 4.5.83 in the Falkland Islands. On 22.1.84 engine cut over the Falklands Range; crashed into the sea. (TFH 1.58; 2 Flights)

ZD192 Dptd Castlereagh 17.8.82 to Larkhill, arrived 20.8.82 and stored. No further details

ZD193 Dptd Castlereagh 1.9.82 to Larkhill and stored; f/f 31.10.83 at the Hebrides Range. Crashed into the sea 22.5.84. (TFH 2.42; 5 Flights)

ZD194 Dptd Castlereagh 1.9.82 to Larkhill and stored; f/f 30.5.84 at the Hebrides Range. Shot down 24.7.84 by a Blowpipe during a shoot with the Royal School of Artillery, RA (TFH 0.40; 2 Flights)

ZD195 Dptd Castlereagh 1.9.82 to Larkhill and stored; f/f 1.11.83 at the Hebrides Range. Last flight 23.5.84. Believed lost in the Hebrides. (TFH 2.53; 4 Flights)

ZD196 Dptd Castlereagh 1.9.82 to Larkhill and stored; f/f 5.11.83 at Manorbier. Crashed into the sea off Manorbier 13.2.84. (TFH 2.26; 3 Flights)

ZD197 Dptd Castlereagh 1.9.82 to Larkhill and stored; f/f 4.5.83 in the Falkland Islands. Shot down 5.5.83, details unkn. Officially w/o 11.5.83. (TFH 0.40; 2 Flights)

ZD198 Dptd Castlereagh 1.9.82 to Larkhill and stored; f/f 5.5.83 in the Falkland Islands. Sustained major damage when it crashed onto a beach in the Falklands during a shoot with 42 Air Defence Battery. Not repaired. (TFH 2.31; 4 Flights)

ZD199 Dptd Castlereagh 1.9.82 to Larkhill and stored. No further details.

ZD200 Dptd Castlereagh 1.9.82 to Larkhill and stored; f/f 5.11.83 at Manorbier. Shot down off Manorbier 24.3.84. (TFH 2.16; 3 Flights)

ZD201 Dptd Castlereagh 1.9.82 to Larkhill and stored. No further details.

ZD202 Dptd Castlereagh 1.9.82 to Larkhill and stored; f/f 5.10.83 in the Falkland Islands. Rtnd to UK c6.84. Crashed into the sea off Manorbier after becoming lost in sea mist during a Javelin shoot with 46 Battery, RA. (TFH 5.12; 8 Flights)

ZD203 Dptd Castlereagh 1.9.82 to Larkhill and stored; f/f 26.11.83 at Manorbier but became lost in cloud after 5 minutes and crashed into the sea.

ZD204 Dptd Castlereagh 1.9.82 to Larkhill and stored; f/f 14.2.84 at Manorbier. Shot down off Manorbier 24.3.84. (TFH 1.41; 2 Flights)

ZD205 Dptd Castlereagh 1.9.82 to Larkhill and stored; f/f 13.2.84 at Manorbier but crashed after 8 minutes.

ZD206 Dptd Castlereagh 1.9.82 to Larkhill and stored. No further details.

ZD207 Dptd Castlereagh 1.9.82 to Larkhill and stored; f/f 17.5.83 at Manorbier. Rtnd to Larkhill damaged; repaired. Next recorded flight at Manorbier 10.2.87. Shot down at Manorbier 17.10.87 by a Javelin missile during a shoot with 104 TA. (TFH 3.03; 4 Flights)

NB. When ZD207 was returned from Manorbier it was described as 'wrecked' and duly written-off charge. At the same time ZB743 was returned as 'repairable' but subsequent close inspection at Larkhill revealed that ZD207 was, in fact, repairable but that ZB743 was not. ZD207 was repaired but in view of the serial having been struck off, the repaired airframe was re-serialled ZB743. (The original ZB743 was 'patch-up', repainted grey overall and used as an anonymous Weslake engine test frame.

ZD208 Dptd Castlereagh 1.9.82 and conveyed to Larkhill and stored; f/f 22.10.83 at Manorbier where, on 13.12.83, it crashed in unknown circumstances. (TFH 1.12; 2 Flights)

ZD209 Dptd Castlereagh 25.10.82 to Larkhill and stored; f/f 17.3.84 at Otterburn but sustained damage when skid-landed after 38 minutes. Conveyed Otterburn-Larkhill 21.3.84 and repaired. To Manorbier where, on 11.12.84, it was shot down by a Blowpipe during a shoot with 46 Battery, RA.

Contract ML11A/1500: 700 Skeet 2

ZF801 Conveyed Thruxton-West Freugh for flight trials; f/f 6.8.87. Rnd to Thruxton. To Larkhill 6.10.87 for parachute trials. To Manorbier 10.87. Shot down by a Javelin missile 2.12.87 during a shoot with 104 Battery, RA. (TFH 2.28; 5 Flights)

ZF802 Conveyed Thruxton-West Freugh for flight trials; f/f 5.8.87. Returned to Thruxton. To Larkhill 6.10.87 for parachute trials. To Manorbier 10.87. Sustained direct hit by a Javelin missile 21.11.87 but later recovered. Rtnd to Thruxton for repair and serialled ZF802R. To Manorbier 6.89. Shot down off Manorbier 4.7.89 by a Javelin missile during a shoot with 10 Battery, RA. Crashed into the sea. (TFH 4.43; 9 Flights)

ZF803 f/f 8.2.88 at Manorbier but shot down after 15 minutes by a Javelin missile during a shoot with 104 Regiment, TA.

Skeet 2 ZF802 seen fully rigged and ready to launch at the Phoenix Range, Larkhill on the occasion of the acceptance trials on 6 October 1987. After the crash of ZF816 the trial was stopped for the day. (Michael I Draper)

258 Sitting Ducks and Peeping Toms

ZF804 Conveyed Thruxton-West Freugh for flight trials; f/f 5.8.87. Rtnd to Thruxton. To Larkhill 6.10.87 and immediately to Manorbier. Shot down 1.12.87 by a Javelin missile during a shoot with 104 Regiment, TA. (TFH 1.35; 3 Flights)

ZF805 f/f 22.2.88 at Manorbier but shot down after 25 minutes by a Javelin missile during a shoot with 21 Battery, RA.

ZF806 f/f 18.12.87 at Manorbier but fail-safed after 2 minutes and crashed into the sea. Recovered and conveyed to Larkhill for repair. Next flown at Manorbier 3.7.89 but fail-safed when changing from launch to Range pilot. Again recovered from the sea and repaired. On its 3rd flight, at Manorbier 21.4.90, became lost in sea mist during a Javelin shoot with 105 Regiment, TA, and fail-safed into the sea. Not recovered. (TFH 0.57; 3 Flights)

ZF807 f/f 6.8.87 at West Freugh as part of manufacturer's trials. Del Thruxton-Larkhill 6.10.87 for parachute trials. In service by 1.12.87. Fail-safed 30 seconds after launch at Manorbier 6.2.88 and crashed into the sea. (TFH 2.14; 7 Flights)

ZF808 f/f 2.12.87 at Manorbier. Shot down 8.2.88 by a Javelin missile during a shoot with Royal School of Artillery, RA. (TFH 2.33; 4 Flights)

ZF809 Del Manorbier 11.87; f/f 11.2.88. Shot down at Manorbier 15.10.88 by a Javelin missile during a shoot with 43 Battery, RA (TFH 11.15; 14 Flights)

ZF810 Del Manorbier 11.87; f/f 23.2.88 but shot down after 19 minutes by a Javelin missile during a shoot with 21 Battery, RA.

ZF811 Del Manorbier 11.87; f/f 6.2.88 but shot down on its 2nd flight of the day by a Javelin missile. Recovered and rebuilt as ZF811R. Shot down at Manorbier 31.7.89 by a Javelin missile during a shoot with Royal School of Artillery, RA. (TFH 1.33; 3 Flights)

ZF812 Del Manorbier 11.87; f/f 10.2.88 but skid-pan caught fire after 31 minutes of a Javelin shoot with the Royal School of Artillery., RA Fail-safe activated and crashed into the sea.

ZF813 Del Manorbier 11.87; f/f 11.2.88. Shot down at Manorbier 15.10.88 by a Javelin missile during a shoot with 103 Regiment, TA (TFH 2.49; 4 Flights)

ZF814 Del Manorbier 11.87; f/f 10.2.88. Shot down at Manorbier 15.10.88 by a Javelin missile during a shoot with 43 Battery, RA. Repaired. On 24.2.88 the engine cut over the Manorbier Range during a Javelin shoot with 21 Battery, RA. Crashed into the sea. (TFH 5.07; 7 Flights)

ZF815 Del Thruxton-Larkhill 6.10.87; f/f 9.10.87. To Manorbier 11.87. Fail-safed during pilot changeover 18.12.87 and crashed into the sea. Recovered and rebuilt as ZF815R. Shot down 31.7.89 by a Javelin missile during a shoot with Royal School of Artillery, RA. (TFH 1.48; 5 Flights)

ZF816 Del Thruxton-Larkhill 6.10.87; launched same date but fail-safed on launch, causing damage to fuselage, fin and wing. Rtnd to Thruxton and repaired with new fuselage as ZF816R. To Manorbier by 7.89. Shot down 9.4.90 by a Javelin missile during a shoot with 10 Battery, RA. (TFH 14.42; 25 Flights)

ZF817 (c/n F.016) To Manorbier 10.87; f/f 2.12.87. W/o 14.2.88 when overshot runway at Manorbier and landed heavily. (TFH 5.00; 7 Flights)

ZF818 (c/n F.017) Initially retained by SBAS Thruxton for demonstrations. Thruxton-Larkhill 30.10.87. To Manorbier; f/f 20.10.88. Shot down 31.10.88 by a Javelin missile during a shoot with 10 Battery, RA. (TFH 6.32; 8 Flights)

ZF819 (c/n F.019) To Manorbier 10.87; f/f 2.12.87. W/o 18.12.87 by a Javelin missile during a shoot with Royal School of Artillery, RA. (TFH 1.24; 2 Flights)

ZF820 (c/n F.022) To Manorbier 10.87; f/f 6.2.88. W/o 10.2.88 by a Javelin missile during a shoot with Royal School of Artillery, RA. (TFH 1.47; 3 Flights)

ZF821 (c/n F.021) To Manorbier 11.87; f/f 18.12.87. Suffered engine failure after 2 minutes of a shoot with Royal School of Artillery, RA 8.2.88 and fail-safed into the sea. Recovered and rebuilt as ZF821R by 6.89. To Manorbier but crashed into the sea 1.8.89 during a Javelin shoot with

Three newly-manufactured Skeet 2 fuselages lean against the wall of Short Brothers Air Services' Thruxton facility on 23 September 1987. All have just arrived from Blandford Forum-based sub-contractor TASUMA Ltd and two (ZF819 & ZF820) are still in their protective polythene wrapping. (Michael I Draper)

The storage rack at Larkhill always contained enough drones for at least six months normal usage. This view, taken on 28 January 1988, shows brand-new Skeet 2s, all with engines fitted and bench-tested. Identifiable aircraft include ZF825, ZF840, ZF841, ZF843 and ZF884 (incorrectly painted as ZF859). (Michael I Draper)

RSA. Recovered and repaired as ZF821RR although the 'RR' suffix was not applied. Shot down at Manorbier 24.9.90 by a Javelin missile of 10 Battery, RA. (TFH 4.51; 10 Flights)

ZF822 To Manorbier 10.87; f/f 24.2.88. W/o 27.3.88 when the aileron jammed to give full 'left stick' making it unable to be flown in straight and level flight. (TFH 1.04; 5 Flights)

ZF823 To Manorbier by 2.88. Shot down at Manorbier 25.2.88 by a Javelin missile. Recovered and rebuilt as ZF823R by 6.89. Shot down at Manorbier 1.8.89 by a Javelin missile during a shoot with the Royal School of Artillery, RA (TFH 2.11; 3 Flights)

ZF824 To Manorbier 10.87; f/f 25.2.88. Shot down 27.3.88 by a Javelin missile during a shoot with 104 Regiment, TA. (TFH 3.30; 6 Flights)

ZF825 To Manorbier 2.88; f/f 18.5.88. Shot down 31.5.88 by a Javelin missile during a shoot with the Royal School of Artillery, RA. (TFH 0.43; 2 Flights)

ZF826 Del Thruxton-Larkhill 30.10.87. To Manorbier; f/f 14.2.88. Shot down 17.5.88 by a Javelin missile during a shoot with the Gibraltar Regiment. Recovered and rtrnd to Larkhill but scrapped. (TFH 3.23; 5 Flights)

ZF827 Del Thruxton-Larkhill 30.10.87. To Manorbier; f/f 26.3.88. Shot down 5.12.88 by a Javelin missile during a shoot with the Royal School of Artillery, RA. (TFH 2.35; 5 Flights)

ZF828 Del Thruxton-Larkhill 30.10.87. To Manorbier; f/f 30.5.88. Damaged 4.6.88 by a Javelin missile during a shoot with 103 Regiment TA. Recovered from sea and repaired as ZF828R. Shot down 2.9.89 by a Javelin missile during a shoot with 103 Regiment, TA (TFH 3.14; 7 Flights)

ZF829 Del Thruxton-Larkhill 30.10.87. To Manorbier; f/f 23.2.88. W/o at Manorbier 4.6.88 when stalled 30 seconds after launch and crashed into the sea during a shoot with 103 Regiment, TA. Recovered and reduced to spares at Larkhill. (TFH 6.28; 9 Flights)

ZF830 Del Thruxton-Larkhill 30.10.87. To Norway 1.88; f/f 8.2.88. Rtnd to UK and on to Falkland Islands where, on 4.9.88, suffered engine-failure and crashed into the sea during a Rapier shoot with 26 Sqdn, RAF Regt. (TFH 1.14; 2 Flights)

ZF831 Del Thruxton-Larkhill 30.10.87. To Manorbier; f/f 25.2.88. Shot down 12.3.88 by a Javelin missile during a shoot with 103 Regiment, TA (TFH 2.46; 4 Flights)

ZF832 Del Thruxton-Larkhill 30.10.87. To Norway 1.88; f/f 7.2.88. Rtnd to UK and on to Manorbier where, on 27.10.88, it was shot down by a Javelin missile during a shoot with 10 Battery, RA. (TFH 2.28; 4 Flights)

ZF833 f/f Manorbier 27.6.88. Shot down 5.7.88 by a Javelin missile during a shoot with 46 Battery, RA. Recovered and conveyed to Larkhill 1.8.88 but scrapped. (TFH 2.53; 5 Flights)

ZF834 f/f Manorbier 12.10.88 but shot down after 9 minutes by a Javelin missile during a shoot with Royal School of Artillery, RA.

ZF835 f/f Manorbier 24.2.88 but stalled off the launcher and crashed into the sea without gaining level flight.

ZF836 (c/n F.026) f/f Manorbier 5.3.88. Shot down 4.7.88 by a Javelin missile during a shoot with 46 Battery, RA. Recovered and conveyed to Larkhill 1.8.88 but scrapped. (TFH 9.10; 13 Flights)

ZF837 f/f Manorbier 19.10.88. Crashed into the sea 27.10.88 after the skid-pan caught fire during a Javelin shoot with 10 Battery, RA. (TFH 4.42; 6 Flights)

ZF838 f/f Manorbier 15.5.88 but stalled off the launcher without gaining level flight. Recovered from the sea and rtnd to Larkhill but scrapped.

ZF839 f/f Manorbier 19.10.88 but shot down on its 2nd flight of the day by a Javelin missile during a shoot with 43 Battery, RA. (TFH 1.15; 2 Flights)

ZF840 f/f Manorbier 14.5.88. Shot down 5.7.88 by a Javelin missile during a shoot with Royal School of Artillery, RA. Recovered and conveyed to Larkhill but scrapped. (TFH 3.53; 7 Flights)

ZF841 f/f Manorbier 12.10.88 but shot down after 16 minutes by a Javelin missile during a shoot with Royal School of Artillery, RA.

ZF842 f/f in the Hebrides 10.9.88 but shot down after 2 minutes by a Rapier during a shoot with 42 Battery, RA.

ZF843 f/f in the Hebrides 8.9.88. To Manorbier 9.88 where, on 10.12.88, it was shot down by a Javelin missile during a shoot with 104 TA. (TFH 1.27; 3 Flights)

ZF844 f/f in the Hebrides 8.9.88. Shot down on its 2nd flight, on 11.9.88, by a Rapier during a shoot with 42 Battery, RA. (Note date also given as 12.9.88.)

ZF845 f/f at Manorbier 15.10.88. Shot down 21.10.88 by a Javelin missile during a shoot with 43 Battery, RA. (TFH 3.30; 5 Flights)

ZF846 f/f at Manorbier 20.10.88. Shot down 21.10.88 by a Javelin missile during a shoot with 43 Battery, RA. (TFH 1.43; 2 Flights)

ZF847 f/f at Manorbier 5.7.88. Shot down 10.10.88 by a Javelin missile during a shoot with Royal School of Artillery, RA. (TFH 3.10; 5 Flights)

ZF848 f/f at Manorbier 19.10.88 but shot down after 25 minutes by a Javelin missile during a shoot with 43 Battery, RA. (TFH 3.10; 5 Flights)

ZF849 f/f in the Hebrides 10.9.88. To Manorbier 10.88 where, on 5.12.88, it was shot down by a Javelin missile during a shoot with Royal School of Artillery, RA (TFH 2.54; 4 Flights)

ZF876 (c/n F.040) Del Thruxton-Larkhill with incorrect serial ZF851; f/f at Manorbier 27.6.88 but shot down after 8 minutes by a Javelin missile during a shoot with 46 Battery, RA. Recovered and returned to Larkhill but scrapped.

ZF877 (c/n F.041) Del Thruxton-Larkhill with incorrect serial ZF852; f/f at Manorbier 18.5.88. Shot down 11.6.88 by a Javelin missile during a shoot with 104 TA. (TFH 1.55; 4 Flights)

ZF878 Del Thruxton-Larkhill with incorrect serial ZF853; f/f in the Hebrides 9.9.88. To Manorbier 10.88 where, on 9.2.89, it failsafed during a shoot with 105 TA and crashed into the sea. (TFH 2.49; 4 Flights)

ZF879 Del Thruxton-Larkhill with incorrect serial ZF854; f/f at Manorbier 5.7.88. Shot down 18.7.88 by a Javelin missile during a shoot with Royal School of Artillery, RA. (TFH 1.39; 3 Flights)

ZF880 Del Thruxton-Larkhill with incorrect serial ZF855; f/f at Manorbier 19.10.88 but shot down after 6 minutes by a Javelin missile during a shoot with 43 Battery, RA.

ZF881 (c/n F.047) Del Thruxton-Larkhill with incorrect serial ZF856; f/f in the Hebrides 8.9.88 but fail-safed immediately after launch and landed in the sea. Recovered and rebuilt as ZF881R. To Manorbier 6.89 and shot down 6.9.89 by Oerlikon 35mm gun during a shoot with 2729 Sqdn, RAF Regiment. (TFH 1.43; 4 Flights)

ZF882 (c/n F.048) Del Thruxton-Larkhill with incorrect serial ZF857; f/f at Manorbier 19.10.88 but control lost after 6 minutes and crashed into the sea.

ZF883 Del Thruxton-Larkhill with incorrect serial ZF858 (later corrected); at Manorbier 5.11.88. Crashed into the sea 10.12.88 after losing power during a Javelin shoot with 104 TA. (TFH 2.56; 4 Flights)

ZF884 (c/n F.050) Del Thruxton-Larkhill with incorrect serial ZF859 (later corrected); f/f at Manorbier 27.10.88. Shot down 28.10.88 by a Javelin missile during a shoot with 10 Battery, RA. (TFH 0.59; 2 Flights)

ZF885 (c/n F.051) Del Thruxton-Larkhill with incorrect serial ZF860 (later corrected); f/f at Manorbier 19.10.88. Shot down 27.10.88 by a Javelin missile during a shoot with 10 Battery, RA. (TFH 2.13; 3 Flights)

ZF886 Del Thruxton-Larkhill with incorrect serial ZF861 (later corrected); f/f at Manorbier 31.10.88 but shot down after 15 minutes by a Javelin missile during a shoot with 10 Battery. RA.

ZF887 Del Thruxton-Larkhill with incorrect serial ZF862 (later corrected); f/f at Manorbier 5.7.88 but shot down after 3 minutes by a Javelin missile during a shoot with 46 Battery, RA. Recovered and rtrnd to Larkhill 1.8.88 for possible repair but scrapped.

ZF888 Del Thruxton-Larkhill with incorrect serial ZF863 (later corrected); f/f at Manorbier 12.4.88. Crashed into the sea 30 seconds after launch on 4.6.88 following loss of control. Later discovered that Clansman was using the same frequency. (TFH 2.03; 4 Flights)

ZF889 (c/n F.055) Del Thruxton-Larkhill with incorrect serial ZF864 (later corrected); f/f at Manorbier 27.6.88. Crashed into the sea 4.7.88 after enginefailure. Recovered and repaired as ZF889R. Shot down off Manorbier 17.10.89 by a Javelin missile during a shoot with 46 Battery, RA. (TFH 3.33; 7 Flights)

ZF890 Originally built with incorrect serial ZF865 but corrected; f/f at Manorbier 4.7.88 but shot down after 38 minutes by a Javelin missile during a shoot with 46 Battery, RA. Recovered and returned to Larkhill 1.8.88 for repair but scrapped.

ZF891 Originally built with incorrect serial ZF866 but corrected; f/f at Manorbier 24.10.88. Shot down 25.10.88 by a Javelin missile during a shoot with 10 Battery, RA. (TFH 1.35; 3 Flights)

ZF892 Originally built with incorrect serial ZF867 but corrected; f/f at Manorbier 27.6.88 but shot down after 36 minutes by a Javelin missile during a shoot with 46 Battery, RA.

ZF893 Originally built with incorrect serial ZF868 but corrected; f/f at Manorbier 11.6.88. Shot down off Manorbier 5.12.88 by a Javelin missile during a shoot with Royal School of Artillery, RA (TFH 2.52; 5 Flights)

ZF894 f/f at Manorbier 31.10.88. Shot down off Manorbier 6.12.88 by a Javelin missile during a shoot with Royal School of Artillery, RA. (TFH 1.30; 3 Flights)

ZF895 f/f at the Hebrides Range 10.9.88. To Manorbier 10.88 where, on 14.2.89, it was shot down by a Javelin missile during a shoot with Royal School of Artillery, RA. (TFH 2.50; 4 Flights)

ZF901 f/f 29.4.88 in the Falkland Islands where it crashed 6.9.88 when stalled on landing after a Rapier shoot with 26 Sqdn, RAF Regt. (TFH 1.18; 2 Flights)

ZF902 f/f 29.4.88 in the Falkland Islands where it was written-off 10.12.90 after radio interference during a Rapier shoot with 27 Sqdn, RAF Regt caused it to crash just 2 minutes after launch. (TFH 1.54; 6 Flights)

ZF903 f/f at Manorbier 10.12.88 but fail-safed into the sea after 5 minutes when the flare system was engaged.

ZF904 f/f in the Hebrides 8.9.88 but shot down following day by a Rapier during a shoot with 42 Battery, RA. (TFH 0.48; 2 Flights)

ZF905 f/f 29.4.88, possibly in the Falkland Islands. Shot down at Manorbier 9.10.89 by a Javelin missile during a shoot with Royal School of Artillery, RA. (TFH 1.34; 3 Flights)

ZF906 f/f in the Falkland Islands 29.4.88 where it was shot down 5.5.89 by a Rapier during a shoot with 16 Sqdn, RAF Regt. (TFH 1.29; 4 Flights)

ZF907 f/f at Manorbier 10.12.88. Shot down off Manorbier 14.2.89 by a Javelin missile during a shoot with Royal School of Artillery, RA. (TFH 2.21; 3 Flights)

ZF908 f/f at Manorbier 31.10.88. Shot down off Manorbier 13.2.89 by a Javelin missile during a shoot with Royal School of Artillery, RA. (TFH 1.17; 3 Flights)

ZF909 f/f in the Falkland Islands 14.12.88. Fail-safed into the sea there 3.4.90 due to suspected local radio interference. (TFH 1.35; 4 Flights)

ZF910 f/f at Manorbier 10.12.88 but shot down after 6 minutes by a Javelin missile during a shoot with 104 TA.

ZF911 f/f 29.4.88, location unkn. Shot down off Manorbier 31.8.89 (or 9.10.89) by a Javelin missile during a shoot with Royal School of Artillery, RA. (TFH 1.04; 2 Flights)

ZF912 f/f in the Falkland Islands 5.9.88. To UK c6.89. Shot down off Manorbier 2.9.89 by a Javelin missile during a shoot with 103 TA. (TFH 1.26; 3 Flights)

ZF913 f/f at Manorbier 5.11.88. Shot down off Manorbier 15.4.89 by a Javelin missile during a shoot with 104 TA. (TFH 8.27; 11 Flights)

ZF914 f/f at Manorbier 25.10.88. Shot down off Manorbier 28.1.88, details unkn. (TFH 2.26; 3 Flights)

ZF915 f/f at Manorbier 29.9.88 but fail-safed into the sea after 10 minutes following a near-miss with a Javelin missile. Recovered and rebuilt as ZF915R. Shot down off Manorbier 24.10.89 by a Javelin missile during a shoot with 21 Battery, RA. (TFH 1.24; 4 Flights)

ZF916 f/f at Manorbier 9.7.88. Shot down off Manorbier 10.10.88 by a Javelin missile during a shoot with Royal School of Artillery, RA. (TFH 1.44; 2 Flights)

ZF917 f/f at Manorbier 9.7.88. Shot down off Manorbier 26.7.88 by a Javelin missile during a shoot with Royal School of Artillery, RA. Conveyed Manorbier-Larkhill 1.8.88 for repair but scrapped. (TFH 3.04; 4 Flights)

ZF918 f/f at Manorbier 29.9.88. Shot down off Manorbier 12.10.88 by a Javelin missile during a shoot with Royal School of Artillery, RA. (TFH 3.36; 6 Flights)

ZF919 f/f at Manorbier 7.7.88. Stalled on launch at Manorbier 29.9.88 and w/o. (TFH 3.24; 7 Flights)

ZF920 f/f at Manorbier 9.7.88. Shot down off Manorbier 28.10.88 by a Javelin missile during a shoot with 10 Battery, RA. (TFH 4.59; 8 Flights)

ZF921 f/f at Manorbier 12.10.88. Crashed into the sea off Manorbier 21.10.88 after the engine failed during a Javelin shoot with 43 Battery, RA. (TFH 1.27; 3 Flights)

ZF922 f/f at Manorbier 9.10.88. Crashed into the sea 10.10.88 after the engine cut during a Javelin shoot with the RSA. Recovered and rebuilt as ZF922R. Shot down at Manorbier 21.10.89 (or 24.10.89) by a Javelin missile during a shoot with 21 Battery, RA. (TFH 6.28; 8 Flights)

ZF923 f/f at Manorbier 17.4.89. Fail-safed into the sea off Manorbier 14.6.89 due to a ground equipment fault during a Javelin shoot with 105 TA. Recovered and repaired as ZF923R but later fail-safed 23.4.90 during a Javelin shoot with 105 TA at Manorbier. Recovered and rebuilt again, as ZF923RR. Conveyed to Saudi Arabia where, on 19.1.91 it was w/o in a heavy landing during a shoot with 12 AD.

ZF924 f/f at Manorbier 8.2.89. Crashed into the sea 9.6.89 after the engine cut during a Javelin shoot with 105 TA. Recovered and rebuilt as ZF924R. Next flown 9.5.90 at Manorbier but crashed into the sea after 30 minutes following another engine failure. (TFH 2.49; 4 Flights)

ZF925 f/f in Norway 4.2.89 where it was shot down, on 7.2.89, by a Rapier missile during an Exercise shoot with 3 Commando RM. (TFH 0.50; 2 Flights)

ZF926 f/f in Norway 8.2.89. Rtnd to UK undamaged and tfd to Manorbier where, on 18.4.89, it stalled immediately after launch and crashed into the sea. (TFH 2.21; 4 Flights)

ZF927 Taken to Norway 1.89 but not flown. To Manorbier where f/f 27.5.89. Fail-safed 5 minutes after launch 7.6.89. Recovered and rebuilt as ZF927R. Shot down at Manorbier 12.6.90 by a Javelin missile during a shoot with 21 Battery, RA. (TFH 2.09; 4 Flights)

ZF928 f/f in Norway 4.2.89 but sustained extensive damage during a heavy landing after 30 minutes. Fuselage and engine w/o for 'spares recovery only'.

ZF929 f/f in Norway 7.2.89. To Manorbier where, on 29.5.89, it was shot down by a Javelin missile during a shoot with the Royal School of Artillery, RA. (TFH 7.14; 10 Flights)

ZF930 f/f 13.12.88 in the Falkland Islands where, on 15.12.88, it was shot down by a Rapier during a shoot with 63 Sqdn, RAF Regt. (TFH 0.52; 2 Flights)

ZF931 f/f 9.5.89 at Manorbier but shot down after 16 minutes by a Javelin missile during a shoot with 7th Royal Horse Artillery, RA.

ZF932 f/f in Norway 7.2.89 but damaged after 7 minutes by a Rapier fired by 20 ADB. Rtnd to UK and repaired. To Manorbier where it later fail-safed during a pilot changeover, on 26.6.89, at the start of a Javelin shoot with 10 Battery, RA. Crashed onto rocks and w/o. (TFH 5.27; 11 Flights)

ZF933 f/f 8.2.89, location unkn. To Manorbier by 5.89 where, on 12.6.89, it sustained damage when the skid-pan caught fire in flight and crashed into the sea. Recovered and rebuilt as ZF933R. Shot down at Manorbier 23.4.90 by a Javelin missile during a shoot with 10 Battery, RA. (TFH 5.21: 8 Flights)

ZF934 f/f 15.12.88 in the Falkland Islands where, on 3.4.90, it fail-safed 5 minutes after launch during a Rapier shoot with 63 Sqdn, RAF Regt and crashed into the sea. (TFH 2.06; 5 Flights)

ZF935 f/f 9.5.89 at Manorbier but shot down after 16 minutes by a Javelin missile during a shoot with 7th Royal Horse Artillery, RA

ZF936 f/f 29.5.89 at Manorbier but fail-safed after 23 minutes and crashed into the sea. Recovered and rebuilt as ZF936R. Shot down at Manorbier 7.6.90 by a Javelin missile during a shoot with 21 Battery, RA. (TFH 5.06; 8 Flights)

ZF937 f/f 20.3.89 in the Hebrides where, on 26.3.89, it was shot down by a Rapier during a shoot with 32 Battery, RA. (TFH 4.32; 8 Flights)

ZF938 f/f 20.3.89 in the Hebrides. Fuselage seriously damaged 4.4.89. Rtnd to Larkhill and repaired. To Manorbier where it was shot down 13.6.89 by a Javelin missile during a shoot with 105 TA. (TFH 6.03; 12 Flights)

ZF939 f/f 20.3.89, location unkn (but possibly Hebrides). Damaged 26.3.89; Rtnd to Larkhill and repaired. To Manorbier 6.89 where, on 10.6.89, it was shot down by a Javelin missile during a shoot with 105 TA. (TFH 3.57; 8 Flights)

ZF940 f/f 23.3.89 in the Hebrides but fail-safed after 19 minutes during a Rapier shoot with 32 Battery, RA.

ZF941 f/f 5.6.89 at Manorbier. Shot down 9.6.89 by a Javelin missile during a shoot with 105 TA. (TFH 2.33; 4 Flights)

ZF942 f/f 21.3.89 in the Hebrides. To Manorbier 6.89 where it was shot down 14.6.89 by a Javelin missile during a shoot with 105 TA. (TFH 6.33; 11 Flights)

ZF943 f/f 11.2.89 at Manorbier where, on 14.2.89, it was shot down by a Javelin missile during a shoot with the Royal School of Artillery, RA. (TFH 1.01; 2 Flights)

ZF944 f/f 11.2.89 at Manorbier where, on 14.2.89, it was shot down by a Javelin missile of the Royal School of Artillery, RA. (TFH 1.20; 2 Flights)

ZF945 f/f 12.12.88 in the Falkland Islands but shot down after 23 minutes by a Rapier during a shoot with 63 Sqdn, RAF Regt.

ZF946 f/f 19.2.89, probably at Manorbier. Shot down at Manorbier 7.6.89 by a Javelin missile during a shoot with 105 TA (TFH 8.17; 13 Flights)

ZF947 f/f 5.3.89, location unkn. Shot down 17.4.89 by a Javelin missile during a shoot with 46 Battery, RA. (TFH 3.21; 5 Flights)

ZF948 f/f 11.2.89 at Manorbier. Shot down 17.4.89 by a Javelin missile during a shoot with the Royal School of Artillery, RA. (TFH 1.19; 2 Flights)

ZF949 f/f 4.3.89 at Manorbier but fail-safed into the sea after 15 minutes during a Javelin shoot with 103 TA.

ZF950 f/f 5.3.89 at Manorbier. Shot down 29.4.89 by a Javelin missile during a shoot with 102 TA. (TFH 4.36; 8 Flights)

ZF961 f/f 5.3.89 at Manorbier. Shot down 29.4.89 by a Javelin missile during a shoot with 102 TA. (TFH 6.46; 10 Flights)

ZF962 f/f 4.3.89, probably at Manorbier. Shot down 27.5.89 by a Javelin missile during a shoot with 102 TA but recovered and later repaired as ZF962R. Shot down at Manorbier 28.7.90 by a Javelin during a shoot with 103 TA. (TFH 11.21; 17 Flights)

ZF963 f/f 3.4.89, probably at Manorbier, but fail-safed after 2 minutes during the first circuit of a Javelin shoot with Royal School of Artillery, RA. Crashed into the sea.

ZF964 f/f 4.5.89 in the Falkland Islands where, on 3.4.90, it fail-safed into the sea during a Rapier shoot with 63 Sqdn, RAF Regt. Likely cause was radio interference. (TFH 1.14; 3 Flights)

ZF965 f/f 4.9.89 in the Falkland Islands where, on 3.4.90, it fail-safed into the sea during a Rapier shoot with 63 Sqdn, RAF Regt. Likely cause was radio interference. (TFH 0.39; 2 Flights)

ZF966 f/f 3.4.90 in the Falkland Islands but was shot down after 6 minutes by a Rapier during a shoot with 63 Sqdn, RAF Regt.

ZF967 f/f 5.5.89 in the Falkland Islands but damaged after 23 minutes when it landed in a former Argentine 'fox-hole'. Rtnd to UK and repaired. To Manorbier 4.90 where, on 31.7.90, it was shot down by a Javelin during a shoot with Royal School of Artillery, RA (TFH 3.03; 7 Flights)

ZF968 f/f 21.3.89 in the Hebrides but shot down on its 2nd flight of the day by a Rapier during a shoot with 35 Battery, RA. (TFH 0.55; 2 Flights)

ZF969 f/f 26.3.89 in the Hebrides but shot down after 12 minutes by a Rapier during a shoot with 32 Battery, RA.

ZF970 f/f 4.5.89 in the Falkland Islands but shot down after 21 minutes by a Rapier during a shoot with 16 Sqdn, RAF Regt.

ZF971 f/f 15.6.89 at Manorbier but shot down after 34 minutes by a Javelin during a shoot with 105 TA.

ZF972 f/f 26.3.89 in the Hebrides where, on 3.4.89, it was shot down by a Rapier during a shoot with 30 Battery, RA. (TFH 3.53; 6 Flights)

ZF973 f/f 31.3.89 in the Hebrides. Rtnd to Larkhill for repairs and to Manorbier 5.89. Shot down 7.6.89 by a Javelin during a shoot with 105 TA. (TFH 2.59; 4 Flights)

ZF974 f/f 13.6.89 at Manorbier but shot down after 39 minutes by a Javelin during a shoot with 105 TA.

ZF975 f/f 15.6.89 at Manorbier where, on 31.7.89 it was shot down by a Javelin during a shoot with the Royal School of Artillery, RA. (TFH 5.33; 9 Flights)

ZF976 f/f 19.6.89 at Manorbier where, on 26.6.89, it was shot down by a Javelin during a shoot with 10 Battery, RA. (TFH 0.35; 2 Flights)

ZF977 f/f 26.6.89 at Manorbier but engine cut whilst approaching to land after a Javelin shoot with 10 Battery, RA. (TFH 0.33; 1 Flights)

ZF978 f/f 14.6.89 at Manorbier where, on 3.7.89, it was shot down by a Javelin during a shoot with 10 Battery, RA. (TFH 2.19; 4 Flights)

ZF979 f/f 26.6.89 at Manorbier where, on 31.7.89, it was shot down by a Javelin during a shoot with Royal School of Artillery, RA. (TFH 0.55; 2 Flights)

ZF980 f/f 27.6.89 at Manorbier but fail-safed after 2 minutes during a Javelin shoot with 10 Battery, RA.

ZF981 f/f 27.6.89 at Manorbier but was shot down after 19 minutes by a Javelin during a shoot with 10 Battery, RA.

ZF982 f/f 1.7.89 at Manorbier but went out of control during its 2nd flight of the day and crashed into the sea. (TFH 1.26; 2 Flights)

ZF983 f/f 27.6.89 at Manorbier but was shot down after 40 minutes by a Javelin during a shoot with 10 Battery, RA.

ZF984 f/f 1.7.89 at Manorbier. Shot down 10.7.89 by a Javelin but later recovered and repaired as ZF984R. Rtnd to Manorbier where it was shot down by a Javelin during a shoot with 21 Battery, RA (TFH 5.15; 8 Flights)

ZF985 f/f 1.7.89 at Manorbier but shot down on its 2nd flight of the day by a Javelin during a shoot with 102 TA. (TFH 0.48; 2 Flights)

ZF986 f/f 31.7.89 at Manorbier where, on 1.8.89, it was shot down by a Javelin during a shoot with Royal School of Artillery, RA. (TFH 1.19; 2 Flights)

ZF987 f/f 12.6.89 at Manorbier but was shot down after 32 minutes by a Javelin during a shoot with 105 TA.

ZF988 f/f 4.7.89 at Manorbier where, on 10.7.89, it was shot down by a Javelin during a shoot with 10 Battery, RA. (TFH 1.45; 3 Flights)

ZF989 f/f 1.7.89 at Manorbier but shot down on its 2nd flight of the day by a Javelin during a shoot with 102 TA. Recovered and repaired as ZF989R. To Manorbier 7.90 but shot down 31.7.90 by a Javelin during a shoot with the Royal School of Artillery, RA. (TFH 2.47; 5 Flights)

ZF990 f/f 31.7.89 at Manorbier but shot down after 23 minutes by a Javelin during a shoot with Royal School of Artillery, RA.

ZG111 (c/n F.139) f/f 2.9.89 at Manorbier where, on 13.9.89, it was shot down by a Javelin during a shoot with 21 Battery, RA. (TFH 2.11; 4 Flights)

ZG112 (c/n F.140) f/f 5.9.89 at Manorbier where, on 19.9.89, it was shot down by a Javelin during a shoot with 21 Battery, RA. (TFH 3.38; 5 Flights)

ZG113 (c/n F.141) f/f 5.9.89 at Manorbier where, on 11.10.89, it was shot down by a Javelin during a shoot with 104 TA. (TFH 8.41; 14 Flights)

ZG114 (c/n F.142) f/f 5.9.89 at Manorbier where, on 13.9.89, it was shot down by a Javelin during a shoot with 21 Battery, RA. (TFH 0.58; 3 Flights)

ZG115 (c/n F.143) f/f 4.9.89 at Manorbier where, on 19.9.89, it was shot down by a Javelin during a shoot with 21 Battery, RA. (TFH 1.35; 2 Flights)

ZG116 (c/n F.144) f/f 16.10.89 at Manorbier where, on 3.2.90, it was shot down by a Javelin during a shoot with 103 TA Regiment, RA. (TFH 4.38; 7 Flights)

ZG117 (c/n F.145) f/f 17.10.89 at Manorbier where, on 19.10.89, it was shot down by a Javelin during a shoot with 43 Battery, RA. (TFH 0.59; 2 Flights)

ZG118 f/f 11.10.89 at Manorbier where, on 16.10.89, it was shot down by a Javelin during a shoot with 43 Battery, RA. (TFH 0.17; 2 Flights)

ZG119 f/f 19.10.89 at Manorbier where, on 25.11.89, it fail-safed into the sea during a Javelin shoot with 105 TA Regt, RA. (TFH 1.24; 3 Flights)

ZG120 f/f 16.10.89 at Manorbier where, on 13.1.90, it fail-safed into the sea during a pilot changeover one minute after launch. (TFH 5.48; 9 Flights)

ZG121 f/f 24.10.89 at Manorbier but on the 3rd flight of the day it was shot down by a Javelin during a shoot with 21 Battery, RA. (TFH 2.03; 3 Flights)

ZG122 f/f 11.10.89 at Manorbier but fail-safed into the sea after 34 minutes. Recovered and repaired as ZG122R. Later shot down 8.9.90 by a Javelin during a shoot with 103 TA. (TFH 3.17; 5 Flights)

ZG123 First launched 19.10.89 at Manorbier but crashed off the launcher without gaining flight, nor responding to commands. Repaired. Shot down at Manorbier 9.5.90 by a Javelin during a shoot with 7th Royal Horse Artillery, RA. (TFH 1.53; 4 Flights)

ZG124 f/f 11.12.89 at Manorbier where, on 12.2.90, it was shot down by a Javelin during a shoot with Royal School of Artillery, RA (TFH 2.05; 4 Flights)

ZG125 f/f 25.11.89 at Manorbier where, on 3.2.90, it was shot down by a Javelin during a shoot with 103 TA. Recovered from the sea and rebuilt as ZG125R. Shot down at Manorbier 7.9.90, possibly by a Dart missile. (TFH 1.57; 6 Flights)

ZG126 f/f 17.10.89 at Manorbier but shot down after 17 minutes by a Javelin during a shoot with 43 Battery, RA. Recovered from the sea and rebuilt as ZG126R. Shot down at Manorbier 7.9.90 by a Javelin during a shoot with 43 Battery, RA.

ZG127 f/f 5.11.89 at Manorbier where, on 3.2.90, it was shot down by a Javelin during a shoot with 103 TA. (TFH 3.37; 6 Flights)

ZG128 f/f 24.10.89 at Manorbier but shot down after 5 minutes by a Javelin during a shoot with 21 Battery, RA.

ZG129 f/f 6.12.89 at Manorbier where, on 24.3.90, it was shot down by a Javelin during a shoot with 103 TA. (TFH 4.34; 8 Flights)

ZG130 f/f 24.10.89 at Manorbier but failed to respond to radio commands after 10 minutes and crashed into the sea.

ZG131 f/f 10.4.90 at Manorbier where, on 11.4.90, it was shot down by a Javelin during a shoot with 10 Battery, RA. (TFH 1.27; 2 Flights)

ZG132 f/f 17.3.90 at Manorbier where, on 24.3.90, it was shot down by a Javelin during a shoot with 103TA. (TFH 1.54; 3 Flights)

ZG133 f/f 13.1.90 at Manorbier but shot down after 24 minutes by a Javelin during a shoot with 103 TA.

ZG134 f/f 12.2.90 at Manorbier where, on 17.3.90, it was shot down by a Javelin during a shoot with 104 TA. (TFH 2.24; 4 Flights)

ZG135 f/f 14.2.90 at Manorbier where, on 9.3.90, it was shot down by a Javelin during a shoot with 104 Regiment TA. (TFH 0.57; 2 Flights)

ZG136 f/f 24.3.90 at Manorbier where, on 9.5.90, it was shot down by a Javelin during a shoot with 7th Royal Horse Artillery, RA. (TFH 5.17; 8 Flights)

ZG137 f/f 10.3.90 at Manorbier where, on 17.3.90, it was shot down by a Javelin during a shoot with 105 TA. (TFH 0.29; 2 Flights)

ZG138 f/f 17.3.90 at Manorbier but was shot down on the 3rd flight of the day by a Javelin during a shoot with 105 TA. (TFH 2.02; 3 Flights)

ZG139 f/f 9.3.90 at Manorbier where, on 12.4.90, it was shot down by a Javelin during a shoot with 10 Battery, RA. (TFH 2.08; 4 Flights)

ZG140 f/f 9.4.90 but engine cut over the Range and crashed into the sea. Recovered and rebuilt as ZG140R. On 18.1.91 it crashed in Saudi Arabia during a shoot with 12 AD

ZG141 f/f 22.1.90 in Norway. Rtnd to UK 2.90. To Manorbier where, on 7.4.90, it fail-safed into the sea one minute after launch during a Javelin shoot with 104 TA. (TFH 1.54; 5 Flights)

ZG142 f/f 10.4.90 at Manorbier where, on 22.5.90, it was shot down by a Javelin during a shoot with 3 Commando RM. (TFH 4.27; 7 Flights)

ZG143 f/f 2.4.90 at Manorbier but shot down after 25 minutes by a Javelin during a shoot with Royal School of Artillery, RA

ZG144 f/f 9.4.90, probably at Manorbier. Shot down 21.4.90; details unkn. (TFH 6.30; 10 Flights)

ZG145 f/f 24.1.90 at Manorbier where, on 21.4.90, it was shot down by a Javelin during a shoot with 105 TA. (TFH 8.06; 10 Flights)

ZG146 f/f 2.4.90 at Manorbier but shot down on the 2nd flight of the day by a Javelin during a shoot with Royal School of Artillery, RA. (TFH 0.59; 2 Flights)

ZG147 f/f 2.4.90 at Manorbier where, on 10.4.90, it was shot down by a Javelin during a shoot with 10 Battery, RA. (TFH 2.44; 5 Flights)

ZG148 f/f 24.1.90 in Norway. Rtnd to UK; to Manorbier where, on 9.5.90, it shot down by a Javelin during a shoot with 7th Royal Horse Artillery, RA. (TFH 2.13; 4 Flights)

ZG149 f/f 11.4.90 at Manorbier but shot down after 27 minutes by a Javelin during a shoot with 10 Battery, RA.

ZG150 f/f 22.1.90 at Manorbier where, on 20.4.90, it was shot down by a Javelin during a shoot with 10 Battery, RA. (TFH 2.05; 4 Flights)

ZG151 f/f 31.5.90 at Manorbier where, on 1.6.90, it was shot down by a Javelin during a shoot with Royal School of Artillery, RA (TFH 0.54; 2 Flights)

ZG152 f/f 15.5.90 at Manorbier where, on 23.5.90, it was shot down by a Javelin during a shoot with 3 Commando RM. (TFH 1.07; 3 Flights)

ZG153 f/f 22.5.90 at Manorbier but shot down after 8 minutes by a Javelin during a shoot with 3 Commando Bde, RM

ZG154 f/f 31.5.90 at Manorbier where, on 23.9.90, it was shot down by a Javelin during a shoot with 10 Battery, RA. (TFH 6.35; 9 Flights)

ZG155 f/f 1.6.90 at Manorbier where, on 12.6.90, it was shot down by a Javelin during a shoot with 21 Battery, RA. (TFH 1.42; 3 Flights)

ZG156 f/f 28.4.90 at Manorbier where, on 24.7.90, it crashed into the sea after engine failure. Recovered and rebuilt as ZG156R. Shot down 8.12.91, probably at Manorbier. (TFH 7.53; 10 Flights)

ZG157 f/f 28.4.90 at Manorbier where, on 4.6.90, it was shot down by a Javelin during a shoot with 21 Battery, RA. (TFH 6.08; 9 Flights)

ZG158 f/f 2.6.90 at Manorbier where, on 5.6.90, it was shot down by a Javelin during a shoot with 21 Battery, RA. (TFH 1.00; 2 Flights)

ZG159 f/f 23.5.90 at Manorbier but shot down after 21 minutes by a Javelin during a shoot with 3 Commando Bde RM.

ZG160 f/f 29.6.90 at Manorbier where, on 24.7.90, it was shot down by a Javelin during a shoot with Royal School of Artillery, RA. (TFH 2.26; 4 Flights)

ZG171 f/f 28.6.90 at Manorbier where, on 29.6.90, it was shot down by a Javelin during a shoot with 102 TA. (TFH 1.05; 2 Flights)

ZG172 f/f 31.5.90 at Manorbier but shot down after 26 minutes by a Javelin during a shoot with Royal School of Artillery, RA.

ZG173 f/f 27.6.90 at Manorbier where, on 25.9.90, it was shot down by a Javelin during a shoot with 10 Battery, RA. (TFH 5.20; 9 Flights)

ZG174 f/f 4.6.90 at Manorbier where, on 10.9.90, it was shot down by a Javelin during a shoot with 43 Battery, RA. (TFH 2.42; 6 Flights)

ZG175 f/f 12.6.90 at Manorbier where, on 13.6.90, it was shot down by a Javelin during a shoot with 21 Battery, RA. (TFH 0.31; 2 Flights)

ZG176 f/f 31.5.90 at Manorbier where, on 4.6.90, it was shot down by a Javelin during a shoot with 21 Battery. (TFH 2.13; 4 Flights)

ZG177 f/f 7.6.90 at Manorbier where, on 28.7.90, it was shot down by a Javelin during a shoot with 103 TA. (TFH 4.13; 6 Flights)

ZG178 f/f 28.6.90 at Manorbier where, on 24.7.90, it fail-safed after 2 minutes and crashed into the sea during a Javelin shoot with Royal School of Artillery, RA. (TFH 1.42; 3 Flights)

ZG179 f/f 28.7.90 at Manorbier but was shot down after 14 minutes by a Javelin during a shoot with 103 TA.

ZG180 f/f 24.1.90 in Saudi Arabia but was landed after 22 minutes due to suspected rear fuselage damage. Rtnd to UK. To Manorbier c3.91 where, on 18.6.91, it was shot down by a Javelin during a shoot with 21 Battery, RA. (TFH 6.14; 11 Flights)

ZG181 f/f 24.7.90 at Manorbier where, on 28.7.90, it was shot down by a Javelin during a shoot with 103 TA. (TFH 0.56; 2 Flights)

ZG182 f/f 10.9.90 at Manorbier where, on 25.9.90, it was shot down by a Javelin during a shoot with 10 Battery, RA. (TFH 2.07; 3 Flights)

ZG183 f/f 24.7.90 at Manorbier but shot down after 11 minutes by a Javelin during a shoot with Royal School of Artillery, RA.

ZG184 f/f 28.7.90 at Manorbier where, on 10.9.90, it was shot down by a Javelin during a shoot with 43 Battery, RA. (TFH 4.02; 6 Flights)

ZG185 f/f 10.12.90, probably at Manorbier. Shot down 24.11.92, possibly also at Manorbier. (TFH 2.48; 5 Flights)

ZG186 f/f 5.9.90, location unkn. W/o 10.12.90 in the Falkland Islands following a heavy landing after a Rapier shoot with 27 Sqdn, RAF Regt. (TFH 0.31; 2 Flights)

ZG187 f/f 18.11.91, location unkn but shot down after 16 minutes. No other details known.

ZG188 f/f 5.9.90 in the Falkland islands but fail-safed after 40 minutes and seriously damaged after landing on scattered rocks. Recovered and rebuilt as ZG188R. Crashed into the sea off the Falklands 13.8.91 when the engine cut during a Rapier shoot. (TFH 0.53; 2 Flights)

ZG189 f/f 4.9.90, possibly at Manorbier. On 27.4.93 a Norton engine (No. 73P846) was installed and test-flown 27.7.93, location unkn. Crashed immediately after launch following lack of response from elevators. (TFH 4.21; 8 Flights)

ZG190 f/f 22.10.90, probably at Manorbier. Shot down 7.3.91, no other details known. (TFH 8.03; 12 Flights)

ZG221 f/f 7.9.90 at Manorbier where, on 8.9.90, it was shot down by a Javelin during a shoot with 103 TA. (TFH 1.37; 3 Flights)

ZG222 f/f 10.9.90 at Manorbier. On 23.9.90 it was shot down by a Javelin during a shoot with 10 Battery, RA. (TFH 2.14; 3 Flights)

ZG223 f/f 6.9.90 at Manorbier but shot down on the 3rd flight of the day by a Javelin during a shoot with 43 Battery, RA. (TFH 1.59; 3 Flights)

ZG224 f/f 4.9.90 in the Falkland Islands but after 16 minutes of a Rapier shoot with 48 Sqdn, RAF Regt the tail section broke off in flight and ZG224 crashed into the sea at Hooker's Point.

ZG225 f/f 7.9.90 at Manorbier. On 23.9.90 it was shot down by a Javelin during a shoot with 10 Battery, RA. (TFH 2.18; 5 Flights)

ZG226 f/f 8.9.90 at Manorbier but stalled on launch without gaining level flight and crashed into the sea.

ZG227 f/f 7.9.90 at Manorbier. On 23.9.90 the engine failed, probably due to fuel shortage, during a Javelin shoot with 10 Battery, RA. Crashed into the sea. (TFH 2.33; 3 Flights)

ZG228 f/f 7.9.90 at Manorbier. On 8.9.90 it was shot down by a Javelin during a shoot with 103 TA. (TFH 1.15; 2 Flights)

ZG229 f/f 5.9.90 at Manorbier. On 6.9.90 it was shot down by a Javelin during a shoot with 43 Battery, RA. (TFH 1.00; 2 Flights)

ZG230 f/f 23.9.90 at Manorbier but fail-safed after 2 minutes on the changeover to optic control. Crashed into the sea.

ZG231 f/f 24.9.90 at Manorbier but shot down after 32 minutes by a Javelin during a shoot with 10 Battery, RA.

ZG232 f/f 16.10.90 at Manorbier. On 3.12.90 it was shot down by a Javelin during a shoot with the Royal School of Artillery, RA. (TFH 6.29; 9 Flights)

ZG233 f/f 25.9.90 at Manorbier but was shot down during the 2nd flight of the day. Recovered from the sea, rebuilt as ZG233R and fitted with a Norton engine. Ground-tested 14.1.92. To Manorbier but shot down 6.3.92 by a Javelin during a shoot with 10 Battery, RA. (TFH 4.26; 5 Flights)

ZG234 f/f 22.9.90 at Manorbier. Shot down 5.12.90 by a Javelin during a shoot with 46 Battery, RA. (TFH 5.37; 8 Flights)

ZG235 f/f 24.9.90 at Manorbier. Shot down 25.9.90 by a Javelin during a shoot with 10 Battery, RA. (TFH 4.16; 6 Flights)

ZG236 f/f 23.9.90 at Manorbier. Shot down 24.9.90 by a Javelin during a shoot with 10 Battery, RA. (TFH 1.39; 2 Flights)

ZG237 f/f 23.9.90 at Manorbier but shot down after 40 minutes by a Javelin during a shoot with 10 Battery, RA.

ZG238 f/f 23.9.90 at Manorbier but shot down after 28 minutes by a Javelin during a shoot with 10 Battery, RA.

ZG239 f/f 23.9.90 at Manorbier. Shot down 24.9.90 by a Javelin during a shoot with 10 Battery, RA. (TFH 1.35; 2 Flights)

ZG240 f/f 22.9.90 at Manorbier. Shot down 7.12.90 by a Javelin during a shoot with 16 AD. (TFH 3.36; 5 Flights)

ZG241 f/f 25.9.90 at Manorbier but stalled on launch during the second flight of the day and cr. (TFH 0.50; 2 Flights)

ZG242 f/f 24.9.90 at Manorbier. Shot down during the second flight of the day by a Javelin during a shoot with 10 Battery, RA. (TFH 0.32; 2 Flights)

ZG243 f/f 24.9.90 at Manorbier but shot down after 16 minutes by a Javelin during a shoot with 10 Battery, RA.

ZG244 f/f 4.10.90 at Manorbier but shot down on its 2nd flight of the day by a Javelin during a shoot with the Royal School of Artillery, RA. (TFH 1.04; 2 Flights)

ZG245 f/f 17.10.90 at Manorbier. Crashed into the sea 22.10.90 after the aileron became detached in flight and the pilot was unable to recover control of the aircraft. (TFH 4.11; 6 Flights)

ZG246 f/f 13.12.90 at Manorbier but shot down after 40 minutes by a Javelin during a shoot with 16 AD.

ZG247 f/f 4.10.90 at Manorbier. Shot down 16.10.90 by a Javelin during a shoot with 46 Battery, RA. (TFH 1.50; 3 Flights)

ZG248 f/f 3.10.90 at Manorbier. Crashed off the launcher 11.12.90 and extensively damaged but appears to have been repaired. Shot down at Manorbier 23.3.91 by a Javelin during a shoot with 105 TA.

ZG249 f/f 3.10.90 at Manorbier but shot down after 3 minutes by a Javelin during a shoot with the Royal School of Artillery, RA.

ZG250 f/f 3.10.90 at Manorbier but stalled off the launcher on its 3rd flight of the day during a shoot with the Royal School of Artillery, RA. (TFH 1.25; 3 Flights)

ZG251 f/f 16.10.90 at Manorbier. Shot down 22.10.90 by a Javelin during a shoot with 46 Battery, RA. (TFH 2.53; 4 Flights)

ZG252 f/f 3.10.90 at Manorbier but shot down after 46 minutes by a Javelin during a shoot with 46 Battery, RA.

ZG253 f/f 16.10.90 at Manorbier but shot down after 28 minutes by a Javelin during a shoot with 46 Battery, RA.

ZG254 f/f 3.10.90 at Manorbier. Shot down 16.10.90 by a Javelin during a shoot with 46 Battery, RA. (TFH 1.46; 3 Flights)

ZG255 f/f 22.10.90 at Manorbier. Shot down 13.12.90 by a Javelin during a shoot with 16 AD. (TFH 1.04; 3 Flights)

ZG256 f/f 16.10.90 at Manorbier but seriously damaged (broken fin and twisted fuselage) on landing. Repaired and declared serviceable 22.11.90. Crashed into the sea off Manorbier on its next flight, on 6.12.90, when its engine cut during a shoot with 46 Battery, RA. (TFH 1.10; 2 Flights)

ZG257 f/f 3.10.90 at Manorbier where, on 4.10.90, it was shot down by a Javelin during a shoot with the Royal School of Artillery, RA. (TFH 1.37; 3 Flights)

ZG258 f/f 1.12.90 at Manorbier where, on 2.12.90, it was shot down by a Javelin during a shoot with the Royal School of Artillery, RA. (TFH 0.59; 2 Flights)

ZG259 f/f 3.12.90 at Manorbier where, on 4.12.90, it was shot down by a Javelin during a shoot with 46 Battery, RA.

ZG260 f/f 7.12.90 at Manorbier where, on 10.12.90, it was shot down by a Javelin during a shoot with 6 AD. (TFH 1.10; 2 Flights)

ZG261 f/f 22.10.90 at Manorbier but crashed onto rocks after engine failed on approach to land during a Javelin shoot with 46 Battery, RA. (TFH 0.44; 1 Flight)

ZG262 f/f 17.10.90 at Manorbier. Shot down 4.12.90 by a Javelin during a shoot with 46 Battery, RA. (TFH 7.46; 11 Flights)

ZG263 f/f 4.12.90 at Manorbier where, on 5.12.90, it was shot down by a Javelin during a shoot with 46 Battery, RA.

ZG264 f/f 7.12.90 at Manorbier where, on 11.12.90, it was shot down by a Javelin during a shoot with 6 AD. (TFH 2.01; 3 Flights)

ZG265 f/f 16.10.90 at Manorbier. Shot down 5.12.90 by a Javelin during a shoot with 46 Battery., RA (TFH 7.22; 10Flights)

ZG266 f/f 8.12.90 at Manorbier. Shot down 26.6.91 by a Javelin during a shoot with 21 Battery, RA. (TFH 14.44; 20 Flights)

ZG267 f/f 6.12.90 at Manorbier. Crashed into the sea 12.12.90 when it ran out of fuel during a Javelin shoot with 6 AD. (TFH 2.32; 3 Flights)

ZG268 f/f 8.12.90 at Manorbier. Shot down 12.12.90 by a Javelin during a shoot with 6 AD. (TFH 3.03; 5 Flights)

ZG269 f/f 13.12.90 at Manorbier. Shot down 21.6.91 by a Javelin during a shoot with 21 Battery, RA. (TFH 7.42; 11 Flights)

ZG270 f/f 12.12.90 at Manorbier. Shot down 2.2.91 by a Javelin during a shoot with 103 TA. (TFH 2.12; 3 Flights)

ZG301 f/f 4.12.90 at Manorbier. Shot down 5.12.90 by a Javelin during a shoot with 46 Battery, RA. (TFH 2.27; 3 Flights)

ZG302 f/f 1.12.90 at Manorbier. Shot down 2.12.90 by a Javelin during a shoot with the Royal School of Artillery, RA. (TFH 1.01; 2 Flights)

ZG303 f/f 3.2.91 at Manorbier. Written-off 6.11.91 when, after a shoot with 7th

RHA, the engine cut too early on approach to land and the aircraft crashed into the sea. (TFH 7.55; 11 Flights)

ZG304 f/f 16.2.91 at Manorbier. Shot down 7.3.92, further details unkn. (TFH 3.19; 6 Flights)

ZG305 f/f 13.2.90 at Manorbier but fail-safed into the sea after 10 minutes and during a Javelin shoot with 16AD.

ZG306 f/f 3.2.91 at Manorbier. Shot down 25.6.91 by a Javelin missile during a shoot by 21 Battery, RA. (TFH 5.33; 10 Flights)

ZG307 f/f 11.12.90 at Manorbier. During its second flight of the day it became lost in poor visibility during a Javelin shoot with 6 AD. Parachute-landed into the sea. Recovered and repaired as ZG307R and fitted with a Norton engine (No.73P754). Shot down 11.2.93, no further details known. (TFH 4.25; 5 Flights)

ZG308 f/f 26.1.91 at Manorbier for a Javelin shoot with 105 TA but after just 3 minutes the engine cut and the aircraft crashed onto rocks. Likely cause was interference by local transmissions.

ZG309 f/f 13.12.90 at Manorbier but landed short of the way (after 51 minutes) causing the fuselage to break into two parts. Repaired and next flown at Manorbier 26.1.91. Later shot down by a Javelin missile on 3.2.91 during a shoot with 103 TA. (TFH 2.36; 4 Flights)

ZG310 f/f 12.12.90 at Manorbier. Shot down 13.12.90 by a Javelin missile during a shoot with 16 AD. (TFH 2.75; 5 Flights)

ZG311 f/f 11.12.90 at Manorbier but was shot down after 48 minutes by a Javelin missile during a shoot with 6 AD.

ZG312 f/f 2.2.91 at Manorbier but shot down by a Javelin missile during its 2nd flight of the day and during a shoot with 103 TA. (TFH 1.25; 2 Flights)

ZG313 f/f 20.1.91 in Saudi Arabia but shot down on the same flight by a Rapier missile during a shoot with 12 AD.

ZG314 f/f 11.5.91 at Manorbier but shot down on its 2nd flight of the day by a Javelin missile during a shoot with 103TA.l (TFH 1.01; 2 Flights)

ZG315 f/f 23.1.91 in Saudi Arabia but shot down on the same flight by a Rapier missile during a shoot with 12 AD.

ZG316 f/f 4.6.91 at Manorbier and believed lost on this flight. No other details known.

ZG317 f/f 14.7.91 at Manorbier. Shot down 16.6.92. (TFH 1.17; 2 Flights)

ZG318 f/f 25.5.91 at Manorbier. Shot down off Manorbier 11.6.91 by a Javelin missile during a shoot with 105TA. (TFH 5.09; 7 Flights)

ZG319 f/f 14.11.91 at Manorbier but shot down after just 3 minutes. Wreckage fell into the sea. No other details known.

ZG320 No details known.

ZG321 f/f 20.6.91 at Manorbier for a Javelin shoot with 21 Battery, RA but engine failed after 23 minutes and the aircraft crashed into the sea.

ZG322 f/f 20.1.91 in Saudi Arabia but shot down on the same flight by a Rapier missile during a shoot with 12 AD.

ZG323 f/f 18.1.91 in Saudi Arabia but shot down on the same flight by a Rapier missile during a shoot with 12 AD.

ZG324 f/f 18.1.91 in Saudi Arabia but crashed after engine failed shortly after launch. Further details unkn.

ZG325 f/f 2.3.91 at Manorbier. On 25.5.91 it stalled on launch from Manorbier and crashed into the sea without gaining level flight. (Date also reported as 12.5.91.) (TFH 3.04; 5 Flights)

ZG326 f/f 22.1.91 (possibly) in Saudi Arabia but sustained damage after 11 minutes when a Rapier missile sliced 2ft off the starboard wing, including the aileron. Landed safely and repaired on site with replacement wing. On 2.3.91 during a shoot with the RAF 150 rounds of cannon fire was expended against it causing loss of control before it crashed into the sea. (TFH 1.22; 3 Flights)

ZG327 f/f 19.1.91 in Saudi Arabia but crashed in unkn circumstances during the same flight.

ZG328 f/f 5.3.91 at Manorbier. On 27.9.91, during a Javelin shoot with 102 TA, the engine cut after 28 minutes and it crashed into the sea. (TFH 1.53; 3 Flights)

ZG329 f/f 9.2.93, possibly in the Hebrides. On its 2nd flight of the day it was shot at by Dart missiles but survived and landed safely. No further flights were made due to a leaking fuel tank. Appears never to have flown again. No further details (TFH 1.35; 2 Flights)

ZG330 f/f 19.1.91, location unkn. On 13.8.91, during a Rapier shoot in the Falkland islands, it fail-safed after 12 minutes and crashed into the sea. (TFH 1.40; 3 Flights)

ZH263 f/f 3.9.91 for a training flight, location unkn, but engine cut after 13 minutes and it crashed into cliffs.

ZH264 f/f 29.5.91 at Manorbier. Shot down on the 2nd flight of the day by a Javelin missile during a shoot with the Royal School of Artillery, RA. Recovered and repaired as ZH264R; next flown 19.2.92. Shot down 6.3.92, location and details unkn. (TFH 2.13; 4 Flights)

ZH265 f/f 5.3.91 at Manorbier. Shot down 7.3.91 off Manorbier by a Javelin missile during a shoot with the Royal School of Artillery, RA. (TFH 3.22; 4 Flights)

ZH266 f/f 9.3.91 at Manorbier. Fail;-safed on 23.3.91 after just 2 minutes flight at the point of pilot changeover ahead of a Javelin shoot with 105 Regiment TA. Aircraft landed in the sea. Recovered and repaired as ZH266R; next flown 18.1.92. Shot down 13.4.92, location and details unkn. (TFH 5.25; 6 Flights)

ZH267 f/f 3.6.91 at Manorbier but shot down after 11 minutes by a Javelin missile during a shoot with 105 Regiment TA.

ZH268 f/f 6.3.91 at Manorbier. Stalled on launch 3.6.91 and failed to gain level flight for a Javelin shoot with 105 Regiment TA. (TFH 2.12; 5 Flights)

ZH269 f/f 5.3.91 at Manorbier. Lost on 6.3.91 when the engine cut during a rainstorm whilst performing a Javelin shoot with the Royal School of Artillery, RA. Crashed into the sea. (TFH 3.05; 4 Flights)

ZH270 No details of any flights recorded.

ZH271 f/f 24.11.92, possibly at Manorbier, but engine failed after 49 minutes due to a fuel tank leak causing fuel starvation.

ZH272 f/f 23.11.92, possibly at Manorbier. On 2.5.94 it fail-safed into the sea over the Falkland Islands Range, possibly due to missile damage. (TFH 2.54; 4 Flights)

ZH273 Built with a Norton engine (No. 73P726) and f/f 28.2.91. Later conveyed

Unmanned Targets for the Army

to Manorbier where, on 12.6.91, it is believed to have run out of fuel after 63 minutes and crashed into the sea. (TFH 1.29; 2 Flights)

Note that all of the following Skeets were built with Norton engines fitted as standard.

ZH274 f/f 11.6.91 at Manorbier. Became unstable in flight on 17.6.91, possibly due to radio interference during a Javelin shoot with 21 Battery, RA. Landed in the sea but recovered and rebuilt as ZH274R. Shot down 16.6.92 off Manorbier, further details unkn. (TFH 2.07; 4 Flights)

ZH275 f/f 28.1.91 at Manorbier for a 17-minute Norton engine trial flight. Next flown as a target on 11.6.91 for a Javelin shoot with 105 Regt TA but became lost in poor visibility. Crashed into the sea.

ZH276 f/f 26.6.91 at Manorbier. Shot down 23.7.91 by a Javelin missile during a shoot with the Royal School of Artillery, RA. (TFH 1.59; 4 Flights)

ZH277 f/f 18.6.91 at Manorbier but sustained a direct hit from a Javelin missile after 53 minutes. Crashed into the sea but was recovered and repaired as ZH277R. Next flown 17.2.92 but engine cut immediately after launch; parachute landed in the sea. Recovered again and repaired (but appears to have been fitted with a non-Norton engine). Conveyed to the Falkland Islands where, on 3.5.94 it fail-safed after 21 minutes and crashed into the sea. (TFH 1.14; 3 Flights)

ZH281 f/f 12.6.91 at Manorbier. Shot down 17.6.91 by a Javelin missile during a shoot with 21 Battery, RA. (TFH 1.02; 2 Flights)

ZH282 f/f 18.6.91 at Manorbier but fail-safed after 2 minutes during pilot changeover. Recovered from the sea and repaired as ZH282R. Next flown 27.7.93 in the Falkland Islands but failed to respond to r/t commands and crashed into the sea after 2 minutes. (TFH 0.04; 2 Flights)

ZH283 f/f 19.6.91 at Manorbier as an engine and smoke (flare) test. Made a 2nd flight on this date but was shot down by a Javelin missile during a shoot with 21 Battery, RA. (TFH 1.17; 2 Flights)

ZH284 f/f 25.10.91 at Manorbier. Shot down 6.7.92, further details unkn. (TFH 5.01; 6 Flights)

ZH285 f/f 26.6.91 at Manorbier. During a routine flight on 7.11.91 the MDI was providing poor signals and a later inspection revealed a cracked fuselage. Repaired but then stored. Next flown 23.7.92 but shot down on 27.7.92, details unkn. (TFH 10.14; 13 Flights)

ZH286 f/f 27.9.91 at Manorbier. Sustained a direct hit by a Javelin missile at Manorbier 6.11.91 during a shoot with 7th RHA, RA. Recovered from the sea and repaired as ZH286R. Next flown 30.11.93, probably at Manorbier, but fail-safed during a flight there on 2.5.94 and crashed into the sea, possibly as a result of a missile strike. (TFH 5.30; 7 Flights)

ZH287 f/f 5.10.91 at Manorbier but was shot down after 49 minutes by a Javelin missile during a shoot with 104 TA.

ZH288 f/f 23.11.91 at Manorbier. On its 2nd flight of the day the smoke flares began igniting themselves over the Range. The pilot attempted a recovery but the engine cut early on approach to land and the target crashed into cliffs. (TFH 1.49; 2 Flights)

ZH289 f/f 7.11.91 at Manorbier. On 9.12.91 it went out of control after 2 minutes without responding to transmissions. Crashed into the sea. (TFH 0.45; 2 Flights)

ZH290 f/f 25.6.91 at Manorbier but was shot down after 8 minutes by a Javelin missile during a shoot with 21 Battery, RA.

ZH302 f/f 17.9.91 at Manorbier but was shot down after 38 minutes by a Javelin missile during a shoot with 3 Commando Bde, RM.

ZH303 f/f 5.10.91 at Manorbier but was shot down after 27 minutes by a Javelin missile during a shoot with 104 TA.

ZH304 f/f 17.9.91 at Manorbier. Shot down 25.10.91 by a Javelin missile during a shoot with 103 TA. (TFH 5.01; 7 Flights)

ZH305 f/f 11.12.91, probably at Manorbier. Shot down 7.3.91, details unkn. (TFH 3.37; 5 Flights)

ZH306 f/f 23.11.91, probably at Manorbier. Shot down 2.2.92, details unkn. (TFH 7.17; 7 Flights)

ZH307 f/f 9.12.91, probably at Manorbier. Shot down 6.3.91, details unkn. (TFH 1.38; 3 Flights)

ZH308 f/f 23.11.91 at Manorbier but fail-safed into the sea after 2 minutes due to aileron flutter causing loss of control. Recovered and repaired as ZH308R and stored. On its 2nd flight, on 30.11.93, it fail-safed into the sea. (TFH 1.04; 2 Flights)

ZH309 f/f 17.2.92 at Manorbier but went out of control after 12 minutes and was landed in the sea by parachute. Recovered and repaired as ZH309R. Next flown 30.11.93 but was shot down on 3.5.94, details unkn. (TFH 3.26; 5 Flights)

ZH310 f/f 8.12.91 at Manorbier but fail-safed into the sea immediately after launch and without achieving level flight.

ZH311 f/f 9.12.91 at Manorbier. Shot down 6.4.92, further details unkn. (TFH 5.09; 5 Flights)

ZH312 f/f 6.3.92 at Manorbier but was shot down on the 2nd flight of the day. (TFH 1.29; 2 Flights)

ZH313 f/f 7.12.91 at Manorbier where, on 6.3.92, it was shot down, details unkn. (TFH 3.54; 6 Flights)

ZH314 f/f 2.11.91 at Manorbier but control was lost just 1 minute after launch for a Javelin shoot with 104 TA. After failing to respond to radio commands the target crashed into the ground.

ZH315 f/f 26.10.91 at Manorbier where, on 6.11.91, it was shot down by a Javelin missile during a shoot with 7 RHA, RA. (TFH 1.19; 3 Flights)

ZH316 f/f 3.8.92 at Manorbier. On its 2nd flight at Manorbier the engine failed during pilot changeover; crashed into the sea. (TFH 1.04; 2 Flights)

ZH336 f/f 4.5.92 at Manorbier but was shot down on the 2nd flight of the day. (TFH 1.43; 2 Flights)

ZH337 f/f 4.5.92 at Manorbier but the engine failed on take-off before gaining level flight. On its second flight, on 4.8.92, the target fail-safed after 5 minutes and crashed into the sea. (TFH 0.05; 2 Flights)

ZH338 f/f 25.6.91 at Manorbier but was shot down by a Javelin missile after 22 minutes during a shoot with 21 Battery, RA.

ZH339 No details known.

ZH340 f/f 4.5.92 at Manorbier but the engine failed after 9 minutes; crashed into the sea.

ZH341 No details known.

ZH342 f/f 19.6.91 at Manorbier but was shot down by a Javelin missile after 15 minutes during a shoot with 21 Battery, RA.

ZH343 f/f 17.6.91 at Manorbier but was shot down by a Javelin missile after 24 minutes during a shoot with 21 Battery, RA.

ZH344 & ZH356 No details known.

ZH357 f/f 9.2.93 in Norway during an exercise shoot but shot down after 18 minutes.

ZH358 f/f 12.2.93 (location unkn) but stalled on launch in zero wind conditions. Never gained level flight and was written-off in the crash that followed.

ZH359 f/f 17.7.92 at Manorbier. Written-off 23.7.92 when it fail-safed into the sea after the skid-pan caught fire. (TFH 2.00; 3 Flights)

ZH360-ZH362 No details known.

ZH363 f/f 16.7.92 at Manorbier. Shot down 21.7.92, details unkn. (TFH 1.14; 3 Flights)

ZH364 f/f 16.2.92 at Manorbier. Engine failed in flight, on 4.7.92, just 9 minutes after launch. Crashed into the sea. (TFH 0.54; 4 Flights)

ZH365 Underwent a pre-flight check at Manorbier 12.2.92 but was not flown. No further details are known and it is suspected that this target has never been flown.

ZH366 f/f 31.5.92 at Manorbier but shot down after 52 minutes.

ZH396 No details known.

ZH397 f/f 22.7.92 at Manorbier but was shot down after 46 minutes.

ZH398 No details known.

ZH399 f/f 15.6.92 at Manorbier but fail-safed into the sea after 33 minutes.

ZH400 & ZH401 No details known.

ZH402 f/f 4.7.92 at Manorbier but crashed into the sea on its 2nd flight of the day following loss of radio control. (TFH 0.55; 2 Flights)

ZH403 f/f 1.6.92 at Manorbier. Shot down 16.6.92 and crashed into the sea off Manorbier. (TFH 4.05; 6 Flights)

ZH404 f/f 10.6.92 at Manorbier. Crashed onto rocks 15.6.92 after the engine cut too early on the landing approach. (TFH 3.06; 3 Flights)

ZH405 No details known.

ZH406 f/f 24.7.92 at Manorbier. Shot down at Manorbier 28.7.92, details unkn.

ZH407 No details known.

ZH408 f/f 6.3.92 at Manorbier. Shot down 7.4.92.

ZH409 f/f 17.2.92 at Manorbier. Aircraft went out of control 11.4.92 during its final circuit to land; fail-safed and crashed into the sea. (TFH 4.41; 7 Flights)

ZH410 f/f 17.2.92 at Manorbier. Engine failed in flight, on 18.2.92, before it crashed into the sea. (TFH 1.52; 2 Flights)

ZH431 f/f 6.4.92 but was shot down after 13 minutes.

ZH432 f/f 2.2.92 at Manorbier. Shot down 29.7.92, further details unkn. (TFH 5.12; 8 Flights)

ZH433 f/f 5.5.93, possibly in the Falkland Islands where, on 27.7.93, it was written-off in a crash after the engine failed just 1 minute from launch. (TFH 0.15; 2 Flights)

ZH434 f/f 3.5.93, probably at Manorbier, but crashed into the sea after 20 minutes following radio transmission problems.

ZH435 f/f 9.2.93, probably at Manorbier. Shot down 11.2.93. (TFH 1.31; 2 Flights)

ZH436 f/f 10.2.93, probably in Norway where it sustained a cracked fuselage when parachute-recovered on 12.2.93. Rtnd to UK for repair and next flown 3.5.93 when it was again damaged. Not repaired and instead reduced to spares at Manorbier. (TFH 5.18; 7 Flights)

ZH437 f/f 10.2.93 in Norway where it was shot down on 11.2.93. (TFH 1.20; 2 Flights)

ZH438 No details known.

ZH439 f/f 10.2.93 in Norway where it was shot down on 11.2.93. (TFH 0.47; 2 Flights)

ZH440 f/f 17.6.92 at Manorbier where, on 27.7.92, it was shot down. No further details known. (TFH 3.57; 6 Flights)

ZH484 f/f 6.4.92 at Manorbier but fail-safed over the Range after 15 minutes.

ZH485 f/f 22.7.92, probably at Manorbier, but was shot down after 8 minutes.

ZH486 f/f 7.4.92, probably at Manorbier, but was shot down after 21 minutes.

ZH487 f/f 20.6.92, probably at Manorbier. Shot down 6.7.92. (TFH 1.13; 2 Flights)

ZH488 f/f 13.4.92 at Manorbier. Shot down off Manorbier 16.6.92. (TFH 9.46; 11 Flights)

ZH489 f/f 17.6.92 at Manorbier but was shot down after 39 minutes.

ZH490 f/f 13.4.92 at Manorbier. Shot down over the sea 16.6.92. (TFH 4.20; 5 Flights)

ZH491 f/f 6.4.92 at Manorbier. On 7.4.92 the aircraft went out of control just one minute after launch and crashed into the sea. (TFH 2.25; 3 Flights)

ZH492 f/f 16.5.92 at Manorbier but fail-safed for no apparent reason during its 2nd flight of the day. Landed in the sea and not recovered. (TFH 1.11; 2 Flights)

ZH493 f/f 7.4.92 at Manorbier but shot down after 64 minutes.

ZH494 f/f 8.4.92 at Manorbier. Shot down 27.7.92. (TFH 5.28; 10 Flights)

ZH495 f/f 7.4.92 at Manorbier. Shot down 31.5.92. (TFH 1.33; 3 Flights)

ZH496 f/f 21.7.92 at Manorbier where, on 27.7.92, it was shot down. (TFH 2.22; 4 Flights)

ZH497 f/f 27.7.93 in the Falkland Islands. On its 2nd flight of the day the aircraft "locked out with left bias" after 10 minutes causing it to crashed uncontrollably into the sea. (TFH 0.54; 2 Flights)

ZH498 No details known.

Banshee ZF714 was repainted in almost black overall scheme with a white upper fin section. This view, taken at Manorbier on 10 November 1986, shows '714 on its launcher, engine at full power and about to launch on its maiden flight. It was shot down by a Javelin missile the following day. (Target Technology Ltd)

Meggitt BTT-3 Banshee

Piper Target Technology of Ashford, Kent entered the world of unmanned target aircraft as a specialist producer of lightweight piston engines for target drones. By 1983, however, the company had developed its first design, a delta-wing UAV weighing 30kg, 9ft long and a wingspan of 7ft. Known from the outset as the Banshee, the first two (of six) prototypes made their initial flights on March 1 and March 2 1983 respectively. By May 1983 the Banshee was beginning to attract interest from several Middle East countries.

Piper Target Technology later changed its title to Target Technology Ltd (TTL) and it was under that parentage that what became referred to as the BTT-3 Banshee entered full-scale production at the company's production facility at Brunswick Industrial Centre in Ashford, Kent. The first production Banshee made its first flight in June 1984.

As its designation implies Banshee is a <u>B</u>asic <u>T</u>raining <u>T</u>arget designed primarily to simulate the threat of missiles (including sea skimming weapons). It was also designed to simulate aircraft for missile and cannon air defence systems both on land and at sea.

Banshee is a low-wing monoplane with cropped-delta wings and sweptback fin. The wings have a 50° sweepback and approximately 3° dihedral. The entire airframe is constructed from glassfibre reinforced plastic and Kevlar. Early production aircraft were powered by a Normalair-Garrett 342cc twin-cylinder two-stroke engine which produced 26bhp for the pusher propeller. The engine is mounted at the base of the rudderless fin. The only flying surfaces are elevons.

By mid-1986 the delay in service entry of Shorts Skeet 2 began to give some rise for concern amongst Army planners. Whilst not grave, the situation did threaten a shortage of available targets for missile training. The same planners turned their attention towards the BTT-3 Banshee target as a temporary stop-gap alternative and placed an immediate 'off-the-shelf' order for 75 examples. The selection process was made easier by the fact that Banshee was already in production for a number of overseas forces and the first public airing of a British Army Banshee occurred at the 1986 Farnborough Show when ZF687 was displayed on the Racal Radar Defence Systems stand.

There is some confusion as to when deliveries of Banshee to the Army started. According to TTL documentation the first delivery was made on 1 July 1986 when a batch of five aircraft, ZF654-658, were conveyed by road to Larkhill. However, contemporary reports at Larkhill suggest that the first delivery to Larkhill was a 'spare fuselage' together with a supply of 'first-line spares' and that these were received on 14 June 1986. There never was any 'spare' fuselage at Larkhill but TTL records describe c/n 273 as a 'spare' fuselage and that this airframe became ZF681. It is just possible, therefore, that this was this airframe that arrived at Larkhill on 14 June 1986. Subsequent deliveries were made by road and normally in batches of ten, the last consignment against the first contract (ZF794-798) being just five targets.[23]

The first flight of a production Banshee in British Army service took place at the Manorbier Range on 17 July 1986 when ZF656 was flown for 15 minutes. Within two hours of landing it made a second flight but on that occasion the servos began to respond too slowly and the controls proved to be over-sensitive. Two flights were made later in the day by ZF655 without any problem. On the following day, 18 July, the same two Banshees were launched again, this time with different results. ZF655 was damaged on landing whilst radio interference affected ZF656 causing it to fail-safe into the sea. It marked the first loss of a British Army Banshee target and

---

23 Correspondence between TTL and Trevor Stone.

Above: *Two Banshee drones (ZF655 and ZF657) are prepared for launch at Manorbier on 9 September 1986. ZF657 is in a standard factory-finish whilst ZF655 has been repainted with black and white patches. (Michael I Draper)*

Right: *Late-1986 trials proved that those Banshee aircraft repainted with black patches were more visible to gunners as targets. Therefore, the next delivery involved aircraft repainted in an almost overall black scheme. This line-up shows ZF749-ZF751 and ZF766-ZF772 at Larkhill on 14 January 1987. Unfortunately a number of these aircraft fail-safed during their initial flights, the cause of which led directly to the revised paint scheme. (Michael I Draper)*

whilst Banshee eventually proved a reliable target drone the start of Banshee operations was not entirely troublefree.

The first live Artillery Camp using Banshee targets involved a three-day shoot at Manorbier (23-25 September 1986), in support of the Blowpipe-equipped 7th Royal Horse Artillery Regiment, RA. A total of six Banshees were written-off (ZF655, 656, 658, 660, 661 and ZF663) although only one (ZF658) was actually shot down. A second Camp at Manorbier took place within a month, on 14-16 October 1986, this time for the Royal School of Artillery, RA. On that occasion ten Banshees (ZF657, 662, 676, 677, 678, 680, 681, 682, 688 and ZF706) were shot down by Javelin missiles but of some concern was the fact that three others (ZF659, 685 and ZF689) were lost in different circumstances.

Many of the ground controllers at Manorbier were old hands at operating target aircraft. They were skilled model aircraft flyers and had built up considerable experience on MATS-B and Skeet. All were fully adept at controlling their aircraft in flight visually. But Banshee presented a very different proposition. It was delta-shaped and had a pusher engine. Not that the aircraft's shape seriously tested the controller's flying skills but what became evident very soon was that the Banshee's bright orange and yellow colour scheme did not offer sufficient contrast against the sky to ensure proper control.

In trying to solve the visibility problem, RCA engineers at Larkhill decided to repaint a number of Banshees with black and yellow portions to create a greater contrast. Several variations of orange, black, yellow, and even white emerged. Aircraft were repainted at both Larkhill and Manorbier and in such a manner that for a while no two aircraft looked the same.

Early test-flights at Manorbier revealed that the repainted targets were markedly more visible. So much so that RCA

Unmanned Targets for the Army   271

instructed TTL to deliver the next batch of production Banshees in a predominantly black scheme. In overall black, but with a yellow nose-cone, the batch ZF749-751/766-772 was delivered to Larkhill on 19 December 1986 in the revised scheme.

Towards the end of January 1987 a number of the newly-repainted Banshees were taken to Manorbier for a shoot with the Shorts Javelin-equipped 21 Battery RA. The shoot got off to a bad start when Banshee ZF684 became lost in sea mist and crashed. For the next 48 hours the weather remained poor and flying was impossible. When the mist fully cleared, flying operations resumed but with curious results. ZF744 fail-safed for no apparent reason. So did four more Banshees on the following day – and at that stage none of the gunners had even lined up a single missile. All four were making their maiden flights.[24] Two days later, Banshee ZF750 fail-safed at Manorbier, just four minutes into its flight. Banshees, it seemed, were beginning to fall out of the sky like autumn leaves.

The search for a cause of these unexplained losses eventually led to an examination of the paint. Only then was it discovered that the high carbon pigment in the black paint had created an excessive static discharge. Discharging static in flight had, it seemed, triggered the fail-safe system. Rather than change the colour scheme again all of the existing Banshees were fitted with an anti-static modification to both the fuselage and the wing. In the meantime it was decided that further new-build aircraft would revert to the standard orange and yellow scheme.

Towards the end of 1987 the difficulties that had dogged Skeet 2 had been overcome and deliveries of production examples began in earnest. It signalled the end of Banshee procurement for the time being.

Before stocks of Skeet 2 began to be exhausted, Shorts had worked on a number of improvements which led to Skeet 3. But Meggitt had also been developing Banshee. By late-1988 the company had completed tests on an improved version and placed the new variant, known as Banshee 300, into production at Ashford. Improved aerodynamics included streamlining the underfuselage smoke pod into the fuselage contours and also deepening the fuselage slightly to offer alternative internal location for a Luneburg lens. The fin was also made detachable to allow better storage and transportation, as well as providing easier access to the rear payload bay. Other improvements were made to the control systems and included a radar altimeter height-lock module to permit simulation of sea-skimming missiles.

When the time came to make a decision about Skeet 2's successor, it was the Banshee 300 that the Army favoured. Large-scale production for the Army began in 1992.

A further development of Banshee 300 was introduced in mid-1996. The main innovation was a thermal nosecone IR augmenter, fuelled by liquid propane gas. Referred to as a 'hot nose', this offered an alternative to the traditional short-burn pyrotechnic flares. The Banshee 400, as the new variant was designated, attracted a contract in 1999 for two-years' supply of Banshee drones.

SERCO had operated Banshees on behalf of the Ministry of Defence for a number of years, the company successfully re-tendering for the Manorbier contract on several successive occasions throughout the 1990s. But towards the end of 2001 Banshee's manufacturer, by now re-named Meggitt, decided to tender for the contract by offering the MoD a fully-inclusive arrangement – not only to provide the Banshee targets but also to operate them across the Ranges as well. Meggitt won the contract and took over the running of target operations at Manorbier Range from SERCO,

---

[24] The four Banshees involved were ZF751 which "fail-safed" after just 9 minutes of flight, ZF742 after 8 minutes, ZF749 after 14 minutes and ZF746 after 17 minutes.

Banshee – Technical & Performance Details

	Original Banshee	Banshee 300	Banshee 400
Length (overall)	2.84 m (9 ft 4 in)	2.95 m (9 ft 8 in)	2.95 m (9 ft 8 in)
Wing Span	2.49 m (8 ft 2 in)	2.49 m (8 ft 2 in)	2.49 m (8 ft 2 in)
Wing Area	2.14 m^2 (23 sq ft)	2.42 m^2 (26 sq ft)	2.42 m^2 (26 sq ft)
Height	0.86 m (2 ft 10 in)	0.89 m (2 ft 11 in)	0.91 m (3 ft 0 in)
Weight (empty)	38.5 kg (85 lb)	47.6 kg (105 lb)	47.6 kg (105 lb)
Max launching weight	72.6 kg (160 lb)	86.2 kg (190 lb)	91.6 kg (202 lb)
Max launch speed	54 kt (100 km/h; 62 mph)	54 kt (100 km/h; 62 mph)	54 kt (100 km/h; 62 mph)
Max level speed	174 kt (322 km/h; 200 mph)	205 kt (380 km/h; 236 mph) *	
Ceiling	7,010 m (23,000 ft)	7,010 m (23,000 ft)	7,010 m (23,000 ft)
Max control range (Optical tracking)	5.4 nautical miles (10 km; 6.2 miles)	5.4 nautical miles (10 km; 6.2 miles)	5.4 nautical miles (10 km; 6.2 miles)
Max control range (Radar tracking)	16.2 nautical miles (30 km; 18.6 miles)	16.2 nautical miles (30 km; 18.6 miles)	16.2 nautical miles (30 km; 18.6 miles)
Max control range (GPS tracking)	27 nautical miles (50 km; 31 miles)	27 nautical miles (50 km; 31 miles)	27 nautical miles (50 km; 31 miles)
Max Endurance	1 hr 15 mins	1 hr 30 mins	1 hr 30 mins

* Data shown for Banshee 300 with AR731 engine; some early-production Banshee 300 were fitted with MDS342 engine. Max level speed on this variant is as original Banshee

Banshee – British Contract Summary

Contract	Date	Serial Range	Allotment Date	Quantity	Remarks
ML22a/1450		ZF654-ZF663 ZF676-ZF691 ZF704-ZF720 ZF741-ZF751 ZF766-ZF779 ZF791-ZF798	20.5.86	75 +1	Delivered between 7.86 and 2.87. ZF681 quoted by TTL as a "spare" fuselage.
ML11A/1602		ZG539-ZG550 ZG580-ZG599	22.4.87	32	Delivered between 5.87 and 7.87

ZG539-548 were delivered ex-factory without serials but with their build numbers (394-400/407-409) applied instead. Shortly afterwards, and upon realising that they should have "ZGxxx" serials, RCA applied the prefix letters "ZG" to the build numbers, eg ZG394-ZG400/ZG407-ZG409. This error was subsequently realised and the surviving aircraft were repainted with the correct serials. ZG549 onwards were delivered correctly marked.

Precise details of aircraft subsequent to Contract ML11A/1602 are unknown but are thought to have involved around 500 units. None were allocated serials within the standard sequence. It is known that the final purchase (Contract AArm(C) 1b/326) accounted for 654 targets; 454 of which were Close Air Defence Weapon System version plus 200 of a Beyond Visual Range version.

effective from 1 January 2002. For Meggitt, however, there was a sting in the tail.

Meggitt had aggressively sold Banshee to the MoD, and a sizeable reserve stock of Banshee drones was still held at Larkhill. In fact, when SERCO relinquished control to Meggitt there was in excess of 150 unflown Banshees in store at Rollestone Camp, Larkhill. As they prepared to wind up their target operation SERCO insisted that Meggitt should be forced to buy back those unflown aircraft. The MoD agreed and Meggitt re-purchased the entire stock.

In taking over the role of target service provider, Meggitt effectively acquired the maintenance base at Rollestone Camp, Larkhill. However, as the majority of Banshee operations was centred at Manorbier it made greater sense to have a maintenance back-up facility at Manorbier. Rollestone

A number of Banshees were given a revised colour scheme in order to help make them more visible over the Range. Several variations were attempted as seen in this view of the Larkhill storage rack, on 30 September 1986. ZF677 has a black and yellow fin; ZF688 and ZF704 sport a yellow fin whilst ZF679 has a more distinctive black and white fin and rear fuselage. (Michael I Draper)

Unmanned Targets for the Army 273

When Banshee entered service as a 'stop-gap' (due to late delivery of Skeet 2) aircraft operated in factory-standard overall orange scheme. But after gunners complained that aircraft were difficult to see, a number were repainted with a range of different schemes. ZF663, seen here at Larkhill on 30 September 1986 and just six days after being severely damaged in a heavy landing at Manorbier, shows the rear fuselage section having been repainted black. (Michael I Draper)

Camp was therefore closed and all Banshee support was transferred to the South Wales Range.

At the end of 2006 the Ministry of Defence introduced a dramatic change to the manner in which target services were provided for the Armed Forces. The Combined Aerial Target Service (CATS) saw their responsibility for providing targets transferred to QinetiQ. A new Banshee variant had been developed to meet the Basic Aerial Target aspect of CATS and which became known simply as the CATS-Banshee. As a result all surviving earlier Banshee variants on MoD charge were withdrawn from service on 31 March 2008 and stored at Manorbier pending disposal by MoD. They involved 26 Banshee 400s (c/ns 2329, 2330, 2349, 2350, 2352, 2353, 2354, 2373, 2378, 2444, 2467, 2468, 2679, 2691, 3032, 3087, 3127, 3150, 3176, 3196, 3198, 3199, 4047, 4049, 4050 and 4051) plus a small number of the higher-performance Banshee 500s (including c/n 4200 and a small number of similar targets located on the Falkland Islands.) It is likely that all of these were sold back to Meggitt.[25]

One Banshee was retained by MoD; that being the 3000th Banshee, a 400 variant that was originally delivered to the MoD on 7 December 2000, and which had survived a number of sorties at Manorbier. For some time c/n 3000 was displayed inside the MoD Abbey Wood complex until November 2007 when it was donated to QinetiQ for use as a 'gate-guardian' at the Manorbier Range.

---

25 Banshee 500, introduced in 2001, was a higher-performance variant with a new 38.8kW (52hp) Meggitt Tempest engine.

Banshee Colour Schemes

Initial deliveries were in a standard factory-finish of overall orange, yellow nose-cone, wing-tips etc

In order to establish an improved visual footprint over Manorbier Range a number of Banshees were repainted at Larkhill with a series of trial schemes, as follows:

ZF656 Black rear fuselage with white vertical band; white horizontal block on upper fin
ZF663, ZF712 Black rear fuselage and two-thirds of fin.
ZF677 Black rear fuselage and fin with yellow horizontal tail band
ZF679 Black rear fuselage and fin with white horizontal tail band
ZF688, ZF704 Standard factory finish with large yellow tail band
ZF714 Black overall with white upper fin and yellow nose
ZF749-751/766-772 Delivered ex-factory in a black overall scheme with white upper fin and yellow nose.
ZF773 onwards Delivered in standard factory-finish of overall orange etc.

ZF654, ZF661, ZF677, ZF684 and ZF686 are also known to have been repainted in a black scheme but precise details are unknown. It is just possible that others were repainted also.

Meggitt BTT-3 Banshee – Individual Aircraft Histories

ZF654 (c/n 262) Del Larkhill 1.7.86. TOC 2.7.86; f/f 4.9.86. W/o at Manorbier 22.11.86 after it crashed into the sea following a Blowpipe missile strike during a shoot with 104 TA Regiment, RA. (TFH 3.23; 7 Flights)

ZF655 (c/n 253) Del Larkhill 1.7.86. TOC 3.7.86; f/f 17.7.86. W/o at Manorbier 25.9.86 when it crashed into the sea following a Blowpipe missile strike during a shoot with the 7th Royal Horse Artillery, RA. (TFH 4.34; 6 Flights)

ZF656 (c/n 254) Del Larkhill 1.7.86. TOC 3.7.86; f/f 17.7.86. Crashed into the sea off Manorbier 23.9.86 after the engine failed during a Blowpipe shoot with the 7th Royal Horse Artillery, RA. (TFH 1.12; 4 Flights)

ZF657 (c/n 260) Del Larkhill 1.7.86. TOC ??..9.86; f/f 9.9.86. Sustained a direct hit by a Javelin missile 16.10.86 during a shoot at Manorbier with the School of Artillery, RA. (TFH 2.24; 3 Flights)

ZF658 (c/n 261) Del Larkhill 1.7.86. TOC 3.7.86; f/f 20.9.86. Sustained a direct hit by a Blowpipe missile at Manorbier 25.9.86 during a shoot with the 7th Royal Horse Artillery, RA. (TFH 2.01; 4 Flights)

ZF659 (c/n 263) Del Larkhill 18.7.86. TOC 3.9.86; f/f 25.9.86 at Manorbier. Destroyed after it crashed into the sea off Manorbier 14.10.86 during a Javelin missile shoot with the Royal School of Artillery, RA. (TFH 2.21; 5 Flights)

ZF660 (c/n 264) Del Larkhill 18.7.86. TOC 8.9.86; f/f 24.9.86 at Manorbier but crashed into the sea off after 4 minutes during a Blowpipe missile shoot with the 7th Royal Horse Artillery, RA.

ZF661 (c/n 265) Del Larkhill 18.7.86. TOC 12.9.86; f/f 23.9.86 at Manorbier but crashed into the sea off after 2 minutes following an engine failure during a Blowpipe missile shoot by 7th Royal Horse Artillery, RA.

ZF662 (c/n 266) Del Larkhill 18.7.86. TOC 8.9.86; f/f 23.9.86 at Manorbier. Shot down over the Manorbier Range 14.10.86 by a Javelin missile during a shoot with the Royal School of Artillery, RA. (TFH 5.42; 8 Flights)

ZF663 (c/n 272) Del Larkhill 18.7.86. TOC 19.8.86. Badly damaged during an unsuccessful launch 4.9.86. Repaired and next flown at Manorbier 23.9.86. W/o 24.9.86 in a heavy skid-landing at Manorbier during a Blowpipe missile shoot with 7th Royal Horse Artillery, RA. (TFH 1.46; 3 Flights)

ZF676 (c/n 268) Del Larkhill 31.8.86. TOC 20.9.86; f/f 22.9.86 at Manorbier. Sustained a direct hit by a Javelin missile at Manorbier 15.10.86 during a shoot with the Royal School of Artillery, RA (TFH 1.00; 3 Flights)

ZF677 (c/n 269) Del Larkhill 31.8.86. TOC 9.10.86; f/f 15.10.86 at Manorbier. Sustained a direct hit by a Javelin missile at Manorbier 16.10.86 during a shoot with the Royal School of Artillery,RA. (TFH 1.46; 2 Flights)

ZF678 (c/n 270) Del Larkhill 31.8.86. TOC 15.9.86; f/f 14.10.86 at Manorbier but sustained a direct hit by a Javelin missile during a shoot with the Royal School of Artillery, RA. (TFH 0.03; 1 Flight)

ZF679 (c/n 271) Del Larkhill 31.8.86. TOC 27.10.86; f/f 3.11.86 at Manorbier for a Javelin shoot with 46 Battery, RA but crashed into the sea after elevon became detached in flight. The pilot attempted to get ZF679 over the mainland for a parachute recovery but failed. (TFH 0.15; 1 Flight)

ZF680 (c/n 278) Del Larkhill 31.8.86. TOC 18.9.86; f/f 15.10.86 at Manorbier. Sustained a direct hit by a Javelin missile at Manorbier 16.10.86 during a shoot with the Royal School of Artillery, RA. (TFH 1.01; 2 Flights)

ZF681 (c/n 273) Del Larkhill unkn. TOC 18.9.86; f/f 14.10.86 at Manorbier. Sustained a direct hit by a Javelin missile at Manorbier 15.10.86 during a shoot with the Royal School of Artillery, RA. (TFH 1.11; 2 Flights)

ZF682 (c/n 274) Del Larkhill 31.8.86. TOC 11.9.86; f/f 22.9.86 at Manorbier. Sustained a direct hit by a Javelin missile at Manorbier 16.10.86 during a shoot with the Royal School of Artillery, RA. (TFH 2.21hrs; 4 Flights)

ZF683 (c/n 275) Del Larkhill 31.8.86. TOC 18.9.86; f/f 3.10.86 at Manorbier. Sustained a direct hit by a Javelin missile at Manorbier 10.11.86 during a shoot with 46 Battery, RA. (TFH 1.01; 2 Flights)

ZF684 (c/n 276) Del Larkhill 31.8.86. TOC 21.11.86; f/f 6.12.86 at Manorbier. W/o 25.1.87 when it became lost in sea mist and crashed into the sea off Manorbier during a shoot with 21 Battery, RA. (TFH 4.39; 7 Flights)

ZF685 (c/n 277) Del Larkhill 31.8.86. TOC 17.9.86; f/f 3.10.86 at Manorbier. Crashed into the sea off Manorbier 15.10.86 after the prop sheared in flight during a shoot with the Royal School of Artillery, RA. (TFH 0.37; 2 Flights)

ZF686 (c/n 282) Del Larkhill 31.8.86. TOC 22.10.86; f/f 3.11.86 at Manorbier but crashed into the sea after aircraft stopped responding to signals during a shoot with 46 Battery, RA (TFH 0.50; 1 Flight)

ZF687 (c/n 291) Statically displayed (by Racal Radar Defence Systems) at Farnborough 9.86. Del Larkhill 30.9.86. TOC 10.10.86; f/f 4.11.86 at Manorbier but sustained a direct hit by a Javelin missile after just 10 minutes during a shoot with 46 Battery, RA.

ZF688 (c/n 292) Del Larkhill 30.9.86. TOC 9.10.86; f/f 15.10.86 at Manorbier but sustained a direct hit by a Javelin missile after just 9 minutes during a shoot with the Royal School of Artillery, RA.

ZF689 (c/n 293) Del Larkhill 30.9.86. TOC 10.10.86; f/f 16.10.86 at Manorbier for a Javelin shoot by the Royal School of Artillery, RA but command was lost after 45 minutes and aircraft crashed into the sea.

ZF690 (c/n 294) Del Larkhill 30.9.86. TOC 20.10.86; f/f 4.11.86 at Manorbier. Crashed into the sea off Manorbier 13.11.86 following loss of response after 15 seconds during a Javelin shoot with 46 Battery, RA.

ZF691 (c/n 295) Del Larkhill 30.9.86. TOC 22.10.86; f/f 4.11.86 at Manorbier but sustained a direct hit by a Javelin missile after 19 minutes during a Dart and Javelin shoot with 46 Battery, RA

ZF704 (c/n 296) Del Larkhill 30.9.86. TOC 22.10.86; f/f 4.11.86 at Manorbier but sustained a direct hit by a Javelin missile after 5 minutes during a shoot with 46 Battery, RA

ZF705 (c/n 297) Del Larkhill 30.9.86. TOC 20.10.86; f/f 4.11.86 at Manorbier. Sustained a direct hit by a Javelin missile 10.6.87 during a shoot with the Royal

Well-battered and bruised, damaged Banshee ZF718 lies on the hangar floor at Larkhill on 24 March 1987 after technicians had completed their investigation into the reasons for so many fail-safe crashes. The engine clearly shows signs of salt water corrosion as a result of its unexplained crash into the sea on 15 December 1986. Note the TTL logo on the aircraft's fin. (Michael I Draper)

School of Artillery, RA. (TFH 7.18; 10 Flights)

ZF706 (c/n 298 Del Larkhill 30.9.86. TOC 9.10.86; f/f 16.10.86 at Manorbier but sustained a direct Javelin missile hit after 11 minutes flight during a shoot by the Royal School of Artillery, RA.

ZF707 (c/n 299) Del Larkhill 30.9.86. TOC 14.10.86; f/f 3.11.86 at Manorbier. Sustained a direct hit by a Javelin missile 11.11.86 during a shoot with 46 Battery, RA. (TFH 0.55; 2 Flights)

ZF708 (c/n 300) Del Larkhill 30.9.86. TOC 20.10.86; f/f 3.11.86 at Manorbier. Sustained a direct hit by a Javelin missile 4.11.86 during a shoot with 46 Battery, RA. (TFH 1.25; 2 Flights)

ZF709 (c/n 313) Del Larkhill 31.10.86. TOC 14.11.86; f/f 15.11.86 at Manorbier but crashed when fail-safe parachute inadvertently deployed during pilot handover during a Blowpipe shoot with 103 TA Regiment, RA (TFH 0.03; 1 Flight)

ZF710 (c/n 314) Del Larkhill 31.10.86; f/f 11.11.86 at Manorbier but crashed after 56 minutes when it ran out of fuel and failed to reach the mainland during a Javelin shoot with 46 Battery, RA.

ZF711 (c/n 315) Del Larkhill 31.10.86; f/f 11.11.86 at Manorbier. Crashed into the sea 9.5.87 during a Javelin shoot with 3 Commando Brigade, RM after the prop was damaged by the launch buffer piston and the aircraft lost its throttle after 12 minutes. (TFH 7.38; 11 Flights)

ZF712 (c/n 316) Del Larkhill 31.10.86. TOC 7.11.86; f/f 13.11.86 at Manorbier but sustained a direct hit after 17 minutes by a Javelin missile during a shoot with 46 Battery, RA.

ZF713 (c/n 317) Del Larkhill 31.10.86. TOC 13.11.86; f/f 15.11.86 at Manorbier. On 6.12.86 and during a Blowpipe shoot with 105 TA Regt, RA it stopped responding to signals and rolled into the sea. (TFH 0.51; 2 Flights)

ZF714 (c/n 318) Del Larkhill 31.10.86. TOC 5.11.86; f/f 10.11.86 at Manorbier. On 11.11.86 it sustained a direct hit by a Javelin missile, during a shoot with 46 Battery, RA. (TFH 1.09; 2 Flights)

ZF715 (c/n 319) Del Larkhill 31.10.86. TOC 5.11.86; f/f 10.11.86 at Manorbier. On 11.11.86 it sustained a direct hit by a Javelin missile, during a shoot with 46 Battery, RA. (TFH 0.56; 2 Flights)

ZF716 (c/n 320) Del Larkhill 31.10.86. TOC 5.11.86; f/f 10.11.86 at Manorbier during a Javelin shoot with 46 Battery, RA but was lost after 3 minutes when the aircraft rolled to port and dived vertically into the sea.

ZF717 (c/n 321) Del Larkhill 31.10.86. TOC 7.11.86; f/f 12.11.86 at Manorbier. On 6.12.86 it crashed into the sea off Manorbier when the fail-safe recovery parachute inadvertently deployed after 13 minutes. (TFH 1.59; 3 Flights)

ZF718 (c/n 322) Del Larkhill 31.10.86. TOC 8.11.86; f/f 13.11.86 at Manorbier. On 15.12.86 it crashed into the sea after the engine failed in flight, during a Blowpipe shoot with the Royal School of Artillery, RA. (TFH 3.11; 4 Flights)

ZF719 (c/n 341) Del Larkhill 28.11.86 and stored. TOC 22.2.87; f/f 28.7.87 at Manorbier during a shoot with the Royal School of Artillery, RA but the fail-safe 'chute inadvertently deployed after 3 minutes and ZF719 crashed into the sea.

ZF720 (c/n 342) Del Larkhill 28.11.86. TOC 4.12.86; f/f 6.12.86 at Manorbier. On 15.12.86 it sustained a direct hit by a Blowpipe missile during a shoot with the Royal School of Artillery, RA.

ZF741 (c/n 343) Del Larkhill 28.11.86. TOC 13.12.86; f/f 16.12.86 at Manorbier. On 22.7.87 it sustained a direct Blowpipe missile hit during a shoot with 10 Battery, RA. (TFH 16.19; 23 Flights)

ZF742 (c/n 344) Del Larkhill 28.11.86. TOC 13.12.86; f/f 28.1.87 at Manorbier for a Javelin missile shoot with 21 Battery, RA but fail-safed into the sea after 8 minutes.

ZF743 (c/n 345) Del Larkhill 28.11.86. TOC 4.12.86; f/f 27.1.87 at Manorbier. On 23.9.87 it sustained a direct hit by a Javelin missile during a shoot by 43 Battery, RA. (TFH 9.56; 14 Flights)

ZF744 (c/n 346) Del Larkhill 28.11.86. TOC 4.12.86; f/f 16.12.86 at Manorbier. On 27.1.87 it was lost during a Javelin shoot with 21 Battery, RA, possibly as a result of a direct missile hit. (TFH 0.51; 2 Flights)

ZF745 (c/n 347) Del Larkhill 28.11.86. TOC 5.12.86; f/f 5.12.86 at Manorbier. On either 5.12.86 or 16.12.86) it fail-safed into the sea during a Blowpipe shoot with the Royal School of Artillery, RA. (TFH 0.44; 1 Flight)

ZF746 (c/n 348) Del Larkhill 28.11.86. TOC 5.12.86; f/f 28.1.87 at Manorbier for a Javelin shoot with 21 Battery, RA but fail-safed into the sea after 17 minutes.

ZF747 (c/n 349) Del Larkhill 28.11.86. TOC 13.12.86; f/f 30.1.87 at Manorbier for a Javelin shoot with 21 Battery, RA but the engine cut after 30 minutes and it crashed into the sea.

ZF748 (c/n 350) Del Larkhill 28.11.86. TOC 13.12.86; f/f 26.1.87 at Manorbier. On 18.7.87, and during a Javelin shoot with 10 Battery, RA the prop sheared off in flight and the aircraft fail-safed into the sea. Sunk before recovery. (TFH 9.28; 13 Flights)

ZF749 (c/n 356) Del Larkhill 19.12.86. TOC 12.1.87; f/f 28.1.87 at Manorbier for a Javelin shoot with 21 Battery, RA but fail-safed after 14 minutes and crashed into the sea. Sunk before recovery.

ZF750 (c/n 357) Del Larkhill 19.12.86. TOC 13.1.87; f/f 30.1.87 at Manorbier for a Javelin shoot with 21 Battery, RA but fail-safed after 4 minutes and crashed into the sea. Sunk before recovery.

ZF751 (c/n 358) Del Larkhill 19.12.86. TOC 13.1.87; f/f 28.1.87 at Manorbier for a Javelin shoot with 21 Battery, RA but fail-safed after 9 minutes and crashed into the sea. Recovered and rtnd to Larkhill for investigation. Later scrapped.

ZF766 (c/n 359) Del Larkhill 19.12.86. TOC 12.1.87; f/f 28.5.87 at Manorbier. On 22.9.87 it sustained a direct hit by a Javelin missile during a shoot with 43 Battery, RA. (TFH 11.13; 14 Flights)

ZF767 (c/n 360) Del Larkhill 19.12.86. TOC 12.1.87; f/f 2.2.87 at Manorbier on a trial flight to determine cause of fail-safing. After 36 minutes one 'smoke flare' was fired and 20 seconds later the aircraft fail-safed into the sea. It was later recovered for investigation at Larkhill, repaired and re-flown 25.5.87 with an anti-static mod. There is some doubt as to whether it flew again but one report (thought to be erroneous) suggests that ZF767 was shot down at Manorbier on 28.5.87 by a Javelin missile from 105 TA Battery, RA.

ZF768 (c/n 361) Del Larkhill 19.12.86. TOC 12.1.87. Aircraft 'water-proofed' at Manorbier 6.2.87 ahead of a trial flight to determine cause of fail-safing; f/f 7.2.87 but after one 'smoke-flare' was fired the aircraft rolled to the left and fail-safed into the sea. Recovered and rtnd to Larkhill for investigation and repair. Rtnd to service at Manorbier and re-flown 9.5.87. On 28.5.87 and during a shoot with 105 TA Battery, RA the prop sheared off in flight and the aircraft crashed into the sea. (TFH 3.05; 5 Flights)

ZF769 (c/n 362) Del Larkhill 19.12.86. TOC 12.1.87. Anti-static mod fitted at Larkhill 24.3.87; f/f 25.5.87 at Manorbier for a Javelin shoot with 105 TA Battery, RA but the pilot lost control on approach to land and the aircraft crashed into the sea. (TFH 0.50; 1 Flight)

ZF770 (c/n 363) Del Larkhill 19.12.86. TOC 13.1.87. Anti-static mod fitted at Larkhill 24.3.87; f/f 16.5.87 at Manorbier for a Javelin shoot with 104 TA Battery, RA. At the end of the flight the pilot attempted a parachute recovery but the 'chute did not fully deploy and the aircraft was w/o on landing.

ZF771 (c/n 364) Del Larkhill 19.12.86. TOC 13.1.87. Anti-static mod fitted at Larkhill 24.3.87; f/f 25.5.87 at Manorbier for a Javelin shoot with 105 TA Battery, RA but sustained a direct hit after 37 minutes.

ZF772 (c/n 365) Del Larkhill 19.12.86. TOC 12.1.87; f/f 12.2.87 at Manorbier and after 5 minutes the pilot pressed for the first flare. 20 seconds later the aircraft fail-safed into the sea. Recovered by boat and rtnd to Larkhill. Anti-static mod fitted at Larkhill 13.4.87. Conveyed back to Manorbier but shot down 9.6.87 by a Javelin missile of the Royal School of Artillery, RA. (TFH 0.19; 2 Flights)

ZF773 (c/n 366) Del Larkhill 30.1.87. TOC 3.2.87. Anti-static mod fitted at Larkhill 7.3.87; f/f 9.5.87 at Manorbier during a Javelin shoot with 103 TA Battery, RA but crashed on landing after 46 minutes.

ZF774 (c/n 367) Del Larkhill 30.1.87, accepted 13.1.87; f/f 24.2.87 at Larkhill but fail-safed on first run and after 30 seconds of smoke (as expected). Repaired and fitted with anti-static mod 10.3.87. Conveyed to Manorbier where, on 23.9.87 and during a Javelin shoot with 43 Battery, RA, the parachute deployed over Range and '774 crashed into the sea. (TFH 6.42; 11 Flights)

ZF775 (c/n 368) Del Larkhill 30.1.87; accepted 4.2.87. Anti-static mod fitted at Larkhill 16.4.87; f/f 25.5.87 at Manorbier for a Javelin shoot with 105 TA Battery, RA but the prop sheared in flight after 3 minutes. Aircraft crashed into the sea.

ZF776 (c/n 369) Del Larkhill 30.1.87. TOC 4.2.87. Anti-static mod fitted at Larkhill 9.3.87; f/f 25.3.87 at Manorbier for a Javelin shoot with the Royal School of Artillery, RA but fail-safed into the sea after 5 minutes.

ZF777 (c/n 370) Del Larkhill 30.1.87. TOC 4.2.87. Anti-static mod fitted at Larkhill 9.3.87; f/f 25.3.87 at Manorbier. On 26.3.87 and during a shoot with the Javelin QA it sustained a direct missile hit and crashed into the sea.

ZF778 (c/n 371) Del Larkhill 30.1.87. TOC 4.2.87. Anti-static mod fitted at Larkhill 9.3.87; f/f 25.3.87 at Manorbier. On 22.9.87 all response was lost immediately after launch for a Javelin shoot with 43 Battery, RA. The recovery parachute deployed but due to strong winds it was w/o on landing. (TFH 8.00; 13 Flights)

ZF779 (c/n 372) Del Larkhill 30.1.87. TOC 4.2.87; f/f 24.2.87 at Larkhill as part of a series of trials to investigate losses. As expected the aircraft fail-safed after 20 seconds of flight but was recovered safely. Anti-static mod fitted at Larkhill 10.3.87. On 6.5.87, and during a Javelin shoot with 3 Commando Bde, RM the

Once the cause of a series of crashes had been realised, all Banshee targets in black and white scheme were fitted with an anti-static mod on the rear of the fin. ZF771 was fitted with the modification on 24 March 1987 at Larkhill, which is where this view was taken. ZF771 was later taken to Manorbier and made its first flight there on 25 May 1987. (Michael I Draper)

A new batch of ten Banshee targets has just been unloaded at Larkhill on 24 June 1987 after delivery from Ashford, Kent. The aircraft involved are ZG549-ZG550, ZG580-ZG587. (Michael I Draper)

aircraft fail-safed into the sea. (TFH 0.38; 2 Flights).

ZF791 (c/n 373) Del Larkhill 30.1.87. TOC 4.2.87; f/f 24.2.87 at Larkhill as part of a series of trials to investigate losses. Landed safely without damage. Anti-static mod fitted at Larkhill 2.3.87; later removed for further trial flight 4.3.87. Aircraft fail-safed after one flare but landed safely. Conveyed to Manorbier where, on 25.3.87 and during a Javelin shoot with the Royal School of Artillery, RA, it sustained a direct hit. (TFH 0.55; 3 Flights).

ZF792 (c/n 374) Del Larkhill 30.1.87. TOC 4.2.87. Anti-static mod fitted at Larkhill 9.3.87; f/f 25.3.87 at Manorbier. On 6.5.87, and during a Javelin shoot with 3 Commando Bde, RM and the Javelin QA, the aircraft sustained a direct hit and crashed into the sea. (TFH 3.43; 6 Flights).

ZF793 (c/n 375) Del Larkhill 30.1.87. TOC 4.2.87; f/f 24.2.87 at Larkhill as part of a series of trial flights to investigate unexplained losses. To Manorbier 3.87. Anti-static mod fitted at Larkhill 2.3.87. Next flown at Manorbier 25.3.87 where, on 17.6.87, and during a Javelin shoot with 'P' Troop & 7th Royal Horse Artillery, RA it lost power and crashed into the sea. (TFH 6.44; 13 Flights).

ZF794 (c/n 377) Del Larkhill 27.2.87. Anti-static mod fitted at Larkhill 9.3.87. TOC 19.3.87; f/f 25.3.87 at Manorbier for a Javelin shoot with the Royal School of Artillery, RA but dived into the sea whilst recovering. W/o. (TFH 0.47; 1 Flight)

ZF795 (c/n 382) Del Larkhill 27.2.87. No further details known.

ZF796 (c/n 383) Del Larkhill 27.2.87. Anti-static mod fitted at Larkhill 3.3.87; f/f 4.3.87 at Larkhill. To Manorbier 3.87. On 15.4.87 the recovery parachute deployed prior to changeover to Range pilot during a Javelin shoot by the Gibraltar Regiment. The aircraft crashed into the sea. W/o. (TFH 2.04; 5 Flights)

ZF797 (c/n 380) Del Larkhill 27.2.87. Anti-static mod fitted at Larkhill 12.3.87; f/f 16.5.87 at Manorbier. On 10.6.87 the aircraft sustained a direct hit by a Javelin missile during a shoot with the Royal School of Artillery, RA. (TFH 3.50; 6 Flights)

ZF798 (c/n 381) Del Larkhill 27.2.87. Anti-static mod fitted at Larkhill 11.3.87. Accepted 21.3.87; f/f Manorbier 25.3.87. On 15.4.87 the aircraft sustained a direct hit by a Javelin missile during a shoot with the Gibraltar Regiment. (TFH 1.38; 3 Flights)

ZG539 (c/n 394) Del Larkhill 22.5.87. TOC 10.7.87; f/f Manorbier 23.7.87 for a Javelin shoot with 10 Battery, RA. After 52 minutes it sustained a direct missile hit.
(Note that ZG539 was delivered as '394'. It is unlikely that the true serial was ever applied.)
The serial ZG539 was later applied to Banshee c/n 2353 for reasons unkn.

ZG540 (c/n 395) Del Larkhill 22.5.87. TOC 10.7.87; f/f Manorbier 22.7.87. On 14.1.89 it was shot down at Otterburn Range by a Javelin missile of 105 TA Battery, RA. (TFH 7.01; 9 Flights). (Note that ZG540 was delivered as '395', later adjusted to 'ZG395' and eventually corrected to ZG540.)

ZG541 (c/n 396) Del Larkhill 22.5.87. TOC 12.6.87; f/f Manorbier 30.6.87. On 17.7.87, and during a Javelin shoot with the Royal School of Artillery, RA, it fail-safed after 2 minutes from launch due to a fault with the ground station. (TFH 1.51; 4 Flights). (Note that ZG541 was delivered as '396', later adjusted to 'ZG396' but thought not to have been corrected.)

ZG542 (c/n 397) Del Larkhill 22.5.87. TOC 10.7.87; f/f Manorbier 24.7.87 but was shot down by a Javelin missile of 10 Battery, RA after 34 minutes. (Note that ZG542 was delivered as '397', later adjusted to 'ZG397' but thought not to have been corrected.)

ZG543 (c/n 398) Del Larkhill 22.5.87; f/f Manorbier 18.7.87. On 22.7.87 it was shot down at by a Javelin missile of 10 Battery, RA. (TFH 1.23; 2 Flights). (Note that ZG543 was delivered as '398', later adjusted to 'ZG398' but thought not to have been corrected.)

ZG544 (c/n 399) Del Larkhill 22.5.87. TOC 12.7.87; f/f Manorbier 21.7.87 but was shot down by a Javelin missile of 10 Battery, RA after 47 minutes. (Note that ZG544 was delivered as '399', later adjusted to 'ZG399' but thought not to have been corrected.)

ZG545 (c/n 400) Del Larkhill 22.5.87. TOC 8.6.87; f/f Manorbier 3.7.87 but was shot down by either a Dart or Javelin missile after 36 minutes during a shoot with the Royal School of Artillery, RA. (Note that ZG545 was delivered as '400', later adjusted to 'ZG400' but thought not to have been corrected.)

ZG546 (c/n 401) Del Larkhill 22.5.87. TOC 11.7.87; f/f Manorbier 18.7.87. On 21.7.87 it was shot down by a Javelin missile of 10 Battery, RA. (TFH 1.02; 2 Flights). (Note that ZG546 was delivered as '401', later adjusted to 'ZG401' but thought not to have been corrected.)

ZG547 (c/n 408) Del Larkhill 22.5.87. TOC 8.6.87; f/f Manorbier 10.6.87 but was shot down after 10 minutes, probably by a Javelin missile of the Royal School of Artillery, RA. (Note that ZG547 was delivered as '408', later adjusted to 'ZG547' but thought not to have been corrected.)

ZG548 (c/n 409) Del Larkhill 22.5.87. TOC 11.6.87; f/f Manorbier 18.7.87. On 23.7.87 it was shot down by a Javelin missile of 10 Battery, RA. (TFH 1.51; 3 Flights). (Note that ZG548 was delivered as '409', later adjusted to 'ZG409' but thought not to have been corrected.)

ZG549 (c/n 416) Del Larkhill 24.6.87. No further details known.

ZG550 (c/n 418) Del Larkhill 24.6.87. TOC 22.9.87; f/f Otterburn 14.2.88 but after 48 minutes control was lost; the aircraft fail-safed but the parachute failed to operate correctly and ZG550 was w/o when it hit the ground.

ZG580 (c/n 419) Del Larkhill 24.6.87. TOC 29.9.87; f/f Manorbier 23.9.87. On 29.9.89 crashed into the sea after the engine failed in flight during a Javelin shoot with 43 Battery, RA (TFH 3.27; 4 Flights).

ZG581 (c/n 420) Del Larkhill 24.6.87. TOC 29.9.87; f/f Manorbier 5.10.87. Tfd to Otterburn Range 11.87. On 14.1.89 it was shot down at Otterburn by a Javelin missile of 105 TA Battery, RA. (TFH 4.50; 8 Flights).

ZG582 (c/n 421) Del Larkhill 24.6.87. No further details known.

ZG583 (c/n 422) Del Larkhill 24.6.87. TOC 3.10.87. To Manorbier but not flown there; instead tfd to Otterburn where it f/f 28.11.87. After 24 minutes of flight it was shot down by a Blowpipe missile of 104 TA Battery, RA

ZG584 (c/n 423) Del Larkhill 24.6.87. TOC 23.9.87; f/f Manorbier 24.9.87 but was shot down after 36 minutes during a Javelin shoot with 43 Battery, RA..

ZG585 (c/n 424) Del Larkhill 24.6.87. TOC 22.9.87; f/f Manorbier 29.9.87. Tfd to Otterburn 11.87 where, on 19.3.88, it was shot down by a Blowpipe missile during a shoot with 105 TA Battery, RA. (TFH 3.04; 4 Flights).

ZG586 (c/n 425) Del Larkhill 24.6.87. TOC 20.10.87; f/f Manorbier 22.10.87 but was shot down by a Javelin missile after 47 minutes during a shoot with 43 Battery, RA.

ZG587 (c/n 431) Del Larkhill 24.6.87. No further details known.

ZG588 (c/n 432) Del Larkhill 31.7.87. TOC 6.8.87; f/f Otterburn 13.2.88 for a Blowpipe shoot with 105 TA Battery, RA. After 3 minutes the aircraft failed to respond to radio commands during the pilot changeover and crashed into the ground.

ZG589-ZG591 (c/n 433-435) Del Larkhill 31.7.87. No further details known.

ZG592 (c/n 436) Del Larkhill 31.7.87. TOC 6.8.87; f/f Hebrides 7.12.87. Tfd to Otterburn prior to 2.88 where, on 19.3.88, the engine failed over the Range during a Javelin shoot with 103 TA Battery, RA. The aircraft is thought to have crashed but officially reported as "Lost or Stolen!" (TFH 1.38; 3 Flights)

ZG593 (c/n 437) Del Larkhill 31.7.87. TOC 6.8.87; f/f Otterburn 19.3.88. On 19.11.88, and during a Javelin shoot with the Royal School of Artillery, RA, the aircraft went into fail-safe mode after smoke was turned on for its 1st Range run of the day and cr. The wreckage was not located and it was subsequently w/o as "Not found". (TFH 3.04; 5 Flights)

ZG594-ZG599 (c/ns 438-443) Del Larkhill 31.7.87. No further details known.

Following the final deliveries of Skeet 2, the contract for supplying further target drones was awarded to Meggitt, who resumed deliveries of Banshee targets during mid-1992. None of these aircraft were allocated serials within the standard alpha-numeric sequence; instead they were identified by their manufacturer's c/n and which remained the sole means of identity. Known examples delivered to SERCO at Larkhill for operational use at Manorbier and/or the Hebrides were as follows:

1309 f/f Manorbier 22.2.93 but caught fire in the air after 15 minutes and was w/o in an emergency landing. (TFH 0.15)

1311 f/f Manorbier 6.10.92. Shot down off Manorbier 14.10.92. (TFH 6.15; 6 Flights)

1312 f/f Manorbier 7.12.92. Shot down into the sea off Manorbier 8.12.92. (TFH 2.24; 3 Flights)

1313 f/f Manorbier 22.2.93. Shot down off Manorbier 28.6.93. (TFH 3.24; 4 Flights)

1314 f/f Manorbier 20.10.92 but shot down after 14 minutes.

1315 f/f Manorbier 12.10.92. Shot down off Manorbier 9.12.92. (TFH 4.55; 5 Flights)

1317 f/f Manorbier 5.9.92. Shot down off Manorbier 27.2.93. (TFH 2.41; 4 Flights)

1318 f/f Manorbier 19.10.92. Crashed into the sea off Manorbier after a missile strike 19.1.93. (TFH 2.07; 2 Flights)

1322 f/f Manorbier 22.2.93 but shot down after 30 minutes.

1324 f/f Manorbier 8.10.92. Shot down off Manorbier 27.2.92. (TFH 2.31; 3 Flights)

1325 f/f Manorbier 14.10.92. Shot down off Manorbier 10.12.92. (TFH 3.43; 5 Flights)

1327 f/f Manorbier 12.10.92. Shot down off Manorbier 9.12.92. (TFH 4.46; 5 Flights)

1328 f/f Manorbier 16.9.92. Shot down off Manorbier 27.2.93. (TFH 3.20; 4 Flights)

1331 f/f Manorbier 12.10.92. Fuselage and wing damaged beyond economical repair whilst landing at Manorbier 9.12.92 after its 6th flight. Rebuilt with a new fuselage and wing and flew 26.5.93. Finally shot down 29.6.93. (TFH 15.21; 15 Flights)

1332 f/f Manorbier 16.9.92. Shot down off Manorbier 19.10.92. (TFH 2.04; 3 Flights)

1334 f/f Manorbier 1.10.92. Shot down off Manorbier 25.9.93. (TFH 2.55; 7 Flights)

1335 f/f Manorbier 1.10.92. Shot down off Manorbier 10.12.92. (TFH 4.51; 6 Flights)

1336 f/f Manorbier 14.10.92. Shot down off Manorbier 8.12.92. (TFH 3.39; 4 Flights)

1337 f/f Manorbier 26.2.93. Shot down off Manorbier 8.5.93. (TFH 3.23; 4 Flights)

1338 f/f Manorbier 23.2.93. Shot down off Manorbier 24.2.93. (TFH 3.16; 3 Flights)

1339 f/f Manorbier 9.5.93. Shot down off Manorbier 12.10.93. (TFH 3.02; 3 Flights)

1340 f/f Manorbier 24.2.93. Shot down off Manorbier 27.2.93. (TFH 2.41; 3 Flights)

1341 f/f Manorbier 5.7.93 but shot down after 20 minutes.

1351 f/f Norway 13.2.93 for 10 minutes. No further record of flights.

1355 f/f Manorbier 27.2.93 but shot down after 27 minutes.

1357 f/f Manorbier 8.5.93. Shot down on its 2nd flight of the day. (TFH 2.03; 2 Flights)

1358 f/f Manorbier 8.5.93. Shot down off Manorbier 6.10.93. (TFH 5.04; 7 Flights)

1359 f/f Manorbier 25.9.93 but shot down after 34 minutes.

Unmanned Targets for the Army

1360 f/f Manorbier 24.4.93. Shot down off Manorbier 12.7.93. (TFH 3.27; 4 Flights)

1361 f/f Manorbier 23.2.93 but shot down after 7 minutes.

1362 f/f Manorbier 22.2.93 but the recovery parachute deployed after 10 seconds, causing the aircraft to crash.

1363 f/f Manorbier 22.2.93 but shot down after 28 minutes.

1364 f/f Manorbier 27.2.93 but shot down after 16 minutes. Repaired to non-flying status and exhibited at the Science Museum, South Kensington.

1373 f/f Manorbier 28.6.93. Shot down off Manorbier 29.6.93. (TFH 2.08; 3 Flights)

1377 f/f Manorbier 5.7.93 but shot down after 26 minutes.

1378 f/f Manorbier 14.3.93. Shot down off Manorbier 29.6.93. (TFH 4.57; 5 Flights)

1379 f/f Manorbier 3.7.93 but shot down after 44 minutes.

1383 f/f Manorbier 24.4.93. Crashed over the Manorbier Range 10.7.93 after the engine cut. (TFH 2.11; 2 Flights)

1385 f/f Manorbier 24.4.93 although engine failed after 10 seconds of flight, causing slight damage on landing. Shot down off Manorbier 30.6.93. (TFH 6.37; 9 Flights)

1394 f/f Manorbier 26.2.93. Shot down off Manorbier 27.2.93. (TFH 1.12; 2 Flights)

1402 f/f Manorbier 4.8.92. Shot down off Manorbier 18.1.93. (TFH 3.54; 5 Flights)

1407 f/f Manorbier 23.2.93. Shot down off Manorbier 27.2.93. (TFH 3.37; 4 Flights)

1408 f/f Manorbier 9.12.92. Shot down off Manorbier 10.12.92. (TFH 2.51; 3 Flights)

1409 f/f Manorbier 18.10.92. Suffered engine failure 10 seconds after launch 24.10.92 and ccrashed into the sea off Manorbier. Not recovered. (TFH 2.12; 3 Flights)

1423 f/f Manorbier 13.3.93. Shot down off Manorbier 29.6.93. (TFH 5.49; 9 Flights)

1425 f/f Hebrides Range 24.3.93. Shot down by Rapier FSC missile 2.4.93. (TFH 1.58; 3 Flights)

1427 f/f Manorbier 22.2.93. Shot down off Manorbier 23.2.93. (TFH 2.58; 3 Flights)

1430 f/f Manorbier 6.11.93. Shot down off Manorbier 27.11.93. (TFH 5.30; 7 Flights)

1431 f/f Manorbier 13.3.93. Ran out of fuel over the Manorbier Range 15.6.93 and crashed into the sea. (TFH 3.43; 4 Flights)

1438 f/f Manorbier 13.10.93. Shot down off Manorbier 4.12.93. (TFH 5.28; 6 Flights)

1459 f/f Manorbier 6.10.93. Damaged by a missile strike 11.10.93 but crashed into sea before recovery procedure was applied. (TFH 2.18; 3 Flights)

1461 f/f Manorbier 6.11.93 but shot down after 23 minutes.

1464 f/f Manorbier 11.10.93 but shot down after 59 minutes.

1465 f/f Hebrides Range 24.3.93. Crashed into the sea off the Hebrides 2.4.93 after fail-safe mode engaged due to local interference. (TFH 0.33; 2 Flights)

1466 f/f Hebrides Range 29.7.93 but shot down after 16 minutes.

1471 f/f Manorbier 19.9.93. Shot down off Manorbier 20.9.93. (TFH 1.07; 2 Flights)

1474 f/f Manorbier 16.9.93. Shot down off Manorbier 23.9.93. (TFH 6.22; 8 Flights)

1477 f/f Hebrides Range 25.3.93. Fail-safed into the sea off the Hebrides 2.4.93 due to local radio interference. (TFH 1.29; 3 Flights)

1478 f/f Hebrides Range 24.3.93. Shot down off Hebrides 4.12.93. (TFH 2.12; 3 Flights)

1479 f/f Manorbier 4.11.93. Lost in mist and low cloud off Manorbier 27.11.93. Presumed crashed and sank. (TFH 1.48; 3 Flights)

1480 f/f Hebrides Range 28.7.93. Shot down into the sea off Hebrides 29.7.93. (TFH 0.23; 2 Flights)

1482 f/f Hebrides Range 27.7.93 but shot down after 11 minutes.

1483 f/f Manorbier 22.7.93 but shot down after 7 minutes.

1488 f/f Manorbier 25.9.93. Shot down off Manorbier 7.10.93. (TFH 1.53; 3 Flights)

1489 f/f Manorbier 10.7.93. Shot down off Manorbier 11.7.93. (TFH 1.24; 2 Flights)

1493 f/f Manorbier 10.7.93. Shot down off Manorbier 25.9.93. (TFH 4.29; 7 Flights)

1494 f/f Manorbier 30.6.93. Crashed off Manorbier 30.9.93 after recovery parachute failed. (TFH 6.19; 7 Flights)

1495 f/f Manorbier 11.7.93. Shot down off Manorbier 12.7.93. (TFH 0.50; 2 Flights)

1496 f/f Manorbier 10.7.93 but shot down after 23 minutes.

1516 f/f Manorbier 27.9.93 but fail-safed after 72 minutes. Crashed into the sea.

1519 f/f Manorbier 24.7.93 but shot down after 18 minutes.

1520 f/f Manorbier 28.9.93 but shot down after 27 minutes.

1522 f/f Manorbier 24.7.93. Crashed into the sea off Manorbier 20.12.93, believed as a result of shoot-down. (TFH 2.47; 3 Flights)

1523 f/f Manorbier 29.9.93. Shot down 7.10.93. (TFH 1.34; 2 Flights)

1530 f/f Manorbier 8.11.93 but crashed after 1 minute following an in-flight engine failure.

1532 f/f Manorbier 25.9.93 but shot down after 28 minutes.

1533 f/f Manorbier 21.7.93. Shot down off Manorbier 22.7.93. (TFH 2.07; 4 Flights)

1537 f/f Manorbier 21.7.93. Shot down off Manorbier 22.7.93. (TFH 1.34; 3 Flights)

1539 f/f Manorbier 7.10.93 but shot down after 39 minutes.

1540 f/f Manorbier 11.10.93. Fail-safed on launch at Manorbier 12.10.93 and crashed into the sea. (TFH 0.47; 2 Flights)

1545 f/f Hebrides Range 25.9.93 but shot down after 36 minutes.

1546 f/f Manorbier 11.6.94 but shot down after 54 minutes.

1572 f/f Manorbier 10.6.94. Shot down off Manorbier 11.6.94. (TFH 2.02; 3 Flights)

1573 f/f Manorbier 9.6.94. Shot down off Manorbier 14.6.94. (TFH 1.53; 3 Flights)

When the CATS-Banshee entered service on 1 April 2008 all existing Banshee targets were withdrawn and stored at Manorbier pending disposal by MoD. These included Banshee 400s and Banshee 500s. In this view, taken inside the Manorbier Store on 3 June 2008, Banshee 400s c/ns 3150, 3032 and 2353 are visible. (Michael I Draper)

1575 f/f Manorbier 13.9.93. Shot down off Manorbier 20.9.93. (TFH 3.22; 4 Flights)

1578 f/f Manorbier 21.9.93. Shot down off Manorbier 6.10.93. (TFH 6.27; 10 Flights)

1579 f/f Manorbier 16.9.93. Fail-safed over the Range 22.9.93 possibly due to missile hit. (TFH 2.59; 5 Flights)

1581 f/f Manorbier 19.9.93. Shot down off Manorbier 30.9.93. (TFH 2.41; 3 Flights)

1582 f/f Manorbier 17.9.93. Shot down off Manorbier 12.10.93. (TFH 7.59; 10 Flights)

1583 f/f Hebrides Range 31.8.94 but shot down after 24 minutes by a Rapier RARH missile.

1584 f/f Manorbier 8.6.94. Crashed into the sea on the 3rd flight of the day after engine failed. (TFH 2.19; 3 Flights)

1585 f/f Manorbier 9.6.94. Damaged beyond economical repair at Manorbier 28.7.94 when it crashed 1 minute after launch. (TFH 7.32; 9 Flights)

1586 f/f Hebrides Range 29.8.94. Shot down by a Rapier missile 1.9.94. (TFH 2.50; 4 Flights)

1587 f/f Hebrides Range 9.6.94 although fail-safed on launch before gaining real flight. Shot down by a Rapier missile off the Hebrides Range 2.9.94. (TFH 1.49; 4 Flights)

1598 f/f Hebrides Range (?) 13.6.94. Shot down into the sea off Manorbier 15.6.94. (TFH 1.06; 3 Flights)

1605 f/f Hebrides Range 29.9.93 but shot down after 5 minutes.

1606 f/f Hebrides Range 27.7.93 but shot down after 26 minutes.

1608 f/f Manorbier 11.10.93 but shot down after 12 minutes.

1609 f/f Hebrides Range 12.10.93 but shot down on its 2nd flight of the day. (TFH 1.30; 2 Flights)

1610 f/f Hebrides Range 26.7.93. Shot down over the Hebrides Range by a Rapier missile 27.7.93. (TFH 1.31; 2 Flights)

1611 f/f Manorbier 28.7.93. Shot down off Manorbier 29.7.93. (TFH 0.49; 2 Flights)

1641 f/f Hebrides Range 7.6.94 but fail-safed after 6 minutes.

1642 f/f Hebrides Range 15.2.94. W/o 7.6.94 at the Hebrides Range after recovery parachute was deployed in 30 knot winds. (TFH 1.54; 3 Flights)

1682 f/f Hebrides Range 21.9.94 but shot down by a Rapier missile after 24 minutes.

1822 f/f Hebrides range 28.7.94. Shot down over the Hebrides Range 5.9.94 by a Rapier missile. (TFH 2.06; 4 Flights)

1833 f/f Hebrides Range 20.9.94. Shot down by a Rapier missile over the Hebrides Range 21.9.94. (TFH 1.17; 3 Flights)

1835 f/f Hebrides Range 13.9.94 but shot down by a Rapier missile after 6 minutes.

1839 f/f Hebrides Range 15.9.94. Shot down off the Hebrides 19.9.94 by a Rapier missile. (TFH 1.14; 2 Flights)

1840 f/f Hebrides Range 13.9.94. Shot down off the Hebrides 19.9.94 by a Rapier missile. (TFH 3.44; 4 Flights)

1841 f/f Hebrides Range 13.9.94. Shot down by a Rapier missile on the 2nd flight of the day. (TFH 1.15; 2 Flights)

1843 f/f Hebrides Range 14.9.94 but shot down by a Rapier missile after 43 minutes.

The following Banshee 400 target drones are also known to have been delivered to Larkhill where they were stored initially: 2231, 2237, 2239, 2240, 2241, 2244, 2254, 2259, 2266, 2284, 2285, 2288, 2289, 2291, 2294, 2308, 2328, 2332, 2334, 2335, 2336, 2337, 2338, 2347, 2354, 2356, 2358, 2359, 2360, 2361, 2370, 2372, 2373, 2374, 2375, 2376, 2379, 2384, 2389, 2394, 2395, 2396, 2397, 2402, 2403, 2416, 2417, 2419, 2444, 2447, 2467, 2468, 2493, 2495, 2496, 2497, 2565, 2576, 2577, 2579, 2581, 2657, 2658, 2659, 2660, 2661, 2662, 2663, 2664, 2665, 2666, 2683, 2684, 2685, 2686, 2736, 2737, 2738, 2739, 2740, 2741, 2742, 2743, 2744, 2745, 2750, 2751, 2752, 2753, 2754, 2755, 2756, 2757, 2758, 2759, 2772, 2773, 2774, 2775, 2776, 2777, 2778, 2779, 2780, 2781, 2782, 2783, 2784, 2785, 2786, 2787, 2788, 2789, 2790, 2791, 2823, 2833, 2834, 2835, 2836, 2837, 2838, 2839, 2840, 2841, 2842, 2849, 2850, 2851, 2852, 2853, 2854, 2858, 2859, 2860, 2861, 2862, 2863, 2864, 2865, 2866, 2867, 2868, 2869, 2870, 2871, 2872, 2873, 2877, 2878, 2879, 2880, 2881, 2882, 2883, 2884, 2885, 2886, 2887, 2889, 2890, 2891, 2892, 2893, 2894, 2895, 2896, 2897, 2898, 2899, 2900, 2901, 2902, 2903, 2888, 2904, 2910, 2911, 2912, plus 19 unidentified.

Flight Refuelling Falconet (ASAT/FR-500)

Of all the modern high-speed expendable aircraft operated by the Army, probably the least-publicised is the Flight Refuelling Falconet target drone.

Design work began on a small turbojet RPV vehicle when the company visualised a likely need for a target to succeed the Royal Navy's Northrop MQM-74A Chukar I targets. A private venture project, Flight Refuelling's projected target was designated FR-500. Powered by a single Noel Penny Turbines NPT 401, the FR-500 was designed for zero-launch with two JATO bottles, each of 2,645lb (1,200 kg st) for launch boost.

Until that time, the Navy had only placed two orders (totalling just 23 Chukar Is) over a 2½ year period. Whilst 'off-the-shelf' purchases often proved to be expensive, the MoD considered that the small number of Chukars procured annually did not warrant the cost of developing an entirely new system. Instead, the Navy chose to procure the MQM-37C Chukar II and, towards the end of 1977, began to place small quantity orders for the new variant. As a result the FR-500 project, which in reality was little more than a feasibility study at that stage, was dropped.

In the meantime the MoD began to survey a number of existing and projected drone systems. The objective was to assess their suitability and long-term viability as a standard target for use on British Ranges through to the mid-1990s. None were considered to be suitable and so, under General Staff Requirement 3700, MoD invited a number of tenders from British manufacturers.

GSR3700 called for a cheap, re-useable and maneuverable aerial target for sole use at the Royal Artillery Hebrides Range. It was intended primarily to be used as a target for Rapier but also as a target for other low-level air defence systems. Realising that it could meet GSR3700, Flight Refuelling resurrected the FR-500 and soon emerged as the leading contender. By now FR-500 was being referred to by the more marketable term, ASAT (Advanced Subsonic Aerial Target).

Of conventional aluminium alloy stressed skin construction, the ASAT was designed as a highly-proven structure, easily maintained and repairable. The powerplant, an AMES Industrial TRS 18-075 turbojet, was also proven and readily available.

What set ASAT apart from other projects was a requirement to be launched without the need for propellant charges, i.e. neither booster rockets or a catapult launcher. That led to the development of the Rotary Carousel Launch System. This involved the air vehicle mounted on a launch trolley travelling round a 5m wide circular asphalt track of some 57.5m radius. The trolley was attached to a central pylon by a 10mm "Kevlar" cable. The turbojet was fired using compressed air from a ground start trolley; the trolley also provided fuel until immediately before launch, enabling take-off with a full (77 litre/17 gallon) fuel tank. Under its own power the aircraft made several circuits to reach take-off speed, at which point it was then released. The one main advantage of the carousel runway was that it gave the opportunity to check out the aircraft in "near flight" conditions before making a final commitment to launch. This factor offered greater reliability, safety and cost advantages over the standard "boost and go" system.

Flight Refuelling constructed a first prototype at Tarrant Rushton, a non-flying ground-test vehicle (GTV) used for testing the carousel launch procedure. The test track was built on the Larkhill Range by the Property Services Agency (PSA) in 1981 where the GTV completed 1,300 laps of the carousel, simulating 100 sorties up to representative launch attitudes and speeds, in both wet and dry conditions.

Six examples development vehicles were built and despatched to Larkhill for flight-testing. The first live launch was successfully achieved on 14 Feb 1982. Ron "Jock" Kyle, a former RAF Mosquito navigator conducted the first flight. In total, the Larkhill trials involved a series of 28 test flights.

Deliveries to the British Army began in late-1983 (against Contract ML11A/1278) with production aircraft being used for continued tests and acceptance trials. Final acceptance and service entry was achieved in June 1986, by which time the six prototypes and 22 production Falconets had amassed just over 100 flights, as follows:

c/n*	Flights	Remarks
001	5	
002	5	
003	?	
004	?	
005	?	
006	?	
051	1	Transferred to ML11A/1362
052	16	
053	1	Transferred to ML11A/1362
054	17	
055	1	Crashed on launch
056	2	Lost on FGA manoeuvre trial
057	3	Destroyed by Rapier missile
058	4	Destroyed on landing due to failure of recovery 'chute
059	3	Destroyed by Rapier missile
060	1	Transferred to ML11A/1362
061	8	
062	5	
063	3	
064	1	Destroyed on landing due to failure of recovery 'chute
065	2	
066	1	
067	10	
068	2	
069	3	
070	3	Destroyed by Rapier missile
071	3	
072	1	

* The full identity of these aircraft was prefixed FRTR- indicating that they had been built by Flight Refuelling at Tarrant Rushton. The 'TR' was later dropped after production switched to Wimborne.

Just ahead of service entry some consideration had been given to installing a more powerful engine and this had led to Contract ML11A/1362 as an 'Alternative Engine Trials

The Name Game

Before it entered service, Flight Refuelling's ASAT drone was officially named Falconet. By most accounts the name rather appropriately referred to a style of gun dating from the Tudor period. But that was coincidental; the thought process that led to the naming of ASAT was far less straightforward.

During one of the regular MoD progress meetings the question of giving ASAT a name was raised. One suggestion was that Francolin would be appropriate as, not only did it continue the use of wildfowl names for targets, (Skeet, Shelduck etc), but that the name would allow Flight Refuelling's publicity department to create artistic licence from the initial letters 'Fr'. The MoD Naming Committee was less supportive of the likely marketing opportunities and, in their private wisdom, chose to reject 'Francolin', preferring instead to name ASAT as the 'Falcon'. It then fell to somebody within MoD Contracts Branch to point out that the US manufacturer, Lockheed, was already producing an F-16 'Falcon' for the USAF and that it was somewhat faster and much more lethal. Acknowledging that fact, the Naming Committee settled for a 'toning-down' of Falcon – hence ASAT became the Falconet!

Contract', involving aircraft 051, 053 and 060. The engine selected was the AMES TJA-24.

MoD also explored the feasibility of operating a recoverable maritime version of Falconet. The notion was first raised in November 1983, necessitating the fitting of twin booster launch rockets for zero-length launching from a ship's deck. A series of trials was conducted over Cardigan Bay from RAE Aberporth.

Upwards of 450 Falconets were produced before the design was upgraded. At that stage the existing Falconet was re-styled Falconet I. The upgraded Falconet II was introduced in 2001.

Falconet remained in service at the Hebrides range but, since it was out of production, spares became an issue and eventually the type was withdrawn from service. The final 'camp' took place towards the end of 2009 with what was effectively a 'turkey shoot'. It is thought that just four aircraft survive and just one, FR164 which was washed up in the Hebrides and later donated to the Museum of Army Flying, Middle Wallop. It carried the name "Isle of Kyle".

Falconet II Technical Data	
Wing span	10 ft 0.0 in (3.05 m)
Wing Area	15.0 sq ft (1.39 m²)
Length overall	12 ft 2.6 in (3.75 m)
Body diameter	1 ft 3.25 in (0.39)
Height overall	5 ft 0 in (1.52 m)
Tailplane span	4 ft 6.7 in (1.39 m)
Basic weight empty	377 lb (171 kg)
Max fuel	132 lb (60 kg)
Payload with max fuel	50.7 lb(23 kg)
Max t-o/launching weight	584 lb (265 kg)
Max level speed (clean)	450 kt (833 km/h; 518 mph)
Min flying speed	150 kt (278 km/h; 173 mph)
Operating height range: min	16 ft (5 m)
Operating height range: max	29,525 ft (9,000 m)
Typical operating radius	10.8 n miles (20 km; 12.4 miles)
Range	67 n miles (125 km; 77 miles)
Typical endurance: clean	1 hour
With subtarget	42 mins

Source: *Jane's Unmanned Aerial Vehicles & Targets*.

Combined Aerial Target Service (CATS)

Towards the end of 2006 the means of providing target facilities for the Army and Navy underwent a dramatic change. Rather than have the Navy providing target drones for the Navy and for the Army to operate a separate dedicated service for the Army, the decision was taken to provide an all-embracing and more flexible service both in the UK and overseas. Referred to as the Combined Aerial Target Service (CATS), the new facility was seen as key to air defence training of the UK's armed forces and was officially declared operational in June 2008. The launch of CATS followed an 18-month preparatory period after the Ministry of Defence confirmed, on 14 December 2006 the award of a contract – valued at the time of up to £308m over a two-year period – to QinetiQ.

The Combined Aerial Target Service comprised four fundamental elements to meet varying needs and demands: a basic aerial target; an intermediate aerial target; an advanced aerial target and a ground-based helicopter target. Target drones selected to meet the first three elements involved the Meggitt Banshee (basic), Meggitt Voodoo (intermediate) and the Mirach 100/5 (advanced) respectively.[26]

Meggitt CATS-Banshee

Since 1992, when the last of the surviving Skeet 2 target drones was expended, the Meggitt Banshee had been the standard basic aerial target for Army live missile training. With the incentive of securing further contracts, and to meet specific requirements for the 21st century, the manufacturer had already embarked on an upgrade of Banshee 400. Several combinations of enhancements were evaluated and tested over the Outer Hebrides Range using four modified Banshee 400 drones. These had originally been built as standard production examples but had been returned to the Ashford factory for modification. Each of the four, being configured differently and using various powerplants, were allocated standard alpha-numeric

---

[26] The remaining element was provided by a "pop-up" target resembling a Mil-24 Hind helicopter. Although it was raised above the ground it was on a fixed but extendable tether and available only at the BATUS Range, in Canada.

At Manorbier, a Kawasaki Mule proved to be the ideal vehicle for towing Banshee targets between the hangar and the launch area. CATS-Banshee ZZ420/009 is seen being towed from the QinetiQ Workshop to the launch site on 3 June 2008. (Michael I Draper)

CATS-Banshee is fitted with the Meggitt Defence Systems Whirlwind engine. Based on the Wankel principle, the engine is water-cooled giving rise to the need for air vents to cool the radiator. This gives CATS-Banshee quite a distinctive change of appearance. (Michael I Draper)

identities on 6 September 2000 as follows: ZK201 (c/n 2400), ZK202 (c/n 2401), ZK203 (c/n 2633) and ZK204 (c/n 2398).[27]

What emerged from the evaluation process was a completely new variant of Banshee, considerably unlike earlier variants, and which eventually became known officially as the Meggitt CATS-Banshee. The principal difference was the introduction of an MDS Whirlwind engine, a design based on the Wankel principle and adapted

---

27 An unconfirmed report claims that a small number of Banshees were evaluated by RAE Bedford on behalf of the Defence Research Agency. Flight trials are said to have been conducted at Lulsgate airfield, Bristol with launches from a flat-bed Ford Transit The report suggests that these "old-Spec" Banshees, two of which had the standard 342cc engine whilst a third had a Norton radial engine. It is claimed that the Norton engine used excessive amounts of oil. Quite what this report, if accurate, relates to is not known.

The reusable IR thermal source – the 'hot nose' – enables CATS-Banshee to produce a 'hot signature' without affecting performance. The nose is ignited just prior to take-off and burns throughout the aircraft's flight. (Michael I Draper)

A vital piece of kit fitted to the CATS-Banshee is the laser pod mounted at the starboard wing-tip. This enables missile-tracking personnel to check the accuracy of the missile aimer as he lines up his missile on the target. If the aim is good the missile is fired; if not, the firer is stood down to spend more time on a simulator until sufficiently proficient. (Michael I Draper)

Banshees operating under the CATS contract have roundels applied and also the legend BANSHEE TARGET across the wing. ZZ420/023 is seen inside the QinetiQ Workshop at Manorbier on 3 June 2008. (Michael I Draper)

by Meggitt Defence Systems. The engine, a 3-cylinder, single-plug rotary engine, is water-cooled and therefore requires air-intakes on each side of the rear fuselage giving CATS-Banshee its distinctively different appearance.

In view of the anticipated large quantity of Banshees required throughout the two-year contract, CATS-Banshee was allocated the 'type serial' ZZ420 on 7 September 2007 with production aircraft allotted suffix digits in the now-standard manner. Deliveries began just ahead of the in-service target date of 1 April 2008 when six examples (ZZ420/001 to ZZ420/006) were deployed to the Falkland Islands. The second deployment was to the main QinetiQ/Meggitt operational facility at Manorbier Range, followed by a third batch, delivered in May 2008, for onward delivery to the BATUS Training Area in Canada.

CATS Banshee Technical Data	
Powerplant	MDS Whirlwind Rotary
Wing Span (without pods)	8 ft 2 in (2.49 m)
Length overall	9 ft 8 in (2.95 m)
Max Launch Weight	202.8 lb (92 kg)
Service Ceiling	16,400 ft (5,000 m)
Endurance at SL	90 mins

CATS Banshee – known production	
ZZ420/001 to ZZ420/006	c/ns not known
ZZ420/007 to ZZ420/045	c/ns 4300-4338
ZZ420/046	c/n not known
ZZ420/047	c/n 4497

Other CATS-Banshees known to have been allocated to QinetiQ include c/ns 4520/4521/4523 & 4525.

Meggitt Voodoo

At one-and-a-half times larger than Banshee, Meggitt Defence Systems' Voodoo target drone was launched at the Paris Air Show, in June 2001. A high-speed aerial target, Voodoo is powered by a 150hp Ilmore Fury (955cc) 4-stroke, water-cooled engine with altitude compensation. It is capable of speeds of up to 348mph.

The airframe is all carbon-fibre and can be equipped with signature enhancement for passive and active IR and chaff dispensing pods (flares and body-heat generator), laser reflectificity, adjustable radar cross-section enhancement and electronic countermeasures (ECM), including pyrotechnic and black body IR augmentation.

Voodoo was put into production in 2002, to meet an initial order from Taiwan. When selected by the Ministry of

Selected by CATS as an Intermediate Aerial Target, the Meggitt Voodoo finally entered British service in March 2010. ZZ422 (c/n 027) is seen at the Hebrides Range where the Voodoo fleet is permanently based. (Meggitt Defence Systems)

Unmanned Targets for the Army

Defence, as part of its CATS Requirement, it was to meet the need for an intermediate aerial target, specifically for use at the Royal Artillery Hebrides Range.

The initial British order was placed in 2008 and accounted for eight aircraft (allocated serials ZZ421-ZZ428 on 17 March 2008), two Robonic launchers and three ground stations. In effect the six Voodoo targets were purchased virtually off-the-shelf but protracted manufacturer's flight trials over the Hebrides Range were beset by a number of difficulties and, as a result, acceptance did not take place until March 2010 when the first four (ZZ421-ZZ424 c/ns 026-029) were formally taken onto charge.

Voodoo Technical Data	
Length (overall)	11 ft 9 in (3.58 m)
Wing Span	10 ft 9 in (3.28 m)
Wing Area	37.46 sq ft (3.48 m²)
Height	3 ft 4 in (1.02 m)
Weight (empty)	340 lb (154 kg)
Max launching weight	440 lb (200 kg)
Max level speed	303 kt (561 km/h; 348 mph)
Operating height range: lower > upper	16.5 ft (5 m) > 20,000 ft (6,100 m)
Max operating radius	>65 n miles (120 km); 75 miles)
Typical endurance	> 1 hr 30 min
Max control range (GPS tracking)	27 nautical miles (50 km; 31 miles)
Max Endurance	1 hr 15 mins

Meteor Mirach 100/5 (CATS)

Apart from functioning as a target for the Royal Navy, Mirach 100/5 was selected to succeed the GAF Jindivik when the latter was withdrawn from service in 2004. The Ministry of Defence selected Mirach 100/5 to fulfill its Replacement Aerial Target System (RATS) and signed a contract with Meteor in February 2004 for fifty aircraft. Allocated serials ZJ725-ZJ774 on 16 February 2004, all were to be operated solely by QinetiQ. They were delivered in several batches, the initial deliveries being made direct to the QinetiQ Range at Aberporth whilst the remainder were consigned to QinetiQ's storage facility at Boscombe Down.

QinetiQ's Mirach drones took a significant step up in tactical realism for USAFE missile training in November 2006 when 555th 'Triple Nickel' Squadron deployed a force of F-16s to RAF Fairford for a week as part of Exercise 'Deployed Titan 06'. Included in the tasking was a programme of simulated combined air combat operations and which involved laser-guided bomb drops against surface targets at the Aberporth Range as well as firing eight AIM-9M Sidewinder missiles against Mirach 100/5 target drones. The exercise marked the first occasion that Mirach had been engaged by the USAF.

A second contract involving Mirach 100/5s for use by QinetiQ accounted for a further fifty targets as part of the Combined Aerial Target Service (CATS) programme. This batch, allocated as ZZ450-ZZ499 on 17 March 2008, is also deployed to the QinetiQ Aberporth Range.

Mirach 100/5 production	
ZJ725-ZJ727	c/n AD138-AD140
ZJ728-ZJ734	c/n AE156-AE162
ZJ735-ZJ737	c/ns not known
ZJ738	c/n AF192
ZJ739-ZJ744	c/ns not known
ZJ745-ZJ749	c/n AF209-AF213
ZJ750-ZJ764	c/ns not known
ZJ765	c/n AG229
ZJ766-ZJ774	c/ns not known
ZZ450-ZZ499	c/ns not known

Note that the first two digits of construction numbers indicate year of build, eg AD=2003, AE=2004, AF=2005 and AG=2006.

The inscription on the side fuselage of Mirach 100/5 ZJ749 underlines the connection with Aberporth. The manufacturer's construction number, AF213, also appears, the prefix letters 'AF' indicate the year of construction as 2005. (Michael I Draper)

Rarely seen beyond the airfield gates are those Mirach 100/5s operated by QinetiQ at Aberporth. ZJ745 is seen just around the corner, at ParcAberporth on 11 July 2007. (Michael I Draper)

Chapter 9
Surveillance Drones for the Army

As any experienced Army commander will acknowledge, Counter Bombardment – the art of locating, attacking and defeating the enemy's artillery – has always been a supremely exacting task. Since war was first waged, the most obvious, yet vital, factor in any successful campaign has been good intelligence of the enemy's position. That was only possibleif the enemy could be accurately located; not an easy task when artillery was traditionally deployed where it could not be easily seen by the other side's observation posts. Tactics have, of course, changed over the years and several methods of locating enemy artillery – through Flash-Spotting, Sound-Ranging and Surveying – have been widely adopted at various times.

The root of Counter Bombardment lies in campaigns fought during World War I when the essence of Flash-Spotting was first introduced. It involved deducing accurate cross-observations of muzzle flashes from at least three different ground positions. Flash-spotting troops, organised into Observation Sections – which, in turn comprised of several observation posts, each reported the bearings to their Troop HQ – who was then able to calculate the enemy position.

The GEC-Marconi Phoenix took the British Army – and notably the Royal Artillery – into a new age of unmanned aerial surveillance. Development of Phoenix was complex and time-consuming, consequently it went into service late and proved to be ill-suited for some of its designated tasks. But it did eventually prove to be an extremely reliable and successful surveillance platform. ZJ447 is seen undertaking a test flight in Kosovo.

The rapid evolution of radio technology in World War I bore fruit in several ways including an entirely new system based, not on pure geometry or formal principles, but by the means of recording various sound waves as an enemy shell was fired. Known as Sound-Ranging it offered an alternative means of detecting an enemy artillery position. The first successful use of Sound-Ranging has been claimed by the Russians who first used the process on a training Range in 1910, but it was to a German officer, in 1913, that a patent was granted for a method of Sound-Ranging. Ideally, the system required the siting of up to six microphones at equidistant positions across the battlefield, each connected to a pen recorder. These microphones recorded the various sound waves as a shell was fired, passed overhead and exploded – thereby offering a means of calculating the point of firing. Various other factors were built into the calculation, including the prevailing meteorological conditions. Few would doubt this to be an exacting task, even needing specialised units to be trained and equipped for reporting meteorological conditions on the battlefield.

During the Second World War the introduction of Air Observation Post (AOP) aircraft made life a little easier for the artillery commander in seeing the 'other side of a hill'. When Operation 'Torch' launched the Allied invasion of North-West Africa in 1942, the Order of Battle included 651 Squadron – the first of sixteen RAF Air Observation Post squadrons. Although commanded and operated under the aegis of the RAF, wartime AOP Austers were flown by experienced gunnery officers. For the artillery commander this was a monumental step forward.

Men of the British 2nd Army use a Crusader tank as an observation post for the guns of a British Armoured Division during the early stages of World War II. Although effective to a degree the modern battlefield has become a very different scenario since the ability to despatch a surveillance drone over enemy lines with the ability to beam back 'real' television images. (Crown Copyright; Neg. No 12991XF)

One development in artillery surveillance during World War II was the introduction of Air Observation Post squadrons, manned largely by artillery Captains who had been trained as pilots. Although the Austers were owned by the RAF, the AOP Squadron – in the field – came under the operational control of the Army. Whilst in flight, the pilot was in direct communication with the Gun Position Officer and passed him corrections as he observed the fall of shot. The G.P.O. then passed on corrections to the gunners. In this view of an Auster AOP.III, Captain Stormonth-Darling poses in full Air OP communications mode. (Crown Copyright)

In historical terms, the connection between aviation and the Army is arguably one of the most complex of subjects and one that is ever-evolving. Much of the Army's current need for an aviation support element is provided by the Army Air Corps, but the prime responsibility for locating enemy targets continues to rest with the Royal Artillery – a situation that is constantly, and hotly, debated to this day.

The original Royal Artillery 'Survey' Regiments were subsequently re-designated as 'observation' Regiments and ultimately, after the end of World War II, they adopted the term 'Locating' Regiments. The notion of using unmanned reconnaissance drones to enhance the Counter Bombardment role was probably first raised during 1959 when a Colonel Cox returned from a visit to US, extolling the virtues of US Army tactics and the deployment of Northrop drones and radars. The Artillery was quick to react and before the end of the year a special Trials Unit had been established at Larkhill as an offshoot of the Royal School of Artillery. Subsequently the Unit, which was effectively an independent unit, was quickly granted 'Troop' status although, in reality, it had grown to almost Battery proportions. Under the command of Lt Col J.J. 'Jim' Cooke the Troop was known simply as Drone Troop although for administrative purposes was attached to 228 Battery, RA., an administrative Battery and part of Artillery Wing, Royal School of Artillery.

Much of the Drone Troop's first eighteen months at Larkhill time was spent welding a very disparate group of personnel (consisting of men from the Royal Ordnance Corps, Royal Electrical & Mechanical Engineers and the Gunners) into something that represented a workable unit, capable of carrying out what later proved to be both a very interesting and often critical series of trials designed to prepare the unit for the introduction of the Northrop AN/USD-1 drone – referred to in British service as simply the SD-1.[1]

---

1 The unit worked up using Northrop OQ-19 target drones, a quantity of which had been purchased by the Ministry of Aviation several years previously but had never been used and had been held in long-term storage. The batch was subsequently allocated the serials XR404-XR428.

Right: *The Drone Troop's Photographic Interpretation Unit was established inside a Commer lorry where personnel studied images retrieved from the drone's cameras. This view, taken during a break in the dash to West Germany in January 1963 illustrates the lack of de-icing equipment fitted to these vehicles. Drivers were forced to proceed with the windscreen almost fully open! (Lt. Col. J.J. Cooke)*

Left: *John Profumo's announcement that the Royal Artillery's new SD-1 surveillance drone was operational in West Germany caused panic in the War Office. The Battery was still working up at Larkhill but received instructions to deploy immediately – despite the atrocious winter 1962/63 weather. It took eight days for the convoy to cross the Channel and through some of the worst conditions ever experienced. In this view the men were allowed a short meal and drink break. (Lt.Col. J.J. Cooke)*

The contract for SD-1 drones involved just the basic airframe, i.e. excluding US radar and camera equipment. Instead, a British radar system was developed and evaluated during the trials period under the personal direction of Mr George Walters, owner and Managing-Director of APT Electronics at Byfleet, Surrey. Ultimately, the Army decided to augment the drone's photographic capability by developing a triple array camera produced by Vinten Ltd.

Although the Larkhill trials went more-or-less to plan, one particularly worrying problem to emerge was, not with the newly developed photographic equipment, but with the SD-1 drone itself and occasionally with embarrassing results. Shortly after training began at Larkhill, the Trials Unit was asked to demonstrate the SD-1 to a group of permanent staff officers. The flight took place over the Knighton Down Range on Salisbury Plain but after performing a few impressive manoeuvres, the drone unexpectedly went out of control, rolled sharply and then entered a steep dive before destroying one of the fences on the nearby Larkhill racecourse! The demonstration was promptly cancelled. Perhaps of greater concern was another incident that took place several weeks afterwards when another SD-1 drone power-dived into the ground from a considerable height, destroying the (then) only set of Vinten prototype cameras.

In spite of the early setbacks, flight training progressed to schedule. Since its formation, the Drone Troop was effectively an independent unit and virtually self-sufficient. Four Bedford 3-ton lorries, each specially-adapted to carry three SD-1 drones, were fitted with a hoist and securing brackets, the three SD-1s being carried in pyramid fashion. Two Commer vehicles were fitted out as photographic developing units, both with vital water tanks fitted onto the roof, giving these vehicles an extremely ungainly appearance. Unfortunately they often became immobile in wet or muddy wooded areas. Other Commer vehicles were fitted out as photographic interpretation units. Three Mk.7 Air Defence Radars (which had been sent to Byfleet for fitment of moving-map displays and height meters) were adapted for use as Drone Tracking units and towed to the Range area by large AEC Matador lorries. It was all a bit of a circus.[2]

Much of the Army's early involvement with surveillance drones was developed away from the public gaze and not until 2 April 1961 did the general public become aware of the SD-1 Drone. It came about when the War Office quietly announced the placing of an order for 32 unmanned aircraft which the press immediately dubbed as 'Pilotless Peeping Toms'. Nothing more was heard or said and the fact that Britain was acquiring unmanned surveillance drones went largely unnoticed for almost a year. What brought the subject back to the fore occurred on 21 February 1962 when War Minister John Profumo announced in a memorandum to the Army Estimates that "training has also begun in the use of pilotless aircraft for photographing enemy-held

---

2 As related to the author by Lt.Col. J.J 'Jim' Cooke, former Commander of the Trials Unit.

Surveillance Drones for the Army   289

XR292 was one of 32 AN/USD-1 surveillance drones ordered in September 1960 (known as the SD-1) and is seen 'at the ready' on its zero-launcher. (Bruce Robertson Collection Neg No. R.20959)

territory. They will find targets far beyond the range of ground observation." The press again ran the story but, as in the past, the story failed to make front-page news, yet despite the existence of the SD-1 having been public knowledge for some time, few people outside Army circles had ever actually seen one. That changed quite dramatically towards the end of November 1962 when the BBC asked the Ministry of Defence if they could do a programme about 'The Spy in the Sky'. The MoD agreed and Lt Col 'Jim' Cooke, the Drone Troop Commander, was instructed to take one of his SD-1s from Larkhill to the BBC's Shepherd's Bush studios where he was interviewed by Peter West. The programme sparked a great deal of interest in Parliament the following day when – and in answer to a member's question – John Profumo stated that this new system was already up and running in West Germany and performing a key role within BAOR. Needless to say, it wasn't – it was still working-up at Larkhill! Nevertheless Profumo's announcement caused near panic at the War Office who immediately fired off a telegram to Larkhill ordering the Drone Troop to "get yourselves out to Germany ASAP – if not before!"[3]

The winter of 1962/63 was one of the worst on record and conditions were far from ideal for the 26-vehicle convoy setting out from Larkhill for the continent. Drones, radars, tools and spares finally left Larkhill early on 1 January 1963 and headed for Dover. The road conditions across southern England were atrocious with snow and ice causing enormous difficulties. The weather on the continent was no better and after landing at Dunkirk the convoy struggled against more black ice and snow. Conditions for the move could not have been worse but eventually, after a grueling eight-day trek, the convoy arrived at Fallingbostel, West Germany. With immediate effect the Troop was attached to 57 (Bhurtpore) Battery, RA.

57 Battery, 94 Locating Regiment, RA

94 Locating Regiment, RA had been long associated with post-war West Germany. Until August 1951 it was titled 94 Observation Regiment, RA and headquartered at Luneburg, later transferring to Dennis Barracks, Munsterlager. Another move, during November 1956, took the Regiment to Taunton Barracks, Celle.

By mid-1960 94 Regiment, RA consisted of four Batteries, as follows:

14 (Cole's Kop) Battery	Survey/Meteorology
73 (Sphinx) Battery	Locating Battery
152 (Inkerman) Battery	Locating Battery
156 (Inkerman) Battery	Locating Battery

Towards the end of 1960 BAOR units underwent a major reorganization resulting in 152 and 156 Batteries becoming short-range locating Batteries with one Radar Troop and one Counter-Bombardment Troop. 73 Battery became a long-range Battery with three long base sound-ranging Troops and one Divisional Counter-Bombardment Troop.

On paper, 94 Regiment, RA also operated a Drone Troop but the arrival of the Regiment's own drone aircraft was still a considerable long way off. In fact, it was not until 29 April 1964, when 57 (Bhurtpore) Battery was transferred in from the disbanded 21 Locating Regiment, RA., that the Regiment acquired its drones. However, although 94 Regiment remained concentrated at Taunton Barracks, 57 Battery's Drone Troop (together with the Troop's workshops and SD-1s (MQM-57A drones in the XR290-XR302 range)

---

3 Conversation with Lt.Col. J.J. 'Jim' Cooke.

290 Sitting Ducks and Peeping Toms

At the edge of a Range in Germany an unidentified SD-1 drone has landed in a small tree, causing some structural damage. (via Lt.Col J.J.Cooke)

took up residence at Goodwood Barracks, Celle. Once 57 Battery, RA was established so 156 Battery, RA was transferred out to the School of Artillery at Larkhill, on 31 August 1964.

22 Battery, 21 Locating Regiment, RA

21 Regiment, RA, one of the oldest Regiments in the British Army, entered the 1960s with several Batteries. These included 22 (Gibraltar 1779-83) Composite Divisional Locating Battery, RA which, on 4 October 1961, was re-styled as 22 (Gibraltar 1779-83) Battery, RA. At the same time the Battery moved into Busigny Barracks, Perham Down, on the edge of Salisbury Plain, Wiltshire.

When delivery of SD-1 (MQM-57A) surveillance drones began in April 1963, the Royal Artillery formed a second Drone unit; this was 'B' Troop, and part of 22 Battery, with drones in the XR894-XR923 range. From Perham Down, the Troop operated exclusively in support of the School of Artillery; not that that restrained further changes in title and structure.

Within a year, the Royal Artillery was again moved to reconsider the title of the Battery when, on 18 March 1964, it was re-styled as 22 Locating Battery, RA. However, at the same time the Battery's parent unit, 21 Locating Regiment, RA (which despite also being re-styled as such) was placed into suspended animation and 22 Locating Battery, RA continued as an independent unit.[4]

---

4 The Royal Artillery has traditionally described the closure or disbandment of a Regiment as being 'placed in suspended animation'.

SD-1 XR923 was operated by 94 Locating Regiment, RA and is seen receiving final pre take-off adjustments by a Sergeant during a Regimental exercise in Denmark. (HQ 1 Div (PR) BAOR Neg. No BV/66/52/4)

Surveillance Drones for the Army   291

Undergoing an engine test-run on a German Range is Northrop SD-1 XR331. In an attempt not to generate lift during an engine-run the wings have not been fitted. However, judging by the expression on the faces of the ground crew, the drone still required a fair degree of holding down. (via Lt.Col. J.J.Cooke)

Drone Operations at the sharp end

Lt.Col (Retd) 'Jim' Cooke's introduction to unarmed surveillance drones was on the Northrop AN/USD-1 (MQM-57A). He later went on to operate CL-89 before becoming deeply involved with the prolonged GEC-Marconi Phoenix trials programme. Of the AN/USD-1 (MQM-57A) surveillance drone, he recalls:

"Flying the 'SD-1 drone was fun – there's no other term for it, even when we were launching against the clock on crash actions. The system was far from foolproof however. Radio control was nowhere near 100%, and even though the control system was supposed to have a fail-safe device that cut off the engine and deployed the parachute when contact was lost, this didn't always work. I recall an occasion when everything failed one fine summer's day over West Germany's Range 5C firing point and the miscreant drone went into a shallow landing pattern all of its own devising, landing in a nearby farmer's potato patch and within yards of the very startled farmer's wife. That cost us a very large bouquet of flowers and a large box of Milk Tray to keep that one out of the press!

The only occasion on which we actually flew under radar control during my term in West Germany as Photo Interpreter was memorable. Launch and handover to the radar went smoothly and soon the radar controller was happily flying the drone in long oval patterns over the length of the Hohne gun deployments and impact areas at a height of 4,000ft (1,219m). Once we had established that all was well, I told him to bring the aircraft down to 2,000ft (610m) and to position it for a photographic run over our designated target area. It seemed to be taking an age to reduce height and no matter what angle the 'pilot' put on his controls, the aircraft didn't seem to want to respond. Then the spot of light on the rolling map disappeared and we knew then that we had lost it. Panic buttons were hit and we proceeded to try and forecast where the parachute landing would have taken place. The recovery crew radioed back that nothing could be found, and no parachute had been seen. Eventually, we sent them to the grid reference where the spot of light had disappeared, and, sure enough there it was – buried in a large hole where it had dived vertically downwards at full throttle! At the subsequent Court of Enquiry, the altimeter display in the rear cabin was found to have been incapable of keeping up with the rate of descent. It could only handle a maximum rate of descent of around 10ft/sec. Thus, while it was still reading 3,000ft (914m), the drone was in fact in a steep dive and about to make a huge impact!"

Lt.Col (Retd) J. 'Jim' J. Cooke, RA

Northrop KD2R-5 (MQM-36A) Technical Data

Powerplant	One 95hp McCulloch O-100-3, 4-cylinder horizontally-opposed engine; two-blade fixed-pitch laminated wooden propeller.
Wing span	3.50 m (11 ft 6 in)
Overall length	3.85 m (12 ft 7½ in)
Overall height	0.76 m (2 ft 6 in)
Empty weight	123 kg (271 lb)
Max launch weight	163 kg (360 lb)
Max speed at sea level	175 kt (324 km/h; 202 mph)
Cruising speed	144 kt (267 km/h; 166 mph)
Stalling speed	58 kt (108 km/h; 67 mph)
Ceiling	7,000 m (23,000 ft)
Range (with max fuel)	180 nm (333 km; 207 miles)

Source: *Jane's All the World's Aircraft*, 1970–71 edition.

Northrop SD-1 (MQM-57A) Technical Data

Powerplant	One 92hp McCulloch O-100-2, 4-cylinder horizontally-opposed engine; two-blade fixed-pitch laminated wooden propeller.
Wing span	3.50 m (11 ft 6 in) without wing pods 4.01 m (13 ft 2 in) with wing pods
Overall length	4.09 m (13 ft 5 in)
Overall height	0.80 m (2 ft 7½ in)
Empty weight	161 kg (354 lb)
Max launch weight	200 kg (442 lb)
Max speed at sea level	174 kt (323 km/h; 201 mph)
Cruising speed	144 kt (267 km/h; 166 mph)
Ceiling	4,570 m (15,000 ft)
Endurance at sea level	35 minutes

Source: *Jane's All the World's Aircraft*, 1970–71 edition.

The Battery existed as an independent unit for almost four years, until late-1967 when 22 received an order to deploy its drone-equipped 'B' Troop to Celle, West Germany and become part of 94 Locating Regiment, RA. The move, which actually took place in March 1968, appears not to have involved the entire Battery as elements of the Troop remained at Larkhill for some time afterwards. The final flight, in support of the Larkhill-based School of Artillery, took place on 26 January 1969 at an Artillery demonstration over the Salisbury Plain Ranges. The occasion, it was said, was a highly emotional day, not least because "the drone disappointed the large crowd in attendance by flying perfectly and not becoming involved in a spectacular crash!"

Northrop's surveillance drone remained in service with the British Army until early 1972 when it was superceded by the Canadair CL-89 (AN/USD-501) Midge drone. The surviving MQM-57As were sold as scrap in 1974 to Larry Bax, late of Aerial Target Services. All were conveyed to Bax's store at nearby Amesbury, Wiltshire where some are thought to have been refurbished and exported to Belgium.[5] Two others (XT581 & XT584) were retained by the Royal School of Artillery but later passed on to Museums, One other (XR898) found its way to a Kent Air Training Corps Squadron whilst the remainder, which comprised damaged fuselages and sundry bits and pieces, eventually came to light some years later in a garden centre at Stapehill, Dorset. It is thought that this was the source of one MQM-57A (XV383) that later turned up at the Bournemouth Aviation Museum but which was sadly broken down to enable the restoration of MQM-36A Shelduck XR346.

---

[5] As related to the author by Larry Bax.

Summary of Contracts involving Northrop KD2R-5 (MQM-36A) Shelduck training drones & AN/USD-1 (MQM-57A) surveillance drones for the Army

Contract	Contract Date	Serial Range	Allotment Date	Quantity	Remarks
KF/5R/08/CB25(b)	1.9.60	XR290-XR315 XR331-XR336	9.11.60	32	AN/USD-1 (MQM-57A)
KD/5R/011/CB25(b)	27.2.61	XR345-XR356	9.11.60	12	KD2R-5 (MQM-36A)
		XR404-XR428	9.11.60	25	OQ-19 (MQM-33)
KK/T/014/CB25(b)	7.12.61	XR927-XR938	2.2.62	12	KD2R-5 (MQM-36A)
KK/T/016/CB25(b)	13.4.62	XR894-XR898 XR916-XR923	2.2.62	13	AN/USD-1 (MQM-57A)
KK/T/038/CB25(b)	27.10.64	XT580-XT589	23.9.64	10	MQM-57A/3
KK/T/048/CB20(a)	20.6.66	XV378-XV389	20.10.66	12	MQM-57A/3
KK/T/059/CB20(c)*	unkn	XW594-XW603	13.12.68	10	MQM-36A
K20C/65/6*	unkn	XW803-XW832	17.7.70	30	MQM-36A

*Contracts KK/T/059/CB20(c) and K20C/65/6 were originally placed on behalf of the Royal Navy's Pilotless Target Association but involved aircraft procured for use by the RAE in connection with Blowpipe trials. A number were later released to the RNPTA.

Northrop KD2R-5 (MQM-36A) and AN/USD-1 (MQM-57A) Individual Aircraft Histories

Contract KF/5R/08/CB25(b): 32 AN/USD-1 (MQM-57A)

Note that whilst the first batch of AN/USD-1s were consigned to Melton Mowbray the former Commanding Officer of the Trials Unit recalls that the aircraft were collected from Southampton docks. It is just possible therefore that the first shipment did not reach its consigned address.

XR290-XR302 Dptd USA (Wilmington, California) aboard SS *Pacific Reliance* 11.5.61; consigned to Tech Stores Sub Depot, Old Dalby, Melton Mowbray. Most, if not all, issued to 22 Locating Battery (eg XR296, XR299 and XR302 noted at Larkhill May 1965); others to 57 Battery, RA. No further details recorded.

XR303-XR315 Dptd USA (Terminal Island, California) aboard SS *California Star* 26.10.61; consigned to Tech Stores Sub depot, Old Dalby, Melton Mowbray. XR304, XR306, XR309 and XR314 noted with 22 Locating Battery, RA in May 1965; others to 57 Battery, RA. No further details recorded.

XR331-XR336 Shipped ex-USA with XR303 etc. XR333 noted with 22 Locating Battery, RA in May 1965; others issued to 57 Battery, RA. No further details recorded.

Contract KF/5R/011/CB25(b): 12 KD2R-5/MQM-36A Shelduck

XR345-XR356 (allocated 'c/ns' UK136 to UK147) were procured for use as basic training aircraft prior to conversion training on MQM-57A. All 12 departed Wilmington, California 19.1.61 aboard SS *Pacific Reliance* 19.1.61 and consigned to Old Dalby, Melton Mowbray. No further details recorded apart from XR346 being restored at the Bournemouth Museum (and by using parts from XV383). Their present whereabouts are unknown.

XR345 Dptd USA 19.1.61 aboard SS *Pacific Reliance*; consigned to Melton Mowbray. SOC 20.6.62 after crashing into the sea, location unkn.

XR346 Shipped ex-USA with XR345 etc. Noted with 22 Locating Battery, RA in May 1965. No operational details known but eventually acquired by Bournemouth Aircraft Museum. Still extant 2009.

XR347-XR351 Shipped ex-USA with XR345 etc. All noted with 22 Locating Battery, RA in May 1965. Details of fates unknown.

XR352 Shipped ex-USA with XR345 etc. Tfd to RNPTA between 1-7.61; f/f with RNPTA 13.3.62. Crashed into the sea immediately after launch 19.6.62. (TFH 2.10; 4 flights)

XR353 Shipped ex-USA with XR345 etc. Noted with 22 Locating Battery, RA in May 1965. Fate unknown.

XR354 Shipped ex-USA with XR345 etc. Stored until tfd to Royal Navy; noted at Portland by 7.61; TOC RNPTA charge 10.61. Lost at sea 14.12.62. SOC 17.12.62. (TFH 5.48; 9 flights)

XR355-XR356 were shipped ex-USA with XR345 etc. XR356 was noted with 22 Locating Battery, RA in May 1965. No further details known.

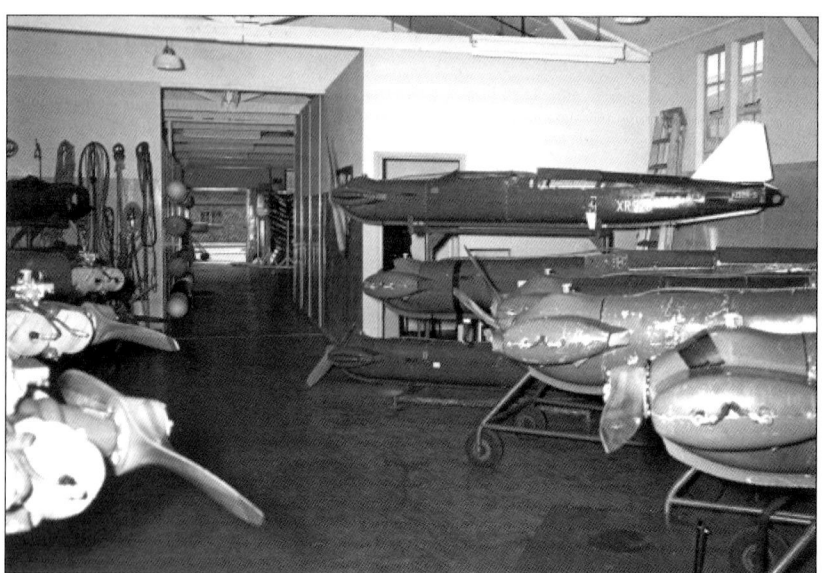

Contract KF/5R/011/CB25(b): 25 OQ-19 Surveillance drones

XR404-XR428 were originally purchased by the MoA (prior to 1957) for a series of trials at RAE Aberporth. These trials were subsequently cancelled before any of the aircraft had been assembled and flown; all were stored. When the Army adopted the Northrop AN/USD-1 drone in 1960 the OQ-19s were added to the initial contract for KD2R-5 training target aircraft and to help with the working-up process. Unfortunately official files remain silent on further details.

Contract KK/T/016/CB25(b): 13 (AN/USD-1) MQM-57A

XR894-XR898 Dptd USA 20.12.62 by ship; consigned to Old Dalby, Melton Mowbray.

XR898 noted with 22 Locating Battery, RA in May 1965. Later passed to Air Training Corps. Presented to the Medway Aircraft Presentation Society (Ltd) 1992 and restored. Statically displayed with spurious serial 'XT005'.

XR916-XR923 Shipped ex-USA with XR894 etc. Most, if not all, allocated to 22 Battery, RA. No further details recorded.

Contract KK/T/014/CB25(b): 12 (KD2R-5) MQM-36A Shelduck

XR927 Dptd USA 13.7.62 by ship; consigned to Tech Stores, Old Dalby, Melton Mowbray. Noted with 22 Locating Battery, RA in May 1965. No further details known.

XR928 Shipped with XR927 etc. Noted with 22 Locating Battery, RA in May 1965. Tfd to RNPTA 1969. Crashed 5.3.70, details and location not known. (TFH 2.10)

XR929-XR933 Shipped with XR927 etc. XR931 & 932 noted with 22 Locating Battery, RA in May 1965. No further details known.

When the Canadair CL-89 Midge drone was selected as a successor to the Army SD-1 (MQM-57A), the surviving KD2R-5 (MQM-36A) Shelduck training drones were also withdrawn from service. These were offered to the Royal Navy PTA who took a number of airworthy examples. One of those, XR928, is seen here in the RNPTA Hangar at Portland on 8 September 1969, shortly after transfer from the Army. (HMS Osprey, Portland; Neg No. G0746)

The annual Army Show held on fields alongside Aldershot's Queen's Avenue Parade Ground almost always included a statically-displayed SD-1 drone from 22 Locating Battery, RA. Drones displayed at Aldershot (such as XT584 shown here) always carried their JATO launchers, unlike at other shows. Strangely, when the US designation was radically overhauled and the AN/USD-1 became the MQM-57A, the Army continued to refer to it as the SD-1. (Peter J. Cooper)

XR934 Shipped with XR927 etc. Transferred to RNPTA 1969. Crashed 6.10.70 immediately after launch.

XR935 Shipped with XR927 etc. Noted with 22 Locating Battery, RA in May 1965. Tfd to RNPTA 1969. Lost 7.7.70, details and location not known (TFH 4.40)

XR936-XR938 Shipped with XR927 etc. XR938 noted with 22 Locating Battery, RA in May 1965. No further details known.

Contract KK/T/038/CB25(b):
10 MQM-57A/3

XT580-XT589 Dptd USA (Terminal Island, California) aboard SS *California Star* 11.5.65; consigned to Tech Stores Sub Depot, Old Dalby, Melton Mowbray.

XT581 was donated by the Central Ordnance Depot, Donnington to the Imperial War Museum, Duxford in August 1978. Currently on static display.

XT584 was donated to the Royal Artillery Museum, Woolwich (London) and statically displayed within the Cold War Exhibition.

Contract KK/T/048/CB20(a):
12 MQM-57A/3

XV378-XV389 Dptd USA (Wilmington, California) aboard SS *Dinteldyk* 31.3.67; consigned to Tech Stores Sub Depot, Old Dalby, Melton Mowbray. No further details recorded.

MQM-57A/3 XV383 was acquired by the Bournemouth Aviation Museum but never exhibited. Parts of it were used in the restoration of MQM-36A Shelduck XR346. The discarded remains were disposed to a private buyer in 2007.

Contract KK/T/59/CB20(b):
10 MQM-36A Shelduck

XW594-XW603 Shipping, consignment and operational details not known. This batch of 10 targets was delivered to the Army solely as basic training aircraft. XW595 and 596 are known to have later transferred from the Army to RNPTA Portland in 9.76. XW596 was used to assist in the rebuild of XW812 at Portland.

(Contract KK/T/59/CB20(b) also involved 10 aircraft for the RNPTA. These were XW571-XW580, details of which are included within Chapter 6.)

Contract K20C/65/6:
10 MQM-36A Shelduck

XW803-XW832 Shipping, consignment and operational details not known. XW812 was later damaged and repaired using XW596 as a component source.

Canadair AN/USD-501 (CL-89) 'Midge'

Canadair entered the unmanned aircraft sector in the late-1950s when the company responded to a Canadian Army Aerial Target Requirement for its 'Honest John' artillery missile. Design work effectively began in 1959 and over a period of time the Canadair CL-89 became an Anglo-Canadian government-inspired project, evolving from an aerial target to a high-speed reconnaissance drone. By June 1963 the Canadian and British governments had formally agreed to sponsor design, development, test and evaluation of a reconnaissance drone variant designed to provide tactical intelligence in forward battle areas. The system was based on studies that Canadair had carried out on target drones for Sparrow missile testing.

Flight-testing began in March 1964, a year before West Germany joined the project. The new partner agreed to share, as part of a tripartite agreement, the cost of design, development, test and evaluation.[6]

After some six years of flight-testing prototypes, tri-service flight trials of production models at Shilo, Manitoba began in early-1970. By the time that production started at Canadair's Cartierville, facility in Montreal, the CL-89 had become re-designated the Canadair AN/USD-501 as part of an US-inspired system of designating NATO drones and missiles within a common sequence; those of Canadian origin were placed within the block 500-599. Deliveries of AN/USD-501 drones began in September 1971 when an initial batch of 282 drones was shipped to Europe.

Despite its US-style designation, Britain always used the manufacturer's designation CL-89. It was occasionally referred to as 'Midge' but for most of its life was known simply as 'Drone'. The first CL-89 trial flights in the UK took place over the Hebrides Range during October 1971 by the reformed 'B' (Drone) Troop of 22 Locating Battery, RA. The flights met with success and the Canadair CL-89 Midge entered service with the British Army in early-1972.

Fired by a 2,065kg British booster rocket from a short rail launcher mounted on the rear of a Bedford 4x4 truck the

---

[6] The Italian manufacturer, Meteor SpA, joined later and the drone was ordered by the Italian armed forces. By mid-1978 production had passed the 500 mark when the French Army became the fifth nation to adopt the AN/USD-501.

Surveillance Drones for the Army   295

The Canadair CL-89 Midge was always known in Army circles as simply 'the drone'. Midge entered British service in early-1972 and served the Royal Artillery for twenty years. One of the few survivors is preserved at Roberts Barracks, Larkhill and is seen on permanent display outside 22 Battery's Headquarters on 14 April 1983. Note the 32 Regiment, RA insignia on the nose. (Michael I Draper)

CL-89 was essentially a recoverable missile capable of performing a reconnaissance mission. As soon as the drone had achieved flying speed the booster was jettisoned and a 57kg thrust Williams Research WR2-6 turbojet took over propulsion. The drone then flew a pre-programmed course, scanned the target area with an infra-red linescan camera before taking photographs or infra-red images at preset intervals. The standard camera fitted to British CL-89s was a Zeiss (automatic exposure control) tri-lens system capable of taking oblique, starboard and vertical pictures at day or night. When its mission was completed it homed to a radio beacon and descended by recovery parachute. During the final descent phase large landing bags inflated automatically to prevent damage on impact. CL-89 was a difficult target for the enemy. It flew at high subsonic speed, its noise and heat levels were low and its flight pattern was pre-programmed and therefore could not be jammed. Not only was it hard to see, it was very hard to shoot down. Expected life of a CL-89 drone was around 10 flights with unit level repair; however some drones survived over 40 flights.

Midge performed well for the Army but it had its limitations, none more so than its operational system which was based on dead-reckoning. The operator, having been advised of the proposed target, pre-plotted the drone's intended course on a map and then calculated a programme based on required action for 'each kilometer' of flight. Midge could only perform a maximum of five fixed radius turns (to left or right) and two camera actions, i.e. "camera-on, camera-off, camera-on, camera-off".

Once the drone's course had been plotted and checked the operator then manually set the drone's Programme Unit which was an electro-mechanically operated unit in the nose section. The operator would simply queue the sequence in by depressing a series of buttons. The programmer also dialled in wind direction and planned changes in altitude. The drone, in the words of one operator, was 'delightfully simple providing the plot had been measured and calculated correctly'.

It was not until the 1991 Gulf War that Midge drones were had the opportunity to be used in a 'real-war' situation. They were operated by 57 (Bhurtpore) Locating Battery although the drones used were in fact loaned from 22 Locating Battery, RA. British CL-89s made some seventy surveillance flights over enemy lines. While results were described at the time as being outstanding, it was also becoming increasingly apparent that fast-moving tank warfare across open desert did not present the unit with a realistic opportunity for deployment. By the time the 'bread wagon' had driven out to retrieve the cameras and the film had been processed as 'wet prints', the tanks had moved on!

Apart from conflict in the Middle East, the political geography of Europe changed dramatically during the late-1980s and early-1990s. East and West Germany had re-unified, Czechoslovakia had been split into two and communist regimes in Hungary, Rumania and Bulgaria were toppled. By the end of 1991 the foundations of the non-aligned communist Federal Republic of Yugoslavia had also began to crumble.

When Slovenia and Croatia broke away from the Serb-dominated Yugoslav republic both countries received international recognition. When, however, the Muslims of Bosnia-Herzogenia tried to do the same the Bosnian Serb minority (supported by Belgrade) resisted fiercely. Because almost one-third of the Bosnian population was ethnic Croatian, the Muslims found themselves as a minority within their own self-proclaimed state. Before long a bitter tripartite civil war broke out.

A UK Artillery force was assembled, the major components of which were 5 (Gibraltar 1779-83) Field Battery,RA and (as it then still was) 22 (Gibraltar 1779-83) Locating Battery, RA. The locating equipment selected was 'C' Troop's sound-ranging microphones with 'A' Troop taking Vaisala as meteorological support. Ironically, 'B' Troop's (now) veteran CL-89 Midge drones, by now long since due for replacement, remained behind at Larkhill.

The last Midge exercise took place in Germany during November and December 1992 at the Scherbenhof Camp, Hohne. The drones of 'B' Troop, 22 Locating Battery, RA flew throughout the exercise, the last flight occurring on 8 December. That flight marked the end of the CL-89 Midge drone in British service.

The surviving drones were sold to the German forces at a time when the drone's successor, the GEC/Marconi Phoenix, was far from ready to replace it.

Canadair CL-89 Midge Technical Data	
Wing span	3 ft 1 in (0.94 m)
Length	8 ft 6 in (2.60m) without booster
	12 ft 2 in (3.71 m) with booster
Body diameter	1 ft 1 in (0.33 m)
Launch weight	342.3 lb (155.6 kg) with booster
	220 lb (100 kg) without booster
Max speed	400 kt (740 km/h; 460 mph)
Max range	56.7 nm (105 km; 65.2 miles)

Units Operating CL-89 Midge

94 (Locating) Regiment, RA

By 1981 94 (Locating) Regiment, RA had three Batteries: 'Q' Battery,RA; 57 Battery, RA; and 156 Battery,RA each of which operated a Drone Troop. Throughout its time in West Germany the Regiment was headquartered at Celle until October 1985 when 94 Regiment transferred back to the UK, to Larkhill, having lost some of its Batteries to other Regiments: 57 Battery, RA was transferred to 32 Heavy Regiment, RA (and based at Dortmund, Germany) and 'Q' Battery moved to 5 Regiment, RA. All that then remained of 94 (Locating) Regiment was 156 Battery, RA.

To restore the Regiment to full complement, 22 (Locating) Battery, which hitherto had been an Independent Battery lost that status and, on 31 January 1986, was absorbed into 94 Regiment, RA. 5 Battery,RA (a light gun unit) was also added, as was HQ Commander, Land Forces (later re-styled AMF/L).

In September 1993 94 Regiment, RA went into suspended animation. A complex series of changes followed: AMF/L and 5 Battery, RA were transferred to 19 Regiment, RA whilst the two remaining Batteries (22 Battery, RA and 156 Battery, RA) were merged and re-titled 22 Battery, RA. The 'new' 22 Battery, RA then became part of 32 Regiment, RA, which at the time was headquartered at Dortmund, Germany. (Since 1985 57 Battery,RA had been 32 Regiment's only Locating Battery, as described earlier. However when 22 Battery, RA joined the Regiment, 57 Battery,RA was transferred out to Paderborn to join 39 Regiment, RA and to become that Regiment's Locating Battery.)

32 Regiment, RA

57 Battery, RA joined the Regiment (ex-94 (Locating) Regiment, RA) in February 1985 and moved from Celle to the Regimental HQ at Dortmund. The Battery later deployed to the Middle East in 1991 to take part in Operation 'Granby'.

In April 1993, 57 Battery,RA was transferred from 32 Regiment, RA to 39 Regiment, RA and took up residence at Paderborn. To maintain a drone element, 22 Battery, RA was transferred from 94 Regiment, RA to 32 Regiment, RA in September 1993. At the same time 32 Regiment, RA transferred from Dortmund to Larkhill.

39 Regiment, RA

Roled as a medium-artillery regiment since 1972, 39 Regiment was located at Paderborn, Germany. In 1993 the drone-equipped 57 Battery, RA was transferred to 39 Regiment. Two years later the Regiment left (Sennelager) Germany and took up residence at Newcastle. 57 Battery was the first battery to be equipped with Phoenix UAV (see later).

In 2003 57 Battery transferred to 32 Regiment, RA whilst 74 Battery left 32 Regiment, RA to join 39 Regiment, RA making 39 Regiment a single capability MLRS Regiment.

Supervisor & Phoenix

In its call for a small, unmanned helicopter capable of carrying out surveillance by live television or a day/night Thermal Imager, the Ministry of Defence (Procurement Executive), in 1974, formally launched its Supervisor programme. The objective was to eventually procure an airborne surveillance vehicle capable of locating enemy targets for attack by either artillery or a Multiple Launch Rocket System (MLRS). An operational range of around fifty kilometers was required.

From the outset Supervisor was fundamentally an already-established joint programme between Marconi and Westland, the proposed air vehicle being simply an upgraded Wideye (see Chapter 10). A prototype had been built and test-flown but Westland was becoming increasingly concerned over Marconi's stabilized television system. So much so, that in 1976, Westland turned instead to Ferranti's Electro-Optics Department (EOD) in Edinburgh. Westland re-designed Supervisor to incorporate the preferred Ferranti system but for reasons that have never been fully-explained were then unable to have the changes approved by the MoD Supervisor Project Office.

By late-1979 the Supervisor project began to suffer numerous technical shortcomings. The on-going reliability of Westland's mini-helicopter was reportedly brought into question, as were apparent oversights in the original General Staff Requirement. In fact, so much concern was being expressed that, in spite of some £28million having already been expended, the entire Supervisor project was cancelled.

In cancelling Supervisor, Britain's quest for a new airborne surveillance system had effectively been thrown back to Square One. However, in an almost uncharacteristically romantic twist, from the ashes of Supervisor arose Phoenix, a title given to a new Feasibility Study RFP (Request for Proposal), announced in June 1981 (which was later built into GSR 3486).[7]

---

7 With the cancellation of SUPERVISOR, MoD Contracts Branch concentrated on two linked Requirements, CASTOR and PHOENIX. CASTOR was an acronym for **C**orps **A**irborne **St**and-**O**ff **R**adar to provide a platform for a medium level battlefield radar with a low grazing angle beyond the Forward Edge of the Battlefield Area (FEBA) That, in turn would provide data back to BATES (**B**attlefield **A**rtillery **T**arget **E**ngagement **S**ystem) which would also receive more refined and low-level data from PHOENIX, a self-recoverable drone system with on-board sensors scanning beyond the FEBA. CASTOR was originally aimed at providing a system to be fitted to the photo-reconnaissance Canberra and shortly afterwards it was decided to disengage CASTOR from the Army and transfer it to RAF control, thus losing the initial 'C' in the process.

What followed was most certainly an extremely complex and often confusing series of proposals and counter proposals that eventually left many to wonder if the end result was actually what the Army genuinely wanted. Fourteen different proposals were considered before the MoD Procurement Executive down-selected to four bidders in what was later seen as the first round in the Phoenix Project selection process. This initial stage was described within Army circles as a 'paper' exercise involving four likely contenders: Ferranti, Marconi-Avionics, British Aerospace Dynamics, and Westland/BHC.

The proposal from British Aerospace Dynamics owed much to experience gained from the company's Stabileye programme. Based on an expendable vehicle it was designed around the company's own infra-red linescan system. However, the British Aerospace Dynamics proposal was dropped at quite an early stage.

Despite the frustration of Westland's experience with Supervisor, the company did respond to the MoD's invitation to propose solutions to the revised Phoenix requirement. The WHL concept was based on a derivative of its WR07/08 configuration but was sufficiently and radically reworked to combine low weight, long endurance, advanced sensors and a sophisticated anti-jamming data link. The programme was designated Westland WR.10 and the proposed prototype was configured as an ultra-low signature airframe that made use of the Wideye rotor system.

Westland undertook an international market survey using a close derivative of Wideye to be known as 'Sharpeye' although the proposal for Phoenix was never specifically (or officially) named. It was always referred to as the WR.10, several models of which were built for wind tunnel radar signature tests.[8] WR.10 would have continued with the Manoeuvre Demand Control System that had initially been proposed for Supervisor but with an added Thermal Imaging Sensor to replace the television sensor previously provided by GEC Marconi. WR.10 also featured a Spread Spectrum Data Link and full integration with the Army's ground-based artillery command and control system (BATES). In searching for a suitable powerplant, Westland turned to Norton Motors and selected the 294cc water-cooled engine rated at 28hp. The Norton Wankel engine was later to become virtually a standard UAV power unit, supplied around the world by UEL. Westland's selection of this engine, combined with a radical rework of the fuselage aerodynamics, allowed the WR10 to achieve double the endurance of the proposed operational Supervisor air vehicle at a reduced gross weight.

The natural choice of a suitable supplier for the Phoenix payload, AFCS and data-link was, of course, GEC Marconi. However, at the time, Westland was not willing to re-establish any collaboration with GEC Marconi and instead selected a 'cut back' Lockheed Aquila link (known in the US as MICNS). A well-proven design by an experienced supplier, MICNS featured an effective anti-jamming facility. (It was claimed by Westland that the GEC link had very little protection from jamming.) Westland's preferred Thermal Imager was a design by Rank-Pullin and after several productive meetings in Edinburgh, the stabilized platform was to be supplied by Ferranti. Smiths Industries was selected as the proposed supplier of an AFCS. However, when it became clear that the Phoenix project was to be based on a fixed-price contract, Westlands – and purely for commercial reasons – withdrew from the MoD project.

Ferranti Phoenix Proposal

Ferranti offered two proposals, one based on a rotary wing concept; the other using a fixed-wing vehicle. For its rotary-wing proposal, Ferranti had teamed up with Canadair and the CL-227 unmanned helicopter. This was not the first time that the CL-227 had figured in British thinking. Back in December 1972 a small team of RAE engineers had visited Canadair to discuss a feasibility study to meet GSR3494. At the time Canadair's CL-89 (AN/USD-501) drone was still in production whilst two months of wind tunnel testing the CL-227, a (then) radical design had just been completed.[9]

The fuselage of the CL-227 (or 'the stack', as Canadair referred to it) consisted of a dumb-bell shaped cylindrical body with a co-axial contra-rotating rotor and four fixed landing struts. It was to be powered by a small shaft horsepower gas turbine engine and to Ferranti engineers the CL-227 was referred to as a 'jet-powered Flying Peanut'.[10]

Ferranti's proposal for a fixed-wing air vehicle was based on a Short Brothers' design, but the Belfast manufacturer argued that, because of its previous experience with unmanned aircraft, any joint venture with Ferranti had to involve Shorts becoming the prime contractor. Ferranti refused to accept these terms and called what they believed to be Shorts' bluff. The Belfast manufacturer promptly withdrew.[11]

Just before Shorts took the decision to pull out of any collaboration, Ferranti was approached by AEL, a small company based at Crawley, West Sussex which, in the past, had produced a range of small-arms target aircraft for the Army. Ferranti asked AEL to produce a study proposal.[12]

From the contenders in the first round, as many as sixteen design proposals were put forward. Curiously, the Ferranti-Canadair proposal emerged as the most favoured project while also finding favour with MoD(PE) was the Ferranti-AEL fixed-wing proposal, so much so that contracts were prepared. Of the other contenders, the Westland project (designated Westland WR.10) was thought to be far too complicated whilst the British Aerospace, GEC and Marconi Avionics' proposals were simply rejected at an early stage.

---

8   One of these models was later permanently loaned to the International Helicopter Museum, Weston-super-Mare.

9   National Archives AVIA6/25537

10 Cynics described the CL-227 turbine power unit as 'expensive and hot'. Furthermore its shape was driven by its stacked layout making it quite a tall air vehicle. The 'peanut' shape never was and never could be a true low-signature design. As an aside it has been claimed that after exploratory talks between Westland and Ferranti – during which Westland emphasised the need for a low-signature design – Ferranti chose to drop the Canadair CL-227 and instead concentrate on its fixed-wing proposal.

11 Much of the detail on Ferranti's Phoenix bid provided to the author by Bill Blain, former Manager, Tactical Systems Group, Ferranti Defence Systems 1966-1990.

12 As reported in *Flight International*, issue dated 2 July 1983.

The Ferranti Phoenix proposal was the only serious contender to compete with the GEC-Marconi project. Several prototypes were built by sub-contractor Slingsby Sailplanes. One of the three Slingsby T.68 Mk.1s is seen here at Charterhall airfield where, because of the restricted runway length, was launched from the roof of a 'souped-up' Land Rover! (Bill Blain)

Believing that politics had played too great a role in the selection process, a number of senior Army officers challenged the MoD's decision to award the contract to Ferranti. In fact, the Army went even further and refused to accept MoD(PE)'s decision. What became an embarrassing stalemate ultimately forced a second competition.

The main contenders for the second round were Ferranti and Marconi Avionics. The Ferranti proposal now involved a fixed-wing air vehicle carrying inertial navigation and wideband datalink equipment, plus a Thermal Imager. Ferranti's board had become nervous about collaborating with AEL (who they felt were too inexperienced in the increasingly sophisticated field of UAVs) and were relieved when AEL withdrew. Ferranti attempted to seek a collaboration with Flight Refuelling Ltd but the Dorset-based company had already become closely involved with Ferranti's main competitor, Marconi. In its search for a suitable air vehicle, Ferranti turned to Slingsby who were fast becoming specialists in the highly-relevant field of composite resin/fibre structures.

MoD was agreeable to having Slingsby involved in the design process but whilst Slingsby was equally agreeable to building an air vehicle to carry Ferranti's equipment, the Kirkbymoorside manufacturer felt that to design a new aircraft with complex launch and recovery requirements as well as a shape that ensured low detection signatures (visual, radar, sound and heat) was somewhat beyond their capability.

Convinced that there were few other British manufacturers that could sub-contract the building of an air vehicle, Ferranti sought collaboration with Lockheed (who, at the time, was involved in the equivalent Aquila programme for the Army). Ferranti also considered using the German manufacturer, Dornier, and at one stage even to buying the Israeli Scout UAV 'off-the-shelf'. (The Scout was dismissed on the grounds that it required a permanent runway for take-off.)

In the end, Ferranti came to the conclusion that the programme was best served if they designed their own air vehicle and built it in-house. Designed by a small team of Ferranti employees, all of whom were keen and experienced model aircraft makers, a prototype was constructed in the Ferranti Carpentry Shop at Robertson Avenue, Edinburgh. Built of wood and plywood, this first example was used for initial aerodynamic testing and made its first flight at Charterhall airfield, near Duns in May 1983.[13]

After flight-testing the initial prototype, four more air vehicles joined the Ferranti test programme. All were built by Slingsby Sailplanes at Kirkbymoorside and constructed in a resin-fibre material. Each was to be powered by a Normalair Garrett WAM342 engine. Three variations were

---

13 Other contractors appointed by Ferranti's Edinburgh-based Electro-Optics Department included Rank Pullin Controls who were to supply the thermal imager and MEL for the datalink.

designed by Slingsby under the general designation Slingsby T.68, two of which attained flight status, as follows:

Slingsby T.68 Mk.1 Three aircraft built (referred to as Aircraft 2, 3 & 4) with a single-piece wing and a tailplane mounted beneath the rear fuselage. Twin fins were angled downwards.

Slingsby T.68 Mk.2 One aircraft built (Aircraft 5) with a wing and tailplane split and plugged into the fuselage sides. Angled downwards, twin fins design retained.

Following test flights on the earlier aircraft, Slingsby made improvements to the electronic systems by combining them into one unit re-positioned just behind the engine. The Sensor Ball was also re-positioned slightly forwards than on earlier examples. In this guise the design was referred to as the T.68 Mk.3 but the improved model never flew; indeed it was never completed.

Although MoD partly funded the 'fly-off', rising production costs led Ferranti not to build a dedicated launcher. Instead the UAVs were mounted onto (and launched from) the roof of a V8-powered long-wheelbase Land Rover. But the first test runs proved that the length of Charterhall's runway to be insufficient in length for the Land Rover to stop. Ferranti's solution was to fit twin turbochargers to the Land Rover's V8 engine. It was, without doubt, the most powerful Land Rover of the day!

GEC-Marconi Phoenix

Ferranti's only competitor in the final selection process was (the now newly-named) GEC-Marconi Avionics contender. This was based on a fixed-wing air vehicle, with the ability to be flown both autonomously or by remote control, carrying a Class III common-module thermal imager (TICM II) and microwave real-time datalink. Ground facilities involved a mobile control station with monopulse datalink tracking system and a remote data terminal. In formulating its bid for the Phoenix contract, GEC-Marconi had already selected Flight Refuelling Ltd to design and build the air vehicle whilst the then GEC-Marconi-Avionics Division was responsible for the flight control and navigation, turret-mounted stabilized Thermal Imager, datalink and overall integration.

Final designs were submitted to the MoD on Friday 1 June 1984, followed by formal bids in the following September.

Of the contenders in the second round, GEC Avionics (as Marconi Avionics had become known) was announced as the winning design on 15 February 1985. The submission found favour essentially as it was based on a fixed-price of around £80million and offered full integration with the planned procurement of the BATES (Battlefield Artillery Target Engagement System) system. Ferranti, convinced that theirs was the preferred tender, later learnt that their bid had been undercut by approximately 27% and that GEC-Marconi had offered delivery some ten months ahead of them, in 1988. Marconi was also considered to be an 'odds-on' bet because of the company's experience in the Supervisor and Machan programmes. What won over the Army in favouring the GEC-Marconi option was that it was to be equipped with Marconi's Thermal Imaging Common Module (TICM II), a system common to the Army's Challenger tank.

Responsibility for design and building the air vehicle rested with Flight Refuelling Ltd and came at a time when production of the company's ASAT target drone was winding down. Phoenix introduced many new concepts including (for a low radar signature) a sandwich composite construction using materials such as Kevlar, glass fibre, carbon reinforced plastics and Nomex honeycomb, something that caused Flight Refuelling's designers a

The first prototype Phoenix (A01) was purely a flight control system trials aircraft and was first flown on 30 May 1986. It was never fitted with a sensor, nor the final datalink. Although it was designed to be recovered conventionally by parachute the fin was representative of the crushable 'hump' that was fitted to the Phoenix B models. Its only function on the prototype was to help achieve correct drag and inertias from a control law viewpoint. The 'lump' on the very bottom represented the TICM II turret but was actually a foam block which the aircraft landed on. Seen at the start of trials at Larkhill, Phoenix Development Team leader Major David Potts stands to the fore (with his ever-faithful spaniel) and with other members of the Team. (via Major D Potts)

A 1987 view of the first Phoenix B, seen as the first of a pre-production batch is close to resembling the final design. (GEC Avionics Ltd Neg. No.C9476, via Ken Munson)

After a safe landing the pod is lifted clear of the aircraft. In this view of Phoenix B02 the modified wing tips can be clearly seen as can be the 'weight and space model' instead of a genuine TICM II turret. Note that the propeller has stopped in the horizontal position; this was designed to prevent damage and was achieved by arranging the propeller to be horizontal at the compression stroke of the simultaneously firing flat-twin engine. The roundel applied beneath the starboard wing was unofficial. (via Major D. Potts)

Phoenix B04 is gently lowered from an Army Land Rover at Larkhill on 13 July 1987. Phoenix was originally designed in such a manner that in a dismantled state it would fit neatly into a standard Land Rover. (via Major D. Potts)

Surveillance Drones for the Army

Phoenix B05 is about to be hoisted onto its launcher in what would be the ideal semi-secluded launch location. It is likely that this is a specially-posed shot, taken for publicity purposes. (GEC-Marconi, Neg No. C10239)

number of headaches. Until then, Flight Refuelling's airframe experience had been almost exclusively with metal aircraft and in many respects, perhaps not surprisingly, the Phoenix air vehicle was designed as if it *was* a metal airframe. That led to a number of difficulties during the early testing phase.

To counter Flight Refuelling's lack of experience in composites, the manufacture of the first batch of five Phoenix prototype Air Vehicles – referred to as Phoenix A and individually identified as A01 to A05 – was sub-contracted to Herman Smith HITCO), a Worcestershire company that specialized in composites. Manufactured parts were then conveyed to Wimborne where, and after software had been delivered from GEC-Marconi's Rochester plant, final assembly and pre-delivery testing took place.

A rig, known as the 'Iron Bird' was constructed at Wimborne which allowed each Phoenix prototype to be fully ground-tested before initial flight tests took place at Lulworth, Dorset in May 1986.[14]

Phoenix, by most accounts, performed well during these flights especially in the recovery stage. Based on experience gained with ASAT Falconet (which recovered in nose-down attitude) it was always intended that Phoenix would recover in the inverted position. An overwing fairing, referred to as a Ground Impact Device (GID), was constructed of an impact-absorbing foam matrix as was the fin, both of which were designed to be crushable on landing. Of greatest importance was the safety of the under-fuselage pod containing camera and imagery equipment. (In the fullness of time, the foam used became subject to the Montreal protocol which caused a re-think and re-design of the impact-absorbing fin and resulted in its replacement with an air bag.)

The original 'Model A' prototypes were fitted with a crushable dome, a sensor with an off-the-shelf home video camera and were flown using standard radio control. Early test flights did not perform to expectations and as a result Phoenix underwent some major design changes. (In fact the Model A was always viewed as a 'stepping stone' for flight control evaluation.) A second batch of prototypes that were planned to incorporate a number of design changes were designated Phoenix B. The changes included replacing the Ground Impact Device with an Air Bag, the fitting of new Antenna Steering algorithms, a new Parachute Carriage and Release and a new Ground Impact detection device. Another feature introduced on Phoenix B was the turned-down wingtips.

One area of contention was that GSR3486 demanded a maximum weight of 130kg. This limit had been set because of the need for Phoenix to be man-maneuverable and able to be transported inside a standard Land Rover. When Full Model

---

14 Flight Refuelling was also awarded design authority for the Phoenix launcher. In a move that was never fully explained (although clearly a politically-inspired decision) the company was directed to use a launcher built in the USA by Philadelphia-based All-American Industries. The launcher had originally been designed for the Lockheed Aquila UAV. Launchers were built for mounting onto a 4-ton lorry; eventually Flight Refuelling produced ten launchers for the Army.

1

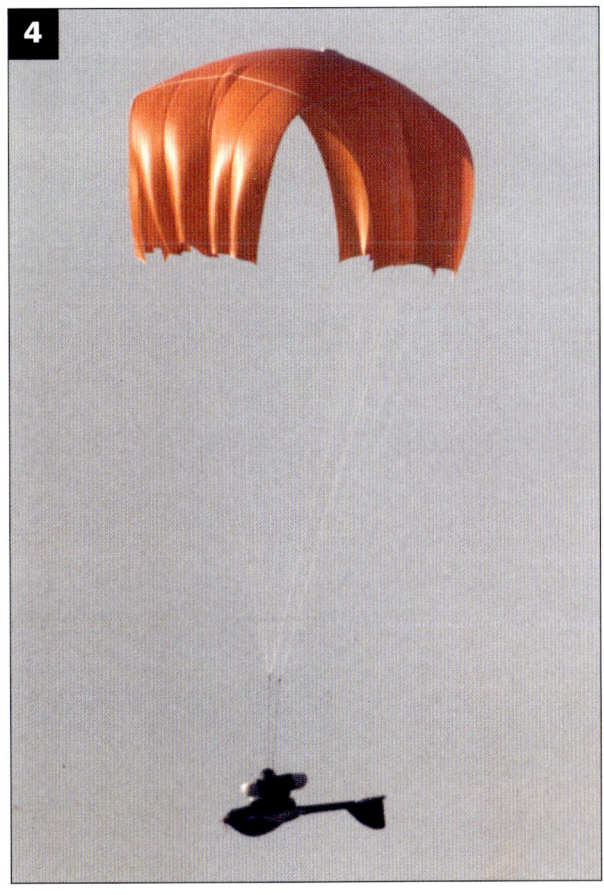

2

3

4

One of the pre-production Phoenix B models (now fitted with the definitive fin shape) recovers by parachute during trials at Larkhill on 16 November 1988. The engine has already stopped and the main 'chute has deployed in such a way that the aircraft adopts its intended inverted position so that the impact of landing is absorbed by the crushable fin and fuselage 'hump'. The camera and pod are, as a consequence, undamaged. (via Major D. Potts)

Surveillance Drones for the Army

With a re-styled fuselage 'hump' and dorsal fin extensions this Phoenix B was probably one of the more attractive variations in Phoenix design development (GEC-Avionics Ltd Neg. No. W3388/8, via Ken Munson)

B aircraft development flight trials began in 1987 at Lavington Folly, on Salisbury Plain not everything came up to specification and within six months it was being predicted, albeit very much off the record, that the aircraft's weight might well end up around 180kg.[15] Naturally, the weight increase had an obvious knock-on effect. The proposed powerplant for Phoenix was a Weslake engine(a fuel-injected engine derived from the Normalair-Garrett WAM342); adequate for an air vehicle weighing up to 130kg, but not 180kg. Not only would Phoenix suffer from some poor flying characteristics, it was likely to be seriously underpowered.[16]

Nevertheless, with the series of 'Model B' Air Vehicles, Phoenix began to mature considerably. During the same period a Ground Control Station was introduced, as well as numerous versions of software. Eventually, by the end of 1994 most of the technical development issues had been overcome.

Although some technical issues had still to be resolved, Army support for the trials programme was notched up to Troop level in 1995, allowing a shift in emphasis towards developing the tactical uses of Phoenix. Manpower for this stage of the trials was provided by 22 Battery, RA (32 Regiment, RA) and 57 Battery, RA (39 Regiment, RA) and lasted until 1997 when the final acceptance tests were completed.

Phoenix had proved to be probably one of the most complex development programmes ever attempted involving parallel development of airframes, datalinks and control software. As a result Phoenix was literally years behind schedule and, ironically, its former competitor, Ferranti, had since become an associate company of Marconi in 1990.

---

15 A Phoenix Trials Team was formed in 1987 and although Phoenix was far from being accepted by the Army, personnel from 22 and 57 Batteries were almost permanently attached to the Team.
16 As related verbally by Major David Potts, RA (Ret'd) to the author 30 March 2006.

The complete and self-contained Phoenix unit equipment and personnel in a specially-commissioned photograph at Larkhill mid-1986. The Land Rover transporter, Control vehicle, Radar receiver, Launcher and Generator provide the backdrop for a pre-production Phoenix B. (via Major D. Potts)

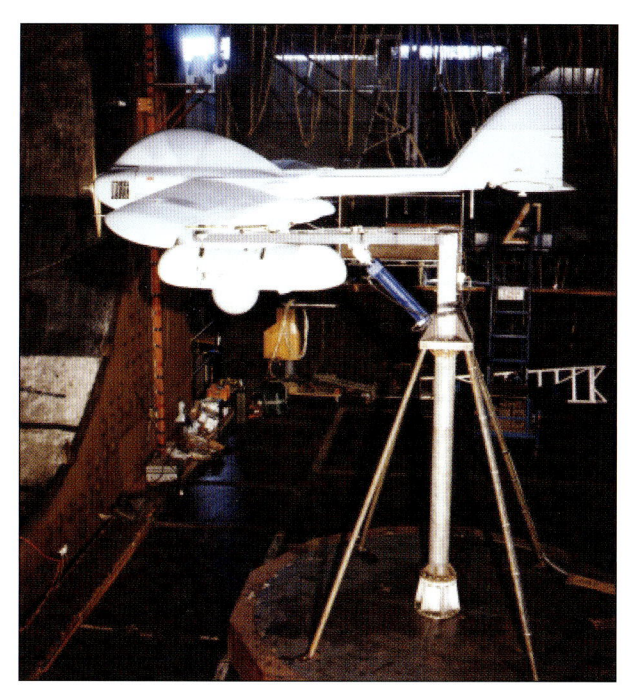

Phoenix B022 was matched with Pod 017 and used for aerodynamic tests inside the huge wind tunnel at RAE Farnborough, where it was photographed on 25 March 1993. This example features the 'gills' on the engine cowling which, combined with a splatter plate at the front, provided for much better cooling of the engine whilst keeping the drag and propeller interference low. The engine, in this instance, was a dummy with no pistons, allowing the propeller free to 'windmill'. The crushable top 'hump' – designed to absorb the shock of landing inverted – was standard before its constituent chemical composition became subject to the Montreal Protocol materials ban. A replacement foam which had the same properties could not be found and that eventually led to the adoption of an air-bag which considerably altered the shape of Phoenix. (Farnborough Air Sciences Trust)

After the MoD's decision to award the Phoenix project to GEC-Marconi, Ferranti had turned to other military projects but with few orders on its book was forced to merge, in 1987, with the American company, International Signals & Controls (ISC). It later emerged that the US operation was nothing short of a commercial scam and in order to avoid insolvency, the Ferranti operation at Edinburgh was sold to GEC, of which Marconi was a part.

By the end of 1997 a total of 23 Phoenix air vehicles had been produced. These were a mix of Phoenix A and Phoenix B – prototype and pre-production examples. At one stage, late in the development of Phoenix, the MoD considered cancelling the entire programme. GEC Avionics even completed the design of an alternative air vehicle, known as the Frigate Bird. But the Government gave the Phoenix project one final chance to be in service by 1998, some nine years behind its original estimate.

Phoenix did, in fact, enter full-scale production in 1998. 200 Phoenix UAVs had been ordered and allocated the consecutive serials ZJ281-ZJ480. Construction of the air vehicle was sub-contracted by Flight Refuelling to British Petroleum Advance Materials (BPAM) at Avonmouth. (During the course of the production run, BPAM was taken over by GKN which in turn became part of GKN-Westland. As a result the Avonmouth factory was closed and this led to some difficulty in manufacturing in-service spares for Phoenix. However, that was resolved when an associate company of Flight Refuelling, Cobham Composites Ltd (of Shepshed, Loughborough), was contracted to build spare parts.)

Initial deliveries of Phoenix drones to the Army began in 1998, the first involving ZJ282 which was handed over to the School of Artillery and first flown at Larkhill on 8 January

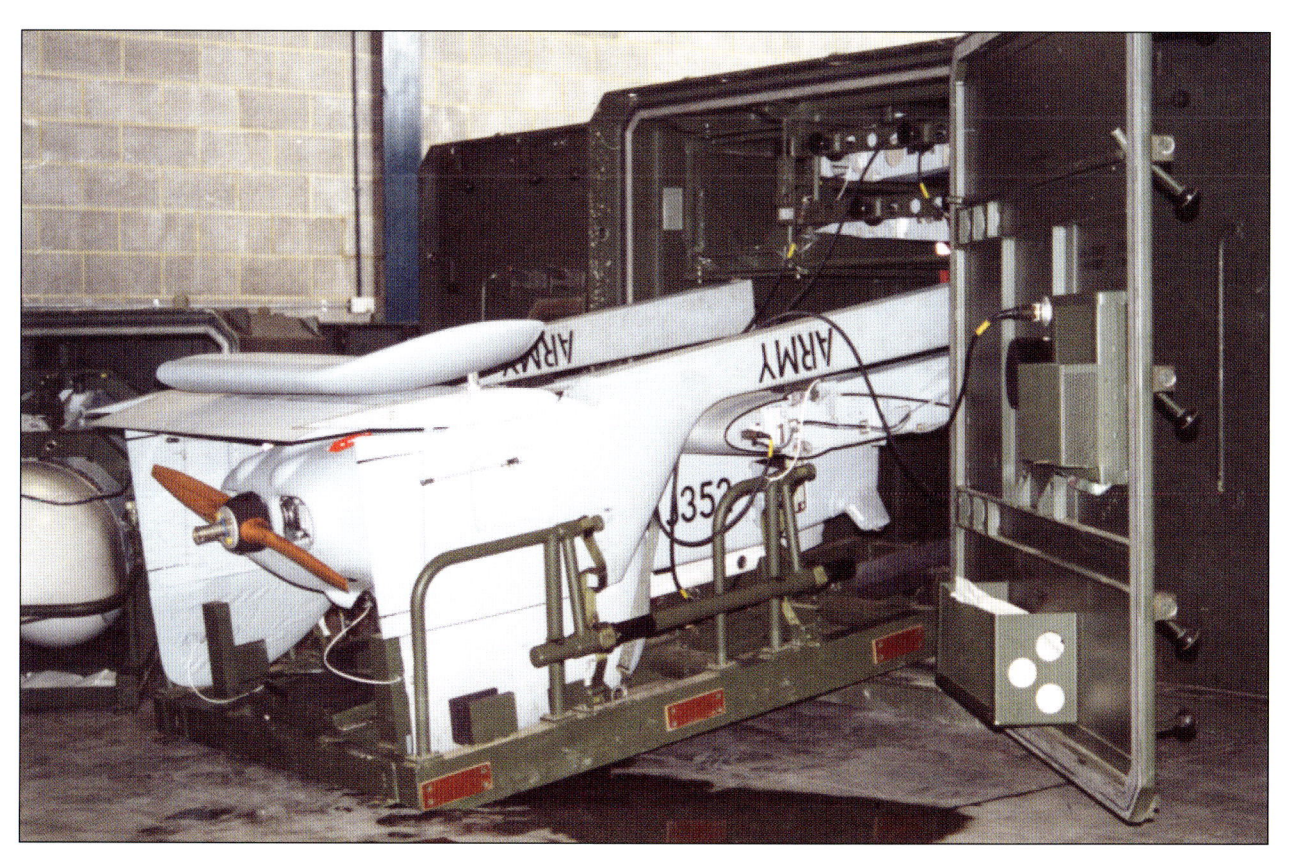

Phoenix ZJ352 is seen dismantled and ready for stowing away inside its transit crate. (Michael I Draper)

Surveillance Drones for the Army   305

22 Battery (32 Regiment, RA) took part in two KFOR tours to Kosovo. This series of images show Phoenix ZJ293 being lifted out of its protective container, through the assembly process and on to the launcher. The second Kosovo tour was cut short when the region called a ceasefire.

1998. The first batch of aircraft were allocated to 57 Battery RA (39 Regiment, RA) at Ouston, near Newcastle-upon-Tyne. At the time the Battery was mid-way through a Roulemont Tour in Northern Ireland and so the UAVs were placed in short-term storage at the Battery's Harlow Hill base.

The second unit to receive Phoenix was 22 Battery (32 Regiment, RA) at Larkhill but with no operational commitments at the time, the Battery was immediately despatched to BATUS/Suffield in June 1998 for two months of training and working-up on Phoenix. When 22 Battery returned to Larkhill it did so as a fully operational UAV unit and just two months later the Battery was deployed as part of the NATO peacekeeping mission in Kosovo.

Although delivery of production examples was finally under way, flight-testing of Phoenix continued throughout 1998. Several of the aircraft involved in these tests sustained damage and Flight Refuelling was asked to provide replacement parts but in such quantity that it was mutually agreed that MoD would offset the cost by allowing Flight Refuelling to build two aircraft less than the contract stipulated. Therefore only 198 aircraft were actually built, the final two (ZJ479/480) being officially cancelled.

Phoenix in Kosovo

The Kosovo War was essentially a conflict between Serbian and Yugoslav security forces and the Kosovo Liberation Army (KLA). By the mid-1990s Serbs had escalated the conflict by using military and paramilitary forces in a widespread ethnic cleansing operation against the Kosovar Albanians. By 1998 it was being reported by the international media that some 300,000 refugees had been displaced.

Eventually, on 24 March 1999 NATO forces launched an air bombardment against Yugoslavia. The initial strikes were carried out by Spanish Air Force F-18s when they bombed Belgrade. It marked the first occasion that NATO had attacked a sovereign country.

For a number of weeks an intensive air campaign was directed against the Yugoslav region until, following considerably strong diplomatic pressure from Russia, the Yugoslav Government agreed to withdraw its forces from Kosovo. The bombardment was suspended on 10 June 1999.

NATO ground troops moved into the Province to establish an interim UN-led civil administration. Allied UAVs supported the initial move into the Province in providing reconnaissance missions to monitor the Serb withdrawal: it was during this phase that Phoenix entered service.

22 Battery, RA took to Kosovo a total of 28 Phoenix UAVs (ZJ310, ZJ324, ZJ329-330, ZJ333-335, ZJ337, ZJ339-340, ZJ342, ZJ344-345, ZJ347-350, ZJ352, ZJ355, ZJ360-363, ZJ365, ZJ367, ZJ384, ZJ389 & ZJ421). Establishing its base in Macedonia the Battery carried out two training flights on 5 June before despatching ZJ360 to make the first live surveillance flight over Kosovo on the following day.

Phoenix had, in many respects, been deployed too late to be an effective surveillance platform during the bombardment phase. Most UAV units left the region as soon as the Allied Kosovo Force (KFOR) was in position and only US Army Hunter UAVs and British Army Phoenix remained in the area. 22 Battery,RA moved up to Kosovo on 13 June 1999 to take on a Force Protection and Area Surveillance role in support of NATO peacekeeping troops. It was during this period that one British Army Phoenix was routed over Pristina airport and unexpectedly relayed back live pictures of eleven Serb Air Force MiG-21s being prepared for take-off to Belgrade.

During the same period a Phoenix night surveillance sortie caught sight of refugees and Serbian troops retreating along three specific roads. The fact that the troops were seen using these particular roads provided clear intelligence that they had not been mined. That in turn allowed NATO ground forces to safely enter the area.

Despite reports to the contrary, Phoenix performed well in Kosovo given the conditions and terrain. Phoenix had originally been designed to operate in 'Cold War' North-West Europe; Kosovo offered a totally different environment. Other factors that made life difficult for 32 Regiment were, to a large extent, beyond their control. Maps, supplied at short notice, were not sufficiently up to date and did not show, for example, all of the ground features and obstacles. True, the contours of hills and mountains were shown but some hills had high-reaching pine trees. Telegraph poles and other similar obstructions were not marked and it was features such as these that led to a number of losses.

By the end of the campaign the Regiment had lost fourteen aircraft. The first had occurred on 10 June 1999 when ZJ360 came down in an unfriendly area. What caused the crash is still unclear but the UAV was later found to have been systematically stripped by local villagers. Another Phoenix, ZJ384, gained a degree of infamy when it was prominently displayed in the Belgrade Aviation Museum after coming down just three miles inside the buffer zone on 15 June 1999. Reports circulating at the time of its loss suggested that ZJ384 had been quickly sent on to Moscow, but in fact it never left the area.

22 Battery's first Kosovo tour concluded after six weeks, the final flight being made on 29 July 1999. Apart from the two Phoenix mentioned above, the Battery lost a dozen other Phoenix: ZJ324, ZJ329, ZJ333, ZJ340, ZJ344, ZJ345, ZJ348, ZJ350, ZJ355, ZJ363, ZJ367 and ZJ389.

No sooner had 22 Battery returned to Larkhill in August 1999, they were assigned for a second tour to Kosovo to commence on 1 October 1999. But with the end of the Kosovo campaign, the Tour only last for two weeks before the Detachment returned to its Wiltshire base.

Whilst the 22 Battery Detachment had re-deployed to Kosovo the main element of the Battery deployed to Egypt to take part in a multi-national joint Exercise 'BRIGHT STAR'. To bring the Battery up to full strength, 57 Battery (39 Regiment, RA) was temporarily detached to 32 Regiment, RA for the duration of the exercise.[17]

Exercise 'SAIF SAREEA II' was held in Oman in August and September 2001 and involved British, American, French and Omani forces. Over 22,500 British servicemen were deployed to Oman, the largest deployment of British Forces since the 1991 Gulf War. 22 Battery was deployed (with 3 Brigade and 7 Armoured Brigade) but mid-way through the Exercise news broke of what was undoubtedly the most radical and extreme act of terrorism ever attempted.

On 11 September 2001 the world changed forever, as Afghanistan visited the world in a brutal, tragic fashion. The nineteen suicide bombers, who hijacked four airliners and then rammed three of them into the twin towers of the World Trade Center in New York and the Pentagon in Washington all belonged to the Al' Qaeda organisation led by the terrorist Osama Bin Laden.[18]

The suicidal attacks had an immediate and major ramification around the world and, at a single stroke, what became universally known as '9-11' moved the goalposts for all future conflicts. 22 Battery's participation in 'SAIF SAREER II' ended abruptly and the Detachment returned to Larkhill. Although 22's exercise had ended prematurely, a number of lessons had been learnt at an early stage and were to prove of immense value for what was to come later. One of the lessons involved the UAV's Bedford launch vehicle which, although adequate in Kosovo, proved to be insufficiently robust to cope with desert conditions. As a result the decision was taken to replace the Bedfords with Foden-DEROPS vehicles, a timely decision for what was to come.

Phoenix in Iraq 2003 – Gulf War II

In strictly military terms, Operation 'TELIC', the military operation to dispose of Saddam Hussein and the Ba'athist gangsters who had terrorised Iraq for 35 years, was a brilliant success. The vast majority of Iraqis were glad to see the back of their vainglorious old tyrant. Conversely, the same majority had no desire to be occupied by a foreign army, which is precisely what happened, with terrible consequences for the entire US-led coalition. General Sir Mike Jackson, the British Army chief during the invasion, later described the approach taken by Donald Rumsfeld, the former US Secretary of State, to the post-Saddam administration of Iraq as 'intellectually bankrupt' and cited as the main reason that a mission that was supposed to last three years ended up taking six.

One of the key factors determined at the earliest planning stage of the campaign was the need, once the shooting started, for non-stop, real-time aerial surveillance of the battlefield. From Larkhill 32 Regiment RA despatched, in January 2003, an Advanced 'TAC Party' Group (made up with men from 18 Battery, RA) to Kuwait City. The task set for the Advanced Group was simply to determine how and where best to deploy Phoenix onto the battlefield. In the meantime 37 Phoenix drones were shipped out through Marchwood Port aboard contracted merchant ships. Further shipments followed.

While 18 Battery examined and prepared suitable launch sites, a second Battery was placed on standby on 1 February 2003. Just five days later 22 Battery flew out from RAF Brize

---

17 Exercise 'BRIGHT STAR' also involved 3 Commando Brigade, RM, 1 Artillery Brigade and 1 Recce Brigade. The US 3 Infantry Division was also involved.

18 A fourth hijacked jet, a United Airlines Boeing 757, crashed in open countryside in Shanksville County, Pennsylvania after passengers and flight crew had attempted to fight the hijackers. It is thought that the hijackers' target was Washington, more precisely, the White House.

Phoenix ZJ421 awaits the order for launch at the height of the Iraq War. Note how the launch vehicle is dug into the desert sand and the 32 Regiment RA flag is proudly attached to the launcher. (Author's Collection)

Norton to join 18 Battery in Kuwait City. The battle plan, having now been drawn up, placed the 22 Battery TAC Group in support of 16 Air Assault Brigade and 18 Battery TAC Group in support of 3 Commando Brigade although in reality the two Batteries worked effectively as a merged composite unit. In the meantime another batch of 11 Phoenix were shipped out from the UK.[19]

Operation 'TELIC' opened with a ground assault on 19 March 2003. The air war was launched early on 20 March with aircraft and cruise missiles targeting military installations in and around Baghdad. During the following day, two British Army battle groups (1st Btn, Black Watch and the 2nd Royal Tank Regiment) from 7 Armoured Brigade crossed the border from Kuwait into Iraq.

When the allied assault began the Phoenix operation was deployed, on 29 January, to two designated Coalition Assembly Areas in four Flight Troops, each Troop allocated with eight UAVs: 1 & 2 Troops to 'CAA VIKING' (in support of 3 Cdo Bde) and 3 & 4 Troops to 'CAA GRYPHON' (with 16 AA Bde). Within the first 36 hours of the campaign Phoenix flew eighteen missions over some of the most hostile Iraqi territory around Basra. These flights successfully provided continuous day and night surveillance cover in support of 'both the Brigade and the Division'.

As ground forces made their advance towards Basra, so Battery HQ re-positioned into Iraq, to Shaibah airfield.

Phoenix was now tasked with providing 7 Brigade with constant surveillance of Basra city, the immediate surrounding areas and the Al Shatetat waterway. At the same time a number of surveillance flights were made over the Al Faw peninsula, on behalf of 3 Commando Brigade, in order to assess the strength of the enemy at the oil fields there as well as providing target cues for US Predator UCAVs. A final tasking was to monitor traffic movements along the main highway between Basra and Baghdad (in support of 16 Air Assault Brigade). In each of the three taskings, Phoenix has been described as 'heavily used' in battle.

By 28 March Phoenix drones had pinpointed three Iraqi SCUD missile sites, all of which were subsequently destroyed by air strikes. Ironically, on the same date a number of international television news channels showed footage of Phoenix UAV ZJ300 being conveyed through the centre of Basra and with local Iraqis symbolically beating it with their shoes. ZJ300 had, in fact, been lost a week beforehand, on 21 March, and had been the first Phoenix loss of the campaign. Iraqi forces claimed to have brought the Phoenix down with small-arms fire but whether or not that was true remains unconfirmed. However, as men of 32 Regiment, RA later (and somewhat cynically) recalled, the television broadcast had brought the Regiment "fame at last!"

The manufacturer's manual has always claimed Phoenix to have an operational endurance of five hours. Although this was correct under normal conditions, as a general rule of thumb a four-hour mission was considered the limit for operations in Iraq. The heat of the Iraqi desert, the air density and frequent strong desert winds were all factors that had a direct bearing on 'time on task'. One effect of the desert heat was an enforced limit on payload, especially the fuel load and most flights carried out during the campaign

---

19 The initial two shipments involved at least 53 Phoenix UAVs: ZJ282, ZJ292, ZJ296, ZJ297, ZJ300, ZJ302, ZJ305, ZJ313, ZJ322, ZJ324, ZJ330, ZJ331, ZJ332, ZJ335, ZJ337, ZJ341, ZJ355, ZJ365, ZJ367, ZJ376, ZJ381, ZJ387, ZJ391, ZJ393, ZJ394, ZJ395, ZJ399, ZJ402, ZJ404, ZJ405, ZJ407, ZJ408, ZJ409, ZJ410, ZJ411, ZJ412, ZJ413, ZJ414, ZJ417, ZJ421, ZJ422, ZJ427, ZJ428, ZJ437, ZJ451, ZJ454, ZJ456, ZJ459, ZJ462, ZJ463, ZJ465, ZJ473 and ZJ475.

Phoenix ZJ331 was one of several 32 Regiment Phoenix UAVs that 'went missing' during early sorties of the Iraq War. However, once British Forces fully recaptured areas around Basra some UAVs were recovered safely, including ZJ331.

Such was the need for continuous surveillance during the battle for Basra that a number of Phoenix were tasked to remain over target until their fuel exhausted. Such was the case with ZJ376 which is seen at Az Zubayr, a few miles south-south-west of Basra. ZJ376, like many others allowed to suffer the same fate, was later regained by advancing forces and passed over to REME for repair and return to service. (S/Sgt John Draper)

Surveillance Drones for the Army 309

Phoenix ZJ367 lies wrecked on Sparrowhawk Airfield, just outside Al Amarah, after possibly suffering a malfunction during Operation 'TELIC'. It has clearly been 'got at' as the camera has been removed, although this is more likely to have been carried out by allied forces. (S/Sgt John Draper)

The lush background offers evidence that this shot of Phoenix ZJ395 lying inverted is on the bank of the river Tigris at Al Amarah. Thought to be the result of an engine malfunction, ZJ395 was later repaired by a REME team and returned to active service. (S/Sgt John Draper)

Phoenix ZJ381 was a casualty in the Iraq War and is seen wrecked where it fell at Camp Condor.

Summary of Phoenix Operational Losses during 2nd Gulf War, 2003*	
Date	Remarks
21.3.03	Crashed over Basra City, possibly shot down.
23.3.03	Missing in action; details unconfirmed
23.3.03	Landed in a hostile area 48km from planned point of recovery. Abandoned after rescue refused
26.3.03	Communications link lost; UAV missing In action
26.3.03	Missing In action, details unconfirmed
28.3.03	Launched 1725; Launch & Recovery Detachment Commander searched 3km radius of planned point of recovery but not found.
29.3.03	Launched 0912; lost over Basra
30.3.03	Launched 1824 but crashed 6mins after launch
30.3.03	Launched 1905; lost over Basra
31.3.03	Launched 2303 but crashed shortly after launch
1.4.03	Launched 2227; crashed immediately after launch
1.4.03	Launched 2332; lost over Basra
2.4.03	Launched 1745; possibly shot down over Basra
2.4.03	Launched 2030; lost, presumably shot down
2.4.03	Launched 2313; lost over Basra.
2.4.03	Launched 2344; lost over Basra, possibly shot down.
3.4.03	Launched 1519; lost over Basra
5.4.03	Launched 1232; communications link lost at 1321; lost over Basra
5.4.03	Launched 1521; last noted 1535 after likely UCLA; lost over Basra
6.4.03	Launched 0057; communications lost 0325; lost over Basra
6.4.03	Launched 0828 but crashed on launch and burnt out
6.4.03	Launched 0858; lost over Basra and vandalized after landing.
6.4.03	Launched 0934; lost over Basra, probably due to UCLA.
6.4.03	Launched 1359; lost over Basra, probably due to UCLA.
6.4.03	Launched 1535; lost over Basra, probably due to UCLA
6.4.03	Launched 1720; lost over Basra, possibly due to communications failure.

*It should be noted that some aircraft declared lost over Basra were despatched on planned one-way missions only. A number were later retrieved undamaged following the capture of Basra and surrounding area.
UCLA = Uncommanded Loss of Altitude due to sudden change in climatic conditions.

had a limit of 30 litres of fuel aboard. Launch Geometry – the distance between launch site and the Ground Data Terminal (GDT) – was also a critical factor. Given such extreme climatic conditions, battle losses were inevitable. But, as so often happens in such situations, the rule book was often ignored.

The order given to 32 Regiment, RA at the start of the campaign was short, sharp and to the point – "gather real-time intelligence at any cost". The order clearly implied that it was far more important to get good intelligence back than the aircraft. In order to maximize surveillance-over-target, a number of Phoenix sorties were planned from the outset as 'one-way missions'. The UAV would remain above the target area until the fuel simply ran out, by which time another UAV was in position to continue aerial surveillance. The Ba'ath Party HQ in Basra was one of those targets that Commanders demanded constant surveillance and as a direct result of live intelligence fed back by Phoenix UAVs, the enemy complex was attacked at precisely the right moment and with the maximum effect.

It is believed that an overall total of 89 Phoenix UAVs were deployed to Iraq for Operation 'TELIC' and that these carried out a total of 138 operational sorties. By the end of the campaign, 23 Phoenix flights had ended in the loss of the UAV. A further thirteen sustained battle damage that was later repaired. Of the losses, at least one was confirmed to have been shot down when the Royal Irish Regiment apparently opened fire on it after intelligence suggested that Iraqi forces were about to deploy unmanned drones equipped with germ weapons. It is strongly suspected that ZJ300 may also have been shot down at the start of the campaign. However, most of the losses were by design, being deliberately allowed to run out of fuel. They were posted as 'Missing in Action' although once the Basra area had been safely secured by British troops some of the missing Phoenix were found lying relatively undamaged in the desert.

In some respects Phoenix did present the Iraqi forces with an easy and visible target. Most sorties were carried out at between 900ft and 1,000ft during hours of daylight, often lower at night. Climatic conditions often presented difficulties as operating over rivers and desert brought sudden changes in air pressure causing the air vehicle's altimeter to give a misleading height. As the air vehicle had been programmed to fly at a pre-determined altitude some losses were narrowly avoided. Such incidents were termed as UnCommanded Loss of Altitude (UCLA), a constant problem facing Phoenix pilots.

On 8 May 2003, for 18 and 22 Batteries it was deemed 'job done' and time to pull out. Once the fighting had stopped, the role of allied forces in Iraq changed to one of peace-keeping and by 7 June 2003 most of the Battery Group was back at Larkhill.

Army Structure & Unit Changes

The 2002 UK Strategic Defence Review announced a number of changes to the structure of those artillery Regiments equipped with UAVs and Multi-Launch Rocket System (MLRS). Prior to the Review the permanent structure was as follows:

32 Regiment, RA (Larkhill)	
18 Battery	MLRS
22 Battery	Phoenix UAV
74 Battery	MLRS

39 Regiment, RA (Harlow Hill, Newcastle)	
57 Battery	Phoenix UAV
132 Battery	MLRS
176 Battery	MLRS

The main change involved 18 Battery, 32 Regiment RA, who re-roled from MLRS to Phoenix just ahead of the Battery's deployment to Iraq. At the same time 74 Battery was transferred from 32 Regiment, RA to 39 Regiment, RA in exchange for 57 Battery which moved from 39 to 32 Regiment, RA. The situation, as at June 30 2003, was therefore as follows:

32 Regiment, RA (Larkhill)	
18 Battery	Phoenix UAV
22 Battery	Phoenix UAV
57 Battery	Phoenix UAV

39 Regiment, RA (Harlow Hill, Newcastle)	
74 Battery	MLRS
132 Battery	MLRS
176 Battery	MLRS

For several months after the end of the Gulf campaign there was no Phoenix presence in Iraq. Back in the UK, 57 Battery settled into Larkhill after its move south from Harlow Hill and in October 2003 was despatched to Iraq for a 5-month 'TELIC II' deployment.

The transfer of 57 Battery had effectively 'tidied up' the respective roles of the Royal Artillery's two Regiments. At the same time, 32 Regiment took on an additional responsibility in Iraq when 57 Battery re-equipped with 24 newly-delivered Lockheed-Martin Desert Hawks, marking the first operational use of the American mini-UAV. A major part of the Battery's activity was surveillance of road-blocks or, perhaps more importantly, tracking those vehicles seen to be trying to evade the road blocks.

32 Regiment, RA added a fourth Battery in early-2004 with the addition of 42 Battery. The Battery, having been briefly placed in suspended animation since 22 Regiment, RA was disbanded in 2003, re-equipped with Phoenix UAV. The Order of Battle, as at March 2004, was as follows:

32 Regiment, RA (Larkhill)	
18 Battery	Phoenix UAV
22 Battery	Phoenix UAV
42 Battery	Phoenix UAV
57 Battery, RA	Desert Hawk MUAV

Phoenix returned to Iraq on 4 April 2004 when 22 Battery was deployed for a 6-month 'TELIC III' tour. The tour lasted until 15 October and for the next two years 32 Regiment, RA provided a continuous presence in Iraq with Phoenix. 'TELIC IV' (October 2004 to March 2005) took 18 Battery, RA back in Iraq; 'TELIC V' (April to September 2005) involved 42 Battery, RA whilst 'TELIC VI' (October 2005 to March 2006) was the turn of 57 Battery, RA.

In April 2006 22 Battery deployed to Iraq for 'TELIC VII', the first time the Battery had returned to Iraq since the conflict ended. Much of the tasking by 22 Battery was by now concentrated on searching for possible insurgents along the north-east Iraq-Iran border. But 'TELIC VII' also marked the final Phoenix tour. The decision had already been taken to withdraw the Phoenix from front-line service and the Battery was already in the process of winding down its deployment when the final operational flight was made on 6 June 2006 by ZJ406, launched from Camp Abu Naji, in Al Amarah for a routine Counter Indirect sortie. That sortie not only marked the end of 22 Battery's 'TELIC VII' tour, but also the end of Phoenix as a front-line surveillance drone.

A farewell parade took place at Roberts Barracks, Larkhill on 20 March 2008 to mark the official withdrawal of Phoenix from Army service. Despite widespread press criticism, Phoenix performed with distinction in the fight for Basra, Iraq, winning high respect from Army commanders in the field. In this view Phoenix ZJ461, on its launcher, is saluted into retirement by men of 32 Regiment, RA (Gunner Publications, Larkhill)

When Phoenix was withdrawn from service several survivors were presented for 'gate-guardian' duty. The farewell parade and Iraq veteran ZJ449 was donated to the REME Museum of Technology at Arborfield Garrison and erected there on 7 October 2008. The Arborfield-Phoenix connection is explained by "Maintained by REME; deployed by the Royal Artillery." (Tony Hyatt)

For some, the decision to replace Phoenix was a decision that could not have come sooner. It had acquired a reputation, generated principally by the media, of having been ill-conceived and poor in performance. Indeed, it was even referred to by some as the 'bugger-off' drone in view of the number that failed to return from surveillance sorties. But all of that was born out of sheer ignorance – true, there were some early shortcomings but for those who operated it on the frontline and for those who relied upon the intelligence it provided, especially in the heat of battle, Phoenix had proved its value and was considered a "very good piece of kit". Furthermore, all the work carried out by 32 Regiment, RA in Kosovo and Iraq over a four-year period had effectively laid down the ground rules for all future British UAV operations.

Until September 2006 32 Regiment, RA had carried out a total of 1,487 flights, including training exercises as well as in battle. Of the original 198 Phoenix UAVs delivered, 124 had been declared Cat.5 for various reasons, leaving some 74 in stock. The greatest accolade bestowed upon Phoenix came at the end of the Iraq War. Three factors were said to have been battle-winning concepts; the Alvis Vickers Challenger 2 battle tank, the Fv510 Warrior armoured infantry fighting vehicle (AIFV) and the Phoenix UAV surveillance system. Any 'go-or-no-go' decision at the height of battle was said to have depended emphatically on the availability of *all* three factors.

Although Watchkeeper, the nominated replacement for Phoenix, was not expected to enter Army service until 2009/10, the decision was taken to finally withdraw Phoenix from service in early 2008. A formal farewell parade was held at Roberts Barracks, Larkhill on Thursday, 20 March 2008 when ZJ461, characteristically positioned on its Foden launcher, formed part of the drive-past. Phoenix was officially withdrawn from service on 31 March 2008.

Most of the surviving Phoenix remained in BAE System's compound at Larkhill for a few months before being disposed of. After a frustrated attempt by the Dutch Army to purchase an undisclosed number, discussions were held between the Disposal Support Agency and the Governments of Jordan and Pakistan but neither took the decision to buy. In the end 32 Regiment, RA chose to retain just four Phoenix UAVs to serve as ground training aids and several others were earmarked for museums throughout the country. One other Phoenix was assembled from various major components and mounted as a 'gate guardian' at Roberts Barracks. In a clear reference to Camp Commandant, Colonel Nick Fitzgerald, the Phoenix was given the fictitious serial 'NF314'; the digits being the last three of the Colonel's Army service number.

Of those donated to various museums and other organisations, ZJ369 passed to the Defence Academy of the UK and held at the Defence College, Shrivenham; ZJ461 was donated to the REME Museum of Technology at Arborfield Garrison whilst ZJ452 passed to The Science Museum and stored at the Museum's out-station at Wroughton. The remains of ZJ325 are also said to be at the AAC Headquarters, Middle Wallop. The remainder of the Phoenix fleet was sold for scrap.

One Phoenix UAV was assembled from various salvageable parts and exhibited statically at the entrance to Roberts Barracks, Larkhill, home of 32 Regiment, RA. A fictitious serial NF314 was applied, it being derived from the initials of Camp Commandant, Colonel Nick Fitzgerald, followed the 'last three' digits of his service number. (Michael I. Draper)

Surveillance Drones for the Army

BAE Systems Phoenix Technical Data	
Powerplant	One 25 hp (18.6 kW) Meggitt MDS 342 two-cylinder two-stroke engine; two-blade fixed-pitch wooden propeller.
Wing span	18 ft ½ in (5.50 m)
Overall length	12 ft 5½ in (3.80 m)
Propeller diameter	2 ft 7 in (0.78 m)
Max payload	110.2 lb (50 kg)
Max fuel weight	44.1 lb (20 kg)
Max launch weight	397 lb (180 kg)
Max level speed	85 kt (157 km/h; 97 mph)
Cruising speed	70 kt (130 km/h; 81 mph)
Ceiling	8,000 ft (2,440 m)
Operational radius	38 nm (70 km; 43.5 miles)
Max endurance	4 hrs 30 mins
Recovery accuracy	330 ft (100 m)

Afghanistan

If proof were needed of the dramatic change in global conflict over the past 20 years one need only turn to the situation in Afghanistan.

In April 1978, Marxist sympathizers in the Army, some of whom had been trained in the Soviet Union, overthrew Sardar Mohammed Daud in a bloody military coup. Daud, together with most of his family and the Royal bodyguard were all massacred. But the Soviets who, since 1956, had largely bolstered the Afghan regime with economic and military aid were divided. The first Afghan President, Nur Mohammed Taraki, was later murdered while his successor, Hafizullah Amin, was killed when Soviet troops invaded Afghanistan in December 1979. Within a few short, dramatic months Afghanistan had been catapulted into the centre of an intensified Cold War between the Soviet Union and the USA.

To a large degree, many western powers remained impartial observers of the post-Soviet invasion although occasionally visiting western officials would express support for those Afghan tribesmen fighting 'the Soviet infidel' with just rifles and bandoliers. Those tribesmen were the Mujaheddin – the so-called freedom fighters and one British Foreign Office Minister, visiting an Afghan refugee camp in Peshawar in 1982, wished the Mujaheddin "well in their struggle to expel the Soviet forces".

The Afghan Mujaheddin were to become the US-backed, anti-Soviet shock troops. But for the Afghans the Soviet invasion was largely seen as yet another attempt by the outside world to subdue them. Jihad took on a new momentum as the USA, China and Arab states poured in money and arms supplies to the Mujaheddin. Out of the conflict, and only when Soviet troops withdrew from Afghanistan in 1989, would emerge a second generation of Mujaheddin who called themselves Taliban.[20]

Before the Taliban, Islamic extremism had never flourished in Afghanistan. Resistance against the Soviet invasion had been complex and based on the tribal network. It meant that many factions with differing ideals fought, not only the Soviets, but also between themselves. Ultimately the traditionalists and the Islamicists fought each other so mercilessly that, by 1994, the traditional leadership in Kandahar, Afghanistan's second largest city, had virtually been eliminated, leaving the field open for even more extreme Islamicists – the Taliban.[21]

The Taliban captured Kandahar in November 1994; two years later, on 27 September 1996, the Afghan capital, Kabul, fell to the Taliban followed immediately by the capture of Jalalabad.

The circumstances surrounding the western intervention were, of course, entirely different to those that led to the Soviet invasion. For the West, the catalyst had been the destruction of New York's 'twin-towers' by Al'Qaida terrorists. In the immediate aftermath of '9/11', intelligence reports confirmed that the Afghan Taliban was providing support, training facilities and a safe haven for the Al'Qaida organisation and had been since Osama Bin Laden was forced to move his base from the hitherto safe haven in Sudan in May 1995 to set up a compound in Afghanistan's mountain redoubt of Tora Bora.[22]

Even before '9-11', the American FBI had, on 8 June 1998, placed Osama Bin Laden at the top of its most-wanted list, subsequently offering a $5m reward for his capture. A month later, on 6 July, the US imposed a trade and economic boycott on the Taliban for refusing to hand over Bin Laden.[23]

US intervention in Afghanistan came within a month of '9-11'; on 7 October 2001 the US launched Operation 'ENDURING FREEDOM' with a hell-bent aim of locating Osama Bin Laden and other senior Al'Qaida members, to destroy the Al Qaeda organisation and to remove the Taliban regime which had supported and gave safe support to it.

Britain's contribution was to support US forces in the fight against the Taliban; UK troops first deployed to Afghanistan in November 2001 when marines from 40 Commando helped to secure the airfield at Bagram. Since 2002 Britain has led its own military operation, Operation 'HERRICK'. But Afghanistan was, in the early stages, a struggle in conditions far removed from the typical terrain that British forces were used to. The 1993 Iraq war had already confirmed a number of shortcomings in British equipment and as strategic objectives became increasingly complex so the tacticians were forced to seek a number of new approaches.

---

20 *Taliban – the Story of the Afghan Warlords* by Ahmed Rashid. (Pan Macmillan Ltd 2001). ISBN 0 330 49221 7. Taliban is a literal translation of 'students of Islam'.)

21 *Ibid* Ahmed Rashid.

22 *Merchant of Death (Viktor Bout)* by Douglas Farah & Stephen Braun (John Wiley & Sons Inc, 2007). ISBN 978-0-470-04866-5.

23 *Ibid* Ahmed Rashid. The bombing of the US Embassies in Kenya and Tanzania, which killed 220 people, made Bin Laden a household name in the Muslim world and the West. Thirteen days later the US retaliated by firing 70 cruise missiles against Bin Laden's Afghan camps around Khost and Jalalabad. Within a few weeks of the Africa bombings, the Clinton administration had demonized Bin Laden to the point of blaming him for just about every atrocity committed against the USA in the Muslim world. In the consequent indictment against him by a New York court, Bin Laden was blamed for the 18 American soldiers killed in Mogadishu, Somalia in 1993; the deaths of five servicemen in a bomb attack in Riyadh in 1995 and the deaths of another 19 US soldiers in Dhahran in 1996 and at least four other bombing incidents that had taken place since 1992. Osama Bin Laden was eventually killed in Pakistan on 1 May 2011.

With the knowledge that Watchkeeper was unlikely to be available until at least 2010, an Urgent Operational Requirement (UOR) was issued in May 2007, calling for a stop-gap UAV. The UOR was met by securing a fleet of Israeli-built Elbit Lydian 450 UAVs (otherwise known as the Hermes 450) and upon which the Army's Watchkeeper is based. ZK505 became the first Hermes 450 to be delivered to Camp Bastion, Afghanistan to join 57 (Bhurtpore) Battery, 32 Regiment RA, on Operation 'HERRICK VI' (Thales Group)

Hermes 450 and Watchkeeper

One factor requiring urgent attention was the need for much better intelligence, surveillance, target acquisition and reconnaissance (ISTAR). As far as the Army was concerned, this was a role previously undertaken, in Bosnia and Iraq, by Phoenix but Phoenix had never been designed to operate in such conditions that Iraq had offered; much less so in Afghanistan. Such considerations were built into the MoD's ambitious Watchkeeper programme.

Four industrial teams led by BAe Systems, Lockheed Martin, Northrop Grumman and Thales UK were considered initially before the MoD, in February 2002, invited just two – Northrop Grumman and Thales UK – to submit bids that emphasised an outline capability rather than specific UAV platforms. Both companies submitted their bids to the MoD in March 2004. Four months later, in July 2004, Thales UK emerged as the preferred bidder and was awarded a £700million contract for the design, development and production of the Watchkeeper UAV system.

Watchkeeper was, in simplistic terms, a re-design of the Israeli Elbit Hermes 450 surveillance UAV. Thales UK's initial proposal had included two UAVs – one large and one smaller example – as well as support equipment and ground stations but, clearly influenced by cost-effectiveness, the MoD selected just the larger WK450 for development.

With the likelihood that production Watchkeeper UAVs would not be available in large numbers until 2010 at the very earliest (and with Phoenix having already been withdrawn from service) an interim measure was urgently required in both Iraq and Afghanistan theatres. Thus a venture company, UAV Tactical Systems Ltd (U-Tacs) was jointly set up by Thales UK and Elbit Systems and in early-2007 U-Tacs signed an initial two-year agreement to supply two Hermes 450 systems, under a 'fly-by-the-hour' service provision arrangement called 'Project Lydian'. Each of the Hermes 450 systems comprised a ground station, line-of-sight data link and up to three air vehicles. One system (involving just two UAVs) was earmarked for deployment to Iraq, where the British still had a large presence as part of Operation 'TELIC'; the other system (involving three UAVs) for Afghanistan (Operation 'HERRICK').

The five Hermes 450s were part of an Urgent Operational Requirement (UOR) involving up to twenty Israeli-built

Hermes 450 ZK505 sits dismantled on its mobile transporter at Camp Bastion, Afghanistan. The ability to pack the Hermes 450 away in such fashion had obvious advantages in storage and maneuverability. (Thales Group)

Surveillance Drones for the Army   315

The first flight of a Watchkeeper in UK airspace took place on 14 April 2010 when WK060 completed a 20-minute sortie at ParcAberporth, West Wales. Noticeable in these two views of WK060 landing at the end of its initial flight is the extent to which the Israeli Hermes 450 UAV influenced the design of Watchkeeper. (Thales UK)

Hermes 450 History in the UK

To mark the signing of the Watchkeeper contract, Thales UK arranged for a flight demonstration of an Elbit Hermes 450 in the UK. The flight took place at ParcAberporth on 7 September 2005 and was the first occasion that a large UAV had been certified to fly in UK airspace, an important milestone in the development of the UK's unmanned system industry.

Watching the demonstration were members of MoD, Department of Transport, the Department of Trade and Industry, the Civil Aviation Authority and other invited guests.

The Civil Air Traffic Movement Log at ParcAberporth recorded the UAV's sortie through civil airspace in the normal fashion. Air Traffic Controllers logged the entry by date, aircraft type, number of passengers and call-sign. The call-sign for the Hermes 450 was 'UAS Silver 01' but for the first time ever the log showed "zero persons on board".

UAVs at a reported cost of £55million. The twenty aircraft were allocated serials ZK501-ZK520 on 18 May 2007 and within a month the first two aircraft, ZK503 and ZK504, were deployed to Basra, Iraq allowing Army capabilities in the south of the country to be 'significantly boosted'. The first in-theatre sortie took place on 14 June 2007 and just three weeks later the Hermes 450 was declared fully operational with 22 Battery, 32 Regiment RA.

In the meanwhile one of 32 Regiment's other components, 57 Battery, RA had deployed to Fort Bastion, Afghanistan in April 2007 to support 12 Mechanised Brigade as part of Operation 'HERRICK VI' (April to October 2007). The Battery, which had converted from Phoenix to Desert Hawk shortly beforehand, took delivery of a complete Hermes 450 system, thus adding a tactical surveillance element for those British troops in central Helmund. Initially, three UAVs (ZK505, ZK507 and ZK509) were delivered to Helmund, Afghanistan. Later, they were supplemented by ZK511, ZK512 and ZK516.

Hermes 450 performed well in theatre despite reports that two had been lost on operations. No reasons were provided for their loss although neither incident was apparently due to any technical defect.

57 Battery, RA completed its tour in Afghanistan on 18 October 2007 and began to return, as planned, to the UK. In fact, only personnel from the Desert Hawk element left theatre immediately; the Battery's three Tactical UAV crews remained in theatre for a further month so as to act as mentor to 18 Battery, RA which had arrived from the UK as 57's replacement. And so continued the rolling 'HERRICK'

The first example of Watchkeeper was shipped out to Israel for initial flight-tests. Given the appropriate out-of-sequence serial WK001, it made its first flight at Megido airfield, northern Israel on 16 April 2008 and for early flights Watchkeeper was also allocated the temporary Israeli civilian identity, 4X-USC. Comparison with the Hermes 450 underlines the origin of Watchkeeper. (Thales UK)

Hermes 450 Technical Data	
Powerplant	One 52 hp (38.8 kW) UEL AR 801 rotary engine; two-blade pusher propeller.
Wing span	34 ft 6 in (10.51 m)
Overall length	20 ft 0 in (6.10 m)
Overall height	7 ft 9 in (2.37 m)
Max payload	331 lb (150 kg)
Weight empty	441 lb (200 kg)
Max take-off weight	992 lb (450 kg)
Take-off run	1,150 ft (350 m)
Max level speed	95 kt (176 km/h; 109 mph)
Cruising speed	70 kt (130 km/h; 80 mph)
Ceiling	18,000 ft (5,480 m)
Mission radius	108 n miles (200 km; 124 miles)
Max endurance	20 hrs 0 mins

deployments by 32 Regiment, RA, including a fifth Battery after 43 ('Lloyd's Battery') Battery, raised during 2009. 22 Battery deployed for 'HERRICK 10'; 18 Battery for 'HERRICK 11' and 42 Battery for 'HERRICK 12'

With Hermes 450 in operational service, work progressed on developing Watchkeeper under a £317million order, awarded in October 2005 to the Leicester-based UAV Tactical Systems Ltd. The total requirement is expected to involve just short of 100 Watchkeeper UAVs to be produced over an eight year period.

Production of Watchkeeper air vehicles began at Thales' Leicester factory in 2005. The initial allocation involved 20 airframes (allocated 'out-of-sequence' serials WK001-WK040 on 14 December 2007 whilst on 25 March 2010 a further single example was allocated the serial WK060 for test-flying in the UK.) By the end of 2008 the Leicester Watchkeeper facility had completed five air vehicles, all of which had been shipped out to Israel for final assembly and flight-testing. The first of these, WK001, made its maiden flight from Megido Airfield, northern Israel on 16 April 2008. Wearing the temporary civil identity 4X-USC, the flight lasted for 25 minutes. A second Watchkeeper, WK002/4X-USD, performed the first autonomous flight in November 2008.[24]

A further milestone occurred on 23 July 2008 when Watchkeeper made the first automated take-off and landing using Thales' MAGIC ATOLS at Megido Airfield. (The flight was made without the aid of GPS; the MAGIC ATOLS functions independently of GPS, day or night, in all weather conditions.)[25]

Further progress was achieved on 14 April 2010 when WK060 marked the first occasion that a Watchkeeper flew in UK airspace. The flight, which took place at ParcAberporth, lasted 20 minutes and was without incident.

Lockheed Martin Desert Hawk

Beneath a veil of utmost secrecy, Desert Hawk was designed and developed at Lockheed-Martin's 'Skunk Works' in 2001. Not until mid-2002 did any details emerge publicly when it was revealed that 'Sentry Owl' – a generic title for a family of mini-UAVs designed for autonomous reconnaissance and surveillance – had been adopted by the US Air Force as part of its 'Force Protection Airborne Surveillance System (FPASS)'

Construction of prototype air vehicles was sub-contracted to Aeromech Engineering Inc at San Luis Obispo, California, the first example being completed in February 2002; two more, with minor design changes, followed shortly afterwards. The first two production

---

24 The first two Watchkeeper (WK001 & WK002) were retained for extensive flight testing. By July 2010 WK002 was effectively grounded to become an exhibition example, appearing (unmarked) on the Thales Exhibition stand at the 2010 Farnborough SBAC show.
25 MAGIC ATOLS is an acronym for **M**icrowave **A**nd **G**PS **I**ntegrated **C**ooperation **A**utomatic **T**ake**O**ff and **L**anding **S**ystem.

Surveillance Drones for the Army

systems (each of which involved six air vehicles) were delivered to the USAF's Electronic Systems Center at Hanscom AFB, Massachusetts in June 2002 followed by six more systems (involving 48 air vehicles) four months later. These had been ordered against a March 2002 Lockheed Martin subcontract to Aeromech by which time the UAV had been named Desert Hawk.

The battery-powered Desert Hawk is constructed of mould-injected expanded polypropylene – a flexible, damage-resistant type of foam. Weighing just 7lb, Desert Hawk is launched by two people using a bungee cord, and flies its mission fully autonomously at between 40-80km/h at a maximum height of 500ft. The 1lb sensor payload is carried in the middle of the fuselage and consists of either a colour video camera or a thermal imaging system for night operations.

Initial deployment to theatre took place in mid-November 2002 when US forces took a number of Desert Hawks to Afghanistan for airbase protection work during Operation 'Enduring Freedom'. Several months later, 28 Desert Hawks of the US 332nd Expeditionary Security Forces Squadron were deployed from Tallil AFB to Iraq during Operation 'Iraqi Freedom'.

Desert Hawk in Iraq

British Army involvement in Desert Hawk began in December 2002 when, as part of an Urgent Operational Requirement (UOR) a group of personnel from 22 Battery, 32 Regiment RA was sent out to Eglin AFB, Florida. After completing a familiarization course the personnel returned to the UK, bringing with them the first batch of British Desert Hawk UAVs. As if to underline the urgency of the requirement, 22 Battery was immediately despatched to Iraq, marking the introduction of British small unmanned air vehicles (SUAVs) to theatre.

Errant Desert Hawks

Shortly after it entered service in Iraq, the British Army's 32 Regiment, RA began experiencing unexplained difficulties with its Desert Hawk UAV. On a number of occasions, the Desert Hawk simply refused to comply with ground command transmissions and began to behave in an erratic manner.

One aircraft, which unexpectedly went out of control, was seen to make a perfect – but uncontrolled – landing in the fast-flowing Shatt al-Arab waterway in Basra. Before personnel had any chance of fishing the UAV out of the water the strong current had quickly pulled it downstream and out of sight. Quick thinking, however, by Battery personnel led to a call to the Royal Navy to seek assistance. The Navy reacted promptly and launched a Rigid Raider craft and chased the errant UAV for several miles down the Waterway before managing to haul it on board. The Desert Hawk was later returned to the Regiment with an 'Invoice Claim' attached, declaring that the Army owed the Royal Navy a significant debt. The claim was for one of most valued of items in the Region – one case of ice-cold beer!

Introduced to the British Army in the wake of the second Iraq War, the Desert Hawk mini-UAV was used by 32 Regiment RA for airborne airfield border patrols as well as surveillance of sensitive areas, such as roadblocks etc. This example, seen at Roberts Barracks, Larkhill on 28 June 2005 shows the 'type' serial ZK102 and a suffix of '019' to represent the revised serial system introduced for UAVs. (Michael I Draper)

Operations with Desert Hawk in Iraq were not without their difficulties and very soon aircraft were being lost in unexplained circumstances. In a number of instances aircraft had begun to behave erratically; some simply refused to comply with ground commands.

What investigations very quickly revealed was the Achilles heel of mini-UAVs in Iraq. It centred around the proliferation of multi-national military operations, as well as non-military and governmental agencies all communicating within the same area. Investigators realised that the root cause of the Desert Hawk problem was that its communications system worked within the same frequency band as one of the mobile telephone networks. Local telephone transmitters, being far stronger than those directing the UAVs, caused considerable interference and in turn caused many flights to become uncontrollable.

Desert Hawk was immediately withdrawn from Iraq and surviving aircraft were returned to the UK and stored at Horne Barracks, Larkhill.[26] Subsequently, and under a contract between the Defence Procurement Agency and Lockheed-Martin, one of the UAVs was returned to the US where the problems were identified during trials at Camp Roberts in October 2005. Only the manufacturer was able to modify the software and so all of the remaining UAVs were returned to the USA where the opportunity was taken, not just to upgrade the software with new frequencies, but also to install GPS Version 2 (with a stronger signal) and finally, a slightly stronger camera. When the upgrade was fitted into these Desert Hawks, the modified UAV was re-designated Desert Hawk 1+ (UK) and returned to service. At the same time a batch of new-build Desert Hawk 1+ was also delivered, all now serialled in the ZK120 range with examples extending to ZK120/64.

---

26 Precisely how many Desert Hawk 1s were lost as a result of these problems has not been revealed. Following Desert Hawk's withdrawal from Iraq, survivors were returned to the UK and placed into storage at Larkhill. Only eleven examples were present in June 2005; however, it is doubtful that as many as thirteen were lost in Iraq.

Right. *'Detachment 3' of 57 Battery, RA was an early deployment of Desert Hawk 1+ to Afghanistan. In this view ZK120/25 is held against the taut bungee rope moments before the point of release. The electric engine starts when the forward velocity reached 15m (50ft) per second. (David Oliver)*

Below. *Desert Hawk 1+ proved not to have the problems that beset the Desert Hawk 1 in Iraq. ZK120/25 is seen at Camp Bastion, Afghanistan in December 2006, just before the variant was withdrawn from service. (David Oliver)*

Desert Hawk in Afghanistan

Above: Former England football captain David Beckham visited Afghanistan 21-24 May 2010 as part of a morale-boosting exercise for troops on operations there before journeying on to South Africa to support his England World Cup colleagues. Appropriately his visit included a visit to the Army's UAV HQ at Camp Bastion where he posed for the camera holding Desert Hawk 3 (ZK150/406), operated at the time by 47 Regiment, RA. Note the angle of the propeller which, although normal for Desert Hawk in rest mode, does rather lend itself to the phrase "Bend It Like Beckham!" (courtesy of Gunner Publications, HQ DRA, Larkhill)

Towards the end of October 2005 a hand-picked team from 18 Battery, RA was sent out to the Afghanistan theatre with Desert Hawk 1+. The Detachment took several aircraft with them and carried out approximately sixty flights without any recurrence of the problems previously experienced in Iraq. By mid-Spring 2006 there were sufficient numbers of Desert Hawk 1+ (in the ZK120 range) available to allow 32 Regiment, RA to deploy 18 Battery for a five-month tour commencing in May 2006 (Operation 'HERRICK IV'). Based at Camp Bastion, the Battery provided UAV support for 16 Air Assault Brigade with six Air Detachments, two of which were mobile. Each of the Detachments consisted of four air vehicles and four soldiers – pilot, commander and two operators. The four non-mobile Detachments were deployed throughout Helmund Province; to Garmsir, Nowzad, Kajaki and Sangin.

In the meantime, the Ministry of Defence announced, on 23 February 2006, a $2.65m contract for eight new Desert Hawk systems for delivery in April 2007. These involved a new variant, the upgraded Block II Desert Hawk 3 although it is believed that some of the initial deliveries involved a "proving batch" until definitive production examples of Desert Hawk 3 were available. All Desert Hawk 3s were serialled in the ZK150 range and with the delivery of the later variant, all surviving Desert Hawk 1+ UAVs were withdrawn from service and returned to Lockheed-Martin.

Unlike the earlier Desert Hawk 1 system – each of which included six – the DH3 system involved eight air vehicles.

Surveillance Drones for the Army

Desert Hawk 3 was also significantly different to earlier models in that it featured a nose-mounted 'pull', rather than a tail-mounted 'push' engine. DH3 also had the traditional 'V'-tail arrangement replaced with a standard single fin design. With better aerodynamics, a turret-mounted imaging system yet being only marginally heavier than existing air vehicles, Desert Hawk 3 proved not only much more reliable in theatre but had an increased range and payload capability.

In October 2006 18 Battery handed over to 42 Battery who remained in theatre (as part of Operation 'HERRICK V') until May 2007 when they were, in turn, replaced by 57 Battery for the six-month 'HERRICK VI' tour.[27]

Operating conditions in Afghanistan could hardly have been more difficult for the Desert Hawk. Despite its robust construction, the harsh Afghan terrain and operating conditions levied a toll on the mini-UAV. Each Desert Hawk had been cleared for 200 launches but only managed to average around 70 per vehicle. By April 2007 six incidents involving Desert Hawks had occurred with two air vehicles being completely written-off. Cannibalisation of parts became commonplace, as complete repair meant sending the individual UAV unit back to Lockheed Martin in California, via the UK, on a 12-16 week turnaround.[28]

As part of the Sustaining Current Operations (SCO) Defence requirement in Afghanistan and Iraq, the responsibility for operating Desert Hawk 3 changed in Autumn 2007 when 47 Regiment, RA, located at Baker Barracks, Thorney Island, re-roled as a UAV Regiment and took over the Desert Hawk role from 32 Regiment, RA. The first of the new Regiment's Batteries to convert was 25/170 (Imjin) Battery who, in late-August 2007 carried out flight training on Desert Hawk at Camp Roberts, California. In the meantime 32 Regiment's 18 Battery had conducted pre-tour training in Israel on Hermes 450 TUAV. Deployment to theatre took place in October 2007 when elements of both Batteries were positioned in Iraq as the Theatre UAV Battery (Iraq) and as part of Operation 'TELIC X'. The hybrid Battery operated in support of 4 Brigade.

25/170 Battery returned to Thorney Island in March 2008, replaced in Iraq by 47 Regiment's 21 Battery, RA, reinforced by elements of 42 Battery, RA. The changeover, however, did not involve new aircraft; the newly-arrived Battery simply took over UAVs from the outgoing 25/170 Battery. The ease with which it was deployed made Desert Hawk an increasingly popular choice for those battle groups conducting operations in eastern Al Basra and Maysaan provinces and down the Al Fawr peninsula. Within a short space of time 47 Regiment's Batteries had completed over 1,000 successful missions – causing one observer to make the judgment "not bad for soldiers whose usual trade was to shoot them down!"

Despite its superiority over earlier variants, Desert Hawk 3 losses were not insignificant. In March 2008, the Defence Secretary acknowledged that, of 160 Desert Hawk 3s delivered, 27 had been lost in Afghanistan since April 2007. All had crashed either as a result of technical failure or following an unexplained loss of signal. Of the 27 lost, one had been subsequently recovered but two had "come into the possession of opposing forces". Many more Desert Hawks had been damaged and patched up locally.[29]

47 Regiment, RA continued to deploy Batteries for 'HERRICK VIII' and 'HERRICK IX' (10 Battery). In the meantime a second mini-UAV regiment came into force when HVM-equipped 12 Regiment, RA re-rolled to become a Close Air Defence/mini-UAV unit. 12 Regiment, RA deployed to Afghanistan for 'HERRICK X' and 'HERRICK XI' before handing over, in April 2010, to 47 Regiment, RA who returned to Afghanistan for 'HERRICK XII' (April-October 2010).

At the time of 47 Regiment's return to the Afghan theatre so the Army restructured its UAV capabilities as part of Operation 'ENTIRETY'. The objective was seen as to optimising both the structure and training in order to sustain pressure in Afghanistan. Prior to the restructure the composition of the two Desert Hawk Regiments was as follows:

12 Regiment, RA – 1 (UK) Armoured Div. (Baker Barracks, Thorney Island)
12 (Minden) Battery
9 (Plessey) Battery
58 (Eyre's) Battery
T (HQ) Battery (Shah Sujah's Troop)

47 Regiment, RA – 3 (UK) Div. (Baker Barracks, Thorney Island)
31 (HQ) Battery
10 (Assaye) Battery
21 (Gibraltar 1779-83) Battery
25/170 (Imjin) Battery

From 10 April 2010, 12 Regiment, RA - which only took Desert Hawk 3 into its inventory in September 2009 - relinquished its UAV activity to focus upon close air defence. At the same time 47 Regiment, RA lost its close air defence role to concentrate wholly on its mini-UAV role. The restructuring also saw 47 Regiment transfer from 3 (UK) Division to 1 Artillery Brigade control as part of the Theatre Troops organisation which oversees the Army's specialist units. 12 Regiment, however, remained subordinate to 1 (UK) Armoured Division.

In a move to enhance the surveillance capabilities of Desert Hawk 3, Lockheed-Martin developed an upgraded variant with a new signal intelligence (SIGINT) payload and a next-generation wing design. Flight testing was completed in the US, in April 2009. The enhanced software allowed Desert Hawk 3 to detect and locate sources of radio frequency emissions.[30] As part of a £3m Urgent Operational Requirement (UOR) a batch of upgraded Desert Hawk 3s

---

27 57 Battery, RA also operated the larger Hermes 450 UAV but these were permanently based at Camp Bastion.
28 'Report from Kandaha' by Andrew Krwiega; *Unmanned Vehicles* June 2007.
29 In response to a Parliamentary question, the Government released the following details: "As at 29 October 2008 the RAF had 14 pilots fully-qualified to fly Reaper UAV with three in training; 74 pilots were fully-trained to fly Hermes 450, with a further 24 undergoing training; whilst 120 people had been fully-qualified (plus 38 in training) to fly the 160 Desert Hawk 3 UAVs."
30 *"Defense Update – International Online Defense Magazine."*

Members of 25/170 Battery, RA show off one of their Desert Hawk 3 MUAVs. The serial, ZK150/62, is clearly visible in this view taken 'somewhere in Iraq' during the Battery's deployment to Iraq as part of Operation 'TELIC XI'. The Battery was part of the Thorney Island-based 47 Regiment, RA. Standing at the extreme left is Battery Commander Lt Rachel Cameron-Dick. (Courtesy of Gunner Publications, HQ DRA, Larkhill)

The CRA 1(UK) Armoured Division holds Desert Hawk 3 ZK150/62 in quasi-launch mode. The location is 'somewhere in Iraq' and whilst the propeller gives the impression of being bent backwards this view does show the engine in the nose, as opposed to the rear, as on Desert Hawk 1. (Courtesy of Gunner Publications, HQ DRA, Larkhill)

was procured for work in Afghanistan, arriving in theatre for 47 Regiment, RA over the weekend 21/22 August 2010.[31]

Honeywell RQ-16A T-Hawk Micro Air Vehicle System

Throughout the post-Iraq campaign and the current Afghanistan conflict, one of the most feared terrorist weapon is the Explosive Ordnance Device (EOD) – the so-called "dirty bomb", referred widely as an IED (Improvised Explosive Device). To meet that threat the US launched a multi-million dollar project to develop a Micro Unmanned Air Vehicle (MUAV) to fulfill the need for a Class 1 platoon-level surveillance drone. Honeywell Defense & Space Electronic Systems was the appointed prime contractor for what emerged as the Honeywell RQ-16A Tarantula Hawk (T-Hawk). The prototype T-Hawk made its first tethered flight in January 2005, followed by an initial free flight in the following June. After an extensive evaluation period by the US Army approximately 20 pre-production YRQ-16A T-Hawks were

---

[31] As announced on the Ministry of Defence website 27 August 2010.

Desert Hawk 1 Technical Data	
Powerplant	Battery-powered electric motor
Wing span	4 ft 4 in (1.32 m)
Length	2 ft 10 in (0.86 m)
Weight	7 lb (3.2 kg)
Operating height range	300–500 ft (90–150 m)
Speed range	30–50 kt (56–93 km/h; 35–58 mph)
Ceiling	1,000 ft (305 m)
Mission radius	5 n miles (9.3 km; 5.8 miles)
Endurance	60–90 mins

Desert Hawk 3 Technical Data	
Powerplant	Battery-powered electric motor
Wing span	4 ft 6 in (1.37 m)
Length	3 ft 0 in (0.91 m)
Weight	6.5 lb (3.0 kg)
Operating height range	300–500 ft (90–150 m)
Mission radius	5 n miles (9.3 km; 5.8 miles)
Endurance	90+ mins

Surveillance Drones for the Army

Desert Hawk Procurement

Desert Hawk was the first UAV to utilize the revised MoD Serial System; 'ZK102' being the 'type' serial with individual aircraft being identified by a three-digit suffix.

Desert Hawk I

Allocated 'Type' serial ZK102 19.12.2003.
Serials range from ZK102/001 to ZK102/024 inclusive. The following survivors from Operation 'TELIC' were noted in store at Larkhill in June 2005: ZK102/004, ZK102/005, ZK102/008, ZK102/011, ZK102/012, ZK102/016, ZK102/018, ZK102/019, ZK102/022, ZK102/023 and ZK102/024. Survivors modified to Desert Hawk 1+ (UK). All withdrawn from use and returned to USA 10.07.

Desert Hawk 1+

Allocated 'Type' serial ZK120 12.5.2006.
ZK120/01 to ZK120/64 at least have been confirmed, purchased for operations in Afghanistan commencing with 'HERRICK IV'. Batch included modified Desert Hawk 1 (ex-ZK102 series) plus new-build examples.

Desert Hawk 3

Allocated 'Type' serial ZK150 18.5.2007
ZK150/1 to ZK150/77 at least confirmed although ZK150/406 has also been noted. Some damaged air vehicles have been rebuilt and reportedly issued with new suffix numbers.

---

deployed to Iraq in 2007 with the US Army 25th Infantry Division, marking the first time a ducted-fan unmanned aerial vehicle had been used during combat missions, being employed on seeking out IEDs and insurgent ambushes.

Weighing just 20lb (8.4kg), T-Hawk is small enough to carry in a backpack and is equipped with video cameras to relay information back to foot soldiers using a portable handheld terminal. It has the ability to take-off and land vertically from complex desert and urban terrains without using runways or helipads. T-Hawk can also operate at an altitude in excess of 10,000ft (3,048m) although it can easily fly down to inspect hazardous areas for threats without exposing soldiers to enemy fire.

In 2008 a British MoD Integrated Project Team conducted a series of trials in the US which led to an announcement, on 3 February 2009, that an order had been placed by the US Navy (under Foreign Military Sales), on behalf of the British MoD, for six Block 2 T-Hawk MAV (otherwise known as RQ-16A) systems. Each system consists of two air vehicles and a portable ground station used to guide the aircraft and receive images from the cameras. The Ground Station can be used to programme a flight-path for the T-Hawk or control it manually.

British T-Hawks have been allocated the "Type Serial" ZK155 and deliveries to UK forces originally chalked for May 2009 with an initial five (ZK155/01 to ZK155/05) air vehicles, the remaining seven (ZK155/06 to ZK155/12) being scheduled for delivery in September 2009. All were delivered and deployed to Afghanistan for evaluation by units of the Royal Engineers.[32] Launched from a Mastiff mine-protected vehicle, T-Hawk can explore a potential IED location without the operator having to leave the cover of his vehicle. However, a re-assessment of operational factors led to a decision that, rather than have men of the Royal Engineers learn to fly MUAVs, the responsibility should rest with a dedicated UAV Royal Artillery Regiment. As a result, and as part of Operation 'ENTIRETY', T-Hawk was transferred to 32 Regiment, RA who undertook the first qualifying flight on 17 April 2010.

The first public announcement of British T-Hawks in service was made on 13 August 2010 when it was stated that men of 15 Field Support Squadron – part of 21 Engineer Regiment, RE – were the first British troops to make use of the T-Hawk system.

Referred to unofficially as a "flying dustbin", the Honeywell T-Hawk Micro Unmanned Air Vehicle is one of the smallest UAVs in British military service. Operational in Afghanistan, this example (ZK155/31) is seen inside its transit case and well illustrates the compact nature of this small UAV.

Honeywell T-Hawk Technical Data	
Powerplant	One 3W-56 56cc Boxer twin-piston engine (4hp kW each)
Diameter	1 ft 2 in (0.35 m)
Weight	20 lb (8.4 kg)
Service ceiling	10,500 ft (3,200 m)
Mission radius	6 n miles (11 km; 6.9 miles)
Endurance	40 mins

---

32 Honeywell announced that the British T-Hawks were deployed to "Operation Enduring Freedom", the official US Government term for the war in Afghanistan.

Chapter 10

The UAV Revolution

Joint UAV Experimentation Programme – JUEP

Established by the Directorate of Equipment Capability (DEC) in Defence Staff and intended to address a number of UAV-related objectives, the first steps towards establishing a Joint UAV Experimentation Programme (JUEP) were taken in February 2002. The programme was led by mid-grade military officers seconded from the Army's Land Command, the Royal Air Force's Air Warfare Centre (AWC) and the Royal Navy's Maritime Warfare Centre (MWC). Operational and technical support was provided by 32 Regiment, RA (which at the time was the only British unit operating unmanned air vehicles, the Phoenix UAV). This partnership involved mutual assistance in conducting field tests with an overall objective of seeking ways to move beyond the land tactical environment and explore UAVs in a joint battle space. The MoD claimed that JUEP was intended to lead to the introduction of a Network Enabled Capability (NEC) for UK Forces. This significantly involved an enhanced intelligence-gathering, surveillance, targeting, and reconnaissance (ISTAR) capability. In short, the programme would identify the contribution UAVs could make to the UK's future overall defence capability.

JUEP was never intended to select UAVs for in-service use; instead its role was more towards informing military planners of new and emerging requirements. To fully understand the potential of second-generation UAVs, the JUEP programme involved the acquisition of a range of UAVs, from Micro UAVs (MUAV) to High Altitude Long Endurance (HALE) UAVs. The range of specific objectives was similarly broad, initially to develop and confirm a viable UAV Concept of Operations (CONOPS) and, in particular, to support time sensitive targeting for network enabled operations. Other objectives were to explore UAVs for maritime operations, close/urban surveillance and, finally, electronic warfare.

Two years after establishing JUEP's credentials, a Joint UAV Experimentation Team (JUET) was formed in April 2004 to plan and carry out a series of flight trials. Drawn from all three services, the JUET Trials Management Team was headquartered at RAF Waddington where it worked under the tactical control of the RAF's Air Warfare Centre (AWC), but reported directly to DEC (ISTAR) located at the MoD Centre, Abbey Wood. The first of the flight trials, conducted in the US under the name 'Desert Rescue XI', actually occurred before the formation of JUET. Subsequently, an initial phase of urban surveillance evaluation trials took place, leading to a series of UK-based trials, examining mini-UAV Systems deployed within an urban operational environment. The programme ended with a series of maritime trials from a Royal Navy Type 23 frigate. The trials, and the UAVs involved, were:

In its final scheme and revised serial presentation, Mi-Tex Buster ZK009-03 is ready for launch from its launcher at Larkhill on 15 January 2007. In some respects all is not quite what it seems to be as the manufacturer's serial number 5044 would suggest that this is, in reality, ZK009-04. In fact, the mini UAV can be assembled in a short space of time and clearly the components have become interchanged at some point. The Mi-Tex logo and manufacturer's numbers were later removed to avoid any subsequent confusion. (Michael I Draper)

One of the first UAVs to be evaluated in the wake of the Iraq War was the EADS/IAI Eagle. After a series of trials in the USA, the Eagle was conveyed to Suffield, Canada for a British Army exercise that took place at BATUS between 7 and 21 October 2003. The serial ZJ989 was applied after arrival, together with an unofficial legend 'ROYAL AIR FORCE'. ZJ989 rests at the Suffield runway on 17 October. Note the c/n 2109 visible on the forward fuselage.

'Mighty Magpie'	Buster, Scorpio-6 and Quadrocopter
'Urban Hummingbird'	Buster & Scorpio 6
'Arkansas Odyssey'	ScanEagle
'Vigilant Viper'	ScanEagle

Although 'Vigilant Viper' effectively marked the end of the Joint UAV Experimentation Programme, evaluation of UAVs did continue and became the focus of activity at the Air Warfare Centre UAV Battlelab at RAF Waddington.

UAVs acquired specifically for the Joint UAV Experimentation Programme were as follows:

EADS/IAI Eagle UAV

The first live trial conducted by JUEP involved, amongst other factors, examining UAV integration into rescue forces for combat search and rescue (CSAR1). Trial 'Desert Rescue XI' took place at Fallon Naval Air Station, Nevada, USA in August 2003. The trial also enabled, for the first time, UK participants to fully integrate a UAV system into a US joint exercise with both manned and unmanned aircraft working in close co-operation.

The UAV selected for 'Desert Rescue XI' was an EADS/IAI Eagle 0 (c/n 2109), on loan from the manufacturer. The Eagle was air-freighted from Israel to NAS Fallon aboard a chartered Antonov An-124 but to avoid any diplomatic difficulties, the flight was routed via the UK.

By the end of 'Desert Rescue XI' the Eagle had flown some 56 flight hours, culminating in a successful first series of operational UAV trials.

A second trial involving the EADS/IAI Eagle took place at the British Army Training Unit at Suffield, Alberta, Canada (BATUS). The UAV and support equipment was conveyed to Canada by road for exercise 'Iron Anvil 03' which involved artillery and close air support to Brigade and Battalion Battle Groups. Specifically for this exercise, which took place between 7 and 21 October 2003, the UAV was placed onto the official military aircraft register as ZJ989, although less official was the controversial legend 'ROYAL AIR FORCE' applied to the fuselage.

ZJ989 completed twelve missions during 'Iron Anvil 03', many of which were carried out during the hours of darkness and in fairly harsh environmental conditions. The exercise exposed the wider utility of Synthetic Aperture Radar/Moving Target Indicator (SAR/MTI) data and also assessed the value of incorporating Electro Optical/Infra Red (EO/IR) sensors on the same air vehicle.[1]

EADS/IAI Eagle UAV – Specifications	
Length	30 ft 6 in (9.3 m)
Wing span	54 ft 6 in (16.6 m)
Max take-off weight	2,756 lb (1,250 kg)
Payload capacity	551 lb (250 kg)
Max speed	112 kt (207 km/h; 130 mph)
Max Operational altitude	25,000 ft (7,620 m)
Endurance	24 hours

Mission Technologies Mi-Tex Buster

The primary function of Trial 'Urban Hummingbird' was to evaluate a number of Mini UAV systems, the first involving the diminutive Mi-Tex Buster system.[2]

Designed and developed by Hondo, Texas-based Mission Technologies Inc, the Mi-Tex Buster system consisted of a Ground Control Station (GCS), a launcher and two air vehicles. The rather unorthodox-looking Buster was fully man- or Humvee-portable and was capable of fully automated missions without the need for piloting. It proved to be a long-endurance vehicle which was capable of flying in strong winds and heavy rain.

The first appearance of Buster in the UK occurred in October 2003 when the manufacturer carried out a series of demonstration flights over the Larkhill Ranges. Emerging as a likely contender for further evaluation, two Buster systems were purchased for the planned 'Urban Hummingbird' trial. The two systems were originally allocated serials ZK009 and ZK010 on 18 June 2004 but when it was realised that each system, in fact, contained two air vehicles, the allocation was

---

1 A usually reliable source has claimed that, prior to the US trial, the EADS/IAI Eagle spent three days undergoing flight demonstrations on Salisbury Plain after which it was conveyed to Newport docks and shipped back to Israel. It has been further reported that it was shipped back to Israel without clearing through customs. However no original source document has been found to support this.
2 Buster was an acronym for "**B**ackpack **U**nmanned air vehicle **S**urveillance **T**arget acquisition **E**nhanced **R**econnaissance".

Evaluation of the Mi-Tex Buster air vehicle began in October 2004 with Trial 'Urban Hummingbird'. Each of the Busters was painted in an overall drab green scheme. The poor quality of this picture, taken at Larkhill during a break in flying, is more than compensated by the fact that it is the only known image of all four Busters in the original scheme and with the original serial presentation.

amended to suit a newly-devised system of allocating 'type' serials to UAVs. As a result the Buster was allocated the 'Type serial' ZK009 and the four UAVs became ZK009-01 to ZK009-04 respectively, although initially they were painted as ZK0091, ZK0092, ZK0093 and ZK0094.[3]

'Urban Hummingbird' began in October 2004 and centred around the need for conducting close surveillance within a complex urban terrain. The trial was carried out in two phases, the first involving Special Forces training at Larkhill.

Reports at the time strongly suggested that the SAS disliked Buster on account of it being a little "too cumbersome" and, perhaps more importantly, "too noisy".[4] Representatives of the American manufacturer, who were also present at both phases of the trial were, it is alleged, also unhappy at Buster's performance on the day. However, although Buster had been rejected for use by Special Forces, the two systems were returned to the manufacturer for modifications pending a second trial phase with the RAF Regiment who had expressed an interest in Buster to fulfill a Force Protection role. This second trial phase took place at Larkhill in March 2005, but for reasons that have never been made clear, the RAF Regiment chose not to adopt the system.

The question of Buster's future at the end of the final Larkhill trial was complex. Technically these UAVs were viewed as being 'SAS kit' because they had been purchased especially for the Special Forces' trial. Despite the SAS not wanting these UAVs, all four were despatched to Hereford where they were simply placed into 'unwanted storage'. But shortly afterwards they were passed over to the Gunnery Training Team at Larkhill's School of Artillery.

All four Busters were again put into long-term storage. Being of sufficient size, they literally sat "on the shelf of the School's Quartermaster" until late 2006 when the Quartermaster set about clearing them from his books because he really did not know what to with them. There

was an easy solution which was simply to hand them over to 32 Regiment RA who at the time was the Royal Artillery's only user of UAVs. In fact the Busters were gratefully received since Desert Hawk (which 32 Regiment, RA were by then operating) had been effectively grounded due to it conflicting with emergency services' radio frequencies. Buster therefore provided an ideal platform to train raw pilots into handling small battlefield UAVs and furthermore came free-of-charge!

Busters began OPTAG training with 32 Regiment at the Senny Bridge Range during January 2007.[5] Later, and after returning to Larkhill, they were regularly flown over the Salisbury Plain Ranges where 22 Battery, 32 Regiment RA offered mini-UAV conversion training for units re-rolling to MUAVs.

Mi-Tex Buster – Specifications	
Length	1.02 m (3 ft 4 in)
Wingspan	1.22 m (4 ft 0 in)
Max take-off weight	4.5 kg (10 lb)
Max speed	65 kt (120 km/h; 75 mph)
Operational altitude	3,050 m (10,000 ft)
Range	8.1 n miles (15 km; 9.3 miles)
Endurance	6 hours

Mi-Tex Buster UAV Individual Aircraft Histories

ZK009-01 c/n 5041 Current with 32 Regiment, RA, Larkhill

ZK009-02 c/n 5042 Current with 32 Regiment, RA, Larkhill

ZK009-03 c/n 5043 Damaged in a crash on Salisbury Plain 9.7.07. Repaired locally but later written-off in a crash on Salisbury Plain 25.1.08.

ZK009-04 c/n 5044 Current with 32 Regiment, RA, Larkhill

EADS Scorpio-6

Produced by the European Aeronautic Defence & Space Company (EADS), Scorpio-6 was a light and robust VTOL UAV system designed for close-range surveillance and tactical intelligence gathering.

One Scorpio-6 system was leased in 2004/05 for a series of trials, but the system included only one UAV which had been allocated the serial ZK103 on 7 December 2004. The first trial, which consisted simply of several de-risking evaluation flights, took place at Larkhill immediately as part of Trial 'Mighty Magpie'. Two months later, between 10–24 February 2005, ZK103 was taken to Copehill Down Village

---

3 An unconfirmed report suggests that these aircraft were delivered as ZK0091, ZK0092, ZK0101 and ZK0102. The 'cancelled' serial ZK010 was re-allocated to the first of 60 Hawk T.2s on 18 November 2004.
4 As related to the author by pilots involved in the Larkhill trial.

5 OPTAG Training (**Op**erational **T**raining & **A**dvisory **G**roup) is compulsory for all soldiers as a lead-up to deployment and is usually tailor-made for a specific theatre. The training involves detailed familiarization and where individual skills are refreshed and where necessary, trained.

on Salisbury Plain for a second evaluation phase as part of Trial 'Urban Hummingbird' (also referred to as 'URBEX II'.)

Results of the trial were described as inconclusive and the sole Scorpio-6, ZK103, was returned to the manufacturer.

Scorpio-6 – Specifications	
Length	5 ft 7 in (1.70 m)
Overall height	2 ft 5½ in (0.75 m)
Main rotor diameter	5 ft 11 in (180 m)
Max take-off weight	29 lb (13 kg)
Payload capacity	13 lb (6 kg)
Max speed	19 kt (35 km/h; 22 mph)
Operational altitude	6,500 ft (2,000 m)
Endurance	1 hour

EADS Quadrocopter

The CPX4 Quadrocopter was initially developed by the Institute National Polytechnique of Grenoble and the Novadem Company before being adopted by EADS. This unusual VTOL UAV was powered by a quadruple rotor, driven by an electrical motor. Fitted with a side camera (although an optional down-looking sensor could also be fitted) Quadrocopter had the ability to remain stationary in a hover for up to 30 minutes. One example was evaluated by the MoD as part of Trial 'Urban Hummingbird' alongside the EADS Scorpio-6.

Allocated the serial ZK104 on 7 December 2004, the single Quadrocopter, together with the Scorpio-6, was immediately flown on a series of de-risking sorties at Larkhill as part of Trial 'Mighty Magpie'. It was later flown at Copehill Down Village between 10–24 February 2005 as part of Trial 'Urban Hummingbird'.

Quadrocopter was quickly assessed as being "too immature" for further evaluation and the single example, ZK104, was returned to the manufacturer's Newport, Gwent facility where, devoid of some parts, it was placed in long-term storage.

Boeing/Insitu ScanEagle UAV

ScanEagle was based on Insitu's SeaScan aircraft, a commercial ship-based surveillance platform. In 1998, Insitu and the University of Washington had demonstrated SeaScan's potential when they co-ordinated the first UAV transatlantic flight from Newfoundland to Scotland, using only 1½ gallons of fuel to do so.

In February 2002 Boeing teamed up with the Insitu Group to build and test ScanEagle. Insitu built the UAV at its Bingen, Washington factory and Boeing provided the systems integration, communications and payload technology expertise. Designed for continuous missions of 15+ hours, ScanEagle has always been conceived as a ship-based (or ship-controlled) system, launched from a 'Sky Wedge' hydraulic launcher and recovered by a novel 'Sky Hook' retrieving system.

A single Boeing/Insitu ScanEagle system was delivered to the UK for evaluation against contract TUAV/0031, which was signed on 4 November 2004 between Thales, Boeing and QinetiQ. The system, which was allocated the 'Type Serial' ZK105 on 22 February 2005, consisted of four ScanEagle UAVs which had all been specially modified by Boeing to comply with UK safety and airworthiness regulations.

'Arkansas Odyssey' was designed to demonstrate the utility of mini-UAVs in support of maritime operations. The ScanEagles were taken to the QinetiQ Hebrides Range where launches and recoveries were carried out from a land site on the island of South Uist. The first ScanEagle flight took place on 2 March; the last on 23 March 2005.

Launched from a pneumatic wedge catapult, ScanEagles flew a series of autonomous 15hr missions, guided by GPS and flown at around 50kts at 1,000 to 3,000ft (104m to 914m). ScanEagle was equipped with an inertially stabilized electro-optical or infra-red video camera and once airborne was operated by a controller aboard the Type 23 Destroyer, HMS *Sutherland*. The trial, which had only limited success, accounted for the loss of two ScanEagle UAVs.[6]

Trial 'Vigilant Viper', which again involved ScanEagle, took place a year later between 20 February and 17 March 2006. The trial achieved ten flights using the surviving two ScanEagle UAVs from 'Arkansas Odyssey' plus two additional new air vehicles. 'Vigilant Viper' was performed from HMS *Sutherland* and involved lashing a launcher onto the Destroyer's foredeck and connecting it to the ship's low-pressure air system. ScanEagle UAVs were launched and recovered from the ship, the aircraft being recovered by

---

[6] The term 'autonomous' has become a key factor in UAV development. Autonomy greatly increases the effectiveness of operations by allowing commanders to focus on the overall task and not on vehicle control.

One of the most unorthodox UAVs to take part in the MoD's Joint UAV Experimentation Programme was the EADS Quadrocopter. This 'sneak shot' of ZK104, taken from the long grass at the Copevill Down Village Range, Larkhill in February 2005 shows just how unusual a design Quadrocopter was. Unfortunately it was considered to be 'too immature' at the time of the trial.

directing the wingtip to a vertical recovery line suspended from a moving derrick.

'Vigilant Viper' marked several 'firsts'. By transferring electro-optical and infra-red imagery to a command control helicopter and via satellite to HQ facilities, it was possible for the first time to control a UAV from an airborne station. The helicopter involved was the QinetiQ-operated Sea King ASaC Mk.7 XV672.

With the conclusion of 'Vigilant Viper' the three surviving ScanEagles had their external identities removed and each was placed into storage. One of the three (ZK105/06) was conveyed to Farnborough in July 2006 and was statically displayed inside the Exhibition Hall.

Boeing/In-Situ ScanEagle – Specifications	
Powerplant	One 0.97kW (1.3hp) piston engine; two-blade propeller
Wingspan	9 ft 11 in (3.04 m)
Length overall	6 ft 7 in (2.00 m)
Weight (empty)	24.3 lb (11.0 kg)
Max payload	7.1 lb (3.2 kg)
Max launching weight	33.0 lb (15.0 kg)
Max level speed	68 kt (126 km/h; 78 mph)
Cruising speed	49 kt (91 km/h; 56 mph)
Max rate of climb at s/l	492 ft (150 m)/min
Ceiling	16,000 ft (4,870 m)
Max range, no reserves	810 n miles (1,500 km; 932 miles)
Max endurance, no reserves	15 hours

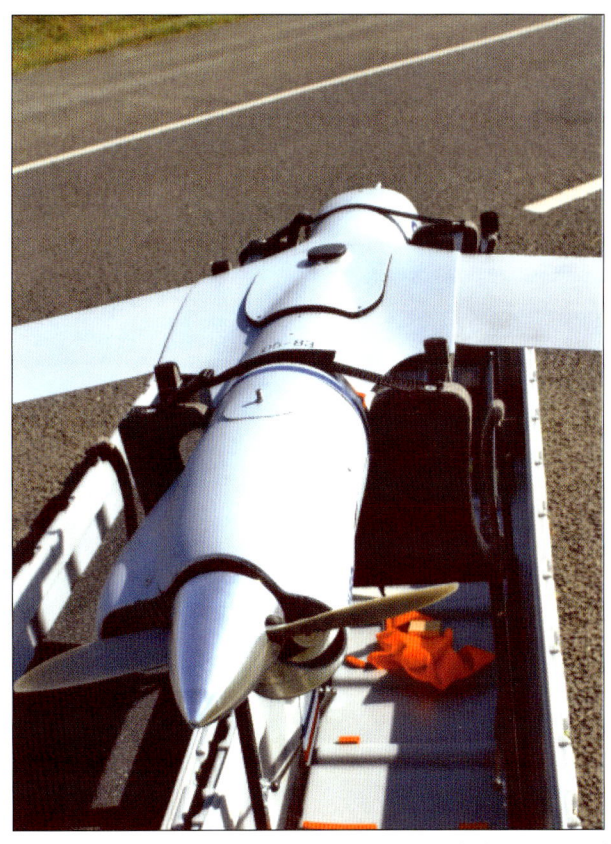

ScanEagle UAVs used for the JUEP trials wore serials that represented a corruption of serial suffix and c/n. ZK105/05 c/n AV.83 carried the identity "05-83" on the upper fuselage as seen in this view, taken at RIAT Fairford on 17 July 2005. (Dave Allen)

Above: *Boeing/In Situ ScanEagle ZK105/04 rests on its display stand prior to making undertaking a public flying demonstration at RIAT Fairford 17 July 2005. Note the ROYAL NAVY titling. (Dave Allen)*

Left: *Boeing/In Situ ScanEagle ZK105/04 was exhibited at RIAT Fairford in July 2005. It was the only public display by the ScanEagles in the UK and is seen performing one of the earliest public flying displays on 17 July 2005. (Dave Allen)*

The UAV Revolution

Boeing/In-Situ ScanEagle
Individual Histories

ZK105/01 c/n AV47 Although conveyed to the Hebrides Range, no evidence has been found that it was ever flown there.

ZK105/02 c/n AV48 Damaged in a minor crash 9.3.05 at the Hebrides Range. Later written-off when crashed into the sea off the Hebrides 21.3.05, possibly due to engine failure.

ZK105/03 c/n AV49 Written-off whilst operating within the Hebrides Range 19.3.05, possibly following a crash immediately after launch.

ZK105/04 c/n AV50 Flown on trials at the Hebrides Range. Later demonstrated at RIAT Fairford 7.05 in an orange scheme.

ZK105/05 c/n AV83 Flown on trials at the Hebrides Range. Later demonstrated at RIAT Fairford 7.05 in a grey scheme.

ZK105/06 c/n AV136 Deployed to Hebrides Range for trials. Later exhibited statically at SBAC Farnborough Show 7.06.

ZK105/07 c/n AV144 Deployed to the Hebrides Range until written-off in the Hebrides 4.3.06.

None of the ScanEagles carried their full serials; instead they were each marked with a corrupted abbreviation of serial suffix and c/n, eg ZK501/01 as 0147; ZK105/02 as 0248; ZK105/03 as 0349; ZK105/04 as 0450; ZK105/05 as 0583. ZK105/06 and ZK105/07 are assumed to have been marked as 0637 and 0744 respectively.

General Atomics MQ-1 Predator A
General Atomics MQ-9 Reaper

Just as the Meteor F.1, the first jet-powered front-line fighter, marked a significant milestone in Royal Air Force history, so the acquisition of Predator and Reaper UAVs has brought about a massive leap forward in RAF capability. What drove the urgency to acquire a modern front-line UAV was the worsening situation in Afghanistan. This led to adopting America's (then) most successful UAV, the General Atomics MQ-9 Reaper.

The origin of Reaper stretches back to the mid-1980s when Leading Systems Inc (LSI) began development of its Amber UAV for the US Department of Defense Joint Program Office. Although it offered great promise almost immediately, Amber proved to be too small to carry sufficient fuel and sensors required for optimum theatre operations. By 1988 Leading Systems Inc had begun to develop a scaled-up version, flight-testing a prototype the following year. However just as construction of production airframes began, it became very obvious that the company's limited resources had been considerably overstretched to the point that LSI faced serious financial difficulties. General Atomics Aeronautical Systems Inc stepped in and, in 1990, acquired the company assets and immediately funded further development of the scaled-up Amber UAV, by now referred to as GNAT-750. By 1993 the US Army was showing a determined interest and GNAT-750 was subsequently bought by several military customers, including the US Army and the CIA. The latter deployed two specially-modified examples to a military base in Albania from where reconnaissance overflights of Bosnia were conducted for a brief period in February 1994. Later in the year they resumed flights from Croatian bases.

In the meantime a US Advanced Concept Technology Demonstration (ACTD) programme to develop a Tier II Medium Altitude Long Endurance (MALE) UAV was awarded to General Atomics. What emerged was an improved version of GNAT-750 (designated I-GNAT) with a more powerful turbo-charged engine, radar altimeter, capability for air-to-air datalink relay payload and, perhaps most notably, provision for external hard points. It was soon re-named Predator and entered service with the USAF in 1995.

Interest by the Royal Air Force in acquiring a small UAV force was partially influenced by the recognised value of the Royal Artillery's Phoenix UAV even though the MoD was acutely aware of the difficulties that Phoenix had experienced in a high temperature theatre. Predator, it was argued, was proven in battle when deployed by US forces during the second Gulf War.

UK experience with the MQ-1A Predator began in January 2004 with the formation of 1115 Flight, RAF as a UAV Evaluation Unit. Operating as a subordinate unit to the USAF's 15th Reconnaissance Squadron, 1115 Flight took up residence at Indian Springs Air Force Auxiliary Field (ISAFAF), Nevada (north-west of Nellis AFB).

Towards the end of 2004, 1115 Flight was deployed to Iraq as part of a 44-man strong US/UK Combined Joint Predator Task Force, operating in support of UK forces around the Basra region. According to other reports, RAF Predators may well have also operated out of Balad, near Baghdad during September 2004.[7] The Balad operation was controlled directly from Nellis, via satellite link, and whilst there is little doubt that the Predator Detachment personnel were fully capable of controlling the aircraft throughout their missions, this unusual arrangement did significantly reduce the number of personnel committed to theatre, especially as many missions were said to have lasted in excess of 18 hours.

By Autumn 2006 plans to raise the status of the RAF drone operation were set in action. In October 2006 crews selected by the Royal Air Force began training on MQ-9A Reaper UAVs with the USAF 42nd Attack Squadron. Shortly afterwards, on 3 January 2007, 39 Squadron, RAF was officially reformed as the RAF's first Unmanned Air Vehicle (UAV) Squadron.[8] Based in the Nevada desert, 39 Squadron was immediately divided into two Flights located

---

7 Although these Predator drones were operated by the RAF in support of British forces, they remained USAF property and operated in standard USAF markings etc.

8 In American military circles the armed MQ-9A Reaper was frequently described as a "Predator on Steroids"!

Unofficially described as a "Predator on Steroids", the Royal Air Force took delivery of a fourth MQ-9 Reaper UAV in 2009. This was ZZ203, seen here at the start of a mission from Camp Bastion, fully equipped with two AGM-114P Hellfire air-to-surface missiles and four GBU-12 226kg (500lb) laser-guided bombs. Note the US fiscal serial 08-133 still visible on the dorsal fin and also the RAF flash on the tailplane undersides. (General Atomics Inc)

at separate US Air Force Bases in Nevada. 'A' Flight was formed by absorbing the Nellis AFB-based evaluation unit, 1115 Flight, whilst 'B' Flight was formed as an MQ-9A Reaper unit and resident at Creech AFB.

Under an Urgent Operational requirement (UOR), the MoD funded an initial five MQ-9As for the RAF. The aircraft were allocated the serials ZZ200 to ZZ204 on 19 March 2007 (although the actual allocation extended to ZZ213 to allow for follow-on orders). In the meantime, 39 Squadron began operations over Afghanistan using USAF Reapers.

The initial cadre of 39 Squadron personnel is reported to have arrived in Afghanistan in September 2007 to prepare for the main deployment the following month. The first RAF MQ-9A Reaper to deploy, ZZ200, arrived at Kandahar airfield in Regional Command South in early-October, joined shortly afterwards by ZZ201.[9]

Operating alongside those of the USAF 42nd Attack Squadron, it has been claimed that for several months the RAF Reapers were flown, on take-off and landing mainly by US aircrew using line-of-sight systems. Once outside the airfield's immediate air traffic zone of responsibility, control was handed over to 39 Squadron aircrew at Creech AFB, Nevada using Ku-Band satellite communications, adding a delay of between one and four seconds. Initially the RAF Reapers operated a surveillance role and were therefore unarmed.

The first operational loss of a 39 Squadron Predator occurred during the evening of 9 April 2008 when, mid-way through a surveillance sortie, ZZ200 made a forced-landing in a remote and unpopulated part of southern Afghanistan. Contemporary reports suggested that the need to have enforced a landing was due to a mechanical malfunction. Published accounts of events immediately afterwards tell of a specialist team of engineers and technicians who made a dramatic dash to the crash site to remove all vital and sensitive equipment before an RAF Harrier was called in to strike and destroy the stranded drone.

The loss of ZZ200 was made up when MQ-9A ZZ202 arrived in theatre during June 2008 but this too was later involved in an accident which occurred on 28 September, although on that occasion the drone was said to be repairable. A fourth MQ-9A Reaper, ZZ203, was handed over to the RAF towards the end of 2009 whilst the fifth, and final MQ-9 funded under UOR, ZZ204, was air-freighted into Kandahar airfield by an RAF C-17 in late-September 2010.[10]

MQ-9 Technical Data & Dimensions	
Powerplant	Honeywell TPE331-10T turboprop engine
Thrust	900 shp (max)
Wingspan	66 ft (20.1 m)
Length	36 ft (11 m)
Height	12 ft 6 in (3.8 m)
Weight (empty):	4,900 lb (2,223 kg)
Max take-off weight	10,500lb (4,780 kg)
Speed	230mph (cruise)
Range	1,000 n miles (1,150miles)
Ceiling	up to 50,000 ft (15,240 m)

Two months later, on 7 December, it was announced that a further five MQ-9A Reapers (and four additional GCSs) had been authorised. Finally, in May 2011, came the news that a reformed 13 Squadron will operate Reaper from RAF Waddington.

---
9 As reported in Air Forces Monthly, June 2008 issue.

10 US Fiscal Serials for the RAF MQ-9A Reapers are reported as 07-109 (ZZ200), 07-111 (ZZ201), 07-117 (ZZ202), 08-133 (ZZ203) and 10-157 (ZZ204).

The BAE Systems Family of UAVs

BAE Systems Soarer

What subsequently led to the High Endurance Rapid Technology Insertion Programme (HERTI) began as a concept in June 2001. Responsibility for this programme was vested with BAE Systems' Concept Engineering Group at Warton and from the earliest stage design work focused upon a finless air vehicle. The first design to emerge from this group was a small, unpowered delta-wing finless vehicle, known as Soarer. The first drawings were supplied to the Warton Mock-up Department in July 2001. Soarer was produced simply to enable the UAV pilot to develop a 'feel' for the flight characteristics of this configuration of vehicle.

Soarer was completed in September 2001. Flight tests began using conventional 'off-the-shelf' radio-control equipment, albeit in a rather unusual manner. Because of the need for strict security BAe Systems chose to take it to Parlick, near Chipping in NW England. Parlick was a popular site for hill soaring for both model and full-size gliders. Nobody, the company thought, would take any special notice of a group launching a glider off the hill-side. And they were right; nobody did take any notice!

Soarer's first flight was made on 24 September 2001; its final flight took place on 22 May 2002. Between these two dates the glider performed thirty-two flights in varying wind speeds from 10 to 50 knots (11 to 58mph). Many different yaw control techniques were tested with differing centre-of-gravity positions. Overall, Soarer proved an extremely cost-effective way of expanding the company's understanding of flying this type of vehicle.

The simplistic design of BAE Systems Soarer is clearly evident in this view, said to be taken in the area of Parlick, in north-west England. Soarer spearheaded a range of innovative UAVs as part of an extensive development study. (BAE Systems)

BAE Systems Kestrel UAV

In developing a semi-autonomous UAV, BAE Systems designed a novel configuration that included a blended-wing body of advanced low-cost composite materials. It was flown semi-autonomously by an advanced fly-by-wire flight-control system that relied almost solely on air-pressure sensors mounted flush to its skin. It was powered by two small jet engines above the trailing edge.

In pursuing development of a semi-autonomous UAV, BAE Systems designed a novel configuration that included a blended-wing body of advanced low-cost composite materials. Working in collaboration with Cranfield University, BAE Systems produced Kestrel UAV as the first of a series of designs. The sole Kestrel is seen here immediately after completion and flanked by the team responsible for its construction. (BAE Systems)

BAE Systems Kestrel became the first jet-powered UAV to fly in UK airspace when, in March 2003, it flew at Machrihanish under Class B conditions, G-8-003. (Ian Wallace Shaw)

Working in collaboration with Cranfield University, the design developed into the Kestrel, a 5.5m (18ft), 140kg (309lb) UAV that, in March 2003, became the first jet-powered UAV to fly in UK airspace under civil registration and approved by the Civil Aviation Authority.

Registered G-8-003 for initial flight trials at Machrihanish, Campbeltown, Kestrel proved to be difficult to control in flight. Nevertheless the Kestrel programme was relatively low-cost and allowed rapid development over a relatively brief flight-test phase of only six months. Furthermore the programme enabled BAE Systems to build up the right experience in manufacture, integration and test of a subscale aircraft while demonstrating the use of advanced low-cost composites. It also inspired BAE Systems towards achieving fully autonomous flight which in turn led to the BAE Systems Raven.

BAE Systems Raven UAV

It took just nine months from the initial design of Raven to its flight trials. Considerably stealthier in appearance and aerodynamically highly unstable, the jet-powered Raven was fully autonomous from take-off to landing and was especially configured to provide agile performance capabilities. As a sub-scale demonstrator for unmanned combat air vehicle (UCAV) technology, Raven proved to be much more agile than Kestrel and was designed to meet the (subsequently cancelled) Future Offensive Air System (FOAS), a programme for exploring the possibility of replacing RAF Tornado fighters with a deep-strike UAV.

The first of two prototype Ravens (identified with c/n DV001 to denote Development Vehicle 1) was air-freighted to Woomera Test Range where, on 17 December 2003, it made its intital test flight. A second prototype flew at Woomera for the first time on 24 November 2004.[11]

Experience with Raven led BAE Systems development team to the Corax UAV.

---

11 At least one reliable source has stated that the 2nd prototype Raven first flew as G-8-004.

BAE Systems Raven proved to be much more agile than Kestrel and was designed to meet a Future Offensive Air System (FOAS). Raven made its first flight at the Woomera Range on 17 December 2003 and is seen here in typical Woomera terrain. (BAE Systems)

The sole BAE Systems Corax was designed as a UAV technology demonstrator and is seen here immediately after roll-out on a wet day at Warton. It was later flight-tested at Woomera in early-2005. (BAE Systems)

BAE Systems CORAX UAV

In 2004 BAE Systems modified the Raven design, keeping the centre fuselage, systems and engine the same but replacing the highly-swept Raven wing surfaces with a larger, higher-aspect ratio composite wing. What was perhaps lost in stealth features was compensated by achieving greater mission endurance. The revised design was named BAE Systems Corax, taking its name from the Latin for 'raven'.

Aimed at creating a highly survivable strategic UAV system, BAE Systems drew on advanced flight control systems technology from Raven in order to stabilize and control what was undoubtedly a highly novel, next generation air vehicle.

Just one Corax was built and was first flown on 25 January 2005 at the Woomera Range under Class B conditions as G-8-005.

Like its predecessors, CORAX was designed solely as a UAV technology demonstrator, intended to explore intelligence, surveillance, target acquisition and reconnaissance roles (ISTAR) as well as survivable designs.

BAE Systems HERTI & Fury UAV

Having developed an impressive autonomous capability with the Raven and Corax programmes, BAE Systems took the logical step of applying that technology to a low-cost vehicle series of UAVs with a multiple applications in both military and civil security fields. The result was the HERTI (High Endurance Rapid Technology Insertion) programme.

Rather than create an original design, BAE Systems based its prototype HERTI vehicle on a motor glider designed by Jaroslaw Janowski of the Polish manufacturer, J & AS Aero Design. One unfinished Janowski J-5 Marco airframe was imported from Poland and modified at Warton, Lancashire to BAE Systems' specification. Known as the HERTI-1D, the prototype used the same BMW jet engine, systems and ground station as the BAE Corax. Within seven months of arriving at Warton the HERTI-1D prototype was completed and air-freighted to Australia and test-flown at the Woomera Range in mid-December 2004, possibly under Class B conditions, as G-8-006.

Initial flight test results were impressive. HERTI-1D achieved a ceiling of 6,000m, an endurance of 25+ hours and an operational radius of over 1,000km (621 miles).

Only one HERTI-1D was built before BAE Systems realised that a piston engine-powered HERTI had a better payload and endurance than the HERTI-1D. Development of the -1D was discontinued and instead the company

HERTI-1A was powered by a BMW twin-cylinder engine. The first example made its first flight, as G-8-008, at Machrihanish on 18 August 2005. (BAE Systems)

Kestrel, Raven and CORAX eventually led to the HERTI series. It is believed that this example, in spite of being marked G-8-007, was a ground trials aircraft. It is seen here at a very wet BAE Systems Warton Families Day.

Throughout its development, the BAE Systems HERTI appeared with various modifications. What was considered to be the ultimate version was displayed at Farnborough 2008 albeit claimed to be only a ground test vehicle. Newly-fitted three-piece ailerons and elevators are evident in this view. (Michael I Draper)

produced the larger HERTI-1A. Powered by a BMW twin cylinder piston engine HERTI-1A was a larger, modified composite airframe based on the J & AS Aero Design J-6 Fregata motor glider. Offering an improved endurance and an increased payload, the J-6 featured redesigned landing gear and a wingspan increased to 12.6m (41ft 4in). It is believed that BAE Systems subsequently funded an initial run of ten HERTI airframes, all based on the Polish J-6. The funding, it has been said, enabled BAE Systems to buy the rights for the J-6 on which was based a scratch design sub-contracted to Slingsby Sailplanes Ltd of Kirkbymoorside.

HERTI-1A made its first flight, as G-8-008, at Macrihanish airfield, Campbeltown on 18 August 2005 and in doing so became the first UAV to fly a fully autonomous mission in UK airspace.

In late-2006 a HERTI vehicle flew several autonomous missions from the Woomera Range to expand the flight envelope, or distance and height limits to which the UAV had flown in real tests. Some months later, in mid-2007, another series of test flights took place, this time from West

Quite what goes through the marshaller's mind when he knows he is facing an oncoming aircraft with no occupant is unimaginable. During the autumn of 2007 this was a regular event at RAF Bastion, Afghanistan whilst BAE Systems HERTI ZZ251 was used for a 3-month evaluation in Afghanistan under the aegis of the Air Warfare Centre (BATTLELAB). Its principle role was as a "hi-definition stills-camera platform". What, at first glance, seems like a ludicrously surreal situation in a ground marshaller guiding an unmanned aircraft can be explained by the video camera mounted on the nose which allows the "pilot" – seated some distance away – to follow the marshaller's instructions. (BAE Systems)

The UAV Revolution 333

One of the twelve airframes imported from Poland for conversion into HERTI UAVs was re-designed with a 'strap on' weapons pylon. Thus evolved a tactical version of the HERTI surveillance UAV for which BAE Systems re-named as a Fury. This unmarked example is seen at Farnborough 2008. (Michael I Draper)

Sale airbase (in south-east Australia) and which were designed to increase the flight envelope even further.

Relatively few test flights were carried out in the UK but one significant event took place at the end of 2007 when a HERTI became the first UAV to fly in the UK with a CAA certification. Appropriately registered as G-HERT on 22 November 2007, the flights were made out of Machrihanish.

Development of HERTI towards what could be termed as the production variant led to the HERTI-1B. Powered by a Rotax 914F engine the -1B variant was controlled by a more advanced autonomous ICE II mission system (payload). Official interest in BAE Systems' development work on HERTI took an important step in early-2006 with Project MORRIGAN, a programme designed to establish a mutually beneficial relationship between Air Warfare Centre UAV Battlelab (AUB) and BAE Systems. A HERTI-1B was taken to Australia where, at the Woomera Range, it made its initial test flight on 5 November 2006, followed by a series of evaluation and test flights between 16 October and 10 December 2006.

The next phase saw HERTI deployed to Afghanistan in August 2007. Allocated the serial ZZ251, it was air-freighted to RAF Bastion where, for three months, it took part in a "war-fighting experiment" in order to help understand the full capability of HERTI. Unlike other UAVs deployed to theatre (which were fitted with a live video link), HERTI ZZ251 used as a hi-definition stills-camera platform. A team of eleven personnel, trained for the Afghanistan operation, helped to produce a mosaic of still images through wide and narrow field of view sensors. Results were said to be encouraging and at the end of the brief trial, ZZ251 was returned to BAE Systems, Warton in November 2007.[12]

Two more HERTI airframes were allocated military identities. Those were ZZ252 and ZZ253, both designated HERTI-XPA denoting Experimental Production Aircraft. A further serial, ZZ254, was allocated to a HERTI XPA-1B.

BAE Systems Fury UAV

BAE Systems chose the 2008 AUVSI North America exhibition to unveil its Fury UAV. Described by the manufacturer as an armed reconnaissance and close support UAV, outwardly Fury was identical to HERTI. What set Fury apart from a standard HERTI was the novel means of strapping a weapons pylon across the wing, thus avoiding any need to drill into the wing or having to build in hard points. Thales' new Lightweight Multi-role Missile (LMM) was selected because of its suitability for lightweight maneuverable platforms and for its "ability to fire on the move while delivering significant precision effects".

Only two examples of Fury were completed, the first of which (reported to be c/n DV008) was used purely for ground tests whilst the second prototype (reported to be c/n DV009) was air-freighted out to Australia and flight-tested at Woomera.[13]

HERTI 1D Known Technical Data & Dimensions	
Powerplant	BMW jet engine
Wing span	26 ft 2 in (8.0 m)
Endurance	25+ hours

HERTI 1A Technical Data & Dimensions	
Powerplant	BMW R1150 RS twin-cyliner, 4-stroke piston engine
Max speed	120 kt (222km/h; 138.2 mph)
Wing span	41 ft 4 in (12.6 m)
Length	16 ft 9 in (5.1 m)
Height	5 ft 6 in (1.7 m)
Weight	40 lb (18 kg)
Cruising Speed	50 kt at 5,000 m (Max: 70 kt)
Endurance	30 hours
Weight	1102.3 lb (500 kg)
Payload Capacity	319.7 lb (145 kg)

---

12 As reported by AWC BattleLab officers at ParAberporth 2008.

13 The marks G-8-007 were carried by a HERTI 1A which was statically displayed at a Warton Families Day. BAE Systems report that this example was never, in fact, fitted with a powerplant. However, the Fury displayed at Farnborough 2008 was unmarked but showed signs of having previously carried the marks G-8-007. BAE Systems personnel present at the show reported the c/ns as quoted.

HERTI 1B Technical Data & Dimensions	
Powerplant	Rotax 914F F4 115hp; 4-cylinder, 4-stroke
Max speed	120 kt (222 km/h; 138.2 mph)
Wingspan	41 ft 4 in (12.6 m)
Length	16 ft 9 in (5.1 m)
Height	5 ft 6 in (1.7 m)
Weight	40 lb (18 kg)
Cruising Speed	50 kt at 5,000 m (Max: 70 kt)
Endurance	20 hours
Weight	1653.5 lb (750 kg)

BAE Systems Mantis UCAV

Jointly funded by BAE Systems and the MoD, Mantis was launched at the 2008 SBAC Farnborough show as the first genuine fly-by-wire, all-electric controlled aircraft. It was designed essentially to meet the MoD's Deep & Persistent (D&P) intelligence, surveillance and reconnaissance needs. The lack of hydraulic systems meant that it could be broken down to fit into a C-130 Hercules, thus allowing for rapid deployment to theatre.

With a wingspan in excess of 20m (65ft) and a fuselage length of over 10m (32.8ft), its size allowed for a significant payload of sensors and potential weaponry. When displayed in mock-up form at Farnborough, it was seen to have six hard-points for underwing stores and weapons although it was mooted that up to eight points could be eventually fitted.

Powered by two Rolls-Royce RR250B-17 turboprop engines, Mantis was said to be able to cruise at around 300mph (483km/h) and to have an endurance of over 24 hours. Its operational altitude was designed to be between 25,000ft (7620m) and 50,000ft (15240m).

The first prototype Mantis was allocated the serial ZK210 in December 2008 ahead of a successful first flight at the Woomera Test Range on 21 October 2009. It is reported to have returned to Warton in June 2010.

BAE Systems Taranis UCAV

When, in March 2005, the UK MoD announced its Strategic Unmanned Air Vehicle (Experiment) programme (SUAVE), what began was a programme to assemble evidence to inform a decision on UK Forces' future use of UAVs and procurement options. By December 2005, when

The BAE Systems stand at Farnborough 2008 contained a full-size mock-up of the Mantis UAV, one of the largest UAVs to emerge as part of the company's ambitious UAV development programme. Although designed essentially to meet an ISTAR role, the underwing stores and weapons clearly show a possible alternative role. (Michael I Draper). The first and only prototype, ZK210, was later flown for the first time at Woomera Range on 21 October 2009. (BAE Systems)

a UK Defence Industry Strategy White Paper was published, the path was clear for targeted investment in UCAV technology demonstrator programmes.

The first of these programmes was announced by the MoD in December 2006 with the awarding of a £124million contract to BAE Systems to develop unmanned systems technology within Project Taranis. Only one Taranis UAV was planned. It was allocated the serial ZZ250 and was designed to act as a Technology Demonstrator Vehicle (TDV). What the programme was intended to achieve was to help increase the understanding of the risks and compromises involved with integrating a number of key Strategic Air Vehicle technologies. It would not be involved in firing live weapons but would have a weapon release system incorporated into the trials programme.

Taranis is likely to be one of the world's largest unmanned air vehicles. Construction of it began at the end of 2007. Roll-out from BAE Systems' Warton facility took place on Monday 12 July 2010. Test flying was due to start at the Woomera Test Range in 2011.

The roll-out ceremony for BAE Systems Taranis, on 12 July 2010, had the air of a Hollywood spectacle with more than a hint of science fiction about it. No identity was carried. (BAE Systems)

Chapter 11

Other UAVs

Since the mid-1960s a number of remotely powered vehicles (RPVs) and unmanned aerial vehicles (UAVs) have been developed in the UK. Many were private venture programmes; others were developed with MoD funding. Some were evaluated by the services and the following is a summary of those known to have been either funded or evaluated by UK forces or in some instances procured for service use.

Skyleader MATS-A

Formed in 1965 specifically to manufacture remote control equipment, Skyleader Radio Control Ltd became one of the leading suppliers of telecommand, remote control and associated electronics systems for use in a wide variety of unmanned aircraft.

Skyleader also entered unmanned aircraft production with the MATS-A aerial target system. Designed by Stewart Unwins, the owner of Skyleader, MATS-A was aimed at providing a cheap target for air defence training. Hand-launched, its size, speed and flight path presented a similar engagement difficulty to that of a fighter ground attack aircraft flying at between 400 and 500 knots. Once the mission was completed MATS-A was belly-landed on its fuselage under-surfaces.

The British Army became the principal user of MATS-A and purchased several hundred for use at a number of Ranges, including Manorbier, Otterburn, and the West German Ranges. The Royal Navy also acquired examples for small-arms practice from ships.[1]

When, in 1986, the Navy declared its MQM-36A Shelduck obsolescent, it was agreed that its replacement should be MATS-A. Used as a close range target for guns of 40mm calibre and below, MATS-A quickly gained an image of "Boys' Toys" yet proved an ideal target for developing aimer skills, giving a challenging Fighter Ground Attack simulation at very low cost. Transported globally with ease, MATS-A required a team of just two personnel to operate. In this 1988 view a naval rating launches a MATS-A while his team-mate takes radio-command. (Fleet Target Group)

---

1 Some published sources describe the MATS-A as the AEL MATS-A, but the only connection between Skyleader and AEL Ltd was that AEL used Skyleader radio equipment. To the best of the author's knowledge AEL Ltd was never involved in MATS-A. Skyleader continued to trade until about 1991 when the business was taken over by two former employees and continued in different premises under the name RCL Ltd. By then MATS-A was out of service. RCL survived for several years until being wound up in approximately 1997.

Apart from Skeet and Banshee, Short Brothers Air Services won a contract to repair and service AEL Snipe target drones. These aircraft operated across Ranges to provide targets for small-arms firepower. Snipe Mk.III c/n SN0492 is seen at Larkhill on 14 August 1987. Note how the overall red scheme is augmented with a black and white fin in the same manner that some Banshees were repainted. (Michael I Draper)

MATS-A – Specifications	
Powerplant	One Merco 10cc single-cylinder piston engine; 2-blade propeller
Wing span	5 ft 8 in (1.73 m)
Length	4 ft 0 in (1.22 m)
Max launch weight	8½ lb (3.85 kg)
Max speed	78 kts (145 km/h; 90 mph)
Operating range	Approx 1.7 n.miles; (2 miles; 3.2 km)
Endurance	15-20 minutes

AEL 4111 Snipe

Aero Electronics (AEL) Ltd became established as a manufacturer of small, low-cost radio- and optically-guided systems for target drones, reconnaissance or other unmanned aircraft applications. The company also developed a range of small remotely-powered vehicles, the Merlin, Falcon, Heron and the AEL 4030 Training Drone. All of these were superceded by the more successful AEL 4111 Snipe range.

The original AEL 4111 Snipe Mk.I was designed as an international target system for air defence guns and close-range missiles. The Snipe system comprised two aircraft, airborne guidance equipment, radio-triggered visual enhancement high-intensity strobe lights and radar-triggered recovery parachutes etc.

Powered by a 56cc single-cylinder piston engine with glo-plug ignition, Snipe Mk.I could achieve a maximum speed of 128mph (206km/h). Launched by a simple rubber bungee catapult it had a maximum controllable range of 3.1 miles (5.0km) and an average sortie endurance of around 45 minutes. Recovery was by normal belly landing (if space permitted) or by an Irvin (GB) 21ft (6.4m) diameter cruciform parachute.

Snipe Mk.I was soon superseded by the Snipe Mk.II; both variants were sold to over 20 countries. The Mk.II was designed to be engaged with 20-40mm ammunition as well as man-portable surface-to-air missiles. Powered by an 8.8hp (6.6kW) Piper P.100 single-cylinder two-stroke engine Snipe Mk.II was just 2mph faster than the Snipe Mk.I but had a greater maximum control range of 5 miles (8km).

In 1981 a larger and faster development of Snipe was introduced, as the AEL 4700 Snipe Mk.III. Powered by the more powerful WAM 342 engine, Snipe III offered a more realistic small target aircraft for gunners. A moderate number were used by the British Army and a number of overseas operators upgraded their target systems to utilise the Snipe Mk.III.

Further developments of Snipe were carried out by Meggitt who acquired AEL Ltd and its design bureau. Meggitt introduced the Mk.4, Mk.5 and Mk.15, the last of which entered service in April 1989. However, it remains unclear to what extent British forces used these variants, if at all.

AEL Snipe Mks I & II – Specifications	
Powerplant	One 56cc single-cylinder piston engine; 2-blade propeller
Wing span	8 ft 2½ in (2.50 m)
Length	6 ft 10¾ in (2.10 m)
Max launch weight	40 lb (18 kg)
Max speed	111 kt (206 km/h; 128 mph)
Operating range	3.1 miles (5.0 km)
Endurance	25-40 minutes

AEL Snipe Mk. III – Specifications	
Powerplant	One 342cc (25hp; 18.6kW) two-cylinder, two-stroke, air-cooled piston engine with electronic ignition; 2-blade propeller
Wing span	10 ft 3½ in (3.14 m)
Max in-service speed	In excess of 150 kts (278 km/h; 173 mph)
Average endurance	1 hour

RCS 4024 Heron

RCS Guided Weapons Systems (a division of Radio Control Specialists Ltd) designed and manufactured a wide range of small, low-cost radio or optically-guided target drones and RPVs in the 1970s. The company enjoyed some success with its catapult-launched, delta-winged RCS 4012 Falcon Target System (as well as the RCS 4015 Falcon Reconnaissance variant and the composite RCS 4017 Falcon).[2]

---

[2] An early customer for RCS 4012 and RCS 4015 was the Libyan Government with deliveries in 1973–74.

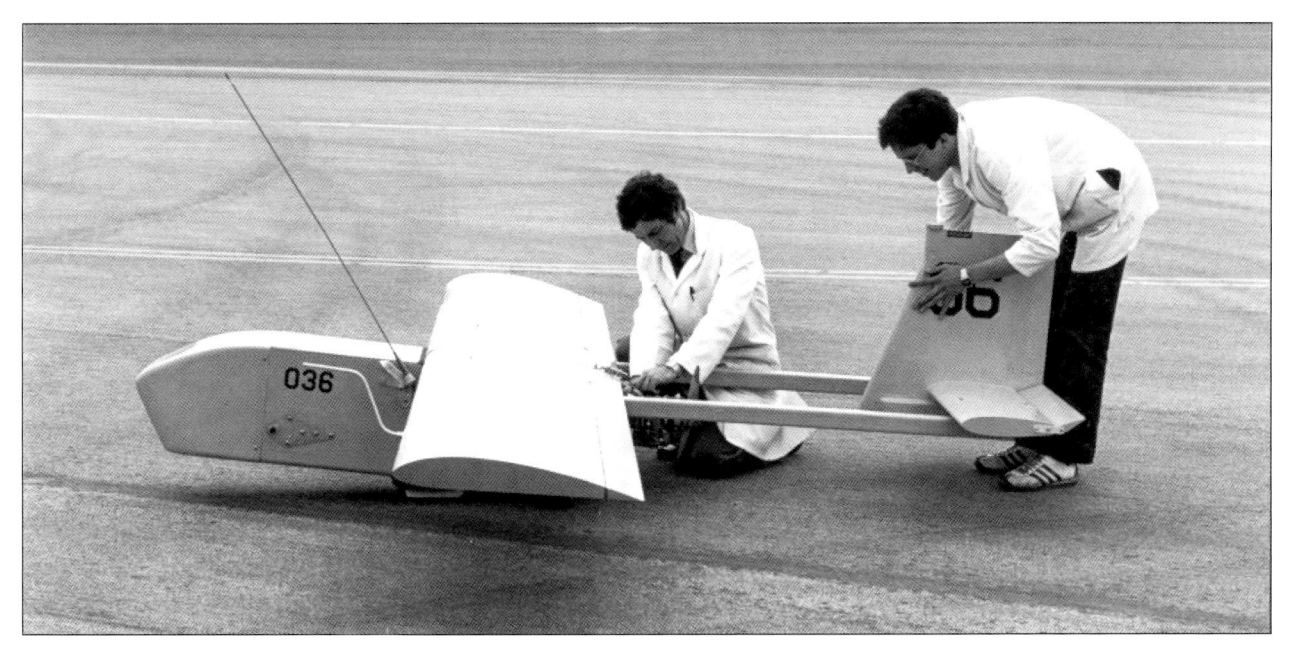

British Aerospace developed the Stabileye as a platform for a variety of reconnaissance tasks. Suitable payloads included the British Aerospace Linescan infra red system as well as conventional photographic and television equipment. Stabileye No.36 is seen being prepared for flight at Filton. (British Aerospace Neg. No.72392)

Of slightly lesser size was the delta-shaped flying-wing RCS Merlin which was manufacturered using polystyrene foam with a plywood skin, Merlin was powered by a 10hp (7.5kW) piston engine and was fitted with a tricycle landing-gear. Three variants were offered: RCS 4018 Target System for training air defence weapons crews; the RCS 4019 Camera System for short-range aerial reconnaissance and the RCS 4020 which, as a composite variant was able to combine the roles of RCS 4018 and 4019.

Altogether of different appearance was the RCS 4024 Heron. It was a high-wing monoplane powered by a 45cc (7.5kW; 10hp) engine which could be flown off from the ground and landed in a similarly orthodox manner. Designed primarily for small-arms target work, but suitable for other applications, the RCS 4024 Heron was ordered by the British Army with deliveries commencing in 1974.

RCS 4024 Heron – Specifications	
Powerplant	One 45cc (7.5kW; 10hp) single-cylinder piston engine; 2-blade propeller
Wing span	9 ft 10 in (3.00 m)
Length	7 ft 0 in (2.13 m)
Max launch weight	34 lb (15.4 kg) (catapult launch) 53 lb (24.0 kg) (ground take-off)
Max payload	15 lb (6.8 kg) (catapult launch) 30 lb (13.6 kg) (ground take-off)
Max speed	104 kt (193 km/h; 120 mph)
Max control range	2.7 n miles (3.1 miles; 5.0 km)
Endurance	30 minutes

BAe Stabileye

The Stabileye family of mini-RPVs was developed over a number of years for various MoD and BAe research programmes. Design work began in 1974 as a private venture project by BAC Dynamics Group in 1974 although the MoD did share the funding of the Stabileye Mk.1 programme. The initial concept was to produce a simple, robust mini-RPV, capable of testing a large variety of sensors and other mission payloads. A key airframe/autopilot design factor of Stabileye (which influenced the choice of name) was its high level of inherent stability which enabled acceptable surveillance images to be recovered from unstabilised sensor packages.

The development of Stabileye was jointly undertaken with RAE Farnborough. BAC was responsible for the airframe design, flight control system and payload installations whilst RAE Farnborough designed and developed the ground control equipment.

The prototype Stabileye Mk.1 made its first flight on 24 October 1974 and was powered by a 3kW (4hp) Rowena 60cc piston engine. It was capable of carrying an 8kg payload. Just twelve Mk.1s were built and between them they carried out over 200 successful flights. All were used primarily as development vehicles with a wide variety of units carried on flight tests, including cameras, homing heads, radar altimeters and other similar devices.

Stabileye Mk.2, which first flew on 20 December 1979, was fundamentally a Mk.1 which was strengthened structurally in order to carry test payloads of up to 15kg. Built mainly of GRP and aluminium alloy, with a steel tube centre fuselage space-frame, Stabileye Mk.2 was powered by a 5.6kW (7.5hp) Weslake T-116 engine.

Fitted with extended wing-tips, the prototype Mk.2 was used for demonstrating a launch from a truck-mounted ramp. Other Mk.2s were fitted with a Luneburg lens in a "thimble" nose to enhance its radar signature. An attempt was made to market Stabileye Mk.2 as an aerial gunnery target but it failed to gain any orders.

In 1980 Stabileye underwent an extensive re-design to improve the payload-carrying capability to at least 25kg and also to make Stabileye suitable for quantity production. Powered by a 7hp (5.2kW) Weslake 116 two-stroke petrol

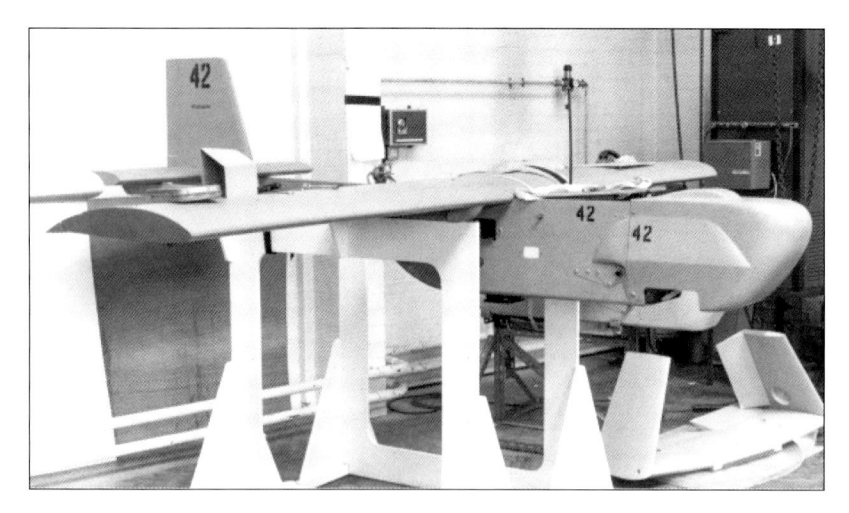

Precisely how many Stabileye UAVs were built remains unconfirmed. The highest known identity is No.42 which is seen here inside the British Aerospace Filton facility on 26 April 1983. (Peter J Cooper)

engine driving a pusher propeller, the prototype Mk.3 (c/n 30) was first flown on 24 September 1980. In December 1981, the Mk.3 won the first of several Ministry of Defence contracts worth a total of £600,000 for an initial batch of ten aircraft (c/ns 30-39). All were used for extended flight trials, including trials of a BAe Dynamics infra-red linescan system. In other trials, Stabileye was to be used to assess the effectiveness of RPVs as anti-radiation weapons.

A second MoD order was announced in May 1983 which accounted for a further eight Stabileyes (c/ns 40-47) to which a ninth was subsequently added. Unconfirmed reports suggest that production reached an eventual fifty aircraft.

Derived rom a design specially prepared for the MoD Phoenix competition, the design philosophy behind Stabileye Mk.4 was to maintain the stable flight platform of earlier marks but also to introduce minimal radar, acoustic and IR signatures. That was achieved by designing a fuselage with a triangular cross-section, formed as a flat floor with two sloping sides.

Initially the Mk.4 incorporated "flip-out" wings which allowed it to be launched from its storage box. However this concept was later dropped and when the prototype made its first flight, in 1985, it was considerably enlarged (to accommodate a stabilized IR imager), had a conventional fixed-wing and was designed to operate from a standard pneumatic rail launcher. It was these factors that helped Stabileye Mk.4 to retain a place in the Phoenix competition until the final contract award stage.

Two engines were considered for Stabileye Mk.4: an 18.6kW (25hp) NGL WAEL 342 two-cylinder, two-stroke engine (installed in the prototype when first flown) and a Lotus 225 two-cylinder, four-stroke engine of the same rating. The engine was mounted in the fuselage centre-section, above the wing, and drove a two-blade pusher propeller through a flexibly coupled shaft.

Recovery was by parachute and airbag in a similar fashion to Stabileye Mk.3, but in the case of the Mk.4 the air vehicle was inverted for the recovery sequence.

When the MoD eventually announced that GEC-Marconi was the successful contender for Phoenix, all work on Stabileye effectively stopped. Just one example of the Stabileye Mk.4 was built.

Although British Aerospace developed the Stabileye Mk.2 as simply a research vehicle it was seen ideally as a target UAV. Nevertheless it was capable of carrying a wide variety of experimental payloads up to 8kg. This static test example, seen in June 1979, shows well the bulbous fuselage section and twin fin arrangement. (British Aerospace Dynamics Group, via Ken Munson.)

Stabileye Mk. 3 – Specifications	
Wing span	12 ft 0 in (3.65 m)
Length	9 ft 4 in (2.87 m)
All-up weight	132.3 lb (60.0 kg)
Max payload	55.1 lb (25.0 kg)
Operational speed range	43–78 kt (80–145 km/h; 50–90 mph)
Max endurance	2 hours at up to 2,000 ft (609.6 m) (max controllable height)

Source: Flight International 12 Dec 1981

Stabileye Mk. 4 – Specifications	
Wing span	12 ft 0 in (3.65 m)
Length	11 ft 2 in (3.42 m)
All-up weight	132.3 lb (60.0 kg)
Max payload	110.0 lb (50.0 kg)
Operational speed range	68–87.5 kt (126–162 km/h; 78–101 mph)
Max endurance	Up to 7 hours, depending on engine and payload.

GEC Avionics Machan
(Cranfield A2 Machan)

Designed and built by the College of Aeronautics at Cranfield, the GEC Avionics Machan (also known as the Cranfield A2 Machan) was a one-off unmanned flight research vehicle funded largely by the Ministry of Defence (via RAE Farnborough). GEC/Marconi Avionics also made a substantial private-venture investment in the Machan programme.

The primary purpose of Machan was the investigation of target recognition and designation as well as navigational, environmental and operational aspects.

Cranfield was responsible for the airframe, power plant and digital flight systems. The airframe was designed by Professor Dennis Howe (Head of Aircraft Design at the College) and featured an aluminium diamond-shaped fuselage for easy manufacture whilst the wing was constructed in fibre-glass with an alloy spar. It was powered by one 13.4kW (18hp) NGL WAM 274-6 flat-twin engine mounted in the rear fuselage and driving a wooden pusher fan within a propulsor duct.[3]

Launched by compressed air, flight control during the early flight stage was by a ground-based pilot. In later flight stages an on-board flight control computer, having been pre-programmed on the ground for whatever mission was required, was used. It is believed that this was the first occasion that a UAV carried its own digital on-board flight control system. The ultimate aim was to achieve a fuller understanding of the possible operational roles that UAVs might undertake in providing information that would lead to cost-effective procurement and deployment of UAVs with enhanced capability.

The first, and only, prototype Machan made its initial flight at RAE Thurleigh on 19 February 1981. By 1984 it had achieved much of what was expected of it and accordingly all flying ceased.

GEC/Cranfield A2 Machan – Specifications	
Wing span	12 ft 0 in (3.65 m)
Length	7 ft 0 in (2.13 m)
Height	1 ft 9½ in (0.55 m)
Mission payload	33 lb (15 kg)
Max take-off weight	180 lb (0.82 kg)
Max speed	115 kt (213 km/h; 132 mph)
Cruising speed	64 kt (119 km/h; 74 mph)
Stalling speed	43 kt (80 kn/h; 50 mph)
Operational ceiling	1,000 ft (304.8 m)
Range	130 n miles (241 km; 150 miles)
Max endurance	2 hours

Intora-Firebird UAV

What made the Firebird helicopter so unique was its unconventional engine which used 85% hydrogen peroxide (H_2O_2) fuel injected into rotor-tip mounted jets. The fuel was designed to break down in the tip jets to produce superheated steam and oxygen. Beyond that there was no pollution.

The original concept dates back to the 1950s when inventor Gilbert W. Magill (of Glendale, California) designed and patented a single-seat helicopter powered by hydrogen peroxide. Magill flew his prototype Rotor-Craft RH-1 Pinwheel in April 1954. Magill formed another company, Aerospace General at Odessa, Texas and continued to develop his design against a USN contract. It is reported that Magill was forced to abandon his work on the project after his assets (including the helicopter design) were seized by the Bank. Subsequently, a former NASA engineers, Elke Mueller, managed to raise $200,000 to pay off the bank. Aerospace General was formed, the basic design was improved and a further prototype was successfully test-flown before Magill's death.

But Mueller could not raise sufficient capital for development and simply abandoned all further work on the project and Aerospace General went into bankruptcy. The rights were acquired by Afibra Handels (later, Liteco Helicopter Systems) of Switzerland, who developed a two-seat, enclosed version, designated ATLAS (Advanced Technology Light Airborne System). Liteco contract Advanced Technologies of the USA to build two new single-seat prototypes (N9042F c/n 00001 and N8186E c/n 00002) as proof-of-concept examples. These were shipped to Switzerland for test-flying. A two-seat variant (F-WGTX) was later built and first flown on 3 May 1990 but all trials work stopped when Liteco failed in 1993.

The British connection began when Intora-Firebird plc was formally registered on 17 October 1997 and acquired the rights and patent, immediately forming a partnership with Innosuisse Corporation in which INSC held 48% and Intora 52%.

Along with the design rights, Intora-Firebird had also acquired the original single-seat version (N8168E) and two French-registered prototypes (F-WGTX and F-WGTY). All were conveyed by road to Intora's base at Southend airport around 1 April 1998. The American-registered prototype was re-registered in the UK (as G-BXZN) on 25 August 1998 – just in time to be launched at the 1998 Farnborough International show.

Intora-Firebird marketed the Firebird in single- and two-seater versions and visitors to the company's stand at Farnborough showed considerable interest in the project, none more so than the Ministry of Defence who urged Intora to explore an unmanned version of Firebird. Details of the Firebird UAV were later unveiled at the 1999 Dubai Air Show.

Interest by the MoD in the Firebird UAV led to an order for two examples to be evaluated and tested at Larkhill. They were placed onto the Military Aircraft Register as ZJ667 and ZJ668 on 24 January 2000 and whilst production began at Southend, neither was completed. Ironically the company had placed too much reliance upon the interest shown by the military and as a result spent too much time, effort and finance in developing the Firebird UAV. To add insult to injury, the company failed to get CAA certification for Firebird, without which the chances of any civilian sales were highly unlikely. What reportedly followed was a bitter

---
3 *Aerogram*, journal of the College of Aeronautics (Volume 2 No.2 May 1981).

Launched at the 1998 Farnborough International Show, the Intora-Firebird UAV was an ambitious project that ultimately led to the company's downfall. G-BXZN is seen in the Farnborough static exhibitors' area. (Bill Teasdale)

dispute between the partners and which led to the end of the Intora company. All of the equipment and surviving helicopters were taken by road from Southend to a store at Wigley Bush Lane, South Weald, near Brentwood, Essex around 28 March 2003.

The company was officially wound up on 12 October 2006.

Westland MOTE, WISP, WIDEYE series

Characterised by remarkable and innovative technical achievement, Britain's association with rotary-wing UAVs has also been dogged by frustrating political set-backs.

As early as 1967 Westland Helicopters' Project Office assembled a small project team under the leadership of Chief Project Engineer Reg Austin to begin a study into the concept of an airborne battlefield surveillance vehicle that was considerably less vulnerable than those that were currently in service. In essence the team was exploring the feasibility of a low-vulnerability successor to the Gazelle AH.1. The helicopter was seen as the most efficient vehicle but it was vulnerable to enemy missile fire.[4]

At an early stage it was realised that removing the aircrew allowed a dramatic reduction in the vehicle's size, rendering it more likely to evade enemy counter measures. The team also moved towards an air vehicle symmetric in plan to increase the stealth measures as well as to enable the vehicle to fly equally well in all directions. By now the concept of a small Plan Symmetric Helicopter was firmly established.[5]

An unsolicited proposal report was submitted to the Ministry of Defence in March 1968 for a detailed design study of an air vehicle referred to as "Westland Wideye".[6] The study generated enthusiasm within the MoD – even with the offer of an eventual contract - but not so within the Westland boardroom who chose not to accept any offer of contract. The MoD responded by requesting proposals from other companies within NATO which were to be submitted by August 1970.[7]

Within a month of the submission deadline the Westland board had a sudden change of heart and instructed the technical team to put forward a proposal. The submission described as a "Wideye System" was for a plan-symmetric vehicle which was shaped essentially as a prolate spheroid with a height to diameter ratio of about 3 to 1. It was to be of 200kg all-up-mass and powered by a 55kW Rover gas turbine engine derived from the starter engine for the Hawker Siddeley Harrier. Thus Westland remained closely "within the loop" and whilst it failed to lead to any production contract, the MoD did award Westland with a feasibility study contract.

Westland favoured a rotary-wing design for a number of other reasons, including the lack of a launcher or catapult, the likelihood of a damage-free recovery and its potential to "stop to loiter and search". Interestingly, Westland not only saw an operational use for WIDEYE by the Army, but also for Police Forces and indeed any other authority requiring an airborne eye in the sky.

By mid-1971 the MoD had clearly retained more than a passing interest in the unmanned rotary-wing concept, so much so that a General Staff Target was formulated and issued, as GST3494, in July 1971. GST3494 outlined a Medium-Range Unmanned Aerial Surveillance Target Acquisition System (MRUASTAS). Westland immediately submitted a proposal, describing the air vehicle as the Westland Wideye.

In March 1972 the MRUASTAS project entered the Phase Two stage when the MoD Project Team awarded

---

4 There was a view within the Westland's Design Office at the time, and possibly a widely-held view at Yeovil, that the Gazelle was a lost opportunity in relation to how long such a helicopter could survive a really high artillery threat or indeed how long it could support long-range artillery on the battlefield.

5 The project team considered a number of alternative concepts, including stand-off systems and translucent balloons, but came to the conclusion that any battlefield surveillance vehicle had to over-fly the area and, if necessary, hover. Correspondence with Reg Austin.

6 Other sources within Westlands suggest that the name 'WIDEYE' did not emerge until a later submission in July 1971.

7 RAeS Yeovil Branch lecture by Jeremy Graham, 18 June 2009.

Westland a feasibility study contract but, because of the high degree of novel and unproven hardware involved, pressed Westland for a demonstrator. The result, after a number of design studies (under the generic designation, Westland WG.25) was PUPIL. This was effectively a private venture vehicle weighing 100lb and powered by a 12hp 4-cylinder model aircraft engine. It had originally been planned to install a Marconi-Elliott stabilized TV into PUPIL but this idea was dropped when it became evident that the air vehicle elements would be completed well ahead of the payload, flight control system and engine becoming available. The decision was therefore taken to conduct a simpler set of experiments to demonstrate the essential control system. Much of this preliminary ground work, including wind tunnel testing and the measurement of radar, optical and infra-red signatures, was completed by the turn of 1974. The next stage was to construct a flyable 'proof-of-concept' test-bed to establish the aerodynamic characteristics and the feasibility of the advanced attitude demand control system. That led to the Westland MOTE.

MOTE was officially known as the Westland WR05 and was designed, built and flown within just eight months. What helped to shorten the timescale was the fact that MOTE was constructed largely from off-the-shelf model helicopter parts and powered by two 1.4hp Veeco (model aircraft) engines.

Only one example of MOTE was built. It was first flown, on a short tether, at Yeovil airfield on 4 June 1975. Superstition put aside, it later made its first free flight at Henstridge airfield on Friday, 13 June 1975, making two more flights on the same day. Representatives of RAE Farnborough's Systems Assessment Division, who had expressed much interest in the project, witnessed the initial Henstridge flights – much to the annoyance of the Westland Board when they got wind of the details. (Eventually MOTE went on to complete 37 flights, all subsequent flights taking place at Yeovil.) Early flights involved no automatic flight control system at all and a number of flights ended with broken rotor blades until an auto-stabiliser was fitted. For electrical power MOTE carried batteries internally and with pitch and roll (vertical gyro) stabilization. With an all-up weight of just over 11kg MOTE flew quite well but as the programme progressed additional equipment eventually was

Marking its first public airing at the 1976 SBAC Farnborough Show was this example of the Westland WISP, a scaled-up version of MOTE. Whether or not the identity 'A3' relates to its Build Sequence is unclear – nor indeed is whether this was a genuine example or a pre-production mock-up. (Malcolm Fillmore, 7 September 1976)

installed which eventually led to a full attitude control system and heading hold. MOTE provided valuable experience (and took full advantage of) the inherently pure cyclic control and very low gust response available with the co-axial rotor configuration. The contra-rotating main rotor system avoided the need for a tail rotor or any complex drive connections and this ensured that piloting MOTE was relatively easy and that piloting skills were minimized in all flight phases.

MOTE successfully convinced the Ministry of Defence that Westland had developed a feasible short-range unmanned aircraft; so much so that in October 1975 the company was provided with funding for a scaled-up version of MOTE under the MoD's 'Project CONGA' which required a surveillance vehicle that involved simplicity, safety, reliability, mobility and the ability to be readied for flight within 30 minutes of arriving on site. The mobility factor required easy handling and operation by a two-man crew from a Land Rover.

The scaled-up version of MOTE emerged as the first true prototype Westland RPH, the Westland WR06, originally referred to as SUPER MOTE but later, and more appropriately, named Westland WISP. The first WISP made its initial free flight at Yeovil on 2 December 1976. Powered by two 5hp two-stroke, two-cylinder Korba piston engines the WISP featured a spheroid body which contained the engines but which also enabled the television surveillance package to make a full 360° scan. This package was produced by the Electro-Optical Division of Marconi-Elliott Avionic Systems enabling Westland to draw upon the company's experience in daylight and low-light sensors, stabilized sensor mountings, secure data and command links, vehicle-tracking and target-location systems, as well as the ground control stations.[8]

The Westland WR.05 MOTE was the first example of a range of unmanned rotary air vehicles. Only one example was built, seen here at Yeovil just prior to making its initial test flight. (Westland Helicopters Ltd)

---

8 *Flight International*, 25 September 1976 reported that WISP was the subject of an MoD contract for a small number of flight vehicles. Elsewhere, it was reported that competitive proposals were unsuccessfully tendered by Canadair and Shorts. Shorts had offered a radical private venture ducted-fan drone known as Skyspy. Tethered flight-tests inside a specially-designed test-rig were carried out at Belfast, followed by

Originally announced on 5 September 1972, Skyspy was a serious attempt by Short Brothers & Harland to enter the unmanned rotary UAV sector. In 1977 Skyspy competed with the Westland WISP to meet the British Army's urgent requirement for a close-range surveillance vehicle in Northern Ireland. Skyspy featured advanced technology in ducted fan engineering and underwent vigorous tethered flight-testing at Belfast. In this view it is seen hovering inside its specially-designed test-rig whilst technicians control the UAV from behind glass. (Short Brothers & Harland; Neg 74117-7)

Because of a delay in producing the flight control system the second prototype WISP did not fly until May 1977, while the third and final WISP followed just three months later. However, hopes for an in-theatre operational trial and possibly putting WISP into limited production were dashed when the Army announced, at the end of 1977, that in its view WISP had too limited a payload capability which they believed would restrict its operational value. The Army had, in fact, seriously considered using WISP in Northern Ireland to assist ground forces in the close scrutiny of suspicious packages and abandoned cars but as it turned out, the now-familiar "wheelbarrow" vehicle was procured which proved to be a much more suitable vehicle for the role. In any case, advances in sensor technology had fast overtaken WISP. The Army's decision not to buy WISP also affected Westland's plans for a production version of WISP, which the company planned to market as VISTA (Visual Intelligence, Surveillance and Target Acquisition). It was a serious setback and as a consequence all work on the WISP was halted.

Despite this setback Westland did continue to develop the WG.25 concept beyond WISP which eventually led to a larger and more sophisticated RPH, assigned the design designation WR07 and known as the WIDEYE. Westland developed WIDEYE specifically to provide a technology demonstrator to support the MoD's MRUASTAS concept. WIDEYE was a much larger and more sophisticated RPH featuring an egg-shaped body with retractable undercarriage legs. (A naval variant of WIDEYE was also considered by Westland which was referred to as the Westland WIGHT.) In the meantime the MRUASTAS concept had evolved into SUPERVISOR, a project that Westland believed WIDEYE might well be suited for. Indeed the MoD proposed that the

The Westland WR.07 WIDEYE which introduced a retractable (upwards) undercarriage legs, a stabilised sensor package and twin 20hp powerplants. This view shows WR.07-03, the last of three built, at Lulworth Range in 1980. (Westland Helicopters Ltd)

WIDEYE airframe be mated with an electro-optic package and a datalink supplied by Marconi. Westland produced a SUPERVISOR demonstrator but to Westland's surprise, when compared with the WG.25 vision, the SUPERVISOR demonstrator programme was significantly less ambitious and with a reduced radius of action. It was powered by gas turbine engine with a gearbox that was grease-lubricated and using straight cut gear teeth and a mix of steel and tufnel materials. The co-axial rotor was retained but the rotors were simplified to be twin-bladed teetering configuration. The rotor diameter was 2.30m and the gross weight just 125kg. Surprisingly the MoD made no demand for specific military handling, transportation or storage features.

Westland's Supervisor demonstrator first flew at Yeovil on 24th August 1978 by which time the concept of an operational derivative had been established and which led to a parallel development of both the demonstrator and a definitive in-service version. Contracts for undisclosed values were placed with Westland Helicopters Ltd (for the airframe, the launch and recovery system as well as the flight control element of the ground station) whilst GEC Marconi was awarded a contract for the electro-optic payload, the data link and the payload control aspects of the ground station). The whole package was to meet the requirements of GSR 3494.[9] The contract covered production of three Wideyes, one being allocated to Marconi for trials, a second

---

wind-tunnel trials at RAE Farnborough to validate data acquired in the tethered flight trials. It is reported that Skyspy was too radical a concept for the British Army's first flirtation with remotely-controlled VTOL vehicles despite a belief that the Skyspy configuration produced a weaker radar signature and hence a greater battlefield survivability than did coaxial-rotor drones. In the event the Westland contract spelt the end of Skyspy.

9   General Staff Target 3494, which was originally issued in 1971, had become a General Staff Requirement by 1976. As a result the SUPERVISOR Extended Feasibility Programme commenced in 1977.

A Westland WIDEYE showing how the undercarriage legs very neatly retracted into the main air vehicle's body. (Westland Helicopters Ltd)

Westland's final foray into unmanned rotary air vehicles produced the WR.09 Sharpeye. Just one non-flyable example was built. Sharpeye certainly introduced a degree of styling, as this view of the prototype at the International Helicopter Museum illustrates. The marking 'ZS782' is completely spurious. (Michael I Draper)

to be retained by Westland and a third was earmarked for IFTU trials with the Army.[10]

Although retaining its basic configuration, the Supervisor system, in its production format, was to have been significantly more sophisticated than the demonstrator. A long-range capability had become an added requirement and other additional features to the control system were planned to reduce still further the piloting skills required for launch and recovery. (In cruise mode and on station the aircraft was computer-controlled from the ground station.) Supervisor was also required to navigate autonomously to its on-task location. However, the strain of completing the demonstrator and designing an operational derivative was such that the demonstrator foundation for the operational system was never able to achieve reliable autonomous flight. Control of the aircraft in flight from the ground station came tantalizingly close but was never actually achieved. Westland had only carried out limited flight testing when the Supervisor programme, in all its guises, was cancelled on Christmas Eve 1979.[11]

Supervisor was cancelled primarily due to escalating costs, the complexity of the air vehicle and its relatively poor performance. Despite the cancellation Westland did undertake an international market survey using a close derivative of Supervisor, to be known as SHARPEYE but no further action was taken. Cancellation of Supervisor did threaten to bring Westland's 15-year involvement in unmanned rotary flight to an immediate end. It had been a period of immense initiative activity and the WG.25 programme had achieved a significant number of firsts. From first flight WIDEYE had flown with a full authority fly-by-wire flight control system which was based on fuselage attitude demand and not on rotor blade pitch demand. The first UK composite main rotor to be built and certified for flight was introduced on WIDEYE. Its modified control system had been configured for the operational system that implemented true manoeuvre demand (speed control) in all three axes combined with a miniature inertial platform and fully digital flight control.

The SUPERVISOR programme was succeeded in 1980 by General Staff Target 3846 which became 'Project Phoenix' (see Chapter 9). Nevertheless Westland did continue limited flight trials using WIDEYE hardware. One short series of trials was conducted at Lulworth Ranges in September 1980 where the only airframe to be lost during the entire programme came to grief following a data link malfunction causing the automatic initiation of the Range safety features. That was the last flight under MoD sponsorship.

---

10 Some sources suggest that four prototypes were ordered. The allocation of the fourth WIDEYE is unknown.
11 There were other difficulties. A boardroom re-shuffle led to internal friction and, it has been said, a difficult working relationship with GEC-Marconi, so much so that the integration of technical work between the two companies was poor. The result was that in contrast to the success of MOTE and WISP, WIDEYE was a failure. Reg Austin left the company on the same date as the MoD cancelled the WIDEYE contract and later joined ML Aviation Ltd, reportedly at the suggestion of the Ministry of Defence, and where he continued to work on unmanned rotary-wing vehicles. See section on ML Aviation SPRITE.

Other UAVs   345

WIDEYE WR.07-03 was written-off at Lulworth Range in September 1980 following an uncontrolled loss of power which was said to have been caused by an over-active fail-safe system. By this time Westland had effectively halted all work on unmanned air vehicles. (Westland Helicopters Ltd)

Some years later, in 1990, Westland was approached by Martin Marietta with a view to establishing a partnered arrangement for a Battlefield Targeting System. One WR07 WIDEYE was assembled by Normalair at Yeovil from spare parts and despatched to California where captive and free flights were conducted in the desert east of San Diego under Martin Marietta control during 1991, but nothing came of the tests. The WIDEYE was later returned to Yeovil and subsequently handed over to the MoD. The San Diego flights marked the last occasion that a Westland unmanned rotary vehicle would fly. All surviving examples were relegated to static exhibition at various museums.

Like many other contractors (including GEC Marconi) Westland Helicopters did respond to the MoD's invitation to propose solutions to 'Project Phoenix'. Westland's concept was, not surprisingly, based on a derivative of the WR07/WR08 configuration but was radically re-worked to combine low weight, long endurance, advanced sensors and a sophisticated anti-jam data link. Westland assigned the designation WR10 to its Phoenix design which was configured as an ultra-low signature airframe making use of the proven WIDEYE rotor system. Wind tunnel and radar signature models were constructed and tested.[12] It was also proposed that WR10 would feature the Manoeuvre Demand Control system that had originally been proposed for Supervisor although the television sensor previously provided by GEC Marconi was replaced by a Ferranti/Rank Pullin thermal imaging sensor. A Harris Corporation spread spectrum data link and full integration with the Army's ground based artillery command and control system (BATES) was also planned.

A search for powerplant options led Westland to select the Norton Motors 294cc single, water-cooled, Wankel engine, rated at 28hp. Engine tests were carried out at RAE Farnborough for what was the first application of a Norton Wankel engine to a UAV. Selection of this engine, combined with a radical rework of the fuselage aerodynamics, allowed WR10 to achieve double the endurance of the proposed operational Supervisor air vehicle and at a much-reduced gross weight.

Although the Westland bid was successful at the first round, the Ministry of Defence announced in March 1983 that a competitive fly-off would take place between two of the bidders. Westland was not one of the two companies selected. It marked the end of the road for Westland's involvement in remotely-powered helicopters. The RPH team was effectively disbanded although did reform occasionally to undertake some project work, including a 1995 study into naval VTOL UAVs.

WR.05 MOTE – Specifications

Rotor span	5 ft 0 in (1.52 m)
Gross weight	18 lb (8 kg)

Source: Jane's All The World's Aircraft

WR.06 WISP – Specifications

Body diameter	2 ft 0 in (0.61 m)
Body depth	1 ft 4 in (0.41 m)
Rotor span (each)	5 ft 0 in (1.52 m)
Take-off weight	Approx 66 lb (30 kg)

Source: Jane's All The World's Aircraft

WR.07 WIDEYE – Specifications

Powerplant	Two 13.5kW (18hp) Weslake 274-3, 2-cylinder, 2-stroke air-cooled piston engine.
Body Diameter	2 ft 5 in (0.74 m)
Rotor span (each)	7 ft 0 in (2.13 m)
Height (landing-gear deployed)	6 ft 0 in (1.83 m)
Height (landing-gear retracted)	5 ft 0 in (1.52 m)
Take-off weight	275 lb (125 kg)

Source: Jane's All The World's Aircraft

---

12 One of the wind tunnel models was later placed on permanent loan to the International Helicopter Museum at Weston-super-Mare.

Individual Aircraft Histories

Westland WR.05 MOTE
No.01 f/f 13.6.75. Completed 37 flights before retired 6.76. Donated to Southampton University 15.2.78 for use as a co-axial rotor research rig. Subsequently acquired by the International Helicopter Museum and deld to Weston-super-Mare 2.5.90.

Westland WR.06 WISP
WR.06-01 Completed Aug 1976 and f/f 2.12.76 at Yeovil. Reported to be at the International Helicopter Museum with c/n WA.01.

WR.06-02 f/f 5.77 at Yeovil. Believed retained at Yeovil and later used as a static rig for WR.10 tests. Fate unknown.

WR.06-03 Believed to be the example statically displayed at SBAC Farnborough 9.76. Later f/f 8.77 at Yeovil. Although unmarked this is almost certainly the Wisp that is statically displayed at the Museum of Army Flying, Middle Wallop.

Note: Two WR.06 WISPS were used to support the Wideye programme, one later moving to Farnborough for flight trials.

Westland WR.07/08 WIDEYE
WR.07-01 f/f 24.8.78. Reportedly acquired by the International Helicopter Museum, Weston-super-Mare.

WR.07-02 f/f 4.79 in a yellow and black chequerboard scheme. To RAE Farnborough 1980. Later to the Museum of Army Flying, Middle Wallop.

WR.07-03 f/f 8.79. Written-off during an uncontrolled landing at Lulworth Range 9.80.

Components for aircraft 04 to 15 were manufactured but of these only airframe 04 was completed. 05 underwent 50hrs of ground-rig-running at Yeovil to demonstrate mechanical reliability but was never fully completed. No WIDEYES beyond No.03 were ever flown as part of the initial trials programme.

One additional WIDEYE was assembled 1990 from sundry parts and despatched to San Diego, California 1991 for flight tests in co-operation with Martin Marietta. It was subsequently returned to Yeovil and passed on to MoD Farnborough. Fate unknown.

Westland WR.09 Sharpeye
Project study configured to support a market survey. One non-flyable example (mock-up) constructed and marked with the spurious serial 'ZS782'. Subsequently acquired by the International Helicopter Museum, Weston-super-Mare.

Westland WR.10 "Phoenix"
Project studies completed in support of the WHL proposals to meet GST3486 "Project Phoenix". Wind tunnel and radar range models built and modified WR06 airframe and rotor system rig tested to demonstrate reliable operation and available performance.

ML Aviation SPRITE

Christmas 1979 was hardly a time for celebrations at Westland when, on Christmas Eve, the MoD announced the cancellation of its Supervisor programme. The team leading the design of rotary UAVs at Yeovil was effectively stood down immediately. Reg Austin, the company's Chief Project Engineer found himself ending the year without a job but within a month he was invited to join ML Aviation Ltd. Aware of the Ministry's intention to continue development of the WIDEYE concept, Austin re-opened negotiations for a new MoD contract and was assured that the MoD would fund ML Aviation to proceed with WIDEYE. Austin also requested that two of the original Westland WISP prototypes be transferred up from storage at Yeovil, but the MoD declined the request, fearing a threat of legal action by Westland. What the MoD was clearly concerned about was that any transfer would likely bring into the open the extent of spending already consumed. As a consequence, ML Aviation Ltd was forced to wait for a MoD decision until "such time that the dust had settled".[13]

Involvement in unmanned rotary-wing RPV development was, for ML Aviation Ltd, a frustrating and ultimately difficult experience.[14] The lack of government

---
13 Westland had been authorized to spend up to £2.75m on the WG.25 programme but had, in fact, spent around £13m, the excess having been paid for out of the public purse. The fear of media-inspired scandal was greater, it seemed, than the need to develop an operational helicopter UAV.

14 ML was effectively established in 1940 when Eric Mobbs and Marcel Lobelle took over the company of R. Malcolm, as Managing Director and Chief Designer respectively. The company continued to trade as R. Malcolm until October 1946 when the White Waltham site was renamed M.L. Aviation. With the establishing of a Holding Company in 1958, M.L. Aviation became a public company.

One of the prototype SPRITE UAVs being prepared for flight. ML Aviation's Land Rover was used as an observation and ground control base. (M.L.Aviation Co Ltd, via Ken Munson)

One of the prototype ML SPRITE UAVs in flight. The contra-rotating system produced an extremely stable platform, a vital factor in battlefield surveillance. (M.L.Aviation Co Ltd Neg. No 21219, via Ken Munson)

financial support was the main factor of frustration, especially after ML had spent a year of design assessment. Nevertheless the ML Aviation Board agreed to proceed with a totally new design of air vehicle, named the ML SPRITE. In fact, although SPRITE was a company-funded venture, the MoD did provide funding for various studies, tests and operational trials. There was also an understanding that, depending on the success of these trials, the UK MoD would purchase the SPRITE system "off the shelf".

Having assembled a small team of professional aeronautical engineers, ML Aviation began work on SPRITE in early 1981. Being a totally new venture, SPRITE gave the opportunity to begin afresh and produce a new, well-considered and integrated system design, making good use of the advance in electronics technology during the 1975-1981 period as well as the lessons learned with MOTE and WISP. In that time, development of silicon chip technology had achieved significant increases in the performance of circuit components and of sub-systems such as power generation, radio equipment, gyros and electric-optic sensors whilst reducing their size and mass and increasing their reliability.

The SPRITE airframe was constructed at White Waltham with electronic modules built at ML Aviation's laboratory in Bristol. The first prototype was test-flown at White Waltham in 1983.

Most of the early test and development flying took place at RAF Hullavington and at Larkhill. Sprite displayed few snags during these flights, a factor that led to renewed MoD interest in possible procurement of the SPRITE system. However, HM Treasury refused to release any funding for SPRITE until the GEC-Marconi Phoenix UAV programme, which was showing signs of consuming public money at an alarming rate, was declared free of problems.

In the meanwhile three European nations, Sweden, France and Germany, expressed interest in SPRITE. Ironically, the greatest interest came, following a demonstration at the Pentagon, from the US Navy who were sufficiently interested to arrange for trials at sea with SPRITE operating from the rear of a US Navy assault ship. The US Army also saw SPRITE as a strong contender for creating a laser-directed artillery shell platform. The US even

sought a series of flight demonstrations and there was talk of a possible requirement of up to 1,000 SPRITES. But that was as far as American interest went.

It is more than likely that US interest in SPRITE was the catalyst for persuading the MoD to award ML Aviation a contract to carry out a design study, under the title 'MERLIN', for a range of larger and faster helicopter UAVs for use by the Royal Navy and other NATO countries' navies.

Development of SPRITE did continue and the company received a firm order from the Swedish Government, involving 65 systems, comprising two UAVs per system. The order prompted ML to establish a SPRITE production line at White Waltham but after only one system had been built and delivered, ML Aviation went into liquidation.

The untimely closure of the ML factory brought SPRITE production to a halt. Cobham plc acquired that part of ML Aviation responsible for producing bomb release systems and in the process also acquired the drawings and production rights for SPRITE.

Cobham plc was, to a large degree, surprised just how much interest was still being shown towards SPRITE; all three British services declared a wish to buy the system and there was even a proposal on the books from the US to acquire SPRITE for power-line inspection tests. However, HM Treasury remained adamant that no further funding would be allowed until the GEC/Marconi Phoenix surveillance drone was ready for service issue.

It is difficult to determine precisely how many SPRITES were built. Because it consisted of four interchangeable major modules any one aircraft at any one time was an assembly of the four and not an equal number of module types were built and some, especially the electronics modules, were often extensively modified as the technology developed and different capabilities were introduced. However, it would be fair to suggest that up to twelve airframes were completed. Only one SPRITE was lost when, towards the end of the programme, it was flown out of sight during a test in Wales and never seen again. An error by the ground crew was the likely cause. It is thought that this may have been one of the examples built for the Swedish Government and that one of the trials aircraft was used as a replacement for consignment to Sweden.[15]

ML SPRITE – Specifications	
Engine power	2 × 5.25 kW
Rotor span (each)	(1.60 m)
All-up mass	36 kg
Max speed	60 km/h
Max endurance	3 hours

Royal Aircraft Establishment XRAE-1, XRAE-2 Flight Refuelling Raven 1 & 2

Designed by RAE Farnborough's Radio & Navigation Department in 1981, the XRAE-1 (pronounced X-Ray One) emerged as an experimental mini-RPV initially for homing head trials. A mid-wing monoplane with pod and

---
15 As described to the author by Reg Austin, January 2011.

Above: *RAE Farnborough designed the XRAE-series (pronounced X-Ray) of UAVs for a range of trials that eventually led to the Flight Refuelling Raven. This example of XRAE-1 No. 31, seen at Farnborough on 8 May 1986, shows the "bug screen" fitted over the payload window. This example appears to be fitted with a 15cc Webber 91 engine. (FAST)*

Right: *A later example of the XRAE-1 UAV, No.35, seen at slow speed on 9 November 1990. The picture reveals a number of modifications. An angle-of-attack vane is fitted to the port wing. Note also the landing skids and what looks like a downward-looking camera built into the lower fuselage between the skids. This was one of the few XRAE-1 aircraft to feature the RAE 'Raspberry Ripple' scheme. (FAST)*

Most of the XRAE-2 flight trials took place at Thorney Island airfield and passed without incident. However, No.206 came to grief with a broken back on 17 March 1986 following a heavy landing. (FAST)

Other UAVs

No.211 was the only known example of XRAE-2 to be painted in "Raspberry Ripple" scheme and was uniquely used for trials with a "mini-mini" UAV tucked neatly beneath the port wing, as seen in this view taken on 26 March 1990. (FAST)

boom fuselage and T-tail, XRAE-1 also carried video and still cameras as well as electronic warfare payloads as part of a programme to explore close-range battlefield surveillance.

Powered, variously, by a 1.9kW (2.5hp) 15cc Webra 91 engine or an OS 90 two-stroke engine, driving a two-blade pusher propeller, a number of examples were built over a relatively short period. XRAE-1 could be launched either by a dedicated trailer-mounted launcher or by stretched elastic cable from suitable sites. Landing was by conventional means using a skid undercarriage.

Design work on a development of XRAE-1 began in late-1982 and which was designated XRAE-2. The first XRAE-2 made its initial flight in October 1984. Its original purpose was to test a British Aerospace miniature infra-red linescan (MIRLS) to demonstrate the feasibility of a low-cost system.

XRAE-2 was powered, variously, by a 2.2kW (*3hp) Quadra 50cc single-cylinder engine or a 3.7kW (5hp) Horner 70cc two-cylinder, two-stroke engine, driving a two-blade pusher propeller. Throughout 1985 and 1986 XRAE-2 was used to evaluate various Marconi Defence Systems' passive and active electronic-warfare systems. Thirteen prototypes were ordered and by early-1986 eleven of these had been completed. At least one is believed to have been lost when it dived vertically into the sea leading to speculation that the powerplant was too heavy and lacked sufficient power for the airframe as built.

In the meantime the concept of XRAE had been acquired by Flight Refuelling Ltd who exploited the design commercially as the FRL Raven I. This was designed as a low-cost RPV surveillance system to provide real-time TV imagery and gathering of still photographs in daylight. FRL also used Raven to evaluate alternative payloads and their roles.

First public awareness of the Raven I came about at the Defence Exhibition in Changi, Singapore in January 1984. Afterwards Raven I was developed under a MoD/Procurement Executive contract as an unmanned aircraft applications demonstrator. Construction of the airframe was contracted to TASUMA from whom the first examples were delivered to FRL in May 1985. In fact, this comprised one Ground Station (including radar tracker) and seven fully-equipped air vehicles. A series of trials was conducted at the British Army's Canadian Training Range (BATUS) at Suffield, Alberta.[16]

Raven 2 was effectively the production version of XRAE-2. The 15cc Webra 91 two-stoke engine that powered Raven I was replaced by a 5.2kW (7hp) engine and later by a 7.5kW (10hp) engine. Flight trials took place at Thorney Island during 1985 whilst later trials were conducted at Kirkcudbright.

Raven 2 was evaluated by the British Army and in a series of exercises, in 1987-88, a Raven 2 was subjected to an estimated 4,000 rounds of small-arms and light anti-aircraft fire but only sustained a direct hit by one round! In the meantime Raven 2 made, on 16 July 1987, what Flight

Clearly showing its XRAE pedigree, the first Flight Refuelling Raven (R001) was built under sub-contract by TASUMA (UK) Ltd at Verwood, Dorset. Bill Longley, TASUMA's Managing Director, holds R001 just prior to it being test-flown at Thorney Island in 1983. (Flight Refuelling Ltd Neg No. 7750/6)

---

16 As described to the author by Bill Longley, June 2008.

Posed in the car park at Flight Refuelling's Sherborne facility, Raven R003 sits on its launcher. Despite taking part in a number of British Army exercises, the Raven failed to capture any orders. (Flight refuelling Ltd Neg No 8447/1)

Refuelling believed to be the first nocturnal demonstration flight by a British Army fixed-wing surveillance UAV.

Two major British Army exercises followed in 1995, involving the 5th Airborne Brigade. During the first of these, Exercise 'Pegasus Fury', Raven 2 completed nine flights over the Otterburn Range. A second major exercise ('Purple Star') was held at Fort Bragg, North Carolina, in 1996, during which Raven 2 successfully completed three flights.

Raven 2 was also marketed as the Raven 201 but despite operating successfully, Raven was never developed for UK forces. The system was acquired by US Missile Command for comparative evaluation against the Canadair CL227.

Whilst it failed to achieve home orders, the British Army found considerable favour with the Raven system and which did much to define the 'look-over-the-next-hill' aspects of future Brigade-level battlefield UAVs.

XRAE-1 – Specifications	
Span	8 ft 10 in (2.70 m)
Length	6 ft 10 in (2.10 m)
Height (over prop)	1 ft 8 in (0.50 m)
Typical launch weight	38.5 lb (17.5 kg)
Max fuel capacity	0.4 US gallons (1.5 litres)
Operational speed range	32–64 kts (60–120 km/h; 37–74 mph)
Max endurance	1 hour

XRAE-2 – Specifications	
Span	11 ft 11 in (3.62 m)
Length	8 ft 6 in (2.58 m)
Height (overall)	2 ft 4 in (0.70 m)
Max launch weight	88 lb (40 kg)
Max payload	22 lb (10 kg)
Max level speed	69.5 kts (129 km/h; 80 mph)
Stalling speed (engine idling)	34.8 kts (65 km/h; 40 mph)

Flight Refuelling Raven 1 – Specifications	
Span	8 ft 10 in (2.70 m)
Length	6 ft 10 in (2.10 m)
Height (over prop)	1 ft 8 in (0.50 m)
Typical launch weight	33.0 lb (15.0 kg)
Max fuel capacity	0.6 US gallons (2.3 litres)
Normal speed range	40–68 kts (74–126 km/h; 46–78 mph)
Operational ceiling	8,000 ft (2,438 m)
Max endurance	100 minutes at 47.5 kts TAS

Flight Refuelling Raven 2 – Specifications	
Span	11 ft 11 in (3.63 m)
Length (overall)	9 ft 4 in (2.85 m)
Height (overall)	2 ft 1 in (0.65 m)
Max payload	33.1 lb (15.0 kg)
Max launch weight	99.2 lb (45.0 kg)
Max fuel capacity	3.2 US gallons (12.0 litres)
Normal speed range	40–90 kts (74–167 km/h; 47–104 mph)
Operational ceiling	8,000 ft (2,438 m)
Max endurance	100 minutes at 47.5 kts TAS

Royal Aircraft Establishment/DERA XRAE-140 Cranfield Aerospace A3 Observer & MinO

Although the Defence Evaluation & Research Agency (DERA) had sold the design rights of XRAE-1 and XRAE-2 to Flight Refuelling, development work on UAVs continued to occupy DERA who, with Cranfield Aerospace Ltd, embarked on a research programme for the acquisition of real-time reconnaissance imagery of ground targets which required minimum operator skill. A UAV system that "de-skilled" the entire operation would, it was claimed, reduce

Not quite what it appears to be. TASUMA (UK) Ltd was contracted to build the Cranfield Aerospace A3 Observer and all five examples were built in Dorset at the company's Verwood facility. One other example was built for static purposes only and given the c/n CA3-0X. It was displayed statically at the 1996 SBAC Farnborough Show and later stored at TASUMA's Blandford Forum site, by which time it had acquired the "genuine but only representative" serial ZJ627. (Michael I Draper, 18 May 2010.)

workload and training costs. The aim was therefore to develop a small, automated, brigade-level system capable of being operated by a single unskilled controller. What initially emerged was a stop-gap concept vehicle, the XRAE-140, with a wing-span of 8ft 6in (2.6m) and very similar in appearance to XRAE-2.[17]

Initially five XRAE-140 air vehicles were built by subcontractor TASUMA (UK) Ltd and delivered to Cranfield in mid-1996. However, not long after they were delivered, a fire broke out in Cranfield's Hangar 3 and all five aircraft were destroyed, bringing the programme to a temporary halt.

TASUMA managed to build five replacement XRAE-140s with the minimum of delay and even managed to incorporate some minor modifications resulting from the few early test flights carried out over the Larkhill Range. In June 1998 XRAE-140 was successfully used to demonstrate a sensor payload planned for XRAE-140's successor.

Cranfield Aerospace Ltd had, in April 1998, been awarded contract ASF/3687 to design and manufacture a delta target of more rugged and higher-performance than the XRAE140 concept air vehicle. Under the terms of the new contract Cranfield Aerospace was responsible for the air vehicle, avionics and design of the control system while DERA Farnborough maintained responsibility for the overall programme. The resultant design was the Cranfield A3 Observer.

Observer featured a bullet-shaped fuselage with pusher engine; mid-mounted, anhedral delta wings with sweptback winglets at the tips. Of all-composites construction, it was designed with an inset rudder in the central fin and each winglet. Elevons were fitted for pitch trim.

Production of air vehicles was again sub-contracted to TASUMA (UK) Ltd (against an order placed on 8 July 1998) although the first example was a purely static airframe that was displayed on the DERA stand at the 1998 SBAC Farnborough exhibition.[18]

The first of five production air vehicles was delivered by road from TASUMA's Verwood facility to Cranfield on 23 December 1998 and later allocated the serial ZJ627 on 16 February 1999. Shortly afterwards '627 was conveyed to Larkhill and successfully launched (using a bungee-launcher also designed and built by TASUMA) and later skid-landed using an external pilot controlling bank and pitch. It was then taken to the DERA Range at Shoeburyness where it was again successfully test-flown on 11 March 1999. As part of developing the de-skilling factor, all further recoveries were made by an automatic parachute/airbag method. In the meantime MoD confirmed go-ahead on the construction of four additional A3 Observers which were allocated serials ZJ628-ZJ631 on 1 March 1999.

Within just eighteen months from receipt of contract to the completion of the initial development phase three A3 Observers had been brought up to full specification and successfully flown. Several modifications were made during the flight-testing phase, including alternately tip fin rudders and a central rudder, both of which proved totally satisfactory. Installing a telemetry antenna inside the fin offered greater protection during ground handling while removing the tip rudders and using only the central rudder enabled a reduction in vehicle structure weight.

One A3 Observer, ZJ627, is known to have been lost during trials when it crashed immediately after take-off at Shoeburyness as a result of the parachute release gear snagging on a small nut as it left the launch ramp. Unusually in such circumstances, but probably due to Observer being the only commercial contract placed for UAVs at that time, an insurance claim for £10,000 was lodged – and reportedly settled.

---

17 This was not the first of Cranfield's association with UAVs. In 1980/1 staff at Cranfield's College of Aeronautics designed and built the Cranfield A2 Machan. Launched by compressed air, Machan made its first flight at RAE Thurleigh on 19 February 1981. At the time Machan was believed to be the first remotely-piloted vehicle to carry its own digital on-board flight control. It was controlled in its first stages of flight by a pilot on the ground using a short control column radio link to the Machan's control surfaces. In later stages, however, the digital computer was used, having been pre-programmed on the ground for whatever mission was required. Cranfield University's College of Aeronautics later formed a wholly-owned company, Cranfield Aerospace Ltd.

18 This example, referred to as "CA3-0X" and carrying the appropriate marks "ZJ627", is currently stored at TASUMA's Blandford Forum facility.

Individual Aircraft Histories

ZJ627 c/n CA3-01 Deld Verwood to Cranfield 23.9.98. Believed f/f at Larkhill (using skid-landing) before conveyed to Shoeburyness where it began test flights on 11.3.99. Damaged beyond repair on its 4th flight at Shoeburyness 24.6.99.

ZJ628 c/n CA3-02 Deld Verwood to Cranfield 30.3.99; f/f Shoeburyness 29.7.99. Completed 20 flghts before placed in long-term storage at Cranfield.

ZJ629 c/n CA3-03 Deld Verwood to Cranfield 30.3.99; f/f Shoeburyness 9.99. Completed 9 flights before transferred to QinetiQ, Farnborough and stored.

ZJ630 c/n CA3-04 Deld Verwood to Cranfield 23.4.99; f/f 9.01 at Shoeburyness. Made 2nd and last flight 11.9.01 before placed in long-term storage at Cranfield.

ZJ631 c/n CA03-5 Deld Verwood to Cranfield 23.4.99. Believed never flown and last known to be in long-term storage at Cranfield.

One of the above was reported as reserved for static display at the Defence College of Management & Technology, Shrivenham, Wiltshire.

One other A3 Observer was built; this was a concept prototype airframe (c/n CA-3-0X) that was statically displayed at the 1998 Farnborough Show. Later stored at TASUMA's Blandford Forum facility and marked (erroneously) as "ZJ627".

The last flight of an A3 Observer took place on 11 September 2001.

Having a proven collaborative record with the Observer system, the QinetiQ UAV Systems Group and Cranfield Aerospace Ltd developed a man-portable UAV system based on Observer. This scaled-down "back-pack" UAV variant was known as MinO, a clever play on its small size. Although based on Observer, MinO had no wing controls, only fuselage control surfaces. At least three examples were built for DERA, all of which were written-off. In fact, only one MinO is thought to have achieved true flight and that was for approximately just one minute. MinO proved to be far too heavy and the concept was swiftly abandoned.

Cranfield A3 Observer – Specifications	
Powerplant	One 4.6kW (6.2 hp) 88cc BH88 2-stroke piston engine; 2-bladed wooden pusher propeller.
Span	7 ft 10½ in (2.40 m)
Max launch weight	66.1 lb (30.0 kg)
Sensor payload	8.8 lb (4.0 kg)
Max level speed	68 kts (126 km/h; 78 mph)
Cruising speed	58 kts (108 km/h; 67 mph)
Max rate of climb at s/l	300 m per min (984 ft/min)
Celing (ISA + 25°C)	8,200 ft (2,500 m)
Range	15.5 miles (25 km)
Endurance	120 minutes

Cranfield MinO – Specifications	
Max take-off weight	22 lb (10.0 kg)
Max speed	78 kts (144 km/h; 89.5 mph)
Endurance	60 minutes

The first Cranfield Observer, ZJ627, sits on its TASUMA-built launcher. ZJ627 began flight-tests at Shoeburyness on 11 March 1999 but only until 24 June when it was damaged beyond repair on just its fourth flight. (TASUMA)

Other UAVs 353

Bristol/Ferranti Bloodhound 1 surface-to-air missiles seen on their launchers at RAF Watton. The nearest example carries the serial E/494/AA. (Bristol Aircraft Ltd. Neg 72664)

Appendix 1
Weapons & Systems

Bloodhound (Red Duster)

Bloodhound Mk. 1

Type	Surface-to-air, medium-to-high level air defence missile
Length	7.7 m (25.3 ft)
Range	30 km (18.6 miles)
Max speed	Mach 2.2
Propulsion	2 Rolls-Royce Bristol Thor ramjets (liquid-fuel) plus 4 Gosling Booster rockets (solid propellant)
Guidance	Semi-active radar homing

Bloodhound Mk. 2

Type	Surface-to-air, medium-to-high level air defence missile
Length	8.45 m (27.7 ft)
Range	85 km (532.8 miles)
Max speed	Mach 2.7
Propulsion	2 Rolls-Royce Bristol Thor ramjets (improved) (liquid-fuel) plus 4 Gosling Booster rockets (solid propellant)
Guidance	Semi-active radar homing

Conceived during the early postwar years by Bristol Aircraft who were awarded a development contract in 1949. A surface-to-air missile deployed in an Air Defence role, Bloodhound – originally known by the code name "Red Duster" – entered service with the RAF in December 1958. However Bloodhound's pulsed rader proved to be very susceptible to enemy jamming; it was vulnerable to gound 'clutter' and performed badly against low-flying targets. An upgrade development programme was quickly undertaken, resulting in Bloodhound Mk.2 which entered RAF service in 1964. When, in 1970, Polaris submarines assumed the nuclear deterrent role, Bloodhound was withdrawn from front-line service with examples variously stored in the UK or transferred to RAF Germany to adopt an air defence role. A subsequent re-appraisal of the perceived threat by low-level attack was the key factor in Bloodhounds being brought out of storage and re-entering service, on 1 July 1976. The last RAF Bloodhound Mk.2 Squadron was eventually stood down in July 1991, it being replaced by the smaller, but more-mobile, Rapier system.

Known drone losses to Bloodhound 1 included Meteor U.15s RA441, RA473, VT142, VT222, VT226, VT230, VT262, VT270, VT319, VW266, & VZ389. Known losses to Bloodhound 2 included U.15s RA421, VT113, VT330, U.21 WK879 and Canberra U.10s WH729, WJ623 and WK110.

Blowpipe

Type	Man-portable shoulder-launched surface-to-air tactical guided missile
Propulsion	2-stage booster-accelertor solid-propellant rocket motor
Guidance	Radio command with optical tracking

Short Brothers and Harland Ltd designed Blowpipe as a light, compact (man-portable) weapon for use in forward battle areas and giving protection against low-level air attack. Blowpipe became the standard British infantry SAM during the Falkland Islands campaign in 1982.

Blowpipe, unusual in a man-portable SAM in being command-guided by the gunner who directed the missile to its target by means of a thumb-operated controller and a radio link. With a burning flare in its tail and a sensor in the aiming unit, the gunner finds the missile with the aid of this flare and then generated commands to gather the missile to the gunner's line of sight. From then on the gunner guided the missile to its target using the controller with up/down, left/right movements. The missile's effective ceiling was 2,000m (6,500ft) and had a range of around 4km (2.48 miles). Javelin was a direct development of Blowpipe.

Confirmed training target losses to Blowpipe are shown in Appendix 2.

Shorts Blowpipe was designed primarily for unit self-defence against close range, low level attack and was effective against both oncoming and receding aircraft targets. Lightweight and shoulder-launched Blowpipe offered immediate firepower and enabled ground forces to engage a variety of targets hitherto invulnerable to individual attack. (Short Brothers & Harland Ltd Neg No. 70476-30)

Fireflash (Blue Sky)

In 1947 Fairey Aviation Ltd started development of Britain's first air-to-air guided missile. Referred to initially by the codename "Blue Sky" Fireflash was designed as a beam-riding missile relying upon radar command guidance from the launch aircraft.

The missile was propelled by a pair of solid-fuelled rocket boosters mounted on the forward missile fuselage and protruding beyond the missile's nose. The boosters generated 1,000kg (2,200lbs) of thrust and were jettisoned 1½ seconds after launch, leaving the missile to coast to its target.

Although as many as 300 are believed to have been produced by 1955, the RAF chose not to go ahead with Fireflash and ordered the de Havilland Firestreak instead.

Firestreak (Blue Jay)

An air-to-air guided missile developed by de Havilland using passive infra-red homing. Originally developed as "Red Hawk" to meet OR.1056 but the programme proved over-ambitious and a lower performance specification was issued in 1951 as OR.1117 and given the MoS codename "Blue Jay".

Blue Jay Mk.1 (by now named Firestreak) entered service in 1957 and became standard armament on Lightning and Sea Vixen.

First airborne launch was made from a RAF Venom F.2 September 1955 against Firefly U.8 WM886 which was successfully shot down.

Known training losses to Firestreak include Jindivik A92-106. In Australia the following Meteor U.15s were lost to Firestreak: VT187, VT256, VW308, VW781 & VZ403.

Two de Havilland Firestreak missiles seen mounted beneath Venom NF.2 WL820. (de Havilland Neg DHP/53)

Javelin

Type	Man-portable shoulder-fired surface-to-air tactical guided missile
Propulsion	2-stage solid-propellant rocket motor
Guidance	Semi-automatic line-of-sight command

Evolved from the Short Blowpipe, Javelin is an electronically more sophisticated system than Blowpipe with a greater range and a night sight. Javelin dispensed with the thumb controller in favour of a control system which, once the missile is gathered to the tracker's line of sight, is kept on target by keeping the tracker pointing in the right direction. Javelin has a higher-impulse rocket motor than the Blowpipe and a new blast fragmentation warhead with a proximity fuse. Javelin proved to be a highly accurate system.

Target practice during Javelin testing in 1985 presented the Army with a problem regarding the numbers of available target drones. So many targets were being destroyed during training that testing had to be slowed down to allow the manufacture of target drones caught up. Confirmed training losses to Javelin are shown in Appendix 2.

Rapier

Type	Mobile surface-to-air, anti-aircraft missile
Propulsion	2-stage solid fuel
Guidance	Command to line-of-sight. Optical tracking; later developed with 'add-on' Blindfire radar tracker

The origin of Rapier stretches back to the late-1950s when English Electric Guided Weapons Division (later part of British Aircraft Corporation) began working on the PT428 project, a sophisticated low-level anti-aircraft system that, at the time, many thought to be too ambitious for the state of art. Few within BAC were therefore surprised when PT428 was cancelled in February 1962. However it did lay the foundation for a 1963 design study for a new low-level anti-aircraft system which by mid-1964 was referred to as ET316 but later named Rapier in 1966. Firing trials began in 1967. Rapier has proved to be an outstanding success and has been considerably developed since its service entry although, largely because of its high lethality and aerodynamic performance, the missile has remained basically unaltered.

To meet a threat of day/night and all-weather attack, a Blindfire radar tracker (designated DN181) was later developed by BAe (in conjunction with Marconi Space and Defence Systems) and which gave Rapier much greater flexibility. Rapier is in service with the British Army and the RAF Regiment.

Confirmed Banshee training losses to Rapier missiles included 1583, 1587, 1610, 1822, 1833, 1835, 1839-1841 and 1843. Other known target losses to Rapier include Shelduck XZ807 and Jindivik A92-722, plus those listed in Appendix 2. Rapier was also responsible for the loss of Meteor U.21 WH460, WK710 and U.21A A77-157, A77-422, A77-510, A77-802 and A77-863.

Seacat (GWS-20)

Type	Surface-to-air, shipborne missile
Propulsion	Two-stage solid fuel
Guidance	Radio command. Optical or radar tracking

Development of Seacat began by Short Brothers and Harland Ltd in the early-1950s, being the first shipborne SAM system designed for close-range air defence in place of rapid-firing guns such as the 40mm Bofors. The first guided

The Shorts Seacat missile became of the most widely used ship-to-air missile systems. It eventually served with the naval forces of over 15 countries. (Short Brothers & Harland Ltd. Neg 69565)

trials took place in 1960 with intial shipboard trials following on board HMS *Decoy* in 1961. A series of full-scale shipboard trials before service acceptance was undertaken in 1962 aboard the same ship. Seacat was designated Guided Weapon System (GWS) Mk.20 in the Royal Navy. Continual in-service improvements led to the GWS-21 and GWS-22 versions with differemnt radars to give darkfire capabilities. Although Seacat entered service with the Royal Navy in the 1960s, it was not until the 1982 Falklands war that it was used in combat.

Confirmed training losses to Seacat include Shelducks XS300, XS304, XS305, XS378, XS398, XT935, XT937, XT968, XT975, XV828, XW107, XW111, XW115, XW118, XW126, XW129, XW134, XW146, XW147, XW149, XW444, XW448, XW452, XW468, XW470, XW473, XW505, XW682, XW697, XW699, XW740, XW976, XW979, XZ746, XZ803, ZA500 and ZA525.

Sea Dart (GWS-30)

Type	Surface-to-air with surface-to-surface and anti-missile capability
Propulsion	Solid booster; liquid fuel ramjet sustainer
Guidance	Semi-active radar

Hawker Siddeley Dynamics Ltd began development work in August 1962 and test firings began three years later. A third-generation area-defence naval SAM capable of engaging aircraft and missiles at very high and, under certain circumstances, very low altitudes. The first Sea Dart system entered Royal Navy service in 1970 aboard HMS *Bristol* but it was not until the 1982 Falklands war that Sea Dart was used in combat.

Confirmed training losses to Sea Dart include Chukars XZ950, XZ956, XZ958, XZ959, ZA156, ZA158, ZA904, ZA912, ZA929, ZB512, ZB513, ZB702, ZD291, ZD295, ZD506, ZD523, ZD524, ZD526, ZD551, ZD679, ZD686. ZG680, ZG683, ZH765, ZH769. Also Mirach 100/5s ZJ588-ZJ593, ZJ595, ZJ596, ZJ598, ZJ600, ZJ606-ZJ608, ZJ616-ZJ618, ZJ658, ZJ661 and Jindivik A92-737.

Seaslug

Type	Long-range beam-riding shipborne surface-to-air guided missile system
Propulsion	Solid-propellant sustainer with 4 wrap-round solid-propellant boosters
Guidance	Beam-riding using Type 901M shipborne radar

Development of Seaslug by Armstrong-Whitworth (later part of the Hawker Siddeley Group) began in the 1950s with prototype trials carried out in HMS *Girdle Ness* in the late-1950s. Seaslug Mk.1 became a standard fit on Royal County-class guided-missile destroyers. A more powerful Seaslug Mk.2 progressively succeeded the Mk.1.

Confirmed target training losses to Seaslug include Chukar ZA155, ZA159, ZA161, ZA162, ZA905, ZA906 and ZB699. Earlier losses to Seaslug 1 involved Meteor U.15s RA371, VT105, VT112, VT177, VT219, VT329, VW273, VW303 & VZ407. U.21 WE902 and U.21A A77-872 and Canberra U.10s WH705 and WH860 were all lost to Seaslug 2.

Sea Sparrow (RIM-7)

Type	Air-to-air and surface-to-air guided missile
Propulsion	Hercules MK-58 solid-propellant rocket motor
Guidance	Raytheon semi-active or continuous wave or pulsed Doppler radar energy

Development of the AIM-7 Sparrow in the 1960s led to the RIM-7 Sea Sparrow, a shipborne, short-range anti-aircraft and anti-missile missile system. Originally developed by Sperry and the US Navy, later versions were produced by Raytheon Company, General Dynamics and Hughes Missile Systems. Apart from the US Navy, several NATO Naval Forces – but not the Royal Navy – procured Sea Sparrow.

Known training losses to Sea Sparrow during NATO exercises include Shelduck XZ774 and XZ796 whilst Jindivik A92-LLAN-1 was destroyed by a Sparrow missile.

Seawolf (GWS-25)

Type	Surface-to-air shipborne weapon with anti-missile capability
Propulsion	Solid fuel
Guidance	Line-of-sight guidance with radar differential tracking

The British Aircraft Corporation began development work on Seawolf in mid-1968 and entered service on Royal Navy Type 22 destroyers and Leander-class frigates. Development of the Seawolf system led to a family of sub system options known as Lightweight Seawolf.

Confirmed training losses to Seawolf include Shelduck XZ425, XZ768 and Chukar ZB709.

Sidewinder (AIM-9)

Type	Air-to-air missile
Propulsion	Solid fuel
Guidance	Infra-red

Developed by the US Navy in the 1950s, the first variant of ther Sidewinder family, the AIM-9B, entered service with the USN and USAF in July 1956. Subsequent variants involved the AIM-9D (USN), AIM-9E (USAF), AIM-9H (USN). Production of the AIM-9L Sidewinder began in 1976 and was extensively exported, including to the UK.

Confirmed training losses to Sidewinder include Chukar ZD676, ZE990, ZG342 and ZG697.

Thunderbird (Red Shoes)

Type	Surface-to-air, mobile medium-to-high level air defence missile
Propulsion	Four jettisonable solid boosters with solid sustainer
Guidance	Semi-active radar

A medium-to-high level air defence system operated either independently or as one unit of a larger air defence system. Thunderbird 1 entered service with the British Army in 1960. British Aircraft Corporation began design studies for Thunderbird 2 in 1956 and it entered service in 1965.

Confirmed training losses to Thunderbird I include Jindiviks A92-109, A92-241, A92-242, A92-243 and A92-245. Thunderbird 2 accounted for the loss of Canberra U.10 WH652, WH742 and WK107.

The English Electric Thunderbird surface-to-air missile was designed to remain at instant readiness on its launcher for long periods, exposed to all weathers and in a wide range of climatic conditions. (Napier. Neg 31539)

AMRAAM (AIM-120)

AMRAAM is a follow-on to the AIM-7 Sparrow missile series. It is a medium-range, air-to-air, supersonic, aerial intercept guided missile employing active radar target tracking, proportional navigation guidance and active Radio Frequency (RF) target detection. Conceived for US armed forces and NATO allies, AMRAAM is produced in the USA by the Hughes Aircraft Co and the Raytheon Co. Deliveries to the US Navy began in 1991. In the UK AMRAAM has equipped Sea Harrier, Tornado and Typhoon.

Confirmed training losses to AMRAAM include Mirach 100/5 ZJ594, ZJ605, ZJ613, ZJ614 and ZJ721.

ASRAAM (AIM-132)

ASRAAM is a short-range infrared-guided missile originally developed by Hawker Siddeley (later part of British Aerospace Dynamics). In January 1995 BAe Dynamics secured governmental funding to develop ASRAAM. Deliveries to the RAF began late-1998 and in service with Tornado F.3 and Harrier GR.7 by 2002.

Appendix 2
Units Equipped with Missiles used against Unmanned Aerial Targets

ROYAL AIR FORCE REGIMENT

Squadrons of the RAF Regiment were responsible for ground-based air defence. On 21 July 2004 it was announced by the Government that the role would transfer to the Army and that the "reassignment of responsibility would be completed by 2008".

16 Squadron, RAF Regiment

Formed at Watchet on 12.1.48, 16 Squadron served at Upavon, Wattisham, Innsworth, Felixstowe, Upwood, Catterick and Wildenrath. When the Squadron returned to UK it re-equipped with Rapier and took up residence at RAF Honington. With the responsibility for ground-based air defence transferred to the Army, 16 Squadron was disbanded on 28.9.06.

Skeet losses to Rapier missiles included ZB749, ZB813, ZB885, ZB917, ZB992, ZF906.

26 Squadron, RAF Regiment

Based at RAF Honington. Amalgamated with 15 Squadron, RAF Regiment as an expedience to form a Field Squadron in August 2007 for deployment to Iraq. The formation was made permanent (as 15 Squadron) in 5.08 and based at Honington.

Skeet losses to Rapier missiles included ZB742, ZB745, ZB795, ZB796, ZB797, ZB798, ZB801, ZB875, ZB881, ZF830, ZF901

27 Squadron, RAF Regiment

Formed at Yatesbury 3.9.51. Later at Nicosia, Akrotiri, Leeming, Akrotiri, North Luffenham, Leuchars and latterly at Honington as the RAF element of the Joint Nuclear, Biological & Chemical Regiment (Joint NBC). Re-titled Joint Chemical, Biological, Radiological & Nuclear Regiment (Joint CBRN) 1.4.99.

Skeet losses to Rapier included ZF902 and ZG186.

37 Squadron, RAF Regiment

Based at RAF Wittering until announced, in July 2004, that disbandment "will take place by March 2006". Skeet losses to Rapier included ZB814, ZB940, ZB943, ZD154

48 Squadron, RAF Regiment

Formed at Chivenor on 3.10.51 and has served at Rudlow Manor, Felixstowe, Upwood and Catterick. Disbanded 1992.

63 Squadron, RAF Regiment

Formed at Gatow 21.8.47 by re-numbering 2865 Squadron. Served at Fassberg, Upavon, Middleton St. George, Pembrey, Ouston, Felixstowe, Malta, Cyprus, Tengah, North Luffenham and Gutersloh. Latterly served at Uxbridge as The Queen's Colour Squadron. 63 Squadron was the first RAF Regiment Squadron to be equipped with Rapier missile.

Target losses to 63 Squadron: ZB863, ZF930, ZF934, ZF945, ZF964 and ZF965.

2729 Squadron, RAF Regiment

Formed (as 729 Sqdn) at Waddington 19.12.41, re-numbered 2729 Sqdn 1.2.42. Disbanded at Gatow 3.46. Reformed at Waddington 1985 to operate ex-Argentine Oerlikon 35mm guns and Skyguard radar captured during the Falklands War. Disbanded 1993.

2729 Squadron is recorded as having shot down Skeet ZF881.

ROYAL ARTILLERY

6 Air Defence Battery, RA

Skeets lost to Javelin missiles included ZG260, ZG264, ZG267, ZG268, ZG307 and ZG311.

10 Air Defence Battery, RA

In 1948, 10 Battery, RA (part of 37 Heavy Anti-Aircraft Regiment, RA) converted to a heavy anti-aircraft role with 3.7" guns. On 1.10.59 the Battery was re-titled 10 Heavy Air Defence Battery and re-equipped with Thunderbird Mk.1, later converting to Thunderbird Mk.2 on 1.4.68. When Thunderbird was withdrawn 10 Battery became an Independent Battery within 45 Regiment, RA at Hohne. Equipped with Blowpipe, and later Javelin, the Battery remained an air defence Battery, passing from 45 Regiment, RA to 40 Regiment, RA in 1993. 10 Battery, RA is now part of 47 Regiment, RA at Thorney Island.

Confirmed Skeet losses to Blowpipe include ZB790, ZB795, ZB819, ZB853, ZB860, ZB902, ZB918, ZB926, ZB938, ZB972, ZB982, ZB984, ZB986, ZB989, ZB990, ZB996. Banshee ZF741 was also lost to Blowpipe. Javelin missiles accounted for the loss of Skeets ZB782, ZB786, ZB787, ZB877, ZB903, ZB914, ZB920, ZB921, ZB971, ZB991, ZF802, ZF816, ZF818, ZF821, ZF832, ZF837, ZF884-ZF886, ZF891, ZF920, ZF932, ZF933, ZF976-ZF978, ZF980, ZF981, ZF983, ZF986, ZG131, ZG139, ZG147, ZG149, ZG150, ZG154, ZG173, ZG182, ZG222, ZG225, ZG227, ZG231, ZG233, ZG235-ZG239, ZG242 and ZG243. Javelins also accounted for the loss of Banshees ZF748, ZG539, ZG542-ZG544, ZG546 and ZG548

11 Battery, RA

When 34 Light Air Defence Regiment (to which 11 Battery had belonged for over 20 years) was disbanded in December 1969, the Battery transferred to 22 Light Air Defence Regiment at Dortmund. In September 1975 the Battery moved (with the Regiment) to Kirton in Lindsey, South Humberside to join 3 (UK) Division. The Battery converted to Towed Rapier in 1976 and moved back to BAOR in 1977. In February 1984 11 Battery became the first to be equipped with Tracked Rapier.

Skeet losses to Rapier included ZB792, ZB802, ZB848, ZB856, ZB865

12 Air Defence Battery, RA

Formerly an anti-tank Battery (within 20 Regiment, RA) and equipped with Swingfire. After the Falkland Islands campaign, 12 (Minden) Battery transferred to BAOR in 1985 as an Air Defence Battery and converted to Tracked Rapier system. Rapier accounted for the loss of Skeets ZB818, ZB857, ZB864, ZB909, ZB913, ZD143, ZG140, ZG313, ZG315, ZG318, ZG322 and ZG323.

16 Air Defence Battery, RA

16 Battery (Sandham's Company) has, since 1947, been part of 26 Regiment, RA. Javelin missiles accounted for the loss of Skeets ZG240, ZG246, ZG255, ZG305 and ZG310. Confirmed Skeet losses include ZB762, ZB783, ZB785, ZB809, ZB810, ZB812, ZB817, ZB821 of which ZB785 and ZB809 are known to have been destroyed by Blindfire Rapier.

21 Air Defence Battery, RA

After a brief 18-month suspension, 21 Battery was reformed at Menden, West Germany in 1960 as part of 50 Regiment, RA and at the same time re-roled as a 'Medium Battery' with Honest John missiles. In 1976 21 Battery joined 27 Regiment, RA at Lippstadt and adopted an Air Defence role with Blowpipe and later Javelin missiles. Subsequently based at Gutersloh. 21 Battery, RA is now part of 47 Regiment, RA at Thorney Island.

Skeet losses to Blowpipe include ZB724, ZB778, ZB820, ZB872. ZB942, ZB944, ZB947, ZB970, ZB973, ZB975, ZB976, ZB977, ZB985, ZB987, ZB998. Losses to Javelin include Skeets ZB751, ZB916, ZB933, ZB949, ZF805, ZF810, ZF814, ZF915, ZF922, ZF927, ZF936,ZF984, ZG111, ZG112, ZG114, ZG115, ZG121, ZG128, ZG155, ZG157, ZG158, ZG175, ZG176, ZG180, ZG266, ZG269, ZG321, ZH274, ZH281, ZH283, ZH290, ZH338, ZH342, ZH343 and Banshees ZF744, ZF746 and ZF747.

30 Air Defence Battery, RA

From 1965 30 Battery (Roger's Company) was based at Munster, West Germany and part of 2 Field Regiment, RA. The Regiment was disbanded in December 1993 whereupon 30 Battery moved to Tidworth as part of 1 Regiment, Royal Horse Artillery. Skeet losses to Rapier included ZB854, ZB931 and ZF972.

32 Air Defence Battery, RA

32 (Minden) Battery was part of 16 Coast Regiment, RA when the Regiment was formed in 1947. The Regiment was re-titled as 16 Light AA Regiment, RA in 1950 and moved from Rosyth to Bulford, Salisbury Plain to become part of 1st Armoured Division. On re-equipping with Rapier c1979 the Regiment was re-styled as 16 Air Defence Regiment, RA.

Skeet losses to Rapier included ZF937, ZF940 and ZF969.

35 Air Defence Battery, RA

After a period of suspended animation, 35 Battery was reformed 1.3.85 as an Air Defence Battery within 22 Air Defence Regiment, RA. Based at Dortmund, the Battery was equipped with Rapier missile system. Skeet losses included ZD157 and ZF968.

42 Air Defence Battery, RA

Skeet losses included ZB732, ZD198. To Rapier included ZF842, ZF844, ZF904

43 Air Defence Battery, RA

In November 1981 43 Battery, RA transferred from 20 regiment to 32 Regiment, RA. Equipped with Swingfire. Transferred to 94 Regiment, RA January 1985 as an Air Defence Battery and equipped with Blowpipe, later Javelin, missiles. In 1992 the Battery transferred to 26 Field Regiment, RA at Thorney Island. Later placed into suspended animation until 1 April 2009 when reformed within 32 Regiment, RA.

Skeet losses by Blowpipe included ZB779, ZB806, ZB880, ZB945. By Javelin included ZB755, ZF809, ZF839, ZF845, ZF848, ZF880, ZF921, ZG117, ZG118, ZG126, ZG174, ZG184, ZG223, ZG229. Banshee losses to Javelin included ZF743, ZF766, ZF774, ZG580, ZG584 and ZG586.

46 Air Defence Battery, RA

Skeet losses to Blowpipe included ZB803, ZB825, ZB827, ZB850, ZB861, ZB876, ZB900, ZD209

To Javelin included ZB782, ZB874, ZB900, ZB916, ZB933, ZD202, ZF833, ZF836, ZF876, ZF887, ZF889, ZF890, ZF892, ZF947, ZG234, ZG247, ZG251-ZG254, ZG256, ZG259, ZG261-ZG263, ZG301. Banshee losses by Javelin included ZF691, ZF704, ZF707, ZF708, ZF710, ZF712, ZF714, ZF715 and ZF716.

53 Battery, RA

53 (Louisburg) Light Air Defence Battery, RA was re-titled as such in 1969 to mark its replacement of Bofors anti-aircraft guns by Rapier missiles. The Battery undertook a number of Northern Ireland tours under Operation 'Banner'. Skeet losses to Rapier included ZD140.

120 Battery, RA

Reformed 1 March 1985 at Dortmund, Germany as an Air Defence Battery within 22nd Air Defence Regiment. Equipped with Rapier system; deployed to Falkland Islands 1986. Moved to Kirton in Lindsey, Lincs 1992. Subsequently disbanded 1 April 2004.

No recorded losses of targets but did participate in a joint camp with AMF(L). See Skeet ZB928.

7th Royal Horse Artillery (7 RHA)

Formed 1962 and served (until 1977) as the artillery regiment of the 16th Independent Parachute Brigade Group. Later, in 1984, it joined the 5th Airmobile Brigade in a close support artillery role. Moved to North Camp, Farnborough, where an Air Defence Troop was incorporated, equipped initially with Blowpipe and later with Javelin.

Blowpipe accounted for the loss of Skeet ZB823 and Banshees ZF655, ZF656, ZF658, ZF660, ZF661, and ZF663. Javelin missiles destroyed Skeets ZF931, ZF935, ZG123, ZG136, ZG148, ZG303, ZH268 and ZH315 and Banshee ZF793.

Royal School of Artillery, RA

In 1961 the Manorbier-based School of Anti-Aircraft Artillery, RA, Manorbier was re-named The School of Artillery, RA. In 1970 it was merged with the School of Artillery, RA at Larkhill, at which point it was re-styled as the Royal School of Artillery, RA.

The role of the Royal School of Artillery has been to train gunners in missile firing. The final part of each gunnery course involved gunners in live firing against aerial targets, thus accounting for the large number of target losses on RSA shoots.

Blowpipe missiles accounted for the loss of Skeets ZB722, ZB780, ZB789, ZB794, ZB811, ZB824, ZB859, ZB908, ZB915 and ZD194. Javelins accounted for the loss of ZB725, ZB788, ZB858, ZB871, ZB910, ZB974, ZB978, ZF808, ZF811, ZF812, ZF815, ZF819, ZF820, ZF823, ZF825, ZF827, ZF834, ZF840, ZF841, ZF847, ZF849, ZF879, ZF893-ZF895, ZF905, ZF907, ZF908, ZF911, ZF916-ZF918, ZF929, ZF943, ZF944, ZF948, ZF963, ZF967, ZF975, ZF979, ZF986, ZF989, ZF990, ZG124, ZG143, ZG146, ZG151, ZG160, ZG172, ZG178, ZG183, ZG232, ZG244, ZG249, ZG250, ZG257, ZG258, ZG302, ZH264, ZH265, ZH269, ZH276. Banshee losses to Javelin included ZF657, ZF659, ZF662, ZF676-ZF678, ZF681, ZF682, ZF685, ZF688, ZF689, ZF705, ZF706, ZF718, ZF720, ZF745, ZF772, ZF794, ZF797, ZG541, ZG545 and ZG547.

Gibraltar Regiment, Royal

On 31 August 1958 the Gibraltar Defence Force was formed into the Gibraltar Regiment. In 1982 the Regiment's L40/780 Anti-Aircraft guns were replaced by Blowpipe missiles; later re-equipping with Javelin.

Blowpipe accounted for Skeet ZB822; Javelin missiles accounted for the loss of Skeet ZF826 and Banshees ZF796 and ZF798.

3 Commando Brigade, RM (3CDO)

Skeet losses to Blowpipe included ZB852, ZB866, ZB873, ZB879, ZB923, ZB924. Losses to Javelin included Skeets ZB805, ZG142, ZG152, ZG153, ZG159, ZH302 and Banshee ZF711. ZB805. 3Cdo is also reported to have destroyed Skeet ZF925 with a Rapier missile.

AMF(L)

Allied Command Europe Mobile Force (Land) is the UK's primary land commitment to NATO. With a field of operations stretching from Bardufoss, northern Norway to the Erzurum area of north-east Turkey the difference in temperatures and conditions requires special operating skills. A number of Skeet losses occurred during AMF(L) exercises in Norway. Blowpipes accounted for the loss of Skeets ZB790, ZB795, ZB853, ZB904, ZB928, ZB948. Javelin missiles accounted for the loss of ZB721, ZB757,

ZB826, ZB901, ZB903, ZB928, ZB971, ZB988, ZB991, ZD185.

TERRITORIAL ARMY & VOLUNTEER RESERVE

1967 saw the disbandment of the Territorial Army and the formation of The Territorial Army and Volunteer Reserve.

102nd (Ulster) Regiment, RA (Volunteers)

Originally titled 102nd (Ulster & Scottish) Regiment, RA(V) until 1.4.86 when the Scottish-based element was reformed as 105th (Scottish) Air Defence Regiment, RA(V). In 1993 the 102nd was absorbed into the 105th and became 206 (Ulster) Battery.

Skeet losses to Blowpipe included ZB764, ZB815. Losses to Javelin included ZF961, ZF962, ZF985, ZF989, ZG171 and ZG328.

103rd Regiment, RA (Volunteers)

The title "103rd (Lancashire Artillery Volunteers) Air Defence Regiment" was adopted in 1972 in anticipation of 103 becoming the first full Regiment to be armed with the Short Blowpipe missile system in 1977.

Based in North-West England, the 103rd accounted for the loss of the following Skeets to Blowpipe: ZB730, ZB735, ZB752, ZB807 and the following to Javelin: ZB718, ZB942, ZF813, ZF828, ZF829, ZF831, ZF912, ZF949, ZF962, ZG116, ZG122, ZG127, ZG129, ZG132, ZG133, ZG177, ZG179, ZG181, ZG221, ZG228, ZG270, ZG309, ZG312, ZG314 and ZH304. Javelin missiles also accounted for the loss of Banshees ZF769 and ZF773.

104th Regiment, RA (Volunteers)

Originally formed on 1 April 1967 with HQ at Raglan Barracks, Newport. In 1986, with a modest expansion of the Territorial Army, the Regiment adopted an Air Defence role. In 2007 the Regiment was re-roled as a UAV General Support Regiment providing TA reinforcements for both mini-UAV and tactical-UAV capabilities.

The 104th accounted for the loss of the following Skeets to Blowpipe: ZB751, ZB867, ZB915, ZB930 and Banshee ZF654. The following Skeets were lost to Javelin missiles: ZB816, ZD118, ZD207, ZF801, ZF803, ZF804, ZF824, ZF843, ZF877, ZF883, ZF910, ZF913, ZG113, ZG134, ZG135, ZG141, ZH287, ZH303, ZH314. Banshees ZF770 and ZG583 were also lost to Javelins.

105th Regiment, RA (Volunteers)

Formed 1 April 1986 at Edinburgh from the Scottish-based element of 102nd (Ulster & Scottish) Regiment, RA(V).

Roled as an Air Defence Regiment, the 105th accounted for the loss of the following Skeets to Javelin: ZF806, ZF878, ZF938, ZF939, ZF942, ZF946, ZF971, ZF973, ZF974, ZF987, ZG119, ZG137, ZG138, ZG145, ZG248, ZG308, ZG318, ZH266-ZH268, and ZH275. Banshees lost to Javelin included ZF767-ZF769, ZF771, ZF775, ZG540 and ZG581 whilst Banshees ZF713 and ZG585 were reportedly also lost to Blowpipe missiles.

MISCELLANEOUS UNITS

MGW3

Military Guided Weapons Branch 3. An MoD Project Branch responsible to the Director(ate) of Military Guided Weapons. Skeets ZB849, ZB941, ZB946 were lost during a trial on behalf of MGW3.

Javelin QA

Until the late-1960s/early-1970s the inspection routine leading to service acceptance was based on two processes, one being a Direct Inspection for contractors who had not been separately assessed for performing their own certification. A revised process led to Quality Assurance (QA) whereby the contractor's entire production system was evaluated and then approved so that they could self-certify their goods as meeting the Specification. One example of this that involved unmanned target drones was the adoption of the Javelin missile. As part of the Javelin QA process the following targets were expended: Skeets ZB791, ZB868, ZB919 and Banshees ZF777 and ZF792.

# Appendix 3
Principle Ranges

The number of bombing and firing Ranges was dramatically increased during the expansion period of the mid-to-late 1930s. All three Services had their own designated Ranges, often requiring aircraft to tow targets for the gunners. For the training of anti-aircraft gunners, a number of Anti-Aircraft Co-operation Units were formed and split into Flights detached to a number of coastal airfields

The following list includes the principle Ranges where unmanned aircraft were used as targets or where tests and development trials were carried out. For a number of years many of the these Ranges were operated by the Royal Aircraft Establishment (RAE) but over the past twenty-five years the RAE has changed identity and structure on a number of occasions, as follows:

Royal Aircraft Establishment (RAE) was officially formed on 1 April 1918 when the Royal Aircraft Factory was re-named so as to avoid confusion with the newly-established Royal Air Force. The RAE remained as such until 1 April 1988 when a cosmetic change brought about the **Royal Aerospace Establishment (RAE)**. On 1 April 1991 the RAE was merged with several other research departments to become the **Defence Research Agency (DRA)**. Four years later, on 1 April 1995, the title was again changed, to **Defence Evaluation & Research Agency (DERA)**, and remained thus until DERA was part-privatised by the MoD in 2001. DERA was separated into two organisations – **DSTL** (Defence Science & Technology Laboratory, a retained agency of the UK Ministry of Defence whilst the privatised element became **QinetiQ**. The formal launch of QinetiQ took place on 2 July 2001.

Aberporth (Cardiganshire)

Aberporth first opened as a weapons Range in 1939 and during the Second World War was effectively two distinct Establishments – the Anti-Aircraft Artillery Range and the Projectile Development Range. They were separated literally by a chain-link fence and their only common feature was that they shared the over water Range Danger Area that extended into most of Cardigan Bay.

The Anti-Aircraft Artillery, an exclusively Army operation, became the first user of the Aberporth Range in August 1939. Weapons employed included 3" (13-pounder); 3.7" (28-pounder) and naval 4.5" (with a 54lb shell) modified for shore use as a heavy anti-aircraft gun.

'X' Flight, 1 AACU began moving in to Aberporth, from Watchet, on 3 September 1940. Remaining a resident unit for a number of years, the Flight was re-designated 1621 Army Co-operation Flight on 1 November 1942.

By 1943 the AAAR began to be referred to as the 1st Heavy Anti-Aircraft Practice Camp and incorporated 'Z' Battery (the anti-aircraft experimental rocket Battery) which, in some senses, was considered to have "jumped the fence" from the Projectile Development Range.

The Projectile Development Range (later the Project Development Establishment) was evacuated from Fort Halstead, Kent in early 1940. Although there is no definitive record of when rocket firings started, by mid-1940 both 2" and 3" rockets were being fired in large numbers.

Targets utilised across the Range, initially by the guns, consisted of towed drogues and banners by aircraft operating out of RAF Carew Cheriton, Pembrokeshire. These were transferred to RAF Blaenannerch (later re-named RAF Aberporth) in 1941. 1621 Flight also flew Queen Bee drones from the airfield to the Range.

With the end of hostilities in 1945 the Army pulled out of Aberporth altogether and the Projectile Development Establishment eventually became the Guided Projectile Establishment and moved most its staff, plus chemical laboratories, workshops and static firing facilities to the wartime airfield at Westcott, Buckinghamshire. This left Aberporth as the primary UK firing site for guided and unguided projectiles whereupon the Range was expanded to occupy the areas vacated by the Army. In 1947, both Westcott and Aberporth were taken over by RAE Farnborough at which time Aberporth became the Guided Weapons Trials Wing of RAE's GW Department.

Throughout the 1947–1951 period the emphasis was on development of test vehicles of almost every description from RAE and other research establishments. Many of these had anti-aircraft applications but it was not until 1952 when target drone aircraft re-appeared at Aberporth. These featured an evaluation batch of French Arsenal 5501 ground-launched target drones that were test-flown at Aberporth (see Chapter 7).

1951 had seen the start of various missile development tests at Aberporth, including Bloodhound, Fireflash, Firestreak, Seaslug and Thunderbird. During the development phases, many initial homing and guidance trials were made against static targets, eg metal spheres suspended from a barrage balloon or tied to a sea anchor or buoy. Subsequently these missiles required a moving target and which led to the provision of a drone target service from RAE Llanbedr. The first Firefly U.8 drone flight took place in February 1954 and the first "kill" was recorded in April 1954 by an RTV1q beam rider.

From 1956, the Superintendent at Aberporth assumed responsibility for Llanbedr, which from then onwards was regarded as Aberporth's Target Group. However, by 1959, when new weapon systems began to enter service the choice of practice/training/in-service R&D Ranges became something of an issue that embroiled all three Services.

As far as the Army was concerned, the Director of Royal Artillery and the RAE Range management could not agree on a number of issues. This resulted in the Royal Artillery developing its own practice Range for Thunderbird Mk.1 at the TEGWRA/TERA Range at Ty Croes, on Anglesey, referred to at one stage as the Joint Guided Weapons Range Unit. The targets used were flown from Llanbedr but routed around the Lleyn Peninsula. Eventually the Army transferred to Aberporth with Thunderbird Mk.2 in 1970.

Despite repeated requests by the Army to use the Ty Croes Range, the RAF chose to use Aberporth from the outset for both air-launched (Fireflash and Firestreak) and ground-launched (Bloodhound Mk.1) service firings.

There are reports that the Royal Navy wished to establish temporary Danger Areas in virtually any offshore location and to use ship-launched targets from escort vessels. But without sufficient numbers of target drones available the Navy was forced to use the Aberporth Range for Firestreak (by FAA Squadrons) and Seaslug Mk.1 (from ships). Eventually, of course, the Navy procured Shelduck and Chukar in large quantities and the escort ship/target solution became viable but the Navy did continue to use Aberporth for first firings from new ships and after re-fits or on other occasions when the exercise featured an R&D element.

From 1963 the responsibility of the Superintendent Aberporth was widened to become Superintendent of RAE Ranges at which point RAE Larkhill and RAE West Freugh came within his remit. The move led to centralized planning – allocation of trials to the most suitable Range – and with economies of scale being applied to the provision of required instrumentation.

The organization of Range responsibility remained unchanged until 1991 when most of the RAE joined the DRA. However, the Ranges were excluded from this change; they became the Air Ranges element of the Directorate General of Test & Evaluation within MoD(PE) alongside the Land Ranges and a number of sea Ranges associated with the measurement of ship signatures, sonar and torpedo work amongst other things.

Eventually, in 1995, all Ranges became an integral part of an enlarged DERA, later privatised as QinetiQ. Together with the A&AEE at Boscombe Down the entire Range organisation became an integrated, test and evaluation facility.

Until November 2004, Aberporth was essentially a missile-launching Range. Apart from some Chukar Detachments from Portland (or, later, Culdrose) target aircraft were traditionally launched from Llanbedr but with the untimely closure of Llanbedr (and the withdrawal of Jindivik) the main air target duties were transferred to the Mirach 100/5 drone, maintained and launched from the Aberporth Range head.

Whilst most of the unmanned target activity was traditionally restricted to Llanbedr-based Jindivik and Stiletto, DERA Hawk T.1 aircraft, also operated out of Llanbedr, often acted as targets for non-firing trials.

Benbecula (Hebrides Range)

Work on converting the original pre-war grass airfield, known locally as Balivanich, began in August 1941. During the war a number of Squadrons, principally RAF Coastal Command units, were based at Benbecula until, in January 1946, the airfield went to Care and Maintenance.

When the Hebrides Range head was being established off the west coast of South Uist, Benbecula was returned to the RAF during 1957/58.

Range D701 extended for some 100 miles into the Atlantic; Falconet and Banshee were both used regularly as Rapier targets on the Inner Range and for brief periods Jindiviks were deployed from Llanbedr to Benbecula on a campaign basis, as required.

Cleave (Cornwall)

RAF Cleave was established as a grass landing ground in February 1939 to provide anti-aircraft Co-operation for Territorial Army Units. Situated on a windy cliff top 5 miles north of Bude, it was an ideal site for an Artillery Practice Camp because of a lack of inshore shipping and offered a good arc for 3.7", 3", Bofors and Lewis guns.

'G' Flight/1AACU was formed in May 1939 to undertake target-towing duties. At the same time Queen Bee-equipped 'V' Flight was also formed at Cleave.

Falkland Islands

Several locations have been used for unmanned target operations before a permanent facility was established at the Harrier Range. This Range has been used for a twice-yearly camp using CATS-Banshee targets.

Larkhill Range (Wiltshire)

The Larkhill Range has always been wholly contained within the Army's Salisbury Plain Training Area (SPTA).

From 1947 both the RAE and the RAF began to deploy to Larkhill on an "as-and-when-required" basis to fire and instrument trials of several recoverable short-range test vehicles. These utilised a relatively small portion of the SPTA whilst a similarly small area was independently instrumented by the A&AEE for various tasks.

RAE Larkhill was formally established in 1958 and from the outset, and operating under a degree of sufferance from the Army, was subjected to stringent limitations on days/hours of operation. It has been said that their instrumentation huts were often "accidentally" damaged by errant shellfire and on at least one occasion broken into during silent hours by soldiers looking for shelter whilst on manoeuvres!

By 1962/63 Larkhill came under the wing of the Superintendent of Ranges, by which time A&AEE had relinquished their small portion of the Range and became users of the RAE Range.

A large number of targets and drones were tested at Larkhill, including the first Royal Navy training flights on Shelduck in 1960. By the early-1980s Larkhill was being regularly used for trials involving drones and UAVs, eg development flight trials of MACHAN by RAE and GEC in 1981/82, RAE Farnborough's XRAE-1 UAV was test-flown there in 1982 and the ASAT Falconet target drone made its initial test flights at Larkhill. Other development flying involved the FRL Raven, the AEL Snipe target, BAe Stabileye, Westland's Wisp and, of course, the GEC-Marconi Phoenix UAV.

Drones became a permanent feature at Larkhill when the Royal Artillery took delivery of the Northrop MQM-57A surveillance drone.

Another long-term drone operator based at Larkhill was the Target Operations Group, transferring in from Llanbedr to Rollestone Camp in April 1981. The Group, a small offshoot of Shorts' Missile Division and operating MATS-B targets on behalf of the Army, was restructured in September 1981 to become Short Brothers Air Services Ltd. When RCA Flying Services Ltd won the contract from SBAS on 1

June 1984 the new operator took over the existing hangar and facilities. Three years later, on 31 July 1987, the company was re-named SERCO Operations Ltd. Eventually, on 1 January 2002, SERCO lost its contract to Meggitt who, on viewing Larkhill as an unnecessary expense and an out-of-the-way location (there being no target flying at Larkhill), transferred the target maintenance and storage facility to Manorbier.

Llanbedr (Gwynedd)

Situated within reach of the extensive sand dunes of Cardigan Bay, Llanbedr is without doubt the one airfield in the UK that is instantly associated with unmanned target aircraft.

RAF Llanbedr was officially opened as a Fighter Command station on 15 June 1941 and became host to several Spitfire squadrons, eg 74, 131 and 232. However, after just two years the airfield's role changed from Fighter Command to No.12 Fighter Gunnery School. It marked the beginning of an association with targets and target aircraft that was to last some 65 years.

Airborne targets were initially drogues towed by Miles Martinets over Cardigan Bay, offering targets for British and American units. In just four days of air gunnery practice, seven USAAF P-47 Thunderbolts from RAF King's Cliffe, Northamptonshire fired some 12,980 rounds, scoring 355 strikes on the drogues.

In July 1943 1486 (Fighter) Gunnery Flight moved from Valley to Llanbedr and shortly afterwards was reformed, on 18 October, as No.12 Armament Practice Camp with Miles Masters, Martinets and Westland Lysanders. On the same date 1492 (Fighter) Gunnery Flight, based at Weston Zoyland, was reformed as No.13 Armament Practice Camp and also moved to Llanbedr, on 20 November 1943. Both Practice Camps were later disbanded on 21 February 1945.

Llanbedr closed for a very brief period after the war but re-opened when No.5 Civilian Anti-Aircraft Co-operation Unit (5 CAACU) was formed on 16 September 1951 to take over the commitment of 20 (AC) Squadron in serving the Army Artillery Ranges at Tonfannau, just to the north of Towyn, and Ty Croes on Anglesey. The airfield was now under the control of RAF Maintenance Command whilst manning of the CAACU was contracted to Short Brothers & Harland Ltd.

Selected as the primary base for UK unmanned target operations, Llanbedr received its first Fairey Firefly in November 1951 when AS.7 WJ147 was positioned to Llanbedr. Much of the Firefly drone development flying – known as 'Q' Trials – was carried out at Llanbedr and the first fully unmanned sortie took place on 3 February 1954 by Firefly U.8 WJ150.

The first air-launch of a fully guided and controlled missile took place on 5 September 1955 when a Firestreak missile was fired at a Firefly U.8 drone over Cardigan Bay. The drone was destroyed.

From 1956, Llanbedr became the responsibility of the Superintendent at the nearby Aberporth Range and by late-January 1957 the first Meteor U.15 drone (VT110) had arrived at Llanbedr. At the same time the Llanbedr target drone facility transferred to Ministry of Supply although aircraft servicing, pilots and ground controllers were provided by Short Bros. A further change saw RAF Llanbedr re-styled as RAE Llanbedr.

4 January 1960 marked the arrival of the first (of an initial sixteen) Jindivik 102s although the first flight under remote control did not occur until late on 26 April. 1960 also saw the arrival of Meteor U.16s, marking the end of Firefly U.8 operations at Llanbedr.

In 1982 the operational responsibility for managing Llanbedr airfield was formally contracted to Airwork Ltd. The arrangement extended to 1990 when Airwork's submission to renew its contract was bettered by FR/SERCO, a company jointly owned by FR Aviation and SERCO and who had successfully tendered to manage a number of UK military bases. The company had its contract renewed in 1998 but four years later, on 12 July 2002, Llanbedr passed to the care of QinetiQ.

In spite of the various changes in tenure Llanbedr became synonymous with Meteor and Jindivik drones for over forty years. Eventually, the airfield was closed on 28 October 2004 with all target operations being transferred to Aberporth. Ownership of Llanbedr later passed to the Welsh Assembly Government.

Manorbier & Castlemartin (Dyfed)

From 1935, when it first came into use, the small airfield at Manorbier, some 4 miles south-west of Tenby in Dyfed, South Wales, became synonymous with target-towing and radio-controlled target flying. In fact it remains the case today; perhaps not as well-known as the North Wales airfield of Llanbedr but Manorbier most certainly has had a longer association with military target aircraft. Almost 1,000 Army target aircraft have, in recent years, been literally catapulted off the Manorbier cliff-tops simply to be shot down by guided missiles over Carmarthen Bay.

"B" Flight of No.1 Anti-Aircraft Co-operation Unit (1AACU) was based at Manorbier during the summer of 1937. Annual practice camps continued until 15 May 1939 when 'Y' Flight, 1AACU moved in as a new resident unit (until 16 August 1942). By that time the Pilotless Aircraft Unit had also moved in to Manorbier (on 5 May 1942) to provide local training of AA gunners.

Manorbier was never a large field despite being enlarged slightly in 1940 but autumn floods frequently made it unserviceable. To overcome that, and to ensure that artillery practice was kept to schedule, Queen Bees were fitted with floats and fired from a catapult mounted on the cliff which fringed the landing ground. Whenever target flying took place, a salvage vessel was to hand to pick up the pilotless drone after its water landing and return to Tenby harbour, from where it was taken to Manorbier by road.

The Pilotless Aircraft Unit officially closed down on 15 March 1946.

From 1982 the newly-styled Short Brothers Air Services Ltd began deploying Skeet targets to Manorbier for Royal Artillery 'camps' were in residence. Use of Manorbier increased significantly by 1986 when Banshee entered service. When Meggitt took over the target service provider role in January 2002 a permanent storage and servicing facility was established at Manorbier to replace the Rollestone Camp, Larkhill base.

364 Sitting Ducks and Peeping Toms

NAMFI (Soudha Bay, Crete)

NATO Missile Firing Installation (NAMFI) is located off the Mediterranean island of Crete. In 1964 a Multilateral Agreement was signed between the nations of Belgium, Denmark, France, Germany, Greece, Netherlands, Norway and the USA. The Agreement established the terms of NAMFI's operation. Funded by NATO, construction of the Range began in 1964 and was complete four years later.

When NAMFI first became operational, American Hawk (and Improved Hawk) missiles were fired against CT-20 drones operated by Nord Aviation. Northrop won the target-supply contract in 1970 and took over the facilities left by the outgoing contractor. Northrop deployed MQM-74A Chukar 1 targets until December 1976 when MQM-74C Chukar IIs took over.

Subsequently, aerial target services were provided at NAMFI by private companies contracted either by NAMFI on behalf or its users, or by the user individually. A number of Mirach 100/5 targets have been detached to NAMFI for live missile training by the RAF.

Otterburn Range (Northumberland)

In 1911 20,000 acres of land in Redesdale was purchased to provide an artillery range and tented camp for the newly formed Territorial Army. Further land was compulsorily purchased during World War II and more in the decades that followed. The current range extends to some 58,000 acres. The Otterburn Training Area (OTA) is now divided into three separate Danger Areas.

Sennelager Range (Germany)

First used towards the end of the 19th Century, the Sennelager Range is situated between Germany's Northern Lowlands and the mountainous Central region, north of Paderburn.

Immediately after the end of World War II Sennelager passed into US control but very soon handed over on a long-term basis to Britain.

The Range was developed principally as an artillery range but has also been used extensively for air-to-ground bombing.

Regular exercises and deployments have been carried out, often including the use of unmanned surveillance drones.

Shoeburyness Range (Essex)

Situated in Essex, beyond Southend, Shoeburyness is the largest land Range site in the UK and has existed since c1850. The size and relative remoteness of Shoeburyness makes it ideal for teaching bomb disposal techniques and much activity involves demolition training by Explosive Ordnance Disposal (EOD) operators.

Shoeburyness has also been used for trials and evaluation of large calibre weapons testing.

Foulness Island is located within the Shoeburyness Range.

Stiffkey (Norfolk)

Situated on the north Norfolk coast, Stiffkey was the location for No.11 Light Anti-Aircraft Practice Camp and range.

During October 1950 a series of flight trials involving OQ-3 Aerial Targets took place at Stiffkey.

The US Army is also reported to have operated Radioplane OQ-19 target drones from Stiffkey for a brief period in the late-1950s. These were flown for US Army artillery units based in the UK and West Germany.

Thorney Island (Hampshire/West Sussex)

RAF Thorney Island officially opened on 3 February 1938 as part of 16 Group, RAF Coastal Command. On 15 July 1947 the airfield passed to RAF Fighter Command (11 Group) and, via various administrative changes, to 38 Group, RAF Transport Command in January 1962.

The RAF moved out of Thorney Island in January 1976 and the airfield officially closed on 30 June 1976. The airfield laid dormant for several years until August 1982 when control passed to the Army and it was taken over by the Royal Artillery. A number of unmanned aircraft trials took place at Thorney Island.

10 (Assaye) Battery, RA moved to Thorney Island in 1993 to become part of 47 Air Defence Regiment RA (together with 21 Battery, 25/170 Battery and 43 Battery).

Watchet (Somerset)

Air Ministry NOTAMS issued in 1925 provide the earliest reference to Watchet as a Royal Artillery Anti-Aircraft Practice Camp.

The extent of the nearby Range was precisely given as "an irregular segment of a circle on the seaward side between the radii, approximately 6 miles in length bearing 289° True and 70° True and having at their centre a point approximately 1½ miles east of Watchet, Somerset. The centre of this circle is approximately 8 miles ENE Minehead, Latitude 51°13´N, Longitude 3°18´W."

The embryonic Queen Bee Flight deployed to Watchet on 27 July 1937 for a Summer Camp, lasting until 16 September 1937. 'Z' Flight, 1 AACU deployed to Watchet between 14 May and 3 October 1938 and again from 13 May 1939 to 9 September 1940. 'X' Flight was also based at Watchet between 14 September 1939 and 30 October 1940.

After the departure of 'X' Flight Watchet was almost permanently used by target-towing aircraft. During postwar years the Light Anti-Aircraft Gunnery School moved in on 15 July 1947. However Watchet, as an airfield, closed in February 1957.

West Freugh

Although viewed upon as meeting a need for a fast jet airfield, West Freugh had, in fact, been an instrumented bombing Range since 1936. It was principally used by No.4 Bombing & Gunnery School and later by the Ministry of Supply Bombing Trials Unit.

In 1957 West Freugh came under RAE management when personnel were transferred in from Aberporth. Subsequently, and in line with most other Ranges, it became the responsibility of the Superintendent of Ranges in 1962.

Involvement with unmanned target aircraft is thought to have first occurred in the 1980s when Blowpipe research &

development work was transferred from Larkhill. Under an MoD contract Shorts used West Freugh for launching Skeet as a target for Blowpipe firings.

Weybourne (Norfolk)

One leading aviation historian claimed that it was "difficult to imagine Weybourne being described as an airfield as such. It was so, in the sense that Queen Bee target aircraft were launched and recovered there but, in reality, the taking-off was from a catapult and landings were usually made in a nearby field."

Situated just three miles west of Sheringham, on the north Norfolk coast, Weybourne first came into use as Gunnery Range during the Summer of 1936 when anti-aircraft gunners at No.5 Heavy Anti-Aircraft Division Practice Camp began using the Range for firing at targets towed by Westland Wallace biplanes operating out of RAF Bircham Newton.

Contemporary NOTAMs give Weybourne's exact position as a "Land and sea area bounded on the North by an arc of a circle radius 12½ statute miles with centre at Latitude 52°56′N, Longitude 1°07′53″E and bounded on the south by lines drawn at 70° and 310° True from the above centre, for a distance of 12½ miles."

Queen Bee activity began in a relatively small way when 'X' Flight, No.1 AACU arrived on 16 May 1939. The first launch of a Queen Bee from Weybourne took place on 6 June 1939 but the site became well-known for an occasion, on 6 June 1941, when Prime Minister Winston Churchill and a large distinguished company attended a special demonstration of rockets being fired by 'Z' Battery against a Queen Bee.

'X' Flight did not remain at Weybourne for long. After the last Queen Bee was despatched to Langham airfield on 30 June 1942 and on the following day the airfield was obstructed and work began on dismantling the single hangar. Weybourne then reverted to the more conventional style of Range when shooting once again became directed solely at towed sleeve or banner targets.

NB. In his book "Action Stations Revisited", Michael J Bowyer describes the visit of Churchill to Weybourne on 6 June 1941 to watch a demonstration. *(Reproduced with permission)*

"The principle under which the batteries operated was for a salvo of rockets to be fired in such a manner as to produce a box barrage with the target being caught up in the centre. As intended the rockets roared away, Queen Bee V4797 ran into a salvo of 160 UP rockets, then landed unscathed on the sea and was retrieved by the salvage boat SS *Radstock*. There was not time for a repeat performance and what thoughts passed through Sir Winston's mind seem nowhere to have been discovered."

"On 18 June 1941 another demonstration of rocket power was held for the Prime Minister. After no less than 45 minutes of firing a near burst put a Queen Bee out of control and it spun into the sea. A repeat demonstration of the weapons resulted in no hits so the Queen Bee was finished off by Bofors fire."

MoD records reveal that the two Queen Bees lost on the day were L5894 and V4797.

Suffield, Alberta, Canada

In 1971 an agreement was signed between the British and Canadian governments permitting the British Army to use over three-quarters of the Canadian Defence Research Establishment, Suffield (DRES) for armoured, infantry and artillery live-firing training. As a result, the British Army Training Unit, Suffield (BATUS) was formally established in January 1972 as the British Army's premier training unit. Located in a large expanse of the sparsely populated part of the Alberta Province prairie, Suffield can accommodate live-firing exercises up to brigade level.

Selected Bibliography

50 Years of Target Drone Aircraft – Richard A. Botzum (Northrop Corporation, 1985)

A Bit of a 'Tiff' – Bill Drake, Cyril Stanley Drake & Jill Field) Platypus Books, 2003)

Aircraft Systems (UVS International, 2006, 2007, 2009, 2010)

Airspeed Aircraft since 1931 – H.A. Taylor (Putnam & Company, 1970)

Airspeed, the Company & its Aeroplanes – D.H. Middleton (Terence Dalton Ltd, 1982)

Armed Forces of the United Kingdom, The – Charles Heyman (Pen & Sword Books 2003, 2007)

Beech Aircraft & their Predecessors – A.J. Pelletier (Putnam Aeronautical Books, 1995)

British Aircraft Corporation – Charles Gardner (BT Batsford Ltd, 1981)

British Aircraft Specifications File, The – K.J. Meekcoms & E.B. Morgan (Air-Britain Historians, 1994)

English Electric Canberra – Ken Delve, Peter Green & John Clemons (Midland Counties Publishing, 1992)

Fairey Firefly, The Operational Record – William Harrison (Airlife Publishing, 1992)

Farnborough and the Fleet Air Arm – Geoffrey Cooper (Midland Publishing 2008)

Fire Across the Desert – Peter Morton (Commonwealth of Australia)

Gloster Meteor – Phil Butler and Tony Buttler (Aerofax, Midland Publishing, 2006)

He Lit the Lamp – Ursula Bloom (Burke Publishing Company Ltd, 1958)

Jane's RPVs: Robot Aircraft Today – John W.R. Taylor & Kenneth Munson (MacDonald & Janes, 1997)

Jane's Unmanned Aerial Vehicles and Targets – Kenneth Munson (Janes)

K File, The – James J. Halley (Air-Britain Historians, 1995)

Meteor – Paolo Valpolini (Meteor C.A.E. S.pA, 2001)

Miles Aircraft Since 1925 – Don L. Brown (Putnam & Company, 1970)

Royal Aircraft Factory, The – Paul R. Hare (Putnam Aeronautical Books, 1990)

Royal Air Force in Galloway, The – A.T. Murchie (G.C. Book Publishers Ltd, 1992)

Royal Air Force Flying Training & Support Units – Ray Sturtivant, John Hamlin & James J. Halley (Air-Britain Historians, 1997)

Ship Strike, the History of Air-to-Sea Weapon Systems – Peter C. Smith (Airlife Publishing, 1998)

Sopwith – the Man and his Aircraft – Bruce Robertson (Harleyford, 1970)

Sopwith Aircraft 1912–1920 – H.F. King (Putnam & Company, 1980)

Target Rolling – Wendy Mills (Midland Counties Publishing, 2002)

UK Flight Testing Accidents 1940–71 – Derek Collier Webb (Air-Britain Historians, 2002)

Unmanned Aircraft – Sir Michael Armitage (Brassey's Defence Publishers, 1988)

Unmanned Air Vehicles – Bill Holder (Schiffer Publishing, 2001)

World Unmanned Aircraft – Kenneth Munson (Jane's Publishing, 1988)

Selected Journals

Aeromilitaria – Quarterly journal of Air-Britain (Historians) Ltd

Aviation Heritage – Journal of the Aviation Historical Society of Australia (AHSA).

Flight Deck – Journal of the Fleet Air Arm.

Flight International – Reed Business Information Ltd

Flypast – Key Publishing Ltd

Gunner – Journal of the Royal Regiment of Artillery.

Phoenix Facts – UAV Operating Standards Cell Newsletter

Roundel – Bi-monthly journal of British Aviation Research Group (BARG)

RAE News – Journal of the Royal Aircraft Establishment

Target – Quarterly journal of QinetiQ Llanbedr

Unmanned Vehicles – The Shepherd Press Ltd.

Index

Index refers only to the main text. Locations contained within the aircraft histories are excluded.

5 Battery, RA   297
14 Battery, RA   290
18 Battery, RA   x, 307, 308, 311, 312, 316, 317, 319, 320
22 Battery, RA   x, 291, 296, 297, 304, 306, 308, 311, 312, 316–318, 325
42 Battery, RA   312, 317, 320
57 Battery, RA   292
73 Battery, RA   292
74 Battery, RA   297, 311, 312
132 Battery, RA   311, 312
152 Battery, RA   290
156 Battery, RA   290
176 Battery, RA   311, 312
228 Battery, RA   288
61st Finsbury Rifles   20
728B Flight   99–103, 106–114, 118–122, 126, 127, 130, 131, 134, 136, 139
1115 Flight, RAF   328, 329
2 Group Support Unit   80
21 Regiment, RA   291
32 Regiment, RA   296, 297, 304, 306–313, 315–320, 322, 323, 325, 360
39 Regiment, RA   297, 304, 306, 307, 311, 312
47 Regiment, RA   319, 321, 359
94 Regiment, RA   290, 297, 360
39 Squadron, RAF   328, 329
704 Naval Air Sqdn   62
728 Sqdn, RNAS   79, 169   *see also 728B Flight*
762 Sqdn, RNAS   61
773 Sqdn, RNAS   61, 62

A

ABC Motors   3, 4, 222
Abu Dhabi   173
Abu Naji   312
AEL (Aero Electronics Ltd)   298, 299, 337, 338
AEL 4111 Snipe   338
Aerospace Technologies Australia (ASTA)   151
Afibra Handels   341
Air Service Training Ltd   88, 89, 92
Airborne Forces Experimental Establishment   80
Airspeed Ltd, Portsmouth   23, 51–60, 67, 87
    AS.30 Queen Wasp   23, 51–60
    AS.37   51
    AS.50 Trainer   55

Air Warfare Centre (UAV Battlelab)   323, 324, 333, 334
Airwork Ltd   152
Aladdin Industries Ltd   58
Al Amarah, Iraq   310, 312
Al Basra, Iraq   320
Al Fawr, Iraq   320
Al Shatetat Waterway, Iraq   308
APT Electronics   289
Aquila   *see Lockheed*
Armstrong-Siddeley
    Adder   144, 146
    Cheetah   53
    Lynx   8
Armstrong-Whitworth
    Meteor TT.20   101, 117
    Seaslug (missile)   92, 93, 100, 112, 113, 117, 136, 171, 357
    Viper   111, 144, 146, 147
ASAT UAV   282, 283, 300, 302
Ashford, Kent   270, 272
Aspin (engine)   58
Aston Down (20 MU)   94, 95
ATLAS   341
Auster Aircraft Ltd   222, 224, 225, 287
    AOP.6   230
    B2   222
    B3   222–224
    C9   223
Austin, Reg   342, 346, 347, 348
Avro
    Bison   72
    Lancaster   92–94, 111
    Lincoln   94, 96, 111
Az Zubayer, Iraq   309

B

Ba'ath Party   311
BAe Sky Flash (missile)   128
    Stabileye   298, 339, 340
BAE Systems
    Corax   331–333
    Fury   332, 334
    HERTI   330, 332–335
    Kestrel   330, 331, 333
    Mantis   335
    Raven   331–333
    Soarer   330
    Taranis   335–337
Baghdad, Iraq   308, 328
Bagram, Afghanistan   314
Ballykelly   235, 236

Basra (Basrah), Iraq   10, 308, 309, 311, 312, 316, 318, 320, 328
BATUS, Canada   283, 285, 306, 324, 350
Beaufighter   *see Bristol*
Beaulieu   80, 85
Beechcraft AQM-37   161–162
Belfast   136, 160, 161, 235, 238, 247, 298, 343, 344
Belgrade   296, 306, 307
Bell, Stanley, Lt Cdr   76, 81
Bembridge Point   70
Benbecula   152, 216, 236
Biggin Hill   6, 20, 21, 24
Bingen, Washington   326
Biscarosse   215
Bison   *see Avro*
Blackburn
    Blackburn   72–74
    Firebrand TF.5   96
    Fleet Spotter   75
Blandford Forum   242, 259, 352
Bloodhound (missile)   *see Bristol*
Blowpipe (missile)   *see Short Bros*
Blue Jay (missile)   *see de Havilland*
Blue Sky (missile)   *see Fairey*
Boeing ScanEagle   324, 326–328
Bosnia   296, 315, 328
Bouchier, Cecil, Fg Off   70, 71
Boulton Paul Defiant   59, 76, 77
Bradshaw, Granville   4
Brawdy, RNAS   61, 62
Bristol Aeroplane Co Ltd (& Bristol Aircraft)   91, 222, 354
Bristol   4, 12, 30, 348
    170   143
    Beaufighter   86, 172
    Bloodhound (missile)   91, 92, 112, 117, 160, 161, 354
    Fighter   67, 68
    F.2B   6, 67, 68, 71
    Mercury (engine)
        VIII   57
        25/30   59
        26/32   59
    Red Duster (missile)   91–93, 354   *see also Bloodhound*
Bristol, Lulsgate   284
Bristol-Siddeley Viper   147
British Aircraft Corporation Rapier (missile)   115, 117, 140, 236, 240, 354, 356, 358–400
    Seawolf (missile)   117, 357

368   Sitting Ducks and Peeping Toms

British Petroleum Advance Materials 305
Brooklands 2, 3
Brooklands Aviation Ltd 78, 79, 82, 88, 89, 151
Burrowhead 21, 22
Buttocks Booth 78, 82, 88

C

Camp Bastion, Afghanistan 315, 319, 320, 329
Camp Condor, Iraq 310
Camp Roberts, USA 318, 320
Canadair 343
   CL-89 (AN/USD-501) Midge 293–298
   CL-227 298, 351
Canberra *see English Electric*
Cardigan Bay 112, 114, 152, 160, 216, 283
Castlemartin Range 228–230
CATS (Combined Aerial Target Service) 216, 274, 281, 283–286
Cattewater Air Station, Plymouth 8
CB Projections 81
CEDEA Test Range, Huelva 215
Celle 290, 291, 293, 297
Centre d'Essais de la Méditerranée 215
Centre d'Essais des Landes (CEL) 215
CERES Test Range 166
Charterhall 299, 300
Chickerell Aerodrome 19
Chukar *see Northrop*
Clayton, Keith 232
Cleave 22
College of Aeronautics 93, 135, 341, 352
Condor *see Focke-Wulf*
Cooke, J.J., Lt Col (Retired) 288–292
Copehill Down, Salisbury Plain 325, 326
Corax *see BAE Systems*
Counter Bombardment 287, 288, 290
Cranfield Aerospace A3 Observer 351–353
Cranfield MinO 351, 353
Creech AFB 329
Culdrose 101, 173, 177, 199, 216, 217
Curtiss-Wright SO3C-1/SO3C-1K Queen Seamew 65

D

Dagnall, R.F. 85
Dale, RNAS 62
Defiant *see Boulton Paul*
Denny A-2 58
Detling 25
Devonport 8
de Havilland
   Blue Jay (missile) 93, 113, 355 *see also Firestreak*
   DH.9A 6, 67–72
   DH.60 Moth (inc DH.60G & DH.60M) 17, 18
   DH.82A Tiger Moth 17, 49, 50
   DH.82 Queen Bee 13, 17–52, 58, 91, 165, 188
   DH.98 Mosquito 92, 111, 282
      B.XXV 61, 62, 64, 80
      TT.35 98
      TT.39 80
   DH.110 Sea Vixen 103, 139–142, 355
   DH.112 Venom 98, 106, 135, 355
   Firestreak (missile) 91–93, 98, 112–114, 117, 355 *see also Blue Jay*
   Gipsy Queen 59
   Gipsy Six 57
   Red Hawk (missile) 355 *see also Firestreak*
Dekheila 23, 40, 41
Directorate of Training 57
Disposal Support Agency 313
Donnington 223
DTGW 140, 141

E

EADS
   Quadrocopter 324, 326
   Scorpio-6 324–326
EADS/IAI Eagle 324, 325
Edgley EA-7 Optica 151
Edinburgh Field 112, 113, 116, 132
Eglin AFB, Florida 318
El Centro Range, California 196
Elliott B4 Autopilot 113, 145
Elliott's of Newbury Ltd 87, 88
English Electric
   Canberra (general) 89, 160, 161, 235, 297
      U.10, U.14 (D.10 & D.14) 114, 135–137
   Red Shoes (missile) 91–93, 112, 357 *see also Thunderbird Missile*
   Thunderbird (missile) 92, 93
Errington, George 53, 55
Evett's Field 112, 117, 144
Exercise Bright Star 305
Exercise Pegasus Fury 351
Exercise Purple Star 351
Exercise Saif Sareea II 307

F

Fairey Aviation Ltd 58, 97, 98, 116, 117, 135, 144–146, 165, 166, 222, 355
   IIID 6, 7, 74, 75
   IIIF 13, 14, 74
   Blue Sky (missile) 91–94, 96, 355 *see also Fireflash*
   Fireflash (missile) 91–94, 355 *see also Blue Sky*
   Firefly
      AS.4, AS.5, AS.6 98, 111
      AS.7 96–98, 111
      T.7 96–98, 101, 110
      T.8 97, 103
      U.8 96–98, 103–105, 110, 112, 114, 146, 149
      U.9 96, 98–103, 106–110, 113, 114
   Fulmar 59
   Gannet AS.1 96
   Queen 13–16
   Stooge 165
Falkland Islands 231, 238, 240, 241, 274, 285, 355, 356, 358–360
Fallingbostel 290
Fallon NAS 324
Farnborough Show, SBAC 82, 88, 89, 103, 104, 106, 108, 153, 154, 225, 229, 230, 317, 328, 335, 343, 347, 352 *see also RAE Farnborough*
Fayid, Royal Navy Aircraft Repair Yard 23
Ferranti 297–300, 304, 305, 346, 354
Ferranti-Canadair 298
FIM-43 Redeye *see General Dynamics*
FIM-92A Stinger *see General Dynamics*
Firebird *see Intora*
Firebrand *see Blackburn*
Fireflash (missile) *see Fairey*
Firefly *see Fairey*
Firestreak (missile) *see de Havilland*
Fisherman's Bend 143
Flash-Spotting 287
Fleet Spotter *see Blackburn*
Flight Refuelling Ltd 92, 95, 111, 116, 139, 140, 187, 299, 300, 350
   FR-500 drone 282 *see also ASAT*
   Raven 348–351
Focke-Wulf Condor 76
Folland Gnat 135
Folland/Vickers Red Dean (missile) 93
Ford, Sussex, RNAS 62
Fort Bastion 316
Fort Benghaisa 167, 169
Fort Bragg, Carolina 351
Free Flying Glider Mk.1 76
FR/SERCO 152
FR-500 drone *see Flight Refuelling*
FROG model aircraft 76
Fulmar *see Fairey*
Fury *see BAE Systems*

G

G.A.F. Jindivik 92–94, 111–113, 117, 135, 139, 141, 143–160
G.A.L.35 51, 57
Gannet *see Fairey*
Gardner, G.W.H. 6, 8, 9, 15, 19
Garner, Harry 70
GEC Avionics Machan UAV 300, 341, 352
GEC-Marconi 287, 299–302, 305, 348
General Atomics
   MQ-1/RQ-1 Predator 308, 328, 329
   MQ-9A Reaper 320, 328, 329
General Dynamics
   FIM-43 Redeye 231
   FIM-92A Stinger 215, 231
   Sea Sparrow (missile) 194, 357 *see also Sparrow missile*
   Sparrow (missile) (including Sea Sparrow) 159, 161, 196, 197, 295, 357, 358
General Electric 240
Gibraltar 15, 16, 101, 161, 169, 171, 198, 201
Gipsy Queen *see de Havilland*
Gipsy Six *see de Havilland*
GKN-Westland 305
Gladiator *see Gloster*
Glasgow, West Campbell Street 22, 26
Glider Target Unit 72, 74
Gloster
   Gladiator 23, 59
   Javelin 111, 112
   Meteor
      F.4 96, 111
      TT.8 98
      NF.12, NF.14 116
      U.15 100, 103, 111–114, 117–125, 135, 136, 354
      U.16 91, 103, 113, 114, 116–118, 126–134, 136, 149, 152
      U.17 116
      U.18 116
      U.19 116
   see also Armstrong-Whitworth
Gnat *see Folland*
Godalming, Surrey 85
Gosport, Hampshire 15, 20, 25, 70–75

Government Aircraft Factory (Australia)   91, 143, 147, 148
"Green Light" (Seacat missile)   171
GSR/GST.3494   342, 344
GSR.3700   282
Guildford   85
Gunnery Conversion Flight   18, 20
Gunnery Training Team   325
Gunnery Wing, School of Anti-Aircraft Artillery   80

H
Hal Far (Malta)   23, 25, 79, 99–103, 113, 114, 118, 136, 137, 168, 169, 171, 175, 177
Hamble   14, 88
Hamm, Gordon   111
Handley Page Ltd   136, 222
Hanscom AFB, Massachusetts   318
Harley, D, Lt(A)   61, 64
Harlow Hill, Newcastle   306, 311, 312
Hart   *see Hawker*
Hatston, RNAS   59
Hawarden (47 MU)   24, 112
Hawker
   Hart   76
   Typhoon   59
Hayes, Middlesex   96, 97, 135
Heath Row   13, 58
Heinkel He 111   76
Heliwells Ltd   222
Helmund *(or Helmand)*, Afghanistan   316, 319
Hendon, RAF   53
Henlow, RAF   14, 20, 22–25
Henstridge   343
Hereford   325
Hermes 450 UAV   *see Thales*
HERTI   *see BAE Systems*
Heston   98, 145
Hills & Son, F   58
Hitco, F.R. Ltd   302
HMS *Achilles*   21, 24, 25
HMS *Argus*   6, 20
HMS *Ark Royal*   54, 103
HMS *Castor*   7
HMS *Centaur*   103
HMS *Charity*   229
HMS *Courageous*   15, 16
HMS *Cumberland*   169
HMS *Decoy*   171, 172
HMS *Duchess*   103
HMS *Eagle*   16
HMS *Girdle Ness*   100, 101, 113. 136
HMS *Malaya*   16
HMS *Nelson*   16
HMS *Newcastle*   198, 209
HMS *Orion*   19
HMS *Pegasus*   28, 54
HMS *Peregrine*   *see Ford, Sussex*
HMS *Rodney*   16, 21
HMS *Sharpshooter*   71, 73
HMS *Shropshire*   16
HMS *Stronghold*   5–9, 73
HMS *Sturdy*   7
HMS *Sutherland*   326
HMS *Thanet*   12
HMS *Tiger*   73–75
HMS *Valiant*   14–16
HMS *Vigo*   229
HMS *Warspite*   16
HMY *Victoria & Albert*   21
Hohne, West Germany   292, 296, 359
Holsworthy, New South Wales   87
Honeywell T-Hawk UAV   321, 322
Howe, Dennis, Professor   341
Hullavington, RAF   24, 95, 348
Hybrid Mk.1/Mk.2   161–163

I
Idris-el-Awal   226
Indian Springs Air Force Auxiliary Field   328
International Alloys Ltd   96
International Model Aircraft Ltd (IMA Ltd)   67, 75–78, 81, 83–85
   Swallow   83–85
International Signals & Controls   305
Intora Firebird UAV   341, 342
Isle of Grain   67, 69, 70

J
J & AS Aero Design   332
   J-6 Fregata   333
Jackson, Sir Michael, Gen   307
Janowski J-5 Marco   332
Javelin (missile)   275, 355, 356
Javelin   *see Gloster*
Javelin   *see Short Bros*
Jeffries, C   57, 58
Jenkins, Maurice   94
Jersey Brow (Farnborough)   29, 54
Jindivik   *see G.A.F.*
Johnson, Frank C., Fg Off   119
Joint UAV Experimentation Programme (JUEP)   323–327
Joint UAV Experimentation Team (JUET)   323

K
Kandahar, Afghanistan   314, 329
Kendal K.1   88
Kestrel   *see BAE Systems*
Kidsdale, RAF   21, 22
Kirkbride, RAF   61
KMB SA-7 Grail   231
Knight, B.J.S., Sqn Ldr   161
Knighton Down   289
Kosovo, Liberation Army   287, 306, 307, 313
Kyle, Ron "Jock"   91, 282

L
Lagonda (sports car)   76
Lancaster   *see Avro*
Langar   94–96
Langstone Harbour   55
Larkhill, Wiltshire   171, 226, 232, 233, 235–238, 240–242, 270–274, 288–291, 293, 296, 297, 300, 301, 303–307, 311–313, 318, 319, 321, 323–326, 338, 341, 348, 352
LARYNX, RAE   8–12
Laverton, Australia   87, 112, 116
Lavington Folly, Salisbury Plain   304
Lee-on-Solent   15, 16, 20, 24, 25, 54, 61, 62, 96, 139, 169, 172, 175
Libya   215, 226, 227
Lincoln   *see Avro*
Lines Bros Ltd   75–83, 221
Llanbedr   91, 97, 98, 101, 110–115, 117–133, 139–163, 197, 199, 220, 236, 238, 243
Lockheed Aquila UAV   298, 299, 302

Long-Range Weapons Establishment   112
Low, Archibald M   1–5, 9
Lulsgate (Bristol)   286
Lyneham (33 MU)   116, 226
Lysander   *see Westland*

M
Machan UAV   300, 341, 352
Macrihanish   331, 332, 334
M.A.E.E. Felixstowe   14, 56, 71
Magill, Gilbert W.   341
Malta   16, 28, 20, 2–25, 100, 102, 103, 167–169, 172, 173, 175   *see also Hal Far*
Manchester   58
Manorbier   22–25, 50, 55, 56, 58, 61, 62, 167–169, 172, 173, 175, 221, 223, 227–231, 237, 239–281, 284
Mansour, Joseph   76
Mantis   *see BAE Systems*
Marconi   117, 148, 198, 240, 297–299, 304, 344
   Defence Systems   350
   -Elliot   139, 140, 343
   Space & Defence Systems   350
Marine & Armament Experimental Establishment   67, 71
Market Drayton, RAF (34 MU)   94
Market Harborough, RAF   61
Marks, Tom   94
Marsaxlokk (Malta)   100, 167
Martinet   *see Miles*
Master   *see Miles*
MATRA/Marconi   197
MATS-A   *see Skyleader*
MATS-B   *see Short*
McCulloch
   O-90-1 (engine)   170
   O-100-2 (engine)   173, 293
   O-100-3 (engine)   293
   123cc (engine)   235, 237, 241
McDonnell Douglas Phantom FG.1, FGR.2   128, 161, 196, 198
McDougall, Flt Lt   54, 55
Meggitt Defence Systems   270, 272–274, 284, 285, 338
   Voodoo UAV   283, 285, 286
Megido Airfield, Israel   317
Melbourne, Australia   112, 116, 143
Mercury (engine) *see Bristol*
Merton, Surrey   75, 76, 83
Mesopotamia   10
Meteor S.p.A   173
   Mirach 100/2   215
   Mirach 100/5   199, 215–220, 286
Meteor   *see Gloster*
Meteor TT.20   *see Armstrong-Whitworth*
Middle Wallop   173, 194, 243, 283, 313, 347
Midge   *see Canadair*
Mikoyan-Guervich
   MiG-21   307
   MiG-29   198, 199
Miles Aircraft Target Glider   90
Miles, George   59
Miles
   M.25 Martinet   51, 67, 76, 77, 80
   Master   59
   M.3D   52
   M.10   51, 52

M.11 Whitney Straight 52
M.28 58, 59, 63
M.47 58, 59
M.49, 49A 58, 59
M.50 Queen Martinet 51, 58–65, 91, 165
Mills, Colin 232, 234
Minifie, Flt Lt 22
Ministry of Aircraft Production 22, 59, 76, 80, 81
Ministry of Defence 144, 148, 196, 215, 216, 235–237, 240, 242, 272, 274, 283, 286, 290, 297, 319, 340–343, 345, 346
Ministry of Technology 231, 233
Mirach see Meteor
Mission Technologies Inc 324
Mi-Tex Buster UAV 323–325
M.L. Aviation Ltd 66, 225–231, 347, 348
  Queen Spitfire 66
  Sprite 348
  U-120D 225–231
Mombasa 171, 176
Morris Motors Ltd 22, 26
Mosquito see de Havilland
MOTE see Westland
Moth see de Havilland
Mount Batten, RAF 8, 19, 25, 27
Mueller, Elke 341
Munsterlager 290

N
Nab Tower 15, 70–72
Naval Aircraft Factory TD2N-1 165
Naval Anti-Aircraft Gunnery Committee 5, 12, 67
Naval Experimental Pilotless Target Unit 169, 171
Nellis AFB 328, 329
Newport, Gwent 324, 326, 361
Noakes, J., Capt 76
Nore lighthouse 69
Normalair-Garrett Ltd 240, 346
  Weslake (engine) 237, 270, 299, 304
  see also Weslake
Northolt, Middlesex 4
Northrop
  AN/USD-1 288, 290–295
  AN/USD-501 293, 295, 298
  Chukar 165, 172, 173, 195–216, 220, 238, 282
  KD2R-2 166, 170, 228, 230
  OQ-2 170
  OQ-3 92, 170, 221–223
  OQ-14 170
  OQ-17 170
Norway, Neville Shute, Lt Cdr 83
Norwood, MA (USA) 170

O
Oakley airfield 77
Oerlikon 35mm gun 261, 358
Old Sarum 151
Oliver, Cyril 231, 232
Onions (Ribbesford Co.) 52
Operation Enduring Freedom 314, 318, 322
Operation Entirety 320, 322
Operation Granby 297
Operation Herrick 314–317, 319, 320, 322
Operation Iraqi Freedom 318
Operation Telic 307, 308, 310–312, 315, 320, 322

Operation Torch 287
Operational Requirements
  48 57
  57 51, 57
  119 58
  1056 355
  1117 355
Optica see Edgley
Otterburn 236–238, 337, 351

P
Panavia Tornado F.3 161, 199, 214, 358
ParcAberporth 286, 316, 317
Paris Air Salon (Show) 89, 145, 153, 285
Parlick, nr Chipping 330
Pembroke Docks 6
Pennie, E.F., Flt Lt 111
Percival
  P.8 & P.8A (Type H) 51, 52
  P.21 & P.21A (Type T) 51, 57
  Provost T.1 228
Perham Down, Wiltshire 291
Peyton, R.A, Lt/Cdr 20
Phantom see McDonnell Douglas
Phillips & Powis Ltd 52, 61
Pika 143
Pilotless Aircraft Committee 8, 10, 13, 17, 18, 58
Pilotless Aircraft Squadron 20
Pilotless Aircraft Unit 20, 22–24, 49, 50, 55, 60, 61
Pilotless Target Aircraft Unit 167
Piper Target Technology Ltd 270
Point Mugu (USN Pacific Missile Range) 145, 160
Pontypridd 222
Portland, Dorset 10, 12, 19, 171–194, 197, 201–215, 233, 234, 294, 295
Port Stanley (Falkland Islands) 240
Portsmouth 5–8, 12, 16, 20, 52, 54–57, 71, 85, 110, 173, 229
Portsmouth Aviation Ltd 111, 122 see also Airspeed
Portsmouth Dockyard 6, 15, 85
Portsmouth, London Road 53
Portsmouth, Southsea & I.O.W. Aviation 56
Praga (engine) 58
Predator see General Atomics
Preston, H.E 4
Profumo, John (MP) 289, 290
Project Conga 343
Project Morrigan 334
Project MRUASTAS 342, 344
Project Phoenix 298, 340, 345, 346
Provost see Percival

Q
QinetiQ 152, 162, 216, 274, 283–286, 326
Quadrocopter see EADS
Queen see Fairey
Queen Bee see de Havilland
Queen Martinet see Miles
Queen Seamew see Curtiss-Wright
Queen Spitfire see M.L. Aviation
Queen Wasp see Airspeed

R
RAAF 87, 112, 116–118, 122–125, 133, 134, 137, 138
Racal Doppler MDI 237

Racal Radar Defence Systems 270, 275
Radioplane
  KD2R-2 166, 170
  KD2R-5 230
  OQ-3 170
  OQ-19 170
  RP-19 170
  RP-76 196
SS Radstock 20
RAE Bedford 15, 198, 284
RAE Factory, Farnborough
RAE Farnborough 2–4, 6–8, 12–15, 18–25, 52, 54–56, 58, 59, 61, 67–72, 74–76, 81–83, 86–89, 92, 96, 97, 111–113, 115, 139, 141, 145, 148, 152, 163, 222, 225, 230, 233, 270, 305, 317, 327, 333–335, 339, 341–344, 346, 348, 349, 352
  see also Farnborough Air Show
RAE
  XRAE-1 UAV 348–352
  XRAE-2 UAV 348–352
  XRAE-140 UAV 351, 352
RAF Carew Cheriton 80
RAF Gosport 70, 75
RAF Kidsdale 21, 22, 25, 58
RAF Regiment 101, 117, 240, 325, 356, 358
Rank Pullen Controls 298, 299, 346
Rapier (missile) See British Aircraft Corporation
Raven see BAE Systems
Raven see Flight Refuelling
Raytheon Sidewinder (missile) 161, 198, 199, 216, 286, 357
RCA Corporation 240, 242, 271, 273
RCS (Radio Control Specialists) Ltd 338
  4012 Falcon 338
  4015 Falcon 338
  4018 Heron 339
  4019 Camera System 339
  4020 Composite 339
  4024 Heron 338, 339
  Guided Weapons Systems 338
Reaper see General Atomics
Red Dean (missile) see Folland
Red Duster (missile) see Bristol
Red Hawk (missile) see de Havilland
Red Heathen (missile) 91
Red Shoes (missile) see English Electric
Redhill, Surrey 23
RFA Sea Salvor 168
RFD Co Ltd 85, 87
Richards, E.J., Professor 88
Richmond, Lt/Cdr(E) 61
Ringway, Manchester 97, 98, 101, 147 see also Stockport
RNPTA 171–173, 175–177, 196, 197, 211, 231
Roberts, Alex 136
Roberts, Silyn, Air Commodore 166
Roberts Barracks, Larkhill 296, 312, 313, 318
Roborough (Plymouth, Devon) 18, 20, 25
Robson, Dennis, Lt Col 236
Rollestone Camp, Larkhill 236, 238, 240, 242, 249, 273
Royal Navy Experimental Unit 98
RTV-1 (missile) 92
Rumsfeld, Donald 307
Ruston Proctor & Co Ltd 3

Index 371

S
SA-7 Grail   *see KMB*
Salisbury (South Australia)   112
Salto di Quirra Range   215, 216
San Carlos   240
San Diego   346, 347
San Nicholas Island   145
Saudi Arabia   199, 214
Saxa Vord   161
Scimitar   *see Vickers-Supermarine*
Scorpio-6   *see EADS*
Scottish Aviation Ltd   22, 23, 26, 46, 222
SD-1 Drone – *see Northrop AN/USD-1*
Seacat (missile)   *see Short*
Seafire   *see Supermarine*
Sea King ASaC Mk.7   *see Westland*
Seaslug (missile)   *see Armstrong-Whitworth*
Sea Sparrow (missile)   *see General Dynamics*
Sea Vixen   *see de Havilland*
Seawolf (missile)   *See British Aircraft Corporation*
Senny Bridge   325
SERCO   152, 240, 242, 272, 273, 279
Shaibah, Iraq   10–12, 309
Sharpeye   *see Westland*
Shatt al-Arab, Iraq   318
Sheerness   69, 70
Shoeburyness (P.E.E.)   94, 352, 353
Short Brothers Air Services Ltd   236, 240, 241, 243, 249, 259, 338
Short Bros & Harland Ltd   113, 117, 121, 222, 235–237, 293, 344, 355, 356
  Blowpipe (missile)   x, 117, 174, 231–233, 235–237, 271, 293, 355, 356
  Javelin   355, 356
  MATS-B   235–238, 240–242, 271
  SC.4   136
  Seacat (missile)   136, 171, 172, 356
    see also 'Green Light'
  Skyspy   344
  Sturgeon TT.2 & TT.3   79, 101, 145
Sidewinder (missile)   *see Raytheon*
Silloth (22 MU)   94
Singapore   25, 117, 165, 171–173, 175–176
Sky Flash (missile)   *see BAe*
Skyleader Radio Control Ltd   337
  MATS-A   173, 337, 338
Skyspy   *see Short Bros*
Slingsby Sailplanes Ltd   76, 81, 87, 232, 299, 300, 333
  T.39   87
  T.68   299, 300
Soarer   *see BAE Systems*
Sopwith AT   3
Sopwith Aviation Company   34
Sound-Ranging   287, 290, 296
Southampton   *see Supermarine*
South Uist   326
Sparrow (including Sea Sparrow)   *see General Dynamics*
Sparrowhawk Airfield, Iraq   310
Specification
  18/33   18
  Q.32/35   51, 52, 53
  Q.8/37   51, 57
  Q.12/38   51, 57
  T.24/40   55
  Q.10/43   51, 58, 59
  D.168D&P   98
  D.169D&P   135, 136
  D.171D&P   94
  D.173D&P   111
  D.174D&P   113
  D.187D&P   116
  D.202D&P   145
  D.208D&P   147
  D.257D&P   148
  UD.243D&P   148
Spitfire   *see Vickers-Supermarine*
Sprite   *see M.L. Aviation*
Stabileye   *see BAe*
Stapehill, Dorset   293
Stearman-Hammond   57
Stiffkey, Norfolk   221
Stockport (Ringway)   97, 98
Stokes Bay   73
Stooge   *see Fairey*
Stretton, RNAS   101
Sturgeon   *see Short Bros*
Summerhayes, Mr. E   111
Supermarine
  Seafire F.17   96
  Southampton   10
Supervisor   297, 298, 300, 344–347
Swallow   *see IMA*
Swanton Morley, RAF   80
Swift   *see Vickers-Supermarine*
Swinderby, RAF   152
Sywell   78, 82

T
Taranis   *see BAE Systems*
Target Operations Group (TOG)   236
Target Technology Ltd (TTL)   240, 270
Tarhuna, Libya   226
Tarrant Rushton, Dorset   91, 92–94, 96, 111–133, 139, 141, 142, 282
TASUMA (UK) Ltd   242, 247, 259, 350, 352, 353
T-Hawk   *see Honeywell*
Thales Watchkeeper UAV   313, 315–317
Thales/Elbit Hermes 450 UAV   315–317, 320
Thompson, Susan   231–234
Thorney Island, Hampshire   320, 350
Thurleigh, RAE   341
Thruxton, Hampshire   247
Thunderbird (missile)   *see English Electric*
Tiger Moth   *see de Havilland*
Tiltman, Hessell   23, 53, 55
Tiltman Langley Laboratories   225
Timbs, S., Lt/Cdr   169
Tom Laing   55
Tonfannau   98
Tornado   *see Panavia*
Treforest   222
Tri-Ang Ltd   76
Trial 'Arkansas Odyssey'   324, 326
Trial 'Desert Rescue'   324
Trial 'Mighty Magpie'   324–326
Trial 'Urban Hummingbird'   324–326
Trial 'Vigilant Viper'   324, 326, 327
Tuskar Rock, County Wexford   162
Twatt, RNAS   59, 77, 82
Ty Croes   24, 98
Typhoon   *see Hawker*

U
UAV Tactical Systems Ltd   315, 317
U.S. Navy   59, 60, 65, 144, 145, 160, 170, 171, 196, 197, 230, 322, 348, 357, 358

V
Varsity T.1   *see Vickers*
Venom   *see de Havilland*
Veritair   213, 216
Vickers
  Varsity T.1   222
  Viscount   119, 162
Vickers-Supermarine
  Scimitar   103, 135
  Spitfire   66
  Swift   90, 135
Villacoublay, France   167
Villiers-Talisman (engine)   223
Vincent (engine)   226
Vinten Ltd   289
Viper (engine)   111, 144, 146, 147
Viper   *see Armstrong-Whitworth*
Viscount   *see Vickers*
Voodoo   *see Meggitt*

W
Waddington, RAF   323, 324, 358
Walrus   *see Westland*
Walter, George (APT Electronics)   291
Watchet   20, 24, 25, 29, 36, 358
Watchkeeper UAV   *see Thales*
Weapons Research Establishment (WRE)   111, 112, 116–118, 135, 144
Weslake
  274-3 (engine)   346
  274-6 (engine)   237, 240, 248, 255, 256, 258
  342 (engine)M240, 304
  T-116 (engine)   339
Westland (including GEC-Westland)   297, 298, 305, 342–345
  Lysander   59
  MOTE   342, 346
  Sea King ASaC Mk.7   327
  Sharpeye   298, 345, 347
  Walrus   11, 72, 73
  WIDEYE   342–347
  Wight   344
  WISP   237, 342–347
Weston-Super-Mare   298, 346
Westwood, C., Flt Lt   161
White Waltham, Berkshire   66, 97, 111, 145, 146, 227, 230, 247, 248
Whitney Straight   *see Miles*
WIDEYE   *see Westland*
Wight   *see Westland*
Wilmot, Charles   76
WISP   *see Westland* Wolseley Scorpio   53, 61, 62
Woodley, Berkshire   52
Woods, W., F/Lt   23
Woodvale, RAF   98, 152
Woolwich   83
Woomera (Range)   94, 112, 113, 116–118, 136, 143, 144, 331–336
Worminghall airfield   76
Worthy Down, Winchester   84
WREBUS flight termination system   160, 161

Y
Yeovil   342–347
Yeovilton, RNAS   101, 187